Education for All

Literacy for life

Education for All

Literacy for life

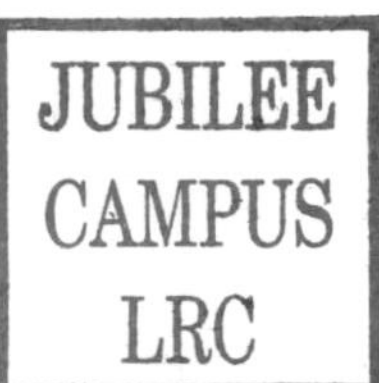

UNESCO Publishing

The analysis and policy recommendations of this Report do not necessarily reflect the views of UNESCO. The Report is an independent publication commissioned by UNESCO on behalf of the international community. It is the product of a collaborative effort involving members of the Report Team and many other people, agencies, institutions and governments. Overall responsibility for the views and opinions expressed in the Report is taken by its Director.

The designations employed and the presentation of the material in this publication do not imply the expression of any opinion whatsoever on the part of UNESCO concerning the legal status of any country, territory, city or area, or of its authorities, or concerning the delimitation of its frontiers or boundaries.

Published in 2005 by the United Nations Educational, Scientific and Cultural Organization
7, Place de Fontenoy, 75352 Paris 07 SP, France

Graphic design by Sylvaine Baeyens
Iconographer: Delphine Gaillard
Maps: INDID
Printed by Graphoprint, Paris
Second printing
ISBN 92-3-104008-1

Printed in France

Foreword

This fourth annual *Education for All Global Monitoring Report*, produced by an independent team housed at UNESCO, invites us to give renewed and bold attention to the global literacy challenge.

There are good reasons why literacy is at the core of Education for All (EFA) – a good quality basic education equips pupils with literacy skills for life and further learning; literate parents are more likely to send their children to school; literate people are better able to access continuing education opportunities; and literate societies are better geared to meet pressing development challenges.

Yet literacy is one of the most neglected EFA goals. The fact that some 770 million adults – about one-fifth of the world's adult population – do not have basic literacy skills is not only morally indefensible but is also an appalling loss of human potential and economic capacity. The *Report* makes a powerful case to end this neglect by affirming that literacy is a right in itself, essential to achieve all the EFA goals and critically important for development. The emergence of knowledge societies makes literacy even more critical than in the past. Achieving widespread literacy can only happen in the context of building literate societies that encourage individuals to acquire and use their literacy skills.

Since its founding, UNESCO has played a lead role in defining literacy, relentlessly affirming its vital importance for development, and supporting country initiatives to expand adult learning. There has been remarkable progress over the past sixty years. The momentous challenge that persists is our collective responsibility. UNESCO is the lead agency and international coordinator of the United Nations Literacy Decade (2003-2012), which states that 'literacy for all is at the heart of basic education for all ... [and] creating literate environments and societies is essential for achieving the goals of eradicating poverty, reducing child mortality, curbing population growth, achieving gender equality and ensuring sustainable development, peace and democracy.' We are giving the Decade concrete support through our programmes, particularly through the Literacy Initiative for Empowerment (LIFE) launched in October 2005 during the 33rd session of UNESCO's General Conference, and more broadly, through our international coordination of Education for All, which we are endeavouring to further strengthen.

The Decade is a framework for promoting international, regional and national efforts aimed at enabling millions of youth and adults to enjoy increased opportunities to acquire literacy skills. To achieve this, countries must commit to literacy at the highest political levels and assign more resources to youth and adult literacy programmes. As this *Report* informs us, literacy typically receives only 1% of the national education budget. International aid for literacy is minuscule as a share of aid to basic education, which is itself too low. Much bolder commitments are urgently required if the EFA goals are to be met.

As in previous years, this *Report* examines progress towards the six EFA goals. The year 2005 has been particularly significant. On the one hand, it is now apparent, as the Report confirms, that the goal to achieve gender parity in primary and secondary education by 2005 has not been met, despite very rapid progress, especially in a number of low-income countries. We must renew our commitment and move forward. On the other hand, resources for basic education are increasing: public spending on education is rising in developing countries and the international community has promised to increase its support, especially to sub-Saharan Africa, as reflected at the G-8 summit in Gleneagles in July 2005 and the United Nations World Summit in New York in September 2005. The challenge now is to translate broad commitments into specific actions in developing countries and to step up the pace of change everywhere. We only have ten years left and we must not fail.

I am confident that this *Report* provides a solid basis to recommit ourselves to achieving the six Education for All goals and, in particular, to making literacy a reality for all people in the world.

Koïchiro Matsuura

Acknowledgements

Former Director Christopher Colclough initiated the work for this Report.

We are indebted to Peter Smith, UNESCO's Assistant Director-General for Education (ADG/ED), to Aïcha Bah Diallo, former Assistant Director-General a.i., and to Abhimanyu Singh, Director of the Division of International Coordination and Monitoring for Education for All, and their colleagues for their support.

The Report benefited strongly from the advice of the international Editorial Board and its chairperson Ingemar Gustafsson, as well as from in-depth guidance from a small advisory group composed of Helen Abadzi, Anita Dighe, Sonja Fagerberg-Diallo, Vera Masagão Ribeiro, Anna Robinson-Pant, Alan Rogers, and Shigeru Aoyagi and Adama Ouane, both from UNESCO. It also profited from the over 120 people who took part in the web-based consultation on the outline, whose comments can be reviewed at: www.efareport.unesco.org

The EFA Report depends greatly on the work of the UNESCO Institute for Statistics (UIS). Former Director Denise Lievesley, Michael Millward, Director a. i., Said Belkachla, Michael Bruneforth, Brian Buffett, Simon Ellis, Alison Kennedy, Olivier Labé, Albert Motivans, Pascale Ratovondrahona, Ioulia Sementchouk, Mamadou Thiam, Subramaniyam Venkatraman, Peter Wallet, Yanhong Zhang and their colleagues contributed significantly to this Report, particularly in the preparation of Chapters 2 and 3 and the statistical tables.

Special thanks are due to all those who prepared background papers, notes and boxes for the Report. These were:

Marifat Abdullaeva, ActionAid, Carlos Aggio, Mark Agranovitch, John Aitchinson, Massimo Amadio, Juan B. Arrien, David Baker, Jill Balescut, Yembuu Batchuluun, Antonio Augusto Gomes Batista, Julien Bayou, Raja Bentaouet-Kattan, Alain Bentolila, Anne Bernard, K. Biswal, Corinne Bitoun, H.S. Bhola, Mohammed Bougroum, Jennifer Bowser, Shoshan Brosh-Vaitz, Don Bundy, Grace Bunyi, Roy Carr-Hill, John Cameron, Stuart Cameron, Nalini Chhetri, Munir Ahmed Choudhry, Roser Cusso, Aimé Damiba, André Delluc, Mark De Maeyer, Kendra Derousseau, Kamal Desai, Chris Duke, Jan Eldred, Karen Erickson, Makhoumy Fall, Iffat Farah, Benjamin Fernandez, Birger Fredriksen, Jonas Frister, Bruno Germain, Christine Glanz, Global Campaign for Education, Christophe Gouel, R. Govinda, Talmadge C. Guy, Aurore Hagel, Hasan Hamomud, Ulrike Hanemann, Heribert Hinzen, Nour Laila Iskandar, Fasli Jalal, Jingjing Lou, Matthew Jukes, Mohamed Abdellatif Kissami, Bidya Nath Koirala, Tatiana Koke, Hanke Koopman, Lisa Krolak, Elaine Lameta, Mirna Lawrence, Aliza Lazerson, Leslie Limage, Wolfgang Lutz, Bryan Maddox, Maria Ester Mancebo, Jean-Claude Mantes, A. Mathew, Markus Maurer, Anne McGill Franzen, Carolyn Medel-Anonuevo, Mario Mouzinho, Khulan Munkh-Erdene, Debora Nandja, Abou Napon, Netherlands Ministry of Foreign Affairs, Bjorn Nordtveit, Pai Obanya, Keichi Ogawa, Anthony Okech, Adama Ouane, Hussain Oujour, Ila Patel, Jason Pennells, Françoise du Pouget, Mastin Prinsloo, Norman Reynolds, Vera Masagão Ribeiro, Lisa Maria Rinna, Clinton Robinson, Anna Robinson-Pant, Alan Rogers, Heidi Ross, Peter Rule, Olga Rybakova, Samuel Sandwidi, Salimata Sanou, Nina Sardjunani, Claude Sauvageot, Julie Schaffner, Amanda Seel, Lynne Sergeant, Inon Shenker, Mammo Kebede Shenkut, Mariko Shiohata, Ronald Siebes, David Sifuentes, Maria Teresa Siniscalco, Penny Smith, John Smyth, Marie-Andrée Somers, Brian Street, Nelly Stromquist, Emmanuelle Suso, Shaizada Tasbulatova, Lucy Thornton, Rosa Maria Torres, Mami Umayahara, Asunción Valderrama, Jan Van Ravens, Consuelo Vélaz de Medrano, Daniel Wagner, Phoeba Wakhunga, Ling Wang, Yaikah Jeng, Yang Lijing and Tidao Zhang.

The Report also benefited considerably from the advice and support of individuals, Divisions and Units within UNESCO's Education Sector, the International Institute for Educational

Planning, the International Bureau of Education, and the UNESCO Institute for Education, including through a consultation on the outline. UNESCO's Regional Bureaux provided helpful advice on country-level activities and helped facilitate commissioned studies. Sue Williams of UNESCO's Bureau for Public Information has provided valuable advice and ongoing support to the promotion and dissemination of the Report.

We are grateful to Rosemary Bellew, Luc-Charles Gacougnolle and Laura Gregory in the Fast Track Initiative secretariat, and to Julia Benn, Valérie Gaveau and Simon Scott in OECD/DAC for their continuing support and helpful advice on international cooperation and aid data.

A number of individuals also contributed valuable advice and comments. These were: Namtip Aksornkool, Massimo Amadio, Shigeru Aoyagi, David Archer, David Atchoarena, Francoise Caillods, Claire Calosci, John Coming, Bridget Crumpton, Roser Cusso, Stephanie Dolata, Marie Dorleans, Birger Fredriksen, Marja Karjalainen, Christine Glanz, Werner Mauch, Adama Ouane, Taeko Okitsu, Muriel Poisson, Kenneth Ross, Mioko Saito, Pierre Runner, Margaret Sachs-Israel, Gaurav Siddhu, Ronald Siebes, Suzanne Stump, Duncan Wilson. Special thanks to John Ryan who provided valuable comments on draft chapters.

The production of the Report benefited greatly from the editorial expertise of Rebecca Brite and Brian Smith. Wenda McNevin, Alison Clayson and Karima Pires also provided valuable editorial support. We would also like to thank Sonia Fernandez-Lauro, Anne Muller, Fouzia Jouot-Bellami, Catherine Ginisty, Judith Roca and their colleagues in the UNESCO Education Documentation Centre for their valuable support throughout the year with the website, distribution and assistance in many matters. Thank-you to Lotfi Ben Khelifa who has played an instrumental role with the timely distribution of the Report. Thanks also to Mary Konin and Chrysanthe Kolia for their logistical support. Special thanks to Richard Cadiou, Vincent Defourny, Igor Nuk and Fabienne Kouadio who facilitated the online consultation in collaboration with colleagues from the Education Documentation Centre.

The EFA Global Monitoring Report Team

Director
Nicholas Burnett

Steve Packer (Deputy Director), Nicole Bella, Aaron Benavot, Lene Buchert, Fadila Caillaud, Vittoria Cavicchioni, Valérie Djioze, Ana Font-Giner, Jude Fransman, Cynthia Guttman, Keith Hinchliffe, François Leclercq, Delphine Nsengimana, Banday Nzomini, Ulrika Peppler Barry, Michelle Phillips, Ikuko Suzuki, Edna Yahil, Alison Kennedy (Head, EFA Observatory, UIS), Agneta Lind (Special Literacy Adviser)

For more information about the Report, please contact:
The Director
EFA Global Monitoring Report Team
c/o UNESCO
7 place de Fontenoy, 75352 Paris 07 SP, France
e-mail: efareport@unesco.org
Tel.: +33 1 45 68 21 28
Fax: +33 1 45 68 56 41
www.efareport.unesco.org

Previous EFA Global Monitoring Reports
2005. Education for All – THE QUALITY IMPERATIVE
2003/4. Gender and Education for All – THE LEAP TO EQUALITY
2002. Education for All – IS THE WORLD ON TRACK?

Contents

List of figures, tables and text boxes

Figures

Tables

Text boxes

The Report at a glance

→ Progress towards Education for All

Steady progress has been made since 1998, especially towards universal primary education (UPE) and gender parity among the poorest countries, but the pace is insufficient for the goals to be met in the remaining ten years to 2015.

Encouraging trends represent considerable achievements in many low-income countries:

- Primary-school enrolments are up sharply in both sub-Saharan Africa and South and West Asia, with nearly 20 million new students in each region.

- Globally, 47 countries have achieved UPE (out of 163 with data available).

- Projections show that 20 additional countries (out of 90 with the relevant data) are on track to achieve UPE by 2015; 44 countries are making good progress but are unlikely to achieve the goal by 2015.

- Girls' primary enrolments have also risen rapidly, especially in some of the lowest-income countries of sub-Saharan Africa, and South and West Asia.

- Gender and educational quality measures are increasingly visible in national education plans.

- Public spending on education has increased as a share of national income in about 70 countries (out of 110 with data).

- Aid for basic education more than doubled between 1999 and 2003 and, following the G8 summit, could rise to US$3.3 billion per year by 2010.

- The Fast Track Initiative has emerged as a key coordinating mechanism for aid agencies.

Major Education for All challenges remain:

- *UPE is not assured:*
  - About 100 million children are still not enrolled in primary school, 55% of them girls.
  - 23 countries are at risk of not achieving UPE by 2015, as their net enrolment ratios are declining.
  - Primary-school fees, a major barrier to access, are still collected in 89 countries (out of 103 surveyed).
  - High fertility rates, HIV/AIDS and armed conflict continue to exert pressure on education systems in the regions with the greatest EFA challenges.

- *The 2005 gender parity target has been missed by 94 countries out of 149 with data:*
  - 86 countries are at risk of not achieving gender parity even by 2015.
  - 76 out of 180 countries have not reached gender parity at primary level, and the disparities are nearly always at the expense of girls.
  - 115 countries (out of 172 with data) still have disparities at secondary level, with boys being under-represented in nearly half, in marked contrast to the primary level.

- *Quality is too low:*
  - Enrolments in early childhood care and education programmes have remained static.
  - Fewer than two-thirds of primary-school pupils reach the last grade in 41 countries (out of 133 with data).
  - In many countries, primary teacher numbers would have to increase by 20% a year to reduce pupil/teacher ratios to 40:1 and to achieve UPE by 2015.
  - Many primary-school teachers lack adequate qualifications.

- *Literacy gets short shrift:*
  - 771 million people aged 15 and above live without basic literacy skills.
  - Governments and aid agencies give insufficient priority and finance to youth and adult literacy programmes.

- *Aid for basic education is still inadequate:*
  - At US$4.7 billion in 2003, bilateral aid to education – 60% of which still goes to post-secondary education – has increased since 1998 but remains well below the 1990 high of US$5.7 billion.
  - Total aid to basic education accounts for only 2.6% of Official Development Assistance; within this category, adult literacy's share is minuscule.
  - While aid to basic education will likely increase in line with overall aid, its share would have to double to reach the estimated US$7 billion a year necessary just to achieve UPE and gender parity.
  - Disproportionate volumes of bilateral aid go to middle-income countries with relatively high primary enrolments.
  - By mid-2005, the Fast Track Initiative had resulted in pledges of only US$298 million.

→ Literacy

Literacy is:

- A right still denied to nearly a fifth of the world's adult population.
- Essential to achieving each of the EFA goals.
- A societal and an individual phenomenon, with attention needed to both dimensions.
- Crucial for economic, social and political participation and development, especially in today's knowledge societies.
- Key to enhancing human capabilities, with wide-ranging benefits including critical thinking, improved health and family planning, HIV/AIDS prevention, children's education, poverty reduction and active citizenship.

The literacy challenge has absolute and relative dimensions, particularly affects the poor, women and marginalized groups, and is much greater than conventional measures indicate:

- In absolute numbers, those without literacy skills are mainly in sub-Saharan Africa, South and West Asia, and East Asia and the Pacific. Prospects for meeting the 2015 goal hinge largely on progress in the 12 countries where 75% of those without literacy skills live.
- In relative terms, the regions with the lowest literacy rates are sub-Saharan Africa, South and West Asia, and the Arab States, all with literacy rates around only 60%, despite increases of more than 10 percentage points since 1990.
- Illiteracy is associated to a significant extent with extreme poverty.
- Women are less literate than men: worldwide, only 88 adult women are considered literate for every 100 adult men, with much lower numbers in low-income countries such as Bangladesh (62 per 100 men) and Pakistan (57 per 100 men).
- 132 of the 771 million people without literacy skills are aged 15 to 24, despite an increase in this group's literacy rate to 85%, from 75% in 1970.
- Direct testing of literacy suggests that the global challenge is much greater than the conventional numbers, based on indirect assessments, would indicate, and that it affects both developed and developing countries.

The literacy challenge can be met only if:

- Political leaders at the highest level commit themselves to action.
- Countries adopt explicit literacy policies to:
  - Expand quality primary and lower-secondary education;
  - Scale up youth and adult literacy programmes;
  - Develop rich literate environments.

Scaling up literacy programmes for youth and adults requires:

- Active government responsibility for adult literacy policy and financing as part of education sector planning.
- Clear frameworks to coordinate public, private and civil society provision of literacy programmes.
- Increased budgetary and aid allocations. Literacy programmes receive a mere 1% of the education budget in many countries. An additional US$2.5 billion a year to 2015 will likely be needed to make significant progress towards the Dakar literacy goal.
- Basing programmes on an understanding of learners' demands, especially their language preferences and their motivations for attending class, in consultation with local communities.
- Curricula that build on these demands, with clearly stated learning objectives and the provision of adequate learning materials.
- Adequate pay, professional status and training opportunities for literacy educators.
- Appropriate language policies, as most countries facing stark literacy challenges are linguistically diverse. The use of mother tongues is pedagogically sound but must offer a smooth transition to learning opportunities in regional and official languages.

Developing literate environments and literate societies requires sustained attention to:

- Language policies.
- Book publishing policies.
- Media policies.
- Access to information.
- Policies to get books and reading materials into schools and homes.

Acquiring, improving and using literacy skills happens at all levels of education, and in multiple formal and non-formal contexts. Achieving each of the EFA goals depends strongly on policies that foster literate societies and set high standards for literacy, the foundation for further learning.

Executive summary

This fourth edition of the *EFA Global Monitoring Report* focuses on literacy, one of the most neglected of the six goals adopted in 2000 by 164 countries at the World Education Forum in Dakar (Senegal). The Report stresses the urgency of devoting increased policy attention and resources to literacy, emphasizing the profound benefits it confers on individuals, communities and nations (Chapter 5). Literacy skills are essential in today's knowledge societies. Understandings of literacy have evolved over the past fifty years to reflect these increasingly complex and demanding needs (Chapter 6). Drawing on a range of data sources, the Report analyses the scale of the literacy challenge (Chapter 7). A historical overview analyses how different societies have made the transition to widespread literacy, taking stock of the broader social context that motivates individuals to acquire and sustain their literacy skills (Chapter 8).

Building literate societies calls for a threefold strategy of quality schooling, youth and adult programmes and the promotion of literate environments (Chapter 9). This approach reflects the interconnected nature of the EFA goals, towards which the Report examines progress, notably the 2005 gender parity goal (Chapter 2). To accelerate the pace of change, sound national policies are required (Chapter 3). The international community must support these efforts: although aid to basic education is on the rise, it remains far short of needs (Chapter 4). The Report concludes by highlighting priority measures for the EFA goals to be achieved in the next ten years (Chapter 10).

Chapter 1

Literacy: the core of Education for All

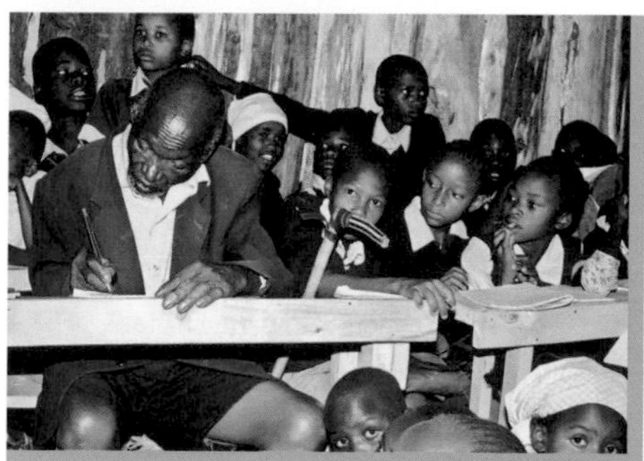

Education for All comprises six inter-related goals that together reflect a holistic conception of educational development. So far, the most dominant attention has focused on the goals that pertain to schooling: universal primary education (UPE), gender parity and quality.

Three key factors have contributed to the neglect of the goals on early childhood care and education, learning programmes for youth and adults, and literacy. First, these are about the creation of new educational opportunities, often through non-formal institutions. Second, national governments and the international community have tended to assume that investing in primary and secondary education and related programmes carries higher political and economic returns. The inclusion of only two EFA goals among the Millennium Development Goals has exacerbated this neglect. Finally, the neglected goals are difficult to define precisely and are stated in qualitative rather than quantitative terms. Monitoring and measurement of progress is correspondingly difficult.

The wording of the literacy goal (goal 4) is itself problematic: strictly speaking, a 50% improvement in levels of literacy is impossible for countries that already have literacy rates above 67%. This Report, therefore, pragmatically interprets the goal as implying a 50% reduction in illiteracy rates, consistent with the wording and intentions of the 1990 Jomtien conference that initiated the entire Education for All movement.

By conventional measurement methods, some 771 million adults are illiterate, two-thirds of them women. This represents a serious violation of human rights for nearly a fifth of the world's adult population. Literacy strengthens the capabilities of individuals, families and communities to take advantage of health, educational, political, economic and cultural opportunities. Women's literacy is of crucial importance in addressing gender inequality.

As the United Nations Literacy Decade (2003–2012) resolution states, 'literacy is at the heart of basic education for all and creating literate environments and societies is essential for achieving the goals of eradicating poverty, reducing child mortality, curbing population growth, achieving gender equality, and ensuring sustainable development, peace and democracy.'

A 'literate' society is more than a society with high literacy rates. Literate societies should enable individuals and groups to acquire, develop, sustain and use relevant literacy skills through basic schooling of good quality, youth and adult literacy programmes and environments in which literacy is valued by individuals, households, schools and communities. This *EFA Global Monitoring Report* aims to stimulate renewed national and international awareness of the crucial importance of literacy for achieving all the EFA goals and, more broadly, for vastly improving the lives of millions of people living in extreme poverty.

Chapter 2

EFA progress: where do we stand?

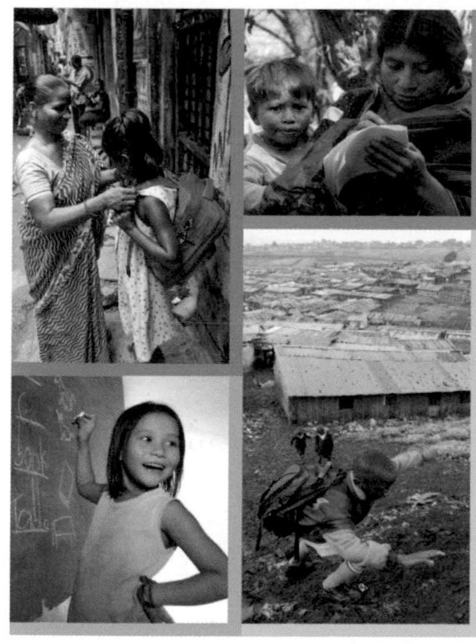

This chapter assesses progress towards the EFA goals, using the most recent global education data, for the 2002/2003 school year.

Progress towards UPE has been slow overall since the World Education Forum in Dakar. A total of 671 million children were enrolled in primary school in 2002, up from 655 million in 1998. Across sub-Saharan Africa, South and West Asia, and the Arab States, however, enrolment ratios are rising rapidly and the gender gap is slowly narrowing, though many countries still combine low enrolment ratios with insufficient capacity to accommodate all children. Despite rising enrolments, about 100 million children of primary school age were still not enrolled in primary schools in 2002, of whom 55% were girls. Sub-Saharan Africa, and South and West Asia accounted for 70% of these out-of-school children. Ensuring that enrolled children remain in school until the last grade of primary schooling is a continuing challenge. In about one-third of countries with data, less than two-thirds of the pupils enrolled in primary school reach the last grade.

School systems are expanding rapidly beyond the primary level. The global number of secondary school students increased four times faster than that of primary school students. This expansion puts education systems under increasing pressure. Newly published data on learning outcomes suggest that average achievement levels have decreased in recent years in sub-Saharan African countries.

Despite rapid progress in several poor countries with low enrolment ratios, the 2005 gender parity goal has been missed in over ninety countries. Gender inequality is concentrated in the Arab States, South and West Asia, and sub-Saharan Africa, where girls continue to face sharp discrimination in access to schooling. At the secondary level, boys are under-represented in over fifty countries. Gender parity is the exception in tertiary education, found in only 4 of the 142 countries with data available.

The vast majority of the world's 771 million adult illiterates live in three regions: South and West Asia, East Asia and the Pacific, and sub-Saharan Africa. Women continue to constitute a majority of the world's illiterates: 64%, unchanged from 1990. At the global level, only 88 adult women are considered literate for every 100 adult men. Regions with relatively low gender parity indices in adult literacy (GPIs) are South and West Asia (0.66), the Arab States (0.69), and sub-Saharan Africa (0.76). In Latin America and the Caribbean, and in East Asia and the Pacific, the GPIs are above the global average of 0.88.

Progress towards mass literacy is especially marked in the 15-24 age group, where expanded access to formal schooling helped raise the global literacy rate from 75% to 88% between 1970 and 2000–2004; the corresponding rates for developing countries were 66% and 85%.

The Education for All Development Index (EDI) provides a summary measure of a country's situation vis-à-vis EFA. It covers four goals: UPE, adult literacy, gender and education quality. The index for 2002 is computed for the 123 countries for which data are available on all four components. Changes in the EDI between 1998 and 2002 were moderate. On average, countries increased their index rating by 1.2%. Twenty-eight countries have very low EDI values; sixteen are in sub-Saharan Africa.

This chapter ends by analysing prospects of achieving by 2015 the goals of UPE, gender equality in primary and secondary education, and reduced levels of adult illiteracy.

Chapter 3

Country efforts: increasing momentum

Accelerating the pace of change to meet the EFA goals in ten years' time requires urgent and sustained attention to planning, strategies to address access and quality, and adequate national resource allocations.

A recent study of national education plans from thirty-two countries showed that those in South Asia and sub-Saharan Africa placed top priority on achieving UPE. Public spending on education as a share of national income increased between 1998 and 2002 in about two-thirds of countries with data, in some cases almost doubling. Higher levels of national expenditure do not in themselves assure good practice and good quality. Efficiency in terms of how resources are used in the education system is key. Several countries have undertaken initiatives to hold education stakeholders accountable for their performance and ensure that financial resources reach designated schools.

Despite increased recognition of the gains that result from eliminating fees at the primary level, 89 of the 103 countries with information available on this topic still charge fees, some legal and some illegal. Making school more affordable, by removing these costs and by providing free or cheap transport and school meals, acts as a powerful incentive for parents to send their children – especially their daughters – to school.

Addressing teacher shortages and training is a top priority for countries that still need to significantly increase the coverage of their primary school systems. In sub-Saharan Africa, pupil/teacher ratios typically exceed 40:1 and are as high as 70:1 in some countries. Projections show that in several countries, the number of teachers would have to increase by 20% per year to achieve UPE by 2015 and bring pupil/teacher ratios to 40:1. In only one-quarter of the approximately 100 developing countries with data available in 2002 have all or almost all primary teachers received some pedagogical training.

The evidence is also very strong that good health and nutrition are prerequisites for effective learning. Iron deficiency occurs among 50% of all children in developing countries, and helminth infections among

25-35% of all children. Low-cost interventions can make a major dent in related educational and human losses, leading to improved school attendance and better overall achievement.

Education for All is about reaching *all* children, youth and adults. The continued exclusion of children who are unregistered at birth, rural children, working children, children with disabilities and girls from disadvantaged backgrounds calls for specific steps to assure them access to school. Successful strategies leading to higher enrolment of girls typically focus on actions inside schools, within the community and at a broader societal level. Women teachers, fee-free schooling, schools closer to home with basic sanitation and separate toilets, protection against sexual violence and community support for girls' schooling are essential elements of a strategy towards greater gender equality.

A major obstacle to the achievement of EFA is the high proportion of countries experiencing, or recently emerged from, conflict, natural disasters and economic instability. Maintaining education systems during conflicts and other emergencies is essential to give children some stability, normality and hope for the future. In sub-Saharan Africa, the HIV/AIDS epidemic, other diseases and political conflict are expected to leave one-tenth of primary school age children orphaned by 2010, necessitating special interventions to provide them with support and learning opportunities.

Chapter 4

International commitments: time to act

The overarching goal of halving the number of people living in extreme poverty galvanized the international community in 2005. The signs are that some significant breakthroughs are being made. The G8 countries agreed to debt relief for some of the world's poorest countries. Donors made commitments that could increase overall aid by more than 50% by 2010. Education should benefit from these developments, but funding still falls short of what is needed to achieve even a limited number of the EFA goals in the world's poorest countries.

Bilateral aid to education reached US$4.65 billion in 2003, a 31% increase over its 2000 low of US$3.55 billion, but still well below the 1990 high of US$5.71 billion (all at constant 2002 prices). The amount for basic education more than doubled between 1998 and 2003, but still accounted for less than 2% of total bilateral Official Development Assistance. Overall, nearly 60% of the bilateral commitments to education is still for the post-secondary level. Basic education's share averaged 28.3%. Disproportionate volumes of aid go to middle-income countries with relatively good social indicators, including primary school enrolment. Only three countries give more than 20% of their aid to South and West Asia, the region facing the largest EFA challenge in terms of numbers of people.

Major multilateral aid agencies committed US$15.9 billion per year on average between 1999 and 2003, with education receiving 9.3%. Basic education received about 60% of that share. Combining both bilateral and multilateral sources, aid to basic education more than doubled between 1999 and 2003 but still only represented about 2.6% of all aid in 2003.

Few bilateral donors and development banks make explicit reference to literacy in their aid policies. There is a strong case for a new international dialogue on literacy, including its place in agency policies and in bilateral and multilateral discussions with governments.

Assuming that the share of funding that goes to basic education remains constant, the increased overall aid flows pledged at the G8 summit could result by 2010 in an annual total of approximately US$3.3 billion for basic education, still far short of the US$7 billion a year estimated as necessary to achieve UPE and gender parity alone. To reach the needed total, basic education's share of total aid would have to more than double from 2.6% to over 5.5%.

The world's poorest countries require predictable, long-term aid to carry through essential policy reforms. Such aid is particularly crucial for meeting recurrent costs – salaries, textbooks, learning materials, day-to-day administrative expenses – in countries with insufficient revenue to finance the steps necessary to achieve EFA. In 2005, the United Nations Millennium Project, the UK Commission for Africa and the G8 summit's Gleneagles Communiqué gave strong endorsement to the Fast Track Initiative (FTI). Although the FTI has taken the lead on better harmonization between donors, it has not directly mobilized significant additional resources for EFA. Efforts to harmonize aid should systematically include attention to technical assistance and cooperation, particularly at the country level, where the proliferation of sources of expertise continues. A premium should be placed on improving the knowledge base and sharing knowledge among countries with comparable problems.

Chapter 5

Why literacy matters

The right to literacy is implicit in the right to education recognized by the 1948 Universal Declaration of Human Rights. Other conventions and international declarations have since restated this right. Several instruments focus on the language of literacy acquisition. Many of these documents allow for an expanded interpretation of literacy, beyond reading and writing skills to, for instance, gaining access to scientific and technical knowledge, legal information, culture and the media. Finally, and importantly, literacy has been recognized as a mechanism for the pursuit of other human rights.

Literacy can be associated with a wide spectrum of benefits. Human benefits are deeply tied to an individual's self-esteem, confidence and personal empowerment. Related to this is the increased civic engagement – whether in labour unions, community activities or politics – found to be correlated with participation in adult literacy programmes. Cultural diversity is enhanced by literacy programmes in minority languages, improving people's ability to engage with their own culture. Research shows that women who participate in literacy programmes have better knowledge of health and family planning, and are more likely to adopt preventive health measures like immunization or to seek medical help for themselves and their children. The correlation between education and lower birth rates is well established, though little research has been done on the impact of adult literacy programmes on reproductive behaviour. Educated parents, especially mothers – whether through formal schooling or adult programmes – are more likely to send their children to school and to help them with their studies.

The economic returns to education have been extensively studied, especially in terms of increased individual income and economic growth. Several studies have attempted to disentangle the impact of literacy on growth from that of the number of years in school. One study on forty-four African countries, for example, found that literacy was among the variables with a positive effect on GDP per capita. The sparse evidence that exists indicates that the returns to investment in adult literacy programmes are generally comparable to those of investment in primary education.

Chapter 6

Understandings of literacy

Definitions and understandings of literacy have broadened considerably over the past fifty years, influenced by academic research, international policy agendas and national priorities. In all understandings, literacy embodies reading and writing skills. Numeracy is generally understood as a supplement to or component of literacy. In the 1960s and 1970s, the notion of 'functional literacy' gained ground and emphasized links among literacy, productivity and overall socio-economic development. Recent perspectives look at the ways in which literacy is used and practised in different social and cultural contexts. Many educators have come to view literacy as an active process of learning involving social awareness and critical reflection, which can empower individuals and groups to promote social change.

Since the 1950s, international organizations – UNESCO in particular – have played an influential role in developing policies on literacy, drawing on emerging conceptual understandings. During the 1960s and 1970s, the international policy community stressed the role of literacy in economic growth and national development, especially in newly independent countries. Reflecting this emerging understanding, UNESCO's General Conference in 1978 adopted a definition of functional literacy still in use today: 'A person is functionally literate who can engage in all those activities in which literacy is required for effective functioning of his (or her) group and community and also for enabling him (or her) to continue to use reading, writing and calculation for his (or her) own and the community's development.' Over the 1980s and 1990s, definitions of literacy broadened to accommodate the challenges of globalization, including the impact of new technology and information media and the emergence of knowledge economies. Greater attention has also been paid to the language or languages in which literacy is learned and practised.

Reflecting these concerns, the World Declaration on Education for All, made in Jomtien in 1990, placed the challenge of literacy within the broader context of meeting the basic learning needs of every child, youth and adult. There is emerging awareness of the broader social context in which literacy is encouraged, acquired, developed and sustained: literacy is no longer exclusively understood as an individual phenomenon, but is seen also as a contextual and societal one.

Chapter 7

Mapping the global literacy challenge

This chapter highlights major trends and patterns of adult and youth literacy at the global, regional, national and subnational levels. It draws upon an array of measures of literacy, including those based on conventional and non-conventional assessments. Conventional cross-national comparisons generally draw upon official national census estimates that are not obtained through direct testing of literacy skills. Censuses vary considerably in how they classify a person as literate, who they consider in the adult population and how frequently they are carried out. For these reasons, census literacy figures should be treated with caution.

Conventional literacy data show that the global literacy rate increased from 56% in 1950 to 70% in 1980, 75% in 1990 and 82% in 2000–2004. It is expected to reach about 86% by 2015. Worldwide, the adult literacy rate increased at a faster pace in the 1970s than in subsequent decades. In sub-Saharan Africa, South and West Asia, and the Arab States, literacy rates increased by more than 10% between 1990 and 2000.

Most of the 771 million adults unable to read and write are concentrated in South and West Asia, sub-Saharan Africa, and East Asia and the Pacific. Prospects for meeting the literacy goal hinge largely on progress in the twelve countries where 75% of those without these skills live.

Illiteracy tends to prevail in low-income countries where severe poverty is widespread. The links between poverty and illiteracy can also be studied at the household level, where evidence from thirty developing countries indicates that literacy levels correlate strongly with wealth. Additional key socio-demographic variables – namely, age, gender, urban/rural residence and schooling – were also found to be highly predictive.

In countries where adult literacy rates are comparatively low, there are significant disparities between – and within – rural and urban areas. Pastoralist and nomadic populations, who number in the tens of millions across the African drylands, the Middle East and parts of Asia, have much lower literacy levels than other rural populations. Indigenous groups, linguistic minorities, migrants and people with disabilities are among populations with lower literacy rates, reflecting exclusion from mainstream society and reduced access to formal education and literacy programmes.

Since the 1980s, concerns about the quality of literacy statistics have gained momentum. Alternative measures incorporate direct assessments that test literacy skills on various scales. They conceive of literacy as a multidimensional phenomenon, embracing several skill domains. Comparative assessments such as the International Adult Literacy Survey, conducted in some twenty developed countries, found that significant proportions of the adult population possessed relatively weak literacy and numeracy skills.

Evidence from direct assessments of literacy show that conventional assessment methods usually overstate actual literacy levels. Several developing countries are designing literacy surveys to provide more accurate knowledge about literacy, including Brazil, China and Botswana. To allow countries to make informed policy decisions, more – and more regular – direct assessments are needed, but they must be relatively simple, rapid and inexpensive to obtain.

Chapter 8

The making of literate societies

Today, more than 80% of the global population over age 15 is reported to possess at least minimal reading and writing skills. This reflects an unprecedented social transformation since the mid-nineteenth century, when only about 10% of the world's adults could read or write. The dramatic increase in adult literacy rates happened despite the quintupling of the world population, from about 1.2 billion in 1850 to over 6.4 billion today.

The spread of formal schooling, well-organized literacy campaigns and policies supporting adult learning opportunities have all played influential roles in enabling people to acquire basic literacy skills. The broader social context is equally powerful: the motivations to become and remain literate are closely related to the quality and variety of the literate environments found at home, at work and in society. Language policies have also had a decisive impact on the spread of literacy.

The expansion of formal schooling is the single most important factor driving the spread of literacy worldwide over the past two centuries, especially during the past fifty years. Its impact spans historical periods and geography. Schools have been, and continue to be, the context in which most people acquire their core literacy skills.

Many countries have also organized mass campaigns to promote literacy, often against a backdrop of nation building, societal transformation and decolonization. Governments of Socialist countries (e.g. the former Soviet Union, China, Viet Nam, Cuba) were particularly active in promoting mass literacy, as were those of some non-Socialist countries (e.g. Thailand, Brazil). The effectiveness of such campaigns in raising literacy rates, however, has varied considerably. Successful campaigns generally involved follow-up initiatives to enrich literate environments and provide adults with continuing learning opportunities.

Widespread literacy can never be considered a won cause. Economic decline and political crisis can lead to stagnation in schooling and literacy, even in countries where educational infrastructures are solid. In addition, pockets of illiteracy persist in most highly literate and schooled societies. International surveys of literacy skills in developed countries reveal that, while most adults perform well, about 10% have substandard skill levels often due to factors such as poverty, low socio-economic status, ill health and disabilities.

Language policies and practices have played, and continue to play, an important role in literacy and the development of literate communities. National language policies – the designation of an official language, the choice of language of instruction in schools and adult learning programmes – can facilitate or hinder language development and literacy acquisition. Research consistently shows that learning to read and write in one's mother tongue enhances access to literacy in other languages. Yet literacy efforts in many countries lack a clear language policy.

Printed and visual materials in households, communities, schools, workplaces and the wider community encourage individuals to become literate and to integrate their skills in everyday life. Comparative studies of academic achievement show that the quantity and use of literacy resources influence achievement levels and literacy proficiency. Policies related to book publishing, the media and access to information play an influential role in developing facilitating environments in which literacy can flourish.

Chapter 9

Good policy, good practice

Literacy is more than a single goal; it is at the centre of the whole EFA endeavour. The Report advocates a three-pronged strategy comprising (a) quality schooling for all children, (b) the scaling up of literacy programmes for youth and adults, and (c) the development of environments conducive to the meaningful use of literacy. Relatively few governments have coherent, long-term national literacy policies encompassing attention to governance, programme design and delivery, human and financial resources and the promotion of an environment in which individuals are encouraged to become literate and to sustain their skills.

Ministries of education have prime responsibility for literacy policy: they are best placed to integrate literacy into education sector strategies, promote lifelong learning, coordinate publicly financed programmes and partnerships, and regulate accreditation systems. In practice, however, responsibility for literacy is often shared by several ministries. Central guidance and coordination has to be dovetailed with local implementation and community ownership.

Initiating literacy campaigns, national programmes and broad partnerships is complex: national, regional and local management structures need to be set up, materials developed, and coordinators and facilitators recruited and trained. Partnerships are very diverse and vital but they are often threatened by fragmentation or even competition. Putting literacy on everyone's agenda, clarifying the roles and responsibilities of different agencies and establishing national coordination mechanisms among and between providers are essential for effective literacy programmes.

Learners' knowledge and wishes should inform adult learning programmes and be their starting point – an axiom that is not applied uniformly. Sensitivity to the adult learner's cultural background, mother tongue and life experience is required. A relevant curriculum that builds on learners' demands and circumstances is conducive to better learning outcomes. It should clearly spell out learning objectives and strike a balance between relevance to local contexts and to wider opportunities. Programmes must have sensible timetables and be sensitive to age and gender issues.

Instructors are vital to the success of literacy programmes, but they are paid little if any regular remuneration, lack job security, have few training opportunities and rarely benefit from ongoing professional support. Unless the professional development of literacy educators and their trainers is taken seriously, progress towards more literate societies will be severely constrained. Training of literacy educators, where it exists, is often in a national or official language while their work is carried out in local ones. Worldwide, conditions of employment for adult literacy educators are very poor, especially compared to those of teachers in formal education. This situation results in frequent turnover, with serious implications for quality.

Distance learning and information and communication technology (ICT) can provide opportunities for informal and non-formal literacy learning by adults, though access to technology is highly uneven in many places. ICT and distance learning have more immediate potential for offering professional development to literacy educators rather than for running programmes per se.

A majority of countries facing salient literacy challenges are linguistically diverse. Decisions on language must balance political and ethnic sensitivity, pedagogical effectiveness, costs and learner preferences. The extra cost of training teachers and developing materials in multiple languages must be weighed against the inefficiency of teaching in languages that learners do not understand. A multilingual policy should also ensure that learners have opportunities to gain literacy skills in a second/official language that may be of wider use.

In many countries, adult literacy programmes represent just 1% of the total national education budget. Policy-makers need to come up with baseline figures for significantly expanding national programmes. Basic costs for good-quality literacy programmes include start-up expenses, training, development and printing of learning materials, payment of literacy educators and operating costs. For a recent sample of twenty-nine literacy programmes, the average cost per learner having completed a programme came to US$68 in sub-Saharan Africa, US$32 in Asia and US$83 in Latin America. Preliminary, broad-brush work suggests that US$26 billion would be required to enable more than 550 million people (nearly half in South and West Asia) to complete a literacy programme of 400 hours. This amounts to at least US$2.5 billion a year from now to 2015, a tall order for countries and the international community.

Chapter 10

Setting priorities for action

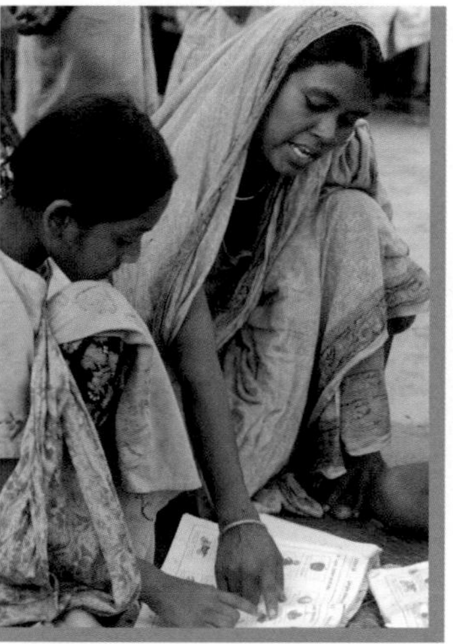

Only ten years are left to achieve the EFA goals. The needs remain enormous at all levels of education, formal and non-formal. Literacy, as this Report argues, must become a cross-cutting political priority at the core of Education for All. If direct measures were used to assess literacy skills, the number of adults with weak or no skills would climb well above the already staggering figure of 771 million as conventionally measured.

This chapter proposes nine areas that require attention if EFA is to be achieved:

1. Sustain attention on achieving good-quality, universal primary education and lower secondary education – abolishing fees, reaching the most disadvantaged, training teachers and implementing low-cost school health and nutrition measures.
2. Recommit to the gender goal.
3. Further increase efficient public spending on education.
4. Move youth and adult literacy up on the national and international agendas.
5. Focus on literate societies, not just on literate individuals.
6. Clearly define government responsibility for youth and adult literacy programmes.
7. Double the aid allocated to basic education to reach US$7 billion.
8. Focus aid on the countries with the greatest educational needs.
9. Complement the flow of funds with analytical and knowledge support.

The groundswell of support for halving the number of people living in extreme poverty in the next decade must translate into long-term commitments that recognize the indispensable role that education – with literacy at its core – plays in bettering the lives of individuals, their communities and nations. ■

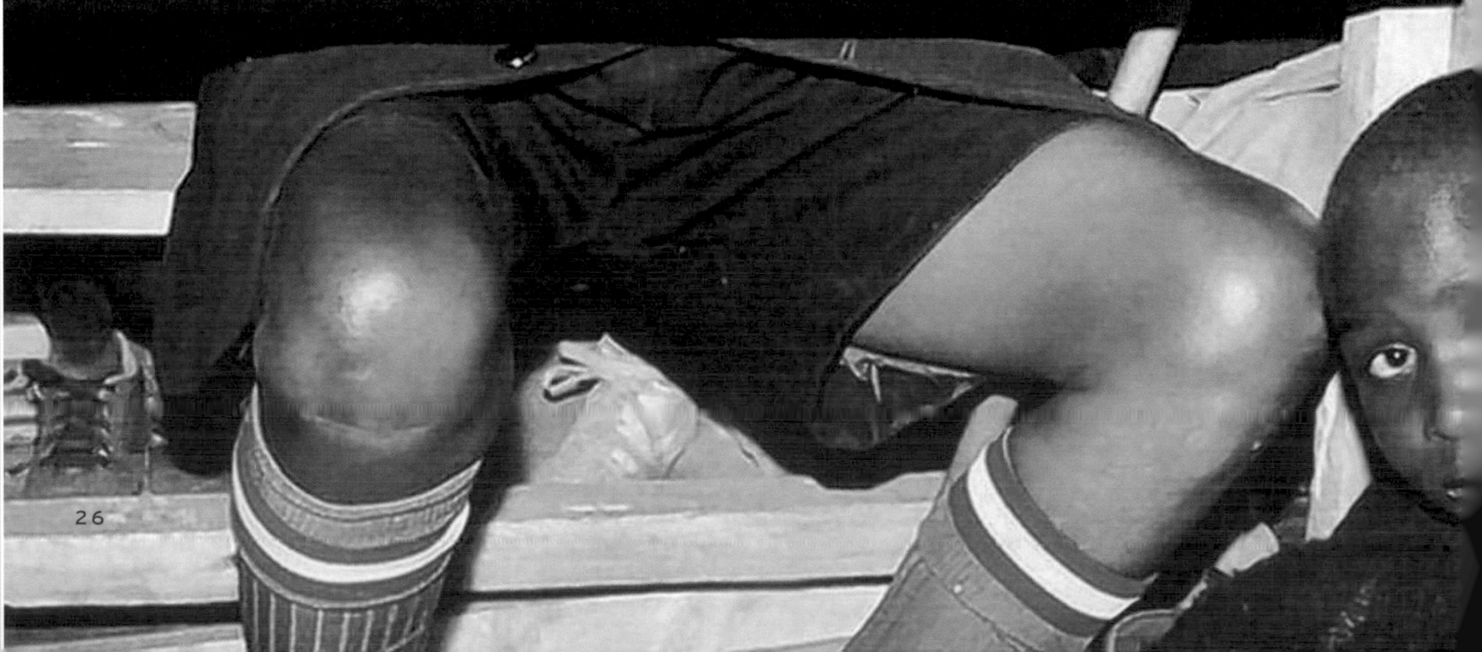

© SIPA / EPA

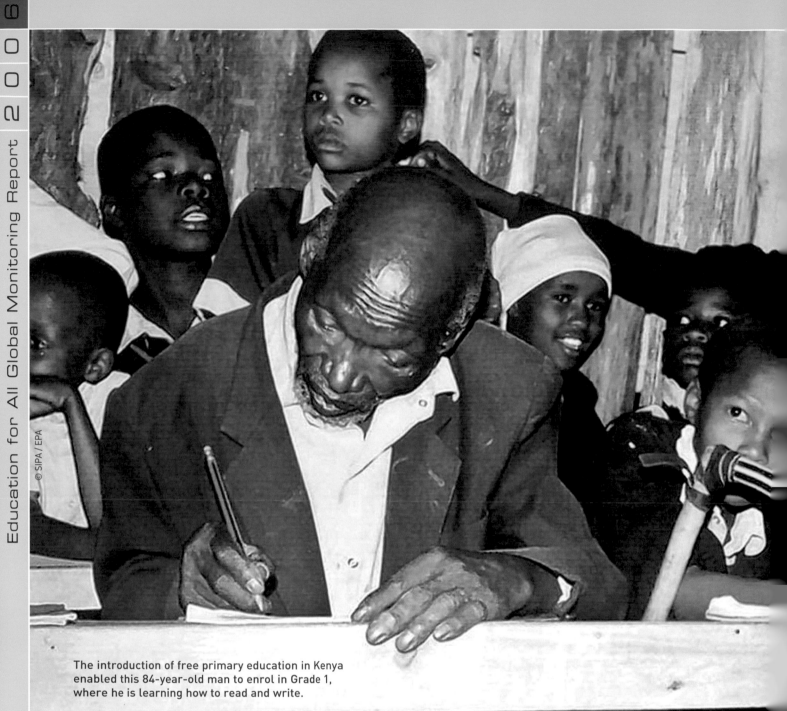

The introduction of free primary education in Kenya enabled this 84-year-old man to enrol in Grade 1, where he is learning how to read and write.

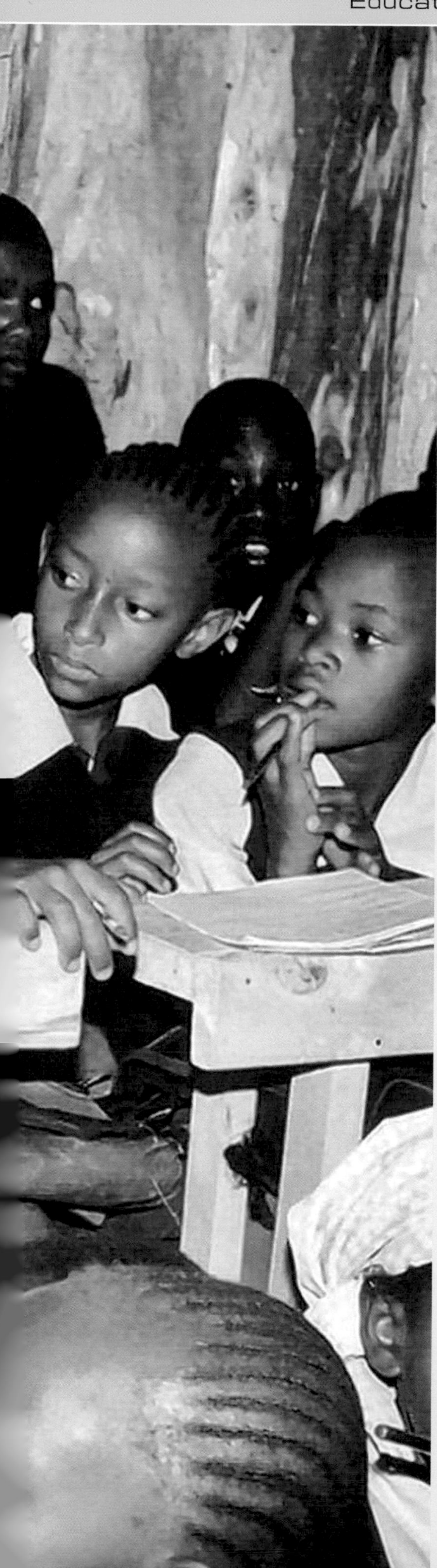

Chapter 1

Literacy: the core of Education for All

This year's *EFA Global Monitoring Report* focuses on literacy, one of the most neglected of the six goals adopted in 2000 by 164 countries at the World Education Forum in Dakar (Senegal). Yet literacy is a human right and at the core of Education for All. Literacy skills are essential in today's knowledge societies, conferring benefits on individuals, communities and nations. This chapter explores some of the reasons for the neglect of literacy, and notes signs of renewed attention. It traces the changing notions of literacy from a narrowly defined concept to one embracing a holistic view of educational development that includes the building of literate societies. Ultimately, literacy's crucial role in achieving each of the other five EFA goals may also provide a key to improving the lives of millions of people living in extreme poverty, and especially women.

A holistic approach to Education for All

Five years after 164 countries agreed on the Dakar Framework for Action, it is time not only to assess progress towards the Education for All goals but also, importantly, to remember that the Framework is not concerned only with universal primary education and gender parity (which are also two of the Millennium Development Goals). Rather, it consists of a set of six goals that, taken together, embrace a holistic conception of educational development (Box 1.1). And yet, since 2000, most attention has been devoted to the three EFA goals that concern the extension and improvement of formal elementary education systems, namely:

The Dakar framework embraces a holistic conception of educational development

- universal primary education (goal 2);
- gender parity (goal 5, the theme of the 2003/4 Report – especially important now, as its first target date was 2005);
- and, more recently, educational quality (goal 6, the theme of the 2005 Report).

The other three EFA goals (goals 1, 3 and 4) have been relatively neglected. Several factors contributed to this neglect.

- Rather than concerning the strengthening of existing formal education systems for school-age children, goals 1, 3 and 4 involve the *creation* of new educational opportunities for very young children (i.e. early childhood care and education), as well as for youth and adults (learning and life-skills programmes, basic and continuing education, and literacy programmes), often through non-formal institutions. As a result, in most countries, implementation responsibility does not fall neatly under the mandate of the Ministry of Education but rather is spread among several ministries.
- National governments and the international community have tended to assume that the political and economic returns from investing in young children, youth and adults are lower than those from investing in school-age children. The resulting neglect has been compounded by the inclusion of only two EFA goals among the Millennium Development Goals and by the decision to limit the Education for All Fast Track Initiative, the only significant multilateral aid vehicle,[1] to universal primary completion.
- The unfounded idea that primary education is more cost effective than youth and adult literacy programmes proved partly a self-fulfilling one. As budget, loan and grant allocations to primary education grew rapidly, adult programmes had their public funding reduced, and responsibility was often transferred from the public sector to non-governmental organizations (NGOs). This reflected a misguided belief that such programmes were the responsibility of NGOs rather than of government, a belief that confused service-delivery mechanisms – in which NGOs play an important role – with broad policy and finance measures, which are the responsibility of government.
- Although the focus on primary education was justified – as this is the principal route to achieving Education for All – it was also limited, for it neglected those who had either not attended school, or who had done so without becoming literate.[2]
- Goals 1, 3 and 4 are difficult to define precisely and are stated in qualitative rather than quantitative terms. Monitoring and measuring progress towards them is thus difficult. For example, early childhood care and education (the theme of next year's Report) potentially includes health, nutrition, education and care interventions, and yet there is no agreed standardized definition. Even more difficult to define, and hence to measure and monitor, are the EFA goals concerned with equitable access to learning and life-skills programmes and to basic and continuing education for all adults (EFA goal 3 and the second part of goal 4). Previous *EFA Global Monitoring Reports* have interpreted these goals differently, and indeed

Box 1.1 The Dakar Framework for

The six EFA Dakar goals

1. Expanding and improving comprehensive early childhood care and education, especially for the most vulnerable and disadvantaged children.
2. Ensuring that by 2015 all children, particularly girls, children in difficult circumstances and those belonging to ethnic minorities, have access to, and complete, free and compulsory primary education of good quality.
3. Ensuring that the learning needs of all young people and adults are met through equitable access to appropriate learning and life-skills programmes.

1. The Fast Track Initiative had been, until recently, exclusively concerned with primary education (see Chapter 4).

2. See Chapter 3. While more schools have been made available, many parents are too poor to afford the costs (direct and indirect) of schooling. In addition, many poor children fail to achieve expected learning outcomes because of poor health, malnutrition, lack of a home or community environment conducive to learning, excessive distance to schools, unfamiliar language of instruction, and so on. Thus, in addition to the children who do not start [illegible] not complete primary education; these will grow up as out-of-school youth and adults, in need of basic education, including literacy skills.

Action and the Millennium Development Goals

4. Achieving a 50 per cent improvement in levels of adult literacy by 2015, especially for women, and equitable access to basic and continuing education for all adults.
5. Eliminating gender disparities in primary and secondary education by 2005, and achieving gender equality in education by 2015, with a focus on ensuring girls' full and equal access to and achievement in basic education of good quality.
6. Improving all aspects of the quality of education and ensuring excellence of all so that recognized and measurable learning outcomes are achieved by all, especially in literacy, numeracy and essential life skills.

Source: UNESCO (2000*b*).

Millennium Development Goals

- Goal 2: Achieve universal primary education.

Target 3: Ensure that by 2015 children everywhere, boys and girls alike, will be able to complete a full course of primary schooling.

- Goal 3: Promote gender equality and empower women.

Target 4: Eliminate gender disparity in primary and secondary education, preferably by 2005, and at all levels of education no later than 2015.

Source: United Nations General Assembly, Resolution A/56/326, 6 September 2001.

Countries have various interpretations of 'life skills', which complicates monitoring

Box 1.2 Interpretation of EFA goals 3 and 4

The interpretation – and hence the monitoring – of EFA goals 3 and 4 has varied (even among past *EFA Global Monitoring Reports*), owing to the lack of consensus over how to define and measure both 'literacy' and 'equitable access to appropriate learning and life-skills programmes'.

Goal 3: Learning and life skills are offered as formal, informal or non-formal programmes. The myriad of institutions delivering programmes follow widely varying guidelines. To limit barriers to access, they all must have flexible options for those groups (which differ in each country) that have been excluded from learning opportunities. Further complicating monitoring is the fact that countries have various interpretations of 'life skills', each prioritizing skills differently. For example, some conceive of life skills as practical and technical skills, others as basic reading and writing skills, and still others as including psycho-social skills. Countries in North America and Western Europe, for instance, tend to emphasize (more than do other countries) critical and conceptual problem-solving skills, considering these to be among the more important skills for everyday life. 'Life skills' can also be interpreted as those tools (e.g. health knowledge) an individual must have in order to change his/her behaviour – raising the question of whether it is the skills or the changes in behaviour that ought to be monitored. In short, a universal interpretation and monitoring of goal 3 has proved elusive.

Goal 4: Traditionally (and in the 2005 Report), two factors set parameters for the literacy rates reported for goal 4: (a) the UNESCO definition of literacy as 'the ability to read and write, with understanding, a short, simple sentence about one's everyday life'; and (b) data on educational attainment. The modes of reporting included self-reporting and head of household responses on surveys, in addition to grade attainment proxy, but this excludes objective measurement, as well as any consideration of the context (see Chapter 7).

The interpretation of terms such as 'learning needs', 'appropriate learning', and 'life skills' can be open to debate, but the essence of goals 3 and 4 concerns equitable access. As such, monitoring these goals should at a minimum involve collecting data on literacy rates and degree of programme participation (enrolment rates) as proxies for equitable access. Future *EFA Global Monitoring Reports* will explore further the monitoring of goals 3 and 4.

Sources: Maurer (2005), OECD (2005*b*).

there are many different understandings of them (Box 1.2); the Report team intends to develop appropriate ways to monitor these important but imprecise goals, consistent with growing interest in this goal among developing countries. In Senegal, for instance, a lively public debate resulted in 2004 in the Éducation qualifiante des jeunes et des adultes (Programme of Skills Development for Youth and Adults) (Box 1.3).

Box 1.3 Senegal's Éducation qualifiante des jeunes et des adultes

In Senegal, the Programme of Skills Development for Youth and Adults (EQJA) seeks to more clearly delineate EFA goal 3, so as to promote equity and much-needed socio-economic integration for groups excluded from literacy opportunities. In light of Senegal's limited experience with educational provision for out-of-school youth and adults, the Ministry of Education, the UNESCO International Institute for Educational Planning (IIEP) and UNESCO's Division of Secondary, Technical and Vocational Education have begun with a coordination centre external to Senegal's Department of Educational Planning and Reform, to gather opinions of various programme partners.

An initial study of programmes targeting three groups – female professionals (in the food and agricultural sector); youth in *daaras* (Koranic schools); and apprentices and those not yet apprenticed – helped to define the initiatives' relevance for a variety of excluded learners. The initial investigation revealed the need for the programmes to pay attention also to factors such as age, gender, data collection, data publication on the Internet and partnerships. The UNESCO/IIEP support particularly targets, and tries to find solutions for, youths who are not apprentices. A key strength of the EQJA lies in its network of partners across sectors, including craftspeople representatives, administrations, local authorities, associations and donors.

Source: Delluc (2005).

Literacy for rights, capabilities and development

As noted above, the special theme of this year's Report is literacy, which is also the object of the first part of goal 4.

Defining literacy

No standard international definition of literacy captures all its facets. Indeed there are numerous different understandings of literacy, some of which are even contradictory.[3] While recognizing that other understandings help illuminate other dimensions, this Report adopts, as its working definition, UNESCO's (1978) definition of 'functional literacy': 'A person is functionally literate who can engage in all those activities in which literacy is required for effective functioning of his group and community and also for enabling him to continue to use reading, writing and calculation for his own and the community's development.' In this Report, therefore, 'literacy' refers to a context-bound continuum of reading, writing and numeracy skills, acquired and developed through processes of learning and application, in schools and in other settings appropriate to youth and adults.

Even with such a pragmatic definition, there is no standard, internationally comparable measurement of literacy; as Chapter 6 also makes clear, the literacy rates reported by the *EFA Global Monitoring Report* are among the weaker international education statistics. There are, moreover, two further problems with the wording of the literacy goal. First, it ignores the crucial question of language (i.e. literacy in which language?).[4] Second, there is a definitional problem with the precise wording of the goal: strictly speaking, a 50% improvement in levels of literacy is impossible for countries with literacy rates already above 67%. This Report therefore pragmatically interprets the goal as implying a 50% reduction in *illiteracy* rates, consistent with the wording and intentions of the 1990 Jomtien World Conference on Education for All that initiated the entire Education for All movement.[5]

Today, by conventional measurements, some 771 million adults are illiterate, two-thirds of them women.[6] This is – for a fifth of the world's adult population – a serious violation of human rights. It also constitutes a major impediment to the realization of human capabilities and the achievement of equity and of economic and social development, particularly for women.

The benefits of literacy

Being literate adds value to a person's life. Literacy can be instrumental in the pursuit of development – at personal, family and community levels, as well as at macro-levels of nations, regions and the world.

A child denied the right to a quality primary education is deprived not only as a child: he/she is also handicapped for life – unable to cope with situations requiring reading, writing and arithmetic – unless given access to educational opportunities as a youth or adult. A lack of literacy is strongly correlated with poverty – both in an economic sense and in the broader sense of a deprivation of capabilities. Literacy strengthens the capabilities of individuals, families and communities to access health, educational, political, economic and cultural opportunities and services. The literacy of women and girls is of crucial importance to the issue of gender inequality. While the benefits accruing from women's formal education are well understood, less well known are those accruing from women's non-formal

3. See Chapter 6.

4. The language question is extensively analysed in Chapters 6, 8 and 9.

5. The Framework for Action to Meet Basic Learning Needs (agreed to at Jomtien, Thailand, 1990) called for the 'reduction of the adult illiteracy rate to one-half its 1990 level by the year 2000.'

6. [illegible] monitoring, literacy is not easy. Chapter 7 discusses this; Chapters 2 and 7 present basic data on world literacy, both for today and historically.

education; literacy contributes positively to women's empowerment, in terms of self-esteem, economic independence and social emancipation. Many women who have benefited from adult basic and literacy education have spoken of feeling a sense of personal empowerment as a result.

Indeed, literacy is at the core of education and especially Education for All with its focus on basic education. Literacy helps people understand decontextualized information and language, verbal as well as written. As such, it paves the way for further learning and, as stated in Article 1 of the World Declaration on Education for All[7] (Jomtien, Thailand, 1990) and reiterated in Dakar (Senegal, 2000), literacy and numeracy are essential learning tools of basic education. The United Nations Literacy Decade (2003–2012) was launched because 'literacy for all is at the heart of basic education for all ... [and] creating literate environments and societies is essential for achieving the goals of eradicating poverty, reducing child mortality, curbing population growth, achieving gender equality and ensuring sustainable development, peace and democracy' (United Nations, 2002*b*).

Literacy is also important for achieving the other EFA goals. Mothers who are educated are more likely to send their children to school than those who have not attended school (Schultz, 1993; Comings et al., 1992). The same is true of parents who have participated in adult literacy programmes. Children's school attendance increased when their parents attended literacy classes in Bangladesh (Cawthera, 1997) and Nepal (Burchfield, 1997). Literate parents are more likely to be able to support their children in practical ways, such as meeting with teachers and discussing progress with their children, as seen in Nepal (Burchfield et al., 2002*a*) and Uganda (Carr-Hill et al., 2001). When literacy courses instruct parents on ways of helping children in school and inform them about the content of the curriculum, the children's education benefit is even greater, as seen in Nepal, South Africa and Turkey (Bekman, 1998; Oxenham, 2004*a*).

It is important to note, however, that these effects are not automatic, but result only when literate individuals are able to exercise their literacy, which requires that broader development and rights policies are in effect and implemented. Indeed, literacy per se is not the sole solution to social ills such as poverty, malnutrition and unemployment, though it is one factor in helping to overcome them.

The right to literacy

Literacy is a right, indeed an essential part of the right of every individual to education, as recognized in the Universal Declaration of Human Rights.[8] It is also a means to achieving other human rights. Those who can use literacy skills to defend their legal rights have a significant advantage over those who cannot. Indeed, it is often the poorest, most socially excluded and least literate individuals (especially women) whose rights are violated by those with more power. Their inability to read, write and calculate keeps them from knowing what they are entitled to, and how to demand it. It limits their ability to participate politically in society. It denies them a voice.

Literacy is a right, indeed an essential part of the right of every individual to education

A renewed emphasis on literacy?

There are signs that literacy is receiving increased attention. As noted above, the United Nations has declared 2003–2012 as the Literacy Decade. The World Bank has in recent years prepared various papers on adult literacy. In addition to international organizations, some governments have recently begun to devote increasing attention to literacy (Box 1.4), joining countries such as Bangladesh, China and India, all of which achieved considerable results in the 1990s.

Literate individuals and literate societies

The Education for All goals and the MDGs concerned with education are expressed in terms of individuals; indeed the literacy part of goal 4 is framed in terms of a quantitative increase in literacy rates. However, education – and literacy within it – does not concern only individuals, as a rights and capabilities framework alone might suggest; it also has a critical social dimension. The types of educational inputs (e.g. material and human resources), outcomes (e.g. reading, writing and numeracy skills), and processes (e.g. curricula, teaching and learning methods) that are relevant to individuals are very much influenced by the social context. Moreover, the degree to which a society enables, promotes and sustains educational outcomes has an overwhelming impact on the demand for, and the value of, these skills.

A 'literate society', then, is more than a society with high literacy rates; rather, it is one 'in which

7. 'Every person – child, youth and adult – shall be able to benefit from educational opportunities designed to meet their basic learning needs. These needs comprise both essential learning tools (such as literacy, oral expression, numeracy and problem solving) and the basic learning content (such as knowledge, skills, values and attitudes) required by human beings to be able to survive, to develop their full capacities, to live and work in dignity, to participate fully in development, to improve the quality of their lives, to make informed decisions, and to continue learning' (World Declaration on Education for All, 1990).

8. Treaty bodies and international and domestic jurisprudence have gone some way to elaborating the requirements – and outlining violations – of the right of all humans to education. As Chapter 5 will show, the right to education is in most cases explicitly or implicitly linked to the right to literacy.

Box 1.4 A renewed attention to literacy

Recent national developments, consistent with the United Nation's Literacy Decade, include:

- Brazil's 2003 launch of an accelerated Literacy Brazil Programme, with significant involvement of local governments and NGOs;
- Burkina Faso's establishment of a national fund for literacy and non-formal education in 2001, and of a Ministry for Literacy and Non-formal Education in 2002;
- Indonesia's 2004 launch of a national literacy movement by the President;
- Morocco's 2002 creation of a State Secretariat for Literacy and Non-formal Education;
- Mozambique's re-establishment of a national directorate for adult literacy in 2000, followed by the launch of a new adult literacy strategy;
- Nicaragua's increasing the share of adult education in the overall education budget from 1.5% in 2000 to 2.2% in 2002;
- Rwanda's moving responsibility for adult literacy to the Ministry of Education in 2004, inventorying of available literacy resources, and outlining of a new literacy policy and strategy;
- Senegal's continuing strong commitment to a private-public partnership approach (called 'faire-faire') to promote adult literacy;
- Venezuela's 2003 launch of the intensive Misión Robinson campaign to extend literacy to all youth and adults and education at least through Grade 6 to all children.

Many of the examples summarized in this box are developed in Chapter 9.

important aspects of social life such as economics, law, science, and government … form what we may call "textual institutions"' (Olson and Torrance, 2001). These institutions should be responsive to the developmental needs and priorities of citizens; and, in turn, the acquisition and use of literacy skills should enable citizens to actively participate in these institutions. As such, 'an understanding of literacy must include how individuals and groups adopt and utilize writing in the pursuit of their goals … [but also how they] come to terms with such textual practices of the dominant (textual) institutions … [B]eing able to read and write a contract is worthless unless there are institutions such as courts to enforce them' (Olson and Torrance, 2001). Box 1.5 gives three examples of countries that have, in different ways, succeeded in creating literate societies.

Though the notion of a literate society is highly context-specific, as Box 1.5 shows, some common lessons have emerged. First, literate societies should enable individuals and groups to acquire, develop, sustain and use relevant literacy skills. This has generally been achieved through a combination of three strategies,[9] which necessarily involve each of the six EFA goals:

- Enabling children to acquire literacy though *basic schooling of good quality*: The principal route to achieving literacy is through quality primary schools in which learning takes place. This requires getting all children – girls as well as boys – into primary schools, ensuring gender parity and equity in initial access to schools,[10] continued enrolment and educational

Box 1.5 Creating literate societies:

Japan

Japan is a highly literate society with near universal literacy rates and a strong sustaining environment. Over its long history (more than one and a half millennia), Japanese literacy evolved in several steps of adapting imported letters. The art of writing first came to Japan in the form of *kanji*, or written Chinese. Over the course of several centuries, a new script called *kana* evolved, in a move to simplify the Chinese characters into sounds, rather than meanings. By the sixteenth century, when the Japanese first learned of Western-style alphabetic letters, a mixed *kanji-kana* orthography was firmly in place. Deliberate interventions for standardizing and simplifying written Japanese were numerous, especially after contacts with the West intensified in the nineteenth century and elements of the Roman alphabet were integrated into Japanese script. However, the alphabetic script has never been adopted and the old systems never fully discarded.

Nevertheless, with new word processing and information and communication technologies, alphabetic letters must now be considered an indispensable part of Japanese literacy. The electronic media in Japan have thus both promoted the alphabet and reinforced the traditional writing system.

The Japanese experience suggests two things: first, that writing systems evolve not just according to practical needs for recording and retrieving information, but also in response to other requirements, such as social control; second, that 'literacy' does not mean simply knowing a script. In Japan, several scripts are involved, each in its proper place; and, as such, the system continues to be too complex for universal literacy to be sustained in the absence of intensive schooling.

[illegible] about these strategies.

10. See the 2003/4 Report, which focused on goal 2: Gender parity and equity in schooling.

Japan, Cuba and Germany

Cuba

In 1961, the Cuban literacy campaign aimed to (a) extend primary education to all children of school age in order to eradicate future illiteracy, (b) wage a national literacy campaign, and (c) wage a post-literacy campaign to prevent relapse into illiteracy through disuse and to introduce systematic lifelong education. In a single year, more than 700,000 people (in a country of only 7.5 million) became literate.

Fuelled by a social-justice-based orientation, the campaign provided many schoolrooms: 10,000 were opened in a single day, and qualified unemployed teachers were assigned to them, together with thousands of well-educated young people who responded to the revolutionary call to serve anywhere (e.g. in remote mountainous areas to which access was difficult) as volunteer teachers. In addition, parents, neighbours, community organizers, and the pupils and teachers themselves helped improvise premises and rudimentary furniture.

Today, free from illiteracy (as Fidel Castro declared in December 1961), Cuba's schools are quite different; the teaching staff is well qualified and universal schooling is guaranteed. Moreover, a strong 'literate environment' has been set in place, with resources for sustaining and developing literacy, and the use of information and communication technologies (mainly through radio, television and video).

Germany

Germany has never been linguistically homogeneous. Yet, in the sixteenth century, a variety of High German began to be dominant, following the shift of the economic centres to the south. Only in the second half of the nineteenth century, with the massive redistribution of the population following industrialization and mass urbanization, did a universally spoken variety of High German come into use. This process was then accelerated in the past century by the electronic mass media – first radio, and then television.

Two factors greatly propelled the development of literacy in Germany: nationalization of culture (which established High German as the official language of administration, education beyond elementary school, and – along with Latin – the Church and literature), and public control of schooling (which, though mainly concentrated on reading, included, towards the end of the seventeenth century, bookkeeping and greater use of writing in activities such as journal and letter writing).

In the nineteenth century, use of Latin diminished, and a German orthography was established and officially regulated. Following enforced compulsory schooling in the latter half of the nineteenth century, literacy rates, by the early twentieth century, reached 90% to 95% of the population. Key to the accomplishment of such high literacy rates was the introduction of a writing system based upon both national language knowledge and local oral varieties. While the more formal uses of High German allow access to literate structures, regional varieties of High German remain in use.

Sources: Coulmas (2001) and Maas (2001), in Olson and Torrance (2001); Keeble (2001).

School today does not solve the problem of achieving literacy for all children

outcomes, and improving the quality of education[11] in these schools (both directly and indirectly, through, for instance, EFA goal 1 – early childhood care and education programmes that enable children from disadvantaged backgrounds to enter primary school well prepared).

- Enabling youth and adults to acquire and develop literacy (including in response to demand for new literacy skills) through *youth and adult literacy programmes*: School today does not solve the problem of achieving literacy for all children and, even less so, for the great number of youth and adults who have been denied basic literacy skills, or who – though having learned to read, write and calculate – are either unable to use their literacy skills or have lost them over time. EFA goals 3 and 4 emphasize the need to provide literacy programmes and adult education/training schemes in response to these challenges.
- Developing *environments in which literacy can flourish* and where its value is recognized by individuals, households, schools and communities.

11. See the 2005 Report, which focused on goal 6: Quality of schooling, especially at the primary level.

Second, literate societies should provide and develop literacy that is of relevance to citizens, communities and the nation, and, at the same time, acknowledge the diverse needs and priorities of different groups – particularly those who are disadvantaged and excluded.[12] Provision and development of literacy should be built on:

- cautious response to demand for literacy, taking into account such factors as gender, age, rural and urban circumstances, levels of motivation and language;
- careful language decisions – including ensuring an orthography that reflects the oral competence of the readers and builds on solid foundations of initial literacy in the mother tongue;
- an appropriate curriculum and teaching/learning methods;
- a well-defined national literacy policy, which addresses issues including languages, books, and other media and information.

Literacy is thus at the core of Education for All, and the implied necessity of developing literate societies provides a link between all six goals. Literacy is simultaneously an outcome (e.g. reading, writing and numeracy), a process (e.g. taught and learned through formal schooling, non-formal programmes or informal networks), and an input (paving the way to: further cognitive skill development; participation in lifelong learning opportunities, including technical and vocational education and training, and continuing education; better education for children; and broader societal developments).

Literate societies should provide and develop literacy that is of relevance to citizens, communities and the nation

Outline of the Report

This *EFA Global Monitoring Report*:

- assesses progress (as have previous Reports) towards the six EFA goals around the world, especially among developing and transitional countries, finding that progress is steady but insufficient if the goals are to be achieved, especially in sub-Saharan Africa, South and West Asia, and the Arab States (Chapter 2);
- examines national commitments to achieve EFA – particularly by looking at national plans, national financing and teacher policies – and reviews crucial issues for achieving EFA, notably policies of inclusion (especially of girls and women), dealing with instability (whether caused by conflict or economic factors), establishing safe and healthy schools in which children can learn, and adapting to the HIV/AIDS pandemic (Chapter 3);
- reviews international commitments to finance EFA in light of the pledge in the Dakar Framework for Action that that 'no countries seriously committed to education for all will be thwarted in their achievement of this goal by a lack of resources', finding that even the various pledges of increased aid made during 2005 – particularly the commitments at the G8 summit in Gleneagles – are still likely to fall short of what is needed (Chapter 4);
- summarizes the crucial importance of literacy, as both a human right and in terms of its contributions to economic and social development (Chapter 5);

12. See Chapter 7 for an overview of such groups.

- argues that there is value in understanding 'literacy' not only as a set of reading, writing and numeracy skills, but also as a set of skills that are socially relevant in terms of the ways they are acquired and applied (or 'practised') (Chapter 6); as discussed above, the goal is thus not only literacy skills for individuals, but also literate societies, which support and are supported by the development and use of these skills;
- summarizes data available on the state of literacy around the world, based on conventional monitoring efforts, which tend to focus on the relative presence or absence of literacy skills in individuals (Chapter 7);
- goes beyond these data to examine the conditions and determinants of literacy, by placing them in a social context, arguing that the creation of rich and dynamic 'literate environments' is a key factor in promoting literacy (both for individuals and societies) (Chapter 8);
- with the ultimate goal of establishing literate societies as its starting point, proposes a three-pronged approach to literacy policy that integrates the expansion (and a renewed commitment to the quality) of schooling, the development of youth and adult literacy programmes, and the promotion and sustaining of rich literate environments (Chapter 9); and
- concludes by summarizing some priority activities, at national and international levels, if the EFA goals, especially literacy, are to be achieved in the ten years that remain until 2015 (Chapter 10). ■

© REUTERS

© UNESCO / Victor Manuel Camacho Victoria

© EPA SIPA

© REUTERS

Chapter 2

EFA progress: where do we stand?

This chapter assesses progress towards the Education for All goals, using the most recent global education data, for the 2002/2003 school year. What has happened since the World Education Forum held in Dakar in 2000? Is there evidence that the goal of gender parity in primary and secondary education is being met in 2005? Is the world on track to achieve Education for All by 2015?

After summarizing the global picture in 2002 as compared to 1998, the chapter examines (a) trends in early childhood care and education; (b) progress towards universal primary education, including the continuing challenge of children out of school; (c) the global increase in participation in secondary and tertiary education; (d) recent assessments of the outcomes of formal schooling; and (e) the evolution of adult literacy rates. In each section, special attention is paid to gender. The final section summarizes overall progress through the EFA Development Index. In addition, it uses projections to analyse country prospects of achieving by 2015 the goals of universal primary education, gender parity in primary and secondary education, and increased levels of adult literacy.

Education: the global story, 1998–2002

A good synthetic measure of enrolment patterns and hence of the evolution of the world education system can be obtained by combining enrolment ratios by age at the different levels of the education system. The resulting indicator, school life expectancy (SLE), represents the average number of years of schooling that individuals can expect to receive.[1]

1. Caution is required in interpreting SLE. Like gross enrolment ratios, it is sensitive to the extent of grade repetition. In at least twenty countries, repetition contributes more than one year to SLE – up to two years in Algeria, Brazil, Gabon, Rwanda and Togo (UNESCO Institute for Statistics, 2004).

Table 2.1: School life expectancy by region in 2002 and change since 1998

	School life expectancy, in years 2002			Change 1998–2002		
	Total	Male	Female	Total	Male	Female
World	10.5	10.8	10.2	+0.7	+0.5	+0.8
Developing countries	9.9	10.3	9.4	+0.8	+0.6	+0.9
Developed countries	16.1	15.2	16.6	+0.4	-0.2	+0.5
Countries in transition	12.6	12.4	12.8	+0.7	+0.6	+0.7
Sub-Saharan Africa	7.8	8.5	7.0	+1.1	+1.1	+1.0
Arab States	10.2	10.7	9.6	+0.4	+0.2	+0.5
Central Asia	11.5	11.6	11.4	+0.7	+0.6	+0.7
East Asia and the Pacific	11.2	11.3	11.0	+1.0	+0.9	+1.1
South and West Asia	9.1	9.7	8.4	+0.6	+0.3	+1.0
Latin America and the Caribbean	13.1	12.8	13.3	+1.0	+0.7	+1.1
North America and Western Europe	16.4	15.3	17.0	+0.2	-0.5	+0.4
Central and Eastern Europe	12.8	12.8	12.8	+1.0	+0.9	+1.0

Source: Statistical annex, Table 4.

Table 2.1 displays regional averages of school life expectancy from primary to tertiary education in 2002 and changes since 1998. The world average is 10.5 years – 9.4 years of primary and secondary education and 1.1 years of post-secondary education. A child in sub-Saharan Africa can expect to attend school for an average of five to nine fewer years than one in Western Europe or the Americas. Children in South and West Asia and in the Arab States also have much lower educational prospects. Significant variations occur within regions; in sub-Saharan Africa and the Arab States, there is a more than fourfold difference between the countries with the highest and lowest school life expectancy (see statistical annex, Table 4).

Overall, the world's children gained 0.7 years of school life expectancy between 1998 and 2002. Encouragingly, progress was greatest in sub-Saharan Africa with 1.1 years, followed by Central and Eastern Europe, East Asia and the Pacific, and Latin America and the Caribbean with a year each. North America and Western Europe, with the highest SLE, experienced the lowest increase (0.2 years).

Early childhood care and education

Early childhood care and education (ECCE) consists of a range of programmes, all aimed at the physical, cognitive and social development

Figure 2.1: Gross and net enrolment ratios in pre-primary education, 2002

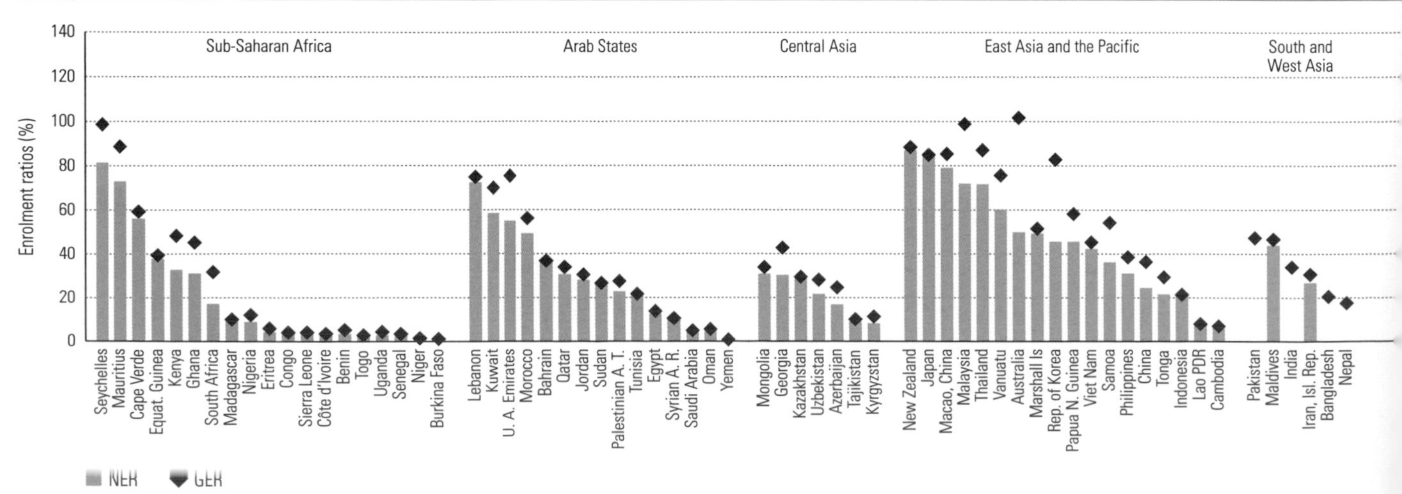

Note: Only countries that have an NER below 95% and for which both the GER and the NER are available (with the exception of Bangladesh, India, Nepal and Pakistan) are displayed. See source table for detailed country notes.
Source: Statistical annex, Table 3.

of children from birth up to their entrance in primary school. The provision of ECCE varies greatly among countries in terms of content, age groups covered, duration in years and number of hours attended. It has yet to become a public policy priority in some countries, which see it as a domain for private initiative. By contrast, at least one year of pre-primary education is compulsory in countries as diverse as Denmark, Israel, Latvia, Myanmar, the Netherlands, the Republic of Moldova and ten Latin American and Caribbean nations (see Umayahara, 2005, and UNESCO-OREALC, 2004).

Monitoring ECCE

The education component of ECCE programmes discussed here is based on pre-primary education data that have been included in UNESCO's surveys of education since the late 1950s. Pre-primary education is defined as level 0 of the International Standard Classification of Education[2] (ISCED) and is normally designed for children aged 3 and above. It constitutes the formal component of ECCE. Monitoring the childhood care component of ECCE is more difficult, as data are scarce. This section focuses on changes in participation in pre-primary education between 1998 and 2002, complementing the discussion of quality in ECCE programmes in the 2005 Report and paving the way for a comprehensive analysis of ECCE, which will be the theme of the 2007 Report.

Participation in pre-primary education

Participation in pre-primary education varies widely both among and within the EFA regions. Figure 2.1, displaying gross enrolment ratios (GERs) and net enrolment ratios (NERs), demonstrates this point. The GER is the ratio of all children enrolled at a given level of education to the population of children in the age range typically covered by that level (e.g. ages 3-5 for pre-primary and 6-11 for primary education). Because it includes younger children who enrol early and older children who enrol late or repeat grades, it can exceed 100%. The NER takes into account only children in the official age range.

Pre-primary education is well developed in most North American and European countries and in several countries of Latin America and the Caribbean and of East Asia and the Pacific. By contrast, it is underdeveloped in sub-Saharan Africa, where the median GER is below 10%, and in the Arab States (median GER about 18%), Central Asia (29%) and South and West Asia (32%) (see statistical annex, Table 3).

Progress between 1998 and 2002 was limited (Figure 2.2). The GER even decreased significantly in several countries, notably Bangladesh, Brunei Darussalam, Iraq, Kuwait, Morocco and the Palestinian Autonomous Territories. On the positive side, sharp increases in the GER (by more than ten percentage points) were observed in countries as diverse as the Islamic Republic of Iran, Panama, Papua New Guinea and the United

Participation in pre-primary education varies widely both among and within the EFA regions

2. See glossary for explanation.

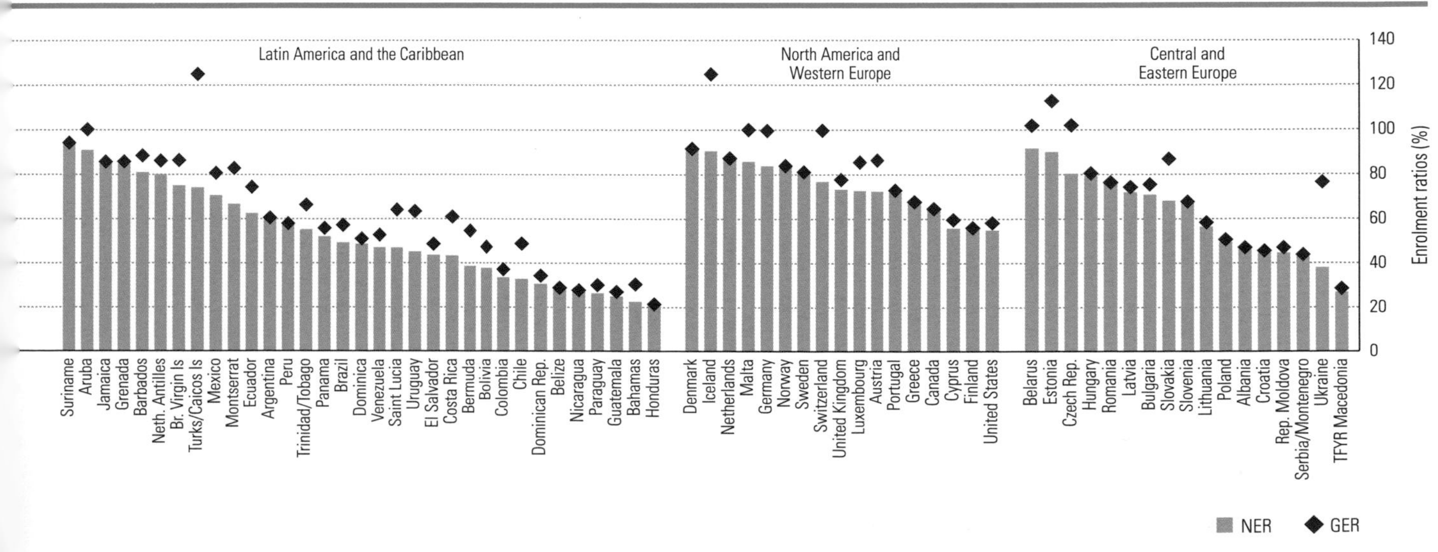

Arab Emirates. India, where efforts are being made to expand the pre-primary facilities through the Integrated Child Development Services and several other programmes, particularly in rural areas (Govinda and Biswal, 2005*a*), also made notable progress, with its GER increasing from 19.5% to 34%.

Gender disparities in ECCE

Gender disparities in pre-primary enrolment (Table 2.2), as measured by the gender parity index (GPI), are less pronounced than at other levels of education. In all countries for which data are available in the Arab States, and Central and

Figure 2.2: Change in gross enrolment ratios in pre-primary education between 1998 and 2002

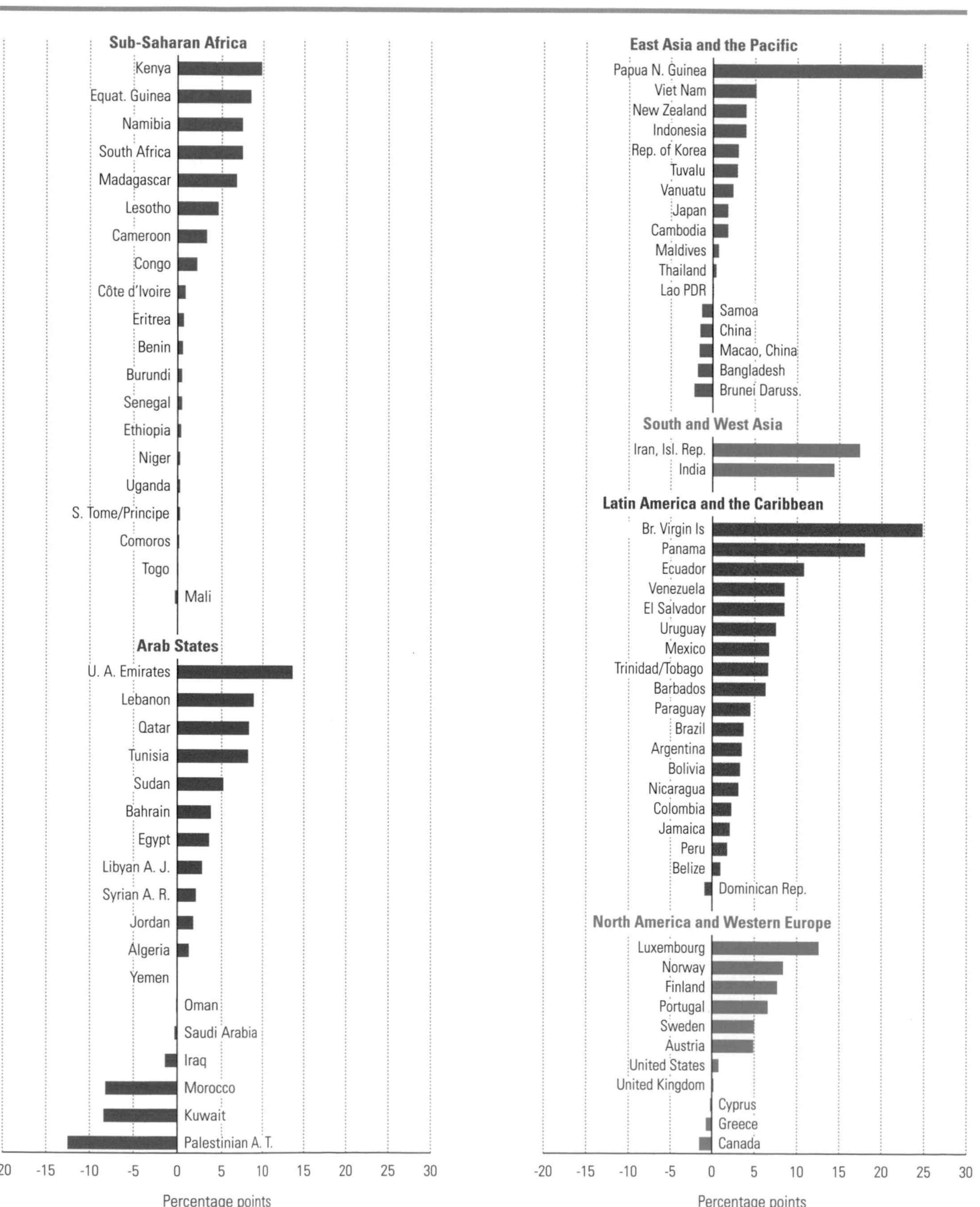

Note: Only countries with a GER below 90% in both years are displayed. See source table for detailed country notes.
Source: Statistical annex, Table 3.

Eastern Europe, boys predominate, while girls predominate in many countries of East Asia and the Pacific, Latin America and the Caribbean and in sub-Saharan Africa. Particularly low GPIs (below 0.90) characterize Morocco, Oman and Sudan, in the Arab States region, and Nepal and Pakistan, in South Asia, though some of them have made significant progress since 1998. Morocco's GPI increased from 0.52 in 1998 to 0.62 in 2002 (though it is still the lowest in the table) and Nepal's from 0.73 to 0.86 (see statistical annex, Table 3).

Primary education

Worldwide, progress towards universal primary education (UPE) has been slow since Dakar – the global NER in primary education increased by only one percentage point, from 83.6% in 1998 to 84.6% in 2002 (Table 2.3). There are still nearly 100 million children of primary school age who are not enrolled in primary schools, and quality remains a major issue worldwide, as discussed in the 2005 Report. Most of sub-Saharan Africa, South and West Asia, and the Arab States still combine low participation with insufficient school supply. At the same time, though, these are the regions where enrolment ratios have been increasing most rapidly and there is evidence that the gender gap is narrowing, albeit too slowly to reach the Dakar goal of parity in primary and secondary school enrolment by 2005.

Access to primary education

Assuring timely access of all children to the first grade is crucial if UPE is to be achieved by 2015. Intake rates provide a measure of access. The gross intake rate (GIR) is the total number of new entrants into the first grade of primary education, regardless of age, expressed as a percentage of the population at the official primary-school entrance age. It can be higher than 100% if younger or older enrolment ages are frequent. The net intake rate (NIR) includes only entrants who are of the official entrance age, and is thus a more accurate measure of timely access to primary schooling.[3]

A wide discrepancy between the two indicators implies that rules defining the official entrance age are not rigidly enforced or that obstacles to access exist, such as high costs or an inadequate supply of schools. GIRs well above 100% are the

Table 2.2: Gender parity index of gross enrolment ratios in pre-primary education, 2002

Disparities in favour of boys (34 countries)		Disparities in favour of girls (29 countries)	
Countries	GPI (F/M)	Countries	GPI (F/M)
Sub-Saharan Africa			
Comoros	0.91	Uganda	1.04
Burkina Faso	0.92	Zimbabwe	1.04
Lesotho	0.94	C. A. R.	1.05
Nigeria	0.94	Guinea-Bissau	1.05
Benin	0.95	Congo	1.06
Seychelles	0.96	Senegal	1.10
		S. Tome/Principe	1.11
		Namibia	1.30
Arab States			
Morocco	0.62		
Oman	0.84		
Sudan	0.86		
Qatar	0.92		
Jordan	0.93		
Yemen	0.93		
Saudi Arabia	0.94		
Syrian A. R.	0.94		
Bahrain	0.94		
Egypt	0.95		
Palestinian A. T.	0.96		
Libyan A. J.	0.96		
Central Asia			
Uzbekistan	0.94	Georgia	1.06
Tajikistan	0.94	Armenia	1.07
Kyrgyzstan	0.95	Mongolia	1.14
East Asia and the Pacific			
China	0.92	Philippines	1.04
Papua N. Guinea	0.93	Lao PDR	1.05
Viet Nam	0.94	Cambodia	1.05
Macao, China	0.95	Malaysia	1.08
		Indonesia	1.09
		Palau	1.12
		Tuvalu	1.16
		Tonga	1.21
		Niue	1.23
		Samoa	1.24
South and West Asia			
Nepal	0.86	Bangladesh	1.07
Pakistan	0.88	Iran, Isl. Rep.	1.12
Latin America and the Caribbean			
St Kitts/Nevis	0.90	Jamaica	1.05
Br. Virgin Is	0.95	Honduras	1.05
		El Salvador	1.06
		Belize	1.07
		Saint Lucia	1.14
North America and Western Europe			
Germany	0.95	Greece	1.04
Central and Eastern Europe			
Turkey	0.94		
Latvia	0.94		
Russian Fed.	0.94		
Slovenia	0.96		

Note: Countries at gender parity (GPI of 0.97 to 1.03) are not included. See source table for detailed country notes.
Source: Statistical annex, Table 3.

Assuring timely access of all children to the first grade is crucial if UPE is to be achieved by 2015

3. However where the official entrance age is not actually the most frequent entrance age, the NIR can seriously underestimate access.

Figure 2.3: Gross and net intake rates in primary education, 2002

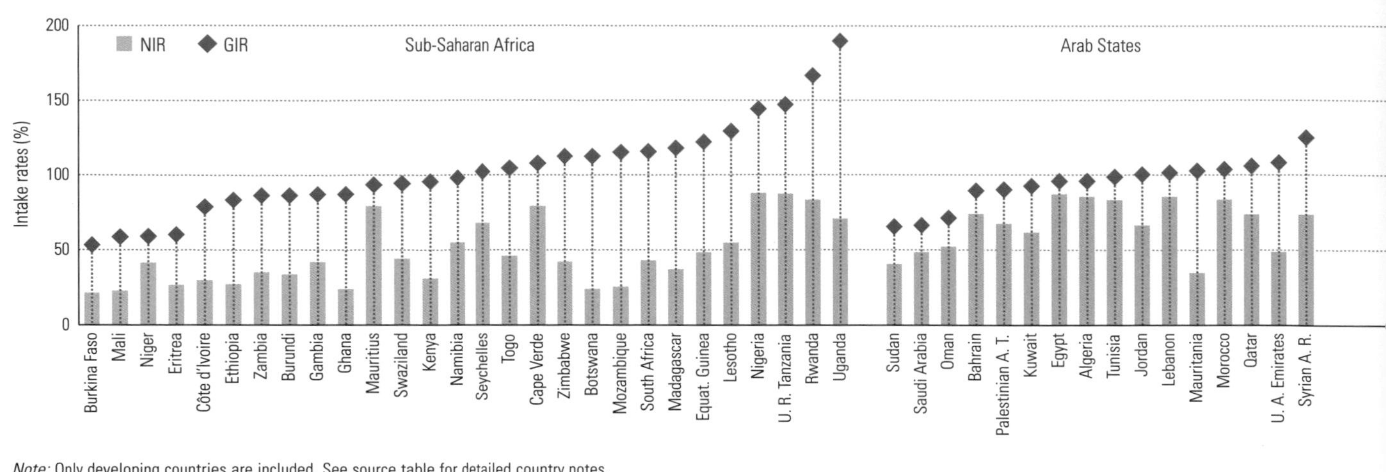

Note: Only developing countries are included. See source table for detailed country notes.
Source: Statistical annex, Table 4.

Figure 2.4: New entrants into primary education: distribution by age group, 2002

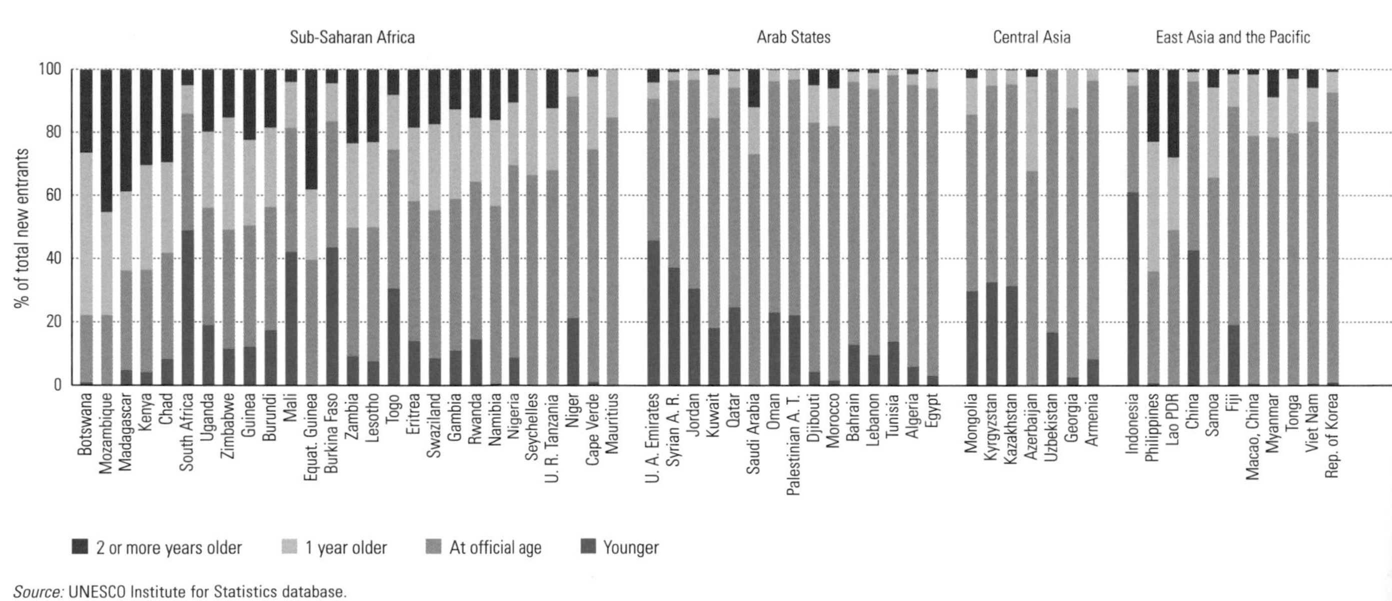

Source: UNESCO Institute for Statistics database.

rule rather than the exception (Figure 2.3). It is quite common for a country to combine a GIR above 100% with an NIR below 50%, particularly in sub-Saharan Africa (e.g. Botswana, Equatorial Guinea, Madagascar, Mozambique, South Africa, Togo and Zimbabwe), but also in some Arab States (e.g. Mauritania and the United Arab Emirates) and in countries with fairly well-developed education systems (e.g. Indonesia, Nicaragua and the Philippines). Delayed entry is very frequent, especially in sub-Saharan Africa, and in Latin America and the Caribbean, while early enrolment is frequent as well in many countries in all regions (Figure 2.4).

Forty per cent of sub-Saharan African countries for which data are available have GIRs below 95%, meaning that access to primary schools remains an issue. This is especially so for poor rural children (particularly girls). Low GIRs are most common in francophone countries (Burkina Faso, Congo, Djibouti, Mali and the Niger have GIRs below

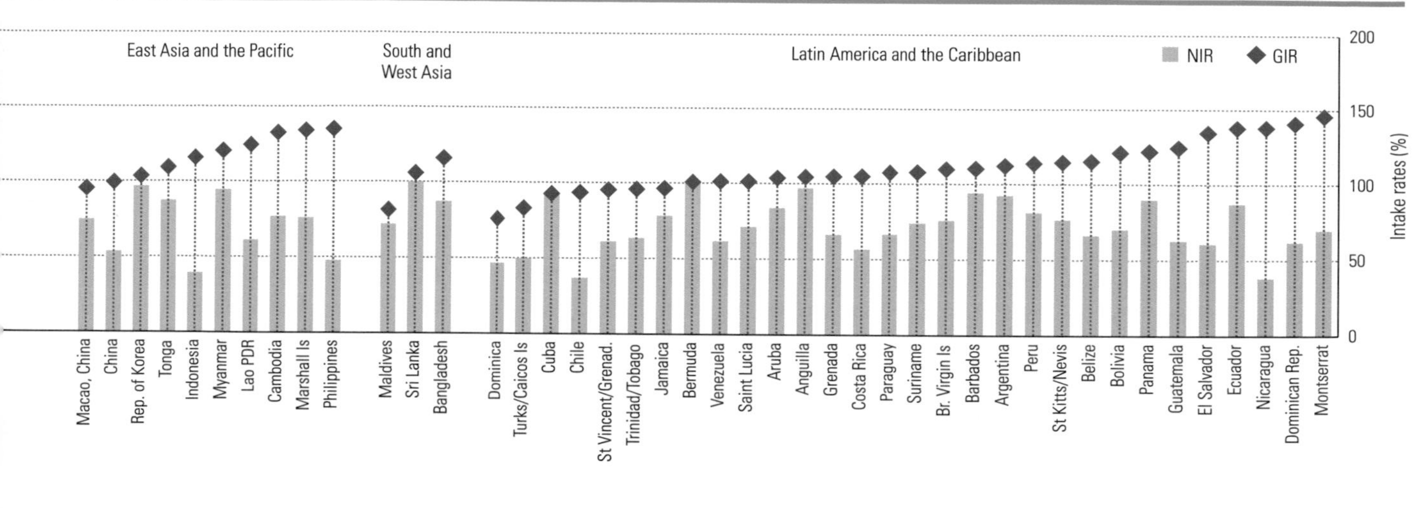

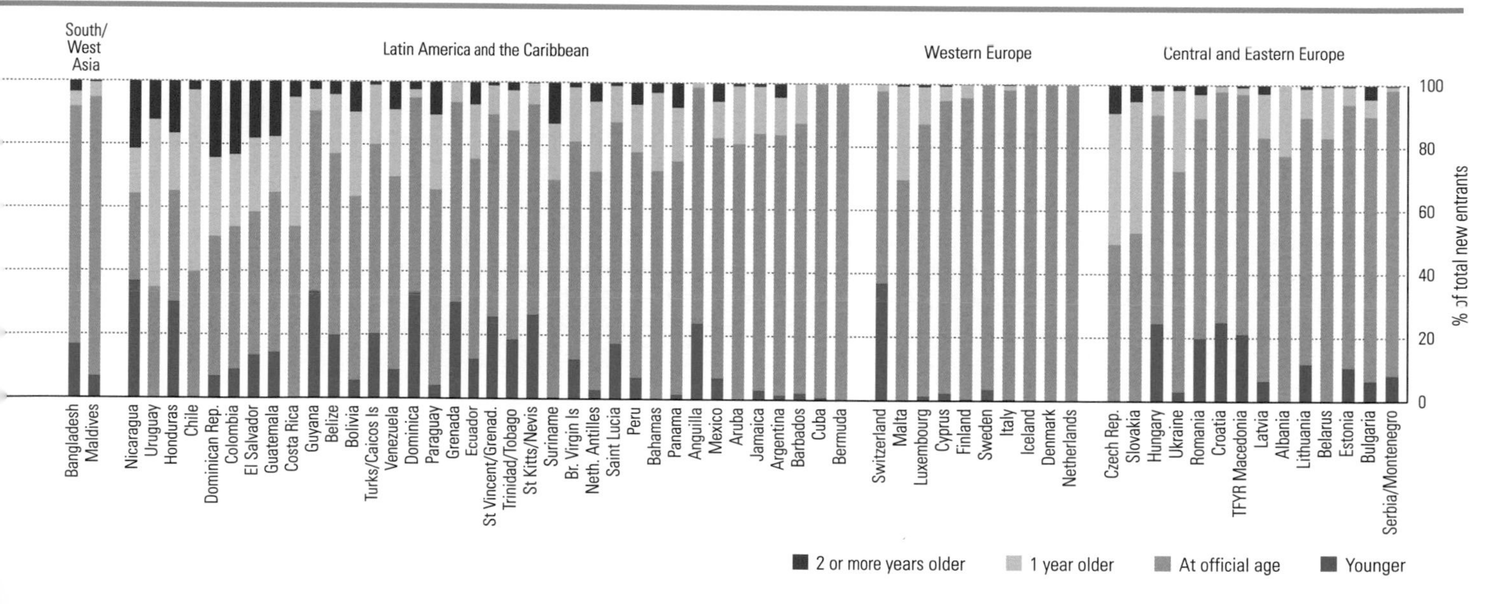

60%). In a majority of countries, however, GIRs rose between 1998 and 2002. This was particularly the case in some of the countries with the lowest rates, which recorded impressive progress over that period: Guinea, the Niger, Senegal, the United Republic of Tanzania and Yemen had increases of 30% or more (see statistical annex, Table 4). Exceptions to this trend include Oman, whose GIR declined by more than 12%.

School participation

Between 1998 and 2002, total enrolment in primary education rose from 655 million to 671 million children (Table 2.3). Encouragingly, sub-Saharan Africa, and South and West Asia saw the highest increases in enrolment, nearly 20 million children each, translating into GER increases of 11.2 percentage points in the former and 7.4 percentage points in the latter. Enrolment remains a challenge in sub-Saharan Africa, still facing high fertility: the region's school-age

Table 2.3: Enrolment in primary education by region, 1998 and 2002

	Total enrolment				Gross enrolment ratios			Net enrolment ratios		
	1998	2002	Difference		1998	2002	Difference	1998	2002	Difference
	(Thousands)			%	%	%	(percentage points)	%	%	(percentage points)
World	655 343	671 359	16 015	2	101	104	3.1	83.6	84.6	1.0
Developing countries	569 072	589 291	20 219	4	100	104	3.6	82.0	83.2	1.2
Developed countries	70 399	67 880	-2 519	-4	102	101	-1.5	96.6	95.6	-0.9
Countries in transition	15 872	14 187	-1 685	-11	101	106	5.1	85.4	89.1	3.7
Sub-Saharan Africa	81 319	100 670	19 351	24	80	91	11.2	56.2	63.5	7.3
Arab States	34 725	37 137	2 411	7	90	94	4.1	78.1	82.6	4.5
Central Asia	6 891	6 396	-495	-7	99	102	2.7	88.9	89.9	1.0
East Asia and the Pacific	217 317	207 054	-10 263	-5	112	111	-0.6	95.7	92.1	-3.7
South and West Asia	158 096	175 527	17 431	11	95	102	7.4	78.6	82.5	3.9
Latin America and the Caribbean	78 656	69 498	-9 158	-12	121	119	-2.0	94.4	96.4	2.0
North America and Western Europe	52 856	51 945	-911	-2	103	101	-1.8	96.3	95.3	-1.0
Central and Eastern Europe	25 484	23 133	-2 351	-9	97	99	2.1	87.2	89.0	1.7

Source: Statistical annex, Table 5.

By 2010, 10% of school-age children in sub-Saharan Africa may be orphaned by HIV/AIDS, other diseases and armed conflict

population is likely to increase by 34 million, or 32%, between 2000 and 2015. The HIV/AIDS epidemic, other diseases and conflict are expected to leave one-tenth of all these children orphaned by 2010 (Fredriksen, 2005*b*). Substantial increases in the school-age population (by about 20%) over this period are also expected in South and West Asia, and the Arab States.

Meanwhile, the school-age population in Latin America and the Caribbean will likely remain constant, and decreases are expected in East Asia and the Pacific (by 4%), Central and Eastern Europe (by 17%), and Central Asia (by 23%). Indeed, enrolment did decline between 1998 and 2002 in East Asia and the Pacific, partly because China's birth rate fell. A decline for that period is also observed in Latin America and the Caribbean, though this resulted principally from a change to the definition of primary education in Brazil.[4]

Figure 2.5 compares GER and NER in primary education by country (also see statistical annex, Table 5). The GER can be understood as a measure of the overall enrolment capacity of school systems, in purely quantitative terms. School systems whose GER is at or above 100%

Figure 2.5: Gross and net enrolment ratios in primary education, 2002

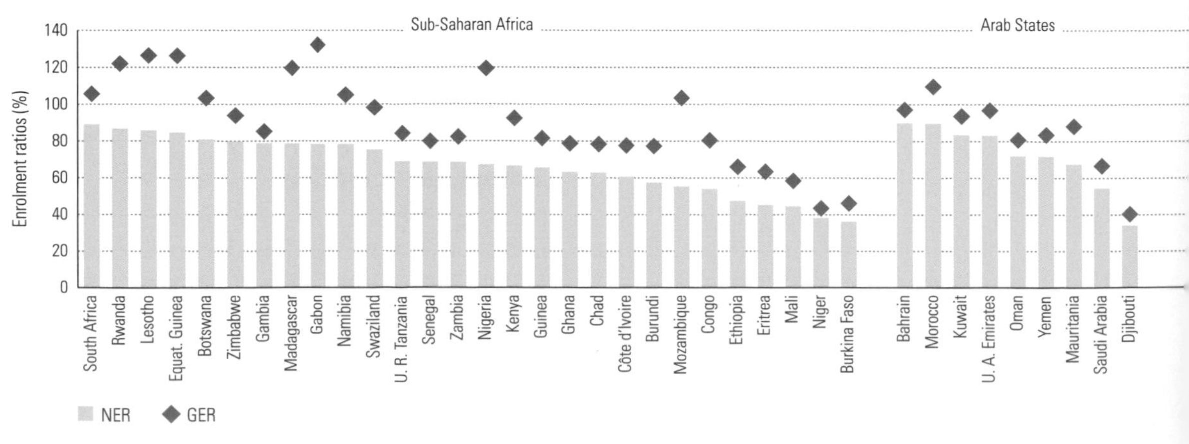

Note: Countries with NER above 90% are excluded. See source table for detailed country notes.
Source: Statistical annex, Table 5.

4. Primary education in Brazil was defined as lasting six years in 1998 but four years in 2002, so data for the two years are not comparable.

can be considered as having the capacity to accommodate all children of primary school age, even if they do not do so, i.e. if the NER is below 100%. A sharp discrepancy between the GER and the NER indicates that enrolled children do not progress regularly through the grades and that the system's internal efficiency could be improved. This is the case in many countries in sub-Saharan Africa (e.g. Equatorial Guinea, Gabon, Lesotho, Madagascar, Mozambique, Nigeria and Rwanda), and in India and Nepal.

Several countries are characterized by GERs considerably below 100% and NERs of 50% or under, e.g. Burkina Faso, Djibouti, Eritrea, Ethiopia, Mali and the Niger.

About two-thirds of the countries with data available registered higher NERs in 2002, including almost all countries that had NERs below 80% in 1998 (Figure 2.6). Increases were particularly substantial (above 20%) in seven sub-Saharan African countries (Eritrea, Ethiopia, Guinea, Lesotho, Madagascar, the Niger and the United Republic of Tanzania) and two Arab States (Morocco and Yemen). Several of the countries recording increases recently abolished school fees, including Guinea, Lesotho and the United Republic of Tanzania. In the Niger, the NER increased by almost one-half, from 26% to 38%, after the government took measures to increase provision in underserved areas, although the country's 2002 ratio remains among the world's lowest. Benin provides another interesting case of policy efforts towards improving school participation among the disadvantaged (Box 2.1).

Figure 2.6: Net enrolment ratios in primary education, 1998 and 2002

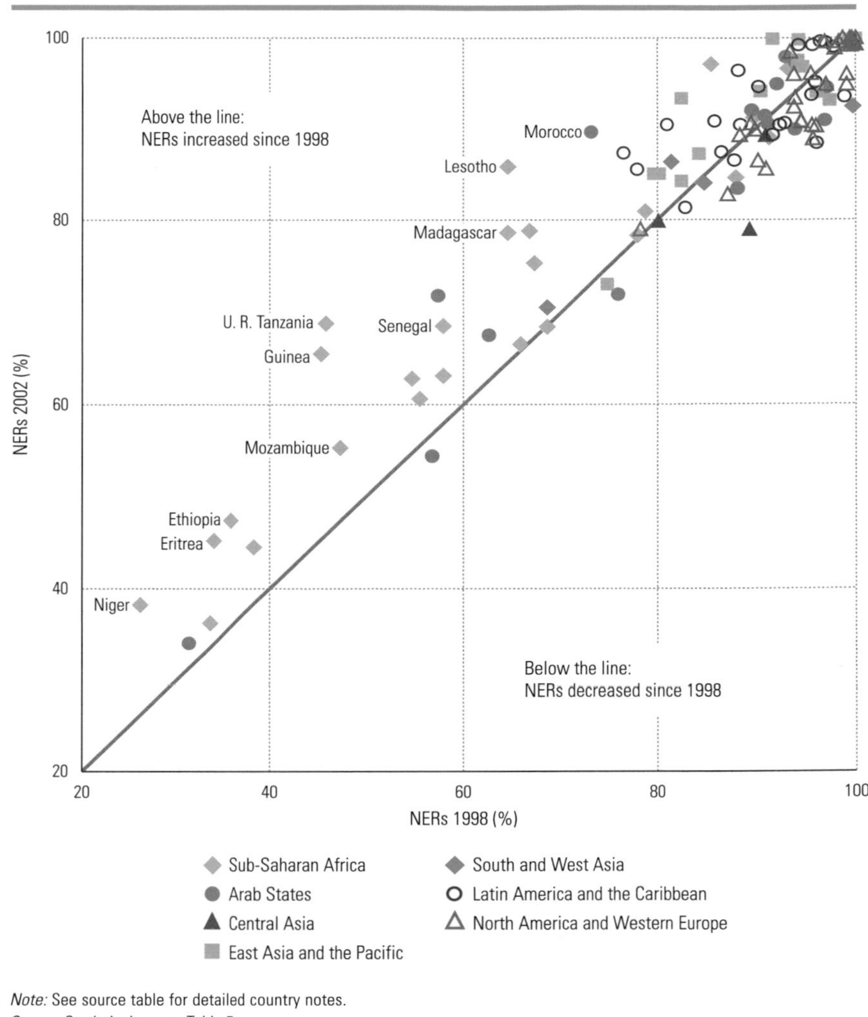

Note: See source table for detailed country notes.
Source: Statistical annex, Table 5.

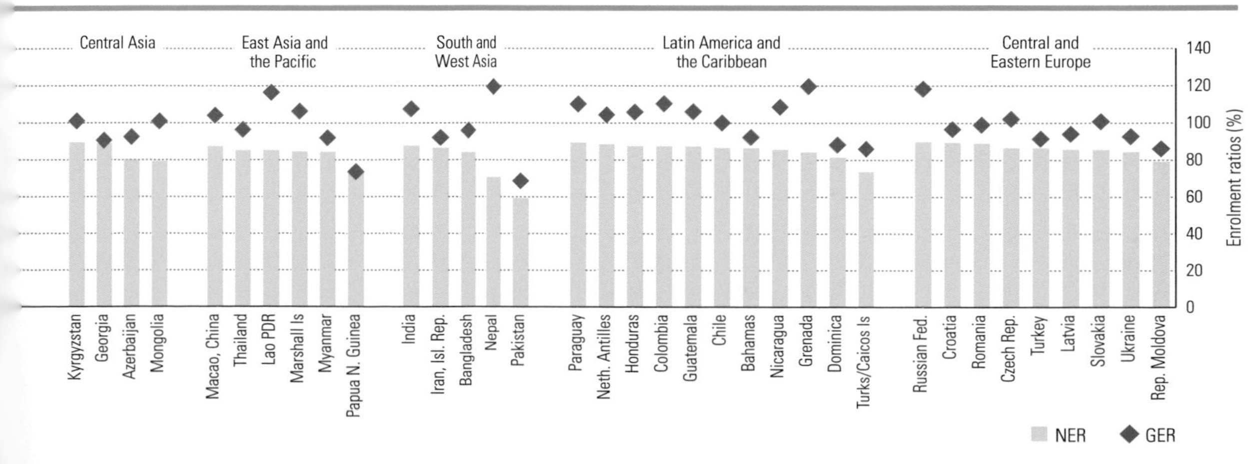

Box 2.1 Closing gaps in participation in primary education: the case of Benin

School attendance by children aged 6 to 14 increased from 44% in 1996 to 55% in 2001, reducing socio-economic disparities in attendance (Figure 2.7). Girls, children living in rural areas, poor children and children living in households whose head had a primary education benefited particularly. This improvement may be the result of the reform of primary education since 1992, which has focused on fostering the education of girls and women. In 1996, school fees were abolished for girls in rural areas and a network of parents, teachers, non-governmental organizations, students and community leaders was set up to change family schooling practices in relation to girls.

Figure 2.7: Changes in net attendance rates by population group in Benin, 1996 and 2001

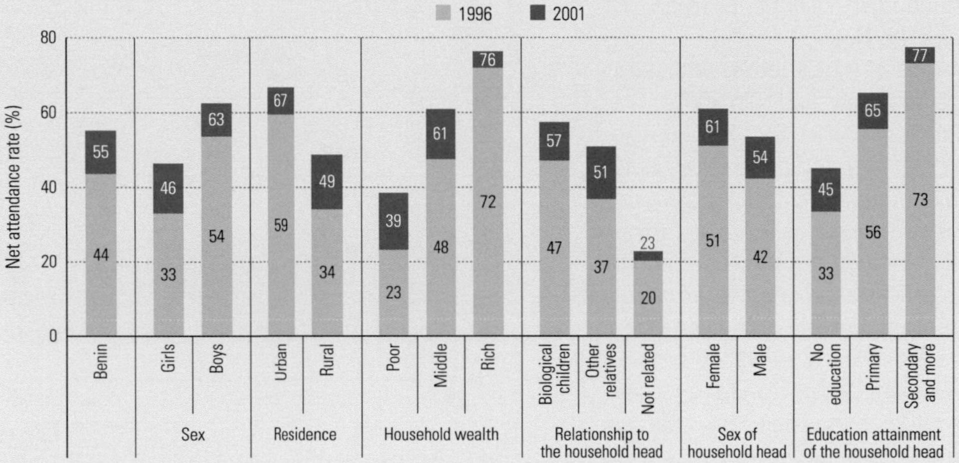

Note: For household wealth, 'poor' refers to the poorest 40% of households, 'middle' to the next 40% and 'rich' to the richest 20%.
Sources: Demographic and Health Survey, Benin, 1996 and 2001; Benin (2001).

Table 2.4: Number of out-of-primary-school children, 1998 and 2002

	1998				2002			
	Total	Male	Female	% female	Total	Male	Female	% female
	Thousands				Thousands			
World	106 724	45 316	61 408	58	99 876	45 030	54 846	55
Developing countries	102 052	42 971	59 081	58	95 459	42 701	52 758	55
Developed countries	2 367	1 210	1 157	49	2 949	1 593	1 356	46
Countries in transition	2 304	1 135	1 170	51	1 468	736	732	50
Sub-Saharan Africa	44 581	20 648	23 933	54	40 370	18 367	22 003	55
Arab States	8 491	3 501	4 991	59	6 906	2 882	4 025	58
Central Asia	775	375	400	52	635	294	341	54
East Asia and the Pacific	8 309	4 158	4 151	50	14 782	7 410	7 372	50
South and West Asia	35 722	12 534	23 189	65	30 109	12 698	17 411	58
Latin America and the Caribbean	3 620	1 623	1 997	55	2 084	858	1 226	59
North America and Western Europe	1 885	967	918	49	2 421	1 320	1 101	45
Central and Eastern Europe	3 340	1 510	1 830	55	2 569	1 203	1 366	53

Note: Figures may not add to totals due to rounding.
Source: Statistical annex, Table 5.

Out-of-primary-school children

Despite the continuing increase in enrolment in primary education, about 100 million children of primary school age were not enrolled in primary school in 2002 (Table 2.4), though the number has decreased by nearly 7 million since 1998. Some 55% of the world's out-of-primary-school children are girls, down from 58% in 1998. Sub-Saharan Africa, and South and West Asia together account for 70% of the global total. Nineteen countries have more than 1 million out-of-primary-school children, including ten in sub-Saharan Africa (where countries with relatively small populations, such as Burkina Faso, Mali or the Niger, thus face a huge challenge) and the largest three South Asian countries (India, Pakistan and Bangladesh).

These figures slightly overstate the actual number of out-of-school children, however, as they include children enrolled at levels other than primary. As Box 2.2 explains, work is under way to improve these statistics.

> **Box 2.2 How many children are out of school?**
>
> The number of out-of-school children is probably the most widely cited education statistic, yet it is difficult to compute accurately. The numbers in Table 2.4, for instance, represent all children of primary school age who are not enrolled in primary schools, whether actually out of the school system or enrolled at other levels. Therefore, they are overestimates.
>
> The UNESCO Institute for Statistics (UIS) and UNICEF have been working together to improve the estimation of the out-of-school figures:
>
> - On the basis of administrative data, the UIS has estimated that, in 2002, 0.8% of all children of primary-school age were enrolled in pre-primary schools, and 2.3% in secondary schools. A first step, then, is to stop including children of primary school age who are actually enrolled in secondary schools, thus reducing the global figure to 85.5 million in 2002. Unfortunately, a lack of reliable data prevents a similar exclusion of children enrolled in pre-primary schools.
> - Administrative data will be supplemented wherever possible with household survey data, which may be more accurate as far as actual attendance (as opposed to enrolment, measured by the number of children registered at the beginning of the school year) is concerned. However, unlike administrative sources, nationally representative household surveys providing cross-comparable education data are not available annually. This raises a challenge in generating the time-series data needed to monitor progress towards UPE.

Internal efficiency of the primary school system

Grade repetition

Once enrolled, most children should progress regularly through the grades, provided they have access to schools of good quality. The incidence of grade repetition can thus be interpreted as a proxy for school quality and student achievement, although repetition depends heavily on promotion policies that make it very context-specific. There is much debate about the pedagogical usefulness of repeating a grade. Some countries automatically promote pupils from one grade to another, while others apply strict promotion rules based on achievement, as the 2005 Report showed. That being said, the incidence of grade repetition deserves examination, and reducing it is a policy priority in many national education plans. The percentage of repeaters in primary education was below 3% in 2002 in a majority of countries for which data are available (see statistical annex, Table 6). However, the percentages are much higher – above 15% – in more than half the countries of sub-Saharan Africa, peaking at 34% in Gabon and 40% in Equatorial Guinea. Proportions of repeaters close to or above 20% are found in Brazil, Guatemala, the Lao People's Democratic Republic, Mauritania, Morocco and Nepal.

Initiatives to reduce grade repetition have been taken in several countries. For example, Burkina Faso, Mali and the Niger have attempted to bring the percentage of repeaters down to 10% by creating three subcycles within the primary education cycle, disallowing repetition within each subcycle and restricting it between them (Damiba, 2005*b*). Only the Niger succeeded in reaching the target, though, reducing the percentage of repeaters from 12.2% in 1998 to 7.3% in 2002. The decrease in Burkina Faso was moderate (from 17.7% to 15.1%), while in Mali the share of repeaters in total enrolment actually rose (from 17.4% to 19.8%), suggesting that the new rules were not effectively implemented.

Retention

Retention of children until the last grade of primary school is another major challenge for education policy. In about one-third of countries for which data are available for 2001, less than two-thirds of a cohort of pupils who had had access to primary school reached the last grade. Such low survival rates to the last grade of primary education are found in nearly 70% of sub-Saharan African countries, as well as in Bangladesh, Cambodia, India, the Lao People's Democratic Republic, Nepal, Papua New Guinea and a few countries of Latin America and the Caribbean. The lowest rate is Malawi's (22%).

Retention of children until the last grade of primary school is a major challenge for education policy

Figure 2.8: Survival rates to the last grade of primary education, 1998/1999 and 2001/2002

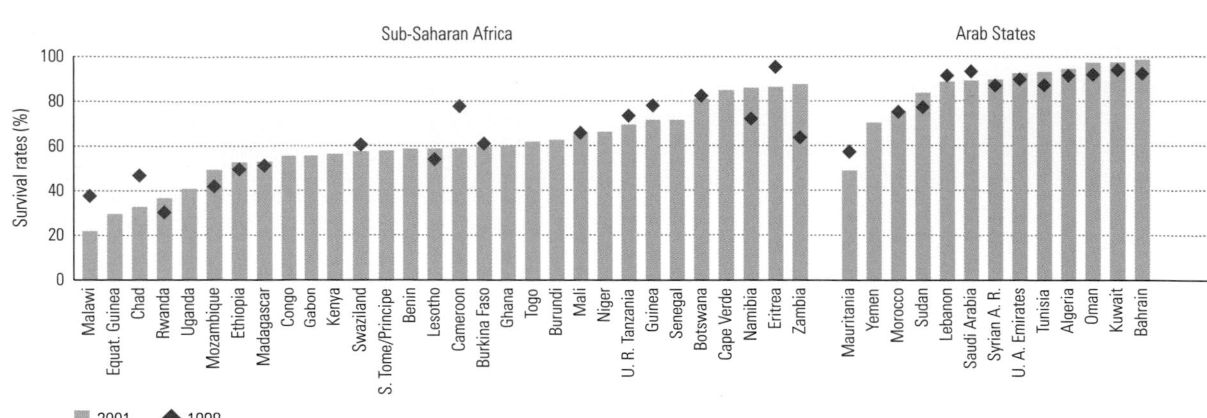

Note: Only countries with a survival rate below 95% in at least one year are included. See source table for detailed country notes.
Source: Statistical annex, Table 7.

Figure 2.8 shows that there has been limited change in survival rates since 1998, although significant improvement took place in several countries, e.g. Cambodia, the Lao People's Democratic Republic, Namibia, Rwanda and Zambia. On the other hand, sharp decreases took place in Cameroon, Chad, Malawi and Papua New Guinea.

School completion

UPE will be achieved only when all children have access to and complete primary school. Estimating completion rates raises methodological issues; indeed, there is no consensus on the very notion of completion. Should one consider as having completed primary education all pupils who reach the last grade of primary education, or only those students who complete it successfully? And how should differences among countries in the definition of 'success' be handled?

Moreover, most completion indicators currently available are gross rates that include all children of a cohort and do not distinguish between children who do not complete primary education because they had no access to it in the first place and those who were enrolled but failed to reach or complete the last grade. Only the latter are relevant to an assessment of the internal efficiency of a school system; as with the computation of survival rates, it is preferable to focus on children who did have access to primary education and to estimate how many of them successfully completed it.[5]

Figure 2.9 thus displays, for selected countries, survival rates to the last grade of primary schooling and the proportion of students in that grade who completed it in 2001. In most countries, not all pupils who reach the last grade of primary education complete it. This phenomenon is particularly marked in sub-Saharan Africa. While both school retention and completion often reflect the state of education quality, in some countries the latter may also indicate that strong selection policies are being applied because the number of places available in lower secondary education is limited. Therefore, improving the quality of education and expanding access to secondary education are conditions for UPE to be fully achieved.

5. Cohort completion rates following this approach are computed as the product of the proportion of graduates from primary school (computed as the number of graduates divided by the percentage of new entrants in the last grade) and survival rates to the last grade.

Figure 2.9: Survival rate to the last grade of primary education and percentage of primary school completers, selected countries, 2001

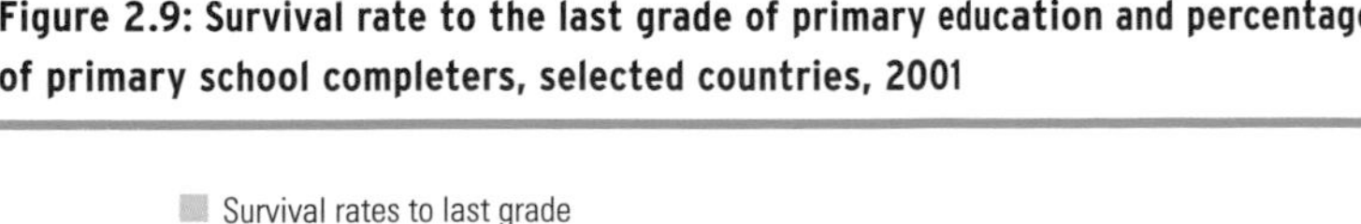

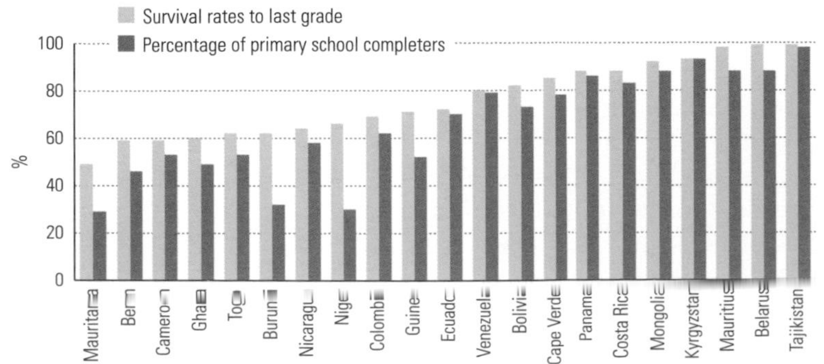

Sources: Statistical annex, Table 7; UNESCO Institute for Statistics database.

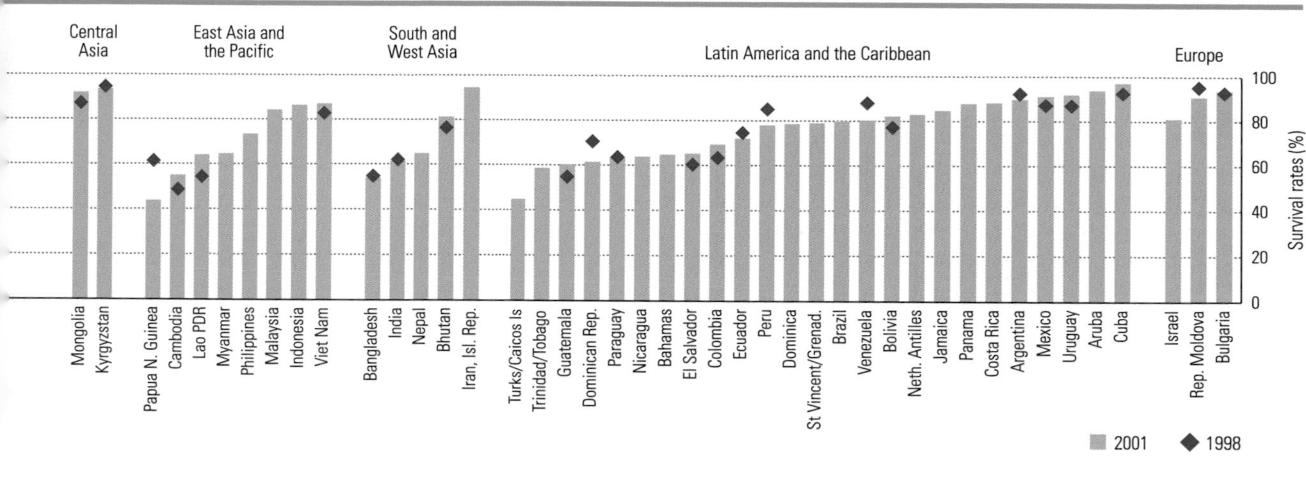

Gender disparities in primary education

Gender disparities in primary education first and foremost stem from disparities in enrolment in the first grade. About 60% of the 159 countries for which data are available had achieved gender parity in the intake rate by 2002 (see statistical annex, Table 4). Most of these countries are in North America and Western Europe, Central and Eastern Europe, Latin America and the Caribbean, Central Asia, and East Asia and the Pacific. Significant gender disparities in intake rate remain in countries such as Burkina Faso, the Central African Republic, Chad and the Niger, with particularly low GPIs (under 0.75). As Figure 2.10 shows, however, dramatic progress was made between 1998 and 2002 in many countries, notably Côte d'Ivoire, Ethiopia, Guinea, Lebanon, Mali, Mozambique and Yemen. There is much variation within South and West Asia: Pakistan has one of the world's lowest GPIs (0.73); India and Nepal have made much progress since 1998 and nearly reached gender parity in 2002 (India's GPI increased from 0.84 to 0.96 and Nepal's from 0.78 to 0.92); Bangladesh, the Islamic Republic of Iran, the Maldives and Sri Lanka had already reached parity by 1998.

Gender disparities in primary education first and foremost stem from disparities in enrolment in the first grade

Figure 2.10: Gender disparities in GIRs in primary education, 1998 and 2002

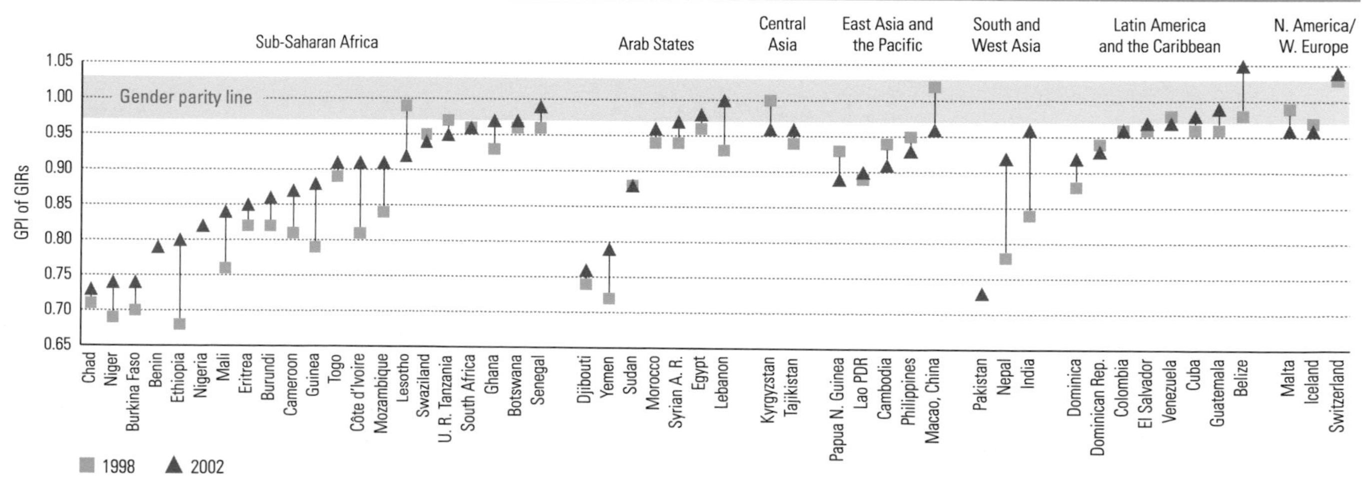

Note: Only countries with GPI below 0.97 or above 1.03 in at least one of the two years are included. No data are available for Pakistan for 1998. See source table for detailed country notes.
Source: Statistical annex, Table 4.

Once enrolled, girls tend to perform better than boys

Progress is being made regarding gender parity in enrolment, as 104 countries out of the 180 for which 2002 data are available have achieved parity in primary education as measured by the GPI of gross enrolment ratios (see statistical annex, Table 5). Major gender disparities that impede girls are now concentrated in the Arab States, South and West Asia and sub-Saharan Africa, though the situation has improved considerably since 1998 (Table 2.5).

Table 2.5: Gross enrolment ratios by gender in primary education, by region, 1998 and 2002

	Gross enrolment ratios					
	1998			2002		
	Male %	Female %	GPI (F/M)	Male %	Female %	GPI (F/M)
World	104.5	96.3	0.92	106.6	100.4	0.94
Developing countries	104.9	95.5	0.91	107.3	100.3	0.93
Developed countries	101.8	102.3	1.00	100.7	100.4	1.00
Countries in transition	101.1	99.9	0.99	106.0	105.1	0.99
Sub-Saharan Africa	86.8	73.1	0.84	97.9	84.3	0.86
Arab States	95.7	83.5	0.87	98.6	88.8	0.90
Central Asia	99.5	98.4	0.99	102.5	100.7	0.98
East Asia and the Pacific	112.1	111.0	0.99	111.7	110.2	0.99
South and West Asia	102.9	85.6	0.83	106.2	97.5	0.92
Latin America and the Caribbean	122.9	119.9	0.98	120.8	118.0	0.98
North America and Western Europe	102.1	103.0	1.01	100.9	100.7	1.00
Central and Eastern Europe	99.3	95.3	0.96	100.8	98.1	0.97

Source: Statistical annex, Table 5.

Figure 2.11 indicates that very rapid progress towards gender parity can be achieved in poor countries with low enrolment ratios, as demonstrated by Afghanistan, Benin, Chad, Ethiopia, the Gambia, Guinea, India, Morocco, Nepal and Yemen. Even so, several of these countries still have GPIs below 0.80 of their GERs. Afghanistan's GPI is the world's lowest, although it recovered from 0.08 in 1998 to 0.52 in 2002.

Once enrolled, girls tend to perform better than boys. This may reflect gender-differentiated attitudes to learning or, more simply, the fact that in countries where fewer girls than boys are enrolled, the average female student tends to come from a more privileged socio-economic background than the average male student. Figure 2.12 shows that repetition rates are higher for boys than for girls, but even in some countries of the three regions where gender disparities favouring boys are most pronounced (sub-Saharan Africa, the Arab States, and South and West Asia), girls' disadvantage is barely significant. In particular, in Latin America and the Caribbean, higher grade repetition and lower survival rates for boys result in girls being in the majority at the secondary and tertiary levels (see statistical annex, Table 7).

Survival rates are also generally higher for girls than for boys everywhere except sub-Saharan Africa and Central Asia, where males' survival rates are higher in a majority of countries (see statistical annex, Table 7).

Figure 2.11: Changes in gender disparities in GERs between 1998 and 2002

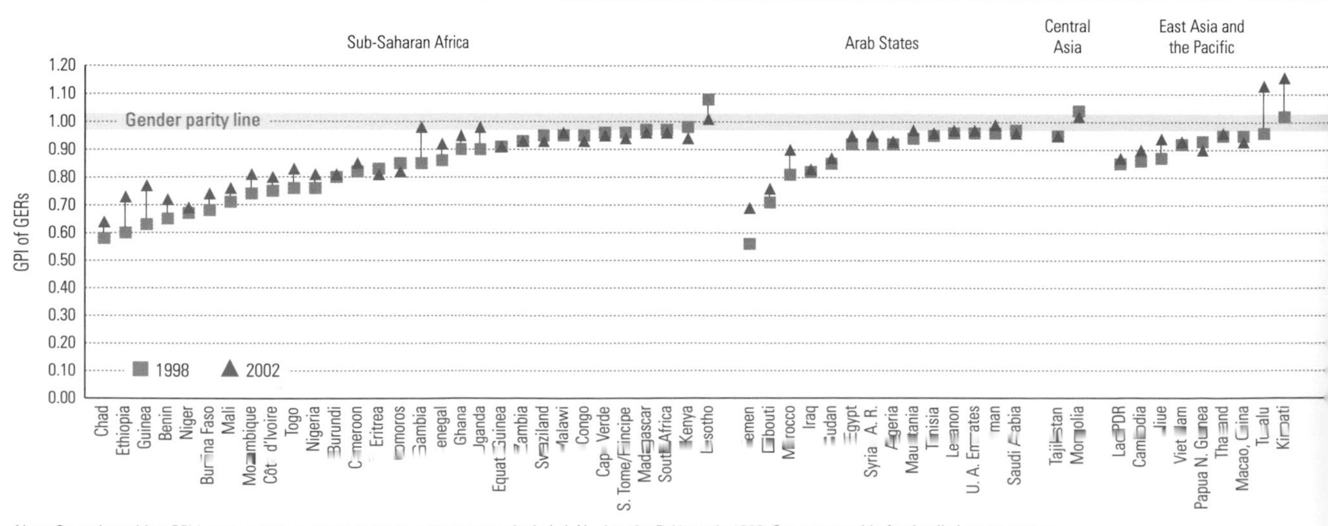

Note: Countries with a GPI between 0.97 and 1.03 in 1998 or 2002 are not included. No data for Pakistan in 1998. See source table for detailed country notes.
Source: Statistical annex, Table 5.

Figure 2.12: Percentage of repeaters in primary education, 2002

Note: Countries whose rate is below 3% are not included. See source table for detailed country notes.
Source: Statistical annex, Table 6.

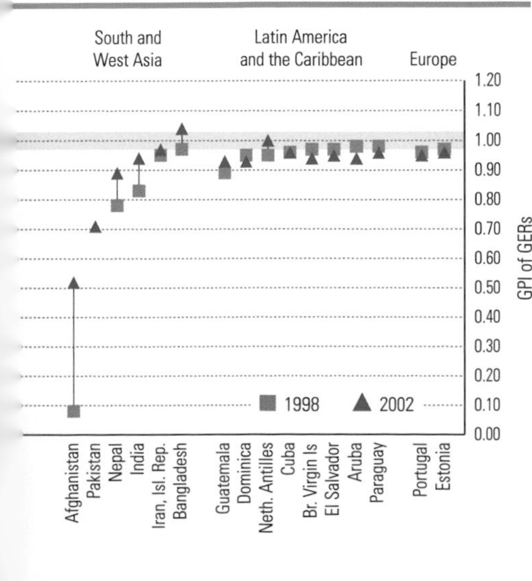

The increases in enrolment ratios and GPIs between 1998 and 2002 are substantial. They are changing the global picture by generating massive demand for secondary and tertiary education. Meeting this demand will be a major education policy challenge in coming decades.

Secondary and tertiary education

The achievement of Education for All depends on progress in secondary and tertiary education as well as in basic education. Both the EFA goals and the Millennium Development Goals include achieving parity in enrolment for girls and boys at the primary and secondary levels by 2005 and gender equality at all levels of education by 2015.

The achievement of Education for All depends on progress in secondary and tertiary education as well as in basic education

Secondary education

The number of secondary students in the world rose substantially between 1998 and 2002, from 430 million to almost 500 million – more than four times the increase in the number of primary-school students. The global GER at this level went up from 60% to 65% as a result of increases in the number of children completing primary school and the proportion going on to secondary school.

The number of secondary students in the world rose substantially between 1998 and 2002, from 430 million to almost 500 million

The transition to and participation in secondary education

Transition rates increased from 1998 to 2002 in most countries (Figure 2.13). High transition rates are now widespread. Half the developing countries for which data are available have transition rates above 80%, and rates generally exceed 90% in developed countries and countries in transition. A small group of countries still had rates below 70% in 2002, as low as 20% in the United Republic of Tanzania. Rates also fell substantially in the Dominican Republic, Ghana, Guinea and Madagascar.

In three out of four countries in the world, home to 80% of children of secondary school age, lower secondary education is compulsory (see statistical annex, Table 4). Nevertheless, of the 109 countries for which data are available and in which lower secondary education is compulsory, 41 have transition rates below 90%.

Regional patterns of participation in secondary education are similar to those observed for primary education, but the contrasts are sharper. Generally, OECD countries have almost achieved universal secondary education. High secondary GERs are found in Central and Eastern Europe, Central Asia, and Latin America and the Caribbean. Levels of participation vary widely in the Arab States (regional average: 65%), and East Asia and the Pacific (71%). The lowest average regional GERs are those of sub-Saharan Africa

Figure 2.13: Transition rates from primary to general secondary education, 1998/1999 and 2001/2002

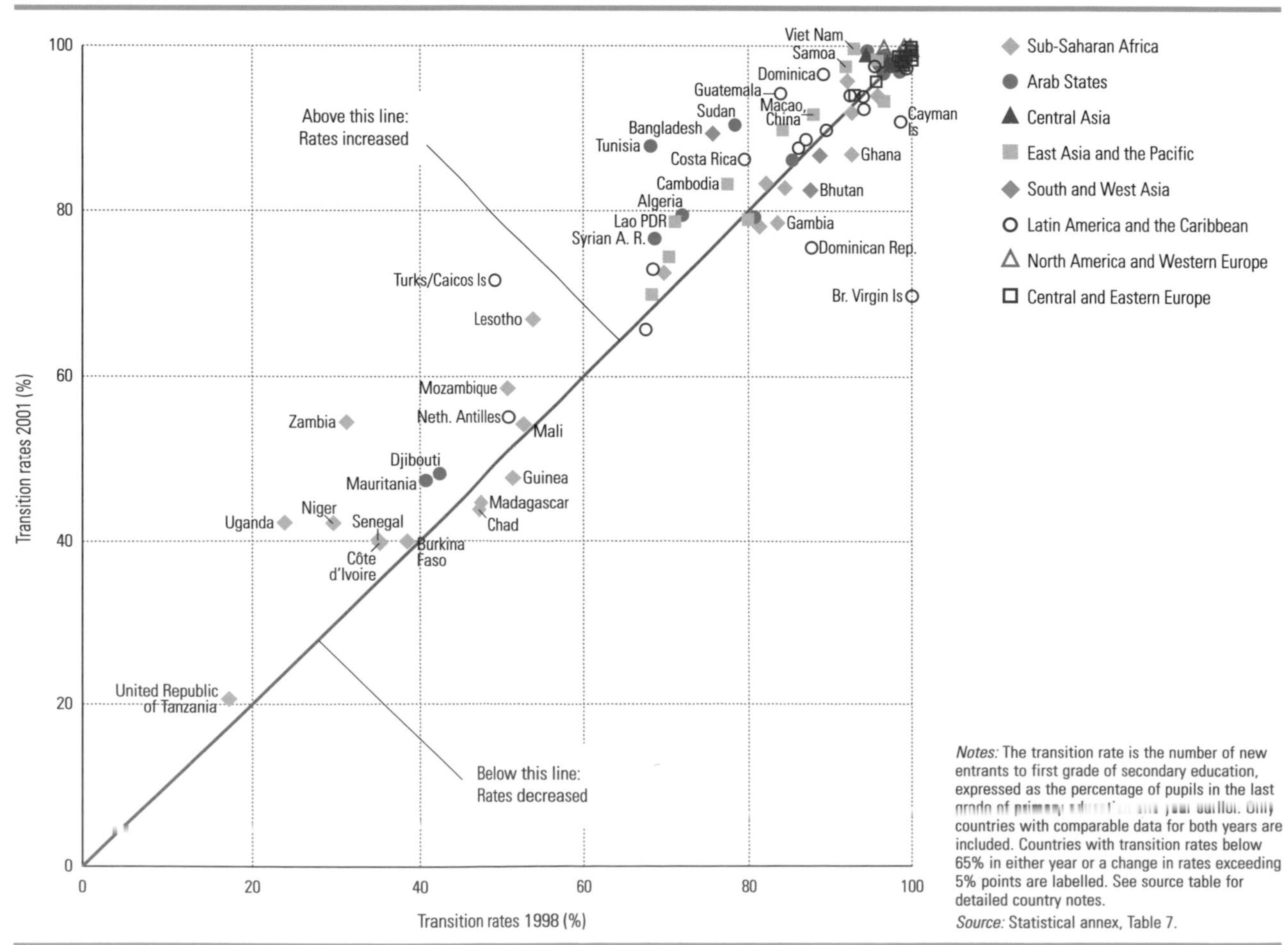

Notes: The transition rate is the number of new entrants to first grade of secondary education, expressed as the percentage of pupils in the last grade of [illegible] year earlier. Only countries with comparable data for both years are included. Countries with transition rates below 65% in either year or a change in rates exceeding 5% points are labelled. See source table for detailed country notes.

Source: Statistical annex, Table 7.

Figure 2.14: Change in secondary gross enrolment ratios between 1998 and 2002

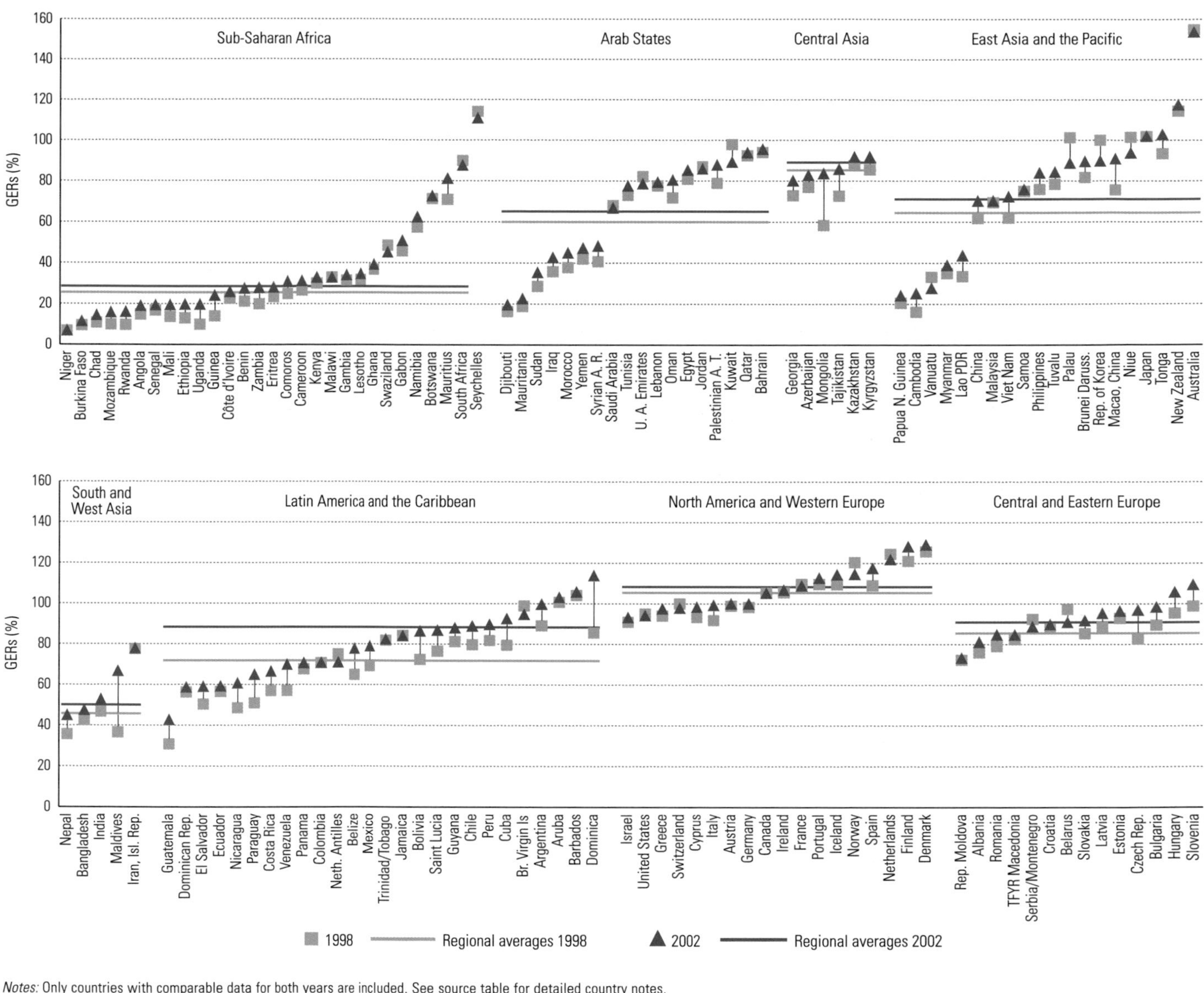

Notes: Only countries with comparable data for both years are included. See source table for detailed country notes.
Source: Statistical annex, Table 8.

(28%), and South and West Asia (50%) (see statistical annex, Table 8).

Figure 2.14 displays changes in GERs between 1998 and 2002 at the country and regional levels. Increases exceeding five percentage points occurred in about half the countries. Increases were especially high in Latin America and the Caribbean, and in East Asia and the Pacific. In sub-Saharan Africa, GERs grew by more than 15% in more than half the countries, including Ethiopia, Guinea, Mali, Mozambique, Rwanda and Zambia, and that of Uganda doubled, albeit from a very low initial level. In contrast to the global trends, substantial decreases were recorded in some countries that already had low enrolment rates in 1998, among them Swaziland and Vanuatu.

Grade repetition in secondary education

Grade repetition is an issue in secondary as well as in primary education. In general, countries with high repetition rates at the primary level also have high rates at secondary level (see statistical annex, Table 8). Grade repetition is especially frequent in sub-Saharan Africa, where the percentage of repeaters exceeds 10% in half the countries. In Burkina Faso, Burundi and Congo, about one-third of secondary students were repeating a grade in 2002.

Tertiary education

Growth rates for tertiary education in developing countries are, on average, more than twice those in developed countries

The number of students in tertiary education worldwide has continued to increase rapidly, from 90 million in 1998 to 121 million in 2002, an average of more than 7% per year. Growth rates for tertiary education in developing countries are, on average, more than twice those observed in developed countries. China's growth of 24% annually accounts for one-third of the global increase.

Access to tertiary education is expanding in the vast majority of countries for which data are available. Two-thirds of all countries had increased their GERs by more than two percentage points between 1998 and 2002 (Figure 2.15). The highest absolute increases were observed in developed countries, but rises of more than ten percentage points were observed in Argentina, Bahrain, Cuba, Mongolia, the Palestinian Autonomous Territories and the United Arab Emirates.

Gender disparities in secondary and tertiary education

Secondary education

Gender disparities at the beginning of secondary education stem from disparities at the primary level as well as from the transition to secondary education. Figure 2.16 illustrates the relationship between gender disparities in the gross intake rate to the last grade of primary education and the transition rate from primary to lower secondary education.[6] Of the 134 countries for which data are available for 2001, 89 have achieved gender parity in the transition rate or are close to doing so. Even countries with relatively weak education systems, such as Benin, Guatemala, Mozambique and the Sudan, have reached gender parity in the transition to secondary schooling, and gender disparities in favour of girls are observed in many countries (India, Morocco and Uganda).

Meanwhile, several countries stand out as having lower intake rates to the last grade of primary education, *and* lower transition rates to secondary education, for girls than for boys. These are the same countries already identified as still having underdeveloped primary school systems, e.g. Burkina Faso, Cambodia, Chad, Djibouti, Eritrea, Ethiopia, Mali, Mauritania, and the Niger. A qualification is that gender disparities in the transition rate are often less pronounced than those in various variables pertaining to primary education. In Burkina Faso, Ethiopia and the Niger, a boy's chances of completing primary education are 1.5 times higher than a girl's, but his chances of making the transition to secondary education are 'only' 1.1 times higher.

Overall, however, progress since 1998 has been slight in countries still experiencing gender disparities in transition rates (see statistical annex, Table 7). Gender disparities in gross

6. See the glossary for detailed definitions.

Figure 2.15: Changes in the tertiary gross enrolment ratios between 1998 and 2002

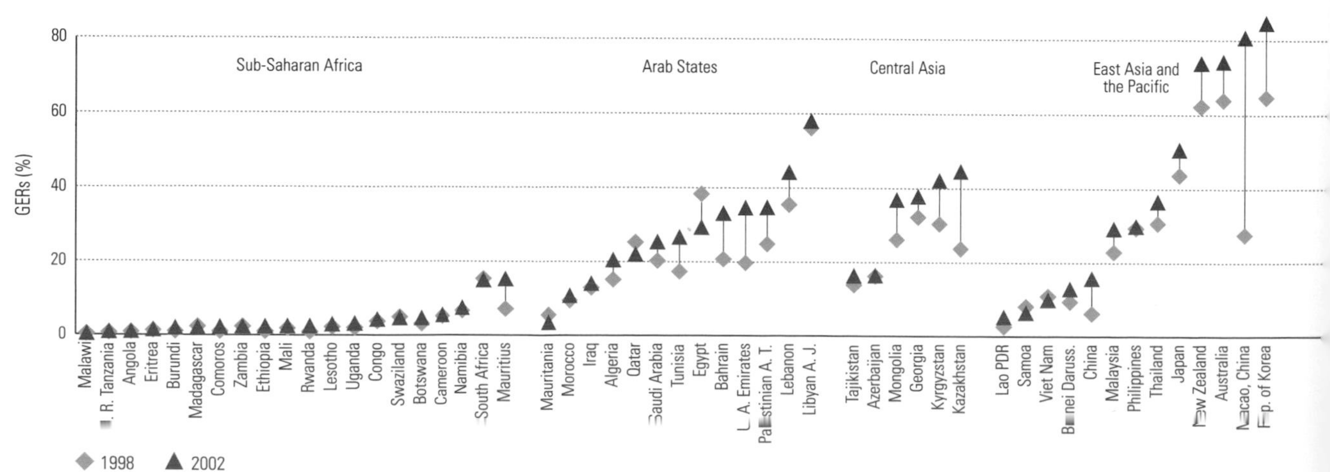

Note: Only countries with comparable data for both years are included. Countries are ranked in ascending order of tertiary GERs in 2002. See source table for detailed country notes.
Source: Statistical annex, Table 9A.

Figure 2.16: Comparison of gender disparities at the end of primary education and in transition to secondary education, 2001

Transition rate from primary to secondary is:

1.4 times higher for girls
1.3 times higher for girls
1.2 times higher for girls
1.1 times higher for girls
Gender parity
1.1 times higher for boys
1.2 times higher for boys
1.3 times higher for boys
1.4 times higher for boys
1.5 times higher for boys
1.6 times higher for boys

Saint Lucia, St Vincent/Grenad., Br. Virgin Is, Mauritius, Uruguay, Bangladesh, Cape Verde, Uganda, Neth. Antilles, India, Comoros, Morocco, Andorra, Sudan, Benin, Aruba, Mozambique, Guatemala, Lesotho, Burkina Faso, Ethiopia, Niger, Nepal, Lao PDR, Senegal, Cameroon, Mali, Eritrea, Cambodia, Myanmar, Togo, Côte d'Ivoire, Mauritania, Chad, Djibouti, U. R. Tanzania, Suriname, Congo

Intake rate to last grade of primary education is: 2.5 times higher for boys; 2 times higher for boys; 1.5 times higher for boys; Gender parity; 1.5 times higher for girls

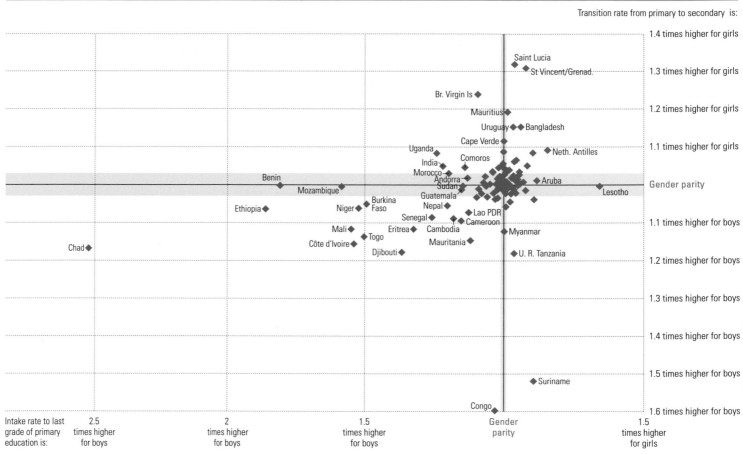

Notes: Only countries with comparable data for both indicators are included. Disparities are presented on a comparable scale for both sexes: those favouring women are expressed as the ratio of the female rates to the male rates while those favouring men are expressed as the ratio of the male rates to the female rates. Countries with disparities above 1.1 for either indicator are labelled. See source table for detailed country notes.

Sources: Statistical annex, Table 7; UNESCO Institute for Statistics (2005), Table 4.

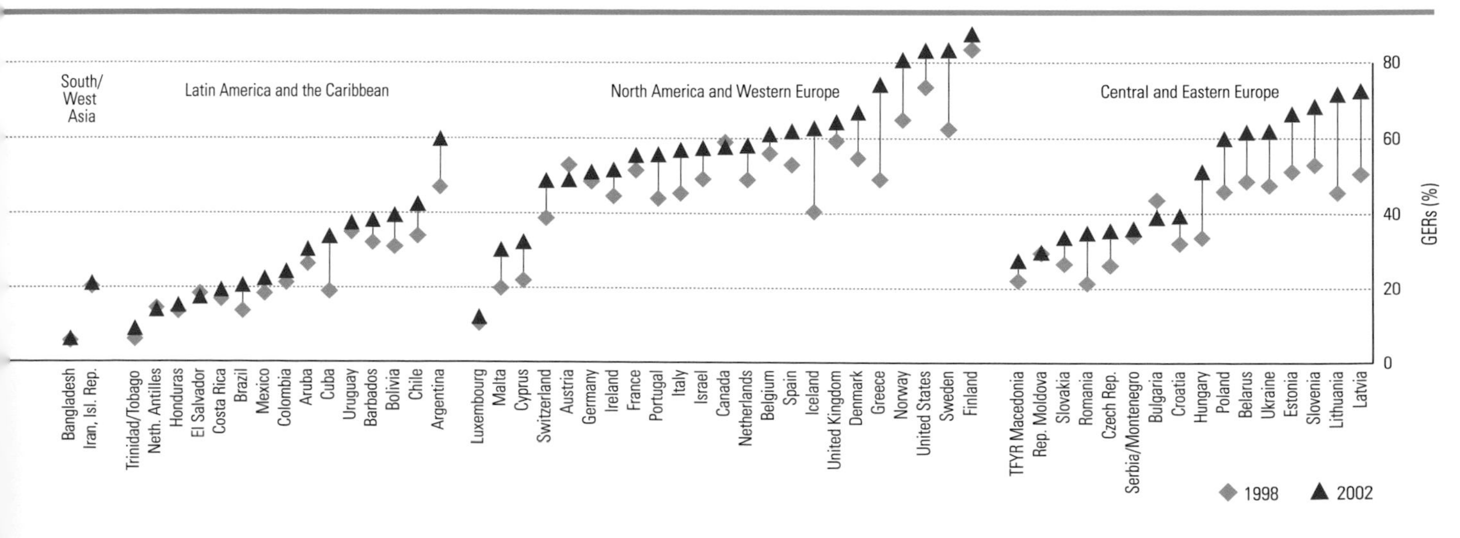

Only 57 of 172 countries for which data are available have reached gender parity in secondary education

enrolment ratios are very common in secondary education, but they can be in favour of girls as well as in favour of boys. Only 57 of 172 countries for which data are available were at gender parity in 2002; most were in Central and Eastern Europe, East Asia and the Pacific, Latin America and the Caribbean, and North America and Western Europe.

Figure 2.17 displays a scatter plot of the GPIs of GER against GNP per capita. Striking patterns obtain. First, gender disparities favouring boys are found almost exclusively in low-income countries: GERs for males exceed those for females by more than 10 percentage points only in countries with GNP per capita of less than PPP US$3,800 (with two exceptions: Equatorial Guinea and Turkey). Second, gender disparities in favour of girls are observed in a large number of countries with very different levels of GNP per capita – ranging from Lesotho to Denmark – which confirms that gender disparities are not the same phenomenon for both genders. Disparities in favour of boys are

Figure 2.17: Gender disparities in secondary gross enrolment ratios and GNP per capita, 2002

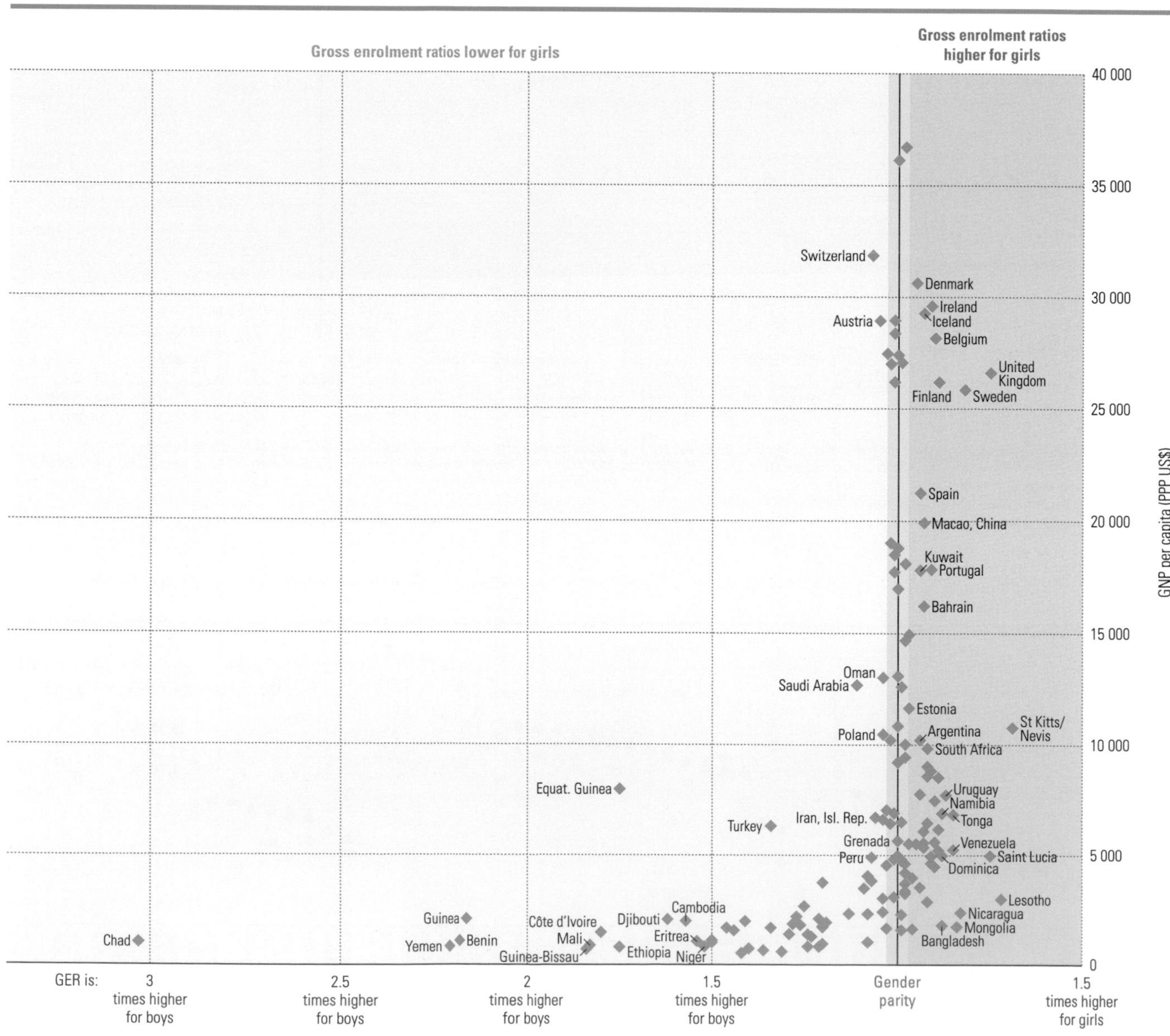

Note: Not included are 25 countries for which no data are available on GNP per capita; nine are at gender parity, twelve have higher GERs for females and four have higher GERs for males. See source tables for detailed country notes.

Source: Statistical annex, Tables 1 and 8.

wide, and tend to be observed in poor countries with underdeveloped school systems. Disparities in favour of girls are much narrower and observed frequently where school systems are well developed (most countries with high GERs have gender imbalances in favour of females). When access to school is limited because of high direct and opportunity costs, girls are less likely than boys to participate in secondary education. When access is not limited by resource constraints, more girls than boys participate, especially at the upper secondary level (UNESCO Institute for Statistics, 2005, Table 5), and they perform better. For example, in countries that participated in the Programme for International Student Assessment (PISA) study, conducted by the OECD (see below), female students are significantly less likely than their male counterparts to be among the lowest-performing students (OECD, 2004). Boys are more likely to participate in shorter and less academic programmes, not leading to tertiary education, and thus leave the school system earlier (OECD, 2001).

The rapid increase in secondary education enrolment thus translated into significant progress towards gender parity between 1998 and 2002, leading to some convergence between countries with low and high GERs: for nearly four out of five countries with a GPI of the secondary GER below 0.80 in 1998, the GPI had improved by 2002, most notably in Cambodia, Chad, Guinea, India, Uganda and Yemen. An opposite trend, however, occurred in Djibouti, Equatorial Guinea, Eritrea, Ethiopia and Rwanda, as well as in Myanmar and Oman, two countries that were at gender parity in 1998.

Girls' higher achievement levels in secondary education are reflected in their lower grade repetition rates (see statistical annex, Table 8). Overall, boys repeat grades more frequently than girls do. Exceptions are found mostly in sub-Saharan Africa, especially in those countries where disparities in enrolment also favour boys.

Tertiary education

At the global level, the numbers of female and male students in tertiary education are almost on a par; at the country level, however, gender parity is exceptional, found in only 4 of the 142 countries for which data for 2002 are available (Cyprus, Georgia, Germany and the Palestinian Autonomous Territories). Gender disparities favouring females are even more frequent than in secondary education, but follow very similar patterns: enrolment ratios for women are higher than those for men in half the developing countries (47 out of 93) and in most developed countries and countries in transition (42 out of 49); they are higher by 50% in one country in 6. Consistent with patterns at primary and secondary level, gender disparities favouring men are found in most countries of sub-Saharan Africa, and South and West Asia, in some of the Arab States, and in a few Central Asian countries. Overall, the expansion of tertiary education between 1998 and 2002 particularly benefited women, as Figure 2.18 shows.

Gender parity is exceptional in tertiary education

Figure 2.18: Change in gender disparities in tertiary gross enrolment ratios between 1998 and 2002

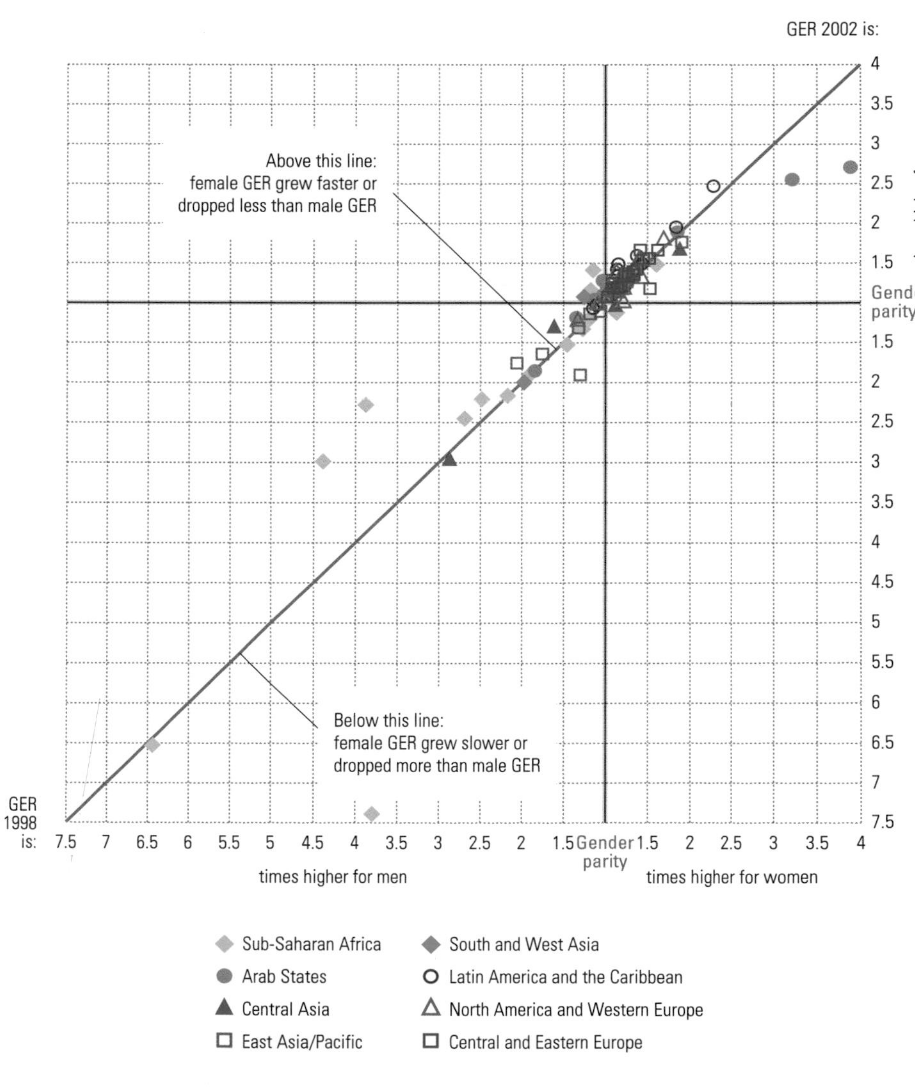

Note: Only countries with comparable data for both years are included. See source table for detailed country notes.
Source: Statistical annex, Table 9A.

Learning outcomes

EFA requires improvements in the quality of learning throughout the school system

Besides progress in terms of school participation, achieving Education for All requires improvements in the quality of learning throughout the school system. As quality was the main theme of the 2005 Report, the discussion here focuses just on newly published data on learning outcomes, in line with the emphasis on measurable achievements in the formulation of the sixth EFA goal. These data come from the 2000–2002 survey of the Southern and Eastern African Consortium for Monitoring Educational Quality (SACMEQ II)[7] and the 2003 rounds of the Trends in International Mathematics and Science Study (TIMSS)[8] and the Programme for International Student Assessment (PISA).[9]

While the quality of education is certainly not limited to learning outcomes, achieving high mastery levels is the ultimate objective of any school system. SACMEQ II data (Figure 2.19) show that quality is a major issue in all the sub-Saharan African countries covered, although to a varying extent. While hardly any student who participated in the survey in Malawi, Lesotho or Zambia reached one of the highest four levels of the SACMEQ numeracy scale, more than one-third did so in Kenya, Mauritius and the Seychelles. As the previous sections show, the two latter have distinctly better quantitative indicators than countries of mainland sub-Saharan Africa.

Low levels of learning achievement are also of concern at higher levels of education. TIMSS 2003 data (Figure 2.20) on Grade 8 students, corresponding to lower secondary education, show a marked contrast between countries that combine high enrolment ratios with high achievement levels (notably those of Europe, North America and some East Asian countries)[10] and countries where lower participation goes hand-in-hand with much lower achievement. Most students do not reach the low benchmark in mathematics in the participating sub-Saharan African countries (Botswana, Ghana, and South Africa) or in Chile, Morocco, the Philippines and Saudi Arabia. Underachievement is a concern not only in other developing countries participating, but also in Central and Eastern Europe, where in several countries about 20% or more of Grade 8 students can be considered low achievers in mathematics.

PISA 2003 data yield similar results (Figure 2.21) and show that much remains to be done to improve achievement in middle-income countries. While the overall share of 15-year-old students performing at or below level 1 of the PISA mathematics scale was 21%, such students made up more than 40% of the 15-year-old student population in Brazil, Indonesia, Mexico, Serbia and Montenegro, Thailand, Tunisia, Turkey and Uruguay. Meanwhile, the high-income countries are not immune to the problem of low

Figure 2.19: Results of SACMEQ II (2000–2002): numeracy skills of Grade 6 students in sub-Saharan Africa

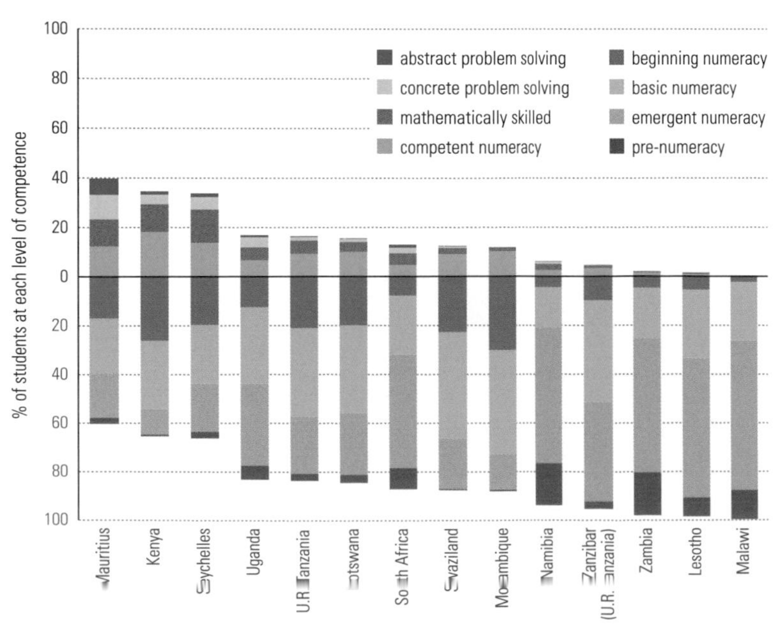

Note: Countries are sorted in increasing order of the proportion scoring at the four lowest levels.
Source: UNESCO Institute for Statistics calculation based on SACMEQ II database.

7. SACMEQ, originating from a survey conducted in Zimbabwe in 1991, has expanded to thirteen countries and one territory. The first series of surveys (SACMEQ I) was conducted in 1995 and 1996. The second series (SACMEQ II), conducted between 2000 and 2002, assesses the reading and mathematics achievement of Grade 6 students and covers around 2,300 schools and 42,000 pupils.

8. TIMSS, carried out in 1995, 1999 and 2003 by the International Association for the Evaluation of Educational Achievement (IEA), assesses the mathematics and science achievement of primary and secondary school students. Data presented in this section pertain to Grade 8 students, typically age 14; the 2003 sample comprises 2,200 to 7,000 such students in each of the 46 participating countries.

9. PISA, carried out in 2000 and 2003 by the OECD, measures the mathematics, science and reading skills of 15-year-old students. It aims to assess their 'preparedness for adult life' towards the end of compulsory schooling, i.e. their 'capacity ... to apply knowledge and skills in key subject areas and to analyse, reason and communicate effectively as they pose, solve and interpret problems in a variety of situations' (cited by Siniscalco, 2005). In 2003, over 275,000 students from 40 countries (including all 30 OECD member countries) participated in PISA.

10. Hong Kong (China), Japan, the Republic of Korea and Singapore stand out for the proportion of their students reaching the advanced benchmark in mathematics.

Figure 2.20: Results of TIMSS 2003: mathematics achievement of Grade 8 students

Reaching advanced benchmark | Reaching high benchmark | Reaching intermediate benchmark | Reaching low benchmark | Not reaching low benchmark

% of students at each international benchmark

100, 80, 60, 40, 20, 0, 20, 40, 60, 80, 100

Low- and middle-income countries

High-income countries

Estonia, Hungary, Latvia, Malaysia, Russian Fed., Slovakia, Lithuania, Armenia, Bulgaria, Serbia/Montenegro, Romania, Rep. Moldova, Lebanon, TFYR Macedonia, Jordan, Indonesia, Iran, Isl. Rep., Tunisia, Egypt, Morocco, Chile, Philippines, Botswana, Saudi Arabia, South Africa, Ghana

Singapore, Canada (Quebec), Hong Kong, China, Rep. of Korea, Japan, Netherlands, Canada (Ontario), Belgium (Flemish), Sweden, Australia, United States, United Kingdom (Scotland), United Kingdom (England), Slovenia, New Zealand, Israel, Italy, Norway, Cyprus, Bahrain

Note: Countries are sorted in increasing order of proportion not reaching the low benchmark.
Source: Mullis et al. (2004), p. 64.

Figure 2.21: Results of PISA 2003: mathematics skills of 15-year-old students

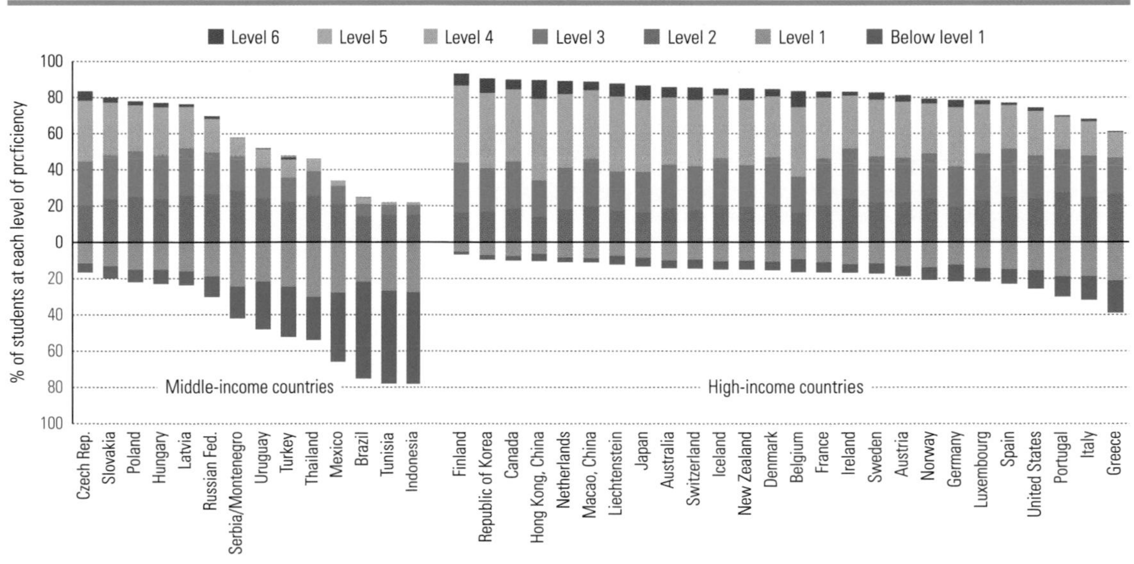

Note: Countries are sorted in increasing order of proportion scoring at and below level 1.
Source: OECD (2004), p. 91.

levels of literacy skills. In eight out of the twenty-six high-income countries and territories participating, 20% or more of the 15-year-old students performed at level 1 or below. In mathematics, the category of low achievers accounts for one-quarter to more than one-third in Greece, Italy, Portugal and the United States.

The evolution of learning outcomes in recent years

There has been no clearly discernible international trend in learning outcomes in recent years. For example, among the twenty-four countries that participated in TIMSS in 1995 and 2003, the proportion of Grade 8 students scoring below the

There has been no clear international trend in learning outcomes in recent years

Figure 2.22: Evolution of TIMSS results between 1995 and 2003

	Proportion of students scoring below the low international benchmark in mathematics in 2003	1995 to 2003 difference	Proportion of students scoring below the low international benchmark in sciences in 2003	1995 to 2003 difference
Iran, Isl. Rep.	45	4	23	4
Cyprus	23	0	29	1
Romania	21	0	22	-1
Norway	19	9	9	3
Bulgaria	18	8	19	12
New Zealand	12	1	6	-5
United States	10	-4	7	-6
Slovenia	10	0	4	-3
Slovakia	10	6	6	1
United Kingdom (Scotland)	10	-3	8	-6
Lithuania	10	-9	5	-16
Australia	10	0	5	-6
Sweden	9	5	5	2
Russian Fed.	8	1	7	-1
Latvia	8	-6	5	-12
Hungary	5	-1	3	-2
Belgium (Flemish)	5	1	6	0
Netherlands	3	-2	2	-2
Canada (Ontario)	3	-6	3	-9
Rep. of Korea	2	-1	2	-3
Japan	2	0	2	-1
Hong Kong, China	2	-2	2	-8
Singapore	1	1	5	4
Canada (Quebec)	1	0	2	-6

Non-significant
Significant

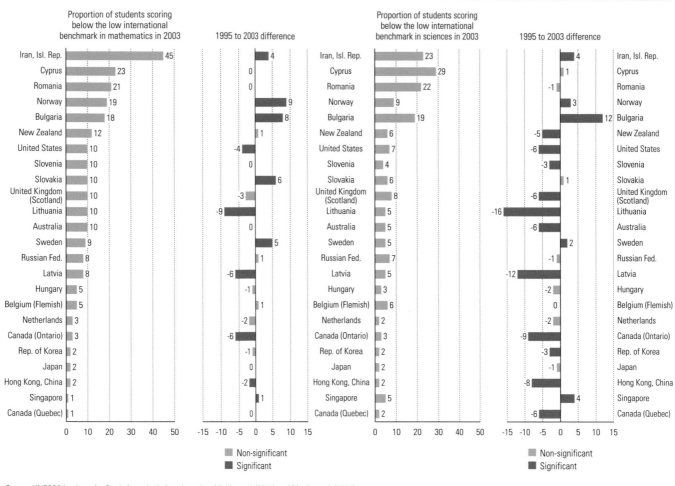

Source: UNESCO Institute for Statistics calculations based on Mullis et al. (2004) and Martin et al. (2004).

Figure 2.23: Evolution of PISA results between 2000 and 2003: reading

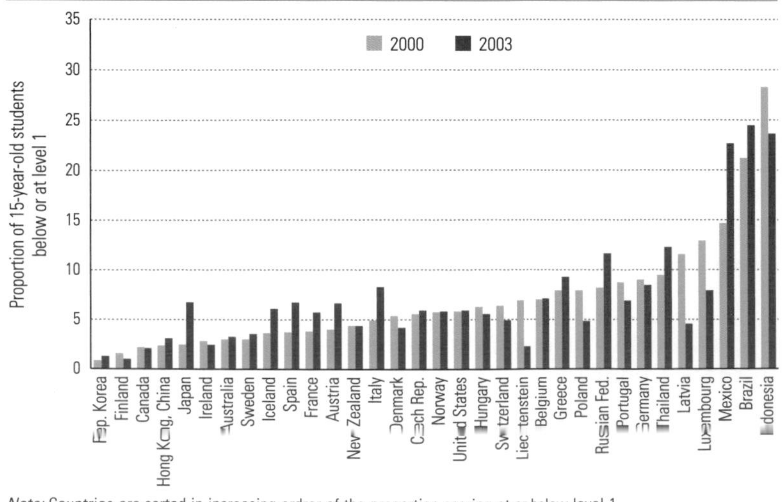

Note: Countries are sorted in increasing ordrer of the proportion scoring at or below level 1.
Sources: OECD/UNESCO Institute for Statistics (2003), p. 274; OECD (2004), p. 443.

low benchmark in mathematics was not significantly changed in thirteen countries, increased in seven and decreased in four (Figure 2.22). The picture for science is slightly better, as the proportion below the low benchmark decreased significantly in eleven countries, although not in those where this proportion was highest in 2000. Similarly, a comparison of the results of PISA for 2000 and 2003 (Figure 2.23) shows typically moderate variations, although the proportion did decrease significantly in a few countries where it was relatively high in 2000 (e.g. Latvia, Indonesia), suggesting some improvement in the quality of the school system during this period.

An important qualification is that Figures 2.22 and 2.23 include few developing countries. There is conclusive evidence that achievement levels have decreased in recent years in several sub-Saharan African countries. As the 2005 Report showed, the results of SACMEQ II were significantly worse than those of SACMEQ I in five of the six countries and territories that participated in both rounds – Malawi, Mauritius, Namibia, Zambia and Zanzibar (United Republic of Tanzania) – and there was no improvement in Kenya. More generally, too few countries are covered by international assessments of student achievement for global trends to emerge. The availability of data that would allow monitoring of the quality of education is still insufficient.

Figure 2.24: Results of SACMEQ II (2000–2002): gender disparities in reading literacy in sub-Saharan African countries

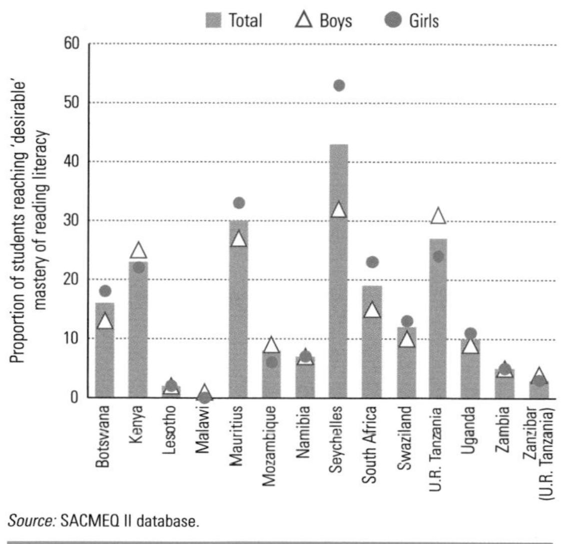

Source: SACMEQ II database.

Gender differences in learning achievements

As the 2003/4 Report emphasized, research shows that girls tend to perform better than boys in countries where they have equal access to the school system (e.g. as measured by GPIs of enrolment ratios), whatever the country's income level.[11] Even in countries where girls are disadvantaged in terms of access, gender differences in learning achievement are often small or insignificant. Thus, in the fourteen SACMEQ II countries and territories, the proportion of girls reaching a 'desirable' mastery in reading literacy is higher (by more than one percentage point) than the proportion of boys in six countries and lower in only three (Figure 2.24). Girls' advantage is largest in reading, however. In mathematics, for example, boys and girls perform similarly in most PISA 2003 countries (Figure 2.25).

Gender patterns of achievement are linked to students' attitudes towards learning, which several recent studies have tried to measure.[12] For example, results of the 2001 Progress in International Reading Literacy Study (PIRLS)[13] show differences in attitudes towards reading among Grade 4 students (Figure 2.26). In virtually all of the thirty-five participating countries, more girls than boys reported very positive attitudes and self-concepts on reading – and students reporting such attitudes also performed better on achievement tests, although the direction of the causality is of course debatable.

Gender patterns of achievement are linked to students' attitudes towards learning

Figure 2.25: Results of PISA 2003: gender disparities in mathematics achievement

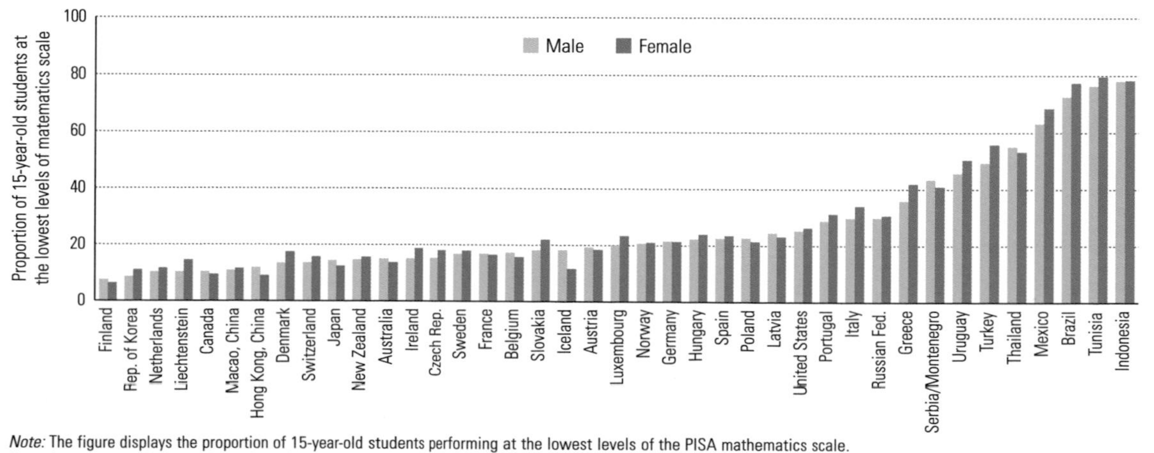

Note: The figure displays the proportion of 15-year-old students performing at the lowest levels of the PISA mathematics scale. Countries are sorted in increasing ordrer of the proportion scoring at or below level 1.
Source: OECD (2004).

11. See UNESCO (2003*b*), pp. 102-5.

12. Caution is needed when interpreting such data, as they are based on self-reports and are thus influenced by country-specific cultural circumstances.

13. Like TIMSS, PIRLS is a survey conducted by the IEA; as its name indicates, it focuses on reading.

Figure 2.26: Gender differences in attitudes towards reading, PIRLS 2001

Attitudes ◆ Self-concept

% girls

% boys

There is no country where boys report more positive attitudes or self-concept towards reading

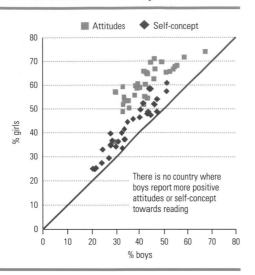

Note: The figure displays the proportion of Grade 4 students reporting very positive 'attitudes' and 'self-concept' in regard to reading. The 'attitudes' variable is based on the degree of agreement with the following statements: 'I read only if I have to'; 'I like talking about books with other people'; 'I would be happy if someone gave me a book as a present'; 'I think reading is boring'; and 'I enjoy reading.'
The 'self-concept' variable is based on the degree of agreement with the following statements: 'Reading is very easy for me'; 'I do not read as well as other students in my class'; and 'Reading aloud is very hard for me.'

Source: UNESCO Institute for Statistics calculations based on PIRLS 2001 database.

In stark contrast, girls are less confident than boys about mathematics in most countries that participated in TIMSS 2003 (Figure 2.27), even though this does not necessarily translate into differences in achievement. Among the forty-five countries concerned, girls performed better in nine and boys in ten, the difference being insignificant in the remaining twenty-six. Yet girls reported lower self-confidence than boys in twenty-five countries, and said they valued mathematics less in twenty-two countries. Girls were more self-confident in only two countries, and valued mathematics more in four.

This mismatch between gender differences in mathematics achievement and differences in self-reported approaches to learning mathematics is also echoed in the findings of

Figure 2.27: Gender differences in mathematics and approaches to learning mathematics, TIMSS 2003

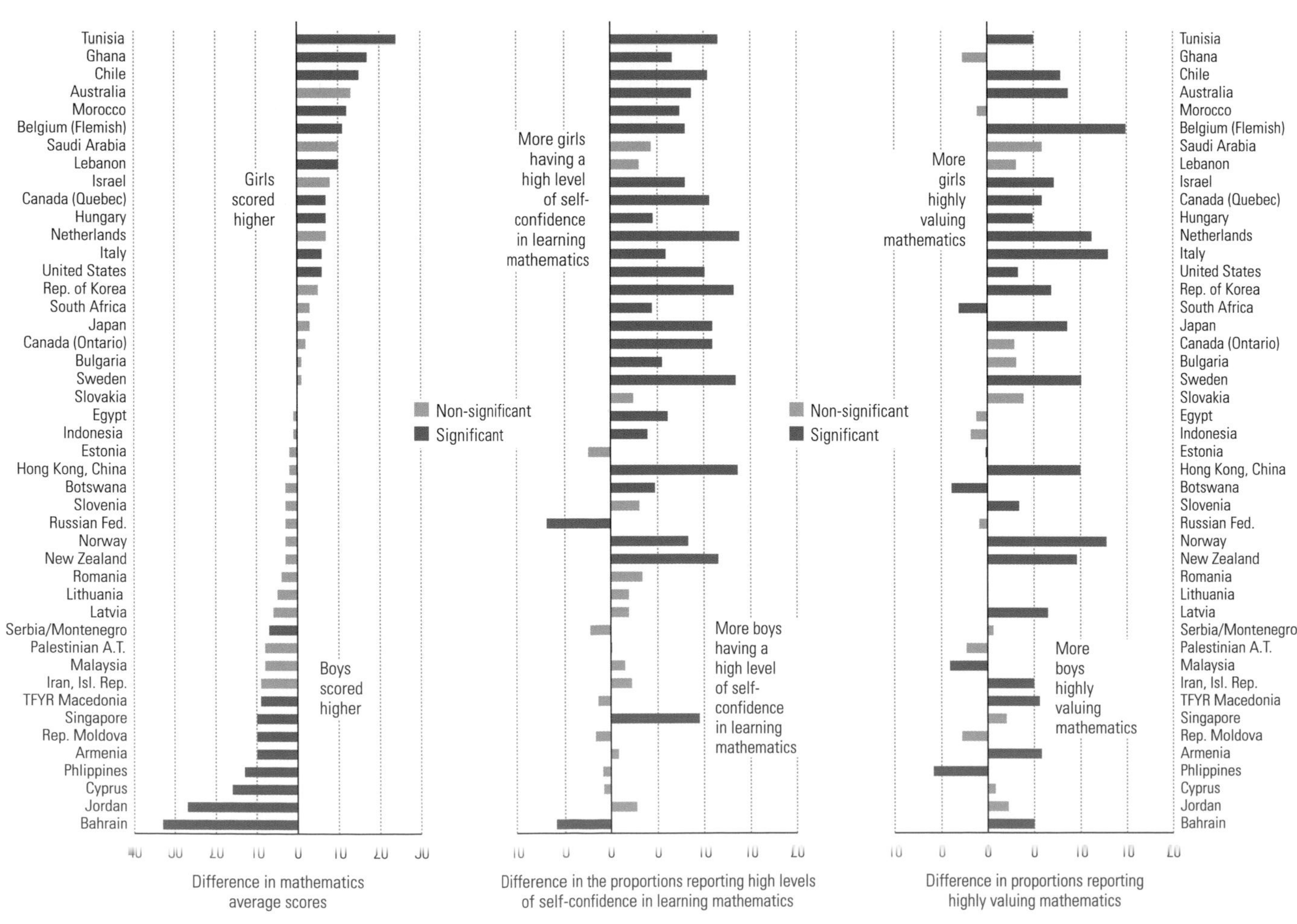

Source: UNESCO Institute for Statistics calculations based on TIMSS 2003 database.

PISA 2003. While gender differences in student performance in mathematics were generally modest, boys expressed much stronger levels of interest and enjoyment in learning mathematics. In addition, boys had stronger beliefs that learning mathematics would help them in their future careers; boys tended to have a more positive view of their abilities than girls in mathematics; and girls reported experiencing significantly more feelings of anxiety, helplessness and stress in mathematics classes (OECD, 2004).

Literacy

Literacy is the focus of the thematic part of this *EFA Global Monitoring Report* and is analysed in Chapters 5 to 9. This section simply reviews key adult literacy patterns in the context of this chapter's general assessment of progress towards Education for All. As Chapter 7 explains, data used here are to be treated with some caution. Based on conventional methods of assessment, they tend to overestimate the actual levels of literacy in countries.

Global patterns of adult literacy

Table 2.6 reports the latest estimates of the number of adult illiterates, along with literacy rates for the population aged 15 and older. The estimates are based on data reported by countries for the most recent year in the 2000–2004 reference period. There are an estimated 771 million illiterate adults globally, or 18% of the world's adult population. Almost all adults who have yet to acquire minimal literacy skills live in developing countries, in particular those in South and West Asia, sub-Saharan Africa and the Arab States, where literacy rates are about 60% (see the world adult literacy map in next pages). Although the East Asia and Pacific region has the highest literacy rate among developing regions (91%), its large population means it remains home to 17% of the world's illiterate adults.

Since 1990, the adult literacy rate has risen from 75% to 82% and the number of illiterates has fallen by 100 million, mainly because of a marked reduction (by 94 million) in China. Declines in the number of illiterates, albeit of much smaller magnitude, occurred in all regions except sub-Saharan Africa and, to a more limited extent, the Arab States. Despite increases in literacy rates of ten percentage points or more in the latter two regions, their absolute numbers of illiterates continued to rise because of high population growth rates. Similarly, in South and West Asia, where the number of adult illiterates declined slightly (by 0.3%), literacy rates increased by eleven percentage points during the period, though the adult literacy rate (59%) still ranks lowest among the world regions, mainly due to the very low levels of Bangladesh and Pakistan (41% and 49%, respectively).

Boys tend to have a more positive view of their abilities than girls in mathematics

Table 2.6: Estimates of adult illiterates and literacy rates (population aged 15+) by region, 1990 and 2000–2004

	Number of illiterates (thousands)		Literacy rates (%)		Change from 1990 to 2000–2004 in: Number of illiterates		Change from 1990 to 2000–2004 in: Literacy rates
	1990	2000-2004	1990	2000-2004	(thousand)	(%)	(percentage points)
World	871 750	771 129	75.4	81.9	-100 621	-12	6.4
Developing countries	855 127	759 199	67.0	76.4	-95 928	-11	9.4
Developed countries	14 864	10 498	98.0	98.7	-4 365	-29	0.7
Countries in transition	1 759	1 431	99.2	99.4	-328	-19	0.2
Sub-Saharan Africa	128 980	140 544	49.9	59.7	11 564	9	9.8
Arab States	63 023	65 128	50.0	62.7	2 105	3	12.6
Central Asia	572	404	98.7	99.2	-168	-29	0.5
East Asia and the Pacific	232 255	129 922	81.8	91.4	-102 333	-44	9.6
South and West Asia	382 353	381 116	47.5	58.6	-1 237	-0.3	11.2
Latin America and the Caribbean	41 742	37 901	85.0	89.7	-3 841	-9	4.7
Central and Eastern Europe	11 500	8 374	96.2	97.4	-3 126	-27	1.2
North America and Western Europe	11 326	7 740	97.9	98.7	-3 585	-32	0.8

Note: Figures may not add to totals because of rounding.
Source: Statistical annex, Table 2A.

Adult literacy rates for the period 2000–2004

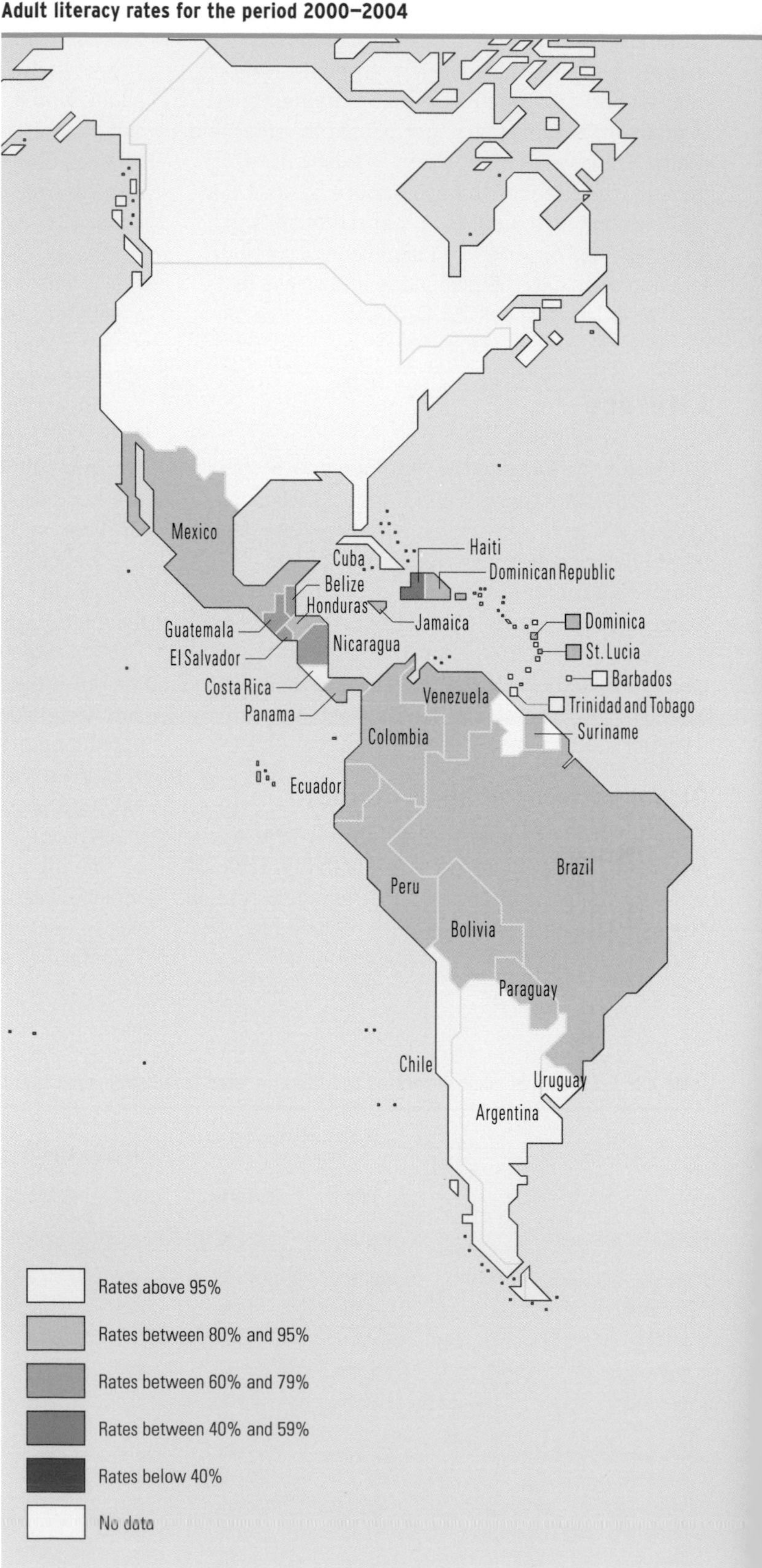

The boundaries and names shown and the designations used on this map do not imply official endorsement or acceptance by UNESCO.

Literacy data refer to the most recent year available during the period specified. They typically use UNESCO's traditional definition of literacy (i.e. the ability to read and/or write, with understanding, a simple short statement on everyday life) and are based on one of three indirect methods of assessment:

a) respondents subjectively report their literacy abilities as part of a census questionnaire or survey instrument (self-declaration);
b) the head of the household (or other adult) reports on the literacy levels of each household member (third-party assessment);
c) the number of years of schooling completed is used to distinguish the 'literate' from the 'non-literate' (educational attainment proxy).

Since the reported data do not directly assess the actual literacy and numeracy skills of the relevant adult population, they tend to overestimate literacy levels and should thus be treated with caution. Literacy data refer to combined male and female rates. See page 184 for a map of literacy challenges in selected countries and territories based on direct methods of assessment.

J. K.: Jammu and Kashmir. Dotted line represents approximately the Line of Control agreed upon by India and Pakistan. The final status of Jammu and Kashmir has not yet been agreed upon by the parties.

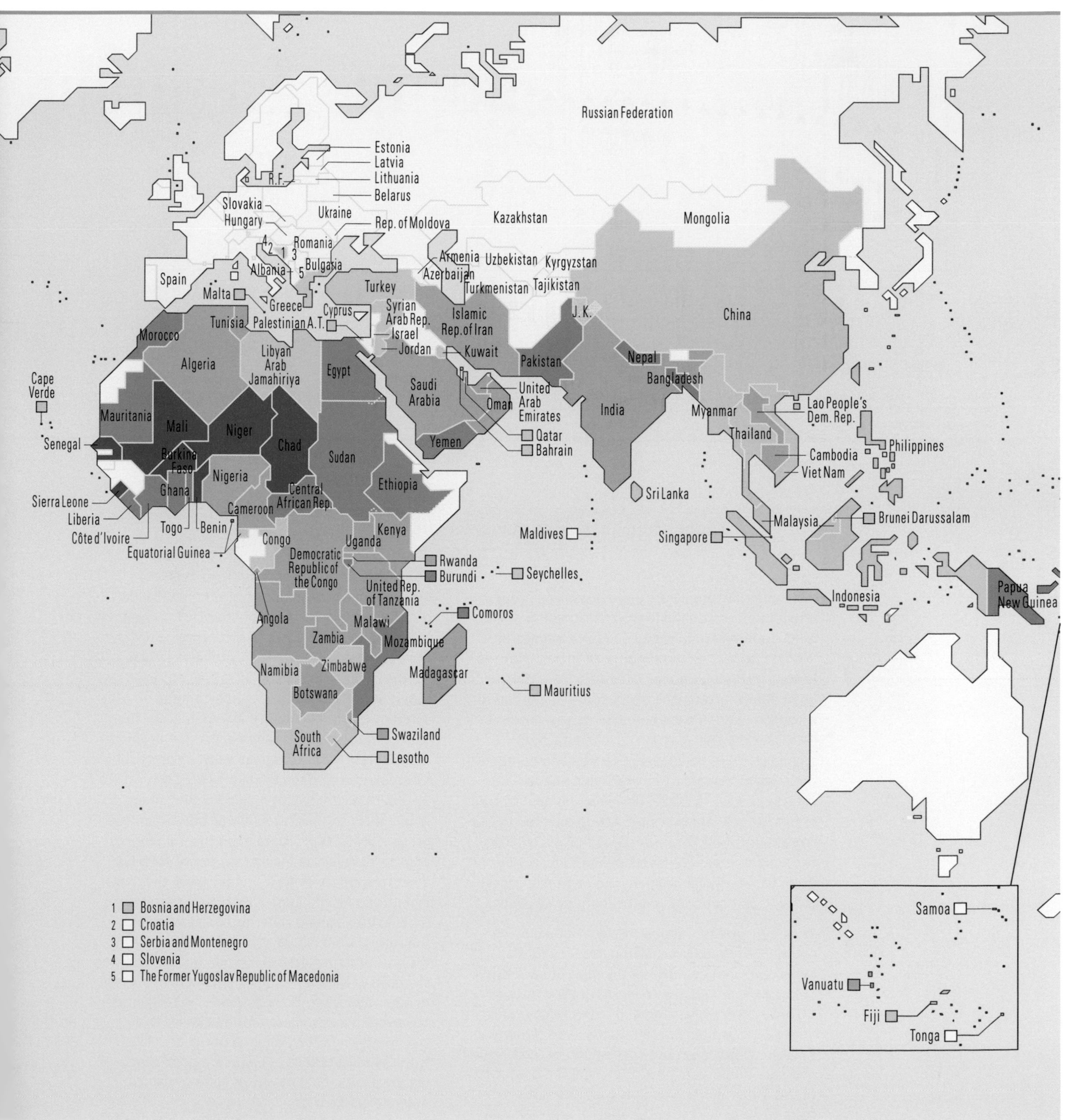

Based on United Nations map

Figure 2.28: Estimated adult literacy rates (15+): 1990, 2000–2004 and 2015 target

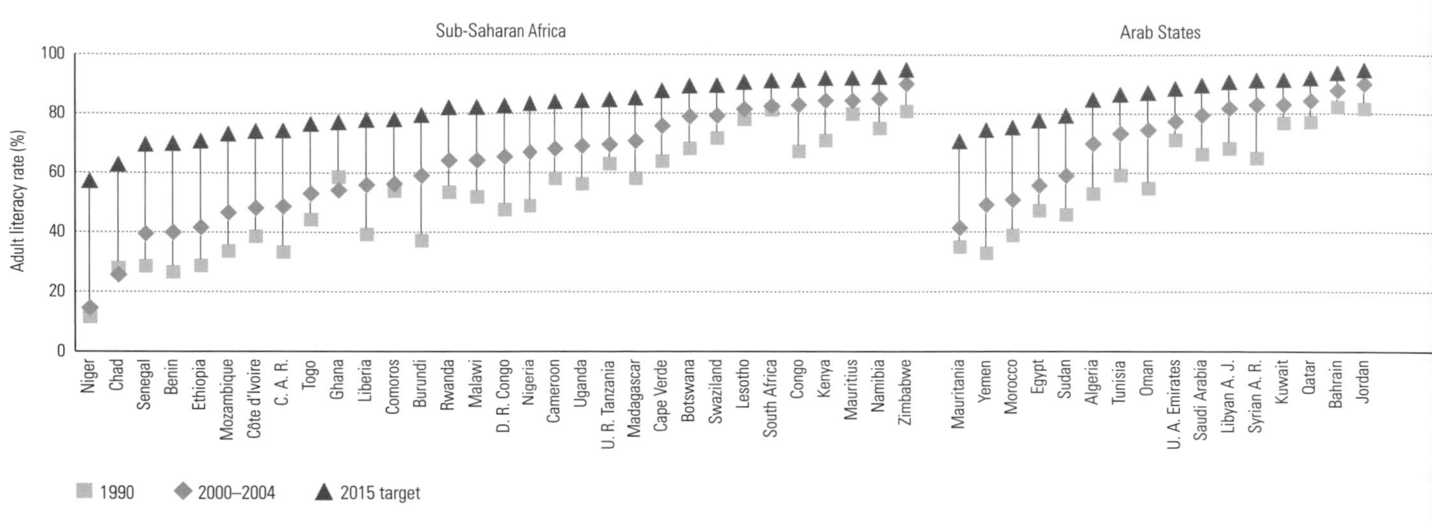

Notes: The 2015 targets are calculated on the basis of illiteracy rates reduced by 50% (see Box 2.4). Countries for which data are available for both 1990 and 2000–2004 are included, except those with literacy rates of 95% and above in 2000–2004. See source table for detailed country notes.
Source: Statistical annex, Table 2A.

Box 2.3 Measuring progress towards the adult literacy target

Early formulations of the literacy goal by the international community were organized around a reduction of adult illiteracy. Paragraph 8 of the 1990 Jomtien Framework for Action suggested 'targets' that 'countries may wish to set ... for the 1990s', including one for illiteracy: 'Reduction of the adult illiteracy rate (the appropriate age group to be determined in each country) to, say, one-half its 1990 level by the year 2000, with sufficient emphasis on female literacy to significantly reduce the current disparity between male and female illiteracy rates.' In 2000, however, the goal included in the Dakar Framework for Action adopted by the World Education Forum read: 'Achieving a 50 per cent improvement in levels of adult literacy by 2015, especially for women, and equitable access to basic and continuing education for all adults.'

Thus interpreted, though, the goal would mean (as the *EFA Global Monitoring Report 2003/4* explained) that countries with adult literacy rates below 66% would aim to increase their rates by 50% by 2015 while countries with literacy rates above 66% would aim to reach universal literacy by 2015, which does not correspond to the EFA goal and may be unrealistic. Concerning the practicality of the Dakar literacy goal, the following passage from UNESCO's first publication of international literacy statistics is relevant: 'Both theoretically and practically, it is not possible to maintain indefinitely any relative rate of progress based on increase in percentage of literacy, for eventually the maximum limit of 100 per cent would be reached where no further progress is possible. On the other hand, any given rate of progress based on the reduction in the percentage of illiteracy can be maintained indefinitely, for the limit of zero per cent is approached but never actually reached. This agrees with the practical situation in regard to illiteracy, where there will always be an irreducible minimum percentage of illiterates in any given country or population age group' (UNESCO, 1953). To allow the monitoring of progress towards the literacy target for all countries, whatever their literacy level, the Global Monitoring Report Team has chosen, therefore, to measure progress in terms of reduction in the rate of adult illiteracy, in accordance with the earlier formulation of the literacy goal: halving the level of illiteracy, rather than improving levels of adult literacy by 50%. It should be recognized, however, that this interpretation implies that the greatest effort is required of the countries with the lowest levels of literacy, a point that demonstrates the difficulty of setting realistic and relevant targets.

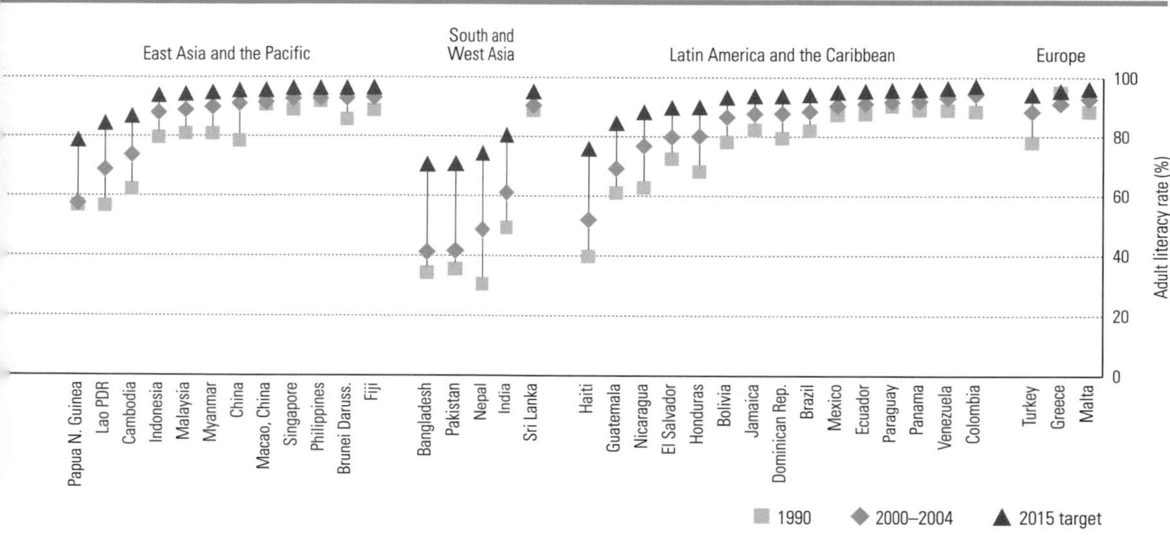

Figure 2.28 reports national progress in literacy rates since 1990 and indicates the efforts required in each country to reach the EFA literacy target by 2015. As Box 2.3 explains, the *EFA Global Monitoring Report* interprets and measures progress towards the EFA adult literacy target in the light of its formulation in the Jomtien Framework for Action, i.e. reducing adult illiteracy rates by 50%. While this interpretation underscores the fact that by far the greatest efforts are needed among countries with low literacy levels, it also enables the goal to be applied to all countries individually regardless of their present literacy rate.

Adult literacy rates in almost all countries have improved since 1990. In many cases, however, the rate of past progress is insufficient for the EFA literacy target to be reached by 2015. This is particularly so for countries with current literacy levels below 50%. Several countries with literacy rates between 50% and 65% – for example, Algeria, Burundi, the Democratic Republic of the Congo, Nigeria and Oman – have made considerable progress but will still find it difficult, on present trends, to reach the EFA literacy goal by 2015.

Gender disparities

Women account for 64% of the adults worldwide who cannot read and write with understanding, virtually unchanged from 63% in 1990. At the global level, only 88 adult women are considered literate for every 100 literate adult men. Regions with the lowest GPIs for adult literacy include South and West Asia (0.66), the Arab States (0.69) and sub-Saharan Africa (0.76). In East Asia and the Pacific, the GPI (0.92) is above the global average, and in the remaining regions, gender parity in adult literacy has been achieved. All regions have experienced increases in the GPI. The increases are especially notable in the three regions where both illiteracy rates and gender disparity are high: sub-Saharan Africa, South and West Asia, and the Arab States (see statistical annex, Table 2A).

Despite steady progress in most countries towards gender parity in adult literacy rates, significant disparities between adult men and women remain. In about one-third of the countries with detailed literacy data, fewer than 80 women are literate for every 100 men. The majority of these countries are in West and Central Africa; they also include Bangladesh, Nepal and Yemen. In several cases, gender disparities favour women over men: e.g. Botswana (1.07), Jamaica (1.09), Lesotho (1.23) and the United Arab Emirates (1.07). There is growing evidence of this trend elsewhere, particularly among the younger age cohorts (see Chapter 7).

Women account for 64% of the adults worldwide who cannot read and write with understanding

Assessing overall progress towards Education for All

The EFA Development Index provides a picture of where countries stand today

This section seeks to assess overall progress towards EFA in two ways: via the EFA Development Index (EDI), which provides a picture of where countries stand today; and by analysing country prospects for the achievement of three goals by 2015.

The Education for All Development Index

The composite EFA Development Index provides one useful summary measure of a country's situation vis-à-vis EFA as a whole. The EDI should ideally be based on progress towards all six goals. As reliable and comparable data pertaining to the achievement of goal 1 (early childhood care and education) are not available for most countries, and goal 3 (learning needs of young people and adults) is not easy to measure and to monitor, the index focuses on:

- universal primary education (goal 2), proxied by the total primary net enrolment ratio;[14]
- adult literacy (goal 4), proxied by the literacy rate for persons aged 15 and above;[15]
- gender (goal 5), proxied by the Gender-specific EFA Index (GEI), an arithmetical mean of the GPIs for primary and secondary gross enrolment ratios and the adult literacy rate;
- quality of education (goal 6), proxied by the survival rate to Grade 5.

The EDI weights the four goals equally. As all four constituents are expressed as rates, the EDI ranges from 0 to 100%, or when expressed as a ratio, from 0 to 1, where 1 represents the achievement of Education for All as summarized by the index. Appendix 1 provides detailed explanations of the EDI rationale and methodology.

14. The total primary NER includes children of primary school age who are enrolled either in primary or in secondary school.

15. The literacy data used are based on 'conventional' assessment methods, as noted earlier, and thus should be interpreted with caution: they are not based on any test, and may overestimate literacy. See Chapter 7 for a fuller explanation.

16. See Appendix 1 for a detailed discussion of the projection methodology.

Table 2.7: Distribution of countries by EDI values, by region, 2002

	Far from EFA: EDI below 0.80	Intermediate position: EDI between 0.80 and 0.94	Close to EFA: EDI between 0.95 and 0.97	EFA achieved: EDI between 0.98 and 1.00
Sub-Saharan Africa	16	7	1	
Arab States	5	10	1	
Central Asia		2	1	2
East Asia and the Pacific	3	7	2	1
South and West Asia	3	1		
Latin America/Caribbean	1	20	4	1
North America/West. Europe		1	7	8
Central and Eastern Europe		1	12	4
Total	28	49	28	16

Source: Appendix 1, Table A1.

Table A1.1 of Appendix 1 displays the EDI for 2002, a year for which it was possible to compute the index for 121 countries. Table 2.7 summarizes this information, breaking it down by category and by region, confirming the patterns discussed in the previous sections:

- Forty-four countries (more than one-third of those for which data are available) have an EDI above 0.95 and are thus in the category of having achieved EFA or being close to doing so. Most are in North America and Western Europe, and Central and Eastern Europe, where compulsory education has been in force for decades.
- Forty-nine countries, across all regions, have EDI values between 0.80 and 0.94. Quality (measured by survival rate to Grade 5) is an issue especially in Latin America and the Caribbean, and adult literacy in the Arab States.
- Twenty-eight countries have EDI values below 0.80. More than half of them are in sub-Saharan Africa. In these countries, all four components of the EDI are at low levels: Achieving EFA would require intervention throughout the school system.

Changes in the EDI between 1998 and 2002 were moderate. On average, the index increased by 1.2%, and the ranking of countries was stable. Significant progress (by more than 10%) was made in Cambodia, Côte d'Ivoire, Ethiopia and Mozambique (Figure 2.29). Several countries registering sharp decreases (between 5% and 11%), resulting from deterioration in the survival rate to Grade 5, include Chad, Guyana, Papua New Guinea and, Trinidad and Tobago. In more than three-quarters of the fifty-eight countries included in the analysis, at least one indicator moved in the opposite direction to the others (see statistical annex, Table 3).

Prospects for the achievement of Education for All by 2015

One way to examine prospects is to project to 2015 on the basis of 1990 and 2002.[16] Projections were made for universal primary education (goal 2), adult literacy (goal 4) and gender parity in primary and secondary education (goal 5). These results are not forecasts and may not reflect the impact of recent changes in policies; but they are a useful monitoring tool nonetheless.

Figure 2.29: The EDI in 2002 and its evolution since 1998 in countries with low EDI

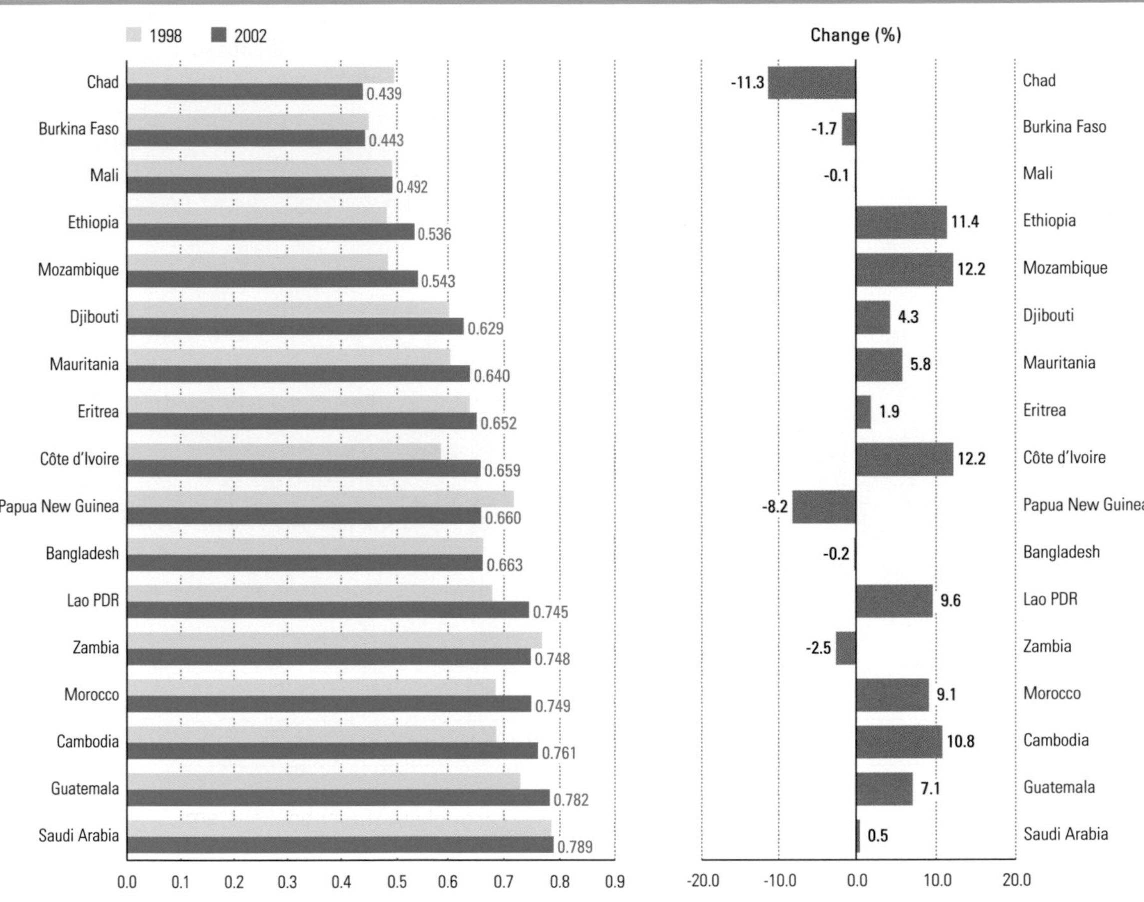

Note: Countries with an EDI below 0.800 in 2002 are included.
Source: Appendix 1, Table A1.3.

Universal primary education

As in the EDI, progress towards UPE is proxied by the total primary NER. Among the 163 countries for which 2002 data were available, 47, mostly in North America and Western Europe, and Latin America and the Caribbean, had achieved UPE by that year. Projections could be run for about 90 of the remaining 116 countries. Table 2.8 displays the results.

- Only twenty countries are likely to achieve UPE by 2015. For example, Colombia's NER increased from 70% to 90% between 1990 and 2002, making it likely that UPE will be achieved by 2015. Indonesia had achieved UPE in 1990 but its NER had decreased to 95% by 1999 due to economic and political crisis; recovery makes it likely that Indonesia will have achieved UPE again by 2015.
- Forty-four countries, most of them starting from low enrolment levels, might not achieve UPE, but are making reasonable progress. For example, Burkina Faso's NER increased rapidly from 26% to 36% between 1990 and 2002, but is still very low. Bangladesh's NER rose from 78% in 1990 to 88% in 1998 but has since stagnated.
- Twenty countries are at risk of not achieving the goal because their NERs are decreasing. These are mostly countries in transition in Central and Eastern Europe, and Central Asia whose school systems have yet to recover from the difficulties they have encountered since 1990.
- Three countries included in the analysis stand out as being at serious risk of not achieving UPE by 2015: Azerbaijan, Papua New Guinea and Saudi Arabia, which have NERs that are below 80% and decreasing.

Only twenty countries are likely to achieve UPE by 2015

Table 2.8: Country prospects for the achievement of universal primary education by 2015

Distance from 100% NER in 2002		Away from the goal	Towards the goal
	Close or in an intermediate position	**QUADRANT I** At risk of not achieving the goal 20 countries Albania, Bahrain, British Virgin Islands, Czech Republic, Equatorial Guinea, Estonia, Georgia, Kuwait, Kyrgyzstan, Slovenia, Maldives, Malaysia, Netherlands Antilles, Palestinian A. T., Paraguay, Romania, South Africa, TFYR of Macedonia, Uruguay, Viet Nam	**QUADRANT II** High chance of achieving the goal 20 countries Algeria, Belarus, Bolivia, Bulgaria, Cambodia, Colombia, Cuba, Guatemala, Indonesia, Ireland, Jamaica, Jordan, Lesotho, Lithuania, Malta, Mauritius, Morocco, Nicaragua, Vanuatu, Venezuela
	Intermediate position or far	**QUADRANT IV** Serious risk of not achieving the goal 3 countries Azerbaijan, Papua New Guinea, Saudi Arabia	**QUADRANT III** Low chance of achieving the goal 44 countries Bangladesh, Benin, Botswana, Burkina Faso, Burundi, Chad, Chile, Costa Rica, Côte d'Ivoire, Croatia, Djibouti, Egypt, El Salvador, Eritrea, Ethiopia, Gambia, Ghana, Guinea, Iran (Isl. Rep.), Kenya, Lao PDR, Latvia, Lebanon, Macao (China), Madagascar, Mali, Mauritania, Mongolia, Mozambique, Myanmar, Namibia, Niger, Oman, Republic of Moldova, Saint Vincent and the Grenadines, Senegal, Swaziland, Thailand, Trinidad and Tobago, United Arab Emirates, U. R. of Tanzania, Yemen, Zambia, Zimbabwe
		Change over the period from 1990 to 2002	

Thirty countries, including India and Pakistan, are at risk of not achieving the literacy goal by 2015

Adult literacy

For this analysis of prospects, countries with current literacy rates above 97% are considered as close to 'universal literacy' (still speaking in terms of data derived from non-direct, non-test assessment) and therefore are not included in the analysis. Such countries account for less than 30% of those with data available for 2000–2004. Most of them are in Central Asia, Central and Eastern Europe, and Western Europe. By contrast, no country in the Arab States, South and West Asia or sub-Saharan Africa is close to 'universal literacy'. As noted earlier, those are the regions with the lowest average adult literacy rates.

As adult literacy rates are increasing everywhere, a distinction is drawn between countries progressing relatively slowly (slow performers) towards high literacy or relatively rapidly (fast performers). Projections could be run for ninety-two countries, including nineteen that have reached literacy rates above 97% (most of them in Europe and Central Asia). Table 2.9 displays the results for the remaining seventy three countries.

- Twenty-three countries stand a fairly high chance of meeting goal 4, as their literacy rates are already relatively high and increasing quite quickly.
- Twenty countries, many of them in Latin America and the Caribbean, are at risk of not meeting the goal given the current pace of increase in their literacy rates, though the rates themselves are quite high.
- Thirty countries are at serious risk of not achieving the goal by 2015 because their very low literacy rates are not increasing fast enough. Most of these countries are in Africa, but the list also includes India, Nepal and Pakistan, and several Latin American countries.

Gender parity in primary and secondary education

Country prospects for the achievement of gender parity are assessed on the basis of trend projections of GERs in primary and secondary education, by gender, for 2005 and 2015 consistent with the formulation of the gender goal. Table 2.10 displays the results for 149 countries.

Table 2.9: Country prospects for the achievement of the adult literacy target by 2015

Level of adult literacy rate in 2000–2004			
	High literacy (between 80% and 97%)	**QUADRANT I** At risk of not achieving the goal 20 countries Brazil, Colombia, Dominican Republic, Ecuador, Honduras, Malaysia, Mauritius, Myanmar, Namibia, Panama, Peru, Philippines, Qatar, Saint Lucia, Sri Lanka, Suriname, Swaziland, Syrian Arab Republic, Turkey, Viet Nam	**QUADRANT II** High chance of achieving the goal 23 countries Bahrain, Bolivia, Bosnia and Herzogovina, Brunei Darussalam, Chile, China, Cyprus, Equatorial Guinea, Greece, Israel, Jordan, Macao (China), Maldives, Mexico, Palestinian Autonomous Territories, Paraguay, Republic of Moldova, Saudi Arabia, Serbia and Montenegro, Singapore, Thailand, TFYR of Macedonia, Venezuela
	Low literacy (below 80%)	**QUADRANT IV** Serious risk of not achieving the goal 30 countries Algeria, Angola, Belize, Benin, Burundi, Cambodia, Central African Republic, Chad, Côte d'Ivoire, Democratic Republic of the Congo, El Salvador, Guatemala, India, Kenya, Lao PDR, Madagascar, Mauritania, Nepal, Nicaragua, Niger, Pakistan, Papua New Guinea, Rwanda, Senegal, Sierra Leone, Sudan, Togo, Tunisia, U. R. Tanzania, Zambia	**QUADRANT III** Low chance of achieving the goal 0 country
		Slow performers	Fast performers
		Increase between 1990 and 2000–2004	

Three main categories emerge:

- Forty-nine countries had achieved gender parity in primary and secondary enrolment by 2002. All EFA regions are represented, and some large Asian countries, including China and Indonesia, are among these forty-nine countries. Six more countries are likely to achieve gender parity in primary and secondary education by 2005 and eight more will likely do so by 2015.
- Forty-three countries that had achieved gender parity in primary education in 2002, and twelve that are likely to do so by 2005 or 2015, will probably not achieve it in secondary education. In most of these fifty-five countries, gender disparities are in favour of girls: in many cases enrolment is high for both sexes and greater success in primary schooling translates into higher transition rates and retention levels in secondary education for girls (Box 2.4). There are also countries, such as India, where girls' enrolment is rapidly increasing at the primary level but their transition rates to secondary school remain low.
- Twenty-four countries are unlikely to achieve parity at either level by 2015. In these countries, disparities are in favour of boys, and the school system is underdeveloped at both the primary and secondary levels.[17]

Thus, of the hundred countries that had not achieved gender parity in either primary or secondary education or both levels in 2002, only six were likely to reach both by 2005, and eight more by 2015, while eighty-six countries are at risk of not achieving gender parity (seven in primary education, fifty-five in secondary education and twenty-four in both). Gender disparities in enrolment remain the rule rather than the exception and present trends are insufficient for the Dakar goals to be met.

Conclusion

The discussion in this chapter has shown that there has been steady but insufficient progress towards the EFA goals. In particular, the gender parity goal for 2005 has been missed, even though the latest data are for the 2002/2003 school year. There has been little change in individual country prospects across the goals since the first two reports. Projections made this year reinforce previous observations that there is a pattern of countries that are, or are not, likely to achieve the UPE, adult literacy and gender goals, although projections were not possible for some key countries and hence the listings in this chapter are not comprehensive. In general, all the evidence continues to point towards the need for

There is need for a continued heavy focus on sub-Saharan Africa, South and West Asia, and the Arab States

17. In addition, seven countries have achieved gender parity at the secondary level, or may achieve it by 2015, without being likely to achieve it at the primary level.

Table 2.10: Country prospects for the achievement of gender parity in primary and secondary education by 2005 and 2015

Gender parity in primary education	Gender parity in secondary education: Achieved in 2002	Likely to be achieved in 2005	Likely to be achieved in 2015	At risk of not achieving the goal by 2015	Number of countries
Achieved in 2002	Albania, Anguilla, Armenia, Australia, Azerbaijan, Bahamas, Barbados, Belarus, Bulgaria, Canada, Chile, China, Croatia, Cyprus, Czech Republic, Ecuador, France, Georgia, Germany, Greece, Hungary, Indonesia, Israel, Italy, Jamaica, Japan, Jordan, Kazakhstan, Kyrgyzstan, Latvia, Lithuania, Malta, Mauritius, Netherlands, Norway, Oman, Republic of Korea, Republic of Moldova, Romania, Russian Federation, Serbia and Montenegro, Seychelles, Slovakia, Slovenia, The former Yugoslav Rep. of Macedonia, Ukraine, United Arab Emirates, United States, Uzbekistan 49	Austria, Bolivia, Guyana, Kenya 4	Switzerland, Argentina, Belize, Botswana 4	Gambia, Mauritania, Myanmar, Peru, Poland, Rwanda, Uganda, Zimbabwe, Bahrain, Bangladesh, Belgium, Brunei Darussalam, Colombia, Costa Rica, Denmark, Dominican Republic, Finland, Iceland, Ireland, Kuwait, Lesotho, Luxembourg, Malaysia, Maldives, Mexico, Mongolia, Namibia, Netherlands Antilles, New Zealand, Nicaragua, Palestinian Autonomous Territories, Philippines, Qatar, Saint Lucia, Saint Vincent and the Grenadines, Samoa, Spain, Suriname, Tonga, Trinidad and Tobago, United Kingdom, Vanuatu, Venezuela 43	100
Likely to be achieved in 2005	Estonia 1	Islamic Republic of Iran 1	Ghana, Saudi Arabia 2	India, Syrian Arab Republic, Lebanon, Panama, Tunisia 5	9
Likely to be achieved in 2015	Cuba 1	Egypt 1		Nepal, Senegal, Tajikistan, Togo, Zambia, Brazil, Portugal 7	9
At risk of not achieving the goal by 2015	El Salvador, Swaziland, Paraguay 3		Cameroon, Macao (China), South Africa, Viet Nam 4	Benin, Burkina Faso, Burundi, Cambodia, Chad, Comoros, Côte d'Ivoire, Djibouti, Eritrea, Ethiopia, Guatemala, Lao People's Democratic Republic, Malawi, Mali, Morocco, Mozambique, Niger, Papua New Guinea, Sudan, Turkey, Yemen, Algeria, Aruba, British Virgin Islands 24	31
Number of countries	54	6	10	79	149

Note: Where countries are shown in blue, enrolment disparities at the expense of boys are observed in secondary education.

Box 2.4 Gender disparities in enrolment ratios

In much of the world, the main challenge in achieving the EFA gender parity goal is still to increase girls' access to schooling. In a growing number of countries, however, enrolment ratios are now *higher* for girls than for boys, especially at the secondary and tertiary levels. Although there are exceptions, such countries are typically either developed countries or developing countries that are close to UPE. Among the seventy-nine countries that are unlikely to achieve gender parity in secondary education by 2015, forty-two have lower enrolment ratios for boys than for girls. Research and results of student assessment worldwide show that boys tend to perform worse than girls, to repeat grades and fail graduation exams, and to leave the school system earlier. This situation, which requires policy attention, is the reason for developed countries such as Denmark, Finland, New Zealand and the United Kingdom appearing in Table 2.10 as being at risk of not achieving gender parity in secondary education by 2015. The problem is also increasingly common in developing countries, especially those of Latin America and the Caribbean.

A qualification is that higher enrolment ratios for girls than for boys may well coexist with persisting inequalities against girls, either in the school system itself (teaching practices, curriculum, etc.) or in other institutions such as the labour market, where women often need higher qualifications than men to reach the same outcomes. Public policies aimed at bringing about gender equality in education thus need to go far beyond initiatives that focus on enrolment ratios alone.

a continued heavy focus on sub-Saharan Africa, South and West Asia, and the Arab States, along with the least developed countries in other regions. Countries most at risk need to redouble their efforts in certain key policy areas, especially domestic resource mobilization (see Chapter 3), and need further external assistance (see Chapter 4). ■

Teaching geography
to young herders
in Ladakh, India.

Chapter 3

Country efforts: increasing momentum

Progress towards the EFA goals is steady, but too slow in terms of the target dates, especially in sub-Saharan Africa, South and West Asia, and the Arab States. The first time-bound goal, gender parity in primary and secondary school by 2005, has already been missed. Accelerating the pace of change sufficiently to meet the goals for 2015 requires more attention to planning, strategies, resources and key policy issues in many countries. This chapter examines selected elements from a sampling of national EFA plans, considers public financing and household costs (with updated information on fees at the primary level) and continues the 2005 Report's attention to teachers, focusing particularly on projected needs. It stresses the necessity of maintaining momentum towards gender parity, despite the disappointment of the missed goal, and the growing urgency of other crucial issues: inclusion, education in difficult country circumstances, response to the HIV/AIDS pandemic, and assuring students' health and safety.

Planning for EFA

National policy priorities and EFA

National education plans must address all the EFA goals

The 2000 Dakar Framework for Action called for comprehensive national EFA plans to be drawn up by 2002. These time-bound, action-oriented plans must include specific reforms addressing each of the six EFA goals, along with a sustainable financial framework.[1] Poverty Reduction Strategy Papers (PRSPs)[2] address the Millennium Development Goals (MDGs) with a similar sense of purpose. One of the two Millennium Project reports on education and gender equality calls on developing country governments to put bold strategies in place by 2006, and recommends that existing PRSPs should be aligned with the MDGs (Millennium Project, 2005*a*).

Previous EFA Global Monitoring Reports have addressed particular aspects of EFA plans and PRSPs. A review of the seventeen PRSPs completed by July 2002 suggested that EFA and the education MDGs were receiving increasing attention in poverty alleviation and education plans (Bagai, 2002). The 2003/4 Report reviewed PRSP content related to education and gender and noted evidence that countries were beginning to set national targets related to EFA and the MDGs (Whitehead, 2003). The 2005 Report highlighted ambitious country policies for delivering EFA and the effective use of aid for national plans. In the present Report, Chapter 9 examines the inclusion of literacy in PRSPs (UNESCO-IIEP, 2005*a*). A review of the education content of the eighteen PRSPs completed by May 2003 (Caillods and Hallak, 2004) finds that, while the papers' education chapters became better and more realistic over time, policy priorities remained insufficiently adapted to individual country circumstances and the education chapters were not well integrated into the broader strategies. The financial sustainability of the PRSP education plans is also a question, since they seem at once too optimistic about domestic financing and heavily dependent on external aid; in addition, the plans devote relatively little attention to literacy or early childhood care and education (ECCE).

To review plans requires analysis of individual papers since there is no database with comprehensive coverage of goals, strategies, financing or other elements of EFA plans, PRSPs and other relevant country education planning documents, such as sector plans. UNESCO collects data on EFA plans only on an occasional basis.[3] Future Reports will further examine PRSPs and other national planning documents. As a first step, this Report uses two new sources from UNESCO institutes: a survey by the International Institute for Educational Planning (IIEP) of EFA plans in thirty-five countries[4] and an analysis by the International Bureau of Education (IBE) of country papers prepared for the 2001 and 2004 sessions of the International Conference on Education. Neither survey, however, can provide information on implementation, financial allocations or general support for national strategies by government or civil society.

Most of the thirty-five EFA plans are relatively recent and long-term: 79% were issued between 2001 and 2005, and 58% cover ten-year periods, especially those of countries in sub-Saharan Africa and the Arab States.[5]

Table 3.1 shows the coverage of individual EFA goals in thirty-two of the plans. The top priority is clearly universal primary education (UPE), addressed by increasing mass schooling in South Asia and sub-Saharan Africa, and by targeting disadvantaged groups in other regions, where enrolment rates are relatively high. Goal 3, meeting the learning needs of young people and adults through equitable access to appropriate learning and life-skills programmes, is apparently the most disregarded, cited in only one-third of the countries in the sample. Of the thirty-two countries, only Benin, India, Indonesia, Kenya, Paraguay, the Sudan and Uzbekistan have plans that include all six goals, while Bangladesh, Brazil, Côte d'Ivoire, Mongolia, Myanmar, Nepal, Nicaragua and the Niger give explicit attention to at least five of the goals. Box 3.1 shows some of the strategies these fifteen countries are adopting.

The IIEP work suggests that central government financing levels may not match countries' ambitious

1. UNESCO has commissioned an evaluation of its role in supporting the development of EFA plans, to be completed by the end of 2005.

2. Fifty-six countries had developed full or interim PRSPs by July 2005; see www.imf.org/external/np/prsp/prsp.asp

3. See UNESCO surveys of EFA plans at http://portal.unesco.org/education/en/ev.php-URL_ID=9328&URL_DO=DO_TOPIC&URL_SECTION=201.html

4. Countries were selected from three groups, derived from work done for the 2002 Report (UNESCO, 2002*b*): those with a high chance of achieving all three quantitative EFA goals by 2015, those likely to miss one of the goals by 2015 and those at serious risk of not achieving any of the three goals by 2015.

5. The UNESCO-IIEP survey also identified some evidence of countries translating their long-term plans into action plans covering three to five years, such as Morocco's 'Medium-Term Action Plan for 2004–2007' and Nicaragua's 'Strategic Priorities for the Period 2005–2008', both issued in 2004 (UNESCO-IIEP, 2005*b*).

Table 3.1: Coverage of the EFA time-bound goals in planning documents of thirty-two countries

Country	Number of countries in the sample	Goal 1 ECCE	Goal 2 UPE	Goal 3 Youth/adult learning	Goal 4 Literacy	Goal 5 Gender	Goal 6 Quality	Number addressing all six goals	Number addressing at least five goals
Sub-Saharan Africa	10	5	10	3	6	8	9	2	4
Arab States	4	3	4	2	4	1	2	1	1
Central Asia	3	3	3	2	3	2	2	1	2
East Asia and the Pacific	3	3	3	1	3	2	3	1	2
South and West Asia	5	4	5	1	4	3	5	1	3
Latin America and the Caribbean	7	6	7	3	5	2	6	1	3
Total	**32**	**24**	**32**	**12**	**25**	**18**	**27**	**7**	**15**

Source: UNESCO-IIEP (2005*b*).

The Plan for the Quality of Brazilian Education focuses on teachers

Box 3.1 National strategies addressing EFA goals: some country examples

Major strategies adopted by some or all of the fifteen countries in the IIEP sample whose EFA plans address at least five of the six EFA goals include:

- ECCE strategies putting priority on underserved and disadvantaged groups (seven countries). Mongolia is developing incentives for home-based ECCE measures for herding populations.
- UPE strategies giving particular attention to removing access barriers to quality schooling (all fifteen countries). Kenya is introducing free primary education, targeted school meal programmes, a textbook fund for poor households and a bursary fund to enable students from poor families to make the transition from primary to secondary education.
- UPE strategies that highlight inclusion and equity of access for severely disadvantaged groups such as street children (eleven countries). In India, strategies aimed at working children include the scaling up of operations such as back-to-school camps, summer schools, bridging courses, continuous academic and emotional support after children join school, and programmes such as the National Child Labour Project initiated by the Ministry of Labour, through which education is provided to working children.
- Strategies to reduce illiteracy (eight countries). Benin's comprehensive approach includes measures to increase demand, improve the quality of literacy programmes, increase funding and strengthen decentralized management systems.
- Strategies to increase women's and girls' access to education (ten countries), particularly incentives to reduce private costs, provision of separate boarding facilities, increased hiring of female teachers, elimination of gender stereotypes in learning materials, and sensitization of teachers and managers to girls' needs and circumstances. Côte d'Ivoire recognizes the importance of legal and policy frameworks to address the many social dimensions of inequality.
- Strategies to improve quality (all fifteen countries). Bangladesh, Benin, Côte d'Ivoire, India, Kenya and the Niger cite the need for new and refurbished classrooms. The Plan for the Quality of Brazilian Education focuses on teachers, including ways to improve the qualifications of underqualified teachers; recruitment; and nationwide professional development, especially in Portuguese and mathematics, for elementary school teachers.

Source: UNESCO-IIEP (2005*b*).

national goals. For the thirty countries for which it was possible to obtain financial data, ten spent less than 3% of GDP on education, fourteen spent 3% to 5% and six spent 5% to 9%. For the thirty countries for which it was possible to examine trends in education expenditure over 2000–2004, budget allocations generally increased in Latin America but declined in sub-Saharan Africa.

The IBE survey analysed reports (rather than planning documents) made by sixty-nine countries participating in the 2001 and 2004 International Conferences on Education (Amadio et al., 2005). Nearly all countries identified UPE and education quality as high priorities on both occasions (Figure 3.1). There was a noticeable increase in attention between 2001 and 2004 to gender parity and equality, and life-skills

Figure 3.1: Policy commitments related to EFA goals in 2001 and 2004 conference reports by sixty-nine countries

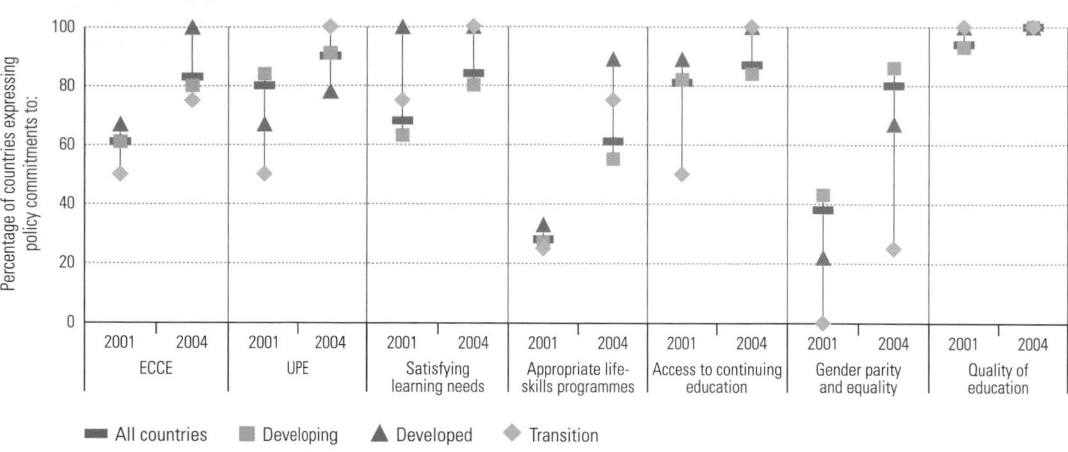

Source: Amadio et al. (2005), drawing on reports to International Conference on Education.

Figure 3.2: Strategies and actions on issues affecting EFA goals reported to 2001 and 2004 conferences by sixty-nine countries

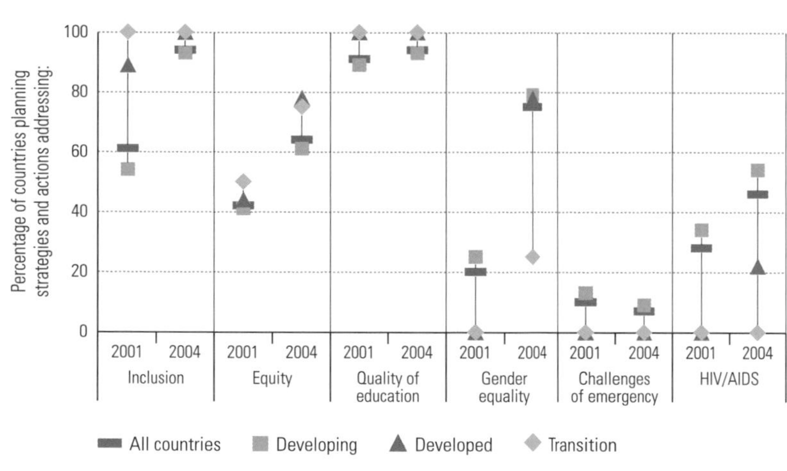

Source: Amadio et al. (2005), drawing on reports to International Conference on Education.

programmes for young people and adults, especially in Central and Eastern Europe, East Asia and the Pacific, and sub-Saharan Africa.[6] References to the importance of the MDGs also increased. Attention is increasingly being paid as well to inclusion, equity, quality, gender equality, situations of emergency and HIV/AIDS (Figure 3.2).

The contribution of civil society

A key strategy identified at Dakar as critical to achieving EFA is assuring the engagement and participation of civil society in the formulation, implementation and monitoring of national strategies (UNESCO, 2000*b*). There is growing evidence from various regions of increasing civil society participation in education policy processes, notably the preparation of national EFA plans (Schnuttgen and Khan, 2004; UNESCO, 2003*b*). Bangladesh is of particular interest (Box 3.2), but there are also developments in Latin America, where civil society organizations (CSOs) in Brazil and El Salvador are involved in monitoring public spending on education (Schnuttgen and Khan, 2004), and in sub-Saharan Africa, where the Global Campaign for Education is initiating activities in West Africa, and CSOs in various countries (notably Malawi, Uganda, the United Republic of Tanzania and Zambia) are monitoring budgets and outputs related to poverty reduction policies, especially those having to do with education.

Despite these initiatives, challenges to full participation by CSOs remain. The most pressing one is the degree of space and opportunity that governments provide. In some countries, this is not available; in many countries, for example, teacher organizations and unions are not fully engaged in national policy discussions (see section below on Teachers for EFA). Even where such space is created, it is often limited to time-bound thematic consultations rather than involving sustained, institutionalized dialogue on national education policy as a whole. Moreover, many CSOs have insufficient capacity and resources to participate in technical and time-consuming policy-related discussions. Overall, it remains uncertain whether the first decade

6. The apparent discrepancy between the IBE survey's finding of increasing priority on learning opportunities and life-skills programmes and the IIEP analysis showing no such trend is probably related to the nature of the conference documents, which reflect conference themes rather than providing comprehensive coverage.

Box 3.2 Civil society involvement in EFA planning and monitoring

In Bangladesh, the Campaign for Popular Education (CAMPE), a national coalition of NGOs, has a reputation for innovation and comprehensive coverage of issues affecting education. It pioneered the Education Watch project, which has sought to track the efficiency of primary education and literacy in Bangladesh. The first Education Watch Report was published in 1999. It and its successors have served as powerful tools, collecting and disseminating assessments of progress in education reform. The main themes of the Education Watch Reports have included internal efficiency, quality of education and literacy. The latest edition is titled *Quality with Equity: The Primary Education Agenda*. External to the government, Education Watch provides a rich database for alternative policy formulation by CSOs. CAMPE not only works closely with research institutions and NGOs in Bangladesh, but has also approached other national NGOs in South Asia as well as a regional network, the Asian South Pacific Bureau of Adult Education, to become its partners in extending the programme across South Asia.

Sources: Campaign for Popular Education (1999, 2001, 2002, 2003, 2005); Schnuttgen and Kahn (2004).

of this century will be characterized by a more participatory approach than was the case in the 1990s (UNESCO, 2002*b* and 2003*b*).

Financing EFA

The importance of public financing

Reaching the EFA goals requires adequate and predictable funding for education (Colclough with Lewin, 1993; Mehrotra, 1998; Bruns et al., 2003). It has been argued that governments should invest at least 6% of GNP in education (Delors et al., 1996). The appropriate level of spending will, in practice, depend on many factors, including countries' demographic, economic, political and educational circumstances and the extent of private financing. There is, however, clearly a minimum level below which government expenditure cannot sink without serious consequences for quality, as the 2005 Report argued.[7] Moreover, the level of public spending is often interpreted as a reflection of government commitment to education and is thus of high political significance.

Figure 3.3 provides a global picture of the volume of public education spending relative to levels of national income.[8] While there is substantial variation within regions, regional medians are highest in North America and Western Europe, and in East Asia and the Pacific. Total public spending on education is close to 2%

The level of public spending on education is of high political significance

7. See, in particular, Chapter 4 (UNESCO, 2004*a*).

8. Because of relatively poor country reporting of financial data to the UNESCO Institute for Statistics, the country coverage in this section on education finance is less extensive than that in the discussion of enrolment in Chapter 2. In addition, as spending by subnational levels of government is generally excluded, public funding is underestimated in some countries, particularly those with federal systems.

Figure 3.3: Public current expenditure on education as percentage of GNP, 2002

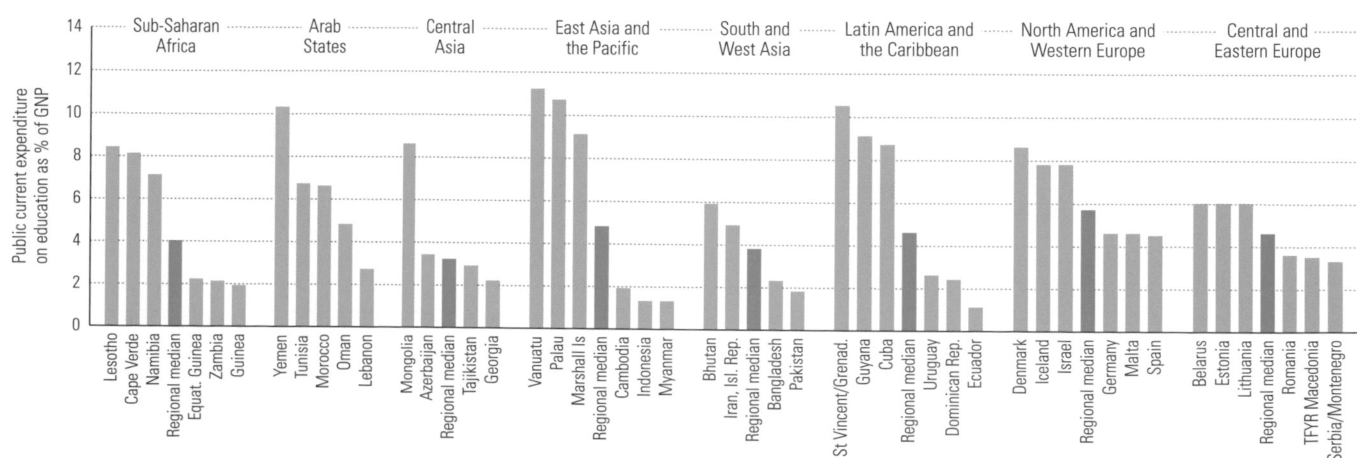

Note: The figure shows regional medians and countries with the highest and lowest values. No regional median was calculated for Arab States because data were available for too few countries. See source table for detailed country notes.

Source: Statistical annex, Table 11.

Figure 3.4: Public expenditure on education as percentage of total government expenditure, 2002

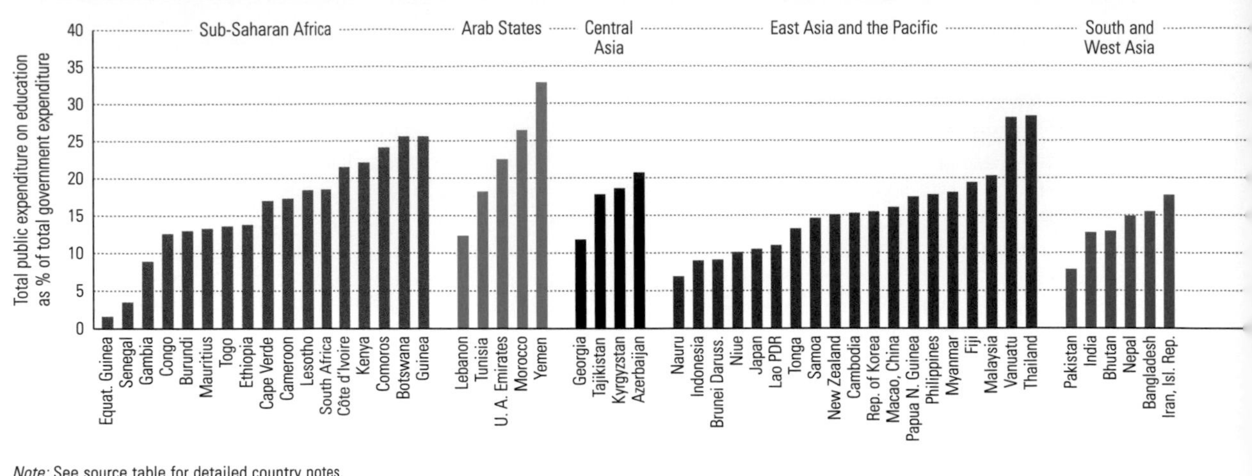

Note: See source table for detailed country notes.
Source: Statistical annex, Table 11.

Figure 3.5: Public education expenditure as a percentage of GNP, 1998 and 2002

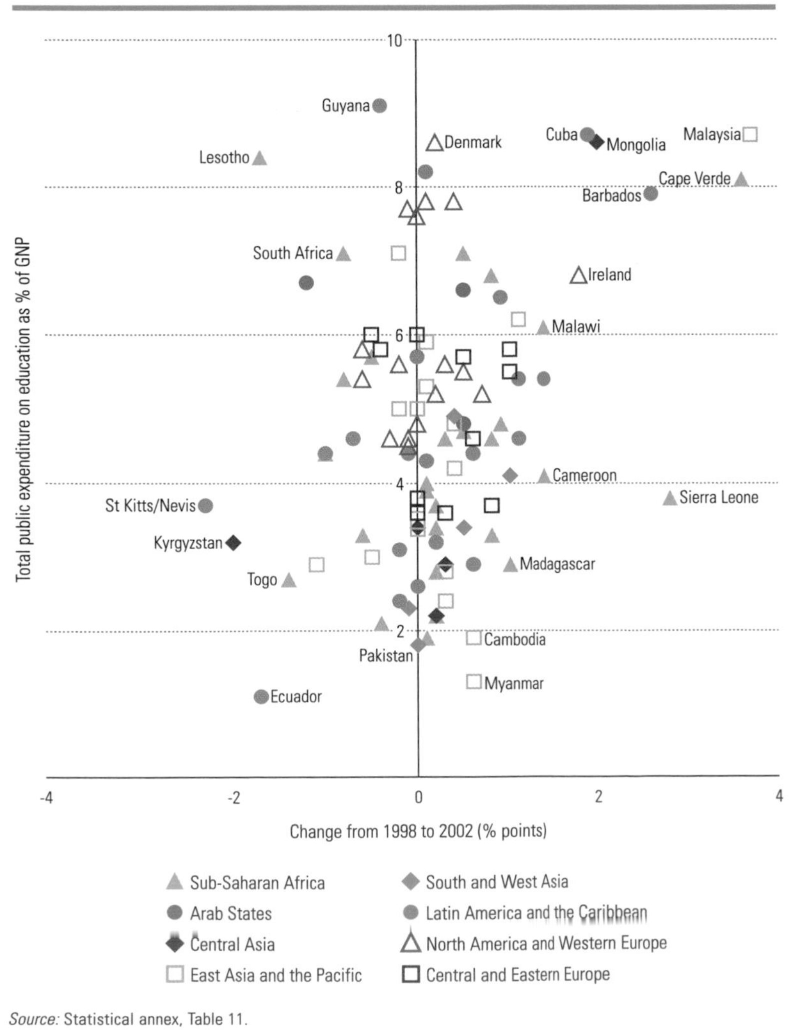

Source: Statistical annex, Table 11.

of GNP in Cambodia, Ecuador, Equatorial Guinea, Georgia, Guinea, Indonesia, Myanmar, Pakistan and Zambia, but exceeds 6% of GNP in about one-quarter of the countries with data available (see statistical annex, Table 11).

The percentage of the government budget allocated to education completes the picture of governments' commitment to education, reflecting the degree of priority they give to education relative to other national expenditure. Figure 3.4 shows that the share of government expenditure devoted to education ranges from about 10% to 30%. While government expenditures on education in high income countries in North America and Western Europe rarely reach 15%, more than half of the countries in sub-Saharan Africa with data available surpass this level. Education accounts for one-quarter or more of total governement budget in Botswana, Guinea, Mexico, Morocco, Thailand, Vanuatu and Yemen. It is interesting to note that some countries like Botswana and Guinea, which allocate a small proportion of their GNP to education, give high priority to it in their government budget.

Spending on education has increased since 1998

The share of education in national income (GNP) increased between 1998 and 2002 in about two-thirds of the countries for which data are available (Figure 3.5). It more than doubled in Cameroon, Cape Verde, Madagascar, Malaysia, and Saint Vincent and the Grenadines. Similarly,

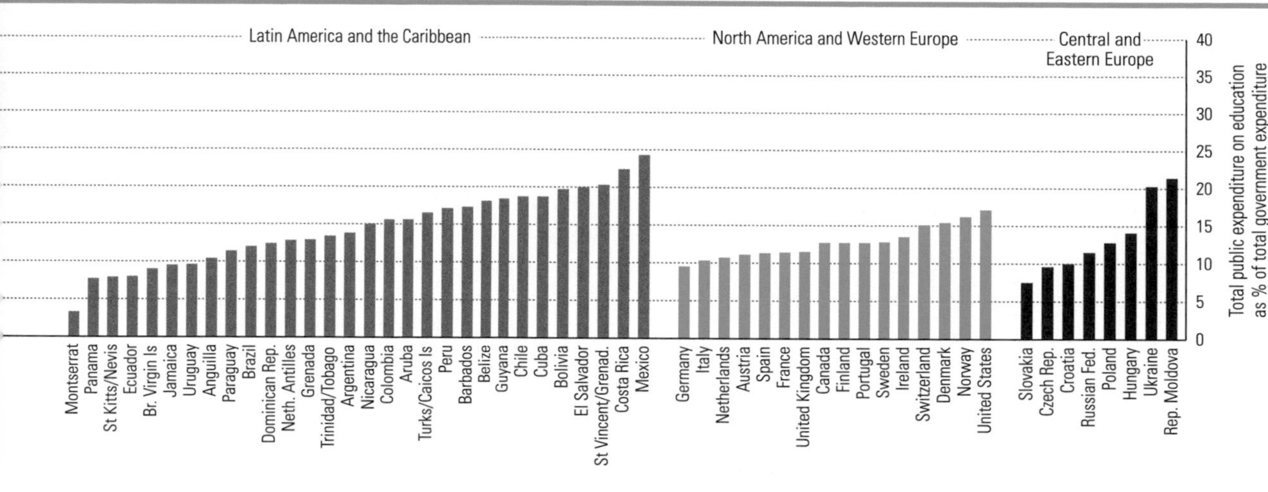

Table 3.2: Primary net enrolment ratios, education expenditure and teachers, 1998 and 2002

	Primary net enrolment ratio (%)		Education expenditure as a % of GNP		Education expenditure as a % of government budget		Primary pupil/teacher ratio	
	1998	2002	1998	2002	1998	2002	1998	2002
Niger	26	38	m	m	12.9	15.9	41:01	42:01
Ethiopia	36	47	4.3	4.6*	13.8**	m	46:01	65:01
Guinea	45	66	1.8	1.9	25.8	25.6**	47:01	45:01
U. R. Tanzania	46	68	3.0	m	21.1***	24.4***	38:01	53:01
Lesotho	65	86	10.2	8.4	25.5	18.4	44:01	47:01
Madagascar	65	79	1.9	2.9	10.2	m	47:01	52:01

Notes: m = missing; * = 2001, ** = 2000, *** = World Bank data.
Sources: Statistical annex, Tables 5, 10A and 11; World Bank database (2004).

education's share in government budget increased in more than half the countries with data available (see statistical annex, Table 11). Data compiled by the International Monetary Fund and the World Bank confirm this trend. After debt relief measures went into effect, seventeen of nineteen highly indebted poor countries in sub-Saharan Africa increased their education expenditure as a share of GDP, and nine increased it as a share of total government expenditure (Hinchliffe, 2004).

This generally positive trend was, however, somewhat offset by declines in some countries. Decreases in spending shares were particularly significant in the Congo, Ecuador, Saint Kitts and Nevis, South Africa and Togo, for both indicators.

Some African countries, including Guinea and Lesotho (Table 3.2), have improved access to education without increasing public spending on education as a share of GDP or of government budget. This has been achieved mainly by raising pupil/teacher ratios, however – dramatically so in Ethiopia and the United Republic of Tanzania.

Distribution across levels of education also matters

If the level of public resources allocated to education is crucial to the achievement of EFA, their distribution matters as well. Figure 3.6 presents the distribution of education expenditure by sub-sector.[9] The set of countries having low primary enrolment rates allocates a relatively high share of total public expenditure to this sub-sector, while countries where UPE is close to being achieved allocate a lower share to primary.

Figure 3.7 shows an emerging shift from primary to secondary education between 1998 and 2002 for countries that have reached UPE. Countries such as Poland and the Republic of

The level of public resources allocated to education is crucial to the achievement of EFA, their distribution matters as well

9. Comparable data exist for only twenty-two countries.

Figure 3.6: Share of public education expenditure by level, 2002

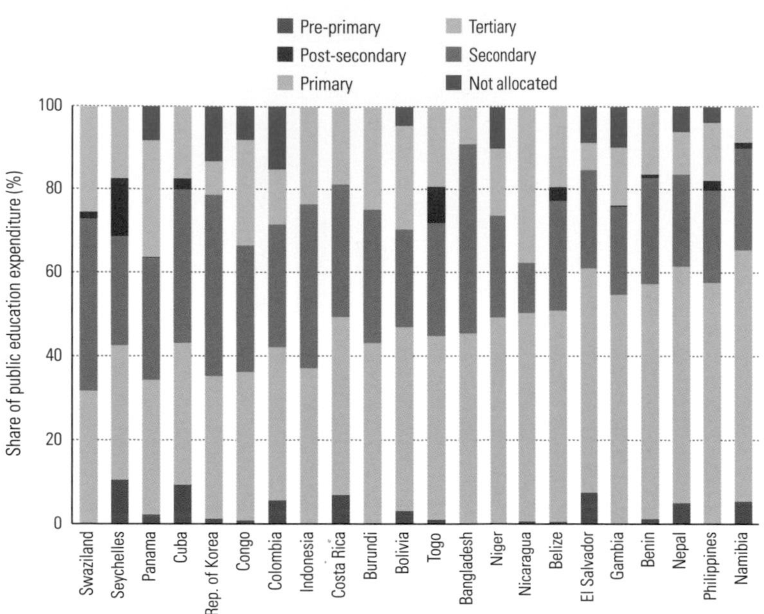

Note: Countries are sorted by increasing share of expenditure on primary education.
Source: UNESCO Institute for Statistics database.

Figure 3.7: Share of primary and secondary education in total public current expenditure on education, percentage change from 1998 to 2002

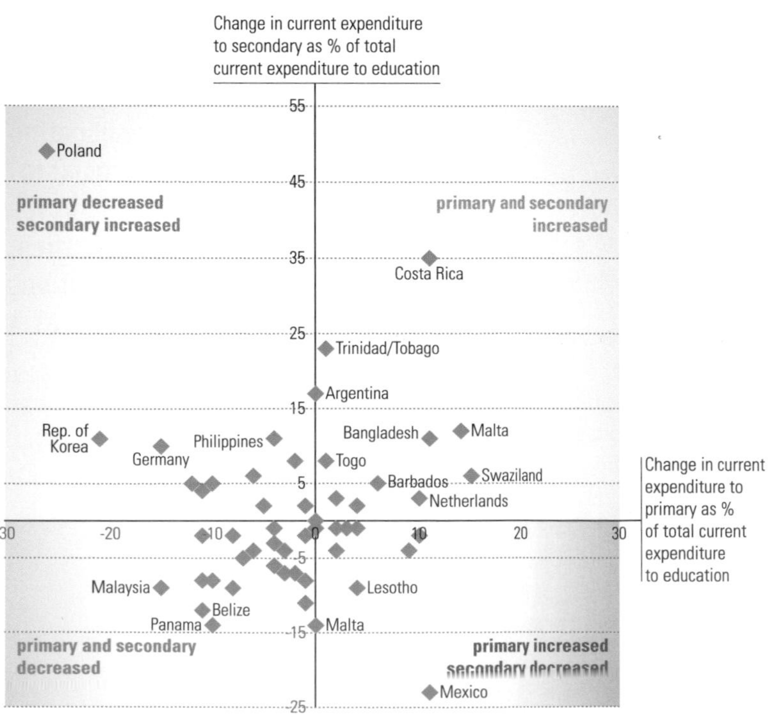

Source: UNESCO Institute for Statistics database.

Korea have clearly increased the priority they give to financing secondary education. Others, like Togo, have managed to improve the share of public education expenditure on secondary education, while maintaining that of primary education.

Efficiency can free up resources

Besides issues of distribution and equity, ways to increase efficiency must be addressed. Where efficiency can be improved, this can free up resources for areas of growing importance, such as investments in quality and access, and in secondary education and adult basic education as well as primary education. Internal efficiency concerns the way in which resources are used in the education system. It includes drop-out and retention (discussed in Chapter 2) as well as the allocation of resources within education levels to teachers and to non-salary inputs such as books and teaching materials (discussed in the 2005 Report, with its emphasis on quality).

Institutional efficiency relates to the institutional context in which public spending takes place. It requires more attention in the education sector than it has so far received. Central education ministry resources do not always reach the schools for which they are intended. The percentage of non-wage public education spending that actually arrived at designated schools was 16% in Senegal (World Bank, 2004*a*) and 40% in Zambia (World Bank, 2003*b*). Various factors are behind this problem, including corruption (UNESCO, 2004*a*). Holding education stakeholders accountable for their performance can help reduce resource leaks and hence increase education efficiency. Extensive examples in the education literature support the idea that community input improves the quality of services and ensures that providers do their job properly (Mookherjee, 2001). A particularly interesting example is that of Uganda (Box 3.3).

Implicit in the various dimensions of efficiency are notions of equity. If public spending is not concentrated where people are geographically concentrated, it is not equitable or efficient. If it subsidizes the more affluent at the expense of the poor, it is not equitable or efficient. Such patterns of inequitable and inefficient education spending are very common. Box 3.4 illustrates the problem, using the example of Mozambique.

Box 3.3 Social accountability to improve education spending in Uganda

Uganda's 1996 Public Expenditure Tracking Survey, the world's first such initiative, was launched because, despite a substantial increase in public spending on education, official reports showed no increase in primary enrolment. The survey provided a stark picture of public funding on the front lines. On average, in 1991–95, 87% of the annual spending (per student) was either diverted for private gain or was used by district officials for purposes unrelated to education. Some 70% of schools received very little or nothing. The picture improved slightly over time, but even in 1995 only 20% of total per capita funding from the central government reached the schools.

Following publication of the findings, the central government began releasing monthly inter-governmental transfers of public funds in the main newspapers and on radio, and requiring primary schools to post information on inflows of funds. A new tracking survey evaluating the information campaign showed a great improvement. While schools on average still did not receive the entire grant and delays continued, misuse of funds was reduced from 78% in 1995 to 18% in 2001. A before-after assessment, comparing outcomes for the same schools in 1995 and 2001 and controlling for a broad range of school-specific factors, suggests that the information campaign can explain two-thirds of this massive improvement.

With a relatively inexpensive policy action – provision of mass information – Uganda managed to reduce dramatically the amount of spending wasted in a public programme aimed at increasing primary education. Poor schools, which before the campaign had been less able to claim their entitlement from district officials, benefited most from the information campaign.

Source: Dehn et al. (2003).

Higher education privatization raises equity issues

The role of private financing

Private contributions, made by parents and by communities, are an integral part of what society invests in education. Private contributions are not only directed to private schools but are also very common at public schools and institutions. Within a group of seven diverse countries, for example, the share of private expenditure in total spending at the primary and secondary levels ranges from 7% in the United States to 47% in Jamaica (Figure 3.8). Private contributions typically increase substantially at the tertiary level, with the proportion up to 81% in Chile. The size of the share signals a significant process of higher education privatization, which raises equity issues, in particular when poor people do not have proper access to financial markets. In India, private contributions are higher at both primary and secondary levels than in tertiary. This could suggest that government subsidies to the tertiary sector come at the expense of improving access and quality in primary and secondary schooling.

Fees are still a major obstacle

The Dakar Framework for Action calls for free and compulsory primary education of good quality, drawing on the 1948 Universal Declaration of Human Rights, which established education as a fundamental human right, and the 1989 Convention on the Rights of the Child, which

Box 3.4 Equity in public education spending in Mozambique

Public spending on education in Mozambique is not equitable geographically or in terms of distribution among income groups. Lower primary education spending is roughly equitably distributed across all income groups, with the poorest 50% benefiting from 51% of the spending. The picture shifts dramatically as the education level increases, however, with the poorest 50% benefiting from only 35% of upper primary spending and only 19% of post-primary spending. Nor is spending aligned geographically with population concentrations (Table 3.3). Maputo, the capital, contains some 6% of the population but receives almost one-third of all public education spending. The North and, especially, Centre regions are severely underfinanced in relative terms, even assuming that some of the Maputo expenditure is for national rather than regional educational institutions, such as secondary schools and the university.

Table 3.3: Regional distribution of population and public education spending

Share (%)	North	Centre	South excluding Maputo	Maputo city	Total
Population	32.5	42.6	18.8	6.1	100
Education	18.8	26.2	22.7	32.2	100

Source: Heltberg et al. (2001).

Figure 3.8: Share of public and private education expenditure by level, 2002

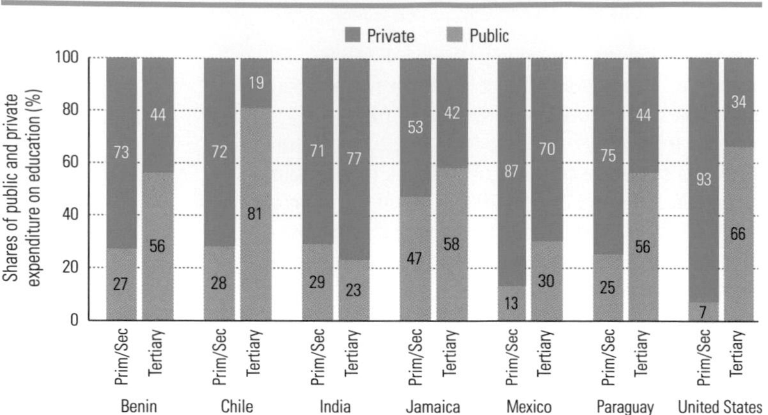

Note: Data for Mexico and United States are from 2001.
Source: UNESCO Institute for Statistics/OECD (2005).

affirms in Article 28 that parties to the convention[10] should make primary education 'compulsory and available free to all'.

Despite increased recognition of the gains that result from eliminating fees at the primary level, and several well-publicized cases of fee reduction (e.g. in Kenya, Uganda and the United Republic of Tanzania), 89 out of 103 countries[11] surveyed by the World Bank for this Report (Bentaouet-Kattan, 2005) still have some type of fees in primary education, whether legal or illegal (Table 3.4).

Since 2000, several countries have reduced or eliminated primary-school fees; they include Cape Verde, Costa Rica, Guatemala, Kenya, Nepal, Peru, Senegal, the United Republic of Tanzania and Zambia. China has announced policy changes in rural areas. Even when direct fees are eliminated, however, other household costs can remain high (Boyle et al., 2002). In Cambodia, for instance, many types of household costs impede access and learning (Box 3.5)

10. The convention has been ratified by 192 countries – that is, all signatories except Somalia and the United States.

11. Only countries for which fee information could be collected are represented in the survey.

12. See, in particular, the section on better teachers in Chapter 4 (UNESCO, 2004*a*).

Table 3.4: Fees still exist in a large number of countries

Legal fees	Albania; Argentina; Armenia; Azerbaijan; Benin; Bhutan; Bosnia/Herzegovina; Bulgaria; Burundi; Cameroon; Cape Verde; Chad; Comoros; Costa Rica; Côte d'Ivoire; Dominica; Dominican Rep.; Egypt; El Salvador; Eritrea; Grenada; Guinea; Guinea-Bissau; Guyana; Haiti; India; Iran, Isl. Rep.; Jordan; Lebanon; Madagascar; Maldives; Mauritania; Morocco; Niger; Papua New Guinea; Paraguay; Peru; Philippines; Romania; Russian Fed.; Rwanda; Solomon Islands; South Africa; Swaziland; Tajikistan; Thailand; TFYR Macedonia; Timor-Leste; Togo; Trinidad/Tobago; Turkey; Uruguay
Illegal fees	Bolivia; Brazil; Colombia; Ethiopia; Ghana; Honduras; Lao PDR; Lesotho; Liberia; Mexico; Mozambique; Namibia; Nigeria; Panama; Tonga; Uganda; Ukraine; Viet Nam
Both types of fees	Burkina Faso; China; D.R. Congo; Djibouti; Ecuador; Georgia; Indonesia; Kenya; Kyrgyzstan; Latvia; Mali; Mauritius; Mongolia; Nicaragua; Palestinian A. T.; Rep. Moldova; Vanuatu; Venezuela; Yemen

Note: Data was collected informally from World Bank task teams and may not reflect the most recent changes in policy and practice at the country level.
Source: Bentaouet-Kattan (2005).

Box 3.5 Household education expenditures in Cambodia

The Priority Action Program (PAP) was launched in Cambodia on a pilot basis in ten provinces in 2000 and expanded to the whole country in 2001. One purpose of the pilot was specifically to 'reduce the cost burden on the poorest to increase participation of their children in Grades 1 to 9 (Cambodia Ministry of Education, Youth and Sport, 2001). Registration charges, formerly common, were prohibited, as were other obligatory contributions. As a consequence of the programme, the share of private recurrent expenditure has been dramatically reduced, particularly for the poorest households.

Households still must cover various expenses, however, related to:

- *registration*: sometimes requires photographs for identity cards, which cost more and are required more often in rural than in urban areas;
- *uniforms*: required in most schools, though enforced less strictly in primary than in secondary schools and in remote rural areas than in urban areas;
- *equipment*: for sports, required in urban and semi-urban areas;

Teachers for EFA

Teachers play a central role in EFA achievement, as the 2005 Report emphasized.[12] Indeed, a long-term vision, strong governmental leadership and a sufficient supply of motivated, respected, supported and supervised teachers are all crucial to the success of education policies and reforms focusing on expansion and quality improvement (UNESCO, 2004*a*). Teachers also represent the bulk of public spending on education (Figure 3.10), and their future supply is a critical issue in assessing both education quality and financial stability. Another important aspect is the provision

- *learning materials*: items such as notebooks, exercise books, pens and pencils;
- *supplementary tutoring*: often needed in urban areas; cost varies, peaking in primary school at grade 6 and in lower secondary school at grade 9;
- *tests and examinations*: charges for testing materials and fees for examinations, charged by the Ministry of Education, Youth and Sport; overall costs were reduced by PAP yet remain substantial, especially in later grades;
- *transport*: bicycle maintenance and repair, with costs varying by region, bicycle use and gender; poor roads in remote and rural areas create higher costs than in urban and semi-urban areas;
- *pocket money*: covering snacks, breakfast, sometimes lunch, with costs varying greatly by socio-economic group; may be offset by school meal programmes such as those offered by the World Food Programme, targeting poor rural communities;
- *other expenditure*: gifts for teachers, collections during various festivals and ceremonies.

As Figure 3.9 shows, pupil expenses increase with grade levels and differ between urban or rural areas.

Figure 3.9: Per-pupil household costs, by grade and area, 2004

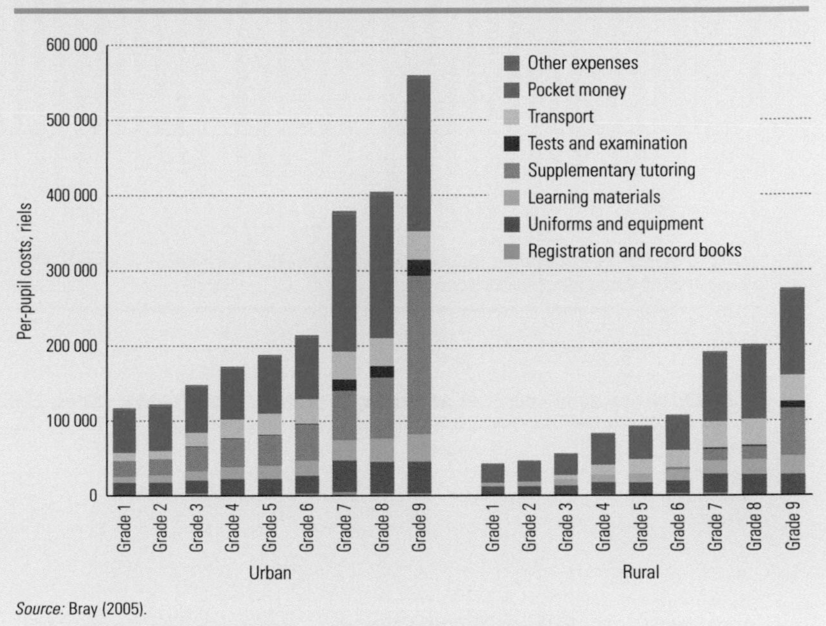

Source: Bray (2005).

of non-salary teaching inputs. This element can sometimes be crowded out in developing countries, where personnel costs often represent over 90% of total public education spending. This section examines issues of teacher supply and quality, mainly at primary level, including projections to 2015.

Pupil/teacher ratios

While the impact of class size on educational outcomes remains a matter of debate, and depends on educational strategies and pedagogical implementation, the pupil/teacher ratio (PTR)[13] is an important indicator of education quality. In general, the ratio is below twenty pupils per teacher in the vast majority of countries in North America and Western Europe, Central and Eastern Europe, and Central Asia, regions where enrolment ratios are also high (Table 3.5).

Most countries in the Arab States, East Asia and the Pacific, and Latin America and the Caribbean have twenty to thirty-four pupils per teacher. PTRs are much higher in sub-Saharan Africa, typically exceeding 40:1 and rising to almost 70:1 in some countries, including Chad, the Congo and Mozambique. Such high PTRs make it difficult to provide primary education of good quality.

The number of pupils per teacher declined between 1998 and 2002 in more than two-thirds of the 143 countries with data available (see statistical annex, Table 10A). Decreases were particularly significant in countries with already low PTRs, but also occurred in high-PTR countries such as Djibouti, Gabon, Nepal and Togo. This generally positive global trend has some key exceptions, however. PTRs were below 40:1 in 1998 in Afghanistan, India and the United Republic of Tanzania, yet had risen well above that level by 2002. The ratio doubled from 32:1 to 61:1 in Afghanistan, where large numbers of new pupils, especially previously excluded girls, enrolled in primary school but few new teachers were hired. PTRs also increased in several countries that eliminated or reduced school fees, including Benin, Cambodia, the Congo, Ethiopia and Uganda. In addition, the number of teachers remains problematic in the very countries that need to increase the coverage of their primary school systems most significantly.

13. Several limitations should be kept in mind when comparing numbers of teachers, percentages of trained teachers and PTRs. For example, the PTR depends on an accurate count of teachers who have teaching responsibilities. In some countries and regions, part of the teaching staff may work part time, and full-time equivalent numbers are not always available. In many resource-constrained countries, forms of schooling organization such as multi-grade and double-shifting may not be taken into account in the PTR, which is a national average. Data on teaching staff may include other education personnel as well, and separate data on the latter are difficult to collect at the international level.

Figure 3.10: Share of personnel costs in total public current expenditure on education by level of national income, 2002

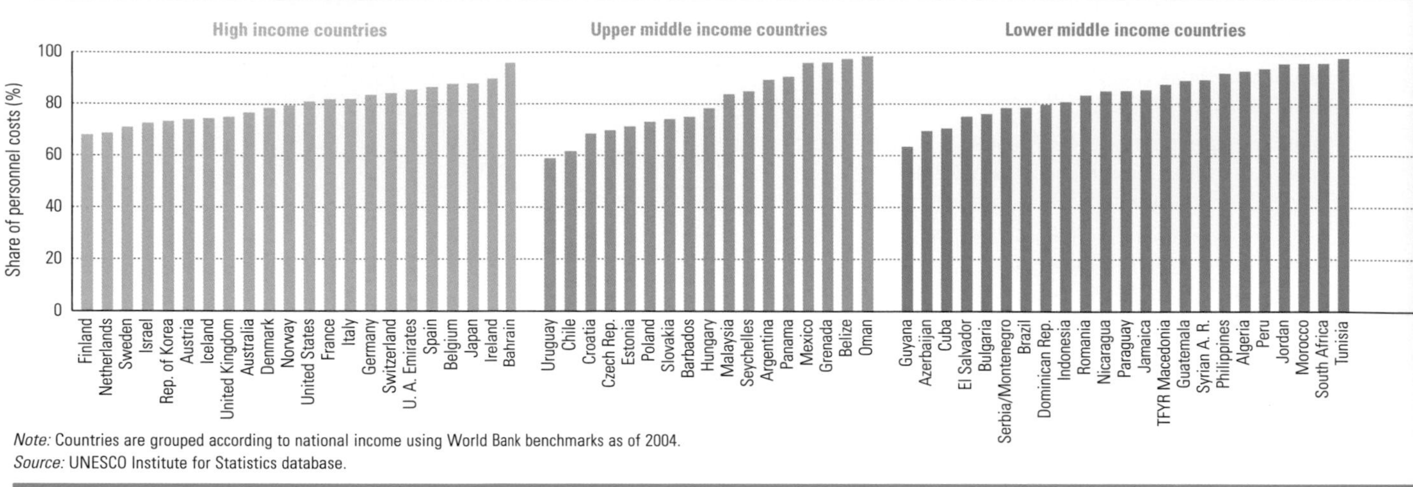

Note: Countries are grouped according to national income using World Bank benchmarks as of 2004.
Source: UNESCO Institute for Statistics database.

Table 3.5: Grouping of countries according to primary pupil/teacher ratios, 2002

Regions	Below 15	15–24	25–34	35–44
Sub-Saharan Africa (40)	Seychelles (1)		Mauritius, Botswana, Cape Verde, Namibia, Swaziland, Ghana, Sao Tome/Principe, Kenya (8)	South Africa, Togo, Gabon, Comoros, Sierra Leone, Gambia, Zimbabwe, Nigeria, Niger, Côte d'Ivoire, Zambia, Equatorial Guinea, Guinea-Bissau (13)
Arab States (18)	Qatar, Saudi Arabia, Kuwait (3)	United Arab Emirates, Bahrain, Lebanon, Iraq, Jordan, Oman, Tunisia, Egypt, Syrian A. R. (9)	Algeria, Morocco, Sudan, Djibouti (4)	Palestinian Autonomous Territories, Mauritania (2)
Central Asia (7)	Georgia (1)	Azerbaijan, Armenia, Kazakhstan, Tajikistan, Kyrgyzstan (5)	Mongolia (1)	
East Asia and the Pacific (25)	Brunei Daruss., Niue (2)	Marshall Is, New Zealand, Cook Islands, Malaysia, Japan, Indonesia, Thailand, China, Tonga, Kiribati (10)	Viet Nam, Tuvalu, Macao, Samoa, Fiji, Vanuatu, Lao PDR, Rep. of Korea, Myanmar (9)	Philippines, Papua New Guinea (2)
South and West Asia (9)		Maldives, Sri Lanka, Islamic Republic of Iran (3)		Nepal, Bhutan, Pakistan, India (4)
Latin America and the Caribbean (37)	Bermuda, Cuba, Br. Virgin Is, Cayman Is (4)	Turks/Caicos Is, Anguilla, Barbados, Bahamas, Argentina, St Kitts/Nevis, St Vincent/Grenad., Aruba, Trinidad/Tobago, Montserrat, Grenada, Dominica, Suriname, Netherlands Antilles, Belize, Uruguay, St Lucia, Costa Rica, Bolivia, Ecuador, Panama (21)	Peru, Brazil, Guyana, Mexico, Colombia, Paraguay, Jamaica, Guatemala, Chile, Honduras (10)	Nicaragua, Dominican Rep. (2)
North America and Western Europe (24)	Denmark, Norway, Iceland, Italy, Portugal, Sweden, Luxembourg, Belgium, Greece, Andorra, Austria, Switzerland, Spain, Germany, Israel, United States (16)	Monaco, Finland, United Kingdom, Canada, Malta, France, Ireland, Cyprus (8)		
Central and Eastern Europe (18)	Hungary, Poland, Slovenia, Latvia, Estonia (5)	Lithuania, Belarus, Czech Republic, Russian Fed., Bulgaria, Romania, Croatia, Slovakia, Ukraine, Rep. Moldova, Serbia/Montenegro, TFYR Macedonia, Albania (13)		
Total	32	69	32	23

Note: Countries are listed in ascending order of PTR. See source table for detailed country notes.
Source: Statistical annex, Table 10A.

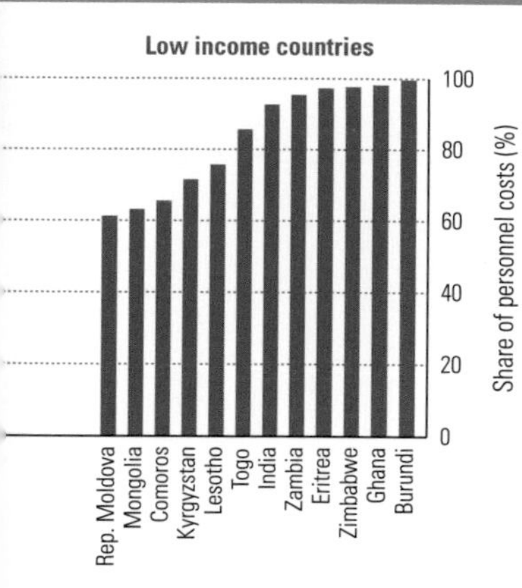

45–54	55 and above
Burkina Faso, Guinea, Eritrea, Lesotho, Senegal, Burundi, Madagascar, Uganda, United Republic of Tanzania (9)	Cameroon, Mali, Rwanda, Benin, Malawi, Ethiopia, Congo, Mozambique, Chad (9)
Timor-Leste (1)	Cambodia (1)
	Bangladesh, Afghanistan (2)
10	12

Are there enough teachers to achieve UPE?

Teacher numbers are generally too low and PTRs generally too high in the countries furthest from attaining the UPE goal. Projections for high-PTR countries indicate that a major teacher shortage is looming (Motivans, 2005). Just maintaining current enrolment ratios while moving to a PTR of 40:1 by 2015 generally requires a faster growth rate for teacher numbers than most of these countries experienced between 1998 and 2002. This situation primarily reflects still-increasing school age populations, especially in sub-Saharan Africa. Growth rates above 9% per year would be needed in Chad, the Congo, Ethiopia, Mali and Uganda, for instance (Figure 3.11).

The numbers of additional teachers needed to increase gross enrolment ratios to 100% and achieve a 40:1 PTR by 2015 are so high that this is probably impossible in several countries. Burkina Faso, Mali and the Niger, where GERs are still low, would each need to increase teacher supply by 20% per year. The number of teachers in the Niger would need to quadruple, from 20,000 to 80,000 in the next ten years or so. Even in countries that would need only moderate teacher supply growth rates, such as Bangladesh (4%) and Cameroon (3%), this would involve huge absolute increases: from 49,000 to 71,000 teachers in Cameroon and from 315,000 to 482,000 in Bangladesh.

To achieve UPE, the Niger will need to quadruple the number of teachers in ten years

The HIV/AIDS pandemic further accentuates the issue of teacher shortages in Africa (Desai and Jukes, 2005). There is ongoing controversy about the impact of HIV/AIDs on education system staffing, reflecting different sources of data on teacher mortality (Boler, 2003).[14] A new study of Eritrea, Kenya, Mozambique, the United Republic of Tanzania and Zambia suggests that HIV/AIDS can considerably exacerbate teacher turnover rates and place significant strain on education ministries' human resource requirements, doubling teacher mortality rates in the worst cases (Box 3.6). Better data on HIV/AIDS prevalence and mortality among teachers are needed, yet only 45% of one major donor's education projects in Africa include specific HIV/AIDS indicators (Boler, 2003).

Teacher qualifications and training

The teacher issue is not just one of numbers; it is also one of training and conditions of service. As the 2005 Report indicated, large proportions of primary school teachers lack adequate academic

14. Two categories of evidence exist: evidence from school-based surveys and educational personnel records, and estimates derived from projection models, which constitute an independent source of evidence. So far the two approaches have produced no agreement on the likely impact of HIV/AIDS on education systems (Bennell, 2005*a* and 2005*b*).

Figure 3.11: Current and projected annual growth rates of teacher numbers, 1998–2002 and 2015

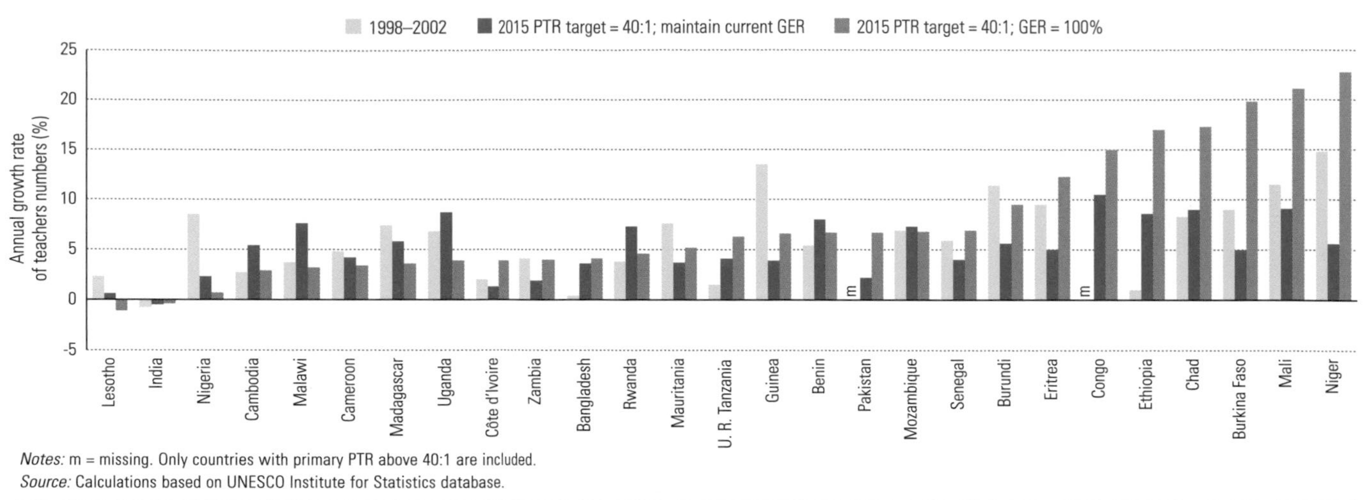

Notes: m = missing. Only countries with primary PTR above 40:1 are included.
Source: Calculations based on UNESCO Institute for Statistics database.

Box 3.6 The impact of HIV/AIDS on education systems in five countries of sub-Saharan Africa

The most common form of data-based evidence of the impact of HIV/AIDS on teachers comes from mortality rates taken from education management information systems, which include personnel and payroll records. A second form of primary data comes from school-based surveys in which randomly selected head teachers and professional staff in education ministries are asked to respond to questionnaires about teacher absenteeism and mortality. Projection models are essential for independently quantifying the potential impact of HIV/AIDS. A projection model was applied to Eritrea, Kenya, Mozambique, the United Republic of Tanzania and Zambia.

Consistent with UNAIDS methodology, the modelling approach allowed teacher infection rates to vary from one-half to double the infection rate in the general population. Baseline population-level HIV prevalence was allowed to vary between the upper and lower ends of the most recent UNAIDS estimates. Where independent estimates were available, they were included in the low-high range of AIDS-related teacher mortality.

In the best-case scenario, Kenya, the United Republic of Tanzania and Zambia will each lose 600 teachers to AIDS in 2005 alone, and Mozambique will lose over 300, based on ~0.5% annual AIDS mortality, the least plausible rate in these countries. In the worst-case scenario, Kenya, the United Republic of Tanzania and Zambia will each lose 1,500 to 3,000 teachers to AIDS in 2005 alone, and Mozambique will lose over 1,100, based on up to 3.1% annual mortality, the highest plausible rate in these countries.

Absenteeism is a significant, rising problem in several service sectors, but data-based research cannot clearly quantify or ascribe absenteeism to AIDS only. In surveys of head teachers in southern Africa, one in five saw AIDS-related absenteeism as a serious problem for the quality of education. They report that 47% of absenteeism is attributed to attending funerals and 30% to sickness. Reliable data on absenteeism due to HIV/AIDS are scarce, not least because of the stigmatization and loss of benefits resulting from declaring one's seropositive status.

Table 3.6: Impact of HIV/AIDS on education in five sub-Saharan countries, 2005

	Eritrea			Kenya			Mozambique			U. R. Tanzania			Zambia		
	medium	low	high	medium	low	high	medium	low	high	medium	low	high	medium	low	high
Total teacher mortalities due to AIDS	35	7.0	130	1 620	700	3 020	675	340	1 150	1 290	605	2 010	1 030	580	1 500
% total attrition	12.4	2.1	30.9	18.0	7.5	29.6	33.2	16.6	43.1	19.9	9.3	31.0	40.4	23.3	48.8
Annual teacher mortality due to AIDS	0.3	0.07	1.5	0.8	0.4	1.8	1.4	0.7	2.3	1.1	0.5	1.9	2.1	1.2	3.1
Teacher-years of absenteeism due to AIDS	37	7	130	1 590	690	2 930	730	370	1 240	1 290	610	2 200	1 090	605	1 580
% of total teacher-years	0.4	0.1	1.5	0.8	0.4	1.8	1.5	0.8	2.9	1.1	0.5	2.3	2.2	1.3	3.9

qualifications, training and mastery of content, especially in developing countries (UNESCO, 2004*a*). New data confirm this. In only one-quarter of the approximately 100 developing countries with data available in 2002 had all or almost all primary teachers received at least some pedagogical training (see statistical annex, Table 10A). More than 20% of primary school teachers lack training in more than half the countries in sub-Saharan Africa, and more than 30% in half the countries of South and West Asia. In South Asia, despite the rather low minimum qualifications in several countries, many teachers have not met the national minimum requirements (Govinda and Biswal, 2005).

Nevertheless, the teacher-training situation is improving. The proportion of trained primary teachers increased between 1998 and 2002 in the majority of the forty-eight countries with data available. It rose by 30% or more in Mozambique, Namibia, Rwanda, South Africa and the Turks and Caicos Islands (Figure 3.12). Despite this general progress, several countries, including Anguilla, Belize, the Congo, Ghana, Nepal[15] and the Niger, experienced a drop in the proportion of trained teachers. In the Niger, the proportion of trained primary teachers fell from 97% to 72% between 1999 and 2002 as a direct result of a government policy to meet increased demand for primary education and keep costs sustainable by hiring large numbers of volunteer teachers without pre-service training, at substantially lower salaries than other teachers, and then providing them with in-service training to upgrade their qualifications. Similar efforts are under way in several other West African countries (Wallet, 2005).

In Mozambique, by contrast, a policy of simultaneously lowering the minimum required primary teacher-training standards from nine to

Figure 3.12: Percentage of trained primary-school teachers, 1998 and 2002

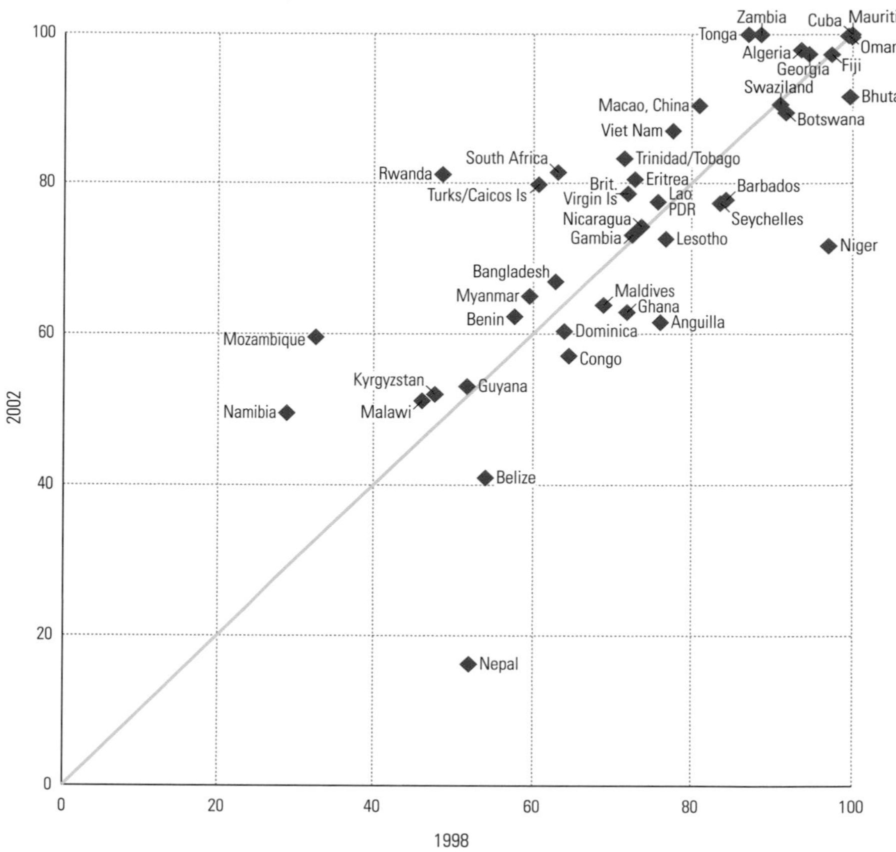

Notes: Data for Belize, the Congo, the Niger and Georgia are for 1999. Data for Rwanda are for 2001.
Source: UNESCO Institute for Statistics database.

Table 3.6 provides estimates of AIDS-related absenteeism. In the best-case scenario, 600 to 700 teacher-years of absenteeism for personal illness due to HIV/AIDS will affect Kenya, the United Republic of Tanzania and Zambia in 2005 alone, while Mozambique will experience a loss of almost 400 teacher-years. In the worst case, these countries will experience 1,200 to 3,000 teacher-years of absenteeism.

It was possible to estimate the financial impact of HIV/AIDS on the education ministries of Mozambique and Zambia. In Mozambique, AIDS-related teacher absenteeism for personal illnesses will likely cost US$3.3 million in 2005 alone, plus US$0.3 million in increased teacher-training costs. In the worst-case scenario, the costs could rise to US$6.0 million per year, in the absence of any behavioural changes or the provision of anti-retroviral drugs to education personnel. In Zambia, the equivalent figures are US$1.7 million for 2005 absenteeism, US$0.7 million for 2005 teacher-training and US$3.4 million per year in the worst-case scenario. Projection data consistently indicate that the cost of absenteeism to employers is substantially greater than the cost of training and recruitment to replace staff lost through AIDS: absenteeism is variously estimated at 24% to 89% of the total HIV/AIDS costs to employers, and training and recruitment at 17% to 24%.

Source: Desai and Jukes (2005).

15. In Nepal, a tremendous drop in the percentage of trained teachers, from 52% to 16%, reflects a stricter definition of training. The most recent data include only teachers who have received at least ten months of training, while data in the past included teachers who might have received as little as 2.5 months of training.

Rwanda increased its proportion of trained teachers from 49% to 81%

seven years of schooling and introducing an accelerated teacher-training programme raised the proportion of trained teachers from 33% to 60% (European Association for International Education, 2003; International Association of Universities/UNESCO, 2005). While the policies of both the Niger and Mozambique largely aimed to reduce the costs of expanding primary education, their implications for quality and learning outcomes remain uncertain (Wallet, 2005). However, other countries succeeded in increasing the percentage of trained teachers without lowering standards. Rwanda increased its proportion of trained teachers from 49% to 81% by reorganizing teacher-training institutions, opening new teacher-training colleges and subsidizing two church-based training institutions that together produce about 1,500 new primary teachers per year (MINEDUC, 2003). However, while the teachers' training status has improved, quantity is still insufficient, as the primary PTR grew from 54:1 to 60:1, with implications for the quality of teaching and learning.

Just as important as teacher qualifications are the status of teachers and the need to involve them in policy development and implementation, as the 2005 Report noted. Yet, salaries remain problematic. In Estonia, for example, despite

Box 3.7 Teacher salaries and working conditions in Latin America

National policy discussions and strategies related to teachers focus on three themes: working conditions, training and performance appraisal. On average, teachers' salaries in OECD countries, including Mexico, start at about the level of GDP per capita and grow steadily to reach 140% of GDP per capita after fifteen years of teaching experience. Teachers in non-OECD Latin American countries, except Chile, start their career with salaries between 60% (Uruguay) and 90% (Peru) of GDP per capita. After fifteen years of service, salaries are 1.4 times the starting level in Argentina and 1.5 times higher in Brazil, while in Chile and Uruguay the ratio between starting and mid-career salaries is a more modest 1.2, and Peru has no increase in base salaries throughout the teaching career (Figure 3.13).

Career progression for teachers in Latin America is very limited, with few opportunities offered except to become, for example, principals and then inspectors. Chile is the only country in Latin America to systematically evaluate public schools and their teachers (both state-run schools and those that are privately run but state-subsidized). It provides monetary rewards to schools and teachers whose performance is evaluated as excellent. In the last two performance evaluations (2003 and 2004), 10% of teachers were assessed as outstanding, 52% as competent, 37% as at the basic level and 3% as unsatisfactory.

Figure 3.13: Primary teacher salaries and comparison with GDP per capita: entry level and after fifteen years' experience (PPP US$, 1999)

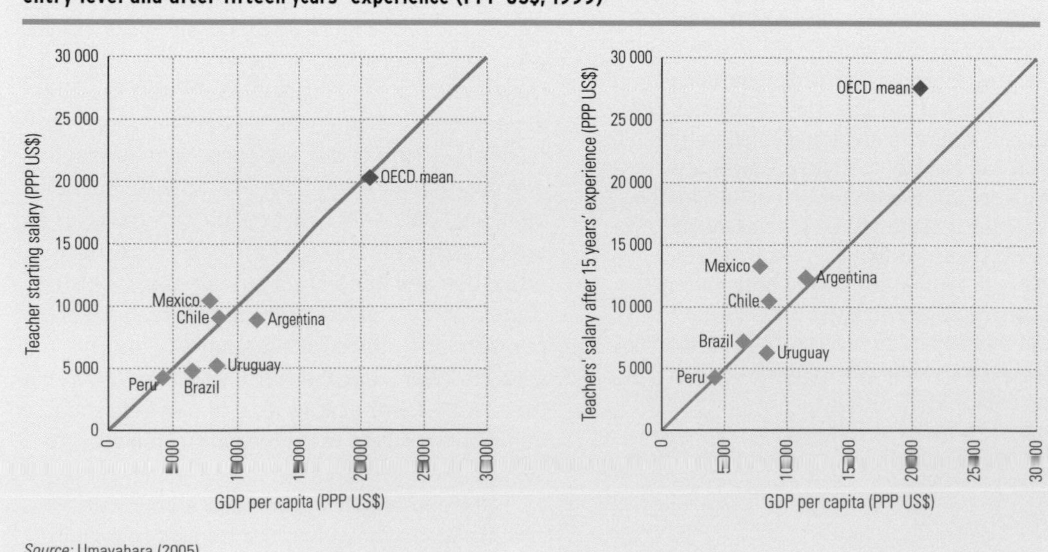

Source: Umayahara (2005).

salary increases in recent years, a junior teacher's pay has not even reached the national average wage (Koke, 2005). Similarly, inadequate teacher salaries in Latin America fail to attract the best candidates (Box 3.7). While teachers may be 'perhaps the most important constituency in education reform', overall in many regions they continue largely to be 'ignored in policy dialogue, monitoring and implementation' (World Economic Forum, 2005). Some countries are trying to improve teachers' status, though. In China, salaries have been increased and a National Teachers Education Network has been launched to provide a 'lifelong learning platform' for strengthening professional skills (Bernard, 2005).

Figure 3.14: Median share of female teachers in various levels of education by region, 2002

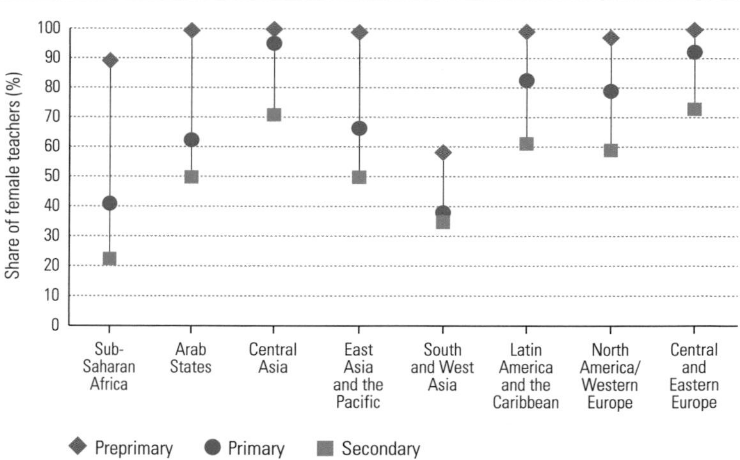

Source: Statistical annex, Tables 10A and 10B.

Women teachers and the gender goal

The proportion of teachers who are women is a potentially crucial indicator for gender outcomes in schooling. In general, women predominate among teachers, the proportion being highest in pre-primary education and somewhat lower at the primary and secondary levels. Important regional differences exist (Figure 3.14): the proportion of women teachers is lowest in South and West Asia and in sub-Saharan Africa, where men outnumber women teachers at both primary and secondary levels. In Benin and Chad, less than one-fifth of primary teachers are women. In countries including Benin, Burkina Faso, the Comoros, the Congo, Eritrea and Senegal, less than 15% of all secondary teachers are women.

Female teachers are fewest in countries where overall enrolment levels are lowest and gender disparities in favour of boys are highest. Equalizing gender balance among teachers will promote girls' enrolment in these countries (UNESCO, 2004*a*). Moving to a very high proportion of female teachers, however, can work to the disadvantage of boys, a phenomenon that also characterizes several Caribbean countries as well as Mongolia, Nicaragua and the United Kingdom.

The need for inclusion

As Chapter 1 noted, Education for All is about all six goals, not just about schooling. It is also about all people – children, youth and adults; women and men; rural and urban residents; the poor and the better-off; ethnic and linguistic minorities and majorities; the disabled and the able; the sick as well as the healthy; the HIV-positive and the HIV-negative; and the chronically hungry and the malnourished as well as those with enough to eat. At school level, given the considerable (albeit insufficient) progress that has been made towards the primary enrolment and gender parity goals in many countries, the EFA challenge now concerns enhancing quality (focus of the 2005 Report) and extending enrolment to include everyone. Among youth and adults, the lack of literacy largely affects excluded groups, and particularly women members of such groups. Chapter 7 discusses literacy among indigenous peoples, migrants and people with disabilities, while this section examines three other types of exclusion that are particularly relevant at school level: the exclusion of unregistered children, rural children and girls.

The proportion of women teachers is lowest in South and West Asia and in sub-Saharan Africa

Unregistered children

According to UNICEF, some 48 million births were not registered in 2003 worldwide – over 30% of all estimated births. In South Asia and sub-Saharan Africa, 63% and 55%, respectively, of total births went unregistered. Reasons for not registering birth vary : it is often not perceived as a fundamental duty and right, it can require a fee that families find hard to afford (e.g. in Indonesia), it sometimes involves travelling far (e.g. in parts of Albania) and it is often especially difficult for ethnic minorities and particular indigenous groups (e.g. Kurds in the Syrian Arab Republic) (UNICEF, 2002 and 2005*c*). Finally, in many countries concerned by this problem, systems of registration are either not in place or not functional.

School enrolment often requires a birth certificate; this is the case, for instance, in Cameroon, Lesotho, the Sudan and Yemen. In other countries, a certificate may not be needed to enrol, but is necessary for obtaining a primary school diploma. Steps are needed, therefore, both to encourage birth registration and to ensure that unregistred children can attend school. Indeed, the right to birth registration is enshrined in the 1989 Convention on the Rights of the Child, and must be guaranteed to all children.

Reaching rural people

About 70% of the world's poorest people live in rural areas

About 70% of the world's poorest people live in rural areas. The supply of education for rural people is generally inadequate. Urban African schools, for instance, are much better equipped than rural ones, especially with regard to electricity and water supplies (Monitoring Learning Achievement Project, 2002). Many rural schools do not offer the full number of primary grades, and teach curricula that are ill adapted to rural circumstances.[16] The language of instruction may differ from children's mother tongues. Rural children also receive less parental supervision and help with homework than do urban ones, as surveys in India and Mexico have found. Demand for schooling in rural areas can be low, particularly because of the opportunity costs of attending school in terms of time lost to working in the fields or the home. Demand can also fluctuate with respect to seasonality of opportunity costs, to agricultural and economic conditions, and to health and nutrition problems. Solutions exist to all these supply and demand problems, including non-formal programmes such as BRAC in Bangladesh, community schools in Mali and the Escuela Nueva programme in Colombia. Non-formal programmes have had a significant impact but are unlikely to reach the scale required to meet the learning needs of large numbers of rural children. To this end, research into formal programmes is needed, which was the rationale for the inter-agency EFA flagship initiative on Education for Rural People, launched in 2002 and led by UNESCO and the Food and Agriculture Organization of the United Nations.[17]

Since the bulk of out-of-school children and those receiving insufficient schooling live in rural areas, it is right to focus attention on the needs of rural children and adults, as the flagship initiative does. Such a focus must, however, avoid three potential traps. The first is to ignore urban children, who are by no means universally better off educationally than their rural counterparts, especially children in peri-urban communities. The second trap is to regard rural areas as homogeneous, which they are not. There is no internationally agreed definition of 'rural', and hence no internationally comparable rural-urban statistical breakdowns can be made. Different countries mean different things by 'rural' and 'urban'. Within the rural parts of countries, moreover, population densities can vary considerably, a fact with important cost implications for rural schools. In remote regions of many countries, access to villages is difficult. As a result, per student costs are high, either because class sizes have to be small or because of transport costs to consolidate children in regional schools. It is important to realize, therefore, not only that there is a need to focus on rural people, but also that the implementation of any policy to include the rural remote entails higher than average unit costs. Solutions exist, such as multigrade teaching and the provision of school meals, but some are resisted in regions without experience of them until very recently, such as Central Asia. The third point, consistent with the concept of Education for All, is to ensure that strategies to reach and educate rural people, taking their geographic circumstances into account, do not involve special curricula that, while adapted to rural children, risk providing them with an education that is more vocational, less flexible and possibly of lower quality than that provided to other children, or that could deny them the choices other children have.

The continuing gender challenge

Previous Reports, especially that of 2003/4, have made the case for gender parity and equality, noting that one is essentially a quantitative and the other a qualitative goal. Though 2005 data are not yet available, we know from the results presented in Chapter 2 that the gender parity goal for 2005 has been missed, especially in South Asia and sub-Saharan Africa, but also elsewhere. Still, some countries, including some of the poorest, have dramatically reduced gender inequality in enrolment and completion in recent years. To stress that successful strategies exist, this section draws on country experiences with enrolling and keeping girls in school.[18] The elements of the strategies are well known, as is the need to integrate actions inside the school with those outside the school at the

16. It should be noted, however, that many parents object to children being taught a special rural curriculum, viewing it as substandard (Moulton, 2001).

17. For details, see www.fao.org/sd/erp/index_en.htm

18. The focus here on girls in primary education is not meant to imply that secondary education is less important or that there are no gender issues for boys. Indeed, increasing girls' enrolment in secondary school is an important strategy for increasing primary enrolment. In middle income countries, as Chapter 2 points out, issues of boys' enrolment and learning, compared to those of girls, are increasingly coming to the fore.

Table 3.7: Strategy framework to assure gender equality in education by 2015

Inside the classroom	Outside the classroom
Component 1: Ensure a girl-friendly environment at all levels of society	
	• Reduce wage and job sex-discrimination in the labour market • Commit at the highest level to promote women's rights to education
Component 2: Make schools girl-friendly	
• Provide school with basic sanitation and separate toilets • Ensure that schools respect girls' safety and privacy • Facilitate the return to school of pregnant girls • Protect girls against violence at school	• Encourage community participation and parental support • Build schools closer to girls' homes and in areas belonging to the same community
Component 3: Make schooling gender-sensitive	
• Eliminate gender bias in teacher attitudes against girls via training • Employ more adequately educated and trained female teachers • Ensure that educational materials are gender sensitive and eliminate gender stereotypes • Provide curricula that are sensitive to present and future needs of girls	
Component 4: Make school more affordable	
• Remove direct costs as fees, but also indirect costs incurred by uniforms or books • Provide free or cheap transportation to schools • Provide breakfasts or meals at schools	• Reduce student domestic workload • Provide targeted scholarships to girls, particularly for secondary education

local level and that of society as a whole. The framework used in this section and presented in Table 3.7 has two particular advantages: (a) it encompasses both demand and supply factors while recognizing that they interact in complex ways, making them difficult to distinguish in practice; and (b) its explicit consideration of actions outside the school highlights that school interventions alone, important though they are, will not assure gender parity and equality. The framework thus builds on the analysis in the 2003/4 Report.

A girl-friendly environment at all levels of society

An environment unfavourable to women is a major impediment to the diffusion of girls' education (Millennium Project, 2005*a*). Broad social measures and reforms beyond the education system are needed to promote women's rights, empowerment and leadership. These are desirable in their own right as well as necessary for facilitating gender equity in education. Attitudes (and even laws and regulations) about women's roles in the labour market and in society – and about the gender-based division of work in the household and on the farm – influence decisions about schooling. Where women face limited employment and income-generation opportunities, families are often reluctant to invest in girls' education. Changing entrenched attitudes against women and promoting women's empowerment at all levels of society, an essential condition for achieving gender equality in education, requires political commitment at the highest level.

However, as Figure 3.1 showed, the inclusion of gender parity in national EFA plans is not systematic, though it is increasingly present. Only eighteen out of thirty-two country plans covered the gender goal, though in some cases, such as countries of Latin America and the Caribbean, this may be because gender parity has largely been achieved at primary and secondary levels. Ten out of fifteen Pacific island countries do not address goal 5 in their plans: the Cook Islands, the Federated States of Micronesia, Kiribati, the Marshall Islands, Nauru, Niue, Palau, Papua New Guinea, Tonga and Tuvalu. In all the countries except Nauru, fewer girls than boys are enrolled in primary school; moreover, the share of girls in total enrolment in secondary school is not only lower than that of boys in all ten countries, it is also less than the share at primary level in Nauru, Niue, Palau and Papua New Guinea. In several Pacific countries, though there may be more boys than girls enrolled, a trend of underachievement by boys is emerging. This is increasingly an issue worldwide (see Chapter 2) and one largely neglected in EFA plans until recently (Lameta, 2005). Even countries that have achieved the gender parity goal are far from gender equality in education, so the exclusion of gender from many of these countries' EFA plans is worrying.

Broad social measures and reforms beyond the education system are needed to promote women's rights

Girl-friendly schools

Like society as a whole, schools need to be girl-friendly. Discriminatory practices are often embedded in school culture. Research in the past decade has endeavoured to understand the link between the school context, the 'informal school environment' and gender differentiation in education.[19] One important example is safety (discussed more generally in the last section of this chapter). Parents' concerns about safety may discourage families from sending children, especially girls, to school, particularly if schooling requires distant travel. Locating schools closer to girls' homes has allowed increased girls' participation in several countries (Herz and Sperling, 2003). Similarly, it seems that the location of schools within a given community is as important as the physical distance, if not more so (Lehman, 2005). Local community involvement can take different forms, from recruiting teachers to designing curricula and discussing pedagogy, and can reduce parents' reluctance to send their daughters to school (Box 3.8). Of course, all children, not only girls, benefit from closer ties between schools and the community.

Parents' concerns about safety may discourage families from sending girls to school

Girls need separate sanitary facilities in schools as well as measures that protect their privacy and safety, and meet community cultural standards. Experience in thirty African countries shows that most young women do not attend school during their menses because of the lack of separate toilets (Herz and Sperling, 2003). In some cultural settings, measures beyond separate sanitary facilities are necessary, such as boundary walls for girls' schools or separate hours for girls and boys in shared school buildings. Once again the school-community link is crucial.

Another important factor is schools' attitude towards girls who marry or become pregnant. A review of several country studies in sub-Saharan Africa found that between 8% and 25% of drop-out among girls was due to pregnancy (Eloundou-Enyegue et al., 2000); other girls leave at marriage. Readmission policies can offer a solution, allowing pregnant girls to resume school after giving birth and married girls to continue their studies. Gender-based violence, discussed further below, can also limit girls' participation.

Gender-sensitive learning

Gender bias in textbooks and in teachers' views, and lack of role models within schools, influence how parents, as well as pupils themselves, make schooling decisions. Considerable effort is still needed in many countries to revise teaching

Box 3.8 The Northern Areas Community Schools Programme in Pakistan

In a remote region of northern Pakistan, extreme poverty, social conservatism and inadequate facilities played a large role in keeping the majority of children, and a disproportionate number of girls, out of school. As of the early 1990s, about 82% of government-run schools were for boys only, and 86% of the teachers in government-run primary and middle schools were male. Very few schools had sanitation and running water.

In the mid-1990s, the Aga Khan Rural Support Programme (AKRSP) developed a proposal for 'community schools' in partnership with village organizations, involving a mutual agreement. The AKRSP would establish either co-educational or girls' primary schools in areas where (a) there was no school; (b) the existing school was too small to meet demand; (c) there was only a boys' school to which parents were unwilling to send their girls; or (d) geographic, political or sectarian constraints prevented parents from sending their children to the local school. For their part, communities would provide a building for classes and hire a teacher meeting the criteria of the Directorate of Education for the Northern Areas. These criteria included preference for female teachers unless there were no females meeting minimum academic requirements. The directorate agreed to help pay, train and supervise the teachers.

Public response to the programme was overwhelmingly positive. Between January and October 1995, a first round of 250 community schools opened. By March 1996, enrolment in these schools had reached 12,088 students, equivalent to about 16% of primary enrolment in the regular government system. Among newly enrolled pupils, almost 61% were girls. Nearly half the teachers were female. The majority of parents seemed comfortable with co-education as long as the community chose the teacher. Another 250 community schools have since opened, with assistance from the directorate.

Source: World Bank (1999c).

19. See, in particular, Gordon (1995), Maimbolwa-Sinyangwe and Chilangwa (1995), Kutnick et al. (1997), Miske and Van Belle-Prouty (1997), Sey (1997) and Swainson et al. (1998).

materials that often display strong role models for boys but few or weak ones for girls, and to make curricula at all levels gender-sensitive and responsive. Girls may receive less attention from teachers, who sometimes have stereotypical, negative perceptions of girls' academic ability. Boys tend to lead groups and have more opportunities to ask and answer questions, limiting girls to more passive roles (Herz and Sperling, 2003). Teachers' attitudes and expectations can deeply influence girls' learning outcomes and course choices, and hence their post-school possibilities. Gender stereotypes often discourage girls from taking courses in technical and scientific fields, for example, as well as reducing job opportunities and reinforcing gender segregation in the labour market (USAID, 1999).

Teacher-training is part of the answer. The presence of women teachers can also draw more girls into school. A randomized evaluation of a programme to hire female teachers in informal schools showed that girls' attendance increased by about half when women teachers were recruited (Banerjee and Kremer, 2002). Increasing the proportion of female teachers in countries where they represent a minority, especially in rural areas, is very important. The overall teacher shortage worldwide (discussed above in the section on teachers), which is especially acute in South Asia and sub-Saharan Africa, presents an opportunity to deal with this situation without risking the careers of existing male teachers. Appropriate measures can include imposing quotas, removing age restrictions, favouring local recruitment and posting, and building rural teacher-training institutions with facilities for women.

Making school more affordable

The direct and indirect costs of formal education, discussed earlier, constitute a significant obstacle to expanded primary school attendance among the poor, and particularly for girls. Family income and the costs of providing education influence family willingness to send girls to school more heavily than they affect the willingness to send boys. In addition, the costs of going to school may be higher for girls. In Ghana, India, Malaysia, Pakistan, Peru and the Philippines, for example, distance to school is a greater deterrent to schooling for girls than for boys (King and Alderman, 2001); parents may have to pay higher transportation costs if they do not want their daughters to walk long distances or walk alone to school. Clothing or uniform costs may be higher where parents are reluctant to send girls to school without proper attire. In the United Republic of Tanzania, for example, households spend as much as 14% more to send a girl to school than to send a boy. (King and Alderman, 2001).

Countries that have removed fees or other direct costs of education have experienced dramatic increases in girls' enrolment. Uganda's UPE programme, begun in 1997, led to a jump in the net enrolment ratio for girls from 63% to 83% in just two years, and the rate for the poorest girls nearly doubled, from 43% to 82%. On average, the gender gap in primary education almost disappeared (Deininger, 2003). The 2003/4 Report also stressed the importance of fee elimination in girls' education, especially in sub-Saharan Africa. Another widely used approach is to provide stipends to parents to cover the costs of schooling. Scholarships for girls' programmes have been successfully used in several countries, including Bangladesh.[20]

Countries that have removed fees have experienced dramatic increases in girls' enrolment

The opportunity cost of children's time in school-related activities is also often higher for girls than for boys, especially in poor and rural areas, where there are strong gender norms for household tasks and where girls tend to work longer hours than boys in both market and non-market work. Investing in early childhood care and education, and in childcare centres at schools and in communities, for instance, can free many girls from poor families to attend school. Such investment not only relieves older girls of sibling care during the day, but also benefits younger siblings directly. Other investments, e.g. in fuel-efficient wood-burning stoves, accessible water wells and simple mechanized grain and grinding mills, have been shown in Nepal, Burkina Faso and the Gambia to reduce demands on girls' time and permit them to attend school (World Bank, 1993).

Priorities and challenges

The various measures that have been discussed in this subsection can be effective only as part of an integrated strategy. Indeed, experience shows it is the convergence of several measures aimed at favouring girls' education that is successful. The national EFA plan of the Niger illustrates the use of this integrated approach (Box 3.9). It should not be forgotten that in some countries it is boys who are the disadvantaged group. Where

20. See UNESCO (2003*b*) for this and other examples.

Box 3.9 The Niger's strategy to eliminate gender bias in schooling

The Niger's strategy to improve girls' participation in the first and second cycle of basic education has eight elements:

- three campaigns between 2003 and 2015 to make parents and school partners aware of the benefits of enrolling girls, with special emphasis on issues relating to registration, retention, graduation rates and the sharing of education costs;
- local action plans to promote the enrolment of girls in rural areas with low girls' enrolment rates, starting with a test phase involving 480 schools and gradually being extended to 1,280 villages;
- tutoring to reduce the drop-out rate in 1,350 schools with the lowest girls' retention indicators;
- gender-based training for 5,410 teachers and 60 academic supervisors;
- revision of texts on the protection of girl students;
- prizes and scholarships for the 400 girls who each year achieve the best grades in science subjects for the primary school completion certificate;
- building of accommodation and provision of support to families that host girls from disadvantaged backgrounds while they attend school;
- capacity-building for the department concerned with the promotion of girls' enrolment (Direction de la promotion de la scolarisation des filles).

Source: Damiba (2005), citing the 2004 action plan of the Niger for its 2000–2015 national plan.

resources are greatly constrained, it is rational to make a special effort to reach the most disadvantaged groups – whether girls or boys – as gender disparities are often greater among the poor (World Bank, 2001; Filmer, 1999). Emergencies, conflict and post-conflict settings should also receive preference in implementing strategic priorities and allocating resources.

Adapting to the context

The discussion thus far in this chapter has related to normal circumstances, implicitly assuming reasonably stable governments and economies. A major obstacle to the achievement of EFA is the high proportion of countries that are in fact in, or recently emerged from, conflict, natural disasters, such as the December 2004 Indian Ocean tsunami, and economic instability. In addition, especially in sub-Saharan Africa, most countries have to confront the HIV/AIDS pandemic. This section initiates a discussion of such issues that future Reports will pursue further.

Figure 3.15: Education and armed conflict

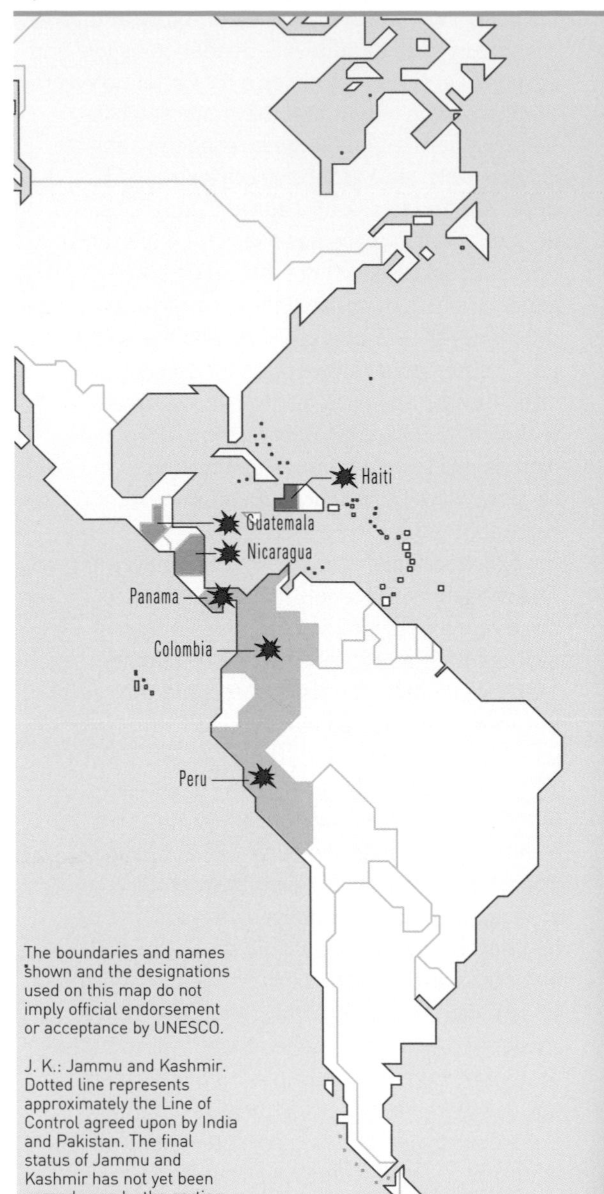
Haiti
Guatemala
Nicaragua
Panama
Colombia
Peru
The boundaries and names shown and the designations used on this map do not imply official endorsement or acceptance by UNESCO.
J. K.: Jammu and Kashmir. Dotted line represents approximately the Line of Control agreed upon by India and Pakistan. The final status of Jammu and Kashmir has not yet been agreed upon by the parties.

Emergencies and EFA

Increasingly war and conflict occur within, rather than between, countries. In 2003, for instance, there were thirty-six armed conflicts, mostly civil wars, in twenty-eight countries, almost all low-income developing countries; 90% of the victims were civilians (Project Ploughshares, 2004). Figure 3.15 plots these conflicts on the world map.

Conflict has important consequences for EFA for two reasons. First, the countries furthest from EFA are the low-income countries, and most conflicts today occur in poorer countries. Second, conflicts and their aftermath directly affect

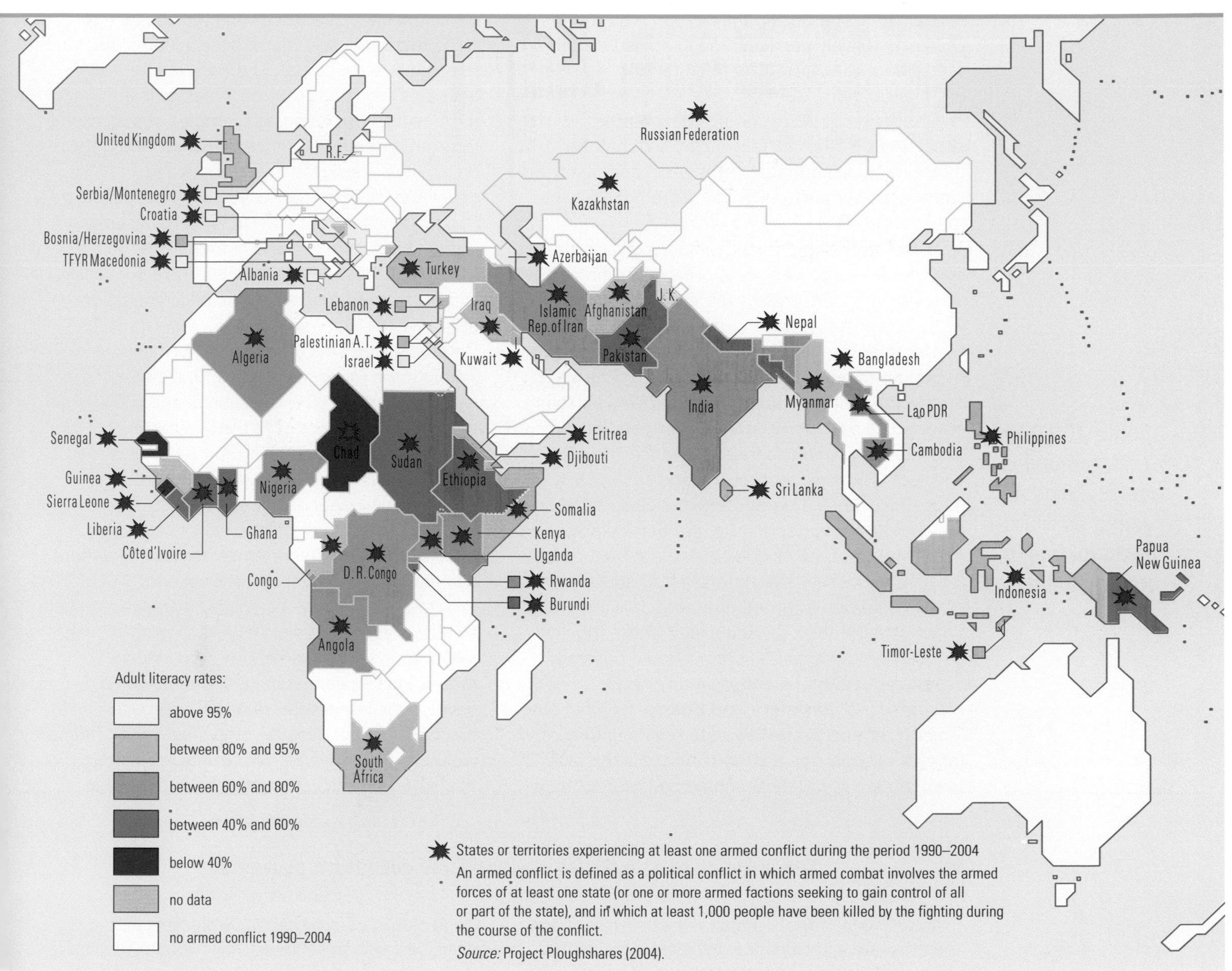

Based on United Nations map

education systems. Schools and other buildings in the education system are common targets, as they are often perceived as a key to power. Schools are also seen as battlefields in the attempt to win hearts and minds. Parents are reluctant to send children, especially girls, to school when there is insufficient security. Children may even be recruited as soldiers. Chechen schools have been bombed during school hours (Nicolai and Triplehorn, 2003). By the end of the genocide in Rwanda only one-third of the country's 1,836 schools were still operational and only 45% of primary school teachers remained (Obura, 2003). In Timor-Leste, 95% of the classrooms were destroyed in the violence that followed independence (Buckland, 2005). Teachers are the targets of murder, threats and displacement in Colombia, where eighty-three teachers were killed in 2003 (Women's Commission for Refugee Children and Women, 2004). Fear of abduction, rape, landmines and crossfire makes travel to school treacherous and parents reluctant to let children go to school during conflicts. Schools are frequent sites of military training and child recruitment, for example by rebel groups in the eastern

Democratic Republic of the Congo. Some 300,000 children under age 18, some as young as 7, are actively participating in armed conflicts throughout the world (Coalition to Stop the Use of Child Soldiers, 2001).

Maintaining education systems during conflicts and other emergencies, like natural disasters, is essential, as education offers some stability, some normality and some hope for the future (Box 3.10).

Soon after being displaced during conflicts, communities often begin to organize rudimentary schools, in basements or under trees, often without funding, teachers or materials. In Guatemala, for instance, so-called Communities of Population in Resistance kept schooling going during the civil war. Learning that takes place in emergency situations can both prepare for the future and have immediate relevance, as in the cases of landmine awareness and HIV/AIDS education. Box 3.11 outlines principles that, while they hold even in peacetime, are particularly important in times of crisis.

Some 300,000 children under age 18, some as young as 7, are participating in armed conflicts

It is, of course, easier to say that education should continue in times of emergency than to ensure that it does so, especially where the government apparatus, which should normally provide education, is either weak or has collapsed. As Sommers and Buckland (2004) note, 'The fundamental challenge to reaching EFA targets in countries during conflicts is the lack of an effective, widely accepted policy or strategy to tackle the dual problems of weakened governments in war zones and the absence of clear mandates and coordinated action plans for international response'. The work of international agencies and NGOs thus becomes crucial. Increasingly, encouraging examples of successful international efforts can be found, including the distribution of education materials and development of teacher education by UNESCO's Programme for Education for Emergencies and Reconstruction in Somalia, Yemen, Djibouti and Ethiopia; UNICEF's community centre support in the southern Sudan, which includes education; and Save the Children Canada's projects in Colombia. The Inter-Agency Network for Education in Emergencies (INEE), a global network of over 100 organizations and 800 individuals, has developed the Minimum Standards for Education in Emergencies, aimed at improving coordination among all those involved in education in emergencies.

The necessary reconstruction of education after conflicts and other emergencies represents considerable potential for renewal and improvement. Policy change, for instance, can be relatively easy, as old structures may have been swept away. At the same time, educational reconstruction cannot be undertaken with a development 'business as usual' approach (Buckland, 2005) because of the legacy of conflict: weakened institutions, civil society in disarray, destroyed infrastructure, unschooled overage

Box 3.10 The impact of the 2004 tsunami on education systems

According to official estimates, the December 2004 earthquake and tsunami killed more than 280,000 people. In India, Indonesia, Malaysia, Maldives, Myanmar, Somalia, Sri Lanka and Thailand, homes, schools, bridges and roads were devastated. UNICEF estimated that 1.5 million children were affected by the disaster and that more than one-third of those killed were children. A month following the disaster, the World Bank estimated damage and loss to the education sector in Indonesia at US$128.4 million. Nearly 1,000 Indonesian schools were destroyed or damaged. The tsunami caused US$21 million in damage to the Sri Lankan education system; 168 public schools were damaged. Teacher unions estimate that up to 75,000 teachers were affected by the tsunami. In Aceh, Indonesia, about 2,500 teachers were killed and 3,000 teachers there were still homeless three months later. In Aceh and the island of Nias, as many as 45,000 students were killed. Despite such hardships, about 750,000 children in tsunami-affected areas returned to school within two months after the disaster, UNICEF reported. In Aceh and Nias, 1,200 temporary primary school teachers were trained and began teaching in July, the beginning of the new school year. School rehabilitation in many cases began with temporary structures, built immediately after the disaster, to maintain continuity of education. The move to more permanent structures has begun, but before rebuilding could begin in earnest, issues such as land rights and safety regulations need to be addressed, and steps taken to ensure that the reconstruction is carried out equitably and sustainably.

Sources: UNICEF (2005*d*); World Bank (2005c).

Box 3.11 Principles of emergency education

Access

- The right of access to education, recreation and related activities must be assured.
- Rapid access to education, recreation and related activities should be followed by steady improvement in quality and coverage, including access to all levels of education and recognition of studies.
- Education programmes should be gender-sensitive, accessible to and inclusive of all groups.
- Education should serve as a tool for child protection and prevention of harm.

Resources

- Education programmes should use a community-based participatory approach, with emphasis on capacity-building.
- Education programmes should include a major component of training for teachers and youth/adult educators, and provide incentives to avoid teacher turnover.
- Crisis and recovery programmes should develop and document locally appropriate resource standards, adequate to meet the programmes' educational and psychosocial objectives.

Activities and curriculum

- All crisis-affected children and young people should have access to education, recreation and related activities, to help meet their psychosocial needs in the short term and longer term.
- Curriculum policy should support the long-term development of individual students and of the society and, for refugee populations, should be supportive of a durable solution, normally repatriation.
- Education programmes should be enriched to include life skills for health, safety and environmental awareness.
- Education programmes should be enriched to include life skills for peace, conflict resolution, tolerance, human rights and citizenship.
- Vocational training programmes should be linked to opportunities for workplace practice of the skills being learned.

Coordination and capacity building

- Governments and assistance agencies should promote coordination among all agencies and stakeholders.
- External assistance programmes should include capacity-building to promote transparent, accountable and inclusive system management by local actors.

Source: Sinclair (2003).

children, demobilized child soldiers, and so on. Above all, there is an immediate need to avoid a relapse into violence.

Experience shows that the most effective reconstruction strategies are participatory, elaborated in full dialogue with the affected community (INEE, 2004). Beyond education systems' reconstruction as such is the role they can play in forging social cohesion and facilitating economic recovery. Rebuilding societies free of discrimination and ethnic bias is a challenge being addressed in several places, including Mozambique, Northern Ireland, Rwanda, South Africa and the countries of the former Yugoslavia, all of which are trying to move away from segregated systems towards inclusive education.

Economic instability and EFA

Economic crises affect education systems. Public finances deteriorate and resources for the public funding of education typically decline. Household incomes fall and resources to meet the private costs of education are less available to families, although not all the effects of economic crisis are to education's detriment: in particular, the lowering of wages in the labour market can reduce the opportunity cost of children attending school rather than working. Hence, an economic and financial crisis often encourages school drop-out, but not invariably. In Costa Rica, economic crises significantly reduced secondary school attendance, especially in rural areas (Funkhouser, 1999). In Pakistan, severe reductions in income increased drop-out from secondary schools and, to a lesser extent, primary schools. In Brazil, by contrast, similarly severe income reduction did not in general reduce school attendance, as they also lowered the wages of children and hence the household cost of attending school (Duryea and Arends-Kuenning, 2001). Mexico experienced both effects, but the income reduction was greater than the drop in opportunity costs, so school attendance fell (Binder, 1999). Patterns similar to these also were

In Costa Rica, economic crises significantly reduced secondary school attendance

found in East Asia during the severe economic and social crisis of the late 1990s.

While economic crises have a mixed impact on school attendance, they more systematically affect quality negatively. Parents may wish to keep their children in school, but may cope by sending their children to a cheaper school and, very commonly, by simply reducing spending on school materials, as occurred in Argentina in 2002 (Box 3.12). It is thus very important for public resources devoted expressly to quality inputs to education to be maintained as much as possible despite economic downturns.

HIV/AIDS and EFA

HIV/AIDS, which caused about 3.1 million deaths in 2004, has a profound impact on education

HIV/AIDS, which caused about 3.1 million deaths in 2004 (UNAIDS/WHO, 2004), has a profound impact on education, and hence on the achievement of the EFA goals, especially in sub-Saharan Africa. Education also has the potential to help mitigate the pandemic. The impact on education results particularly from increases in the numbers of orphans, which education systems must accommodate, especially in sub-Saharan Africa, and from the effects of the pandemic on school system employees, including teachers (discussed above) and administrators. Education can help mitigate the pandemic through providing information to students about HIV/AIDS and developing their ability to respond.

Box 3.12 Economic shocks and the quality of education: the Argentine case

Argentina experienced a major economic and social crisis in 2002. Household income fell by roughly one-third in real terms, and about half of all households also experienced a drop in nominal income. The proportion of the population categorized as poor grew by roughly 15% and the number of the extreme poor nearly doubled between October 2001 and May 2002. Families tried very hard to keep children in school (De Ferranti et al., 2000). However, they made adjustments that had implications for quality, opting for less expensive private schools (3%), moving from private to public schools (2%) and reducing purchases of school materials (72%), an option taken particularly by the poor: while 90% of households in the lowest income quintile reduced spending on school materials, only 43% of those in the highest quintile did so.

Source: Fiszbein et al. (2002).

Impact on education systems

The HIV/AIDS crisis has left many children orphaned (having lost either or both parents). Particularly affected are eastern and southern Africa, where 31% to 77% of all orphans are AIDS orphans, compared to 4% to 39% in the rest of Africa (Desai and Jukes, 2005). AIDS orphans who have lost a mother outnumber those who have lost a father, creating a particular gap in childcare and household continuity. AIDS orphans may be unable to attend school because they or the extended family and community members caring for them cannot afford the household costs; even when they attend, they may need a wider range of support services than children with both parents and may also lack parental support with their learning.

While the needs of orphans and the impact of HIV/AIDS on teachers have been fairly widely reported, a particular gap has concerned the impact of HIV/AIDS upon education administrations and their responses to the pandemic. As with teachers, the impact on administrations stems more from the absenteeism of the sick than from the direct replacement and training costs that follow the death of personnel. 'Absenteeism is variously estimated at 24% to 89% of the total HIV/AIDS costs to employers, and training and recruitment at 17% to 24%' (Desai and Jukes, 2005, citing Grant et al., 2004, and Grassly et al., 2003). There appear to be no estimates of the impact of HIV/AIDS on education administrations specifically, however.

How well prepared are education systems to deal with AIDS? A recent survey reported that only 43% of countries with an education management information system had amended it to include HIV/AIDS-sensitive indicators through measures such as modifying annual school censuses to monitor illness and death among teachers, orphaning, and reasons for teacher attrition and pupil drop-out (HEARD and MTT, 2005). Of the seventy-one countries surveyed, 12% had no education management information system at all, much less one adapted to HIV/AIDS information.

Impact of education on HIV/AIDS

It is generally believed that the higher the level of educational attainment, the lower the rate of HIV infection within a population. In practice, the situation is more complicated. The relationship between education and HIV/AIDS appears to vary according to the stage of the pandemic. At the early stages, more educated people are more vulnerable to infection. Once information becomes available, however, the most educated members of society are more likely to access and internalize it. A survey of African countries confirms this behaviour, notably in Uganda (Desai and Jukes, 2005). As a result of these trends, African countries with higher levels of educational attainment initially have higher rates of HIV/AIDS infection than those with lower levels, but the pattern is beginning to shift. Infection rates were initially higher among the educated because of other socio-economic characteristics of these populations, such as higher income, geographic mobility, more sexual partners and more access to commercial sex partners. As information spread on such crucial topics as HIV transmission routes and ways to block them, however, educated people responded.

Recent developments confirm this pattern. A study in thirty-two countries, for example, found that literate women were three times more likely than illiterate ones to know that a healthy looking person can have HIV, and four times more likely to know the main ways to avoid AIDS (Vandermoortele and Delamonica, 2000). In Thailand – where, in contrast to most of Africa, information spread before the disease appeared – several large studies of HIV prevalence among army recruits confirmed that those with more education had lower HIV infection rates (Desai and Jukes, 2005). In Zambia, HIV infection rates have fallen by almost half among educated women but show little decline for women with no formal schooling (Schenker, 2005). In Uganda, by the end of the 1990s both women and men who had finished secondary school were seven times less likely to contract HIV than those with little or no schooling (Millennium Project, 2005*b*). In Zimbabwe, 15- to 18-year-old girls who were enrolled in school showed an HIV prevalence rate of 1.3%, just over one-sixth of the rate (7.2%) among girls of a similar age who had dropped out (Gregson et al., 2001).

Thus, educational attainment reduce the risk of HIV infection. But schools can do more to stem the spread of the disease. Particularly important are the provision of reliable HIV/AIDS information and the measures discussed above to encourage girls to enrol and stay in school. Formal schooling offers students the opportunity to gain scientific and practical information about HIV/AIDS, and offers society the possibility of people's changing their sexual behaviour as a result (Schenker, 2005). Keeping girls in school is an important strategy because it helps delay initial sexual activity. For example, in eight sub-Saharan countries, women with eight or more years of schooling were 47% to 87% less likely to have sex before the age of 18 than women with no schooling (Schenker, 2005). An analysis based on data from Uganda suggests that universal primary education could save 700,000 young adults from HIV infection. Another analysis from the United Republic of Tanzania suggests that investments in expanded school enrolment for girls is cost effective purely in terms of the effect this increased enrolment will have on the HIV epidemic (Desai and Jukes, 2005).

Data from Uganda suggest that universal primary education could save 700,000 young adults from HIV infection

Not only can schools provide information and a safe, sensitive learning environment, but, at least in countries with higher per capita incomes, they can also offer health services such as voluntary counselling and training. The Ministry of Education in Israel formally encourages all students between ages 15 and 18 to volunteer to undergo HIV testing and counselling. The ministry launched an HIV/AIDS literacy campaign to this effect in March 2005 (Schenker, 2005). Schools can provide on-site health counselling and testing.

Safe and healthy schools

If voluntary counselling and training is one method by which schools can help assure the health of their students, others of great importance in developing countries include keeping schools safe so that students can enrol and learn, and keeping students healthy so that they are ready and able to learn. This subsection draws attention to the need to eliminate violence, including corporal punishment, from schools, and to the importance of simple, cost-effective health and nutrition measures that improve learning and, hence, educational attainment and quality.

Keeping schools safe

Where violence is ever-present in schools, it is a formidable obstacle to achieving EFA, given its negative impact on participation and achievement. It is also, of course, a serious violation of human rights. Children are all too often subject to violence and harassment (Human Rights Watch, 1999): corporal punishment, verbal abuse, sexual harassment, even rape by teachers. Contrary to popular belief, boys are the targets of school violence more often than girls, the exception being sexual violence.

Numerous studies document the fact that corporal punishment is the most widely reported form of violence in schools worldwide. It occurs even in countries that ban it, such as Zimbabwe (Leach and Machakanja, 2000). Cases are on record of teachers forcing students to discipline their peers via corporal punishment (Anderson-Levitt et al., 1998). In South Asia, excessive corporal punishment such as twisting of ears and slapping has been reported. Higher-caste teachers in India have physically and verbally abused lower-caste students, and children in Bangladesh and in Pakistan have reportedly been put in chains and fetters (UNICEF, 2001). Verbal abuse also abounds, especially among female teachers, who may be less inclined to use corporal punishment. Students often perceive verbal abuse as more hurtful than corporal punishment, as it can result in loss of self-esteem.

A wide range of strategies is required to combat all forms of violence in schools

Gender violence can be both explicit and implicit. Explicit violence may be perpetrated both by male teachers and by male students with teacher endorsement. While much of the documented evidence comes from sub-Saharan Africa, explicit violence has also been reported in other countries such as Australia, Brazil, the United Kingdom and the United States, among others (Homel, 1999; Dunne et al., 2005; AAUW, 2001). Implicit violence is more complex and stems from a general school culture that perpetuates gender differences and inequalities to such an extent that the school promotes inappropriate boundaries for gender relations as the norm (Leach, 2003).

A wide range of strategies, including national policies, school discipline rules and codes of conduct for teachers, is required to combat all forms of violence in schools. Australia, South Africa, the United Kingdom and the United States have addressed the issue at national level in recent years (Mirsky, 2003). Many countries have established school discipline codes and codes of conduct for teachers, yet they are often not enforced. Head teachers often hesitate to report cases, as they know it will both generate paperwork and attract unwelcome media attention. Similarly, parents are often reluctant to bring charges due to the onerous nature of court procedures. A research project in Ghana, Malawi and Zimbabwe suggests that an effective approach involves bringing together teachers, parents, students, government officials and representations of civil society (Leach et al., 2003). The Stepping Stones training programme, promoted by UNAIDS, offers a successful approach to sexual violence. Used since 1995 in Africa, Asia and Latin America, it promotes gender equity, inter-generational respect, and solidarity with HIV positive people, in a human rights framework.

Keeping schools healthy

Good health and nutrition are prerequisites for effective learning. There is strong evidence of their direct impact on cognition, learning and educational achievement (Jukes et al., forthcoming). The promotion of health and nutrition supports not only effective learning but also social inclusion, as it is the poorest who suffer the most malnutrition and ill health.

Infectious diseases affecting school age children include helminth infections, which directly impede learning (25% to 35% of all children in developing countries are infected with worms); malaria, which creates a massive absenteeism problem; and acute respiratory infections and HIV/AIDS. Malnutrition and hunger are common in developing countries, and micronutrient deficiencies pose a serious problem. Iron deficiency, caused by malaria and hookworms, occurs among 50% of all children in developing countries. Iodine and vitamin A deficiencies are also very prevalent. Typically low test scores indicate that the total losses from stunting, anaemia and helminthiasis alone in children in developing countries amount to some 600 to 1,800 million IQ points, 15 to 45 million additional cases of mental retardation and 200 to 524 million years of primary schooling (Bundy et al., forthcoming).

Yet, cost-effective, low-cost interventions by teachers (Table 3.8) can make a major dent in these extraordinarily high educational and human losses, improving IQ by 4 to 6 points, school attendance by 10%, and overall school achievement. If schools carry out these actions, the costs are much less than if the health system does so, though this comparison excludes the extra cost of training teachers. Each typical school health intervention in the table will result in at least a 0.25 standard deviation increase in IQ and about an additional 2.5 student-years of primary schooling (Bundy et al., forthcoming). Combining the low cost and the high impact of these interventions makes them very cost-effective compared to traditional educational inputs such as books (Miguel and Kremer, 2004).

The Focus Resources on Effective School Health, or FRESH, is an EFA flagship framework encompassing these and other interventions. Undertaking mass delivery of services such as deworming and micronutrient supplementation avoids the high cost of diagnostic screening that would have to accompany targeted service delivery. Large-scale school health and nutrition programmes thus can have a major impact on learning. Developing countries increasingly recognize this, but implementation is far from complete. ■

Table 3.8: Annual per capita costs of school-based health and nutrition interventions delivered by teachers

Condition	Intervention	Cost US$
Intestinal worms	Albendazole or mebendazole	0.03-0.20
Schistosomiasis	Praziquantel	0.20-0.71
Vitamin A deficiency	Vitamin A supplementation	0.04
Iodine deficiency	Iodine supplementation	0.30-0.40
Iron deficiency and anaemia	Iron folate supplementation	0.1
Refractive errors of vision	Spectacles	2.50-3.50
Clinically diagnosed conditions	Physical examination	11.5
Undernutrition, hunger	School feeding	21.30-151.20

Source: Bundy et al. (forthcoming).

Large-scale school health and nutrition programmes can have a major impact on learning

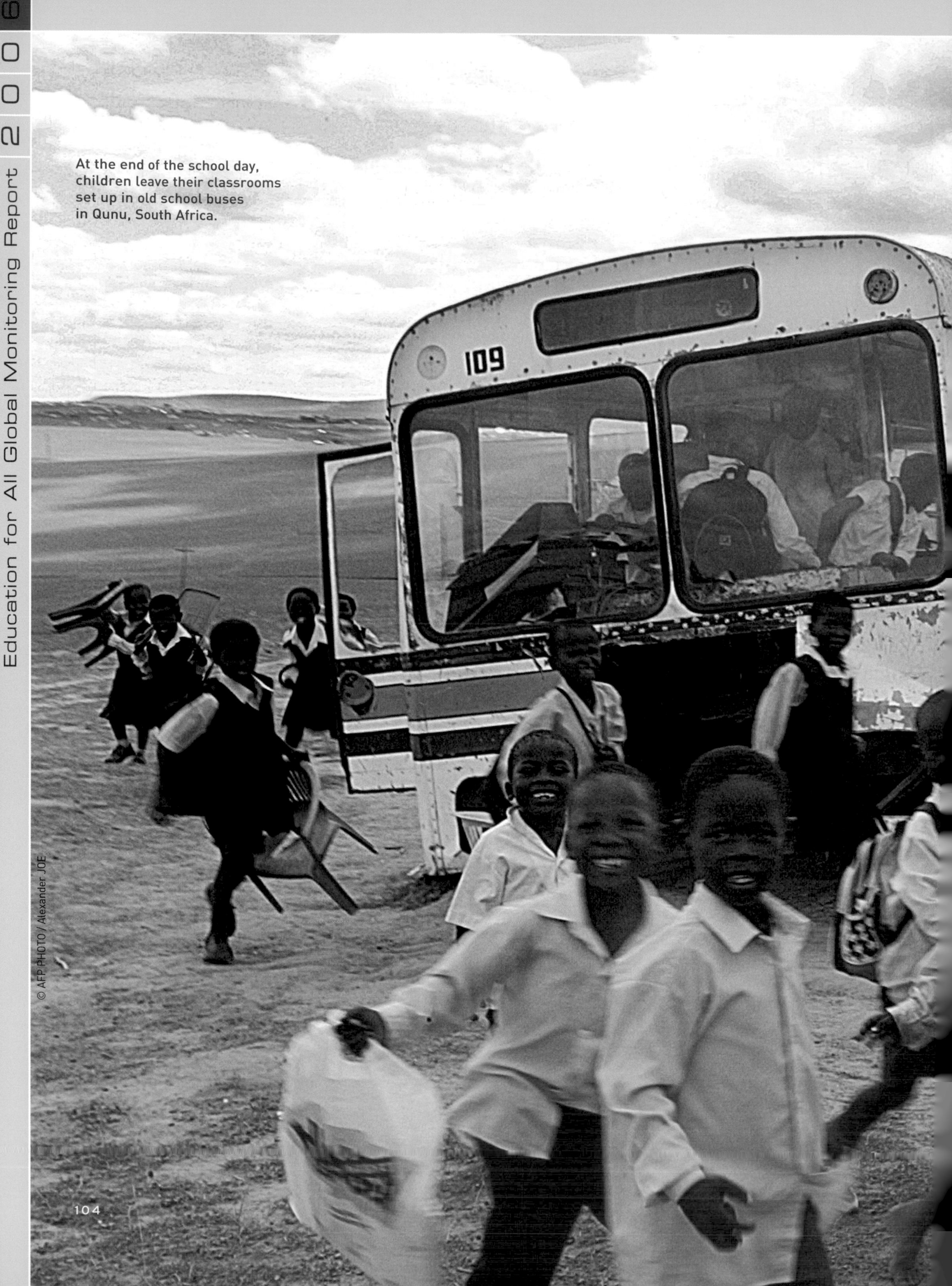

At the end of the school day, children leave their classrooms set up in old school buses in Qunu, South Africa.

Chapter 4

International commitments: time to act

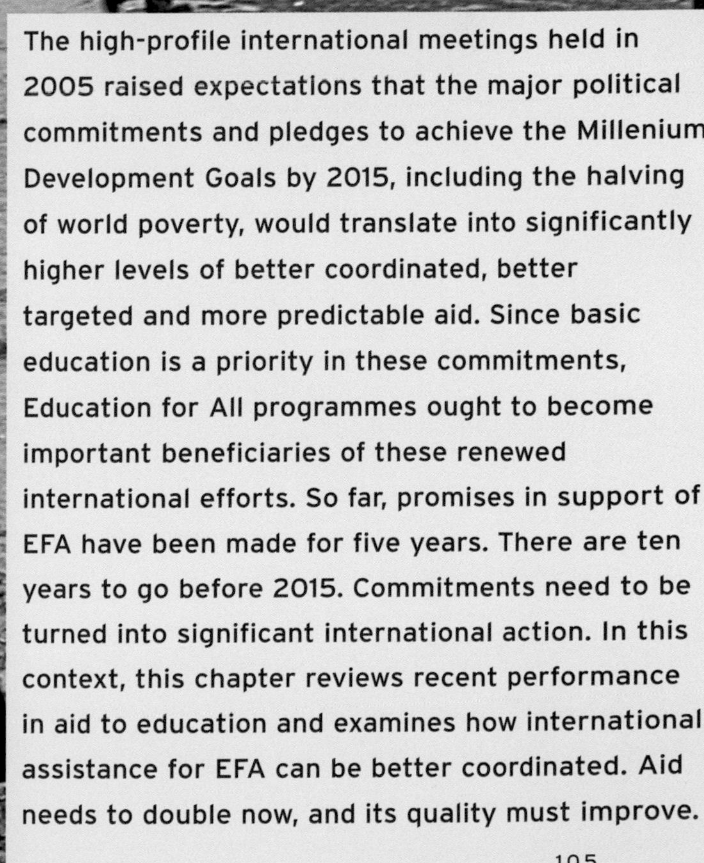

The high-profile international meetings held in 2005 raised expectations that the major political commitments and pledges to achieve the Millenium Development Goals by 2015, including the halving of world poverty, would translate into significantly higher levels of better coordinated, better targeted and more predictable aid. Since basic education is a priority in these commitments, Education for All programmes ought to become important beneficiaries of these renewed international efforts. So far, promises in support of EFA have been made for five years. There are ten years to go before 2015. Commitments need to be turned into significant international action. In this context, this chapter reviews recent performance in aid to education and examines how international assistance for EFA can be better coordinated. Aid needs to double now, and its quality must improve.

New but uncertain international momentum in 2005

The G8 agreed to cancel all outstanding multilateral debts of eligible heavily indebted poor countries

Expectations were raised in 2005 that the international community would step up its support for the eradication of poverty and the achievement of the Millennium Development Goals (MDGs). A number of high-profile reports made the case for more, better targeted and better coordinated aid (Table 4.1). The Group of Eight countries (G8) and other donors made commitments that should increase aid by approximately US$50 billion a year by 2010 compared with 2004 when total bilateral aid was approximately US$80 billion. The G8 also agreed to cancel all outstanding multilateral debts of eligible heavily indebted poor countries. The United Nations World Summit was designed to reach a set of collective agreements to halve global poverty by 2015.

Education should benefit from these and other developments. The G8, for example, intended to give priority to basic education and endorsed the Fast Track Initiative as a mechanism for promoting increased and better aid for education for all.

This chapter reviews the efforts and achievements made by the donor community since Dakar to commit additional financial resources for the expansion of basic education in low income countries, and the evolution of the institutional infrastructure which is being designed in response to calls for more and better targeted and coordinated aid. The first section deals with total flows of aid from both bilateral donors and the multilateral donor agencies to the education sector in general and to basic education. Differences in the relative priority given to education by individual donors are described, together with an account of the geographic distribution of this type of aid. The section ends with a reference to the potential impact of further debt relief on education expenditures and a call for higher levels of more predictable, longer term, aid. The second section deals with the equally important set of issues surrounding the

Table 4.1: 2005 – Major international reports

International reports 2005	Selected points of relevance for EFA
World Economic Forum: *Global Governance Initiative Annual Report 2005.*	• There has been insufficient action on the education goals (a score of 3 out of 10 for 2004 in the GGI report). With only a decade left to get all children through six to eight years of primary school, 2005 is a crucial year for securing much-needed political and financial commitment.
World Bank: *Global Monitoring Report 2005. Millennium Development Goals: From Consensus to Momentum.*	• Without faster progress, the MDGs will be seriously jeopardized. Sub-Saharan Africa is off track on all goals. • Action to achieve the MDGs must be anchored in country-led strategies. • A major scaling up of education and health services is required. • The scaling up of education services requires: rapidly increased supplies of skilled service providers; increased, flexible and predictable financing for recurrent-cost-intensive services; and managing the service delivery chain to achieve results. • The Fast Track Initiative should be strengthened. Partners should make monitorable, long-term commitments to major annual increases in funding for primary education.
Commission for Africa: *Our Common Interest, Report of the Commission for Africa.*	• Donors and African governments should meet their commitments to EFA, ensuring that every child goes to school. • Donors should provide an additional US$7–8 billion per year as African governments develop comprehensive national plans to deliver quality education.
The Millennium Project: *Investing in Development: A Practical Plan to Achieve the Millennium Development Goals.*	• Developing country governments should have development strategies in place by 2006, bold enough to meet the MDG targets. • These strategies require the scaling up of public investments, capacity-building, domestic resource mobilization and development assistance. They should provide a framework for strengthening governance, promoting human rights, engaging civil society and promoting the private sector. • International donors should identify at least twelve MDG 'fast track' countries for a rapid scale up of ODA in 2005. • Governments should launch 'quick wins' strategies (e.g. ending user fees for primary schools), compensated by increased donor aid as necessary, no later than the end of 2006. • High-income countries should increase ODA to 0.44% GDP by 2006 and 0.54% GDP by 2010, to support low-income countries with improved ODA quality. Each donor should reach 0.7 percent no later than 2015. • The UN Secretary-General and the UN Development Group should strengthen the coordination of UN agencies, funds and programmes to support the MDGs at headquarters and country levels.

Sources: ActionAid (2005); Commission for Africa (2005); IMF/World Bank (2005); Millennium Project (2005*a*); OECD-DAC (2005*e*); UNAIDS (2005); UNICEF (2005*b*); United Nations (2005); World Economic Forum (2005); World Bank (2005*b*).

harmonization and effectiveness of aid. Important initiatives have been taken over the past year. These will need to be extended and applied consistently before their full potential is realized. The initiatives are described together with suggestions for their further development.

Aid flows to education

Each year the *EFA Global Monitoring Report* analyses the level and the distribution of aid to education, particularly to basic education.[1]

At the outset, it needs to be made clear that some of the reporting practices of donors and the trends away from discrete project financing towards broad sectoral and budget support complicate these analyses, as described in the sub sections below. While the implications are not sufficient to undermine any of the major conclusions, further effort to more accurately report aid flows would increase the accuracy of assessments of aid needs and gaps, and also provide a more complete picture of the donor support for the achievement of EFA. For a glossary of the terms on types of aid, donors and data presentation, see the introduction to the annex on aid data (p. 408).

Total aid – moving in the right direction

Total net Official Development Assistance (ODA) increased by 4% in real terms from 2002 to 2003 (Figure 4.1) and by a further 5% (preliminary data) from 2003 to 2004.[2] The 2004 estimate of US$79 billion (at current prices) is the highest level of ODA ever recorded in either real or nominal terms,[3] though as a share of the gross national income of DAC member countries (0.25%) it is still well below the average level recorded up to the early 1990s (0.33%). Three quarters of total ODA is contributed directly by donor countries and one quarter is distributed through the multinational agencies. Donors represented in the OECD's Development Assistance Committee (OECD-DAC) contributed over 95% of reported bilateral aid flows.[4]

The 2004 estimate of US$79 billion is the highest level of ODA ever recorded

International reports 2005	Selected points of relevance for EFA
Report of the UN Secretary General: *In Larger Freedom: Towards Development, Security and Human Rights for All.*	• Broad-based actions should be taken to achieve the MDG goals backed by a doubling of global development assistance in the next few years. • Developed countries that have not already done so should establish timetables to achieve the 0.7% of ODA target no later than 2015, starting with significant increases no later than 2006 and reaching 0.5% by 2009.
OECD-DAC: *The Paris Declaration on Aid Effectiveness.*	• Far-reaching and monitorable actions to reform the ways we deliver and manage aid as we look ahead to the UN five-year review of the Millennium Declaration and the MDGs. • An acceleration in the pace of change by implementing, in a spirit of mutual accountability, the Partnership Commitments [on Ownership, Alignment, Harmonization and Managing for Results] • Internationally, we call on the partnership of donors and partner countries ... to broaden partner country participation and, by the end of 2005, to propose arrangements for the monitoring of the Declaration's commitments.
UN AIDS: *AIDS in Africa; Three Scenarios to 2025.*	• Major increases in spending will be needed to produce significantly better outcomes to curb the spread of HIV, extending treatment access and mitigating impact – but more resources without effective coordination ... may do more harm than good. • Measures to improve the status of women are needed, such as universal education for girls. • The resilience of communities to care for orphaned children has been considerable, but the ongoing, cyclical nature of the AIDS crisis means that this may be worn away. Investing in children as a resource for the future, and in keeping their parents uninfected and alive, contributes significantly to the overall outcome of the epidemic.
UNICEF: *Progress for Children: A Report Card on Gender Parity and Primary Education.*	• It is still possible that by 2015 every girl and boy in the world will attend and complete primary school. The litmus test remains the elimination of gender disparity in primary and secondary education by the end of 2005, or as soon as possible thereafter. • There are three major initiatives ... straining to achieve the education goals, each complementing the other... the Fast Track Initiative, UNICEF's '25 by 2005' Initiative, and the United Nation's Girls Education Initiative.
ActionAid International: *Real Aid; An Agenda for Making Aid Work.*	• Aid donors must commit to providing at least 0.7% of their national income in 'real aid', by 2010 at the latest. There must be a new international aid agreement, in which donors and recipients are held mutually accountable.

1. The *EFA Global Monitoring Report* draws primarily on the online databases of the International Development Statistics (IDS) of the OECD's Development Assistance Committee (DAC): the DAC database and the CRS database. This year the analysis benefits from close cooperation with the Secretariat of the Fast Track Initiative, based at the World Bank.

2. In this Report, aid data are expressed in constant 2002 US dollars, unless otherwise indicated (see introduction to the annex on aid data for details).

3. As reported by OECD-DAC on 11 April 2005 (OECD-DAC, 2005*d*). This increase is accounted for primarily by new contributions to international organizations by the DAC members, aid to Afghanistan and Iraq and increases in technical cooperation grants.

4. It is, however, important to note that China and India appear to be giving increasing amounts of aid, though they have disclosed no aggregate figures.

Figure 4.1: Total ODA 1990–2003 (net disbursements in constant 2002 US$ billions)

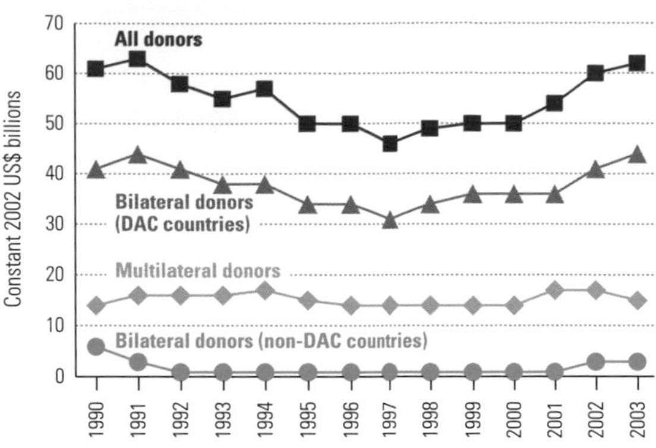

Source: DAC online database (OECD-DAC 2005*c*, Table 2*a*).

Figure 4.2: Proportion of ODA to least developed countries in total ODA, 1990–2003

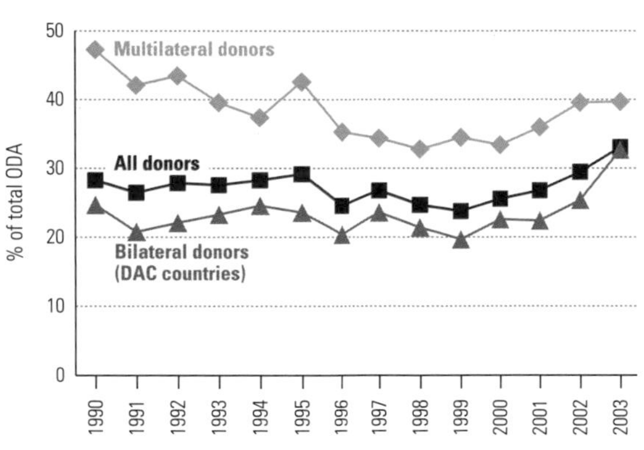

Source: DAC online database (OECD-DAC 2005*c*, Table 2*a*).

Least developed countries receive just one-third of total ODA

Debt relief and technical cooperation, neither of which necessarily increases resources directly available to developing countries, accounted for the major part of the increase in ODA from 2001 to 2003.

The proportion of ODA going to the least developed countries (LDCs) in 2003 rose by 3.6 percentage points (Figure 4.2),[5] largely owing to a 7.3 percentage point increase in bilateral ODA to LDCs. However, multilateral donor agencies allocate a greater share of aid to the LDCs than do the bilateral donors and, overall, LDCs receive just one-third of total ODA. With some exceptions, these countries have the poorest EFA indicators.

Bilateral aid to education – partial recovery since 2000

Five years have passed since the World Education Forum in Dakar in 2000, but aid data for education are only available up to and including 2003. Nevertheless, this allows an initial assessment of whether international commitments to education made at Dakar, the UN Millennium Summit, Kananaskis[6] and Monterrey[7] have resulted in higher aid flows. More recent commitments in 2005 are assessed in the last section of this chapter.

As last year's Report anticipated, bilateral aid to education increased in 2003 to US$4.65 billion, a 31% real increase over its 2000 low of US$3.55 billion, but still well below the 1990 high of US$5.71 billion (Figure 4.3). While the absolute and real levels increased, education's share declined from 8.8% of total ODA in 2002 to 7.4% in 2003, the lowest figure in the last ten years.

A similar situation characterizes bilateral aid to basic education. Between 1998 and 2003, the amount in real terms almost tripled (from US$0.42 billion to US$1.16 billion) and as a share of total ODA it increased from 1.0% to 2.2% before falling back somewhat in 2003 (Figure 4.4). Overall, basic education still only accounts for a small share of total bilateral aid flows.

The priority given to education generally, and to basic education, continues to vary considerably across donors (Table 4.2). From 1999 to 2003[8] the share of aid to education as a percentage of overall ODA averaged 9.7%, ranging from 2.8% (the United States) to 35.7% (New Zealand) (Table 4.2). The share of basic education in total education averaged 28.3%, ranging from 1.4% (Italy) to 88.6% (the United Kingdom). So, while the overall trend of aid to basic education is upwards, this is not reflected uniformly in the aid practice of all DAC members.

5. There are fifty Least Devoloped Countries classified by the United Nations and listed in the DAC's List of Aid Recipients. The data in this Report are based on the list as of 1 January 2003 (http://www1.oecd.org/scripts/cde/members/DACAuthenticate.asp).

6. At the G8 summit in Kananaskis in Canada (2002) it was agreed that G8 countries would assist developing countries to achieve universal primary education for all children and equal access to education for girls. Echoing Dakar, bilateral assistance would increase significantly for countries that demonstrated a strong and credible policy and financial commitment to the goals (Canada, 2003).

7. United Nations (2002).

8. Whereas, in previous Reports, two-year annual averages were used, the data now permit five-year annual averages to be calculated. This should offset somewhat the effect of fluctuation in aid figures year by year and allow for a more accurate assessment of trends by donor and across donors.

Figure 4.3: Bilateral aid commitments to education, 1990–2003 (amounts in constant 2002 US$ billions, and the share of education in total bilateral ODA)

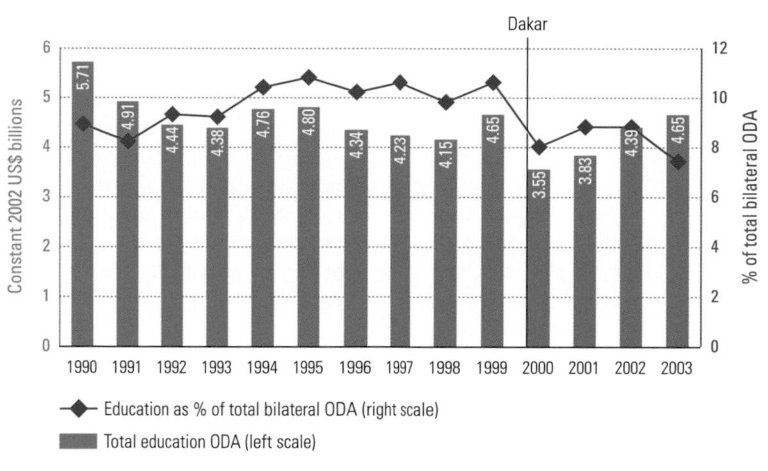

Source: DAC online database (OECD-DAC 2005*c*, Table 5).

Figure 4.5: Contribution of individual DAC countries to total bilateral aid to education, 1999–2003

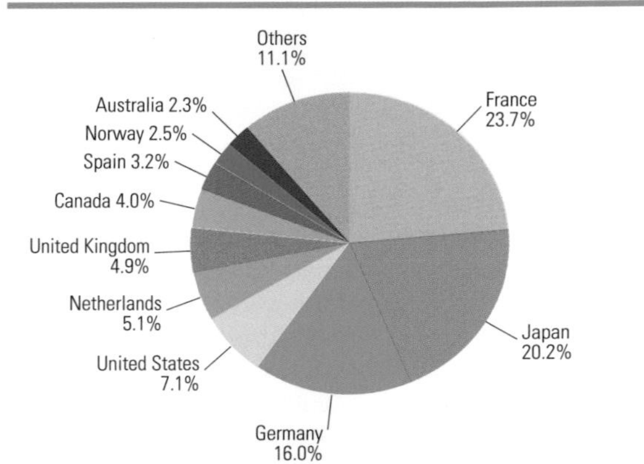

Notes: 'Others' are Austria, Belgium, Denmark, Finland, Greece, Italy, Ireland, New Zealand, Portugal, Sweden and Switzerland. These countries contributed less than 2% each of total bilateral aid to education. Comparable data are not available for Luxembourg.
Source: Computed from DAC online database (OECD-DAC 2005*c*, Table 5).

Figure 4.4: Bilateral aid commitments to basic education, 1993–2003 (amounts in constant 2002 US$ billions, and the share of basic education in total bilateral ODA)

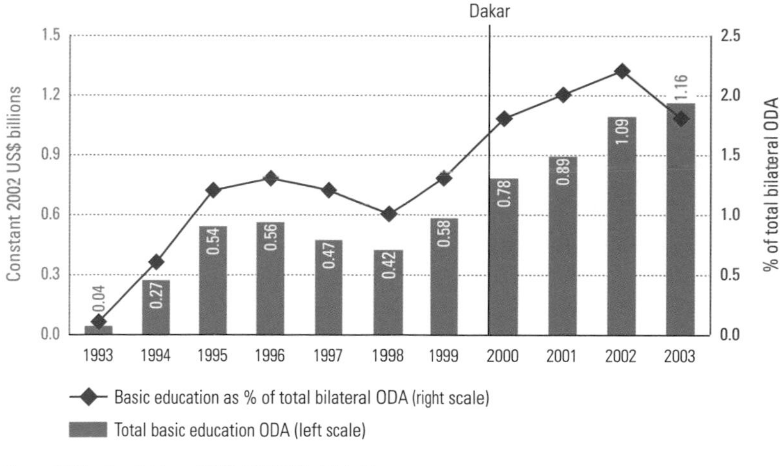

Source: DAC online database (OECD-DAC 2005*c*, Table 5).

Figure 4.6: Contribution of individual DAC countries to total bilateral aid to basic education, 1999–2003

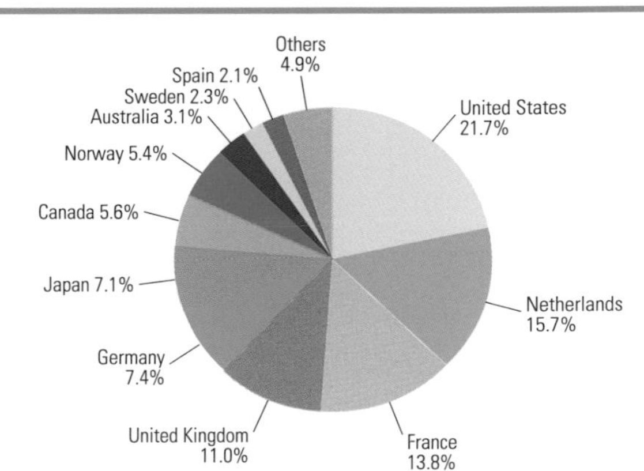

Notes: 'Others' are Austria, Belgium, Denmark, Finland, Italy, New Zealand, Portugal and Switzerland. These countries contributed less than 2% each to total bilateral aid to basic education. Comparable data are not available for Luxembourg, Greece and Ireland.
Source: Computed from DAC online database (OECD-DAC 2005*c*, Table 5).

It is important to record actual levels of aid as well as the relative priorities accorded to education and to basic education. From 1999 to 2003, France, Japan and Germany accounted for almost 60% of total bilateral aid to education (Figure 4.5), while the United States, the Netherlands, France and the United Kingdom made up 62% of bilateral aid to basic education (Figure 4.6). In both categories there is a high degree of concentration in a small group of countries.

Overall nearly 60% of bilateral commitments are for post-secondary education,[9] twice what is assigned to basic education (Figure 4.7). Only four countries (Denmark, the Netherlands, the United Kingdom and the United States) allocated an average of over 60% of their sector aid to basic education between 1999 and 2003, whereas fifteen DAC countries committed less than 50%.

Six countries (the United Kingdom, the Netherlands, the United States, Denmark, Sweden and Norway) give relatively high priority to basic education in an overall aid portfolio that accords education relatively low priority (Figure 4.8). In contrast, Germany, France, Austria

9. Post-secondary education includes higher education and advanced technical and managerial training (OECD-DAC, 2002).

Table 4.2: Bilateral aid commitments to basic education, 1999–2003 (amount and share of basic education in total ODA)

	Amount (annual average, constant 2002 US$ millions)			Share (%)		Relative priority[3] assigned to	
	Education (total)	Basic education[2]	Total ODA	Education as % of total aid[1]	Basic education as % of total education[2]	Education aid	Basic education aid
France	996.6	123.5	4 473.0	24.3	15.4	2.5	0.5
Japan	851.4	63.1	11 636.1	7.9	12.7	0.8	0.4
Germany	673.9	66.0	4 024.8	19.0	10.3	2.0	0.4
United States	298.2	194.0	12 708.0	2.8	67.4	0.3	2.4
Netherlands	212.6	140.3	2 930.4	8.1	78.4	0.8	2.8
United Kingdom	207.9	98.1	3 057.3	7.3	88.6	0.8	3.1
Canada	166.7	50.0	1 421.4	12.8	41.2	1.3	1.5
Spain	133.5	18.5	1 069.2	13.6	21.7	1.4	0.8
Norway	103.1	48.1	1 156.0	10.0	56.1	1.0	2.0
Australia	94.8	27.7	742.6	14.9	31.4	1.5	1.1
Austria	73.8	1.9	423.2	18.3	2.7	1.9	0.1
Belgium	73.1	5.4	695.9	11.5	9.0	1.2	0.3
Sweden	58.6	20.3	1 190.0	5.6	59.6	0.6	2.1
Denmark	43.0	17.3	848.5	5.6	66.6	0.6	2.4
Italy	40.5	0.2	865.5	5.1	1.4	0.5	0.1
Ireland[4]	38.4	...	217.3	18.7	–	1.9	–
Portugal	34.1	3.1	236.2	16.5	11.5	1.7	0.4
Switzerland	31.0	10.1	741.6	5.8	43.1	0.6	1.5
New Zealand	28.8	2.2	94.6	35.7	7.8	3.7	0.3
Finland	26.3	3.2	279.2	11.3	39.6	1.2	1.4
Luxembourg[5]	19.3	5.3	90.7	21.9	47.0	2.3	1.7
Greece[5]	18.6	13.2	112.6	17.8	44.0	1.8	1.6
Total DAC Countries	**4 224.8**	**911.5**	**49 014.1**	**9.7**	**28.3**	**1.0**	**1.0**

Notes: Countries are sorted in descending order by the amount of aid to education.

1. The share of education in total ODA less sector unallocable aid, i.e. multi-sector and general programme assistance that is not shown in this table. These data are different from the share of education shown in Figure 4.3, which are based on total ODA with no differentiation for sector unallocable aid.

2. Aid to basic education in this table is the amount reported directly under this category. It does not include commitments to basic education that may have been reported under 'education, level unspecified'. Accordingly, the share of basic education as a proportion of total education aid omits 'education, level unspecified'. See the Aid Annex Table 1.1 for the total amount of 'education, level unspecified' for each bilateral donor.

3. Relative priority is the ratio between the proportion of total aid assigned to education or basic education by each agency and the mean for all agencies. The indicator is calculated as follows:

$$\text{Relative priority assigned to education aid} = \frac{EA_i / TA_i}{\sum_{i=1}^{22} EA_i \Big/ \sum_{i=1}^{22} TA_i}$$

where: i = a DAC country; EA = Education aid; TA = Total aid

The average for all donors is therefore 1. A score above 1 indicates that the donor gives education a higher priority than the average for all donors; a score below 1 indicates that it gives education a lower priority than the average for all donors.

4. Sub-sector breakdown is not available for Ireland.

5. Data coverage is limited for Luxembourg and Greece; therefore the figures shown here are not comparable with other donors. (Luxembourg: 1999 and 2000 figures are used for education and basic education. Greece: 2000 and 2003 figures are used for the average for basic education.)

Source: Computed from DAC online database (OECD-DAC 2005*c*, Table 5).

and New Zealand give education relatively high priority, but within this basic education has a low priority. Canada, Finland and Australia accord relatively high priority to both.[10] A major shift by France, Germany and Japan towards basic education would have a significant effect on overall resource levels, a move that is underway for France (Box 4.4). If the United States, the United Kingdom, Germany and Japan were also to increase their aid to education to over 0.04% of Gross National Income (GNI), already met by Luxembourg, France, New Zealand, Norway, the Netherlands and Ireland (Figure 4.9), the effect would be dramatic.[11]

The analysis thus far suggests that in international commitments the priorities accorded to education in general, and to basic education in particular, are not reflected in the actual level of bilateral aid. However, there are several reasons to suggest that the data cited above may be a significant underestimate for those donor countries that channel a relatively

10. These patterns, based on five-year averages, broadly confirm the analysis in the 2005 *EFA Global Monitoring Report*, which was based on two-year averages (see UNESCO, 2004*a*, p.191–2).

11. Given the limited coverage, the data for Luxembourg should be interpreted with caution.

Figure 4.7: Bilateral commitments to education: sub-sector breakdown excluding 'education, level unspecified', 1999–2003

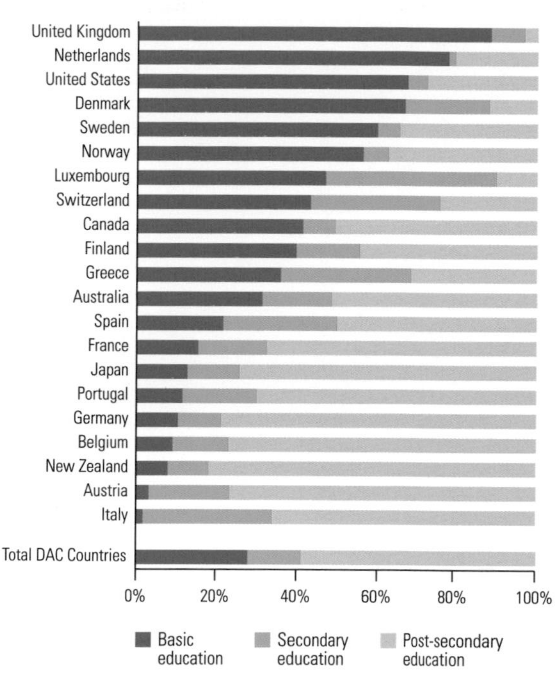

Note: Data for Luxembourg are for 1999 and 2000 only; Greece for 2000 and 2003 only. Ireland does not record data sub-sector breakdown.
Source: Computed from DAC online database (OECD-DAC 2005*c*, Table 5).

Figure 4.8: Relative priorities given to education and basic education by each bilateral donor country, 1999–2003

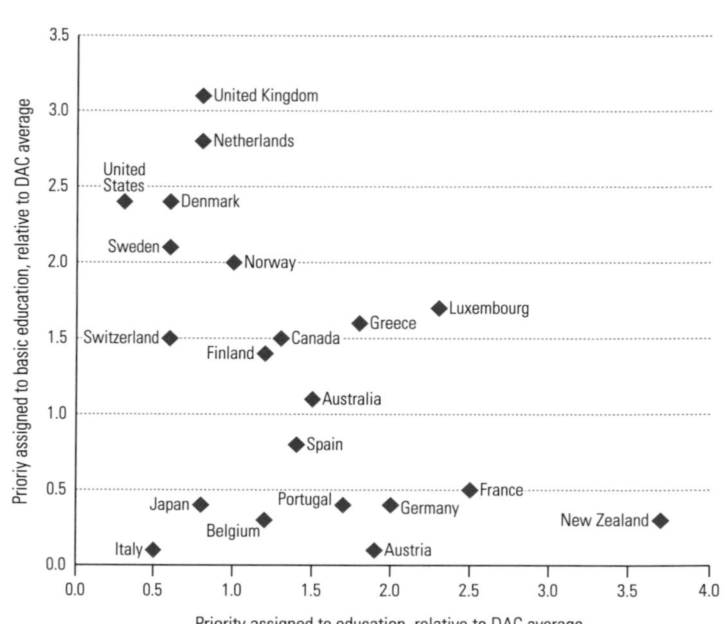

Note: Data for Luxembourg are for 1999 and 2000 only; Greece for 2000 and 2003 only. Ireland does not record data sub-sector breakdown.
Source: Table 4.2.

Figure 4.9: Aid to education and basic education as percentages of GNI, five-year annual averages, 1999–2003

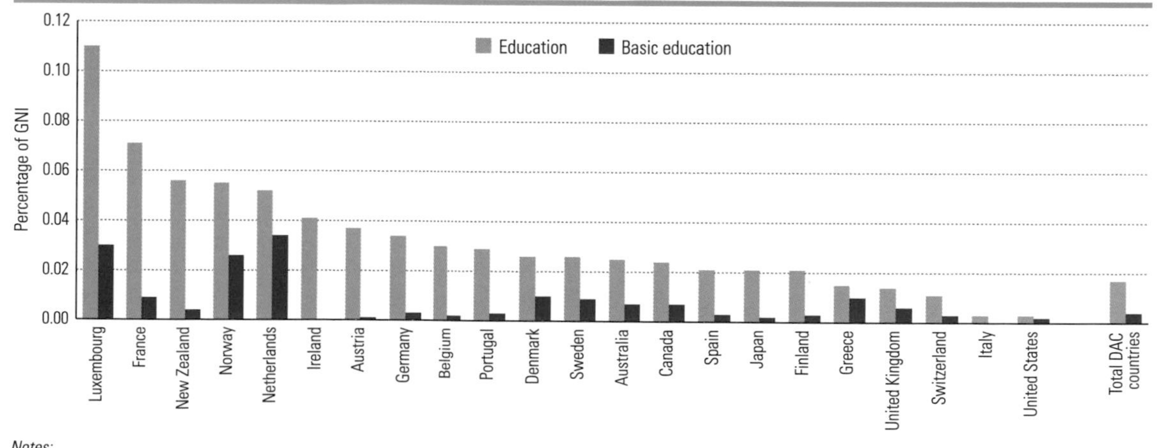

Notes:
1. Aid to basic education does not include allocations from 'education, level unspecified'. Data for Luxembourg are for 1999 and 2000 only; Greece for 2000 and 2003 only. Ireland does not record data on basic education.
2. Gross National Income (GNI) is used here instead of Gross Domestic Product for reasons of data availability. For DAC countries the two figures are very similar.
Sources: OECD-DAC (2005*b*), statistical annex of the 2004 Development Co-operation Report, Table 4; and OECD-DAC (2005*c*), DAC online database, Table 5.

high proportion of their aid through budget support.[12] Overall, budget support accounted for 5% of total bilateral ODA in 1999–2003, some of which went to basic education (Figure 4.10). The Fast Track Initiative (FTI) Secretariat estimates that 15% of budget support can be ascribed to education, half of which goes to basic education (FTI Secretariat, 2004). Based on the data

12. See the introduction to the annex on aid data.

Figure 4.10: Proportion of budget support in total ODA, 1999–2003, by type of donor

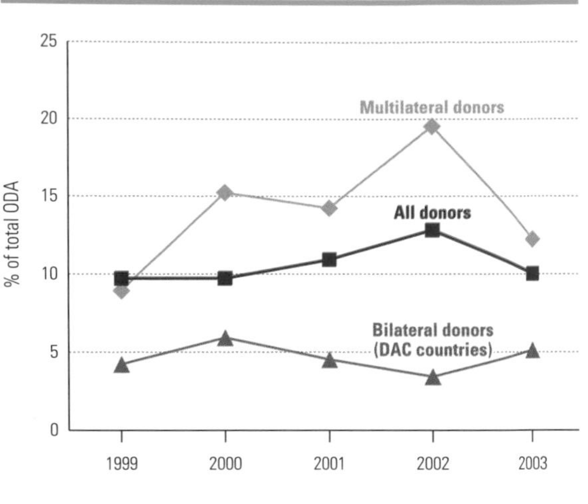

Source: CRS database (OECD-DAC, 2005*c*, Tables 1 and 2).

Table 4.3: Comparison between commitments and disbursements (current US$ millions)

	Commitments			Disbursements		
	annual average					
	1999–2000	2001–2002	2003	2001	2002	2003
Aid for education						
Australia	160.4	46.9	100.8	116.7	90.8	81.2
Austria	91.1	63.4	75.6	72.0	20.9	76.4
Germany	645.9	633.0	982.3	223.6	630.7	1 001.8
Netherlands	159.5	267.6	126.6	85.2	213.8	187.3
Sweden	34.1	55.6	153.6	41.5	50.0	74.0
United Kingdom	232.5	157.3	313.0	106.7	101.4	173.4
Aid for basic education						
Australia	43.8	20.4	66.4	22.8	21.0	25.8
Austria	2.5	0.9	3.4	0.7	10.4	3.1
Germany	72.0	58.0	86.5	69.7	60.4	84.0
Netherlands	85.89	195.6	44.5	36.8	142.5	97.5
Sweden	18.3	23.2	43.7	18.6	12.7	26.7
United Kingdom	167.5	85.1	241.6	64.3	63.5	120.3

Source: OECD-DAC (2005*a*).

Figure 4.11: Share of disbursements in 2003 for education by Australia, Sweden and the United Kingdom, by original year of commitments

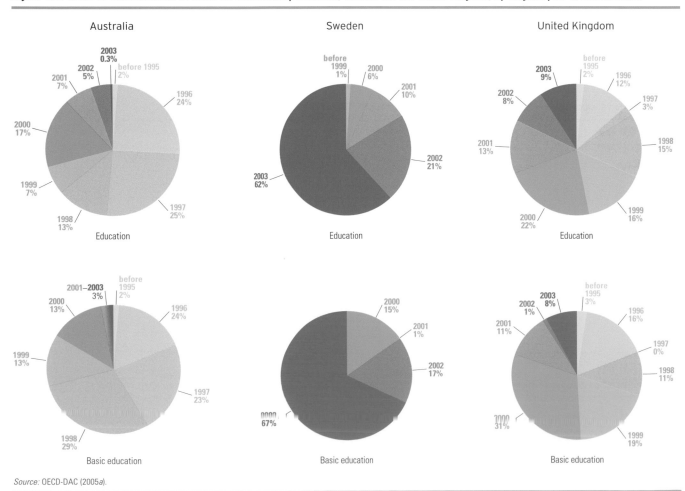

Australia

2003 0.3%, before 1995 2%, 1996 24%, 1997 25%, 1998 13%, 1999 7%, 2000 17%, 2001 7%, 2002 5%

Education

Sweden

before 1999 1%, 2000 6%, 2001 10%, 2002 21%, 2003 62%

Education

United Kingdom

before 1995 2%, 1996 12%, 1997 3%, 1998 15%, 1999 16%, 2000 22%, 2001 13%, 2002 8%, 2003 9%

Education

Australia

before 1995 2%, 1996 24%, 1997 23%, 1998 29%, 1999 13%, 2000 13%, 2001–2003 3%

Basic education

Sweden

2000 15%, 2001 1%, 2002 17%, 67%

Basic education

United Kingdom

before 1995 3%, 1996 16%, 1997 0%, 1998 11%, 1999 19%, 31%, 2001 11%, 2002 1%, 2003 8%

Basic education

Source: OECD-DAC (2005*a*).

available from the CRS database pertaining to budget support, this would represent an additional US$466 million from DAC countries and US$337 million from multilateral donors going to education as a whole in 2003.

In addition, twelve DAC countries report allocating an average of more than 20% of their aid to education as general budget support, or 'education, level unspecified' in 1999–2003,[13] over a third for the United Kingdom, Japan, Sweden and Denmark, and almost 70% for Finland.[14] Again, accounting for how much of this can be allocated to basic education is problematic.[15] The FTI Secretariat (2004) suggests that most or all could be assigned to basic education, but given that continuing education and scholarships are often found in this category also this seems a questionable proposition.

Aid to education is also under-represented to the extent that aid for education and training activities in other sectors is absent from aid totals. One estimate for 2003 suggests that including the aid for education that is reported under other sectors would increase total education ODA by 10% (13% for 2001 to 2003).[16]

Another difficulty posed by the data is that of comparing commitment levels with disbursements.[17] In Table 4.3, all six countries sampled show apparent discrepancies between levels of commitment and disbursement. While the United Kingdom appears to have disbursed less than it committed in all three years (2001 to 2003), there is no apparent common pattern among the other countries. Part of the aid disbursed by the United Kingdom in 2003 goes back to commitments made in the 1990s (Figure 4.11). This suggests that the United Kingdom is able to make long-term commitments in ways that do not appear to be possible in other countries, such as Sweden, for example, which disbursed over 50% of its 2003 commitment in the same year.[18]

Given the importance of good data for estimating need and predicting aid flows, the OECD-DAC should continue to encourage its members to look at ways of reporting their aid to education more accurately and more precisely. Current practices are probably leading to an underestimate of donors' support for basic education – a situation which donor country governments would surely wish to reserve.

Distribution of bilateral aid to education: the neediest miss out

The regional priorities of most donors reflect historical and political factors as well as aid policy. Nine countries allocate over 40% of their aid to education to sub-Saharan Africa, while three (Australia, New Zealand and Japan) give priority to East Asia and the Pacific. Some DAC members, such as Germany, spread their aid more broadly (Figure 4.12). It is striking that only three donors (Norway, Switzerland and the United Kingdom) allocate more than 20% of their aid to

The regional priorities of most donors reflect historical and political factors as well as aid policy

Figure 4.12: Regional distribution of bilateral aid to education, 1999-2003

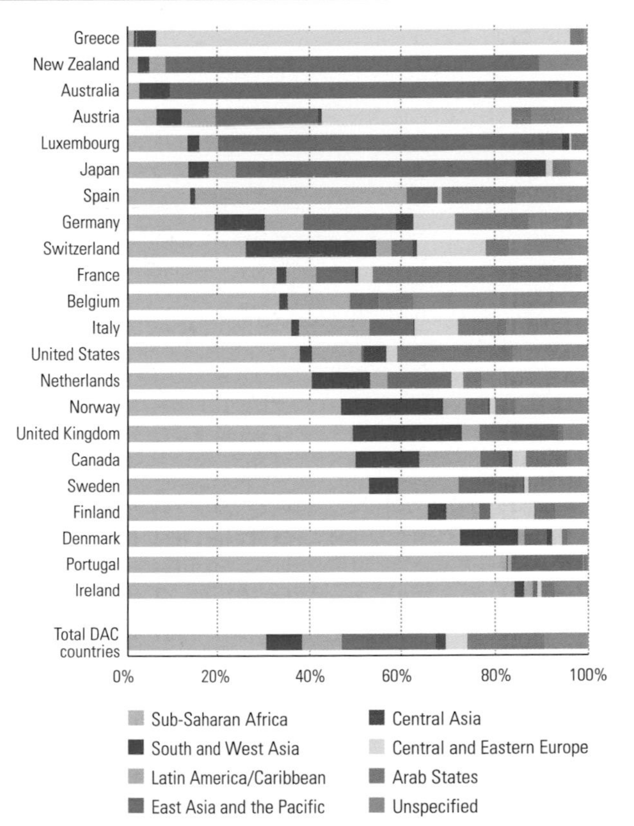

Note: Countries are sorted in descending order by sub-Saharan Africa's share of total education aid.
Source: Computed from CRS database (OECD-DAC, 2005c, Table 2).

13. See the introduction to the annex on aid data for the definition of 'education, level unspecified' in the IDS database.

14. For DAC countries overall 'education, level unspecified' is 24% over the period 1999-2003 (from 69% in Finland to 3.5% in the United States). For the top six providers of aid to basic education it is only 3.5% in the United States but rises to 47% in the United Kingdom.

15. Some of the aid activities reported as 'education, level unspecified' can be attributed to education sub-sectors.

16. This is an FTI calculation based on an analysis of the CRS database.

17. The ability to do so is complicated by the fact that some donors report disbursement figures, whereas others report commitments to OECD-DAC.

18. A variety of factors can explain these patterns, including slow disbursement, delays in implementation, and carefully scheduled long-term programming.

education to South and West Asia – which represent a huge EFA challenge; and most countries give less than 10%. The Dakar Framework for Action makes clear that priority should be given to those countries in greatest need – sub-Saharan Africa, South Asia, and the least developed countries. 'Accordingly, while no country in need should be denied international assistance, priority should be given to these regions and countries' (UNESCO, 2000*b*).

An analysis of the distribution of aid to education by recipient countries identifies wide disparities compared to need. Using the *EFA Global Monitoring Report*'s EFA Development Index (EDI) as a proxy measure of need, it is evident that countries with the lowest EDI are not necessarily accorded priority in aid to education (Table 4.4). These data confirm other analyses that find that aid is not necessarily provided to the poorest and most needy countries. Rather, disproportionate volumes go to middle-income countries with relatively better social indicators, including primary school enrolment (Baulch, 2004; OECD-DAC, 2005*b*; Jones et al., 2004). Although poverty reduction may be an objective, for many donors it is only one of several competing objectives, among which geopolitical and regional considerations appear to be of decisive significance (Jones et al., 2004). Moreover, some donors have explicit commitments to specific groups of countries. For some (such as Japan and Germany), policy-making processes involve several agencies with different mandates and commitments, resulting in competition over the priorities in aid allocation.

Aid to basic education with a gender focus declined from 1999 to 2002, although it rose significantly in 2003. One recent study of DAC countries concluded that, on average, 13% of aid to basic education had gender equality as the principal objective, and about 50% had gender equality as a significant objective (OECD, 2005*a*). However, it is of course not easy to disaggregate aid by gender, and the picture may be incomplete.[19]

Table 4.4: Annual average bilateral aid to education and to basic education received by countries with an Education Development Index (EDI) below 0.8, 1999–2003 (constant 2002 US$)

		Aid to education		Aid to basic education	
Country	EDI (2002)	Average amount received (millions)	Per inhabitant	Average amount received (millions)	Per primary-school-aged child
Chad	0.439	16.0	1.9	12.5	8.8
Burkina Faso	0.443	38.9	3.1	31.7	14.5
Niger	0.458	23.0	2.0	20.0	10.2
Mali	0.492	57.4	4.5	50.9	23.0
Ethiopia	0.536	54.0	0.8	38.0	3.3
Mozambique	0.543	87.1	4.7	65.6	25.1
Yemen	0.622	33.5	1.7	28.6	8.1
Djibouti	0.629	17.8	25.8	9.6	85.0
Mauritania	0.640	25.3	9.0	20.4	45.6
Eritrea	0.652	21.5	5.4	18.4	32.5
Nepal	0.652	32.1	1.3	20.4	6.2
Burundi	0.653	4.9	0.7	3.8	3.3
Senegal	0.653	71.9	7.3	50.2	31.1
Côte d'Ivoire	0.659	42.1	2.6	26.1	9.9
Papua New Guinea	0.660	39.6	7.1	30.7	34.7
Ghana	0.662	56.9	2.8	39.7	12.4
Bangladesh	0.663	135.9	0.9	77.7	4.2
Equat. Guinea	0.689	5.7	11.9	4.0	62.1
Rwanda	0.715	23.3	2.8	18.4	13.7
Congo	0.717	13.9	3.8	7.0	11.0
Kenya	0.731	41.2	1.3	31.8	5.2
India	0.741	225.6	0.2	138.0	1.2
Lao PDR	0.745	20.8	3.8	7.0	9.2
Zambia	0.748	71.1	6.6	66.3	31.5
Morocco	0.749	163.9	5.5	68.2	18.2
Cambodia	0.761	27.3	2.0	18.8	0.4
Guatemala	0.782	21.0	1.7	13.7	7.0

Note: Aid to education and basic education in this table does not include general budget support and 'education, level unspecified'.

Sources: EDI: Annex Table A1; population: statistical annex Table 1 (2002 figures); primary-school-age population: statistical annex Table 5 (2002 figures); aid to education and basic education: CRS online database (OECD-DAC 2005*c*, Table 2).

Multilateral aid to education – a stronger focus on basic education

Between 1990 and 2003, total multilateral ODA disbursements were between US$13 billion and US$18 billion per annum (Figure 4.1). Between 1999 and 2003, commitments by the major multilateral agencies averaged US$15.9 billion per annum (Table 4.5).

Aid to education averaged US$1.3 billion (1999–2003), comprising 9.3% of total ODA, a figure that is broadly comparable with bilateral agencies (7.4%). But the proportion allocated to basic education is significantly higher at 62.6%. The most important multilateral donor to education is the World Bank, through the International Development Association (IDA), which committed an average of US$543 million a year from 1999 to 2003, accounting for over 40% of total multilateral commitments. To arrive at a detailed analysis for the other multilateral agencies is difficult, given data limitations. In particular, the European Commission is an

19. Several donors do not report the degree of gender sensitivity in their aid activities; this is another area where there is a lack of reliable data (see also: Braithwaite et al., 2003, on European Commission aid; and Rose and Subrahmanian, 2005, on DFID).

important donor, whose aid is increasingly through budget support, making it difficult to track by sector. World Bank lending is discussed in more detail below.

The data on the World Bank (IDA) in Table 4.5 are for concessional assistance only. When non-concessional lending is added to IDA commitments, the figures rise by a factor of three or four, depending on the year (Figure 4.13).[20] Within an upward trend overall, total annual lending has fluctuated somewhat; for example, from a high of US$2.35 billion in 2003 (after a sharp drop in 2000 to US$728 million), the figure for 2004 fell back again to US$1.68 billion. Similarly, the share of education in total lending, which increased from 4.8% in 2000 to 12.7% in 2003, dropped back to 8.4% in 2004.

Fluctuation in lending is also apparent in sub-sector allocations (Figure 4.14). Primary education (and not the wider 'basic education' in DAC data) fell below 40% in the years immediately after Jomtien (1990), then rose to 50% of the total in the mid-1990s, but has fallen back to its 1990 levels in recent years. On the other hand, lending for general education increased from 5.8% of the total in 1990 to nearly 40% in 2001. This suggests increased lending for sector programmes that include primary and other forms of basic

Table 4.5: Multilateral ODA: commitments of major donors, five-year annual averages, 1999–2003

	Total ODA	Aid to education		Aid to basic education	
Donors[1]	(Constant 2002 US$ millions)	Amount (constant 2002 US$ millions)	Education as % of total ODA[2]	Amount (constant 2002 US$ millions)	Basic education as % of aid to education[3]
IDA[4]	6 783.6	542.9	8.5	196.9	57.8
EC	6 695.7	347.1	6.3	128.8	50.8
AsDF[4]	1 240.7	135.4	12.7	36.9	33.8
AfDF[4]	968.5	90.7	10.4	39.4	73.5
UNICEF	601.8	52.2	11	52.2	100
UNDP	460.2	11	2.7	1.8	46.4
IDB Special Fund[4]	391.1	21	6.3	6	74.6
UNRWA	358.5	179.5	55.5	154.4	90.3
Nordic Development Fund[4]	64.6	2.5	4.1	0	0
Caribbean Development Bank[4]	47.9	5.3	19.2	1	25
Total[5]	15 886.2	1 307.2	9.3	589.8	62.6

Notes: No data are available for the European Commission for 1999 or for the Caribbean Development Bank for 2001 and 2002. Data for UNDP are for 1999 only. Due to missing data, the total line may not match the total of figures for each donor.

1. There are no comparable data on aid to education for UNESCO. Between 1998 and 2003, annual average expenditure on education and basic education was US$13.8 million and US$7.6 million respectively (based on biannual budget documents). These figures do not include the staff costs and the budgets of UNESCO Institutes.

2. Education as percentage of total ODA less multi-sector and general programme assistance (which are not shown in this table).

3. Basic education as percentage of total education less 'education level unspecified' (which is not shown in this table.)

4. Data for grants and concessional loans to developing countries. (IDA is part of the World Bank; AfDF is part of the African Development Bank; AsDF is part of the Asian Development Bank; and the IDB Special Fund is in the Inter-American Development Bank.)

5. This total is for donors included in this table. The data are based on commitments and are different from the disbursements shown in Figure 4.1.

Sources: For IDA, AsDF, AfDF, IDB Special Fund and UNDP: CRS online database (OECD-DAC, 2005*c*, Table 2). For other donors: DAC online database (OECD-DAC, 2005*c*, Table 5).

Figure 4.13: World Bank education lending, amount and as percentage of World Bank total lending per year, 1963–2004

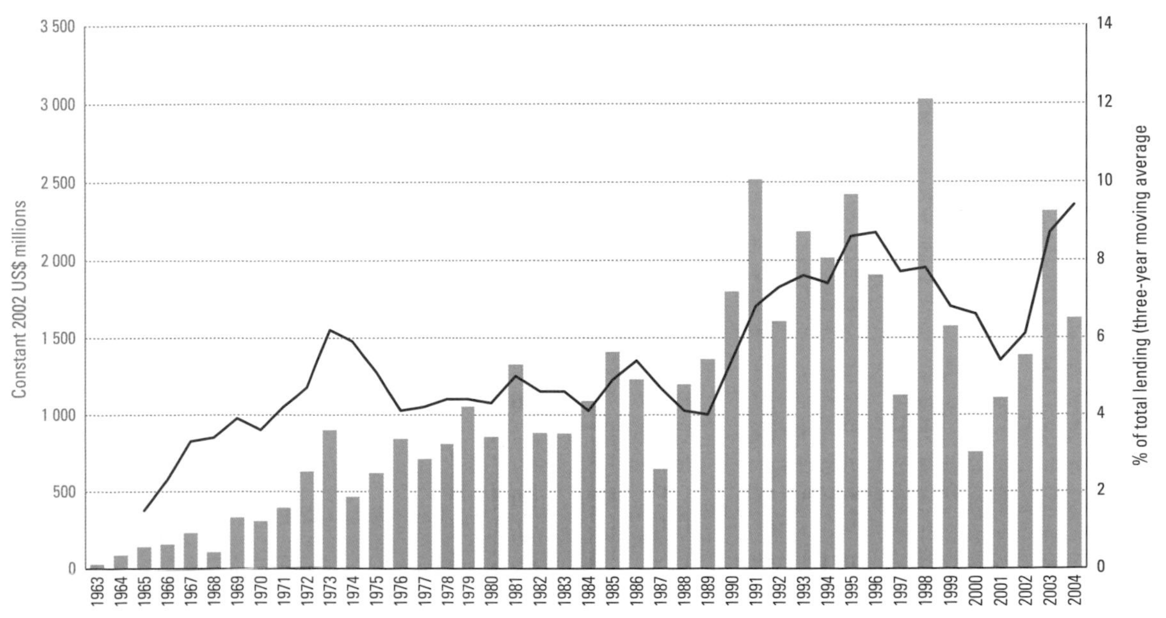

Notes: There is a break in the series in 1990 because a new coding system for sector analysis was introduced in Fiscal Year 2003 and backdated to 1990. The DAC deflator for the United States has been used to produce constant price series.

Source: Computed from World Bank (2005*a*). Deflator: OECD statistical annex of the 2004 Development Co-operation Report, Table 36 (OECD-DAC, 2005*b*).

20. World Bank loans are concessional (ODA) and non-concessional (Official Assistance). The IDA handles the former; the International Bank for Reconstruction and Development, the latter.

Figure 4.14: Composition of total World Bank education lending for 1990–2004

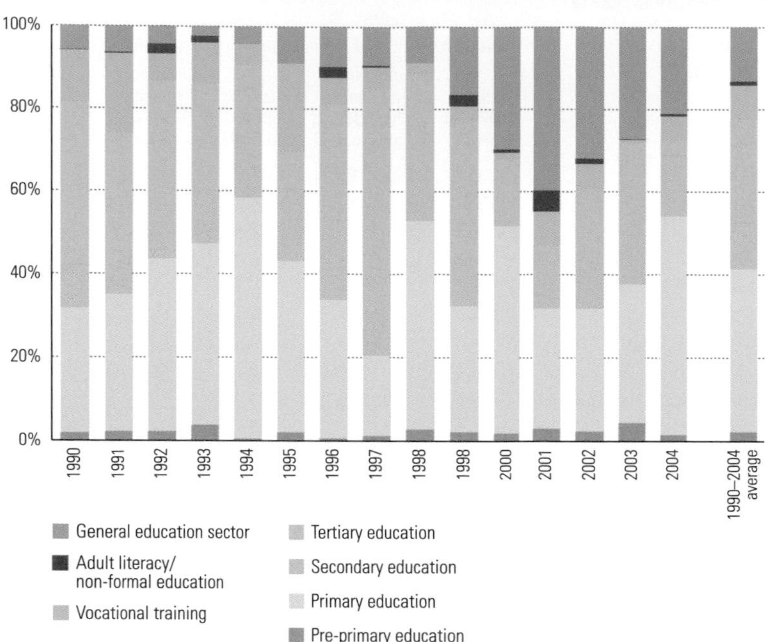

Note: General education sector includes lending to more than one sub-sector.
Source: World Bank (2005*a*).

Figure 4.15: Regional distribution of World Bank education lending (new commitments), annual averages, 1990–2004

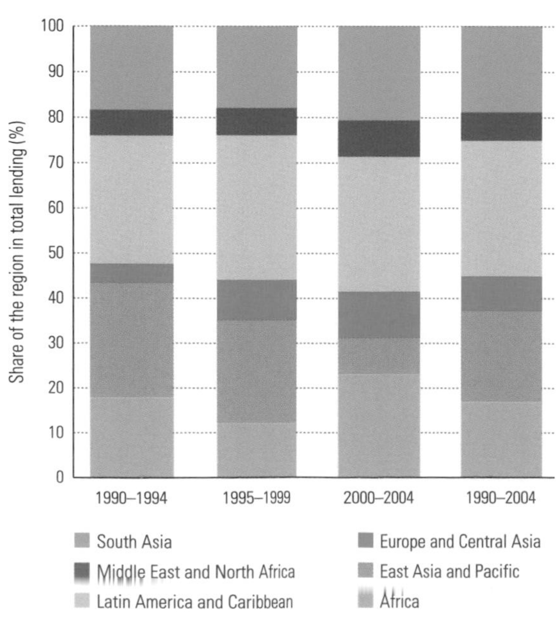

Note: The regions here are those used by the World Bank and different from the EFA regions used in other part of this Report. For the composition of each region, see http://www1.worldbank.org/education/regions.asp.
Source: World Bank (2005*a*).

education. More recently, however, this share has started to fall, for reasons that are not immediately apparent. Notable in the context of this Report is the extremely low level of lending for adult literacy and non-formal education (see Chapter 9).

Since 1990, the distribution of both concessionary and non-concessionary World Bank lending shows that Latin America and the Caribbean received the largest share, at around 30%. East Asia and the Pacific used to occupy 25% of the total lending, but its share has shrunk to 8% in the past five years, while lending to Africa has increased to over 20% (Figure 4.15). South Asia has never exceeded 20% since 1990.

Debt relief, an indirect benefit

US$5.9 billion of the nominal increase in bilateral aid between 2001 and 2003 was debt relief (World Bank, 2005*b*). This debt relief can benefit EFA. For countries to receive irrevocable debt relief under the Heavily Indebted Poor Countries (HIPC) Initiative, social sector policy reforms and associated performance criteria have to be established (to reach the 'completion point').[21] Thus, one possible measure of the benefits of debt relief is real increases in levels of national educational expenditure. At the aggregate level, several HIPC countries have increased government expenditure on poverty reduction,[22] and indicated that they would use approximately 40% of debt relief for the education sector. However, preliminary comparisons of total debt relief and increases in education expenditures demonstrate no very clear pattern. In sub-Saharan Africa, HIPC has had a broadly positive effect on the funding levels of both education and health, but there is a lack of data to demonstrate a direct and causal relationship (Hinchliffe, 2004).[23]

21. According to the World Bank (2005*b*), by March 2005, fifteen countries had reached their 'completion points', and twenty-seven had reached their 'decision points', at which point they receive interim debt relief.

22. The poverty-reducing expenditure of twenty African HIPC countries is estimated to have increased by US$2.7 billion between 1999 and 2003. These aggregate figures mask huge variations between countries and across years. Thirteen countries showed a significant increase in the level of poverty-related expenditures; in three, the share remained constant; but there was a decrease in Chad, Ghana, Sao Tome and Principe, and Zambia (IMF/IDA, 2003, 2004, cited in Hinchliffe, 2004).

23. For a selection of HIPC African countries between 1998 and 2002, the percentage of GDP devoted to education [illegible] from 3.0% to 4.2% (average for nineteen countries), and the share of education in total government expenditures rose from 12.8% to 15.5% (average for twenty-one countries). This suggests that 'in the period since the reform of the HIPC initiative in 1999, expenditures on education and health in a large majority of African HIPCs have increased faster than overall government expenditure and overall economic activity' (Hinchliffe, 2004, p.16).

Other benefits of debt relief may be reflected in the outcomes of policy-related processes. Table 4.6 shows the education-related indicators (or 'triggers') agreed for HIPC completion in four sub-Saharan Africa countries. The focus is clearly on primary education. If these policy commitments are fulfilled, then the HIPC process should lead to increased resources becoming available for basic education.

Some analysts, however, question the effectiveness of enhanced HIPC debt relief in increasing financial resources for the most needy countries (e.g. Killick, 2004), suggesting that, despite the principle of additionality to existing and planned aid, the increase in debt relief has actually resulted in a decrease in net transfers.[24] They note that even if debt relief continues for some years and increases government expenditures in the social sector, it is likely to be a one-off benefit.[25]

Other approaches to debt relief and education are more direct. Some Latin American governments are actively promoting education debt swaps.[26] Argentina provides an interesting and recent example (Box 4.1).

Table 4.6: HIPC completion-point triggers for education in four African Heavily Indebted Poor Countries

Country	Triggers
Benin	• Establish a medium term expenditure programme to increase resources for basic education • Eliminate school fees. Provide grants to schools to compensate for lost revenue • Provide grants to school communities to hire teachers • Eliminate repetition at Grade 1
Burkina Faso	• Adoption and endorsement of organization and budgetary measures of the 1998 civil service reform • Link between teacher training colleges and civil service employment abolished • New categories of teachers established for community hiring • School promotion and grade repetition consolidated
Malawi	• Target set for education's share of the total recurrent budget • Target set for number of teachers to be trained and for in-service training • Reallocation of expenditure from boarding provision to teaching/learning materials • Donor supplied textbooks to be sent directly from suppliers to schools
Rwanda	• Set target for primary gross enrolment ratio • Operationalize six teacher training colleges • Establish a framework for community participation in primary and secondary schools • Design and implement a capacity building programme for the management of education

Source: Hinchliffe (2004).

Box 4.1 A debt swap for education in Argentina

At the turn of the century, Argentina experienced a major economic crisis. Income per capita fell by 20%, inflation was rampant, the peso fell against the US dollar, the banking system was paralyzed, and the government defaulted on its debt. As a result, social sector spending fell dramatically. In 2003, total public expenditure on education was two-thirds of its 1998 level.

One consequence of all this was that Argentina started to canvass the cancellation of debt with international donors in exchange for a commitment to mobilize additional domestic resources for education. In 2004, Spain expressed support for this idea, announcing its intention to engage in debt exchange in support of social development, and of primary education in particular. This policy then became enshrined in Spanish development policy for 2005–2008.[a]

An early expression of this policy in 2005 is an agreement whereby US$100 million will be transferred by the Argentine government to a special and protected education account, in lieu of debt payments to Spain.[b] This will be disbursed over four years to two existing scholarship programmes: Programa Nacional de Becas Estudiantes and Programa Nacional de Inclusion Escolar. The new funds will be used to help 215,000 students in three of the poorest parts of the country (the north-east, the north-west, and the suburbs of Buenos Aires) to complete lower secondary education, by cash transfers of 400 pesos (about US$140 at August 2005 exchange rates) per student per year for three years, money that will be paid directly to the families.

Relative to both the overall level of debt (US$1.3 billion to Spain alone) and to the national basic education budget (US$3.3 billion), US$100 million is a very small sum, although relative to total non-salary elements of the education budget it is not insignificant. The Ministry of Education and Culture in Argentina states that, while this debt swap is not the solution to education financing constraints, it is a valid means of securing resources to meet specific education objectives.

Notes:

a. Spain has also agreed a US$50 million debt swap for education and health in Ecuador.

b. Under the rules of the Paris Club, this agreement depends on the debtor country having an appropriate programme agreed with the International Monetary Fund (IMF). As yet, the IMF has not approved the debt restructuring in Argentina.

Source: Aggio (2005).

24. An evaluation study by the World Bank's Operations Evaluation Department (2003, cited in Killick, 2004, and Hinchliffe, 2004) found a strong decline in net transfers between 1995 and 1997 followed by an increase to 1999 and a fall in 2000 back to the 1997 level. However, IMF/IDA (2003, 2004, cited in Hinchliffe, 2004) reported that the overall totals of loans, grants and debt relief across 27 HIPC countries increased from US$8 billion in 1997 to almost US$12 billion in 2002, suggesting no reversal impact of debt relief on total aid flow.

25. Killick (2004) also questions the rationale for shifting government resources to the social sector at the expense of investment in economic development, which will not solve the fundamental causes of poverty.

26. A debt swap, sometimes called debt conversion or debt exchange, 'involves the voluntary exchange, by a creditor with its debtor, of debt for cash, another asset or a new obligation with different repayment terms' (Moye, 2001). While initially the focus was on swapping commercial debt, the mechanism was later used for financing nature conservation and development programmes. Non-governmental organizations and UN agencies played an important role in promoting and implementing debt swaps for development in the 1990s.

Long-term, predictable aid is essential

Although aid data on education are problematic, some broad global conclusions can be drawn (Table 4.7). Between 1999 and 2003, a period that straddles the World Education Forum and the Millennium Summit, overall aid to education averaged US$5.5 billion, of which US$1.5 billion went to basic education. The figures in 2003 for both education and basic education were significantly higher than the average for both categories (US$6.3 billion and US$2.1 billion respectively), signalling a potentially important upward trend.

In addition, for the reasons noted above, these figures excluded aid to education through budget support and the category 'education, level unspecified' and both of these types of aid have been expanding. Table 4.7 also excludes non-DAC bilateral donors and non-concessional lending by the multilateral donor agencies, private flows and aid to education in other sectors. If the FTI estimates of budget support adduced above were added to the totals in Table 4.7, overall aid to education in 2003 would increase by approximately US$800 million. If half of this is assigned to basic education, and if all of 'education, level unspecified' from DAC bilateral donors (based on 1999-2003 averages) is allocated to basic education – the FTI Secretariat proposition – a further US$1.2 billion would accrue to basic education in 2003, giving a total of about US$3.3 billion. However, these figures should be treated with the utmost caution for the reasons given earlier.

A significant EFA external financing gap remains

Regardless of whether the low or the high estimates are taken, a significant EFA external financing gap remains. In 2002, this Report estimated that US$7 billion was needed each year for the universal primary education (UPE) and gender parity goals to be achieved. This required an additional US$5.6 billion annually on top of aid levels at the beginning of this decade. Thus, even the higher figure for basic education in 2003 is still well short of the estimated need for meeting two of the EFA goals, let alone for adult literacy and the other EFA goals (UNESCO, 2002*b*).

Aid is not the miracle cure for achieving EFA; domestic resources are key. But aid is important, and since Dakar there has been a welcome increase in commitments for basic education. Nevertheless, there is a considerable way to go before the Dakar commitments will be met in full and needy countries will be able to rely on a predictable flow of aid to ensure their necessary recurrent costs can be met (Sperling and Balu, 2005).

This is especially important in those African countries with tax revenues insufficient to achieve UPE, provide publicly financed secondary education and meet the other EFA goals, as well as to generate the modern sector jobs that school graduates seek. A low skills base is a constraint on economic growth, while low growth limits both the financial opportunities to improve skills levels and the political opportunities to introduce reforms to achieve EFA (Fredriksen, 2005*a*). In circumstances such as these, aid can assist governments in taking politically sensitive sector-reform decisions, as long as it is predictable, long-term and can be used to meet recurrent costs. Such decisions include:

- *School fee elimination*: Aid can enable governments to finance the transition to free primary education that is key to the achievement of UPE.
- *Budget trade-offs*: Aid (combined with policy dialogue on poverty reduction) can permit governments to make difficult budgetary trade-offs that allow more equitable allocations to basic education, particularly in rural areas.
- *Teachers' salaries*: Aid can help satisfy demands from teacher unions to increase salaries, which have declined in real income over the past thirty years (UNESCO, 2004*a*), and enable governments to recruit badly needed additional teachers. Where new contract teachers have been recruited at salaries below civil service pay scales (e.g. in francophone Africa), aid can finance the professional development of these new and usually under-qualified teachers.
- *Secondary and higher education*: Aid can facilitate an expansion and financing of secondary and tertiary education that does not adversely affect the financing of basic education. (Major policy

Table 4.7: Total ODA to education and basic education, five-year annual averages for 1999–2003 and 2003 (constant 2002 US$ billions)

	1999–2003 average		2003	
	Education	Basic education	Education	Basic education
Bilateral donors (DAC countries)	[illegible]	[illegible]	4.65	1.16
Major multilateral donors	1.31	0.59	1.66	0.94
Total ODA	5.53	1.50	6.31	2.10

Note: Multilateral donors are those included in Table 4.5.
Source: Aid data annex, Tables 1.1 and 2.

issues will remain of course. Should access be open or selective? Should students be subsidized, or fees and charges levied?)[27]

It is argued in some circles that aid should not be increased because the absorptive capacity of countries is limited, or because aid is misused through corrupt practices. Clearly, where corruption and misadministration are rife, additional aid does not make sense. But to defer aid because absorptive capacity is weak does not contribute to long-term solutions. Long-term predictable aid that enables recurrent costs to be met permits governments to make essential policy changes for EFA, which would otherwise be untenable. Questions about absorptive capacity properly concern the quality and harmonization of aid and its contribution to capacity-building, and not the delaying or denying of assistance. It is to these issues that this chapter now turns.

Opportunities for improving international coordination of EFA

More aid to basic education is needed. Recent increases – primarily from bilateral donors – are promising but insufficient. And as the capacity of many bilateral agencies to move larger volumes of aid effectively is limited, more attention should be given to:

- better harmonization of aid;
- effective use of multilateral channels, notably the Fast Track Initiative;
- promoting silent partnerships;
- improving technical assistance; and
- strengthening UNESCO's role.

These topics are treated in this section.

The need to harmonize aid for education

This Report has argued consistently that efforts to improve international coordination for EFA should be better integrated into wider international endeavours to enhance aid effectiveness. The work of the OECD-DAC, which has moved forward significantly in 2005 with the Paris Declaration on Aid Effectiveness (OECD-DAC, 2005*e*), is important in this regard.[28] The Declaration is designed to enhance mutual accountability of developing-country governments and donors in support of the ownership of national development policies, to align external assistance to national development strategies, to better harmonize donor practice, and to give a strong focus to managing for results. Indicators of progress and good practice are being developed, and targets are being set for 2010, to be endorsed by the UN Special Assembly on the Millennium Development Goals in September 2005.[29]

This is work of direct relevance to the achievement of EFA. Education is an important component of ODA, and aid practice in the education sector should be consistent with wider aid developments. The Fast Track Initiative has been active in this regard, piloting a Donor Indicative Framework (DIF) for education (FTI Harmonization Working Group, 2005).[30] Designed to help donors meet their commitments in terms of more aid and better coordinated aid for education, the DIF is meant to assist the measurement of levels of harmonization (nationally and internationally) and to foster sector dialogue and good practice within countries. Use of the DIF – in pilot programmes in 2004 in Burkina Faso, Ethiopia, Mozambique and the Niger – confirmed that alignment to policy priorities, well-managed budget and implementation processes, capacity-building for country leadership, and performance-based disbursement are all key to monitoring harmonization. The pilot also identified the need for an indicator of the level of harmonization of dialogue between Poverty Reduction Strategy Paper (PRSP) development and education sector planning[31] and suggested that a tool like the DIF should be flexible and country specific (FTI Harmonization Working Group, 2004). At the same time, the FTI is increasingly aligning itself to the DAC's work on harmonization – a welcome development.[32]

Aid practice in the education sector should be consistent with wider aid developments

27. The growing interest in secondary education is reflected in the World Bank strategy paper Expanding Opportunities and Building Competencies for Young People: A New Agenda for Secondary Education (World Bank, 2005*d*). See also Lewin and Caillods (2001).

28. Over 100 countries endorsed *The Paris Declaration*. Twenty organizations participated in the Forum, including the EFA Fast Track Initiative and the United Nations Development Group. The Declaration builds on the International Conference on Financing for Development (United Nations, 2002*a*), the Rome Declaration on Harmonization (Aid Harmonization and Alignment, 2003) and the Second Round Table on Managing for Results held in Marrakech in 2004.

29. The draft Indicators of Progress and associated methodological notes are an appendix to the *Paris Declaration on Aid Effectiveness* (OECD-DAC, 2005*e*). A baseline for the indicators is being developed and a monitoring process defined (see DAC Working Party on Aid Effectiveness and Donor Practice website, http://www.oecd.org/dac/effectiveness).

30. The FTI's work builds on earlier work undertaken by the European Commission and EU Member States (European Commission, 2003).

31. In a more general overview, Norway's aid agency, NORAD, examined different donor approaches to de-linking sector support from sector dialogue, a matter of growing debate in a number of agencies (NORAD, 2004).

32. The FTI's Technical Committee has concluded that: (a) the FTI should work closely with the OECD-DAC Working Party on Aid Effectiveness; (b) the DIF indicators should be aligned to those being agreed under the Paris Declaration; (c) a paper should be developed on lessons that are being learned about harmonization at the country level; and (d) in the future the *EFA Global Monitoring Report* should be a vehicle for some detailed reporting on donor progress on harmonization. Discussions are underway with the FTI Secretariat to give force to this last proposal, with detailed attention to this issue in the 2007 *EFA Global Monitoring Report*.

Maximizing the effectiveness of the Fast Track Initiative

The FTI's work on monitoring aid effectiveness reflects its emergence as an important forum for promoting policy dialogue and initiating technical work on a range of education issues extending beyond its initial objectives of resource mobilization for universal primary completion (UPC) (Box 4.2). The FTI gained political visibility and support in 2005 from the Millennium Project (2005c), the Development Committee of the World Bank/IMF (IMF/World Bank, 2005), the Commission for Africa (2005), and the G8 summit – whose Gleneagles Communiqué stated: 'Our aim is that every FTI-elected country will develop the capacity and have the resources necessary to implement their sustainable education strategies' (G8 Gleneagles, 2005). Individual donor governments have also made strong statements in support of the Initiative.[33]

Although these endorsements have given the FTI a prominent place in EFA coordination, they have not yet resulted in a significant increase in aid to basic education. As of March 2005, the

Developing countries expect the FTI to provide new resources

Box 4.2 The Fast Track Initiative – building an international compact

The Education for All Fast Track Initiative (FTI) is a global partnership between developing and developed countries and funding and technical assistance agencies. Established in 2002 by the Development Committee of the World Bank/International Monetary Fund to accelerate progress towards universal completion of quality primary education by 2015, it is one direct response to the promise made in Dakar that 'no countries seriously committed to education for all will be thwarted in their achievement of this goal by a lack of resources' (UNESCO, 2000*b*).

The FTI is conceived as a compact in line with the Compact agreed at the United Nations conference on Financing for Development (United Nations, 2002*a*), which commits governments to policy and institutional reforms and to accountability for their results against receiving additional and better coordinated external assistance in support of their development plans. The FTI seeks to influence agency and partner country behaviour in the following ways:

- Agencies should: (a) increase support in a predictable manner; (b) align with country development priorities; (c) coordinate support around one education plan; and (d) harmonize procedures as much as possible.
- Partner countries should: (a) develop sound education sector programmes through broad-based consultation; (b) demonstrate results on key performance indicators; and (c) exercise leadership in developing and implementing the programme and coordinating support from technical and financing agencies.

The FTI development partners include over 30 multilateral and bilateral agencies and regional development banks that fulfil different roles and have different levels of commitment with respect to both level of funding and comparative impact on agenda-setting and the direction of the FTI.

The FTI is now open to all low-income countries (eligible for assistance from the IDA) whose poverty reduction strategy and education sector plan are endorsed through a country-based process under the leadership of a locally agreed coordinating agency. The endorsement process should follow appraisal procedures according to guidelines approved in 2005. These encourage in-country dialogue on key policy issues including data, knowledge, financing and capacity gaps, ownership and strategies to achieve the Millennium Development education goals. Central to the assessment are seven policy benchmarks that should be applied flexibly, rather than rigidly, according to country context.

The FTI is governed through annual partnership meetings with representatives from agencies, countries and non-governmental organizations that set its strategic direction. Its ongoing implementation is considered in technical agency meetings supported by the work of multi-agency working groups on Harmonization, Finance and Communications. The partnership and technical meetings are supported by a Steering Committee with membership drawn from the World Bank, UNESCO, two Co-Chairs from donor countries (one from a non-G8 country), and the last outgoing Co-Chair. The daily work is undertaken by the FTI Secretariat housed at the World Bank in Washington, DC. Since last year's *EFA Global Monitoring Report*, there has been one partnership meeting organized in conjunction with the meeting of the EFA High-Level Group in Brasilia (November 2004) and two technical meetings (Brasilia, November 2004, and London, March 2005). The next partnership meeting will take place in conjunction with the EFA High-Level Group meeting (Beijing, November 2005).

Source: Drawn from the FTI website: http://www1.worldbank.org/education/efafti/

33. For example, the UK's Department for International Development has stated that the FTI is pivotal to the achievement of the education MDGs and is establishing entirely new approaches to donor financing that would meet the need for predictability, transparency and country leadership (IMF/World Bank, 2005).

equivalent of US$292 million had been pledged to the FTI Catalytic Fund for 2003–2007 (Box 4.3);[34] and the Education Programme Development Fund had attracted US$6 million for 2005–2007. This relatively low level of financing makes very limited direct inroads into the EFA funding deficit. Importantly, however, the FTI may help to leverage additional funds for basic education within individual agencies (see Box 4.4 for France and the Netherlands).

The FTI guidelines and suggested planning processes have had some influence on sector plans in Mozambique and Yemen (Box 4.5 and Box 4.6), which have received resources from the FTI Catalytic Fund. But, for developing countries in general, the expectation remains that the FTI should be a key channel for providing new and additional resources. This is not yet the case. Burkina Faso expressed concern at the FTI partnership meeting in 2004 that the FTI has not brought the additional funding that would make a significant difference to the implementation of its national plan. Ethiopia has found the process of engagement with the FTI problematic, while Pakistan has felt excluded (Fast Track Initiative, 2004).

While the ability of the FTI to mobilize significant additional resources remains unproven, its role in promoting donor coordination at the international level has become much more significant. It is now clearly the key mechanism for international donor coordination in education for low-income countries. Valuable joint technical work is underway, albeit with relatively high transaction costs, to:

- assist countries via the FTI's Education Programme Development Fund to access technical assistance to develop credible education sector plans, facilitating additional aid;[35]
- develop benchmark criteria to guide the process by which low-income countries are endorsed for the FTI (FTI Secretariat, 2005*b*);
- understand financing modalities including budget support, undertake technical work on costing the MDG education goals,[36] and analyse aid data to reach a better understanding of the nature and targeting of aid to education;
- analyse low-income countries under stress, recognizing the need to give greater emphasis to gender analysis and responsiveness, to HIV/AIDS and to the quality of education.

The development of the FTI in these directions is beginning to respond to concerns that it had been ignoring those countries unable to fulfil the established criteria for FTI eligibility, that it took an overly narrow position on UPC, and was unrealistic about domestic policy reform possibilities in many countries, especially those under stress and affected by emergencies and the HIV/AIDS pandemic (UNESCO, 2002*b*, 2003*b*).

However, these positive developments at the international level are not yet equally matched at country level. There is some evidence (partly anecdotal) of agencies' in-country education advisers questioning the value added of the Initiative, in terms both of extra funding and FTI-related policy dialogue between agencies and national governments (see Fast Track Initiative, 2005*b*). This may be a problem of intra-agency

Box 4.3 Resource mobilization and capacity-building by the FTI

The FTI Catalytic Fund resources* are granted to FTI-endorsed countries in the form of transitional assistance for periods of one to three years. As of June 2005, US$35.5 million from the US$45 million allocated for 2003/4 had been disbursed, as well as US$4 million from the 2005 allocation of US$53 million. Of the first tranche of FTI-endorsed countries, four (Guyana, Mauritania, Nicaragua and Yemen) had received their entire 2004 allocations. In the Gambia, Guyana and the Niger, the assistance that is being provided is sufficient to cover the identified financing needs set out in national FTI plans. In Mauritania, Nicaragua and Yemen, a financing gap remains after FTI help. In the first-tranche countries yet to receive direct Catalytic Fund assistance – Mozambique, Ethiopia and Viet Nam – the funding gaps are between US$100 and US$200 million. The extent to which the Catalytic Fund can (or indeed should seek to) bridge these gaps, as distinct from helping to leverage additional bilateral and multilateral funds, is a key question for the FTI.

In addition to its limited overall resources, the Catalytic Fund has experienced some delay in the time between pledging, actual receipt of the funds from the donors, and the allocation and disbursement to countries. In order to make informed decisions about country choices, allocations are made once a year, leading to a de facto disbursement one year later. Out of the total amount pledged for 2005, equivalent to US$80 million, the contributions as of June 2005 totalled only US$37.7 million. FTI plans to move to a once a year decision making process for 2006 allocations if it appears that demand will exceed the funds available in order to ensure equity in the distribution of funds.

There are now ongoing discussions concerning an exit strategy from the Fund after three years of commitment. These involve considerations about raising alternative financing for countries whose financing gap has not been filled, and for possible reduced funding from the Catalytic Fund for a third year (Fast Track Initiative, 2005*a*).

* The FTI Catalytic Fund home page is at http://www1.worldbank.org/education/efafti/catalytic_fund.asp

34. Since March 2005, the United Kingdom Government has announced that it will contribute an additional £40 million (about €59 million) to the FTI over the period 2006/7 to 2008/9 primarily for the Catalytic Fund, and the Netherlands announced a further US$22.96 million for the Catalytic Fund.

35. The EPDF has limited financing from a small number of agencies, with commitments from Norway (through the Norwegian Education Trust Fund in the African Region) and the United Kingdom amounting to US$5.8 million in 2005 (FTI Secretariat, 2005*a*).

36. The product of the FTI Finance Working Group can be found at http://www1.worldbank.org/education/efafti/finance_wg.asp.

Box 4.4 The Netherlands and France in support of the FTI

Dutch commitments to basic education and the FTI

In 2002, the Dutch Parliament adopted a motion on basic education in developing countries. It declares that 'accessible, good quality education for all, both boys and girls, is so crucial for poverty reduction and sustainable economic, political and social development that the Netherlands must spend 15% of Official Development Assistance (ODA) on basic education by 2005.'

This motion triggered a growth of expenditure on basic education that is scheduled to reach the 15% goal by 2007. From a budget of €156 million on basic education in 2000, €600 million is planned by 2007, when 70% of the total annual budget for basic education will be spent, through bilateral support for:

- education reform in sixteen partner countries (€270 million);
- the FTI Catalytic Fund (€82 million): the Netherlands recognizes the need for additional support for countries that still have a financing gap after short-term FTI funding. It advocates work to identify new donors, increase support for silent partnerships, and open a second window for the Catalytic Fund for which it has already made a financial reservation.
- silent partnerships (€56 million); and
- general budget support for education expenditures (€49 million).

French commitments to basic education and the FTI

France has restructured its aid programme around the Millennium Development Goals (MDGs) and committed to increase its ODA from 0.42% of GDP in 2004 to 0.5% in 2007 and 0.7% in 2012. The €80 million per annum provided to basic education will double to €160 million in 2007. Ninety percent of bilateral ODA is concentrated on low-income countries of sub-Saharan Africa, particularly French-speaking countries.

France supports the Fast Track Initiative Partnership, as part of the 'Monterrey Consensus' by: (a) increasing its funding for basic education; (b) backing improvements in the coordination and harmonization of assistance; and (c) by helping beneficiary countries draw up sustainable and credible sector strategies. Technical support and financial backing of €54 million over three years is being provided to Burkina Faso, Mauritania and the Niger. This commitment will continue as new states are endorsed by the FTI. Funds will be made available for programme aid under the auspices of the Fast Track Initiative.

France is moving from project aid to a sector-wide approach and promoting the incorporation of education policy into wider development and poverty-reduction strategies. Yet project aid remains necessary for countries that lack a coherent, sustainable sector policy. Since 2002 France has provided programme aid in the form of basket funds or budgetary aid to Mauritania (€9.76 million in 2002) and to the United Republic of Tanzania (€4.25 million in 2004).

Sources: Netherlands Ministry of Foreign Affairs (2005) and Mantes (2005).

The issue is whether developing countries are getting value added from the FTI

communication or, more fundamentally, it may reflect the limited need for the FTI in countries with existing sector programmes and well-established policy dialogue.

The FTI has today become an important coordinating mechanism for agencies working in education. Indeed, it is now fulfilling a significant part of the EFA coordination role mandated to UNESCO. The knowledge that it generates and systematizes through its Secretariat and Working Groups serves an immediate function for donors, by providing direction for their individual policies and actions.

But the larger, long-term issue is whether developing countries are getting significant value added from it. Partner countries are not overly influential in the FTI's technical dialogue. Their primary concern is whether the Initiative will be able to deliver (directly or through leverage) more and better-coordinated aid, aligned to credible national plans, thereby fulfilling the Dakar pledge and the Monterrey compact. This is especially so for countries lacking capacity and resources. It is clearly the expectation of the major 2005 reports and political statements that the FTI should do this.

Box 4.5 The FTI in Mozambique – the donors' view

In Mozambique, the proposal to develop an FTI plan coincided with work to develop a new five-year strategic plan (Education Sector Strategic Plan: ESSP2) in 2003. The FTI indicative framework provided a useful frame of reference for assessing achievements under the first five-year plan and the key issues still to be addressed.

It was agreed by the Ministry of Education (MINED) and Cooperating Partners (CPs) that the FTI should be an integral part of the new ESSP2 and that the FTI plan should form the basis for the primary education component of the broader strategy. It was agreed too that any additional FTI leveraged funding would be moved through existing government channels – preferably the common sector fund – rather than through new mechanisms.

The FTI process contributed positively to dialogue on key issues such as teacher training and deployment, school construction costs, and the teacher/pupil ratio within a context of reaching out to the poor.

While the FTI process made a significant contribution to policy dialogue, it is less clear what impact it has had on resource mobilization. After the HIPC completion point was reached, overall government budget allocations to education (and other social sectors) increased, enhanced by the availability of budget support contributed to this increase, although neither development can be attributed directly to the FTI. At the sector level, the endorsement of the FTI plan in 2003 did lead to additional pledges from a number of donors, but a crisis in confidence about financial management in the ministry in early 2004 affected the overall level of disbursements in that year. Even should donors make increased financial commitments to the sector once the ESSP2 has been finalized, it will not be clear whether these will be directly attributable to the FTI.

However there is consensus among the CPs that even with (a) incremental increases in the state budget allocation to education, (b) increased internal efficiency in the functioning of the sector (e.g. reduced drop-outs and repetitions), (c) improved financial management and efficiency in MINED's allocation of resources, and (d) increased aid effectiveness, there will still be a financing gap between the resources available and those required to meet the goals of EFA-FTI. For this reason, the CPs are seeking clarification on how or whether the FTI process could assist in mobilizing additional resources for education in Mozambique.

Source: Drawn from a note prepared and endorsed in 2005 by donors working for education in Mozambique.

Box 4.6 Yemen benefits from the FTI

Yemen was the only Arab state in the first tranche of countries invited to participate in the FTI. Since 2004, the FTI has committed US$20 million to Yemen through its Catalytic Fund.

In 2002, the World Bank and the Netherlands conducted a joint FTI mission to reach consensus across government and donor partners and to agree baseline indicators and assumptions used for estimating financial shortfalls. At first, the FTI was not well received because of its apparent focus on Grades 1–6, rather than the entire basic education cycle of Grades 1–9. But agreement was reached, and the Ministry of Education drafted an FTI proposal with technical support from the World Bank. This was reviewed and endorsed by the local donor community in February 2003 and then by the international donor community in Paris. Eventually US$10 million from the FTI Catalytic fund became available (August 2004), and a further US$10 million is expected for 2005.

The FTI indicative framework has been used to set targets for monitoring and evaluating the progress of Yemen's Basic Education Development Project (BEDP). This has helped the government to identify priority areas for action and to initiate planning at the governorate levels. Funds from the Catalytic Fund have aided school construction, teacher training and capacity-building. FTI has contributed to the development of a Memorandum of Understanding to strengthen donor harmonization and support to the Ministry of Education with the intention of moving towards a common basket of support. The UK Department for International Development and the Netherlands appraised the BEDP with the World Bank in June 2004, and a US$120 million programme will now be co-financed. FTI's contribution has encouraged donors to support specific components of the basic education sub-sector.

Source: Ogawa (2005).

Technical assistance does not have a strong track record

Silent partnerships are efficient

Silent partnerships[37] are those where donors move some of their own funds through other agencies in support of the development programmes of a country where they are not working. In the education sector, such arrangements are a relatively recent development, led by the Nordic agencies after Dakar, meant to lessen the burden of aid procedures and to promote greater harmonization of aid practice.[38] They are particularly suitable for smaller countries with disproportionately large assistance budgets.

There are a number of potential benefits that come with these partnerships. After initial investments of time, transaction costs are reduced for partner countries. For the active donor partner, work on arranging the partnership has initial costs, but 'learning by doing' lessens these for new partnerships. In addition, the active donor's position tends to be enhanced in policy dialogue, reviews and negotiations. The silent partner benefits by being able to make financial contributions without deploying staff and experts or setting up in-country infrastructure. No fees are involved, and, where aid is through budget support, the timing of disbursements can be set in advance, and funds released against jointly agreed indicators of progress.[39]

Box 4.7 illustrates two silent partnerships involving the Netherlands and identifies some of the lessons that are being learned.[40] Benefiting from these early experiences, new partnerships are under construction. Norway intends to support education in Mali through the Swedish International Development Cooperation Agency (Sida) within the framework of the current arrangement with the Netherlands. The Canadian International Development Agency (CIDA) and the European Commission have expressed interest in this modality in Senegal, Namibia, Nicaragua and Ghana. The French Ministry of Foreign Affairs and the UK Department for International Development (DFID) are developing an Anglo-French FTI strategic partnership in the Niger, a new departure for both countries and one inspired by working together within the FTI.

Improving technical assistance – the case of Africa

Technical assistance has been an integral part of development aid since its inception. More than one-quarter of bilateral aid to Africa is channelled directly into capacity-building (Commission for Africa, 2005). But technical assistance does not have a strong track record. It needs to be refocused so that assistance is provided in ways that both accelerate progress towards EFA and, in the process, help to strengthen capacity.

One recent overview of technical assistance in Africa suggests that 'the capacity of the international community to provide high-quality technical support in a well-coordinated fashion may be declining' (Fredriksen, 2005*a*).[41] With many funding agencies moving towards direct budget support, in-country technical and advisory capacities have been reduced, as has the number of specialist education advisers working in-country. At the same time, there is a proliferation of individual suppliers in the technical assistance market; not all of these are familiar with new aid modalities and some are closely linked to their home country donor agency.[42]

As a consequence of these trends, governments find it increasingly difficult to make informed decisions about expertise to match their requirements.[43] With the advent of budget

37. Early definitions of 'silent partnerships' come from Sweden (Sida, 2000, 2002). The Netherlands defines a silent partnership as: 'An arrangement between two or more like-minded funding agencies which allows one or more partners to channel a financial contribution to the education sector of a country with which they do not have a bilateral relationship, through a partner which is active in that country and in the sector [where] ... the partner country concerned is in full agreement with this construction and needs the financial support' (Netherlands Ministry of Foreign Affairs, 2002). A broader term is 'Delegated Cooperation'. One donor (a 'lead donor') acts with authority on behalf of one or more other donors (the 'delegating donors' or 'silent partners'). The level and form of delegation may range from responsibility for one element of the project cycle for a specific project, to a complete sector programme or even a country programme (OECD-DAC, 2003).

38. The Nordic countries have comparable education sector policies, a strong degree of mutual trust and a joint desire to be flexible and to act swiftly and efficiently, especially where (a) the education sector is a priority in PRSPs, (b) sector plans target EFA goals, (c) there is a realistic and manageable financing gap, and (d) financing is through (sub) sector budget support or a pooled funding mechanism (Koopman, 2005).

39. In the Malawi example (Box 4.7), this is not the case. The indicators were set against progress at the micro-level in the different programmes. The disbursements of both the active and the silent partner lagged behind as a result.

40. For the donors, new legal procedures had to be developed to authorize the active partner to act on behalf of the silent one. In Sweden, a mandate regarding the delegation of funds had to be drawn up and included in the partnership agreements. Cooperation between Britain and the Netherlands in Malawi was hindered by internal financial procedures in the banking system with which the UK Department for International Development had to work in order to merge the Dutch grant with the British programme. Sweden and the Netherlands had to overcome initial concerns about the mandates of embassies and agencies, on the one hand, and headquarters, on the other. Field level participants had to grow accustomed to their new roles and responsibilities.

41. Fredriksen notes the decline of UNESCO in this regard. He argues that while UNESCO continues to provide good quality, operationally relevant technical support through its Institutes and regional offices, its capacity overall has been severely constrained by its limited budget and the proliferation of small projects and programmes.

42. A recent and contested report from the international non-governmental agency ActionAid argues that much aid is 'phantom aid', in that it does not actually benefit those who need it but is tied to a range of donor-related costs and services which deflate its value. The report suggests that technical assistance is strongly tied to donor country firms, overpriced, and often ineffective [illegible]. It estimates that 75% of technical assistance is 'phantom aid', worth US$13.8 billion per year (ActionAid, 2005).

43. This is largely, though not exclusively, an African problem. Many Asian and Latin American countries have succeeded in creating and retaining national technical capacity in the process of developing their national education systems. Countries in these regions are much less dependent on external expertise.

Box 4.7 Silent partnerships at work in Mali and Malawi

The Netherlands and Sweden in Mali

Sweden wished to support education in Mali. The Netherlands already had a development programme there, so Sweden asked it to manage its proposed new education support.

Mali had developed a ten-year education sector plan, was working on an investment strategy and foresaw a shortage of finance despite increasing its own education budget and benefiting from higher donor commitments. It attached importance to donor harmonization and better coordination to reduce its own transaction costs and to enhance its own internal efficiency. In September 2001, the Cadre Partenarial (code of conduct) was signed by the government of Mali and most donors. This regulated joint reviews, endorsed a sector-wide approach as the guiding principle for projects and programmes, and indicated the intention to work towards (sub) sector support for the ten-year Education Development Plan (PRODEC). Within this framework, the Dutch focused on quality improvement, expanded access and improved decentralized management through Mali's sector investment plan for 2001–2004. They had an in-country education adviser, and their embassy in Bamako had a delegated mandate for Dutch aid to Mali.

An analysis of Swedish and Dutch education policies, priorities and aid procedures was undertaken in Stockholm and the Hague. Sida screened Dutch aid modalities, including their monitoring and evaluation practices. Based on these findings, Sida's Chief Controller agreed that the Netherlands could oversee financial and administrative arrangements through the Dutch Embassy in Mali. Mali's own administrative and financial mechanisms would be used to transfer Swedish and Dutch support to a special budget line of its Ministry of Finance.

A set of mutual obligations was then agreed:

- Countries will agree on funding levels for the first phase of the investment plan.
- An interest-bearing bank account will be opened for the Sida contribution in the Netherlands and be operated by the Dutch Embassy in Bamako.
- Formal biannual requests will be made for the transfer of funds to Sweden, based on a call for funds from the Mali government.
- Sweden will receive the annual audit report from Mali through the Dutch embassy.
- The education ministry in Mali will provide progress and evaluation reports.
- The three countries will participate in the joint annual reviews of the Sector Programme.
- The Netherlands and Sweden will conduct annual meetings.

From 2002 to 2005, Dutch financial support was €44 million and Sida's €10 million for three years. The partnership's share of the financing of the education plan was 35%, constituting 22% of total external financing in 2004, the largest single external contribution to education in Mali.

The Netherlands and the United Kingdom in Malawi

The Netherlands had neither a diplomatic presence in, nor bilateral relationships with, Malawi. But under Dutch policy it is possible to support education outside of its 'concentration countries', because basic education is a priority and a Silent Partnership is an accepted aid modality.

DFID has had a long and extensive development cooperation relationship with Malawi, including in the education sector. The Malawi government had indicated the need for greater donor cooperation. Ten donors supported education, many through projects. The possibility of a silent partnership was welcomed as a step towards a more coherent sector-wide approach. Already, the donor group was undertaking a joint review of progress and the development of a common code of conduct.

The education sector plan gives priority to basic education. DFID supports three key components of the plan: strengthening the Ministry of Education, Science and Technology in its planning and management capacities; improved teaching of literacy and numeracy in the primary sector; and the decentralization of primary education to districts. The overall programme was financed from a special government account for basic education.

It was agreed that Dutch funds should be channelled to DFID, which would transfer these funds jointly with their own. This was a new procedure for DFID. The arrangement stipulates the modes of monitoring, reporting and evaluation, as well as an annual meeting between the two donors in Malawi.

DFID support for education is £78.7 million (about €125 million) over seven years, while the Netherlands has committed €29.2 million for four years. Together this constitutes the second biggest donor commitment in Malawi and the first in terms of disbursements in 2003–2004.

Source: Koopman (2005).

support, education ministries increasingly have to find ways of accessing and financing high-quality technical assistance directly from the education sector budget, rather than through discrete technical assistance projects. While this is a desirable shift in many respects, in the short term, securing funds may be difficult, especially if capacity-building activities are not part of mainstream education strategies or there is no provision in the budget for them.

Options for change

New thinking is needed about ways of using technical assistance to strengthen education sector capacities. What are the options?

Substantive reform and increased salaries may be needed to retain national capacity

First, strategies for strengthening existing capacity should be an integral component of sector policy. If additional aid comes in the form of budget support, provision should be made within the budget for capacity-building activities. There is some evidence that capacity-building is not receiving the attention it deserves in sector plans, or that it is primarily defined as better teacher training. But, by making capacity-building and institutional development an integral part of sector policy, the relationship between donor and government can become more client-driven and help promote systemic reform (Bossuyt, 2001).

Second, technical assistance and cooperation should be a significant part of aid harmonization, particularly at the country level, where the proliferation of different sources of expertise continues. Recent studies point to the value of pooling technical assistance funds and resources, as well as of joint frameworks for the design, management and monitoring of technical assistance for capacity development (e.g. Baser and Morgan, 2002; Browne, 2002; Fukuda-Parr et al., 2001). Work of this type in the education sector cannot ignore the major structural difficulties that confront the public sector as a whole (see, for example, Pavignani and Hauck, 2002).[44]

Third, the purposes and practice of technical assistance need to be reshaped so as to focus on the constraints to sector policy development and programme implementation, as well as on the potential to scale up EFA strategies. Technical assistance should place more emphasis on improving the knowledge base, sharing knowledge among those countries with comparable problems, and sustaining a cooperative process of dialogue and sharing of experience. These are not new ideas,[45] but neither are they central to the current practices in technical assistance. Two examples of this new approach at work today in Africa are shown in Boxes 4.8 and 4.9.

These examples illustrate ways of providing technical support that help to mobilize, strengthen and utilize existing local capacity. They do not pretend to address how to retain capacity. Even where very strong national competence has been created, poor working conditions, low salaries and budget constraints make it difficult for education ministries and others to retain key people and to sustain progress. Some of the actions required are not primarily economic in nature. New institutional and management approaches to recruitment, promotion, and security of employment – as well as more 'evidence-based' decision-making – make a difference. But in some countries more substantive reforms are needed, backed by external, long-term financial support to ensure 'acceptable' salaries over a transition period for an essential cadre of civil servants and educators (another example of more aid for recurrent costs).

A more focused international debate on how to better coordinate technical assistance and capacity-building in education is needed, concentrating on how to mobilize, strengthen and utilize existing national and regional capacity.[46] Within this, aid agencies need to examine how best to build existing capacities within their overall assistance programmes, how to improve the international management of technical assistance, and how UNESCO might play a more central role.[47, 48]

44. Gunnarsson (2001) notes that efforts to strengthen institutional capacity must also take account of governments' regulatory frameworks, including those of the civil service. Changing administrative and management behaviour does not in itself bring about development. It is necessary therefore to look at the viability of whole systems.

45. For example, the Commonwealth Secretariat's work on teachers and school management http://publications.thecommonwealth.org/publications/html/DynaLink/cat_id/?9/subcat_id/29/category_details.asp

46. The FTI Technical Committee has established a task team of agencies to promote the idea of a network on capacity-building (Fast Track Initiative, 2005*b*). UNESCO-IIEP has developed some proposals for the scaling up of training in educational planning and management (UNESCO-IIEP, 2005*d*). See also UNDP's work on Capacity 2015, at http://www.capacity.undp.org/

47. Fredriksen (2005*a*) proposes that aid agencies should consider establishing a special team of high-quality education specialists for Africa, designed as an integral part of the overall assistance provided by agencies. The team might comprise three to five high-quality specialists in five to seven focus areas where implementation constraints are severe. The team would have a strong 'public good' function. Its annual costs would be small compared with total education assistance to Africa. Without such assistance, the expected impact of increases in financial aid is likely to fall short of expectations. Accelerated progress towards EFA hinges crucially on a country's ability to use both domestic and external technical assistance effectively.

48. This brief analysis has focused on sub-Saharan Africa, but much of it is applicable to other regions and countries where aid is a not-insignificant part of education budgets and programmes. In this context, see the work of UNESCO Bangkok's Education Policy and Reform Unit in Asia (http://www.unescobkk.org/index.php?id=9); and the Asian Development Bank's programme on Managing for Development Results (http://www.adb.org/MfDR/default.asp).

Box 4.8 Building capacity to meet demand

Norwegian Education Trust Fund: Technical support for sector programmes[a]

NETF-supported work identified six areas where the Fund could provide technical support to countries in Africa to implement critical components of their sector programmes: textbooks and training materials; training of, and support for, teachers; system and school level management; the impact of HIV/AIDS on education; education simulation models for preparing sector programmes and budgets; and decentralization. Each area is critical to quality improvement and to accelerating the implementation of sector programmes. Work is progressing in the first five areas, in close cooperation with other partners, including the Association for the Development of Education in Africa (ADEA).[b]

The programme on textbooks and training materials illustrates NETF's approach. The objective is to help countries develop sustainable systems for the development, procurement, financing, distribution and use of textbooks at the school level. After decades of donor support, most low-income sub-Saharan African countries continue to have a severe shortage of learning materials. The main constraint is not financing (most sector programs provide support, and more would have been provided had implementation been better) but poor policies, weak national publishing capacity, insufficient support from external publishers for the development of capacity in Africa, and weak implementation capacity in education ministries.

A major review of the World Bank's support for textbooks from 1985 to 2000 (World Bank, 2002*b*) served as an instrument for working with countries in regional workshops (Burkina Faso in 2003; Uganda in 2004; Mozambique in 2005) to address weaknesses and develop national plans to achieve an 'adequate' supply of materials over a two- to three-year period, implemented as part of the countries' ongoing sector programmes. After the workshops, NETF provides support for systematic follow-up at the country level, at national workshops in large countries, and through punctual support for national teams through the work of two textbook specialists, one of whom was recruited to help countries resolve problems in implementing national programmes.

NETF's approach seeks to:

- *Create national ownership*: by giving priority for assistance to countries actively engaged in solving a problem in an area critical to the success of their education programme.
- *Give help to countries when their programmes need assistance*: by ensuring that the assistance is of a high quality, is easily available, fully grant-funded and additional to other support received under sector programmes. The local donor group can assist in identifying bottlenecks in programme implementation that requires technical support.
- *Help mobilize, strengthen and utilize existing capacity* by: (a) providing punctual (not resident) assistance by a specialist or team of specialists 'on call', over several years if needed, to assist when a national team needs support; (b) using, as much as possible, national and regional specialists and institutions; and (c) promoting regional cooperation and knowledge-exchange (e.g. facilitating building of 'quality node networks' among countries working to address a particular implementation problem).

Notes:

a. Set up in 1998, the NETF supports the preparation of high-quality, poverty-focused, education sector development programmes in sub-Saharan Africa. It is managed by the Human Development Department of the Africa Region of the World Bank. It has three medium-term objectives: (a) to strengthen governments' political commitment, national consensus and ownership; (b) to support the development of technical and analytical capacity; and (c) to enhance institutional and systemic capacity for sector development. Total receipts to NETF amounted to $34.5 million (June 2004) of which $29.4 million had been disbursed (85%). For a full review of the work of NETF see World Bank (2004*b*).

b. Established in 1988, ADEA is a network of African Ministers of Education, development agencies, education specialists, researchers, and NGOs. Based in UNESCO-IIEP in Paris, its work is described at http://www.adeanet.org/about/en_aboutADEA.html

Source: Fredriksen (2005*a*).

Strengthening UNESCO's role

UNESCO's mandate to provide international leadership for EFA stands firm

UNESCO's mandate to provide international leadership for EFA stands firm, although the *EFA Global Monitoring Report* has suggested that UNESCO has interpreted its role rather conservatively (UNESCO, 2002*b*), has missed some opportunities to create a politically influential platform for EFA (UNESCO, 2003*b*), and needs to develop a stronger international policy voice (UNESCO, 2004*a*). These judgements were made with an understanding of the resource constraints under which UNESCO operates, of its growing attention to EFA in its national and regional programmes, and of the inherent difficulties of coordinating a very diverse set of EFA stakeholders.

Box 4.9 Working together for better-quality schooling

After the Association for the Development of Education in Africa (ADEA) Biennial Conference in Mauritius (December 2003), a pilot on school quality was launched. Prior to the Conference, ADEA had conducted an extensive study of quality improvement interventions in African schools (Verspoor, forthcoming). Following discussions of the findings of this study, ADEA surveyed member countries to identify potential areas of interest for follow-up work, with technical support facilitated by ADEA. Five main areas were identified: professional development of teachers and pedagogical renewal; implementation of reforms at the school and classroom levels; decentralization/diversification of education provision; curricula/language of instruction; and equity in education financing. Work is now underway to create 'quality nodes' to facilitate cooperation among countries expressing interest in working on a particular topic, teaming them up with institutions that can provide technical support as needed. A progress report of this pilot will be presented at ADEA's next Biennial Conference in 2006.

Source: Fredriksen (2005*a*).

The EFA Working Group offers a broad platform for discussion of EFA related issues

Since the World Education Forum, UNESCO has sought to fulfil its international coordination mandate in two main ways. First, during 2000–2002, it developed frameworks to guide the action of the international community towards achieving the EFA goals. One framework, The Global Initiative Towards Education for All: A Framework for Mutual Understanding (UNESCO, 2001), was designed to give impetus to the global initiative called for in the Dakar Framework for Action.[49] The other, the International Strategy to Put the Dakar Framework for Action into Operation (UNESCO, 2002*a*), while building upon the former, identified concrete actions and strategies for the international community. Neither document created any strong momentum for action, although some of the underlying ideas of the first framework are now being played out in the Fast Track Initiative.

Second, rather than work through the implications of the frameworks and understand why they did not carry weight, UNESCO put its main effort into the EFA Working Group (from 2000) and the EFA High-Level Group (from 2001). The Working Group, an information forum, offers a broad platform for discussion of EFA related issues. Through the creation of a Sherpa Group (ten members representing international agencies, NGOs and developed and developing countries), a bridge is being built to the EFA High-Level Group. This group sets out to achieve sustained political commitment for EFA and to set some strategic directions for international action. Both the High-Level Group and the Working Group have provided some general impetus and annual visibility to international coordination, but neither has yet succeeded in securing specific international commitments within the United Nations system, or elsewhere. While the discourse of the EFA High-Level Group has improved since 2001, its lack of significant outcomes continues to limit its global impact.

These limited achievements have not lessened the view of the international community that UNESCO should strengthen its leadership and coordination role. The Fourth Meeting of the EFA High-Level Group in Brasilia in 2004 concluded that UNESCO should: consult 'with key stakeholders to achieve greater clarity, cohesion and mutual recognition regarding their respective roles as partners in reaching the EFA goals and the education related Millennium Development Goals. ... [and] facilitate the preparation of a comprehensive mapping exercise and implementation plan of the current and future contributions of each partner towards reaching these goals' (UNESCO, 2004*a*).

UNESCO's Executive Board has requested that UNESCO should intensify its consultations with key international stakeholders – particularly the World Bank, the United Nations Development Programme (UNDP), the United Nations Children's Fund (UNICEF) and the United Nations Population Fund (UNFPA) – to agree on the specific roles, responsibilities and contributions of each stakeholder for 2005 to 2015, and to prepare 'a concise global plan to achieve the EFA goals, including resource mobilization' (UNESCO, 2005*b*). These are high – and probably unrealistic – expectations of UNESCO for three main reasons:

First, unlike before Dakar, the five convening agencies for the World Education Forum (UNESCO, the World Bank, UNICEF, UNDP and

49. The Global Initiative in the Dakar Framework for Action called for: increasing external finance for education, in particular basic education; ensuring greater predictability in the flow of external assistance; facilitating more effective donor coordination; strengthening sector-wide approaches; providing earlier, more extensive and broader debt relief and/or debt cancellation for poverty reduction with a strong commitment to basic education; and undertaking more effective and regular monitoring of progress towards EFA goals and targets, including periodic assessments (UNESCO, 2000*b*).

UNFPA) no longer have a joint responsibility for coordinating follow-up through a common secretariat. UNICEF and the World Bank have tended to focus on their own programmes and coordination mechanisms. UNFPA has had a lower, but supportive profile, while UNDP has been largely absent. Kofi Annan, Secretary-General of the United Nations, gave strong support for EFA at Dakar and has reiterated the importance of UNESCO's mandate and its role as the technical agency for education. But, as a recent study of the United Nations and education observes, there is a diversity of rationales for UN work in education, and while many of its approaches to education are complementary, others appear to be in competition (Jones with Coleman, 2005).[50]

Second, work in support of the Millennium Development Goals and the broader EFA agenda are not supported equally. The World Bank and UNICEF explicitly address the education MDGs and have reinforced their leadership in the international initiatives for which they have direct responsibilities – the Fast Track Initiative and the United Nations Girls' Education Initiative (UNGEI). There are, however, attempts to promote synergy across these initiatives through discussions at the FTI and UNESCO coordination meetings. Many of the difficulties experienced by UNESCO in promoting international action and coordination have also been experienced by UNGEI, whose purposes have neither been entirely clear, nor easily distinguishable from the work and programming of UNICEF (Box 4.10).

Third, the request for further mapping and planning at the global level may be considered as having been overtaken by events. Many countries have already developed sector plans, and the FTI is mapping country needs. This Report monitors progress towards the EFA goals, and the FTI is undertaking detailed technical work on aid flows and their distribution. Most agencies have defined their policies and their priorities. Thus, if a new mapping exercise is to add value to international programming for EFA, it will need to be thorough, based on sound data, and sustained over time; and it should be clearly endorsed by all key partners as an essential tool for better international action.

50. The study recognizes the tension that has existed within UNESCO since its inception, in the emphasis that has been given to reflection, action and standard-setting, but it does not apply this analysis explicitly to EFA since Dakar. It also identifies the challenge for UNESCO in working on education when other UN bodies (with finance) have the sector as part of their remit as well.

Box 4.10 The Ten-Year United Nations Girls' Education Initiative

UNGEI was launched at the World Education Forum in Dakar in 2000, by the Secretary-General of the United Nations, with UNICEF as the lead agency. It is a partnership mechanism aimed at reinforcing work on educating girls, in order to reach EFA and MDG goals, in particular those on gender parity. Networking, partnership building, advocacy, knowledge generation and sharing, and programme and project activities in countries are its stated ways of working.

Recently, UNGEI has reinforced its work at all three levels at which it operates – global, regional and national. In addition to the Global Advisory Committee, there is now a Regional Advisory Committee for Africa and UNICEF – appointed regional and sub-regional coordinators in Africa and Asia. These committees provide strategic direction and recommend specific programmes within government plans and Common Country Assessment-UN Development Assistance Framework processes. Steps have been taken to increase the understanding of UNGEI as a partnership, as distinct from UNICEF's independent work in the areas of girls' education. These steps include an UNGEI strategy and implementation plan, communications materials, an UNGEI website, and UNGEI technical meetings, reports and studies, with ongoing attempts to strengthen the UNGEI Secretariat at UNICEF Headquarters.

UNGEI has used the EFA High-Level Group meetings in New Delhi (November 2003) and Brasilia (November 2004) to organize side events to highlight the importance of girls' education and seek greater commitment from policy-makers. It will continue to do so at the High-Level Group meeting in Beijing (November 2005). UNGEI has placed girls' education on the agenda of the FTI, so that gender-sensitive EFA planning is recognized in the FTI appraisal instruments.

Despite these efforts, some difficulties continue at the regional and national levels. No UNGEI global advisory committee has been established for Asia. Some partners continue to be unable to distinguish between UNICEF and UNGEI. The underlying issue, as in the case of the Fast Track Initiative, is what constitutes its value added globally, both for the individual partners and for governments.

The Millennium Development Goals and the broader EFA agenda are not supported equally

Five opportunities for UNESCO

In both its coordination and technical roles, UNESCO will have some specific opportunities to place EFA at the forefront of international efforts to meet the Millennium Goals (especially given new senior management for education), and to encourage bolder steps. Some of these opportunities will come in 2005.

First, within the United Nations Development Group and with the support of the UN Secretary-General, UNESCO is well placed to articulate a strong case for EFA at the global level, especially at the UN Special Assembly on the Millennium Goals in September 2005.[51] The benefits of basic education for poverty reduction need to be constantly defined and defended in international forums. This is a critical function within UNESCO's coordination mandate. There is no other international voice able to undertake this role.[52]

Second, the connections between UNESCO, the FTI, UNGEI, the E-9 countries[53] and other coordinating mechanisms could be strengthened, including in the design and the development of the High-Level Group meetings. The bringing together of the High-Level Group and the FTI Partnership Meeting in Brasilia in 2004 was a good step forward. Now, a more complete integration of objectives and dialogue is required and, in due course, a merging of separate groups. UNESCO is best placed to promote this approach.

The High-Level Group could bring together in a forceful way what the events and commitments of 2005 mean for EFA

Third, the High-Level Group could bring together in a bold and forceful way what the events and commitments of 2005 mean for EFA. It could translate the G8 decisions and the outcomes of the UN Special Assembly into a well-defined set of international actions for EFA for the next ten years. This could be incorporated in the Joint Action Plan for EFA that UNESCO is preparing for endorsement at the EFA High-Level Group in November 2005.

Fourth, as the lead technical agency for education, UNESCO should exercise leadership in promoting harmonization and good practice of technical cooperation, in close consultation with the FTI. As noted above, there is a strong case for international dialogue on improving the quality of technical assistance in a well-coordinated manner. The pooling of assistance, building of regional capacity and rebuilding of UNESCO's own place in this field are all topics worthy of attention.

Fifth, UNESCO is the lead agency for the United Nations Literacy Decade 2003–2012, the United Nations Decade of Education for Sustainable Development 2005–2014, and for three major programmes: the Literacy Initiative for Empowerment, the Teacher Training Initiative in sub-Saharan Africa, and the Global Initiative on HIV/AIDS and Education (Box 4.11). It also leads and coordinates work on EFA Flagship programmes (Box 4.12). These give UNESCO the possibility to demonstrate in a very practical way that separate initiatives can be both well-coordinated internationally and integrated into national plans and programmes. However, to do so will require a major upgrading of UNESCO's technical capacity.

2005 and beyond: from commitment to action

There are promising signs that the coming years will bring increased commitment and progress. More international resources are being pledged (Figure 4.16) – up to approximately US$120 billion (2003 prices) per annum by 2010.[54] This should, in turn, ensure an increase in the level of resources for education in general and for basic education in particular: but, if the proportion of ODA for basic education continues at its current modest levels, the increase will be insufficient to meet the

51. In which context there are opportunities through the work of ECOSOC and its High-Level Meeting in preparing a Declaration for the UN Special Assembly. See http://www.un.org/docs/ecosoc/.

52. By way of a comparative example, the European Commission is developing a contribution to the review of the MDGs at the UN Special Assembly that focuses on long-term MDG contracts between donors and selected countries to ensure predictability of aid flows. UNESCO should be able to articulate approaches to encompassing the full EFA agenda within the new modalities of aid.

53. See www.unesco.org/education/e9/index.shtml.

54. Early in 2005, the European Commission set a new objective, for its fifteen longer-term member states, of 0.51% of GNI for ODA by 2010 and 0.7% by 2015 (EUROPA, 2005). If this commitment is honoured, an additional €20 billion would become available by 2010 (against €43 billion in 2005). In July, G8 leaders agreed to cancel 100% of the outstanding debts of eligible HIPC countries to the IMF, IDA and the African Development Fund. On the basis of both commitments, the G8 concluded that ODA to Africa will increase by US$20 billion a year by 2010 (doubling 2004 disbursements) and that, globally, ODA should increase by approximately US$50 billion by the same year. In addition: (a) France intends to reach 0.7% of GNI in addition to its European Commission commitments by 2007 (two-thirds to Africa); (b) the United Kingdom plans to reach 0.7% of GNI by 2013 (it will double bilateral spending in Africa between 2003/04 and 2007/08); (c) the United States proposes to double aid to sub-Saharan Africa between 2004 and 2010 (the Millennium Challenge Account is scheduled to provide up to US$5 billion a year); the United States has also committed to double the funding to its African Education Initiative (US$400 million) to train 500,000 teachers and grant scholarships to 300,000 young people (primarily girls) over the next four years (US Department of State, 2005); (d) Japan intends to increase ODA by US$10 billion in the next five years and to double its Africa commitments in three years; (e) Canada is doubling its ODA from 2001 to 2010, doubling its assistance to Africa from 2003/04 to 2008/09; and (f) Russia will cancel debt worth US$750 million (G8 Gleneagles, 2005).

Box 4.11 Windows of opportunities through UNESCO-led initiatives

The United Nations Literacy Decade 2003–2012

Expected outcomes:

- Significant progress towards the 2015 Dakar goals (3, 4 and 5), in particular, a recognizable increase in the absolute numbers of those who are literate among women (accompanied by reduction in gender disparities); excluded pockets in countries that are otherwise considered to have high literacy rates; and regions of greatest need (sub-Saharan Africa, South Asia and E-9 countries).
- Attainment by all learners, including children in school, of a mastery level of learning in reading, writing, numeracy, critical thinking, positive citizenship values and other life skills.
- Dynamic literate environments, especially in schools and communities of the priority groups, so that literacy will be sustained and expanded beyond the Literacy Decade.
- Improved quality of life (poverty reduction, increased income, improved health, greater participation, citizenship awareness and gender sensitivity) among those who have participated in the various educational programmes under EFA.

The United Nations Decade of Education for Sustainable Development 2005–2014

Globally to:

- Give an enhanced profile to the central role of education and learning in the common pursuit of sustainable development.
- Facilitate links and networking, exchange and interaction among stakeholders in education for sustainable development (ESD).
- Provide a space and an opportunity for refining and promoting the vision of, and transition to, sustainable development – through all forms of learning and public awareness.
- Foster increased quality of teaching and learning in ESD.
- Develop strategies at every level to strengthen capacity in ESD.

The Literacy Initiative for Empowerment 2005–2015

- Promote literacy policies and practices within existing national education and development frameworks (in up to thirty-four countries).
- Provide target groups with quality and relevant literacy learning opportunities linked to development programmes.

The Teacher Training Initiative in sub-Saharan Africa 2006–2015

For up to forty-six countries to:

- More directly relate teacher policy to national development goals.
- Improve the quality of teacher education.
- Improve the delivery of quality teacher education.
- Augment teacher recruitment and retention to stem teacher shortage.

The Global Initiative on HIV/AIDS and Education

- Support governments (of up to thirty countries by 2010) to prepare a comprehensive educational response to HIV and AIDS, aiming at both risk and vulnerability.
- Mitigate the impact of HIV and AIDS on education.
- Address the structural causes of vulnerability in and around the learning environment.

Sources: UNESCO (2003*f*, 2005*b*, 2005*c*).

estimated US$7 billion of aid per annum that was required from 2000 to achieve UPE and gender equity in schools. It follows that additional bold commitments are needed now. A doubling of aid to basic education would bring the international community closer to meeting its commitments and to achieving the EFA 2015 goals. Consequently, it is vital that the case be made strongly for EFA in the follow-up to the G8 decisions and the outcomes of the UN Special Assembly. UNESCO has a major role to play in this regard.

These additional resources need to be delivered in more predictable, better coordinated and targeted ways to countries which have developed effective strategies and programmes. Predictability is required for effective planning and for taking decisions with long-term implications, including for recurrent costs; and better coordination and targeting are required to reduce both duplication and the reporting demands on recipient countries, and to ensure that aid is directed to countries most in need. Much can be done to improve the ways in which the

Additional resources need to be delivered in more predictable, better coordinated and targeted ways

Box 4.12 Nine EFA Flagships

Nine EFA flagship programmes were launched in Dakar to consolidate international cooperation on themes identified as critical to the achievement of the EFA goals (UNESCO, 2002*b*, 2003*b*): The Initiative on HIV/AIDS and Education; Early Childhood Care and Education; The Right to Education for Persons with Disabilities: Towards Inclusion; Education for Rural People; Education in Situations of Emergency and Crisis; Focusing Resources on Effective School Health (FRESH); Teachers and the Quality of Education; the United Nations Girls' Education Initiative (UNGEI); and Literacy in the Framework of the United Nations Literacy Decade (UNLD).

UNESCO has now integrated its work on the UNLD, HIV/AIDS and education, and teacher training in sub-Saharan Africa into its core EFA programme. UNICEF and FAO – which are lead agencies for, respectively, UNGEI and Education for Rural People – are moving in a similar direction.

The HIV/AIDS and Education Initiative is undertaking work to accelerate the education sector's response to HIV/AIDS in thirty African countries. A survey of the capacity and readiness of seventy-one countries to manage the impact of HIV/AIDS on their education sectors has been undertaken (UNESCO-IIEP, 2005*c*. A study of eighteen of these countries, from a civil society perspective, supplemented the survey results (Global Campaign for Education, 2005). The reports will result in the first international benchmark for examining official responses to the threat to education systems and a challenge to teaching and learning everywhere.

The Right to Education for Persons with Disabilities: Towards Inclusion is a catalyst to ensure that the right to education, and the goals of the Dakar Framework, are realized for individuals with disabilities (Lawrence, 2004). It builds on the International Working Group on Disability and Development, an alliance of twenty agencies and NGOs, including UNESCO, UNICEF and the World Bank. It encourages agencies to define a common vision, defend it and work towards its realization. The new Human Rights Convention on Disabilities (decided by UN General Assembly in June 2003) and its Article 17 on education provides an authoritative global reference point for domestic laws and policies, provides mechanisms for monitoring, establishes a standard of assessment and achievement and provides a framework for international cooperation. Collaborative work is undertaken to review indicators of disability and special need in order to provide a complete picture of disability issues in education.

Education for Rural People: Led by FAO, this programme has undertaken consultative and capacity-building activities in Asia, in nine Latin America countries and in Kosovo and Mozambique, targeting decision-makers from agriculture and education ministries, aid agencies and NGOs. It has a publications programme with UNESCO-IIEP.

international community supports EFA. Joined-up ways of working are necessary. Parallel and competing initiatives should be linked or integrated.

Five years have passed since Dakar. Progress is being made, but not quickly enough. ■

Figure 4.16: DAC members' ODA:[1] 1990–2004[2] and simulations to 2006 and 2010[3] (Amount in constant 2003 US$ billions and % share of GNI)

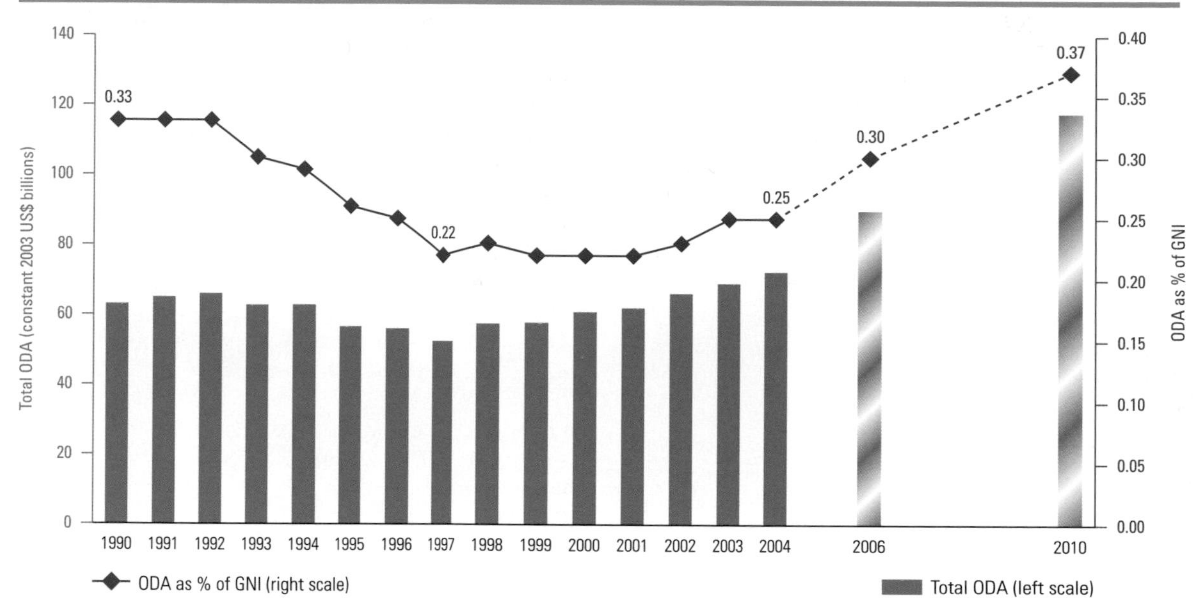

Notes:

1. DAC members' ODA is the sum of bilateral aid and contributions to multilateral donors. Therefore the figures are different from the total ODA in Fig 4.1 which shows total aid received from DAC donors, multilateral donors and non-DAC bilateral donors.
2. The total DAC ODA for 1991, 1992 and 1993 excludes debt forgiveness of non-ODA claims. It is included in the individual donors' data, and thus the total of individual donors for these years will be higher than the figures shown in this graph.
3. Simulations are based on donors' ODA undertakings and estimated growth rates.

Source: Communication from OECD-DAC, August 2005.

Students and parents browse through used school books for sale in Bac Ninh, Viet Nam.

Chapter 5

Why literacy matters

This chapter explores the case for literacy, especially for youth and adults. It summarizes the foundations of the right to literacy through a review of international agreements, noting that literacy is both a right in itself and an instrument for achieving other rights. The chapter then reviews the broader benefits that result from literacy, in human, economic, social and cultural terms. Since literacy is a key outcome of education, it is difficult to separate the right to literacy from the right to education or the benefits of literacy from those of education.

Literacy as a right

Literacy is a right. It is implicit in the right to education. It is recognized as a right, explicitly for both children and adults, in certain international conventions. It is included in key international declarations.

The 1948 Universal Declaration of Human Rights recognizes the right to education, as do other binding international conventions. These include the International Covenant on Civil and Political Rights (ICCPR) and the International Covenant on Economic, Social and Cultural Rights, both adopted in 1966, which, together with the Universal Declaration of Human Rights, were proclaimed by the United Nations as constituting the International Bill of Human Rights. Other important instruments include the 1979 Convention on the Elimination of all Forms of Discrimination against Women (CEDAW) and the 1989 Convention on the Rights of the Child (CRC).[1]

Literacy should be understood within a rights-based approach and among principles of inclusion for human development

The 1975 Persepolis Declaration, the CRC and CEDAW further recognize literacy, rather than just education, as a right. The 1960 Convention against Discrimination in Education (CDE) specifically tackles the issue of those who have not attended or completed primary education. The Persepolis Declaration states: 'Literacy is not an end in itself. It is a fundamental human right' (UNESCO, 1975*a*). Both the CRC and CEDAW refer to the promotion of literacy and the eradication of illiteracy. For example, Article 10(e) of CEDAW, which entered into force in 1981, recognizes the right of adults to literacy, calling on parties to ensure that men and women have 'the same opportunities for access to programmes of continuing education, including adult and functional literacy programmes'. The CRC characterizes literacy as a basic skill to which children are entitled and stresses the need to rid the world of illiteracy (UNHCHR, 1989). A strategic objective of the 1995 Beijing Declaration and Platform for Action is to 'eradicate illiteracy among women'. The CDE directs states to 'encourage and intensify by appropriate methods the education of persons who have not received any primary education or who have not completed the entire primary education course and the continuation of their education on the basis of individual capacity' (UNESCO, 1960). The CDE further mandates increasing opportunities for literacy via continuing education.

There is considerable pressure for a renewed emphasis on literacy as a right. The Hamburg Declaration states under Resolution 11: 'Literacy, broadly conceived as the basic knowledge and skills needed by all in a rapidly changing world, is a fundamental human right' (UNESCO, 1997). The UNESCO round-table report *Literacy as Freedom* recommends that literacy be understood within a rights-based approach and among principles of inclusion for human development (UNESCO, 2003*c*).

Less clear than the right to literacy has been the understanding of literacy in these various conventions and declarations. Couching the right mainly in terms of eradicating illiteracy, as in CEDAW and the Beijing Declaration, implies the equivalence of literacy with knowledge or of illiteracy with ignorance. Where literacy as a right derives from the right to education, it is seen more as a set of skills that constitute *fundamental or basic education*, as the CDE implies. From the founding of UNESCO, the term 'fundamental education' has signified the skills of reading, writing and calculating, with a heavy emphasis on reading and writing (UNESCO, 2003*d*). While numeracy is usually mentioned alongside literacy in legal instruments, the word 'literacy' itself is generally limited to reading and writing skills. General Comment 1 of the CRC (Article 29), for example, establishes that 'basic skills include not only literacy and numeracy but also life skills' (UNHCHR, 1989). In this context, 'literacy' means reading and writing only. The World Declaration on Education for All (Jomtien, Thailand, 1990) in Article I.1, includes 'literacy, oral expression, numeracy, and problem solving' as essential learning tools that comprise the basic learning needs of every person (UNESCO, 1990).

Key to the interpretation of literacy as reading and writing skills is the issue of the language in which one learns to read or write. The right to learn a language is quite different from the right to learn *in* that language. Article 27 of the ICCPR sets forth the right of persons belonging to minorities to use their own language; this would mean at least the right to speak minority languages in private. International law makes clear that the state has the right to determine official languages, which will rarely if ever encompass all or most minority languages. Public education may well be provided in a variety of languages beyond the official ones. In Namibia, for example, the national literacy programme has three stages, the first two in mother tongue and the third introducing basic English, so that learners with different levels of literacy can be accommodated. Where public education is provided only in the official language, it should be

1. See Chapter 1 of the 2003/4 Report for a detailed discussion of the right to education.

more widely recognized that human rights standards presuppose the possibility of pluralism in education, including in language of instruction, with the freedom to establish private schools secured. The increasing emphasis on bilingual formal education (Box 5.1) has also influenced adult and youth programmes in the non-formal sector.

Many documents, including the Persepolis and Hamburg Declarations, allow for an expanded interpretation of literacy beyond the skills of reading and writing. Literacy can include access to scientific and technical knowledge, to legal information, to means of enjoying the benefits of culture and to the use of media, both for those seeking greater access and those with no access (Organization of American States, 1948; United Nations, 1995; UNHCHR, 1969). Literacy is also interpreted as a foundational, universal life skill for those in adverse circumstances; for example, Article 22 of the Convention relating to the Status of Refugees guarantees refugees the 'same treatment as is accorded to nationals with respect to elementary education' (UNHCHR, 1951). As a tool, literacy has the potential to meet people's most vital needs and to stimulate social, cultural, political and economic participation, especially on the part of disadvantaged groups. Emphasis on inclusive lifelong educational provision reflects the international community's recognition of the universal human need for and right to literacy (UNESCO, 1975*b* and 1997).

An additional noteworthy trend concerns literacy in relation to technology, civic engagement and lifelong learning. UNESCO's B@bel Initiative seeks to encourage information dissemination, placing particular emphasis on the potential of communication technologies to maintain and advance cultural and linguistic diversity (UNESCO, 2005*a*). The United Nations Development Programme (UNDP) asserts that possessing knowledge, having access to resources for a decent standard of living and participating in community life constitute basic capabilities for human development (UNDP, 2004*a*). Access to these tools, skills and resources lends greater assurance to the development of literacy. Literacy is inextricably linked to a process of continual education or lifelong learning.

Finally, literacy has been recognized not only as a right in itself but also as a mechanism for the pursuit of other human rights, just as human rights education is a tool for combating illiteracy.

Box 5.1 The right to choose the language of learning

UNESCO promotes bilingual education not only because it encourages multilingualism but also because it permits children from minority and indigenous groups to learn alongside those of majority groups (UNESCO, 2003*a*). Promoting bilingual education is not the same as saying there is a *right* to either bilingual education or mother tongue education, however; these are keenly contested issues, upon which international treaties are much more circumspect. The two main treaty provisions relating to linguistic rights in education are Article 14 of the 1995 Council of Europe Framework Convention for the Protection of National Minorities and Article 28 of the 1989 ILO Convention 169 concerning Indigenous and Tribal Peoples in Independent Countries. The latter states:

- Children belonging to the peoples concerned shall, wherever practicable, be taught to read and write in their own indigenous language or in the language most commonly used by the group to which they belong. When this is not practicable, the competent authorities shall undertake consultations with these peoples with a view to the adoption of measures to achieve this objective.
- Adequate measures shall be taken to ensure that these peoples have the opportunity to attain fluency in the national language or in one of the official languages of the country.
- Measures shall be taken to preserve and promote the development and practice of the indigenous languages of the peoples concerned.

The Vienna Declaration and Programme of Action calls on states to eradicate illiteracy, linking such efforts to greater respect and protection for human rights and personal liberties; it also emphasizes the use of human rights-informed education as a means of combating illiteracy (UNHCHR, 1993). Particularly significant in this respect are the rights of women, who currently constitute the majority of the world's illiterates.

The benefits of literacy[2]

The rationale for recognizing literacy as a right is the set of benefits it confers on individuals, families, communities and nations

The rationale for recognizing literacy as a right is the set of benefits it confers on individuals, families, communities and nations. Indeed, it is widely reckoned that, in modern societies, 'literacy skills are fundamental to informed decision-making, personal empowerment, active and passive participation in local and global social community' (Stromquist, 2005, p. 12). As Chapter 1 noted, however, the benefits of literacy ensue only when broader rights and development frameworks are in place and operating effectively. Individual benefits, for example, accrue only when written material is available to the newly literate person, and overall economic benefits only when

2. This section is based on the following papers, commissioned for the Report: Cameron and Cameron (2005), Farah (2005), Patel (2005), Robinson-Pant (2005) and Stromquist (2005).

there is also sound macroeconomic management, investment in infrastructure and other appropriate development policy measures. Similarly, certain benefits, such as women's empowerment, will result only if the socio-cultural environment is accommodating of them.

The extent to which literacy has negative effects is keenly contested and has more to do with how literacy is acquired than with literacy itself – an important reminder that benefits also depend on the *channels* through which literacy is acquired and practised. Some channels can have effects that some consider detrimental. For example, the forced acquisition of literacy in official languages can lead to the loss of oral languages. Literacy programmes and written materials can be a mechanism to indoctrinate people to participate uncritically in a political system (Graff, 1987*a*). Complex value judgements are involved here, which this Report points out but does not enter into.

The successful completion of adult literacy programmes yields benefits similar to formal schooling

Providing a systematic, evidence-based account of the benefits of literacy is not easy, for several reasons.

- Most research has not separated the benefits of literacy per se from those of attending school or participating in adult literacy programmes. More generally, there is a 'tendency to conflate schooling, education, literacy and knowledge' (Robinson-Pant 2005).
- Little research has been devoted to adult literacy programmes (as opposed to formal schooling) and existing studies focus mainly on women; the benefits of acquiring literacy in adulthood are thus less clearly established than those of acquiring cognitive skills through education in childhood.
- Research has focused on the impact of literacy upon the individual: few authors have examined the impact at the family/household, community, national or international level.
- Some effects of literacy, e.g. those on culture, are intrinsically difficult to define and measure.
- Literacy is not defined consistently across studies and literacy data are frequently flawed.[3]

This section thus briefly rehearses the benefits of education in general[4] and, whenever possible, examines the specific benefits of adult literacy programmes. The limited available evidence suggests that, as far as cognitive outcomes are concerned, the successful completion of adult literacy programmes yields benefits similar to formal schooling. A qualification is that few rigorous assessments of adult literacy programmes in terms of cognitive achievement have been made; nor, usually, has there been any attempt to assess how long effects last after programmes end (Oxenham and Aoki, 2002). Providing such evidence clearly should be a research priority. In addition, adult literacy programmes can produce more adult-specific outcomes, such as political awareness, empowerment, critical reflection and community action, which are not so much identified with formal schooling. Indeed, learners' statements on the benefits of participating in adult literacy programmes include the positive experiences of the process and the social meeting space of literacy groups.[5] Less measurable benefits such as these are about human development dimensions, including social cohesion, social inclusion and social capital.

The benefits of literacy can be conveniently, if arbitrarily, classified as human, political, cultural, social[6] and economic.

Human benefits

The human benefits from literature are related to factors such as the improved self-esteem, empowerment, creativity and critical reflection that participation in adult literacy programmes and the practice of literacy may produce. Human benefits are intrinsically valuable and may also be instrumental in realizing other benefits of literacy: improved health, increased political participation and so on.[7]

Self-esteem

There is extensive reference to the positive impact of literacy on self-esteem. Improved self-esteem has been reported in studies of literacy programmes in Brazil, India, Nigeria, the United States, and several African and South Asian countries.[8] A review of forty-four studies on the behavioural changes involved in literacy training (Bown, 1990) also provides many examples. Statements such as 'I have more self-confidence', quoted by Canieso-Doronila (1996) in a study of the Philippines, are typical.

Empowerment

Literacy may empower learners – especially women – to take individual and collective action in various contexts, such as household, workplace and community, in two related ways. First, literacy programmes themselves may be designed and conducted so as to make participants 'into authors of their own learning, developers of their own knowledge and partners in dialogue about

3. See Chapter 7 for an extensive discussion of literacy data.

4. A principal source for the benefits of education is Hannum and Buchmann (2003).

5. See, for instance, Robinson-Pant (2005) and Stromquist (2005).

6. 'Social' as used here includes health and education benefits, also discussed in Chapter 1 (education) and Chapter 3 (HIV/AIDS).

7. See Drèze and Sen (2002; pp. 38-41) for a fuller discussion of the intrinsic value and instrumental roles, both individual and social, of health and education, which applies as well to literacy.

8. See, in particular, Young et al. (1980,1994), Bingman (2000), Greenleigh Associates (1968), Beder (1999), Stromquist (1997), Egbo (2000), Farrell (2004), Abadzi (2003*b*) and Lauglo (2001).

limit situations in their lives' (Easton, 2005). Second, literacy programmes can contribute to broader socio-economic processes of empowerment, provided they take place in a supportive environment. Recent evidence exists for Turkey, Nepal, India and Bolivia (respectively, Kagitcibasi et al., 2005; Burchfield, 1996; Dighe, 2004; and Burchfield et al., 2002*b*).[9] Many learners of both genders surveyed in Namibia – explaining why they wanted to be able to read and write letters, deal with money and master English – mentioned a wish to be self-reliant and to exert control over everyday-life situations, citing, for instance, 'keeping secrets' and 'not being cheated' (Lind, 1996).

Political benefits

The empowering potential of literacy can translate into increased political participation and thus contribute to the quality of public policies and to democracy.

Political participation

The relationship between education and political participation is well established. Educated people are to some extent more likely to vote and voice more tolerant attitudes and democratic values (Hannum and Buchmann, 2003). Participation in adult literacy programmes is also correlated with increased participation in trade unions, community action and national political life, especially when empowerment is at the core of programme design. For example:

- An adult literacy programme set up by workers at a Brazilian construction site increased participation in union activities (Ireland, 1994).
- Literacy programme participants in the United States reported an increase in community participation (Greenleigh Associates, 1968; Becker et al., 1976) and were more likely than non-participants to register to vote, though they did not actually vote more than non-participants (Boggs et al., 1979).
- Literacy programme graduates in Kenya participated more in elections and local associations than did illiterates (Carron et al., 1989).
- Women who took part in literacy programmes in Turkey voted more and participated more in community organizations than did illiterate women (Kagitcibasi et al., 2005).
- Among Nepalese women, those who had spent two years in state-run literacy programmes demonstrated more political knowledge than those not in the programmes and were more likely to believe they could serve as political representatives (Burchfield et al., 2002*a*). On various measures of political participation, the more intense participation in a literacy programme was, the larger the proportion of women reporting changes in their political attitudes, except as regards voter registration (Table 5.1). Much the same results held for NGO-run programmes in Bolivia (Burchfield et al., 2002*b*).
- Qualitative studies yield similar results to these quantitative analyses. Literate women in Nigeria, for example, reported being confident enough to participate in community meetings, unlike illiterate women (Egbo, 2000).
- Rural women who participated in literacy programmes in El Salvador claimed a voice in community meetings and several were able to engage in sophisticated socio-political analysis (Purcell-Gates and Waterman, 2000).

The empowering potential of literacy can translate into increased political participation

Table 5.1: Political and community participation and literacy among Nepalese women

	Participation in adult literacy programmes			
	Intensity of participation			Non-participants
	Low	Medium	High	
Political awareness and participation				
Knows national policy on electing women representatives	82	84	95	78
Knows minimum voting age	24	31	41	14
Knows name of member of parliament in their area	24	42	53	19
Knows name of village development committee	84	85	94	94
Has registered to vote	97	95	94	94
Thinks it possible for her to become a local political representative	24	31	35	13
Is interested in becoming a political representative	21	18	20	11
Community participation				
Is a member of a community group	33	40	56	16
Participates in community development activities	12	16	21	12

Note: Each figure represents the percentage of women in each category of participation in adult literacy programmes for whom the statement about political or community participation in the left-hand column is true.
Source: Burchfield et al., 2002*a*.

Democracy

The expansion of education may contribute to the expansion of democracy and vice versa, yet the precise nature of the relationship between education and democracy remains unclear and difficult to measure accurately (Hannum and Buchmann, 2003). For example, a comparison of countries over 1965–80 and 1980–88 found no impact from expansion of primary and secondary schooling on various measures of democracy,

9. It has also been claimed for the Reflect method in Bangladesh, El Salvador, Lesotho and Uganda but the evidence is somewhat contentious (Riddell, 2001).

controlling for such factors as economic development and ethnic homogeneity (Benavot, 1996). The role of civic education as such is also unclear, although it is typically included in the curriculum of formal schools and adult literacy programmes. The Civic Education Study by the International Association for the Evaluation of Educational Achievement (IEA), covering 14-year-old students in twenty-eight countries in 1999 and 17- to 19-year-old students in sixteen countries in 2000, found that the more students knew about democratic institutions, the more likely they were to plan on voting as adults. The IEA study also found that democratic classroom practices were the most effective means of promoting civic knowledge and engagement among students. It can be surmized, although it has not been established, that the same may be true of literacy programmes for youth and adults.

The more students know about democratic institutions, the more likely they are to plan on voting as adults

Ethnic equality

There appears to be no research into the impact on ethnic equality of either literacy or participation in adult literacy programmes. It is probably reasonable to assume, however, that the impact of literacy is likely similar to that of educational expansion, i.e. that it has the potential to benefit disadvantaged ethnic groups but will not necessarily do so. A range of experiences appears to support the statement that 'It is not safe to assume that expansion in access to education will allow disadvantaged minorities to "catch up" with initially advanced ethnic groups, at least in the short run' (Hannum and Buchmann, 2003, p. 11).

- Ethnic disparities in formal education have persisted in Israel, Nepal and China, for example (respectively, Shavit and Kraus, 1990; Stash and Hannum, 2001; and Hannum, 2002). Similarly, education does not consistently reduce ethnic occupational inequality.
- Racial inequality decreased with educational expansion in Brazil for most occupations but increased in the professions and other white-collar sectors (Telles, 1994).
- Rising ethnic disparities in north-west China are explained by rising ethnic differences in education, despite improved educational access for ethnic minorities (Telles, 1994; Hannum and Xie, 1998).

Post-conflict situations

Literacy programmes can have an impact on peace and reconciliation in post-conflict contexts. For example, CLEBA, a Colombian non-governmental organization providing literacy programmes in Medellín, emphasizes the 'pedagogy of the text' approach, in which learners write texts based on their own experiences. About 900 men and women, who migrated to Medellín from rural communities heavily affected by armed conflict, participated in an adult literacy project whose key themes were citizenship and peace education (ProLiteracy Worldwide, 2004). Mobilizing people's capacity for resilience by having them write down their experiences and share them with others appeared to be a promising approach, helping them come to terms with multiple traumas and shift towards constructive action (Hanemann, 2005*b*).

Cultural benefits

The cultural benefits of literacy are harder to identify clearly than benefits in terms of political participation. Adult literacy programmes may facilitate the transmission of certain values and promote transformation of other values, attitudes and behaviours through critical reflection. They also provide access to written culture, which the newly literate may choose to explore independently of the cultural orientation of the literacy programmes in which they participated. Adult literacy programmes can thus be instrumental in preserving and promoting cultural openness and diversity. However, 'any effect that literacy may have on the culture (i.e. what people believe and how they do things) of an individual or group will be slow, will not be easily and immediately accessible, and will be difficult to identify as the outcome of a single intervention such as a literacy and adult education programme' (Farah, 2005).

Cultural change

Literacy programmes can help challenge attitudes and behavioural patterns. Indeed, this type of cultural transformation is central to the Freirean approach, which aims to develop skills of critical reflection (Freire, 1985). This approach is often used in conjunction with active 'experiential learning' or learning by doing (Mezirow, 1996). Many programmes also aim to promote values such as equity, inclusion, respect for cultural diversity, peace and active democracy. However, such transformation typically is limited.

- In Uganda, it was observed that the difference in attitudes between participants and non-participants was less than the difference in knowledge (Carr-Hill et al., 2001).

- In Nepal, adult literacy programmes influenced women's attitudes towards family planning and made them more open to speaking up for change. Women's ability to translate their new attitudes into new fertility practices, however, was limited by household structures (Robinson-Pant, 2001).

Both of these studies emphasized the possible impact of adult literacy programmes on gender relations. In Pakistan, women's access to reading and writing resulted in a norm of privacy that had been non-existent in the culture (Box 5.2).

Preservation of cultural diversity

Adult literacy programmes can help preserve cultural diversity. In particular, literacy programmes that make use of minority languages have the potential to improve people's ability to participate in their own culture. This has been observed in programmes whose outcomes included the writing down of folk tales in Botswana (Chebanne et al., 2001), in an Orang Asli community in Malaysia (Chupil, 2003), the Karen in Myanmar (Norwood, 2003), the Limbu in Nepal (Subba and Subba, 2003) and among the Maori in New Zealand (Tarawa, 2003).

The UNESCO Institute for Education has interpreted the 'four pillars of lifelong learning for the twenty-first century', outlined in the report of the International Commission on Education for the Twenty-first Century (Delors et al., 1996), in terms of the human rights situation of indigenous people. The 'four pillars' provide principles that should be followed in the design of carefully planned and culturally relevant adult literacy programmes aimed at contributing to the protection of the cultural rights of indigenous peoples (Table 5.2).

Social benefits

The practice of literacy can be instrumental in people's achievement of a range of capabilities such as maintaining good health and living longer, learning throughout life, controlling reproductive behaviour, raising healthy children and educating them. Improving literacy levels thus has potentially large social benefits, such as increased life expectancy, reduced child mortality and improved children's health. The evidence has often focused on the benefits of education, as opposed to literacy per se, but evidence on the effects of adult literacy programmes is beginning to accumulate.

Box 5.2 Effects of literacy on leisure time and privacy in Pakistan

Once women in Pakistan are able to read and write in Urdu (the national language) and in English, the quality of their leisure time changes and they create a new norm of privacy, according to studies of two different rural communities. Younger women create private time when they can read news, romantic fiction and women's magazines, and write diaries. Reading and writing do not remain mere leisure activities but become means of creating private space, freeing imagination, and engaging in reflection and emotional expression. Through leisure reading and writing, women begin to question, challenge, resist and renegotiate values and their own roles.

Sources: Zubair (2001, 2004).

Table 5.2: UNESCO's four pillars of learning with regard to indigenous peoples

Learning to be: the right to self-definition and self-identification	The right of indigenous peoples to their own interpretation of their history as well as the right to learn in their own languages.
Learning to know: the right to self-knowledge	Indigenous peoples have their own informal learning systems, which are compatible with their livelihood systems. This knowledge has often been denied to them through formal education and the imposition of foreign values on their societies.
Learning to do: the right to self-development	Indigenous concepts of development are inextricably linked to culture, education, environment and self-determination. Sustainable development for indigenous peoples is possible only when indigenous languages and cultures are protected.
Learning to live together: the right to self-determination	This implies the right to be able to organize the relationships between indigenous peoples and the wider society, not on terms defined unilaterally by the dominant society, but on terms defined in consultation with the indigenous peoples.

Source: UIE (1997*a*).

Health

A growing body of longitudinal research evaluating the health benefits of literacy programmes points to the same impact as that of education, and indeed in some cases, to a greater impact. For example, infant mortality was less, by a statistically significant amount, among Nicaraguan mothers who had participated in an adult literacy campaign than among those who had not, and the reduction was greater for those made literate in the campaign than for those made literate in primary school (Sandiford et al., 1995). Bolivian women who attended literacy and basic education programmes displayed gains in health-related knowledge and behaviour, unlike women who had not participated in such programmes; the former group was more likely, for instance, to seek medical help for themselves and sick children, adopt preventive health measures such as immunization and know more about family planning methods (Burchfield et al., 2002*b*). A survey in Nepal found similar effects but was less able to link these to programme participation, because women in the control group of non-participants, like women in the programmes, had been exposed to radio broadcasts and other health interventions (Burchfield et al., 2002*a*). In Mexico, women with no or low literacy had the most difficulty following verbal health explanations by medical personnel (Dexter et al., 1998).

In Mexico, women with no or low literacy had difficulty following verbal health explanations by medical personnel

Small-scale qualitative studies provide evidence about how literacy affects cultural beliefs that in turn affect health, e.g. concerning female circumcision in Nigeria (Egbo, 2000). Studies indicate, however, that literacy programmes that themselves attempt to transmit health information have not been particularly successful, as the participants value reading and writing over receiving health knowledge (Robinson-Pant, 2005). Behaviour change is more dependent on changing attitudes and values than on gaining new knowledge. Chapter 3 explores the relationship between education, literacy and HIV/AIDS.

Reproductive behaviour

The negative correlation between education (in particular that of females) and fertility is well established. It was demonstrated by Cochrane (1979) and Wheeler (1980), and has consistently been reported since in studies both within and between countries. For example, studies based on Demographic and Health Surveys find that, on average, a 10% expansion in the primary gross enrolment ratio (GER) lowers the total fertility rate by 0.1 child and a 10% increase in the secondary GER by 0.2 child (Hannum and Buchmann, 2003, p. 13). However, there is much debate about how this correlation arises and the extent to which it is causal. The mechanisms whereby education may reduce fertility include its effects on women's autonomy, infant mortality and child health, spouse choice, marriage age, female employment outside the home and the costs of educating children.

Some of the same mechanisms may also apply to adult literacy programmes, depending on participants' age. Unfortunately, however, little research into the impact of adult literacy programmes on fertility has been done.

Education

Literacy has important educational benefits. These were largely discussed in Chapter 1, where the interconnectedness of all six EFA goals was established, in particular the fact that parents who themselves are educated, whether through schooling or adult programmes, are more likely to send their children to school and more able to help the children in the course of their schooling.

It used to be thought that literacy contributed to the development of abstract reasoning. This now appears less likely. Studies in Liberia, Morocco, the Philippines and the United States indicate, rather, that abstract reasoning is the result of formal schooling (respectively, Scribner and Cole, 1981; Wagner, 1993; Bernardo, 1998; and Heath, 1983). In general, 'the effects of literacy are more likely to be determined by formal schooling, socialisation, and the cultural practices of a particular society than by literacy per se' (Patel, 2005).[10] However, literacy does help people understand decontextualized information and language, verbal as well as written.

Gender equality

Most literacy programmes have targeted women rather than both sexes, limiting the ways in which gender equality can be addressed holistically and directly through the programmes themselves. The programmes have thus tended to concentrate specifically on women's inequality rather than gender equality. Participation in adult literacy programmes does enable women to gain access to and challenge male domains by, for instance, entering male-dominated areas of work, learning languages of power previously associated with men (where only men had access to formal education) and participating in household finances. Examples of elite languages newly available to women include English in Uganda and 'posh Bangla' in Bangladesh (Fiedrich and Jellema, 2003). In some Bangladesh households, literacy has enabled women to become involved in the financial management of the household, previously controlled by men (Maddox, 2005). In India, an evaluation of a literacy programme using the Total Literacy Campaign approach showed that 'women learners had a strong desire to learn. They liked to go to the literacy classes because this gave them an opportunity to meet others and study collectively. Thus, literacy classes

10. This finding raises important questions about the design of adult literacy programmes, where it is deemed desirable for such programmes also to develop abstract reasoning.

provided women with a social space, away from home' (Patel in UNESCO, 2003*c*, p. 142). Many women have reported that acquiring literacy and attending a class is in itself a threat to existing gender relations (Horsman, 1990; Rockhill, 1987).

Literacy programme participants can gain more voice in household discussions through their experience of speaking in the 'public' space of the class, though this may vary according to context and the kind of decisions involved. Detailed case studies reviewed by Robinson-Pant (2005) indicate that, while a newly literate woman may be able to decide whether to send her daughter to school, for example, she may not feel able to assert herself regarding family planning. Similarly, women may become aware of further education possibilities or of information about AIDS prevention through literacy programmes but still find it difficult to make actual changes in the household. The same social barriers that kept these women from attending school in the first place may, for example, impede their access to education beyond literacy programmes. There are, however, many instances of social mobilization due to literacy programmes' tackling of gender issues at the community level, including campaigns against men's alcohol use in India (Dighe, 1995; Khandekar, 2004) and the use of legal measures to address abuse (D'Souza, 2003; Monga, 2000).

Economic benefits[11]

The economic returns to education have been extensively studied, especially in terms of increased individual income and economic growth.

Economic growth

Education has been consistently shown to be a major determinant of individual income, alongside professional experience. While the number of years of schooling remains the most frequently used variable, recent studies tend also to use assessments of cognitive skills, typically literacy and numeracy test scores. These studies show that literacy has a positive impact on earnings, beyond the impact of the quantity of schooling; studies of the impact of adult literacy programmes are much rarer, however. The relationship between educational expansion and economic growth in the aggregate has proven surprisingly difficult to establish, for several reasons. Hannum and Buchmann (2003), in their literature review, propose that the apparently inconsistent findings may result from the 'difficulty of distinguishing the effects of growth on education from the effects of education on growth, and the possibility that other factors drive both educational expansion and economic growth.' Krueger and Lindahl (2000) suggest that the issue has more to do with measurement errors in education data and with the time horizon: they show an increase in schooling having no short-term impact on growth, but a statistically significant effect over the longer term (ten to twenty years). Several studies nevertheless find that economies with a larger stock of human capital or rate of human capital accumulation do experience faster growth.[12] An influential paper by Pritchett (2001), however, concludes that educational expansion has failed to contribute to economic growth owing to the lack of an adequate institutional environment.

Literacy programme participants can gain more voice in household discussions through their experience of speaking in the 'public' space of the class

Several studies have taken on the difficult task of trying to disentangle the impact of literacy on growth from that of education. Most recently, Coulombe et al. (2004), using data from the International Adult Literacy Survey (IALS)[13] to investigate the relationship between literacy skills and economic growth, concluded that differences in average skill levels among OECD countries explained fully 55% of the differences in economic growth over 1960–94. This implies that investments in raising the average level of skills could yield large economic returns. Furthermore, the study found that direct measures of human capital based on literacy scores performed better than years-of-schooling indicators in explaining growth in output per capita and per worker.

Other studies that have examined specifically the relationship between literacy and economic growth include:

- Barro (1991), which, using cross-country data for 1960–85, found that adult literacy rates, as well as school enrolment rates, exert a positive impact on growth;
- Bashir and Darrat (1994), which found the same relationship for the same period for thirty-two Islamic developing countries;
- Hanushek and Kimko (2000), which identifies a relationship between student achievement in mathematics and science and economic growth that is consistently strong across thirty-one countries. However, the apparent relationship is reduced: a) when South Korea, Singapore, Hong Kong and Taiwan, with high growth and high scores during the period, are removed from the analysis; and b) in the most recent period when many Asian countries went into a slow-growth phase. This suggests that the overall effect between mathematics and

11. This section is based on Cameron and Cameron (2005).

12. See, for instance, Barro (1991), Petrakis and Stamatakis (2002), Poot (2000), Sylwester (2000) and Loening (2002).

13. See Chapter 7 for a presentation of IALS and other literacy surveys.

The average literacy score in a given population is a better indicator of growth than the percentage of the population with very high literacy scores

science achievement and economic growth may not be a causal one (Ramirez et al. 2003).

- Naudé (2004), which, using panel data for 1970–90 for forty-four African countries, found that literacy was among the variables with a positive effect on GDP per capita growth.

Two studies suggest that the impact of literacy on economic growth depends on the initial literacy level. Azariadis and Drazen (1990) found a threshold effect: countries that experienced rapid economic growth based on technology transfers had first achieved a literacy rate of at least 40%, a finding reminiscent of the 1960s economic history studies of modernization.[14] Sachs and Warner (1997) found a statistically significant S-shaped relationship with maximum effect when literacy rates were neither very high nor very low. This suggests that small changes at high and low levels might not affect economic growth, but small changes at the intermediate levels characteristic of many developing countries do have an important effect.

Thus, while there is evidence relating literacy and education to economic growth, the mechanisms are not well explained. Today the contribution of education to economic efficiency lies to some extent in the very nature of the growth process, in which new technology and skilled labour complement each other. Box 5.3 illustrates the importance of literacy for technology transfer and use in the case of Viet Nam. Economies are increasingly based on knowledge and less on physical capital or natural resources, and knowledge is characterized by strong network effects. The more people with access to knowledge, the greater its likely economic benefits. Thus, the average literacy score in a given population is a better indicator of growth than the percentage of the population with very high literacy scores (Coulombe et al., 2004). In other words, a country that focuses on promoting strong literacy skills widely throughout its population will be more successful in fostering growth and well-being than one in which the gap between high-skill and low-skill groups is large.

Besides its relationship with economic growth, literacy is related to economic inequality, as Figure 5.1 illustrates for twelve countries that participated in IALS: greater disparities in literacy rates between the richest and the poorest deciles are associated with higher degrees of income inequality. This phenomenon may reflect an impact of literacy on inequality, or simply indicate that countries that are less tolerant of economic inequality also tend to have stronger literacy policies benefiting the deprived.

Returns to investment

Whether the returns to investing in adult basic education are higher or lower than those to investing in formal schooling is an important question that remains difficult to answer from

14. See, for example, Rostow (1960).

Box 5.3 Investment and literacy in Viet Nam

Low wages combined with high literacy have helped make parts of Viet Nam more attractive than others as investment destinations. An analysis of the country's regional variations in investment and in literacy rates over 1988–93 shows that the two are related. Although Viet Nam has provided basic education to a large proportion of its overall population, training and educational attainment vary among provinces or regions (for example, the South ranks lower than the North). Different parts of the country differ, therefore, in the capacity of their labour forces to participate in the modernized sectors in which foreign direct investment is involved. It appears that for foreign investors in manufacturing the top priority was good infrastructure, but that they remained very sensitive to human capital considerations: projected investment was greatest in the provinces with the highest literacy rates.

Source: Anh and Meyer (1999).

Figure 5.1: Inequality in income and inequality in literacy in OECD countries, 1994–98

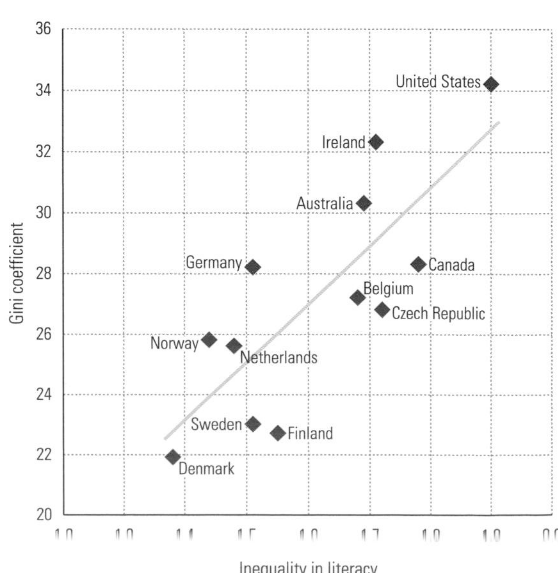

Note: The Gini coefficient is an indicator of income inequality. Inequality in literacy is measured by the ratio of the literacy rate for the ninth decile of the income distribution to the rate for the first decile.
Sources: International Adult Literacy Survey, 1994–98; OECD (1999).

the existing research. In some countries, adults spending a year in a basic education course outperform primary school children from Grades 3 and 4 in standardized tests (Oxenham and Aoki, 2002). Thus, depending on relative costs, adult basic education may well be cost-effective. Indeed, it has been suggested that the level of cognitive achievement of literacy programme trainees is the equivalent of that resulting from four years of schooling (Oxenham, 2003).

A review of four literacy projects in three countries (Bangladesh, Ghana and Senegal) conducted between 1997 and 2002 estimated that the cost per successful learner lay within a range of 13% to 33% of the cost of four years of primary education (Table 5.3). In practice, it takes more than four years to complete four years of primary school in most of these countries, so the actual schooling cost is likely higher. Interestingly, the findings are consistent with, albeit less dramatic than, those comparing the relative costs thirty years earlier during the Experimental World Literacy Programme (UNESCO/UNDP, 1976): in seven out of eight countries, literacy was cheaper per successful adult learner by significant margins, ranging from 85% to 2%; only in one country was primary school cheaper.

Table 5.3: Costs of adult literacy compared to primary school

Country	Cost per successful learner (constant 1996 US$)	Cost per successful learner as ratio of estimated cost of four years of primary education
Bangladesh	20.40	33.3
Ghana – programme 1	27.59	13.3
Ghana – programme 2	37.07	17.8
Senegal	97.78	15.0

Source: Oxenham (2003).

The relative returns to investment in primary education compared to other levels of education have been hotly contested in recent years; moreover, the returns to education may have been overestimated. Nonetheless, a recent review of the literature concludes that the effect of education on individual earnings is unambiguously positive and large, relative to returns on other investments (Harmon et al., 2003). One of the rare attempts to estimate the specific returns to adult literacy programmes covers three countries with World Bank-financed projects (Oxenham, 2003). The Ghana National Functional Literacy Program of 1999 had a private rate of return of 43% for women and 24% for men, with social rates of 18% and 14%, respectively; benefits were estimated on the basis of differentials in earnings profiles. A programme in Indonesia produced returns of around 25%, compared to 22% for primary education, though in this case the returns were estimated by measuring the rate of growth of individual income compared to the rate of growth of the cost of training. A Bangladesh programme had an average private rate of return as high as 37%. However uncertain these estimates, they suggest, first, that the investments are productive and, second, that what poor people learn from literacy programmes does help them raise their incomes and move out of poverty. Further insight comes from a study of the effects of adult literacy programme participation on household consumption in Ghana. Programme participation made no difference to households in which at least one member had already had some formal education. However, among households in which no member had any formal education, the difference was dramatic: households with a member in a literacy programme consumed 57% more than those without, controlling for all other relevant variables (Blunch and Pörtner, 2004). In Ghana generally, only the most educated household member's level of education appears to matter for income generation (Joliffe, 2002).

Adult programmes yield benefits that go beyond those that result from schooling

The sparse evidence that exists indicates, therefore, that the returns to investment in adult literacy programmes are generally comparable to, and compare favourably with, those from investments in primary education. In practice, the opportunity cost for a child to attend school is typically lower than for an adult to attend a literacy programme. Yet, the opportunity to realize the benefits is more immediate for an adult who is already in some way involved in the world of work.

Conclusion

As this chapter has shown, literacy is a right and confers distinct benefits, whether acquired through schooling or through participation in adult literacy programmes. Adult programmes appear to yield some benefits, particularly in terms of self-esteem and empowerment, that go beyond those that result just from schooling; the very scant evidence also indicates that adult programmes are as cost-effective as primary schooling, raising important questions as to why investment in adult programmes has been relatively neglected until recently.[15] ■

15. See Chapter 1 for a discussion of the relative neglect of the EFA literacy goal and certain other EFA goals.

Migrant construction workers read the newspaper during their lunch break in Beijing, China.

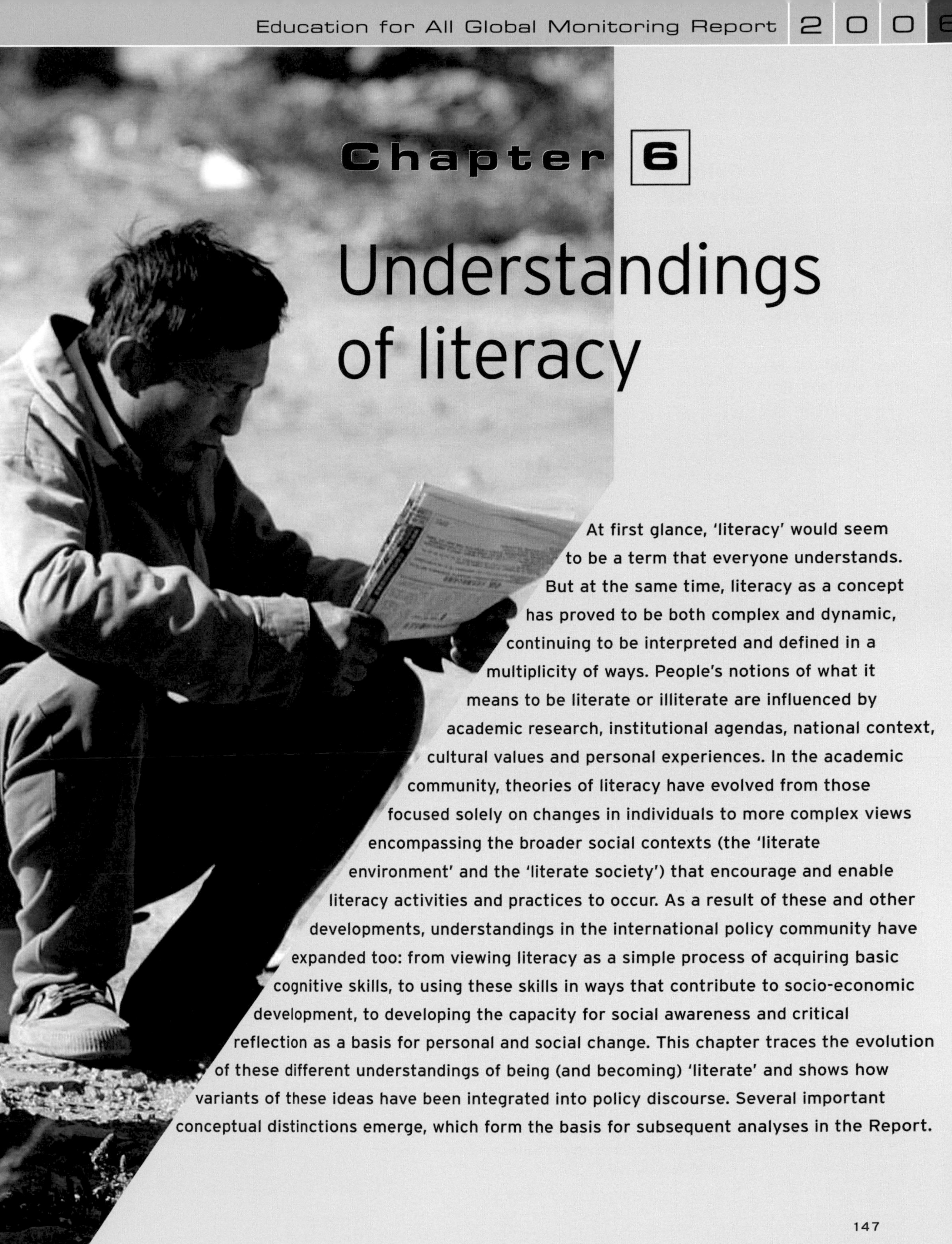

Chapter 6

Understandings of literacy

At first glance, 'literacy' would seem to be a term that everyone understands. But at the same time, literacy as a concept has proved to be both complex and dynamic, continuing to be interpreted and defined in a multiplicity of ways. People's notions of what it means to be literate or illiterate are influenced by academic research, institutional agendas, national context, cultural values and personal experiences. In the academic community, theories of literacy have evolved from those focused solely on changes in individuals to more complex views encompassing the broader social contexts (the 'literate environment' and the 'literate society') that encourage and enable literacy activities and practices to occur. As a result of these and other developments, understandings in the international policy community have expanded too: from viewing literacy as a simple process of acquiring basic cognitive skills, to using these skills in ways that contribute to socio-economic development, to developing the capacity for social awareness and critical reflection as a basis for personal and social change. This chapter traces the evolution of these different understandings of being (and becoming) 'literate' and shows how variants of these ideas have been integrated into policy discourse. Several important conceptual distinctions emerge, which form the basis for subsequent analyses in the Report.

Defining and conceptualizing literacy

The original meaning of the English word 'literacy' is different from its translations in several other languages

For most of its history in English, the word 'literate' meant to be 'familiar with literature' or, more generally, 'well educated, learned'. Only since the late nineteenth century has it also come to refer to the abilities to read and write text, while maintaining its broader meaning of being 'knowledgeable or educated in a particular field or fields'. Thus, the original meaning of the English word 'literacy' is different from its translations in several other languages (see Box 6.1, for French terms).

Since the mid-twentieth century, scholars have devoted considerable attention to defining literacy, and their work has had direct implications for approaches to practice and policy (Fransman, 2005).[1] Academics from such wide-ranging disciplines as psychology, economics, linguistics, sociology, anthropology, philosophy and history have engaged in an ongoing and, at times, highly contested debate over the meaning and definition of the term 'literacy' and how it is related to the broader notions of education and knowledge. Taking into account these evolving debates, including the major traditions, critiques and approaches to literacy, this section presents four discrete understandings of literacy:

- literacy as an autonomous set of skills;
- literacy as applied, practised and situated;
- literacy as a learning process;
- literacy as text.

These broad areas of enquiry accommodate almost all theoretical understandings of literacy.[2]

Box 6.1 French terms for 'literacy'

In French, *alphabétisme* and *analphabétisme* are the terms generally used to designate 'literacy' and 'illiteracy', while *alphabétisation* refers to 'literacy learning' and is used in France to denote the process of literacy acquisition. Until the early 1980s, France had perceived illiteracy as an issue concerning the immigrant population from North and sub-Saharan Africa. Yet, while the French used the terms *analphabétisme* (illiteracy) and *alphabétisation* (literacy learning) to refer to what they perceived as a literacy problem of immigrants, the issue was, in reality, one of poor reading and writing skills in French as a second language (which concerned second-generation immigrants and, to a lesser extent, immigrants as well as French nationals with a regional language, such as Basques, Catalans and Bretons).

In 1981, the Oheix Report on Poverty underscored the limited reading and writing skills of many French nationals. At the same time, the French charity ATD Quart Monde coined the term *illetrisme*, so that the poor French with limited reading and writing skills would not feel they were being compared to the immigrant workers labelled as *analphabètes*. Thus, the term *illettrisme* evolved to refer to those who had been through part or all of the French primary school system without gaining adequate skills. Subsequently, an interministerial body (the Groupe interministériel permanent de lutte contre l'illettrisme) was established to address this issue.

More recently, international (particularly anglophone) discourses contributed to new understandings of literacy and, in Canada, the International Adult Literacy Survey provided a new meaning for the term *alphabétisme*. Here, 'literacy' refers to broader learning and the mastery of information 'to work within the knowledge (information) societies that will dominate the twenty-first century' (OECD, 1997). In this view, literacy has a clear functional role within the context of a globalizing world.

The latest revision of the francophone concept of literacy has emerged (originally in Quebec) through the terms *littératie* and, less commonly, *littératies*. While the former derives from anglophone understandings of literacy championed by OECD (referring to competencies deemed important for 'information societies'), the latter (employed, for example, by the Centre de Recherche et de Développement en Éducation of the University of Moncton, New Brunswick) is akin to the anglophone concept of multi-literacies advanced by the New Literacy Studies movement. (See the section *Literacy as applied, practised and situated.)*

In August 2005, France adopted the term *littérisme* as referring to 'the ability to read and understand a simple text, and to use and transmit written information of everyday life'. *Littérisme*, meant to be the opposite of *illettrisme*, would thus be a close equivalent to the English concept of literacy, encompassing also numeracy.

Sources: Fernandez (2005), Limage (1986, 2005), Ministère de la culture et de la communication (2005), OECD/HRDC/Statistics Canada (1997).

1. This section relies heavily on academic research from the anglophone tradition, which has had by far the most significant influence on international policy. Other notable theoretical traditions come from the hispanophone, lusophone and sinophone countries.

2. Excluded is a postmodernist theory of literacy that views it as an instrument of power and oppression legitimating dominant discourses and endangering languages, cultures and local knowledge. This view, according to which literacy is a 'meaning-making' tool, pays attention to the ultimate vision and direction of the 'literacy project', which, it claims, aims to standardize the Western notion of education (Shikshantar, 2003).

Literacy as skills

Reading, writing and oral skills

The most common understanding of literacy is that it is a set of tangible skills – particularly the cognitive skills of reading and writing – that are independent of the context in which they are acquired and the background of the person who acquires them. Scholars continue to disagree on the best way to acquire literacy, with some advocating the 'phonetic' approach and others 'reading for meaning', resulting in what has sometimes been called the 'reading wars' (Adams, 1993; Goodman, 1996; and see discussion in Street, 2004). The emphasis on meaning has recently given way to a 'scientific' attention to phonetics, word recognition, spelling and vocabulary. This approach has lately turned to research in the cognitive sciences on important features of human memory (e.g. how the brain processes reading patterns) and to techniques such as phonological awareness training and giving increasingly faster reading tasks (Abadzi, 2003*b*, 2004).

A tendency to favour the 'scientific' principles of phonetics has given rise to claims that writing is the transcription of speech and hence 'superior' to it. Similarly, some claim the alphabetic system is technologically superior to other script forms, since it is phonetic, rather than reliant on pictures to denote meaning (Olson, 1994). Street (2004) notes that many such views are founded on deeper assumptions about the cognitive consequences of learning to read and write. The cognitive argument has been linked to broader societal development, so that literacy becomes a condition (or instrument) for economic growth, 'progress' and the transition from 'oral' to 'literate' cultures (Goody, 1977; Ong, 1982; Olson, 1977, 1994).

The transition from oral to literate modes has a fundamental impact on human consciousness. Not only does it allow for the representation of words by signs, but it gives a linear shape to thought, providing a critical framework within which to think analytically. While rational consciousness is often taken to be a given good, it derives from a classical epistemology, which may be less appropriate for societies founded on different patterns of thought and interaction. Consequently, an understanding of literacy that maintains some focus on oral skills is desirable (Box 6.2).

In the 1970s, some social psychologists argued that many of the assumptions about literacy in general were linked to school-based writing, resulting in serious limitations in accounts of literacy – particularly in the claim that it improves faculties of reasoning (Scribner and Cole, 1978; Olson, 1977).

Box 6.2 Oral expression

Earlier notions of a 'great divide' between oral and literate societies have given way to the concept of a 'continuum' of communication modes in different societies and an ongoing dynamic interaction between various media (Finnegan, 1988). Within a single society, a variety of modes of 'orality' and 'literacy' exist. Even the practices of individuals in their use of these modes may vary from situation to situation.

Taking into account oral competencies as well as reading and writing skills has important consequences for securing benefits from literacy programmes. For example, since efforts to empower women and girls involve developing their oral expression skills (i.e. confidence in speaking), these should build upon the oral knowledge that they already possess (Robinson, 2003). In terms of numeracy, most adult learners already know oral counting and some mathematical structures, and have an art of mental arithmetic more or less adequate for their daily life; in fact, many 'illiterate' adults (especially those involved in trade) are better at mental arithmetic than are more 'educated' people (Archer and Cottingham, 1996*a*). These skills should be taken into account and built upon.

Maintaining and developing oral skills can be a means of language preservation, since many languages do not have (or are less compatible with) equivalent textual scripts and thus run the risk of extinction as younger generations adapt to written languages employed in schools.

Numeracy skills

Numeracy – and the competencies it comprises – is usually understood either as a supplement to the set of skills encompassed by 'literacy' or as a component of literacy itself. A recent research review notes that the English term 'numeracy' was first coined in 1959 (in the Crowther report submitted to the United Kingdom's Ministry of Education), as the 'mirror image of literacy', to refer to a relatively sophisticated level of what we now call 'scientific literacy' (Coben et al., 2003).

Numeracy is most often assumed to depend upon a solid mathematical education and innumeracy to be the result of poor schooling. This 'limited proficiency' conception of numeracy, which emphasizes equipping the workforce with minimum skills, continues to dominate and has been adopted by many national and international assessment agencies (Coben et al., 2003).

The most common understanding of literacy is that it is a set of tangible skills – particularly the cognitive skills of reading and writing

Scholars have suggested that a useful concept would be that of multiple literacies

Challengers to this view note that the competence-based agenda for adult mathematics/numeracy education is dangerously limited (FitzSimons, 2002, cited in Coben et al., 2003). They distinguish between concepts of numeracy with narrowly defined learning outcomes, which they characterize as approaching numeracy from a human resources perspective, and approaches that would allow for the development of critical citizenship (Johnston et al., 2002, cited in Coben et al., 2003).

More recently, 'numeracy' has been used to refer to the ability to process, interpret and communicate numerical, quantitative, spatial, statistical and even mathematical information in ways that are appropriate for a variety of contexts (Box 6.3). The term increasingly refers to a competence allowing more effective participation in relevant social activities (Evans, 2000).

Skills enabling access to knowledge and information

The word 'literacy' has begun to be used in a much broader, metaphorical sense, to refer to other skills and competencies, for example 'information literacy', 'visual literacy', 'media literacy' and 'scientific literacy'. International organizations – notably the OECD through publications such as *Literacy in the Information Age* (2000) and *Literacy Skills for the Knowledge Society* (1997) – have given impetus to the use of such terms, eventually giving rise to a new French term, *littératie* (Fernandez, 2005). The meaning of these concepts tends to be diverse and shifting, ranging from the view of literacy as a set of largely technical skills (the OECD perspective) to the idea that these skills should be applied in critical ways to examine one's surroundings (e.g. the workplace and the media) and push for social change (Hull, 2003). For instance, 'information literacy' broadly refers to the ability to access and use a variety of information sources to solve an information need. Yet, it can also be defined as the development of a complex set of *critical* skills that allow people to express, explore, question, communicate and understand the flow of ideas among individuals and groups in quickly changing technological environments.

Some scholars have suggested that a more useful concept would be that of multiple literacies – that is, ways of 'reading the world' in specific contexts: technological, health, information, media, visual, scientific, and so on (see Street, 2003; Lankshear and Knobel, 2003; Cope and Kalantzis, 2000). This concept has recently been adopted in the francophone world (most prominently, in Quebec) through the term *littératies* and has been used to understand the multiple forms of literacy among minority communities with shifting cultural identities (see the work cited in Fernandez, 2005).

Yet the notion of multiple literacies is not without controversy. By attracting a long list of modifiers, 'literacy' has become a debased term, its core reference to reading skills undermined (Jones, 1997; Hull, 2003). Some respond to this critique by emphasizing that *reading*, in the broadest sense of the word, remains integral to the notion of literacy. Thus, reading may mean not only the decoding and understanding of

Box 6.3 Numeracy situations

A recent approach to the issue of numeracy describes three different types of 'numeracy situations' (Gal, 2000):

- *Generative situations* require people to count, quantify, compute and otherwise manipulate numbers, quantities, items or visual elements – all of which involve language skills to varying degrees.
- *Interpretive situations* require people to make sense of verbal or text-based messages that, while based on quantitative data, require no manipulation of numbers.
- *Decision situations* 'demand that people find and consider multiple pieces of information in order to determine a course of action, typically in the presence of conflicting goals, constraints or uncertainty'.

Teaching adults numeracy means enabling them 'to manage effectively multiple types of numeracy situations'. As such, numeracy should be seen as a semi-autonomous area at the intersection between literacy and mathematics and address not only purely cognitive issues, but also students' dispositions and cognitive styles.

Sources: Gal (2000), Coben et al. (2003).

words, but also the interpreting of signs, symbols, pictures and sounds, which vary by social context (Cope and Kalantzis, 2000). In short, different everyday contexts present different literacy demands, perceptions of literacy, and types of power relations and hierarchies of knowledge (Barton et al., 1999; Street, 2003).

Literacy as applied, practised and situated

Acknowledging the limitations of a skills-based approach to literacy, some scholars have tried to focus on the *application* of these skills in 'relevant' ways. One of the first coordinated efforts to do so was through the development of the notion of 'functional literacy'. In the 1960s and 1970s, this concept initially emphasized the impact of literacy on socio-economic development.[3] Views of functional literacy often assumed literacy could be taught as a universal set of skills (applicable everywhere) and that there was only one literacy, which everyone should learn in the same way. Literacy was seen as neutral and independent of social context.

This understanding evolved as scholars argued that the ways in which literacy is *practised* vary by social and cultural context (Barton, 1994). Ethnographic research into literacy practices in particular settings was particularly instrumental in the development of this approach, typically known as 'New Literacy Studies' (NLS) (Gee, 1999; Barton and Hamilton, 1999; Collins, 1995; Heath, 1993; Street, 1998). Rather than see literacy as a technical skill independent of context, the NLS approach argues it is a social practice, embedded in social settings and, further, that even a presumably 'objective' skill such as numeracy can be socially situated (Box 6.4).

Among key concepts in this view of literacy are *literacy events* ('any occasion in which a piece of writing is integral to the nature of the participants' interactions and their interpretative processes') and *literacy practices* ('the social practices and conceptions of reading and writing') (Street, 1984). The *literacy as applied, practised and situated* approach questions the validity of designations of individuals as 'literate' or 'illiterate', as many who are labelled illiterate are found to make significant use of literacy practices for specific purposes in their everyday lives (Doronilla, 1996).

Yet, this approach has been criticized by some scholars, who claim it overemphasizes local exigencies and insufficiently recognizes how external forces (e.g. colonial administrations, missionaries, international communication and economic globalization) have impinged upon the 'local' experiences of specific communities (Brandt and Clinton, 2002; Collins and Blot, 2003). Maddox (2001) and Stromquist (2004) question the reluctance of advocates of this approach to examine the potential of literacy to help people move out of 'local' positions into fuller economic, social and political participation.

Box 6.4 Ethnomathematics

The term 'ethnomathematics' encompasses both 'the mathematics which is practised among identifiable cultural groups' (Coben et al., 2003) and educational approaches geared to engagement with these forms of mathematics. It is a field of anthropological, political and educational research and a practice championed since the mid-1970s by Brazilian educationalist Ubiratan D'Ambrosio and since developed by Paulus Gerdes, Gelsa Knijnik and others. Although mathematics is sometimes claimed to be a universal language, much of mathematics education depends on Western assumptions and values. The development of ethnomathematics as an active area of research and practice has encouraged a growing recognition that mathematics may, like literacy, be embedded in a range of practices. Studies on folk mathematics, for example, have examined the methods by which members of various indigenous groups acquire numeracy skills. For instance, despite being officialy illiterate, adults in rural Tamil Nadu acquire sophisticated numeracy skills, including the ability to calculate time and seasonal changes on the basis of the length of the sun's shadow; likewise, village women must know how to count in order to make sophisticated geometrical patterns in the rice-paste designs known as *kolums*.

Sources: Coben et al. (2003), Dighe (2004).

Literacy as a learning process

Literacy can be viewed as an active and broad-based learning process

As individuals learn, they become literate. This idea is at the core of a third approach, which views literacy as an active and broad-based learning process, rather than as a product of a more limited and focused educational intervention. Building on the scholarship of Dewey and Piaget, constructivist educators focus on ways in which individual learners, especially children, make sense of their learning experiences. In the field of adult education, some scholars see personal experience as a central resource for learning. Experience is one of Knowles's (1980) five principles of 'andragogy', or adult learning theory, in which he argues for

3. Subsequently, the term has evolved considerably to acknowledge other dimensions (e.g. personal, cultural and political).

Central to Paulo Freire's pedagogy is the notion of 'critical literacy'

a learner-centred educational process, with critical reflection as central. Kolb (1984) developed an experiential learning cycle, with 'concrete experience' as the starting point for learning, based on critical reflection.

More recently, social psychologists and anthropologists have used terms such as 'collaborative learning', 'distributed learning' and 'communities of practice' to shift the focus away from the individual mind and towards more social practices building on newer understandings of literacy (Rogoff and Lave, 1984; Lave, 1988; Rogoff, 2003; Lave and Wenger, 1991). For example, Rogers (2003) distinguishes between 'task-conscious' learning, typically evaluated by test-based task completion, and 'learning-conscious learning', which is assessed from the perspective of the learner. The more traditional learning methods of children ('task-conscious' test learning) are often used for adults, as is evident in many adult literacy programmes.

Paulo Freire is perhaps the most famous adult literacy educator whose work integrated notions of active learning within socio-cultural settings (Box 6.5). Freire emphasized the importance of bringing the learner's socio-cultural realities into the learning process itself and then using the learning process to challenge these social processes. Central to his pedagogy is the notion of 'critical literacy', a goal to be attained in part through engaging with books and other written texts, but, more profoundly, through 'reading' (i.e. interpreting, reflecting on, interrogating, theorizing, investigating, exploring, probing and questioning) and 'writing' (acting on and dialogically transforming) the social world.

Freire's ideas have been used as pedagogical tools to support learners who have been oppressed, excluded or disadvantaged, due to gender, ethnicity or socio-economic status. In francophone Africa, scholars such as Joseph Ki-Zerbo from Burkina Faso have documented mobilization for an 'Africanized' literacy that would directly respond to the pressing communication needs of the continent. This movement has motivated the introduction of Freirean methodologies by several NGOs (Fernandez, 2005).

Box 6.5 Paulo Freire: reading the world

Every reading of the word is preceded by a reading of the world. Starting from the reading of the world that the reader brings to literacy programs (a social- and class-determined reading), the reading of the word sends the reader back to the previous reading of the world, which is, in fact, a rereading.

Paulo Freire, *Pedagogy of the City* (1993, translated by D. Macedo)

According to Paulo Freire, dialogue provides the link between oral and literate forms of interpreting, understanding and transforming the world. It is not a matter of speaking first, then developing reading skills and then learning to write. Rather, speaking, reading and writing are interconnected parts of an active learning process and of social transformation. The words that people use in order to give meaning to their lives are fashioned, created and conditioned by the world which they inhabit.

Sources: Freire (1995), Gadotti (1994).

Literacy as text

A fourth way of understanding literacy is to look at it in terms of the 'subject matter' (Bhola, 1994) and the nature of the texts that are produced and consumed by literate individuals. Texts vary by subject and genre (e.g. textbooks, technical/professional publications and fiction), by complexity of the language used and by ideological content (explicit or hidden).[4]

This approach pays particular attention to the analysis of discrete passages of text, referred to by socio-linguists as 'discourse'. Influenced by broader social theories (e.g. those of Michel Foucault), it locates literacy within wider communicative and socio-political practices that construct, legitimate and reproduce existing power structures (see Gee, 1990; Fairclough, 1991)[5]. Language represents one of several modes through which communication is conducted (Kress and van Leeuwen, 2001). The broader policy question raised by this work is whether the types of literacy taught in schools and adult programmes are relevant to the present and future lives of learners (Gee et al., 1996).[6]
In summary, these four approaches broadly reflect the evolution of the meaning of 'literacy' in different disciplinary traditions. While international policy has not evolved in direct response to these views, there has been a mutual influence between evolving theories and policy-oriented approaches to literacy, as the following section shows.

4. Certain recent linguistic analyses have adopted the view that language is constructed historically, is constructed again when the learner learns it, and is reconstructed whenever someone uses it (Barton, 1994). Since the reader is also constructed (as there are limited subject positions for a reader), texts have the power to legitimate and reproduce social inequalities, such as gender relations.

5. See [Box 9.3], on the hidden curriculum.

6. Critical approaches to literacy such as these maintain that the movement to universalize literacy may have negative implications: for example, it can unwittingly label and rank people, it may reduce cultural diversity, and it may confine motivation for learning to exams, certificates and getting a job (Shikshantar, 2003).

Understandings of literacy in the international community

Since the 1950s, international organizations have promoted policy discussions and decisions that have incorporated, in various ways, the conceptual understandings of literacy explored above. UNESCO in particular has played a leading role in developing international policies on literacy and has influenced the changing policy discourse among stakeholders in the international community. A key issue for the international community during this period has been the question of what emphasis and funding priority literacy-enhancing programmes and campaigns should be given in international policy agendas. Even when literacy became the focal point of international conferences, there was often a gap between the rhetoric of literacy-related policy statements and the realities of the investment in, and the implementation and evaluation of, literacy programmes. The discussion below pays particular attention to understandings of literacy as articulated in official policy discussions in international organizations. The practical application of these understandings is explored in Chapter 9.

The 'eradication of illiteracy' (1950s–1960s)

Following the Second World War, UNESCO supported the international drive to spread literacy as part of its concerted effort to promote basic education.[7] In 1947, UNESCO recognized a wide range of skills, including the acquisition of literacy, as fundamental aspects of individual development and human rights (UNESCO, 1947). UNESCO supported the idea of a 'fundamental education', centred mainly upon the skills of reading and writing, and which was reflected in UNESCO's (1958) statement that 'a literate person is one who can, with understanding, both read and write a short simple statement on his or her everyday life.' The onset of the Cold War and the resulting political tensions weakened interest in a worldwide campaign for universal literacy.[8] Nevertheless, the international community agreed on the need to 'eradicate illiteracy' and promote ways to help individuals acquire a basic set of autonomous literacy skills (Jones, 1990*b*; Chabbott, 2003; UNESCO, 2004*b*).

An important development in the international effort to promote universal literacy emerged during the Second International Conference on Adult Education in Montreal, Canada, in 1960. Participants in this conference advocated the organization of a major international campaign to 'eradicate illiteracy in just a few years' that would bolster isolated national efforts in developing countries, with the financial support of industrialized countries. In addition, the Convention and the Recommendation against Discrimination in Education, adopted by UNESCO's General Conference in 1960, sought 'to encourage and intensify by appropriate methods the education of persons who have not received any primary education' (Yousif, 2003). Despite these decisions and recommendations, actions on the ground were limited, with the exception of isolated national campaigns (e.g. in Cuba in 1961).

Efforts to promote universal literacy started in the 1950s

Functional literacy and the Experimental World Literacy Programme (1960s–1970s)

Most international organizations abandoned their support for mass literacy campaigns in the 1960s and 1970s and embraced human capital models of education. Increasingly, literacy came to be viewed as a necessary condition for economic growth and national development. For example, the World Congress of Ministers of Education on the Eradication of Illiteracy (held in Tehran, 1965) stressed for the first time the interrelationship between literacy and development, and highlighted the concept of functional literacy: 'Rather than an end in itself, literacy should be regarded as a way of preparing man for a social, civic and economic role that goes beyond the limits of rudimentary literacy training consisting merely in the teaching of reading and writing' (cited in Yousif, 2003).[9]

The notion of functional literacy became a linchpin of UNESCO's Experimental World Literacy Programme (EWLP), initiated at the General Conference in 1966, implemented in eleven countries and discontinued in 1973.[10] The EWLP, funded by the United Nations Development Programme (UNDP) and other agencies, aimed to provide literacy acquisition via experimentation and work-oriented learning. In parallel, the UNDP took a leading role in financing technical assistance that incorporated ideas of functional literacy (Jones, 1990*b*).

Although initially focused on enhanced efficiency and productivity, the concept of functional literacy was later expanded in light of EWLP experiences to include a broader array of human concerns and aspirations:

7. The post-war period was also characterized by national movements for liberation from colonial rule. One of the first countries engaged in the struggle for independence was India, where literacy and basic education formed the core of a vast programme for community development under Gandhi (Yousif, 2003).

8. Smyth suggests that the representatives of Western countries in UNESCO's governing bodies and influential members of the World Bank associated mass literacy campaigns with the culture and policies of Eastern Bloc countries. As such the decision to limit the funding of a major international campaign to 'eradicate illiteracy' stemmed, in part, from the perception that the political content of mass literacy campaigns would help spread Communism (personal communication, see also Smyth 2005).

9. Throughout this chapter the lack of gender neutrality reflects usage in historical international agreements and declarations.

10. Four projects were implemented in 1967 (in Algeria, Ecuador, the Islamic Republic of Iran and Mali), five in 1968 (Ethiopia, Guinea, Madagascar, the United Republic of Tanzania and Venezuela) and two in 1971 (India and the Syrian Arab Republic). The EWLP paid particular attention to organization, methodology, financing, international cooperation and monitoring and evaluation (Yousif, 2003); unfortunately, overall, it was commonly regarded as a failure.

> It is with reference to the whole range of people's functions, whether as citizens, as producers, as private householders in their families, villages or home neighbourhoods, or as individuals seeking answers to the questions they ask themselves about the physical, social, moral and intellectual world in which they live, that the role of literacy training is to be perceived and manifests itself. It is from this standpoint that functional literacy is seen to be identical with lifelong education, insofar as the latter concept also encompasses everything which enters into life (UNESCO/UNDP, 1976, cited in Yousif, 2003).

International agencies' interest in literacy programmes declined during the 1980s and the early 1990s

In 1978, UNESCO's General Conference adopted a definition of functional literacy – still in use today – which states: 'A person is functionally literate who can engage in all those activities in which literacy is required for effective functioning of his group and community and also for enabling him to continue to use reading, writing and calculation for his own and the community's development.'

Paulo Freire and literacy as transformative (1970s)

During the 1970s, Paulo Freire's theory of 'conscientization' – which stated, among other things, that social awareness and critical enquiry are key factors in social change – gained popularity in developing countries. It also heavily influenced evolving conceptions of literacy in UNESCO and other international organizations. In 1975, during an International Symposium for Literacy held in Persepolis (Iran), Freire was awarded the Mohamed Reza Pahlavi Prize for literacy by UNESCO. The Persepolis Declaration reflected this influence and posited that literacy must go beyond the process of learning the skills of reading, writing and arithmetic, and contribute to the 'liberation of man' and to his full development:

> Thus conceived, literacy creates the conditions for the acquisition of a critical consciousness of the contradictions of society in which man lives and of its aims; it also stimulates initiative and his participation in the creation of projects capable of acting upon the world, of transforming it, and of defining the aims of an authentic human development. It should open the way to a mastery of techniques and human relations. Literacy is not an end in itself. It is a fundamental human right (Bataille, 1976).

International recognition of Freire's approach to literacy was considerable during this period.

Reduced investment and the impact of Jomtien (1980s–1990s)

International agencies' interest in, and funding of, literacy programmes declined during the 1980s and the early 1990s. The World Bank in particular began to focus heavily on primary schooling to the relative neglect of adult education. With increased pressure on national budgets, investments in non-formal education and adult literacy programmes decreased, whereas those for primary education programmes increased (Torres, 2004). UNICEF and UNESCO established a working group on the Universalization of Primary Education and Literacy in 1982, which gave rise to annual consultation meetings involving international NGOs and, eventually, a new focus on literacy and education for all (Chabbott, 2003).

During the late 1980s, definitions of literacy broadened to accommodate the demands of globalization, including the significance of new technologies and other information media. The Toronto Seminar on Literacy in Industrialized Countries, held in 1987, declared: 'Literacy is more than the ability to read, write and compute. The demands created by advancing technology require increased levels of knowledge, skills and understanding to achieve basic literacy' (cited in Yousif, 2003).

Important conceptual clarifications were made during this period, in conjunction with the International Literacy Year (1990) and the World Declaration on Education for All adopted in Jomtien, Thailand (1990). For example, UNESCO distinguished between literacy as a skill and literacy as a set of culturally and socially determined practices, and later endorsed efforts to promote the acquisition of literacy – newly conceived as 'basic learning needs' – on a continuum including formal and non-formal education, extended to people of all ages (UNESCO, 2004*b*). Indeed, the value of lifelong learning gained momentum when the 1996 Report of the International Commission on Education for the Twenty-first Century and the 1997 Hamburg Declaration endorsed literacy as essential for lifelong learning and as a catalyst for active community engagement (UNESCO, 1997, 2004*b*). However, there is little evidence that these clarifications and endorsements had an impact on the ground (Yousif, 2003). As the final report of the Mid-Decade Forum on Education for All (Amman, Jordan, 1996) stated: 'While there has been progress in primary school enrolments, the unschooled and illiterate youths and adults are still forgotten.' International attention remained focused on primary education and even UNESCO was unable to maintain its pre-Jomtien level of support for literacy (Yousif, 2003).

Dakar to the present

Since 2000, international involvement in literacy has revolved around the six Dakar goals and the Millennium Development Goals (MDGs) (see Chapter 1). The International Monetary Fund, the OECD, the World Bank and the United Nations have all committed themselves to work toward the realization of the MDGs, and thus, to achieve universal primary education, to promote gender equality and to empower women at all levels of education. Following the adoption of the Dakar Framework for Action, literacy-related discussions among international planners and stakeholders have been characterized by a focus on improving literacy levels and on new understandings of literacy (UNESCO, 2003*d*). Many international organizations and NGOs have recognized the problems that illiteracy poses and are seeking to improve access to literacy (ILO, 2004; OECD, 2004; UNESCO, 2004*b*; UNICEF, 2005*a*; World Bank, 2003; UNDP, 2004). Perhaps the strongest assertion of renewed commitment to literacy has been the declaration of the United Nations Literacy Decade (Box 6.6). While advocacy and activity have increased in the international arena, literacy efforts (as well as definitions and measures of literacy, and beneficiaries) vary across organizations. Factors such as language, gender, HIV/AIDS, and emergency and conflict situations complicate and intensify the need for understanding, promoting and securing literacy for all. They also reflect the difficulty of formulating a unified international policy approach to literacy.

International conceptions of literacy have evolved since the mid-twentieth century, often reflecting dominant strands of (largely anglophone) academic research. The international policy community, led by UNESCO, has moved from interpretations of literacy and illiteracy as autonomous skills to an emphasis on literacy as functional, incorporating Freirean principles, and, more recently, embracing the notions of multiple literacies, literacy as a continuum, and literate environments and societies. Regional networks have emphasized understandings of literacy that more closely resonate with national policy priorities. The next section briefly looks at understandings of literacy of other actors in the international policy community, including national governments, aid agencies and members of civil society.

Box 6.6 UNESCO and literacy today

In 2002, the United Nations declared 2003–2012 the United Nations Literacy Decade.* Resolution 56/116 acknowledged the place of literacy at the heart of lifelong learning, affirming that: 'literacy is crucial to the acquisition, by every child, youth and adult, of essential life skills that enable them to address the challenges they can face in life, and represents an essential step in basic education, which is an indispensable means for effective participation in the societies and economies of the twenty-first century' (United Nations, 2002*b*).

The Resolution also embraced the social dimension of literacy, recognizing that 'creating literate environments and societies is essential for achieving the goals of eradicating poverty, reducing child mortality, curbing population growth, achieving gender equality and ensuring sustainable development, peace and democracy.' UNESCO emphasizes the goal of universal literacy under the motto 'Literacy as Freedom,' reflecting the evolution of the conception of literacy:

> beyond its simple notion as the set of technical skills of reading, writing and calculating . . . to a plural notion encompassing the manifold meanings and dimensions of these undeniably vital competencies. Such a view, responding to recent economic, political and social transformations, including globalization, and the advancement of information and communication technologies, recognizes that there are many practices of literacy embedded in different cultural processes, personal circumstances and collective structures (UNESCO, 2004*b*).

The United Nations Literacy Decade aims to achieve the following four outcomes by 2012:

- making significant progress towards Dakar Goals 3, 4 and 5;
- enabling all learners to attain a mastery level in literacy and life skills;
- creating sustainable and expandable literate environments; and
- improving the quality of life.

While calling for an understanding of literacy based on its 'pluralities', UNESCO nonetheless excludes such skills as 'computer literacy', 'media literacy', 'health literacy', 'eco-literacy' and 'emotional literacy' from this definition (UNESCO, 2004*b*).

* For the Resolution as adopted by the General Assembly on the report of the Third Committee [A/56/572], see: http://portal.unesco.org/education/en/ev.php-URL_ID=11559&URL_DO=DO_PRINTPAGE&URL_SECTION=201.html

The declaration of the United Nations Literacy Decade is a strong assertion of renewed commitment to literacy

Box 6.7 The promotion of literacy in regional associations

The new Pan African Association for Literacy and Adult Education, supported by UNESCO and the International council for Adult Education, specifically addresses the Dakar literacy goal. In 1993, the Arab League Educational, Cultural and Scientific Organization stated its aim to liberate the region from 'alphabetical and cultural illiteracy'; current priorities include an array of issues, ranging from training for primary school teachers to contemporary views of functional literacy. In Asia and the Pacific, UNESCO's Regional Bureau for Education and its cultural centre have become involved in non-formal education, and materials production for literacy teaching, neo-literates and literacy personnel.

The Regional Cooperation Center for Adult Education in Latin America and the Caribbean was created in 1951. Beginning in 1979, the Major Project in the Field of Education in Latin America and the Caribbean sought to increase access to basic education and adult literacy programmes throughout the 1980s and, in the 1990s, to increase quality and equity of opportunity (UNESCO/OREALC, 2001). While illiteracy rates declined in the region, a continued problem of inequity necessitated the design of the new Regional Education Project for Latin America and the Caribbean 2002–2017, addressing youth and adult education.

Source: Torres (2004).

Other views of literacy

Regional and national definitions

Besides major global institutional initiatives to promote literacy, programmes also took shape regionally, generally in line with the understandings of literacy adopted by UNESCO (Box 6.7).

Country-level understandings of literacy also tend to echo the conceptual themes summarized above, particularly over the past decade, though there remain some interesting variations (Box 6.8).

Based upon data compiled by the UNESCO Institute for Statistics, Table 6.1 shows national definitions of literacy drawn from various

Box 6.8 Some national understandings of literacy

Brazil

- The Brazilian Geographical and Statistics Institute defines as 'functionally literate' those individuals who have completed four grades of schooling, and as 'functionally illiterate' those who have not. NGOs and education advocacy groups have lobbied authorities to redefine functional literacy based on eight years of schooling, the amount currently guaranteed to all citizens by the Constitution.

India

- The national census defines a 'literate' person as one having the ability to read and write in any language.

Israel

- Literacy is defined as the ability to 'acquire the essential knowledge and skills that enable [individuals] to actively participate in all the activities for which reading and writing are needed'.
- The Ministry of Education uses the local terms *oryanut* (reading comprehension, writing and other language skills) and *boryanut* (someone lacking education or knowledge, or who has learned nothing, or who cannot read nor write – analphabetic) in official directives and documents.

Kenya

- The 1994 Central Bureau of Statistics survey defined as 'literate' those persons aged 15 and over who responded that they could read and write.
- The 1999 national census gathered data on education, from which literacy information was inferred; four years of primary education were regarded as necessary for sustainable literacy development.

Nepal

- Literacy is traditionally defined as 'the three Rs' (reading, writing and arithmetic) plus functionality.
- Literacy is defined by the Basic Primary Education Programme as: basic literacy, updating skills and continuing education.
- Literacy must be in Nepali, although the Non-Formal Education Council, the policy-making body for literacy education, recognizes literacy in one's mother tongue.

Sources: Masagão Ribeiro and Gomes Batista (2005), Brosh-Vaitz (2005), Bunyi (2005), Govinda and Biswal (2005*b*), Koirala and Aryal (2005).

Table 6.1: National definitions of literacy/illiteracy

'Ability to *read* easily or with difficulty a letter or a newspaper'	
	Angola, Bosnia and Herzegovina, Burundi, the Central African Republic, Chad, Côte d'Ivoire, the Democratic Republic of the Congo, Equatorial Guinea, Kenya, Madagascar, Myanmar, the Republic of Moldova, Rwanda, Sierra Leone, Sudan, Suriname, Swaziland, Togo, Zambia
Ability to *read and write* simple sentences	
Language criteria	• No mention of language: Algeria, Bahrain (illiterate: 'persons who cannot read or write, as well as persons who can read only, for example a person who studied the Koran'), Belarus, Bulgaria, Macao (China), Colombia, Cuba, Cyprus, Dominican Republic, Ecuador, Egypt, Honduras, Lesotho, Malta, Mauritius, Mexico, Nicaragua, the Russian Federation, Tajikistan • Ability to read and write simple sentences *in specified languages:* Argentina, Azerbaijan ('literacy is acceptable in any language having written form'), Cameroon (in French or English, for those aged 15 and above), Lao PDR, Malawi, Mauritania ('in the language specified'), Niger, Sri Lanka (in Sinhalese, Tamil and English), the Syrian Arab Republic (in Arabic), Turkey (for Turkish citizens: in current Turkish alphabet; for non-citizens: in native language) • Ability to read and write *in any language:* Benin, Brazil, Brunei Darussalam, Burkina Faso, Cambodia, Croatia, Iran (Islamic Republic of) ('in Farsi or any other language'), Maldives (in 'Dhivehi, English, Arabic, etc.'), Mongolia, Pakistan, Palestinian Autonomous Territories, Papua New Guinea, Philippines, Saudi Arabia (with allowance for blind reading by Braille), Senegal, Tonga, United Republic of Tanzania, Viet Nam
Age criteria	Thailand (over 5); Armenia, Guatemala, India and Turkmenistan (over 7); El Salvador (over 10); Seychelles (over 12); Bolivia and Jordan (over 15)
School attainment (by increasing levels of attainment)	
Estonia	"No primary education, illiterate" was recorded for a person who had not completed the level corresponding to primary education and cannot, with understanding, both read and write a simple text on his/her everyday life at least in one language.
Lithuania	Literate (no formal schooling) is a person who does not attend school but can read (with understanding) and/or write a simple sentence on topics of everyday life.
Mali	Illiterate is a person who never attend school even if that person can read and write.
Ukraine	[Literate] 'Those who have a definite level of education. For people who do not have education – reading or writing ability in any language or only reading ability'.
School attainment (by increasing levels of attainment)	
Slovakia	[Illiterate] 'Data on the number of persons who do not have formal education'.
Malaysia	[Literate] 'Population 10 years and above who have been to school in any language'.
Hungary	'Persons not having completed the first grade of general (primary, elementary) school have been considered as illiterate.'
Paraguay	'Illiterates are defined as people aged 15+ who have not attained Grade 2.'
TFYR of Macedonia	'Persons having completed more than three grades of primary school were considered literate. In addition, literate was a person without school qualification and with 1–3 grades of primary school, if he/she can read and write a composition (text) in relation to everyday life, i.e. read and write a letter, regardless of the language'.
Israel	[Literate] 'Population at least having primary school'.
Greece	'As illiterate are considered those who have never been in school (organic illiterate) as well as those who have not finished the six years of primary education (functional illiterate).'
Saint Lucia	Data submitted were based on 7 years of schooling.
Belize	'Illiterate: Persons who are 14+ years of age and have completed at most seven or eight years of primary education.'
Romania	'Literates: primary level + secondary level + post-secondary level and people who read and write. Illiterates: people who read but cannot write and people who can neither read nor write.'
Other definitions	
China	'In urban areas: literate refers to a person who knows a minimum of 2,000 characters. In rural areas: literate refers to a person who knows a minimum of 1,500 characters.'
Namibia	'[Literacy:] The ability to write with understanding in any language. Persons who could read and not write were classified as non-literate. Similarly, persons who were able to write and not read were classified as non-literate.'
Singapore	Literacy refers to a person's ability to read with understanding, eg a newspaper, in the language specified.
Tunisia	Literate is a person who know how to read and write at least one language.

Note: For source of country definitions of literacy, see introduction to the statistical annex.

assessment instruments, including household surveys and population censuses, administered in 107 different countries from 1995 to 2004. In most cases, national data come from indirect assessments based on self-declarations, household surveys, or educational attainment proxies.[11] About 80% of the listed countries define literacy as the ability to read and/or write simple statements in either a national or native language.[12]

Aid agencies

In general, bilateral aid agencies' definitions of literacy have remained relatively consistent with UNESCO's evolving understanding of literacy (see Table 6.2); although, because of their objectives, their definitions are often narrower and more 'pragmatic'. For the industrialized world, there is a greater emphasis on the type of literacy skills relevant for the global economy. For example, in 1997, the OECD report *Literacy Skills for the Knowledge Society* defined literacy as: 'A particular skill, namely the ability to understand and employ printed information in daily activities at home, at work and in the community, to achieve one's goals, and to develop one's knowledge and potential.' In referring to a broad

11. See Chapter 7 for an in-depth discussion of measuring literacy.

12. Note that Table 6.1 shows a second set of literacy definitions for three of the five countries listed in Box 6.8 – Brazil, India and Israel. These overlapping and possibly contradictory definitions provide an indication of the variety of understandings and ways of measuring literacy and of the difficulty of making even subnational comparisons of literacy, much less cross-national ones.

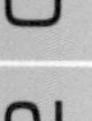
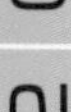
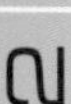

Table 6.2: Aid agencies' definitions of literacy

Organization	Definition of literacy
UNICEF	*Functional literacy* is the ability to use **reading, writing and numeracy** skills for **effective functioning and development** of the individual and the community. Literacy is according to the UNESCO definition ('A person is literate who can, with understanding, both read and write a short statement on his or her everyday life.').
Department for International Development (UK); United States Agency for International Development; World Bank	*Literacy* is a **basic set of skills** (reading, writing and counting) or **competencies**.
Canadian International Development Agency; Danish International Development Assistance; New Zealand's International Aid and Development Agency	*Literacy* is one of the skills that basic education should provide or a **component of basic education**.
BMZ (German Federal Ministry for Economic Cooperation and Development); the Netherlands	*Literacy* is reading and writing skills, and it indicates the **capacity for further learning**.
Swedish International Development Cooperation Agency	*Literacy* is about **learning to read and write** (text and numbers) and also about **reading, writing and counting to learn**, and developing these skills and using them effectively for **meeting basic needs**.

Source: EFA Global Monitoring Report Team.

set of information-processing competencies, this definition points to the multiplicity of skills that constitute literacy in advanced industrialized countries.

The vast majority of NGOs that prioritize educational issues neglect adult education and literacy

Civil society

Few international NGOs have adopted understandings of literacy that differ radically from those discussed above. In fact, the vast majority of NGOs that prioritize educational issues tend to neglect adult education and literacy. Oxfam, for instance, has framed its education policy within the MDGs and, as a result, focuses on gender equality and the financing of primary education, with little attention given to youth or adult literacy. Among the few NGOs that emphasize adult literacy, the majority focus on reading and writing skills, fewer on functional literacy and a minority on 'transformative' interpretations (Box 6.9).

Box 6.9 Different understandings of literacy among NGOs

Plan Philippines focuses in part on the alternative learning system of the Basic Literacy Program, seeking to provide both children and adults with 'basic literacy skills in reading and numeracy'. Their core programmes concentrate on two areas – basic learning and life skills – so learners can reach their full potential and contribute to the development of their societies.

World Vision offers literacy programmes using a broad approach to education that encourages support for out-of-school youth and vulnerable adults. The programmes focus on vocational and livelihood education and target children in crisis, as well as youth, women and adults.

ActionAid's Reflect (Regenerated Freirean Literacy through Empowering Community Techniques) programme has had considerable influence on the literacy policies and practices of NGOs around the world. In its discussion of 'New concepts of literacy: the ideological approach', the 1996 edition of Reflect's manual states:

> Literacy is no longer seen as a simple skill or competency but as a process. It is more than just the technology by which we presently know it (whether pen, paper, computer, etc.) ... Freire provides a social, political and economic analysis of the processes which affect people's knowledge and beliefs (forming their 'consciousness' of their situation). For Freire no educational or developmental process can be neutral' (Archer and Cottingham, 1996*a*).

Sources: EFA Global Monitoring Report Team; Archer and Cottingham (1996*a*).

A 'global consensus' on literacy?

Definitions and understandings of literacy have broadened considerably over the past fifty years. As early as 1949, the United Nations General Assembly envisioned the minimum requirements for fundamental education as including domestic skills, knowledge of other cultures and an opportunity to develop personal attributes such as initiative and freedom (Jones, 1990*b*). The deeper, conceptual aspects of literacy have been understood for years yet have not been articulated in official national or international definitions. As definitions of literacy shifted – from a discrete set of technical skills, to human resource skills for economic growth, to capabilities for socio-cultural and political change – international organizations acknowledged broader understandings of literacy, which encompass 'conscientization,' literacy practices, lifelong learning, orality, and information and communication technology literacy.

The growing international awareness of the broader social contexts in which literacy is encouraged, acquired, developed and sustained is especially significant. Indeed, literacy is no longer exclusively understood as an individual transformation, but as a contextual and societal one. Increasingly, reference is made to the importance of rich literate environments – public or private milieux with abundant written documents (e.g. books, magazines and newspapers), visual materials (e.g. signs, posters and handbills), or communication and electronic media (e.g. radios, televisions, computers and mobile phones). Whether in households, communities, schools or workplaces, the quality of literate environments affects how literacy skills are practised and how literacy is understood.

As text becomes an integral part of basic social, political and economic institutions – for example, in offices, law courts, libraries, banks and training centres – then the notion of 'literate societies' becomes pertinent (see, for example, Olson and Torrance, 2001). Literate societies are more than locales offering access to printed matter, written records, visual materials and advanced technologies; ideally, they enable the free exchange of text-based information and provide an array of opportunities for lifelong learning. These broader understandings of literacy provide fertile ground for further research, innovation and progress toward the development of effective literacy programmes for all, and they inform the content of the next three chapters. ■

Literate societies enable the free exchange of text-based information and provide an array of opportunities for lifelong learning

Chapter 7

Mapping the global literacy challenge

Enhancing the literacy skills and practices of all individuals worldwide is the overarching objective of the EFA literacy goal, with a particular focus on developing countries. Drawing upon an array of measures and assessments, this chapter highlights major trends and patterns of adult and youth literacy in different regions, nations and locales. Though the trends are positive, they are insufficient to meet the literacy goal.

Illiteracy remains prevalent among women, the elderly, in rural communities and among members of poor households. Opportunities for acquiring literacy are especially limited among socially excluded groups such as the indigenous, the nomadic, the migrant, the homeless, the internally displaced and people with disabilities. New, direct measures of literacy that go beyond conventional ones – which have been based largely on self-assessments, and expressed as a dichotomy between 'illiterates' and 'literates' – indicate that the scale and scope of the global literacy challenge are greater than previously thought.

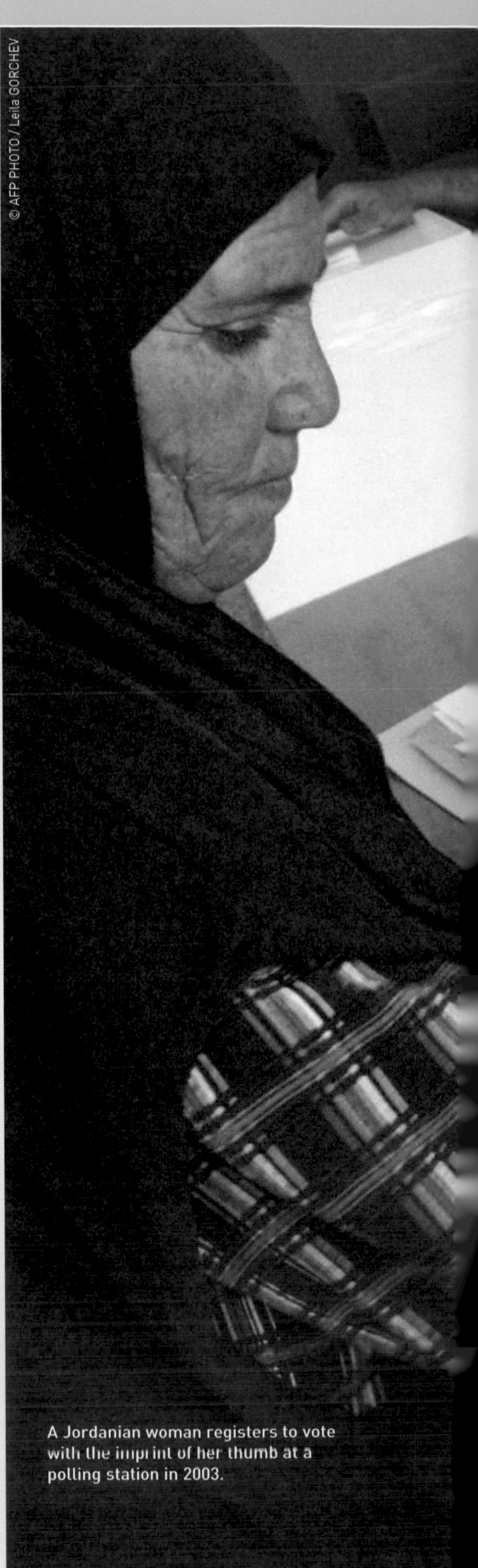

A Jordanian woman registers to vote with the imprint of her thumb at a polling station in 2003.

Reducing significantly all forms of illiteracy and enabling young and old alike to enrich their literacy skills and practices are the core challenges raised by the EFA goal. To address these formidable challenges, national and international policy-makers must have state-of-the-art knowledge of where literacy has been more or less achieved, how it has been (and could be better) measured and monitored, and why certain groups have successfully acquired strong literacy competency while others have not. An understanding of the states of literacy is essential if stakeholders are to meet the Dakar EFA goals by 2015.

An understanding of the states of literacy is essential if the Dakar EFA goals are to be met by 2015

With these aims in mind, this chapter examines global, regional, national and subnational patterns of literacy, some over time.[1] It describes how literacy and illiteracy have been 'conventionally' assessed – as a dichotomy that is based on self-declaration, third-party opinion or educational proxy. It discusses serious concerns raised about the validity and comparability of conventional literacy data and pays particular attention to new assessment techniques. The chapter then summarizes major findings resulting from alternative measurement strategies, including those of direct assessments in developing countries and large-scale, comparative studies in developed countries.

Measuring and monitoring literacy

International compilations of literacy data

During the 1950s and 1960s, scholars and international organizations used comparative data on adult literacy as a means of assessing economic progress and national development.[2] Literacy statistics were considered an important indicator of the extent to which individuals could effectively participate in and benefit from a modernizing economy and society. A national literacy threshold, for example, was viewed as a critical condition for economic 'take-off' and modernization (Rostow, 1960). In international organizations, the 'great divide' between the 'literate' and 'illiterate' provided policy-makers with tools to pinpoint where and among which social groups policy measures and literacy programmes were most warranted. Indeed, 'eradicate illiteracy' became a rallying cry for the international community (Smyth, 2005).

In the 1950s, UNESCO addressed the growing demand for comparative data on literacy. An early publication, *Progress of Literacy in Various Countries* (1953), compiled figures from about thirty pre-Second World War national censuses. *World Illiteracy at Mid-Century* (1957) reported census data from over sixty countries, mainly gathered after 1945, and estimated illiteracy rates for all countries of the world. Subsequent publications updated national estimates and included projections of global and regional trends (UNESCO, 1970, 1978, 1980, 1988, 1995).

The first publications contributed to a standard definition of literacy, adopted by UNESCO's General Conference in 1958, as follows: 'A person is literate/illiterate who can/cannot with understanding both read and write a short simple statement on his [or her] everyday life.' This definition became a guidepost for national censuses and contributed to the generation of more comparable literacy statistics.

Thus, within this framework of measurement standards, literacy came to be viewed as a limited set of cognitive skills (typically, the abilities to read and write printed text), which individuals acquire in various ways (mainly at school, but also through literacy 'campaigns' and non-formal programmes) and which can be measured independently of the context in which they were acquired (see Chapter 6).

UNESCO publications on literacy consistently aimed at worldwide coverage. For policy-makers and analysts alike, the usefulness of such statistics outweighed doubts concerning their validity (do they measure what they purport to measure?) and comparability (can they be compared across and within nations?). The principal challenge for UNESCO was to ensure that published literacy data conveyed a reasonably accurate picture of global trends and regional patterns of illiteracy.

Compilations of illiteracy data reinforced the growing international consensus that illiteracy affected most countries and posed a serious problem with important social and economic ramifications.[3] Literacy, on the other hand, presented a more ambiguous issue. How much literacy was needed? And what purposes of literacy should be targeted? In countries where almost all adults became literate (by conventional assessments), the challenge to 'eradicate illiteracy' evolved into more complex concerns: spreading 'functional literacy', assessing literacy as a continuum of skills, meeting everyone's basic

1. The chapter focuses on trends and patterns in literacy within and across societies, and only indirectly considers the impact of literacy-enhancing frameworks (e.g. schools, adult education programmes, literacy campaigns and 'literate environments') and broader societal forces that affected the development of literacy in the past. Chapter 8 includes a more systematic discussion of these issues.

2. See, for instance, Cipolla (1969), UNESCO (1957), McClelland (1961, 1966), Anderson and Bowman (1965, 1976).

3. Illiteracy was typically depicted as a scourge to be eradicated or a disease that unfortunates should be cured of. The highly negative connotations of illiteracy inadvertently stigmatized those with weak writing skills and contributed to a dichotomized concept as opposed to a notion of literacy as a spectrum.

learning needs and providing opportunities for lifelong learning.

In sum, the incidence of illiteracy – not literacy – remained the focal point of international policies until the late 1980s.[4] While many in the international community acknowledged that literacy and numeracy deserved sustained attention, only after the Jomtien (1990) and Dakar (2000) conferences was the challenge to eradicate illiteracy placed within a broader context of meeting the basic learning needs of all children and adults (Smyth, 2005).

Measurement and monitoring approaches

Until quite recently, all cross-national literacy assessments were based on official national census figures. Alternative sources (e.g. demographic or economic surveys with limited literacy information, or specialized studies of literacy)[5] were rarely used.

In practice, experts determined an individual's literacy level by one of three methods:

- Respondents reported their literacy level as part of a census questionnaire or survey instrument (self-declaration).
- Another individual – typically, the head of the household – reported on the literacy level of household members (third-party assessment).
- The number of years of schooling completed was used as a proxy measure to distinguish the 'literate' from the 'non-literate' (educational attainment proxy).

Each of these 'conventional' methods provided an estimate of the total number of 'literates' and 'illiterates' in a society. Interestingly, even if the method used included multiple categories to assess an individual's literacy skills, the reported data were usually collapsed into a simple dichotomy: literate or illiterate.

Adult literacy rates took national census figures on the number of 'literate' persons – typically above the age of 10 or 15 – and divided them by the total number of adults in that same age category. In most cases, overall rates were then disaggregated by sex, age and urban/rural residency. For decades these 'comparable' literacy rates provided a reasonable strategy for monitoring the prevalence of illiteracy across nations, regions and selected social groups, as well as changes over time.[6]

Beginning in the 1980s, concerns about the credibility and comparability of census-based literacy statistics gained momentum (Box 7.1).[7] Conventional methods for monitoring literacy, using indirect assessments to classify adults dichotomously, were seriously questioned. Since few countries had carefully measured individuals' actual skills in large or broad enough population samples, the validity and reliability of reported literacy levels were uncertain (Wagner, 2004).[8]

Since the 1980s, a variety of household-based surveys have been carried out in developing countries. Some have been directly related to literacy (see below); others (e.g. World Fertility Survey, Living Standards Measurement Study, and Demographic and Health Survey) have included some literacy-related questions. The advantages of these surveys included their cost-effectiveness, efficiency, timeliness and flexibility. The literacy-related surveys also had the advantage of being designed to investigate targeted – often disadvantaged – social groups or recent policy priorities. Some surveys included both direct tests of literacy skills and conventional indirect assessments, providing additional measuring and monitoring tools (Schaffner, 2005).[9]

Until quite recently, all cross-national literacy assessments were based on official national census figures

Only in the past five years have international compilations of literacy statistics drawn upon household-based surveys. Almost 40% of official literacy rates in the statistical annex of this Report are based on household surveys. The limitations of census-based literacy estimates, the increasing availability and reliability of new data sources and the growing demand for comprehensive, up-to-date international literacy data are among the reasons for this shift.

Language diversity has always posed a special problem for assessing and comparing literacy levels within and across countries. In many

4. See, for example, Bataille (1976), UNESCO Regional Office for Education in Africa (1983).

5. Both types of survey are typically based on household sampling designs and thus are referred to as 'household surveys'.

6. As Wagner (2004) notes, the notion of *monitoring*, from the Latin *monere*, means 'to warn' or to observe. Thus, to the extent that international statistics on literacy have been used in the past to gather sufficient information in order to judge whether there is a problem necessitating a warning, they have fulfilled a monitoring function. As self-assessments, assessments by others and proxy variables tell little about the actual literacy skills of individuals or groups, however, their use obscures the nature and extent of the problem being monitored.

7. In 1986, UNESCO and the United Nations Statistical Office held a joint seminar in Paris to discuss the use of household surveys to improve the collection of adult literacy statistics (see United Nations Statistical Office, 1989). Similar discussions ensued over the next two decades (see, for example, ILI/UNESCO, 1999, 2001, 2002*a*, 2002*b*).

8. While many specialists agree that exclusive reliance on traditional indirect measures of literacy may be flawed, there is renewed discussion of the utility of proxy measures, since they may be sufficient and cost less (Desjardins and Murray [in press]; Murray, 1997).

9. Household surveys are not without their shortcomings, including some of the problems listed above (Carr-Hill, 2005*a*).

Box 7.1 Determining literacy from census data

The widespread use of census data to estimate literacy (or illiteracy) is not without problems, both substantive and methodological. These problems – which vary from country to country and have diminished in recent years – include:

■ *The paucity of census data:* This problem occurs particularly in countries with high literacy rates, since some have never included questions on literacy in their census surveys (e.g. the Netherlands, Sweden and Switzerland), and others discontinued their use at some point (e.g. Australia, Austria, Canada and New Zealand). Many developing countries, where illiteracy was understood to be widespread, have begun only in recent decades to include census provisions to measure its extent.

■ *Widely diverging operational definitions:* Among current census definitions of literacy are those that classify a person as literate if they: 'can read or write' (e.g. in Bulgaria, El Salvador and Egypt); 'can read a newspaper and write a simple letter' (e.g. Pakistan); 'can read and write, understanding the text, in any language having a written form' (Azerbaijan); 'can read and write or only read, no matter the language used' (Turkmenistan); or 'can both read and write with understanding in any language' (India). In past censuses, the ability to sign one's name was sometimes considered as sufficient evidence of literacy. Depending on the country, persons who could only read or only write might be classified as literate, illiterate or 'semi-literate' (UNESCO, 1953). Even within the same country, census definitions changed rapidly: for example, in each of Pakistan's five national censuses a different definition of literacy was used (Choudhry, 2005). Overall, the evidence suggests that while operational definitions continue to vary, the extent of cross-national variation has decreased in recent years as international definitions have become institutionalized.

■ *Varying definitions of 'adult' population:* Most censuses define the adult population as 15 years and older. Yet in some cases the lower age limits of the adult population have been set at 10, 7 or even 5 years. Persons of unknown age may or may not be included in the total count of literates and illiterates. There have even been instances in which no age limits were defined, meaning that even pre-verbal children were included (UNESCO, 1953). Another problem is infrequent censuses and reliance on outdated data. While censuses typically are conducted every ten years in developed countries, they are less frequent in many developing countries. Literacy statistics can thus be outdated by as much as two decades.

■ *Indirect vs direct assessment:* Conventional measurement strategies do not directly assess the actual literacy skills and practices of the individuals studied. Rather, they rely on self-assessments or third-party assessments, which are indirect. As such, they provide inaccurate and, in many ways, incomplete depictions of literacy levels. They can also produce overestimations of literacy rates. As discussed below, direct assessments of reading and writing skills generally provide a more realistic picture of individual literacy levels and their distribution in society.

■ *The validity of educational attainment as a proxy:* Many censuses consider years in school (typically, four or five years) as a valid proxy measure to determine literacy. As will be shown, estimating the number of illiterates/literates based on educational attainment is increasingly problematic. Some students attain 'literacy' (conventionally assessed) before completing four years in school; others remain 'illiterate' despite having completed five or more years of schooling.

contexts, the languages in which individuals' literacy skills are measured touch upon sensitive and often controversial issues.[10]

The changing scale and scope of the global challenge[11]

UNESCO's first 'global' survey of literacy estimated that 44% of the world's adults (15 years and older) – about 690–720 million people – lacked minimum literacy skills in a written language (UNESCO, 1957). Global illiteracy was concentrated in Asia (74%), particularly in China, Pakistan, India, Nepal, Afghanistan and Sri Lanka. The remainder of the world's illiterate adults lived in Africa (15%), the Americas (7%), and in Europe, Oceania, and the former USSR (4%).

Subsequent assessments estimated that the overall number of illiterates increased from about 700 million in 1950 to 871 million in 1980 (Table 7.1). During the 1980s, the illiterate population stabilized, and it began to decrease in the 1990s – from 872 million in 1990 to 771 million today.[12]

10. Chapter 6 discussed current national policies regarding language and literacy assessment. The interrelationship of language and literacy issues is discussed more thoroughly in Chapter 8.

11. This section examines literacy trends and patterns, using data compiled by UNESCO from national literacy estimates based on conventional (i.e. dichotomous and indirect) assessments. Later sections examine findings resulting from other assessment methods.

12. Overall, the reliability and comparability of census data on literacy improved during this period and the number of countries compiling such information increased, enhancing the quality of UNESCO's estimates. Nevertheless, beyond the problems noted in Box 7.1, analysing trends in (il)literacy rates or in numbers of illiterates entails collating data from [illegible] assessment exercises, which may have involved different methods and sources. Thus, the trends over time discussed in this section should be interpreted with caution, since the various segments of the trend line are not always strictly comparable.

Important trends concerning the world's illiterate population (Table 7.2) include:

- The vast majority of the illiterate population is concentrated in developing countries.
- The percentage living in South and West Asia, sub-Saharan Africa and the Arab States has increased since 1970, partly owing to population growth rates, while there has been a pronounced decline in East Asia and the Pacific, particularly due to the efforts and achievements of China.[13]
- Women continue to constitute a majority of the illiterate: their percentage has increased from 58% in 1960 to 64% today.
- Young adults (aged 15–24) comprise a decreasing minority: from about 20% in 1970 to 17% today.

The bulk of this chapter is devoted to the analysis of literacy in developing countries; the relatively small but persistent developed country challenge is addressed below in relation to the International Adult Literacy Survey (IALS), and again in Chapter 8.

Trends in literacy rates, 1950–2004

At the global level, the adult literacy rate increased throughout the post-1950 period: from 56% in 1950 to 70% in 1980, and to 82% in the most recent period (Table 7.3).[14] While the more developed countries had already attained over 90% adult literacy rates in the 1950s, rates in developing countries then averaged lower than 50% but have since increased to over 75%. On average, the world literacy rate increased at a faster pace in the 1970s than in subsequent decades. Based on current projections, the adult literacy rate should reach about 86% in 2015 (see Chapter 2).

Adult literacy rates increased quite rapidly in regions where initial literacy rates were lowest, especially in the 1970s – doubling in sub-Saharan Africa, the Arab States, and South and West Asia from 1970 to 2000. The regional literacy rate in East Asia and the Pacific grew from 58% to 91%, while in Latin America and the Caribbean the increase was more moderate (74% to 90%), owing to the region's relatively high starting point.

13. According to official census estimates, the number of adults who had not mastered at least 1,500 characters in Chinese (the operational definition of illiteracy) declined from 320 million in 1949 to 230 million in 1982 and is now at 87 million (Zhang and Wang, 2005), though several scholars (e.g. Banister, 1987; Hagemann, 1988; Henze, 1987; Seeberg, 2000; World Bank, 1983) have questioned the accuracy of the statistics prior to the 1990s.

14. Past increases in the adult literacy rate did not translate into a reduction of the overall number of illiterates until the 1990s, due to continuing population growth.

Table 7.1: Global and regional trends in number of illiterates, 1950 to 2000–2004

	Adult illiterates (15 and over) (millions)					
	1950	1960	1970	1980	1990	2000–2004
World	700	735	847	871	872	771
Developing countries	…	…	804	839	855	759
Developed and transition countries	…	…	43	32	17	12
Selected regions						
Sub-Saharan Africa	…	…	108	120	129	141
Arab States	…	19	48	55	63	65
East Asia and the Pacific	…	…	295	267	232	130
South and West Asia	…	…	301	344	382	381
Latin America and the Caribbean	…	…	43	44	42	38

Note: See the introduction to the statistical annex for a broader explanation of national literacy definitions, sources and years of data.
Sources: For 1950 and 1960: UNESCO (1978) Estimates and Projections of Illiteracy, CSR-E-29. Data refer to the 1972 assessment and are not necessarily comparable with data for subsequent years. For 1970 and 1980: UIS 2002 assessment based on the UN Population estimates and projections (2000 assessment). For 1990 and 2000–2004: data are from this Report's statistical annex, Table 2A.

Table 7.2: Percentage distribution of global illiterate population, by country development status, region, gender and age

	Adult illiterates (15 and over)					
	1950	1960	1970	1980	1990	2000–2004
Global estimate of illiterate population (in millions)	700	735	847	871	872	771
Distribution (%)						
Developing countries	…	…	94.9	96.3	98.1	98.4
Developed and transition countries	…	…	5.1	3.7	1.9	1.6
Selected regions						
Sub-Saharan Africa	…	…	12.8	13.8	14.8	18.3
Arab States	…	2.6	5.7	6.3	7.2	8.4
East Asia and the Pacific	…	…	34.8	30.7	26.6	16.9
South and West Asia	…	…	35.5	39.5	43.8	49.4
Latin America and the Caribbean	…	…	5.1	5.1	4.8	4.9
Gender						
Women	…	58.0	61.0	62.0	63.0	64.0
Men	…	42.0	39.0	38.0	37.0	36.0
Age						
Youth aged 15–24	…	…	19.8	19.1	17.9	17.2
All other adults (25+)	…	…	80.2	80.9	82.1	82.8

Sources: Same as Table 7.1.

Gender disparities in literacy, 1970–2004

During the past three decades, women have comprised three-fifths or more of the adult illiterate population. However, this fact provides only partial information about gender disparities, since women may outnumber men because of differential mortality rates in older age groups. Thus, the gender parity index (GPI) is a preferable measure.[15]

15. The GPI calculates the ratio between female and male literacy rates. A GPI of 1.0 indicates gender parity; GPIs below or above 1.0 indicate that literacy rates are higher among men or women, respectively.

Table 7.3: Global and regional trends in adult literacy rates, 1950 to 2000–2004

	Adult literacy rates (%)						Increase in literacy rates (%)		
	1950	1960	1970	1980	1990	2000–2004	1970 to 1980	1980 to 1990	1990 to 2000–2004
World	55.7	60.7	63.4	69.7	75.4	81.9	9.9	8.2	8.5
Developing countries	…	…	47.7	58.0	67.0	76.4	21.6	15.6	14.0
Developed and transition countries	…	…	94.5	96.4	98.6	99.0	2.0	1.8	0.5
Selected regions									
Sub-Saharan Africa	…	…	27.8	37.8	49.9	59.7	36.0	32.1	19.6
Arab States	…	18.9	28.8	39.2	50.0	62.7	36.1	27.7	25.3
East Asia and the Pacific	…	…	57.5	70.3	81.8	91.4	22.3	16.4	11.7
South and West Asia	…	…	31.6	39.3	47.5	58.6	24.4	20.8	23.5
Latin America and the Caribbean	…	…	73.7	80.0	85.0	89.7	8.5	6.3	5.5

Sources: Same as Table 7.1.

Figure 7.1: Adult literacy rates: global and regional trends in gender parity, 1970 to 2000–2004

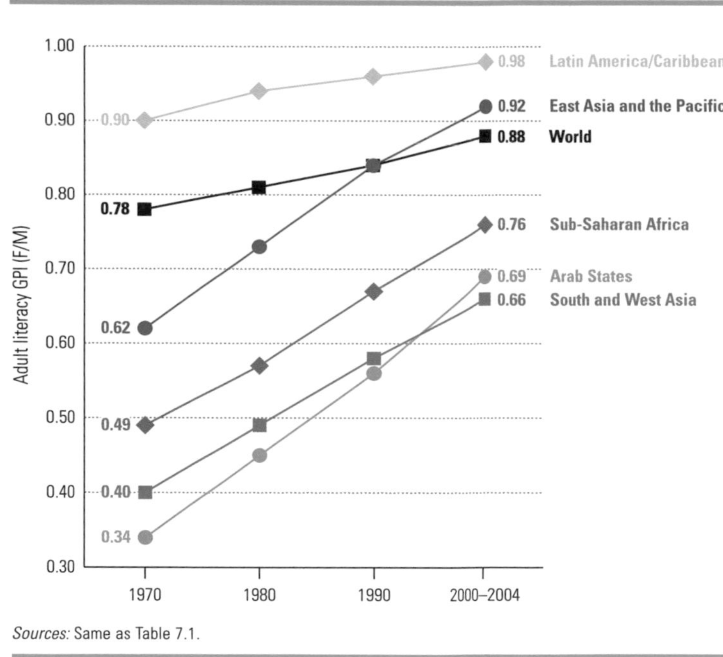

Sources: Same as Table 7.1.

Worldwide, gender disparities in literacy have declined significantly since 1970, with the GPI increasing from 0.78 to 0.88 (Figure 7.1). This reduction occurred in all regions, notably in the Arab States, South and West Asia, and sub-Saharan Africa. The GPIs in these three regions were below 0.50 in 1970 and are today all above 0.65. Adult literacy rates in Latin America and the Caribbean (GPI = 0.98) and East Asia and the Pacific (GPI = 0.92) are approaching gender parity.

Improvements in youth literacy

Recent progress towards mass literacy is especially marked among people aged 15 to 24: expanded access to formal schooling contributed to an increase in the global youth literacy rate from 75% to 88% between 1970 and 2000–2004 (Table 7.4). In developing countries, the respective figures were 66% and 85%. Almost all youth are now literate in East Asia and the Pacific, and in Latin America and the Caribbean. Nevertheless, more than 132 million young people worldwide are still unable to communicate in a written language.

Table 7.4: Youth literacy rates by country development status and region, 1970 to 2000–2004, with percent increases in each decade

	Youth literacy rates (%)				Increase in literacy rates (%)		
	1970	1980	1990	2000–2004	1970 to 1980	1980 to 1990	1990 to 2000–2004
World	74.7	80.2	84.3	87.5	7.4	5.1	3.8
Developing countries	66.0	74.4	80.9	85.0	12.7	8.7	5.1
Developed and transition countries	99.0	99.3	99.5	99.7	0.3	0.2	0.2
Selected regions							
Sub-Saharan Africa	41.3	54.3	67.5	72.0	31.5	24.3	6.6
Arab States	42.7	54.7	66.6	70.0	28.1	21.8	17.6
East Asia and the Pacific	83.2	91.3	95.4	97.9	9.7	4.5	2.6
South and West Asia	43.3	52.6	61.5	73.1	21.6	16.8	18.9
Latin America and the Caribbean	84.2	89.5	92.7	95.9	6.2	3.6	3.4

Sources: Same as Table 7.1.

Increases in youth literacy rates have, on average, been slower than for adult literacy rates, due to their higher starting point. In developing countries, the youth literacy rate increased during each of the past three decades by about thirteen, nine and five percentage points, respectively. The corresponding figures for the adult literacy rates were twenty-two, sixteen and fourteen percentage points. Gender disparities in youth literacy are less pronounced than in adult literacy, with a global GPI of 0.93 in 2000–2004.

Throughout the developing world, levels of youth literacy are higher than levels of adult literacy – a sign of future progress. Still, youth literacy rates vary considerably among countries with low adult literacy rates (Figure 7.2). In several cases, mainly in sub-Saharan Africa (e.g. Burkina Faso, the Niger and Mali), both adult and youth literacy levels are extremely low and improvements in literacy levels are expected to be slow. In many such contexts, young women have yet to acquire minimal literacy skills. For example, in Benin, Burkina Faso, Chad, Mali, the Niger and Yemen, the GPIs are below 0.60 for the younger generation (see statistical annex, Table 12).

Overall, considerable global progress in adult and youth literacy rates has occurred during the past fifty years. Nevertheless, the challenge to improve the quantity and quality of literacy worldwide has not diminished: indeed, unless progress is significantly accelerated, the 2015 targets fixed at Dakar will not be achieved (see Chapter 2). To better understand the enormous intra-regional variation in literacy trends and patterns, the next section presents evidence and analyses at the national and subnational levels.

Figure 7.2: Youth and adult literacy rates for selected countries, 2000–2004

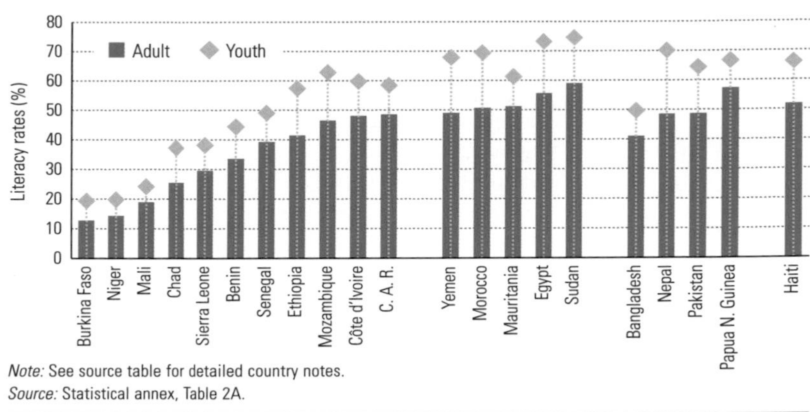

Note: See source table for detailed country notes.
Source: Statistical annex, Table 2A.

Figure 7.3: Distribution of global adult illiterate population, 2000–2004

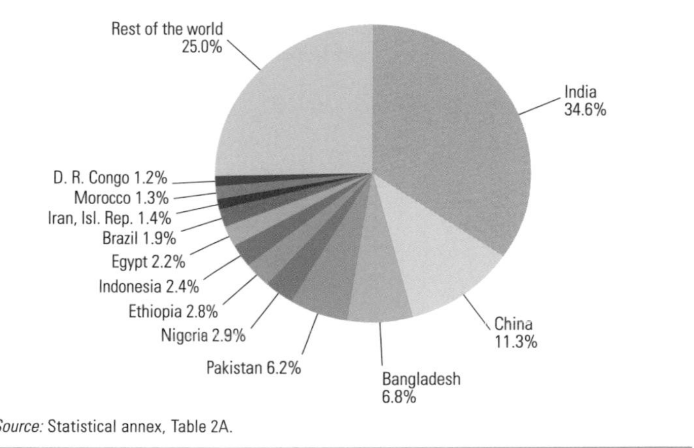

Source: Statistical annex, Table 2A.

Where is the literacy challenge most pressing?

The vast majority of the 771 million adults who lack minimal literacy skills live in three regions: South and West Asia, East Asia and the Pacific, and sub-Saharan Africa. In fact, as Figure 7.3 shows, three-quarters of the world's illiterate population live in just twelve countries.[16]

Since 1990, the illiterate population in eight of these twelve countries has decreased (Table 7.5),

Table 7.5: Change in the illiterate population, 1990 to 2000–2004, in countries with the greatest numbers of illiterates

Country	Total 1990 (000)	Total 2000–2004 (000)	Share of world total 1990 (%)	Share of world total 2000–2004 (%)	Change from 1990 to 2000–2004 (000)
India	272 279	267 002	31.2	34.6	-5 277
China	181 331	87 038	20.8	11.3	-94 293
Bangladesh	41 606	52 209	4.8	6.8	10 603
Pakistan	41 368	47 577	4.7	6.2	6 209
Nigeria	23 678	22 167	2.7	2.9	-1 511
Ethiopia	18 993	21 955	2.2	2.8	2 962
Indonesia	23 800	18 432	2.7	2.4	-5 368
Egypt	17 432	17 270	2.0	2.2	-162
Brazil	17 336	14 870	2.0	1.9	-2 466
Iran, Isl. Rep.	11 506	10 543	1.7	1.8	-963
Morocco	9 089	10 108	1.4	1.7	1 019
D.R. Congo	10 400	9 131	1.6	1.6	-1 269
Total	**668 818**	**578 302**	**77.8**	**76.2**	**-90 516**

Note: See source table for detailed country notes.
Source: Statistical annex, Table 2A.

16. After these twelve countries, the largest illiterate populations in decreasing order of number of illiterates, are found in the Sudan, Nepal, Mexico, Algeria, the United Republic of Tanzania, Turkey, Mozambique, Ghana, Yemen, Viet Nam, the Niger, Burkina Faso, South Africa, Mali, Côte d'Ivoire, Kenya, Uganda and the Philippines, with an estimated 3–8 million each. Extrapolations from earlier literacy data indicate that Afghanistan and Iraq should also be on this list.

though only in China was the reduction very significant; Brazil, the Democratic Republic of the Congo, Egypt, India, Indonesia, Nigeria and the Islamic Republic of Iran recorded small decreases. By contrast, the illiterate populations in Bangladesh, Ethiopia, Morocco and Pakistan have increased since 1990, despite improvements in adult literacy rates, indicating that progress in the latter was insufficient to offset the effect of continuing population growth.

Adult literacy rates remain relatively low in South and West Asia, sub-Saharan Africa and the Arab States

In which countries are adult literacy rates especially low?

While adult literacy rates have improved in all world regions, they remain relatively low (around 60%) in South and West Asia, sub-Saharan Africa and the Arab States. Within these regions there are considerable differences in adult literacy rates. For example, in South and West Asia, rates are especially low in Bangladesh, Nepal and Pakistan, and quite high in the Maldives and Sri Lanka. In sub-Saharan Africa, literacy rates are extremely low in Benin, Burkina Faso, Chad, Mali, Mozambique, the Niger, Senegal and Sierra Leone, and relatively high in the Congo, Equatorial Guinea, Lesotho, Mauritius and Namibia. Literacy skills are very limited in Egypt, Mauritania, Morocco, Sudan and the Yemen, but more widespread in Bahrain, Jordan, Qatar and the Syrian Arab Republic. Figure 7.4 ranks the fifty-five countries that have the world's lowest adult literacy rates – ranging from 13% (Burkina Faso) to 80% (Honduras) – and are thus at risk of not meeting the 2015 goal.

Figure 7.4: Adult literacy rates by gender in fifty-five low-literacy developing countries, 2000–2004

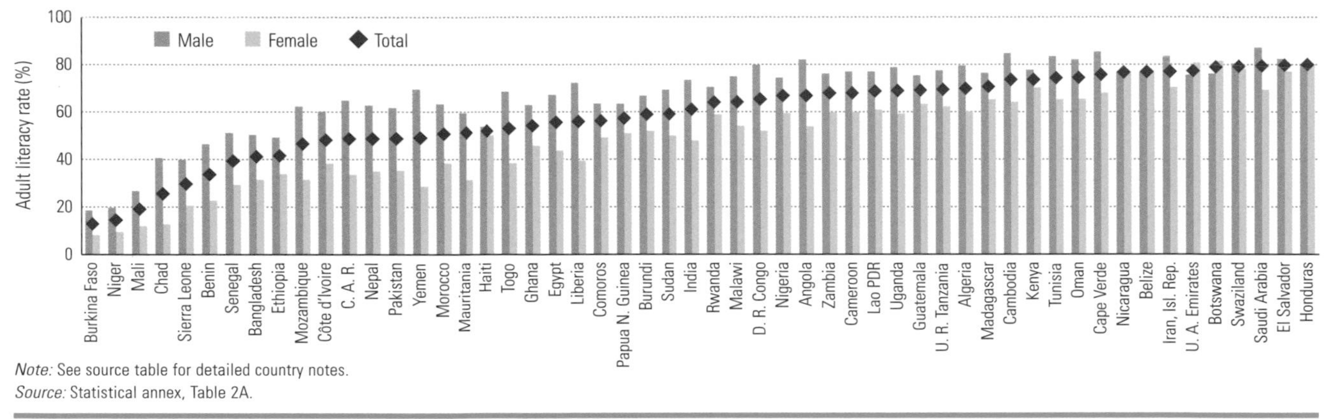

Note: See source table for detailed country notes.
Source: Statistical annex, Table 2A.

Table 7.6: The literacy challenge compounded: many illiterates, low adult literacy rates, 2000–2004

	Adult literacy rate is < 63%	Adult literacy rate is > 63%
Number of illiterates is greater than 5 million	Bangladesh; Egypt; Ethiopia; Ghana; India; Morocco; Mozambique; Nepal; Pakistan; Sudan; Yemen	Afghanistan;[1] Algeria; Brazil; China; D.R. Congo; Indonesia; Iraq;[2] Iran, Isl. Rep.; Mexico; Nigeria; Turkey; U.R. Tanzania
Number of illiterates is between 1 and 5 million	Benin; Burkina Faso; Burundi; Central African Republic; Chad; Côte d'Ivoire; Haiti; Mali; Niger; Papua New Guinea; Senegal; Sierra Leone; Togo	Angola; Cambodia; Cameroon; Guatemala; Kenya; Madagascar; Malawi; Malaysia; Myanmar; Peru; Rwanda; Saudi Arabia; South Africa; Syrian A.R.; Tunisia; Uganda; Zambia
Number of illiterates is less than 1 million	Comoros; Liberia; Mauritania	Bahrain; Belize; Bolivia; Botswana; Cape Verde; Congo; Dominican Republic; El Salvador; Equatorial Guinea; Honduras; Jamaica; Jordan; Kuwait; Lao PDR; Lesotho; Libyan A.J.; Malta; Mauritius; Namibia; Nicaragua; Oman; Qatar; Suriname; Swaziland; U.A. Emirates; Vanuatu

Note: The figure of 63% to distinguish between high and low adult literacy rates is based on an examination of the distribution of all countries with rates below 95% and a calculation of the median. See source table for detailed country notes.
1. Data for Afghanistan based on estimates from CIA (2005).
2. Data for Iraq based on estimates from UNDP (2004*c*).
Source: Statistical annex, Table 2A.

By comparing the size of each country's illiterate population with its overall adult literacy rate, countries with especially significant literacy challenges can be identified. India, Bangladesh, Ethiopia, Egypt, Ghana, Morocco, Mozambique, Nepal, Pakistan, the Sudan and Yemen fall into this category, with relatively large numbers of illiterates (more than 5 million) and relatively low adult literacy rates (less than 63%) (Table 7.6). By contrast, countries such as Burkina Faso, Chad, Côte d'Ivoire, Haiti, the Niger, Papua New Guinea and Senegal have low literacy levels, but also have smaller illiterate populations (1–5 million).

The link with poverty

The magnitude of the literacy challenge facing many countries today is further complicated by the strong links between illiteracy and poverty. For example, there is a significant negative correlation between measures of poverty and the adult literacy rate, at both the international level (Figure 7.5) and at the subnational level in countries such as India (Figure 7.6); that is, where poverty rates are higher, literacy rates tend to be lower. Noteworthy exceptions include countries such as the Islamic Republic of Iran, Morocco and Tunisia, which have relatively low poverty and literacy rates.

Table 7.7 provides additional evidence of the illiteracy–poverty link by reporting estimates of per

Where poverty rates are higher, literacy rates tend to be lower

Table 7.7: The literacy challenge compounded: links to poverty

	Gross national income per capita, 2003 (in PPP US$)	Percent of population living below US$2 a day (most recent figures)	Belongs to HIPC countries
Number of illiterates is greater than 5 million and adult literacy rate is < 63%			
Bangladesh	1 870	83	
Egypt	3 940	44	
Ethiopia	710	78	X
Ghana	2 190	79	X
India	2 880	81	
Morocco	3 940	14	
Mozambique	1 060	78	X
Nepal	1 420	81	
Pakistan	2 040	66	
Sudan	1 760	–	X
Yemen	820	45	
Number of illiterates is greater than 5 million and adult literacy rate is > 63%			
Algeria	5 930	15	
Brazil	7 510	22	
China	4 980	–	
D.R. Congo	660	–	X
Indonesia	3 210	52	
Iran, Isl. Rep.	7 000	7	
Mexico	8 980	26	
Nigeria	900	91	
Turkey	6 710	10	
Number of illiterates is between 1 and 5 million and adult literacy rate is < 63%			
Burkina Faso	1 170	81	X
Côte d'Ivoire	1 400	38	X
Mali	960	91	X
Niger	830	86	X

Note: The categorization of countries in this table is based on Table 7.6.
Source: World Bank Development Indicators Database (http://www1.worldbank.org/prem/poverty/data/, accessed April 2005).

Figure 7.5: Literacy rate and poverty

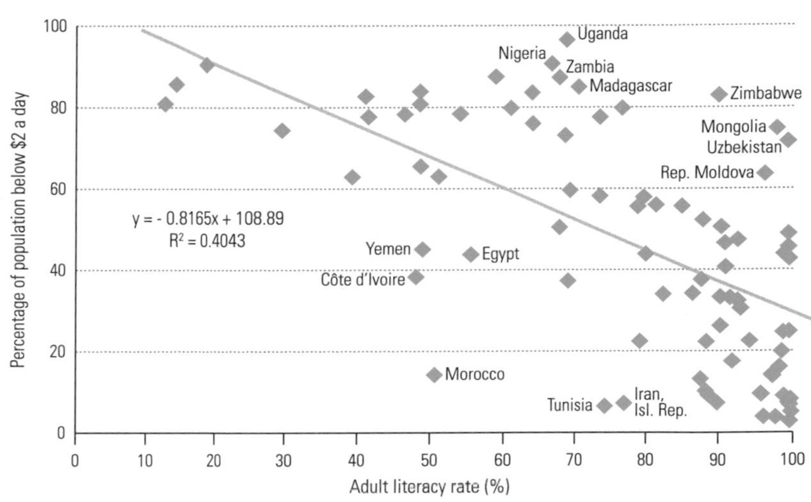

Sources: Statistical annex, Table 2A, and World Bank Development Indicators Database (http://www1.worldbank.org/prem/poverty/data/, accessed April 2005).

Figure 7.6: Relationship between adult literacy and average household expenditure in India, by selected states

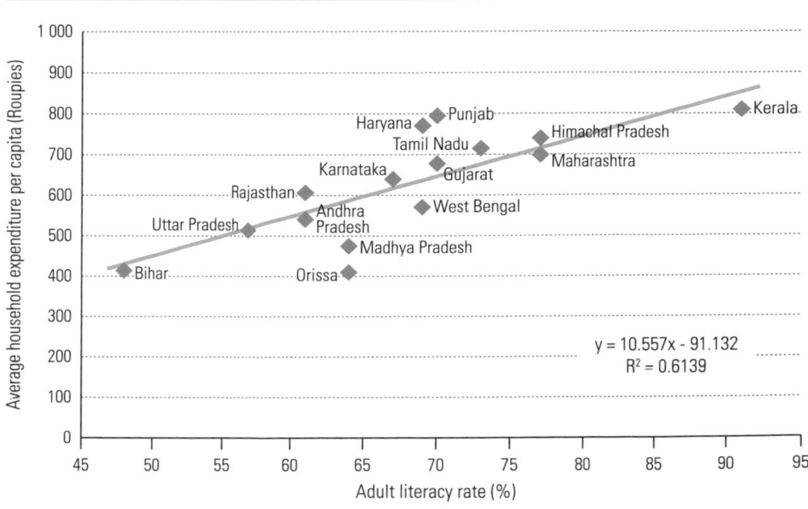

Source: Drèze and Sen (2002).

capita income and poverty rates for countries with large illiterate populations and low adult literacy rates. This table illustrates that illiteracy tends to prevail in low-income, often heavily indebted countries with widespread household poverty.

Social and demographic disparities in literacy rates

Gender

Gender disparities are either non-existent or minimal in countries with adult literacy rates at 95% or above. In almost all other countries, men have better reading and writing skills than women. On average, the literacy gaps between adult men and women are largest in South and West Asia (70% vs 46%), the Arab States (73% vs 51%) and sub-Saharan Africa (68% vs 52%). The gap between the female and male literacy rates is considerably greater in countries where the overall adult literacy rate is lower (Figure 7.4).[17]

Interestingly, literacy disparities *favouring* young women over young men (aged 15–24) occur in an increasing number of countries. For example, the GPIs in Botswana, Honduras, Jamaica, Malta, Nicaragua and the United Arab Emirates are above 1.03 for the younger age group. Overall, the number of countries (with relevant data) for which the GPI favours young women over young men increased from fifteen to twenty-two between 1990 and 2000–2004. This trend is more pronounced in Latin America and the Caribbean, in eastern and southern Africa, and in countries with higher literacy rates.[18]

Age

In all countries, literacy rates vary across age groups. Typically, individuals aged 15–34 have higher literacy levels than those aged 45 and older, reflecting in large part the expansion of mass schooling throughout the world. In some countries, there are small decreases in literacy rates among younger age groups and then sharp declines among older age groups, especially after the age of 45. In other cases, the decline in literacy rates across age groups is fairly linear. Unsurprisingly, age disparities are smaller in high-literacy countries and larger in low-literacy countries. In countries with comparatively low literacy levels (e.g. Angola, Burundi, the Gambia, the Lao People's Democratic Republic, Nepal, Pakistan, Rwanda and Zambia), the literacy rate among 25- to 34-year-olds is twice that of those aged 65 and older.

Further evidence of age disparities in adult literacy can be seen in Figure 7.7, which plots literacy rates among four select age groups in several developing regions. Age disparities in adult literacy tend to be more prominent in the Arab States than in Asia or in Latin America and the Caribbean.

Six countries in eastern and southern Africa (Angola, the Democratic Republic of the Congo, Zambia, the United Republic of Tanzania, Madagascar and Kenya) have *lower* literacy rates among 15- to 24-year-olds than among 25- to

17. Among developing countries, there are several interesting exceptions to the tendency for female literacy rates to be lower than those for men. For example, in Brazil, Colombia, Honduras, Jamaica, Lesotho, Malta, Nicaragua, the Philippines, Saint Lucia and Seychelles, the differences between the male and the female literacy rates are either insignificant or favour women (see Chapter 2).

18. This emergent tendency of gender disparities in favour of young women should be examined in relation to similar tendencies in educational achievement and educational attainment, including primary completion rates.

Figure 7.7: Literacy rates for selected age groups, 2000–2004

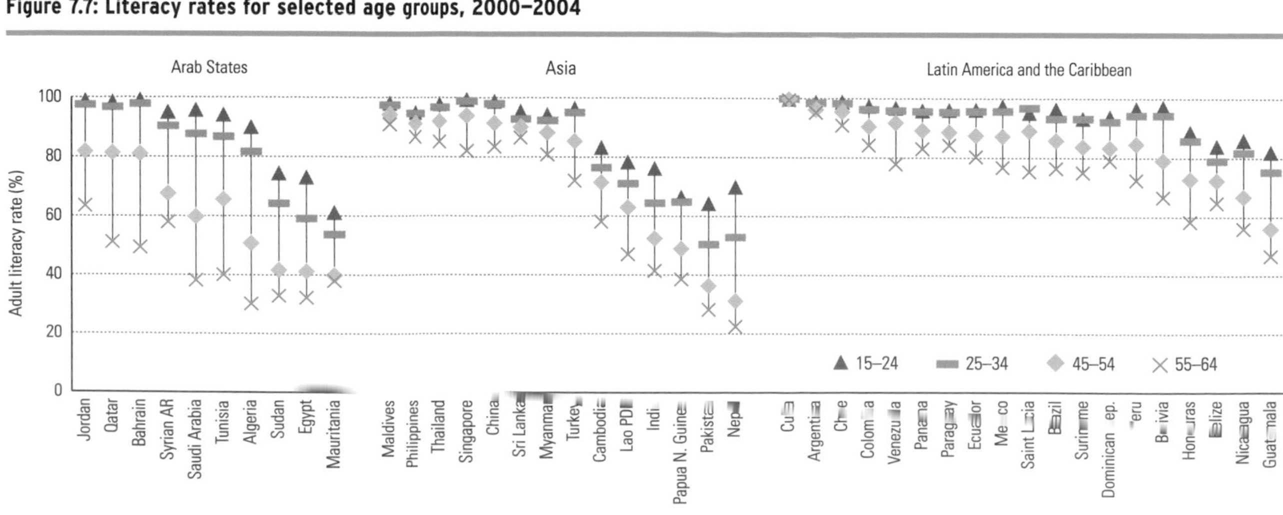

Source: UNICEF Multiple Indicator Cluster Surveys (MICS) 2000, taken from Carr-Hill (2005*a*).

Figure 7.8: Adult literacy rates by urban/rural residence, 2000–2004

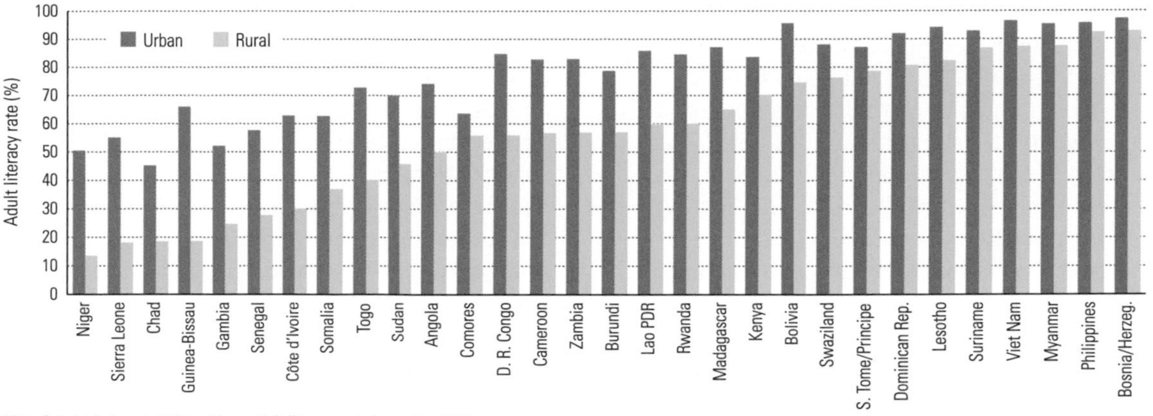

Note: Only includes countries with an adult literacy rate lower than 95%.
Source: UNICEF MICS 2000, taken from Carr-Hill (2005*a*).

34-year-olds. This exceptional pattern is mainly prevalent among younger men.[19] Apparently, severe political and economic conditions contributed to this literacy decline, including armed conflict, unemployment, rising household costs of schooling and perceptions of limited future income prospects from becoming literate (see Chapter 8).

Geographical disparities

Rural residents have lower literacy levels than urban residents, whether measured from census data (e.g. Wagner, 2000) or from household data (Figure 7.8).[20] The disparities between urban and rural populations tend to be greater in those poorer countries in which overall literacy rates are comparatively low. In large measure, the influence of urbanization on literacy acquisition and retention reflects differences in access to formal schooling, higher-quality education and non-formal education programmes. Urban residents, in contrast to rural residents, tend also to reside in more literate environments, which are more demanding of literacy skills in written languages, and which offer greater rewards to those who possess them (see Chapter 8).

Regional or provincial differences in literacy are particularly prevalent in countries with large illiterate populations. For example, census figures for Pakistan report an adult literacy rate of 72% in urban areas (e.g. the Islamabad Capital Territory), as compared with 44% in rural areas such as Baluchistan and Sindh (Choudhry, 2005). This rural/urban ratio of 0.61, while relatively low, has nearly doubled since 1972, when it stood at just 0.34. In Ethiopia, regional disparities in literacy rates range from 83% in the Addis Ababa region to 25% in the Amhara region. The overall literacy rate in rural Ethiopia is estimated at 23%, only one-third of the urban rate of 74% (Shenkut, 2005). In Morocco, rural–urban literacy disparities are extensive and compounded by gender (Table 7.8).

In Morocco, rural–urban literacy disparities are extensive and compounded by gender

Table 7.8: Morocco: Adult literacy rates by gender and urban/rural residence, 1990/91 and 1998/99

		Adult literacy rate			
		%			GPI
		Total	Male	Female	(F/M)
All country	1990/91	45.3	60.5	31.7	0.52
	1998/99	51.7	66.2	38.1	0.58
Urban	1990/91	63.3	76.5	51.4	0.67
	1998/99	66.3	79.0	54.5	0.69
Rural	1990/91	28.2	45.3	12.8	0.28
	1998/99	33.1	50.1	17.0	0.34
Rural/urban ratio	1990/91	0.45	0.59	0.25	0.42
	1998/99	0.50	0.63	0.31	0.49

Source: Direction de la Statistique, cited in Bougroum et al. (2005).

19. These analyses draw upon data from the UNICEF Multiple Indicator Cluster Surveys (MICS), carried out in 2000; literacy figures are based on the respondent's self-assessment of his/her ability to read easily or with difficulty a letter or a newspaper.

20. Census definitions of 'urban' and 'rural' areas vary considerably and increasingly add a third category – 'peri-urban' or 'suburban' – to further distinguish geographical entities in contrast to urban and rural areas. Many countries define an urban area in terms of (minimum) population size, a definition which varies from country to country: ranging from at least 1,000 and 2,000 residents (in Canada and Bolivia, respectively) to 10,000 (Spain) and 20,000 (Turkey), up to at least 50,000 residents (Republic of Korea). In other countries, where the status of an 'urban area' involves a binding legal decision approved through legislative or bureaucratic processes, definitions also vary. This lack of definitional uniformity confounds comparisons of urban literacy rates across countries and weakens comparative accounts of urban–rural literacy gaps.

These disparities improved only slightly during the 1990s. Similar trends can be found in Iraq, where, for example, 72% of the women in the Baghdad area are literate, compared to 46% in the northern region (UNDP, 2004*d*).

In China, regional variation has been, and continues to be, widespread (Ross et al., 2005). Illiteracy is concentrated in the country's rural, western regions, which have high percentages of minority populations and lower levels of economic development.[21] China's most literate areas are the three urban municipalities of Shanghai, Beijing and Tianjin, the economically developed Guangdong province, and the three north-east provinces, which benefited from rapid industrialization in the past.

In India, adult literacy rates in 2001 varied from 91% in the state of Kerala to 48% in Bihar

Among states in India, adult literacy rates in 2001 varied from 91% in the state of Kerala to 48% in Bihar (Biswal and Govinda, 2005). Variations were even more pronounced at the district level: according to the 2001 census, in about one-fifth of all 591 districts[22] less than half of the adult population was literate; another one-fifth of the districts have literacy rates in the range of 50% to 60%; 29% of districts have literacy rates in the 60% to 70% range; and the remaining districts have literacy rates over 70% (Biswal and Govinda, 2005).

Additional insights are gained by going beyond the traditional urban–rural dichotomy. Indeed, in many developing countries *intra-urban* and *intra-rural* differences in literacy rates can be as significant, if not more so, than urban–rural differences. In China, for example, the China Adult Literacy Survey found substantial differences in the literacy skills of native and migrant workers in five cities (Giles et al., 2003).[23] Literacy levels among urban-resident men and women were, on average, one-quarter of a standard deviation higher than among migrant men and women.

In other countries, intra-urban literacy disparities follow 'core–periphery' patterns, with central urban districts having higher literacy rates than peripheral ones, where poor families and migrants reside. In Egypt, for example, rural migrants with weak literacy skills flocked to Cairo and peri-urban areas seeking employment, but usually found themselves in substandard housing, working long hours in the informal sector with little access to training, credit or community safety nets; opportunities for literacy acquisition or skills upgrading were severely limited (Iskandar, 2005). In addition, many residents of urban peripheries live in unauthorized or illegal areas, which are typically excluded from the sampling frame of household surveys (Carr-Hill, 2005*a*). In such cases, the literacy rate of urban areas may be inflated due to the undercounting of poor or rural migrant populations.

The urban–rural dichotomy also masks important *rural-based differences* between regions. For example, the rural literacy rate in southern (Upper) Egypt (47%) is considerably lower than that of northern (Lower) Egypt (62%) (Iskandar, 2005).[24] Nomadic populations (such as the Bedouin in Arab States) tend to have lower literacy levels, lower enrolment and higher drop-out rates than other rural populations (Hammoud, 2005). Likewise, children of pastoralists in the arid and semi-arid regions of Kenya have significantly lower enrolment rates than children in other rural regions (Bunyi, 2005).

In sum, urban–rural disparities in literacy rates apparently mask as much as they reveal. The evidence, although limited, suggests that geographical disparities in literacy are considerably more complex than conventionally portrayed.

Household wealth and poverty

The links between poverty and illiteracy, previously examined at the national level, can also be studied at the household level. Considerable evidence suggests that household socio-economic status is strongly associated with literacy acquisition and retention. People who live (or have grown up) in low-income households, and lack sufficient nutritional intake or access to clean water, are less likely to acquire and use literacy skills.

Adult literacy rates by household wealth quintiles[25] in thirty developing countries show that literacy rates are lower in the poorer quintiles and higher in the richer quintiles (see Carr-Hill, 2005*a*).[26] Furthermore, as Figure 7.9 shows, disparities in adult literacy rates between households belonging to the poorest and richest

21. In 2000, the national literacy rate was 93.3%, whereas in Tibet, Qinghai, Gansu, Guizhou and Ningxia, the rates were, respectively, 67.5%, 81.9%, 85.7%, 86.1% and 86.6%.

22. The 2001 census of India was conducted in 591 districts out of the total 593 districts (Biswal and Govinda, 2005).

23. The China Adult Literacy Survey was a direct assessment of literacy skills among men and women, from 15 to 60 years of age, residing in Shanghai, Shenyang, Xian, Wuhan and Fuzhon.

24. In contrast, there is only a slight difference between the *urban* literacy rates of these two regions in Egypt (80% vs 82%).

25. Recognizing the difficulties of comparing household assets across and within countries (due to differences in climate, infrastructure and cultural notions about ownership), the UNICEF MICS surveys grouped possessed assets into a measure of household wealth, then divided this into quintile scores. These scores measure the *relative wealth* (or relative poverty) of the household; in other words, regardless of the country, all those living in households belonging to a certain quintile are in the same *relative* position within their own country, even though their income levels or assets may differ greatly.

26. In Chad, Guinea, Madagascar, Sao Tome and Principe, the Lao People's Democratic Republic and Myanmar the relationship between poverty/wealth and literacy was negative but not linear.

Figure 7.9: Comparison of adult literacy rates by poorest and richest wealth quintiles

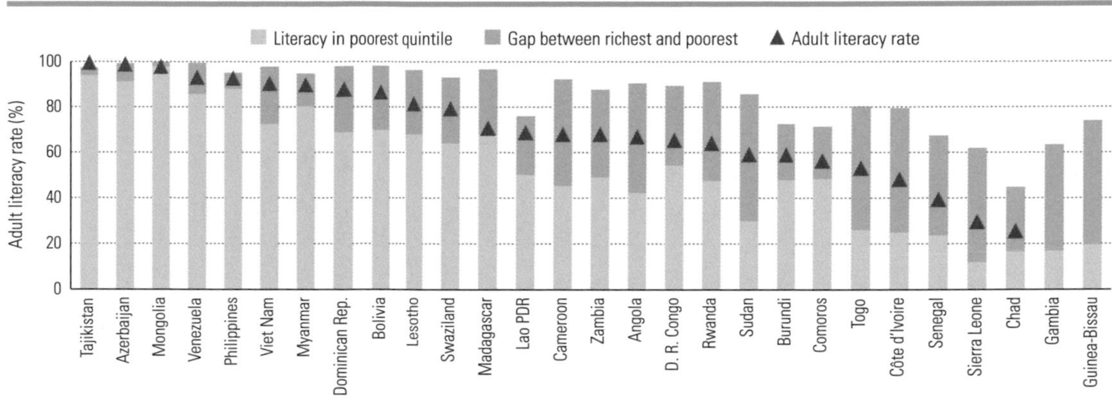

Note: The official adult literacy rates for Guinea-Bissau and the Gambia were not available.
Source: UNICEF MICS 2000, taken from Carr-Hill (2005*a*).

quintiles are quite large, especially where the overall literacy rate is low. In countries such as Côte d'Ivoire, Guinea-Bissau, Rwanda, Senegal, Sierra Leone, the Sudan and Togo, the literacy gap between the poorest and wealthiest households is more than forty percentage points. Even in countries where the overall rate is above 90%, literacy disparities by household wealth exist (e.g. Azerbaijan, the Philippines and Venezuela).[27]

The literacy gaps between the poorest and richest quintiles are nearly always greater for women than for men.[28] In other words, women who reside in wealthier households acquire much stronger literacy skills than women in poorer households. These wealth/poverty differences are less significant for men.

Literacy and schooling

Literacy rates increase significantly as the levels of completed schooling increase. The very strong relationship between educational attainment and literacy obtains in both developing and developed countries.[29] How many years of schooling are needed to acquire and sustain basic literacy skills? In the past, many asserted that minimal literacy was achieved among individuals who completed at least four to five years of primary schooling.[30] According to a recent report on education in Latin America (Chile Ministry of Education and UNESCO/OREALC, 2002), functional literacy requires at least six to seven years of schooling. Census data in many countries showed that 90% literacy levels were found (based on self-declarations) among those with four to six years of primary schooling. Such findings became the basis for setting a specific educational threshold to estimate the number of literates/illiterates.

In fact, the impact of completed schooling on self-declared literacy is more immediate and more varied than previously thought. Figure 7.10 reports adult literacy rates by three school attainment levels (no schooling, one to three years of schooling and four to six years) in over thirty developing countries and shows that:

- The sharpest increase in literacy is between adults with 'no schooling' and those reporting having completed only one to three years of primary education.
- In some countries (e.g. Albania, the Democratic Republic of the Congo, the Niger, Senegal, Sierra Leone, Sudan and Zambia), many individuals who completed four to six years of schooling remain illiterate.
- A relatively high percentage of respondents indicate that they can easily read a letter or a newspaper (i.e. are 'literate') even though they either never attended primary school or did not complete the first grade.

No firm conclusions can be drawn from these analyses, but they reinforce the notion that the quality of schooling matters for literacy and that uniform schooling thresholds warrant caution.

Literacy rates increase significantly as the levels of completed schooling increase

27. The literacy gap between the poorest and richest households tends to decrease as a country's literacy rate approaches 100% (the 'ceiling effect'). This strong negative association between a country's overall literacy rate and the disparities by wealth is apparent in the Carr-Hill (2005*a*) study.

28. Three exceptions are Chad, the Niger and Sierra Leone, where the gap is greater among men than women.

29. Indeed, the fact that census experts and statisticians have used the number of years of schooling as a proxy variable for individual literacy is due to the implicit assumption that the two processes are closely intertwined.

30. The apparent origins of this assertion can be traced back to the 1920s when certificates of literacy were required for residents of the State of New York who wished to exercise their right to vote. A committee was appointed to devise a reading test, the successful completion of which entitled a resident to a literacy certificate. The committee concluded that a voter's ability to comprehend what they read and to write intelligibly corresponded to the median achievement of Grade 4 pupils in city schools (UNESCO, 1957).

Figure 7.10: Adult literacy rates by three educational levels: no schooling, 1–3 years of schooling and 4–6 years of schooling, 2000

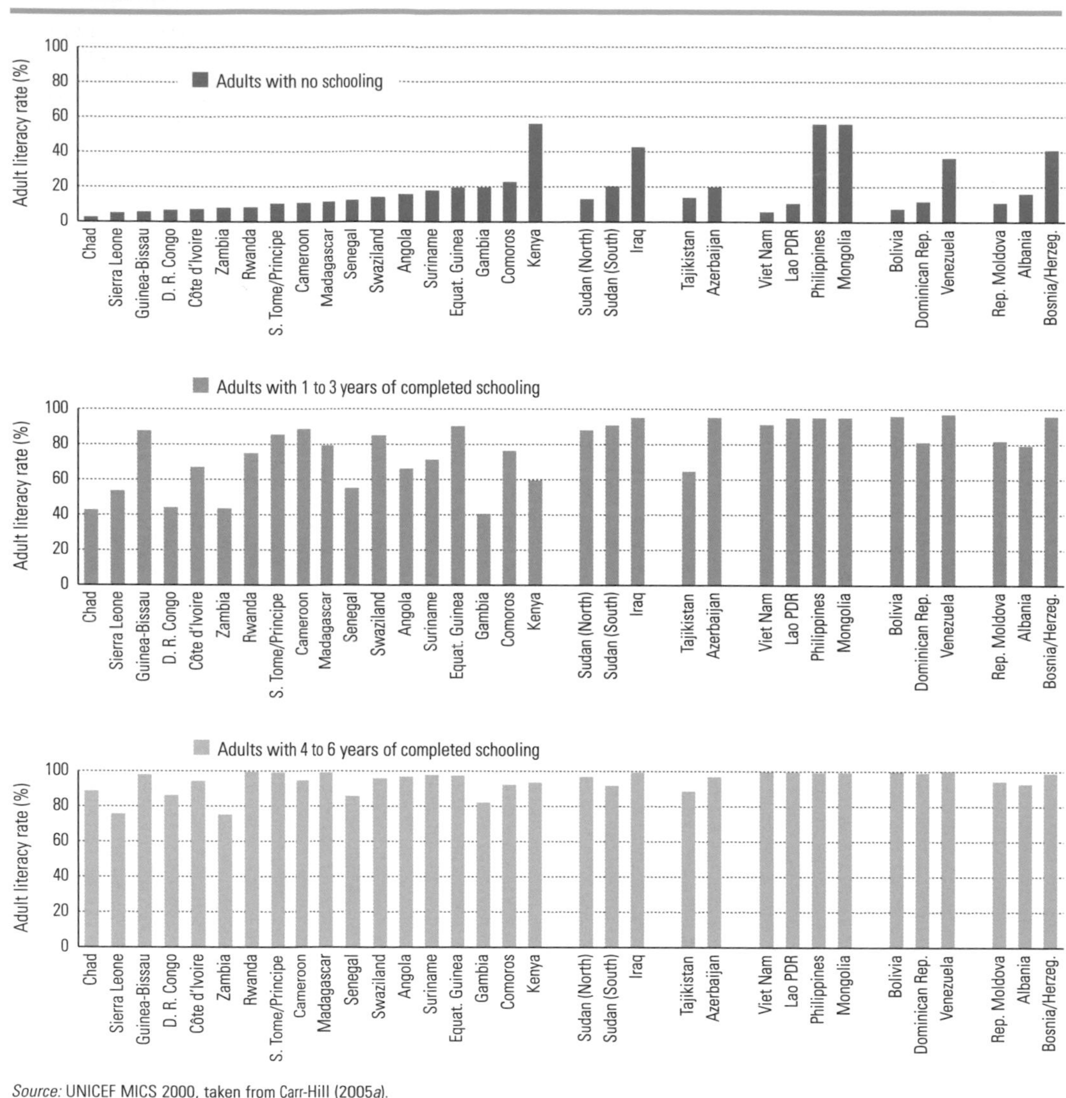

Source: UNICEF MICS 2000, taken from Carr-Hill (2005*a*).

Each additional year of schooling above zero can have a lasting effect on reducing illiteracy

Overall, the tentative conclusion is that each additional year of schooling above zero can have a lasting effect on reducing illiteracy, as conventionally assessed.[31] This conclusion, however, needs further confirmation in at least two respects. First, there may be doubts about the accuracy of self-reports of years of schooling completed: some respondents may have conflated *attended* years of schooling with *completed* years of schooling. Additional analyses of literacy rates by single years of primary schooling indicate that there is a relatively steep gradient between those with one year, two years, three years and four years of schooling in almost all sampled countries.[32] This pattern holds for both men and women. Second, it is important to carefully examine whether the effect of additional years of schooling remains after controlling for other variables such as sex, age and wealth (see below).

31. Alternative explanations to consider: (a) many low-schooled and 'illiterate' individuals have been excluded from the household-based sampling frame; (b) schooling refers to years completed, not years attended; high repetition rates or interrupted schooling might mask literacy gains among those who complete few years of school; and (c) according to cultural norms, everyone who attends school is considered literate, and schooled individuals should not refer to themselves as illiterates.

32. The exceptional cases, in which literacy rates do not increase with each and every year of formal schooling (between Grades 1 and 4), include Azerbaijan, and to a lesser extent, Cameroon, Comoros, Lesotho and Sierra Leone.

Which background characteristics are most associated with literacy?

Based on multivariate and multilevel analyses, this section explores the importance of gender, age, household size, area of residence, school experience, highest grade completed and wealth quintile on self-assessed literacy in twenty-eight developing countries, using the UNICEF Multiple Indicator Cluster Surveys database (Carr-Hill, 2005*a*).[33] In nearly all countries, key socio-demographic variables are highly predictive of illiteracy, with a substantial degree of variation explained in nearly every country context (Table 7.9).

In particular, the pattern of results confirms earlier findings and indicates that, net of other factors:

- Women are significantly less likely to be literate than men.
- Age is nearly always a significant factor, with older people more likely to be illiterate than younger people (this relationship is weaker than the association with gender).
- In most countries household size was not associated with literacy; however, in a limited number of cases, individuals living in larger households are less likely to be literate.
- Individuals from wealthier households are more likely to be literate than those from poorer households, but the strength and significance of this association vary.
- Urban residents are more likely to be literate than rural residents, although this factor is weaker than others.
- Whether or not an individual *ever went to school* has the strongest and most significant effect on literacy. Between the remaining two school variables – grouped years of schooling (e.g. 0, 1–3, 4–6) and the highest grade achieved – the latter is more important than the former.[34]

Finally, this pattern of results is not substantially altered when multilevel models are analysed for each country, which shows that the factors associated with individual-level literacy assessments are not substantively different at the household and 'sampling' cluster levels (Carr-Hill, 2005*a*).[35]

33. Multilevel models are used because different factors may be more or less significant depending on the unit of analysis that is, individual, household or country.

34. For further elucidation of the influence of each educational variable on self-assessed literacy, see Carr-Hill (2005*a*).

Table 7.9: Factors significantly associated with adult literacy rates in twenty-eight developing countries: results from multivariate analyses, 2000

	Number of countries in which factor is *significantly related* to adult literacy rate		Number of countries in which factor is *unrelated* to adult literacy rate
Socio-demographic factor	Positive association	Negative association	
Male	23	0	5
Age	1	20	7
Household size	4	7	17
Resides in urban area	16	3	9
Completed at least one year of schooling	26	0	2
Grouped levels of formal schooling	17	3	8
Highest grade completed	24	1	3
Wealth quintile of household	18	1	9

Source: UNICEF MICS 2000, taken from Carr-Hill (2005*a*).

Literacy in excluded groups

The present section focuses on a set of groups that – for complex social, cultural or political reasons – have been excluded from mainstream society and whose skills and practices in written languages remain severely restricted.[36] Such social exclusion may be due to disability, to ascribed characteristics such as ethnicity, caste or religion (in addition to gender and age), or to 'acquired' characteristics such as poverty, migration, displacement or incarceration. For example, in relatively closed caste societies such as Nepal, a number of types of ascribed attributes – including caste (e.g. Dalit), ethnicity (e.g. Janajati) and religion (e.g. Muslim) – act as barriers (in addition to those of gender and rural residence) to literacy acquisition (Table 7.10).

Urban residents are more likely to be literate than rural residents

Exclusion from a society's mainstream may result from a lack of recognition or respect for a certain group's cultural heritage, or from negative stereotypes that characterize group members as in some way inferior, primitive, backward or

35. Household surveys using third-party assessments of literacy may be biased since a single respondent (typically the head of household) may provide inaccurate literacy assessments about other household members. Multilevel analyses of literacy (i.e. for individuals, households and sampling 'clusters') found that: (a) the sign, size and statistical significance of coefficients associated with major independent variables were similar at the household and 'cluster' levels to those at the individual level (see Carr-Hill, 2005*a*) (this is to be expected given the large sample sizes involved); and (b) comparisons of the variances attributable to each of the three levels show that household-level variance is always smaller than both that attributable to the individual and to the cluster. This suggests, though it does not confirm, that the aforementioned household-level bias is relatively small.

36. Although most literature refers to the Minorities at Risk (MAR) data set (http://www.cidcm.umd.edu/inscr/mar/) – which estimates that approximately 900 million people worldwide (or 1 in 7) are subject to some form of exclusion – the MAR definition of excluded groups is not consistent with the one used here.

Table 7.10: Nepalese adult literacy rates by caste/ethnicity, 1991 and 2001

Caste/Ethnicity*	Literacy rate for those aged 6 years and over (%)		Increase in literacy rate (percentage points)
	1991	2001	
Hill/Terai B/C+	53.1	67.5	14.4
Terai Middle Caste	29.6	41.7	12.1
Dalit	22.6	33.8	11.2
Janajati	39.9	53.6	13.6
Religious minorities	23.1	34.5	11.3
Others	25.6	50.1	24.5
Total	**40.1**	**53.7**	**13.7**

* 'Hill/Terai B/C+' refers to upper castes; 'Dalit' refers to twenty-two 'untouchable' caste groups; and 'Janajati' to sixty indigenous groups.
Source: Koirala and Aryal (2005).

Discrimination towards members of excluded groups can trap them in a cycle of illiteracy

uncivilized. Subtle or overt discrimination towards members of these groups often results in reduced access to formal education and literacy programmes, thereby trapping them in a cycle of illiteracy. Yet, knowledge about the literacy levels of these groups is limited since they often go undetected in, or omitted from, census- or household-based literacy assessments (Carr-Hill, 2005*a*). The homeless, illegal migrants and street children, for example, cannot easily access public services, including education, and are excluded from household-based samples. Another neglected population is the institutionalized – be they in care facilities, on military bases or in prisons (see Box 7.2, on prisoners). Additional examples of undercounted and excluded groups (whose numbers vary considerably among different societies) include internally displaced persons and refugees, as well as nomadic, pastoralist and highly mobile populations.

Even when such excluded groups are included in literacy assessments, response rates are often low, owing to a variety of factors including security concerns, transportation difficulties and unstable households due to HIV/AIDS, immigration or natural disasters. In Asia, Latin America and sub-Saharan Africa, poor households in peri-urban areas are widely under-represented in national censuses. Unstable or hard-to-reach households impede

Box 7.2 Prisoners

There are approximately 10 million individuals incarcerated worldwide. Countries with the largest prison populations are the United States, China, the Russian Federation, Brazil, India, Ukraine, Mexico and South Africa (International Centre for Prison Studies, 2005). Prisoners, as a group, have had limited learning opportunities and often belong to socially disenfranchised groups prior to incarceration. Prison populations tend to be disproportionately poor and male. Unsurprisingly, the educational levels of inmates are lower than national averages. In Canada, for example, more than eight out of ten prisoners have not completed secondary school. In the United Kingdom and Portugal, a majority of prisoners have obtained no more than a primary-school education. In Romania and Brazil, a majority of prisoners are illiterate or have not completed primary school. Finally, foreigners and national minorities are overrepresented in prison populations. In Malaysia, Saudi Arabia and the European Union, over a quarter of all prisoners are foreign nationals (European Offenders Employment Forum, 2003).

International data on prison-based literacy or educational programmes are difficult to obtain and rarely comparable. Multiple actors are involved in such programmes, including trainers from the Ministry of Education, social workers, religious workers and volunteers. Literacy provision for prisoners is fraught with challenges. Prison-based educational activities tend to be organized by volunteers or on an ad hoc basis by community associations, NGOs, religious groups and civil society organizations. Literacy or basic skills classes are usually not provided in the mother tongue. In some countries (e.g. United Kingdom, New Zealand and South Africa), prisoners are charged for courses, which acts as an additional disincentive.
In other places (e.g. Brazil, France, New Delhi), while authorities claim educational opportunities are available to all prisoners, actual participation rates in such programmes vary greatly (Hanemann and Mauch, 2005). Unlike 'conventional' adult literacy programmes, educational activities in prison rarely meet minimum requirements for successful learning (de Maeyer, 2005). Conditions of overcrowding, lack of classroom space and inappropriate literacy materials are not conducive either to learning or to practising literacy skills.

the measurement and monitoring of literacy, since lists of sampled households become quickly out of date.[37] The context in which the assessment occurs (e.g. crowded, cramped or noisy homes) can also reduce data quality. On the other hand, if respondents are requested to come to assessment centres – where 'standard' conditions prevail – response rates decline. Adjustments can be made for some of these problems, but literacy assessments of excluded groups are rarely complete or of high quality.

Indigenous peoples[38]

There are approximately 300 to 350 million indigenous people, who speak between 4,000 and 5,000 languages, live in more than 70 countries and account for 5% of the world's population (UNDP, 2004*a*).[39] Over 60% of indigenous or tribal peoples live in Asia, about 17% in Latin America, and the remainder in Africa, Europe and North America (UNDP, 2004*a*). India, for example, is home to 90 million indigenous people (about 8% of its population), who belong to some 400 tribal groups (UIE, 1999). Large indigenous populations reside particularly in Mexico, Bolivia, Peru, Ecuador, Guatemala, Canada and the United States (UNDP, 2004*a*). Many other indigenous communities are scattered throughout Oceania, in particular Papua New Guinea.

More often than not, population censuses disregard, or are not allowed to assess, the ethnicity of their populations, thereby limiting knowledge on these groups' literacy and educational circumstances.[40] Available evidence suggests that significant disparities exist between indigenous and non-indigenous populations. For example, the national literacy rate in Ecuador was 91% (based on 2001 census figures), but was only 72% for indigenous groups (Torres, 2005). In Bangladesh, only 18% of indigenous peoples were literate (1991 census figures), as compared to the national figure of 40% (Rao and Robinson-Pant, 2003). In Namibia, the adult literacy rate among the San population is approximately 20%, as compared to the 95% rate among the Afrikaans population (UNDP, 2004*a*). Viet Nam has a national literacy rate of 87%, but it has a literacy rate of only 4% for some indigenous groups such as the Lolos. Nepal's Dalit population has a significantly lower adult literacy rate than the rest of the population (Table 7.10).[41] According to the 1996 Adult Literacy Survey in New Zealand, significantly higher percentages of Maoris than non-Maoris scored below the minimum level required to meet the 'complex demands of everyday life and work' in prose, document and quantitative literacy.[42] Literacy rates among the Roma in Central Europe are lower than those of majority populations (Ringold et al., 2004).

There are also substantial literacy gender gaps among indigenous peoples. In Cambodia, for example, the literacy rate among indigenous communities in the Ratanakiri and Mondulkiri provinces is a mere 2% for women, but 20% for men. In Viet Nam, the lowest literacy rates are found among indigenous girls and women (UNESCO/PROAP, 2001). In Rajasthan, India, the literacy rate among indigenous women was 8%, compared to 39% among indigenous men (Rao and Robinson-Pant, 2003). Likewise, female literacy rates among Peruvian and Bolivian indigenous populations are much lower than those for men (UNESCO/OREALC, 2004).

No (or limited) access to formal schooling has clearly resulted in lower literacy levels among indigenous populations. Ecuador's indigenous population (aged 24 and older) has completed, on average, 3.3 years of formal schooling; the corresponding figure for the non-indigenous population is 7.3 (Torres, 2005). Seventeen per cent of Canada's indigenous 15- to 49-year-olds reported no formal schooling or less than Grade 9 as their highest level of education, in contrast to 6% in the non-indigenous population. Disparities in educational attainment were even larger among older age groups according to Ningwakwe (2002). Recent census figures in Australia indicate

In Namibia, the adult literacy rate among the San population is approximately 20%, as compared to the 95% rate among the Afrikaans population

37. Such households may include: elderly household heads with young children, grandparent households; large households with unrelated fostered or orphaned children attached; child-headed households; single-parent, mother- or father-headed households; cluster foster care – where a group of children is cared for formally or informally by neighbouring adult households; children in subservient, exploited or abusive fostering relationships; itinerant, displaced or homeless children; neglected, displaced children in groups or gangs (Hunter and Fall, 1998).

38. Indigenous peoples are descendants of the original habitants of a region, prior to colonization, who have maintained some or all of their linguistic, cultural and organizational characteristics. International organizations including the United Nations, the International Labour Office and the World Bank have applied the following four criteria to distinguish indigenous peoples:

- They usually live within or maintain an attachment to geographically distinct ancestral territories.
- They tend to maintain distinct social, economic and political institutions within their territories.
- They typically aspire to remain distinct culturally, geographically and institutionally, rather than to assimilate fully into national society.
- They self-identify as indigenous or tribal (UNDP, 2005).

Self-identification is regarded as a fundamental criterion for determining an indigenous status, which is being claimed by many 'politically marginalized, territorially based ethnic groups ... who are culturally distinct from the majority populations of the states where they live' (Minority Rights Group website, 2003, cited in Rao and Robinson-Pant, 2003).

39. Indigenous groups account for approximately two-thirds of the world's 6,700 mostly oral languages (Skutnabb-Kangas, 2001).

40. Important exceptions include Bolivia, Brazil, Mexico and Peru. Namibia is the only country to calculate the human development index by linguistic group (UNDP, 2004*a*). Indigenous organizations repeatedly emphasize that data collection and data disaggregation are critical tools for advocacy and policy development concerning indigenous issues such as literacy (see, for instance, http://www.unhchr.ch/indigenous/forum.htm).

41. The National Dalit Commission defines as *Dalit* those communities which, by virtue of caste-based discrimination and 'untouchability', are less developed in the social, economic, educational, political and religious spheres and are deprived of human dignity and social justice (UNDP, 2004*a*).

42. Percentages of Maoris who scored below the minimum level were: in prose literacy, 67%; in document literacy, 72%; and in quantitative literacy or numeracy, 72%. The respective figures for non-Maoris were 42%, 47% and 46% (Statistics New Zealand [Te Tari Tatau], http://www.stats.govt.nz/, accessed 16 February 2005.)

that 3% of indigenous adults never attended school, compared with only 1% of non-indigenous adults (Australian Bureau of Statistics, 2003). Roma throughout Europe have attended school less than non-Roma (Ringold et al., 2003) (Box 7.3).

Box 7.3 Roma in Spain

Roma have lived in Spain for over six centuries but still remain excluded from society. The Spanish Roma community numbers approximately 650,000, half of whom are under 18, out of a total population of 40 million inhabitants. Levels of education attainment among Roma children have been low due to late commencement of schooling, irregular attendance and early drop-out rates. Since 1994, however, there have been improvements in primary school attendance, with more than 90% of Roma children officially entering infant or primary schools. Increasingly, Roma families are deciding themselves to send their children to school, rather than being directed to do so by social services. While growing numbers of Roma youth are enrolled in secondary education, their need to support their families and assume adult responsibilities continues to result in high drop-out rates

Source: Vélaz de Medrano (2005).

Migration flows raise the demand for literacy skills among both the migrants and those family members who remain behind

Nomadic or pastoralist populations

Nomads or pastoralists, who number in the tens of millions, are geographically mobile groups found primarily in the African drylands, the Middle East and parts of Asia. In Nigeria, for example, approximately 10 million people (8% of the total population), including about 3.6 million school-aged children, are pastoralist nomads or members of migrant fishing communities. The National Commission for Nomadic Education, Nigeria, has estimated that, in 1990, the literacy rate among Nigerian nomads was 0.02%, and among migrant fishermen, 2%. In the Afar region of Ethiopia, the literacy rate for adults was 25% in 1999, but only 8% in the rural pastoralist areas (Carr-Hill, 2005*b*).

In general, the mobile lifestyles of nomadic groups have hindered their access to education (Ezeomah, 1997). The low population density and the high cost of providing formal schooling to nomadic and pastoralist children has led many countries such as Mongolia to use education as a means of sedentarization and settlement (Kratli, 2000). The development of boarding schools and hostels (e.g. in Kenya) represents another strategy to reach these children. The issue of cultural opportunities lost through such programmes has been recognized, but there has been little systematic response to these communities' needs (Carr-Hill, 2005*a*).

Migrants

Worldwide, migration has grown dramatically in recent decades. According to the International Organization for Migration, the number of international migrants has increased from 76 million in 1960 to over 185 million today, with a wider range of sending and receiving countries (UNDP, 2004*a*). Economic betterment remains the overwhelming motive for the massive migration from the South to the North. The break-up of the former Soviet Union, greater economic interdependence, cheaper and more accessible transportation, and increases in refugees and displaced persons due to wars and political conflicts have also been significant factors.

Internal migrant flows typically exceed international flows. In China, for example, over 120 million rural residents had moved into urban areas, whereas 'only' 550,000 Chinese nationals were living and working abroad (International Organization for Migration, 2005). Internal migration also predominates in Bangladesh, Cambodia, Ethiopia, India, Mongolia, Pakistan, Viet Nam and most of sub-Saharan Africa (International Organization for Migration, 2005).[43]

Migration flows tend to raise the demand for literacy skills among both the migrants and those family members who remain behind. For example, male Senegalese migrants living in France write home to their families, using French. Then their wives, many of whom cannot read French, must often ask others in their communities to translate their husbands' letters for them. Today, as the cost of international calls decreases, mobile phones are increasingly being used by migrant families to send short written messages, a factor that appears to be adding to the demand for literacy.

Yet it is difficult to generalize about the varying literacy situations and learning needs of heterogeneous migrant populations. For example, between 500,000 and 1 million adults in the United Kingdom do not speak English as their first language (Department for Education and Skills, 2001). Their literacy skills and second-

43. Figures for internal migration should be treated with caution since movement into cities in most countries is neither well regulated nor visible.

language levels vary by country of origin, as well as gender. Among Somali in the United Kingdom, 90% of men, but only 60% of women, can read in Somali. Yet most language courses assume that participants are already literate in their mother tongue or that illiterate immigrant adults can be taught to read and write in English at the same time as acquiring skills in first languages (Martinez Nateras, 2003).

Literacy training for international migrants can be impeded by a variety of factors, including instruction in a foreign language, lack of programmatic flexibility, and the location and provision of the courses. The problematic legal status of migrants – and their fear of deportation – can act as powerful deterrents to participating in literacy courses. Many of these issues also apply to internal migrants, who face considerable difficulties when moving from one region to another. A literate migrant from a rural community might become 'illiterate' in an urban community that uses different written languages and more technologically advanced communication systems. For instance, in practical terms, the literacy ability of rural Tamils who move to New Delhi will worsen if they cannot read and write in Hindi. In some countries, internal migrants who live in impoverished urban areas face long-term insecurity and therefore have little incentive to invest in long-term learning programmes. Thus, even if the provision and management of urban-based literacy programmes are easier than rural-based ones, there may be little uptake (Sharma et al., 2002).

Persons with disabilities

Over 600 million people (about 10% of the world's population) – two-thirds of whom live in low-income countries – have a disability of one form or another. The World Health Organization (WHO) points out that health risks such as poverty, malnutrition, armed conflict and natural disasters – together with increased life expectancy in industrial countries – will increase the number of people with disabilities (WHO, 2005). The OECD has established three categories of disability: disabilities for which there is substantive normative agreement (e.g. blindness, deafness and severe intellectual impairment); disabilities that are manifested as learning difficulties; and disabilities that are the result of socio-economic, cultural and linguistic disadvantages.[44] The UN is addressing these multiple needs by drafting a Convention on the Protection and Promotion of the Rights and Dignity of Persons with Disabilities.

People with disabilities are often invisible in official statistics. It is estimated that about 35% of all out-of-school children have disabilities (Erickson, 2005) and that fewer than 2% of children with a disability are enrolled in school (Disability Awareness in Action [DAA], 2001). In Africa, more than 90% of all disabled children have never gone to school (Balescut, 2005). In Canada and Australia, more than 40% of disabled children have only completed primary education (DAA, 1998).

People with disabilities are often invisible in official statistics

Gender also influences the relationship between disabilities and illiteracy: limited data suggest that gender disparities in literacy rates are greater for people with disabilities (DAA, 1994). In 1998, for example, a large proportion of blind and other disabled girls in South Asia remained illiterate, while the general rate of literacy among women increased considerably in all South Asian countries. In India in the same year, more than 95% of disabled male children received no education. Educational exclusion is thought to be higher among disabled female children (DAA, 1998).

There is little comparative information regarding the literacy achievements of students with disabilities. National assessments in the United States suggest that only half of the students who receive special education services participated in the National Assessment of Educational Progress (NAEP) and even fewer participate in state-wide testing (Elliot et al., 1995).

Towards an expanded understanding of literacy

The global challenge of literacy is much greater, both quantitatively and qualitatively, than the analysis so far presented in this chapter would seem to imply. The results are based almost exclusively on conventional indirect assessments and a dichotomy between 'literate' and 'illiterate', which are now considered to be quite inaccurate, and overly simplistic, so that large-scale adult literacy surveys no longer rely on them.

The present section highlights alternative measures and assessments of literacy and seeks to demonstrate the value of 'non-conventional' approaches that:

- incorporate direct (rather than indirect) assessments of literacy;

44. This framework should be applied cautiously; it runs the risk of enabling authorities to claim to be addressing the different needs of these categories, while only skimming the surface of each. Without careful attention to the range of individual needs represented by each category, categorization can serve to exclude the most needy (Erickson, 2005).

- measure literacy with ordinal or continuous scales (rather than as dichotomies); and/or
- conceive of literacy as a multidimensional (rather than a uni-dimensional) phenomenon.

It is important to note that these more recent and 'non-conventional' studies of literacy still have much in common with previous research. For instance, recent comparative assessments continue to view literacy as a set of cognitive skills acquired by individuals, that can be measured independently of the context in which the acquisition process occurred. The change in approach is more one of nuance – a growing emphasis on the application of literacy skills in everyday life or, 'how adults use printed and written information [such as news stories, editorials, poems, forms, books, maps, transportation schedules and job applications] to function in society' (OECD/HRDC, 1997). While the notion of *functional literacy* has been disseminated widely since the 1970s, it is only now being practically assessed with multiple dimensions, each measured along continuous scales.

Direct assessments of literacy in developing countries

Indirect assessments usually overstate 'true' literacy levels

For over a decade, calls have circulated for improved literacy measures, especially for developing countries, (e.g. Terryn, 2003; United Nations Statistical Office, 1989; Wagner, 2005). So, too, has the recognition that such measurement strategies must be simpler and cheaper than those used in OECD countries (Wagner, 2003). Yet, until recently, there was little consensus about how best to measure and monitor literacy in the developing world.

Concurrently, various countries and agencies have carried out household surveys with direct assessments of literacy (Table 7.11 and Box 7.4). These assessments evolved in a decentralized fashion, frequently under severe resource constraints. Not surprisingly, the resulting reports vary in quality, and often provide limited information about the survey's design and implementation (Schaffner, 2005).

Despite these limitations, these studies clearly show that indirect assessments usually overstate 'true' literacy levels. In Morocco, while 45% of sampled respondents reported being literate (self-assessment), only 33% demonstrated a basic literacy competence and only 24% demonstrated a full competence. In Bangladesh, only 83% of those who indicated they could read actually achieved the minimal reading level when asked to complete a simple test. In the United Republic of Tanzania, household reports tended to overstate literacy rates (Schaffner, 2005).

The upward bias of indirectly assessed literacy tends to be greater among individuals with few years of schooling. In the Demographic and Health Surveys[45] conducted in Ethiopia (2000) and Nicaragua (2001), there was a strong tendency for conventional assessments to overstate literacy

Table 7.11: Developing country household-based surveys with direct literacy assessments

Survey	Year*
Zimbabwe Literacy Survey	1986
Kenya Literacy Survey	1988
Ghana Living Standards Measurement Survey	1988–89
Morocco Literacy Survey	1991–92
Bangladesh: Assessment of Basic Learning Skills	1992
Botswana: National Survey on Literacy	1993
U.R. Tanzania Human Resource Survey	1993
Namibia: Adult Literacy in Ondangwa and Windhoek	1994
Indonesia Family Life Survey (Wave 3)	2000
Ethiopia Demographic and Health Survey	2000
Nicaragua Demographic and Health Survey	2001
Lao PDR National Literacy Survey	2001
Ghana Household and School Survey	2003
Additional household surveys with direct assessments	
Jamaica National Literacy Survey	1994
Trinidad and Tobago National Literacy Survey	1995
Jamaica Adult Literacy Survey	1999
Chile International Adult Literacy Survey	1998
Malta National Literacy Survey	1999
Cambodia National Literacy Survey	1999
Bermuda Population Census	2000

* *Note:* The year indicates the year of the survey, not the year of survey-based reports/publications.

Sources: General: Schaffner (2005). See also Chilisa (2003); Knight and Sabot (1990); Bangladesh: Greaney et al. (1998); Bermuda: Blum et al. (2001); Botswana: Commeyras and Chilisa (2001); Cambodia: ACCU (1999); Chile: Blum et al. (2001); Ethiopia: http://www.measuredhs.com; Ghana: Operations Evaluation Department (2004); World Bank (1999); Indonesia: Strauss et al. (2004); Jamaica: Statistical Institute of Jamaica (1995); Lao PDR: Lao People's Democratic Republic, Ministry of Education. Department of Non-formal Education (2004); Malta: Mifsud et al. (2000*a*, 2000*b*); Morocco: Lavy et al. (1995); Namibia: Namibia Ministry of Education and Culture and University of Namibia (1994); Nicaragua: http://www.measuredhs.com; U. R. Tanzania: http://www.worldbank.org/html/prdph/lsms/country/tza/tanzdocs.html; Trinidad and Tobago: St Bernard and Salim (1995); Zimbabwe and Kenya: United Nations Statistical Office (1989).

45. The Demographic and Health Survey (DHS) programme, funded by the United States Agency for International Development (USAID) and administered by ORC Macro, has implemented nearly 200 household surveys in over seventy countries since 1984 (http://www.measuredhs.com). Most DHS instruments prior to 2000 collected only household reports on literacy. After a significant revision of the model questionnaire in 2000, DHS instruments now contain simple direct assessments of reading skills. Respondents are asked to read a simple sentence in their mother tongue, and the interviewer records whether the respondent was able to read some, all, or none of the sentences. Sentences include: 'Parents love their children', 'Farming is hard work', 'The child is reading a book', and 'Children work hard at school.' According to DHS documents, the process of revising the questionnaires involved a large number of experts and users from a variety of international organizations.

Box 7.4 Direct assessments of 'literacy as skills'

Many view literacy as the possession of skills related to the interpretation or use of written language and symbols. Yet conceptions of 'literacy as skills' differ as regards the types and levels of skills individuals must possess in order to be considered literate. Direct assessments of literacy typically involve a two-stage approach: first, skill domains are identified and then the skills are categorized into literacy levels.

Determining skill domains necessitates choices about whether the required skills relate to:

- reading, writing, oral or written mathematical calculations, or the interpretation of visual information other than words;
- tasks commonly performed in school contexts or in everyday life;
- the use of 'any' written language (including various mother tongues), or only the use of a specific official, national or international language.

Then, within each skill domain, individuals are categorized into one of several skill levels or categories. For example, those who are able to identify letters and sound out words, read aloud a simple sentence, or read a letter with understanding, may be placed in the respective categories of 'pre-literate', 'basic literacy' and 'functional literacy'. Those who cannot complete any of these tasks may be labelled 'illiterate'. Alternative strategies view literacy as a continuum and measure literacy levels with a continuous score in each skill domain.

Some important lessons from direct assessments of literacy skills:

- The key skill domains to assess literacy are: reading/writing in the official language, reading/writing in the local language, oral mathematics and written mathematics. These six domains constitute distinct competencies.
- Interpreting results about a particular literacy skill based only on a single test item is extremely problematic. Several questions should be used to measure each skill domain.
- Sorting respondents into a small number of clearly defined categories of skill levels appears more useful than assessments aimed at giving respondents continuous cognitive skill scores.
- Determining whether individuals can 'decode' a written language by having them read aloud a simple sentence can be done simply and with reasonable accuracy. By contrast, attempts to assess higher skill levels involving comprehension and interpretation of prose or documents are more problematic, especially if comparability across countries or ethno-linguistic groups is sought. In short, the quality, ease and comparability of direct literacy assessments decrease as the level and range of literacy skills to be measured increases.
- Establishing a clear protocol for test administration, which minimizes the amount of discretion on the part of interviewers or test administrators, is important. So too is extensive pre-testing in local contexts.

Source: Schaffner (2005).

among minimally schooled populations. Among Ethiopian women with one year of schooling, 59% were considered literate by household assessments, while only 27% passed a simple reading test. Among Ethiopian men with one year of schooling, the literacy rate was 65% based on household assessments, but only 33% based on direct assessments. In Nicaragua, indirectly assessed literacy rates were higher than directly assessed rates in all education groups. Though the differences were smaller than in Ethiopia, they were especially high for individuals with only a few years of schooling. This tendency, however, is not universal: in Botswana, for example, it was found that only 2% of those who said they could read or write in English or Setswana failed the related direct test (Schaffner, 2005).

In short, the extent to which indirect literacy assessments overstate actual reading and writing skills varies from country to country. The evidence suggests that these biases are larger in countries where educational attainment is lower and school quality weaker. Additionally, in those countries where conventional assessments tend to greatly overstate actual literacy levels, the overstatement is greater for men than for women. This is true even when the direct assessment is based on simple measures of rudimentary reading skills.

Among Ethiopian women with one year of schooling, 59% were considered literate by household assessments, while only 27% passed a simple reading test

Box 7.5 Literacy surveys in Botswana and Brazil

■ Several attempts to include literacy-related questions in **Botswana**'s national censuses of 1981 and 1991 were rejected on the grounds that the census questionnaire would be too long. The first national survey to establish the literacy rate in Botswana was carried out in 1993 and covered a total population of 1.5 million people (46% male and 54% female). In the survey, 'objective literacy' was defined as 'the ability to read and write in either Setswana, English, or both; and the ability to carry out simple mathematical computations'. 'Ability' was ascertained through the results of literacy tests, and respondents who scored above 50% were categorized as literate. The second national literacy survey, carried out ten years later, expanded the target group to cover all citizens aged 10 to 70. The total population estimated from this second survey was 1.9 million (47% male, 53% female). A total of 7,280 households (46% rural and 55% urban) were selected for the survey, with a response rate of 94%. The two national literacy surveys constitute a milestone in the effort to provide a reliable database for politicians and decision-makers, as well as managers of the Botswana National Literary Programme. They mirror an innovative policy to systematically monitor the evolution of literacy in the country. Botswana's policy now is that literacy surveys are to be conducted every ten years, when new National Population Census data are available.

■ In **Brazil**, surveys of the literacy levels of the adult population based on skills testing are conducted at the initiative of the National Functional Literacy Index (NFLI). With the objective of fomenting a debate and public engagement in the literacy issue, NFLI has been divulging, ever since 2001, the results of annual household surveys done with sample groups representing the Brazilian population, aged 15 to 64 (Masagão Ribeiro, 2003; Fonseca, 2004). Four surveys have been carried out: two for reading and writing, and two for mathematics. Besides skills testing, detailed questionnaires have been administered on reading, writing and mathematics practices in various contexts: home, work, religious, community participation and continuing education. NFLI uses a comprehensive concept of literacy, understood as the skills involved in the use of written language and numeric calculation, and its actual use in social practices, by individuals, social groups and societies, as well as the meaning those individuals and groups attribute to the development of those skills and practices.

Sources: Masagão Ribeiro and Gomes Batista (2005); Hanemann (2005*a*).

Direct assessments show that there is no uniform educational threshold at which 90% of adults achieve literacy

Direct assessments of literacy also challenge assumptions about the number of school years needed for literacy skills to be acquired and retained. As discussed above, sorting individuals into 'literate' and 'illiterate' categories based on the completion of a predetermined educational threshold (say, four, five or six years) is a highly inaccurate procedure. Direct assessments of literacy carried out in different contexts show that there is no uniform educational threshold at which 90% of adults achieve literacy. In some cases, the vast majority of adults attain basic literacy after four years of schooling, and, in others, only after nine years, reflecting in large measure the quality of schooling they receive. In short, direct assessments of literacy indicate that: (a) a standard educational attainment proxy for literacy across developing countries does not exist; and (b) educational thresholds for widespread literacy tend to be *higher* than previously assumed.

Large-scale comparative surveys of adult literacy

The International Adult Literacy Survey (IALS) represents the largest comparative survey of adult literacy ever undertaken. Carried out in three phases (1994, 1996 and 1998), in some twenty developed countries,[46] it incorporates each of the aforementioned 'non-conventional' components (Box 7.6).

The findings indicate the extent to which significant segments of the adult populations in many developed countries possess only low levels of literacy skills (such as being able to read and understand newspapers and brochures) that many consider necessary for productive

46. The first survey took place in 1994 and covered nine countries: Canada (English- and French-speaking), France, Germany, Ireland, the Netherlands, Poland, Sweden, Switzerland (German- and French-speaking regions) and the United States, with France withdrawing from the survey in November 1994. A second study was conducted in 1996, which included samples from Austria, the Flemish Community of Belgium, New Zealand and the United Kingdom. A third round of data collection (1998) was carried out in Chile, the Czech Republic, Denmark, Finland, Hungary, Italy, Norway and the Italian-speaking region of Switzerland (OECD/HRDC, 1997; OECD/Statistics Canada, 1995, 2000).

Box 7.6 Literacy assessment in the International Adult Literacy Survey

Nationally representative samples of adults aged 16–65 responded to two questionnaires: one measuring literacy knowledge and skills in three domains (prose, document and quantitative literacy) and the other asking for background information on education, labour force participation, income, language proficiencies and literacy practices. Trained interviewers carried out the two phases of the survey at the respondent's home, which typically took about forty-five minutes to complete the background questions and sixty minutes for the literacy tasks. In each literacy domain, IALS developed a series of tasks, which were intended to minimize cultural and linguistic differences, and which became the basis for placing individuals on a continuous scale ranging from 0 to 500 points. Scores on this scale were categorized into five literacy levels: from levels 1 and 2, for individuals with relatively poor literacy skills, to levels 4 and 5, where individuals command higher-order information-processing skills. Literacy ability was defined as the point in each domain where an individual has an 80% chance of successful completion of a set of tasks of varying difficulty.

Source: OECD/Statistics Canada (2000).

Figure 7.11: Distribution of adults by level of prose literacy proficiency, 1994–1998

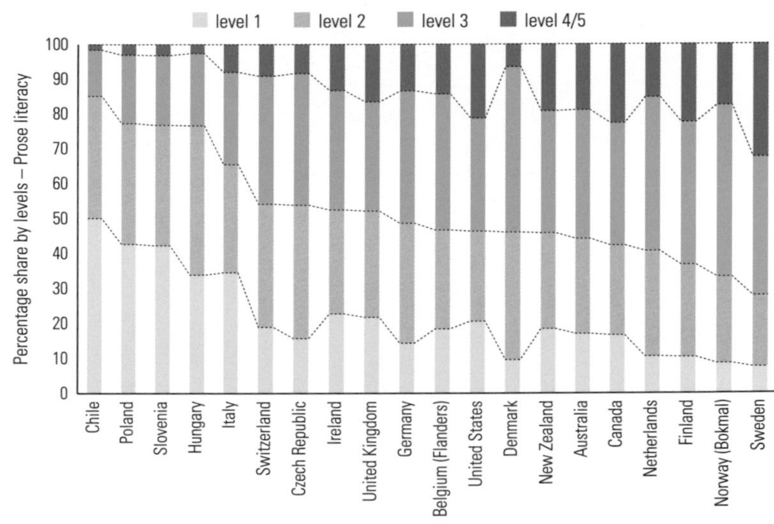

Note: The figure shows the distribution of adults by level of prose literacy proficiency, defined as the ability to understand and use information from texts such as news articles or fiction. Results were categorized into five different levels (1 being the lowest and 5 the highest), based on an analysis of the skills represented by the type of tasks successfully completed by the reader. Countries are listed in ascending order based on mean results for prose literacy.
Source: OECD/Statistics Canada (2000).

employment and prosperity in knowledge-based societies (Figure 7.11). Even in the Nordic countries, where most adults performed well in all three literacy areas (prose, document and quantitative), there were significant proportions whose skill levels were barely above the minimal threshold. In other areas, notably in Eastern Europe and Chile, more than two-thirds of adults aged 15–65 have relatively weak literacy and numeracy skills, and literacy levels tend to be distributed in a highly unequal manner. (See the map *Literacy challenges in selected countries*, p. 184)

A more recent comparative adult literacy project, the Adult Literacy and Life Skills Survey (ALL), was conducted in six countries in 2003.[47] Like IALS, the ALL survey defined literacy and numeracy in functional terms and described the distribution of these skills among adults in each participating country.[48] The basic findings from the ALL survey are very similar to those from IALS.

Much of the distribution of literacy and numeracy skills among adults in industrialized countries is related to the distribution of completed schooling in each country (Somers, 2005).[49] However, the level of literacy skills of individuals with low levels of education varies greatly from country to country, while individuals with high levels of schooling have fairly high literacy skills no matter what their country. Countries with large immigrant populations, many linguistic minorities, low labour force participation rates and limited access to adult education were more likely to have adult literacy skills dip below the levels expected based on completed schooling (Somers, 2005). Thus, improving school quality for the least advantaged socio-economic groups, offering high-quality language training to immigrants and their children (as well as to other linguistic minorities),

Even in the Nordic countries, there were significant proportions whose skill levels were barely above the minimal threshold

47. Participating countries were Bermuda, Canada, Italy, Norway, Switzerland and the United States. Adults surveyed ranged in age from 16 to 65 (Statistics Canada/OECD, 2005). Currently, a second phase of ALL is underway.

48. Literacy was defined as the knowledge and skills needed to understand and use information from text and other written formats. Numeracy was defined as the knowledge and skills necessary to manage mathematical demands of diverse situations.

49. The shape and strength of the relationship between educational attainment and literacy varies by literacy component and country.

Literacy challenges in selected countries and territories
Percentage of adults aged 16 to 65 with very poor skills in prose literacy

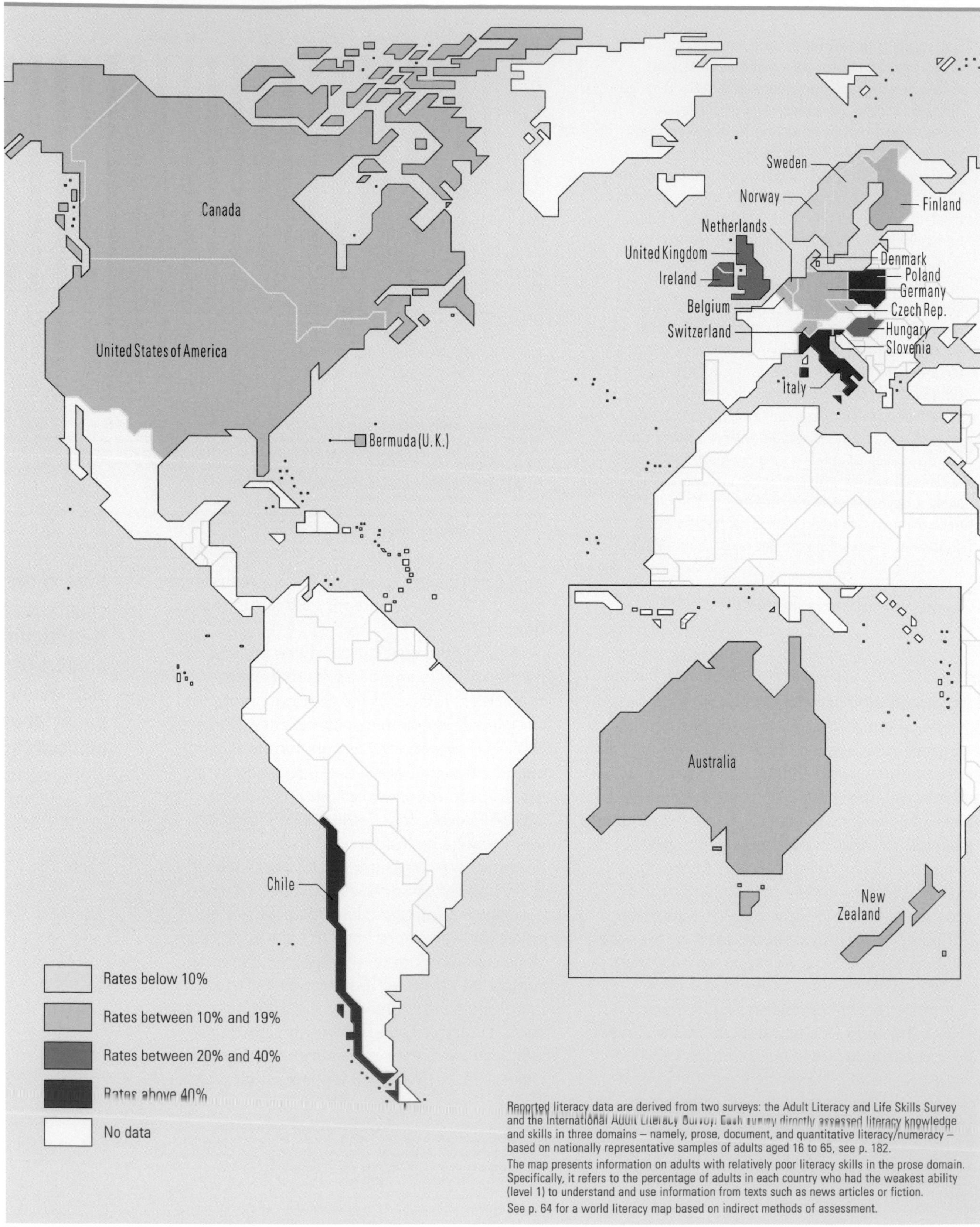

Reported literacy data are derived from two surveys: the Adult Literacy and Life Skills Survey and the International Adult Literacy Survey. Each survey directly assessed literacy knowledge and skills in three domains – namely, prose, document, and quantitative literacy/numeracy – based on nationally representative samples of adults aged 16 to 65, see p. 182.

The map presents information on adults with relatively poor literacy skills in the prose domain. Specifically, it refers to the percentage of adults in each country who had the weakest ability (level 1) to understand and use information from texts such as news articles or fiction.

See p. 64 for a world literacy map based on indirect methods of assessment.

The boundaries and names shown and the designations used on this map do not imply official endorsement or acceptance by UNESCO.

Based on United Nations map

improving access to affordable training options for adults and publicizing the importance of lifelong learning, are all ways to improve the levels and equitable distribution of adult literacy in developed countries.

Adult literacy in urban China

In December 2001, an IALS-like survey designed to assess the literacy skills of urban Chinese workers (including migrants) was carried out in five cities, as part of a labour force survey (see Giles et al., 2003). The China Adult Literacy Survey (CALS) measured prose, document and quantitative literacy, using a continuous-scale approach, and represented the first survey of its kind in China.[50] Among other things, CALS reported the skill levels of different subpopulations in the urban Chinese labour force, by gender, migrant status and region, and underscored areas in which migrants and women are discriminated against in the labour market. In addition to identifying mechanisms for increasing opportunities for lifelong learning, CALS noted important policy implications regarding adult skill training, especially for disadvantaged groups in the labour market (Ross et al., 2005).

The Literacy Assessment and Monitoring Programme

The Literacy Assessment and Monitoring Programme (LAMP) is a cross-national and comparable direct literacy assessment project, mainly for developing countries, being designed by the UNESCO Institute for Statistics (UIS). The overall aim is twofold: first, to provide reliable and comparable estimates of the levels and distribution of functional literacy and numeracy skills; and, second, to contribute to national and international policy needs and decision-making processes. When fully implemented, LAMP surveys are intended to replace indirect assessments of literacy in censuses or household surveys. Plans are for LAMP surveys to be piloted in several countries (El Salvador, Kenya, Mongolia, Morocco and the Niger) towards the end of 2005, after which LAMP will be expanded to other countries.

A critical assessment

Alternative literacy assessments have expanded the conventional classification system beyond the literate/illiterate dichotomy by directly measuring literacy in multiple domains, using ordinal or continuous scales. These assessments have enabled comparisons within and across countries over time. In contrast to self-declarations and third-party assessments, direct literacy assessments provide literacy stakeholders with more accurate information on literacy trends and patterns. Moreover, countries involved in large-scale surveys such as IALS and LAMP benefit from capacity-building, given the design, implementation and dissemination demands of such surveys. Supporters of such literacy surveys recognize that there are trade-offs from such a complex and costly assessment exercises: the need for substantial human and financial resources; the time needed for item development, data collection and report preparation; and the complexity of the methodologies employed.

Direct literacy assessments provide more accurate information on literacy trends and patterns

A common critique of large-scale, alternative assessments is their high costs (including hidden costs to national governments) and the limited sense of 'ownership' by local and national agencies.[51] Others raise concerns over language and translation issues (Blum et al., 2001) and note problems with sampling frames, operational definitions and response rates (Carey, 2000). The time required to run large-scale assessments does not always permit governments and decision-makers to respond to literacy needs with timely policies.[52]

Some critics question key assumptions inherent in existing or proposed literacy assessments like IALS and LAMP. For example, some scholars dispute whether a common measurement instrument can be developed to compare individuals from different education systems, using standard translation and psychometric scaling techniques (Goldstein, 2004). Others argue that cross-national literacy assessments assume incorrectly that literacy skills and practices have the same meaning across cultures, and that attempts to ground literacy survey items in real-life situations across

50. The China Adult Literacy Survey was developed with the support of the World Bank, the Chinese Academy of Social Sciences, the University of Michigan and Michigan State University. The study was conducted in the same cities that were part of the China Urban Labour Study, in 2001. The Chinese team drew upon the IALS project at Statistics Canada for a part of the study. (For a detailed explanation of the survey, see Giles et al., 2003.)

51. Cost estimates of the IALS surveys run into the tens of millions of US dollars. The cost of a national literacy survey in Zimbabwe in 1989 was estimated at US$100,000 (Wagner, 2003).

52. Wagner (2003) suggests three parameters should be considered when developing assessment tools in developing countries: smaller, quicker and cheaper.

Box 7.7 Implications for measuring and monitoring literacy

The measurement and monitoring of literacy and illiteracy has evolved considerably during the past fifty years. Today, more than ever, it is important to:

- clarify what is meant by 'literacy', including distinguishing among different types and levels of literacy;
- improve the measurement of literacy in both developing and developed countries, in part by moving away from census-based data to survey-based data;
- strengthen the direct assessment of literacy skills and practices;
- enhance technical capacities for measuring and monitoring adult literacy in developing countries.

From the perspective of the global monitoring of literacy, the present infrastructure for measuring and assessing literacy is inadequate. Proposals put forth by the UIS, in particular the LAMP strategy, while achieving considerable scientific rigour and cross-case comparability, raise difficult feasibility questions. As such, they contribute very little to monitoring progress towards the EFA literacy goal and, more broadly, to expanding literate environments and sustaining literacy competencies and practices. There is value in staking out – and legitimizing – a middle territory, one which goes beyond conventional approaches to measuring literacy and provides a feasible strategy for examining progress towards a significant improvement in adult literacy rates by 2015.

Tentatively, the *EFA Global Monitoring Report* calls for the construction of several types of self-standing literacy modules that would:

- address concerns of national policy-makers as well as those of international monitoring agencies by offering multiple measurement and assessment strategies;
- be easily incorporated into ongoing household surveys (e.g. on living standards, the labour force and consumption) carried out in developing countries;
- measure literacy and numeracy in the entire adult population (aged 15+);
- minimize the exclusion of groups often excluded from literacy surveys;
- constitute a relatively short (20- to 30-minutes) but sophisticated assessment tool, building on the accumulation of expertise in this field.

This is in line with new initiatives undertaken by the UIS to provide literacy assessment tools complementary to LAMP. In particular, there is considerable value in the Literacy Questionnaire Module Project, which consists of about ten questions for monitoring literacy trends that can be attached to existing surveys (either census or household surveys). Items on self-declaration, use of literacy skills, literacy environment and languages, along with two or three simple tests, would be included.

Some literacy tests neglect the cultural specificity of literacy skills and practices and inadvertently incorporate cultural biases

countries have been unsuccessful (Street, 2005). Yet another criticism is that IALS-like literacy tests neglect the cultural specificity of literacy skills and practices and inadvertently incorporate cultural biases (Hamilton and Barton, 2000; Street, 1996).

Overall, the development of comparable international statistics on literacy to monitor progress (or the lack thereof) poses special problems, which will continue to be debated among scholars, donors and policy-makers.

In response to earlier concerns over the validity, reliability and comparability of existing literacy data, new methods and data sources have been developed. There is considerable consensus (Box 7.7) that conventional assessments must be complemented with more detailed and nuanced literacy information. Indeed, to fully appreciate and address the enormous challenges of illiteracy, stakeholders and analysts must insist on feasible, timely, affordable *and* scientifically robust assessments of literacy.

Global literacy: the emerging challenge

This chapter has shown that adult literacy rates, as conventionally measured, have been steadily rising over the past decades, but that enormous challenges remain, especially in South and West Asia, the Arab States and sub-Saharan Africa. It has also shown that conventional measures of literacy overestimate the actual reading and writing skills of adults worldwide and therefore understate the global literacy challenge. More direct literacy assessments are needed more regularly, in order to allow countries to make informed decisions about alternative literacy policies; but these assessments must be relatively simple and inexpensive to obtain.

Moreover, the demand for improved literacy skills, beyond a necessary minimal level, is growing, especially in the wake of economic globalization, increasing internal and international migration, rapid technological change (including for information and communication technology) and the shift towards knowledge-based societies. These global trends imply an increased need to focus on reducing illiteracy, particularly for poor countries and for excluded groups everywhere – the EFA literacy goal – but also a need to continuously upgrade the quality of literacy skills of all adults. Chapter 8 will explore the broader social context for literacy, as well as how various factors have influenced changes in literacy throughout history. ■

In Garissa, Kenya, a mobile librarian unloads his camel laden with books.

Chapter 8

The making of literate societies

In the mid-nineteenth century, only 10% of the world's adult population could read or write. At the dawn of the twenty-first century, UNESCO estimates that over 80% of adults worldwide can read and write at some minimum level. This unprecedented social transformation occurred despite the world's population quintupling from about 1.2 billion in 1850 to over 6.4 billion today.

The transition to widespread literacy was not uniform across societies, as the historical overview in this chapter shows. The spread of formal schooling, well-organized literacy campaigns and expanded adult learning opportunities have all played a role. The broader social context is equally important: the motivations for acquiring literacy, and the ability to sustain it, are closely related to the literate environments found at home, at work and in society more generally. The social character of literacy is revealed in the variety of ways – and languages – in which it is practised. Literacy today, in its many manifestations, has become a vital set of competencies and practices, interwoven in the fabric of contemporary societies.

Introduction

The aim of this chapter is twofold. First, it reviews the history of various countries' transitions to widespread literacy, examining the factors that have accelerated this process (formal schooling, literacy campaigns and adult learning opportunities) and, more briefly, those that have hindered it (protracted conflict, economic decline and social dislocation). Second, it examines the broader social context of literacy: how it is acquired and practised in particular social settings, and used in particular languages, how it serves different individual and societal purposes, and how it is influenced by public policies and family circumstances. In particular, the chapter focuses on language issues, literacy practices and literate environments.

The origins of literacy can be traced back thousands of years

Literacy in historical perspective

The rise of literacy

The origins of literacy can be traced back thousands of years through a multiplicity of civilizations and institutions (Collins, 2000). In ancient Mesopotamia, the Sumerian and Babylonian cultures developed the cuneiform script for administrative purposes. In the sixth century BCE, the Chinese Confucian movement spawned communities of devotees with a distinctive identity, known as *ju* (meaning 'scholars'). Although not the only literati in Chinese society, they were the custodians of valued books and teachings. In ancient Greece, religious brotherhoods (e.g. the Pythagoreans and Epicureans) emerged as closed communities of learning. Teaching as a profession – including fee payments and a short-term relationship with students – was pioneered by the Sophists. Formally organized schools, initially founded by several of Socrates's disciples to teach adults, later replaced the military, athletic and aesthetic training received by adolescents. The Brahmin priests of ancient India created guilds in which texts were recited at ceremonies; later, under Buddhism and Jainism, these priest-guilds became frameworks within which teachers and apprentices studied and commented on the ancient Veda texts. Jewish communities in the diaspora, cut off from the leadership of temple priests, developed a class of educated leaders – or rabbis – who possessed knowledge of the Torah and a growing body of interpretative texts, later codified in the Talmud.

As the Islamic civilization expanded, centres for higher learning, or madrasas, were established; these provided extensive instruction in Islamic law, Arabic language and literature and, to a lesser extent, in secular subjects such as philosophy, mathematics and science (Herrera, 2006).[1] At the same time, prominent Muslim intellectuals and court physicians contributed to the preservation and elaboration of new knowledge. In Christian Europe, beginning in the eleventh century, collectives of teachers acquired monopolistic rights from the Pope to teach certain professions. By 1600, they had founded more than three dozen universities, including those at Bologna, Paris, Oxford, Cambridge, Salamanca, Padua, Toulouse, Coimbra, Kraków and Leipzig. From the fifteenth century onwards, degree-granting universities were also established in Turkey (1453), Santo Domingo (1538), Peru (1551) and the Philippines (1611).[2] Most universities not only conferred professional licences but also became centres of higher learning in religion, law, philosophy, public administration and certain scientific fields.[3]

Across the Saharan desert, along the Asian silk routes and European rivers, and up and down the African coasts, merchants and traders developed and used an array of literacy and numeracy skills (Curtin, 1990, 2000*b*). Finally, as state (and imperial) bureaucracies grew, with their emphasis on record-keeping, text reproduction and accounting, so too did the demand for literate administrators and public officials.

And yet, despite this diverse array of literacy activities and growing interest in scholarly inquiry, the spread of reading, writing and calculating skills remained limited. As Graff (1987*b*) notes: 'In earliest times, literacy was highly restricted and a relatively unprestigious craft; it carried little of the association with wealth, power, status and knowledge that it later acquired. It was a tool, useful firstly to the needs of state and bureaucracy, church and trade.' In short, the spread of literacy skills was, until the eighteenth century, primarily limited to religious leaders, state servants, far-travelling traders, members of specialized guilds and certain nobility. The vast majority of adults had little involvement with written texts – sacred or secular.

Europe and North America

Transitions from largely illiterate to predominantly literate societies occurred earliest in Europe and North America. Using wide-ranging sources,[4]

1. The first madrasa, which housed over 6,000 volumes, was established by the Fatimid caliphs in 1005 in Egypt.

2. During the late nineteenth and early twentieth centuries, various universities, many beginning as missionary colleges, were established in India (1857), Lebanon (1866), Japan (1877), Korea (1885–56), Hong Kong (1910), Thailand (1917) and Israel (1925).

3. Other institutions of higher learning that did not originally grant university degrees were established even earlier in China (Nanjing) and Egypt (Al-Azhar).

4. These include censuses, military records, wills, deeds, depositions, petitions, marriage records, book circulation, posted law[illegible] job applications, business records and catechetical examinations. They also include 'aggregate data sources' such as educational surveys, statistical society reports, social surveys, government commissions and prison records.

social historians of literacy[5] have identified three historical periods (pre-1800, 1800–1860s, post-1860s) and three groups of countries to discuss the history of these literacy transitions (Graff, 1987*b*; Vincent, 2000).

Prior to 1800, reading (though not always writing) skills were widespread in several northern European countries (e.g. Denmark, Finland, Iceland, Scotland, Sweden and Prussia), as well as in parts of England, France and Switzerland. In a second group – Belgium, Ireland, the Netherlands, and the remaining parts of England, France and Switzerland – literacy skills were used by members of the higher social classes and were more limited among other social strata, except in scattered communities, monasteries or households that possessed books and other printed matter. Finally, in most of eastern and southern Europe (Russia, the Balkans, the eastern Austro-Hungarian empire, the Iberian Peninsula and southern Italy), illiteracy was widespread, especially outside the cities and towns, and written materials were almost non-existent. Throughout Europe, gender disparities in literacy were the norm.

From 1800 to 1860, the more advanced and industrialized European countries made modest progress in reducing illiteracy, with more adults who could affix full signatures (rather than simple marks) to legal documents, provide written responses to census questions and pass literacy tests in army recruitment centres. Other countries in northern and western Europe saw significant reductions in male illiteracy, with similar (though varying) trends for female illiteracy (Vincent, 2000). The relative literacy ranking of countries changed little (although, in Sweden, the early neglect of writing skills, due to the Protestant Church's emphasis on the importance of reading, was overcome during the nineteenth century). By the 1860s, only a minority of adults in industrializing countries lacked rudimentary literacy skills. In eastern and southern Europe, however, the pace of change in literacy was slow and mainly extended to certain professions and elite populations.

In the latter decades of the nineteenth century, the spread of adult literacy in most of northern and western Europe was extensive. Yet in some countries, such as Belgium and Ireland, only three-quarters of all males could sign their full names. Around 1900, literacy levels in Hungary, Italy, Russia, Spain and the Balkan countries were significantly below those in other parts of Europe. During the First World War, many European countries encouraged the acquisition of literacy skills among military recruits so they would be able to read instructions on weaponry use and to correspond with their families (Limage, 2005*b*).

While literacy levels improved in much of Europe during the late nineteenth century, subnational disparities in literacy by gender, age, social class, ethnicity and area of residence continued. For example, urban areas had a distinct advantage in literacy over rural areas. Books – and the social institutions encouraging their use – were more prevalent in cities and towns than in rural communities. Religious, secular, professional and private forms of learning were more available to urban residents, as was the supply of print media. The greater prevalence of literacy in urban areas had in turn an impact on the nature of the labour market and scale of commercial transactions. Thus, the dynamics of literacy acquisition and the forces of industrialization and urbanization tended to reinforce one another (Limage, 2005*b*).

Prior to 1800, reading skills were widespread in several northern European countries

During the early twentieth century, literacy levels increased throughout Europe, with few changes in the ranking of countries. By mid-century, central and northern Europe were reported to have achieved over 95% literacy; western Europe, over 80%; Austria and Hungary, over 70%; and Italy, Poland and Spain, over 50% literacy. In Portugal and the Eastern Orthodox countries, adult literacy rates were not above 25%; only after 1945 did the ability to use written languages extend to the masses (Johansson, cited in Graff, 1987*b*; Vincent, 2000).

In the United States and Canada, literacy levels increased steadily during the nineteenth and early twentieth centuries. In the United States, 80% of adults were estimated to be literate in 1870 and over 95% in 1940; in Canada, the literacy rate rose from 83% in 1901 to 95% in 1931 (UNESCO, 1957). Disparities in adult literacy levels by race, region, labour force participation, household economic status and foreign birth remained. By the 1960s, these disparities had lessened, with the exception of certain groups, such as those with disabilities and Native Americans.

Overall, the historical record in Europe and North America suggests that there was no single route to widespread mass literacy. In many Nordic countries and Protestant areas, high literacy levels *preceded* the expansion of formal schooling and reflected religious inclinations and pressures.

5. See, for example, the pioneering work of Stone (1969) and Cipolla (1969), as well as important studies such as Furet and Ozouf (1977), Graff (1987*b*, 1991), Houston (1985), Johansson (1977, 1981), Schofield (1968) and Lockridge (1974). In addition to establishing major chronological trends in literacy, historical scholarship seeks to develop historically grounded interpretations of changing patterns of literacy in different places and to examine connections between literacy and social and economic development.

In other areas, the growing provision of public and private instruction, administered by centralizing nation-states or religious organizations, contributed to the spread of literacy. Among early industrializing countries, the transition to widespread literacy was a gradual process spanning centuries; among late industrializing countries the spread of literacy came later but at a more rapid pace. The literacy gaps between early and late industrializers only began to close during the twentieth century, with growing popular demand for, and increased public supply of, literacy (Mitch, 1992).

Africa, Asia, Latin America and the Arab States

Historical information about literacy trends in other world regions, many of them under colonial rule in the nineteenth and twentieth centuries, is limited. Population censuses – a major source of literacy data – were usually conducted in the wake of national independence (Barrett and Frank, 1999), and few were carried out in the territories of European empires. Consequently, historical literacy data are available for only certain parts of Africa, Asia and the Middle East, though rather more widely for Latin America.

Trends in adult literacy rates for 1900–1950, based on census figures compiled by UNESCO (1953, 1957), are reported in Figure 8.1.[6] A few countries (Argentina, Chile and Cuba) had literacy levels between 35% and 45% at the start of the twentieth century, which steadily increased during the next five decades. Others (Brazil, Ceylon [Sri Lanka], Colombia, Mexico, the Philippines and Turkey) had lower levels (20% to 35%) prior to the First World War, which rose modestly in the interwar period. In most other developing countries, the pace of change was slow: in Burma (Myanmar) and Honduras, literacy rates rose slightly in the interwar period; in Egypt, India and the Union of South Africa, literacy levels were very low and progress was minimal.

Moreover, rising literacy rates during 1900–1950 did not necessarily reduce the illiterate population. In many cases, modest increases in literacy levels (less than 10% over ten years), together with strong population growth, actually resulted in *increases* in the number of illiterates.[7] Outcomes were mixed among countries reporting moderate progress in literacy rates. For example, while the adult literacy rate rose from 47% to 65% in Argentina between 1895 and 1914, the number of illiterates increased by over 450,000 during the same period. Only in countries where literacy rates increased significantly (i.e. by at least 25%), did the number of illiterates decline.[8]

By 1950, a more complete assessment of regional and national differences in adult literacy rates was possible. Figure 8.2, which presents UNESCO (1957) compilations of adult literacy rates, shows that many countries had made great strides by mid-century. Argentina, Barbados, British Guiana (Guyana), Ceylon (Sri Lanka), Chile, Costa

Figure 8.1: Trends in literacy rates in developing countries, 1900–1950

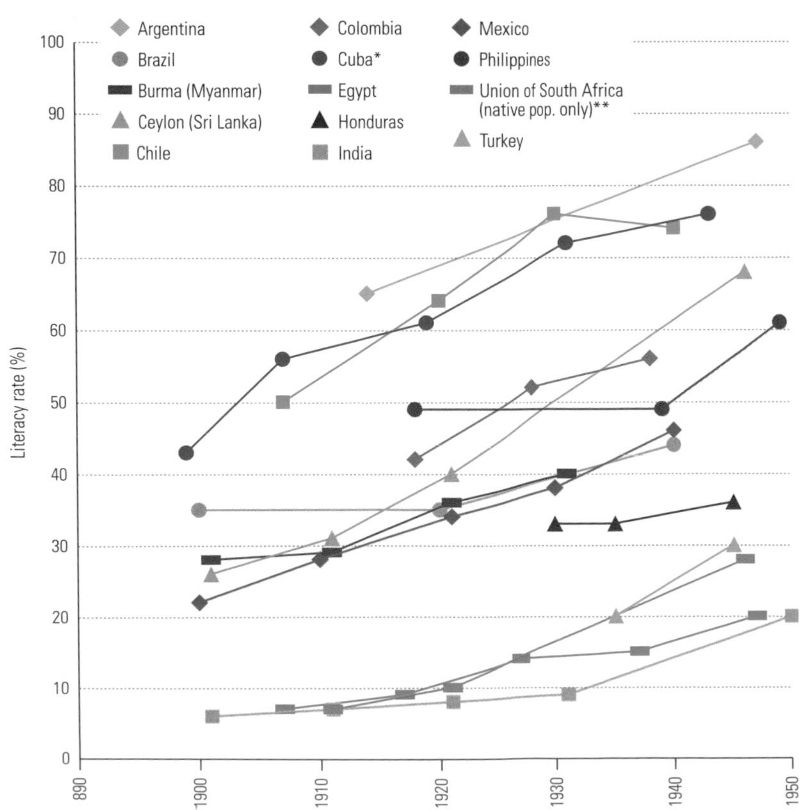

Note: For Ceylon (Sri Lanka), the adult population is defined as 5 years or older; for Burma (Myanmar), Chile, Colombia, Cuba, Egypt, India, Mexico, the Philippines, Turkey and the Union of South Africa, it is defined as 10 years or older; for Argentina, Brazil and Honduras, it is defined as 15 years or older.

* In the 1899, 1907 and 1919 censuses, all persons aged 10 and older who attended school were counted as among the literate population.

** The literacy rate of the adult white population was about 95% in 1904 and 98% in 1918.

Source: UNESCO (1957).

6. Because of a lack of historical census data, many countries with large illiterate populations (e.g. China) are excluded from this figure. In addition, caution is warranted when comparing literacy rates across countries, given different operational definitions of the adult population and of literacy.

7. This was true in Brazil, Burma, Ceylon, Chile, Colombia, Cuba, Egypt, Honduras, India, Mexico, Portugal and the majority population of the Union of South Africa.

8. Examples include Chile and Cuba, as well as (in Europe) Belgium, Bulgaria, Finland, France, Hungary, Italy and Spain, and (in North America) Canada and the United States.

Rica, Cuba, Israel, Japan, Panama, and Trindidad and Tobago all achieved adult literacy rates above 75% by 1950. In parts of Asia (Burma [Myanmar], China, Fiji, the Korean peninsula, Malaya [now part of Malaysia], the Philippines and Thailand) and the rest of Latin America and the Caribbean, literacy rates were in the middle range (35% to 75%). They were relatively low in Afghanistan, India, Iran and Pakistan, and throughout Africa (except Mauritius) and the Arab States.

Based on 1950 estimates, UNESCO (1957) also reported that:

- Adult literacy rates were almost invariably higher among men than among women. On average, gender disparities were smaller in Latin America than in Africa or Asia.
- The prevalence of literacy, and the rate at which it increased, tended to be higher in urban areas than in rural areas.
- In developing countries for which subnational literacy rates were available, significant disparities in literacy levels were found between different linguistic, ethnic, religious and racial groups.[9]

Overall, the historical evidence suggests that, prior to 1950, there were already substantial inter- and intraregional differences in literacy transitions in Asia, Africa, the Arab States and Latin America. In Latin America, political independence led to changes in adult literacy levels but with a lag until the twentieth century. In the other regions, progress in adult literacy was generally limited to the specific cases discussed above. For the vast majority of adults residing in these regions, there was little, if any, access to literacy-acquiring opportunities.

Major determinants of literacy transitions

Keeping in mind the diverse and complex origins of literacy, this section examines those factors that have broadened access to literacy opportunities and featured prominently in the creation of literate societies (both historically and in the recent past) – the establishment and expansion of formal schooling, mass literacy campaigns,

9. For example, in the Union of South Africa in 1904, only 5% of the black population was literate, in contrast to 95% of the white population. In the United States in 1900, the literacy rate was 95% for US-born whites, 86% for foreign-born whites, and 55% for blacks; by 1920, the rates had increased to 98%, 87% and 77%, respectively. In 1920, among Bulgarian adults above the age of 10, the literacy rate was 48% for Bulgarians, 7% among the Turkish, Tartar and Roma populations, and 73% for Jews; by 1934, the rates had increased to 75%, 18% and 82%, respectively.

Figure 8.2: Estimated adult literacy rates for selected countries circa 1950

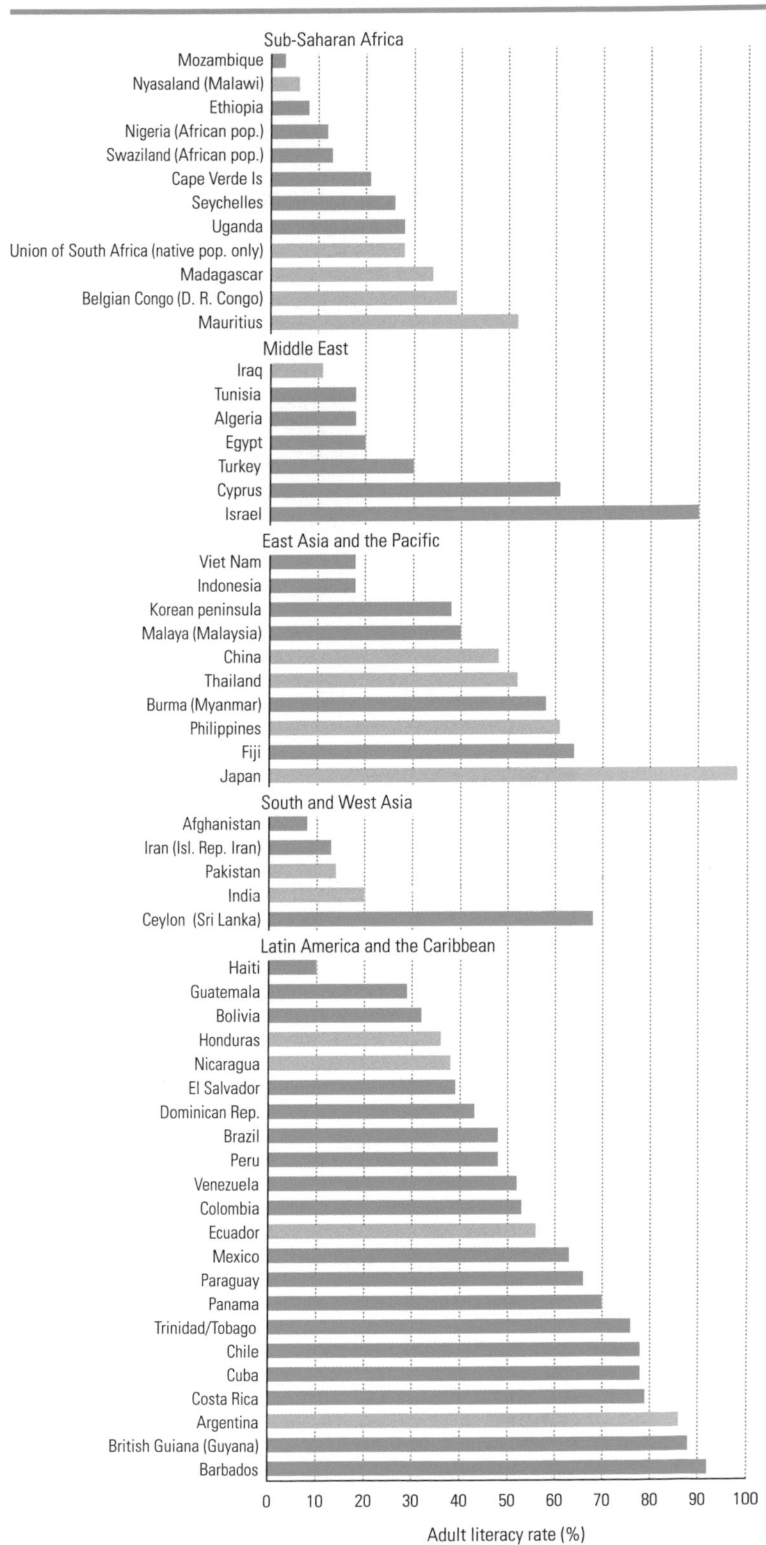

Notes:

1. Literacy rates in **blue** are based on national census figures, and were calculated as the percentage of adults in the listed age levels who could read *and* write, based on self-declarations or third-party assessments. Literacy rates in **orange** are estimates prepared by UNESCO statisticians in the mid-1950s based on diverse sources.
2. Composition of world regions is different from United Nations in the 1950s and also from present-day EFA regions.

Source: UNESCO (1957).

The single most significant factor influencing the spread of literacy worldwide over the past two centuries has been the expansion of formal schooling

and adult education and learning policies and programmes. It also looks at conditions that have hindered literacy transitions and resulted in literacy stagnation and pockets of illiteracy. The impact of language on literacy is discussed later (see *Languages and literacy* section).[10]

Establishing schools and increasing enrolment rates

The single most significant factor influencing the spread of literacy worldwide over the past two centuries has been the *expansion of formal schooling*. Schools have been, and continue to be, the sites in which most people acquire their core literacy skills – reading, writing and 'reckoning'.

There have been, however, historical exceptions to this pattern. During the seventeenth century, in certain Nordic countries, German principalities and North American colonies, the Protestant Churches supported the *compulsory education* (not schooling) of children to ensure the piety of families. Out of religious conviction, parents saw to it that their children learned to read and write at home (with or without a tutor) and in church. Here the historical transition to widespread literacy *pre-dated* the consolidation of state school systems.

Only in the eighteenth century did communities in Norway, various Swiss cantons, Dutch provinces and German *Länder* establish local schools, with largely religious curricula emphasizing literacy, biblical knowledge and moral character. This movement towards *mass schooling* was intended to replace home- and church-based instruction. Later in the nineteenth and early twentieth centuries, systems of *compulsory mass schooling* were established – first in Western and then Eastern Europe (Ramirez and Boli, 1994; Benavot and Resnik, 2005). By legally establishing the principle of compulsory attendance, nascent states became the initiator, guarantor and administrator of a system of schools. At the same time, in the United States, northern states and western territories passed statutes requiring parents to send their children to school, although primary enrolment rates, even in rural areas, were already relatively high. The southern states eventually followed suit in the twentieth century (Richardson, 1980). Thus, with the exception of the mainly Protestant areas noted above, as formal schooling became more available and enrolments increased during the nineteenth century, adult literacy rates slowly began to rise.

Elsewhere, the interrelationship of compulsory schooling, enrolment expansion and adult literacy evolved differently. Countries in South and Central America, for example, passed compulsory attendance laws in the nineteenth and early twentieth centuries, but enrolment realities lagged behind legislative ideals (Benavot and Riddle, 1988). In many of these countries, compulsory laws went unenforced (Garcia Garrido, 1986). Overall, the cross-national association between the passage of compulsory school laws and primary enrolment rates is weak (Ramirez and Ventresca, 1992). The evidence suggests that countries tend to pass compulsory education laws in the wake of political independence, a legal move reflecting official intentions, but with limited impact on actual enrolment expansion.[11]

In Asia, Africa and the Arab world, various forms of formal education were well established prior to contact with the West (Collins, 2000; Craig, 1981; Herrera, 2004). Indigenous, non-Western schools (e.g. Koranic, pagoda, temple and native schools) had existed for generations, albeit with enrolments usually limited to young boys. These forms of indigenous education, mostly oriented towards inculcating religious and traditional cultural knowledge and ideals, were transformed, assimilated or destroyed as they came into contact with European school models introduced by missionary groups or colonial authorities.[12] In parts of Asia, modernizing regimes adapted European models to local contexts (e.g. Japan in the 1870s, and the Korean peninsula between 1885 and 1910). The historical record suggests that contacts between indigenous and European models of education (although characterized by unequal power relations) initiated a process of expanding access to formal schooling, especially for children from households where there was no reading or writing. As such, they represent a major turning point in the transition to widespread literacy.

The unleashed dynamic of growing access to 'modern' forms of public and private schooling

10. Several economic, political, cultural and demographic factors, some of which are associated with cross-national differences in adult literacy rates, are left unexamined in this section. Poverty (or per capita product) and urbanization, for example, are correlated with literacy levels and were discussed in greater detail in Chapter 7. Conditions of high fertility and rapid population growth have slowed the rise in literacy rates and, in some cases, contributed to a growing illiterate population. The impacts of manufacturing, rising living standards, and increased availability of newspapers and inexpensive books have been, at least in Europe, mixed (Graff, 1987*b*; Mitch 1992). In short, different sets of factors have combined in different contexts to influence the transition to widespread literacy (or the lack thereof). Here the emphasis is on *major* determinants of literacy, whose impact has been substantial and consistent across a multiplicity of contexts.

11. Of the sixty countries that were independent by 1945, 60% had enacted compulsory education laws. Between 1945 and 2004, 125 former colonies and non-governing territories became independent in Africa, Asia, Europe and parts of the Americas; 85% of these countries had passed compulsory education laws by 2000 (Benavot and Resnik, 2005). Ramirez and Boli (1982) show that with each wave of political independence, the time lag between independence and compulsory schooling got smaller. It was between twenty-five and fifty years in the nineteenth century and decreased to less than six years in the first half of the twentieth century. After the Second World War, most countries passed compulsory school laws within a year of independence.

12. The diffusion and influence of the United States-based school models were more limited geographically.

Figure 8.3: Mean unadjusted primary enrolment rates in developing regions, 1880 to 1935–40

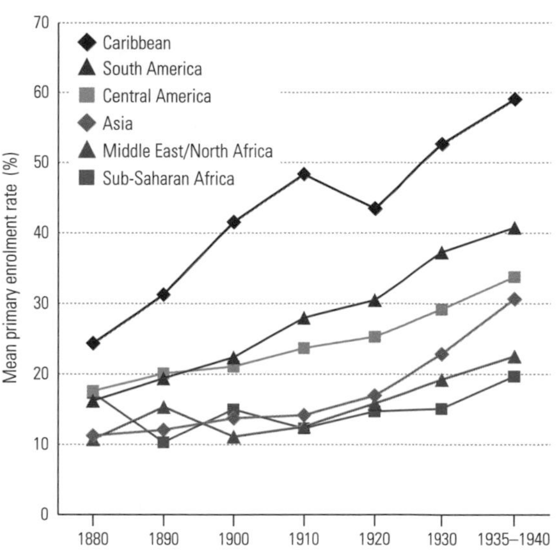

Note: Unadjusted enrolment rates refer to the number of pupils enrolled in primary schools divided by the 5-14 year-old population.
Source: Benavot and Riddle (1988).

can be seen in Figure 8.3, which presents regional estimates of primary enrolment rates from 1880 to 1940.[13] In South and Central America, about two out of ten school-age children attended school in 1880, whereas three to four out of ten did so by 1940. Increases in enrolment rates during this period were even greater in the Caribbean (from 24% to 59%), especially in British colonies. In Africa, Asia and the Middle East, where colonial rule predominated, the pace of primary school expansion was slow. Nevertheless, some countries (Ceylon [Sri Lanka], Japan, Lebanon, Lesotho, Malawi, Mozambique, the Philippines, Seychelles and Thailand) experienced relatively rapid school expansion before 1940. Not surprisingly, in many of the same countries adult literacy rates were on the rise.

Evidence of the strong association between educational expansion and adult literacy levels can be seen in Figure 8.4, which plots historical primary school enrolments (in the late-1930s) with subsequent adult literacy rates (circa 1950) for thirty-nine countries or territories.

Contemporary evidence for the education–literacy association is reported in Table 8.1, which shows that:

- Both net primary enrolment rates and measures of adult educational attainment are strongly correlated with both adult and youth literacy rates.

Figure 8.4: Association between unadjusted primary enrolment rate (1935–40) and adult literacy rate (circa 1950), for thirty-nine countries or territories

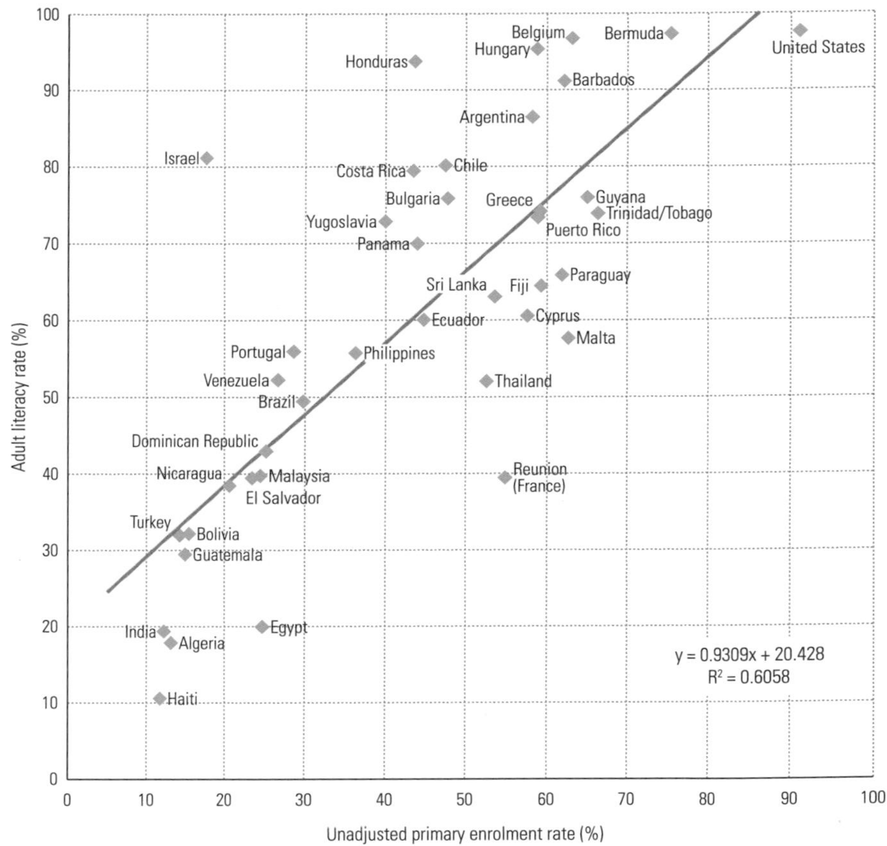

Sources: UNESCO (1957), Benavot and Riddle (1988).

Table 8.1: Correlations between measures of educational expansion and educational attainment, and literacy rates (Number of countries in parentheses)

	Adult literacy rates 2000–2004			Youth literacy rates 2000–2004		
	Total	Male	Female	Total	Male	Female
Net primary enrolment rate, 1998 (n = 52)	0.83	0.78	0.86	0.85	0.79	0.88
Percentage of relevant population with no schooling, circa 1990 (n = 74-78)	-0.92	-0.85	-0.94	-0.85	-0.79	-0.85
Percentage of relevant population with some primary education, circa 1990 (n = 74-78)	0.60	0.42	0.72	0.56	0.38	0.65
Percentage of relevant population who completed primary education, circa 1990 (n = 74-78)	0.56	0.46	0.58	0.51	0.40	0.52

Note: The relevant population refers to one of three groups: all adults, all adult males or all adult females. Thus, for example, the correlation of -0.94 refers to the cross-national association between the percentage of all females with no schooling and the female adult literacy rate.
Sources: Adult and youth literacy rates are the most recent estimates from the UNESCO Institute for Statistics (UIS). Data on education attainment (for 15+ population) come from Barro and Lee (1990). Net enrolment ratios are UIS estimates from 1998.

13. The regions in this figure are different from the EFA regions.

- Literacy rates are most strongly associated with the population which has had *at least some exposure to formal schooling*.
- The interrelationships between measures of schooling and literacy rates are stronger among women than among men.[14]

Recent studies of literacy transitions using multivariate models conclude that educational expansion has been one of the most (if not *the* most) important determinant of historical rises in literacy rates (Verner, 2005; Wils, 2002).[15] Notwithstanding certain methodological caveats (see Chapter 7), the significant impact of mass school expansion on the spread of literacy spans historical periods and geographical boundaries.

Overall, the historical record suggests that the emergence, consolidation and expansion of formal education systems were major forces in the reduction of adult illiteracy, with the exception of limited parts of Europe and North America. In most world regions, the spread of mass primary schooling in the nineteenth and early twentieth centuries became the motor for rising adult literacy.

Mobilization for mass literacy: organized campaigns

Many countries promoted literacy by organizing massive campaigns. This section examines two types of mobilizations – *sustained literacy campaigns over several years and short-term or one-off literacy campaigns* – both of which tended to complement the provision of primary education. Mass literacy campaigns sought to produce broad-based improvements in the literacy skills of adults for whom literacy had previously been inaccessible or unattainable. Unlike that of schooling, the influence of literacy campaigns has been limited to specific cases and historical periods.

In addition to the teaching of basic literacy skills, mass literacy campaigns have included an array of government actions: reformulating literacy policies, reforming administrative authority over literacy activities, creating new national or regional institutions to train literacy educators, creating new laws in support of literacy and setting up targeted partnerships with universities, schools and NGOs. Usually, countries initiated mass literacy campaigns as a means of promoting nation-building and national unity, and of expanding the base of their moral authority.[16]

Most *sustained mass literacy campaigns* were initiated by Socialist/Communist governments and/or followed in the wake of decolonization. The Soviet literacy campaign between 1919 and 1939 represents the earliest and one of the most effective (Bhola, 1984). Only 30% of the Soviet population was literate in 1919; by the end of the campaign, this had risen to 85% (94% for men, 82% for women).[17] Viet Nam initiated four well-integrated literacy campaigns, three in the north (1945–58) and, later, one in the south (1976–78), which provided expanded learning opportunities and basic skills training for most adults (Bhola, 1984; Limage, 2005*b*). China organized several campaigns from the 1950s to the 1980s to combat widespread illiteracy.[18] Sustained campaigns were also carried out in Algeria, Brazil, Ethiopia, Indonesia, Japan, Mexico, Mozambique, Somalia, the United Republic of Tanzania and Thailand (see Box 8.1).

The effectiveness of mass campaigns in raising literacy rates has varied considerably. In addition to those in the former USSR, campaigns in China, the United Republic of Tanzania and Viet Nam succeeded in reaching large segments of the illiterate adult population. Elsewhere, adult participation in such campaigns was less extensive (Graff, 1987*b*). In several cases, the goals were never realized or the achievements were greatly exaggerated. For example, Mozambique ran four successive campaigns between 1978 and 1982; while over 500,000 adults participated in the first two, far fewer did so in the last two (Lind, 1988). The goal of the 1971–72 literacy campaign in the Philippines was to provide instruction to 2 million people; yet only 200,000 became literate during this period (UNESCO, 1978).

Short-term or one-off mass literacy campaigns, a second type of mass mobilization, have sometimes resulted in significant reductions in illiteracy over relatively brief time frames. For example, literacy rates increased in Cuba (1961) from 76% to 96%; in Somalia (1974–75) from 5% to 20%; in southern Viet Nam (1976–78) from 75% to 86%; in Nicaragua (1980) from 50% to 77%; and in Ecuador (1988–89) from about 85% to 89%. Several conditions appear to have contributed to the success of certain one-off campaigns (Lind and Johnston, 1990): First, except for Somalia, initial literacy levels tended to be high and the targeted populations limited before the campaigns began. Second, these campaigns were often initiated by newly installed political regimes when popular enthusiasm was high. Third, they occurred in countries with a principal majority language,

14. A possible explanation for this finding: cultural restrictions reduce women's exposure to, and interaction with, written and visual materials in the surrounding public environment. Thus, schooling becomes a more critical context for the acquisition and practice of literacy skills for women than for men, who encounter a wider range of literacy-enhancing settings.

15. As Wils concludes: 'The main key to rising adult literacy has historically been child school enrollment, with adult education programs being a secondary force.' Additional, but less important, variables facilitating the rise of adult literacy include: the age-structure of the population, levels of school expenditure per school-age child, adults with post primary education in general and those who become teachers in particular.

16. The history, ideological motivation and rationale for these campaigns are discussed in greater detail in Arnove and Graff (1987) and Bhola (1984). Other factors that have at times influenced such campaigns – e.g. industrial development, urbanization and democratization – are beyond the scope of this Report.

17. General compulsory education was introduced in the former USSR in 1930. In 1927, only half of children aged 8–11 attended school; by 1932 this had risen to 98% (Shadrikov and Pakhomov, 1990). The Soviet experience served as a reference point for later campaigns in Cuba and Nicaragua (Kenez, 1982). On Cuba, see Leiner (1987) and Bhola (1984); on Nicaragua, Arnove (1987), Miller (1985) and Arrien (2005).

18. Bhola (1984) divides anti-illiteracy work in China into three distinct phases: (1) from 1949 to mid-1966, (2) May 1966 to October 1976 (the Cultural Revolution) and (3) October 1976 to the present. Others (e.g. Hayford, 1987; Ross et al., 2005) use different periodizations.

Box 8.1 Mass literacy campaigns: the United Republic of Tanzania, Somalia, Ethiopia, Thailand and Brazil

■ In 1970, eight years after he became president of the country, Julius Nyerere declared that **the United Republic of Tanzania**'s 5.5 million illiterate adults (of which 56% were women) should learn to read and write. Teachers and other literacy educators were recruited, large quantities of books and documents were printed, vehicles and bicycles were donated, and a million pairs of eyeglasses were distributed (UNESCO, 1980). Enormous in scale, the campaign – which grew out of a Socialist development ideology emphasizing education and literacy – advanced with significant assistance from Nordic countries and Germany. Primary education expanded and, by 1980, more than 90% of school-age children attended school. It is estimated that the literacy rate increased from 33% in 1967 to 61% by 1975 (Bhola, 1984).*

■ The literacy campaign in **Somalia** was largely driven by language and development politics (Bhola, 1984). In 1973, the government introduced written Somali and launched the National Literacy Campaign. Educated Somalis were mobilized under the motto 'If you know, teach; if you do not know, learn' (UNESCO, 1980). Despite organizational difficulties, skilled teacher shortages, and the lack of classrooms and textbooks, about 400,000 adults successfully completed literacy training during the initial campaign. The overall programme was extended another five years to further reduce illiteracy (Mohamed, 1975; UNESCO, 1980).

■ **Ethiopia**'s literacy campaign (1979–83) was also tied to language policies, which until 1974 had privileged Amharic over other languages. At the time of the revolution in 1974, the literacy rate for adults (aged 10–45) was 40% in urban areas and 8% in rural areas (National Literacy Campaign Coordinating Committee [Ethiopia], 1984). The campaign established over 450,000 literacy centres and reached over 22 million people (52% female), of which over 20 million (51% female) passed a beginners' literacy test. More than 5 million textbooks were produced, in over a dozen languages, and a large quantity of learning materials (blackboards, exercise books) were distributed (Department of Adult Education and National Literacy Campaign Office [Ethiopia], 1989, cited in Shenkut, 2005). The vast majority of campaign participants continued through the post-literacy stage and successfully completed the programme (Mammo, 2005).

■ **Thailand** exemplifies a non-Socialist country that successfully carried out several mass literacy campaigns (Sunanchai, 1988, 1989; Varavarn, 1989). In 1937, only an estimated 30% of the population had minimal literacy skills. During the first national campaign (1942-45), 1.4 million people learned to read. A second campaign was organized during 1983–87.

■ During the twentieth century, **Brazil** carried out several adult education initiatives and literacy campaigns, offering short-term courses and mobilizing non-professional literacy monitors. Among the more significant campaigns were those of 1947–50, which were attended by over 800,000 adults (Beisiegel, 1974), and the 1970–72 Brazilian Literacy Movement (Mobral), in which 7.3 million adults participated (Corrêa, 1973). Census figures estimated the Brazilian adult literacy rate at 35% in 1920, 49% in 1950, 64% in 1970 and 74% in 1980. Only in the past twenty years has the illiterate population decreased. The evidence suggests that the great campaigns to eradicate illiteracy had a limited impact on raising literacy rates (Ferraro, 2002). Rather, increases in literacy rates were, first and foremost, a result of the constant expansion of Brazil's public education systems and, second, of gradual gains in adult education (Masagão Ribeiro and Gomes Batista, 2005).

For a discussion of the impact and effectiveness of these campaigns on literacy outcomes, see Chapter 9.

* For a critique of the United Republic of Tanzania literacy campaign, see Unsicker (1987).

which eased the mobilization of teachers and the preparation of literacy materials. Finally, many one-off campaigns involved follow-up literacy initiatives to increase adult learning opportunities.

Public policies in support of adult learning

In addition to the expansion of primary schooling and mass literacy campaigns, a third approach has also played a role in reducing illiteracy – the expansion of adult education and learning opportunities.[19] As with mass literacy campaigns, the establishment and broadening of adult learning opportunities typically complemented the expansion of primary schooling. Yet, unlike such campaigns, which were (in general) characterized by ideological fervour and a sense of urgency to 'eradicate' the 'scourge' of illiteracy, the implementation of relatively large-scale adult education programmes in Botswana, Brazil, Burkina Faso, Cape Verde, India, Kenya, Mexico and Zimbabwe sought to gradually expand adult access to learning opportunities within the context of various development plans, cultural policies or human rights initiatives (Lind and Johnston, 1990). These programmes constituted one part of broader governmental policies to address multiple objectives, including raising literacy levels.

19. An earlier variation involved national development policies or projects that incorporated a literacy component. During the 1960s and 1970s, and especially after the Tehran Conference in 1965, several developing countries (e.g. Burkina Faso, Gabon, Iraq, the Niger and Pakistan) embarked on rural development initiatives that included efforts to raise literacy levels. In Algeria and Tunisia, agricultural and industrial development projects also incorporated literacy efforts.

In other cases, literacy-supporting policies or projects were introduced on a much smaller scale, sometimes in conjunction with other policy aims (Lind and Johnston, 1990). Examples include decentralized participatory projects incorporating local traditional institutions in areas of Madagascar, Mali, Peru and the Philippines. In the United Republic of Tanzania, the Ujamaa Village – a small, democratic rural unit – directly assumed responsibility for literacy activities (UNESCO, 1975*b*). Other countries (e.g. Guinea, Mexico and Viet Nam) focused on the role of language (see 'Languages and literacy' section, below) and implemented programmes in minority languages to increase learner accessibility to literacy. For example, Mali began literacy courses in Bambaram, Mandé, Peul, Songhay and Tamasheq. In Burundi, the Niger and Togo, literacy texts were prepared in different local languages. In Somalia, the local language was transcribed into Latin script, which was easier to read. Zambia used seven languages for instructional purposes. In certain regions, Peru adopted a system of literacy education that began in vernacular Quechua and switched to Spanish.

The transition to widespread literacy, once initiated, is not inevitable and may stagnate

By their very nature, small-scale programmes reached out to targeted, often excluded segments of the adult population and therefore had a limited role in reducing illiteracy, unless combined with the expansion of formal schooling and other public policies. They broadened access to literacy on a more voluntary and self-motivated basis (see Chapter 9).

Literacy stagnation and pockets of persistent illiteracy

The transition to widespread literacy, once initiated, is not inevitable and may stagnate. Moreover, the speed of literacy transitions can vary considerably due to societal factors such as industrialization, urbanization and political independence, as well as policies concerning formal schooling, mass literacy campaigns, and the demand for, and provision of, adult learning opportunities. In addition, there exist important pockets of persistent illiteracy, even in highly literate or schooled societies, which often go unrecognized or ignored in the debate over literacy transitions.[20] This section focuses on these issues and highlights factors that have slowed progress towards widespread literacy or contributed to pockets of illiteracy. Protracted political conflicts, civil or ethnic warfare, prolonged economic decline and massive social dislocations are important examples of such factors.

Literacy stagnation can occur on a national scale or among certain social and demographic groups. Chapter 7 reported apparent examples of this among youth cohorts in six countries: Angola, the Democratic Republic of the Congo, Kenya, Madagascar, the United Republic of Tanzania and Zambia. Similar processes are likely occurring in countries (e.g. Afghanistan and Iraq) for which statistical information is lacking. Box 8.2 reports examples of literacy stagnation and renewal in Uganda and Mongolia.

A type of literacy stagnation occurred recently in the Trans-Caucasus and Central Asia region, which, prior to the collapse of the Soviet Union in 1990, had had high literacy levels. Several interrelated factors contributed to the literacy crisis. First, there was a severe reduction in industrial output, followed by inflation and economic decline in much of the region. The economic downturn resulted in drastic cuts in government expenditures for education and health, and increases in poverty rates and economic inequalities.[21] Second, in some areas (e.g. Georgia, Tajikistan and the Nagorny-Karabakh region), ethnic and military conflicts interrupted the provision of educational services and training programmes. Third, new laws governing language policy brought about a sharp transfer from the extensive use of Russian, especially in the workplace, to various national languages. Many Russian-speaking families emigrated, which contributed to a loss of highly skilled professionals. Speakers of national languages became, in relative terms, 'functionally illiterate', as their languages often lacked specialized scientific terminologies; and there were neither the skilled translators nor the educational materials needed to ease the transition from Russian in a wide spectrum of economic and social arenas (Abdullaeva, 2005).

The impact of armed conflict and political crises

Acute economic crises and violent conflicts have had deleterious effects on the quality of, and access to, schooling (World Bank, 2005*c*). Rarely, however, do such economic or political shocks result in irreversible literacy losses for an entire generation (UNESCO, 2000*a*). Prolonged armed conflicts, however, can result in school buildings being damaged or destroyed, qualified teachers

20. The poor literacy skills among members of excluded groups, discussed extensively in Chapter 7, are clear examples of these pockets of persistent illiteracy.

21. The one exception in the region is Uzbekistan, where in 2000 educational spending was at approximately 70% of the pre-independence rate (UNESCO, 2000*a*). On literacy in this region in general, see Meredith and Steele (2000).

Box 8.2 Literacy stagnation and renewal in Uganda and Mongolia

■ Following independence in 1962, **Uganda** developed a relatively well-organized system of formal schooling and, although education was neither free nor compulsory, literacy levels began to rise. In 1964, a national mass literacy campaign was launched. However, civil strife and economic decline during the 1970s and 1980s substantially weakened the campaign and progress came to a halt.

In the 1990s, the Ugandan government introduced several measures to address the literacy stagnation. Adult literacy programmes were promoted in eight representative districts of the country beginning in 1992. The universalization of primary education was introduced in 1997 by eliminating fees. While it initially applied to only four children per family, it was later extended to all children. Primary enrolments rose from 2.9 million in 1996 to over 7 million in 2000. All of these measures contributed to wider literacy acquisition.

■ **Mongolia** experienced reversals in school participation and literacy levels in the aftermath of massive political and economic changes beginning in 1990. Public educational expenditures substantially declined, leading to (among other things) the closure of dormitories for nomadic children. Many children from rural areas left school to help their families look after the privatized livestock. A devaluation of education and literacy ensued. Drop-out rates increased and reached a high of almost 9% in 1992/93. Literacy rates among young adults (aged 15–19) also declined and, by 2000, were lower than those for older adults.[a]

Several initiatives by the Mongolian government have sought to halt these negative trends. New programmes targeted hard-to-reach rural learners scattered over vast distances. In 1993, the Government, in partnership with UNESCO and the Danish International Development Assistance, developed the Gobi Women's Project to develop national capacity through non-formal education, and open and distance learning.[b] Books and radios were distributed to women. Teaching was done over the radio, together with follow-up visits by volunteer teachers. The literacy achievements of older adults, combined with a relatively developed literate environment, enabled Mongolia to recover from earlier shocks, and literacy rates are now improving. Remaining challenges include providing literacy opportunities in scattered rural areas and creating a decentralized system of lifelong learning in a historical context of centralized planning and control.

Notes:
a. For educational figures see UNESCO (2000*a*).
b. See http://www.unescobkk.org/index.php?id=1625 or Undrakh (2002).
Sources: Batchuluun and Khulan (2005); Okech et al. (2001).

being displaced or maimed, and parents being prevented from sending their children (particularly their daughters) to school because of the lack of security. Chronic violent conflict in parts of Burundi, the Democratic Republic of the Congo, Somalia and southern Sudan significantly reduced access to education. In Somalia in 2000, only 21% of school-age boys and 13% of girls were enrolled in primary school; among those enrolled, 80% never reached Grade 5 (Sommers, 2002). In such contexts, efforts to address the EFA goals are hindered.

Prolonged armed conflicts and the fear of persecution have pushed millions of families to flee their homes and seek safety in refugee or displaced persons camps coordinated by the international community (Hanemann and Mauch, 2005; Sommers, 2002; Waters and Leblanc, 2005). Not surprisingly, under such conditions, children's access to educational services is usually severely diminished. The United Nations recent Refugee Education Indicators and Gap Analysis (UNHCR, 2004), which covers 118 refugee camps in 23 asylum countries, sets forth a basic standard on five educational indicators[22] and quantifies the gaps between current educational programmes and these standards.

As might be expected, none of the standards in any of the five indicators is being met. For example, only two-thirds of the camps achieved the standard of enabling 90% of students to successfully complete the school year. Some 50,000 refugee children dropped out during the school year, contributing to increased rates of out-of-school children and illiterates. Drop-out rates are critical in many camps in the Democratic Republic of the Congo, Guinea, Pakistan and the United Republic of Tanzania. Only one-quarter of the 860 schools studied have girl retention initiatives to prevent girls from dropping out of school because of household responsibilities, obligations to contribute to family income, or religious or cultural constraints.

Some 50,000 refugee children in refugee camps dropped out during the school year, contributing to increased rates of out-of-school children and illiterates

Pockets of persistent illiteracy

A different problem occurs in highly literate and schooled societies, in which pockets of persistent illiteracy continue from one generation to the next (Limage, 1986; Vélaz de Medrano, 2005; Guy, 2005). Although these countries have largely completed their literacy transition and have well-established systems of universal primary education (as well as higher education), many school graduates possess only rudimentary

22. Percentage of the population aged 5–17 enrolled in school (standard: 100%); percentage of students who successfully completed the school year (standard: 90%); student to teacher ratio (standard: 40 to 1); percentage of qualified or trained teachers (standard: 80%); and percentage of schools with structured retention initiatives for girls (standard: 80%) (UNHCR, 2004).

literacy skills. Indeed, recent international studies have revealed that significant proportions of the adult population in these highly literate countries have substandard literacy skills (see Chapter 7), results which are typically greeted with shock and disbelief by the public and government officials (Guy, 2005; Bailey, 2004).

Literacy acquisition in highly schooled or literate countries should not be taken for granted

Several factors may contribute to such illiteracy pockets. For example, adults whose mother tongues are different from the language of instruction tend to have lower literacy levels than other groups; immigrants (both legal and illegal) typically must contend with this problem. Illiteracy is also prominent among those native-born adults who have had to struggle with poverty, ill health or discrimination (Box 8.3). Individuals with disabilities and prisoners (discussed in Chapter 7) are additional examples of groups with literacy problems. High drop-out rates, low-quality schooling and lack of support for special needs further exacerbate literacy problems among these groups (Bailey, 2004; Benseman and Tobias, 2003).

In short, literacy acquisition in highly schooled or literate countries should not be taken for granted. The damage of missed opportunities to acquire sustainable literacy skills during childhood and adolescence may be compounded during adulthood, especially among those with limited employment opportunities.

Box 8.3 Illiteracy in Japan

The Burakumin are descendants of a formerly excluded caste created during Japan's feudal period and are among the 50,000 people in Osaka prefecture (population 8.8 million in 2000) who have substantial difficulties in everyday reading and writing. Although the caste was abolished in 1871, Burakumin are still subject to social discrimination, particularly in education and employment, and live in difficult conditions of poverty. Educational attainment and average income for members of this group are significantly lower than the national average. According to a 1980 study, illiteracy among this group in the Osaka prefecture was over 8%. Their situation is an example of how discrimination reduces literacy opportunities and incentives to acquire literacy among socially disadvantaged groups in highly literate societies.

Sources: Shikiji Nihongo Centre, 2005; Burakukaihou Jinken Kenkyusho, 2005; New Media Jinken Kikou, 2005.

Placing literacy in a social context

The spread of formal schooling, adult learning opportunities and (in some countries) organized literacy campaigns have played a significant role in historical literacy transitions. By contrast, political strife, warfare and economic decline have hindered progress towards widespread literacy. Today, illiteracy continues to affect those groups which were denied opportunities to acquire literacy in the past. In more developed regions, such groups typically constitute a minority of the population. In those developing countries where educational access is limited and social exclusion is pervasive, however, these groups constitute a majority.

In practice, one's literacy skills and competencies are largely determined by a complex interplay between one's own motivations and the available learning opportunities. This relationship between the demand and supply of literacy opportunities is itself influenced by the broader social context. The next sections discuss three critical issues – multilingualism and linguistic diversity, the social character of literacy practices and the importance of literate environments – in order to illuminate the social contexts of literacy and to suggest improvements for existing policy interventions (see Chapter 9).

Languages and literacy

Language policies and practices have played – and continue to play – an important role in literacy transitions and the development of literate communities. Despite the fact that, in practice, literacy skills are *applied* or *used* in a specific language, most definitions of literacy view it as a generic set of skills that are comparable across languages. According to this dominant view, whether a person acquires or practises literacy skills in Urdu, Modern Standard Arabic, Mandarin Chinese, Swahili, Portuguese, Amharic or English makes little substantive difference. Given the longstanding interest in measuring, monitoring and comparing literacy levels across diverse language contexts, this position is understandable.

Yet, in reality, the nature of literacy is not homogeneous across all languages, just as the features of different languages are not homogeneous. Thus, linguists use the notion of 'language development' to talk about the level and status of a language – e.g. whether it is written, how widely it is in use and its official or non-official status (see Walter, 2004; Sadembouo and Watters, 1987). The majority of living languages in Africa and Asia are spoken but not written. Conversely, some languages are no longer spoken but survive in written form (e.g. Coptic and Latin). Other languages are written for some purposes (e.g. religious rituals), but not for others. The oral and written forms of a language (e.g. Arabic) sometimes serve different purposes, so that the skills commonly used in the oral form do not necessarily provide access to the language's written form (Box 8.4). Moreover, the actual skills involved in reading or writing a text depend on the language in which they are applied. Different skills are required to master different script systems (e.g. for alphabets vs ideograms) (Box 8.5). Finally, other non-conventional semiotic systems – namely, sign language and Braille – allow communication and the conveyance of meaning without conventional scripts (Box 8.6).

Box 8.4 Arabic

Arabic, which has been an official United Nations language since 1974, is spoken by over 200 million people in the Middle East, in North Africa and in countries with significant Muslim populations. There are three types of Arabic: Classical (found in the Koran and religious texts), Modern Standard (used by many countries as the national or official language) and over thirty forms of colloquial, or modern spoken Arabic. Speakers of various Arabic dialects do not necessarily understand one another; thus many must learn Modern Standard Arabic (MSA) or use another language to communicate. Nevertheless, while MSA is the official language of the Arab States, many inhabitants do not have access to it. In the Sudan, for example, MSA is the official language, used in most written materials and taught in public schools. Spoken Sudanese Arabic, however, is quite distinct from MSA. Many Sudanese master neither language, but use local languages and dialects instead. This means that learners have to perform two distinct operations: first, learn the standard or classical form of Arabic; and, second, master the skills of encoding the oral language *into* a script and of decoding the spoken language *from* the script (see Maamouri, 1998). For adults in short literacy courses, the lack of correspondence between the spoken and written languages poses a particular problem.

Sources: Gordon (2005), Hammoud (2005).

Box 8.5 Script diversity

Each major script type – ideographic (Chinese), syllabic (Ethiopian languages and to some extent Burmese), and alphabetic (Latin, Cyrillic, Devanagari and other Indian alphabets) – has a long history. The acquisition of literacy is complicated not only by the challenges of particular scripts, but also by the common necessity to master a number of different scripts. The following are some examples of script diversity:

- **China:** Though Chinese languages all use the same ideographic script, they each require the recognition of 2,000 basic characters for literacy (1,500 characters for rural residents). Children gain access to literacy in this script via a romanized representation of Mandarin (Putonghua), which was adopted as the national dialect in the 1950s and, since then, has been used in the first years of primary schooling. The Bai minority writes its own language, with a Latin script, while also learning the ideographic script of Chinese.
- **Myanmar:** The Lahu minority writes its own language in Latin script, and learns Burmese (in Burmese script), as well as English; some other minorities use Burmese script for their own language.
- **Ethiopia:** A Wolaitta person may learn Wolatigna in either the Ethiopic syllabary or in Latin script – both are in use: the Ethiopic script is used by older people, while school children are taught the language using the Latin alphabet. Students are also likely to learn Amharic (Ethiopic script) and English. Some language groups, including the largest, Oromo, have opted to replace the Ethiopic syllabary with the Latin alphabet, so as to make a clear distinction with the past when Amharic was the dominant language (it is still the prevailing lingua franca).
- **Mongolia:** The Cyrillic alphabet is used today, although there is also an older, Mongolian one (the only one written vertically down, from left to right across the page). In the 1990s, schools introduced literacy learning in the older Mongolian script, but this proved too difficult to sustain in an environment where the Cyrillic alphabet was dominant. Now Cyrillic script is again used for basic literacy, but children are also taught the Mongolian script.

Cultural and political factors have played a role in the choice, maintenance, simplification and evolution of a script. The use of Latin scripts attests to the impact of European languages; on a smaller scale, the Cyrillic script reflects Russian influences. Chinese characters and foreign words (from English and Japanese) increased script and language diversity in the Republic of Korea, while a 'Koreanization' of the language occurred in the Democratic People's Republic of Korea.

While they may present certain difficulties to learners, language scripts are rarely the decisive obstacle in language acquisition. Learner motivation, practice and opportunities for use are more influential factors for achieving and sustaining literacy.

Source: Robinson (2005).

Box 8.6 Sign languages

Deaf communities are an important linguistic minority, who are served by various sign languages, the exact number of which is unknown. A sign language that a deaf child acquires early in life becomes a 'mother tongue' and contributes to the acquisition of other languages, both signed and non-signed. A sign language and an oral language in the same environment (e.g. British Sign Language and British English) are entirely different languages, with their own grammars and linguistic structures. A deaf person may also access the oral language through lip-reading, as a second language. Many deaf children do not have the opportunity to learn a sign language at an early age and are obliged to follow the same schooling as their hearing counterparts, with negative effects on learning and literacy.

Source: Skutnabb-Kangas (2000).

National language policies have a significant impact on language development and literacy acquisition

National language policies – in particular, the designation of an official language (or languages), the choice of languages of instruction in schools and adult learning programmes and the languages pupils are required to learn – have a significant impact on language development and literacy acquisition. Yet, surprisingly, there is a paucity of detailed knowledge about national language policies and their application in educational settings.[23] Countries privilege certain languages by designating them as national, regional or official languages (UNESCO, 2003*a*). The authority of a 'national' or 'official' language is reflected in its widespread use in governmental affairs, legal activities and public institutions. Most countries have one or two official languages, some three or more.[24] In the past, the designation of an official language was a politically charged and contentious issue, reflecting prior colonial ties, existing power relations and the languages used by dominant ethnic and cultural groups (Ouane, 2003). It remains so today.

Colonial language policies, especially in Africa, have impeded the development of literacy (Coulmas, 1992; Mazrui, 1996). While many African languages developed orthographies during the colonial period, their use was often limited to the religious domain (including missionary educational programmes). European languages, by contrast, served wider purposes, had abundant literatures, and facilitated international ties; consequently, many were retained after independence as official languages. This policy reverberated throughout the post-colonial world; except for an elite minority, becoming literate meant first learning literacy in a new (typically European) language.

Language standardization has long been considered an essential means of unifying culturally diverse communities (as in early modern France). Although Indonesia has over 800 distinct languages, it designated Bahasa-Indonesia – a hybrid of several languages – as its official state language.[25] Swahili was meant to serve a similar function in the United Republic of Tanzania. Israel's language-as-nation-building process was reflected in the *ulpans* – intensive Hebrew language programmes for adults – which helped create a national identity among diverse Jewish immigrants, many of whom were illiterate (Brosh-Vaitz and Lazerson, 2005).[26] Chinese authorities pursued a single-language policy based on Mandarin (Putonghua) to enable minority groups to communicate with, and assimilate into, Chinese (Han) society, and to unify speakers of other Han varieties. In some countries, the move to adopt a single national language (e.g. Hindi in India, or Urdu in Pakistan) was resisted by speakers of other languages. In Ethiopia, initial modernization favoured Amharic as the national language, but language priorities shifted following subsequent regime changes (Shenkut, 2005).

Despite attempts at language consolidation, linguistic diversity remains a significant factor in language policies and literacy acquisition (Spolsky, 2004).[27] At the national level, where language policies are set, monolingualism is a rarity, and most countries are home to many

23. Kosonen (2004) addresses language policies in education in East and South-East Asia. Surprisingly little research has examined the relationship between language policies and literacy acquisition in schools or adult literacy programmes in the developing world (Robinson, 2005). Williams and Cooke (2002) argue that there has been little research on language and development policies in general.

24. All together, there are 225 languages that have been designated as 'official' in at least one country (UNESCO, 2006*b*, Table 6). Countries with three or more official languages include India (with nineteen), South Africa (eleven), Singapore and Switzerland (four each), and Belgium, Bolivia, Egypt and Sri Lanka (with three each).

25. Bahasa-Indonesia is a product of nation-building efforts: it was a custom-built language, designed to meet the needs of a multilingual community and to unify it. It combines several national languages with a simplified grammar and is relatively easy to use.

26. Arabic is also an official language in Israel.

27. *Ethnologue*, a major reference work cataloguing the world's languages, estimates that there are over 6,900 living languages worldwide. One-third of these are found in Asia, 30% in Africa, 19% in the Pacific, 14% in the Americas and 4% in Europe. A majority of the world's living languages have no written form and are used by numerically small populations. In fact, more than half of all living languages have less than 10,000 mother tongue speakers; an additional one-quarter of languages have between 10,000 to 100,000 speakers. From a different perspective, there are a small number of dominant lingua francas: 85 languages constitute the first languages of 80% of the world's population. Many exclusively oral languages are disappearing, and, consequently, language diversity at the *global* level is declining. (Data are from http://www.ethnologue.com/ [accessed 10 July 2005] [see Gordon, 2005].) It is estimated that, each year, ten languages become extinct and that the population of mother tongue speakers for languages with less than 10,000 speakers is declining rapidly (Wurm, 2001; UNESCO, 2003*e*).

Table 8.2: Literacy needs and languages

Country	Percentage of world's non-literate population	Adult literacy rate* (15 and over) (%)	Number of living languages	Official languages	
				Number	Names
Twelve countries with 75% of world's non-literate population					
India	34.6	60.1	415	19	Assamese, Bengali, English, Gujarati, Hindi, Kannada, Kashmiri, Konkani, Malayalam, Manipuri, Marathi, Nepali, Oriya, Punjabi, Sanskrit, Sindhi, Tamil, Telugu, Urdu
China	11.3	90.9	235	1	Mandarin
Bangladesh	6.8	41.1	39	1	Bangla
Pakistan	6.2	48.7	72	2	Urdu, English
Nigeria	2.9	66.8	510	1	English
Ethiopia	2.8	41.5	84	1	Amharic
Indonesia	2.4	87.9	737	1	Bahasa Indonesia
Egypt	2.2	55.6	11	3	Arabic, English, French
Brazil	1.9	88.4	188	1	Portuguese
Iran, Isl. Rep.	1.4	77.0	75	1	Farsi
Morocco	1.3	50.7	9	1	Arabic
D.R. Congo	1.2	65.3	214	1	French
Five countries with lowest adult literacy rates					
Burkina Faso		12.8	68	1	French
Niger		14.4	21	1	French
Mali		19.0	50	1	French
Benin		33.6	54	1	French
Senegal		39.3	36	1	French

* In almost all the countries listed, literacy rates are based on literacy in an official language and/or at least one non-official language.
Sources: Literacy rates are from the statistical annex, Table 2; the number of living languages, from Gordon (2005); official languages and languages in daily use, from UNESCO (2000*c*).

Initial learning in the mother tongue has cognitive, psychological and pedagogical advantages

languages.[28] Even where language use has been standardized, regional languages persist (e.g. Breton, Basque and Occitan). Migrant communities, linguistic minorities and expatriates constitute important sources of on-going linguistic diversity.

Table 8.2 illustrates these issues by presenting comparative information on linguistic diversity for countries identified in Chapter 7 as facing especially significant literacy challenges. Each of the listed countries is linguistically diverse (ranging from 9 spoken languages in Morocco to 737 languages in Indonesia), and there is a notable disjunction between the great number of spoken languages in a country and the relatively small number of lingua francas that have obtained 'official' status. In some of these linguistically diverse countries, large majorities speak the national or 'official' language: in the Islamic Republic of Iran over 70% speak Western Farsi, in Brazil 95% speak Portuguese, in Bangladesh 98% speak Bangla. Thus, linguistic diversity in many countries is concentrated in particular regions or among specific minority communities.

Language, literacy and schooling are closely intertwined. The languages used in school (languages of instruction) are either officially or legally defined. Mother tongue education is advocated as a human right, language being recognized as an integral part of one's cultural identity (UNESCO, 2003*a*, 2003*b*). In addition, acquiring literacy in one's mother tongue is thought to facilitate the social participation of minorities.

Research has consistently shown that learning to read and write in one's mother tongue facilitates access to literacy in other languages (Ouane, 2003; Brock-Utne, 2000; Goody and Bennett, 2001; Heugh, 2003; Grin, 2005; Reh, 1981; Geva and Ryan, 1993). Literacy provision that uses initial learning in the mother tongue and then moves to a second language has cognitive, psychological and pedagogical advantages. Mother tongue education is advocated as a preferred policy in developing countries (see Ouane, 2003). Papua New Guinea is an interesting example, since over 800 languages are spoken and vernacular education is widespread. Primary school pupils begin in their mother tongue, then gradually shift to English (see UNESCO, 2004*a*, pp. 156–7). This

28. Such languages can be usefully classified in a three-tier scheme: a category of local languages used for everyday social intercourse; a second category of regional languages or lingua francas used for commerce and communication over wider geographical areas; and a third category of national, usually 'official', languages, some of which have an international dimension.

Adult literacy learners often prefer to learn regional or national languages

example shows that language diversity does not necessarily impede literacy acquisition, especially if language and literacy policies are calibrated.

Yet, despite its recognized value, this two-step language policy is not always successfully implemented or implemented at all (Dutcher and Tucker, 1997; Benson, 2004). The lack of specialized training and instructional materials for teachers who have to implement mother tongue education at school is a serious problem, particularly in developing countries (Chatry-Komarek, 2003). Even more problematic is how to facilitate the transition from literacy obtained in a mother tongue to literacy in a national or official language (Walter, 2004).

Learning literacy skills in minority languages can be more difficult than doing so in dominant languages (see Walter, 2004). Some linguistic minorities end up with weak literacy skills in both their own *and* the second language (Gordon, 2005). Where literacy programmes in the mother tongue are judged too costly, language minorities must either learn literacy in their second language or be left behind; thus many remain illiterate (see Walter, 2004). On the other hand, if the mother tongue is the only language of instruction, and pupil retention rates are low, it can result in:

- reduced access to wider sources of information, including electronic media;
- barriers to participation in the broader social, economic and political life of the country;
- the possible 'ghettoization' of a minority-language population;
- reduced intercultural contact and learning;
- greater chance of exploitation by unethical mediators within the wider society (e.g. economic intermediaries).

Language and adult literacy

A major challenge for adult literacy efforts has been the lack of a clear language policy for literacy programmes. While adult literacy programmes tend to have more flexibility than schools in choosing the language of instruction, this issue often involves practical problems and political sensitivities for national decision-makers. Many learners end up following lessons that are provided in a language different than their own. As a result, knowledge acquisition and literacy acquisition are mixed, lowering learner motivation and achievement, and contributing to higher drop-out rates (Robinson, 2005).

There is a strong case for decentralization and experimentation at the local level, with the involvement of non-governmental organizations, which would allow learners to choose the language(s) in which learning is to take place (see Chapter 9). The demand for language in literacy programmes is a complex issue. Potential learners are likely to feel more comfortable if they are taught in their mother tongue, at least initially. This may involve using unwritten local languages in the classroom, to facilitate the acquisition of literacy in another (i.e. regional or national) language; it may also involve developing written materials in a local language. Minority peoples whose language is threatened may also prefer learning in their own language (e.g. Quechua-speaking people in Andean countries).

On the other hand, potential adult literacy learners often prefer to learn regional or national languages, which will yield more immediate returns and which may also be easier to teach, given the greater availability of teaching materials and the presence of a more developed literate environment. In the United Republic of Tanzania, for example, literacy programmes in Swahili proved to be far more popular than those in local languages. In Bolivia, many adult learners prefer to learn in Spanish.

Multilingualism and literacy

The key question is not whether multilingualism predominates in countries facing literacy challenges. It does. The central issue is how and in what ways multilingualism can be integrated into formal schools and adult learning programmes so as to enhance the literacy prospects of all. Literacy policies and multilingualism are deeply intermeshed. Literacy policies can be an instrument of language policies, by either promoting multilingualism or imposing monolingualism. Language policies cannot but influence literacy policies (an extreme example being languages banned from the public sphere, including the media and educational institutions). In short, given the nexus between language and literacy, policy decisions need to be well informed in this area, keeping in mind the following questions:

- In how many languages are literacy opportunities available?
- Which groups use major languages to acquire literacy skills and competencies?
- Which communities should be considered as linguistic minorities and therefore have access to literacy acquisition in their own language?

At present, the multilingualism found in most societies is absent from schools and literacy programmes. Languages that are spoken by relatively few speakers are largely excluded from publicly supported educational frameworks. Data from *Ethnologue* (Walter, 2004) show that the size of a language group has a significant impact on access to mother tongue education. Stated differently, communities who speak minority languages have far fewer opportunities to be educated in their mother tongue.

The core problem is that, while teaching literacy in the mother tongue is supported by research, and often by policy, educational realities are complex. Schools and adult education programmes often do not know in advance what the mother tongues of their pupils are; they often lack the teachers, learning materials and tried pedagogical practices in such languages; and often they find that the learners themselves (or their parents) prefer literacy skills to be acquired in official, national or even international languages, which are perceived as having greater value. Although teaching a 'transitional literacy in the mother tongue' may be a good approach, further research is needed on how to implement it, so as to ensure a smooth transition to literacy in other languages (Spolsky, 2004).

In sum, while language diversity is commonly considered an important cultural asset, it poses problems for literacy policies: training teachers in multiple languages can be difficult and developing materials in different languages is costly. Yet these difficulties must be weighed against the inefficiency of teaching in languages that learners do not understand and against the creative potential of multilingual teaching, which reproduces situations encountered by learners in their everyday lives.

Literacy practices

How do people commonly use the literacy skills they have acquired in a given language? How are literacy skills actually practised in different settings: at home, in markets, at work, while participating in religious activities or political movements, in government offices, or during warfare? How do such literacy practices evolve? How, and in what ways, do societies regulate the practice of literacy? Who is expected to perform different literacy practices and what meanings do they attach to them? This section briefly addresses these questions, by paying particular attention to *the actual uses and applications of literacy in different contexts*. Drawing upon ethnographic research, it illustrates how the social embeddedness of literacy has important implications for both policy-makers and practitioners, at international, national and local levels.[29] Key insights from this literature are outlined below.

Individuals apply literacy skills to serve a multiplicity of purposes in their lives. While literacy skills are used for practical purposes (e.g. to communicate with government offices and officials, read medical instructions, complete applications, pay bills and extract information from newspapers), they are also practised for a diverse range of cultural, social and emotional purposes (Box 8.7). People use their literacy skills to read religious texts, strengthen ties with family and friends, read literature, keep diaries, get involved politically, and learn about their ancestors and cultural heritage. These literacy practices are an integral part of people's lives and contribute to their sense of identity and self-worth.

Gender or ethnic discrimination in the labour market can delimit how and where literacy skills are practised

Societies and communities regulate the practice of literacy – especially for women. Historically, many social groups have been (and still are) denied access to literacy in written languages. Today, new forms of exclusion have evolved: many individuals are provided ample opportunities to acquire literacy skills but then learn that their practice is inappropriate, improper or even illegal in certain cases.

The social regulation of literacy practices is often gender specific: in many societies, it is men, not women, who are expected to practise literacy skills in public (e.g. in government offices and religious institutions), while women are expected to practise their skills in private. In Bangladesh, for example, the discovery and circulation of a woman's personal writings can result in humiliation or even physical violence (Maddox, 2005). Gender or ethnic discrimination in the labour market can also delimit how and where literacy skills are practised.

Literacy practices influence the literacy skills individuals hope to acquire, and their motivations for doing so. Studies highlight how the practice of literacy affects the totality of people's lives, especially

29. Most ethnographic studies of literacy published over the past two decades belong to the so-called 'New Literacy Studies.' (This section draws on the work of: Barton, 1994; Barton and Hamilton, 1998; Barton et al., 2000; Bett, 2003; Dyer and Choksi, 2001; Kell, 1995, 1999; Maddox, 2005; Papen, 2004, 2005; Robinson-Pant, 2000; Street, 1993, 2001*a*, 2001*b*, 2003.)

Box 8.7 The diversity of literacy practices in Ghana

The purposes to which Ghanaian individuals apply literacy skills differ widely, especially by gender, age, marital status, social class and residence. Among other things, literacy skills can serve practical, political, religious or cultural purposes. A recent study in Ghana by SIL UK, an NGO, gave examples of how learners actually used the skills they acquired:

- write in their mother tongue such things as stories, songs, children's names, letters to family and friends, letters to newspapers;
- use immunization clinics, attend antenatal and post-natal clinics, practise exclusive breast-feeding;
- properly administer medications to their children;
- help children with their homework and follow their progress in school by reading school reports;
- know about Ghana's laws, be more informed about rights and responsibilities;
- understand government policies and citizens' rights;
- understand family planning programmes, increase awareness of HIV/AIDS and STDs;
- properly apply fertilizer and chemicals to crops;
- read the Bible for oneself;
- see and read husband's pay slip, so he cannot claim not to have been paid;
- challenge husband's relatives when he dies, so that widows are not cheated out of husband's property or their own;
- use money; read prices, bills and receipts; calculate expenses; keep proper records; develop family budgets;
- improve chances of obtaining a loan, keep written records of payments, and open a savings account;
- interact in the wider society and with other communities;
- learn other languages (such as English, so as to be able to participate in discussions in which only English is used).

Sources: SIL UK (2004), Street (2003).

The real benefits of practising literacy skills are in their transformative power

their sense of self and social identity. In Guinea, as in many other countries,[30] women participating in literacy classes report increases in confidence, responsibility and autonomy (Aide et Action, 2005). It is largely because literacy practices affect core aspects of people's lives and social identity that there is such a strong demand for literacy. Becoming educated and acquiring literacy give expression to an individual's (and a family's) deep hopes, aspirations and plans for the future. Indeed, many studies indicate that the real benefits of practising literacy skills are in their transformative power, the ways they empower individuals to 'read' (and reread) their worlds. And, as Freire has demonstrated, literacy programmes have the potential to alter broader power relations by enhancing the assets and capabilities of the poor, as well as their sense of empowerment (Freire and Macedo, 1987).

Knowledge about literacy practices can improve policy design to support literacy acquisition and retention.

Formal schooling and adult learning programmes make many assumptions about literacy practices, if only implicitly. Schools typically emphasize skills such as the understanding of scholarly materials (what is termed 'schooled literacy') and the demonstration of knowledge in examinations. Much less emphasis (if any) is usually placed on skills commonly used in real-life situations. By contrast, programmes targeting out-of-school youth and adults tend to have more practical and/or political orientations, such as providing marketable skills, strengthening political solidarity, helping generate income and improving reproductive health or childcare.

Analyses of literacy practices, and the social contexts in which they are embedded, provide policy-makers and designers of programmes with information about learner demands and motivations. Schools and adult literacy programmes are more likely to enhance learner participation and outcomes if they calibrate contents with learner demands. Learners in southern Africa placed priority on obtaining the status and labour opportunities available to those with formal schooling, rather than acquiring literacy skills for everyday needs. In El Salvador (Bett, 2003), India (Dyer and Choksi, 2001) and South Africa (Mpopiya and Prinsloo, 1996), many literacy programme participants insisted on receiving a school-like education, with its accompanying benefits, an indication of the importance of formal schooling in their societies.

30. See Chapter 5 for additional examples.

Literate environments and literacy

The social and cultural environments in which people live and work can be characterized as being either more or less supportive of the acquisition and practice of literacy. Undoubtedly, schools are meant to be especially supportive settings, containing diverse written and visual materials, enabling the acquisition of literacy skills and practices. What about other environments? How prevalent and valued are printed and visual materials in households, workplaces, occupational groups and communities? And do these environments make a significant contribution to the spread of literacy? To what extent do literate environments, which are more or less rich in written documents and visual materials, encourage individuals to become literate and help them to sustain and integrate their newly acquired skills in their everyday lives?[31]

The specific contents of literate environments vary from setting to setting. For example, in households, a stimulating literate environment would have an abundance of reading materials (e.g. books, magazines or newspapers) and/or communication and electronic media (e.g. radios, mobile phones, televisions or computers). In neighbourhoods and communities, a rich literate environment would have numerous signs, posters and handbills, as well as literacy-promoting institutions such as schools, offices, courts, libraries, banks and training centres. And yet literate environments are more than places offering access to printed matter, written records, visual materials or advanced technologies; ideally, they should enable the free exchange of information and provide an array of opportunities for lifelong learning. Indeed, whether they be in households, neighbourhoods, workplaces or communities, literate environments influence not only those directly exposed to them but also other members of the society.

In high-income countries, rich literate environments are common, whereas in low- and medium-income countries, literate environments vary considerably across and within countries. Cultures promoting reading and writing are often concentrated among privileged members of society (e.g. political leaders, educated professionals, cultural and religious elites). In many developing countries, existing printed materials are unevenly distributed and the production of new ones is limited (Altbach, 1992). For example, Africa is home to 12% of the world's population, but produces only 2% of the world's books (Krolak, 2005). In many remote rural communities in Africa, Asia and Latin America, the circulation of newspapers, books, magazines or even posters is severely limited. Schools represent special settings – sometimes the only setting – in which books and written materials are (or should be) readily available, although access to them among adults and out-of-school youth may be restricted, thus further impoverishing their literate environment.[32]

Scholarly interest in the effects of literate environments has increased in recent years, although the conditions under which literate environments spread and sustain literacy (and the mechanisms involved) remain under-studied (Chhetri and Baker, 2005). Many commentators associate stimulating literate environments with the demand for literacy: individuals residing in such environments are more motivated to become literate and practise their literacy skills (Oxenham et al., 2002). Less understood and empirically grounded are how these links emerge in different families, communities, language groups, work settings and societies.

Overall, measuring literate environments and their impact remains elusive, owing in large part to different conceptual and operational definitions. Moreover, studies with clear specifications of literate environments indicate that learning outcomes vary considerably within low-income communities (Neuman and Celano, 2001). With this in mind, the following sections review key insights from studies of the nature and impact of literate environments, with an eye to the appropriateness and effectiveness of national policy initiatives in this area.

Literate environments should enable the free exchange of information and provide an array of opportunities for lifelong learning

Environments for literacy among school-age children

Comparative studies of educational achievement in developed countries have shown that students from homes with a greater quantity of literacy resources including books, magazines and computers attain higher achievements in reading and other subjects than those from homes with fewer literacy resources (e.g. Elley, 1992). According to the recent International Association for the Evaluation of Educational Achievement (IEA) study *Progress in International Reading Literacy Study (PIRLS)*, exposure to home-based literacy activities (i.e. access to and use of reading

31. The term *literate environment* has been used extensively in the early-child-development literature to describe how the surroundings of young children influence literacy outcomes such as language acquisition, school readiness and reading skills (Dickinson and Tabors, 2001; Nielsen and Monson, 1996). The critical role of the home environment for pre-school children, where initial language learning occurs, has received particular attention (Burgess, 1999). In addition to the physical surroundings of children, the child-development literature suggests that human relationships determine when, how often and in which kinds of situations young children use their newly acquired literacy tools (Neuman and Ruskos, 1997).

32. See the UNESCO/Danida Basic Learning Materials Initiative website: http://www.unesco.org/education/blm/blmintro_en.php

Figure 8.5: Percentage of Grade 4 students in high-level home literacy environments (HLE) and average reading achievement score, by country, 2001

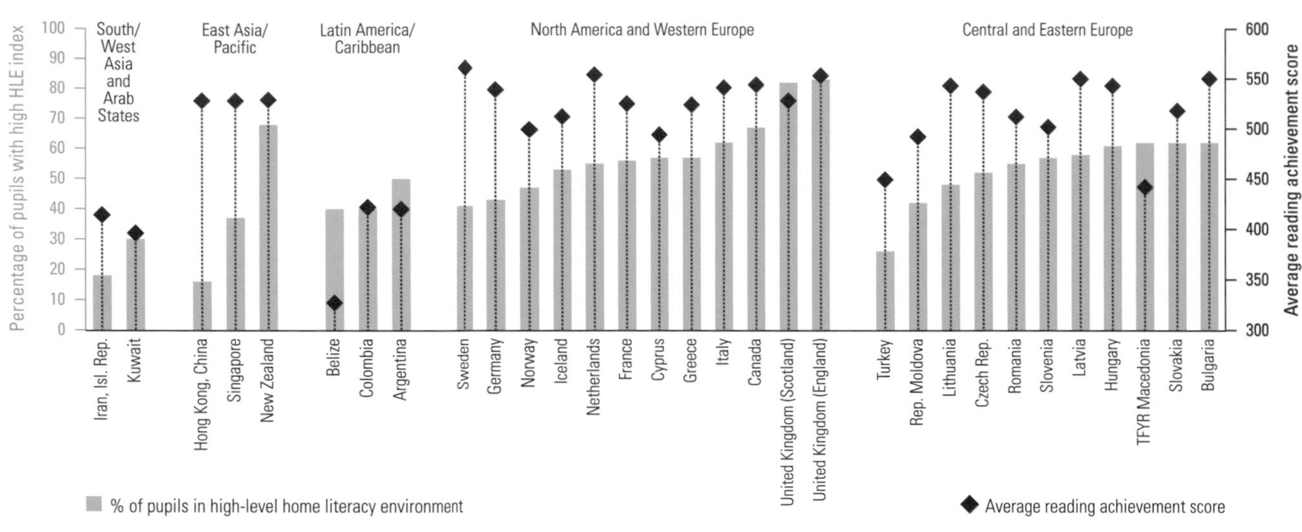

Note: The index of early home literacy activities used in the Progress in International Reading Literacy Study was constructed from parental reports on six activities: reading books, telling stories, singing songs, playing with alphabet toys, playing word games and reading aloud signs and labels.
Source: Mullis et al. (2003*a*).

materials, literacy-related play, television programmes emphasizing reading, reference books and information and computer technologies) was positively related to Grade 4 reading achievement (see Figure 8.5).

In Latin America, results from the UNESCO-sponsored Primer Estudio Internacional Comparativo found that the two most important predictors of language and mathematics achievement were parents' education and the presence of ten or more books in the home (Willms and Somers, 2001, 2005; Carnoy and Marshall, 2005). In short, there is considerable evidence that home environments with significant literacy resources have a positive effect on pupil literacy acquisition.

In reality, however, the environments of many households in developing countries have few literacy resources. For example, The Southern and Eastern Africa Consortium on Monitoring Educational Quality (SACMEQ) (see Chapter 2) compiled data on the prevalence of books, newspapers, magazines, radios and televisions in the homes of Grade 6 students.[33] The SACMEQ survey found that the vast majority of student homes had a radio, with (in all but three of the African countries studied) at least 80% of student homes having one. In comparison, book ownership is limited: in twelve of the fifteen cases, at least 70% of students reported having fewer than ten books in the home (Figure 8.6). Only in Mauritius, Seychelles and (to a lesser degree) South Africa did student homes have a significant number of books (eleven or more).

In all countries except Mauritius, newspapers were more prevalent in student homes than magazines, with considerable cross-national

33. The reports of Grade 6 pupils are less representative in countries where primary enrolment rates are relatively low (e.g. Mozambique and, to a lesser extent, the United Republic of Tanzania and Zambia).

Figure 8.6: Grade 6 student reports of quantity of books in their homes in fifteen African education systems, 2000*

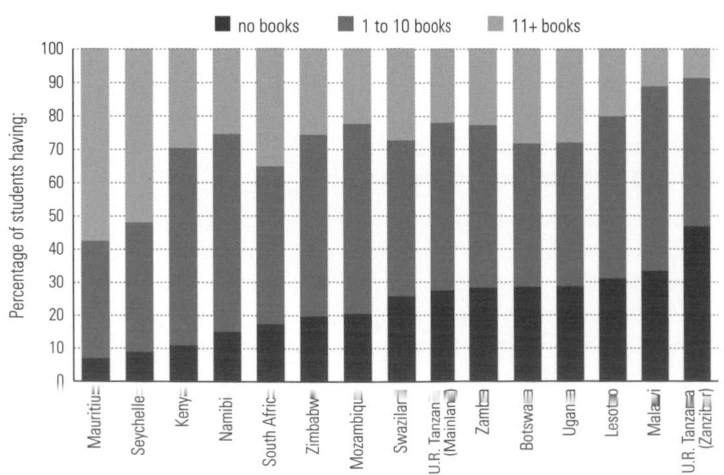

* There are fifteen education systems comprising fourteen countries. All data are from SACMEQ II archives (2000) except Zimbabwe, which is based on SACMEQ I archives (1995).
Source: Ross et al. (2004).

differences (Figure 8.7). The presence of newspapers in student homes ranged from 20% (in the United Republic of Tanzania) to over 60% (in Botswana and Swaziland); the range for magazines was somewhat greater (from 10% in Uganda to nearly 60% in Mauritius). While newspaper and magazine prevalence were fairly similar in each country, television prevalence varied to a much greater extent, most likely due to differential household access to electricity. The results also show that, between 1995 and 2000, the percentage of southern African homes with magazines and newspapers declined, whereas the percentage with a television increased.

The SACMEQ survey also provided information about the *literate environments of schools*, considering, for example, whether or not a school has a library (from pupil reports) and the number of books in the classroom (from teacher reports). The first measure provides an indication of a school's overall literate environment; the latter assesses the availability of literacy resources where instruction takes place. As Figure 8.8 shows, most Grade 6 pupils in Mauritius, Seychelles, Uganda and (to a lesser extent) Namibia attend schools with libraries. In the other countries, however, only 20% to 40% of Grade 6 pupils have access to a school or classroom library, with substantial differences among rural communities, small towns and large cities.

Of greater concern still are the large percentages of Grade 6 pupils whose classrooms have no books (Figure 8.9). In fact, over half of the Grade 6 pupils in Kenya, Malawi, Mozambique, the United Republic of Tanzania, Uganda and Zambia learn in *classrooms in which there is not a single textbook*. Thus, while research clearly shows that home and school literate environments significantly influence student reading and language achievement, the school literate environments of many pupils are impoverished, lacking even the bare minimum of written materials, a situation that has a negative impact on their literacy acquisition and retention.

Significantly improving textbook publishing and provision in developing countries has been on the agenda of aid agencies for several decades (Limage, 2005c). Yet, there is little sign of a coherent strategy of book investment at either national or regional levels (Read, 1995). Investments in textbook production have often been one-shot, short-term projects, doing little to sustain local publishing capacity over time. In addition, ensuring that available textbooks actually find their way into the hands of learners remains an elusive target in many places. Studies have indicated, for example, that only about one-third of primary-school children in Bolivia, Brazil, Chile, Colombia, Ecuador, Panama, Peru and Venezuela actually had access to textbooks (Montagnes, 2000). Sustainable literacy and effective learning require extensive use of written and visual materials; yet many classrooms in developing countries must still do without them.

Figure 8.7: Prevalence of newspapers, magazines and televisions in students' homes in fifteen African education systems, 2000*

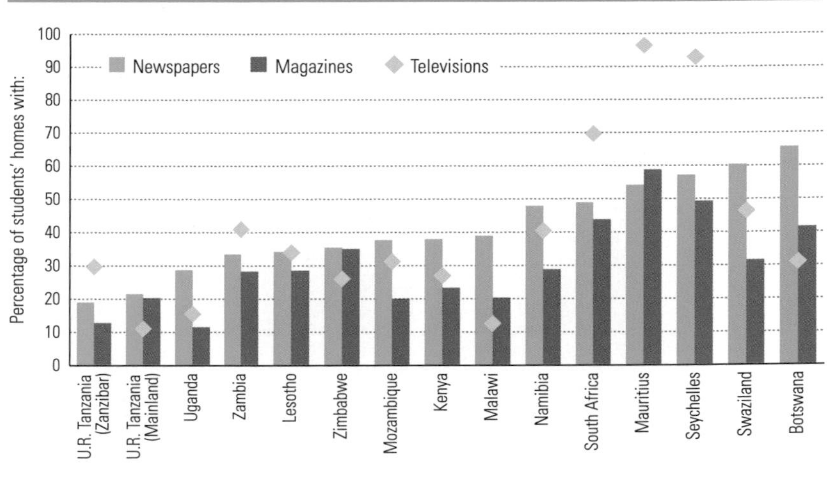

* See note to Figure 8.6.
Source: Ross et al. (2004).

Figure 8.8: Percentage of Grade 6 students attending schools where there is no school or classroom library, by country, and area of residence, 2000*

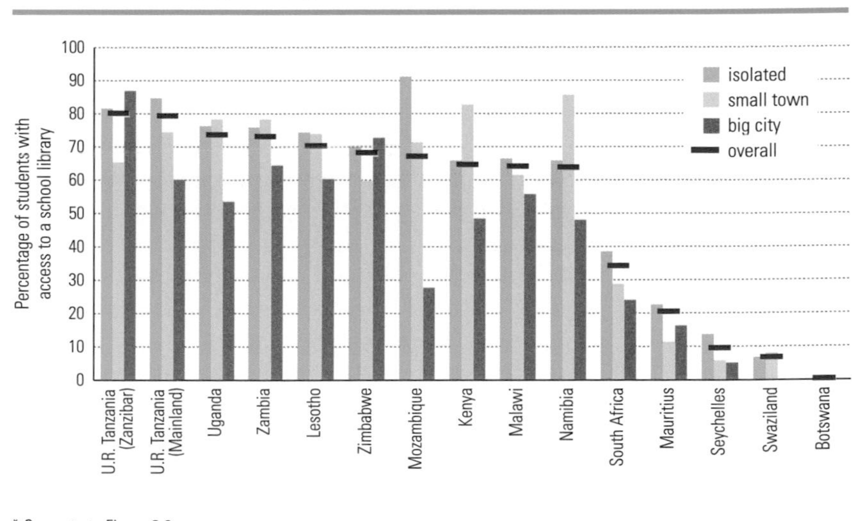

* See note to Figure 8.6.
Source: Ross et al. (2004).

The school literate environments of many pupils are impoverished

Figure 8.9: Percentage of Grade 6 pupils in classrooms where there are no books available, by country and area of residence, 2000*

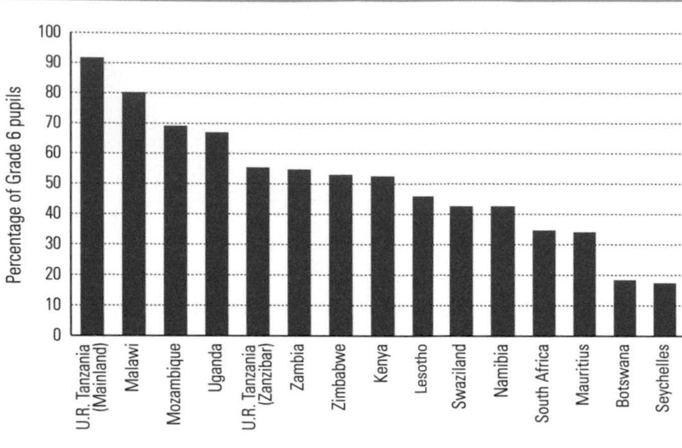

* See note to Figure 8.6.
Source: Ross et al. (2004).

Environments for literacy among adults

The International Adult Literacy Survey (IALS) examined factors associated with literacy proficiencies – including socio-economic background, educational attainment, labour force experience, and various home and work activities reflecting the richness of respondents' literate environments – in twenty OECD countries (OECD, 2000).[34] Concerning their home environment, respondents provided information about their participation in literacy-promoting activities (e.g. reading books and newspapers, visiting public libraries), the presence of various print media and the time spent watching television. For their workplace, they provided information about the frequency and variety of reading, writing, and mathematical activities. The IALS study found that literacy practices at work and home (in addition to formal educational attainment, labour force participation and formal adult training) were significantly associated with literacy proficiency. The study concluded that home and work environments with substantive literacy-requiring activities promote higher levels of prose, document and numerical literacy.

National literate environments and literacy

In the past, many countries attempted to create sustainable environments for literacy through print and broadcast media (Box 8.8 describes the case of China). Quite a few countries developed special publications for individuals with minimal proficiency in written language (UNESCO, 1975*b*). Journals in Thailand, Tunisia, the United Republic of Tanzania, Venezuela and Zambia prepared special articles for 'neo-literates'. During the 1960s and 1970s, several periodicals were developed with the aim of expanding literacy in local languages.[35] In Brazil, the literacy movement Mobral published two newspapers: the *Journal do Mobral* (with a circulation of 2 million) for learners in literacy courses and *Integração* for new literates (Bataille, 1976).

The mobilization of mass media in support of literacy and literacy programmes has also been a common strategy. During the 1930s, directors such as Sergey Eisenstein produced popular films to promote the Soviet literacy campaign. During 1965–72, the number of developing countries using radio or television in conjunction with literacy programmes more than doubled (from ten to twenty-two). Many Latin American countries formed listening groups (e.g. ACPO in Colombia) to maximize the literacy impact of radio broadcasts. In Côte d'Ivoire, the Democratic Republic of the Congo, Ghana, the Niger, Nigeria, Senegal, Togo and the United Republic of Tanzania, radio clubs and listening groups were also initiated (Bataille, 1976).

Few studies have examined the overall effectiveness of changes in a nation's literate environment. Box 8.9 describes a cross-national study of the influence of print materials, mass media or advanced technologies on literacy rates.

Box 8.8 Literate environments in China

Literate environments in China have developed dramatically in recent decades. For example, the number of periodicals in China has grown from about 250 in 1949 to more than 8,500 in 2001. During the past half century, the number of newspapers increased nearly tenfold. Today, China is home to over 400 daily newspapers, with print runs of 80–85 million copies. It has some 560 publishing houses, which send about 100,000 (new and old) book titles to the market each year. There are scores of electronic publishing units, thousands of radio and television stations, and a press corps of well over half a million. Estimates this year suggest that there are as many as 40 million computers in China connected to the Internet and 200 million users of data, multimedia and the Internet (Ross et al., 2005).

34. Not surprisingly, level of formal education attainment was the main determinant of literacy proficiency, serving as the first and strongest predictor in seventeen out of twenty countries, with each year of schooling increasing the literacy score by ten points, on average. Age and occupation were also major determinants of literacy.

35. Examples include the *Bekham Bidan* in Afghanistan, *Sengo* in the Democratic Republic of [illegible] in India, *Ruz-Now* in the Islamic Republic of Iran, *News for All* in Jamaica, *New-Day* in Liberia, *Kibaru* in Mali, *Saabon Ra'avili* in the Niger, and *Game-Su* in Togo, and *Elimu-Haina-Mwishe* in the United Republic of Tanzania.

Box 8.9 Does the prevalence of print materials, mass media and advanced technologies influence literacy rates?

In a recent exploratory, cross-national study including over 100 countries, the correlations between measures of national literate environments and literacy rates were examined. Indicators of the quality of literate environments included, first, the prevalence of reading and learning materials, as measured by newspaper circulation, book production and registered library users per 1,000 inhabitants; and, second, the availability of information and communication technologies (ICTs), measured by the percentage of households with radios and televisions, and the number of personal computers per 1,000 people. Controlling for the net primary enrolment rate, this study found that there was a positive relationship between high ICT prevalence (televisions, radios and personal computers) and both adult and youth literacy rates, with the association between adult literacy rates and television prevalence being strongest, followed by personal computer use and radio use. These preliminary findings suggest visual media may be more influential than audio-based (especially in developing countries), although the mechanisms involved need further study.

High prevalences of books, newspapers and libraries have long been considered key indicators of healthy literate environments and as central to the processes of literacy acquisition and sustainability. Yet, as for books, multivariate analyses indicate that national indicators of book production are only weakly related to literacy rates. It may be that the ubiquity of 'mundane' forms of print and writing (i.e. application forms, brochures, signs, banners, letters and medical instructions) is more influential on literacy than that of specialized literatures and textbooks. However, there is a significant positive relationship between newspaper circulation per capita and literacy rates. This is unsurprising, given the lower cost, greater availability and wider distribution of newspapers.

Overall, the evidence suggests that stimulating literate environments encourage individuals to become literate and provide a basis for new literates to sustain and develop literate practices over the course of their lives. Further analyses of the impact of literate environments might examine these processes among different ethnic groups, age groups, geographical locations and occupational categories, and would require detailed data on budgetary allocation in literacy programmes.

Source: Chhetri and Baker (2005).

Most people live in communities in which they have some access to the literacy skills of others

Overall, the evidence suggests that different components of literate environments have different impacts on aggregate literacy levels.

Equity issues: access to literacy in households and communities

In the developed world, widespread literacy is the norm: almost all adults have acquired basic skills in reading and writing, even though the quality of those skills and the frequency with which they are practised vary considerably (just as with numeracy). In the developing world, where literacy needs are most pronounced, the spatial and social distribution of literacy skills are highly uneven (see Chapter 7). This section focuses on the social geography of literacy, probes the relative inaccessibility of literacy for households in literate-impoverished communities and examines the extent to which individuals with weaker literacy skills interact with, or have access to, individuals with stronger skills.

Apart from extremely poor or remote rural communities in which not a single adult can read or write, most people live in communities in which they have some access to the literacy skills of others. Basu and Foster (1998) refer to individuals in the first group as *isolated illiterates*[36] and to those in the latter as *proximate illiterates*. To the extent that proximate illiterates are inclined to request the help of people with stronger literacy skills, they can effectively perform some 'demanding' or complex literacy tasks (e.g. filling out applications, understanding administrative documents, reading medical instructions and writing letters to family members).[37] For example, older adults with weak literacy skills often call upon younger members of the household to carry out literacy-demanding tasks. Likewise, foreign migrants may request literacy-related assistance from extended family networks or ethnic associations. Gibson (1998) studied intra-household literacy dynamics and argued that the presence of even one literate member in an 'illiterate' household can have various external benefits. Gibson (2001) also showed how regional rankings of adult literacy rates in Papua New Guinea change if proximate illiterates are factored in and an 'effective' literacy rate calculated.

36. At present, few studies have examined in detail the characteristics of isolated illiterates or possible ways to overcome the literacy challenges faced by their communities.

37. The IALS survey also asked respondents to indicate the frequency with which they requested assistance from others in carrying out various literacy-related tasks (OECD, 2000).

Table 8.3 shows that, while the South Coast region of Papua New Guinea has a higher literacy rate than the North Coast region, it has a lower level in terms of its effective literacy rate.

Rarely do studies examine the distribution of literate individuals across households. In a case where individuals with basic literacy skills are evenly distributed across households, the percentage of households with access to literacy skills could reach 100%, even though the individual-level literacy might be much lower. On the other hand, in a case where literate individuals are 'perfectly concentrated' within households, and all household sizes are the same, the percentage of households with literate members would be equal to the percentage of individuals who are literate. A percentage of households with any literate member that is only a little higher than the percentage of literate individuals would suggest a high degree of concentration of literacy within households and poor 'spread' of literacy over the population. It would be valuable to know both the causes and the effects of such concentration.[38]

In less than two centuries, the nature and social functions of literacy have changed dramatically

Table 8.3: Reported and effective adult literacy in Papua New Guinea, 1996

Region	% of adult population who are:				Effective adult literacy rate (%)
	Literates	Proximate illiterates	Isolated illiterates	Gender gap in literacy	
National Capital District	85.8	12.1	2.1	5.3	95.0
New Guinea Islands	77.7	15.2	7.1	5.8	89.3
South Coast (Papua)	59.0	23.4	17.6	15.8	76.7
North Coast	56.3	28.6	15.1	25.1	78.0
Highlands	34.6	37.7	27.7	17.8	63.2
Papua New Guinea	51.9	29.1	19.0	18.2	74.0

Source: The 1996 Papua New Guinea Household Survey, cited in Gibson (2001).
Estimates are for the population aged 15 years and older.

Conclusion

In less than two centuries, the nature and social functions of literacy have changed dramatically: from a means of understanding religious precepts and selecting military recruits to an essential building block of information processing and worker productivity; from a specialized tool of merchants, administrators and professionals to a vital instrument for cultural intercourse and global commerce; and from a way of enforcing legal contracts and determining voter rights to a basis for linking individuals and families to public institutions and international networks. Literacy today has become essential.

The expansion of formal schooling was the single most significant factor in past transitions to widespread literacy. For social, cultural and economic reasons, these transitions occurred earliest in Western Europe and North America. More recently, organized literacy campaigns and increased opportunities for adult learning and education (e.g. in Latin America, Africa and Asia) were two additional factors, which, together with school expansion, contributed to rising literacy rates. On the other hand, protracted political conflict and acute economic decline have resulted in stagnating literacy rates; and exclusion and discrimination continue to contribute to pockets of illiteracy, even within developed countries.

38. This discussion benefited from comments by Julie Schaffner.

Language issues, literacy practices and literate environments underscore the importance of the broader social context in which literacy is acquired and sustained. The evidence suggests:

- There is value in providing youth and adults with learning opportunities that more closely suit their literacy needs and reflect the actual uses to which literacy is put in their communities.
- The challenge is how to do this in ways that carefully consider the complex language situations of teacher and learners, while enabling learners to enrich their literacy skills in both their mother tongue and additional languages.
- Creating (and maintaining) a stimulating literate environment is an effective way of generating motivation to acquire literacy and of encouraging its uses and practices.

Chapter 9 discusses the policy and programme implications of these findings. ■

© AFP / Juan Barreto

A woman deeply engaged in a literacy class in Venezuela, part of a national literacy drive.

Chapter 9

Good policy, good practice

The preceding chapters, particularly Chapters 2 and 7, show that the global literacy challenge is huge in terms of the hundreds of millions of people who do not benefit from literacy. Scale is therefore an important aspect of any policy response to this challenge. The challenge is not just one of scale, however. It is also one of scope. The thrust of this Report is that literacy policy should have the goal not only of literate individuals but also the much broader goal of literate societies, in which all people can use their literacy to pursue freedoms, opportunities and personal development and in which literacy contributes to the development of the economy and the society. This chapter suggests policy priorities and good practices for countries and for the international community to assist them in meeting the literacy challenge. It advocates a three-pronged approach to literacy – assuring quality schooling, scaling up literacy programmes for youth and adults, and developing literate environments. The chapter focuses particularly on youth and adult literacy programmes, as school quality was covered in the 2005 Report and the importance of the literate environment is discussed in Chapter 8.

Four policy directions

The evidence of this Report suggests four major policy directions for governments and other literacy stakeholders, especially in developing countries: to consider literacy policy as central to the entire EFA framework; to develop a three-pronged policy for literate societies; to take careful account of multilingualism; and to place literacy firmly within education sector plans and poverty reduction strategies.

Literacy is at the **core of EFA** as a learning tool, a learning process and a learning outcome, all contributing to the achievement of broader human development goals.

Literacy policy is central to the entire EFA framework

A **three-pronged policy for literate societies** is essential. Quality schooling for all children is necessary if the entire next generation of adults is to be literate – this means not just universal primary enrolment but also universal primary completion and good-quality primary education. Scaled-up youth and adult literacy programmes are necessary if the hundreds of millions of adults without literacy skills are to have the means to acquire and use these skills; simply waiting for universal primary completion is not the answer. Nor are 'one size fits all' solutions: strategies need to respond to diverse needs and contexts. Rich literate environments are necessary both for the acquisition and the retention and use of literacy skills; literate environments in turn depend on language, book, media and information policies. The weight accorded to each of the three prongs will vary across countries, reflecting relative needs and the availability of resources. The challenge is further compounded by the fact that the countries in which the majority of adults lack minimal literacy skills are also those in which the attainment of a good basic education for all children is still many years away, at current rates of progress. These countries are mainly in sub-Saharan Africa and South and West Asia.

Multilingualism is a crucial factor for all three prongs of literacy policy. Use of mother tongues is pedagogically sound, encourages community mobilization and social development, and provides for political voice. At the same time, there is strong demand for learning dominant languages to increase economic opportunity, mobility and engagement in national development processes. Consistency and coherence must shape language, literacy and education policy.

Only if literacy and the goal of literate societies are placed firmly within **education sector plans and poverty reduction strategies** are the necessary institutional, human and financial resources likely to be provided. This direction is also important if the international community is to recognize the magnitude and complexity of the task and include literacy within aid programme frameworks.

Three strategic considerations

To achieve the policy directions outlined above, there are three important strategic considerations. First, strong and sustained political commitment to literacy is essential. The general absence of such commitment and the resulting lack of sufficient resources for developing holistic literacy policies partly explain the failure to reach higher levels of literacy (Jones, 1990; Lind and Johnston, 1990). In evaluating the Experimental World Literacy Programme (1967–1973), UNESCO concluded that unless the political will to implement literacy programmes was explicit in both theory and practice, individual programmes would have limited success (UNESCO/UNDP, 1976, cited in Lind and Johnston, 1990).[1]

Where significant national gains in levels of adult literacy have been achieved, both national and local leaders have stressed the value of literacy for nation-building and/or for the achievement of particular aspects of human and economic development. Financial and other resources have been allocated and responsibilities have been shared. The public has supported adult learning. This was true in the United Republic of Tanzania after independence[2] and Mozambique in the 1970s, and it is true today in countries undergoing rapid economic growth and transformation, including China and India.

Local community leaders are well placed to acknowledge the real constraints on people's participation in literacy activities. In Indonesia, for example, support for learning groups in a literacy campaign was sought through endorsement by village chiefs. The groups did well where the chiefs were aware of the need for literacy, and much less so where they were not (Downing, 1987, cited in Lind and Johnston, 1996).

The second strategic consideration is partnership. Outside schools, literacy programmes are diverse, and their providers varied and often institutionally insecure. But the involvement of the media, universities, ministries

1. The majority of the enrolled learners who became literate in the eleven countries participating in the Experimental World Literacy Programme were in the United Republic of Tanzania: 96,900 out of 120,000, or 81% (Lind and Johnston, 1990).

2. In the United Republic of Tanzania, literacy was clearly identified as a national priority. President Julius Nyerere was a strong advocate of adult education. Illiteracy fell from 67% to 20% between 1971 and 1983 (Lind and Johnston, 1990).

other than education, local authorities, civil society and the private sector is a strength. Different types of competence and capacity are brought to bear. Brokering national partnerships to promote institutional development, enhance programme sustainability and make literacy more visible can increase cohesion in national literacy efforts. In addition, clarifying the roles and responsibilities of agencies, and establishing national and local coordination among providers enhance the national literacy resource base.

The third important strategic consideration is that responding to demand and creating motivation for literacy are critical. A basic principle of adult education, albeit one not applied uniformly, is that the knowledge and wishes of learners should both inform learning programmes and be their starting point. Gender, age, rural and urban circumstances, levels of motivation and language are important facets of demand, as are longer-term expectations. In Uganda, initial literacy graduates sought continuing education in advanced literacy, English, vocational skills and modern agricultural methods (Carr-Hill, 2001). People who have never acquired basic literacy skills need different channels from those that respond to the demands of people looking to continue their education beyond schooling. It is important to build links between literacy programmes and continuing education.

Building on the above directions and strategic considerations, this chapter gives particular attention to the challenge represented by one of the three prongs of literacy policy – investment in youth and adult literacy. The chapter focuses on:

- promoting good practice in the learning and teaching of literacy;
- scaling up adult literacy programmes;
- bringing greater coherence to national policies on adult literacy;
- engaging the international community.

In so doing, the intent is not to obscure the importance of the literate environment, an issue addressed in Chapter 8. The link between adult literacy and the environments in which learners use their literacy skills receives regular attention in the sections that follow. The relationship between literate environments and types and levels of adult learning is complex and not always direct, but it seems clear that literate environments encourage individuals to become literate and enable those with newly acquired skills to sustain and develop their literacy (see Box 8.9).

Some specialists suggest that opportunities to use and develop literacy should be in place before literacy programmes are offered, arguing that literacy skills are learned and developed throughout life in literate societies.[3] The retention of literacy and numeracy skills might in that case depend more on their continued use than on the provision of additional courses (Lauglo, 2001). Accordingly, the importance of providing and disseminating reading materials for newly literate adults is critical, especially where the opportunity to use new literacy skills is otherwise limited (Carron et al., 1989; Carr-Hill, 2001). Several reviews highlight the lack of reading materials in local languages in multilingual contexts (Riddell, 2001; Lind and Johnston, 1996).

Providing and disseminating reading materials for newly literate adults is critical

Policies related to book publishing,[4] the media and access to information also play an influential role in developing environments in which literacy can flourish. This Report does not discuss the policies in detail, in part because they are so specific to particular contexts and countries. They require policy-makers' attention, however.

The creation of literate societies involves the promotion of a broad range of policies and activities. Good schools should exist in every community. The reading habit should be supported and acknowledged.[5] Access to the media and to printed matter in general should be extensive. Time should be made for women and for men to read and write, and explicit links between oral and written cultures and different languages should be encouraged. There should be support for enhancing visual literacy. Multiple paths to learning and to the creation of learning and of literate environments are required (Box 9.1).

Promoting good practice in the learning and teaching of literacy

Sound policy and planning require an understanding of good practice in the learning and teaching of literacy. The diversity of practice in schools, adult literacy classes, homes, workplaces and meeting places is a challenge for government policy-makers and planners more familiar with a one-track approach to provision of formal education. Appreciation of this fact is an important point of departure for policy development.

3. See, for instance, Dumont (1990), Ouane (1989), and Lind and Johnston (1990).

4. Despite numerous textbook and curriculum development projects in the 1990s, the establishment of book provision systems has been ineffective in many developing countries (Salzano, 2002). There have been strong calls for the creation of national book development bodies and for national book policies favouring the development, publication and dissemination of printed materials (e.g. Montagnes, 2000; Salzano, 2002; UNESCO, 2004*a*).

5. Broad reading of self-selected material is associated with the acquisition of vocabulary and comprehension skills, and with the development of the reading habit and of creative imagination. It provides experience in the use and retrieval of information, essential for problem-solving and lifelong learning (Rosenberg, 2000).

Box 9.1 Nijera Shikhi's literacy programme in Bangladesh

An evaluation of the impact of a literacy programme organized by the people's movement Nijera Shikhi in **Bangladesh** showed that the majority of learners acquired functional and sustainable literacy and numeracy skills even when villages lacked reading materials. A key factor identified as contributing to retention and other gains was the 'post-literacy' part of the course. This third stage of the programme consisted of organized self-education study groups in which learners read, and helped each other read, books on development themes. The sixty-one books, provided by Nijera Shikhi, constituted a 'mini-library' managed by the local 'committee for mass education' and expanded through broad involvement by the whole village.

Source: Cawthera (1997 and 2003).

Adult literacy programmes are normally oriented around some or all of three main goals: acquisition of basic literacy skills; literacy for particular uses and applications; and literacy for empowerment or 'conscientization', a transformative approach to learning that encourages collective action, and social and political engagement.[6] These approaches overlap. Indeed, the first necessarily underpins or informs the other two.

Literacy programmes can also be grouped by the strategies they employ. Some are literacy-*led*, focusing primarily on specific and basic literacy skills. Others are literacy-*informed*, aiming mainly at non-literacy goals such as better health, rural development, self-employment and women's empowerment. Literacy-*creating* and *-sustaining* activities, designed to encourage the use and development of literacy practices, may involve support for literacy through use of the media, books, multiple languages, information and communication technology (ICT), and cultural and library-based activities. Here too, the categories are by no means discrete.

These goals and strategies can be combined to form part of a basic framework for policy dialogue on the learning and teaching of literacy (Table 9.1). This framework suggests some measure of correspondence between the goal of acquiring basic skills and certain literacy-led strategies, and between the goal of literacy for specific applications and strategies related to literacy-informed programmes. The framework is a conceptual aid, not a firm categorization of programmes, and is used accordingly in this chapter. Few literacy programmes fit neatly into a simplified framework. For example, family literacy programmes combine pre-school experience for children, focusing on cognitive outcomes for school readiness, with parenting and literacy skills for parents.[7]

The framework also identifies wider development goals and some economic, social, political and cultural dimensions of literacy. This is not meant to suggest that literacy per se can meet specific non-literacy objectives. Important relationships exist, but literacy itself does not achieve development without other economic and social policies (Lauglo, 2001).

Whatever the objectives and strategies, all literacy programmes require attention to (a) the literacy curriculum; (b) pedagogy; (c) the composition and organization of learning groups; (d) the recruitment, training, use and professional development of literacy educators and trainers; (e) learning technology; and (f) language. These are discussed in the following sections.

Table 9.1: Three approaches to literacy acquisition

	Learning outcomes	Strategies	Wider policy goals
Literacy skills	Reading, writing and numeracy skills in a given language or languages.	Largely through formal schooling and national adult programmes and campaigns. Primarily **literacy-led**.	Mass literacy; equity in opportunity; development and human rights.
Application of literacy for specific purposes	The application of skills to meet specific needs and priorities; life skills.	Largely through non-formal adult programmes. Often **literacy-informed**, or part of development programmes.	A competitive workforce; political participation and citizenship; ability to respond to the demands of globalization; a range of social benefits.
Empowerment and transformation	Empowerment; critical skills; social transformation.	Freirean or participatory techniques; learner-designed. **Literacy-led and -informed**.	Human and social empowerment; active citizenship; critical participation; social mobilization.

The literacy curriculum

Different objectives for literacy programmes place different demands on the literacy curriculum, whether it is interpreted as the content of a subject to be taught or as a total learning experience, direct and indirect.[8] Direct learning experiences are realized through planned curricula. These should offer a varied menu of learning opportunities for diverse

6. See, for instance, Lind and Johnston (1996) and Beder (2003).

7. Such programmes are of growing importance in the United States and other industrialized countries, and are being tested in some low-income countries. The approach serves broad social groups rather than targeting individual learners.

8. Indirect learning experiences, sometimes referred to as the 'hidden curriculum', can include anything that is unintentionally taught or learned. This might occur through a teacher's biases or sociocultural assumptions, or through those of textbooks. See Box 9.3 for an example related to gender.

participants in a well-organized and flexible way, using resources that directly respond to learners' needs and interests. Teaching and learning strategies should reflect the learning outcomes and objectives that provide the rationale for the literacy programme.[9]

A well-planned curriculum respects the demand and motivation for literacy. It takes account of the circumstances of young people and adults, including the poverty that pervades many learners' lives. All too often it needs to address disability, HIV/AIDS, conflict or other emergencies, migration and exclusion, as Chapter 7 notes. Fundamentally, the curriculum must be useful and relevant to learners' everyday lives.[10] A relevant curriculum is conducive to better learning outcomes.

Whether literacy-led, -informed or -sustaining, the curriculum should reflect and build on the individual and social contexts underlying the demand for literacy. These include what the learner already knows, wants and brings to the learning experience; the learner's mother tongue and his/her other languages; his/her cultural background (including family, local culture, oral traditions and indigenous knowledge) and its relationship to the literacy being acquired; and the identity of the learner in relation to gender, class, religion and race (Ouane and Glanz, 2005). Some commentators also emphasize helping learners move out of their current context through, for example, knowledge of an official or international language. Balancing the curriculum in ways that are relevant to local context and wider opportunity is a significant curriculum development challenge.

To respond to these diverse needs and motivations, clear, appropriate and realistic goals should define the 'why' of the curriculum (Hendricks, 1996). From this should flow the 'what' – the specific learning objectives and results that provide clear statements of intent for learners, couched in terms of skills and their application or wider social engagement (Hendricks, 1996; Posner and Rudnitsky, 1982, cited in Otto, 1997).

The 'who' in these processes is also important. Specialists tend to predominate in defining functional or skills-based programmes, while a more participatory and less prescribed approach generally characterizes transformative activities. When the primary objective is literacy-informed development of a job-specific skill, the vocational subject specialist usually determines the curriculum (Otto, 1997). A broader, team-based approach is required when a range of skills is targeted. Other literacy stakeholders who may participate in curriculum design include government officials, literacy or education experts, representatives of civil society organizations, educators (teachers, facilitators, trainers and supervisors) and learners. Another approach increasingly taken is the integration of adult education (including literacy-informed programmes) into the formal education system and the expansion of credentials for adult education. This involves a greater degree of curriculum determination by formal agencies.

A well-planned curriculum respects the demand and motivation for literacy

The core of a literacy curriculum, often directed to the attainment of the cognitive skills of reading, writing and calculation, tends to be taught the same way in all contexts.[11] The centrality of this approach may be challenged if critical analysis and confidence-building are seen as primary learning outcomes, and learners participate in determining programme objectives and content (Streumer and Tuijnman, 1996). ActionAid's Reflect initiative is guided by the goal of having literacy programmes taken over fully by their host communities.[12] This requires a much more open approach to curriculum development but also a large number of very committed, well-trained educators and trainers, which is often impossible to provide where resources are limited.

Programme rationale has an impact on the choice and sequencing of subject matter and the uses to which primers, educators' manuals and other learning materials are put. Again, choices are influenced by the degree to which reading, writing and numeracy are approached as ends in themselves or as means to realize other goals. Programmes that stress empowerment may give priority to literacy and civic education, and to rights and responsibilities. Those geared to poverty reduction may focus on health education or other socio-economic life skills. The development and choice of learning materials will reflect such wider goals.

Many literacy programmes, notably in Africa, describe themselves as 'functional'. Literacy is combined with health practices, agriculture, marketing, environmental issues, and other life skills or livelihood skills. Senegal's Women's Literacy Programme (1996–2001) combined basic education with opportunities for training in income-generating activities, such as soap-making, dyeing, poultry, shop-keeping and other

9. See, for instance, Bondi and Bondi (1989, cited in Otto, 1997).

10. This observation is supported at least rhetorically by nearly all the country background papers commissioned for this Report.

11. Skills-based approaches often follow the memorization and 'chalk and talk' methods used in many schools.

12. Reflect (the name is an acronym, standing for 'Regenerated Freirean Literacy through Empowering Community Techniques') combines Freirean and participatory methods. Begun with pilot projects in Bangladesh, El Salvador and Uganda in 1995, it has since been adopted by over 350 organizations in more than 60 countries.

undertakings that the learners proposed. Learners had a choice regarding the language of instruction and the class schedule (Nordtveit, 2005*b*).

The experience of functional programmes is mixed. Some run literacy and income-generation activities in parallel, others separately. A literacy course may be followed by income-generation activities. A common mistake seems to be to combine the two, in too short a time, with educators insufficiently qualified to deal with both. Each element needs sufficient learning time, and cross- or multi-sector collaboration should be undertaken so that a given group of learners has different educators for the two components (Oxenham et al., 2002). It also appears easier to offer livelihood-related training to those who already have basic literacy skills.

High-quality literacy primers remain key to programme success

The use of literacy primers and manuals, common in many programmes, can become too rigid (Riddell, 2001).[13] High-quality literacy primers and manuals, and their interpretation by well-trained educators, remain key to programme success, but materials that are too prescriptive and 'top-down' in approach, and insufficiently responsive to local needs and priorities, have limited value. ActionAid's Reflect Mother Manual was created to be a resource that would generate new, locally produced and locally relevant manuals. The experience of this approach in South Asia (Box 9.2) highlights the importance of flexible application in response to local demand and capacity, as well as coherence and consistency between curriculum, pedagogy and training.

Even where programmes follow a well-designed primer-based approach, literacy teaching is often hindered by the insufficiency of texts or scarcity of learning materials. In Senegal, many literacy classes are taught orally. The few books available are poorly designed and written. The lack of good materials is most obvious in mathematics teaching, where poor results are due largely to poor materials and to educator training that fails to address how to teach various calculation methods in a clear, step-by-step way (Fagerberg-Diallo, 1999).

Indeed, the numeracy dimension of literacy curricula tends to ignore the contextual realities of learners even more than the reading and writing components do. Yet, most adults have numeracy skills, including oral counting. They possess some mathematical structures and mental arithmetic skills that are more or less adequate for daily life. This is important knowledge and should be (but rarely is) surveyed before numeracy programmes are developed (Archer and Cottingham, 1996*a*). Still, written numeracy is important. People are aware of the limitations of memory for storing complex numbers and managing household accounts. The teaching of numerical calculations in ways

Box 9.2 Three responses to the Reflect Mother Manual in South Asia

For many years in **Nepal**, primer-based literacy programmes have published manuals or guidebooks for literacy facilitators. Significant investment has gone into preparing the manuals, but less to developing the capacities of rural practitioners, who after a couple of weeks of training are expected to run literacy centres with little help. As a result, the programmes experience problems of drop-out and poor performance, leading to facilitators' rapid disillusionment and departure.

The Reflect Mother Manual suggests that a local team should prepare the local facilitators' manual, and recruit and train facilitators in its use. This approach was rejected in Nepal because it was feared that the result would be a manual not unlike the existing ones, with people told what to do but rarely able to do it. Instead, the focus has been on training facilitators in the ideas and methods of Reflect so that they can internalize the approach and make it their own.

In **Bangladesh**, by contrast, the Reflect Mother Manual and the manual from the Reflect pilot programme were heavily relied upon in the production of local manuals, with little variation or adaptation. Now diversification is being emphasized, indicating that the weight of a 'definitive manual' was distorting the very philosophy of the manual itself.

A third way is taken in **India**. Facilitators produce their own local manual during initial and ongoing training. Having been introduced to basic participatory tools, they adapt the tools to address critical local issues in writing their own manual. Because they have written it, they are less likely to regard it as sacred and are more able to adapt the approach to their individual contexts. The guideline they produce is loose-leaf, so it can be updated and revised, and never becomes a fixed or frozen text.

Source: Gautam (1998).

13. A primer is a textbook for learners, while a manual is a handbook for facilitators. ActionAid argues that in many circumstances using a manual has not helped facilitators teach creatively. If used, the argument goes, the manual becomes prescriptive rather than a guide to good contextual practice (Gautam, 1998).

14. Most existing research on the selective transmission and reproduction of values and beliefs highlights how class, race and gender inequalities work their way through the content and organization of the school curriculum (Apple, 1996).

that relate to the social tasks and texts that adult learners actually encounter needs more attention. This means better training of literacy educators, backed by curriculum resources that develop their expertise in numeracy (Coben et al., 2003).

Literacy curricula are not immune to instances of the 'hidden curriculum', a topic well researched in formal education but largely neglected in adult literacy.[14] As in any educational activity, learning materials should be scrutinized for images, symbols and messages that might legitimize inequalities. An analysis of literacy materials developed several years ago by World Education, an international non-governmental organization (NGO), discovered that while Freirean terminology was used consistently, the primers perpetuated ideas of dependence and subordination (Kidd and Kumar, 1981, cited in Dighe, 2004). Box 9.3 looks at the 'hidden curriculum' in literacy curricula through a gender lens.

In 1998, drawing on Indian experience, UNESCO Bangkok identified six important dimensions of the literacy curriculum: awareness, functionality, flexibility, diversity, appropriateness of the learning relationship and action orientation. These dimensions bridge the skills-based, functional and transformative approaches. They emphasize contextual relevance but leave space for ambitions of upwards social and economic mobility. They recognize the critical need for consistency between *what* is taught and learned, and *how* it is taught and learned.

Pedagogy for adults

Teaching adults is not the same as teaching children. The study of adult learning, or 'andragogy', asserts that adults:

- need to know why they should learn something before they undertake to learn it;
- conceive of themselves as responsible for their lives and need to be treated by others as such;
- come to educational activity with a range of life experiences;
- are ready to learn how to cope with real-life situations effectively;
- are task- or problem-centred (unlike children in school, who are subject-oriented):
- respond to extrinsic motivation (e.g. better jobs, promotions and salary increases) but even more to intrinsic motivation (e.g. increased self-esteem, quality of life, responsibility and job satisfaction) (Knowles, 1989, cited in Dighe, 2004).

Box 9.3 Gender in the 'hidden curriculum'

Repetitive images and themes characterize the content of literacy primers. In an Indian study, literacy primers were shown to have ignored women as productive workers and focused exclusively on them as wives and mothers. They reinforced traditional definitions of women and propagated the ideal of Indian women as passive, submissive and self-sacrificing. There was no attempt to challenge or question the existing sexual division of labour and discriminatory practices against women in society (Bhasin, 1984; Patel, 1987).

In the words of a researcher on the content of an adult literacy textbook in Egypt:

'I leafed through the whole textbook looking for pictures of women and found only one, though every story was accompanied by a picture. In this picture, every woman was pregnant or accompanied by small children or both. I asked what the story was about and was told the subject was family planning. The agricultural work Egyptian women undertake, participation in the paid labour force in a variety of capacities, food preparation, household work, beer brewing, and all the other types of work with which women engage, were completely ignored' (Greenberg, 2002).

Source: Dighe (2004).

These understandings are important. They point to the significance of participatory and learner-centred adult teaching and learning methods, which find expression in a number of learning paradigms (e.g. Box 9.4)

While such approaches are desirable in principle, their success depends heavily on the skills and ability of the literacy educators and the quality of their training. A lesson from most reviews is that adults must be treated with respect and patience; another is that if the chosen learning approach is not within the reach of educators, there is increased risk that 'they will relapse even more easily into the methods they remember from their own school experience' (Lind and Johnston, 1990).

Success depends heavily on the skills and ability of the literacy educators and the quality of their training

Much of this debate relates to reading, writing and written text. As noted earlier, although numeracy is usually considered an important component of literacy, in practice the methods for teaching and learning numeracy receive much less attention.

The teaching and learning of visual literacy tends to be similarly neglected. Research into visual literacy has challenged the assumption that people can understand posters and leaflets more easily than words. People who lack exposure to two-dimensional images and are unfamiliar with their conventions can find photographs to be cluttered and their perspective confusing, or line

Box 9.4 Learner-centred learning paradigms for literacy

Critical learning

Feminist learning

Feminist education theorists, building on critical learning theories, argue that the focus on class-based oppression has neglected gender, race and interlocking systems of oppression (Dighe, 2004). In this view, inadequate attention has been paid to how women learn and the barriers to their learning. It is well known that women starting or returning to education programmes often suffer from a lack of self-confidence and low self-esteem. To learn effectively, women need to know they are intelligent and capable of learning, so educators should be trained to give positive, constructive feedback to ensure that confidence is enhanced. Research is also beginning to show that women seem to do best in learning environments where forms of knowledge that come from life experiences are valued (Belenky et al., 1986). In Mahila Samakhya, an education programme for women's equality in India, women have generated their own learning materials on the basis of their experiences. Niranter, a feminist NGO in India, developed a curriculum collaboratively with village women around issues affecting their lives (Windows to the World, 1997; Dighe, 2004).

Cultural learning

This approach contends that traditional adult learning theories neglect types of learning suited to people of various races and class backgrounds, those who are unemployed, etc. Culture is regarded as central to shaping education processes. The way people think, communicate, learn and relate to others is a product of the value system of their home, community and culture. People from different cultures have different ways of thinking and learning (Dighe, 2004). Ethnographic research (Street, 2001*b*) can lead to curricula differing from those in traditional programmes. The 'local literacies' used every day by marginalized groups help identify specific literacy skills focused on immediate tasks. An example is ethnomathematics, which reveals indigenous methods for acquiring numeracy skills. Many illiterate people of rural Tamil Nadu in India, for instance, have sophisticated numeracy skills, including the ability to make complicated geometrical patterns (Rampal et al., 1997) (Box 6.4).

drawings and cartoons to be full of 'strange' conventions such as bubbles and arrows.[15] It has been observed that people 'learn to read pictures just as they learn to read the pages in a book. This is not recognized because education in reading pictures is an informal process. It goes on automatically in societies where a variety of pictures are presented daily through a variety of media. In social environments with no pictorial tradition or very few pictorial representations ... the informal process of learning to read pictures simply does not occur' (Fuglesang, 1982, cited in Archer and Cottingham, 1996*a*).

While the argument for participatory, learner-centred programmes is powerful, a formal 'basic skills' approach to literacy is widespread, focusing on the teaching of specific reading, writing and numeracy skills.[16] Mastery of these skills is deemed to constitute a form of literacy that can be generalized to various contexts. Quality is defined in terms of speed and efficiency in learning basic skills. Efficiency is important because many learners can take part in only a limited number of hours of classes (Beder, 2003). This philosophy is evident in the first phase of the Joint Programme for the Promotion of Basic Education for All Malagasy Children in Madagascar.[17]

Approaches to literacy acquisition (particularly reading) based on efficiency have been analysed in the field of cognitive science. This research involves important features of the human memory, a field little known by literacy educators. A review of the research indicates that it has improved understanding of how the brain processes reading patterns, that increasingly faster reading tasks reinforce the retention of messages and their meaning, and that educators' unfamiliarity with such issues and techniques

15. [illegible] Murray Bradley (1994) and Fuglesang (1982), cited in Archer and Cottingham [illegible].

16. The vast literature on conventional methods of teaching reading and writing skills to children is not explored here beyond recognizing the distinction between, on the one hand, teaching reading through initial emphasis on the elements of words and their sounds as aids to word recognition, and, on the other, the use of words or larger language units to put the initial emphasis on the meaning of what is read; see Gray (1969).

17. The programme, whose sponsors include the United Nations and the Government of Madagascar (with assistance and technical coordination by UNESCO), lets out-of-school children and illiterate adults complete the traditional primary education cycle in ten months instead of five years. Adults and [illegible] 'intensive functional literacy for development' courses. In the initial forty-eight-day course, [illegible] become familiar with reading, writing and numeracy; a second phase (thirty-six days) focuses on basic technical and professional training. An evaluation midway through the programme showed that 76.4% of those completing the first phase could be considered literate and 35.5% reached the advanced level (UNESCO, 2004*c*).

contributes to the relative lack of success in many literacy programmes (Abadzi, 2003*a* and 2004).

Organizing learning groups

Organizing literacy programmes to enable women and men to participate in ways and at times that suit their needs and circumstances is critical to programme effectiveness. Adult learners are largely voluntary participants. The demands of work and family can affect attendance and lead to drop-out. The cyclical patterns of life in rural areas determine when investment in learning is practical. At the same time, adults usually have pragmatic, focused reasons for taking such courses, and will stop participating if they feel their goals have been met or if the programme is not addressing their needs.

Some commentators have used drop-out rates as an indicator of programme inefficiency (Abadzi, 2003*a*). Care needs to be taken in the measurement of these rates since irregular attendance or 'drop-in/drop-out' may be common. Whatever the circumstances, organizational strategies should promote appropriate grouping of learners, sensible organization of their time and a friendly, suitable location.

Gender considerations matter greatly. In societies where men are assumed to be the principal family decision-makers, it is often as important to gain their agreement to the participation of their wives and daughters in literacy courses as it is to appeal to the interest of the women themselves. An understanding of the cultural constraints under which both men and women operate is important. In parts of rural Morocco, a husband would lose face if his wife attended classes taught by a male instructor or where other safeguards were not provided. In most cases, husbands are not actively opposed to their wives attending classes, but they require that the classes conform to the social practices and conventions of the community. If a woman instructor is not available, classes might still be possible if they meet in a mosque or the home of a respected community leader (Bougroum, 2005).

In Uganda, the training of women as literacy educators is a basic requirement for reaching out to potential women learners, especially in the more rural and conservative areas. Current plans call for 40,000 literacy educators to be trained and at least half of these will be women. This is in response to a situation in which 70% of adult learners are women but most existing educators are men (Okech, 2005). In contrast, in Namibia's National Literacy Programme in the 1990s, the majority of both learners and literacy educators were women (Lind, 1996). In this case, men were disinclined to participate in the classes because of the numbers of women; moreover, the course was seen as a woman's activity, with a focus on childcare, nutrition and health.

In Namibia's National Literacy Programme in the 1990s, the majority of both learners and literacy educators were women

While gender analysis is essential, attention to age, prior learning experiences and other sociocultural factors is also important. The Alternative Basic Education programme in Karamoja, Uganda, serves both adults and children, though the latter are the primary target (Okech, 2005). Another Ugandan study revealed that learners' opinions about the desirability of class homogeneity were mixed (Box 9.5).

The duration of instruction needs to be flexible: long enough to achieve agreed outcomes, but short enough to reduce irregular attendance and drop-out (Lind and Johnston, 1996). In Burkina Faso, class schedules respond to the needs of female participants. Childcare is provided to enable mothers to concentrate on their courses (Napon and Sanou/Zerbo, 2005). In Eritrea, programmes are scheduled at different times of the year to reflect patterns

Box 9.5 Opinions on the composition of learning groups in Uganda

Some learners believed classes worked best when participants were of similar age and background. 'Most of us learners are women aged between 30 and 40 years of age. We interacted freely and could ask our instructors any questions.' For others, a mix of ages was an advantage: 'The age difference brought cooperation and love among us, with the younger [ones] helping the older and vice versa.' In the latter group, however, some felt the age difference impeded learning, with younger learners saying the older ones held them back, while older learners observed: 'Some male youth are stubborn, they refuse to interact with us, saying you old people are rigid.' Younger participants felt uneasy when family matters were being discussed. Some felt the learning groups would assist only the older adults. There were learners who suggested that it would be best to have separate days or classes for different age groups, with, for example, older and slower learners in one class and younger, faster learners in another, and that there should be two facilitators. Self-confidence was another theme: 'The old are the ones who always answer. The young are always shy. Those who have been to school have a higher reasoning capacity than we who did not go to school. In family affairs such as cooking, it is women who always answer.'

Source: Carr-Hill (2001).

of climate and agricultural activity. Courses in rural areas usually run for two hours a day, five days a week for six months. In the more remote areas, where the population is scattered and often mobile, the courses are shorter. In urban areas, and for the army, courses are held daily throughout the year (Ghebrezghi, 2003).

Because contexts are so divergent, it is difficult to establish general benchmarks for the scheduling, duration and intensity of literacy programmes. Data from Bangladesh, Ghana and Senegal indicate that most adult literacy programmes last about 300 to 400 hours (Oxenham, 2004*b*). Another survey reported similar findings for initial literacy programmes but concluded that, for literacy to be sustainable, around 600 hours is desirable (Global Campaign for Education[GCE]/ActionAid International, 2005).[18]

How these hours are distributed is another matter. The programme managers who responded to the GCE/ActionAid survey were asked how long their programmes lasted. The average was over two years,[19] with the initial literacy phase lasting nine to twelve months in sixteen programmes and eighteen to thirty months in twenty programmes.

Another critical factor is the regularity of classes. The GCE/ActionAid survey suggests that the most common pattern is two or three sessions a week. It concludes that classes held two or three times a week, for about two hours each, over two to three years, represents good practice in good programmes. But many programmes struggle to achieve as much, invariably because funds are short and/or programmes depend on external donors with aid tied to specific time-bound projects (GCE/Action Aid, 2005).

With regard to the location of literacy classes, a recent survey in Rwanda found that many take place in less than ideal conditions: 'Classes are held in: churches/mosques 33%; sector offices 26%; schools 13%; under a tree 13%; special shelter 6%; someone's home 4%; and others 4%. Only 32% rate the venue as appropriate, especially considering accessibility and equipment' (MINEDUC, 2005).

For first time women learners, a non-threatening environment is crucial. In India, the Women's Development Programme in Rajasthan (Sharma and Srivastava, 1991; Patel 1991) and the Mahila Samakhya programme in the Banda district of Uttar Pradesh (Nirantar 1997) found ten-day residential literacy camps to be an effective strategy for women's literacy. The camps allowed women to learn in an environment free from the pressures of their household responsibilities. However, for women who cannot leave home, a centre-based approach is necessary, in which case classes need to be conducted at a suitable time, and innovative teaching-learning methods and learner-centred materials used (Patel, 2001).

Although often under-resourced, libraries and community learning centres can offer easy access to all the learning materials needed to run an adult literacy programme, including printed and recorded books, magazines for all reading levels, videos and newspapers. They can supply space for learners and tutors, and are usually centrally located and accessible by public transport. Adults with low literacy levels often have bad memories of schools and a negative attitude towards formal education, but they can be invited into libraries to enjoy non-print activities, such as lectures, movies and discussion groups, to facilitate their first step back into learning. In Botswana, village reading rooms providing library services were established to support literacy graduates in rural areas where no traditional libraries operate. The library is an ideal place to offer family literacy programmes, as it provides materials and services for all age groups and reading levels. In Slovenia, public libraries enabled intergenerational lifelong learning processes that included children, youth and adults who came together and learned from each other by exchanging knowledge, experiences and viewpoints (Adams et al., 2002).

Literacy educators[20]

Those who facilitate learning classes and groups are vital to the success of adult literacy programmes. '[T]he quality and effectiveness of any adult education programme obviously depend crucially on the "coal face" workers, namely the class instructors or facilitators: it is they who actually teach and interact with the intended beneficiaries' (John Oxenham, quoted in Rogers, 2005). But they are one of the least supported groups of educators worldwide. They receive little (if any) regular remuneration, lack job security, and receive few training opportunities and little ongoing professional support. This is a poor basis for major improvements in adult literacy. Unless the professional development of literacy educators and their trainers is taken seriously,

18. The GCE/ActionAid survey gathered data from sixty-seven programmes in thirty-five countries with 4 million learners. Literacy specialists from around the world identified the programmes as being of good quality. Fifty were NGO programmes. Twenty-six had over 300 learning groups.

19. Programmes are often divided into literacy and post-literacy phases, and it was not easy to consolidate the data. The survey asked about contact-hours in the initial phase, but not in post-literacy phases, so data about the overall length of good-quality programmes were incomplete.

20. This section is largely based on a background paper for this Report (Rogers, 2005) on the training of trainers of adult literacy educators. In line with the terms defined in this paper, those who teach literacy to adults (called variously facilitators, animators, monitors, mobilizers, tutors, etc.) are mostly referred to as 'adult literacy educators', with the term 'teacher' restricted to those who are formally trained and accredited as teachers in adult education. The term 'trainers' is used for the people who train adult literacy educators.

Box 9.6 Approaches to the training of literacy educators

The many approaches to training adult literacy educators vary according to the type of educator trained (e.g. voluntary or part-time facilitators with no formal qualifications, qualified schoolteachers who teach adults after hours, formally qualified adult educators, NGO staff with no education qualification) and the type of training (e.g. non-formal, often unaccredited, training or formal and accredited). Rodgers (2005) summarizes these approaches in two main categories.

Training of adult literacy facilitators

The existence of considerable variety among programmes to train adult literacy facilitators would seem to reflect (a) the ideologies of different programme providers; (b) attempts by most providers to adapt courses to the perceived needs of trainees; and (c) the voluntary nature of the courses, and the need to attract and retain trainees. Most courses are short, intensive, one-shot activities lasting one or two weeks, more or less full time.

Accreditation is generally absent. Brazil's Solidarity in Literacy programme does provide certificates, but the facilitators may be employed for only six months at most and may not be able to obtain the certification to become formal teachers. In another programme in Brazil, however, students who complete training courses offered by Unitrabalho, an inter-university network, are certified as specialist teachers in adult and youth education. Few programmes use any form of assessment, although in Botswana and some other countries in Africa, literacy instructors are tested to make sure they are able to teach effectively.

Training of 'adult basic education and training' teachers

Programmes in this category take two main forms: institutional-based training, and open and distance learning. A few programmes combine the two. Most offer a one-year certificate, two-year diploma or three-year degree, and are based at institutions of further or higher education. Such formal courses are strong in southern Africa and parts of Latin America, and are starting in parts of Asia for non-formal education programmes. Some also exist in francophone Africa, emphasizing social psychology. Formal assessments are held and formal qualifications awarded. Such training may recognize trainees' previous educational experience. In some cases, relationships exist between this form of training and primary-school teacher training.

Source: Rogers (2005).

progress towards more literate societies will be severely constrained.

Literacy educators are a diverse group. Many come from the communities in which their programmes are situated. They may be broadly categorized into four groups:

- Local people with no formal qualifications, engaged part-time and on a casual basis – the largest of the four groups. Many in this category have no previous experience of teaching.[21] Some are unpaid. The group includes students working for credit in formal education programmes. People in this category may have limited formal education, though some are well educated.
- Full-time or part-time NGO staff or other development workers, such as extension staff who teach literacy incidentally. Some NGO staff have come up through social movements and have high levels of commitment (e.g. in South Africa and Latin America) while others are pressed into service. Their qualifications are usually in areas other than adult literacy.
- Full-time teachers in other sectors of education who teach literacy voluntarily or as part of their duties. They are qualified schoolteachers, but their qualifications are not in adult education.
- Full-time, formally qualified adult educators, employed within wider programmes of adult basic education and training or non-formal education.

Given this diversity, and the range of goals and objectives characterizing literacy programmes, national training strategies vary considerably. The practice of training, where it exists – formal and non-formal – is equally diverse (Box 9.6). But some important principles, having to do with professional development and motivation, underpin approaches to good quality.

Professional development[22]

Relatively little research into the training of trainers of literacy educators has been conducted. Evaluation reports, where they exist, suggest that training is a major area of weakness. For training

Evaluation reports suggest that training is a major area of weakness

21. A survey of India's Total Literacy Campaigns reported that 'more than 70% of the volunteer teachers interviewed ... had no previous experience of teaching literacy' (Rogers, 2005).

22. All direct quotations in this subsection are from Rogers (2005).

Evidence suggests that even where training policies exist, implementation is flawed

to be taken seriously, policies are needed that take into account 'the average base of competence, the type and time of training required to secure the adoption of appropriate instructional habits, and the likely need for periodic review, reinforcement and moral support'. A key to success is the ability to work in support of the realization of individual programme objectives. Where general training is at odds with specific programme objectives, the quality of learning outcomes will at best remain stagnant and at worse decline. Training that is formal and rigid, for instance, is unlikely to be helpful in participatory programmes designed to promote community activities. Even when training is carried out directly by programme providers, there is often a failure to address the gap between programme goals, and the ability and capacity of literacy educators to meet them. The tendency is to take a one-size-fits-all approach. In Bangladesh, for example, 'a comparison of the curricula, methodologies and training presented by NGOs and government agencies reveals no fundamental difference between the various providers with regard to the training presented to grassroots level facilitators'.

Other evidence suggests that even where training policies exist, implementation is flawed. The training in the Ugandan Government's Functional Adult Literacy programme, for instance, was 'particularly limited': '[M]any of the educators had been trained only once for just three days and had never had any refresher training. This inadequacy in training is particularly serious in view of the very little supervisory support given. In most cases, ... the supervisors themselves received no training in adult education and literacy methodology.'

As with literacy programmes generally, the language of training is a controversial topic. Training is often conducted in a nationally approved language, frequently an international language, while the work of literacy educators is invariably in a local language. The result is the 'awkward and difficult task of asking an instructor to take training in one language and then apply it in another, with no indication of how that process might work'. Training in numeracy is also rare. Literacy educators need to be able to transcend cultural barriers to teach mathematics according to local norms, but are rarely taught how to do so. These challenges again point to the absolute necessity of ensuring that the content, methodologies and envisaged outcomes of training are consistent with the intentions and goals of locally defined literacy needs and programmes.

The link between accreditation and teaching quality is important but ambiguous. Qualifications do not necessarily mean better teaching and learning, particularly where the trainers of literacy educators have no direct experience themselves of teaching literacy to adults.

Despite this, interesting innovations in training are being carried out (Box 9.7). Distance learning and ICT form a relatively new channel for the training and support of literacy educators. A potential benefit of this approach is that it can offer continuous professional development and support (Pennells, 2005).

Some training programmes include provision for follow-up training and ongoing support, which are widely recognized as essential: 'If there are major gaps in their initial training, as is common in the training of teachers of youths and adults, continuing development must be of a very high standard if it is to successfully help teachers improve their performance.' Follow-up can include monthly meetings of educators from a given area; refresher courses; regular or occasional workshops on specific topics; and provision of continuing-education materials.

Among sixty programmes responding to the GCE/ActionAid survey, over a third offered some follow-up or refresher training every three months, while fourteen had activities at least once a month. Many respondents emphasized that formal follow-up training was less important than informal support structures in which educators generally meet regularly (even weekly) at first and less regularly as new programmes settle down. Such forums not only allow educators to share problems with peers, but also give them a sense of belonging to a larger structure (GCE/ActionAid, 2005).

Clearly, the professional development of literacy educators, and of their trainers and supervisors, needs much more attention in national literacy policy and practice. Cultivating the long-term capacity of national research institutions in the field of literacy can facilitate the development and testing of training curricula, instructional materials and training strategies.

Incentives and motivation

Conditions of employment for adult educators are poor. Most literacy educators and trainers are not employed full time. Namibia is an example of a country where all literacy facilitators work on contract (though the contracts are annual and part-time). Worldwide, most facilitators 'are not assured of another literacy class when the one they are teaching is completed. In part, this is the result of the agreed approach to recruit literacy facilitators locally (often by the local community) rather than centrally' (Rogers, 2005). The result is major, regular turnover of facilitators with the inevitable implications for programme quality.

An associated issue is one of the most sensitive in the literacy policy debate: remuneration for literacy educators. While many literacy campaigns have celebrated the volunteer spirit, for underfunded literacy programmes volunteerism can become an economic necessity rather than a philosophy.

The GCE/ActionAid survey, covering sixty-seven programmes worldwide, revealed that half of the literacy educators involved were paid an honorarium or stipend, 25% received the national minimum wage and about 20% were unpaid. Most programmes paid 25% to 50% of a basic primary-school teacher salary (for hours worked); almost all others paid less than 25%. Given these levels of pay, it is not at all surprising that many programmes suffer from rapid turnover (GCE/ActionAid, 2005; Rogers, 2005).

As Table 9.2 shows, there are other forms of reward or incentives that programmes offer their educators. Non-material benefits, including increased status, are important, but not necessarily primary motivations for long-term service. When asked about investment priorities, those surveyed cited 'increasing the pay of facilitators' as one of their three primary concerns, along with training and reading materials (GCE/ActionAid, 2005). Clearly, a more coherent approach to the remuneration of literacy educators is required at national level, one that allows for diversity but encourages payment of enough to live on.

New learning technologies

Beyond the use of technology in formal education programmes for adults, where computer skills and other components of 'digital literacy' are often defined learning objectives, distance learning and ICTs can provide significant opportunities for informal and non-formal continuing literacy learning in adult and youth basic education programmes, as examples from four high-population countries show (Box 9.8).

Distance learning and ICTs can enable interaction and practice, use learner-generated materials, stimulate awareness-raising and learner motivation, support and train literacy workers, facilitate the distribution of materials and information to resource centres, and gather feedback from centres and individual learners regarding available materials and programmes (Pennells, 2005). It is rare, however, for adult literacy programmes to be conducted solely through these media, which instead are used primarily in support of conventional programmes, as in the Cuban example described in Box 9.9.

Some writers recognize that access to technology does not guarantee that its use will be meaningful or empowering. The real challenge is

Box 9.7 Innovations in the training of adult literacy educators

A group of non-literate women founded the **Zimbabwe** Adult Learners' Association in 1994. It has achieved such a reputation for training literacy educators that its trainees are hired for both government and NGO activities. In addition to raising the association's profile, this achievement reduced 'government hegemonic control of the literacy curriculum'.

Another innovation relates to the enhancement of literacy educators' formal education. 'In **Mozambique**, literacy instructors with Grade 7 [schooling] are allowed to upgrade to Grade 9 through a fulltime course, receive some training as literacy teachers and can be employed as fulltime teachers in the programme'.

The Reflect programme's current approach to training emphasizes the importance of both the trainers' and the participants' learning contributing to the overall learning environment, highlighting the ability of both to create knowledge. The approach covers all forms of training, from orientation and initial or pre-service training (which generally lasts twelve days) to ongoing support through Reflect forums, exchange visits and refresher training on themes such as gender analysis and facilitation skills.

Source: Rogers (2005).

Table 9.2: Ranking of incentives other than basic pay for literacy educators in 67 programmes

Main incentives	Cited first*
Additional pay for results	8
Access to credit	7
Access to further education	8
Training certificates	8
Increased status in the community	11
Show of appreciation by learners	20
Provision of food parcels	5

* Number of programmes ranking the incentive first, after regular wage employment.
Source: GCE/ActionAid (2005).

It is rare for adult literacy programmes to be conducted solely through distance learning and ICTs

Box 9.8 Major distance education projects in four E-9 countries

China

Audience/purpose: Adult basic education (equivalence programmes and non-formal education)

Project/institution and date: Liaoyuan television and Broadcasting University (satellite-based television programmes), 1986–97

Scale: 150,000 rurally based adults trained per year, 137,500 of whom become qualified agricultural workers (Green Certificate)

Outcomes: 2,000+ hours of training materials on practical rural vocational and technical skills

India

Audience/purpose: Adult basic education (equivalence programmes and non-formal education)

Project/institution and date: 1. The National Open School (NOS), 1989; 2. Open Basic Education Project, 1999

Scale: (NOS only) In 1998–99, some 130,000 enrolled from most states and Union Territories in India; 900 study centres, 8 regional centres

Outcomes:

- NOS: Learner-selected courses in academic and vocational subjects at foundation, junior and senior-secondary levels, targeting disadvantaged groups aged 14–29, the majority 18–24. Launch of study centres in Dubai and Abu Dhabi. In 1998–99, some 6.5 million books produced; 140,796 certified students at junior secondary level in 1998. Cost per learner US$10
- Open Basic Education Project: Equivalence programme for adults

Box 9.9 Cuba's 'Yo, sí puedo' method

The 'Yo, sí puedo' (Yes, I can) approach has its roots in the literacy campaign begun in Cuba in 1961. Its basic concept is to use the broadcast media and video as an inclusive approach to literacy teaching for all. In principle, a learner can acquire a basic level of literacy skills in sixty-five sessions over two months for a maximum of two hours a day. The learner is introduced to reading and writing via numbers, which the method assumes are familiar to learners through their daily transactions with money.

A thirty-minute video per session trains student and educator simultaneously. Then an educator manual and separate student workbooks guide exploration (reflection), experimentation (practice) and generalization (consolidation and evaluation of skills). Educators guide groups of no more than twenty students, encouraging them to reflect upon and discuss the video's lessons for their lives, thus making learning highly contextualized. Bilingual/bicultural programmes are being developed, though they take longer than two months. Crucial to the method's success are the learner's relationship with the educator and consistent attendance to give a sense of identification with the sociocultural context.

'Yo, sí puedo' has been introduced in pilot projects in Argentina, Ecuador, Mexico, New Zealand, Venezuela (where it was adopted nationally and 1 million people learned to read and write between July and December 2003) and, more recently, Bolivia, Mozambique and Nigeria. The average cost is US$33 per learner. In April 2005, Ecuador's Cotacachi province declared itself free of illiteracy after having used a 'Yo, sí puedo' programme for one year. 'Yo, sí puedo' claims a roughly 90% success rate.

Sources: Cuban Libraries Solidarity Group (2004); Juventud Rebelde (2005); 'Yo, sí puedo' presentation at UNESCO in Paris on 29 March 2005.

to shift from acquisition of technical skills to addressing 'how digital technologies enable people and groups to engage in particular social practices' (Hayes, 2003). Emphasizing individual instruction and individual ownership of technology could widen rather than bridge the 'digital divide'. Given such pedagogical and resource constraints, ICTs and distance learning have more immediate potential for the professional development of literacy educators than for literacy programmes per se.

The unevenness of access to technology constrains its use in many contexts. Most potential literacy learners do not have access to electricity, let alone new technology. Thus the use of ICT and other electronic media in literacy learning has to be examined in context (Box 9.10). Still, Cuba's 'Yo, sí puedo' provides an interesting example of the use of radio, television, audiocassettes and video at the heart of a literacy programme.

The language of literacy

National policy must take account of the linguistic context of literacy-building and -sustaining activities, for which there are many different purposes and strategies, as Chapter 8 delineates in detail. Literacy policy that enables people to learn in a language that facilitates daily communication, and literacy programmes that provide initial learning in the mother tongue and

Mexico

Audience/purpose: Adult basic education (equivalence lower secondary education)

Project/institution and date: 1. Secundaria a distancia para adultos, since 1998; 2. Education for Society, since 1999; 3. SEPa English Programme, since 1998

Scale:

- Education for Society: National (transmitted by commercial television)
- SEPa: 22 states, 183 advisers, 9,000 users in 358 groups

Outcomes:

- Secundaria a distancia para adultos: Self-study text materials + advisers and television programmes. Two levels (beginners and advanced) in five subjects
- Education for Society: Citizenship television programmes for general public
- SEPa: 61 English-language learning television programmes at 4 levels, 60 audiocassettes and 600,000 self-study packages

Nigeria

Audience/purpose: Nomadic adults and youth (non-formal education)

Project/institution and date: Nomadic Education Programme, 1999

Scale: 1-year pilot in Kaduna

Outcomes: Radio-listening groups for functional literacy and numeracy, income-generating activities, agricultural extension, citizenship, vocational skills. Radio, mobile cinema, flip charts, print, audiocassettes. Regular monitoring. Outreach/support centres for contact and distribution of materials

Source: Creed and Perraton (2001).

Box 9.10 A range of media for literacy acquisition

Deciding which are the most useful and effective media depends on cost, access and control, in addition to educational values and benefits.

Telecommunications infrastructure and use are expanding rapidly. The popularity and relative affordability of text messaging, for instance, suggest that it could be used for mass distribution of messages to learners and for communication among learners and between learners and distance trainers. Nevertheless, even the lowest-priced mobile phone handsets and connection time are out of reach for most non-literate people, and it is beyond the scope of literacy programmes to provide them for participants. Many people remain excluded from mobile telephone use by barriers of cost (including import duties, taxes and other government-imposed charges), skills, electricity supply (to charge batteries) and network coverage. Moreover, the kind of literacy learning available through reading and writing text messages on a mobile phone, while potentially useful, is extremely limited.

Radio has continuing potential for use in literacy development. Locally produced interactive radio instruction, along with community radio for locally specific programme support, can allow two-way engagement among learners and programme providers, especially where potential learners are widely scattered or are mobile (such as nomads).

Cassettes offer still more potential for genuine multimedia pedagogy to enrich functional teaching in literacy courses. In some cases, they could even serve as direct tools in the teaching of basic literacy skills. Support in the form of cassettes relies on fairly simple technology, albeit one that includes a system of making and distributing recordings. It also requires extra visits by local coordinators/supervisors to distribute cassettes, but these can also be used for other in-service support purposes.

In **South Africa**, experiments have begun in the use of computer software for teaching literacy, with backup from a teacher. Whatever the potential of such technology in countries that can afford it and provide logistical support, computer-assisted literacy teaching is not yet an affordable option for large-scale provision in the countries where the literacy rates are lowest and the need for programmes is greatest.

Although television is not accessible to much of the world's population, it does reach very large audiences in many countries. Its potential use as a channel for promoting literacy is considerable.

Sources: Pennells (2005); Lauglo (2001).

Radio has continuing potential for use in literacy development

then add a second language, offer social, cognitive, psychological and pedagogical advantages.

An inclusive multilingual policy will address language group needs and available resources, and will have the following key features, applied in ways suited to local context (Robinson, 2005):

- Studies of the linguistic and sociolinguistic situation will be the basis for understanding which languages should be used in learning. The studies will include data on the attitudes of communities towards the languages they use.
- Consultations with local communities to establish links between literacy providers and local institutions will lead to input into learning and to local governance and management of programmes, especially with respect to choice of language of literacy.
- Local writing and production of material must be the basis for sustainable development of the literate environment and for the incorporation of local knowledge as learning content.
- Specific issues of linguistic structure and language use must be considered in designing the learning of second (third, etc.) languages, so that the addition of languages in oral and written form is readily available to large numbers of people. In other words, the learning of additional languages must take into account learners' existing language patterns, skills and knowledge.

Progress requires strong leadership, good governance, efficient organization and adequate financing

Conclusion

The diversity of literacy acquisition processes, depending on context, and on learner and educator backgrounds, poses technical challenges in curricula, and in teaching and learning approaches that need much more professional attention at the national level. Adult literacy-led and literacy-informed programmes need to take better account of the principles of adult education and learners' experience, knowledge and motivations. Meeting the challenges requires much more investment in human resources and sustainable training systems, which should include adequately paid, qualified and motivated literacy educators, trainers and supervisors. Similarly, the importance of careful monitoring, evaluation and research, and an experimental spirit based on adapting and improving teaching and learning processes along the way, cannot be understated.

Scaling up adult literacy programmes: the role of government

In Chapter 8 it was shown that in certain circumstances mass literacy campaigns, whether sustained over time or short one-off programmes, made a difference to levels of literacy. Political commitment and direction, popular enthusiasm, realistic targeting and attention to the language of instruction all played their part. Elsewhere, national programmes as part of wider development initiatives have been preferred vehicles for change.

Whatever the route chosen, the scaling up of literacy programmes has to be part of a major national endeavour, even if it finds practical expression in a diversity of programme activities. There is no chance of progress at a level consistent with the Dakar goal without government action on four policy directions set out at the beginning of this chapter. This in turn requires strong leadership, good governance, efficient organization and adequate financing of national literacy strategies.

Who leads?

Ministries of education normally have a major responsibility for literacy policy and for coordinating its implementation. In practice, though, the home for adult literacy is not always the education ministry.[23] Even when it is, capacity may be weak, influence limited and resources scarce. The locus for literacy may change within a given ministry or even move from ministry to ministry. But a comitment to increased youth and adult literacy requires a secure and suitably resourced base in government. Fortunately, evidence of good practice exists or is emerging in this regard.

Morocco merged the departments of adult literacy from the Ministry of Employment and Social Affairs and non-formal education from Education to form a State Secretariat for Literacy and Non-Formal Education. It is designed to coordinate the growing number of public, private and civil society literacy providers. Its decentralized management structure includes national and local coordination committees chaired by senior political authorities (Bougroum, 2005). In **Brazil**'s decentralized education system, youth and adult education is provided by twenty-six state school administrations and 5,000 municipalities, using teachers from the formal

23. Botswana, Eritrea, Namibia and Thailand are among the countries with well-established adult or non-formal education units in the education ministry overseeing adult literacy programmes. More recently, Burkina Faso has established a separate Ministry for Literacy and Non-Formal Education. On the other hand, in Madagascar and Kenya, for example, the Ministries of Population and Social Affairs, respectively, have overall responsibility for adult literacy programmes.

system. The federal government, some sub-national governments and civil society also run adult literacy programmes outside the school system, using non-professionals as educators (Masagão Ribeiro and Gomes Batista, 2005). In **Indonesia**, a literacy movement launched by the President in 2004 is designed to strengthen cooperation within government, encourage community participation and promote political awareness of the importance of literacy (Jalal and Sardjunani, 2005).[24]

If ministries of education implement programmes, these are often initial literacy courses or literacy-led activities. Literacy-informed and more development-oriented programmes, continuing adult education and literacy-sustaining activities usually involve other government sectors, along with community projects, cultural activities, library services, vocational training and adult night schools. In part, this is because some education ministries, like some education NGOs, lack the resources and expertise to undertake programmes that do more than introduce initial, basic skills (Riddell, 2001; Govinda and Biswal, 2005*b*). Moreover, literacy-informed programmes often have objectives that are the responsibility of sectors other than education.

Botswana's Ministry of Education cooperates with the national library to sustain literacy through village reading rooms, which essentially are mini-libraries in rural areas. An inter-agency committee prepares reading materials for newly literate adults and children in Setswana, the national language, and in simplified English for extension programmes in literacy. This works well, although a recent evaluation of Botswana's literacy programme concluded that the reading rooms could be better integrated with the literacy courses, and recommended establishing resource centres incorporating the reading rooms and other activities (UIE, 2004).

Elsewhere, independent national agencies oversee adult literacy. In **Ireland**, a government-funded, non-profit membership organization, the National Adult Literacy Agency, leads coordination, policy and training (Bailey, 2004; see www.nala.ie). Its activities are based on learner and tutor participation, and implemented through a network of vocational education committees linked to the Irish Vocational Education Association, a body representing employers. The agency thus links literacy learners with labour market training and further education opportunities.

For most developing countries, however, it is the ministry of education that is best placed to integrate literacy into overall education sector policy, promote lifelong learning strategies, coordinate publicly financed non-formal adult programmes run by civil society organizations (CSOs), and regulate systems for the recognition, validation and accreditation of prior learning and of organized learning programmes.[25]

At the same time, as lifelong education policies in some European Union countries illustrate, embedding adult learning and education in public policies and sharing responsibilities across a range of sectors helps in the development of more effective literacy strategies (Duke and Hinzen, 2005). Spain's recent experience illustrates this point.[26] Flexibility should also allow local-level implementation through local partnerships and coordination as a complement to, rather than a substitute for, state leadership.

Strategies for planning and organizing literacy

Planning and organizing major literacy campaigns, national programmes and broader-based national partnerships is complex. Good planning takes time and resources. Establishing national, regional and local management, and implementation structures is politically and technically demanding, particularly if wider government reforms relating to decentralization and subcontracting of services are being undertaken.

When a clear strategy and institutional framework is in place, trainers and coordinators have to be trained, curricula developed, textbooks and teachers' manuals written, printed and distributed, other learning materials provided, local monitoring committees established and advocacy undertaken for the mobilization of resources, partners, providers, teachers and learners. Local coordinators have to recruit and train teachers/educators, who in turn recruit learners, organize literacy groups, distribute materials and monitor programmes.

India's district-level Total Literacy Campaigns, launched in 1992, focused on initial literacy. The carefully targeted campaigns mobilized community resources, backed up by coordination mechanisms at state and local levels.[27] Centres managed by communities, with the help of public grants, offered post-literacy and continuing education activities. In **Ecuador**, a national literacy

24. The Ministry of Education in Indonesia has a four-pronged policy strategy to ensure that (a) all children become literate through formal and non-formal education; (b) all adults have equal access to the equivalent of primary and junior secondary education; (c) there is 'functional literacy education' for people over 15, including 'productivity enhancement' and 'child-rearing;' and (d) literacy competence is retained through the provision of reading materials and community libraries (Jalal and Sardjunani, 2005).

25. Increasingly, policies on lifelong learning and adult education and literacy must address learner demand for certification and for flexible learning entry and exit points. While progress has been slow, some developing countries, such as South Africa, have established national qualification authorities (Duke and Hinzen, 2005). In Mozambique, school and adult education examinations have been opened to the general public, so that self-study or resumption of interrupted studies can be tested and certified.

26. The 2002 Act on Qualifications and Vocational Training, sponsored by the Ministries of Education and of Labour and Social Affairs in Spain, created a system based on the lifelong learning principle, establishing a direct relationship between training and employment. Notable programmes include accreditation for adult training, and professional experience, compulsory on-the-job training and an information and counselling service.

27. By March 2003, some 98 million adults were reported to have acquired literacy, 75% through Total Literacy Campaigns and 25% by other means (Govinda and Biswal, 2005*b*). While these estimates may be high, the campaigns clearly had a significant impact.

campaign was planned and organized within eight months and conducted in four to five months in 1988/89 (Torres, 2005). Around 70,000 literacy teachers were trained, partly face-to-face (aided by videos demonstrating teaching methodology) and partly by distance training. Over 25,000 literacy circles were established in homes and workplaces. Of some 300,000 learners, 200,000 completed the courses, 85% of whom wrote the final test with satisfactory results. The campaign provided important lessons regarding mobilization, pedagogy and the engagement of young students in literacy work (Box 9.11).

In Ecuador, 70,000 teachers were trained for a national literacy campaign

After **Namibian** independence in 1990, the Ministry of Education developed policy guidelines and literacy primers and manuals, and recruited fifty district literacy organizers who were trained for three months and then posted across the country to recruit, contract and train literacy educators (called promoters). The programme was well planned and financed, although the promoters lacked adequate ongoing support (Lind, 1996). **Eritrea**'s Enhanced Adult Literacy Programme (2002–2006) is charged with developing basic literacy and numeracy skills for 450,000 adults in their mother tongue. Special efforts are made to assure the participation of those disabilities, women, the internally displaced, refugees returning from the Sudan and demobilized members of the Eritrean Defence Forces. The Adult Education Division of the Ministry of Education plans, manages, monitors and evaluates the programme in partnership with other ministries, United Nations agencies, local and international NGOs, and public and private partners. Learning is supported by educational broadcasting and small rural libraries or reading rooms. Day care is provided for children of women learners (Ghebrezghi, 2003).

These examples concern large national programmes. But many literacy activities are small and often relatively isolated, run by NGOs, religious bodies and other CSOs. While they are likely to have more intensive contact with learners, they face challenges similar to those of larger programmes: finding stable funding, training and motivating staff, obtaining appropriate materials and, above all, eliciting community support.

A still greater challenge is the scaling up of local good practice. Maintaining staff quality and training capacity, sustaining access to learning materials and managing greater distances between coordinators and learner groups present significant problems, as the experience of Reflect programmes demonstrates. In **Ghana**, keeping Reflect's approach to training and supervision was found to be unaffordable for an expanded programme. The incentives built into the pilot, such as transport and meal allowances, required strong political backing for widespread replication, and high teacher turnover was a severe constraint on large-scale programming (Riddell, 2001).

The extent to which different programmes and activities are coordinated and integrated within a comprehensive national policy varies considerably. Fragmentation, even competition, operates against the creation of genuine partnerships in which literacy becomes the universal concern. Thus, how to share resources, and divide roles and responsibilities among stakeholders, is a major consideration in the planning and designing of literacy policies and strategies.

A recent evaluation of literacy programmes supported by the World Bank concluded that intensive government training and supervision of NGOs was important: 'though many NGOs can carry out quality literacy programmes, others need considerable support and monitoring' (Abadzi, 2003*a*). Some commentators see a danger of community-based organizations becoming dependent on government funds and having to adopt practices at odds with their programme philosophy (Duke and Hinzen, 2005).

Box 9.11 Selected lessons from Ecuador's literacy campaign

- Mass literacy campaigns with the enthusiastic participation of broad sectors of the population are possible in societies with democratically elected or popular governments.
- Acceptable learning results in reading and writing can be achieved if enough emphasis is given to pedagogical issues rather than ideological ones and if quality is made at least as important as quantity.
- Young students can be turned into effective literacy facilitators and enthusiastic organizers, given enough guidance, pedagogical training and instillation of self-confidence.
- Public opinion and participation can be won by demonstration of good practices.

Source: Torres (2005).

The Ugandan Government has encouraged pluralism in the delivery of educational services. This policy has resulted in many small, autonomous initiatives with limited coverage, operating largely in isolation from each other. There is an agreed framework for cooperation between government and civil society in adult literacy, but many groups work outside it. Consequently, their work adds little to the government's overall literacy efforts. The impact of all the initiatives would be greater if they were to work together more, building a common provision structure (Okech, 2005).

Partnerships can be more or less informal. In Senegal, the outsourcing model called 'faire-faire' is managed by an agency set up to encourage adult literacy provision by NGOs and small entrepreneurs. This public-private partnership approach is spreading to other West African countries. Its initial success in Senegal was due largely to 'the government's strong commitments to the approach – and to literacy. Hence, the outsourcing approach is not a substitute for public involvement' (Nordtveit, 2004, cited in Duke and Hinzen, 2005). However, programme quality has suffered because 'some providers were more interested in obtaining funds than in providing high quality literacy courses' (Nordtveit, 2005*b*). In Brazil, partnerships involve local authorities, universities, large NGOs, companies and community-based organizations (Box 9.12). According to Masagão Ribeiro and Gomes Batista (2005), this has shown the need for:

- increased government resources for the poorest regions;
- technical assistance to help local authorities manage, deliver, monitor and evaluate programmes;
- greater civil society participation as a complement to state provision, to encourage independent monitoring of public policies and to help reach marginalized targets groups, and because partnerships with community-based organizations are more easily mediated by local government;
- reduced emphasis on large corporate- and church-related organizations.

Community learning centres can provide constructive partnerships among sectors and between government and civil society. In Asia, such centres have been supported and documented via UNESCO's Asia and Pacific Programme of Education All (APPEAL). They 'combine education with community development activities, preferably with strong participation of the people, young and old, including literacy classes and skills training, within a network of traditional and modern structures of Government and NGOs' (Duke and Hinzen, 2005).

Box 9.12 Literacy partnership models in Brazil

The Literacy Movement (MOVA), under Paulo Freire, was launched in São Paulo in the early 1990s. Partnerships gave community-based organizations responsibility for recruiting learners and facilitators, and providing group meeting sites. The city council provided funds to pay facilitators and was responsible for pedagogical supervision and monitoring. In 1992, some 18,000 adult learners participated in programmes implemented by 73 community organizations. After closing because of changes in the city government, the programme was revived in 2001 and spread to other cities, with local adaptations and new partners such as trade unions and companies.

In 1996, the federal government launched the Solidarity in Literacy Programme as part of its poverty reduction policies, with institutions of higher education coordinating the work of engaging municipalities, and training and supervising facilitators; municipal authorities recruited learners and provided facilities. In 1998, Solidarity in Literacy was transformed into an NGO but it continued to receive most of its funding from the federal government. Between 1997 and 2004, partners included 2,050 municipalities, 144 companies and 209 higher education institutions. The cost per learner was US$62, including grants to facilitators, local coordinators, snacks and textbooks for learners, and training and evaluation.

In 2003, a new Brazilian Government launched an accelerated initiative, Literate Brazil, which funds government agencies and NGOs with experience in adult literacy to enable them to expand their coverage. In 2004, the initiative expanded its partnerships with local governments. Further decentralization was planned for 2005.

Source: Masagão Ribeiro and Gomes Batista (2005).

Community learning centres can provide partnerships between government and civil society

Clearly, no single model for campaigns, programmes or partnerships can be replicated everywhere. The approach has to be tailored to context. Whatever the model, sustained national and local political commitment, and strong community participation are required. Investment in the quality of human resources is also essential, as is the engagement of CSOs (especially at the community level), local authorities and higher education institutions in the planning and implementation of national strategies.

Financing literacy

A major scaling up of adult literacy programmes requires additional financing. Although reliable data on levels of funding for youth and adult literacy are scarce, the available evidence suggests that they are very low in most developing countries, both overall and in terms of priority in national and education-sector budgets.[28] In many countries, literacy programmes secure just 1% of the national education budget (DFID, 2000). There are exceptions,[29] but the examples shown in Table 9.3 are more representative of the norm.

In many countries, literacy programmes secure just 1% of the national education budget

Any attempt to calculate overall financial support for literacy is complicated. Central government funds may go to multiple ministries and responsibility for resource mobilization is devolved increasingly to lower tiers of government. Moreover, it is almost impossible to aggregate funds from NGOs, employers and donors.[30] It is true that more is spent on literacy than government figures suggest, but this does not alter the fact that new and additional resources are required.

What are the financing options and strategies that should be considered? How can long-term, sustainable financing strategies be developed? To answer these questions requires an assessment of some basic cost parameters for good-quality literacy programmes and attention to strategies for mobilizing resources.

Table 9.3: Examples of financial allocations to non-formal education and literacy

Botswana	The government is fully responsible for the costs of the National Literacy Programme. Aid is sought for particular activities but no effort is made to generate income from learners, communities or NGOs. The total budget of the Department for Non-Formal Education is just over 1% of the Ministry of Education's 2001–2004 estimates; 43% of this goes to the Botswana College of Distance and Open Learning, and the African Association of Correspondence Education (Hanemann, 2005).
Brazil	In 1995, youth and adult education received 1.4% of public expenditure on education, broken down as follows: federal, 9.2%; state, 62.3%; municipal, 28.4%. (No subsequent data allow for such a breakdown.) In 1996, the Fund for the Development of Elementary Education and Promotion of Teaching was introduced to increase equity in the provision of primary education. This reduced state and municipal spending on adult education. Since 2001, the federal government has compensated for this in the 14 poorest states and 398 municipalities with low human development indices. In 2003, the Ministry of Education began negotiating with state and municipal governments to set up a fund covering all levels of basic education, including youth and adult literacy (Masagão and Batista, 2005).
Nepal	From 1995/96 to 2002/2003, the proportion of the total education budget allocated to non-formal education ranged from 0.50% to 1.48% (and to literacy from 0.50% to 0.75%) (Koirala and Aryal, 2005).
Nicaragua	The Ministry of Education, Culture and Sport spent 1.5% of its budget (US$[illegible] million) on adult education in 2000 and 2.2% (US$34.4 million) in 2002. The Literacy and Adult Basic Education Programme, funded by Spanish donors from 1997 to 2003, has been taken over by the government, which has secured its continuity with an Inter-American Development Bank loan of US$10 million over 2004-2006 (Arrien, 2005).

Note: It is difficult to disaggregate spending on literacy from adult education more generally.
Sources: As shown in the table.

Costing literacy programmes

The constituent parts of any literacy programme are no different in most respects from those of other education activities. There are start-up costs to be met, teachers and educators to be trained and paid, learning materials to be developed and provided, and operating costs to be met[31] (Oxenham et al., 2002; Abadzi, 2003*a*). If literacy is part of wider development activities, such as improving health or livelihoods, then additional costs are incurred, for example for 'specialist' non-literacy facilitators and savings and credit facilities (Oxenham et al., 2002).

None of the costs can easily be standardized.[32] They vary according to levels of remuneration for trainers and educators, types of learning materials, programme duration, training costs, the existence or otherwise of back-up support and the extent to which continuing education opportunities are provided. If new technology is used, it has its own costs. Furthermore, costs vary within and among countries.

Caution should be used in comparing figures from country to country because purchasing power levels and programme types differ, but it is interesting to note the results of some such exercises. For a small sample of twenty-nine literacy programmes, the estimated average cost per learner is US$47 in sub-Saharan Africa, US$30 in Asia and US$61 in Latin America (GCE/Action Aid, 2005).[33] When the cost is computed for 'successful' learners or completers, the respective averages are US$68, US$32 and US$83 (Table 9.4). Costs per enrolled learner (excluding developed countries) range from US$16 to US$167 and per successful learner

28. A recent overview of literacy in Poverty Reduction Strategy Papers, prepared for this Report, found little if any reference to levels of financing for literacy (UNESCO-IIEP, 2005*a*).

29. The United Republic of Tanzania (1961–86) and Cape Verde (1975–99) allocated about 10% of their national education budgets to non-formal education (Abadzi, 2003*a*).

30. It is as difficult to collect data on financing for literacy from donors as it is from governments. The OECD-DAC databases are not conducive to disaggregating information on literacy. World Bank lending to adult education as a percentage of total education lending from 1% to 9% over 1990–2002 (Abadzi, 2003*a*).

31. Although adult literacy programmes do not require the construction of school buildings, resource centres, possibly combined with training facilities, may be needed.

32. One could argue, however, that the 'basics' include blackboards, [illegible] stationery, exercise books, and eyeglasses for learners with a sight problem.

33. Of the sixty-seven programmes covered by the GCE/ActionAid survey, only twenty-nine were able to provide financial data allowing the type of calculation made in Table 9.4, and even those results are not necessarily comparable. Many programmes indicated they were working at less than optimum levels because of a lack of resources.

from US$18 to US$199. A World Bank review of adult education programmes calculated costs ranging from US$6 to US$58 per enrolled participant and US$12 to US$74 per successful learner (Oxenham, 2003). In Senegal's literacy and poverty alleviation programme, the cost for one adult learner is US$50 (broadly equivalent to the cost of one year of primary schooling).

These figures are instructive at the international level but in themselves offer little assistance to those faced with determining baseline figures for a significant expansion of a national literacy programme. Are there guidelines or benchmarks that would help in this regard? A key consideration is the cost associated with literacy educators. Unless they are volunteers, this is likely to be the main cost. While many commentators applaud the spirit of volunteerism, most argue that long-term sustainability depends upon a level of remuneration that will retain and help develop literacy educators.[34] Literacy educators need to be paid, and their training needs to be financed.

The GCE/ActionAid study concludes that facilitators should be paid at least the equivalent of the minimum wage of a primary-school teacher for all hours worked, including time for training, preparation and follow-up. But given the pressure many governments are under to find sufficient funds to pay primary-school teachers an adequate salary, this potential benchmark raises important and difficult questions. For adult literacy to be taken as a serious component of education policy and overall development policy, financial allocations will have to be at a level that will give both non-government and government programmes enough resources to improve teaching quality. This is an issue for national policy and budget dialogue that extends beyond literacy policy alone.

'The success of adult literacy and basic education largely depends on the facilitators, and their efficiency depends on the training they are given' (Rogers, 2005). Clearly a minimum period of initial training is required. The GCE/Action Aid study recommends giving facilitators at least fourteen days of initial training and regular refresher training, as well as ongoing opportunities for exchange with other facilitators. The costs would vary considerably by country. A recent budget in post-war Afghanistan put the cost of training on a par with that of producing all necessary teaching and learning materials. Recently, the Brazilian Government proposed that 20% to 30% of staff costs should be devoted to training. Costs of this order represent a major investment item in scaling up programmes.

Table 9.4: Literacy programme costs per learner

Region/Country	Enrolled learner US$	Successful learner US$	Organization or programme
Asia/Pacific			
Average (n = 4)	**30**	**32**	
Nepal	16	18	International Nepal Fellowship
Pakistan	30	30	Bunyad Literacy Community Council
Solomon Islands	40	40	Literacy Association Solomon Islands
Viet Nam	35	38	ActionAid Vietnam
Latin America/Caribbean			
Average (n = 12)	**61**	**83**	
Bolivia	20	29	Fundación IRFA
Bolivia	22	27	Fundación de Población
Bolivia	167	199	Ayuda en Acción
Brazil	38	38	Ministry of Education
Brazil	57	73	Serviço Social da Indústria (SESI)
Brazil	125	167	Projeto Escola Zé Peão
Brazil	56	58	Centro Josué de Castro: Estudos e Pesquisas
Ecuador	31	40	Centro de Alfabetización
Guatemala	19	53	Comité Nacional de Alfabetización
Peru	61	125	National Literacy Programme
Peru	90	110	Fundación Ayuda en Acción
Peru	67	72	Escuela Campesina de Educación y Salud (ESCAES)
Sub-Saharan Africa			
Average (n = 14)	**47**	**68**	
Angola	30	36	AAEA
Burkina Faso	20	...	TinTua
Gambia	60	80	Community Skills Development Project
Ghana	20	31	ActionAid
Kenya	43	80	EPID
Lesotho	118	178	University of the Witwatersrand
Malawi	63	100	Work for Rural Health
Mali	55	89	Jeunesse et Développement
Niger	39	118	VIE
Senegal	32	38	Tostan
Somalia	28	...	Africa Educational Trust
Sudan	75	115	ADRA
U.R. Tanzania	50	51	ActionAid International
Zambia	22	31	People's Action Forum
Other			
Belgium	1 423	...	Lire et Ecrire
Canada	2 646	2 646	East End Literacy
Ireland	742	742	NALA

Note: These data should be treated with caution, notably where enrolled learner costs and 'successful' learner costs are identical, but they offer indications of unit costs for a set of relatively successful programmes.
Source: GCE/ActionAid (2005).

34. Abdazi (2003*a*) notes that an Indonesian programme depended on 170,000 volunteers but that turnover was high and limited demands could be placed on their time. '[T]he effectiveness of cheaper versus more expensive programmes has not been systematically evaluated but experience shows that few have both low per participant costs and stable, well-performing teachers. Programme costs and effectiveness need to be considered with a long-term strategic perspective in order to avoid a trap of low cost and low effectiveness.'

They will have to be met by government, or through government encouragement of the private sector and others, including donors, to be major financiers of training (Box 9.13).

Another major future cost is production of learning materials. These costs vary considerably depending on programme pedagogy, the extent to which learning resources are self-generated in the learning process, the availability of existing materials and the use of ICTs. Furthermore, to assure much wider availability of texts and other learning materials, investment in the literate environment takes on considerable importance. While some of these materials may be included in individual literacy programmes, many are not. In this case, the materials then depend on the extent to which government and other stakeholders are prepared to invest in free or subsidized newspapers, local and national language editions of materials, provision of travelling libraries and the like. These costs are additional to the normal costs of individual programmes.

A major cost is production of learning materials

Further financing costs include start-up, management and overhead, and – although they are all too rare in many programmes – monitoring and evaluation. Abadzi (2003*a*) concludes that management costs are sizable and should not be underestimated. Moreover, they can become regular and significant if the longer-term view is taken that the benefits of short-term literacy programmes should be extended though access to continuing non-formal education. '[C]ountries that decide to engage in adult literacy should consider their long-term commitment and should determine the extent to which they are willing to fund more effective but also [relatively] more expensive programmes' (Abadzi, 2003*a*).

Again, none of these costs are easy to standardize, but in an endeavour to obtain further insights into the order of magnitude of the additional costs that might have to be incurred if major progress is to be made towards the Dakar literacy goal, preliminary work was commissioned for this Report, in association with the UNESCO-LIFE project (Van Ravens and Aggio, 2005). Two sets of data were brought together. First, approximate estimates were derived for the number of people recorded as illiterate who would need to acquire basic literacy skills for the global Dakar literacy target to be achieved. Table 9.5 presents these data, which identify a global target group of over 550 million people, almost half of them in South and West Asia.

The second strand of the analysis calculates the cost per learner of completing a time-bound literacy programme, defined by the quality of its inputs, as a percentage of per capita GNP by country. Table 9.6 shows the aggregate results of this work at the regional and global levels. With several qualifications, the study arrives at an average regional cost per completer not dissimilar to the GCE/ActionAid results: US$41 for sub-Saharan Africa (ActionAid, US$47), US$60 for Latin America (US$61) and US$30 for Asia (US$30).

The data in Table 9.6 suggest that US$26 billion, or some US$2 billion per year, would have been required over the thirteen years to 2015 to enable over 550 million people to complete a literacy programme of 400 hours. Since some years have already passed, at least US$2.5 billion a year would now be needed. Though this would not be a continuing cost, it would entail increased demand for further education and more supportive literate environments. At the regional level, the numerical and financial challenge is greatest in South and West Asia, but relative costs are highest in the Arab States.

This is a very rough estimate. Any variation in the assumptions will result in significant shifts in the final figures. For example, if a uniform unit cost of US$20 is applied (assuming very low educator costs), the total global cost estimate is just over one-third of the total in the table. If the range of inputs and/or their quality is significantly enhanced, the costs increase accordingly. An estimate of US$10 to US$50 billion over ten years

Box 9.13 Funding the training of literacy educators and their trainers

A large share of funding for training often comes from donors. In the Pacific, while governments often have training budgets, international agencies such as UNESCO (PROAP and ACCU), Germany's IIZ/DVV and Japan Funds-in-Trust cover many of the costs. NGOs in the Lao People's Democratic Republic, oil, rubber and mobile phone companies in Brazil, lotteries and charitable bodies in Ireland, and businesses in South Africa support training. In some instances, local communities and trainee literacy facilitators find their own funds for training activities, while governments and NGOs use their staff as trainers.

Source: Rogers (2005).

Table 9.5: The scale of the Dakar challenge, by region and development level

	Adult illiteracy rate 2000–2004 (simple average)	Number of adult illiterates 2000–2004 (thousands)	Dakar challenge	
			Target literacy rate (average)	Number of illiterates to be reached (thousands)
Arab States (13)	30.2	54 662	92.2	38 191
Central and Eastern Europe (18)	2.2	8 180	100.0	8 180
Central Asia (8)	1.0	385	100.0	385
East Asia and the Pacific (15)	13.9	123 742	99.1	123 306
Latin America and the Caribbean (24)	12.5	37 171	99.1	36 061
South and West Asia (7)	33.7	385 974	85.6	265 021
Sub-Saharan Africa (37)	40.4	132 083	82.3	86 538
Developing countries (122)	**22.0**	**742 196**	**92.7**	**557 681**

Notes: Calculated from data in the statistical annex tables. The number of countries in each group is in brackets and differs from those in Table 2.6.
Source: Van Ravens and Aggio (2005).

Investing in the broader literacy environment is important

captures both the order of magnitude and the wide range involved.

The potential advantage of this work, akin to that of the GCE/ActionAid study, is that it offers a framework to help stimulate a policy debate at global and country level, where the assumptions can be varied and applied according to context.[35]

Mobilizing additional resources for literacy

People in low-income countries have a very limited ability to pay for educational activities, so resource mobilization strategies are required, most notably (Oxenham et al., 2002):

- Budgetary allocations to literacy need to be increased, separately or as part of wider attention to continuing adult education, though *not* at the expense of investment in the quality of schooling. Diversification of funding across government should reap dividends in terms of overall funding levels but has implications for coordination. Investing in the broader literacy environment to stimulate the production and distribution of a wide variety of materials suitable for new readers is also important.
- To the extent possible, mechanisms should be developed to mobilize resources within the lower tiers of government and within communities, though never in ways that deny anyone the opportunity to benefit from literacy programmes because of cost.
- In many countries, governments and possibly national NGOs can form consortia or partnerships with the private sector, donor agencies and international NGOs. This might lead to public-private partnerships of the sort that exist in Senegal ('faire-faire'), the Gambia and Guinea.[36] An international variant would be for international donors to fill financing gaps, in line with the commitment in the Dakar Framework for Action that no countries 'seriously committed to education for all will be thwarted in their achievement of this goal by a lack of resources'. This statement is used extensively in relation to UPE, but rarely, if at all, about literacy.

Table 9.6: Estimated costs of achieving the literacy component of Dakar goal 4

Region	Total costs (US$ millions)
Arab States (13)	4 017
Central Asia (8)	11
East Asia and the Pacific (15)	6 552
Latin America and the Caribbean (24)	4 948
South and West Asia (7)	7 214
Sub-Saharan Africa (37)	3 208
Developing countries total	**25 951**
Developing countries annual average*	**1 996**

* Calculated for the thirteen years to 2015.
Source: Van Ravens and Aggio (2005).

The balance among these strategies in any given country and/or for any one significant programme will be context-specific. It is clear, however, that the scaling up of youth and adult literacy programmes in poor countries requires a national financing strategy that taps a variety of sources in a coordinated way. This requirement becomes all the more pressing if adult literacy programmes have to shoulder the responsibility for meeting the needs of those who, for whatever reason, have been failed by schooling (Abadzi, 2003*a*).

35. A dynamic presentation of the Van Ravens/Aggio study is available at www.efareport.unesco.org It enables readers to alter the costing assumptions for individual countries on a spreadsheet and develop tailored estimates of the costs of achieving the Dakar literacy goal.

36. Public private-partnerships do have certain disadvantages, including low fixed transaction costs being offset by high variable transaction costs (contract compliance, supervision and monitoring, information costs, provider selection, etc.) and providers taking advantage of weak government leadership and management, e.g. to exclude population groups that incur higher unit costs. In addition, some critics maintain that such arrangements pose a risk of CSOs' missions becoming diluted (Nordtveit, 2005*a*).

Few governments have set out coherent, long-term national literacy policies

This section has highlighted the paucity of data and research on the financing of literacy. A strong evidence base on cost-effective, sustainable approaches to delivering good-quality literacy programmes and promoting literate environments is badly needed. Examples of such work exist in Bangladesh, Brazil, Mexico and South Africa. A major initiative to build capacity for monitoring and evaluation in literacy programmes should be undertaken systematically at all relevant levels of national systems (Bhola, 2005). Support for such work would be a valuable contribution of and to the United Nations Literacy Decade.

Bringing greater coherence to national literacy policies

Governments have made commitments to improve levels of adult literacy but relatively few have set out coherent, long-term national literacy policies, either because this is not deemed a priority for political or economic reasons or because coordinating programme delivery and/or creating more enabling and proactive literate environments is found to be difficult, complex and potentially costly. Accordingly, in most countries policy on literacy is less than the sum of its parts. A cohesive, comprehensive approach is required to promote literacy for literate societies, firmly embedded in national education and poverty reduction strategies. How might such a policy process be stimulated?

The Indicative Framework developed by the World Bank to promote focused policy and planning dialogue for achieving UPE through the Fast track Initiative has given rise to substantive debate worldwide (Chapter 4). Despite disagreements regarding the choice of indicators and their benchmark values, the concept of the framework is a useful policy tool. A similar approach to stimulate dialogue on literacy – and adult literacy in particular – could be worthwhile. GCE and ActionAid developed twelve baseline statements of good practice ('benchmark statements') designed to serve this purpose, summarized in Box 9.14.

This benchmarking work is very useful but necessarily incomplete. The understandings represented in statements 1 and 2 are very much in line with the thrust of this Report. So is statement 3, though its considerable implications for developing human resource capacity within government would have to be factored into national policy, including the need to work productively with civil society.[37] There is a strong case for decentralization, given the superior local knowledge of literacy needs, though caution is required as the success of decentralization in many fields has been mixed.

The emphasis on evaluation of adult literacy programmes (statement 4) is wise and highlights an area that is weak in many literacy programmes where resources and knowledge are limited (Bhola, 2005).

A major plank in the framework is a unified approach to investment in human resources (statements 5, 6 and 7). The underlying premise is that, although good practice may exist in individual programmes, a national approach is needed to scale up and sustain improvements in literacy. Since meeting that need necessitates new resources and a significant increase in training capacity, this is the issue most likely to test the willingness of many governments to engage seriously in major new literacy initiatives, especially when volunteerism and the payment of honorariums keep many literacy programmes alive. In essence, it means recognition of a new cadre of education professionals.

The statements on teaching and learning (8, 9 and 10) rehearse many of the arguments in this Report and have implications for other aspects of government policy, including policy on language, rights to information and books, all areas that are politically charged as well as technically challenging.

More detailed work is needed to assess the cost benchmark (11). The proposed dedication of at least 3% of national education budgets to adult literacy programmes (statement 12) is arbitrary, the study acknowledges. The arguments in favour of allowing national need, rather than a set figure, to drive strategy and policy are much stronger.

Four major weaknesses characterize the proposed framework. First, it underplays the place of gender in literacy and the importance of gendered strategies in literacy policies.[38] Second, by assuming a relatively steady state of national circumstances, it underestimates the incidence of conflict and other emergencies, and, to a lesser extent, the urgent demands stemming from the HIV/AIDS pandemic. Third, it does not prioritize the benchmarks. Promoting a three-year literacy programme cycle, with its attendant costs, may be unrealistic, and setting budget targets in a vacuum may serve limited purposes. Fourth,

37. The literacy programme contributors to the GCE/ActionAid study (most of them from NGOs) made clear that the relationships between government and CSOs should not be one-way, with governments telling CSOs how to deliver programmes. With their local knowledge and experience, CSOs have much to contribute in the definition and design of literacy strategies. The programme representatives also made clear that government-led coordination could be counterproductive where relationships between government and civil society were weak or strained.

38. For example, in relation to same-sex facilitators in single-sex learner groups and gender-equitable teaching and learning materials.

Box 9.14 GCE/ActionAid 'Benchmark statements' to help define literacy policy

A: Understanding literacy

1. Literacy: the acquisition and use of reading, writing and numeracy skills, and thereby the development of active citizenship, improved livelihoods and gender equality. The goals of literacy programmes should reflect this understanding.

2. Literacy: a continuous process that requires sustained learning and practice. Policies and programmes should encourage sustained participation and celebrate progressive achievement.

B: Governing literacy

3. Governments have lead responsibility in fulfilling the right to literacy and in providing leadership, policy frameworks and resources. They should:

- assure cooperation among relevant ministries and links to all relevant development programmes;
- work in systematic collaboration with experienced CSOs;
- assure links between all these stakeholders, especially at the local level;
- assure relevance to the issues in learners' lives by promoting decentralization of budgets and of decision-making on curriculum, methods and materials.

C: Evaluating literacy programmes

4. It is important to invest in ongoing feedback and evaluation mechanisms, data systematization and strategic research. The focus of evaluations should be on the practical application of what has been learned and the impact on active citizenship, improved health and livelihoods, and gender equality.

D: Facilitators, supervisors and trainers

5. Facilitators should be paid at least the equivalent of the minimum wage of a primary-school teacher for all hours worked (including time for training, preparation and follow-up).

6. Facilitators should be local people who receive substantial initial training and regular refresher training, as well as ongoing opportunities for exchanges with other facilitators. Governments should put in place a framework for professional development of the sector, including trainers/supervisors, with full access to facilitators (e.g. through distance education).

7. There should be a ratio of at least one facilitator to thirty learners and at least one trainer/supervisor to fifteen learner groups (1:10 in remote areas), with a minimum of one support visit per month. Programmes should have timetables that flexibly respond to learners' daily lives but provide for regular and sustained contact (e.g. twice a week for at least two years).

E: Teaching, learning and the wider literate environment

8. In multilingual contexts it is important at all stages for learners to be given an active choice about the language in which they learn. Active efforts should be made to encourage and sustain bilingual learning.

9. A wide range of participatory methods should be used in the learning process to assure active engagement of learners and relevance to their lives. These same participatory methods and processes should be used at all levels of training of trainers and facilitators.

10. Governments should take responsibility to stimulate the market for production and distribution of a wide variety of materials suitable for new readers, for example working with publishers and newspaper producers. They should balance this with funding for local production of materials, especially by learners, facilitators and trainers.

F: Financing literacy

11. It should be assumed that a good-quality literacy programme that respects all these benchmarks will cost between US$50 and US$100 per learner per year for at least three years (two years of initial learning and ensuring that further learning opportunities are available for all).

12. Governments should dedicate at least 3% of their national education-sector budgets to adult literacy programmes as conceived in these benchmarks. Where governments meet this target, international donors should fill any remaining resource gaps (e.g. by including adult literacy in the Fast Track Initiative).

Note: For the full 'benchmark statements' see the source document.
Source: GCE/ActionAid (2005).

while the framework is potentially an important tool for countries with a major literacy deficit, it is less useful where the objective is to meet the needs of a relatively small but diverse target population.

Despite these weaknesses, the framework can help stimulate policy debate. It is not a solution in itself but a contribution to a dialogue that should be situated in broader policy frameworks. Youth and adult literacy, and the promotion of literate environments are key to poverty reduction, education-sector development and other strategies devoted to human development. If this is not recognized and acted upon, those efforts will not prosper.

Literacy and government strategies

Poverty Reduction Strategy Papers (PRSPs)[39]

An analysis of fifty-six full PRSPs (thirty from sub-Saharan Africa) and eleven interim PRSPs undertaken in the first half of 2005 assessed the extent to which literacy[40] is part of development policy (UNESCO-IIEP, 2005*a*).

Care is needed in interpreting this analysis. Literacy policies do not invariably gain attention in PRSPs. Education sector plans may highlight actions that PRSPs leave out. On the other hand, if literacy policies are not included in PRSPs, it can be assumed that their priority is not high.

In over 80% of the PRSPs and I-PRSPs, literacy appears in the poverty diagnosis as an indicator, and illiteracy as a significant factor in the perpetuation of poverty. The Mali PRSP states that 'poverty is characterized by illiteracy'. Cambodia recognizes that illiteracy excludes people from development. In Djibouti, illiteracy is seen as helping explain rural poverty. Mozambique draws correlations between child mortality, illiteracy and gender disparities.

Some countries, (e.g. Burundi, Chad, Mauritania and the Lao People's Democratic Republic) list literacy among their overall development goals. Cambodia, envisaging a socially connected, educationally advanced and culturally vibrant society, notes that this requires 'dealing with the problems of poverty, illiteracy, and health'. Some human development strategies seek to bridge the literacy gender gap, e.g. through women's learning centres in Mali, increased scholarships for girls in Nepal and functional literacy programmes for girls and women in Zambia. Bolivia and Nicaragua link gender and literacy with better nutrition.

Most references to literacy appear in the education section. Countries giving some priority to literacy make reference both to youth (primarily in relation to UPE) and to adult literacy. There are instances of adult literacy being treated in other sections (gender, health and nutrition, and, more rarely, agricultural development and employment). In Honduras and the Lao People's Democratic Republic there is reference to literacy and good governance, civic awareness and participation, and in the Lao People's Democratic Republic and Malawi to literacy and the environment.

In recognizing the needs of particular groups of people, most attention is paid to gender inequalities. Virtually all PRSPs identify lack of literacy as a factor impeding women's empowerment. Some mention is also made of particularly vulnerable groups. Bolivia correlates urban poverty, indigenous households and levels of education. Bosnia and Herzegovina establishes a similar link with regard to its Roma population.

When PRSPS are examined for a more precise indication of strategies related to literacy, relatively little detail is found. Most attention is given to improving the quality of schooling for all children. Box 9.15 sets out some broad lines of action in three countries where literacy does receive some focused attention.

Twelve PRSPs include plans to launch literacy campaigns, all in countries with low recorded literacy rates. The Chad PRSP refers to 'the weakness of Chad's human resources', notes that 'over 80% of the population is illiterate and only a small percentage of people over 15 years of age has received an education' and states that a 'vast literacy campaign is therefore urgently needed'.

Few PRSPs analyse the costs of the plans and proposals they contain, although eighteen mention costing exercises and twelve provide figures, the most detailed of which come from Mozambique. Table 9.7 shows countries that state their intent to allocate funds to literacy in their budgets and/or to projects that depend primarily on external financing.

The PRSP picture is mixed. The lack of literacy is taken into account relatively well in the poverty diagnosis, but the case for investing in youth and adult literacy seems less well made, either for literacy in its own right or as part of a three-pronged strategy of the type advanced in this Report.

Education sector plans

In the analysis of education sector plans discussed in Chapter 3, attention was drawn to whether governments are covering the full range of EFA goals, including literacy and adult education. That evidence is revisited here very briefly to see to what extent education sector plans shed more light on literacy than do PRSPs. Details from the twenty-five countries listed in Table 9.8 show that a significant sample of them are setting explicit and often ambitious short- to medium-term literacy targets, many of which cannot be achieved by schooling alone.

The table shows statements of intent for which governments can be held to some account. Whether these targets are grounded in true assessments of the nature and extent of illiteracy and realistic appraisals of what is possible in

39. PRSPs are the strategy and implementation documents of national poverty reduction strategies. They provide a poverty diagnosis, define key strategies for growth, poverty reduction and human development, and set out approaches to institutional strengthening. Education and literacy usually receive the most attention in the human development chapter. PRSPs were initially developed as part of the HIPC initiative for debt relief.

40. Few PRSPs define literacy; even the eleven papers that do are not very specific. The main approaches are to equate literacy with a level of schooling (e.g. in Cameroon, five years of primary school) or to use definitions that explicitly mention adult literacy (Albania, Djibouti, Ethiopia, the Niger, Senegal, Sierra Leone, Sri Lanka) and reading and writing skills. Madagascar and Pakistan take both approaches. A few countries, mainly those in transition, refer to literacy in information technology, and Kenya's PRSP sees IT literacy as a prerequisite for civil servants to be able to handle e-government.

relatively little time is unclear, as in some cases the Dakar goal is itself the country policy.

Despite the limitations of the evidence of PRSPs and sector plans, the main messages suggest that literacy, including youth and adult literacy, may be experiencing some resurgence of interest and concern.[41] What is less clear is the extent to which there are well-developed national policies for meeting the specific literacy targets and objectives in ways that are grounded in realistic, well-conceived, long-term strategies for literacy – and the extent to which the type of policy dialogue proposed above is taking place.

Conclusion

Most governments need to be much more active in researching, defining, financing, scaling up, implementing, coordinating and monitoring literacy policy and practice in schools, youth and adult literacy programmes, and literate environments. In the field of adult literacy, what is required is a national strategy for adult literacy, adult learning and the literate environment, set within wider education and development plans. Whether this strategy is implemented through a mass campaign, national literacy programmes, better coordinated government literacy programming and investment, or strong and well-coordinated national partnerships (vertical and horizontal) with a wide array of literacy stakeholders – or a combination of these approaches – will depend on political commitment, technical capacity, financing levels and strong public support. Whatever the choice, it should not be delayed. It should be driven by the need to meet the sort of ambitious targets that many governments have begun to set.

Engaging the international community

In the poorest countries, implementing the three-pronged approach to literacy will require international assistance. Yet literacy is not high on the agenda of most international agencies, beyond strong support for UPE. A survey of bilateral donors and development banks shows that few explicitly refer to literacy in their aid policies.[42] United Nations bodies consider literacy with non-formal and informal education, and international NGOs either stress schooling or conceive literacy to be a part of a rights-based approach to EFA for the poorest in society.[43]

Box 9.15 Three national literacy strategies

■ **Mauritania**'s size and the nomadic life of many of its people limit the effectiveness of literacy campaigns. The long-term objective is to eradicate illiteracy; the short-term aim is to reduce illiteracy to 20% by strengthening the financial and logistical resource base, boosting the skills of literacy campaign staff, improving the curriculum of literacy programmes and gaining greater participation by the *mahadra* (Koranic schools) through extension, training and logistical support. Extensive involvement of CSOs in the design, execution and monitoring of literacy programmes is expected. Ten new functional literacy centres are planned, 10,000 literacy classrooms are to be equipped each year and an incentive fund for literacy promoters is to be established.

■ **Malawi** intends to improve the quality and relevance of primary education, emphasizing literacy, numeracy and life skills. It also plans to increase levels of adult literacy and numeracy through improved access to more effective adult literacy classes and equitable participation of women. The Ministry of Gender, Youth and Community services will provide learning materials and appropriate honorariums for trainers, review adult literacy policy, undertake social mobilization campaigns, revise curricula, recruit and train additional instructors, strengthen monitoring, print and distribute manuals, and open more rural instruction centres in existing community buildings.

■ **Nepal** plans to improve livelihoods by integrating literacy programmes with community-based organizations and their income-generating activities. Increasing the engagement of community-based organizations, local NGOs and other local bodies should strengthen literacy campaigns. Community learning centres will be expanded.

Source: UNESCO-IIEP (2005*a*).

Table 9.7: Two approaches to financing literacy programmes

Money explicitly allocated to literacy in proposed budgets	Literacy projects dependent on external finance
Burkina Faso, Cambodia, Djibouti,[1] Ghana, Guinea,[2] Honduras, Malawi, Mozambique, Nepal, Nicaragua, Rwanda, Uganda	Burkina Faso, Djibouti, Ethiopia, Ghana, Guyana, Malawi, Mali, Mauritania, Mozambique, Nepal, Nicaragua, Pakistan, Rwanda, Yemen

1. Funds available for girls' literacy.
2. Funds available for growth sector and rural development.
Source: UNESCO-IIEP (2005*a*).

As Table 9.9 shows, most bilateral agencies and banks refer to literacy as an instrument for attaining other ends, such as eradicating poverty (e.g. the European Commission, New Zealand, and Norway). Sweden sees literacy at the heart of basic education and any economic and social development effort, but also part of broader adult basic education needs and learning activities (Sida, 2003). Most donors endorse EFA without

41. It should be noted, however, that an analysis of sixty-nine country reports to the International Conference on Education for 2001 and 2004 does not appear to back this up. The synthesis study does conclude that between the two sessions the emphasis on goals related to appropriate life-skills programmes for all young people and adults, and to satisfying the learning needs of young people, significantly increased. But there is no specific reference to literacy per se (Mancebo, 2005).

42. The survey was conducted by the Global Monitoring Report Team from November 2004 to January 2005. Seventy organizations were contacted and replies were received from fifteen bilateral agencies (seven of which gave partial responses), three development banks, six United Nations agencies and nine international NGOs.

43. Germany, New Zealand, Sweden and the Netherlands use specific definitions of literacy. The United Kingdom, United States and World Bank define literacy as a basic set of skills. Canada, Denmark, Germany, New Zealand and the United States refer to literacy in the context of basic education. The Netherlands sees it within a framework of adult education. Sweden relates literacy skills to social development. The United Nations bodies follow UNESCO's definition of literacy.

Table 9.8: Adult literacy targets in twenty-five developing and transition countries

Country	Target
Bangladesh	For all ages, literacy to increase from 53% (2002) to 81% (2015); for ages 15 to 45, from 56% to 80%; for ages 15 to 24, from 66% to 90%, through a combination of equitable access to quality basic education and continuing education for all adults.
Benin	Raise the adult literacy rate by 50% by 2015. Ensure equal access to basic and permanent education programmes for all adults.
Brazil	Establish literacy programmes for 10 million youth and adults within five years, and eradicate illiteracy by 2010.
China	Achieve 95% literacy for adults and young adults by 2005.
Côte d'Ivoire	Increase the current literacy rate by 50% and assure equitable access to basic education for adults and seniors by 2015.
Egypt	Eliminate 50% of current adult illiteracy for those 15 years and above by 2015/16. Give priority to younger age groups, women and girls, and residents of poor rural and urban areas.
Guatemala	Lower the illiteracy rate from 29% to 22% between 2004 and 2008, including through post-literacy training.
India	Achieve a sustainable threshold of 75% literacy by 2007 and a 50% improvement in levels of adult literacy by 2015.
Indonesia	A 50% decrease in the illiteracy rate by 2015. A decrease in illiteracy levels among people over 15 from 10.81% (15.5 million people) in 2000 to 5.41% (9.9 million) in 2015 (a fall from 6.7% to 3.3% for males and from 14.7% to 7.3% for females).
Kazakhstan	Achieve a 50% improvement in levels of adult literacy by 2015, especially for women, and equitable access to basic and continuing education for all adults.
Kenya	Achieve 50% improvement in levels of adult literacy by 2010 and universal adult literacy (especially for women) by 2015.
Mongolia	By 2005, 58.8% of the illiterate population will become literate.
Morocco	Reduce the illiteracy rate to less than 20% by 2010 and eradicate illiteracy by 2015.
Myanmar	The adult literacy rate (92.8% in 2002) will be 99% in 2015. Intermediate targets are set for 2005 and 2010. Achieve significant improvement in the levels of functional literacy and continuing education for all by 2015.
Nepal	By the end of the Tenth Plan to achieve literacy targets of 63% (age 15+) with a female literacy rate of 55%.
Nicaragua	Reduce illiteracy rate from 18.7% in 2004 to 10% in 2015.
Niger	Raise literacy rates for people above 15 years of age to 20% in 2002 and 40% in 2015.
Nigeria	By 2015, the Universal Basic Education policy aims to eradicate illiteracy.
Pakistan	From a base of adult literacy of 50.5% (male 63%, female 38%; rural 39%, urban 70%), the education sector plan targets adult literacy rate of 61% by 2005, 71% by 2010 and 86% by 2015. Gender equity (86% literacy rate for both male and female) is a target for the end of the sector plan period. A 50% reduction in illiteracy is planned for 2010 with a focus on raising rural literacy rates from 38% to 83% by 2015.
Paraguay	Raise the number of literate adults aged 15 to 24 by 6,450 through lifelong education for work programmes in 2003–2005, by 16,100 in 2006–10 and by 17,600 in 2011–15. Reduce overall numbers of illiterates over age 15 by 76,700, 96,000 and 102,000, respectively. Reduce illiteracy among rural women from 15.4% (2000/2001) to 12.5% and for rural men from 10.7% to 8.5% by 2005, and then by 8.2% and 6.4% by 2010 and 5.2% and 4.4% by 2015.
Sudan	Raise literacy rates among those age 15 and above to 60% by 2007 and to 82.5% by 2015.
Tunisia	Decrease the overall illiteracy rate from 20% (targeted in 2004) to 16% in 2006 and to 10% in 2010. Eradicate illiteracy in the age group below 30 by 2006.
Uzbekistan	100% functionally literate adults by 2015, especially women, and provision to all adults of equal access to basic and continuous education.
Venezuela	Eliminate illiteracy by 2005.
Zimbabwe	Increase the adult literacy rate from 87% to 100% by 2015.

Source: UNESCO-IIEP (2005*a*).

explicit reference to literacy, although some see it as a primary goal of good schooling (e.g. Canada, the European Commission and the United Kingdom) or as a skill at the heart of basic education (e.g. the United States). The Danish, German and Japanese agencies, and the World Bank and the Asian Development Bank discuss literacy in the context of non-formal education, even when they have a priority for UPE, and see no obvious synergy between the two. Denmark argues for integrating literacy for youth and adults into the programming of other sectors. Japan's aid agency emphasizes the importance of literacy for advancing development projects, while Sweden's is guided by education sector priorities with emphasis on the EFA goals; one of these priorities is 'enhancing literacy for all – children, youth and adults – through formal and non-formal education, as well as informal means, such as books, newspapers, and libraries' (Sida, 2001).

The United Nations agencies understandably approach literacy in relation to their specific mandates. For UNFPA, literacy is important in increasing demand for reproductive health services and women's empowerment. For the ILO, literacy is a core work skill. UNICEF considers literacy a key outcome of a high-quality education, especially for girls. These and other approaches come together in the International

Table 9.9: Literacy in bilateral and development bank aid policies

Countries	Agencies	How literacy is addressed in aid policy
Canada	Canadian International Development Agency	Canada supports EFA globally and with developing country partners. It has three main goals: (a) universal primary completion; (b) gender equality; and (c) improved quality 'as reflected in recognized and measurable learning outcomes, especially in literacy, numeracy and life skills for learners of all ages' (CIDA, 2002).
Denmark	Danish International Development Assistance	The EFA goals are at the heart of Danish support for education. Danida sees basic education as developing essential skills for social and economic life: literacy, numeracy, social skills, life skills (e.g. related to nutrition, sexual and reproductive health, subsistence production), critical and reflective thinking skills, and community-oriented skills.
Germany	Federal Ministry for Economic Cooperation and Development	Aid to basic education is informed by international commitments (e.g. Dakar goals, MDGs, United Nations Literacy Decade). Literacy is defined as a fundamental aspect of basic education. Literacy programmes for youth and adults are part of non-formal education projects (BMZ, 2004).
Japan	Japan Bank for International Cooperation	The Medium-term Strategy for Overseas Economic Cooperation specifies that support is geared towards human resource development for poverty reduction and human development. Literacy is implicit in human resource development (JBIC, 2002).
	Ministry of Foreign Affairs	The Basic Education for Growth Initiative, BEGIN, is designed to help realize the EFA goals. A priority area is access to education, including non-formal. Literacy projects are promoted, with some focus on raising literacy levels of adult women and using ICT for education, e.g. in remote areas (2002).
	Japan International Cooperation Agency	A strategy paper on non-formal education identifies literacy for youth and adults as a priority for cooperation in basic education. Literacy, both basic and functional, is recognized as a key life skill regardless of sex, age, ethnic origin or socio-economic status (2004).
New Zealand	New Zealand Agency for International Development	Aid to education is intended to support partner countries in achieving the EFA goals. A further aim of NZAID is to both influence and learn from the international debates on EFA (NZAID, 2002).
Norway	Norwegian Agency for Development Cooperation	Norad has a role in implementing the Norwegian Strategy for Delivering Education for All by 2015, which calls education 'Job Number 1' in eliminating poverty. The strategy is based on the Dakar Framework for Action and contains explicit references to literacy training (Norwegian Ministry of Foreign Affairs, 2003).
Sweden	Swedish International Development Cooperation Agency	Sida's education policy builds on United Nations rights conventions and declarations, including the Dakar Framework for Action. The relevant policy goal: 'enhance the right to ... an education that empowers the poor and excluded parts of the population to participate as active and informed citizens in all aspects of development' (Sida, 2001*b*).
United Kingdom	Department for International Development	DFID supports EFA goals by promoting international commitment and action, implementing country programmes and supporting knowledge and research strategies. It emphasizes formal education, particularly UPE, as the building block of literacy, and recognizes the importance of adult literacy programmes. It endorses country-led education-sector plans, of which adult literacy may be a key component (DFID, 2001).
United States	United States Agency for International Development	At the heart of USAID's education strategy is support for basic education and facilitating acquisition of basic skills such as literacy, numeracy and critical thinking, including for adults and out-of-school youth. The US government backs the United Nations Literacy Decade (USAID, 2005).
European Union	European Commission	EFA goals are part of EU development policy on education. Support for literacy comes through a focus on basic education, particularly formal primary schooling. The policy emphasizes holistic sector strategies, including for vocational education and adult literacy (European Commission, 2002).
World Bank		The World Bank supports country implementation of reforms and programmes within education sector and national development plans. It sees achieving EFA as multidimensional, including adult literacy and non-formal education for all children and youth, and literacy as a foundation skill comprising numeracy, reasoning and social skills, as well as a major component of non-formal education for youth and adults (World Bank, 1999). (www1.worldbank.org/education/adultoutreach/introduction.asp).
Asian Development Bank		The education sector policy refers to the World Declaration on Education For All (Jomtien, Thailand, 1990) and reiterates support for achieving EFA (ADB, 2003). Literacy and non-formal education are identified as priorities. Support for literacy for youth and adults (women in particular) is seen in the context of poverty reduction. Collaboration with NGOs is proposed.
Inter-American Development Bank		Forthcoming education strategy refers to the MDGs and the challenges associated with meeting them throughout Latin America and the Caribbean.

Note: Descriptions are based on the documents cited and/or agency replies to a survey conducted from November 2004 to January 2005. Where no reference is cited, the date of the policy information, if available, is given in brackets at the end of the description.
Source: EFA Global Monitoring Report Team.

Plan of Action for the United Nations Literacy Decade (United Nations, 2002c), with literacy seen as a crucial element of the right to education. The small sample of international NGOs illustrates a strong on-the-ground programme approach focusing on women and on literacy for better livelihoods.

Very few agencies have disbursement data on literacy

Assessing how these broad statements translate into programmes and funding allocations is problematic. It is almost impossible to extract literacy-focused or -related programme data from the OECD-DAC databases, as literacy is part of 'basic skills for youth and adults' and some donors support it within broader integrated projects. Very few agencies have disbursement data on literacy, and those that do give caveats regarding its accuracy (e.g. the Japanese agencies and that of Norway). Similar difficulties apply to the United Nations agencies. The data in Table 9.10 give some indication of the level of funding for a range of activities, including literacy, for some agencies. The data must be interpreted with caution, as each agency used different criteria.

Table 9.10: Average annual funding for literacy, selected agencies

	Amount (000 US$)	Period	Notes
Japanese Ministry of Foreign Affairs	553	1995–2004	Disbursements for support to literacy through NGOs. Judgement based on short project descriptions.
Japan International Cooperation Agency	17,802	1996–2003	Disbursements for non-formal education; includes adult education and literacy, provision of information and education to general public (e.g. museums, libraries).
Norwegian Agency for Development Cooperation	5,072	1999–2003	Based on figures reported to OECD-DAC in the category 'basic skills for youth and adults'.
World Bank	11,089	1995–2003	Disbursements recorded under the category 'adult literacy and non-formal education'.
Asian Development Bank	10,000	2001–2003	Figure based on commitments.
UNICEF	2,803	1995–2003	Disbursements under the categories 'youth and adult education', 'primary education' and 'girl child initiatives'.
UNESCO	2,829 (regular budget) 5,087 (extrabudgetary resources)	2000–2005 [illegible]	Regular budget: commitments; [illegible]budgetary resources: disbursement-based.

Note: Taken from agency replies to a survey conducted from November 2004 to January 2005. Original data for Japan and Norway were in national currencies, converted at United Nations exchange rates for April 2005: JPY 1=US$107; NOK 1=US$6.08.
Source: EFA Global Monitoring Report Team.

Similar problems arise in assessing literacy projects and programmes. Table 9.11 is derived from information provided by agencies on major programmes specifically dedicated to adult literacy. The data again have to be approached with caution, but it appears there is strong emphasis on literacy for women and girls, particularly in programmes supported by United Nations agencies. The emphasis on school-age children may reflect agencies' focus on UPE. Sub-Saharan Africa has been the main project recipient and, in one-third of the projects, NGOs were primary programme providers.

From these limited data sets it is clear that literacy in the broad policy sense of literate societies is not widely embraced by donor agencies. For some, youth and adult literacy, and the promotion of literate environments are simply not priorities for aid budgets. For others, literacy is judged as a tool for specific development ends, or receives only marginal attention in policies and programmes, much as in national PRSPs and sector plans. Whatever the reason, the fact that no agency surveyed could quote with confidence a single figure to illustrate its level of funding to literacy indicates the low priority assigned to literacy in aid budgets.

There is a strong case for a new international discussion of literacy, including its place in agencies' policies and their education sector dialogues with governments, and the degree to which agencies can give support to adult literacy and to literate environments that accords much more closely with the scale and scope of the Dakar literacy challenge.

Two opportunities for such a dialogue are led by UNESCO. The United Nations Literacy Decade (2003–2012) has a set of major international goals covering the full range of objectives that appear in this Report (see Box 4.11). Its International Plan of Action (United Nations, 2002c) has a menu of strategies and key areas for action that include international support and coordination. The plan states:

UNESCO will work within the Education for All Coordination mechanism already established ... to identify literacy components in ongoing development programmes of various international and bilateral agencies and forge joint mobilization and maximum use of resources among these agencies in support of the Decade ... In consultation with United Nations agencies UNESCO will work towards creating meaningful and goal oriented partnerships ... The World Bank will work with UNESCO on literacy assessment and cost and financing analysis for literacy, for which OECD and UNICEF can also be key partners.

Potentially, this is important work, and UNESCO's programme on literacy practices and environments, and literacy for all is another valuable resource. If the Literacy Decade can generate political and technical visibility for literacy internationally, strengthen evidence-based research and serve as an advocate for literacy in education sector and poverty strategies, it will make a signal contribution to putting literacy back into the core of EFA.

The second opportunity is provided by the UNESCO Literacy Initiative for Empowerment (LIFE) programme (2005–2015), designed to operate within the framework of the Literacy Decade. Its primary goal is to empower women and girls through literacy in thirty-four countries with a recorded literacy rate of below 50% or with more than 10 million people without basic literacy skills. This ambitious programme, relying on advocacy, capacity-building and the promotion of innovation, will need to be well coordinated within the framework of national sector policies and will almost certainly require significant levels of additional funding if the desired impact is to be achieved. It is unlikely to be successful as a standardized model but can serve as a framework for working flexibly in individual countries. There are obvious opportunities to work with the United Nations Girls' Education Initiative (UNGEI) as well as with regional bodies and initiatives, such as the Association for the Development of Education in Africa (ADEA) and the African Union.

Conclusion

No one questions the goal of the literate society, but far too many people are denied the opportunity to contribute and gain from its benefits. There is sufficient evidence around the world – historical and current – to show that the goal is attainable if the right policies are put in place, and sufficient national and international political, public and professional energy and resources drive the process. The policies are not an add-on to the Millennium Development Goals but a necessary if understated part of their achievement. And they lie at the core of EFA. ■

Table 9.11: Trends in major aid-financed literacy projects and programmes

Survey	Total	Bilateral & banks	UN agencies
Description of target population[1]			
Women	65	25	40
Girls	36	11	25
Youth	35	21	4
Children	33	19	14
Adults	23	11	12
School-age	17	17	0
Rural	15	14	1
Out-of-school	12	1	11
Teachers	9	7	2
Poor	8	8	0
Boys	6	6	0
Trainers	6	6	0
Indigenous	5	4	1
Minority	4	4	0
Ministry	3	3	0
Parents	2	0	2
Refugee	2	1	1
Disadvantaged	2	0	2
Regional distribution[2]			
Arab States	19	6	13
Central Asia	3	1	2
Central and Eastern Europe	8	0	8
East Asia and the Pacific	65	35	30
Latin America and the Caribbean	36	19	17
Sub-Saharan Africa	93	57	36
South and West Asia	43	33	10
Multiregional	27	12	15
No data	4	0	4
Type of partner/implementing organization[3]			
Government	92	42	50
NGO	99	84	15
Government and NGO	14	5	9
NPO	5	5	0
United Nations[4]	59	9	50
Others and unknown	29	18	11

1. Derived from counting the frequency of words describing the characteristics of populations appearing in project descriptions for 208 projects. Some projects had more than one target group.
2. Project countries and regions are categorized by EFA region.
3. 'Government' = central and local government and government institutions; NGO = local and international civil society organizations.
4. Of 50 United Nations projects, 48 are UNESCO extrabudgetary programmes, financed by other private, bilateral or multilateral donors but executed by UNESCO. Some are implemented by government or NGOs.
Source: EFA Global Monitoring Report Team.

In Dhaka, Bangladesh, a mother helps her daughter with a reading lesson.

Chapter 10

Setting priorities for action

Only ten years are left until 2015, the target date for achieving the Education for All goals. The year 2005 has been one of promising developments, whose potential must now be realized. Some progress towards EFA has become evident, especially in many low-income countries. The international community has focused renewed attention on global poverty, especially in sub-Saharan Africa. The importance of EFA has become even clearer in the context of globalization and the emergence of the knowledge society. The G8 summit in Gleneagles and the annual meeting of the World Bank and the International Monetary Fund have promised increased international support, including more aid and more debt relief. What must be done now to support EFA is to translate these broad pro-development moves at the international level into specific measures for the education sector within individual countries. This chapter suggests some high-priority areas for national and international action, if EFA, including the literacy goal, is to be achieved. Attaining the goals by 2015 remains feasible, but can only be accomplished by accelerating immediately the current pace.

The EFA balance sheet

This Report has reviewed changes in EFA since the World Education Forum in 2000 (in Dakar, Senegal) by comparing 2002 data (the most recent available) with those for 1998. Some progress has been made, particularly among girls, resulting in improved gender parity at the primary level. Encouragingly, this progress is most evident for several countries in both sub-Saharan Africa and South and West Asia. Forty-seven countries have achieved universal primary education (UPE) and another twenty will likely do so by 2015. A further forty-four countries are making solid progress but will not reach UPE until after 2015. Secondary education has expanded very rapidly, in part reflecting past success at the primary level. There is more attention to quality in national planning. Public spending on education has increased as a share of national income in two-thirds of countries for which data exist. Aid to basic education has more than doubled since 1999 and, optimistically, could rise to US$3.3 billion a year by 2010 following the G8 summit. The Education for All Fast Track Initiative, established only in 2002, has already emerged as a key coordinating mechanism for aid agencies.

Universal primary education by 2015 is not assured. About 100 million children are still not enrolled in primary school, 55% of them girls

Yet, however promising, these positive developments will not be enough to achieve all six EFA goals. It is now urgent to do so, as the emerging global economy and knowledge society make education – and literacy – an even more pressing need. Full participation in the knowledge society and economy – and hence reduced poverty and enhanced citizenship – is predicated on education, with literacy at its core.

The imperative of building literate societies necessitates simultaneous action on three fronts:

1) continuing to increase enrolments while reducing gender disparities and improving quality in basic education (at least at the primary and lower secondary levels);
2) scaling up programmes for youth and adult literacy; and
3) investing in literate environments at home, school, and throughout communities.

This will not be easy. EFA challenges remain enormous. For example:

- Universal primary education by 2015 is not assured. About 100 million children are still not enrolled in primary school, 55% of them girls. In 23 countries, primary net enrolment rates have been declining. Fees are still collected at the primary level in 89 out of the 103 countries surveyed. High fertility rates, HIV/AIDS and conflict continue to exert pressure on education systems in the regions with the greatest EFA challenges.
- The 2005 gender parity target has been missed. Ninety-four countries have not met the goal, and eighty-six are at risk of not doing so even by 2015. At the primary-school level, where seventy-six countries have not reached gender parity, the issue is principally one of girls' enrolment. At the secondary level, on the other hand, girls predominate in almost half of the countries that have not achieved parity, reflecting high drop-out rates among boys.
- Education quality is too low. In forty-one countries, less than two-thirds of primary-school pupils reach the last grade. There are too few teachers, too few women teachers, and too few trained and qualified teachers; in many countries, primary teacher numbers would have to increase by 20% a year to reduce pupil/teacher ratios to 40:1 and to achieve UPE by 2015. In addition, enrolments have not increased significantly in early childhood care and education programmes, one of the keys to enhanced performance at primary school.
- Literacy has been neglected. Over 770 million youth and adults – about one-fifth of the world's adult population – are without basic literacy skills, mostly in sub-Saharan Africa and Asia. Moreover, as this Report has shown, this number actually underestimates the size of the global problem, as it is based on conventional, but flawed, methods of assessing literacy. Literacy is not prominent in most education plans and typically accounts for only 1% of public spending on education. Yet the goal is central to the achievement of other EFA goals.
- Aid to basic education is inadequate: despite recent increases, it still represents only about 2.6% of Official Development Assistance (and within this, aid for adult literacy is minuscule). It will fall far short of the US$7 billion a year estimated to be needed just for achieving UPE and gender parity. Aid is not allocated sufficiently to the countries with the greatest need – in terms of absolute numbers of children and youth facing the EFA challenge, and in terms of ranking according to the Education for All Development Index (EDI). The Fast Track Initiative, launched in 2002, had resulted in only US$298 million in new pledges by mid-2005, although it may also have leveraged some additional bilateral funding.

Priorities for action

To meet these challenges and to consolidate the progress that has already been made, nine areas must be adressed:

Broad EFA measures

1. *Accelerating efforts towards UPE and quality in primary education.* Particularly important are attention to: (a) reducing and eliminating fees; (b) policies to include rural children, minorities, those affected by HIV/AIDS and those living with disabilities; (c) increasing the teacher supply and improving teacher training; (d) expanding enrolments in early childhood care and education programmes, especially for the disadvantaged; and (e) implementing low-cost school health and nutrition measures that can increase access and learning.
2. *Recommitting to the gender goal.* Although the 2005 goal has been missed, considerable progress has been made, and often in the countries where the challenge is greatest. This progress must be celebrated and reinforced. It is important therefore that the EFA movement renew its commitment to the gender goal and push ahead.
3. *Spending more on education, and spending more efficiently.* Spending is increasing but remains low as a percentage of national income. In some countries, this reflects the low share in national income of public spending in general, and broad revenue measures are needed rather than actions specific to the education sector. In others, allocations to education are too low. In many countries, improving the efficiency of spending also has considerable potential.

Literacy measures

4. *Making youth and adult literacy a higher priority on national and international agendas.* For literacy to be achieved, political commitment from the highest level is essential, as are clear government policies that include literacy in education sector plans and other relevant documents, such as Poverty Reduction Strategy Papers. There are encouraging signs of change in some countries, but these are still too few. At the international level, adult literacy remains largely neglected by aid agencies and the United Nations Literacy Decade has yet to take specific form, though again there are some early signs of possible change.
5. *Focusing on literate societies, not just on literate individuals.* It is very clear that the EFA goals can be met only through the development of literate societies, in which all literate individuals have the means and the opportunity to benefit from rich and dynamic literate environments. Policies to develop rich literate environments – alongside schooling and programmes that ensure that youth and adults become literate – are thus important. Such policies can include support for libraries, local-language newspapers, book publishing, access of adults to school libraries and radio listening groups.
6. *Defining government responsibility for youth and adult literacy.* Governments must clearly define responsibility for adult literacy, which is often diffused across several ministries. It also involves many partnerships at all levels of government and with civil society organizations. Adequate public financing is needed. It is essential to professionalize literacy educators and provide them with adequate pay and training.

International measures

7. *Doubling aid to basic education to reach US$7 billion.* The increases in aid announced during 2005 have yet to be allocated by sector. It is essential that the share of aid to basic education – including to literacy – increase even faster than aid as a whole. It should at least double, from 2.6% to over 5% of total aid.
8. *Targeting aid to the greatest educational needs.* Aid must be aligned more closely with need, must be more predictable and long-term, and should flow more to those countries furthest from achieving the EFA goals. Efforts to harmonize aid to education should continue, including through the Fast Track Initiative.
9. *Complementing the flow of funds with knowledge and technical support.* For many EFA goals, and especially for literacy, developing countries need access to technical knowledge and expertise. There is significant potential for UNESCO and other agencies to play a greater role in organizing and providing this knowledge and technical support, complementing the financial aid provided by donors.

Achieving EFA – with literacy at its core – is ever more pressing. The needs are clear. It is up to the world community to make it happen. ■

For literacy to be achieved, political commitment from the highest level is essential, as are clear government policies

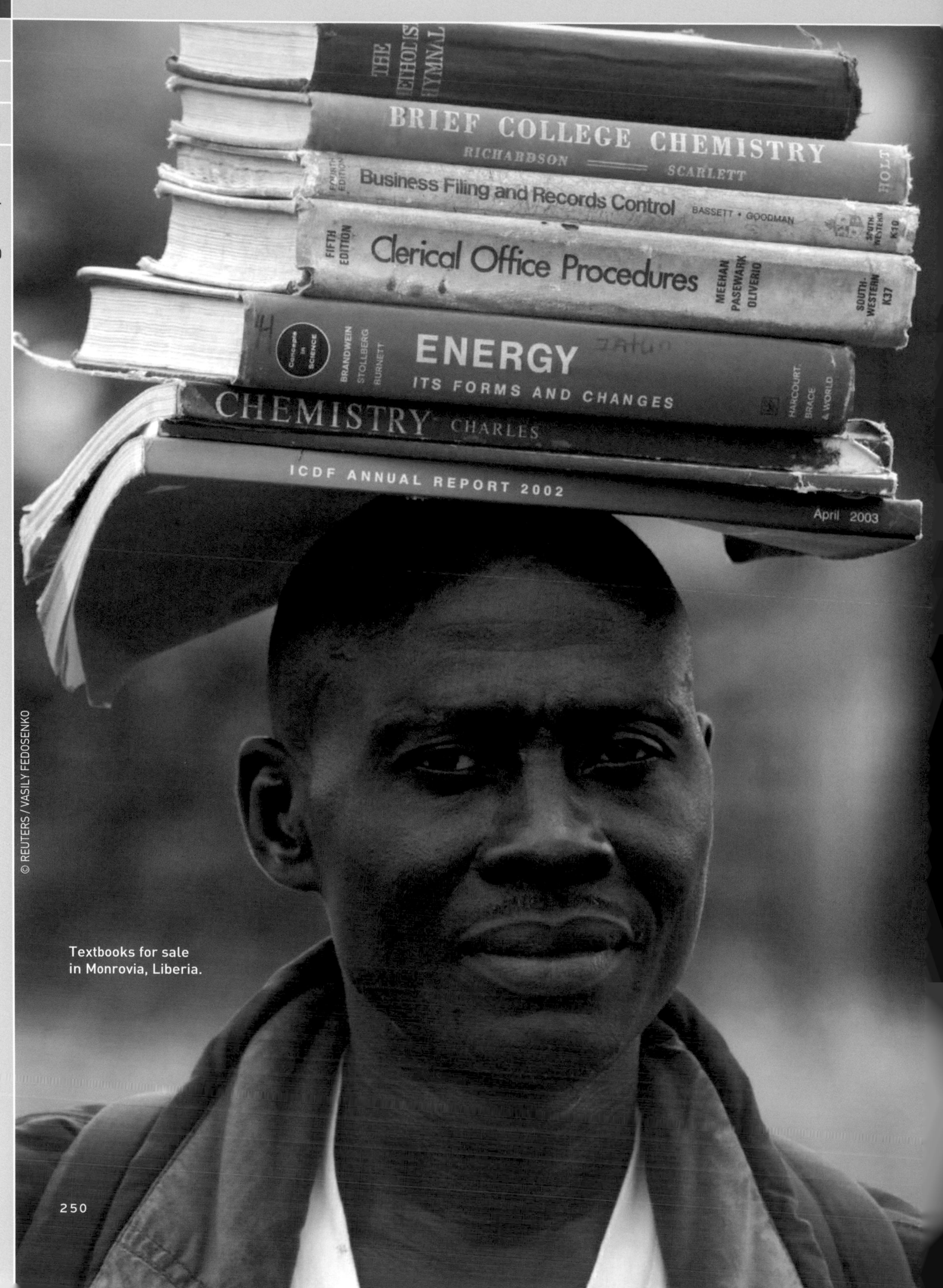

Textbooks for sale in Monrovia, Liberia.

Annex

Appendices: EDI and prospects for the achievement of EFA

Statistical annex

Aid data annex

Appendices: EDI and prospects for the achievement of EFA

Appendix 1
The Education for All Development Index

While each of the six EFA goals is individually important, it is also useful to a have a means of indicating progress towards EFA as a whole. The EFA Development Index (EDI), a composite of relevant indicators, provides one way of doing so, at least for four of the goals: universal primary education (UPE), adult literacy, gender parity and the quality of education.

The two goals not included in the EDI are goals 1 and 3. Indicators on goal 1 (Early childhood care and education) cannot easily be incorporated because national data are insufficiently standardized and reliable and comparable data are not available for most countries. As for goal 3 (learning needs of youth and adults), it has not yet been sufficiently defined for quantitative measurement.

In accordance with the principle of considering each goal to be equally important, one indicator is used as a proxy measure for each of the four EDI components,[1] and each component is assigned equal weight in the overall index. The EDI value for a particular country is thus the arithmetic mean of the observed values for each component. Since the components are all expressed as percentages, the EDI value can vary from 0 to 100% or, when expressed as a ratio, from 0 to 1. The closer a country's EDI value is to the maximum, the greater the extent of its overall EFA achievement and the nearer the country is to the EFA goal as a whole.

1. The EDI's gender component is itself a composite index.

Choice of indicators as proxy measures of EDI components

In selecting indicators, relevance has to be balanced with data availability.

Universal primary education

The indicator selected to measure UPE achievement (goal 2) is the total primary net enrolment ratio (NER), which reflects the percentage of primary-school-age children who are enrolled in either primary or secondary school. Its value varies from 0 to 100%. A NER of 100% means that all eligible children are enrolled in school.

Adult literacy

The adult literacy rate is used as a proxy to measure progress towards goal 4. The existing data on literacy are not entirely satisfactory, however; new methodologies are being developed (see Chapter 7). Moreover, as the adult literacy indicator is a statement about the stock of human capital, it is slow to change, and thus it could be argued that it is not a good 'leading indicator' of year-by-year progress towards improvement in literacy levels. Providing a new data series of good quality for all countries will take many years, though; the literacy rates now used are the best currently available internationally.

Quality of education

Measures of students' learning outcomes are widely used as a proxy for the quality of education, particularly among countries at similar levels of development. They are incomplete, as they do not include values, capacities and other non-cognitive skills that are also important aims of education, beyond cognitive skills (UNESCO, 2004*a*: pp. 43–4). They also tell nothing about the cognitive value added by schooling, (as opposed to home background), or the distribution of ability among children enrolled in school.[2] Despite these drawbacks, learning outcomes would likely be the most appropriate single proxy for the average quality of education, but as they are not available as comparable data for a large number of countries, it is not yet possible to use them in the EDI.

Among the feasible proxies available for a large number of countries, the survival rate to Grade 5 was selected as being the best available for the quality component for the EDI.[3] Figure A1.1 shows that there is a clear positive link between such survival rates and educational achievement in sub-Saharan African countries participating in the Southern and Eastern African Consortium for Monitoring Educational Quality (SACMEQ II) assessment. The coefficient of determination is around 31%. Education systems capable of retaining a larger proportion of their pupils to Grade 5 are performing better, on average, on international tests.

The survival rate to Grade 5 is associated even more strongly with learning outcomes in lower secondary school. Figure A1.2 shows that the variation in one variable explains about 38% of the variation in the other one in the results of the third Trends in International Mathematics and Science Study (TIMSS), and up to 68% in the Programme for International Student Assessment (PISA) study.

Another possible proxy for quality is the pupil/teacher ratio (PTR). Indeed, among SACMEQ II countries, the proportion of variation in learning outcomes explained by the PTR (35%) is slightly higher than that explained by survival rates to Grade 5 (31%). Many other studies, however, produce much more ambiguous evidence of the relationship between the PTR and learning outcomes (UNESCO, 2004*a*). In a multivariate context, PTRs are associated with higher learning outcomes in some studies, but not in many others. In addition, the relationship seems to vary by the level of mean test scores. For low levels of test scores, a decrease in pupils per teacher has a positive impact on learning outcomes, but for higher levels of test scores, additional teachers have only limited impact. For these reasons, the survival rate was chosen as a safer proxy for learning outcomes, and hence for education quality.[4]

Figure A1.1: Survival rate to Grade 5 and learning outcomes at primary level

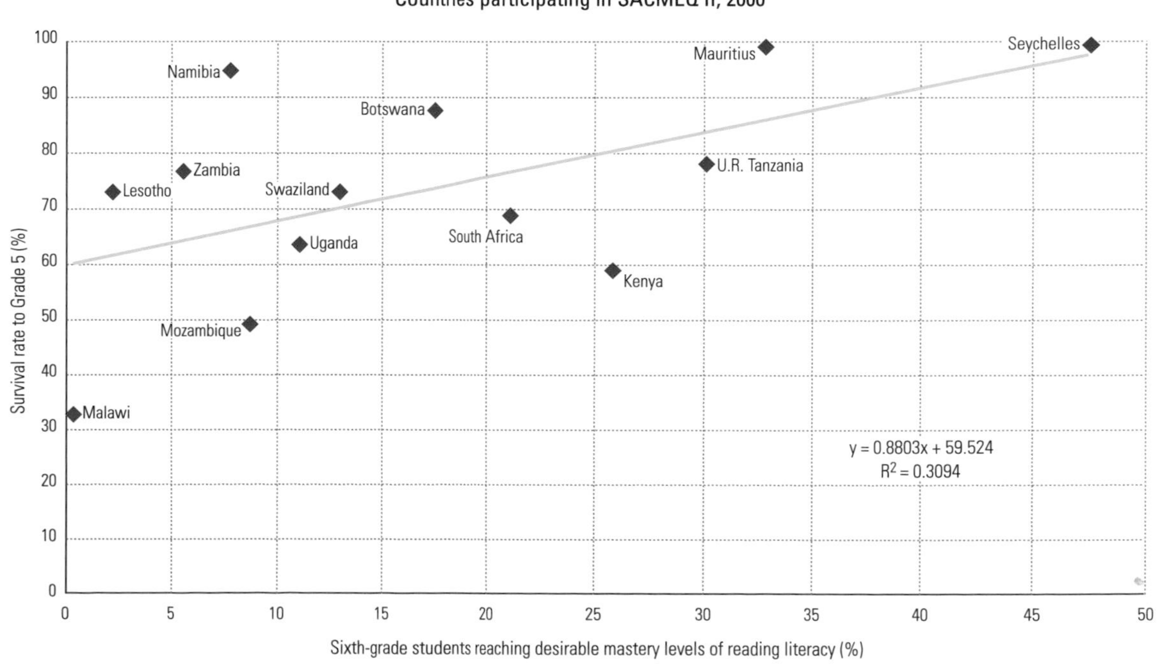

Sources: UNESCO Institute for Statistics calculation, based on SACMEQ II database; statistical annex, Table 7.

2. Strictly speaking, it would be necessary to compare average levels of cognitive achievement for pupils completing a given school grade across countries with similar levels and distributions of income and with similar levels of NER, so as to account for home background and ability cohort effects.

3. See *EFA Global Monitoring Report 2003/4*, Appendix 2, for background.

4. Another reason is that, unlike PTRs, survival rates, like the other EDI components, range from 0 to 100%. Therefore, the use of the survival rate to Grade 5 in the EDI avoids a need to rescale the data.

Figure A1.2: Survival rate to Grade 5 and learning outcomes at lower secondary level

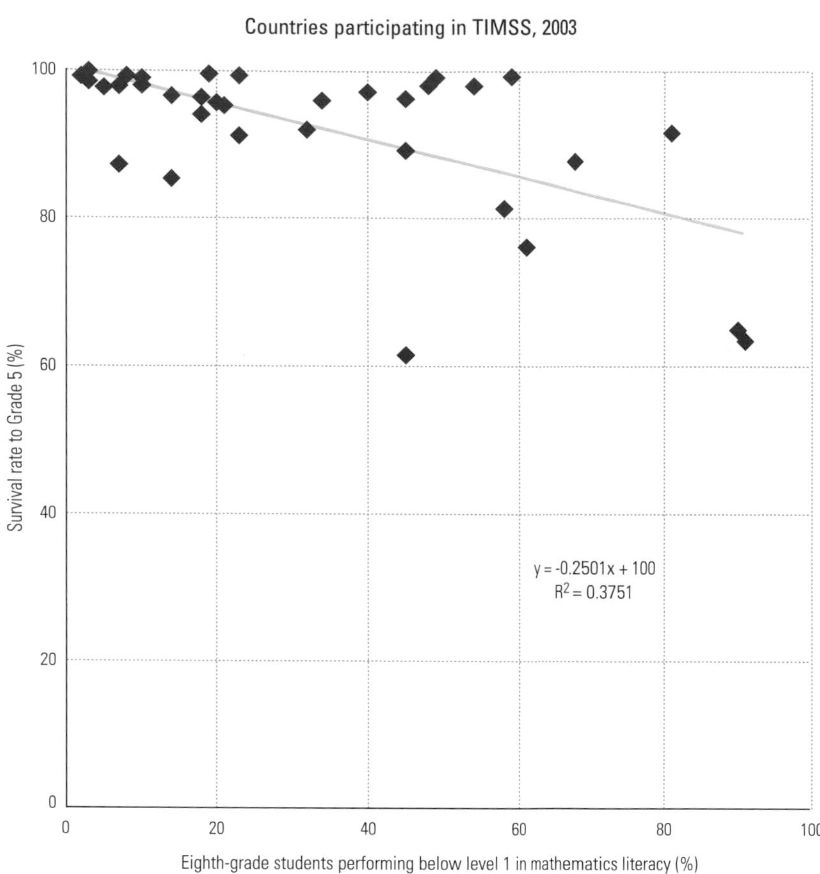

Sources: Mullis et al. (2004); statistical annex, Table 7.

Figure A1.2 (continued)

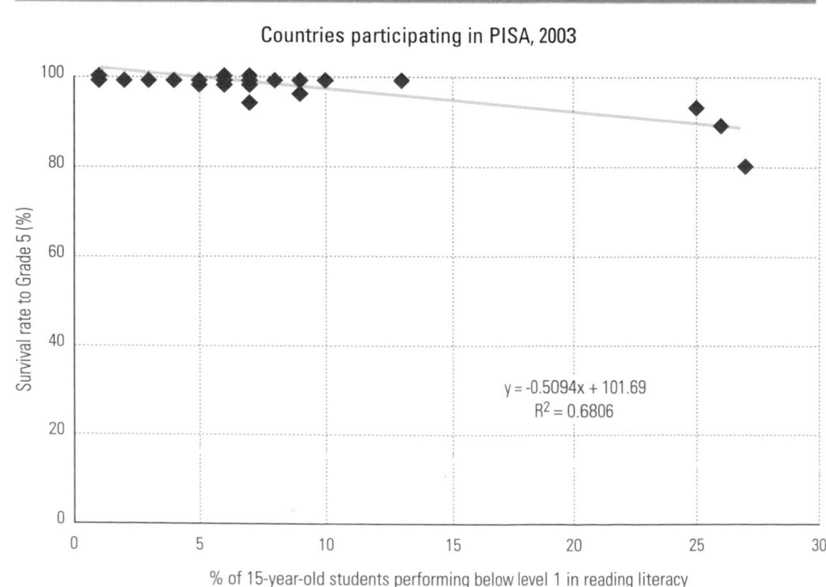

Sources: OECD (2004); statistical annex, Table 7.

Gender

The fourth EDI component is measured by a composite index, the gender-specific EFA index (GEI). Ideally, the GEI should reflect the whole gender-related EFA goal, which calls for 'eliminating gender disparities in primary and secondary education by 2005, and achieving gender equality in education by 2015, with a focus on ensuring girls' full and equal access to and achievement in basic education of good quality'. There are thus two sub-goals: gender parity (achieving equal participation of girls and boys in primary and secondary education) and gender equality (ensuring that educational equality exists between boys and girls).

The first sub-goal is measured by the gender parity indexes (GPIs) for the gross enrolment ratios at primary and secondary levels. Measuring and monitoring the broader aspects of equality in education is difficult, as the 2003/4 Report demonstrated (UNESCO, 2003*b*). Essentially, outcome measures, disaggregated by sex, are needed for a range of educational levels. No such measures are available on an internationally comparable basis. As a step in that direction, however, the GEI includes gender parity for adult literacy. Thus, the GEI is calculated as a simple average of three GPIs: for the gross enrolment ratio in primary education, for the gross enrolment ratio in secondary education and for the adult literacy rate. This means the GEI does not fully reflect the second, equality aspect, of the EFA gender goal.

The GPI, when expressed as the ratio of females to males in enrolment ratios or the literacy rate, can exceed unity when more girls/women are enrolled or literate than boys/men. For the purposes of the index, the F/M formula is inverted to M/F in cases where the GPI is higher than 1. This solves mathematically the problem of including the GEI in the EDI (where all components have a theoretical limit of 1, or 100%) while maintaining the GEI's ability to show gender disparity. Figure A1.3 shows how 'transformed GPIs' are arrived at to highlight gender disparities that disadvantage males. Once all three GPI values have been calculated and converted into 'transformed GPIs' (from 0 to 1) where needed, the composite GEI is obtained by calculating a simple average of the three GPIs, with each being weighted equally.

Figure A1.4 illustrates the calculation for Tunisia, using 2002 data. The GPIs in primary education, secondary education and adult literacy were 0.964, 1.082 and 0.784, respectively, resulting in a GEI of 0.891:

GEI = 1/3 (transformed GPI in primary)
+ 1/3 (transformed GPI in secondary)
+ 1/3 (transformed GPI in adult literacy)

GEI = 1/3 (0.964) + 1/3 (0.924) + 1/3 (0.784) = 0.891

Calculating the EDI

The EDI is the arithmetic mean of its four components – total primary NER, adult literacy rate, GEI and survival rate to Grade 5. As a simple average, the EDI may mask important variations among its components: for example, results for goals on which a country has made less progress can offset its advances on others. Since all the EFA goals are equally important, a synthetic indicator such as the EDI is thus very useful to inform the policy debate on the prominence of all the EFA goals and to highlight the synergy among them.

Figure A1.5 illustrates the calculation of the EDI, again using Tunisia as an example. The total primary NER, adult literacy rate, value of the GEI and survival rate to Grade 5 in 2002 were 0.984, 0.748, 0.891 and 0.925, respectively, resulting in an EDI of 0.886:

EDI = 1/4 (NER)
+ 1/4 (adult literacy rate)
+ 1/4 (GEI)
+ 1/4 (survival rate to Grade 5)

EDI = 1/4 (0.984) + 1/4 (0.743) + 1/4 (0.891) + 1/4 (0.925)
= 0.886

Data sources and country coverage

All data used to calculate the EDI for 1998 and 2002 (or 2001, where more recent data were not available) are from the UNESCO Institute for Statistics (UIS) database, with one exception. Adult literacy data for some OECD countries, for which UIS estimates are not available, are based on the results of the 2003 European Labour Force Survey.

Only the 121 countries with a complete set of the indicators required to calculate the EDI are included in this analysis. Many countries are thus not included in the EDI. Coupled with the exclusion of goals 1 and 3, the EDI does not yet therefore provide a comprehensive global overview of overall progress towards the EFA goals.

Figure A1.3: Calculating 'transformed' GPIs

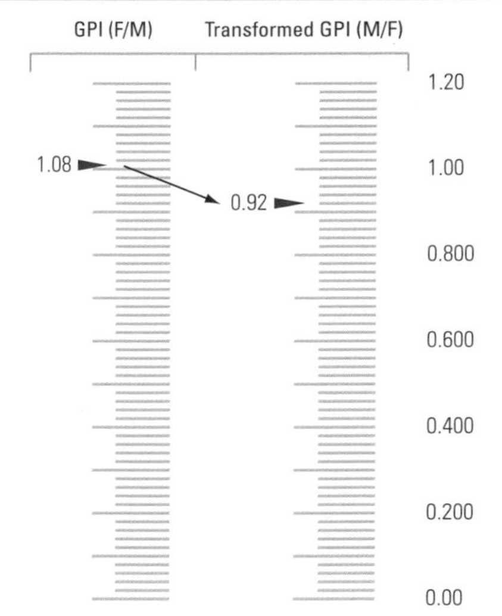

Figure A1.4: Calculating the GEI

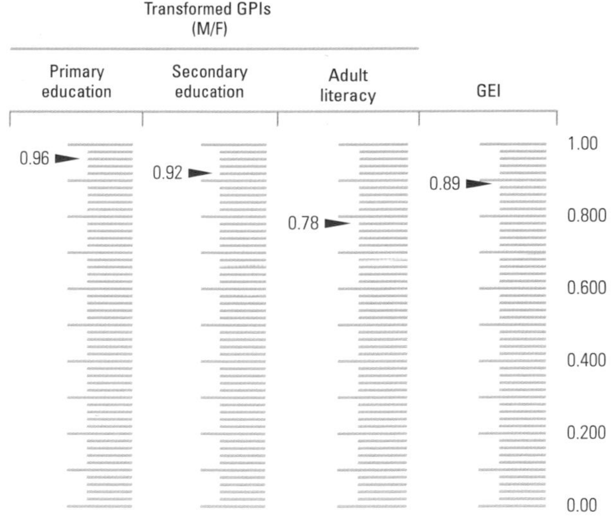

Figure A1.5: Calculating the EDI

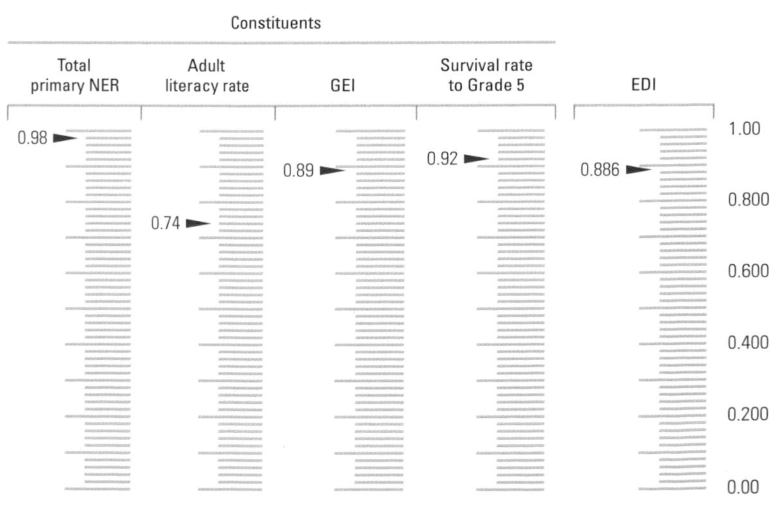

Table A1.1: The EFA Development Index and its components, 2002

Ranking according to level of EDI	Countries	EDI	Total primary NER[1]	Adult literacy rate	Gender-related EFA index (GEI)	Survival rate to Grade 5
High EDI						
1	Barbados	0.994	1.000	0.997	0.991	0.988
2	Norway	0.993	1.000	0.983	0.993	0.995
3	France	0.992	0.999	0.987	0.993	0.990
4	Switzerland	0.992	1.000	1.000	0.977	0.990
5	Finland	0.991	1.000	1.000	0.965	0.999
6	Republic of Korea	0.990	0.998	0.980	0.991	0.991
7	Belgium	0.989	1.000	1.000	0.965	0.990
8	Kazakhstan	0.989	0.982	0.995	0.996	0.982
9	Hungary	0.987	0.980	0.993	0.997	0.976
10	Estonia	0.984	0.976	0.998	0.977	0.984
11	Slovenia	0.983	0.954	0.997	0.995	0.989
12	Armenia	0.983	0.991	0.994	0.983	0.963
13	Cyprus	0.983	0.986	0.968	0.984	0.993
14	Poland	0.983	0.980	0.978	0.979	0.993
15	Spain	0.982	0.997	0.971	0.969	0.990
16	United Kingdom	0.980	1.000	0.997	0.932	0.990
17	Ireland	0.979	0.960	0.993	0.973	0.992
18	Denmark	0.979	1.000	0.950	0.976	0.990
19	Belarus	0.978	0.949	0.996	0.984	0.985
20	Croatia	0.978	0.951	0.981	0.985	0.996
21	Cuba	0.976	0.947	0.969	0.980	0.979
22	Lithuania	0.976	0.936	0.996	0.991	0.979
23	Seychelles	0.975	0.996	0.919	0.993	0.993
24	Italy	0.971	1.000	0.940	0.981	0.965
25	Serbia and Montenegro	0.970	0.979	0.964	0.980	0.956
26	Greece	0.970	1.000	0.910	0.978	0.990
27	Argentina	0.968	0.998	0.972	0.981	0.922
28	Kyrgyzstan	0.965	0.953	0.987	0.985	0.935
29	Samoa	0.965	0.975	0.987	0.959	0.938
30	Luxembourg	0.964	0.913	0.975	0.979	0.990
31	Latvia	0.961	0.877	0.997	0.991	0.978
32	Ukraine	0.958	0.858	0.994	0.995	0.986
33	Romania	0.957	0.921	0.973	0.981	0.952
34	Albania	0.957	0.949	0.987	0.992	0.900
35	Czech Republic	0.956	0.865	0.998	0.986	0.977
36	Bulgaria	0.956	0.923	0.982	0.980	0.939
37	Slovakia	0.956	0.855	0.996	0.992	0.979
38	China	0.954	0.957	0.909	0.959	0.990
39	Malta	0.954	0.961	0.879	0.982	0.993
40	TFYR Macedonia	0.952	0.908	0.961	0.980	0.959
41	Chile	0.952	0.865	0.957	0.985	0.999
42	Saint Lucia	0.950	0.998	0.901	0.935	0.966
43	Israel	0.950	0.993	0.969	0.984	0.852
44	Palestinian A.T.	0.950	0.948	0.919	0.952	0.979
Medium EDI						
45	Jordan	0.946	0.955	0.899	0.959	0.971
46	Mexico	0.946	0.994	0.903	0.957	0.930
47	Fiji	0.944	0.998	0.929	0.965	0.885
48	Panama	0.944	0.996	0.919	0.964	0.898
49	Mauritius	0.943	0.966	0.843	0.973	0.989
50	Uruguay	0.941	0.907	0.977	0.952	0.929
51	Portugal	0.938	1.000	0.842	0.922	0.990
52	Costa Rica	0.938	0.905	0.958	0.971	0.916
53	Azerbaijan	0.932	0.799	0.988	0.974	0.966
54	Guyana	0.930	0.992	0.987	0.971	0.772
55	Bahrain	0.930	0.909	0.877	0.944	0.991
56	Macao, China	[illegible]	0.873	0.913	0.928	0.997
57	Netherlands Antilles	0.927	0.889	0.967	0.968	[illegible]
58	Indonesia	0.923	0.968	0.879	0.956	0.891
59	Jamaica	0.923	0.954	0.876	0.963	0.897
60	Bahamas	0.921	0.998	0.956	0.980	0.752
61	Mongolia	0.916	0.822	0.978	0.946	0.920
62	Kuwait	0.914	0.884	0.829	0.969	0.975
63	Peru	0.911	0.997	0.877	0.935	0.836

Table A1.1 (continued)

Ranking according to level of EDI	Countries	EDI	Total primary NER[1]	Adult literacy rate	Gender-related EFA index (GEI)	Survival rate to Grade 5
Medium EDI						
64	Venezuela	0.911	0.926	0.930	0.947	0.842
65	Viet Nam	0.910	0.941	0.903	0.927	0.871
66	Republic of Moldova	0.910	0.790	0.962	0.977	0.911
67	Lebanon	0.909	0.926	0.869	0.923	0.919
68	Ecuador	0.908	0.995	0.910	0.984	0.744
69	Syrian Arab Republic	0.908	0.997	0.829	0.892	0.914
70	Malaysia	0.908	0.931	0.887	0.943	0.871
71	Brazil	0.905	0.983	0.884	0.954	0.799
72	Bolivia	0.904	0.965	0.865	0.940	0.844
73	Trinidad and Tobago	0.904	0.955	0.985	0.963	0.712
74	Philippines	0.898	0.943	0.926	0.964	0.760
75	Tunisia	0.895	0.984	0.743	0.891	0.962
76	Belize	0.888	0.992	0.769	0.975	0.815
77	United Arab Emirates	0.886	0.886	0.773	0.959	0.925
78	Namibia	0.883	0.784	0.850	0.949	0.947
79	Cape Verde	0.879	0.992	0.757	0.889	0.880
80	Algeria	0.877	0.969	0.698	0.872	0.970
81	Colombia	0.876	0.901	0.942	0.969	0.694
82	Iran, Islamic Republic of	0.874	0.863	0.770	0.917	0.946
83	Paraguay	0.870	0.899	0.916	0.970	0.697
84	Dominican Republic	0.865	0.964	0.877	0.928	0.691
85	Botswana	0.859	0.811	0.789	0.959	0.876
86	Oman	0.843	0.736	0.744	0.914	0.980
87	El Salvador	0.842	0.923	0.797	0.959	0.689
88	South Africa	0.840	0.937	0.824	0.952	0.648
89	Myanmar	0.834	0.842	0.897	0.951	0.646
90	Egypt	0.828	0.932	0.556	0.844	0.980
91	Nicaragua	0.817	0.908	0.767	0.947	0.648
92	Lesotho	0.817	0.862	0.814	0.861	0.730
93	Swaziland	0.810	0.756	0.792	0.961	0.732
Low EDI						
94	Saudi Arabia	0.789	0.560	0.794	0.887	0.915
95	Guatemala	0.782	0.886	0.691	0.900	0.652
96	Cambodia	0.761	0.935	0.736	0.765	0.609
97	Morocco	0.749	0.898	0.507	0.778	0.812
98	Zambia	0.748	0.699	0.679	0.848	0.767
99	Lao PDR	0.745	0.850	0.687	0.801	0.641
100	India	0.741	0.937	0.610	0.802	0.614
101	Kenya	0.731	0.676	0.736	0.923	0.590
102	Congo	0.717	0.540	0.828	0.837	0.663
103	Rwanda	0.715	0.870	0.640	0.883	0.466
104	Equatorial Guinea	0.689	0.850	0.842	0.770	0.295
105	Bangladesh	0.663	0.875	0.411	0.828	0.539
106	Ghana	0.662	0.639	0.541	0.835	0.633
107	Papua New Guinea	0.660	0.730	0.573	0.829	0.506
108	Côte d'Ivoire	0.659	0.617	0.481	0.663	0.876
109	Senegal	0.653	0.690	0.393	0.729	0.800
110	Burundi	0.653	0.575	0.589	0.771	0.675
111	Nepal	0.652	0.732	0.486	0.741	0.649
112	Eritrea	0.652	0.456	0.576	0.712	0.863
113	Mauritania	0.640	0.679	0.512	0.763	0.606
114	Djibouti	0.629	0.343	0.665	0.705	0.802
115	Yemen	0.622	0.723	0.490	0.518	0.759
116	Mozambique	0.543	0.553	0.465	0.661	0.492
117	Ethiopia	0.536	0.482	0.415	0.662	0.587
118	Mali	0.492	0.445	0.190	0.585	0.746
119	Niger	0.458	0.385	0.144	0.611	0.691
120	Burkina Faso	0.443	0.366	0.128	0.614	0.662
121	Chad	0.439	0.629	0.255	0.429	0.443

1. Total primary NER includes children of primary-school age who are enrolled in either primary or secondary school.

Note: Data in blue indicate that gender disparities are at the expense of boys or men, particularly at secondary education level.

Sources: Statistical annex, Tables 2A, 5, 7 and 8; UNESCO Institute for Statistics database; European Labour Force Survey 2003, for proxy literacy measure for European countries.

Table A1.2: Countries ranked according to value of EDI and components, 2002

Countries	EDI	Total primary NER[1]	Adult literacy rate	Gender-related EFA index (GEI)	Survival rate to Grade 5
Barbados	1	10	8	11	25
Norway	2	8	25	6	5
France	3	11	23	7	14
Switzerland	4	2	1	36	14
Finland	5	2	1	52	2
Republic of Korea	6	12	28	12	11
Belgium	7	2	1	50	14
Kazakhstan	8	32	13	2	29
Hungary	9	34	17	1	39
Estonia	10	36	4	37	28
Slovenia	11	49	9	3	24
Armenia	12	28	15	22	45
Cyprus	13	29	38	20	9
Poland	14	33	29	32	8
Spain	15	19	35	46	14
United Kingdom	16	9	7	80	14
Ireland	17	44	16	42	10
Denmark	18	1	46	38	14
Belarus	19	53	12	18	27
Croatia	20	51	27	16	4
Cuba	21	55	37	30	33
Lithuania	22	60	10	10	35
Seychelles	23	21	54	5	7
Italy	24	2	48	25	44
Serbia/Montenegro	25	35	40	27	48
Greece	26	2	57	34	14
Argentina	27	15	34	26	58
Kyrgyzstan	28	50	20	17	54
Samoa	29	37	21	62	53
Luxembourg	30	69	32	33	22
Latvia	31	82	6	13	36
Ukraine	32	90	14	4	26
Romania	33	68	33	24	49
Albania	34	52	19	9	65
Czech Republic	35	86	5	14	37
Bulgaria	36	67	26	29	52
Slovakia	37	91	11	8	34
China	38	45	59	59	13
Malta	39	43	68	23	6
TFYR. Macedonia	40	71	42	31	47
Chile	41	87	44	15	1
Saint Lucia	42	14	62	78	43
Israel	43	24	36	21	77
Palestinian A.T.	44	54	53	69	32
Jordan	45	47	63	58	40
Mexico	46	23	61	64	55
Fiji	47	16	50	51	70
Panama	48	20	52	54	66
Mauritius	49	40	76	41	23
Uruguay	50	73	31	67	56
Portugal	51	2	78	86	14
Costa Rica	52	74	43	43	61
Azerbaijan	53	97	18	40	42
Guyana	54	25	22	44	86
Bahrain	55	70	[illegible]	[illegible]	12
Macao, China	56	84	56	82	3
Netherlands Antilles	57	78	39	49	69
Indonesia	58	39	67	65	68
Jamaica	59	48	72	55	67
Bahamas	60	13	45	28	90
Mongolia	61	95	30	74	59
Kuwait	62	81	79	47	39
Peru	63	17	71	79	80
Venezuela	64	65	49	72	79
Viet Nam	65	57	60	83	75
Republic of Moldova	66	98	41	35	64
Lebanon	67	64	73	85	60
Ecuador	68	22	58	19	92
Syrian Arab Republic	69	18	80	90	63
Malaysia	70	63	65	76	74
Brazil	71	31	66	66	85
Bolivia	72	41	74	77	78
Trinidad and Tobago	73	46	24	56	95
Philippines	74	56	51	53	88
Tunisia	75	30	94	91	46
Belize	76	27	90	39	81
United Arab Emirates	77	79	88	61	57
Namibia	78	99	75	71	50
Cape Verde	79	26	92	92	71
Algeria	80	38	97	95	41
Colombia	81	75	47	48	97
Iran, Isl. Rep.	82	88	89	87	51
Paraguay	83	76	55	45	96
Dominican Republic	84	42	70	81	98
Botswana	85	96	87	63	73
Oman	86	101	93	88	31
El Salvador	87	66	84	60	100
South Africa	88	59	82	68	107
Myanmar	89	94	64	70	108
Egypt	90	62	107	98	30
Nicaragua	91	72	91	73	106
Lesotho	92	89	83	96	94
Swaziland	93	100	86	57	93
Saudi Arabia	94	113	85	93	62
Guatemala	95	80	98	89	104
Cambodia	96	61	96	108	112
Morocco	97	77	110	105	82
Zambia	98	105	100	97	87
Lao PDR	99	93	99	104	109
India	100	58	103	103	111
Kenya	101	108	95	84	114
Congo	102	115	81	99	102
Rwanda	103	85	102	94	119
Equatorial Guinea	104	92	77	107	121
Bangladesh	105	83	116	102	116
Ghana	106	109	108	100	110
Papua New Guinea	107	103	106	101	117
Côte d'Ivoire	108	111	113	114	72
Senegal	109	106	117	111	84
Burundi	110	112	104	106	101
Nepal	111	102	112	110	105
Eritrea	112	117	105	112	76
Mauritania	113	107	109	109	113
Djibouti	114	121	101	113	83
Yemen	115	104	111	120	89
Mozambique	116	114	114	116	118
Ethiopia	117	116	[illegible]	[illegible]	115
Mali	118	118	119	119	91
Niger	119	119	120	118	99
Burkina Faso	120	120	121	117	103
Chad	121	110	118	121	120

1. Total primary NER includes children of primary-school age who are enrolled in either primary or secondary school.

Sources: Statistical annex, Tables 2A, 5, 7 and 8; UNESCO Institute for Statistics database; European Labour Force Survey 2003.

Table A1.3: Change in EDI and its components between 1998 and 2002

	EFA Development Index		Variation	Change in the EDI constituents between 1998 and 2002 (% in relative terms)			
Countries	1998	2002	1998-2002	Total primary NER[1]	Adult literacy rate	Gender-related EFA index (GEI)	Survival rate to Grade 5
High EDI							
Barbados	0.979	0.994	1.6	0.3	0.1	1.1	5.0
Republic of Korea	0.976	0.990	1.5	5.8	0.6	0.5	-0.8
Estonia	0.991	0.984	-0.7	-2.4	0.0	0.1	-0.7
Cyprus	0.971	0.983	1.2	0.6	0.2	0.8	3.3
Croatia	0.977	0.978	0.1	0.0	0.1	0.4	-0.1
Cuba	0.967	0.976	1.0	-5.2	0.6	1.2	4.4
Lithuania	0.989	0.976	-1.3	-3.9	0.1	-0.1	-1.5
Italy	0.985	0.971	-1.3	0.0	-4.4	-0.9	-0.1
Samoa	0.936	0.965	3.1	0.5	0.2	-0.3	13.5
Latvia	0.969	0.961	-0.8	-5.4	0.0	1.0	0.9
Romania	0.980	0.957	-2.3	-7.8	-0.6	-0.2	-0.4
Bulgaria	0.967	0.956	-1.2	-5.5	0.0	-0.1	1.0
Chile	0.952	0.952	0.0	-1.6	0.3	1.0	0.1
Medium EDI							
Jordan	0.936	0.946	1.1	2.6	1.6	0.9	-0.6
Mexico	0.940	0.946	0.6	-0.2	-0.2	-1.4	4.5
Mauritius	0.934	0.943	1.0	3.6	0.8	0.1	-0.6
Guyana	0.979	0.930	-5.0	1.8	0.5	-1.5	-20.8
Bahrain	0.936	0.930	-0.7	-5.8	1.2	0.4	1.7
Mongolia	0.923	0.916	-0.7	-10.7	-0.6	3.2	5.5
Peru	0.927	0.911	-1.7	0.0	-1.5	-0.7	-4.8
Venezuela	0.907	0.911	0.5	6.0	1.2	2.1	-7.3
Viet Nam	0.909	0.910	0.1	-2.3	-2.0	0.2	5.1
Republic of Moldova	0.929	0.910	-2.0	1.0	-2.5	-1.5	-4.5
Lebanon	0.892	0.909	1.9	3.5	2.3	1.1	0.7
Ecuador	0.910	0.908	-0.2	1.0	0.2	0.7	-3.4
Syrian Arab Republic	0.858	0.908	5.8	3.9	14.1	7.5	-0.3
Bolivia	0.882	0.904	2.5	-0.6	2.9	2.2	6.3
Trinidad and Tobago	0.979	0.904	-7.7	-1.6	0.4	-0.3	-28.8
Tunisia	0.859	0.895	4.1	4.0	8.5	0.6	4.4
Belize	0.906	0.888	-2.0	3.5	-17.0	1.3	4.8
United Arab Emirates	0.857	0.886	3.4	10.0	3.0	1.2	0.2
Namibia	0.841	0.883	5.0	0.5	5.5	0.6	13.5
Colombia	0.849	0.876	3.2	0.7	3.4	1.3	9.4
Paraguay	0.879	0.870	-1.0	-2.4	-1.2	0.1	-0.5
Dominican Republic	0.850	0.865	1.8	7.4	5.8	0.7	-7.9
Botswana	0.841	0.859	2.1	2.9	4.7	1.2	0.1
Oman	0.824	0.843	2.4	-5.2	8.7	1.8	4.5
El Salvador	0.792	0.842	6.3	13.0	2.7	-0.5	12.4
South Africa	0.878	0.840	-4.3	-2.4	-2.4	0.5	-14.7
Lesotho	0.740	0.817	10.3	33.6	-1.3	7.3	6.0
Swaziland	0.814	0.810	-0.5	9.5	1.4	-0.9	-10.2
Low EDI							
Saudi Arabia	0.785	0.789	0.5	-2.2	7.0	1.7	-4.0
Guatemala	0.730	0.782	7.1	14.2	3.0	3.4	7.9
Cambodia	0.687	0.761	10.8	13.2	10.6	10.1	8.3
Morocco	0.686	0.749	9.1	22.3	8.1	7.6	-0.7
Zambia	0.768	0.748	-2.5	1.6	-11.0	1.2	-1.9
Lao PDR	0.680	0.745	9.6	6.0	8.8	8.0	18.0
Bangladesh	0.664	0.663	-0.2	-0.6	5.7	-1.6	-1.5
Papua New Guinea	0.718	0.660	-8.2	-2.3	-8.2	0.8	-25.6
Côte d'Ivoire	0.588	0.659	12.2	9.4	3.2	5.4	26.8
Eritrea	0.640	0.652	1.9	33.5	6.8	-1.7	-9.5
Mauritania	0.605	0.640	5.8	8.3	30.6	1.9	-7.1
Djibouti	0.603	0.629	4.3	9.0	6.7	-0.2	4.5
Mozambique	0.484	0.543	12.2	16.8	11.4	5.5	17.7
Ethiopia	0.482	0.536	11.4	32.7	12.6	3.9	5.3
Mali	0.492	0.492	-0.1	15.2	-21.3	4.9	-4.7
Burkina Faso	0.450	0.443	-1.7	9.1	-42.2	9.4	-3.0
Chad	0.496	0.439	-11.3	15.0	-35.2	-12.4	-19.6

1. Total primary NER includes children of primary-school age who are enrolled in either primary or secondary school.

Sources: Statistical annex, Tables 2A, 5, 7 and 8; UNESCO Institute for Statistics database; European Labour Force Survey 2003, for proxy literacy measure for European countries.

Appendix 2
Prospects for the achievement of Education for All by 2015: methodology

Chapter 2 includes projections to 2015 for three of the six EFA goals: UPE, gender parity and adult literacy. National prospects of reaching each of the three goals are based on trend projections of enrolment and adult literacy rates.

Projection methodology for UPE and gender parity

Prospects for achievement of these two EFA goals are based on extrapolation into the future of trends in enrolment ratios between 1990 and 2002 (for further details, see Bayou et al., 2005). Particular emphasis was given to trends during the most recent period, 1998-2002, which provide a picture of the possible effects of education policies implemented since the Dakar forum in 2000. These projections do not aim or claim to forecast enrolment rates, but only to show how the rates would change in the future if past trends were to continue. The projections do not, therefore, take account of recently implemented policy changes that may affect enrolments but have not yet done so. Despite this limitation, trend projections are useful as an analysis and monitoring tool and as a baseline to reflect on educational policy changes that may be needed for countries to achieve the various EFA goals.

In general, only countries that have a sufficiently complete set of data and that have not yet achieved UPE and primary- and secondary-school gender parity goals were included in the projections, that is, 90 for the first goal and 150 for the second one.

Projecting net enrolment ratios

The NER is one of the two most relevant indicators widely used to measure progress towards UPE, the other being the completion rate. The decision was made to base the projections on the total primary-school-age NER (N1), which takes into account all children of primary-school age enrolled either in primary (N1P) or secondary (N1S) school. As primary-school-age children enrolled in secondary school have, by definition, already attended primary school, including them takes fuller account of the reality of UPE than does the primary education NER.

Total primary-school-age children NERs (N1) were projected separately for each sex using the logistic function, particularly when rates were rising. The choice of this method is based on the very nature of the rates, which tend towards a natural maximum of 100%, which they should not exceed. In addition, their marginal rate of increase falls as a country approaches the 100% limit of UPE. For countries in which rates were decreasing, the projections employed a linear regression in order to keep projected rates from falling to unrealistically low levels, as might have happened had the logistic function been used.

Once N1 was projected, projections of N1P and N1S were calculated, based on their respective shares in N1 in 2002.

Projecting the gender parity index in primary and secondary education

Achievement of gender parity is defined as having reached a GPI value between 0.97 and 1.03 (Chapter 2). The 3% tolerance is to allow for statistical measurement errors and does not imply any judgement about the acceptability of any particular level of disparity (UNESCO, 2003).

Country prospects for the achievement of gender parity are assessed on the basis of trend projections of GERs in primary and secondary education, by gender, for 2005 and 2015. Projected primary GERs by gender are reconstructed, based on the N1P projections by sex. As the GER/N1P ratio was fairly constant between 1990 and 2002 for most of the countries, it was not projected, so the 2002 ratio was used for 2015 as well.

Primary $GER_{2015} = N1P_{2015} * (GER_{2002}/N1P_{2002})$.

Once the GER by gender is projected, the projected GPI is calculated as the ratio of the girls' rate to that for boys.

GERs by gender for secondary education are projected directly using a linear regression.

Projection methodology for adult literacy

Adult literacy rates in 2015 are projected using a standard demographic projection methodology – the cohort-component method and its extension to multi-state projections. In other words, future proportions of literates are derived largely from the current age distribution of literacy in the population, together with explicit assumptions concerning the transition rates to literacy for the youngest cohorts. Two important principles of this demographic approach are (a) the explicit consideration of the population by age, sex and literacy status at different points in time; and (b) the clear distinction between stocks (people who are literate) and flows (transitions from illiterate to literate states).

More specifically, projections of adult literacy rates are based on a trend scenario which assumes that future transition rates to literacy will increase at the same rate as in the past, i.e. the increase in the proportion of literates from higher to younger age groups is taken as a proxy for the increase in transition rates over time. Extrapolations were made of trends in proportions of literates (separately for men and women) only for the age groups 25–29, 20–24 and 15–19 in 2000, as older age groups would not reflect the effect of recent policy changes.

Figure A2.1 illustrates this, based on a logarithmic extrapolation that results in proportions of literates in the age group 15–19 over the five-year periods 2000–2005, 2005–2010 and 2010–2015. The result of the projection is a full age pyramid (starting at age 15) giving the literate and illiterate populations by five-year age groups and sex up to 2015.

Prospect analysis for achievement of the goals

The methodology used to assess countries' chances of achieving the three EFA goals takes into account two dimensions, one static and one dynamic. The first represents a country's current situation: it may have reached a goal, or be close to or far from it. Each country is also moving

Figure A2.1. Proportion of literates in age group 15–19 up to 2015

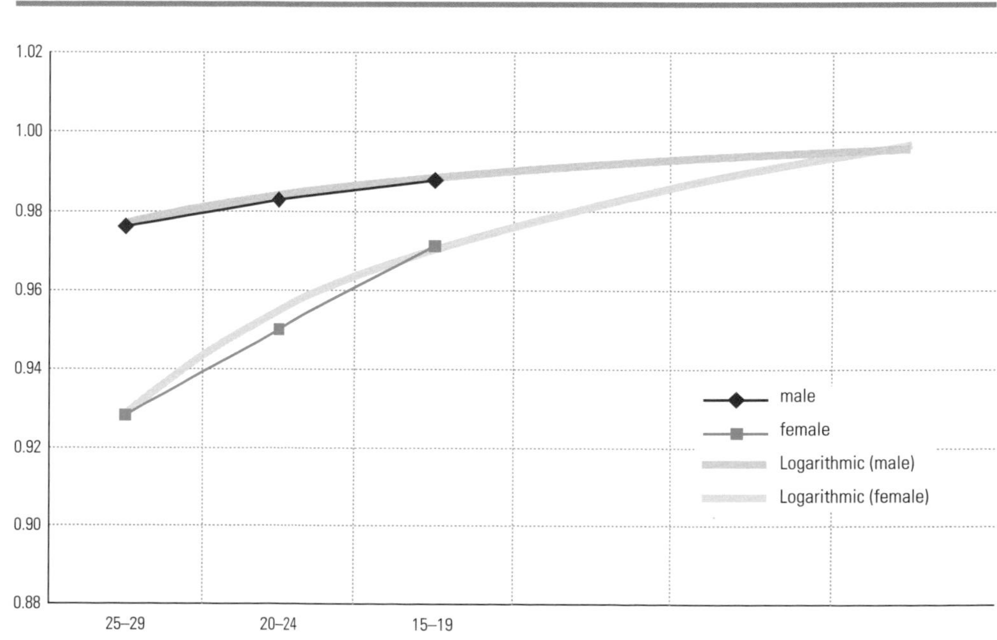

Source: Lutz and Goujon (2005).

towards or away from the goal – the dynamic dimension. The two dimensions are integrated and compared on the basis of explicit criteria, forming a matrix containing four quadrants (Table A2.1).

Countries that have already achieved a particular goal are not included in the matrix for that goal, with the exception of the gender parity goal (see Table 2.10), which has two target dates: 2005 and 2015.

The quadrant also shows a country's chance of achieving a goal by the target date set in Dakar. Thus, quadrant II, labelled 'High chance of achieving the goal', includes countries currently either close to the goal or not yet there but moving towards it. Quadrant III contains countries that have a low chance of achieving a goal because of their current position far from the goal, but that are nonetheless moving towards it. Other countries far from the goal, but moving in the wrong direction (away from it), are in quadrant IV, labelled 'Serious risk of not achieving the goal'. Finally, quadrant I comprises countries that, though close to the goal, are moving away from it and are therefore at risk of not achieving it.

For the adult literacy goal, a slightly different methodology was used to determine the dynamic dimension in the quadrants. As almost all countries reduced their adult illiteracy rates from 1990 to 2000-2004, there was no point in distinguishing between movements towards or away from the goal. This is all the more the case because the target for 2015 – halving the illiteracy rate – varies in quantitative terms from country to country according to its rate in 2000.

For example, a country with a literacy rate of 70% in 2000 would have as the target for 2015 a rate of 85%; one with an initial rate of 80% would have a target of 90% to reach by 2015, and so on. The *rate* of progress is thus used as a criterion for the dynamic dimension in this analysis. On the basis of their current literacy levels, countries progressing rapidly enough to reach the target in 2015 are considered 'fast performers', while those at risk or serious risk of not achieving the target, given their current pace, are labelled 'slow performers'.

Table A2.1: Analytical framework

Distance from the goal in 2002			
	Close	**QUADRANT I** At risk of not achieving the goal Countries close to the goal but moving away from it	**QUADRANT II** High chance of achieving the goal Countries close to the goal and moving towards it
	Far	**QUADRANT IV** Serious risk of not achieving the goal Countries far from the goal and moving away from it	**QUADRANT III** Low chance of achieving the goal Countries far from the goal but moving towards it
		Away from the goal	**Towards the goal**
		Change over the period from 1990 to 2002	

Statistical annex

Introduction

The most recent data on pupils, students, teachers and expenditure presented in these statistical tables refer to the school year 2002/2003. They are based on survey results reported to and processed by the UNESCO Institute for Statistics (UIS) before the end of May 2005. Data received after this date will be used in the next *EFA Global Monitoring Report*. A small number of countries (Chile, Djibouti, Ethiopia, Ghana, Republic of Korea, Sri Lanka, Thailand, United Republic of Tanzania, Zimbabwe) have submitted data for more recent years that are presented in bold in the statistical tables. These statistics refer to all formal schools, both public and private, by level of education. They are supplemented by demographic and economic statistics collected or produced by other international organizations, including the United Nations Development Programme (UNDP), the United Nations Population Division (UNPD) and the World Bank.

A total of 203 countries and territories are listed in the statistical tables. Most of them report their data to UIS using standard questionnaires issued by the institute. For some countries, however, education data are collected via surveys carried out under the auspices of the World Education Indicators (WEI) project funded by the World Bank, or are provided by the Organisation for Economic Co-operation and Development (OECD) and the Statistical Office of the European Communities (Eurostat).

Population

The indicators on access and participation in the statistical tables were calculated using the population estimates produced by the United Nations Population Division, in its 2002 revision. Thus, because of possible differences between national population estimates and those of the United Nations, these indicators may differ from those published by individual countries or by other organizations. UNPD does not provide data by single year of age for countries with a total population of less than 80,000. Where no UNPD estimates exist, national population, when available, was used to calculate enrolment ratios.

ISCED classification

Education data reported to UIS are in conformity with the 1997 revision of the International Standard Classification of Education (ISCED). In some cases, data have been adjusted to comply with the ISCED97 classification. Data for 1990/1991 may conform to the previous version of the classification, ISCED76, and therefore may not be comparable in some countries to those for years after 1997. ISCED is used to harmonize data and introduce more international comparability among national education systems. Countries may have their own definitions of education levels that do not correspond to ISCED, however, some differences between nationally and internationally reported enrolment ratios may be due to the use of nationally defined education levels rather than the ISCED standard, in addition to the population issue raised above.

Adult participation in basic education

ISCED does not classify education programmes by participants' age. For example, any programme with a content equivalent to primary education, or ISCED 1, may be classed as ISCED 1 even if provided to adults. However, the guidance provided by UIS for respondents to the regular annual education survey asks countries to exclude 'data on programmes designed for people beyond regular school age'. On the other hand, the guidance for UNESCO/OECD/Eurostat (UOE) and WEI questionnaires states that 'activities classified as "continuing", "adult" or "non-formal" education should be included' if they 'involve studies with subject content similar to regular educational programmes' or if 'the underlying programmes lead to similar potential qualifications' as do the regular programmes.

As a result of these distinctions, data from WEI countries and those for which statistics are collected via the UOE questionnaires, particularly concerning secondary education, may include programmes for older students. Despite the UIS instructions, data from countries in the regular UIS survey may also include pupils who are substantially above the official age for basic education.

Literacy data

UNESCO has long defined literacy as the ability to read and write, with understanding, a short simple statement related to one's daily life.

In many cases, the UIS current literacy statistics rely on this definition and are largely based on the 'self-declaration' method: respondents are asked to say whether they are literate or not, as opposed to being asked a more comprehensive question or to demonstrate the skill. Some countries assume that children who complete a certain level of schooling are literate. As definitions and methodologies used for data collection differ by country, data need to be used with caution.

Literacy data in this report cover adults of 15 years and over as well as youth of 15–24 years. They refer to 1990, 2000-2004 and 2015:

1) 1990 data represent the UIS estimates used in earlier EFA reports, rebased to the 2002 UN population revision. The UIS estimation methodology can be reviewed at the UIS website (www.uis.unesco.org).

2) 2000–2004 data are derived from the May 2005 UIS Literacy Assessment, which uses directly reported national figures together with UIS estimates. National literacy estimates are published in the statistical tables when available. They were obtained from national censuses or surveys taken between 1995 and 2004; the reference year and literacy definition for each country are presented after this introduction. Figures dated before 2000 will be replaced as soon as UIS gets more recent national estimates. For countries that did not report literacy data for the most recent year available during the 2000–2004 reference period, the tables publish UIS estimates for 2002, generated in July 2002 and based on national data collected before 1995. All literacy figures were rebased to the 2002 UN population revision.

3) Projections to 2015 data were produced using empirical information on national literate/illiterate population provided by countries. The description of the projection methodology is provided on page 261 in Appendix 2.

In many countries, there is growing interest in assessing the literacy skills of the population. In response to this need, UIS is developing a new methodology and data collection instrument called the Literacy Assessment and Monitoring Programme (LAMP). Following the example of the International Adult Assessment Survey, LAMP is based on actual, functional assessment of literacy skills. It aims to provide literacy data of higher quality and in line with the concept of a continuum of literacy skills rather than the common literate/illiterate dichotomy.

Estimates and missing data

Both actual and estimated data are presented throughout the statistical tables. When data are not reported to UIS using the standard questionnaires, estimates are often necessary. Wherever possible, UIS encourages countries to make their own estimates, which are presented as national estimates. Where this does not happen, UIS may make its own estimates if sufficient supplementary information is available.

Gaps in the tables may also arise where data submitted by a country are found to be inconsistent. UIS makes every attempt to resolve such problems with the countries concerned, but reserves the final decision to omit data it regards as problematic.

To fill the gaps in the annex tables, data for previous school years were included when information for 2002/2003 was not available. Such cases are indicated by footnote.

Data processing timetable

The timetable for collection and publication of data used in this report was as follows.

■ June 2003: the final school year in the data collection period ended.

■ November 2003 for UIS and May 2004 for UOE and WEI: questionnaires were sent to countries asking for data submission, with deadlines of 31 March 2004, 30 September 2004 and 1 August 2004, respectively.

■ June 2004: after sending reminders by e-mail, fax and post, UIS began to process data and calculate indicators.

■ December 2004: provisional statistical tables were produced and draft indicators sent to member states.

■ February 2005: the first draft tables were produced for the *EFA Global Monitoring Report*.

■ April 2005: the final statistical tables were sent to the *EFA Global Monitoring Report* team.

Regional averages

Regional figures for gross and net enrolment ratios, and school life expectancy, are overall weighted averages, taking into account the relative size of the school-age population of each country in each region. The averages are derived from both published data and broad estimates for countries for which no reliable data are available. The figures for the countries with higher population thus have a proportionately greater influence on the regional aggregates. Where not enough reliable data are available to produce an overall weighted mean, a median figure is calculated for countries with available data in the statistical tables.

Capped figures

There are cases where an indicator theoretically should not exceed 100 (the net enrolment ratio, for example), but data inconsistencies may have resulted nonetheless in the indicator exceeding the theoretical limit. In those cases the indicator is 'capped' at 100 but the gender balance is maintained (the highest value, whether for male or female, is set equal to 100 and the other two indicators are then recalculated) so that the gender parity index for the capped figures is the same as that for the uncapped figures.

Footnotes to the tables, along with the glossary following the statistical tables, provide additional help in interpreting the data and information.

Symbols used in this annex

* National estimate

** UIS estimate

... Missing data

– Magnitude nil or negligible

. Category not applicable

./. Data included under another category

o Countries whose education data are collected through UOE questionnaires

w World Education Indicators (WEI) project countries

Composition of regions

World classification

■ Countries in transition:
Countries of the Commonwealth of Independent States, including 4 in Central and Eastern Europe (Belarus, Republic of Moldova, Russian Federation, Ukraine) and the countries of Central Asia (minus Mongolia).

■ Developed countries:
North America and Western Europe (minus Cyprus and Israel); Central and Eastern Europe (minus Belarus, Republic of Moldova, Russian Federation, Ukraine and Turkey); Australia, Bermuda, Japan and New Zealand.

■ Developing countries:
Arab States; East Asia and the Pacific (minus Australia, Japan and New Zealand); Latin America and the Caribbean (minus Bermuda); South and West Asia; sub-Saharan Africa; Cyprus, Israel, Mongolia and Turkey.

EFA regions

■ Arab States (20 countries/territories)
Algeria, Bahrain, Djibouti, Egypt[W], Iraq, Jordan[W], Kuwait, Lebanon, Libyan Arab Jamahiriya, Mauritania, Morocco, Oman, Palestinian Autonomous Territories, Qatar, Saudi Arabia, Sudan, Syrian Arab Republic, Tunisia[W], United Arab Emirates, Yemen.

■ Central and Eastern Europe (20 countries)
Albania[O], Belarus, Bosnia and Herzegovina[O], Bulgaria[O], Croatia, Czech Republic[O], Estonia[O], Hungary[O], Latvia[O], Lithuania[O], Poland[O], Republic of Moldova, Romania[O], Russian Federation[W], Serbia and Montenegro, Slovakia, Slovenia[O], The former Yugoslav Republic of Macedonia[O], Turkey[O], Ukraine.

■ Central Asia (9 countries)
Armenia, Azerbaijan, Georgia, Kazakhstan, Kyrgyzstan, Mongolia, Tajikistan, Turkmenistan, Uzbekistan.

■ East Asia and the Pacific
(33 countries/territories)
Australia[O], Brunei Darussalam, Cambodia, China[W], Cook Islands, Democratic People's Republic of Korea, Fiji, Indonesia, Japan[O], Kiribati, Lao People's Democratic Republic, Macao (China), Malaysia[W], Marshall Islands, Micronesia (Federated States of), Myanmar, Nauru, New Zealand[O], Niue, Palau, Papua New Guinea, Philippines[W], Republic of Korea[O], Samoa, Singapore, Solomon Islands, Thailand[W], Timor-Leste, Tokelau, Tonga, Tuvalu, Vanuatu, Viet Nam.

■ Latin America and the Caribbean
(41 countries/territories)
Anguilla, Antigua and Barbuda, Argentina[W], Aruba, Bahamas, Barbados, Belize, Bermuda, Bolivia, Brazil[W], British Virgin Islands, Cayman Islands, Chile[W], Colombia, Costa Rica, Cuba, Dominica, Dominican Republic, Ecuador, El Salvador, Grenada, Guatemala, Guyana, Haiti, Honduras, Jamaica[W], Mexico[O], Montserrat, Netherlands Antilles, Nicaragua, Panama, Paraguay[W], Peru[W], Saint Kitts and Nevis, Saint Lucia, Saint Vincent and the Grenadines, Suriname, Trinidad and Tobago, Turks and Caicos Islands, Uruguay[W], Venezuela.

■ North America and Western Europe
(26 countries)
Andorra, Austria[O], Belgium[O], Canada[O], Cyprus[O], Denmark[O], Finland[O], France[O], Germany[O], Greece[O], Iceland[O], Ireland[O], Israel[O], Italy[O], Luxembourg[O], Malta[O], Monaco, Netherlands[O], Norway[O], Portugal[O], San Marino, Spain[O], Sweden[O], Switzerland[O], United Kingdom[O], United States[O].

■ South and West Asia (9 countries)
Afghanistan, Bangladesh, Bhutan, India[W], Islamic Republic of Iran, Maldives, Nepal, Pakistan, Sri Lanka[W].

■ Sub-Saharan Africa (45 countries)
Angola, Benin, Botswana, Burkina Faso, Burundi, Cameroon, Cape Verde, Central African Republic, Chad, Comoros, Congo, Côte d'Ivoire, Democratic Republic of the Congo, Equatorial Guinea, Eritrea, Ethiopia, Gabon, Gambia, Ghana, Guinea, Guinea-Bissau, Kenya, Lesotho, Liberia, Madagascar, Malawi, Mali, Mauritius, Mozambique, Namibia, Niger, Nigeria, Rwanda, Sao Tome and Principe, Senegal, Seychelles, Sierra Leone, Somalia, South Africa, Swaziland, Togo, Uganda, United Republic of Tanzania, Zambia, Zimbabwe[W].

Metadata for national literacy data

Year	Country	Data source	Literacy definition	Mode
2001	Albania	Population Census	Literate is a person who acquires the capacities of reading and writing by himself and never attends any kind of educational programme. Is also considered literate a person who acquires those capacities from schooling, literacy programmes.	Household declaration
2002	Algeria	Health Survey	The capacity to read and write.	Self declaration
2001	Angola	MICS	Literacy is defined as the ability to read easily or with difficulty a letter or a newspaper.	Self declaration
2001	Argentina	Population Census	Literate is a person who can read and write in spanish.	Household declaration
2001	Armenia	Population Census	Corresponds to those individuals aged 7 years old and higher who can read and understand it, in any language.	Household declaration
1999	Azerbaijan	Population Census	Literates are persons who can read and write, understanding the text. Literacy is acceptable to any language having written form.	Household declaration
2001	Bahrain	Population Census	Persons who cannot read or write, as well as persons who can read only, for example a person who studied Qur'an.	Household declaration
1999	Belarus	Population Census	Persons who could not read and write were referred to the category of illiterate.	Household declaration
2000	Belize	Population Census	Illiterate: Persons who are 14+ years of age and have completed at most 7 or 8 years of primary education.	Educational attainment proxy
2002	Benin	Population Census	The ability to read and write with understanding in any language.	Household declaration
2001	Bolivia	Population Census	Percentage of people aged 15 years and over who know how to read and write.	Household declaration
2000	Bosnia & Herzegovina	MICS	Literacy is defined as the ability to read easily or with difficulty a letter or a newspaper.	Self declaration
2003	Brazil	Household Survey	A person who can both read and write at least a simple statement in a language he or she knows.	Self declaration
2001	Brunei Darussalam	Population Census	The ability of a person to read and write a simple letter or to read a newspaper column in one or two languages.	Household declaration
2001	Bulgaria	Population Census	Persons who can read and write.	Household declaration
1996	Burkina Faso	Population Census	Literates are persons who declare that they can read and write in either a national language or a foreign language.	Household declaration
2000	Burundi	MICS	Literacy is defined as the ability to read easily or with difficulty a letter or a newspaper.	Self declaration
2004	Cambodia	Inter-censual population survey	The ability to read and write with understanding in any language. A person is literate when he can read and write a simple message in any language or dialect. A person who both cannot read and write a simple message is considered illiterate. Also to be considered illiterate is that person who is capable of reading only his own name or number, as well as persons who can read but not write. Children aged 0-9 were treated as illiterate by definition even if a few of them could read and write.	Self declaration
2001	Cameroon	Second Household Survey (Deuxième Enquête auprès des Ménages – ECAMII)	Literacy is the ability of people aged 15+ to read and write in French or in English.	Self declaration
2000	Central African Republic	MICS	Literacy is defined as the ability to read easily or with difficulty a letter or a newspaper.	Self declaration
2000	Chad	MICS	Literacy is defined as the ability to read easily or with difficulty a letter or a newspaper.	Self declaration
2002	Chile	Population Census	m	m
2000	China	Population Census	In urban areas: literate refers to a person who knows a minimum of 2,000 characters. In rural areas: literate refers to a person who knows a minimum of 1,500 characters.	Household declaration

(Continued)

Year	Country	Data source	Literacy definition	Mode
2003	Colombia	Household Survey	The capacity to read and write.	Self declaration
2000	Cote d'Ivoire	MICS	Literacy is defined as the ability to read easily or with difficulty a letter or a newspaper.	Self declaration
2001	Croatia	Population Census	A literate person is any person with or without schooling, who is able to read and write a composition concerning everyday life, that is, who is able to read and write a letter, irrespective of the language or scripture he or she reads or writes in.	Household declaration
2002	Cuba	Population Census	Literate is a person capable to read and write at least a simple text related to facts of everyday life. Illiterate is a person who does not fulfill the previous definition and who is therefore unable to either read or write a simple text related to facts of everyday life.	Household declaration
2001	Cyprus	Population Census	Persons who can read and write simple sentences.	Household declaration
2001	Democratic Republic of Congo	MICS	Literacy is defined as the ability to read easily or with difficulty a letter or a newspaper.	Self declaration
2002	Dominican Republic	Population Census	Literate is a person who can read and write.	Household declaration
2001	Ecuador	Population Census	The capacity to read and write.	Household declaration
1996	Egypt	Population Census	Literates are persons who can read and write.	Household declaration
2000	Equatorial Guinea	MICS	Literacy is defined as the ability to read easily or with difficulty a letter or a newspaper.	Self declaration
2000	Estonia	Population Census	"No primary education, illiterate" was recorded for a person who had not completed the level corresponding to primary education and cannot, with understanding, both read and write a simple text on his/her everyday life at least in one language.	Educational attainment proxy
1996	Fiji	Population Census	m	m
2000	Ghana	Population Census	m	m
2003	Greece	Labour Force Survey	As illiterate are considered those who have never been in school (organic illiterate) as well as those who have not finished the six years of primary education (functional illiterate).	Educational attainment proxy
2002	Guatemala	Population Census	Literate: a person who can read and write in a specific language. This capacity includes persons who are 7 years and over.	Household declaration
2001	Honduras	Population Census	Literate refers to those who can read and write.	Household declaration
2001	Hungary	Population Census	Persons not having completed the first grade of general (primary, elementary) school, have been considered as illiterate.	Educational attainment proxy
2001	India	Population Census	A person aged 7 and above who can both read and write with understanding in any language.	Household declaration
2002	Iran, Islamic Rep. of	Household Survey	Literate is an individual who can read and write a simple sentence in Farsi or any other language.	Self declaration
2003	Israel	Labour Force Survey	Population having at least primary schooling.	Educational attainment proxy
2003	Jordan	Household Expenditure & Income survey	Persons aged 15 years and above who can read and write in any language.	Self declaration
1999	Kazakhstan	Population Census	m	m
2000	Kenya	MICS	Literacy is defined as the ability to read easily or with difficulty a letter or a newspaper.	Self declaration
1999	Kyrgyzstan	Population Census	m	m
2001	Lao PDR	National Literacy Survey	A literate person was defined as a person who can read, write and understand simple sentences in Lao, and perform simple arithmetic calculations (numeracy). All household members aged 6 and above were asked whether they can read, write and perform simple calculations.	Self declaration

(Continued)

Year	Country	Data source	Literacy definition	Mode
2000	Latvia	Population Census	Literate is a person who is able to read and write.	Household declaration
2001	Lesotho	Demographic Survey	Literates are persons who can read and write.	Self declaration
2001	Lithuania	Population Census	Literate (no formal schooling) is a person who does not attend school but can read (with understanding) and/or write a simple sentence on topics of everyday life.	Household declaration
2001	Macao, China	Population Census	A person is defined as literate if he/she can, with understanding, both read or write a short, simple statement on his/her everyday life.	Household declaration
2000	Madagascar	MICS	Literacy is defined as the ability to read easily or with difficulty a letter or a newspaper.	Self declaration
1998	Malawi	Population Census	The ability of an individual to read and write a simple statement in Chichewa, English or any other language.	Household declaration
2000	Malaysia	Population Census	Population, 10 years and over who have been to school in any language.	Household declaration (school attendance)
2000	Maldives	Population Census	Literate is a person who can read and write with understanding in any language: Maldivian language (Dhivehi), English, Arabic etc.	Household declaration
1998	Mali	Population Census	Illiterate is a person who never attend school even if that person can read and write.	Household declaration (school attendance)
1995	Malta	Population Census	Literacy is defined as the ability both to read and to write. A person, who can, with understanding, both read and write a short, simple statement on his everyday life is literate. A person who cannot, with understanding, both read and write a short, simple statement on his everyday life is illiterate.	Household declaration
2000	Mauritania	Population Census	All persons who are able to read and write in the language specified.	Household declaration
2000	Mauritius	Population Census	A person was considered as literate if he or she was able with understanding to both read and write a simple statement in his/her everyday life.	Household declaration
2002	Mexico	Household Survey	Literate is a household member who has the ability to read and write a message in Spanish.	Self declaration
2000	Mongolia	Population Census	Individuals who are not educated, but are able to read and write and understand short, simple statements in Mongolian or any other language are considered as literate.	Household declaration
2000	Myanmar	MICS	Literacy is defined as the ability to read easily or with difficulty a letter or a newspaper.	Self declaration
2001	Namibia	Population Census	The ability to write with understanding in any language. Persons who could read and not write were classified as non-literate. Similarly, persons who were able to write and not read were classified as non-literate.	Household declaration
2001	Nepal	Population Census	m	m
2001	Nicaragua	National Survey	Literate is a person who can read and write; illiterate is a person who can only read or who cannot read and write.	Self declaration
2001	Niger	Population Census	A person is literate when he/she can, with understanding, read and write a simple text (in French, Arabic or any other language), on everyday life.	Household declaration
2004	Pakistan	Labour Force Survey	Persons 10 years and older who can read and write in any language with understanding is called literate.	Self declaration
2003	Palestinian Autonomous Territories	Household Survey	Literate is a person who is able to read and write in any language.	Self declaration
2000	Panama	Population Census	m	m

(Continued)

Year	Country	Data source	Literacy definition	Mode
2000	Papua New Guinea	Population Census	The definition of literacy: those who have the ability to read and write a language with understanding.	Household declaration
2001	Paraguay	Household Survey	Illiterates are defined as people aged 15+ who have not attained grade 2 of education.	Educational attainment proxy
2004	Peru	Household Survey	m	m
2000	Philippines	Population Census	In Census 2000: Simple literacy is the ability to read and write a simple message. A person is literate when he can both read and write a simple message in any language or dialect. A person who knows how to read and write but at the time of the census, he/she can no longer read and/or write due to some physical defects or illness, is considered literate. Disabled persons who can read and write through any means such as Braille are considered literate.	Household declaration
2004	Qatar	Household Survey	m	m
2000	Republic of Moldova	MICS	Literacy is defined as the ability to read easily or with difficulty a letter or a newspaper.	Self declaration
2002	Romania	Population Census	Literates: primary level + secondary level+ post-secondary level+ people who read and write. Illiterates: people who read but cannot write + people who can neither read nor write.	Educational attainment proxy
2002	Russian Federation	Population Census	Persons indicated that they could neither read nor write and were referred to as illiterate.	Household declaration
2000	Rwanda	MICS	Literacy is defined as the ability to read easily or with difficulty a letter or a newspaper.	Self declaration
2001	Saint Lucia	Population Census	The data submitted was based on 7 years of schooling, no question was asked on literacy.	Educational attainment proxy
2000	Saudi Arabia	Household Survey	A person is considered literate if he/she can read and write in any language. A blind person is considered literate if he/she can read and write with so called 'Braille' method.	Household declaration
2002	Senegal	Household Survey	Literate: persons who are able to read and write in any language.	Self declaration
2002	Serbia Montenegro	Population Census	m	m
2003	Seychelles	Population Census	A person aged 12 or more who can read and write a simple sentence in any language.	Household declaration
2000	Sierra Leone	MICS	Literacy is defined as the ability to read easily or with difficulty a letter or a newspaper.	Self declaration
2000	Singapore	Population Census	Literacy refers to a person's ability to read with understanding, eg a newspaper, in the language specified.	Household declaration
2001	Slovakia	Population Census	Data on the number of persons who do not have formal education.	Educational attainment proxy
1996	South Africa	Population Census	m	m
2001	Sri Lanka	Population Census	The census schedule provided for recording the ability to speak, read and write Sinhalese, Tamil and English. A person was regarded as able to read and write a language only if he could both read with understanding and write a short letter or paragraph in that language. A person who is able to read and write at least one language was regarded as literate.	Household declaration
2000	Sudan	MICS	Literacy is defined as the ability to read easily or with difficulty a letter or a newspaper.	Self declaration
2000	Suriname	MICS	Literacy is defined as the ability to read easily or with difficulty a letter or a newspaper.	Self declaration

(Continued)

Year	Country	Data source	Literacy definition	Mode
2000	Swaziland	MICS	Literacy is defined as the ability to read easily or with difficulty a letter or a newspaper.	Self declaration
2002	Syrian Arab Republic	Labour Force Survey	Ability to read and write. Each Arab Syrian who reads and writes in Arabic language.	Self declaration
2000	Tajikistan	Population Census	A literate person is an individual who can read and write.	Household declaration
2000	Thailand	Population Census	Literate persons are defined as persons aged 5 and over who are able to read and write simple statements with understanding, in any language. If a person can read but cannot write, then he/she is classified as illiterate.	Household declaration
2002	The Former Yugoslav Rep. of Macedonia	Population Census	Persons having completed more than three grades of primary school were considered literate. In addition, literate was a person without school qualification and with 1-3 grades of primary school, if he/she can read and write a composition (text) in relation to everyday life, i.e. read and write a letter, regardless of the language and alphabet he can read.	Educational attainment proxy/ Household declaration
2000	Togo	MICS	Literacy is defined as the ability to read easily or with difficulty a letter or a newspaper.	Self declaration
1996	Tonga	Population Census	For a person to be considered as literate in a language, that person must be able to read and write in that Language	Household declaration
2004	Tunisia	Population Census	Literate is a person who know how to read and write at least one language.	Household declaration
2003	Turkey	Labour Force Survey	Person should know reading and writing in the Turkish alphabet. When the person is not a Republic of Turkey citizen, if she/he knows reading or writing in his/her native languages, she/he should be accepted as literate. If the person knows reading in Turkish, but not writing, she/he should not be accepted as literate. If the person knows reading and writing in the former Turkish alphabet, she/he should not be accepted as literate. To know reading and writing, there is no condition for completing any formal education. She/he may have learned reading or writing via courses or other learning method or by him/herself.	Self declaration
1995	Turkmenistan	Population Census	Literate is a person aged 7 and above who can read and write or only read, no matter the language used; illiterate is a person who cannot read.	Household declaration
2001	Ukraine	Population Census	Those who have a definite level of education. For people who do not have education – reading or writing ability in any language or only reading ability (at least slowly).	Educational attainment/ Household declaration
2002	United Republic of Tanzania	Population Census	Literacy is defined as the ability both to read and to write with understanding, a short, simple statement on everyday life. The ability to read and write may be in any language.	Household declaration
1999	Vanuatu	Population Census	m	m
2001	Venezuela	Population Census	m	m
1999	Vietnam	Population Census	A person who knows how to read and write with understanding simple sentences in his/her national or ethnic language or foreign language.	Household declaration
1999	Zambia	MICS	Literacy is defined as the ability to read easily or with difficulty a letter or a newspaper.	Self declaration

m: missing

Table 1
Background statistics

Country or territory	DEMOGRAPHY[1]						HIV/AIDS[2]		
	Total population (000)	Average annual growth rate (%)	Life expectancy at birth (years)		Total fertility rate (children per woman)	Infant mortality rate (‰)	HIV prevalence rate (%) in adults (15-49)		Number of children orphaned by AIDS (000)
	2002	2000-2005	2000-2005		2000-2005	2000-2005	2003		2003
			Total	Female			Total	% Female	
Arab States									
Algeria	31 266	1.7	69.7	71.3	2.8	43.9	0.1	15.6	...
Bahrain	709	2.2	74.0	75.9	2.7	14.2	0.2	...	...
Djibouti	693	1.6	45.7	46.8	5.7	102.4	2.9	56.0	5
Egypt	70 507	2.0	68.8	71.0	3.3	40.6	<0.1	13.3	...
Iraq	24 510	2.7	60.7	62.3	4.8	83.3	<0.1	...	...
Jordan	5 329	2.7	71.0	72.5	3.6	23.9	<0.1	...	...
Kuwait	2 443	3.5	76.6	79.0	2.7	10.8	...	...	...
Lebanon	3 596	1.6	73.5	75.1	2.2	17.2	0.1	...	...
Libyan Arab Jamahiriya	5 445	1.9	72.8	75.4	3.0	20.7	0.3	...	...
Mauritania	2 807	3.0	52.5	54.1	5.8	96.7	0.6	57.3	2
Morocco	30 072	1.6	68.7	70.5	2.7	42.1	0.1	...	...
Oman	2 768	2.9	72.4	74.4	5.0	19.7	0.1	...	...
Palestinian Autonomous Territories	3 433	3.6	72.4	74.0	5.6	20.7	...	...	...
Qatar	601	1.5	72.2	75.4	3.2	12.3	...	...	...
Saudi Arabia	23 520	2.9	72.3	73.7	4.5	20.6	...	...	...
Sudan	32 878	2.2	55.6	57.1	4.4	77.0	2.3	57.9	...
Syrian Arab Republic	17 381	2.4	71.9	73.1	3.3	22.3	<0.1	...	...
Tunisia	9 728	1.1	72.8	74.9	2.0	23.3	<0.1	...	...
United Arab Emirates	2 937	1.9	74.7	77.4	2.8	13.6	...	...	...
Yemen	19 315	3.5	60.0	61.1	7.0	70.6	0.1	...	...
Central and Eastern Europe									
Albania	3 141	0.7	73.7	76.7	2.3	25.0	...	...	...
Belarus	9 940	-0.5	70.1	75.3	1.2	11.3	...	...	...
Bosnia and Herzegovina	4 126	1.1	74.0	76.7	1.3	13.5	<0.1	...	...
Bulgaria	7 965	-0.8	70.9	74.6	1.1	15.2	<0.1	...	...
Croatia	4 439	-0.2	74.2	78.1	1.7	8.1	<0.1	...	...
Czech Republic	10 246	-0.1	75.4	78.7	1.2	5.6	0.1	32.0	...
Estonia	1 338	-1.1	71.7	76.8	1.2	9.4	1.1	33.8	...
Hungary	9 923	-0.5	71.9	76.0	1.2	8.8	0.1	...	...
Latvia	2 329	-0.9	71.0	76.2	1.1	14.2	0.6	33.3	...
Lithuania	3 465	-0.6	72.7	77.6	1.3	8.7	0.1	...	...
Poland	38 622	-0.1	73.9	78.0	1.3	9.1	0.1	...	...
Republic of Moldova	4 270	-0.1	68.9	72.2	1.4	18.1	0.2	...	...
Romania	22 387	-0.2	70.5	74.2	1.3	20.0	<0.1	...	...
Russian Federation	144 082	-0.6	66.8	73.1	1.1	15.9	1.1	33.7	...
Serbia and Montenegro	10 535	-0.1	73.2	75.6	1.7	13.0	0.2	20.0	...
Slovakia	5 398	0.1	73.7	77.6	1.3	8.0	<0.1	...	...
Slovenia	1 986	-0.1	76.3	79.8	1.1	5.5	<0.1	...	...
The former Yugoslav Rep. of Macedonia	2 046	0.5	73.6	75.8	1.9	16.0	<0.1	...	...
Turkey	70 318	1.4	70.5	73.2	2.4	39.5	...	...	...
Ukraine	48 902	-0.8	69.7	74.7	1.2	13.8	1.4	33.3	...
Central Asia									
Armenia	3 072	-0.5	72.4	75.6	1.2	17.3	0.1	36.0	...
Azerbaijan	8 297	0.9	72.2	75.5	2.1	29.3	<0.1	...	...
Georgia	5 177	-0.9	73.6	77.6	1.4	17.6	0.1	33.3	...
Kazakhstan	15 469	-0.4	66.3	71.9	2.0	51.7	0.2	33.5	...
Kyrgyzstan	5 067	1.4	68.6	72.3	2.6	37.0	0.1	...	...
Mongolia	2 559	1.3	63.9	65.9	2.4	58.2	<0.1	...	...
Tajikistan	6 195	0.9	68.8	71.4	3.1	50.0	<0.1	...	...
Turkmenistan	4 781	1.5	67.1	70.4	2.7	48.6	<0.1	...	...
Uzbekistan	25 705	1.5	69.7	72.5	2.4	[illegible]	0.1	[illegible]	...
East Asia and the Pacific									
Australia	19 544	1.0	79.2	82.0	1.7	5.5	0.1	7.1	...
Brunei Darussalam	350	2.3	76.3	78.9	2.5	6.1	<0.1	...	...
Cambodia	13 810	2.4	57.4	59.5	4.8	73.2	2.6	30.0	...
China	1 294 867	0.7	71.0	73.3	1.8	36.6	0.1	22.9	...

GNP[3]				AID AND POVERTY[4]		EXTERNAL DEBT[3]					
GNP per capita											
current US$		PPP US$		Net aid per capita (US$)	Population living on less than US$2 per day (%)	Total debt, (US$ millions)	Total debt service, (US$ millions)	Total debt as % of GNP	Public debt service as % of government current revenue	Total debt service as % of exports	
1998	2002	1998	2002	2002	1990-2002[5]	2002	2002	2002	2002	2002	**Country or territory**
											Arab States
1 560	1 720	4 850	5 530	11.5	15.1	22 800	4 166	7.8	21.3 z	...	Algeria
9 610	10 500	14 180	16 190	99.5	...	...	...	...	...	...	Bahrain
790	850	1 950	2 040	112.3	...	335	12	2.0	...	...	Djibouti
1 270	1 470	3 210	3 810	18.2	43.9	30 750	2 066	2.3	...	10.3	Egypt
...	...	...	...	5.1 z	...	...	...	...	...	...	Iraq
1 590	1 760	3 730	4 180	100.3	7.4	8 094	585	6.3	26.0 z	8.7	Jordan
17 390	16 340	19 020	17 780	1.9	...	...	...	...	...	...	Kuwait
3 670	3 990	4 400	4 600	126.8	...	17 077	2 188	12.0	...	51.0	Lebanon
...	...	...	...	1.9	...	...	...	...	...	...	Libyan Arab Jamahiriya
420	280	1 560	1 790	126.6	63.1	2 309	64	8.2	...	...	Mauritania
1 260	1 170	3 350	3 730	21.2	14.3	18 601	3 691	10.4	...	23.9	Morocco
6 420	7 830	11 620	13 000	14.7	...	4 639	1 748	8.8	14.7 z	...	Oman
...	...	...	...	470.9	...	...	...	...	...	...	Palestinian Autonomous Territories
...	...	...	...	3.7	...	...	...	...	...	...	Qatar
8 120	8 530	12 320	12 660	1.1	...	...	...	...	...	...	Saudi Arabia
340	370	1 400	1 740	10.7	...	16 389	23	0.2	...	0.8	Sudan
930	1 130	3 250	3 470	4.7	...	21 504	258	1.3	...	3.0	Syrian Arab Republic
2 050	1 990	5 320	6 440	48.8	6.6	12 625	1 438	7.2	...	13.5	Tunisia
19 550	...	22 620	...	1.4	...	...	...	...	...	...	United Arab Emirates
390	490	710	800	30.2	45.2	5 290	171	1.9	...	3.3	Yemen
											Central and Eastern Europe
890	1 450	3 210	4 960	100.9	...	1 312	58	1.2	...	3.4	Albania
1 560	1 360	4 220	5 500	4.0	...	908	197	1.4	5.4 z	2.1	Belarus
1 190	1 310	...	...	142.3	...	2 515	158	2.7	...	6.9	Bosnia and Herzegovina
1 270	1 770	5 380	7 030	47.9	...	10 462	1 368	9.0	19.1 z	15.9	Bulgaria
4 690	4 540	8 450	10 000	37.5	...	15 347	3 018	13.8	16.9 z	25.9	Croatia
5 160	5 480	12 650	14 920	38.3	...	26 419	4 534	6.9	9.7 z	9.5	Czech Republic
3 490	4 190	8 830	11 630	51.5	...	4 741	783	12.7	2.3 z	13.7	Estonia
4 480	5 290	10 410	13 070	47.5	...	34 958	14 870	23.1	...	33.9	Hungary
2 430	3 480	6 610	9 190	37.1	...	6 690	650	7.8	4.9 z	15.8	Latvia
2 700	3 670	7 990	10 190	42.4	...	6 199	1 281	9.4	11.1 z	16.6	Lithuania
3 860	4 570	8 780	10 450	30.0	...	69 521	13 489	7.2	11.4 z	22.5	Poland
470	460	1 320	1 600	33.2	...	1 349	229	12.9	29.4	19.9	Republic of Moldova
1 520	1 870	5 490	6 490	31.3	...	14 683	3 088	6.8	16.4 z	18.6	Romania
2 140	2 130	5 770	8 080	9.0	...	147 541	14 330	4.2	12.0 z	11.3	Russian Federation
...	1 400	...	...	122.6 z	...	12 688	150	1.0	...	2.8	Serbia and Montenegro
4 000	3 970	10 490	12 590	35.1	...	13 013	3 377	14.5	14.0 z	19.3	Slovakia
9 740	10 370	14 660	18 480	86.1	...	...	...	...	...	...	Slovenia
1 920	1 710	5 790	6 420	135.2	...	1 619	238	6.3	...	15.8	The former Yugoslav Rep. of Macedonia
3 060	2 490	6 150	6 300	9.0	10.3	131 556	27 604	15.2	26.0 z	46.8	Turkey
850	780	3 590	4 800	9.9	...	13 555	3 243	7.9	8.2 z	13.7	Ukraine
											Central Asia
570	790	2 150	3 230	95.5	...	1 149	74	3.0	...	8.8	Armenia
510	710	2 000	3 010	42.1	...	1 398	187	3.3	...	6.5	Azerbaijan
700	650	1 780	2 270	60.4	...	1 838	129	3.8	18.0	11.0	Georgia
1 350	1 520	3 580	5 630	12.2	...	17 538	4 115	17.4	18.6 z	34.4	Kazakhstan
350	290	1 330	1 560	36.7	...	1 797	173	11.2	...	25.3	Kyrgyzstan
410	430	1 510	1 710	81.5	50.0	1 037	52	4.7	11.6 z	6.7	Mongolia
180	180	660	930	27.2	...	1 153	79	6.9	25.5 z	10.2	Tajikistan
580	...	2 500	...	8.5	...	...	...	...	...	...	Turkmenistan
490	310	1 360	1 640	7.4	...	4 568	733	9.4	...	24.3	Uzbekistan
											East Asia and the Pacific
21 240	19 530	23 730	27 440	...	...	...	...	...	...	...	Australia
...	...	...	...	-5.0	...	...	...	...	...	...	Brunei Darussalam
290	300	1 510	1 970	35.3	77.7	2 907	21	0.5	...	0.8	Cambodia
740	960	3 240	4 520	1.1	46.7	168 255	30 616	2.4	...	8.2	China

Table 1 (continued)

Country or territory	DEMOGRAPHY[1]						HIV/AIDS[2]		
	Total population (000)	Average annual growth rate (%)	Life expectancy at birth (years)		Total fertility rate (children per woman)	Infant mortality rate (‰)	HIV prevalence rate (%) in adults (15-49)		Number of children orphaned by AIDS (000)
	2002	2000-2005	2000-2005		2000-2005	2000-2005	2003		2003
			Total	Female			Total	% Female	
Cook Islands	18	0.2	...	...	...	...	...	...	...
Democratic People's Republic of Korea	22 541	0.5	63.1	66.0	2.0	45.1	...	...	...
Fiji	831	1.0	69.8	71.5	2.9	17.8	0.1	...	...
Indonesia	217 131	1.3	66.8	68.8	2.4	41.6	0.1	13.6	...
Japan	127 478	0.1	81.6	85.1	1.3	3.2	<0.1	24.2	...
Kiribati	87	1.4	...	...	...	...	...	...	...
Lao People's Democratic Republic	5 529	2.3	54.5	55.8	4.8	88.0	0.1	...	...
Macao, China	460	0.9	78.9	81.2	1.1	8.6	...	...	...
Malaysia	23 965	1.9	73.1	75.7	2.9	10.1	0.4	16.7	...
Marshall Islands	52	1.2	...	...	...	...	...	...	...
Micronesia (Federated States of)	108	0.8	68.6	69.1	3.8	33.9	...	...	...
Myanmar	48 852	1.3	57.3	60.2	2.9	83.5	1.2	30.3	...
Nauru	13	2.3	...	...	...	...	...	...	...
New Zealand	3 846	0.8	78.3	80.7	2.0	5.8	0.1	...	...
Niue	2	-1.2	...	...	...	...	...	...	...
Palau	20	2.1	...	...	...	...	...	...	...
Papua New Guinea	5 586	2.2	57.6	58.7	4.1	62.1	0.6	30.0	...
Philippines	78 580	1.8	70.0	72.0	3.2	29.0	<0.1	22.5	...
Republic of Korea	47 430	0.6	75.5	79.3	1.4	5.0	<0.1	10.8	...
Samoa	176	1.0	70.0	73.4	4.1	26.1	...	...	...
Singapore	4 183	1.7	78.1	80.3	1.4	2.9	0.2	24.4	...
Solomon Islands	463	2.9	69.2	70.7	4.4	20.7	...	...	...
Thailand	62 193	1.0	69.3	73.5	1.9	19.8	1.5	35.7	...
Timor-Leste	739	4.0	49.5	50.4	3.8	123.7	...	...	...
Tokelau	2	-0.1	...	...	...	...	...	...	...
Tonga	103	1.0	68.6	69.1	3.7	33.9	...	...	...
Tuvalu	10	1.2	...	...	...	...	...	...	...
Vanuatu	207	2.4	68.8	70.5	4.1	28.5	...	...	...
Viet Nam	80 278	1.3	69.2	71.6	2.3	33.6	0.4	32.5	...
Latin America and the Caribbean									
Anguilla	12	1.7	...	...	...	...	...	...	...
Antigua and Barbuda	73	0.5	...	...	...	...	...	...	...
Argentina	37 981	1.2	74.2	77.7	2.4	20.0	0.7	20.0	...
Aruba	98	2.0	...	...	...	...	...	...	...
Bahamas	310	1.1	67.1	70.3	2.3	17.7	3.0	48.1	...
Barbados	269	0.4	77.2	79.5	1.5	10.9	1.5	32.0	...
Belize	251	2.1	71.4	73.0	3.2	31.1	2.4	37.1	...
Bermuda	81	0.7	...	...	...	...	...	...	...
Bolivia	8 645	1.9	63.9	66.0	3.8	55.6	0.1	27.1	...
Brazil	176 257	1.2	68.1	72.6	2.2	38.4	0.7	36.9	...
British Virgin Islands	21	1.8	...	...	...	...	...	...	...
Cayman Islands	39	3.0	...	...	...	...	...	...	...
Chile	15 613	1.2	76.1	79.0	2.4	11.6	0.3	33.5	...
Colombia	43 526	1.6	72.2	75.3	2.6	25.6	0.7	34.4	...
Costa Rica	4 094	1.9	78.1	80.6	2.3	10.5	0.6	33.3	...
Cuba	11 271	0.3	76.7	78.7	1.6	7.3	0.1	33.3	...
Dominica	78	0.3	...	...	...	...	...	...	...
Dominican Republic	8 616	1.5	66.7	69.2	2.7	35.7	1.7	27.1	...
Ecuador	12 810	1.5	70.8	73.5	2.8	41.5	0.3	34.0	...
El Salvador	6 415	1.6	70.7	73.7	2.9	26.4	0.7	34.3	...
Grenada	80	-0.3	...	...	...	...	...	...	...
Guatemala	12 036	2.6	65.8	68.9	4.4	41.2	1.1	41.9	...
Guyana	764	0.2	63.2	66.3	2.3	51.0	2.5	55.5	...
Haiti	8 218	1.3	49.5	50.0	4.0	63.2	5.6	57.7	...
Honduras	6 781	2.3	68.9	71.4	3.7	32.1	1.8	55.9	...
Jamaica	2 627	0.9	75.7	77.8	2.4	19.9	1.2	47.6	...
Mexico	101 965	1.5	73.4	76.4	2.5	28.2	0.3	33.1	...
Montserrat	3	0.3			...	...	...	...	...
Netherlands Antilles	219	0.8	76.3	79.2	2.1	12.6	...	...	...

GNP[3]				AID AND POVERTY[4]		EXTERNAL DEBT[3]					
GNP per capita											
current US$		PPP US$		Net aid per capita (US$)	Population living on less than US$2 per day (%)	Total debt, (US$ millions)	Total debt service, (US$ millions)	Total debt as % of GNP	Public debt service as % of government current revenue	Total debt service as % of exports	
1998	2002	1998	2002	2002	1990-2002[5]	2002	2002	2002	2002	2002	**Country or territory**
…	…	…	…	…	…	…	…	…	…	…	Cook Islands
…	…	…	…	…	…	…	…	…	…	…	Democratic People's Republic of Korea
2 300	2 130	4 580	5 330	41.0	…	210	28	1.5	…	5.9	Fiji
670	710	2 660	3 070	6.0	52.4	132 208	16 971	10.3	22.4[z]	24.8	Indonesia
33 780	34 010	24 760	27 380	…	…	…	…	…	…	…	Japan
1 150	960	…	…	…	…	…	…	…	…	…	Kiribati
310	310	1 350	1 660	50.3	73.2	2 665	45	2.8	…	…	Lao People's Democratic Republic
15 220	14 600[z]	18 470	19 890[z]	…	…	…	…	…	…	…	Macao, China
3 630	3 540	7 220	8 500	3.6	9.3	48 557	8 082	9.1	…	7.3	Malaysia
2 110	2 380	…	…	…	…	…	…	…	…	…	Marshall Islands
1 910	1 970	…	…	…	…	…	…	…	…	…	Micronesia (Federated States of)
…	…	…	…	2.5	…	6 556	113	…	…	…	Myanmar
…	…	…	…	…	…	…	…	…	…	…	Nauru
15 310	13 260	17 000	20 550	…	…	…	…	…	…	…	New Zealand
…	…	…	…	…	…	…	…	…	…	…	Niue
…	…	…	…	…	…	…	…	…	…	…	Palau
840	530	2 200	2 180	36.4	…	2 485	278	10.2	…	…	Papua New Guinea
1 080	1 030	3 850	4 450	7.1	46.4	59 343	9 192	11.1	49.4[z]	20.2	Philippines
8 500	9 930	12 240	16 960	-1.7	<2	…	…	…	…	…	Republic of Korea
1 380	1 430	4 560	5 570	214.2	…	234	8	3.0	…	…	Samoa
23 510	20 690	20 200	23 730	1.8	…	…	…	…	…	…	Singapore
870	580	2 210	1 590	56.8	…	180	6	2.4	…	…	Solomon Islands
2 110	2 000	5 620	6 890	4.8	32.5	59 212	19 738	15.8	24.3[z]	23.1	Thailand
…	520	…	…	297.6	…	…	…	…	…	…	Timor-Leste
…	…	…	…	…	…	…	…	…	…	…	Tokelau
1 720	1 440	5 640	6 820	217.2	…	74	3	2.0	…	5.9	Tonga
…	…	…	…	…	…	…	…	…	…	…	Tuvalu
1 240	1 070	3 000	2 850	133.0	…	84	2	1.0	…	…	Vanuatu
350	430	1 760	2 300	15.9	63.7	13 349	1 181	3.4	16.1	6.0	Viet Nam
											Latin America and the Caribbean
…	…	…	…	…	…	…	…	…	…	…	Anguilla
8 430	9 720	8 970	10 390	192.1	…	…	…	…	…	…	Antigua and Barbuda
8 230	4 220	12 220	10 190	4.0[z]	14.3	132 314	5 826	6.1	43.6[z]	18.3	Argentina
…	…	…	…	…	…	…	…	…	…	…	Aruba
12 940	…	14 640	…	17.2	…	…	…	…	…	…	Bahamas
8 230	8 790	13 780	14 660	12.8	…	…	…	…	…	…	Barbados
2 700	2 970	4 580	5 490	88.6	…	835	188	24.7	…	36.5	Belize
…	…	…	…	…	…	…	…	…	…	…	Bermuda
990	900	2 270	2 390	78.8	34.3	4 867	476	6.3	17.4[z]	27.7	Bolivia
4 610	2 830	6 740	7 450	2.1	22.4	227 932	51 632	11.9	…	68.9	Brazil
…	…	…	…	…	…	…	…	…	…	…	British Virgin Islands
…	…	…	…	…	…	…	…	…	…	…	Cayman Islands
4 890	4 250	8 530	9 420	-1.5	9.6	41 945	7 729	12.6	8.0[z]	32.9	Chile
2 410	1 820	6 040	6 150	10.1	22.6	33 853	6 921	8.9	…	40.2	Colombia
3 590	4 070	7 500	8 560	1.3	9.5	4 834	670	4.1	16.9[z]	8.9	Costa Rica
…	…	…	…	5.4	…	…	…	…	…	…	Cuba
3 270	3 000	5 000	4 960	381.7	…	207	11	5.1	…	7.9	Dominica
1 870	…	5 030	…	18.2	<2.0	6 256	671	3.3	…	6.4	Dominican Republic
1 800	1 490	3 170	3 340	16.9	40.8	16 452	2 193	9.7	…	28.7	Ecuador
1 860	2 110	4 340	4 790	36.4	58.0	5 828	453	3.2	…	7.7	El Salvador
3 150	3 530	5 760	6 600	117.5	…	339	26	6.8	…	13.6	Grenada
1 660	1 760	3 710	4 030	20.7	37.4	4 676	412	1.8	…	7.5	Guatemala
860	860	3 600	3 940	84.9	…	1 459	78	11.7	…	10.7	Guyana
430	440	1 600	1 610	18.9	…	1 248	28	0.8	…	…	Haiti
740	930	2 400	2 540	64.1	44.4	5 395	397	6.2	…	12.3	Honduras
2 450	2 690	3 380	3 680	9.2	13.3	5 477	842	11.6	21.6[z]	18.4	Jamaica
4 020	5 920	7 820	8 800	1.3	26.3	141 264	43 536	7.0	…	23.2	Mexico
…	…	…	…	…	…	…	…	…	…	…	Montserrat
…	…	…	…	…	…	…	…	…	…	…	Netherlands Antilles

Table 1 (continued)

Country or territory	DEMOGRAPHY[1] Total population (000) 2002	Average annual growth rate (%) 2000-2005	Life expectancy at birth (years) 2000-2005 Total	Life expectancy at birth (years) 2000-2005 Female	Total fertility rate (children per woman) 2000-2005	Infant mortality rate (‰) 2000-2005	HIV/AIDS[2] HIV prevalence rate (%) in adults (15-49) 2003 Total	HIV prevalence rate (%) in adults (15-49) 2003 % Female	Number of children orphaned by AIDS (000) 2003
Nicaragua	5335	2.4	69.5	71.9	3.7	35.7	0.2	33.9	…
Panama	3064	1.8	74.7	77.4	2.7	20.6	0.9	41.3	…
Paraguay	5740	2.4	70.9	73.1	3.8	37.0	0.5	26.0	…
Peru	26767	1.5	69.8	72.4	2.9	33.4	0.5	33.8	…
Saint Kitts and Nevis	42	-0.3	…	…	…	…	…	…	…
Saint Lucia	148	0.8	72.5	74.1	2.3	14.8	…	…	…
Saint Vincent and the Grenadines	119	0.6	74.1	75.6	2.2	15.7	…	…	…
Suriname	432	0.8	71.1	73.7	2.5	25.7	1.7	34.0	…
Trinidad and Tobago	1298	0.3	71.3	74.4	1.6	14.1	3.2	50.0	…
Turks and Caicos Islands	20	3.5	…	…	…	…	…	…	…
Uruguay	3391	0.7	75.3	78.9	2.3	13.1	0.3	32.8	…
Venezuela	25226	1.9	73.7	76.7	2.7	18.9	0.7	32.0	…
North America and Western Europe									
Andorra	69	2.6	…	…	…	…	…	…	…
Austria	8111	0.05	78.5	81.5	1.3	4.7	0.3	22.0	…
Belgium	10296	0.2	78.8	81.9	1.7	4.2	0.2	35.0	…
Canada	31271	0.8	79.3	81.9	1.5	5.3	0.3	23.6	…
Cyprus	796	0.8	78.3	80.5	1.9	7.7	…	…	…
Denmark	5351	0.2	76.6	79.1	1.8	5.0	0.2	18.0	…
Finland	5197	0.2	78.0	81.5	1.7	4.0	0.1	…	…
France	59850	0.5	79.0	82.8	1.9	5.0	0.4	26.7	…
Germany	82414	0.1	78.3	81.2	1.4	4.5	0.1	22.1	…
Greece	10970	0.1	78.3	80.9	1.3	6.4	0.2	20.0	…
Iceland	287	0.8	79.8	81.9	2.0	3.4	0.2	…	…
Ireland	3911	1.1	77.0	79.6	1.9	5.8	0.1	30.8	…
Israel	6304	2.0	79.2	81.0	2.7	5.9	0.1	…	…
Italy	57482	-0.1	78.7	81.9	1.2	5.4	0.5	32.1	…
Luxembourg	447	1.3	78.4	81.4	1.7	5.4	0.2	…	…
Malta	393	0.4	78.4	80.7	1.8	7.1	0.2	…	…
Monaco	34	0.9	…	…	…	…	…	…	…
Netherlands	16067	0.5	78.3	81.0	1.7	4.5	0.2	20.0	…
Norway	4514	0.4	78.9	81.9	1.8	4.5	0.1	…	…
Portugal	10049	0.1	76.2	79.6	1.5	6.1	0.4	19.5	…
San Marin	27	1.0	…	…	…	…	…	…	…
Spain	40977	0.2	79.3	82.8	1.2	5.1	0.7	20.8	…
Sweden	8867	0.1	80.1	82.6	1.6	3.4	0.1	25.7	…
Switzerland	7171	0.0	79.1	82.3	1.4	4.8	0.4	30.0	…
United Kingdom	59068	0.3	78.2	80.7	1.6	5.4	0.2	29.8	…
United States	291038	1.0	77.1	79.9	2.1	6.7	0.6	25.5	…
South and West Asia									
Afghanistan	22930	3.9	43.1	43.3	6.8	161.7	…	…	…
Bangladesh	143809	2.0	61.4	61.8	3.5	64.0	…	…	…
Bhutan	2190	3.0	63.2	64.5	5.0	53.6	…	…	…
India	1049549	1.5	63.9	64.6	3.0	64.5	0.9	38.0	…
Iran, Islamic Republic of	68070	1.2	70.3	71.9	2.3	33.3	0.1	12.3	…
Maldives	309	3.0	67.4	67.0	5.3	38.3	…	…	…
Nepal	24609	2.2	59.9	59.6	4.3	70.9	0.5	26.7	…
Pakistan	149911	2.4	61.0	60.9	5.1	86.5	0.1	12.2	…
Sri Lanka	18910	0.8	72.6	75.9	2.0	20.1	<0.1	17.1	…
Sub-Saharan Africa									
Angola	13184	3.2	40.1	41.5	7.2	140.3	[illegible]	[illegible]	110
Benin	6558	2.6	50.6	53.0	5.7	92.7	1.9	56.5	34
Botswana	1770	0.9	39.7	40.5	3.7	56.6	37.3	57.6	120
Burkina Faso	12624	3.0	45.7	46.2	6.7	93.2	4.2	55.6	260
Burundi	6602	3.1	40.9	41.4	6.8	107.4	6.0	59.1	200
Cameroon	15729	1.8	46.2	47.4	4.6	88.1	6.9	55.8	240
Cape Verde	454	2.0	70.2	72.8	3.3	29.7	…	…	…

GNP[3]				AID AND POVERTY[4]		EXTERNAL DEBT[3]					
GNP per capita											
current US$		PPP US$		Net aid per capita (US$)	Population living on less than US$2 per day (%)	Total debt, (US$ millions)	Total debt service, (US$ millions)	Total debt as % of GNP	Public debt service as % of government current revenue	Total debt service as % of exports	
1998	2002	1998	2002	2002	1990-2002[5]	2002	2002	2002	2002	2002	Country or territory
380	710	1 930	2 350	97.0	79.9	6 485	151	4.0	...	11.7	Nicaragua
3 590	4 020	5 520	6 060	11.5	17.6	8 298	1 677	13.9	...	19.7	Panama
1 810	1 170	4 660	4 590	9.9	30.3	2 967	327	6.0	22.7[z]	10.5	Paraguay
2 210	2 020	4 430	4 880	18.4	37.7	28 167	3 357	6.1	20.5[z]	32.8	Peru
5 750	6 540	9 650	10 750	683.8	...	255	38	12.4	...	22.6	Saint Kitts and Nevis
3 700	3 750	5 090	4 950	226.5	...	415	26	4.2	...	7.2	Saint Lucia
2 590	2 820	4 710	5 190	40.1	...	206	13	3.9	...	7.6	Saint Vincent and the Grenadines
2 310	1 940	...	...	26.9	...	...	...	...	...	...	Suriname
4 540	6 750	7 370	9 000	-5.6	39.0	2 672	265	2.9	...	5.7	Trinidad and Tobago
...	...	...	...	...	...	...	...	...	...	...	Turks and Caicos Islands
6 620	4 340	8 900	7 710	4.0	3.9	10 736	1 280	10.7	26.3[z]	40.0	Uruguay
3 540	4 080	5 780	5 220	2.3	32.0	32 563	7 487	8.2	23.1[z]	25.6	Venezuela
											North America and Western Europe
...	...	...	...	...	...	...	...	...	...	...	Andorra
27 040	23 860	25 130	28 910	...	...	...	...	...	...	...	Austria
25 590	22 940	24 460	28 130	...	...	...	...	...	...	...	Belgium
20 000	22 390	24 200	28 930	...	...	...	...	...	...	...	Canada
12 110	12 320[z]	15 150	18 080[z]	62.3	...	...	...	...	...	...	Cyprus
32 770	30 260	26 450	30 600	...	...	...	...	...	...	...	Denmark
24 750	23 890	22 040	26 160	...	...	...	...	...	...	...	Finland
24 770	22 240	23 200	27 040	...	...	...	...	...	...	...	France
26 630	22 740	23 920	26 980	...	...	...	...	...	...	...	Germany
12 130	11 660	15 140	18 770	...	...	...	...	...	...	...	Greece
27 390	27 960	25 150	29 240	...	...	...	...	...	...	...	Iceland
20 630	23 030	21 080	29 570	...	...	...	...	...	...	...	Ireland
16 730	16 020	17 950	19 000	119.6	...	...	...	...	...	...	Israel
20 560	19 080	22 810	26 170	...	...	...	...	...	...	...	Italy
44 810	39 470	42 620	53 290	...	...	...	...	...	...	...	Luxembourg
8 790	9 260	15 340	17 710	28.8	...	...	...	...	...	...	Malta
...	...	...	...	...	...	...	...	...	...	...	Monaco
25 160	23 390	24 920	28 350	...	...	...	...	...	...	...	Netherlands
35 240	38 730	32 400	36 690	...	...	...	...	...	...	...	Norway
11 030	10 720	15 290	17 820	...	...	...	...	...	...	...	Portugal
...	...	...	...	...	...	...	...	...	...	...	San Marin
14 840	14 580	17 850	21 210	...	...	...	...	...	...	...	Spain
28 710	25 970	21 570	25 820	...	...	...	...	...	...	...	Sweden
40 820	36 170	28 770	31 840	...	...	...	...	...	...	...	Switzerland
22 790	25 510	22 820	26 580	...	...	...	...	...	...	...	United Kingdom
30 700	35 400	31 790	36 110	...	...	...	...	...	...	...	United States
											South and West Asia
...	...	...	...	14.7[z]	...	...	...	...	...	...	Afghanistan
360	380	1 450	1 770	6.3	82.8	17 037	722	1.5	...	7.3	Bangladesh
450	600	...	...	33.5	...	377	6	1.2	6.1	4.6	Bhutan
420	470	2 150	2 650	1.4	79.9	104 429	13 128	2.6	13.1[z]	14.9	India
1 650	1 720	5 440	6 690	1.7	7.3	9 154	1 460	1.3	...	4.1	Iran, Islamic Republic of
1 950	2 170	...	...	88.9	...	270	22	3.7	10.1	4.5	Maldives
220	230	1 220	1 370	14.9	82.5	2 953	98	1.8	14.9	8.8	Nepal
470	420	1 760	1 960	14.3	65.6	33 672	2 844	4.8	19.6	17.8	Pakistan
850	850	3 060	3 510	18.2	45.4	9 611	716	4.4	19.5[z]	9.8	Sri Lanka
											Sub-Saharan Africa
520	710	1 520	1 840	32.0	...	10 134	863	8.9	...	10.0	Angola
390	380	890	1 060	33.6	...	1 843	63	2.4	...	9.6	Benin
3 290	3 010	6 220	7 740	21.2	50.1	480	60	1.2	...	2.0	Botswana
250	250	950	1 090	37.4	81.0	1 580	53	1.7	...	16.0	Burkina Faso
140	100	600	630	26.1	89.2	1 204	23	3.3	...	59.0	Burundi
600	550	1 620	1 910	40.2	50.6	8 503	358	4.1	...	...	Cameroon
1 300	1 250	4 050	4 920	203.1	...	414	22	3.6	...	7.6	Cape Verde

Table 1 (continued)

Country or territory	DEMOGRAPHY[1]						HIV/AIDS[2]		
	Total population (000)	Average annual growth rate (%)	Life expectancy at birth (years)		Total fertility rate (children per woman)	Infant mortality rate (‰)	HIV prevalence rate (%) in adults (15-49)		Number of children orphaned by AIDS (000)
	2002	2000-2005	2000-2005		2000-2005	2000-2005	2003		2003
			Total	Female			Total	% Female	
Central African Republic	3 819	1.3	39.5	40.6	4.9	100.4	13.5	54.2	110
Chad	8 348	3.0	44.7	45.7	6.7	115.3	4.8	55.6	96
Comoros	747	2.8	60.8	62.2	4.9	67.0	...	...	...
Congo	3 633	2.6	48.2	49.7	6.3	84.0	4.9	56.3	97
Côte d'Ivoire	16 365	1.6	41.0	41.2	4.7	101.3	7.0	56.6	310
Democratic Rep. of the Congo	51 201	2.9	41.8	42.8	6.7	119.6	4.2	57.0	770
Equatorial Guinea	481	2.6	49.1	50.5	5.9	100.9	...	...	...
Eritrea	3 991	3.7	52.7	54.2	5.4	73.0	2.7	56.4	39
Ethiopia	68 961	2.5	45.5	46.3	6.1	100.4	4.4	55.0	720
Gabon	1 306	1.8	56.6	57.5	4.0	56.8	8.1	57.8	14
Gambia	1 388	2.7	54.1	55.5	4.7	80.5	1.2	57.1	2
Ghana	20 471	2.2	57.9	59.3	4.1	57.8	3.1	56.3	170
Guinea	8 359	1.6	49.1	49.5	5.8	101.7	3.2	55.4	35
Guinea-Bissau	1 449	2.9	45.3	46.9	7.1	120.0	...	...	...
Kenya	31 540	1.5	44.6	45.6	4.0	69.3	6.7	65.5	650
Lesotho	1 800	0.1	35.1	37.7	3.8	92.1	28.9	56.7	100
Liberia	3 239	4.0	41.4	42.2	6.8	147.4	5.9	56.3	36
Madagascar	16 916	2.8	53.6	54.8	5.7	91.5	1.7	58.5	30
Malawi	11 871	2.0	37.5	37.7	6.1	115.4	14.2	56.8	500
Mali	12 623	3.0	48.6	49.1	7.0	118.7	1.9	59.2	75
Mauritius	1 210	1.0	72.0	75.8	1.9	16.0	...	...	...
Mozambique	18 537	1.8	38.1	39.6	5.6	122.0	12.2	55.8	470
Namibia	1 961	1.4	44.3	45.6	4.6	59.8	21.3	55.0	57
Niger	11 544	3.6	46.2	46.5	8.0	125.7	1.2	56.3	24
Nigeria	120 911	2.5	51.5	51.8	5.4	78.8	5.4	57.6	1 800
Rwanda	8 272	2.2	39.3	39.7	5.7	111.5	5.1	56.5	160
Sao Tome and Principe	157	2.5	69.9	72.8	4.0	31.6	...	...	...
Senegal	9 855	2.4	52.9	55.1	5.0	60.7	0.8	56.1	17
Seychelles	80	0.9	...	...	...	...	...	...	...
Sierra Leone	4 764	3.8	34.2	35.5	6.5	177.2	...	...	...
Somalia	9 480	4.2	47.9	49.5	7.3	117.7	...	...	...
South Africa	44 759	0.6	47.7	50.7	2.6	47.9	21.5	56.9	1 100
Swaziland	1 069	0.8	34.4	35.4	4.5	78.3	38.8	55.0	65
Togo	4 801	2.3	49.7	51.1	5.3	81.5	4.1	56.3	54
Uganda	25 004	3.2	46.2	46.9	7.1	86.1	4.1	60.0	940
United Republic of Tanzania	36 276	1.9	43.3	44.1	5.1	99.8	8.8	56.0	980
Zambia	10 698	1.2	32.4	32.1	5.6	104.8	16.5	56.6	630
Zimbabwe	12 835	0.5	33.1	32.6	3.9	58.4	24.6	58.1	980

	Sum	Weighted average					Weighted average		
World	6 210 815	1.2	67.0	69.2	2.7	43.9	1.1	47.6	15 000
Countries in transition	280 970	-0.3	68.1	73.3	1.4	21.7	...	...	...
Developed countries	992 756	0.4	77.8	80.9	1.6	6.2	...	...	...
Developing countries	4 937 089	1.5	64.7	66.4	2.9	52.8	...	...	...
Arab States	289 938	2.2	66.9	68.6	3.7	46.2	...	...	...
Central and Eastern Europe	405 457	-0.1	69.8	74.5	1.4	18.4	...	...	...
Central Asia	76 336	0.8	69.1	72.7	2.3	39.4	...	...	...
East Asia and the Pacific	2 059 455	0.9	70.7	73.2	2.0	34.4	...	...	...
Latin America and the Caribbean	530 734	1.4	70.6	74.0	2.5	31.2	...	...	...
North America and Western Europe	[illegible]	0.6	78.0	80.9	1.8	5.7	...	...	...
South and West Asia	1 480 287	1.7	63.4	64.0	3.3	66.3	...	[illegible]	
Sub-Saharan Africa	647 645	2.3	46.1	47.0	5.4	91.6	...	...	12 000

1. United Nations Population Division statistics, 2002 revision, medium variant.
2. Joint United Nations Programme on HIV/AIDS (UNAIDS).
3. World Bank statistics.
4. *Human Development Report 2004.*
5. Data refer to the most recent year available during the period specified.

(z) Data are for 2001.

GNP[3]				AID AND POVERTY[4]		EXTERNAL DEBT[3]					
GNP per capita											
current US$		PPP US$		Net aid per capita (US$)	Population living on less than US$2 per day (%)	Total debt, (US$ millions)	Total debt service, (US$ millions)	Total debt as % of GNP	Public debt service as % of government current revenue	Total debt service as % of exports	
1998	2002	1998	2002	2002	1990-2002[5]	2002	2002	2002	2002	2002	Country or territory
290	250	1 080	1 170	15.7	84.0	1 066	1	0.1	...	...	Central African Republic
220	210	890	1 010	27.9	...	1 281	29	1.5	...	...	Chad
410	390	1 640	1 690	43.5	...	270	5	1.9	...	...	Comoros
530	610	670	710	115.5	...	5 152	24	1.1	9.2[z]	1.0	Congo
780	620	1 520	1 450	65.3	50.4	11 816	832	7.5	16.6[z]	14.1	Côte d'Ivoire
110	100	710	630	15.8	...	8 726	927	16.8	...	...	Democratic Rep. of the Congo
1 060	930[z]	3 530	7 950[z]	42.0	...	260	4	...	...	...	Equatorial Guinea
220	190	1 100	1 040	57.7	...	528	9	1.2	...	4.7	Eritrea
110	100	630	780	18.9	80.7	6 523	108	1.8	...	9.7	Ethiopia
3 870	3 060	5 590	5 530	55.1	...	3 534	410	9.8	...	11.7	Gabon
330	270	1 520	1 660	43.6	82.9	573	19	5.5	...	...	Gambia
380	270	1 770	2 080	31.9	78.5	7 338	211	3.5	...	8.0	Ghana
520	410	1 820	2 060	29.9	6.1	3 401	136	4.3	...	13.6	Guinea
140	130	660	680	41.0	...	699	15	7.6	...	...	Guinea-Bissau
360	360	990	1 010	12.5	58.6	6 031	452	3.7	...	13.6	Kenya
690	550	2 650	2 970	42.5	56.1	637	67	7.7	...	11.8	Lesotho
110	140	...	...	11.5[z]	...	2 324	1	0.2	...	0.6	Liberia
260	230	760	730	22.0	83.3	4 518	73	1.7	...	9.9	Madagascar
220	160	560	570	31.8	76.1	2 912	36	1.9	...	7.6	Malawi
250	240	720	860	37.4	90.6	2 803	90	2.9	...	7.0	Mali
3 760	3 860	8 640	10 820	19.8	...	1 803	251	5.5	15.8[z]	8.2	Mauritius
200	200	760	990	111.0	78.4	4 609	76	2.2	...	6.1	Mozambique
2 160	1 790	6 370	6 880	68.9	55.8	...	...	...	...	...	Namibia
200	180	780	800	25.9	85.3	1 797	28	1.3	...	...	Niger
260	300	760	800	2.6	90.8	30 476	1 490	3.7	...	8.6	Nigeria
250	230	990	1 260	43.1	84.6	1 435	22	1.3	...	14.9	Rwanda
270	300	...	...	166.	...	333	6	13.1	...	31.8	Sao Tome and Principe
520	470	1 340	1 540	45.5	67.8	3 918	219	4.5	20.0[z]	12.6	Senegal
7 300	6 780	...	...	97.8	...	253	15	2.3	...	2.6	Seychelles
150	140	480	500	74.2	74.5	1 448	23	3.1	...	...	Sierra Leone
...	...	...	...	16.4[z]	...	2 688	0.2	...	...	...	Somalia
3 290	2 500	8 850	9 810	14.7	23.8	25 041	4 692	4.6	8.1[z]	12.5	South Africa
1 400	1 240	4 350	4 730	23.1	...	342	20	1.6	...	1.7	Swaziland
330	270	1 450	1 450	10.6	...	1 581	13	1.0	...	2.5	Togo
290	240	1 110	1 360	25.5	...	4 100	79	1.4	4.9[z]	7.1	Uganda
230	290	480	580	34.0	59.7	7 244	145	1.6	...	8.9	United Republic of Tanzania
330	340	700	800	59.9	87.4	5 969	309	8.7	...	27.1	Zambia
560	480[z]	2 660	2 310[z]	15.6	64.2	4 066	58	...	...	...	Zimbabwe

Weighted average				Weighted average		Weighted average					
5 060	5 120	6 730	7 820	9.7	...	...	...	...	...	...	World
...	...	...	...	...	...	...	...	...	...	...	Countries in transition
...	...	...	...	...	...	...	...	...	...	...	Developed countries
...	...	...	...	8.8	...	...	...	...	...	...	Developing countries
2 080	2 240	4 960	5 670	24.2	...	189 010	21 459	...	...	9.6	Arab States
...	...	...	...	31.2	...	...	...	...	...	...	Central and Eastern Europe
...	...	...	...	...	...	...	...	...	...	...	Central Asia
800	960	3 200	4 280	3.9	...	497 354	86 335	4.9	...	12.1	East Asia and the Pacific
3 860	3 280	6 590	6 950	8.6	...	727 944	136 709	8.5	...	30.7	Latin America and the Caribbean
...	...	...	...	...	...	...	...	...	...	...	North America and Western Europe
...	...	...	...	...	...	...	...	...	...	...	South and West Asia
520	450	1 550	1 700	26.3	...	210 350	12 422	4.2	...	10.5	Sub-Saharan Africa

Table 2A
Adult and youth literacy[1]

	Country or territory	ADULT LITERACY RATE (15 and over) (%)									ADULT ILLITERATES (15 and over)					
		1990			2000-2004[2]			2015			1990		2000-2004[2]		2015	
		Total	Male	Female	Total	Male	Female	Total	Male	Female	Total (000)	% F	Total (000)	% F	Total (000)	% F
	Arab States															
1	Algeria	52.9	64.3	41.3	69.8 *	79.5 *	60.1*	79.8	87.4	72.1	6 799	62	6 280	66 *	5 596	69
2	Bahrain	82.1	86.8	74.6	87.7 *	92.5 *	83.0*	93.2	95.6	90.1	60	55	55	60 *	47	60
3	Djibouti	53.0	66.8	39.7	...	...	...	...	...	...	141	65	...	...	...	...
4	Egypt	47.1	60.4	33.6	55.6 *	67.2 *	43.6*	...	...	...	17 432	63	17 270	64 *	...	...
5	Iraq	35.7	51.3	19.7	...	...	...	...	...	...	6 208	62	...	...	...	...
6	Jordan	81.5	90.0	72.1	89.9 *	95.1 *	84.7*	95.2	97.8	92.3	320	72	336	74 *	229	77
7	Kuwait	76.7	79.3	72.6	82.9	84.7	81.0	...	...	...	317	47	301	42	...	...
8	Lebanon	80.3	88.3	73.1	...	...	...	...	...	...	347	72	...	...	...	...
9	Libyan Arab Jamahiriya	68.1	82.8	51.1	81.7	91.8	70.7	...	...	...	773	71	685	77	...	...
10	Mauritania	34.8	46.3	23.9	51.2 *	59.5 *	31.3*	58.9	65.7	52.4	743	60	732	60 *	955	59
11	Morocco	38.7	52.7	24.9	50.7	63.3	38.3	...	...	...	9 089	62	10 108	63	...	...
12	Oman	54.7	67.3	38.3	74.4	82.0	65.4	...	...	...	457	57	423	55	...	...
13	Palestinian Autonomous Territories	...	...	...	91.9*	96.3*	87.4*	96.6	98.3	94.8	...	...	156	77 *	104	75
14	Qatar	77.0	77.4	76.0	89.2 *	...	...	91.4			78	28	50	...	48	...
15	Saudi Arabia	66.2	76.2	50.2	79.4 *	87.1 *	69.3*	89.2	93.7	84.0	3 287	59	2 776	65 *	2 315	68
16	Sudan[3]	45.8	60.0	31.5	59.0 *	69.3 *	49.9*	71.3	79.3	63.4	7 836	63	7 621	62 *	7 757	64
17	Syrian Arab Republic	64.8	81.8	47.5	82.9 *	91.0 *	74.2*	89.6	95.3	84.0	2 351	75	1 864	74 *	1 622	77
18	Tunisia	59.1	71.6	46.5	74.3 *	83.4 *	65.3*	82.2	89.7	74.8	2 081	65	1 864	68 *	1 532	71
19	United Arab Emirates	71.0	71.2	70.6	77.3	75.6	80.7	...	...	...	421	28	497	25	...	...
20	Yemen	32.7	55.2	12.9	49.0	69.5	28.5	...	...	...	3 820	66	5 032	70	...	...
	Central and Eastern Europe															
21	Albania	77.0	86.8	66.7	98.7 *	99.2 *	98.3*	...	...	...	509	71	28	67 *	...	...
22	Belarus	99.5	99.7	99.3	99.6 *	99.8 *	99.4*	99.8	99.8	99.8	42	76	33	77 *	16	54
23	Bosnia and Herzegovina	...	...	...	94.6 *	98.4 *	91.1*	97.3	99.1	95.6	...	...	172	85 *	99	83
24	Bulgaria	97.2	98.3	96.2	98.2 *	98.7 *	97.7*	98.4	98.7	98.1	195	70	122	66 *	100	62
25	Croatia	96.9	99.0	94.9	98.1 *	99.3 *	97.1*	99.0	99.5	98.6	121	85	68	83 *	36	73
26	Czech Republic	...	...	...	...	...	...	...	...	...	...	...	...	...	...	...
27	Estonia	99.8	99.8	99.8	99.8 *	99.8 *	99.8*	99.8	99.8	99.8	3	53	3	56 *	2	55
28	Hungary	99.1	99.3	98.9	99.3 *	99.4 *	99.3*	99.4	99.4	99.4	78	63	54	57 *	49	53
29	Latvia	...	...	...	99.7 *	99.8 *	99.7*	99.8	99.8	99.8	...	...	5	63 *	4	55
30	Lithuania	99.3	99.5	99.1	99.6 *	99.6 *	99.6*	99.7	99.7	99.7	20	67	10	54 *	8	55
31	Poland	...	...	...	...	...	...	...	...	...	...	...	...	...	...	...
32	Republic of Moldova	97.5	99.1	96.1	96.2 *	97.5 *	95.0*	98.5	98.6	98.5	80	83	126	69 *	53	53
33	Romania	97.1	98.6	95.6	97.3 *	98.4 *	96.3*	97.7	98.3	97.2	519	77	501	71 *	421	63
34	Russian Federation	99.2	99.6	98.9	99.4 *	99.7 *	99.2*	99.7	99.7	99.7	857	76	672	75 *	346	54
35	Serbia and Montenegro	...	...	...	96.4 *	98.9 *	94.1*	98.4	99.3	97.5	...	...	302	85 *	139	79
36	Slovakia	...	...	...	99.6 *	99.7 *	99.6*	99.6	99.6	99.6	...	...	16	54 *	18	52
37	Slovenia	99.6	99.6	99.5	99.7	99.7	99.6	...	...	...	7	58	6	56	...	...
38	The former Yugoslav Rep. of Macedonia	...	...	...	96.1 *	98.2 *	94.1*	97.6	98.8	96.5	...	...	62	77 *	41	74
39	Turkey	77.9	89.2	66.4	88.3 *	95.7 *	81.1*	92.4	97.4	87.4	8 066	75	5 768	81 *	4 686	83
40	Ukraine	99.4	99.7	99.2	99.4 *	99.7 *	99.2*	99.8	99.8	99.7	237	77	232	80 *	77	81
	Central Asia															
41	Armenia	97.5	98.9	96.1	99.4 *	99.7 *	99.2*	99.9	99.9	99.8	63	80	14	74 *	3	104
42	Azerbaijan	...	...	...	98.8 *	99.5 *	98.2*	99.7	99.9	99.5	...	...	66	79 *	22	87
43	Georgia	...	...	...	...	...	...	...	...	...	...	...	...	...	...	...
44	Kazakhstan	98.8	99.5	98.2	99.5 *	99.8 *	99.3*	99.8	99.8	99.8	136	79	55	77 *	24	53
45	Kyrgyzstan	...	...	...	98.7 *	99.3 *	98.1*	99.6	99.7	99.4	...	...	41	74 *	18	77
46	Mongolia	...	...	...	97.8 *	98.0 *	97.5*	97.6	97.1	98.1	...	...	36	56 *	54	40
47	Tajikistan	98.2	99.2	97.2	99.5 *	99.7 *	99.3*	99.9	99.9	99.9	55	77	19	68 *	5	50
48	Turkmenistan	...	...	...	98.8 *	99.3 *	98.3*	...	...	...	...	...	31	73 *	...	...
49	Uzbekistan	98.7	99.5	97.9	99.3	99.6	98.9	...	...	...	164	80	122	74	...	...
	East Asia and the Pacific															
50	Australia	...	...	...	...	...	...	...	...	...	...	...	...	...	...	...
51	Brunei Darussalam	85.5	91.0	79.4	92.7 *	95.2 *	90.2*	95.9	97.3	94.4	24	66	17	65 *	14	66
52	Cambodia	62.0	77.7	48.8	73.6 *	84.7 *	64.1*	79.6	87.4	72.4	2 032	73	2 235	72 *	2 351	70
53	China	78.3	87.2	68.9	90.9 *	95.1 *	80.5*	95.7	97.8	93.4	181 331	70	87 038	73 *	48 626	76
54	Cook Islands	...	...	...	...	...	...	...	...	...	...	...	...	...	...	...

YOUTH LITERACY RATE (15-24) (%)									YOUTH ILLITERATES (15-24)						
1990			2000-2004[2]			2015			1990		2000-2004[2]		2015		
Total	Male	Female	Total	Male	Female	Total	Male	Female	Total (000)	% F	Total (000)	% F	Total (000)	% F	
													Arab States		
77.3	86.1	68.1	90.1*	94.1*	86.1*	94.1	94.4	93.9	1 158	69	673	69*	397	51	1
95.6	96.2	95.0	99.3*	99.2*	99.3*	99.9	99.9	99.9	3	54	0.8	43*	0.2	48	2
73.2	82.2	64.2	...	...	...	...	...	...	28	67	...	...	...	...	3
61.3	70.9	51.0	73.2*	79.0*	66.9*	...	...	...	3 970	62	3 286	61*	...	...	4
41.0	56.4	24.9	...	...	...	...	...	...	2 063	62	...	...	...	...	5
96.7	97.9	95.3	99.1*	99.3*	98.9*	99.6	99.6	99.7	23	66	10	61*	5	37	6
87.5	87.9	87.2	93.1	92.2	93.9	...	...	...	46	51	25	40	...	...	7
92.1	95.5	88.6	...	...	...	...	...	...	48	71	...	...	...	...	8
91.0	98.9	82.7	97.0	99.8	94.0	...	...	...	78	94	39	97	...	...	9
45.8	55.5	36.1	61.3*	67.7*	55.5*	66.4	70.3	62.5	214	59	199	58*	258	56	10
55.3	68.0	42.0	69.5	77.4	61.3	...	...	...	2 254	64	1 923	62	...	...	11
85.6	95.4	75.4	98.5	99.6	97.3	...	...	...	43	82	8	87	...	...	12
...	...	...	98.7*	98.7*	98.6*	99.0	98.7	99.4	...	...	9	51*	11	29	13
90.3	88.3	93.0	98.6*	...	...	99.6	...	...	6	29	1	...	0.4	...	14
85.4	91.2	78.6	95.9*	98.1*	93.7*	99.8	99.9	99.8	446	68	162	76*	12	49	15
65.0	75.6	54.0	74.6*	81.6*	69.2*	81.7	85.2	78.1	1 752	65	1 526	62*	1 546	59	16
79.9	92.2	66.9	95.2*	97.1*	93.0*	97.3	97.8	96.8	520	81	199	70*	117	58	17
84.1	92.8	75.2	94.3*	96.4*	92.2*	97.8	97.9	97.6	264	77	117	67*	39	53	18
84.7	81.7	88.6	91.4	88.2	95.0	...	...	...	48	27	36	25	...	...	19
50.0	73.5	25.0	67.9	84.3	50.9	...	...	...	1 134	73	1 244	75	...	...	20
													Central and Eastern Europe		
94.8	97.4	91.9	99.4*	99.4*	99.5*	...	...	...	34	75	3	42*	...	...	21
99.8	99.8	99.8	99.8*	99.8*	99.8*	99.8	99.7	99.8	3	50	3	40*	2	49	22
...	...	...	99.6*	99.6*	99.7*	99.9	99.9	99.9	...	...	2	41*	0.5	48	23
99.4	99.5	99.3	98.2*	98.3*	98.1*	97.4	97.6	97.2	7	59	21	52*	19	53	24
99.6	99.7	99.6	99.6*	99.6*	99.7*	99.6	99.6	99.7	2	52	2	48*	2	37	25
...	...	...	...	...	...	...	...	...	...	...	...	...	...	...	26
99.8	99.7	99.8	99.8*	99.7*	99.8*	99.8	99.7	99.8	0.5	42	0.5	40*	0.2	48	27
99.7	99.8	99.7	99.5*	99.4*	99.6*	99.5	99.5	99.5	4	56	7	39*	5	49	28
...	...	...	99.7*	99.7*	99.8*	99.7	99.7	99.8	...	...	0.8	43*	0.7	32	29
99.8	99.8	99.8	99.7*	99.7*	99.7*	99.8	99.8	99.8	1	45	1.5	42*	0.8	49	30
...	...	...	...	...	...	...	...	...	...	...	...	...	...	...	31
99.8	99.8	99.8	98.7*	98.3*	99.1*	98.7	98.2	99.2	1	48	10	34*	7	30	32
99.3	99.3	99.2	97.8*	97.7*	97.8*	97.2	97.1	97.4	28	54	79	49*	65	45	33
99.8	99.8	99.8	99.7*	99.7*	99.8*	99.7	99.6	99.8	42	47	64	41*	43	33	34
...	...	...	99.4*	99.4*	99.3*	99.4	99.4	99.4	...	...	10	51*	8	48	35
...	...	...	99.6*	99.6*	99.7*	99.4	99.4	99.4	...	...	3	42*	4	49	36
99.8	99.7	99.8	99.8	99.8	99.8	...	...	...	0.7	45	0.6	50	...	...	37
...	...	...	98.7*	99.0*	98.5*	98.7	98.9	98.5	...	...	4	59*	4	56	38
92.7	97.1	88.3	96.6*	98.4*	94.8*	97.6	98.8	96.3	838	79	466	76*	338	76	39
99.8	99.8	99.9	99.8*	99.8*	99.8*	99.8	99.7	99.8	11	43	14	42*	10	49	40
													Central Asia		
99.5	99.7	99.4	99.8*	99.8*	99.9*	99.9	99.9	99.9	3	63	1	35*	0.4	49	41
...	...	...	99.9*	99.9*	99.9*	99.9	99.9	99.9	...	...	2	44*	2	49	42
...	...	...	...	...	...	...	...	...	...	...	...	...	...	...	43
99.8	99.8	99.8	99.8*	99.8*	99.9*	99.8	99.8	99.8	6	45	4	40*	4	49	44
...	...	...	99.7*	99.7*	99.7*	99.6	99.6	99.6	...	...	3	42*	4	50	45
...	...	...	97.7*	97.0*	98.4*	96.3	94.9	97.7	...	...	12	34*	20	30	46
99.8	99.8	99.8	99.8*	99.8*	99.8*	99.9	99.9	99.9	2	55	2	49*	1	49	47
...	...	...	99.8*	99.8*	99.8*	...	...	...	...	...	2	49*	...	...	48
99.6	99.7	99.6	99.7	99.7	99.6	...	...	...	14	57	17	59	...	...	49
													East Asia and the Pacific		
...	...	...	...	...	...	...	...	...	...	...	...	...	...	...	50
97.9	97.6	98.1	98.9*	98.9*	98.9*	99.9	99.9	99.8	1	43	0.7	48*	0.1	95	51
73.5	81.5	65.6	83.4*	87.9*	78.9*	90.3	92.8	87.8	476	65	555	63*	367	62	52
95.3	97.5	93.1	98.9*	99.2*	98.5*	99.5	99.5	99.5	11 709	72	2 260	63*	985	47	53
...	...	...	...	...	...	...	...	...	...	...	...	...	...	...	54

Table 2A (continued)

	Country or territory	ADULT LITERACY RATE (15 and over) (%)									ADULT ILLITERATES (15 and over)					
		1990			2000-2004[2]			2015			1990		2000-2004[2]		2015	
		Total	Male	Female	Total	Male	Female	Total	Male	Female	Total (000)	% F	Total (000)	% F	Total (000)	% F
55	Democratic People's Republic of Korea	...	...	...	...	...	...	...	...	...	...	...	...	...	...	...
56	Fiji	88.6	91.6	85.5	92.9 *	94.5 *	91.4*	...	...	...	51	63	36	60 *	...	...
57	Indonesia	79.5	86.7	72.5	87.9	92.5	83.4	...	...	...	23 800	68	18 432	69	...	...
58	Japan	...	...	...	...	...	...	...	...	...	...	...	...	...	...	...
59	Kiribati	...	...	...	...	...	...	...	...	...	...	...	...	...	...	...
60	Lao People's Democratic Republic	56.5	70.3	42.8	68.7 *	77.0 *	60.9*	76.8	82.2	71.5	1 017	67	970	64 *	1 067	62
61	Macao, China	90.5	94.6	86.8	91.3 *	95.3 *	87.8*	95.1	97.2	93.1	26	73	31	75 *	22	75
62	Malaysia	80.7	86.9	74.4	88.7 *	92.0 *	85.4*	93.3	95.2	91.4	2 190	66	1 723	64 *	1 442	64
63	Marshall Islands	...	...	...	...	...	...	...	...	...	...	...	...	...	...	...
64	Micronesia (Federated States of)	...	...	...	...	...	...	...	...	...	...	...	...	...	...	...
65	Myanmar	80.7	87.4	74.2	89.7 *	93.7 *	86.2*	93.3	95.0	91.7	4 905	68	3 224	69 *	2 733	64
66	Nauru	30.4	47.4	14.0	...	...	...	...	...	...	7 546	61	...	...	...	...
67	New Zealand	...	...	...	...	...	...	...	...	...	...	...	...	...	...	...
68	Niue	...	...	...	...	...	...	...	...	...	...	...	...	...	...	...
69	Palau	...	...	...	...	...	...	...	...	...	...	...	...	...	...	...
70	Papua New Guinea	56.6	64.4	48.2	57.3 *	63.4 *	50.9*	62.9	66.2	59.5	1 046	57	1 330	56 *	1 755	53
71	Philippines	91.7	92.2	91.2	92.6 *	92.5 *	92.7*	94.2	93.7	94.6	2 986	53	3 500	50 *	3 919	47
72	Republic of Korea	...	...	...	...	...	...	...	...	...	...	...	...	...	...	...
73	Samoa	98.0	98.5	97.4	98.7	98.9	98.4	...	...	...	2	61	1	57	...	...
74	Singapore	88.8	94.4	83.2	92.5 *	96.6 *	88.6*	96.4	98.1	94.7	265	75	232	77 *	148	74
75	Solomon Islands	...	...	...	...	...	...	...	...	...	...	...	...	...	...	...
76	Thailand	...	...	...	92.6 *	94.9 *	90.5*	95.7	96.9	94.5	...	...	3 298	66 *	2 334	66
77	Timor-Leste	...	...	...	...	...	...	...	...	...	...	...	...	...	...	...
78	Tokelau	...	...	...	...	...	...	...	...	...	...	...	...	...	...	...
79	Tonga	...	...	...	98.9 *	98.8 *	99.0*	...	...	...	...	...	0.7	46 *	...	...
80	Tuvalu	...	...	...	...	...	...	...	...	...	...	...	...	...	...	...
81	Vanuatu	...	...	...	74.0 *	...	...	...	...	...	...	...	29	...	...	...
82	Viet Nam	...	...	...	90.3 *	93.9 *	86.9*	93.8	94.7	92.9	...	...	4 887	69 *	4 386	58
	Latin America and the Caribbean															
83	Anguilla	...	...	...	...	...	...	...	...	...	...	...	...	...	...	...
84	Antigua and Barbuda	...	...	...	...	...	...	...	...	...	...	...	...	...	...	...
85	Argentina	95.7	95.9	95.6	97.2 *	97.2 *	97.2*	98.1	98.0	98.2	964	54	764	52 *	624	49
86	Aruba	...	...	...	...	...	...	...	...	...	...	...	...	...	...	...
87	Bahamas	94.4	93.6	95.2	...	...	...	...	...	...	10	44	...	...	...	...
88	Barbados	99.4	99.4	99.3	99.7	99.7	99.7	...	...	...	1	57	0.6	50	...	...
89	Belize	...	...	...	76.9 *	76.7 *	77.1*	81.9	81.6	82.2	...	...	34	49 *	39	49
90	Bermuda	...	...	...	...	...	...	...	...	...	...	...	...	...	...	...
91	Bolivia	78.1	86.8	69.8	86.5 *	92.9 *	80.4*	93.4	96.8	90.0	862	71	693	74 *	480	77
92	Brazil	82.0	82.9	81.2	88.4 *	88.3 *	88.6*	92.3	91.9	92.6	17 336	53	14 870	51 *	11 807	50
93	British Virgin Islands	...	...	...	...	...	...	...	...	...	...	...	...	...	...	...
94	Cayman Islands	...	...	...	...	...	...	...	...	...	...	...	...	...	...	...
95	Chile	94.0	94.4	93.6	95.7 *	95.8 *	95.6*	97.2	97.3	97.2	550	55	483	52 *	385	51
96	Colombia	88.4	88.8	88.1	94.2 *	93.7 *	94.6*	95.2	94.8	95.6	2 584	53	1 765	47 *	1 829	47
97	Costa Rica	93.9	93.9	93.8	95.8	95.7	95.9	...	...	...	121	50	118	48	...	...
98	Cuba	95.1	95.2	95.1	99.8 *	99.8 *	99.8*	99.9	99.9	99.9	398	51	18	52 *	8.3	63
99	Dominica	...	...	...	...	...	...	...	...	...	...	...	...	...	...	...
100	Dominican Republic	79.4	79.8	79.0	87.7 *	88.0 *	87.3*	92.6	92.0	93.3	894	50	684	51 *	537	45
101	Ecuador	87.6	90.2	85.1	91.0 *	92.3 *	89.7*	94.1	94.8	93.4	775	60	753	57 *	652	56
102	El Salvador	72.4	76.1	69.1	79.7	82.4	77.1	88.5	90.3	86.8	835	59	847	58	614	59
103	Grenada	...	...	...	...	...	...	...	...	...	...	...	...	...	...	...
104	Guatemala	61.0	68.8	53.2	69.1 *	75.4 *	63.3*	77.9	83.2	72.9	1 843	60	2 103	60 *	2 242	62
105	Guyana	97.2	98.0	96.4	...	...	...	...	...	...	13	66	...	...	...	...
106	Haiti	39.7	42.6	36.9	51.9	53.8	50.0	...	...	...	2 328	54	2 407	54	...	...
107	Honduras	[illegible]	[illegible]	[illegible]	[illegible]	[illegible]	[illegible]	86.0	84.8	87.2	851	51	779	49 *	816	46
108	Jamaica	82.2	78.0	86.1	87.6	83.8	91.4	...	...	...	274	40	223	36	...	...
109	Mexico	87.3	90.6	84.3	90.3 *	92.0 *	88.7*	94.6	95.8	93.4	6 471	64	6 640	60 *	4 755	63
110	Montserrat	...	...	...	...	...	...	...	...	...	...	...	...	...	...	...
111	Netherlands Antilles	95.6	95.6	95.7	96.7	96.7	96.7	...	...	...	6	53	6	53	...	...
112	Nicaragua	62.7	62.7	62.8	76.7 *	76.8 *	76.6*	84.0	82.6	85.4	764	51	701	51 *	732	46
113	Panama	89.0	89.7	88.4	91.9 *	92.5 *	91.2*	94.3	95.0	93.7	171	53	164	54 *	157	55
114	Paraguay	90.3	92.4	88.3	91.6 *	93.1 *	90.2*	94.8	95.4	94.2	237	60	285	59 *	262	56

YOUTH LITERACY RATE (15-24) (%)									YOUTH ILLITERATES (15-24)						
1990			2000-2004[2]			2015			1990		2000-2004[2]		2015		
Total	Male	Female	Total	Male	Female	Total	Male	Female	Total (000)	% F	Total (000)	% F	Total (000)	% F	
…	…	…	…	…	…	…	…	…	…	…	…	…	…	…	55
97.8	98.1	97.6	99.3*	99.1*	99.4*	…	…	…	3	54	1	39*	…	…	56
95.0	96.6	93.4	98.0	98.5	97.6	…	…	…	1 873	65	834	62	…	…	57
…	…	…	…	…	…	…	…	…	…	…	…	…	…	…	58
…	…	…	…	…	…	…	…	…	…	…	…	…	…	…	59
70.1	79.47	60.56	78.5*	82.6*	74.7*	83.9	86.8	80.8	235	66	225	59*	238	59	60
97.2	99.2	95.8	99.6*	99.4*	99.8*	99.9	99.9	99.9	2	88	0.3	26*	0.1	49	61
94.8	95.3	94.2	97.2*	97.2*	97.3*	98.8	98.6	98.9	179	55	120	48*	66	45	62
…	…	…	…	…	…	…	…	…	…	…	…	…	…	…	63
…	…	…	…	…	…	…	…	…	…	…	…	…	…	…	64
88.2	90.1	86.2	94.4*	95.6*	93.2*	96.7	96.1	97.3	972	58	531	60*	340	41	65
46.6	67.0	27.3	…	…	…	…	…	…	1 867	67	…	…	…	…	66
…	…	…	…	…	…	…	…	…	…	…	…	…	…	…	67
…	…	…	…	…	…	…	…	…	…	…	…	…	…	…	68
…	…	…	…	…	…	…	…	…	…	…	…	…	…	…	69
68.6	74.4	62.4	66.7*	69.1*	64.1*	67.5	66.3	68.8	277	60	343	52*	504	47	70
97.3	97.1	97.4	95.1*	94.5*	95.7*	95.0	94.2	95.9	342	46	759	43*	946	40	71
…	…	…	…	…	…	…	…	…	…	…	…	…	…	…	72
99.0	99.1	98.9	99.5	99.4	99.5	…	…	…	0.3	50	0.2	50	…	…	73
99.0	98.8	99.2	99.5*	99.4*	99.6*	99.7	99.4	99.9	6	39	2	38*	2	16	74
…	…	…	…	…	…	…	…	…	…	…	…	…	…	…	75
…	…	…	98.0*	98.1*	97.8*	98.6	98.6	98.6	…	…	236	53*	147	49	76
…	…	…	…	…	…	…	…	…	…	…	…	…	…	…	77
…	…	…	…	…	…	…	…	…	…	…	…	…	…	…	78
…	…	…	99.3*	99.2*	99.4*	…	…	…	…	…	0.1	45*	…	…	79
…	…	…	…	…	…	…	…	…	…	…	…	…	…	…	80
…	…	…	…	…	…	…	…	…	…	…	…	…	…	…	81
94.1	94.5	93.6	…	…	…	95.6	95.1	96.1	801	54	…	…	727	44	82
Latin America and the Caribbean															
…	…	…	…	…	…	…	…	…	…	…	…	…	…	…	83
…	…	…	…	…	…	…	…	…	…	…	…	…	…	…	84
98.2	98.0	98.4	98.9*	98.7*	99.1*	99.2	99.0	99.3	97	44	72	40*	55	43	85
…	…	…	…	…	…	…	…	…	…	…	…	…	…	…	86
96.5	95.4	97.5	…	…	…	…	…	…	2	34	…	…	…	…	87
99.8	99.8	99.8	99.8	99.8	99.8	…	…	…	0.1	49	0.1	50	…	…	88
…	…	…	84.2*	83.9*	84.5*	86.9	85.8	88.0	…	…	8	48*	8	45	89
…	…	…	…	…	…	…	…	…	…	…	…	…	…	…	90
92.6	96.2	89.0	97.3*	98.5*	96.1*	99.0	99.1	99.0	98	74	43	72*	22	49	91
91.8	90.5	93.1	96.6*	95.6*	97.7*	98.6	97.9	99.4	2 363	42	1 180	34*	455	21	92
…	…	…	…	…	…	…	…	…	…	…	…	…	…	…	93
…	…	…	…	…	…	…	…	…	…	…	…	…	…	…	94
98.1	97.9	98.3	99.0*	98.8*	99.2*	99.3	99.1	99.4	48	44	26	40*	20	42	95
94.9	94.3	95.5	97.6*	96.7*	98.4*	98.2	97.1	99.3	369	44	201	32*	167	19	96
97.4	97.1	97.7	98.4	98.1	98.7	…	…	…	15	43	12	42	…	…	97
99.3	99.3	99.2	100.0*	100.0*	100.0*	100.0	100.0	100.0	17	51	0.7	51*	0.6	51	98
…	…	…	…	…	…	…	…	…	…	…	…	…	…	…	99
87.5	86.8	88.2	94.0*	93.1*	95.0*	95.9	93.9	98.0	184	46	100	41*	72	24	100
95.5	96.0	94.9	96.4*	96.4*	96.5*	96.7	96.3	97.1	95	56	91	48*	91	43	101
83.8	85.1	82.6	88.9	89.6	88.1	95.7	95.1	96.2	172	55	143	53	60	44	102
…	…	…	…	…	…	…	…	…	…	…	…	…	…	…	103
73.4	80.5	66.2	82.2*	86.4*	78.4*	87.0	89.4	84.6	457	63	440	60*	437	58	104
99.8	99.8	99.8	…	…	…	…	…	…	0.3	51	…	…	…	…	105
54.8	55.8	53.8	66.2	65.8	66.5	…	…	…	580	51	637	49	…	…	106
79.7	78.5	80.8	88.9*	86.9*	90.9*	91.2	88.2	94.3	201	47	153	40*	160	32	107
91.2	87.1	95.2	94.5	91.3	97.8	…	…	…	42	28	27	19	…	…	108
95.2	95.9	94.4	97.6*	97.9*	97.3*	98.8	98.9	98.8	889	58	486	57*	254	50	109
…	…	…	…	…	…	…	…	…	…	…	…	…	…	…	110
97.5	97.3	97.7	98.3	98.2	98.5	…	…	…	0.7	46	0.6	50	…	…	111
68.2	67.7	68.7	86.2*	83.6*	88.8*	90.9	87.1	94.8	246	50	154	40*	134	28	112
95.3	95.7	94.8	96.1*	96.5*	95.6*	96.4	96.6	96.2	24	54	21	55*	23	52	113
95.6	95.9	95.2	96.3*	96.2*	96.5*	97.1	97.0	97.2	36	53	41	47*	43	48	114

Table 2A (continued)

	Country or territory	ADULT LITERACY RATE (15 and over) (%) 1990 Total	1990 Male	1990 Female	2000-2004[2] Total	2000-2004[2] Male	2000-2004[2] Female	2015 Total	2015 Male	2015 Female	ADULT ILLITERATES (15 and over) 1990 Total (000)	1990 % F	2000-2004[2] Total (000)	2000-2004[2] % F	2015 Total (000)	2015 % F
115	Peru	…	…	…	87.7 *	93.5 *	82.1*	92.4	96.0	88.9	…	…	2 271	73 *	1 762	73
116	Saint Kitts and Nevis	…	…	…	…	…	…	…	…	…	…	…	…	…	…	…
117	Saint Lucia	…	…	…	90.1 *	89.5 *	90.6*	93.0	92.3	93.6	…	…	10	49 *	8	47
118	Saint Vincent and the Grenadines	…	…	…	…	…	…	…	…	…	…	…	…	…	…	…
119	Suriname	…	…	…	88.0 *	92.3 *	84.1*	90.0	92.6	87.5	…	…	34	68 *	34	63
120	Trinidad and Tobago	96.8	98.1	95.6	98.5	99.0	97.9	…	…	…	26	70	15	67	…	…
121	Turks and Caicos Islands	…	…	…	…	…	…	…	…	…	…	…	…	…	…	…
122	Uruguay	96.5	96.0	97.0	97.7	97.3	98.1	…	…	…	80	46	57	42	…	…
123	Venezuela	88.9	90.1	87.7	93.0 *	93.3 *	92.7*	95.7	95.4	96.0	1 340	55	1 154	52 *	972	47
	North America and Western Europe															
124	Andorra	…	…	…	…	…	…	…	…	…	…	…	…	…	…	…
125	Austria	…	…	…	…	…	…	…	…	…	…	…	…	…	…	…
126	Belgium	…	…	…	…	…	…	…	…	…	…	…	…	…	…	…
127	Canada	…	…	…	…	…	…	…	…	…	…	…	…	…	…	…
128	Cyprus	94.3	97.7	91.0	96.8 *	98.6 *	95.1*	98.6	99.4	98.0	29	80	19	79 *	10	72
129	Denmark	…	…	…	…	…	…	…	…	…	…	…	…	…	…	…
130	Finland	…	…	…	…	…	…	…	…	…	…	…	…	…	…	…
131	France	…	…	…	…	…	…	…	…	…	…	…	…	…	…	…
132	Germany	…	…	…	…	…	…	…	…	…	…	…	…	…	…	…
133	Greece	94.9	97.6	92.3	91.0 *	94.0 *	88.3*	95.7	97.3	94.1	419	77	836	67 *	408	70
134	Iceland	…	…	…	…	…	…	…	…	…	…	…	…	…	…	…
135	Ireland	…	…	…	…	…	…	…	…	…	…	…	…	…	…	…
136	Israel	91.4	94.9	88.0	96.9 *	98.3 *	95.6*	98.0	99.0	97.1	267	71	145	73 *	117	74
137	Italy	…	…	…	…	…	…	…	…	…	…	…	…	…	…	…
138	Luxembourg	…	…	…	…	…	…	…	…	…	…	…	…	…	…	…
139	Malta	88.4	87.9	88.9	87.9 *	86.4 *	89.2*	…	…	…	32	49	36	45 *	…	…
140	Monaco	…	…	…	…	…	…	…	…	…	…	…	…	…	…	…
141	Netherlands	…	…	…	…	…	…	…	…	…	…	…	…	…	…	…
142	Norway	…	…	…	…	…	…	…	…	…	…	…	…	…	…	…
143	Portugal	…	…	…	…	…	…	…	…	…	…	…	…	…	…	…
144	San Marin	…	…	…	…	…	…	…	…	…	…	…	…	…	…	…
145	Spain	…	…	…	97.1 *	98.1 *	96.1*	…	…	…	…	…	1 030	69 *	…	…
146	Sweden	…	…	…	…	…	…	…	…	…	…	…	…	…	…	…
147	Switzerland	…	…	…	…	…	…	…	…	…	…	…	…	…	…	…
148	United Kingdom	…	…	…	…	…	…	…	…	…	…	…	…	…	…	…
149	United States	…	…	…	…	…	…	…	…	…	…	…	…	…	…	…
	South and West Asia															
150	Afghanistan	…	…	…	…	…	…	…	…	…	…	…	…	…	…	…
151	Bangladesh	34.2	44.3	23.7	41.1	50.3	31.4	…	…	…	41 606	56	52 209	57	…	…
152	Bhutan	…	…	…	…	…	…	…	…	…	…	…	…	…	…	…
153	India[4]	49.3	61.9	35.9	61.0 *	73.4 *	47.8*	69.7	79.5	59.5	272 279	61	267 002	65 *	273 107	65
154	Iran, Islamic Republic of	63.2	72.2	54.0	77.0 *	83.5 *	70.4*	…	…	…	11 506	61	10 543	64 *	…	…
155	Maldives	94.8	95.0	94.6	96.3 *	96.2 *	96.4*	97.5	97.4	97.7	6	50	6	47 *	6.7	46
156	Nepal	30.4	47.4	14.0	48.6 *	62.7 *	34.9*	63.4	75.5	51.5	7 546	61	7 308	63 *	7 548	65
157	Pakistan	35.4	49.3	20.1	48.7 *	61.7 *	35.2*	57.1	68.8	44.8	41 368	60	47 577	62 *	54 259	63
158	Sri Lanka[3]	88.7	92.9	84.7	90.4 *	92.2 *	88.6*	92.8	93.6	92.1	1 262	65	1 331	57 *	1 169	54
	Sub-Saharan Africa															
159	Angola	…	…	…	66.8 *	82.1 *	53.8*	70.2	81.1	59.8	…	…	2 174	73 *	2 993	69
160	Benin	26.4	38.1	15.5	33.6 *	46.4 *	22.6*	42.9	55.7	30.1	1 773	59	2 352	61 *	3 006	63
161	Botswana	68.1	65.7	70.3	78.9	76.1	81.5	…	…	…	234	49	223	45	…	…
162	Burkina Faso	…	…	…	12.8 *	18.5 *	8.1*	…	…	…	…	…	4 726	56 *	…	…
163	Burundi	37.0	[illegible]	[illegible]	[illegible]	[illegible]	51.9*	69.7	74.0	65.6	1 929	61	1 338	62 *	1 615	58
164	Cameroon	57.9	68.7	47.5	67.9 *	77.0 *	59.8*	…	…	…	2 701	64	2 807	64	[illegible]	[illegible]
165	Cape Verde	63.8	76.2	54.3	75.7	85.4	68.0	…	…	…	67	71	64	72	…	…
166	Central African Republic	33.2	47.1	20.7	48.6 *	64.8 *	33.5*	55.9	68.9	43.5	1 119	63	1 093	68 *	1 206	66
167	Chad	27.7	37.0	18.8	25.5 *	40.6 *	12.7*	37.9	54.3	21.9	2 299	58	3 097	61 *	4 031	64
168	Comoros	53.8	61.4	46.4	56.2	63.5	49.1	…	…	…	129	59	187	58	…	…
169	Congo	67.1	77.1	57.9	82.8	88.9	77.1	…	…	…	443	66	330	68	…	…
170	Côte d'Ivoire	38.5	50.5	25.7	48.1 *	60.1 *	38.2*	58.2	67.3	48.8	4 119	57	4 579	59 *	5 200	60

YOUTH LITERACY RATE (15-24) (%)									YOUTH ILLITERATES (15-24)						
1990			2000-2004[2]			2015			1990		2000-2004[2]		2015		
Total	Male	Female	Total	Male	Female	Total	Male	Female	Total (000)	% F	Total (000)	% F	Total (000)	% F	
94.5	96.9	92.1	96.8*	97.8*	95.7*	97.9	97.8	97.9	243	71	174	66*	124	49	115
…	…	…	…	…	…	…	…	…	…	…	…	…	…	…	116
…	…	…	95.4*	94.8*	95.9*	93.0	92.5	93.5	…	…	1	44*	2	45	117
…	…	…	…	…	…	…	…	…	…	…	…	…	…	…	118
…	…	…	93.5*	95.1*	92.1*	92.1	91.4	92.8	…	…	6	61*	7	45	119
99.6	99.7	99.6	99.8	99.8	99.8	…	…	…	0.8	51	0.6	50	…	…	120
…	…	…	…	…	…	…	…	…	…	…	…	…	…	…	121
98.7	98.3	99.1	99.1	98.8	99.4	…	…	…	6	34	5	33	…	…	122
96.0	95.4	96.6	97.2*	96.3*	98.1*	97.8	96.9	98.8	153	42	136	34*	122	27	123
North America and Western Europe															
…	…	…	…	…	…	…	…	…	…	…	…	…	…	…	124
…	…	…	…	…	…	…	…	…	…	…	…	…	…	…	125
…	…	…	…	…	…	…	…	…	…	…	…	…	…	…	126
…	…	…	…	…	…	…	…	…	…	…	…	…	…	…	127
99.7	99.5	99.8	99.8*	99.7*	99.8*	99.9	99.9	99.9	0.3	29	0.3	40*	0.1	48	128
…	…	…	…	…	…	…	…	…	…	…	…	…	…	…	129
…	…	…	…	…	…	…	…	…	…	…	…	…	…	…	130
…	…	…	…	…	…	…	…	…	…	…	…	…	…	…	131
…	…	…	…	…	…	…	…	…	…	…	…	…	…	…	132
99.5	99.4	99.7	99.5*	99.4*	99.5*	99.1	99.2	99.1	7	37	7	43*	10	48	133
…	…	…	…	…	…	…	…	…	…	…	…	…	…	…	134
…	…	…	…	…	…	…	…	…	…	…	…	…	…	…	135
98.7	99.0	98.4	99.6*	99.7*	99.4*	99.8	99.8	99.8	10	61	5	66*	2	49	136
…	…	…	…	…	…	…	…	…	…	…	…	…	…	…	137
…	…	…	…	…	…	…	…	…	…	…	…	…	…	…	138
97.5	96.0	99.1	96.0*	94.4*	97.8*	…	…	…	1	18	2	27*	…	…	139
…	…	…	…	…	…	…	…	…	…	…	…	…	…	…	140
…	…	…	…	…	…	…	…	…	…	…	…	…	…	…	141
…	…	…	…	…	…	…	…	…	…	…	…	…	…	…	142
…	…	…	…	…	…	…	…	…	…	…	…	…	…	…	143
…	…	…	…	…	…	…	…	…	…	…	…	…	…	…	144
…	…	…	99.6*	99.6*	99.6*	…	…	…	…	…	21	54*	…	…	145
…	…	…	…	…	…	…	…	…	…	…	…	…	…	…	146
…	…	…	…	…	…	…	…	…	…	…	…	…	…	…	147
…	…	…	…	…	…	…	…	…	…	…	…	…	…	…	148
…	…	…	…	…	…	…	…	…	…	…	…	…	…	…	149
South and West Asia															
…	…	…	…	…	…	…	…	…	…	…	…	…	…	…	150
42.0	50.7	33.2	49.7	57.8	41.1	…	…	…	12 842	56	14 740	57 …	…		151
…	…	…	…	…	…	…	…	…	…	…	…	…	…	…	152
64.3	73.4	54.2	76.4*	84.2*	67.7*	83.7	87.9	79.2	58 555	61	45 781	65*	37 517	62	153
86.3	91.7	80.8	…	…	…	…	…	…	1 425	68	…	…	…	…	154
98.1	98.1	98.1	98.2*	98.0*	98.3*	98.3	98.0	98.6	0.7	48	1	46*	1	41	155
46.6	67.0	27.3	70.1*	80.6*	60.1*	82.5	88.0	76.8	1 867	67	1 370	66*	1 133	64	156
47.4	62.5	30.6	64.5*	74.8*	53.9*	72.1	78.9	64.9	10 697	63	11 122	63*	11 318	61	157
95.1	95.9	94.2	95.6*	95.1*	96.0*	97.0	96.5	97.6	157	57	157	44*	91	39	158
Sub-Saharan Africa															
…	…	…	71.4*	82.7*	62.6*	70.3	76.9	63.8	…	…	669	69*	1 148	61	159
40.4	56.6	24.7	44.4*	58.2*	32.5*	52.6	65.0	39.9	497	64	750	62*	891	63	160
83.3	79.3	87.2	89.1	85.5	92.8	…	…	…	48	38	43	33	…	…	161
…	…	…	19.4*	25.5*	14.0*	…	…	…	…	…	1 753	54*	…	…	162
51.6	58.4	44.8	72.3*	75.6*	69.5*	78.0	77.7	78.4	517	57	358	56*	420	49	163
81.1	86.4	75.9	…	…	…	…	…	…	414	64	…	…	…	…	164
81.5	87.1	76.2	89.1	92.0	86.3	…	…	…	13	65	11	64	…	…	165
52.1	65.6	39.4	58.5*	70.3*	46.8*	61.8	70.3	53.5	258	65	306	65*	389	62	166
48.0	58.4	37.7	37.3*	55.4*	23.1*	46.0	61.4	30.5	569	60	912	63*	1 305	64	167
56.7	63.8	49.6	59.0	65.6	52.2	…	…	…	45	58	64	58	…	…	168
92.5	94.9	90.3	97.8	98.4	97.3	…	…	…	36	66	14	64	…	…	169
52.6	64.9	40.3	59.8*	69.5*	51.5*	65.5	71.6	59.3	1 046	62	1 326	61*	1 449	59	170

Table 2A (continued)

	Country or territory	ADULT LITERACY RATE (15 and over) (%)									ADULT ILLITERATES (15 and over)					
		1990			2000-2004[2]			2015			1990		2000-2004[2]		2015	
		Total	Male	Female	Total	Male	Female	Total	Male	Female	Total (000)	% F	Total (000)	% F	Total (000)	% F
171	Democratic Rep. of the Congo	47.5	61.4	34.4	65.3 *	79.8 *	51.9*	67.1	76.3	58.1	10 400	64	9 131	71 *	12 885	64
172	Equatorial Guinea	73.3	85.8	61.1	84.2 *	92.1 *	76.4*	91.8	93.9	89.7	55	74	41	76 *	31	64
173	Eritrea	46.4	58.5	34.8	...	...	...	...	...	...	900	62	...	...	...	...
174	Ethiopia	28.6	37.3	19.8	41.5	49.2	33.8	...	...	...	18 993	57	21 955	57	...	...
175	Gabon	...	...	...	...	...	...	...	...	...	...	...	...	...	...	...
176	Gambia	25.6	31.7	19.7	...	...	...	...	...	...	397	55	...	...	...	...
177	Ghana	58.5	70.1	47.2	54.1 *	62.9 *	45.7*	...	...	...	3 455	65	5 290	60 *	...	...
178	Guinea	27.2	42.3	12.9	...	...	...	...	...	...	406	61	...	...	...	...
179	Guinea-Bissau	...	...	...	...	...	...	...	...	...	...	...	...	...	...	...
180	Kenya	70.8	80.9	60.8	73.6 *	77.7 *	70.2*	77.4	78.2	76.5	3 489	68	4 523	58 *	5 294	52
181	Lesotho	78.0	65.4	89.5	81.4 *	73.7 *	90.3*	...	...	...	184	28	182	32 *	...	...
182	Liberia	39.2	55.4	22.8	55.9	72.3	39.3	...	...	...	691	64	765	69	...	...
183	Madagascar	58.0	66.4	49.8	70.6 *	76.4 *	65.2*	70.6	73.5	67.8	2 768	60	2 583	60 *	4 111	55
184	Malawi	51.8	68.8	36.2	64.1 *	74.9 *	54.0*	...	...	...	2 450	69	2 137	66 *	...	...
185	Mali	...	...	...	19.0 *	26.7 *	11.9*	...	...	...	...	...	4 647	56 *	...	...
186	Mauritius	79.8	84.8	75.0	84.3 *	88.2 *	80.5*	89.7	91.4	88.0	150	62	138	63 *	109	59
187	Mozambique	33.5	49.3	18.4	46.5	62.3	31.4	...	...	...	4 867	65	5 637	68	...	...
188	Namibia	74.9	77.4	72.4	85.0 *	86.8 *	83.5*	90.3	90.0	90.6	201	57	164	58 *	133	49
189	Niger	11.4	18.0	5.1	14.4 *	19.6 *	9.4*	19.2	24.8	13.4	3 391	54	4 765	53 *	7 440	53
190	Nigeria	48.7	59.4	38.4	66.8	74.4	59.4	...	...	...	23 678	61	22 167	61	...	...
191	Rwanda	53.3	62.9	44.0	64.0 *	70.5 *	58.8*	73.3	76.1	70.8	1 660	61	1 514	63 *	1 594	57
192	Sao Tome and Principe	...	...	...	...	...	...	...	...	...	...	...	...	...	...	...
193	Senegal	28.4	38.2	18.6	39.3 *	51.1 *	29.2*	46.3	56.4	36.6	2 822	58	3 345	60 *	4 308	60
194	Seychelles	...	...	...	91.9 *	91.4 *	92.3*	...	...	...	...	...	...	...	...	...
195	Sierra Leone	...	...	...	29.6 *	39.8 *	20.5*	36.4	45.5	27.5	...	...	1 735	58 *	2 275	58
196	Somalia	...	...	...	...	...	...	...	...	...	...	...	...	...	...	...
197	South Africa	81.2	82.2	80.2	82.4 *	84.1 *	80.9*	...	...	...	4 252	54	4 666	56 *	...	...
198	Swaziland	71.6	73.7	69.9	79.2 *	80.4 *	78.1*	86.3	85.8	86.8	129	58	121	57 *	89	50
199	Togo	44.2	60.5	28.7	53.0 *	68.5 *	38.3*	70.6	80.5	61.1	1 049	65	1 193	67 *	1 115	67
200	Uganda	56.1	69.3	43.5	68.9	78.8	59.2	...	...	...	3 940	66	3 889	67	...	...
201	United Republic of Tanzania	62.9	75.5	51.0	69.4 *	77.5 *	62.2*	75.4	79.7	71.1	5 128	68	6 017	64 *	6 757	59
202	Zambia	68.2	78.6	58.7	67.9 *	76.1 *	59.7*	68.7	73.2	64.1	1 400	67	1 779	64 *	2 194	57
203	Zimbabwe	80.7	86.6	75.0	90.0	93.8	86.3	...	...	...	1 085	66	730	69	...	...

		Weighted average									Sum	% F	Sum	% F	Sum	% F
I	World	75.4	81.8	69.1	81.9	86.9	76.8	85.8	89.6	82.0	871 750	63	771 129	64	764 475	63
II	Countries in transition	99.2	99.6	98.8	99.4	99.7	99.1	99.7	99.7	99.7	1 759	78	1 431	75	683	53
III	Developed countries	98.0	98.5	97.5	98.7	99.0	98.4	98.9	99.4	98.3	14 864	64	10 498	62	9 684	77
IV	Developing countries	67.0	75.9	57.9	76.4	83.2	69.5	82.4	87.2	77.5	855 127	63	759 199	64	754 109	63
V	Arab States	50.0	63.7	35.6	62.7	73.8	51.1	75.5	82.8	68.2	63 023	63	65 128	64	62 245	64
VI	Central and Eastern Europe	96.2	98.0	94.6	97.4	98.9	96.2	97.9	99.1	96.9	11 500	75	8 374	79	6 994	78
VII	Central Asia	98.7	99.4	98.0	99.2	99.6	98.9	99.6	99.7	99.5	572	79	404	73	258	64
VIII	East Asia and the Pacific	81.8	88.9	74.5	91.4	95.0	87.7	94.9	97.0	92.8	232 255	69	129 922	71	91 851	70
IX	Latin America and the Caribbean	85.0	86.7	83.3	89.7	90.5	88.9	93.5	93.9	93.1	41 742	56	37 901	55	30 780	54
X	North America and Western Europe	97.9	98.4	97.4	98.7	99.0	98.4	99.4	99.6	99.1	11 326	64	7 740	62	3 821	77
XI	South and West Asia	47.5	59.7	34.4	58.6	70.5	46.2	67.2	76.7	57.3	382 353	60	381 116	64	416 647.5	64
XII	Sub-Saharan Africa	49.9	60.0	40.3	59.7	68.2	51.8	69.4	75.0	63.9	128 980	61	140 544	61	151 879	59

General note: The population used to generate the number of illiterates is from the United Nations Population Division estimates (2002 Revision). For countries with national observed literacy data, the population corresponding to the year of the census or survey was used. For countries with UIS estimates, the population used was that of 2002.

1. For countries indicated with (*), national observed literacy data are used. For all others, UIS literacy estimates (July 2002 assessment) are used.

YOUTH LITERACY RATE (15-24) (%)									YOUTH ILLITERATES (15-24)						
1990			2000-2004[2]			2015			1990		2000-2004[2]		2015		
Total	Male	Female	Total	Male	Female	Total	Male	Female	Total (000)	% F	Total (000)	% F	Total (000)	% F	
68.9	80.3	57.6	68.7*	76.7*	61.1*	66.5	71.3	61.8	2 213	68	3 132	63*	4 868	57	171
92.7	96.6	88.8	93.8*	93.9*	93.7*	94.9	93.2	96.6	5	77	5	51*	7	33	172
60.9	72.5	49.3	...	...	...	...	...	...	236	65	...	...	...	...	173
43.0	51.5	34.1	57.4	63.0	51.8	...	...	...	5 326	58	5 751	57	...	...	174
...	...	...	...	...	...	...	...	...	...	...	13	59*	...	...	175
42.2	50.5	34.1	...	...	...	...	...	...	95	58	...	...	...	...	176
81.8	88.2	75.4	...	...	...	...	...	...	538	67	...	...	...	...	177
44.1	62.2	26.5	...	...	...	...	...	...	107	66	...	...	...	...	178
...	...	...	...	...	...	...	...	...	...	...	...	...	...	...	179
89.8	92.9	86.7	80.3*	79.8*	80.7*	77.2	74.3	80.2	473	65	1 374	49*	1 880	43	180
87.2	77.2	97.1	...	...	...	...	...	...	38	12	...	...	...	...	181
57.2	75.4	38.6	70.8	86.3	55.4	...	...	...	176	71	189	76	...	...	182
72.2	77.8	66.6	70.1*	72.4*	68.1*	68.5	69.0	68.0	635	60	912	54*	1 520	51	183
63.2	75.7	51.2	76.3*	82.1*	70.7*	...	...	...	643	68	501	63*	...	...	184
...	...	...	24.2*	32.3*	16.9*	...	...	...	...	...	1 720	55*	...	...	185
91.1	91.2	91.1	94.5*	93.7*	95.4*	96.6	95.2	98.0	18	49	12	42*	7	29	186
48.8	66.1	31.7	62.8	76.6	49.2	...	...	...	1 365	68	1 363	69	...	...	187
87.4	85.9	89.0	92.3*	91.2*	93.5*	93.1	91.3	94.9	36	44	29	42*	38	37	188
17.0	24.9	9.3	19.8*	26.2*	14.2*	22.1	28.3	15.5	1 211	54	1 724	53*	2 767	53	189
73.6	80.8	66.5	88.6	90.7	86.5	...	...	...	4 243	63	2 779	58	...	...	190
72.7	78.0	67.4	76.5*	77.2*	75.9*	78.4	78.1	78.7	363	60	386	56*	473	50	191
...	...	...	...	...	...	...	...	...	...	...	...	...	...	...	192
40.1	50.0	30.2	49.1*	58.5*	41.0*	52.7	59.6	45.7	829	58	1 025	59*	1 264	57	193
...	...	...	99.1*	98.8*	99.4*	...	...	...	...	...	...	...	...	...	194
...	...	...	38.2*	46.9*	29.9*	42.1	49.1	35.1	...	...	523	57*	753	56	195
...	...	...	...	...	...	...	...	...	...	...	...	...	...	...	196
88.5	88.6	88.4	93.9*	93.5*	94.3*	...	...	...	882	51	518	47*	...	...	197
85.1	84.7	85.5	88.1*	86.8*	89.4*	88.8	87.0	90.6	25	52	27	45*	32	42	198
63.5	79.4	47.7	74.0*	83.1*	63.3*	83.7	87.1	80.4	242	72	246	69*	218	60	199
70.1	79.8	60.5	80.2	86.3	74.0	...	...	...	1 003	66	1 000	66	...	...	200
03.1	89.2	77.2	78.4*	80.9*	76.2*	78.1	77.8	78.3	882	69	1 634	56*	2 236	50	201
81.2	86.4	76.2	69.4*	72.6*	66.1*	66.8	68.2	65.3	311	64	656	55*	1 000	52	202
93.9	96.6	91.3	97.6	98.9	96.2	...	...	...	128	72	73	78	...	...	203

Weighted average									Sum	% F	Sum	% F	Sum	% F	
84.3	88.2	80.1	87.5	90.5	84.2	89.5	91.4	87.5	156 430	62	132 909	61	128 364	57	I
99.2	99.2	99.2	99.7	99.7	99.8	99.7	99.7	99.8	332	49	125	43	105	33	II
99.7	99.7	99.6	99.7	99.7	99.7	99.5	99.6	99.4	471	51	419	49	672	53	III
80.9	85.8	75.8	85.0	88.7	81.1	88.0	90.1	85.7	155 627	62	132 364	61	127 587	57	IV
66.6	77.3	55.3	78.3	84.7	71.9	88.2	89.6	86.8	14 203	66	12 212	64	8 230	55	V
98.3	99.2	97.4	98.9	99.3	98.6	98.8	99.2	98.5	1 023	75	710	66	592	61	VI
97.7	97.8	97.7	99.7	99.7	99.7	99.7	99.6	99.7	281	50	46	47	44	49	VII
95.4	97.2	93.6	97.9	98.3	97.4	98.5	98.5	98.5	17 383	68	7 146	59	5 045	48	VIII
92.7	92.7	92.7	95.9	95.6	96.3	97.8	97.4	98.3	6 351	50	4 164	46	2 370	38	IX
99.7	99.7	99.7	99.8	99.8	99.8	99.8	99.8	99.8	310	49	217	49	191	49	X
61.5	71.1	51.0	73.1	81.0	64.8	79.9	84.6	74.9	87 276	61	72 329	64	67 962	60	XI
67.5	74.8	60.2	72.0	76.6	67.5	75.6	78.3	72.9	29 603	61	36 085	58	43 931	55	XII

2. Data refer to the most recent year available during the period specified. See introduction to the Statistical annex for broader explanation of national literacy definitions, assessment methods, sources and years of data.

3. Literacy data for the most recent year do not include some geographic regions.

4. Literacy rates for the most recent year were derived from the absolute numbers of illiterates and literates provided to the UIS through its literacy questionnaire.

Table 2B
Literate environment

		PERIODICALS CIRCULATION[1]								
		Daily newspapers			Non-daily newspapers			Other periodicals		
			Circulation			Circulation			Circulation	
		Number of titles	Total (000)	per 1,000 inhabitants	Number of titles	Total (000)	per 1,000 inhabitants	Number of titles	Total (000)	per 1,000 inhabitants
	Country or territory	2000	2000	2000	2000	2000	2000	2000	2000	2000
	Arab States									
1	Algeria	24[V]	796[V]	27	82[V]	909[V]	31[V]	106[V]	...	...
2	Bahrain	...	...	...	...	...	...	...	...	...
3	Djibouti	...	...	...	...	...	...	...	...	...
4	Egypt	16[X]	2 080[X]	31	45[X]	1 371[X]	21[X]	235[X]	2 773[X]	42[X]
5	Iraq	...	...	...	...	...	...	...	...	...
6	Jordan	5	352[V]	74	20	155[V]	33[V]	270[V]	148[V]	31[V]
7	Kuwait	...	...	...	...	...	...	...	...	...
8	Lebanon[3]	13	220	63	7	...	...	49	...	...
9	Libyan Arab Jamahiriya	4[**,V]	71[**,V]	14	...	...	...	...	...	...
10	Mauritania	...	...	...	...	...	...	...	...	...
11	Morocco[4]	23	846	29	507	4 108	141	364	4 956	170
12	Oman	5[V]	...	...	...	...	...	29[V]	...	...
13	Palestinian Autonomous Territories	3	...	...	13	2 058	645	62	1 854	581
14	Qatar	...	...	...	...	...	...	...	...	...
15	Saudi Arabia	...	...	...	...	...	...	...	...	...
16	Sudan	...	...	...	11[V]	5 644[V]	188[V]	54[V]	68[V]	2[V]
17	Syrian Arab Republic	...	...	...	...	...	...	...	...	...
18	Tunisia	7	180	19	29	940	99	182	525	55
19	United Arab Emirates	...	...	...	...	...	...	...	...	...
20	Yemen	...	...	...	...	...	...	...	...	...
	Central and Eastern Europe									
21	Albania	...	...	...	...	...	...	...	...	...
22	Belarus[5]	20[V]	1 559[V]	154[V]	600	10 339	1 030	318[V]	1 687[V]	167
23	Bosnia and Herzegovina	...	...	...	...	...	...	...	...	...
24	Bulgaria[3]	43	1 400	173	527[X]	2 649[X]	325[X]	619[X]	1 247[X]	153[X]
25	Croatia[3, 5]	12	595	134	229	568[V]	128[V]	2 003	...	...
26	Czech Republic	103	...	...	712	...	...	2 437	...	...
27	Estonia[3]	13	262	192	93	...	...	956	2 144	1 569
28	Hungary[3, 5, 6]	40	1 625	162	167	...	...	433[V]	...	...
29	Latvia	26	327	138	201	1 754	739	325	1 856	782
30	Lithuania	22	108	31	339	949	271	753	...	...
31	Poland	42	3 928	102	24	583	15	5 468	67 820	1 754
32	Republic of Moldova	6[V]	660[V]	153[V]	170	915	214	99	258	60
33	Romania	145[**]	...	...	320[*]	...	...	1 608[*]	...	...
34	Russian Federation[3, 5]	333	...	...	10 188	...	...	...	...	...
35	Serbia and Montenegro	...	...	...	...	...	...	...	...	...
36	Slovakia	16	705	131	435	2 651	492	1 014	13 823	2 564
37	Slovenia	5	335	168	200	...	...	1 278	...	...
38	The former Yugoslav Rep. of Macedonia	5	108	54	33	121	60	116	235	116
39	Turkey	542	...	...	688	...	...	1 635	...	...
40	Ukraine	61	8 683	175	2 606	38 985	785	1 245	3 988	80
	Central Asia									
41	Armenia	8	...	...	83	...	...	41	114	36
42	Azerbaijan[3, 5]	15[X]	80[X]	10[X]	329[X]	122[X]	15	38[V]	50[V]	6[V]
43	Georgia	35	26	5	122[X]	...	...	149	728	138
44	Kazakhstan	...	...	...	...	...	...	...	...	...
45	Kyrgyzstan	3	...	...	181	...	...	36	170	35
46	Mongolia[3, 5]	5	44	18	27	94[V]	38[V]	38	85	34
47	Tajikistan	...	...	...	...	...	...	...	...	...
48	Turkmenistan	2	32	[illegible]	[illegible]	338	73	20	47	10
49	Uzbekistan	...	...	...	...	...	...	...	...	
	East Asia and the Pacific									
50	Australia[3, 5]	48	3 083	161	97	381	20	...	...	...
51	Brunei Darussalam	...	...		...	...	...	...	...	...
52	Cambodia	...	...	...	...	...	...	...		...

BOOK PRODUCTION[1]		NATIONAL LIBRARIES[1]			INFORMATION AND COMMUNICATION TECHNOLOGY								
Number of titles of non-periodic printed publications (books and pamphlets)					Radio receivers			Television receivers					
Total (000)	per 1,000 inhabitants	Number of volumes (books) (000)	Registered users (000)	Loans to users (000)	Total[1] (000)	per 1,000 inhabitants[1]	% of households with a radio[2]	Total[1] (000)	per 1,000 inhabitants[1]	% of households with a television[2]	PCs[2] per 1,000 inhabitants	Internet users (estimated)[2] per 1,000 inhabitants	
1999	1999	1999	1999	1999	1997	1997	2002	1997	1997	2002	2002	2002	
												Arab States	
133	0.4	...	...	3	7 100	246	71	3 100	107	88	8	16	1
92 v	14 v	...	...	...	338	541	99 x	275	441	95	151	173	2
...	...	...	...	...	52	86	57	28	46	41	14	6	3
1 410 v	2 v	1 001 v	456 v	...	20 500	320	88	7 700	120	89	16	27	4
...	...	...	...	...	4 850	227	...	1 750	82	...	8	1	5
...	...	...	...	...	1 660	362	83 x	500	109	93	38	58	6
219 **	10	270	...	...	1 175	643	...	875	478	95	117	102	7
289 v	9 v	...	...	...	2 850	864	98 z	1 180	358	93	76	111	8
...	...	...	...	...	1 350	273	91 x	730	148	95 y	24	23	9
...	...	...	...	...	360	148	50	62	26	21	10	4	10
386	1	...	...	...	6 640	239	89	3 100	112	76	17	23	11
12	0.5	115	15 **	194	1 400	586	79	1 600	670	79	34	65	12
...	...	...	...	...	...	...	83	...	...	94	...	...	13
...	...	...	...	...	256	469	...	230	421	90	183	116	14
...	...	...	...	...	6 250	310	90 x	5 100	253	99	128	60	15
...	...	...	...	...	7 550	257	80	2 380	81	49	6	3	16
...	...	...	85	162	4 150	270	...	1 050	68	80	19	13	17
1 260	13.4	...	...	...	2 060	224	77	920	100	92	34	52	18
...	...	1 000	15	365	820	311	91 x	310	117	86	153	346	19
...	...	...	...	...	1 050	64	60 x	470	29	43	8	5	20
												Central and Eastern Europe	
...	...	...	...	...	810	258	82	405	129	90	11	4	21
6 073 v	60 v	...	...	...	3 020	297	48	2 520	248	88 z	...	81	22
...	...	...	...	...	940	267	...	1	0.3	87	...	24	23
4 971	61	2 522	22	758	4 510	544	...	3 310	400	79 z	51	79	24
2 309	52	2 505	220	738	1 510	342	94 x	1 220	277	94 y	171	178	25
12 551	122	5 603	36	597	8 270	802	80	5 470	530	99	176	254	26
3 265	237	2 285	60	486	1 010	718	97	605	430	92	213	332	27
10 352	103	7 554	28	2	7 010	691	93 x	4 420	436	96 y	111	161	28
2 178	91	2 185 v	43 v	3 042 v	1 760	723	80	1 220	501	79	172	133	29
4 097	117	5 761	15	1 562	1 900	539	98 x	1 700	482	97	110	144	30
19 192	50	2 731	40	543	20 200	522	95 y	13 050	337	91	106	230	31
1 166	27	2 666	27	1 392	3 220	746	70 x	1 260	292	...	18	35	32
7 874	35	19 035	77	738	7 200	319	41	5 250	233	97	80	98	33
...	...	73 632	100	22 729	61 500	417	...	60 500	411	98	90	42	34
...	...	5 977 v	295 v	512 v	3 150	298	...	2 750	260	92	28	61	35
3 153	59	6 035	31	863	3 120	580	90	2 620	487	100	180	160	36
3 450	173	1 360	11	228	805	403	92	710	356	91	302	378	37
733	36	2 983 v	760 v	947 v	410	206	...	510	257	82 y	...	49	38
2 920	4	1 553	27	...	11 300	173	49 x	20 900	321	...	43	61	39
6 282	13	4 122	26	2 645	45 050	885	...	18 050	355	97	19	18	40
												Central Asia	
516	16	6 847	2 088	2	850	264	42	825	256	91	20	20	41
444 v	6 v	3 695	27	796	175	22	...	170	21	...	...	36	42
697	13	...	447	...	3 020	568	82	2 570	483	76	30	14	43
1 223	8	3 780	41	2 180	6 470	400	41 x	3 880	240	92 x	...	16	44
420 v	9 v	...	...	...	520	111	45 x	210	45	84 x	13	30	45
...	...	3 272	53	...	360	148	...	118	48	29	27	20	46
...	...	...	2	14	850	144	...	20	3	79 z	...	0.5	47
...	...	...	...	...	1 225	279	46 y	820	186	94 y	...	2 z	48
...	...	...	...	...	10 800	457	61 x	6 400	271	90 x	...	11	49
												East Asia and the Pacific	
...	...	...	...	...	25 500	1 377	96	10 150	548	96	568	537	50
38 v	12 v	...	...	...	93	299	...	77	248	98 z	77	102 z	51
...	...	...	...	...	1 340	110	43 x	94	8	41	2	2	52

Table 2B (continued)

	Country or territory	PERIODICALS CIRCULATION[1]								
		Daily newspapers			Non-daily newspapers			Other periodicals		
			Circulation			Circulation			Circulation	
		Number of titles	Total (000)	per 1,000 inhabitants	Number of titles	Total (000)	per 1,000 inhabitants	Number of titles	Total (000)	per 1,000 inhabitants
		2000	2000	2000	2000	2000	2000	2000	2000	2000
53	China[3, 5]	909	75 603	59	1 098	103 284	81	...	...	...
54	Cook Islands[7]	...	...	...	...	...	...	...	...	...
55	Democratic People's Republic of Korea	...	...	...	...	...	...	...	...	...
56	Fiji	...	...	...	...	...	...	...	...	...
57	Indonesia[3, 5]	396 x	4 782 x	23 x	746	7 758 x	37 x	266 v	4 156 v	20 v
58	Japan[3]	110	71 896	566	...	...	...	...	...	...
59	Kiribati[7]	...	...	...	...	...	...	...	...	...
60	Lao People's Democratic Republic	...	...	...	...	...	...	...	...	...
61	Macao, China	10	167	372	7	20	44	188	...	...
62	Malaysia[3]	31	2 191	95	...	...	...	...	...	...
63	Marshall Islands	...	...	...	...	...	...	...	...	...
64	Micronesia (Federated States of)	...	...	...	...	...	...	...	...	...
65	Myanmar	4 v	400 v	9 v	...	...	...	38 v	3 397	74 v
66	Nauru[7]	...	...	...	...	...	...	...	...	...
67	New Zealand	28	765	202	123	3 076	813	188 v	5 500	1 479 v
68	Niue[7]	...	...	...	...	...	...	...	...	...
69	Palau	...	...	...	...	...	...	...	...	...
70	Papua New Guinea	...	...	...	...	...	...	...	...	...
71	Philippines	...	...	...	...	...	...	...	...	...
72	Republic of Korea[3, 5]	116	...	...	4 708	...	...	...	...	...
73	Samoa	...	...	...	...	...	...	...	...	...
74	Singapore[3, 5]	9	1 096	273	3	115	29	...	...	...
75	Solomon Islands	...	...	...	...	...	...	...	...	...
76	Thailand[3]	34 v	11 753 v	197 v	...	...	...	...	...	...
77	Timor-Leste[3, 5]	1	...	...	1	...	...	...	...	...
78	Tokelau[7]	...	...	...	...	...	...	...	...	...
79	Tonga	...	...	...	...	...	...	...	...	...
80	Tuvalu[7]	...	...	...	...	...	...	...	...	...
81	Vanuatu	...	...	...	...	...	...	...	...	...
82	Viet Nam	5 x	450 **,x	6 **,x	...	...	...	...	...	...
	Latin America and the Caribbean									
83	Anguilla[7]	...	...	...	...	...	...	...	...	...
84	Antigua and Barbuda[7]	...	...	...	...	...	...	...	...	...
85	Argentina[3]	106	1 500	40	...	1 933 v	53 v	113	4 936	133
86	Aruba[7]	...	...	...	...	...	...	...	...	...
87	Bahamas	...	...	...	...	...	...	...	...	...
88	Barbados	...	...	...	...	...	...	...	...	...
89	Belize	...	...	...	...	...	...	...	...	...
90	Bermuda[7]	1	15	...	3	29	...	...	...	...
91	Bolivia	29 v	788 *,v	99 v	10 v	7 884 v	988 v	...	...	...
92	Brazil[3, 5]	465	7 883	46	2 020	...	...	...	...	...
93	British Virgin Islands[7]	...	...	...	...	...	...	...	...	...
94	Cayman Islands[7]	...	...	...	...	...	...	...	...	...
95	Chile[3, 5]	53	...	...	9	...	...	...	...	...
96	Colombia[3, 5]	24 x	1 093 x	26 x	4 x	131 x	3 x	...	...	...
97	Costa Rica[3]	6	275	70	27	...	...	306	...	...
98	Cuba	2	600	54	31	923	82	205	1 166	104
99	Dominica[7]	...	...	...	...	...	...	...	...	...
100	Dominican Republic	9	230	28	8	215	26	188	6 274 v	776 v
101	Ecuador	36	1 220	98	40	175 v	15 v	27	1 086	87
102	El Salvador	4 v	171 v	29 v	...	...	...	...	...	...
103	Grenada		...	...	...	...	...	...	...	...
104	Guatemala	...	...	...	...			...	...	...
105	Guyana	2	57	75	4	48	63	24	131	173
106	Haiti	...	...	...	...	...	...	...	...	...
107	Honduras	...	...	...	...	...	...	...	...	...
108	Jamaica	...	...	...	...	...	...	...	...	...
109	Mexico	311	9 251	94	26	614	6	278	20 362	206
110	Montserrat[7]	...	...	...	1 v	1 v	...	...	...	...

BOOK PRODUCTION[1]		NATIONAL LIBRARIES[1]			INFORMATION AND COMMUNICATION TECHNOLOGY								
Number of titles of non-periodic printed publications (books and pamphlets)					Radio receivers			Television receivers					
Total (000)	per 1,000 inhabitants	Number of volumes (books) (000)	Registered users (000)	Loans to users (000)	Total[1] (000)	per 1,000 inhabitants[1]	% of households with a radio[2]	Total[1] (000)	per 1,000 inhabitants[1]	% of households with a television[2]	PCs[2] per 1,000 inhabitants	Internet users (estimated)[2] per 1,000 inhabitants	
1999	1999	1999	1999	1999	1997	1997	2002	1997	1997	2002	2002	2002	
...	...	...	...	...	417 000	336	...	400 000	322	89	27	46	53
...	...	...	...	...	14	...	...	4	...	...	...	...	54
...	...	...	...	...	3 360	154	...	1 200	55	...	...	– z	55
...	...	...	...	...	500	636	93	21	27	57	48	60	56
121	0.1	...	...	...	31 500	155	74	13 750	68	56	12	21	57
...	...	7 312	...	...	120 500	955	99 x	86 500	686	100	382	449	58
...	...	...	...	...	17	...	56	1	...	24	...	...	59
...	...	...	...	...	730	148	52 x	52	11	30	3	3	60
340	77	...	...	...	...	...	68 x	...	...	93	200	250	61
5 084	23	...	...	...	9 100	425	77 y	3 600	168	89	150	327	62
...	...	...	...	...	82	217	...	66	174	...	...	...	63
...	...	...	...	...	...	...	51	...	...	15	...	11	64
227	0.5	...	...	...	4 200	92	2	260	6	3	5	0.5	65
...	...	...	...	...	7	...	...	1	...	...	...	...	66
5 405	144	...	...	...	3 750	1 018	99	1 926	523	98	424	496	67
...	...	...	...	...	1	...	...	–	...	...	...	...	68
...	...	...	...	...	...	...	...	...	...	...	...	...	69
...	...	...	...	...	410	83	25	42	8	9	57	13	70
1 380	2	...	...	...	11 500	161	83	3 700	52	76	28	45	71
...	...	...	...	...	47 500	1 037	...	15 900	347	92	496	554	72
...	...	...	...	...	178	1 057	99	11	62	96	7	23	73
...	...	5 420	1 720	24 757	2 550	689	98 x	1 330	360	99	619	502	74
...	...	...	...	...	57	143	74	3	6	4	39	5	75
...	...	...	...	...	13 959	236	77 y	15 190	257	92	40	77	76
...	...	...	...	...	18	22	...	–	–	...	...	...	77
...	...	...	...	...	1	...	...	–	...	...	...	...	78
...	...	...	...	...	61	608	...	2	21	...	20	28	79
...	...	...	...	...	4	...	...	–	...	...	...	...	80
...	...	...	...	...	62	341	...	2	13	6	15	34	81
...	...	...	...	...	8 200	109	53 x	3 570	48	83	10	19	82
										Latin America and the Caribbean			
...	...	...	...	...	3	...	...	1	...	...	...	...	83
...	...	...	...	...	36	...	90 x	31	...	91 z	...	...	84
11 991 v	33 v	...	...	...	24 300	681	81 x	7 950	223	97 z	79	108	85
...	...	...	...	...	50	...	...	20	...	...	...	...	86
...	...	...	...	...	215	736	...	67	229	...	...	193	87
...	...	...	...	...	237	896	99 y	76	287	93	104	111	88
...	...	...	...	...	133	591	80 x	41	183	37	140	120	89
...	...	...	...	...	82	...	...	66	...	...	...	...	90
...	...	125	18	38	5 250	672	85 x	900	115	46 y	22	31	91
21 689 v	13 v	...	...	...	71 000	430	88	36 500	221	90	74	81	92
...	...	...	...	...	9	...	...	4	...	...	...	...	93
...	...	...	...	...	36	...	...	7	...	...	...	...	94
1 443	10	101	...	447	5 180	354	99	3 150	215	95	115	229	95
...	...	429	5	...	21 000	525	...	4 590	115	92	49	46	96
1 464 v	39 v	825	...	225	980	268	100 x	525	144	84 z	200	195	97
952	9	3 000	9	173	3 900	352	...	2 640	238	...	32	11 z	98
...	...	...	...	...	46	...	87 z	6	...	76 z	...	...	99
...	...	...	...	...	1 440	181	71 x	770	97	77 x	...	58	100
996	8	...	...	...	4 150	351	...	1 550	131	89	31	42	101
663 v	11 v	...	...	...	2 750	467	...	4 000	679	85 z	25	47	102
...	...	...	...	...	113	271	94 y	118	283	94 y	...	...	103
...	...	...	...	...	835	79	80 x	640	61	40 z	14	33	104
...	...	...	...	...	420	561	...	46	61	...	31	164	105
...	...	...	...	...	415	54	52	38	5	26	...	10	106
...	...	...	...	...	2 450	411	74 z	570	96	47	13	25	107
...	...	...	...	...	1 215	483	...	460	183	70	54	228	108
6 952 v	7 v	539	...	29	31 000	329	82 y	25 600	272	94	82	98	109
...	...	...	...	...	7	...	...	3	...	...	...	...	110

Table 2B (continued)

	Country or territory	PERIODICALS CIRCULATION[1]								
		Daily newspapers			Non-daily newspapers			Other periodicals		
			Circulation			Circulation			Circulation	
		Number of titles	Total (000)	per 1,000 inhabitants	Number of titles	Total (000)	per 1,000 inhabitants	Number of titles	Total (000)	per 1,000 inhabitants
		2000	2000	2000	2000	2000	2000	2000	2000	2000
111	Netherlands Antilles	...	...	...	...	...	...	...	...	...
112	Nicaragua	...	...	...	...	...	...	...	...	...
113	Panama	...	...	...	...	...	...	...	...	...
114	Paraguay	...	...	...	...	...	...	...	...	...
115	Peru[3]	57[v]	570[v]	23[v]	...	...	...	43[v]	...	...
116	Saint Kitts and Nevis[7]	...	...	...	...	...	...	...	...	...
117	Saint Lucia	...	...	...	...	...	...	...	...	...
118	Saint Vincent and the Grenadines	...	...	...	...	...	...	...	...	...
119	Suriname	2[v]	28[v]	67[v]	9[v]	63[v]	152[v]	8[v]	8[v]	20[v]
120	Trinidad and Tobago	...	...	...	...	...	...	...	...	...
121	Turks and Caicos Islands[7]	...	...	...	...	...	...	...	...	...
122	Uruguay[3]	4	...	...	...	...	...	...	...	...
123	Venezuela[8]	...	...	...	...	...	...	...	...	...
	North America and Western Europe									
124	Andorra[7]	2	...	...	...	...	...	...	...	...
125	Austria[3,5,9]	16	2 503	309	120	...	...	2 685[v]	...	...
126	Belgium[3]	29	1 568	153	...	...	...	...	...	...
127	Canada[3]	104	5 167	168	...	...	...	...	...	...
128	Cyprus[7]	8	87	...	38	200	...	50	372	...
129	Denmark	33	1 507	283	10	1 415	266	117	...	...
130	Finland[10,11,12]	55	2 304	445	149	924	178	5 711	...	...
131	France[3,5,12]	84	8 424	142	245[x]	2 236[x]	38[x]	...	...	...
132	Germany[3,5]	382	23 946	291	25	2 021	25	...	...	...
133	Greece[5,12]	207[v]	...	...	14	441	40	...	...	...
134	Iceland[3,5]	3	91	322	20	57	202	938[**,x]	...	...
135	Ireland[3,5,12]	6	564	148	61	1 354	355	...	...	...
136	Israel	...	...	...	...	...	...	...	...	...
137	Italy[3]	89	6 273	109	...	...	...	...	...	...
138	Luxembourg[3,5]	5	120	276	10	86[x]	200[x]	...	...	...
139	Malta	4[v]	...	...	11[v]	...	...	523[v]	...	...
140	Monaco[7]	...	...	...	...	...	...	...	...	...
141	Netherlands[3,5,12]	35	4 443	279	49	317	20	...	...	...
142	Norway[13]	82	2 545	569	70	367	82	...	...	...
143	Portugal[3,5]	28	1 026	102	242[x]	1 134	113	1 065[x]	15 762[x]	1 577[x]
144	San Marino[7]	3[v]	2[v]	...	8[v]	12[v]	...	...	...	...
145	Spain	87	4 003	98	11[x]	5 371[x]	132[x]	...	...	...
146	Sweden	90	3 627	410	71	382	43	389	22 112	2 497
147	Switzerland[3]	104	2 666	372	120[x]	1 190[x]	166[x]	...	...	...
148	United Kingdom[3,5]	108	19 159	326	467	6 246	106	...	...	...
149	United States[3]	1 476	55 945	196	...	...	...	...	...	...
	South and West Asia									
150	Afghanistan	...	...	...	...	...	...	...	...	...
151	Bangladesh	...	...	...	...	...	...	...	...	...
152	Bhutan	...	...	...	...	...	...	...	...	...
153	India[14]	5 221[v]	59 023[v]	60[v]	38 607[v]	67 826[v]	69[v]	...	...	...
154	Iran, Islamic Republic of	112	...	...	906	...	...	...	...	...
155	Maldives	...	...	...	...	...	...	...	...	...
156	Nepal	...	...	...	2 288[v]	...	...	...	...	...
157	Pakistan[3]	306	5 600	39	560[x]	1 782[x]	13[x]	559[x]	1 713	12[x]
158	Sri Lanka[3,5]	12	536	29	36	1 322	71	...	...	...
	Sub-Saharan Africa									
159	Angola	5[**,v]	133[**,v]	11[**,v]	...	...	...	...	...	...
160	Benin	13[x]	33[x]	5[x]	2[x]	44[x]	7[x]	62[x]	110[x]	18[x]
161	Botswana	1[**,v]	41[**,v]	25[**,v]	...	...	...	...	...	...
162	Burkina Faso	4[**,v]	15[**,v]	1[**,v]	...	...	...	...	...	...
163	Burundi	1	15[**,v]	2[**,v]	5[v]	8[v]	1[v]	...	...	...
164	Cameroon[5]	2[**,v]	92[**,v]	6[**,v]	12[v]	69[v]	5[v]	...	...	...

BOOK PRODUCTION[1]		NATIONAL LIBRARIES[1]			INFORMATION AND COMMUNICATION TECHNOLOGY								
Number of titles of non-periodic printed publications (books and pamphlets)					Radio receivers			Television receivers					
Total (000)	per 1,000 inhabitants	Number of volumes (books) (000)	Registered users (000)	Loans to users (000)	Total[1] (000)	per 1,000 inhabitants[1]	% of households with a radio[2]	Total[1] (000)	per 1,000 inhabitants[1]	% of households with a television[2]	PCs[2] per 1,000 inhabitants	Internet users (estimated)[2] per 1,000 inhabitants	
1999	1999	1999	1999	1999	1997	1997	2002	1997	1997	2002	2002	2002	
…	…	…	…	…	217	1 034	…	69	329	…	…	9[x]	111
…	…	…	…	…	1 240	265	78[x]	320	68	60[z]	28	17	112
…	…	…	…	…	815	293	83	510	183	77	38	61	113
…	…	…	…	…	925	182	…	515	101	69[z]	35	17	114
1 942[v]	8[v]	…	…	…	6 650	269	74[z]	3 060	124	65[z]	43	90	115
…	…	…	…	…	28	…	90[z]	10	…	71[z]	…	…	116
…	…	…	…	…	111	775	93[z]	32	221	79[z]	162	89[z]	117
…	…	…	…	…	77	666	…	18	157	…	118	59	118
…	…	…	…	…	300	724	79[x]	63	152	66	47[z]	46	119
…	…	…	…	…	680	534	98[z]	425	334	88	80	106	120
…	…	…	…	…	8	…	…	–	…	…	…	…	121
674	20	…	…	…	1 970	603	95[z]	782	239	93[z]	110[z]	119[z]	122
…	…	…	…	…	10 750	471	85	4 100	179	83	61	51	123
North America and Western Europe													
173	…	…	…	…	16	…	…	27	…	…	…	…	124
…	…	…	…	…	6 080	751	87	4 250	525	98	371	412	125
…	…	…	…	…	8 075	793	71[z]	4 720	463	99	272	330	126
22 941	75	6 955	5	81	32 300	1 079	99[x]	21 500	718	99[z]	489	515	127
931	…	66	7	14	310	407	99	248	325	97	243	264	128
14 455	272	4 617	…	483	6 020	1 143	93[y]	3 121	592	97[z]	579	515	129
13 173	255	2 150	…	451	7 700	1 498	96	3 200	622	91	443	511	130
39 083	66	…	…	…	55 300	944	…	34 800	594	95	346	313	131
78 042[v]	95[v]	34 688[v]	169[v]	…	77 800	948	76	46 500	567	94	432	437	132
…	…	…	…	…	5 020	472	…	2 540	239	98[z]	82	135	133
1 796[v]	650[v]	840	5	83	260	951	97[z]	98	359	97	452	649	134
…	…	…	…	…	2 550	692	95	1 470	399	97	423	282	135
1 969[v]	34[v]	…	…	…	3 070	544	…	1 690	299	93	255	317	136
32 365	56	13 186[v]	592[v]	1 081[v]	50 500	879	…	30 300	527	97[z]	227	346	137
…	…	800	45	20	285	683	99[z]	163	391	94	593	369	138
237[v]	62[v]	…	…	…	255	666	…	280	731	93	257	306	139
72	…	…	…	…	34	…	…	25	…	…	…	…	140
…	…	2 656[v]	…	…	15 300	978	99	8 100	518	99	470	510	141
4 985	112	1 841	146	60	4 030	915	99[z]	2 030	461	100	533	310	142
2 186[v]	22[v]	2 684	67	423[v]	3 020	303	88[y]	3 310	333	100[z]	139	199	143
…	…	…	…	…	16	…	…	9	…	…	…	…	144
59 174	146	5 822[v]	…	…	13 100	325	95[z]	16 200	402	99	195	192	145
12 547[v]	142[v]	3 663[v]	…	130	8 250	931	93	4 600	519	94	627	578	146
18 273	255	3 109	12	98	7 100	991	91[y]	3 310	462	100	720	356	147
110 965[v]	190[v]	27 900	66	…	84 500	1 454	79[z]	30 500	525	98[z]	406	423	148
…	…	…	…	…	575 000	2 084	99[y]	219 000	794	98	653	546	149
South and West Asia													
…	…	…	…	…	2 750	136	58[z]	270	13	6[z]	…	–	150
…	…	…	…	…	6 150	48	32	770	6	29	3	1	151
…	…	…	…	…	37	19	21	11	6	3	5	5	152
14 085[v]	1[v]	…	…	…	116 000	120	35	63 000	65	32	7	16	153
14 783	23	…	…	…	17 000	265	83	4 610	72	77	72	47	154
…	…	…	…	…	34	128	…	7	28	68	65	49	155
…	…	…	…	…	840	38	43[z]	130	6	13[z]	3	3	156
…	…	…	…	…	13 500	102	35	3 100	24	39	4[z]	10	157
4 655	25	…	…	…	3 850	213	63	1 530	84	32	13	11	158
Sub-Saharan Africa													
…	…	…	…	…	630	55	18	150	13	9	2	3	159
9[v]	0.2[v]	…	…	…	620	107	91	60	10	20	2	8	160
…		…	…	…	237	146	92	31	19	15	40	34	161
…	…	…	…	…	370	34	65	100	9	7	2	2	162
…	…	…	…	…	440	72	61	25	4	14	0.8	1	163
52 *	0.4	…	…	…	2 270	161	54	450	32	18	6	4	164

Table 2B (continued)

	Country or territory	PERIODICALS CIRCULATION[1]								
		Daily newspapers			Non-daily newspapers			Other periodicals		
			Circulation			Circulation			Circulation	
		Number of titles	Total (000)	per 1,000 inhabitants	Number of titles	Total (000)	per 1,000 inhabitants	Number of titles	Total (000)	per 1,000 inhabitants
		2000	2000	2000	2000	2000	2000	2000	2000	2000
165	Cape Verde	...	...	...	...	...	...	...	...	...
166	Central African Republic	3 **,v	6 **,v	2 **,v	...	...	...	...	...	...
167	Chad	2	2 **,v	0.2 **,v	10 v	...	...	32 v	...	...
168	Comoros	...	...	...	...	...	...	...	...	...
169	Congo	6 **,v	21 **,v	6 **,v	...	...	...	...	...	...
170	Côte d'Ivoire	12 **,v	238 **,v	16 **,v	...	...	...	...	...	...
171	Democratic Rep. of the Congo	9 **,v	129 **,v	3 **,v	...	...	...	...	...	...
172	Equatorial Guinea	1 **,v	2 **,v	5 **,v	...	...	...	...	...	...
173	Eritrea	...	...	...	...	...	...	...	...	...
174	Ethiopia	2 v	23 v	0.4 v	78 v	402 v	6 v	15	688 v	11 v
175	Gabon	2 **,v	35 **,v	29 **,v	...	...	...	...	...	...
176	Gambia	1 v	2 **,v	2 **,v	...	...	...	...	...	...
177	Ghana	4 **,v	260 **,v	14 **,v	...	...	...	...	...	...
178	Guinea	...	...	...	...	...	...	...	...	...
179	Guinea-Bissau	1 **,v	6 **,v	5 **,v	...	...	...	...	...	...
180	Kenya[3, 5]	4 x	250 x	8 x	10 x	110 x	4 x	...	...	...
181	Lesotho	2 **,v	16 **,v	9 **,v	...	...	...	...	...	...
182	Liberia	6 **,v	37 **,v	14 **,v	...	...	...	...	...	...
183	Madagascar	5 **,v	68 **,v	5 **,v	...	...	...	...	...	...
184	Malawi	5 **,v	26 **,v	2 **,v	...	...	...	...	...	...
185	Mali	3 **,v	13 **,v	1 **,v	...	...	...	...	...	...
186	Mauritius	5	138	116	33	150	127	64	65	55
187	Mozambique	12 v	43 v	3 v	40 v	206 v	12 v	32 v	83 v	5 v
188	Namibia	4 **,v	31 **,v	17 **,v	...	...	...	...	...	...
189	Niger	1 **,v	2 **,v	0.2 **,v	...	...	...	...	...	...
190	Nigeria	25 **,v	2 760 **,v	25 **,v	...	...	...	...	...	...
191	Rwanda	1 **,v	1 **,v	0.1 **,v	8	13	2	10 **	...	...
192	Sao Tome and Principe	...	...	...	...	...	...	...	...	...
193	Senegal	5 v	...	...	...	...	...	...	...	...
194	Seychelles[7]	5 **,v	46 **,v	...	...	...	...	...	...	...
195	Sierra Leone	...	...	...	...	...	...	...	...	...
196	Somalia	...	...	...	...	...	...	...	...	...
197	South Africa[3, 5]	16	1 118	25	261	4 230	96	...	...	...
198	Swaziland	...	...	...	...	...	...	...	...	...
199	Togo	1	10	2	52	5 184	1 136	24	2 496	547
200	Uganda[3, 5]	3	63	3	9	...	...	...	...	...
201	United Republic of Tanzania	...	...	...	...	...	...	...	...	...
202	Zambia	...	228	22	...	...	...	...	...	...
203	Zimbabwe	...	...	...	...	...	...	...	...	...
I	World	...	...	...	...	...	...	...	...	...
II	Countries in transition	...	...	...	...	...	...	...	...	...
III	Developed countries	...	...	...	...	...	...	...	...	...
IV	Developing countries	...	...	...	...	...	...	...	...	...
V	Arab States	...	...	...	...	...	...	...	...	...
VI	Central and Eastern Europe	...	...	...	...	...	...	...	...	...
VII	Central Asia	...	...	...	...	...	...	...	...	...
VIII	East Asia and the Pacific	...	...	...	...	...	...	...	...	...
IX	Latin America and the Caribbean	...	...	...	...	...	...	...	...	...
X	North America and Western Europe	...	...	...	...	...	...	...	...	...
XI	South and West Asia	...	...	...			...	...	...	...
XII	Sub-Saharan Africa	...	...	...	...	...	...	...	...	...

General note: Data on book production, national libraries, radio and television receivers are primarily based on survey results reported to the UNESCO Institute for Statistics. Data on newspaper circulation combine survey results reported to the UIS as well as survey results from the World Association of Newspapers (WAN, 2004). Both institutions use similar methodologies and definitions.

Data on information and communication technology (except those pertaining to radio and televison receivers) are from the International Telecommunication Union's World Telecommunication Indicators Database (ITU, 2004).

1. UNESCO Institute for Statistics, Culture and Communication Database.
2. ITU 2004.
3. Data on the daily newspaper titles and circulation are from the WAN.
4. Data do not include non-dailies issued 2 or 3 times a week.
5. Data on the non-daily newspaper titles and circulation are from the WAN. They do not include newspapers published on Sunday only.
6. Data include number of volumes of books and bound periodicals, manuscripts, microforms, audiovisual documents and other library materials.

Table 2B

BOOK PRODUCTION[1]		NATIONAL LIBRARIES[1]			INFORMATION AND COMMUNICATION TECHNOLOGY								
Number of titles of non-periodic printed publications (books and pamphlets)					Radio receivers			Television receivers					
Total (000)	per 1,000 inhabitants	Number of volumes (books) (000)	Registered users (000)	Loans to users (000)	Total[1] (000)	per 1,000 inhabitants[1]	% of households with a radio[2]	Total[1] (000)	per 1,000 inhabitants[1]	% of households with a television[2]	PCs[2] per 1,000 inhabitants	Internet users (estimated)[2] per 1,000 inhabitants	
1999	1999	1999	1999	1999	1997	1997	2002	1997	1997	2002	2002	2002	
...	...	...	...	...	73	179	66	2	4	40	77	35	165
...	...	...	...	...	283	80	51	18	5	2	2	1	166
...	...	...	...	...	1 670	233	44	10	1	2	2	2	167
...	...	...	...	...	90	139	59	1	2	11	6	4	168
...	...	...	...	...	341	108	32	33	11	6	4	1	169
...	...	...	...	...	2 260	151	79	900	60	35	9	5	170
...	...	...	...	...	18 030	391	15	6 478	140	2	...	1	171
...	...	...	...	...	180	427	...	4	10	...	7	4	172
...	...	...	...	...	345	103	76	1	0.4	13	3	2	173
444	0.7	...	...	...	11 750	194	21	320	5	2	1	0.7	174
...	...	...	...	...	208	178	77	63	54	54	19	19	175
10 [v]	0.8 [v]	...	...	...	196	164	73	4	4	12	14	18	176
7 [v]	– [v]	...	...	...	4 400	240	57	1 730	94	21	4	8	177
...	...	...	...	...	357	46	56	85	11	9	5	4	178
...	...	...	...	...	49	39	28	–	–	26	...	10	179
...	...	...	...	...	3 070	107	87	730	25	17	6	13	180
...	...	...	...	...	104	60	29	54	31	17	...	12	181
...	...	...	...	...	790	330	...	70	29	...	...	0.3 [z]	182
...	...	...	...	...	3 050	209	41	325	22	8	4	3	183
...	...	...	...	...	2 600	248	56	–	–	2	1	2	184
33 [v]	0.3 [v]	...	...	...	570	52	71	45	4	15	1	2	185
55 [v]	5 [v]	...	...	...	420	365	90	258	224	93	149	103	186
...	...	...	...	...	730	43	46	90	5	6	4	3	187
...	...	...	...	...	232	133	89	60	34	39	68	25	188
...	...	...	...	...	680	70	33	125	13	5	0.6	1	189
...	...	...	...	...	23 500	223	62	6 900	65	26	7	3	190
...	...	1	...	0.1	601	102	41	0.6	0.1	2	...	3	191
...	...	9	...	0.2	38	273	54	23	163	36	...	70	192
...	...	...	...	...	1 240	142	73	361	41	29	20	11	193
...	...	...	...	...	42	...	93	11	...	89	...	...	194
...	...	20	10	...	1 120	270	53	53	13	7	...	2	195
...	...	...	...	...	470	61	17	135	17	8	...	9	196
...	...	...	...	...	13 750	325	73	5 200	123	54	74	69	197
...	...	...	...	...	155	158	58	21	21	18	23	19	198
5 [v]	0.1 [v]	...	...	...	940	228	86	73	18	51	31	42	199
...	...	...	...	...	2 600	121	54	315	15	6	3	4	200
...	...	...	...	...	8 800	270	52	103	3	14	4	2	201
...	...	...	...	...	1 030	105	61	277	28	26	7	5	202
...	...	101	13	31	1 140	94	64	370	30	26	47	39	203
...	...	...	...	...	...	...	...	...	...	...	...	...	I
...	...	...	...	...	...	...	...	...	...	...	...	...	II
...	...	...	...	...	...	...	...	...	...	...	...	...	III
...	...	...	...	...	...	...	...	...	...	...	...	...	IV
...	...	...	...	...	...	...	...	...	...	...	...	...	V
...	...	...	...	...	...	...	...	...	...	...	...	...	VI
...	...	...	...	...	...	...	...	...	...	...	...	...	VII
...	...	...	...	...	...	...	...	...	...	...	...	...	VIII
...	...	...	...	...	...	...	...	...	...	...	...	...	IX
...	...	...	...	...	...	...	...	...	...	...	...	...	X
...	...	...	...	...	...	...	...	...	...	...	...	...	XI
...	...	...	...	...	...	...	...	...	...	...	...	...	XII

7. Indicators were not calculated due to lack of population data for the specified year.
8. Number of titles of non-periodic printed publications consists of first editions only.
9. Data are not available for registered users. Data refer to the number of visits, including visits to exhibitions.
10. Data on daily newspaper titles do not include non-members of the Finnish Newspaper Association.
11. Data on non-daily newspaper titles do not include non-members of the Finnish Newspaper Association (non-members: 9 non-dailies in 2000).
12. Data are not available for registered users. Data refer only to the number of visits to the library.
13. Data on daily newspaper titles do not include Sunday issues.
14. Data on daily newspapers circulation include tri-weeklies and bi-weeklies.

(z) Data are for 2001.
(y) Data are for 2000.
(x) Data are for 1999.
(v) Data are for 1998.

Table 3
Early childhood care and education (ECCE)

	Country or territory	Age group 2002/2003	GROSS ENROLMENT RATIO (GER) IN PRE-PRIMARY EDUCATION (%) 1998/1999 Total	Male	Female	GPI (F/M)	2002/2003 Total	Male	Female	GPI (F/M)	NET ENROLMENT RATIO (GER) IN PRE-PRIMARY EDUCATION (%) 2002/2003 Total	Male	Female	GPI (F/M)
	Arab States													
1	Algeria	4-5	2.5	2.5	2.5	1.01	3.8	3.8	3.8	0.99	…	…	…	…
2	Bahrain	3-5	32.9	33.7	32.0	0.95	36.7	37.7	35.5	0.94	35.8	36.6	34.9	0.95
3	Djibouti	3-5	0.4	0.4	0.5	1.50	**1.2**	**1.2**	**1.2**	**0.99**	**1.2**	**1.2**	**1.2**	**0.99**
4	Egypt	4-5	10.1	10.4	9.8	0.95	13.7	14.1	13.3	0.95	12.5	12.9	12.1	0.94
5	Iraq	4-5	5.2	5.3	5.2	0.98	3.8	3.9	3.8	0.98	…	…	…	…
6	Jordan	4-5	28.6	29.9	27.2	0.91	30.4	31.5	29.2	0.93	28.0	28.9	26.9	0.93
7	Kuwait	4-5	78.3	77.8	78.8	1.01	69.9	70.0	69.8	1.00	58.4	58.4	58.4	1.00
8	Lebanon	3-5	66.0	66.9	65.0	0.97	74.8	75.4	74.1	0.98	72.4	72.7	72.0	0.99
9	Libyan Arab Jamahiriya	4-5	5.0	5.0**	4.9**	0.98**	7.8**	8.0**	7.7**	0.96**	…	…	…	…
10	Mauritania	3-5	…	…	…	…	1.9	…	…	…	…	…	…	…
11	Morocco	4-5	64.3	83.9	44.0	0.52	56.1	69.1	42.5	0.62	49.2	60.3	37.7	0.62
12	Oman	4-5	5.6	6.0	5.2	0.87	5.5	5.9	5.0	0.84	4.7	5.1	4.3	0.83
13	Palestinian A. T.	4-5	39.9	40.6	39.1	0.97	27.4	27.9	26.8	0.96	22.7	23.5	22.0	0.94
14	Qatar	3-5	25.6	26.0	25.3	0.98	33.9	35.3	32.4	0.92	30.6	31.8	29.3	0.92
15	Saudi Arabia	3-5	5.1	5.4	4.9	0.91	4.9	5.0**	4.7**	0.94**	4.9	5.0**	4.7**	0.94**
16	Sudan	4-5	21.3	…	…	…	26.6	28.4	24.6	0.86	26.6	28.4	24.6	0.86
17	Syrian Arab Republic	3-5	8.4	8.8	7.9	0.90	10.5	10.9	10.2	0.94	10.5	10.9	10.2	0.94
18	Tunisia	3-5	13.5	13.9	13.2	0.95	21.6**	21.7**	21.5**	0.99**	21.6**	21.7**	21.5**	0.99**
19	United Arab Emirates	4-5	61.6	62.4	60.8	0.97	75.3	75.8	74.8	0.99	54.9	55.3	54.5	0.98
20	Yemen	3-5	0.7	0.7	0.6	0.87	0.7	0.7	0.7	0.93	0.5**	0.5**	0.4**	0.94**
	Central and Eastern Europe													
21	Albania	3-5	41.7**	40.0**	43.5**	1.09**	47.0	46.4	47.7	1.03	47.0	46.4	47.7	1.03
22	Belarus	3-5	81.2	84.5	77.7	0.92	101.9	102.7	101.0	0.98	91.7	92.1	91.2	0.99
23	Bosnia and Herzegovina	3-5	…	…	…	…	…	…	…	…	…	…	…	…
24	Bulgaria	3-6	64.3	64.7	63.8	0.99	75.5	76.3	74.8	0.98	70.9	71.6	70.1	0.98
25	Croatia	3-6	41.1	41.6	40.6	0.98	45.5	46.1	44.9	0.97	44.5	45.1	43.9	0.97
26	Czech Republic	3-5	90.5	87.8	93.4	1.06	102.0	102.1	101.9	1.00	80.4	80.4	80.3	1.00
27	Estonia	3-6	86.8	87.5	86.0	0.98	112.9	113.1	112.5	0.99	90.1	89.9	90.4	1.01
28	Hungary	3-6	79.4	80.1	78.6	0.98	80.5	81.5	79.4	0.97	79.3	80.2	78.4	0.98
29	Latvia	3-6	50.9	52.1	49.6	0.95	74.3	76.5	72.0	0.94	72.0	73.8	70.1	0.95
30	Lithuania	3-6	50.2	51.0	49.4	0.97	58.3	59.1	57.4	0.97	56.4	56.9	55.8	0.98
31	Poland	3-6	49.8	49.7	50.0	1.01	50.6	50.5	50.6	1.00	49.4	49.3	49.5	1.00
32	Republic of Moldova	3-6	40.3	41.1	39.5	0.96	46.9	47.5	46.2	0.97	44.5	45.1	43.8	0.97
33	Romania	3-6	61.8	61.1	62.6	1.02	76.4	75.2	77.6	1.03	76.4	75.2	77.6	1.03
34	Russian Federation	4-6	…	…	…	…	93.9	96.6**	91.1**	0.94**	…	…	…	…
35	Serbia and Montenegro[1]	3-6	44.1	44.3	43.8	0.99	43.7[y]	43.5[y]	44.0[y]	1.01[y]	42.7[y]	42.4[y]	43.0[y]	1.01[y]
36	Slovakia	3-5	81.7	…	…	…	86.9	87.9	85.8	0.98	68.1	68.3	68.0	1.00
37	Slovenia	3-6	72.0	75.3	68.6	0.91	67.7	69.0	66.3	0.96	67.7	69.0	66.3	0.96
38	TFYR Macedonia	3-6	27.3	27.2	27.5	1.01	28.5	28.3	28.7	1.01	26.8	26.5	27.0	1.02
39	Turkey	3-5	6.0	6.2	5.8	0.94	7.6	7.8	7.3	0.94	…	…	…	…
40	Ukraine	3-5	47.5	47.9	47.1	0.98	76.4	77.2	75.4	0.98	37.9	38.1	37.6	0.99
	Central Asia													
41	Armenia	3-6	…	…	…	…	34.6	33.5	35.7	1.07	…	…	…	…
42	Azerbaijan	3-5	20.9	22.0	19.6	0.89	24.6	24.6	24.6	1.00	16.8	16.7	17.1	1.02
43	Georgia	3-5	35.4	35.6	35.3	0.99	42.7	41.4	44.0	1.06	30.3	29.1	31.6	1.09
44	Kazakhstan	3-6	13.9	14.3	13.6	0.95	29.4	29.7	29.1	0.98	28.5	28.7	28.2	0.99
45	Kyrgyzstan	3-6	10.5	11.8	9.2	0.78	11.3	11.6	11.1	0.95	8.2	8.4	8.0	0.95
46	Mongolia	3-7	24.7	22.4	27.1	1.21	33.8	31.6	36.0	1.14	30.8	…	…	…
47	Tajikistan	3-6	8.5	9.6	7.3	0.76	10.1	10.4	9.8	0.94	9.0	9.3	8.8	0.94
48	Turkmenistan	3-6	…	…	…	…	…	…	…	…	…	…	…	…
49	Uzbekistan	3-6	…	…	…	…	28.1	29.0	27.1	0.94	21.6	22.3**	20.8**	0.94**
	East Asia and the Pacific													
50	Australia	4-4	…	…	…	…	101.7	101.5	101.8	1.00	49.9	49.7	50.0	1.01
51	Brunei Darussalam	3-5	50.6	50.0	51.3	1.03	48.5	48.3	48.6	1.01	…	…	…	…
52	Cambodia	3-5	5.2**	5.1**	5.3**	1.03**	7.0	6.8	7.2	1.05	6.3	6.2	6.5	1.05
53	China	4-6	37.9	38.5	37.2	0.97	36.4	37.8	34.9	0.92	24.5**	…	…	…
54	Cook Islands	4-4	…	…	…	…	…	…	…	…	…	…	…	…

GROSS ENROLMENT RATIO (GER) IN PRE-PRIMARY EDUCATION AND OTHER ECCE PROGRAMMES (%)								NEW ENTRANTS TO THE FIRST GRADE OF PRIMARY EDUCATION WITH ECCE EXPERIENCE (%)						
1998/1999				2002/2003				1998/1999			2002/2003			
Total	Male	Female	GPI (F/M)	Total	Male	Female	GPI (F/M)	Total	Male	Female	Total	Male	Female	
													Arab States	
…	…	…	…	…	…	…	…	…	…	…	3.9	3.9	3.8	1
…	…	…	…	38.8	40.0	37.5	0.94	…	…	…	70.5	65.9	75.2	2
0.4	0.4	0.5	1.50	**1.2**	**1.2**	**1.2**	**0.99**	…	…	…	2.7[y]	2.2[y]	3.5[y]	3
…	…	…	…	…	…	…	…	…	…	…	…	…	…	4
…	…	…	…	…	…	…	…	…	…	…	…	…	…	5
…	…	…	…	…	…	…	…	…	…	…	44.2	46.2	42.1	6
…	…	…	…	…	…	…	…	87.2	87.8	86.5	84.1	84.4	83.7	7
…	…	…	…	…	…	…	…	…	…	…	94.0	93.9	94.1	8
…	…	…	…	…	…	…	…	…	…	…	…	…	…	9
…	…	…	…	…	…	…	…	…	…	…	…	…	…	10
65.4	84.9	45.1	0.53	57.2	70.4	43.6	0.62	…	…	…	…	…	…	11
…	…	…	…	…	…	…	…	…	…	…	…	…	…	12
…	…	…	…	…	…	…	…	…	…	…	76.4[y]	81.0[y]	71.6[y]	13
…	…	…	…	…	…	…	…	…	…	…	…	…	…	14
…	…	…	…	…	…	…	…	…	…	…	…	…	…	15
21.3	…	…	…	26.6	28.4	24.6	0.86	…	…	…	45.6	45.6	45.6	16
…	…	…	…	…	…	…	…	…	…	…	12.1	12.0	12.3	17
…	…	…	…	…	…	…	…	…	…	…	…	…	…	18
…	…	…	…	…	…	…	…	…	…	…	74.2	74.0	74.3	19
…	…	…	…	…	…	…	…	1.6	1.5	1.6	…	…	…	20
													Central and Eastern Europe	
41.7**	40.0**	43.5**	1.09**	47.0	46.4	47.7	1.03	…	…	…	…	…	…	21
…	…	…	…	…	…	…	…	…	…	…	…	…	…	22
…	…	…	…	…	…	…	…	…	…	…	…	…	…	23
64.3	64.7	63.8	0.99	75.5	76.3	74.8	0.98	…	…	…	…	…	…	24
…	…	…	…	…	…	…	…	…	…	…	98.0*	98.0*	98.0*	25
90.5	87.8	93.4	1.06	102.0	102.1	101.9	1.00	…	…	…	…	…	…	26
86.8	87.5	86.0	0.98	112.9	113.1	112.5	0.99	…	…	…	…	…	…	27
…	…	…	…	…	…	…	…	…	…	…	…	…	…	28
50.9	52.1	49.6	0.95	74.3	76.5	72.0	0.94	…	…	…	…	…	…	29
55.5	56.3	54.6	0.97	58.3	59.1	57.4	0.97	…	…	…	…	…	…	30
49.8	49.7	50.0	1.01	50.6	50.5	50.6	1.00	…	…	…	…	…	…	31
…	…	…	…	…	…	…	…	…	…	…	…	…	…	32
61.8	61.1	62.6	1.02	76.4	75.2	77.6	1.03	…	…	…	…	…	…	33
…	…	…	…	…	…	…	…	…	…	…	…	…	…	34
…	…	…	…	…	…	…	…	…	…	…	…	…	…	35
…	…	…	…	…	…	…	…	…	…	…	…	…	…	36
…	…	…	…	…	…	…	…	…	…	…	…	…	…	37
31.0	30.9	31.2	1.01	31.3	31.2	31.5	1.01	…	…	…	…	…	…	38
6.0	6.2	5.8	0.94	7.6	7.8	7.3	0.94	…	…	…	…	…	…	39
…	…	…	…	…	…	…	…	38.9	…	…	45.8[z]	…	…	40
													Central Asia	
…	…	…	…	…	…	…	…	…	…	…	…	…	…	41
21.1	22.4	19.8	0.89	24.9	25.0	24.9	1.00	…	…	…	8.8	8.5	9.2	42
…	…	…	…	…	…	…	…	…	…	…	…	…	…	43
…	…	…	…	…	…	…	…	…	…	…	…	…	…	44
…	…	…	…	…	…	…	…	8.7*	9.7*	7.6*	7.7	7.5	7.8	45
…	…	…	…	…	…	…	…	…	…	…	…	…	…	46
…	…	…	…	…	…	…	…	…	…	…	…	…	…	47
…	…	…	…	…	…	…	…	…	…	…	…	…	…	48
…	…	…	…	…	…	…	…	…	…	…	…	…	…	49
													East Asia and the Pacific	
…	…	…	…	101.7	101.5	101.8	1.00	…	…	…	…	…	…	50
…	…	…	…	…	…	…	…	88.2*	86.5*	90.1*	87.7	87.8	87.6	51
…	…	…	…	…	…	…	…	…	…	…	11.9	10.7	13.2	52
…	…	…	…	…	…	…	…	…	…	…	…	…	…	53
…	…	…	…	…	…	…	…	…	…	…	…	…	…	54

Table 3 (continued)

	Country or territory	Age group 2002/2003	GROSS ENROLMENT RATIO (GER) IN PRE-PRIMARY EDUCATION (%) 1998/1999 Total	Male	Female	GPI (F/M)	2002/2003 Total	Male	Female	GPI (F/M)	NET ENROLMENT RATIO (GER) IN PRE-PRIMARY EDUCATION (%) 2002/2003 Total	Male	Female	GPI (F/M)
55	DPR Korea	4-5	…	…	…	…	…	…	…	…	…	…	…	…
56	Fiji	3-5	15.4**	15.2**	15.5**	1.02**	…	…	…	…	…	…	…	…
57	Indonesia	5-6	17.5**	17.5**	17.6**	1.01**	21.4	20.5	22.3	1.09	21.4	20.5	22.3	1.09
58	Japan	3-5	83.1	82.2**	84.0**	1.02**	84.9	83.8**	86.1**	1.03**	84.8	83.7**	86.0**	1.03**
59	Kiribati	3-5	…	…	…	…	…	…	…	…	…	…	…	…
60	Lao PDR	3-5	7.9	7.5	8.3	1.11	8.0	7.8	8.2	1.05	7.5	7.3	7.7	1.06
61	Macao, China	3-5	86.9	89.0	84.7	0.95	85.3	87.6	82.9	0.95	79.0	80.6	77.2	0.96
62	Malaysia	5-5	109.5	110.2	108.8	0.99	98.8	95.3	102.5	1.08	71.9	69.9	74.0	1.06
63	Marshall Islands[1]	4-5	…	…	…	…	51.5[z]	52.1[z]	50.8[z]	0.97[z]	49.3[z]	50.0[z]	48.6[z]	0.97[z]
64	Micronesia (Fed. States of)	3-5	36.6	…	…	…	…	…	…	…	…	…	…	…
65	Myanmar	3-4	1.9	…	…	…	…	…	…	…	…	…	…	…
66	Nauru[1]	5-5	140.9**	143.9**	137.9**	0.96**	…	…	…	…	…	…	…	…
67	New Zealand	3-4	84.5	84.3	84.6	1.00	88.4	88.0	88.7	1.01	87.0	86.6	87.5	1.01
68	Niue[1]	4-4	128.6	120.8	138.9	1.15	147.8[z]	133.3[z]	163.6[z]	1.23[z]	…	…	…	…
69	Palau[1]	3-5	62.5	56.2	69.2	1.23	65.5**[y]	61.9**[y]	69.5**[y]	1.12**[y]	…	…	…	…
70	Papua New Guinea	6-6	33.5	34.3	32.6	0.95	58.2	60.1	56.1	0.93	45.6[z]	48.5[z]	42.5[z]	0.88[z]
71	Philippines	5-5	30.7	30.0	31.5	1.05	38.5	37.8	39.3	1.04	31.1**	31.6**	30.6**	0.97**
72	Republic of Korea	5-5	79.8	79.8	79.8	1.00	**85.8**	**85.4**	**86.3**	**1.01**	**47.1**	**46.6**	**47.6**	**1.02**
73	Samoa	3-4	55.5	51.9	59.3	1.14	54.2**	48.6**	60.1**	1.24**	36.2**[z]	33.1**[z]	39.5**[z]	1.19**[z]
74	Singapore	3-5	…	…	…	…	…	…	…	…	…	…	…	…
75	Solomon Islands	5-5	…	…	…	…	20.5				…	…	…	…
76	Thailand	3-5	86.6	87.5	85.6	0.98	**88.2****	**88.5****	**87.8****	**0.99****	**85.1****	**85.5****	**84.8****	**0.99****
77	Timor-Leste	4-5	…	…	…	…	11.2[z]	…	…	…	…	…	…	…
78	Tokelau	3-4	…	…	…	…	…	…	…	…	…	…	…	…
79	Tonga	3-4	21.7	20.2	23.3	1.15	29.4**[y]	26.7**[y]	32.2**[y]	1.21**[y]	21.6**[y]	14.1**[y]	29.4**[y]	2.08**[y]
80	Tuvalu[1]	3-5	79.5**	71.2**	89.2**	1.25**	82.4[z]	76.6[z]	89.2[z]	1.16[z]	…	…	…	…
81	Vanuatu	4-5	73.2**	69.6**	77.1**	1.11**	75.6[z]	74.6[z]	76.8[z]	1.03[z]	60.1[z]	59.0[z]	61.4[z]	1.04[z]
82	Viet Nam	3-5	40.2	41.5	38.8	0.94	45.3	46.6	43.9	0.94	42.3[z]	…	…	…
	Latin America and the Caribbean													
83	Anguilla[1]	3-4	…	…	…	…	116.1[z]	117.8[z]	114.6[z]	0.97[z]	95.0**[z]	95.8**[z]	94.3**[z]	0.98**[z]
84	Antigua and Barbuda[2]	3-4	…	…	…	…	…	…	…	…	…	…	…	…
85	Argentina	3-5	57.0	56.3	57.6	1.02	60.5	60.0	60.9	1.01	60.2	59.7	60.6	1.02
86	Aruba[1]	4-5	96.9	96.8	97.0	1.00	100.2	100.8	99.6	0.99	90.9[z]	93.5[z]	88.2[z]	0.94[z]
87	Bahamas	3-4	…	…	…	…	30.4**	30.6**	30.2**	0.99**	22.5[z]	23.2[z]	21.8[z]	0.94[z]
88	Barbados	3-4	82.2	82.9	81.5	0.98	88.5	88.3	88.7	1.00	81.0	80.3	81.7	1.02
89	Belize	3-4	27.8	27.4	28.2	1.03	28.8	27.7	29.8	1.07	27.8	26.8	28.8	1.07
90	Bermuda[1]	4-4	…	…	…	…	54.6[y]	…	…	…	38.6[y]	…	…	…
91	Bolivia	4-5	44.1	43.9	44.3	1.01	47.3	46.9	47.8	1.02	37.7	37.3	38.2	1.02
92	Brazil	4-6	53.5	53.3	53.7	1.01	57.2	57.2	57.2	1.00	49.2	…	…	…
93	British Virgin Islands[1]	3-4	61.6	57.0	66.3	1.16	86.4	88.4	84.3	0.95	75.0	75.3	74.7	0.99
94	Cayman Islands[2]	3-4	…	…	…	…	…	…	…	…	…	…	…	…
95	Chile	3-5	73.6	74.0	73.3	0.99	**45.8**	**46.1**	**45.6**	**0.99**	**31.3**	**31.4**	**31.3**	**1.00**
96	Colombia	3-5	34.8	34.4	35.2	1.02	37.1	37.0	37.3	1.01	33.5	33.3**	33.6**	1.01**
97	Costa Rica	4-5	80.5	79.8	81.2	1.02	60.9	60.4	61.4	1.02	43.3	42.7	44.0	1.03
98	Cuba	3-5	102.0	100.2	103.9	1.04	114.6	115.4	113.8	0.99	100.0	…	…	…
99	Dominica[1]	3-4	76.1	72.1	80.3	1.11	51.0	54.2	47.9	0.88	48.6**	51.7**	45.6**	0.88**
100	Dominican Republic	3-5	35.2	35.0	35.4	1.01	34.3	34.1	34.5	1.01	30.6	30.6	30.6	1.00
101	Ecuador	5-5	63.6	62.5	64.7	1.04	74.4	73.3	75.6	1.03	62.5	61.7	63.3	1.03
102	El Salvador	4-6	40.2	39.3	41.1	1.05	48.6	47.3	50.1	1.06	43.6	42.3**	45.0**	1.07**
103	Grenada[1]	3-4	…	…	…	…	85.8	86.3	85.2	0.99	84.8	85.2	84.4	0.99
104	Guatemala	5-6	37.3*	37.5*	37.1*	0.99*	55.2[z]	54.8[z]	55.6[z]	1.01[z]	41.1[z]	41.0[z]	41.2[z]	1.00[z]
105	Guyana	4-5	120.2	120.6	119.9	0.99	120.2	120.4**	120.0**	1.00**	95.3**[z]	95.6**[z]	95.1**[z]	1.00**[z]
106	Haiti	3-5	…	…	…	…	…	…	…	…	…	…	…	…
107	Honduras	4-6	…	…	…	…	21.4**[z]	20.9**[z]	22.0**[z]	1.05**[z]	21.4**[z]	…	…	…
108	Jamaica	3-5	83.6	80.5	86.8	1.08	[illegible]	[illegible]	[illegible]	1.05	85.0**	83.2**	87.0**	1.05**
109	Mexico	4-5	74.0	73.1	74.9	1.02	80.7	79.9	81.6	1.02	70.6	70.1	71.2	1.02
110	Montserrat[1]	3-4	…	…	…	…	82.9[z]	…	…	…	66.7[z]	…	…	…
111	Netherlands Antilles	4-5	100.3	99.0	101.6	1.03	86.2**	86.5**	85.9**	0.99**	80.0**	79.7**	80.4**	1.01**
112	Nicaragua	3-6	24.7	24.4	24.9	1.02	27.7	27.3	28.2	1.03	27.7	27.3	28.2	1.03
113	Panama	4-5	37.7**	38.5**	36.9**	0.96**	55.8	55.5	56.1	1.01	52.0	51.7	52.3	1.01
114	Paraguay	3-5	25.5	25.1	25.9	1.03	30.0	29.9	30.1	1.01	26.3	25.9	26.6	1.03

GROSS ENROLMENT RATIO (GER) IN PRE-PRIMARY EDUCATION AND OTHER ECCE PROGRAMMES (%)								NEW ENTRANTS TO THE FIRST GRADE OF PRIMARY EDUCATION WITH ECCE EXPERIENCE (%)						
1998/1999				2002/2003				1998/1999			2002/2003			
Total	Male	Female	GPI (F/M)	Total	Male	Female	GPI (F/M)	Total	Male	Female	Total	Male	Female	
...	...	...	...	...	...	...	...	...	...	...	...	...	...	55
...	...	...	...	...	...	...	...	...	...	...	...	...	...	56
...	...	...	...	...	...	...	...	...	...	...	...	...	...	57
...	...	...	...	...	...	...	...	...	...	...	...	...	...	58
...	...	...	...	...	...	...	...	...	...	...	...	...	...	59
...	...	...	...	...	...	...	...	...	...	...	7.9	7.2	8.6	60
...	...	...	...	...	...	...	...	96.4	96.6	96.2	96.0	96.2	95.8	61
...	...	...	...	...	...	...	...	...	...	...	78.4	76.0	80.9	62
...	...	...	...	...	...	...	...	...	...	...	...	...	...	63
...	...	...	...	...	...	...	...	...	...	...	...	...	...	64
...	...	...	...	...	...	...	...	...	...	...	...	...	...	65
...	...	...	...	...	...	...	...	...	...	...	...	...	...	66
84.5	84.3	84.6	1.00	88.4	88.0	88.7	1.01	...	...	...	...	...	...	67
...	...	...	...	...	...	...	...	...	...	...	...	...	...	68
...	...	...	...	...	...	...	...	...	...	...	...	...	...	69
...	...	...	...	...	...	...	...	...	...	...	43.8[z]	42.8[z]	45.1[z]	70
...	...	...	...	...	...	...	...	...	...	...	56.8	56.5	57.1	71
...	...	...	...	**85.8**	**85.4**	**86.3**	**1.01**	...	...	...	...	...	...	72
...	...	...	...	...	...	...	...	...	...	...	59.9[y]	55.6[y]	64.6[y]	73
...	...	...	...	...	...	...	...	...	...	...	...	...	...	74
...	...	...	...	...	...	...	...	...	...	...	...	...	...	75
...	...	...	...	...	...	...	...	...	...	...	...	...	...	76
...	...	...	...	...	...	...	...	...	...	...	...	...	...	77
...	...	...	...	...	...	...	...	...	...	...	...	...	...	78
...	...	...	...	...	...	...	...	...	...	...	...	...	...	79
...	...	...	...	...	...	...	...	–	–	–	...	...	...	80
...	...	...	...	...	...	...	...	...	...	...	...	...	...	81
...	...	...	...	...	...	...	...	...	...	...	...	...	...	82
Latin America and the Caribbean														
...	...	...	...	...	...	...	...	100.0	100.0	100.0	100.0[z]	100.0[z]	100.0[z]	83
...	...	...	...	...	...	...	...	...	...	...	...	...	...	84
...	...	...	...	...	...	...	...	...	...	...	89.1	88.8	89.4	85
...	...	...	...	...	...	...	...	84.9	84.7	85.1	88.8	88.7	89.0	86
...	...	...	...	...	...	...	...	...	...	...	...	...	...	87
...	...	...	...	...	...	...	...	...	...	...	100.0	100.0	100.0	88
...	...	...	...	...	...	...	...	...	...	...	...	...	...	89
...	...	...	...	...	...	...	...	...	...	...	50.4[y]	45.6[y]	54.8[y]	90
44.1	43.9	44.3	1.01	47.3	46.9	47.8	1.02	...	...	...	59.9	59.9	60.0	91
...	...	...	...	...	...	...	...	...	...	...	...	...	...	92
...	...	...	...	...	...	...	...	...	...	...	79.6	72.1	88.9	93
...	...	...	...	...	...	...	...	...	...	...	89.3[z]	90.5[z]	88.1[z]	94
...	...	...	...	...	...	...	...	...	...	...	...	...	...	95
...	...	...	...	...	...	...	...	...	...	...	...	...	...	96
...	...	...	...	...	...	...	...	...	...	...	85.1	84.8	85.3	97
...	...	...	...	...	...	...	...	...	...	...	99.5	99.5	99.4	98
...	...	...	...	...	...	...	...	...	...	...	100.0	100.0	100.0	99
35.2	35.0	35.4	1.01	34.3	34.1	34.5	1.01	...	...	...	...	...	...	100
...	...	...	...	...	...	...	...	...	...	...	53.2	52.0	54.4	101
...	...	...	...	...	...	...	...	...	...	...	...	...	...	102
...	...	...	...	...	...	...	...	...	...	...	...	...	...	103
...	...	...	...	...	...	...	...	...	...	...	79.9	78.4	81.6	104
...	...	...	...	...	...	...	...	...	...	...	...	...	...	105
...	...	...	...	...	...	...	...	...	...	...	...	...	...	106
...	...	...	...	...	...	...	...	...	...	...	...	...	...	107
...	...	...	...	...	...	...	...	...	...	...	...	...	...	108
74.0	73.1	74.9	1.02	80.7	79.9	81.6	1.02	...	...	...	...	...	...	109
...	...	...	...	...	...	...	...	...	...	...	...	...	...	110
...	...	...	...	...	...	...	...	100.0 **	100.0 **	100.0 **	...	...	...	111
...	...	...	...	...	...	...	...	...	...	...	38.9*	37.6*	40.3*	112
...	...	...	...	...	...	...	...	...	...	...	61.0	59.6	62.6	113
...	...	...	...	...	...	...	...	...	...	...	74.0	72.5	75.5	114

Table 3 (continued)

	Country or territory	Age group	GROSS ENROLMENT RATIO (GER) IN PRE-PRIMARY EDUCATION (%)								NET ENROLMENT RATIO (GER) IN PRE-PRIMARY EDUCATION (%)			
			1998/1999				2002/2003				2002/2003			
		2002/2003	Total	Male	Female	GPI (F/M)	Total	Male	Female	GPI (F/M)	Total	Male	Female	GPI (F/M)
115	Peru	3-5	56.1	55.5	56.8	1.02	57.9	57.3	58.5	1.02	57.9	57.3	58.5	1.02
116	Saint Kitts and Nevis[1]	3-4	...	...	...	...	163.5	172.1	154.5	0.90	...	...	...	...
117	Saint Lucia	3-4	85.2	85.6	84.8	0.99	64.1	60.0	68.5	1.14	46.9	43.8	50.3	1.15
118	Saint Vincent/Grenad.	3-4	...	...	...	...	...	...	...	...	...	...	...	...
119	Suriname	4-5	...	...	...	...	94.2**	95.1**	93.2**	0.98**	94.2**	95.1**	93.2**	0.98**
120	Trinidad and Tobago	3-4	59.8**	59.5**	60.2**	1.01**	66.4*	65.4**	67.4**	1.03**	55.2**	53.6**	56.9**	1.06**
121	Turks and Caicos Islands[1]	4-5	...	...	...	...	125.0	124.9	125.1	1.00	74.1	72.9	75.2	1.03
122	Uruguay	3-5	56.0	55.6	56.4	1.01	63.4	62.8	64.1	1.02	45.1	44.7	45.6	1.02
123	Venezuela	3-5	44.2	43.6	44.7	1.03	52.7	52.4	52.9	1.01	47.0	46.6	47.5	1.02
	North America and Western Europe													
124	Andorra[2]	3-5	...	...	...	...	...	...	...	...	...	...	...	...
125	Austria	3-5	81.5	81.7	81.3	0.99	86.4	86.4	86.3	1.00	72.4	71.7	73.2	1.02
126	Belgium	3-5	109.9	110.7	109.1	0.99	116.1	116.5	115.6	0.99	99.8	100.0	99.6	1.00
127	Canada	4-5	66.0	65.8	66.3	1.01	64.6**,z	65.1**,z	64.1**,z	0.98**,z	64.6**,z	65.1**,z	64.1**,z	0.98**,z
128	Cyprus[1]	3-5	59.8	59.2	60.4	1.02	59.6	59.5	59.8	1.00	55.8	55.4	56.2	1.02
129	Denmark	3-6	91.0	90.9	91.0	1.00	91.6	91.6	91.5	1.00	91.6	91.6	91.5	1.00
130	Finland	3-6	48.3	48.5	48.1	0.99	56.0	56.2	55.8	0.99	55.5	55.6	55.5	1.00
131	France	3-5	110.6	110.7	110.6	1.00	112.7	112.7	112.7	1.00	100.0	100.0	99.9	1.00
132	Germany	3-5	93.6	94.4	92.7	0.98	99.6	101.9	97.2	0.95	83.8	84.8	82.7	0.98
133	Greece	4-5	68.4	67.8	69.1	1.02	67.7	66.5	69.0	1.04	67.7	66.5	69.0	1.04
134	Iceland	3-5	108.3	108.7	108.0	0.99	124.8	123.4	126.3	1.02	90.5	89.3	91.7	1.03
135	Ireland	3-3	...	...	...	...	...	...	...	...	...	...	...	...
136	Israel	3-5	106.0	106.8	105.2	0.98	112.2	112.1	112.3	1.00	97.4	97.0	97.8	1.01
137	Italy	3-5	95.4	96.1	94.6	0.98	101.4	102.2	100.5	0.98	99.2	99.9	98.4	0.98
138	Luxembourg	3-5	72.9	73.4	72.4	0.99	85.5	85.0	85.9	1.01	72.7	71.9	73.6	1.02
139	Malta	3-4	102.7	103.0	102.4	0.99	100.0	98.8	101.3	1.03	85.8	84.8	86.8	1.02
140	Monaco[2]	3-5	...	...	...	...	...	...	...	...	...	...	...	...
141	Netherlands	4-5	97.8	98.3	97.3	0.99	87.3	87.8	86.8	0.99	87.3	87.7	86.8	0.99
142	Norway	3-5	75.4	73.4	77.6	1.06	83.9	...	...	...	83.5			
143	Portugal	3-5	66.3	66.4	66.1	1.00	72.9	72.1	73.6	1.02	71.9	70.9	73.0	1.03
144	San Marino[2]	3-5	...	...	...	...	...	...	...	...	...	...	...	...
145	Spain	3-5	99.4	99.8	99.0	0.99	111.3	111.6	111.1	1.00	98.9	98.9	98.9	1.00
146	Sweden	3-6	76.1	75.7	76.5	1.01	81.1	81.2	80.9	1.00	80.7	80.8	80.7	1.00
147	Switzerland	5-6	93.9	94.5	93.2	0.99	99.7	99.8	99.7	1.00	76.8	77.2	76.5	0.99
148	United Kingdom	3-4	77.5	77.1	77.9	1.01	77.7	77.4	77.9	1.01	73.3	73.1	73.4	1.00
149	United States	3-5	57.4	58.3	56.5	0.97	58.2	...	...	...	54.9	57.7	51.8	0.90
	South and West Asia													
150	Afghanistan	3-6	...	...	...	...	...	...	...	...	...	...	...	...
151	Bangladesh	3-5	22.3	21.6	23.2	1.08	20.6	19.9	21.3	1.07	...	...	...	...
152	Bhutan[3]	4-5	...	...	...	...	...	...	...	...	...	...	...	...
153	India	3-5	19.5	19.6	19.4	0.99	34.0	33.8	34.1	1.01	...	...	...	...
154	Iran, Islamic Republic of	5-5	13.3	13.0	13.6	1.05	30.7	29.0	32.4	1.12	26.9	25.3	28.5	1.13
155	Maldives	3-5	45.9	46.0	45.9	1.00	46.6	46.2	47.1	1.02	43.9	43.5	44.4	1.02
156	Nepal	3-4	12.1**	13.9**	10.2**	0.73**	17.6	18.8	16.2	0.86	...	...	...	...
157	Pakistan	3-4	...	...	...	...	47.3	50.1	44.3	0.88	...	...	...	...
158	Sri Lanka	4-4	...	...	...	...	...	...	...	...	...	...	...	...
	Sub-Saharan Africa													
159	Angola	3-5	25.5	33.5	17.6	0.53	...	...	...	...	...	...	...	...
160	Benin	4-5	4.6	4.7	4.5	0.94	5.2	5.4	5.1	0.95	3.4**	3.6**	3.3**	0.93**
161	Botswana	3-5	...	...	...	...	...	...	...	...	...	...	...	...
162	Burkina Faso	4-6	1.7	1.7	1.7	1.01	1.1**,z	1.1**,z	1.1**,z	0.92**,z	1.1**,z	1.1**,z	1.1**,z	0.92**,z
163	Burundi	[illegible]	0.8	0.8	0.8	1.01	1.3	1.3	1.3	0.98	...	...	...	...
164	Cameroon	4-5	11.6	11.9	11.3	0.95	14.9	[illegible]	[illegible]	1.01	...	...	...	...
165	Cape Verde	3-5	...	...	...	...	59.2	58.6	59.9	1.02	56.0	55.2	56.8	1.03
166	Central African Republic	4-5	...	...	...	...	2.6	2.5	2.6	1.05	...	...	...	...
167	Chad	3-5	...	...	...	...	...	...	...	...	...	...	...	...
168	Comoros	3-5	2.2	2.1	2.2	1.07	2.4	2.5	2.3	0.91	...	...	...	...
169	Congo	3-5	1.8	1.4	2.2	1.59	4.1**	4.0**	4.2**	1.06**	4.1**	4.0**	4.2**	1.06**
170	Côte d'Ivoire	3-5	2.6	2.6	2.5	0.97	3.5*	3.5*	3.4*	0.97*	3.5*	3.5*	3.4*	0.97*

GROSS ENROLMENT RATIO (GER) IN PRE-PRIMARY EDUCATION AND OTHER ECCE PROGRAMMES (%)								NEW ENTRANTS TO THE FIRST GRADE OF PRIMARY EDUCATION WITH ECCE EXPERIENCE (%)						
1998/1999				2002/2003				1998/1999			2002/2003			
Total	Male	Female	GPI (F/M)	Total	Male	Female	GPI (F/M)	Total	Male	Female	Total	Male	Female	
…	…	…	…	…	…	…	…	…	…	…	…	…	…	115
…	…	…	…	189.6	197.9	181.1	0.91	…	…	…	…	…	…	116
…	…	…	…	…	…	…	…	…	…	…	…	…	…	117
…	…	…	…	…	…	…	…	…	…	…	…	…	…	118
…	…	…	…	…	…	…	…	…	…	…	…	…	…	119
…	…	…	…	…	…	…	…	…	…	…	77.5	76.3	78.8	120
…	…	…	…	…	…	…	…	…	…	…	100.0	100.0	100.0	121
…	…	…	…	…	…	…	…	…	…	…	95.0	95.0	95.0	122
52.8	52.4	53.2	1.02	56.6	56.3	56.8	1.01	…	…	…	…	…	…	123
North America and Western Europe														
…	…	…	…	…	…	…	…	…	…	…	…	…	…	124
…	…	…	…	…	…	…	…	…	…	…	…	…	…	125
109.9	110.7	109.1	0.99	116.1	116.5	115.6	0.99	…	…	…	…	…	…	126
66.0	65.8	66.3	1.01	64.6**,z	65.1**,z	64.1**,z	0.98**,z	…	…	…	…	…	…	127
…	…	…	…	…	…	…	…	…	…	…	…	…	…	128
91.0	90.9	91.0	1.00	91.6	91.6	91.5	1.00	…	…	…	…	…	…	129
48.3	48.5	48.1	0.99	56.0	56.2	55.8	0.99	…	…	…	…	…	…	130
110.6	110.7	110.6	1.00	112.7	112.7	112.7	1.00	…	…	…	…	…	…	131
93.6	94.4	92.7	0.98	99.6	101.9	97.2	0.95	…	…	…	…	…	…	132
68.4	67.8	69.1	1.02	67.7	66.5	69.0	1.04	…	…	…	…	…	…	133
108.3	108.7	108.0	0.99	124.8	123.4	126.3	1.02	…	…	…	…	…	…	134
5.6	…	…	…	…	…	…	…	…	…	…	…	…	…	135
106.0	106.8	105.2	0.98	112.2	112.1	112.3	1.00	…	…	…	…	…	…	136
95.4	96.1	94.6	0.98	101.4	102.2	100.5	0.98	…	…	…	…	…	…	137
72.9	73.4	72.4	0.99	85.5	85.0	85.9	1.01	…	…	…	…	…	…	138
102.7	103.0	102.4	0.99	100.0	98.8	101.3	1.03	…	…	…	…	…	…	139
…	…	…	…	…	…	…	…	…	…	…	…	…	…	140
97.8	98.3	97.3	0.99	87.3	87.8	86.8	0.99	…	…	…	…	…	…	141
75.4	73.4	77.6	1.06	83.9	…	…	…	…	…	…	…	…	…	142
66.3	66.4	66.1	1.00	72.9	72.1	73.6	1.02	…	…	…	…	…	…	143
…	…	…	…	…	…	…	…	…	…	…	…	…	…	144
99.4	99.8	99.0	0.99	111.3	111.6	111.1	1.00	…	…	…	…	…	…	145
76.1	75.7	76.5	1.01	81.1	81.2	80.9	1.00	…	…	…	…	…	…	146
93.9	94.5	93.2	0.99	99.7	99.8	99.7	1.00	…	…	…	…	…	…	147
77.5	77.1	77.9	1.01	77.7	77.4	77.9	1.01	…	…	…	…	…	…	148
57.4	58.3	56.5	0.97	58.2	61.7	54.6	0.88	…	…	…	…	…	…	149
South and West Asia														
…	…	…	…	…	…	…	…	…	…	…	…	…	…	150
…	…	…	…	…	…	…	…	…	…	…	23.3	24.3	22.3	151
…	…	…	…	…	…	…	…	…	…	…	…	…	…	152
…	…	…	…	…	…	…	…	…	…	…	…	…	…	153
…	…	…	…	…	…	…	…	…	…	…	21.3**	21.4**	21.2**	154
…	…	…	…	…	…	…	…	…	…	…	90.0	90.5	89.5	155
…	…	…	…	…	…	…	…	…	…	…	9.6	8.7	10.6	156
…	…	…	…	…	…	…	…	…	…	…	…	…	…	157
…	…	…	…	…	…	…	…	…	…	…	…	…	…	158
Sub-Saharan Africa														
…	…	…	…	…	…	…	…	…	…	…	…	…	…	159
4.6	4.7	4.5	0.94	5.9	6.1	5.8	0.95	…	…	…	…	…	…	160
…	…	…	…	…	…	…	…	…	…	…	…	…	…	161
…	…	…	…	…	…	…	…	…	…	…	4.1y	3.7y	4.7y	162
…	…	…	…	…	…	…	…	…	…	…	2.7z	2.4z	3.1z	163
11.6	11.9	11.3	0.95	14.9	14.9	15.0	1.01	…	…	…	…	…	…	164
…	…	…	…	59.2	58.6	59.9	1.02	…	…	…	73.5	71.9	75.2	165
…	…	…	…	2.6	2.5	2.6	1.05	…	…	…	…	…	…	166
…	…	…	…	…	…	…	…	…	…	…	…	…	…	167
…	…	…	…	…	…	…	…	…	…	…	…	…	…	168
1.8	1.4	2.2	1.59	4.1**	4.0**	4.2**	1.06**	…	…	…	13.5	13.1	13.9	169
2.6	2.6	2.5	0.97	3.5*	3.5*	3.4*	0.97*	…	…	…	11.4**,y	10.5**,y	12.6**,y	170

Table 3 (continued)

	Country or territory	Age group 2002/2003	GROSS ENROLMENT RATIO (GER) IN PRE-PRIMARY EDUCATION (%) 1998/1999 Total	Male	Female	GPI (F/M)	2002/2003 Total	Male	Female	GPI (F/M)	NET ENROLMENT RATIO (GER) IN PRE-PRIMARY EDUCATION (%) 2002/2003 Total	Male	Female	GPI (F/M)
171	D. R. Congo	3-5	...	...	...	...	0.8**,z	0.8**,z	0.8**,z	0.98**,z	...	...	...	...
172	Equatorial Guinea	3-6	30.9	30.2	31.5	1.04	...	...	...	...	...	...	...	...
173	Eritrea	5-6	5.3	5.6	5.0	0.89	5.9	6.0	5.9	1.00	4.2	4.2	4.3	1.01
174	Ethiopia	4-6	1.5	1.5	1.5	0.97	**2.1**	**2.1**	**2.0**	**0.95**	...	...	...	...
175	Gabon	3-5	...	...	...	...	13.9**,z	...	...	...	...	...	...	...
176	Gambia	3-6	19.7	20.7	18.7	0.91	18.3	18.1	18.6	1.03	...	...	...	...
177	Ghana	3-5	37.0	37.2	36.9	0.99	**47.0**	**47.7**	**46.3**	**0.97**	**31.2**	**31.0**	**31.4**	**1.01**
178	Guinea	3-6	...	...	...	...	...	...	...	...	...	...	...	...
179	Guinea-Bissau	4-6	3.2**	3.1**	3.3**	1.05**	3.2**,y	3.1**,y	3.3**,y	1.05**,y	...	...	...	...
180	Kenya	3-5	38.3	37.1	39.6	1.07	48.2	48.4	48.0	0.99	32.7	32.5	33.0	1.02
181	Lesotho	3-5	24.9	23.4*	26.5*	1.13*	29.6	30.5	28.6	0.94	...	...	...	...
182	Liberia	3-5	43.3	49.8	36.8	0.74	...	...	...	...	...	...	...	...
183	Madagascar	3-5	3.4**	3.3**	3.4**	1.02**	10.0	...	...	...	10.0	...	...	...
184	Malawi	3-5	...	...	...	...	...	...	...	...	...	...	...	...
185	Mali	4-6	1.9	1.8	1.9	1.08	1.6**	1.6**	1.6**	1.00**	...	...	...	...
186	Mauritius	3-4	98.0	97.1	99.0	1.02	88.6	88.2	89.0	1.01	72.9	72.5	73.2	1.01
187	Mozambique	3-5	...	...	...	...	...	...	...	...	...	...	...	...
188	Namibia	3-5	20.1**	19.1**	21.2**	1.11**	27.5	24.0	31.1	1.30	...	...	...	...
189	Niger	4-6	1.1	1.1	1.1	1.03	1.4	1.4	1.4	1.01	1.2	1.2	1.2	1.01
190	Nigeria	3-5	...	...	...	...	12.0	12.4	11.7	0.94	8.9	9.3	8.5	0.92
191	Rwanda	4-6	...	...	...	...	2.5**,z	2.5**,z	2.5**,z	0.99**,z	...	...	...	...
192	Sao Tome and Principe	3-6	25.5**	24.8**	26.2**	1.06**	25.8**	24.5**	27.1**	1.11**	...	...	...	...
193	Senegal	4-6	2.9	2.9	2.9	1.00	3.4	3.2	3.5	1.10	2.6y	2.4y	2.7y	1.14y
194	Seychelles[1]	4-5	112.8	111.3	114.3	1.03	98.6	100.6	96.5	0.96	81.4	82.8	80.1	0.97
195	Sierra Leone	3-5	...	...	...	...	4.1y	...	...	...	4.1y	...	...	...
196	Somalia	...	...	...	...	...	...	...	...	...	...	...	...	...
197	South Africa	6-6	24.2*	24.3*	24.1*	0.99*	31.6	31.2	32.0	1.02	17.1	16.6	17.5	1.05
198	Swaziland	3-5	...	...	...	...	...	...	...	...	...	...	...	...
199	Togo	3-5	2.7	2.7	2.7	1.00	2.8	2.8	2.8	0.99	2.8	2.8	2.8	0.99
200	Uganda	4-5	4.0	4.0	4.0	1.00	4.3	4.2	4.4	1.04	2.8	2.8	2.9	1.04
201	United Republic of Tanzania	5-6	...	...	...	...	**23.9****	**24.0****	**23.8****	**0.99****	**22.8****	**22.9****	**22.7****	**0.99****
202	Zambia	3-6	2.3*	2.1*	2.5*	1.19*	...	...	...	...	...	...	...	...
203	Zimbabwe	3-5	...	...	...	...	**39.8**	...	...	...	...	...	...	...
I	World[4]	...	42.5	43.9	43.8	1.00	48.6	47.8	49.3	1.03	47.0	46.4	47.7	1.03
II	Countries in transition	...	28.1	28.8	27.4	0.95	34.6	33.5	35.7	1.07	28.5	28.7	28.2	0.99
III	Developed countries	...	76.1	75.7	76.5	1.01	81.1	81.2	80.9	1.00	73.0	72.5	73.5	1.0
IV	Developing countries	...	32.9	33.7	32.0	0.95	34.3	34.1	34.5	1.01	30.6	30.6	30.6	1.00
V	Arab States	...	13.5	13.9	13.2	0.95	17.7	17.9	17.4	0.98	17.1	17.3	16.8	0.97
VI	Central and Eastern Europe	...	50.5	51.6	49.5	0.96	74.3	76.5	72.0	0.94	67.7	69.0	66.3	0.96
VII	Central Asia	...	17.4	18.2	16.6	0.91	28.8	29.4	28.1	0.96	21.6	22.3	20.8	0.94
VIII	East Asia and the Pacific	...	53.1	51.0	55.3	1.08	56.2	54.4	58.1	1.07	45.6	46.9	44.1	0.94
IX	Latin America and the Caribbean	...	58.4	57.9	58.9	1.02	60.9	60.4	61.4	1.02	50.6	...	...	...
X	North America and Western Europe	...	81.5	81.7	81.3	0.99	86.8	87.1	86.6	0.99	80.7	80.8	80.7	1.00
XI	South and West Asia	...	19.5	19.6	19.4	0.99	32.3	31.4	33.3	1.06	...	...	...	...
XII	Sub-Saharan Africa	...	4.6	4.7	4.5	0.94	5.6	5.7	5.5	0.98	...	...	...	...

1. National population data were used to calculate enrolment ratios.
2. Enrolment ratios were not calculated due to lack of United Nations population data by age.
3. Enrolment ratios were not calculated due to inconsistencies between enrolment and the United Nations population data.

GROSS ENROLMENT RATIO (GER) IN PRE-PRIMARY EDUCATION AND OTHER ECCE PROGRAMMES (%)								NEW ENTRANTS TO THE FIRST GRADE OF PRIMARY EDUCATION WITH ECCE EXPERIENCE (%)						
1998/1999				2002/2003				1998/1999			2002/2003			
Total	Male	Female	GPI (F/M)	Total	Male	Female	GPI (F/M)	Total	Male	Female	Total	Male	Female	
…	…	…	…	…	…	…	…	…	…	…	…	…	…	171
30.9	30.2	31.5	1.04	…	…	…	…	…	…	…	…	…	…	172
5.3	5.6	5.0	0.89	5.9	6.0	5.9	1.00	…	…	…	…	…	…	173
…	…	…	…	…	…	…	…	…	…	…	…	…	…	174
…	…	…	…	…	…	…	…	…	…	…	…	…	…	175
…	…	…	…	…	…	…	…	…	…	…	…	…	…	176
…	…	…	…	…	…	…	…	…	…	…	…	…	…	177
…	…	…	…	…	…	…	…	…	…	…	…	…	…	178
3.2**	3.1**	3.3**	1.05	3.2**,y	3.1**,y	3.3**,y	1.05**,y	…	…	…	…	…	…	179
…	…	…	…	…	…	…	…	…	…	…	…	…	…	180
24.9	23.4*	26.5*	1.13*	29.6	30.5	28.6	0.94	…	…	…	…	…	…	181
…	…	…	…	…	…	…	…	…	…	…	…	…	…	182
…	…	…	…	…	…	…	…	…	…	…	…	…	…	183
…	…	…	…	…	…	…	…	…	…	…	…	…	…	184
…	…	…	…	…	…	…	…	…	…	…	…	…	…	185
98.0	97.1	99.0	1.02	88.6	88.2	89.0	1.01	…	…	…	100.0y	100.0y	100.0y	186
…	…	…	…	…	…	…	…	…	…	…	…	…	…	187
…	…	…	…	…	…	…	…	…	…	…	…	…	…	188
1.1	1.1	1.1	1.03	1.4	1.4	1.4	1.01	…	…	…	19.0	18.9	19.2	189
…	…	…	…	…	…	…	…	…	…	…	…	…	…	190
…	…	…	…	…	…	…	…	…	…	…	…	…	…	191
…	…	…	…	…	…	…	…	…	…	…	…	…	…	192
…	…	…	…	3.4	3.2	3.6	1.10	…	…	…	…	…	…	193
112.8	111.3	114.3	1.03	98.6	100.6	96.5	0.96	…	…	…	100.0	100.0	100.0	194
…	…	…	…	…	…	…	…	…	…	…	…	…	…	195
…	…	…	…	…	…	…	…	…	…	…	…	…	…	196
…	…	…	…	…	…	…	…	…	…	…	…	…	…	197
…	…	…	…	…	…	…	…	…	…	…	…	…	…	198
2.7	2.7	2.7	1.00	2.8	2.8	2.8	0.99	…	…	…	1.9y	1.7y	2.1y	199
…	…	…	…	…	…	…	…	…	…	…	…	…	…	200
…	…	…	…	…	…	…	…	…	…	…	…	…	…	201
…	…	…	…	…	…	…	…	…	…	…	12.8	12.1	13.5	202
…	…	…	…	…	…	…	…	…	…	…	…	…	…	203
…	…	…	…	…	…	…	…	…	…	…	…	…	…	I
…	…	…	…	…	…	…	…	…	…	…	…	…	…	II
…	…	…	…	…	…	…	…	…	…	…	…	…	…	III
…	…	…	…	…	…	…	…	…	…	…	…	…	…	IV
…	…	…	…	…	…	…	…	…	…	…	…	…	…	V
…	…	…	…	…	…	…	…	…	…	…	…	…	…	VI
…	…	…	…	…	…	…	…	…	…	…	…	…	…	VII
…	…	…	…	…	…	…	…	…	…	…	…	…	…	VIII
…	…	…	…	…	…	…	…	…	…	…	…	…	…	IX
…	…	…	…	…	…	…	…	…	…	…	…	…	…	X
…	…	…	…	…	…	…	…	…	…	…	…	…	…	XI
…	…	…	…	…	…	…	…	…	…	…	…	…	…	XII

4. All values shown are medians.
Data in bold are for 2003/2004.

(z) Data are for 2001/2002.
(y) Data are for 2000/2001.

Table 4
Access to primary education

	Country or territory	Compulsory education (age group)	Legal guarantee of free education[1]	New entrants (000)		GROSS INTAKE RATE (GIR) IN PRIMARY EDUCATION (%)							
						1998/1999				2002/2003			
				1998/1999	2002/2003	Total	Male	Female	GPI (F/M)	Total	Male	Female	GPI (F/M)
	Arab States												
1	Algeria[2]	6-16	Yes	745	646	101.3	102.2	100.2	0.98	95.8	97.0	94.5	0.97
2	Bahrain	...	Yes	13	13	95.9	94.3	97.5	1.03	89.3	89.2	89.4	1.00
3	Djibouti	6-15	No	6	**8**	32.1	36.9**	27.3**	0.74**	**40.7**	**44.7**	**36.8**	**0.82**
4	Egypt[3]	6-13	Yes	1 449**	1 541**	88.8**	90.5**	87.1**	0.96**	95.7**	96.5**	94.8**	0.98**
5	Iraq	6-11	Yes	709**	720[**,y]	112.1**	119.3**	104.5**	0.88**	111.0[**,y]	117.9[**,y]	103.8[**,y]	0.88[**,y]
6	Jordan[2]	6-16	Yes	126	139	99.0	98.9	99.2	1.00	100.2	99.8	100.5	1.01
7	Kuwait[2]	6-14	Yes	35	40	99.0	98.9	99.0	1.00	92.4	91.9	93.0	1.01
8	Lebanon[2,3]	6-12	Yes	71	71	96.5	100.0	92.8	0.93	101.4	101.4	101.3	1.00
9	Libyan Arab Jamahiriya[2]	6-15	Yes	...	...	...	...	...	...	...	...	...	...
10	Mauritania[3]	6-14	Yes	...	84	...	...	...	...	102.7	102.8	102.6	1.00
11	Morocco[3]	6-14	Yes	731	638	115.8	119.2	112.2	0.94	103.7	105.9	101.5	0.96
12	Oman	...	Yes	52	49	81.1	81.2	80.9	1.00	71.1	71.6	70.5	0.98
13	Palestinian A. T.	6-15	...	95	96	104.2	103.5	104.9	1.01	90.1	90.3	90.0	1.00
14	Qatar[3]	6-14	Yes	11**	12**	113.8**	115.0**	112.4**	0.98**	105.8**	105.7**	106.0**	1.00**
15	Saudi Arabia[3]	6-11	Yes	379	407	65.2	65.5	64.9	0.99	66.2	66.6	65.8	0.99
16	Sudan[3]	6-13	Yes	...	584	...	...	...	...	65.3	69.4	61.0	0.88
17	Syrian Arab Republic[2]	6-12	Yes	466	537	107.6	110.7	104.4	0.94	124.8	126.4	123.1	0.97
18	Tunisia	6-16	Yes	204	182[z]	100.6	100.8	100.5	1.00	98.5[z]	97.8[z]	99.3[z]	1.01[z]
19	United Arab Emirates[3]	6-15	Yes	47	54	89.7	91.0	88.4	0.97	108.0	107.9	108.2	1.00
20	Yemen[3]	6-14	Yes	440	653	77.3	89.8	64.3	0.72	102.8	114.7	90.3	0.79
	Central and Eastern Europe												
21	Albania	6-13	Yes	67**	60	99.9**	100.6**	99.2**	0.99**	100.4	101.1	99.6	0.99
22	Belarus[3]	6-16	Yes	173	96	130.6	131.4	129.6	0.99	102.7	103.7	101.8	0.98
23	Bosnia and Herzegovina[3]	...	Yes	...	...	...	...	...	...	...	...	...	...
24	Bulgaria[2,3]	7-16	Yes	93	77	97.9	98.8	96.9	0.98	100.8	101.1	100.4	0.99
25	Croatia	7-15	Yes	50	49	97.1	98.3	96.0	0.98	99.4	100.5	98.3	0.98
26	Czech Republic	6-15	Yes	124**	95	100.8**	101.8**	99.9**	0.98**	93.5	94.1	93.0	0.99
27	Estonia	7-15	Yes	18	13	99.7	100.5	98.8	0.98	97.3	97.0	97.6	1.01
28	Hungary	7-16	Yes	127	112	104.0	105.7	102.3	0.97	100.0	100.4	99.5	0.99
29	Latvia[3]	7-15	Yes	32	22	96.2	96.5**	95.9**	0.99**	88.4	89.5	87.3	0.98
30	Lithuania[2]	7-16	Yes	54	41	104.0	104.5	103.5	0.99	93.6	93.6	93.6	1.00
31	Poland[2,4]	7-18	Yes	535	434	100.6	...	...	...	95.4	...	...	...
32	Republic of Moldova[3]	6-16	Yes	62	51	85.1	85.3**	85.0**	1.00**	90.6	91.2	89.9	0.99
33	Romania[3]	7-14	Yes	269	235	93.7	94.1	93.4	0.99	104.9	105.4	104.4	0.99
34	Russian Federation[3]	6-15	Yes	1 659	1 393	87.2	...	...	...	99.8	...	...	...
35	Serbia and Montenegro[5]	7-14	...	...	92[y]	...	...	...	...	98.3[y]	98.0[**,y]	98.6[**,y]	1.01[**,y]
36	Slovakia[2]	6-16	Yes	75	60	101.5	102.1	100.8	0.99	95.3	96.4	94.2	0.98
37	Slovenia[2]	7-15	Yes	21	22	95.3	95.7	94.9	0.99	117.1	118.2	115.9	0.98
38	TFYR Macedonia[2,3]	7-15	Yes	32	28	103.3	103.3	103.2	1.00	94.7	95.8	93.6	0.98
39	Turkey[3]	6-14	Yes	...	...	...	...	...	...	...	...	...	...
40	Ukraine[3]	6-17	Yes	623	500	93.6	94.0	93.2	0.99	105.3	105.6	105.1	0.99
	Central Asia												
41	Armenia[3]	7-15	Yes	...	41	...	...	...	...	97.8	98.5	97.1	0.99
42	Azerbaijan[3]	6-17	Yes	172	143	91.0	90.2	91.8	1.02	88.2	89.7	86.7	0.97
43	Georgia[3]	6-14	Yes	74	58	98.0	97.3**	98.7**	1.01**	94.1	95.6	92.5	0.97
44	Kazakhstan	7-17	Yes	305	259	93.7	92.7	94.8	1.02	102.6	102.7	102.5	1.00
45	Kyrgyzstan[3]	7-15	Yes	120*	116	103.6*	103.3*	103.8*	1.00*	107.3	109.6	105.0	0.96
46	Mongolia	8-16	No	70	64	110.4	110.4	110.4	1.00	115.0	114.7	115.3	1.00
47	Tajikistan[3]	7-15	Yes	177	184	105.8	108.8	102.7	0.94	120.5	122.9	118.1	0.96
48	Turkmenistan	7-15	Yes	...	...	...	...	...	...	...	...	...	...
49	Uzbekistan[3]	7-16	Yes	...	622	...	...	...	...	104.9	104.9	105.0	1.00
	East Asia and the Pacific												
50	Australia	5-15	Yes	...	...	...	...	...	...	...	...	...	...
51	Brunei Darussalam	5-16	No	8	7	109.8	110.6	108.9	0.99	98.6	98.7	98.4	1.00
52	Cambodia[3]	...	Yes	404**	521	111.4**	114.6**	108.1**	0.94**	132.3	138.2	126.3	0.91
53	China[3,6]	6-14	Yes	...	19 528	...	...	...	...	99.3	99.8	98.7	0.99
54	Cook Islands[7]	5-15	...	0.7	0.6[**,y]	...	...	...	...	...	...	...	...

NET INTAKE RATE (NIR) IN PRIMARY EDUCATION (%)								SCHOOL LIFE EXPECTANCY (expected number of years of formal schooling)						
1998/1999				2002/2003				1998/1999			2002/2003			
Total	Male	Female	GPI (F/M)	Total	Male	Female	GPI (F/M)	Total	Male	Female	Total	Male	Female	
Arab States														
77.7	78.7	76.6	0.97	85.4	86.2	84.5	0.98	…	…	…	12.4**	…	…	1
81.2	79.2	83.3	1.05	73.9	74.2	73.6	0.99	12.8**	12.3**	13.4**	13.5**	12.9**	14.2**	2
23.6	27.0	20.1	0.75	**32.1**	**35.7**	**28.5**	**0.80**	3.5**	…	…	4.4**	5.1**	3.8**	3
…	…	…	…	87.0**	87.9**	86.0**	0.98**	12.4**	…	…	11.6**	…	…	4
86.5**	91.1**	81.8**	0.90**	84.0**,y	88.1**,y	79.8**,y	0.91**,y	8.9**	10.1**	7.5**	…	…	…	5
66.5**	65.9**	67.2**	1.02**	66.3	65.7	67.1	1.02	…	…	…	12.8**	12.7**	13.0**	6
63.0	64.1	61.8	0.96	61.5	60.3	62.8	1.04	13.5**	12.9**	14.3**	…	…	…	7
71.1**	72.6**	69.6**	0.96**	85.4	85.5	85.2	1.00	12.6**	12.4**	12.7**	13.2**	12.9**	13.5**	8
…	…	…	…	…	…	…	…	…	…	…	16.4**	15.9**	17.0**	9
…	…	…	…	34.7	35.4	34.0	0.96	6.9**	…	…	7.1**	7.4**	6.7**	10
52.4	54.4	50.4	0.93	83.4	85.4	81.4	0.95	8.2**	9.1**	7.3**	9.9**	10.5**	9.2**	11
65.6	65.3	65.9	1.01	52.0	52.3	51.8	0.99	…	…	…	10.4**,z	10.5**,z	10.4**,z	12
…	…	…	…	67.3**	68.2**	66.4**	0.97**	11.9	11.7	11.9	12.9	12.4	13.1	13
…	…	…	…	73.6**	73.4**	73.8**	1.01**	13.3**	12.6**	14.3**	13.1**	12.6**	13.7**	14
39.9	47.2	32.2	0.68	48.3	49.3	47.4	0.96	9.7**	9.8**	9.5**	9.6**	9.7**	9.5**	15
…	…	…	…	40.5	43.0	37.8	0.88	5.1**	…	…	…	…	…	16
60.7	61.3	60.1	0.98	73.5	73.7	73.2	0.99	…	…	…	…	…	…	17
85.5**	86.0**	85.1**	0.99**	83.2z	82.8z	83.6z	1.01z	12.7**	12.8**	12.5**	13.3**	13.0**	13.6**	18
46.7	46.7	46.7	1.00	48.6	48.3	48.9	1.01	11.2**	10.7**	12.1**	12.1**	11.4**	13.1**	19
25.7	30.4	20.8	0.68	…	…	…	…	7.8**	10.6**	4.9**	…	…	…	20
Central and Eastern Europe														
77.6**	77.7**	77.5**	1.00**	79.0**,y	79.2**,y	78.9**,y	1.00**,y	…	…	…	11.4	11.2	11.6	21
76.1	76.6	75.5	0.99	85.5	86.3	84.7	0.98	13.8**	13.6**	14.0**	14.2	13.7	14.6	22
…	…	…	…	…	…	…	…	…	…	…	…	…	…	23
…	…	…	…	82.1z	81.9z	82.3z	1.00z	12.7	12.2	13.1	12.8	12.7	12.8	24
70.0	71.2	68.7	0.97	72.7	74.5	70.9	0.95	12.5	12.2	12.6	13.1	12.8	13.3	25
…	…	…	…	50.3**,y	47.1**,y	53.7**,y	1.14**,y	…	…	…	14.9	14.6	15.1	26
…	…	…	…	78.8**,z	78.4**,z	79.3**,z	1.01**,z	13.9	13.2	14.6	15.8	14.4	16.7	27
…	…	…	…	66.0**	67.4**	64.6**	0.96**	14.0**	13.8**	14.3**	15.6	14.9	16.1	28
…	…	…	…	69.0**,z	69.0**,z	69.0**,z	1.00**,z	13.7	12.8	14.4	15.2	13.8	16.1	29
…	…	…	…	72.0**,z	72.9**,z	71.1**,z	0.98**,z	…	…	…	15.8	14.9	16.5	30
…	…	…	…	…	…	…	…	…	…	…	15.6	14.9	16.1	31
…	…	…	…	…	…	…	…	9.9**	9.7**	10.1**	10.1	9.8	10.4	32
…	…	…	…	76.7z	77.2z	76.2z	0.99z	11.8	11.6	12.0	12.7	12.3	13.0	33
…	…	…	…	…	…	…	…	…	…	…	13.5**	…	…	34
…	…	…	…	88.8**,y	88.5**,y	89.2**,y	1.01**,y	13.3	13.2	13.4	12.9**,y	12.7**,y	13.1**,y	35
53.5**	50.6**	56.5**	1.12**	50.6**	48.6**	52.7**	1.08**	13.1**	13.0**	13.3**	14.0	13.7	14.1	36
…	…	…	…	…	…	…	…	14.3**	13.6**	14.8**	16.3**	15.5**	16.8**	37
…	…	…	…	74.1z	75.0z	73.2z	0.98z	11.9	11.9	11.9	11.2**	11.0**	11.5**	38
…	…	…	…	…	…	…	…	…	…	…	10.9**	11.8**	9.9**	39
66.5	…	…	…	73.4	73.6	73.2	0.99	…	…	…	13.4	13.0*	13.7*	40
Central Asia														
…	…	…	…	86.3	86.3	86.2	1.00	…	…	…	10.9	10.5	11.2	41
…	…	…	…	59.7	61.2	58.1	0.95	10.0	10.1	9.9	10.6	10.7	10.4	42
67.5	67.1**	68.0**	1.01**	80.2	80.4	79.9	0.99	10.8**	10.6**	10.9**	11.3**	11.2**	11.3**	43
…	…	…	…	65.7**	66.8**	64.5**	0.96**	11.5	11.3	11.7	13.5**	13.1**	13.9**	44
60.7*	61.4*	60.0*	0.98*	66.9	69.8	64.1	0.92	11.6	11.3	11.8	12.8	12.5	13.1	45
82.2	82.4	82.0	1.00	64.3	64.4	64.3	1.00	8.7**	7.8**	9.6**	11.0	10.0	11.9	46
71.0	73.0	69.0	0.95	…	…	…	…	9.9**	10.7**	9.1**	11.3	12.2	10.2	47
…	…	…	…	…	…	…	…	…	…	…	…	…	…	48
…	…	…	…	87.3	87.2**	87.4**	1.00**	…	…	…	11.6**	11.8**	11.4**	49
East Asia and the Pacific														
…	…	…	…	…	…	…	…	19.6**	19.0**	19.9**	20.6	19.4	20.8	50
…	…	…	…	…	…	…	…	13.1**	12.7**	13.4**	13.4**	13.1**	13.8**	51
65.3**	66.5**	64.0**	0.96**	76.5	78.3	74.5	0.95	…	…	…	9.1**	9.9**	8.3**	52
…	…	…	…	53.2**	…	…	…	…	…	…	10.8**	10.9**	10.6**	53
…	…	…	…	…	…	…	…	…	…	…	…	…	…	54

Table 4 (continued)

	Country or territory	Compulsory education (age group)	Legal guarantee of free education[1]	New entrants (000)		GROSS INTAKE RATE (GIR) IN PRIMARY EDUCATION (%)							
						1998/1999				2002/2003			
				1998/1999	2002/2003	Total	Male	Female	GPI (F/M)	Total	Male	Female	GPI (F/M)
55	DPR Korea	6-15	Yes	…	…	…	…	…	…	…	…	…	…
56	Fiji	6-15	No	22**	20**,z	122.5**	123.9**	121.0**	0.98**	111.7**,z	114.7**,z	108.5**,z	0.95**,z
57	Indonesia	7-15	No	…	4 985	…	…	…	…	115.5	115.3	115.7	1.00
58	Japan[4]	6-15	Yes	…	…	…	…	…	…	…	…	…	…
59	Kiribati	6-15	No	…	…	…	…	…	…	…	…	…	…
60	Lao PDR	6-10	No	180	193	121.0	127.8	114.0	0.89	124.2	130.7	117.4	0.90
61	Macao, China	5-14	…	6	5	88.1	87.4	88.8	1.02	95.1	97.0	93.1	0.96
62	Malaysia	…	No	…	525	…	…	…	…	92.4	92.5	92.2	1.00
63	Marshall Islands[2,5]	6-14	No	1	2z	…	…	…	…	133.8z	140.8z	126.8z	0.90z
64	Micronesia (Fed. States of)	6-13	No	…	…	…	…	…	…	…	…	…	…
65	Myanmar	5-9	No	1 226	1 289	113.9	112.7	115.0	1.02	120.1	119.4	120.8	1.01
66	Nauru[5]	6-16	No	…	…	…	…	…	…	…	…	…	…
67	New Zealand[4]	5-16	Yes	…	…	…	…	…	…	…	…	…	…
68	Niue[5]	5-16	…	0.04	0.03z	95.3	112.5	73.7	0.65	110.0z	123.1z	100.0z	0.81z
69	Palau[2,5]	6-17	Yes	0.4	…	120.2	119.8	120.7	1.01	…	…	…	…
70	Papua New Guinea	6-14	No	152	151	106.6	110.5	102.3	0.93	94.3	99.7	88.5	0.89
71	Philippines[3]	6-12	Yes	2 551**	2 637	133.5**	136.8**	129.9**	0.95**	134.8	139.7	129.6	0.93
72	Republic of Korea[2,4]	6-15	Yes	711	**668**	105.9	105.0	106.9	1.02	**103.0**	**103.2**	**102.8**	**1.00**
73	Samoa	5-14	No	5	6z	107.9	107.3	108.5	1.01	116.3z	115.5z	117.1z	1.01z
74	Singapore	6-16	No	…	…	…	…	…	…	…	…	…	…
75	Solomon Islands	…	No	…	…	…	…	…	…	…	…	…	…
76	Thailand	6-14	No	1 037**	…	97.4**	101.0**	93.6**	0.93**	…	…	…	…
77	Timor-Leste	7-15	…	…	…	…	…	…	…	…	…	…	…
78	Tokelau	…	…	…	…	…	…	…	…	…	…	…	…
79	Tonga	6-14	No	3	3z	110.4	111.0	109.7	0.99	109.1z	110.6z	107.6z	0.97z
80	Tuvalu[5]	7-14	No	0.2**	…	86.0**	84.8**	87.5**	1.03**	…	…	…	…
81	Vanuatu	6-12	No	6**	7**,z	104.9**	101.3**	108.8**	1.07**	121.2**,z	118.9**,z	123.8**,z	1.04**,z
82	Viet Nam[3]	6-14	Yes	2 035	1 649**	108.4	112.5	104.2	0.93	99.2**	102.2**	96.2**	0.94**
	Latin America and the Caribbean												
83	Anguilla[5]	5-17	…	0.2	0.2z	…	…	…	…	104.3z	88.2z	127.3z	1.44z
84	Antigua and Barbuda	5-16	Yes	…	…	…	…	…	…	…	…	…	…
85	Argentina[2,3]	5-15	Yes	793	777	116.2	115.7	116.8	1.01	112.1	112.1	112.1	1.00
86	Aruba[5]	6-16	…	1	2	106.2	109.4	102.9	0.94	103.6	103.3	103.9	1.01
87	Bahamas	5-16	No	…	7**	…	…	…	…	113.4**	117.0**	109.6**	0.94**
88	Barbados	4-16	Yes	4	4	109.3	109.8	108.9	0.99	110.2	110.8	109.6	0.99
89	Belize	5-14	Yes	8	8	129.0	130.3	127.8	0.98	115.1	112.4	118.0	1.05
90	Bermuda	5-16	…	…	1z	…	…	…	…	100.6z	…	…	…
91	Bolivia[3]	6-13	Yes	272	282	122.7	122.8	122.6	1.00	121.0	120.8	121.3	1.00
92	Brazil[3]	7-14	Yes	4 227	4 067	125.5	…	…	…	124.6	130.3**	118.7**	0.91**
93	British Virgin Islands[5]	5-16	…	0.4	0.4	105.7	108.6	102.7	0.95	109.7	119.6	99.4	0.83
94	Cayman Islands[7]	5-16	…	0.6	0.6z	…	…	…	…	…	…	…	…
95	Chile[2]	6-14	Yes	288	**266**	97.7	98.2	97.2	0.99	**92.2**	**92.9**	**91.4**	**0.98**
96	Colombia[2,3]	5-15	No	1 258**	1 234	135.1**	137.7**	132.4**	0.96**	128.9	131.7	126.0	0.96
97	Costa Rica[3]	6-15	Yes	86	86	101.9	102.6	101.1	0.98	104.8	104.6	105.1	1.01
98	Cuba	6-14	Yes	161**	135	97.2**	99.1**	95.3**	0.96**	92.5	93.4	91.6	0.98
99	Dominica[5]	5-16	No	2	1	105.1	111.4	98.6	0.88	75.7	79.0	72.6	0.92
100	Dominican Republic[3]	5-13	Yes	259	258**	139.6	144.0	135.0	0.94	140.7**	145.7**	135.5**	0.93**
101	Ecuador[3]	5-14	Yes	374	394	132.1	132.4	131.9	1.00	137.7	138.4	136.9	0.99
102	El Salvador[3]	4-15	Yes	186	205	128.2	130.6	125.8	0.96	134.5	136.8	132.2	0.97
103	Grenada[5]	5-16	No	…	2	…	…	…	…	104.6	106.6	102.5	0.96
104	Guatemala	7-15	Yes	393**	430	123.8**	126.2**	121.2**	0.96**	124.3	125.0	123.6	0.99
105	Guyana[3]	6-15	Yes	18	24**,z	121.0	118.0	124.1	1.05	154.5**,z	156.1**,z	152.9**,z	0.98**,z
106	Haiti	6-11	No	…	…	…	…	…	…	…	…	…	…
107	Honduras[2,3]	6-13	[illegible]	[illegible]	257**,z	…	…	…	…	138.7**,z	138.7**,z	138.8**,z	1.00**,z
108	Jamaica	6-11	No	…	52	…	…	[illegible]		96.[illegible]	97.3**	95.2**	0.98**
109	Mexico[3]	6-15	Yes	2 509	2 440	111.3	111.2	111.5	1.00	108.3	108.0	108.5	1.01
110	Montserrat[5]	5-14	…	0.1	0.1**	…	…	…	…	145.7**	…	…	…
111	Netherlands Antilles	6-15	…	4**	3**	100.8**	97.5**	104.1**	1.07**	90.7**	86.9**	94.6**	1.09**
112	Nicaragua[3]	6-16	Yes	…	210	…	…	…	…	137.8	142.0	133.5	0.94
113	Panama[3]	6-11	Yes	…	78	…	…	…	…	121.8	123.5	120.0	0.97
114	Paraguay[3]	6-14	Yes	173	162	120.4	121.7	119.1	0.98	107.4	108.6	106.2	0.98

NET INTAKE RATE (NIR) IN PRIMARY EDUCATION (%)								SCHOOL LIFE EXPECTANCY (expected number of years of formal schooling)						
1998/1999				2002/2003				1998/1999			2002/2003			
Total	Male	Female	GPI (F/M)	Total	Male	Female	GPI (F/M)	Total	Male	Female	Total	Male	Female	
...	...	...	...	...	...	...	...	...	...	...	...	...	...	55
80.5**	81.2**	79.9**	0.98**	77.3**,z	79.3**,z	75.1**,z	0.95**,z	...	...	...	...	...	...	56
...	...	...	...	39.1	39.4**	38.8**	0.99**	...	...	...	11.1	11.3	11.0	57
...	...	...	...	...	...	...	...	14.3**	14.5**	14.2**	14.7**	14.8**	14.5**	58
...	...	...	...	...	...	...	...	...	...	...	...	...	...	59
54.7	55.7	53.7	0.96	60.9	61.7	60.1	0.97	8.4**	9.4	7.4**	9.1**	10.1**	8.1**	60
62.5	60.3	64.7	1.07	74.4	75.1	73.7	0.98	12.1**	12.3**	11.9**	15.1	13.9	14.0	61
...	...	...	...	...	...	...	...	12.0**	11.7**	12.2**	12.3	11.8	12.8	62
...	...	...	...	75.7z	75.9z	75.5z	0.99z	...	...	...	...	...	...	63
...	...	...	...	...	...	...	...	...	...	...	...	...	...	64
78.0**	...	...	...	94.2	93.7	94.7	1.01	...	...	...	7.4**,z	...	...	65
...	...	...	...	...	...	...	...	8.1**	...	...	...	...	...	66
...	...	...	...	...	...	...	...	17.5**	17.0**	17.9**	18.9	...	...	67
95.3	...	...	...	...	...	...	...	12.3	...	...	12.8z	13.3z	12.4z	68
...	...	...	...	...	...	...	...	...	...	...	15.0**,y	14.5**,y	15.6**,y	69
...	...	...	...	...	...	...	...	5.7**	6.1**	5.3**	...	...	...	70
46.5**	47.7**	45.3**	0.95**	47.6	45.5	49.9	1.10	11.7**	11.4**	11.9**	12.0**	11.7**	12.3**	71
99.1	98.2	100.0	1.02	94.5**	94.2**	94.9**	1.01**	14.9**	15.7**	14.0**	**16.9**	**17.5**	**15.9**	72
79.4	81.5	77.2	0.95	76.3**,z	74.1**,z	78.6**,z	1.06**,z	11.7**	11.5**	12.0**	11.8**,z	11.6**,z	12.0**,z	73
...	...	...	...	...	...	...	...	...	...	...	...	...	...	74
...	...	...	...	...	...	...	...	...	...	...	8.7	...	...	75
...	...	...	...	...	...	...	...	...	...	...	12.5**,y	12.7**,y	12.3**,y	76
...	...	...	...	...	...	...	...	...	...	...	11.4**,z	...	...	77
...	...	...	...	...	...	...	...	...	...	...	...	...	...	78
60.9	60.4	61.6	1.02	87.0z	84.9z	89.1z	1.05z	...	...	...	13.5**,z	13.3**,z	13.7**,z	79
86.0**	84.8**	87.5**	1.03**	...	...	...	...	10.9**	...	...	10.8z	10.6z	11.1z	80
...	...	...	...	55.1**,z	54.1**,z	56.3**,z	1.04**,z	...	...	...	9.4**,z	...	...	81
80.8	...	...	...	82.9**,z	...	...	...	10.4**	10.9**	9.8**	10.6**	11.0**	10.1**	82
											Latin America and the Caribbean			
...	...	...	...	96.8z	...	...	...	...	...	...	12.5z	...	...	83
...	...	...	...	...	...	...	...	...	...	...	...	...	...	84
...	...	...	...	92.3	92.3	92.3	1.00	14.9**	14.3**	15.6**	16.4	15.2	17.2	85
87.6	88.6	86.5	0.98	83.6	84.5	82.7	0.98	13.3**	13.2**	13.4**	13.5z	13.2z	13.7z	86
...	...	...	...	80.8**,z	81.1**,z	80.6**,z	0.99**,z	...	...	...	...	...	...	87
85.4**	85.8**	84.9**	0.99**	94.1	93.9	94.4	1.01	15.0**	14.4**	15.6**	14.3**,y	13.6**,y	15.1**,y	88
78.9**	80.6**	77.2**	0.96**	66.1**	64.2**	68.0**	1.06**	...	...	...	12.5**	12.4**	12.7**	89
...	...	...	...	100.0z	...	...	...	...	...	...	15.3**,z	...	...	90
64.2**	63.9**	64.4**	1.01**	70.0	69.8	70.3	1.01	12.8**	13.5**	12.1**	14.2**	...	...	91
...	...	...	...	...	...	...	...	...	...	...	14.7	14.1	15.0	92
73.3**	70.3**	76.4**	1.09**	75.7**	75.1**	76.2**	1.01**	15.8**	...	...	14.7**	13.7**	15.8**	93
...	...	...	...	...	...	...	...	...	...	...	...	...	...	94
37.7**	37.3**	38.1**	1.02**	36.9**	36.5**	37.2**	1.02**	12.7**	12.8**	12.6**	15.0**	15.2**	14.9**	95
55.8**	...	...	...	57.3**,z	58.5**,z	55.9**,z	0.96**,z	11.1**	10.9**	11.3**	11.0**	10.8**	11.3**	96
58.8**	58.2**	59.4**	1.02**	56.5	55.5	57.5	1.04	10.1**	9.9**	10.3**	10.7**	10.6**	10.9**	97
95.4**	97.0**	93.6**	0.96**	91.8	92.7	90.8	0.98	12.1**	...	...	13.3**	13.1**	13.4**	98
76.2	78.4	73.8	0.94	46.5	48.6	44.6	0.92	11.8**	...	...	13.1**	12.6**	13.6**	99
61.0	60.9	61.2	1.01	61.8**	64.2**	59.3**	0.92**	...	...	...	12.7**	11.9**	13.6**	100
82.8	82.3	83.3	1.01	87.2	86.9	87.5	1.01	...	...	...	...	...	...	101
...	...	...	...	60.6**	60.4**	60.9**	1.01**	10.7**	10.8**	10.6**	11.3**	11.4**	11.1**	102
...	...	...	...	66.1**	66.4**	65.9**	0.99**	...	...	...	...	...	...	103
...	...	...	...	62.7	63.1	62.4	0.99	...	...	...	9.1**	9.5**	8.7**	104
88.0**	86.4**	89.6**	1.04**	89.0**,y	90.0**,y	88.0**,y	0.98**,y	...	...	...	...	...	...	105
...	...	...	...	...	...	...	...	...	...	...	...	...	...	106
...	...	...	...	48.6**,z	48.6**,z	48.6**,z	1.00**,z	...	...	...	...	...	...	107
...	...	...	...	78.1**	76.8**	79.6**	1.04**	...	...	...	11.8**	11.3**	12.3**	108
...	...	...	...	83.1**,z	81.5**,z	84.8**,z	1.04**,z	11.8**	11.8**	11.7**	12.6	12.3	12.7	109
...	...	...	...	69.6**	...	...	...	...	...	...	13.6z	...	...	110
69.2**	64.6**	74.0**	1.15**	61.5**,z	54.8**,z	68.4**,z	1.25**,z	12.3**	12.0**	12.6**	11.5z	11.0z	11.9z	111
...	...	...	...	38.1	39.1	37.1	0.95	...	...	...	10.5**	10.3**	10.8**	112
...	...	...	...	89.8**	89.1**	90.5**	1.02**	...	...	...	13.2**	12.6**	13.8**	113
70.8**	69.8**	71.9**	1.03**	66.4	65.3	67.5	1.03	...	...	...	12.1**	12.0**	12.3**	114

Table 4 (continued)

	Country or territory	Compulsory education (age group)	Legal guarantee of free education[1]	New entrants (000)		GROSS INTAKE RATE (GIR) IN PRIMARY EDUCATION (%)							
						1998/1999				2002/2003			
				1998/1999	2002/2003	Total	Male	Female	GPI (F/M)	Total	Male	Female	GPI (F/M)
115	Peru[3]	6-16	Yes	726	696	120.1	119.7	120.5	1.01	113.7	113.4	114.1	1.01
116	Saint Kitts and Nevis[5]	5-16	No	...	0.9	...	...	...	...	114.4	112.4	116.5	1.04
117	Saint Lucia	5-16	No	4**	3	106.1**	106.0**	106.3**	1.00**	101.1	100.2	102.1	1.02
118	Saint Vincent/Grenad.	5-15	No	...	2	...	...	...	...	95.1	96.4	93.7	0.97
119	Suriname[3]	6-11	Yes	...	10**	...	...	...	...	107.7**	115.0**	100.1**	0.87**
120	Trinidad and Tobago[2,3]	5-12	Yes	20	17	97.2	96.7**	97.6**	1.01**	95.7	95.1	96.3	1.01
121	Turks and Caicos Islands[5]	4-16	...	0.3**	0.3	...	...	...	...	82.9	94.5	72.2	0.76
122	Uruguay[3]	6-15	Yes	57	61	102.1	99.3	105.0	1.06	108.2	108.9	107.4	0.99
123	Venezuela[3]	6-15	Yes	547**	562	99.1**	100.2**	97.8**	0.98**	101.0	102.4	99.5	0.97
	North America and Western Europe												
124	Andorra[2,7]	6-16	...	...	0.7	...	...	...	...	...	...	...	...
125	Austria[2,4]	6-15	Yes	100	100**,y	105.3	106.4	104.2	0.98	106.4**,y	107.6**,y	105.2**,y	0.98**,y
126	Belgium[4]	6-18	Yes	...	122	...	...	...	...	103.6	103.2	104.0	1.01
127	Canada	6-16	Yes	...	...	...	...	...	...	...	...	...	...
128	Cyprus[2,5]	6-15	Yes	...	10	...	...	...	...	99.1	99.1	99.0	1.00
129	Denmark	7-16	Yes	66**	69	100.2**	100.2**	100.2**	1.00**	100.1	99.9	100.3	1.00
130	Finland	7-16	Yes	65**	63	100.4**	100.4**	100.4**	1.00**	98.9	99.5	98.2	0.99
131	France	6-16	Yes	736	...	100.8	...	...	...	...	...	...	...
132	Germany	6-18	Yes	869**	807	100.3**	100.5**	100.2**	1.00**	100.6	100.7	100.4	1.00
133	Greece[2]	6-15	Yes	...	...	...	...	...	...	...	...	...	...
134	Iceland	6-16	Yes	4	4	98.4	99.8	96.8	0.97	96.5	98.3	94.7	0.96
135	Ireland	6-15	Yes	51	56	100.9	101.6	100.1	0.99	106.4	105.5	107.4	1.02
136	Israel[3]	5-15	Yes	...	116	...	...	...	...	97.7	97.0	98.5	1.02
137	Italy[2]	6-16	Yes	558**	532	100.0**	100.6**	99.3**	0.99**	97.9	98.4	97.3	0.99
138	Luxembourg	6-15	Yes	...	6**,z	...	...	...	...	99.9**,z	99.4**,z	100.4**,z	1.01**,z
139	Malta[2]	5-16	Yes	5	5	102.0	102.2	101.7	0.99	100.0	101.8	98.0	0.96
140	Monaco[2]	6-16	No	...	...	...	...	...	...	...	...	...	...
141	Netherlands[2,4]	6-17	Yes	199	194	99.9	100.6	99.2	0.99	97.5	98.4	96.7	0.98
142	Norway	6-16	Yes	61**	62	100.3**	101.1**	99.6**	0.99**	101.9	101.9	102.0	1.00
143	Portugal[2]	6-15	Yes	...	...	...	...	...	...	...	...	...	...
144	San Marino[2]	6-16	No	...	...	...	...	...	...	...	...	...	...
145	Spain	6-16	Yes	...	...	...	...	...	...	...	...	...	...
146	Sweden	7-16	Yes	127**	114z	103.9**	104.9**	102.9**	0.98**	98.5z	98.3z	98.7z	1.00z
147	Switzerland	7-15	Yes	82**	77	97.6**	96.0**	99.3**	1.03**	95.7	94.0	97.5	1.04
148	United Kingdom	5-16	Yes	...	...	...	...	...	...	...	...	...	...
149	United States	6-17	No	4 322	...	103.4	106.0	100.6	0.95	...	...	...	...
	South and West Asia												
150	Afghanistan	7-12	...	...	...	...	...	...	...	...	...	...	...
151	Bangladesh	6-10	Yes	3 986**	4 356	111.1**	112.6**	109.6**	0.97**	115.7	115.0	116.5	1.01
152	Bhutan[3,8]	6-16	Yes	12	13z	...	...	...	...	...	...	...	...
153	India[3]	6-14	Yes	29 639	31 184	127.7	138.5	116.2	0.84	131.6	134.0	129.1	0.96
154	Iran, Islamic Republic of	6-10	Yes	1 563	1 199**	90.3	90.5	90.0	0.99	86.7**	85.9**	87.6**	1.02**
155	Maldives	6-12	No	8**	7	102.4**	103.0**	101.7**	0.99**	81.3	80.9	81.8	1.01
156	Nepal	6-10	Yes	641**	798	102.4**	114.9**	89.1**	0.78**	116.5	121.3	111.4	0.92
157	Pakistan	5-9	No	...	3 891**,y	...	...	...	...	93.9**,y	108.1**,y	78.8**,y	0.73**,y
158	Sri Lanka[2]	5-14	Yes	346	**323****	107.7	107.5	107.9	1.00	**106.7****	**107.1****	**106.4****	**0.99****
	Sub-Saharan Africa												
159	Angola[2,3]	6-14	Yes	348	...	94.4	107.5	81.4	0.76	...	...	...	...
160	Benin	6-11	No	...	231	...	...	...	...	115.2	128.4	102.0	0.79
161	Botswana	6-15	Yes	51	53**	110.3	112.6	108.0	0.96	112.4**	114.4**	110.5**	0.97**
162	Burkina Faso	6-15	No	154	213	43.5	51.0	35.9	0.70	53.2	61.0	45.3	0.74
163	Burundi	7-12	No	118**	177	74.2**	81.3**	67.1**	0.82**	86.4	92.8	80.1	0.86
164	Cameroon	6-11	No	335**	454	77.4**	85.3**	69.4**	0.81**	100.2	107.0	99.0	0.87
165	Cape Verde[2]	6-16	No	13**	13	106.3**	107.4**	105.2**	0.98**	107.7	109.1	106.4	0.97
166	Central African Republic	6-15	No	...	71*,z	...	...	...	...	64.4*,z	76.1*,z	52.9*,z	0.70*,z
167	Chad[2,3]	6-14	Yes	175	239**	75.9	88.9	62.8	0.71	91.0**	105.1**	76.9**	0.73**
168	Comoros[2]	6-14	No	13	17z	69.5	75.6	63.3	0.84	80.5z	87.3z	73.4z	0.84z
169	Congo[3]	6-15	Yes	...	64	...	...	...	...	55.5	57.0	54.0	0.95
170	Côte d'Ivoire	6-15	No	309	354*	69.0	76.4	61.6	0.81	78.8*	82.3*	75.2*	0.91*

NET INTAKE RATE (NIR) IN PRIMARY EDUCATION (%)								SCHOOL LIFE EXPECTANCY (expected number of years of formal schooling)						
1998/1999				2002/2003				1998/1999			2002/2003			
Total	Male	Female	GPI (F/M)	Total	Male	Female	GPI (F/M)	Total	Male	Female	Total	Male	Female	
...	...	...	...	81.0	81.0	81.1	1.00	...	...	...	13.8**	13.8**	13.8**	115
...	...	...	...	76.3	75.6	76.9	1.02	...	...	...	15.9**,y	...	...	116
74.8**	74.0**	75.5**	1.02**	71.0**	69.9**	72.2**	1.03**	...	...	...	...	...	...	117
...	...	...	...	61.0**	60.5**	61.4**	1.01**	...	...	...	...	...	...	118
...	...	...	...	73.9**	75.4**	72.4**	0.96**	...	...	...	12.5**,z	11.6**,z	13.4**,z	119
69.2	68.0**	70.5**	1.04**	63.3**	62.1**	64.6**	1.04**	11.8**	11.5**	12.0**	11.8**	11.6**	12.1**	120
...	...	...	...	49.7	59.1	40.9	0.69	...	...	...	12.8**,z	12.2**,z	13.3**,z	121
38.1**	36.2**	40.1**	1.11**	34.8**,z	33.4**,z	36.4**,z	1.09**,z	...	...	...	14.9**	14.0**	15.8**	122
61.0**	60.8**	61.2**	1.01**	61.5	61.2	61.9	1.01	...	...	...	11.8**	11.5**	12.0**	123
North America and Western Europe														
...	...	...	...	...	...	...	...	...	...	...	...	...	...	124
...	...	...	...	...	...	...	...	15.2**	15.2**	15.1**	14.9	14.5	15.1	125
...	...	...	...	...	...	...	...	17.8**	17.4**	18.2**	19.2	18.3	19.9	126
...	...	...	...	...	...	...	...	16.0**	15.7**	16.3**	16.0**,z	15.7**,z	16.4**,z	127
...	...	...	...	91.0z	90.3z	91.8z	1.02z	12.5	12.3	12.7	13.4	13.3	13.5	128
...	...	...	...	99.8z	99.7z	100.0z	1.00z	16.1**	15.6**	16.6**	16.9	15.8	17.6	129
...	...	...	...	94.3**	93.6**	95.0**	1.02**	17.5**	16.7**	18.2**	18.3	16.8	19.1	130
...	...	...	...	...	...	...	...	15.6**	15.3**	15.8**	15.6	15.1	15.9	131
...	...	...	...	...	...	...	...	16.0**	16.2**	15.8**	15.8	15.5	15.7	132
...	...	...	...	...	...	...	...	14.2**	14.0**	14.4**	15.8	15.5	16.0	133
...	...	...	...	96.4	98.2	94.5	0.96	16.7**	16.0**	17.3**	18.3	16.6	19.4	134
...	...	...	...	49.3**	46.2**	52.6**	1.14**	16.3**	15.6**	16.7**	17.0	16.1	17.7	135
...	...	...	...	...	...	...	...	14.8**	14.4**	15.2**	15.6	14.7	16.0	136
...	...	...	...	95.8	96.0	95.7	1.00	14.7**	14.5**	14.9**	15.6	15.1**	16.0**	137
...	...	...	...	85.9**,z	85.5**,z	86.3**,z	1.01**,z	...	...	...	13.5**	13.3**	13.7**	138
...	...	...	...	69.7**	71.4**	67.8**	0.95**	...	...	...	14.5	14.1	14.6	139
...	...	...	...	...	...	...	...	...	...	...	...	...	...	140
99.3	100.0	98.6	0.99	97.5	98.4	96.7	0.98	16.5**	16.7**	16.2**	16.6	16.4	16.6	141
...	...	...	...	...	...	...	...	17.5**	16.9**	10.0**	17.8	16.4	18.5	142
...	...	...	...	...	...	...	...	15.8**	15.4**	16.1**	16.1	15.3	16.6	143
...	...	...	...	...	...	...	...	...	...	...	...	...	...	144
...	...	...	...	...	...	...	...	15.7**	15.4**	16.0**	16.2	15.5	16.6	145
...	...	...	...	95.1z	95.3z	94.8z	0.99z	19.0**	17.3**	20.8**	19.1	16.8	20.7	146
...	...	...	...	58.4	58.2	58.6	1.01	15.5**	16.0**	15.0**	15.9	15.8	15.6	147
...	...	...	...	...	...	...	...	20.0**	19.3**	20.7**	22.0	19.8	23.5	148
...	...	...	...	...	...	...	...	...	...	...	15.7**	14.4**	16.3**	149
South and West Asia														
...	...	...	...	...	...	...	...	...	...	...	...	...	...	150
83.3**	83.5**	83.2**	1.00**	87.0	85.6	88.5	1.03	8.5**	8.7**	8.2**	8.4	8.2	8.5	151
...	...	...	...	...	...	...	...	...	...	...	...	...	...	152
...	...	...	...	...	...	...	...	...	...	...	9.7**	10.3**	8.9**	153
43.8**	44.3**	43.2**	0.97**	41.4**,y	41.9**,y	40.8**,y	0.97**,y	11.6**	12.2**	10.9**	11.6**	12.1**	11.1**	154
...	...	...	...	71.8	71.9	71.7	1.00	11.6	...	...	11.9	11.8	12.1	155
...	...	...	...	...	...	...	...	...	...	...	9.7**	10.6**	8.8**	156
...	...	...	...	...	...	...	...	...	...	...	5.4**	6.3**	4.5**	157
95.1	94.5	95.7	1.01	99.8**	...	...	...	...	...	...	...	...	...	158
Sub-Saharan Africa														
25.8**	28.7**	22.9**	0.80**	...	...	...	...	5.2**	5.8**	4.6**	...	...	...	159
...	...	...	...	...	...	...	...	6.9**	8.7**	5.1**	...	...	...	160
21.5	20.2	22.9	1.14	24.0**	22.4**	25.6**	1.14**	11.4**	11.3**	11.5**	11.3**	11.2**	11.3**	161
18.6	21.9	15.2	0.69	21.3	24.6	17.9	0.73	...	...	...	3.7**	4.3**	3.0**	162
...	...	...	...	33.7	34.1	33.4	0.98	...	...	...	5.6**	6.3**	4.9**	163
...	...	...	...	...	...	...	...	7.6**	...	...	9.2**	10.0**	8.4**	164
68.6**	67.8**	69.5**	1.03**	79.2	78.4	80.0	1.02	...	...	...	11.8**	11.8**	11.8**	165
...	...	...	...	...	...	...	...	...	...	...	...	...	...	166
23.0	26.8	19.1	0.71	30.5z	35.3z	25.7z	0.73z	...	...	...	...	...	...	167
15.5	18.2**	12.7**	0.70**	...	...	...	...	6.5**	7.0**	5.9**	7.9**	8.7**	7.2**	168
...	...	...	...	...	...	...	...	...	...	...	7.7**,z	8.4**,z	7.0**,z	169
28.2	31.4	25.0	0.80	29.8*	30.7*	28.9*	0.94*	6.4**	7.7**	5.1**	...	...	...	170

Table 4 (continued)

	Country or territory	Compulsory education (age group)	Legal guarantee of free education[1]	New entrants (000)		GROSS INTAKE RATE (GIR) IN PRIMARY EDUCATION (%)							
						1998/1999				2002/2003			
				1998/1999	2002/2003	Total	Male	Female	GPI (F/M)	Total	Male	Female	GPI (F/M)
171	D. R. Congo[3]	6-13	Yes	767	...	52.2	50.5	54.0	1.07	...	...	...	...
172	Equatorial Guinea	7-11	Yes	...	16[z]	...	...	...	...	121.9[z]	135.2[z]	108.6[z]	0.80[z]
173	Eritrea	7-13	No	57	72	54.9	60.3	49.3	0.82	60.2	65.0	55.2	0.85
174	Ethiopia	7-12	No	1 537	**2 026****	81.6	96.8	66.3	0.68	**95.9****	**101.0****	**90.8****	**0.90****
175	Gabon	6-16	No	...	35**	...	...	...	...	95.8**	95.9**	95.7**	1.00**
176	Gambia	...	Yes	30	32**	89.5	91.6	87.4	0.95	87.2**	85.1**	89.2**	1.05**
177	Ghana[2,3]	6-15	Yes	469	**495****	87.9	90.9	84.9	0.93	**89.2****	**89.5****	**89.0****	**0.99****
178	Guinea	6-12	No	119	195	53.6	59.6	47.3	0.79	81.1	86.2	75.8	0.88
179	Guinea-Bissau[3]	7-12	Yes	36**	...	93.1**	110.0**	76.3**	0.69**	...	...	...	...
180	Kenya[3]	6-13	Yes	916	826**	104.6	107.3	101.9	0.95	95.7**	96.5**	94.9**	0.98**
181	Lesotho	6-12	No	52	60	108.9	109.3	108.5	0.99	129.2	134.2	124.1	0.92
182	Liberia[2]	6-16	No	50	...	63.0	77.0	48.8	0.63	...	...	...	...
183	Madagascar[3]	6-14	Yes	495	586[z]	109.4	110.6	108.2	0.98	117.9[z]	119.4[z]	116.4[z]	0.98[z]
184	Malawi	6-13	Yes	...	658	...	...	...	...	172.2	169.5	174.9	1.03
185	Mali[3]	7-15	Yes	173**	235	48.5**	55.0**	41.9**	0.76**	58.5	63.4	53.4	0.84
186	Mauritius[3]	...	Yes	22	20	104.3	104.0	104.5	1.00	93.5	92.4	94.7	1.02
187	Mozambique	6-12	No	521**	631	100.5**	109.0**	92.0**	0.84**	115.1	120.2	110.0	0.91
188	Namibia[3]	6-15	Yes	55	58	101.2	100.3	102.0	1.02	97.9	98.4	97.3	0.99
189	Niger[3]	7-12	Yes	133	216	42.1	49.6	34.4	0.69	59.0	67.8	49.9	0.74
190	Nigeria[3]	6-11	Yes	...	5 291	...	...	...	...	144.1	158.4	129.4	0.82
191	Rwanda[3]	6-12	Yes	295	404	153.7	136.0	171.3	1.26	166.6	166.3	166.9	1.00
192	Sao Tome and Principe	7-12	Yes	4	5[z]	105.5	107.9	103.1	0.96	109.3[z]	112.1[z]	106.5[z]	0.95[z]
193	Senegal	7-12	Yes	190	266	71.0	72.5**	69.4**	0.96**	94.5	95.1	93.9	0.99
194	Seychelles[5]	6-15	Yes	2	2	113.4	111.2	115.7	1.04	102.2	102.2	102.2	1.00
195	Sierra Leone	...	No	...	...	...	...	...	...	...	...	...	...
196	Somalia	6-13	...	...	...	...	...	...	...	...	...	...	...
197	South Africa	7-15	No	1 265	1 169	123.6	126.0	121.1	0.96	115.7	117.9	113.5	0.96
198	Swaziland	6-12	No	31	30	101.0	103.6	98.4	0.95	94.5	97.2	91.7	0.94
199	Togo	6-15	No	139	149	107.7	113.9	101.3	0.89	104.5	109.6	99.4	0.91
200	Uganda	...	No	...	1 613	...	...	...	...	189.8	187.4	192.2	1.03
201	U. R. Tanzania[3]	7-13	Yes	669	**1 332****	65.9	66.8	65.0	0.97	**120.1****	**123.3****	**116.9****	**0.95****
202	Zambia	7-13	No	249	286	82.2	83.1	81.3	0.98	86.4	86.4	86.5	1.00
203	Zimbabwe	6-12	No	...	**417**	...	...	...	...	**112.4**	**113.9**	**110.9**	**0.97**

						Median							
I	World	...	...	...	...	101.1	102.0	100.2	0.98	101.1	100.2	102.1	1.02
II	Countries in transition	...	...	...	...	93.7	92.7	94.8	1.02	102.6	102.7	102.5	1.00
III	Developed countries	...	...	...	...	100.3	101.1	99.6	0.99	99.4	100.5	98.3	0.98
IV	Developing countries	...	...	...	...	104.2	104	104.7	1.01	104.3	106	102.1	0.96
V	Arab States	...	...	...	...	99.0	98.9	99.0	1.00	98.5	97.8	99.3	1.01
VI	Central and Eastern Europe	...	...	...	...	99.7	100.5	98.8	0.98	98.8	99.2	98.4	0.99
VII	Central Asia	...	...	...	...	100.8	100.3	101.3	1.01	103.8	103.8	103.7	1.00
VIII	East Asia and the Pacific	...	...	...	...	108.4	112.5	104.2	0.93	110.8	115.0	108.0	0.94
IX	Latin America and the Caribbean	...	...	...	...	111.3	111.2	111.5	1.00	109.0	111.4	109.1	0.98
X	North America and Western Europe	...	...	...	...	100.4	100.8	100.0	0.99	99.5	99.3	99.7	1.00
XI	South and West Asia	...	...	...	...	105.1	111.2	98.5	0.89	105.6	108.1	105.6	0.98
XII	Sub-Saharan Africa	...	...	...	...	88.7	91.3	86.1	0.94	95.8	98.4	94.9	0.96

1. *Source:* Tomasevsky (2003). Background paper for the *EFA Global Monitoring Report 2003/4.*

2. Information on compulsory education comes from the Reports under the United Nations Human Rights Treaties.
3. Some primary school fees continue to be charged despite the legal guarantee for free education (World Bank, 2002*a*; Bentaouet-Kattan, 2005).
4. No tuition fees are charged but some direct costs have been reported (World Bank, 2002*a*; Bentaouet-Kattan, 2005).

NET INTAKE RATE (NIR) IN PRIMARY EDUCATION (%)								SCHOOL LIFE EXPECTANCY (expected number of years of formal schooling)						
1998/1999				2002/2003				1998/1999			2002/2003			
Total	Male	Female	GPI (F/M)	Total	Male	Female	GPI (F/M)	Total	Male	Female	Total	Male	Female	
23.5	22.5	24.5	1.09	…	…	…	…	4.4**	…	…	…	…	…	171
…	…	…	…	48.3[z]	61.2[z]	35.3[z]	0.58[z]	…	…	…	…	…	…	172
17.4	18.3	16.5	0.90	26.6	28.2	25.1	0.89	4.4**	5.0**	3.7**	5.1**	5.9**	4.3**	173
21.4	23.8	19.0	0.80	27.1	28.8	25.4	0.88	4.0**	5.0**	3.0**	**5.9****	**6.9****	**4.8****	174
…	…	…	…	…	…	…	…	12.1**	12.5**	11.7**	…	…	…	175
43.0**	43.8**	42.2**	0.96**	41.9**	40.7**	43.1**	1.06**	…	…	…	…	…	…	176
29.8**	30.2**	29.4**	0.97**	**24.5****	**24.2****	**24.8****	**1.02****	…	…	…	7.3**	7.7**	6.9**	177
20.4	21.9	18.9	0.86	27.6[z]	29.0[z]	26.2[z]	0.90[z]	…	…	…	…	…	…	178
…	…	…	…	…	…	…	…	…	…	…	…	…	…	179
30.5**	30.0**	31.0**	1.03**	31.0**	30.1**	31.9**	1.06**	…	…	…	8.5**[z]	8.7**[z]	8.3**[z]	180
18.1	18.3	17.9	0.97	54.7	53.7	55.8	1.04	9.7	9.2	10.3	10.8**	10.5	11.1**	181
…	…	…	…	…	…	…	…	…	…	…	…	…	…	182
…	…	…	…	37.1[z]	36.1[z]	38.2[z]	1.06[z]	6.2**	6.3**	6.0**	…	…	…	183
…	…	…	…	…	…	…	…	…	…	…	10.9**	11.4**	10.4**	184
…	…	…	…	22.7	25.0	20.3	0.81	3.9**	…	…	4.9**	…	…	185
76.3	75.9	76.6	1.01	79.2	78.0	80.4	1.03	11.9**	11.9**	11.8**	12.7**	12.5**	12.8**	186
17.4**	18.1**	16.8**	0.93**	25.5	25.7	25.2	0.98	…	…	…	…	…	…	187
56.1	54.6	57.6	1.06	54.9	53.5	56.3	1.05	12.1**	12.0**	12.3**	11.5**	11.4**	11.6**	188
26.8	32.0	21.3	0.67	41.4	48.3	34.4	0.71	…	…	…	2.9**[z]	3.5**[z]	2.3**[z]	189
…	…	…	…	87.8**	95.0**	80.2**	0.84**	…	…	…	10.2**	11.3**	9.0**	190
…	…	…	…	83.2	81.9	84.5	1.03	7.9**	…	…	8.6**	8.9**	8.4**	191
…	…	…	…	…	…	…	…	…	…	…	9.6**[z]	10.0**[z]	9.2**[z]	192
39.5	40.3**	38.6**	0.96**	…	…	…	…	5.6**	…	…	…	…	…	193
68.2	67.6	68.7	1.02	67.9	65.0	70.9	1.09	13.4	…	…	13.4**	13.3**	13.5**	194
…	…	…	…	…	…	…	…	…	…	…	6.8**[y]	7.9**[y]	5.7**[y]	195
…	…	…	…	…	…	…	…	…	…	…	…	…	…	196
46.8	46.4	47.1	1.02	43.0	43.9	42.0	0.96	13.5**	13.3**	13.7**	13.1**	12.8**	13.1**	197
38.7	37.4	39.9	1.06	44.1	43.8	44.4	1.01	10.4**	10.8**	10.1**	9.6**	9.9**	9.3**	198
43.7	46.4	40.9	0.88	46.0	48.5	43.4	0.89	10.8**	13.1**	8.5**	…	…	…	199
…	…	…	…	70.6	68.9	72.3	1.05	11.9**	12.7**	11.0**	12.0**	12.3**	11.7**	200
11.3	10.5	12.2	1.15	**81.3****	**82.1****	**80.5****	**0.98****	5.0**	5.1**	4.9**	…	…	…	201
36.9	36.2	37.5	1.04	35.1	34.0	36.1	1.06	6.9**	7.4**	6.5**	6.9**[y]	7.3**[y]	6.5**[y]	202
…	…	…	…	**42.3**	**41.6**	**43.0**	**1.03**	…	…	…	**10.1****	…	…	203

Median								Weighted average						
…	…	…	…	69.6	…	…	…	9.8	10.3	9.4	10.5	10.8	10.2	I
…	…	…	…	76.8	77.0	76.6	0.99	11.9	11.8	12.0	12.6	12.4	12.8	II
…	…	…	…	78.8	78.4	79.3	1.01	15.7	15.4	16.1	16.1	15.2	16.6	III
61.0	60.8	61.2	1.01	65.2	64.2	64.6	1.01	9.1	9.7	8.5	9.9	10.3	9.4	IV
64.3	64.7	63.8	0.99	70.4	70.8	70.1	0.99	9.8	10.6	9.0	10.2	10.7	9.6	V
…	…	…	…	73.8	74.7	73.2	0.98	11.8	11.9	11.8	12.8	12.8	12.8	VI
…	…	…	…	66.9	69.8	64.5	0.92	10.9	11.0	10.8	11.5	11.6	11.4	VII
…	…	…	…	…	…	…	…	10.2	10.4	9.9	11.2	11.3	11.0	VIII
…	…	…	…	69.6	…	…	…	12.2	12.1	12.2	13.1	12.8	13.3	IX
…	…	…	…	…	…	…	…	16.2	15.8	16.6	16.4	15.3	17.0	X
…	…	…	…	…	…	…	…	8.4	9.4	7.4	9.1	9.7	8.4	XI
27.5	30.1	24.8	0.82	41.6	40.9	37.2	0.91	6.7	7.4	6.0	7.8	8.5	7.0	XII

5. National population data were used to calculate enrolment ratios.
6. Children can enter primary school at age 6 or 7.
7. Enrolment ratios were not calculated due to lack of United Nations population data by age.
8. Enrolment ratios were not calculated due to inconsistencies between enrolment and the United Nations population data.

Data in bold are for 2003/2004.
(z) Data are for 2001/2002.
(y) Data are for 2000/2001.

Table 5
Participation in primary education

	Country or territory	Age group 2002/2003	School-age population (000) 2002	ENROLMENT IN PRIMARY EDUCATION 1998/1999 Total (000)	% F	ENROLMENT IN PRIMARY EDUCATION 2002/2003 Total (000)	% F	GROSS ENROLMENT RATIO (GER) IN PRIMARY EDUCATION (%) 1998/1999 Total	Male	Female	GPI (F/M)	GER 2002/2003 Total	Male	Female	GPI (F/M)
	Arab States														
1	Algeria	6-11	4 242	4 779	47	4 613	47	106.8	111.4	102.0	0.92	108.7	112.8	104.5	0.93
2	Bahrain	6-11	84	76	49	82	49	100.7	100.4	101.0	1.01	97.1	97.2	97.0	1.00
3	Djibouti	6-11	113	38	41	**49**	**44**	38.1	44.6	31.5	0.71	**42.5**	**47.5**	**37.4**	**0.79**
4	Egypt	6-10	8 085	8 086**	47**	7 874**	48**	98.6**	102.9**	94.2**	0.92**	97.4**	100.0**	94.7**	0.95**
5	Iraq	6-11	3 887	3 604	44	4 281	44	99.5	109.2	89.3	0.82	110.1	120.1	99.8	0.83
6	Jordan	6-11	794	706	49	786	49	96.5	96.4	96.7	1.00	99.1	98.7	99.5	1.01
7	Kuwait	6-9	165	140	49	154	49	101.9	101.5	102.2	1.01	93.6	93.4	93.7	1.00
8	Lebanon	6-11	435	395	48	449	48	106.7	108.9	104.3	0.96	103.4	105.0	101.7	0.97
9	Libyan Arab Jamahiriya	6-11	652	822	48	744**	49**	115.7	116.6	114.8	0.98	114.1**	114.2**	114.1**	1.00**
10	Mauritania	6-11	447	346	48	394	49	86.5	89.1	83.9	0.94	88.1	89.4	86.9	0.97
11	Morocco	6-11	3 742	3 462	44	4 101	46	89.2	98.2	79.9	0.81	109.6	115.3	103.7	0.90
12	Oman	6-11	389	316	48	314	48	85.7	87.2	84.1	0.96	80.8	81.3	80.2	0.99
13	Palestinian A. T.	6-9	406	368	49	401	49	105.7	104.9	106.4	1.01	98.8	98.6	99.0	1.00
14	Qatar	6-11	63	61	48	66	48	108.0	109.9	106.1	0.97	105.7	107.0	104.3	0.97
15	Saudi Arabia	6-11	3 514	2 260	48	2 342	48	68.7	69.9	67.6	0.97	66.6	67.8	65.4	0.96
16	Sudan	6-11	5 034	2 513**	45**	3 028	46	54.5**	58.7**	50.1**	0.85**	60.2	64.3	55.8	0.87
17	Syrian Arab Republic	6-11	2 598	2 738	47	2 985	48	103.6	108.0	98.9	0.92	114.9	118.1	111.6	0.95
18	Tunisia	6-11	1 154	1 443	47	1 277	48	114.9	118.0	111.6	0.95	110.7	112.6	108.6	0.96
19	United Arab Emirates	6-10	256	270	48	248	48	89.1	90.9	87.2	0.96	96.8	98.3	95.4	0.97
20	Yemen	6-11	3 535	2 303	35	2 950	40	73.3	93.2	52.5	0.56	83.5	98.3	68.0	0.69
	Central and Eastern Europe														
21	Albania	6-9	244	287**	48**	253	48	108.2**	108.7**	107.7**	0.99**	103.5	104.6	102.4	0.98
22	Belarus	6-9	429	632	48	437	48	108.9	109.8	108.0	0.98	101.9	102.6	101.1	0.99
23	Bosnia and Herzegovina	6-9	188	...	...	...	...	...	...	...	...	...	...	...	...
24	Bulgaria	7-10	332	412	48	333	48	103.4	104.7	102.0	0.97	100.3	101.4	99.1	0.98
25	Croatia	7-10	199	203	49	192	49	95.7	96.4	94.9	0.98	96.5	96.9	96.2	0.99
26	Czech Republic	6-10	556	655	49	567	48	104.0	104.5	103.5	0.99	102.0	102.8	101.1	0.98
27	Estonia	7-12	99	127	48	100	48	102.2	104.0	100.4	0.97	100.7	102.5	98.8	0.96
28	Hungary	7-10	463	503	48	464	48	103.5	104.4	102.5	0.98	100.3	100.9	99.6	0.99
29	Latvia	7-10	110	141	48	103	48	99.1	100.1	98.0	0.98	94.0	95.2	92.7	0.97
30	Lithuania	7-10	187	220	48	184	49	101.5	102.3	100.6	0.98	98.1	98.7	97.5	0.99
31	Poland	7-12	2 998	...	...	2 983	49	...	...	...	...	99.5	99.8	99.2	0.99
32	Republic of Moldova	7-10	251	262	49	215	49	84.3	84.2	84.4	1.00	86.0	86.3	85.7	0.99
33	Romania	7-10	1 001	1 285	49	991	48	104.3	105.2	103.3	0.98	99.0	100.1	97.9	0.98
34	Russian Federation[1]	7-9	4 582	6 138	49	5 417	49	100.5	101.0	99.9	0.99	118.2	118.2	118.3	1.00
35	Serbia and Montenegro[2]	7-10	...	418	49	380y	49y	103.9	104.6	103.1	0.99	98.3y	98.3y	98.3y	1.00y
36	Slovakia	6-9	268	317	49	270	48	102.5	103.3	101.8	0.99	100.7	101.5	100.0	0.99
37	Slovenia	7-10	81	92	48	87	49	97.7	98.2	97.2	0.99	107.8	108.2	107.4	0.99
38	TFYR Macedonia	7-10	121	130	48	117	48	101.8	102.7	100.8	0.98	96.5	96.4	96.6	1.00
39	Turkey	6-11	8 647	...	...	7 904**	47**	...	...	...	...	91.4**	94.5**	88.2**	0.93**
40	Ukraine	6-9	2 116	2 200	49	1 961	49	105.7	106.4	105.0	0.99	92.7	92.6	92.7	1.00
	Central Asia														
41	Armenia	7-9	137	...	...	135	48	...	...	...	...	98.5	99.6	97.4	0.98
42	Azerbaijan	6-9	689	691	49	636	48	90.9	90.9	90.9	1.00	92.3	93.6	90.8	0.97
43	Georgia	6-9	263	302	49	238	48	95.3	95.3	95.4	1.00	90.5	91.4	89.6	0.98
44	Kazakhstan	7-10	1 103	1 249	49	1 120	49	93.0	93.0	93.0	1.00	101.5	101.9	101.1	0.99
45	Kyrgyzstan	7-10	445	470	49	449	49	101.1	102.0	100.2	0.98	100.9	102.2	99.6	0.97
46	Mongolia	8-11	237	251	50	239	50	98.2	96.4	99.9	1.04	100.8	99.8	101.9	1.02
47	Tajikistan	7-10	628	690	48	695	48	102.8	105.7	99.9	0.95	110.6	113.5	107.7	0.95
48	Turkmenistan	7-9	346	...	...	...	...	...	...	...	...	...	...	...	...
49	Uzbekistan	7-10	2 447	...	...	2 513	49	...	...	...	...	102.7	103.0	102.3	0.99
	East Asia and the Pacific														
50	Australia	5-11	1 866	1 870	49	1 934	49	100.8	100.9	100.8	1.00	103.6	103.7	[illegible]	1.00
51	Brunei Darussalam	6-11	42	45	47	45	48	114.5	115.7	113.1	0.98	106.1	106.1	106.1	1.00
52	Cambodia	6-11	2 239	2 127	46	2 772	47	96.5	103.5	89.2	0.86	123.8	130.0	117.4	0.90
53	China[3, 4]	7-11	105 580	...	...	121 662	47	...	...	...	...	115.2	115.4	115.0	1.00
54	Cook Islands[5]	5-10	...	3	48	3**,y	46**,y	...	...	...	...	...	...	...	...

NET ENROLMENT RATIO (NER) IN PRIMARY EDUCATION (%)								OUT-OF-PRIMARY-SCHOOL CHILDREN (000)						
1998/1999				2002/2003				1998/1999			2002/2003			
Total	Male	Female	GPI (F/M)	Total	Male	Female	GPI (F/M)	Total	Male	Female	Total	Male	Female	
													Arab States	
92.1	94.0	90.2	0.96	94.9	96.0	93.6	0.97	353	138	215	218	86	132	1
93.9	93.0	94.9	1.02	89.9	89.2	90.6	1.02	5	3	2	9	5	4	2
31.3	36.3	26.2	0.72	**35.6**	**39.5**	**31.7**	**0.80**	69	32	37	**74**	**35**	**39**	3
90.9**	94.0**	87.6**	0.93**	91.4**	93.1**	89.7**	0.96**	746**	250**	496**	692**	283**	409**	4
91.2	98.2	83.8	0.85	90.5**,y	97.6**,y	83.2**,y	0.85**,y	320	33	287	355**,y	46**,y	308**,y	5
89.6	89.2	89.9	1.01	92.0	91.3	92.7	1.02	76	40	36	63	35	28	6
88.2	88.1	88.3	1.00	83.4	82.4	84.4	1.02	16	8	8	27	15	13	7
87.5**	89.0**	85.9**	0.97**	90.6	90.8	90.4	0.99	46**	21**	26**	41	20	21	8
…	…	…	…	…	…	…	…	…	…	…	…	…	…	9
62.6**	64.5**	60.7**	0.94**	67.5	68.4	66.6	0.97	150**	71**	78**	145	71	74	10
73.1	78.6	67.3	0.86	89.6	92.4	86.8	0.94	1 045	422	622	388	145	243	11
75.9	76.0	75.8	1.00	71.9	71.6	72.2	1.01	89	45	44	109	56	53	12
96.9	96.5	97.4	1.01	90.9	90.8	90.9	1.00	11	6	4	37	19	18	13
97.1	96.6	97.7	1.01	94.5	94.6	94.3	1.00	2	1	1	3.5	1.7	1.7	14
56.8	58.7	54.8	0.93	54.4	54.7	54.2	0.99	1 420	695	725	1 602	815	786	15
…	…	…	…	…	…	…	…	…	…	…	…	…	…	16
93.0**	96.4**	89.5**	0.93**	97.9	100.0	95.7	0.96	185**	48**	137**	54	–	54	17
94.0	95.1	92.9	0.98	97.3	97.3	97.3	1.00	75	32	44	31	16	15	18
78.2	79.1	77.3	0.98	83.1	83.9	82.3	0.98	66	32	34	43	21	22	19
57.4	71.8	42.4	0.59	71.8	83.6	59.4	0.71	1 337	453	883	997	296	701	20
													Central and Eastern Europe	
99.1**	99.4**	98.7**	0.99**	94.9	95.8	94.0	0.98	2**	1**	2**	12	5	7	21
…	…	…	…	94.3	94.7**	93.9**	0.99**	…	…	…	25	12**	13**	22
…	…	…	…	…	…	…	…	…	…	…	…	…	…	23
95.6	96.5	94.8	0.98	90.4	90.9	89.9	0.99	17	7	10	32	15	16	24
88.4	89.0	87.6	0.98	89.3	89.8	88.8	0.99	25	12	13	21	10	11	25
90.2	89.9	90.6	1.01	86.5	86.5	86.6	1.00	61	33	29	75	38	36	26
97.0**	97.9**	96.1**	0.98**	94.9	95.3	94.5	0.99	3.7**	1.4**	2.3**	5	2	3	27
89.5	89.8	89.2	0.99	90.6	91.1	90.0	0.99	51	25	26	44	21	23	28
91.0	91.6	90.5	0.99	85.6	86.0	85.2	0.99	13	6	7	16	8	8	29
94.5	95.0	94.0	0.99	90.9	91.0	90.8	1.00	12	6	6	17	9	8	30
…	…	…	…	97.9	97.7	98.1	1.00	…	…	…	63	35	28	31
78.2**	…	…	…	79.0	79.4	78.6	0.99	68**	…	…	53	26	26	32
95.7	96.0	95.4	0.99	88.9	89.4	88.5	0.99	53	25	28	111	55	56	33
…	…	…	…	89.7**	88.9**	90.4**	1.02**	…	…	…	474**	260**	214**	34
…	…	…	…	95.8y	95.7y	95.9y	1.00y	…	…	…	16y	8y	8y	35
…	…	…	…	85.5	85.2	85.8	1.01	…	…	…	39	20	19	36
93.9	94.4	93.5	0.99	93.4	93.6	93.1	0.99	6	3	3	5.3	2.6	2.7	37
94.5	95.6	93.4	0.98	90.8	90.8	90.8	1.00	7	3	4	11	6	5	38
…	…	…	…	86.4	89.1	83.5	0.94	…	…	…	1 179	477	702	39
…	…	…	…	84.3	84.3**	84.4**	1.00**	…	…	…	331	170**	161**	40
													Central Asia	
…	…	…	…	94.4	95.3	93.5	0.98	…	…	…	7.6	3.3	4.4	41
80.1**	80.0**	80.2**	1.00**	79.9	81.1	78.6	0.97	151**	78**	73**	139	67	72	42
…	…	…	…	88.7	89.5	88.0	0.98	…	…	…	30	14	15	43
…	…	…	…	91.5	91.9	91.0	0.99	…	…	…	94	46	49	44
91.0*	92.0*	90.0*	0.98*	89.3	90.9	87.6	0.96	42*	19*	23*	48	20	27	45
89.4	87.8	91.1	1.04	79.0	78.0	80.0	1.03	27	16	11	50	27	23	46
94.3	97.2	91.3	0.94	…	…	…	…	38	10	29	…	…	…	47
…	…	…	…	…	…	…	…	…	…	…	…	…	…	48
…	…	…	…	…	…	…	…	…	…	…	…	…	…	49
													East Asia and the Pacific	
94.7	94.3	95.1	1.01	96.8	96.4	97.2	1.01	99	55	45	60	35	26	50
…	…	…	…	…	…	…	…	…	…	…	…	…	…	51
82.5**	86.5**	78.4**	0.91**	93.3	95.5	90.9	0.95	387**	151**	236**	151	51	100	52
…	…	…	…	94.6**,z	94.3**,z	95.0**,z	1.01**,z	…	…	…	5 819.9**,z	3 261.8**,z	2 558.1**,z	53
…	…	…	…	…	…	…	…	…	…	…	…	…	…	54

Table 5 (continued)

	Country or territory	Age group 2002/2003	School-age population (000) 2002	ENROLMENT IN PRIMARY EDUCATION 1998/1999 Total (000)	% F	2002/2003 Total (000)	% F	GROSS ENROLMENT RATIO (GER) IN PRIMARY EDUCATION (%) 1998/1999 Total	Male	Female	GPI (F/M)	2002/2003 Total	Male	Female	GPI (F/M)
55	DPR Korea	6-9	1 624	...	...	...	...	...	...	...	...	...	...	...	...
56	Fiji	6-11	106	116**	48**	115**,z	48**,z	110.5**	111.0**	110.0**	0.99**	108.8**,z	109.1**,z	108.6**,z	1.00**,z
57	Indonesia	7-12	26 011	...	...	29 051	49	...	...	...	...	111.7	112.7	110.6	0.98
58	Japan	6-11	7 240	7 692	49	7 269	49	101.4	101.4	101.3	1.00	100.4	100.3	100.5	1.00
59	Kiribati[2]	6-11	...	18	49	15	51	130.8	129.6	132.1	1.02	110.9	102.9	119.7	1.16
60	Lao PDR	6-10	752	828	45	875	46	116.7	126.0	107.0	0.85	116.4	124.4	108.1	0.87
61	Macao, China	6-11	40	47	47	42	47	99.1	101.4	96.6	0.95	104.0	107.9	99.9	0.93
62	Malaysia	6-11	3 232	2 877	49	3 009	49	97.4	97.4	97.4	1.00	93.1	93.1	93.1	1.00
63	Marshall Islands[2]	6-11	...	8	48	9z	47z	...	...	...	...	106.4z	110.0z	102.6z	0.93z
64	Micronesia (Fed. States of)	6-11	17	...	...	...	...	...	...	...	...	...	...	...	...
65	Myanmar	5-9	5 321	4 733	49	4 889	50	90.1	90.9	89.3	0.98	91.9	91.5	92.3	1.01
66	Nauru[2]	6-11	...	2**	51**	...	...	81.0**	79.6**	82.4**	1.04**	...	...	...	...
67	New Zealand	5-10	356	362	49	362	48**	102.6	102.7	102.4	1.00	101.7	102.0**	101.3**	0.99**
68	Niue[2]	5-10	...	0.3	43	0.2z	46z	102.9	109.6	95.3	0.87	117.6z	121.0z	113.8z	0.94z
69	Palau[2]	6-10	...	2	47	2**,y	48**,y	113.8	118.0	109.4	0.93	115.8**,y	119.8**,y	111.8**,y	0.93**,y
70	Papua New Guinea	7-12	885	581	45	628z	45z	74.8	77.4	71.8	0.93	73.4z	77.2z	69.3z	0.90z
71	Philippines	6-11	11 533	12 503	49	12 971	49	113.1	113.3	113.0	1.00	112.5	113.2	111.7	0.99
72	Republic of Korea	6-11	3 994	3 845	47	**4 185**	**47**	95.3	94.9	95.8	1.01	**105.5**	**105.8**	**105.2**	**0.99**
73	Samoa	5-10	29	27	49	30**	48**	99.4	98.9	99.9	1.01	105.4**	107.0**	103.7**	0.97**
74	Singapore	6-11	389	...	...	...	...	...	...	...	...	...	...	...	...
75	Solomon Islands	6-11	77	...	...	55	...	...	...	...	...	71.6	...	...	...
76	Thailand	6-11	6 342	6 120	48	**6 113**	**48**	94.1	96.5	91.8	0.95	**96.8**	**98.8**	**94.7**	**0.96**
77	Timor-Leste	6-11	123	...	...	184z	...	...	...	...	...	143.3z	...	...	...
78	Tokelau	5-10	...	...	...	...	...	...	...	...	...	...	...	...	...
79	Tonga	5-10	15	16	46	17	47	110.4	112.2	108.5	0.97	112.3	113.8	110.7	0.97
80	Tuvalu[2]	6-11	...	1**	46**	1z	50z	103.6**	105.8**	101.1**	0.96**	102.2z	96.2z	109.0z	1.13z
81	Vanuatu	6-11	33	34	48	37	48	110.4	111.0	109.7	0.99	112.7	112.7	112.7	1.00
82	Viet Nam	6-10	8 749	10 250	47	8 841	47	109.4	113.8	104.9	0.92	101.0	104.6	97.4	0.93
	Latin America and the Caribbean														
83	Anguilla[2]	5-11	...	2	50	1	50	...	...	...	...	99.9	99.3	100.6	1.01
84	Antigua and Barbuda	5-11	...	...	...	...	...	...	...	...	...	...	...	...	...
85	Argentina	6-11	4 116	4 821	49	4 914	49	119.7	119.6	119.8	1.00	119.4	119.5	119.3	1.00
86	Aruba[2]	6-11	...	9	49	10	48	112.2	113.5	110.8	0.98	115.1	118.6	111.6	0.94
87	Bahamas	5-10	37	...	...	34**	50**	...	...	...	...	92.2**	91.6**	92.8**	1.01**
88	Barbados	5-10	21	28	49	23	49	104.3	104.8	103.8	0.99	108.7	109.4	108.0	0.99
89	Belize	5-10	39	44	48	47	49	118.1	119.8	116.3	0.97	122.0	123.1	120.9	0.98
90	Bermuda[2]	5-10	...	...	...	5z	50z	...	...	...	...	102.2z	...	...	...
91	Bolivia	6-11	1 339	1 400	49	1 544	49	112.5	113.7	111.2	0.98	115.3	115.9	114.7	0.99
92	Brazil	7-10	13 188	...	...	19 380	48	...	...	...	...	147.0	150.8	143.0	0.95
93	British Virgin Islands[2]	5-11	...	3	49	3	48	111.6	113.5	109.8	0.97	106.6	109.7	103.3	0.94
94	Cayman Islands[5]	5-10	...	3	47	4z	49z	...	...	...	...	...	...	...	...
95	Chile	6-11	1 754	1 777	48	**1 714**	**48**	102.7	104.1	101.2	0.97	**98.0**	**99.2**	**96.7**	**0.97**
96	Colombia	6-10	4 708	5 136	48	5 193	49	113.7	115.3	112.0	0.97	110.3	110.8	109.8	0.99
97	Costa Rica	6-11	507	530	49	546	48	104.3	104.5	104.1	1.00	107.6	108.5	106.7	0.98
98	Cuba	6-11	946	1 074	48	925	48	105.3	107.2	103.2	0.96	97.8	99.7	95.8	0.96
99	Dominica[2]	5-11	...	12	48	10	48	98.8	101.2	96.3	0.95	88.2	91.4	85.0	0.93
100	Dominican Republic	6-11	1 106	1 315**	49**	1 375**	50**	116.7**	117.7**	115.6**	0.98**	124.3**	123.2**	125.5**	1.02**
101	Ecuador	6-11	1 700	1 899	49	1 987	49	113.4	113.5	113.3	1.00	116.9	117.1	116.8	1.00
102	El Salvador	7-12	878	926	48	988	48	111.6	113.3	109.9	0.97	112.5	115.5	109.4	0.95
103	Grenada[2]	5-11	...	...	...	17	50	...	...	...	...	119.6	120.6	118.6	0.98
104	Guatemala	7-12	1 956	1 685*	46*	2 076	47	94.0*	99.3*	88.4*	0.89*	106.1	109.7	102.4	0.93
105	Guyana	6-11	90	107	49	112	49**	116.9	117.9	115.9	0.98	124.8	126.2**	123.4**	0.98**
106	Haiti	6-11	1 243	...	...	...	...	...	...	...	...	...	...	...	...
107	Honduras	7-12	1 073	...	...	1 116**,z	50**,z	...	...	...	...	105.8**,z	104.8**,z	106.9**,z	1.02**,z
108	Jamaica	6-11	326	310	[illegible]	[illegible]	49	95.4**	95.6**	95.3**	1.00**	99.8	100.0	99.5	0.99
109	Mexico	6-11	13 459	14 698	49	14 857	49	110.9	111.7	110.1	[illegible]	[illegible]	[illegible]	[illegible]	0.99
110	Montserrat[2]	5-11	...	0.4	44	0.5**	45**	...	...	...	...	118.3**	...	...	...
111	Netherlands Antilles	6-11	22	25	48	23**	49**	115.5	118.2	112.7	0.95	104.3**	104.2**	104.4**	1.00**
112	Nicaragua	7-12	851	783	50	923	49	99.9	98.6	101.2	1.03	108.5	109.0	108.0	0.99
113	Panama	6-11	375	391**	48**	420	48	108.1**	109.9**	106.3**	0.97**	112.0	113.7	110.2	0.97
114	Paraguay	6-11	874	909**	49**	963	48	109.6**	110.4**	108.7**	0.98**	110.1	112.1	108.1	0.96

NET ENROLMENT RATIO (NER) IN PRIMARY EDUCATION (%)								OUT-OF-PRIMARY-SCHOOL CHILDREN (000)						
1998/1999				2002/2003				1998/1999			2002/2003			
Total	Male	Female	GPI (F/M)	Total	Male	Female	GPI (F/M)	Total	Male	Female	Total	Male	Female	
…	…	…	…	…	…	…	…	…	…	…	…	…	…	55
99.4**	99.3**	99.5**	1.00**	99.8**,z	99.6**,z	100.0**,z	1.00**,z	0.6**	0.4**	0.2**	0.2**,z	0.2**,z	–**,z	56
…	…	…	…	92.4	93.3	91.5	0.98	…	…	…	1 970	884	1 085	57
100.0	100.0	99.9	1.00	99.9	99.8	100.0	1.00	3	–	3	6	6	–	58
…	…	…	…	…	…	…	…	…	…	…	…	…	…	59
80.2	83.6	76.6	0.92	85.0	88.2	81.6	0.93	141	59	82	113	45	68	60
84.3	83.9	84.6	1.01	87.2	87.9	86.4	0.98	7.4	3.9	3.5	5.2	2.5	2.7	61
97.4	97.4	97.4	1.00	93.1	93.1	93.1	1.00	76	39	38	223	114	109	62
…	…	…	…	84.4z	85.0z	83.8z	0.99z	…	…	…	1.3z	0.6z	0.7z	63
…	…	…	…	…	…	…	…	…	…	…	…	…	…	64
82.5**	83.1**	81.8**	0.99**	84.2	83.8	84.5	1.01	921**	448**	472**	843	436	407	65
81.0**	79.6**	82.4**	1.04**	…	…	…	…	0.4**	0.2**	0.2**	…	…	…	66
…	…	…	…	99.7**	100.0**	99.4**	0.99**	…	…	…	1**	–**	1**	67
…	…	…	…	…	…	…	…	…	…	…	…	…	…	68
96.8**	99.4**	93.9**	0.94**	96.1**,y	100.0**,y	92.1**,y	0.92**,y	0.05**	0.00**	0.05**	0.1**,y	–**,y	0.1**,y	69
74.8*	77.4*	71.8*	0.93*	73.0**,z	76.8**,z	68.9**,z	0.90**,z	196*	93*	103*	231**,z	104**,z	127**,z	70
…	…	…	…	93.7	92.9	94.6	1.02	…	…	…	722	416	306	71
94.3	93.9	94.8	1.01	**99.8**	**100.0**	**99.5**	**1.00**	229	129	99	**9**	**–**	**9**	72
94.2	93.2	95.2	1.02	97.5**	98.6**	96.4**	0.98**	2	1	1	0.7**	0.2**	0.5**	73
…	…	…	…	…	…	…	…	…	…	…	…	…	…	74
…	…	…	…	…	…	…	…	…	…	…	…	…	…	75
79.6**	81.6**	77.6**	0.95**	**85.4**	**86.6**	**84.1**	**0.97**	1 327**	606**	721**	**922**	**427**	**495**	76
…	…	…	…	…	…	…	…	…	…	…	…	…	…	77
…	…	…	…	…	…	…	…	…	…	…	…	…	…	78
91.7	91.9	91.6	1.00	99.9z	100.0z	99.7z	1.00z	1.2	0.6	0.6	0.02z	–z	0.02z	79
…	…	…	…	…	…	…	…	…	…	…	…	…	…	80
90.5**	90.3**	90.7**	1.00**	94.1**	93.0**	95.2**	1.02**	3**	2**	1**	2**	1**	1**	81
96.1	…	…	…	94.0**,z	…	…	…	361	…	…	544**,z	…	…	82
Latin America and the Caribbean														
…	…	…	…	95.2	94.4	96.1	1.02	…	…	…	0.1	0.04	0.03	83
…	…	…	…	…	…	…	…	…	…	…	…	…	…	84
…	…	…	…	…	…	…	…	…	…	…	…	…	…	85
97.8	97.4	98.1	1.01	99.0	99.7	98.2	0.99	0.2	0.1	0.1	0.1	0.0	0.1	86
…	…	…	…	86.4**	85.1**	87.6**	1.03**	…	…	…	5**	3**	2**	87
99.7**	100.0**	99.3**	0.99**	100.0	99.9	100.0	1.00	0.1**	–**	0.1**	0.01	0.01	–	88
94.3**	94.5**	94.1**	1.00**	99.2	98.4	100.0	1.02	2**	1**	1**	0.3	0.3	–	89
…	…	…	…	100.0**,z	…	…	…	…	…	…	–**,z	…	…	90
96.0	96.3	95.7	0.99	95.1	94.9	95.3	1.00	50	23	27	66	35	31	91
…	…	…	…	97.3	…	…	…	…	…	…	359	…	…	92
95.6**	94.5**	96.7**	1.02**	93.7	94.5	92.9	0.98	0.1**	0.07**	0.04**	0.2	0.1	0.1	93
…	…	…	…	…	…	…	…	…	…	…	…	…	…	94
87.9	88.4	87.4	0.99	**84.8**	**85.4**	**84.3**	**0.99**	210	102	107	**265**	**130**	**135**	95
86.6	…	…	…	87.4	87.9**	86.9**	0.99**	603	…	…	593	291**	302**	96
88.5**	87.6**	89.6**	1.02**	90.4	89.7	91.2	1.02	58**	32**	26**	49	27	22	97
98.9	100.0	97.8	0.98	93.5	94.1	92.9	0.99	11	–	11	62	29	33	98
82.9**	85.9**	79.9**	0.93**	81.3	83.4	79.2	0.95	2**	1**	1**	2	1	1	99
88.3**	87.5**	89.2**	1.02**	96.4	98.7**	94.1**	0.95**	131**	72**	60**	40	8**	32**	100
97.0	96.4	97.5	1.01	99.5	99.1	100.0	1.01	51	30	20	8	8	–	101
81.0	74.7	87.5	1.17	90.4	90.4	90.4	1.00	158	107	51	84	43	41	102
…	…	…	…	84.2**,y	88.7**,y	79.7**,y	0.90**,y	…	…	…	3**,y	1**,y	2**,y	103
76.5**	79.0**	73.8**	0.93**	87.3	88.8	85.7	0.97	422**	192**	230**	249	112	137	104
95.7**	96.2**	95.2**	0.99**	99.2**	100.0**	98.4**	0.98**	4**	2**	2**	1**	–**	1**	105
…	…	…	…	…	…	…	…	…	…	…	…	…	…	106
…	…	…	…	87.4**,z	86.7**,z	88.3**,z	1.02**,z	…	…	…	132**,z	72**,z	61**,z	107
90.3**	90.2**	90.4**	1.00**	94.6	94.4	94.8	1.00	32**	16**	16**	18	9	8	108
99.5	99.1	100.0	1.01	99.4	98.8	100.0	1.01	61	61	–	83	83	–	109
…	…	…	…	…	…	…	…	…	…	…	…	…	…	110
96.1	95.7	96.5	1.01	88.4**	86.1**	90.7**	1.05**	0.9	0.5	0.4	3**	2**	1**	111
77.9**	76.9**	79.0**	1.03**	85.5	85.7	85.3	1.00	173**	92**	81**	124	62	62	112
96.5**	96.7**	96.2**	0.99**	99.6	100.0	99.2	0.99	13**	6**	7**	1	–	1	113
91.7**	91.3**	92.1**	1.01**	89.3	89.1	89.5	1.00	69**	37**	32**	93	48	45	114

Table 5 (continued)

	Country or territory	Age group	School-age population (000)	ENROLMENT IN PRIMARY EDUCATION				GROSS ENROLMENT RATIO (GER) IN PRIMARY EDUCATION (%)							
				1998/1999		2002/2003		1998/1999				2002/2003			
		2002/ 2003	2002	Total (000)	% F	Total (000)	% F	Total	Male	Female	GPI (F/M)	Total	Male	Female	GPI (F/M)
115	Peru	6-11	3 616	4 299	49	4 283	49	122.6	123.4	121.7	0.99	118.4	118.7	118.2	1.00
116	Saint Kitts and Nevis[2]	5-11	...	...	...	6	49	...	...	...	...	111.8	108.9	114.9	1.06
117	Saint Lucia	5-11	22	26	49	25	48	114.8	115.9	113.6	0.98	111.8	112.0	111.5	1.00
118	Saint Vincent/Grenad.	5-11	17	...	...	19	49	...	...	...	...	107.3	108.8	105.9	0.97
119	Suriname	6-11	51	...	...	65**	49**	...	...	...	...	125.8**	126.7**	124.8**	0.98**
120	Trinidad and Tobago	5-11	141	172	49	141	49	101.7	102.3	101.1	0.99	100.1	101.4	98.7	0.97
121	Turks and Caicos Islands[2]	6-11	...	2	49	2	49	...	...	...	...	85.9	87.9	83.8	0.95
122	Uruguay	6-11	334	365	49	365	48	112.8	113.5	112.2	0.99	109.3	110.4	108.1	0.98
123	Venezuela	6-11	3 322	3 261	49	3 450	48	100.3	101.2	99.4	0.98	103.9	104.9	102.8	0.98
	North America and Western Europe														
124	Andorra[5]	6-11	...	...	...	4	47	...	...	...	...	...	...	...	...
125	Austria	6-9	368	389	48	380	49	102.2	102.6	101.8	0.99	103.2	103.4	103.1	1.00
126	Belgium	6-11	723	763	49	762	49	103.8	104.3	103.2	0.99	105.3	105.8	104.8	0.99
127	Canada	6-11	2 420	2 404	49	2 482**,z	49**,z	97.7	97.7	97.7	1.00	101.3**,z	101.1**,z	101.6**,z	1.00**,z
128	Cyprus[2]	6-11	...	64	48	63	49	97.4	97.6	97.2	1.00	97.6	97.4	97.8	1.00
129	Denmark	7-12	404	372	49	420	49	101.9	102.1	101.8	1.00	103.9	103.9	103.9	1.00
130	Finland	7-12	385	383	49	393	49	99.2	99.4	99.0	1.00	102.0	102.3	101.6	0.99
131	France	6-10	3 635	3 944	49	3 792	49	105.6	106.2	104.9	0.99	104.3	104.8	103.8	0.99
132	Germany	6-9	3 323	3 767	49	3 304	49	105.7	106.0	105.3	0.99	99.4	99.6	99.2	1.00
133	Greece	6-11	647	646	48	652	48	95.5	95.7	95.3	1.00	100.8	100.9	100.7	1.00
134	Iceland	6-12	32	30	48	31	48	98.5	99.4	97.6	0.98	99.7	100.1	99.3	0.99
135	Ireland	4-11	424	457	49	448	48	104.1	104.2	103.9	1.00	105.6	105.5	105.7	1.00
136	Israel	6-11	686	722	49	770	49	112.9	113.4	112.3	0.99	112.2	112.3	112.1	1.00
137	Italy	6-10	2 748	2 876	48	2 779	48	102.5	103.1	102.0	0.99	101.1	101.5	100.7	0.99
138	Luxembourg	6-11	34	31	49	34	49	99.6	99.0	100.3	1.01	99.2	99.4	98.9	0.99
139	Malta	5-10	30	35	49	32	48	106.3	106.0	106.7	1.01	104.4	105.1	103.7	0.99
140	Monaco[5]	6-10	...	2	50	2y	49y	...	...	...	...	...	...	...	...
141	Netherlands	6-11	1 196	1 268	48	1 291	48	108.3	109.5	107.0	0.98	107.9	109.2	106.6	0.98
142	Norway	6-12	427	412	49	433	49	101.1	101.1	101.0	1.00	101.3	101.3	101.4	1.00
143	Portugal	6-11	666	815	48	768	48	123.1	125.7	120.3	0.96	115.3	118.0	112.4	0.95
144	San Marino	6-10	...	...	...	...	...	...	...	...	...	...	...	...	...
145	Spain	6-11	2 313	2 580	48	2 488	48	107.4	108.4	106.4	0.98	107.6	108.6	106.6	0.98
146	Sweden	7-12	701	763	49	775	49	109.7	108.1	111.3	1.03	110.5	109.1	112.0	1.03
147	Switzerland	7-12	497	530	49	536	49	106.3	106.9	105.7	0.99	107.7	108.1	107.2	0.99
148	United Kingdom	5-10	4 484	4 661	49	4 488	49	101.8	101.4	102.3	1.01	100.1	100.1	100.0	1.00
149	United States	6-11	25 329	24 938	49	24 849	49	100.6	99.3	102.0	1.03	98.1	97.9	98.3	1.00
	South and West Asia														
150	Afghanistan	7-12	3 540	1 046	7**	3 267	33	32.7	59.0**	4.5**	0.08**	92.3	119.9	62.8	0.52
151	Bangladesh	6-10	18 320	18 361	48	17 562	50	106.0	107.7	104.2	0.97	95.9	94.1	97.7	1.04
152	Bhutan[6]	6-12	...	78	45	91**	47**	...	...	...	...	...	...	...	...
153	India	6-10	116 787	110 986	43	125 569	47	97.9	106.9	88.2	0.83	107.5	110.6	104.2	0.94
154	Iran, Islamic Republic of	6-10	7 648	8 667	47	7 029	48	95.6	98.1	93.0	0.95	91.9	93.3	90.4	0.97
155	Maldives	6-12	58	74	49	68	48	134.1	133.5	134.6	1.01	118.0	119.0	117.0	0.98
156	Nepal	5-9	3 294	3 349**	42**	3 929	45	112.3**	125.7**	97.9**	0.78**	119.3	126.1	112.0	0.89
157	Pakistan	5-9	20 508	...	...	14 045	40	...	...	...	...	68.5	79.6	56.6	0.71
158	Sri Lanka	5-9	1 569	1 802	48	1 702**	49**	109.2	110.7	107.6	0.97	110.5**	110.8**	110.1**	0.99**
	Sub-Saharan Africa														
159	Angola	6-9	1 564	1 342	46	...	...	97.1	106.1	88.1	0.83	...	...	...	...
160	Benin	6-11	1 128	872	39	1 233	42	82.7	100.4	65.0	0.65	109.3	126.9	91.6	0.72
161	Botswana	6-12	321	321	50	331**	50**	102.8	102.8	102.9	1.00	103.3**	103.2**	103.4**	1.00**
162	Burkina Faso	7-12	2 192	816	40	1 012	42	41.8	49.6	34.0	0.68	46.2	53.1	39.2	0.74
163	Burundi	7-12	1 158	702**	44**	895	45	62.7**	69.7**	55.8**	0.80**	77.3	85.7	69.0	0.81
164	Cameroon	6-11	2 601	2 134	45	2 799	40	87.6	95.9	79.0	0.82	107.6	116.1	99.0	0.85
165	Cape Verde	6-11	73	92	49	88	49	125.6	128.5	122.7	0.96	120.6	123.6	117.5	0.95
166	Central African Republic	6-11	633	...	...	415	41	...	...	...	...	65.5	77.9	53.3	0.68
167	Chad	6-11	1 429	840	37	1 119**	39**	67.0	84.8	49.3	0.58	78.3**	95.3**	61.4**	0.64**
168	Comoros	6-11	119	83	45	107**	44**	75.2	81.2	69.0	0.85	89.6**	98.3**	80.7**	0.82**
169	Congo	6-11	634	276	49	510	48	49.6	50.8	48.4	0.95	80.4	83.3	77.5	0.93
170	Côte d'Ivoire	6-11	2 637	1 911	43	2 046*	44*	73.1	83.7	62.4	0.75	77.6*	86.3*	68.8*	0.80*

NET ENROLMENT RATIO (NER) IN PRIMARY EDUCATION (%)								OUT-OF-PRIMARY-SCHOOL CHILDREN (000)						
1998/1999				2002/2003				1998/1999			2002/2003			
Total	Male	Female	GPI (F/M)	Total	Male	Female	GPI (F/M)	Total	Male	Female	Total	Male	Female	
99.8	100.0	99.6	1.00	99.7	99.7	99.8	1.00	7	–	7	9	5	4	115
…	…	…	…	100.0	…	…	…	…	…	…	–	…	…	116
…	…	…	…	99.4	98.9	100.0	1.01	0.04**	–**	0.04**	0.1	0.1	–	117
…	…	…	…	90.0	90.3	89.7	0.99	…	…	…	2	1	1	118
…	…	…	…	97.0**	95.8**	98.2**	1.02**	…	…	…	1.5**	1**	0.5**	119
92.9	92.9	92.9	1.00	90.6	90.9	90.3	0.99	12	6	6	13	7	7	120
…	…	…	…	73.5	74.3	72.7	0.98	…	…	…	0.6	0.3	0.3	121
92.4	92.1	92.7	1.01	90.4	90.2	90.5	1.00	25	13	12	32	17	15	122
85.9	85.5	86.4	1.01	90.8	90.5	91.1	1.01	457	241	217	307	162	145	123
North America and Western Europe														
…	…	…	…	…	…	…	…	…	…	…	…	…	…	124
89.9	89.2	90.5	1.01	89.9	89.0	90.8	1.02	39	21	18	37	21	16	125
99.4	99.5	99.4	1.00	100.0	100.0	99.9	1.00	4	2	2	0.3	–	0.3	126
96.9	96.9	96.9	1.00	99.6**,y	99.5**,y	99.7**,y	1.00**,y	75	39	37	10**,y	6**,y	4**,y	127
95.5	95.5	95.5	1.00	96.1	96.0	96.3	1.00	3	2	1	2	1	1	128
99.4	99.4	99.4	1.00	100.0	100.0	100.0	1.00	2	1	1	0.03	0.03	–	129
98.7	98.9	98.5	1.00	100.0	100.0	100.0	1.00	5	2	3	0.03	–	0.03	130
100.0	100.0	99.9	1.00	99.3	99.3	99.4	1.00	1	–	1	24	14	11	131
…	…	…	…	…	…	…	…	…	…	…	…	…	…	132
93.4	93.5	93.3	1.00	98.5	98.5	98.5	1.00	45	23	22	10	5	5	133
98.3	99.2	97.5	0.98	99.6	100.0	99.3	0.99	0.5	0.1	0.4	0.1	–	0.1	134
93.8	93.3	94.4	1.01	96.0	95.2	96.8	1.02	27	15	12	17	10	7	135
99.9	100.0	99.8	1.00	99.3	99.1	99.4	1.00	0.7	–	0.7	5	3	2	136
99.7	100.0	99.3	0.99	99.5	99.7	99.2	0.99	10	–	10	14	4	11	137
96.0	95.1	97.0	1.02	90.3	90.1	90.6	1.01	1.3	0.8	0.5	3.3	1.7	1.6	138
99.1	98.3	100.0	1.02	96.0	96.2	95.8	0.99	0.3	0.3	–	1.2	0.6	0.6	139
…	…	…	…	…	…	…	…	…	…	…	…	…	…	140
99.5	100.0	98.9	0.99	99.2	99.8	98.6	0.99	6	–	6	9.7	1.4	8.3	141
100.0	100.0	99.9	1.00	100.0	99.9	100.0	1.00	0.2	–	0.2	0.1	0.1	–	142
…	…	…	…	99.5	100.0	99.1	0.99	…	…	…	3	–	3	143
…	…	…	…	…	…	…	…	…	…	…	…	…	…	144
99.6	100.0	99.2	0.99	99.7	100.0	99.3	0.99	9	–	9	8	–	8	145
99.8	100.0	99.5	1.00	99.7	100.0	99.4	0.99	2	–	2	2	–	2	146
97.9	98.4	97.4	0.99	98.9	99.1	98.6	0.99	10	4	6	5.6	2.2	3.4	147
99.6	99.2	100.0	1.01	100.0	100.0	99.9	1.00	20	20	–	2	–	2	148
93.8	93.8	93.8	1.00	92.4	91.9	93.0	1.01	1 527	782	745	1 922	1 057	865	149
South and West Asia														
…	…	…	…	…	…	…	…	…	…	…	…	…	…	150
84.8**	85.6**	83.9**	0.98**	84.0	82.4	85.7	1.04	2 632**	1 277**	1 355**	2 925	1 652	1 273	151
…	…	…	…	…	…	…	…	…	…	…	…	…	…	152
…	…	…	…	87.5[g]	90.0[g]	84.8[g]	0.94[g]	…	…	…	14 586	6 040	8 546	153
81.4**	82.6**	80.2**	0.97**	86.3	87.5	85.0	0.97	1 682**	807**	875**	1 048	489	559	154
99.7**	99.4**	100.0**	1.01**	92.4	92.2	92.6	1.00	0.2**	0.2**	–**	4	2	2	155
68.5*	76.1*	60.3*	0.79*	70.5**,y	74.6**,y	66.0**,y	0.88**,y	940*	370*	570*	918**,y	408**,y	510**,y	156
…	…	…	…	59.1**,y	67.5**,y	50.0**,y	0.74**,y	…	…	…	8 145**,y	3 332**,y	4 813**,y	157
…	…	…	…	…	…	…	…	…	…	…	…	…	…	158
Sub-Saharan Africa														
61.3**	65.8**	56.8**	0.86**	…	…	…	…	536**	235**	300**	…	…	…	159
55.4*	66.7*	44.0*	0.66*	…	…	…	…	470*	175*	295*	…	…	…	160
78.7	77.0	80.4	1.04	80.9**	79.2**	82.7**	1.04**	67	36	30	61**	34**	28**	161
33.5	39.8	27.1	0.68	36.2	41.7	30.6	0.73	1 299	590	709	1 398	643	756	162
…	…	…	…	57.4	62.4	52.3	0.84	…	…	…	494	218	276	163
…	…	…	…	…	…	…	…	…	…	…	…	…	…	164
99.1**	100.0**	98.3**	0.98**	99.2	100.0	98.4	0.98	0.6**	–**	0.6**	0.6	–	0.6	165
…	…	…	…	…	…	…	…	…	…	…	…	…	…	166
54.7	67.6	41.8	0.62	62.8**	74.9**	50.6**	0.68**	568	203	365	532**	180**	352**	167
49.2	53.2	45.1	0.85	…	…	…	…	56	26	30	…	…	…	168
…	…	…	…	54.0	55.1	52.9	0.96	…	…	…	292	142	149	169
55.5	63.2	47.8	0.76	60.6*	67.1*	54.0*	0.81*	1 163	483	681	1 040*	435*	605*	170

Table 5 (continued)

	Country or territory	Age group 2002/2003	School-age population (000) 2002	ENROLMENT IN PRIMARY EDUCATION 1998/1999 Total (000)	% F	2002/2003 Total (000)	% F	GROSS ENROLMENT RATIO (GER) IN PRIMARY EDUCATION (%) 1998/1999 Total	Male	Female	GPI (F/M)	2002/2003 Total	Male	Female	GPI (F/M)
171	D. R. Congo	6-11	8 696	4 022	47	...	...	49.6	52.2	47.1	0.90	...	...	...	...
172	Equatorial Guinea	7-11	64	75	48**	78[z]	48[z]	131.3	137.5**	125.0**	0.91**	126.2[z]	132.2[z]	120.2[z]	0.91[z]
173	Eritrea	7-11	567	262	45	359	44	53.2	58.0	48.4	0.83	63.4	69.9	56.8	0.81
174	Ethiopia	7-12	11 557	5 168	38	**8 270**	**43**	49.9	62.1	37.6	0.60	**70.0**	**78.9**	**61.0**	**0.77**
175	Gabon	6-11	212	265	50	280	49	134.1	134.1	134.1	1.00	132.2	132.6	131.8	0.99
176	Gambia	7-12	209	150	46	178	49**	79.9	86.2	73.6	0.85	85.2	86.0**	84.4**	0.98**
177	Ghana	6-11	3 203	2 377	47	**2 679**	**47**	76.8	81.0	72.5	0.90	**83.0**	**86.7**	**79.2**	**0.91**
178	Guinea	7-12	1 317	727	38	1 073	43	58.4	71.3	45.1	0.63	81.5	92.1	70.6	0.77
179	Guinea-Bissau	7-12	238	...	...	155[**,y]	40[**,y]	...	...	...	...	69.7[**,y]	83.6[**,y]	55.9[**,y]	0.67[**,y]
180	Kenya	6-12	6 050	5 481	49	5 590	48	90.2	90.9	89.5	0.98	92.4	95.1	89.7	0.94
181	Lesotho	6-12	331	370	52	419	50	109.2	104.9	113.6	1.08	126.4	125.5	127.3	1.01
182	Liberia	6-11	549	396	42	...	...	89.6	102.9	76.2	0.74	...	...	...	...
183	Madagascar	6-10	2 389	2 012	49	2 856	49	95.6	97.3	93.9	0.97	119.6	122.0	117.1	0.96
184	Malawi	6-11	2 032	2 525	49**	2 847	49	146.2	150.1**	142.3**	0.95**	140.1	142.7	137.3	0.96
185	Mali	7-12	2 217	959	41	1 295	43	48.8	56.9	40.5	0.71	58.4	66.1	50.5	0.76
186	Mauritius	5-10	128	131	49	132	49	107.6	107.5	107.6	1.00	103.8	103.4	104.2	1.01
187	Mozambique	6-10	2 617	1 968**	42**	2 705	45	81.2**	93.2**	69.1**	0.74**	103.4	113.9	92.7	0.81
188	Namibia	6-12	385	387	50	405	50	113.9	113.5	114.3	1.01	105.0	104.5	105.5	1.01
189	Niger	7-12	1 971	530	39	858	40	30.9	37.0	24.7	0.67	43.5	51.2	35.5	0.69
190	Nigeria	6-11	20 572	16 046**	42**	24 563	44	86.1**	97.5**	74.3**	0.76**	119.4	131.6	106.8	0.81
191	Rwanda	7-12	1 341	1 289	50	1 637	50	118.6	120.2	117.1	0.97	122.0	121.9	122.2	1.00
192	Sao Tome and Principe	7-12	23	24	49	29[**,z]	48[**,z]	107.1	109.3	104.9	0.96	126.4[**,z]	130.4[**,z]	122.4[**,z]	0.94[**,z]
193	Senegal	7-12	1 611	1 034	46**	1 287	48	68.6	73.6**	63.5**	0.86**	79.9	83.1	76.6	0.92
194	Seychelles[2]	6-11	...	10	49	9	49	112.8	113.8	111.8	0.98	109.6	110.2	108.9	0.99
195	Sierra Leone	6-11	761	...	...	554[y]	42[y]	...	...	...	...	78.9[y]	92.9[y]	65.2[y]	0.70[y]
196	Somalia	...	...	...	...	...	...	...	...	...	...	...	...	...	...
197	South Africa	7-13	7 067	7 998*	49*	7 466	49	114.4*	116.1*	112.8*	0.97*	105.6	107.5	103.7	0.96
198	Swaziland	6-12	213	212	49	209	48	104.3	107.1	101.4	0.95	98.2	102.0	94.4	0.93
199	Togo	6-11	804	954	43	975	45	132.3	150.2	114.3	0.76	121.2	132.3	110.0	0.83
200	Uganda	6-12	5 226	6 591	47	7 354	49	143.3	150.4	136.1	0.90	140.7	142.0	139.5	0.98
201	U. R. Tanzania	7-13	7 107	4 043	50	**6 563**	**49**	61.8	61.9	61.6	0.99	**90.8**	**92.8**	**88.8**	**0.96**
202	Zambia	7-13	2 107	1 557	48	1 732	48	81.2	84.3	78.1	0.93	82.2	85.1	79.3	0.93
203	Zimbabwe	6-12	2 555	...	...	**2 362**	**49**	...	...	...	...	**92.9**	**93.6**	**92.1**	**0.98**

			Sum	Sum	% F	Sum	% F	Weighted average							
I	World	...	648 064	655 343	47	671 359	47	100.5	104.5	96.3	0.92	103.6	106.6	100.4	0.94
II	Countries in transition	...	13 437	15 872	49	14 187	49	100.5	101.1	99.9	0.99	105.6	106.0	105.1	0.99
III	Developed countries	...	67 488	70 399	49	67 880	49	102.1	101.8	102.3	1.00	100.6	100.7	100.4	1.00
IV	Developing countries	...	567 139	569 072	46	589 291	47	100.3	104.9	95.5	0.91	103.9	107.3	100.3	0.93
V	Arab States	...	39 593	34 725	46	37 137	46	89.7	95.7	83.5	0.87	93.8	98.6	88.8	0.90
VI	Central and Eastern Europe	...	23 255	25 484	48	23 133	48	97.3	99.3	95.3	0.96	99.5	100.8	98.1	0.97
VII	Central Asia	...	6 296	6 891	49	6 396	49	98.9	99.5	98.4	0.99	101.6	102.5	100.7	0.98
VIII	East Asia and the Pacific	...	186 616	217 317	48	207 054	48	111.6	112.1	111.0	0.99	110.9	111.7	110.2	0.99
IX	Latin America and the Caribbean	...	58 162	78 656	49	69 498	48	121.4	122.9	119.9	0.98	119.5	120.8	118.0	0.98
X	North America and Western Europe	...	51 542	52 856	49	51 945	49	102.5	102.1	103.0	1.01	100.8	100.9	100.7	1.00
XI	South and West Asia	...	172 133	158 096	44	175 527	46	94.5	102.9	85.6	0.83	102.0	106.2	97.5	0.92
XII	Sub-Saharan Africa	...	110 467	81 319	45	100 670	46	80.0	86.8	73.1	0.84	91.1	97.9	84.3	0.86

1. In countries where two or more education structures exist, indicators were calculated on the basis of the most common or widespread structure. In the Russian Federation this is three grades of primary education starting at age 7. However, a four-grade structure also exists, in which about one-third of primary pupils are enrolled. Gross enrolment ratios may be overestimated.

2. National population data were used to calculate enrolment ratios.

3. Children enter primary school at age 6 or 7. Since 7 is the most common entrance age, enrolment ratios were calculated using the 7-11 age group for both enrolment and population.

NET ENROLMENT RATIO (NER) IN PRIMARY EDUCATION (%)								OUT-OF-PRIMARY-SCHOOL CHILDREN (000)						
1998/1999				2002/2003				1998/1999			2002/2003			
Total	Male	Female	GPI (F/M)	Total	Male	Female	GPI (F/M)	Total	Male	Female	Total	Male	Female	
...	...	...	...	...	...	...	...	...	...	...	...	...	...	171
88.0	96.4**	79.7**	0.83**	84.6[z]	91.4[z]	77.8[z]	0.85[z]	7	1**	6**	10[z]	3[z]	7[z]	172
33.9	36.2	31.6	0.87	45.2	48.7	41.7	0.86	325	158	167	310	147	164	173
35.8	42.4	29.2	0.69	**51.1**	**55.2**	**46.9**	**0.85**	6 651	2 987	3 664	**5 780**	**2 653**	**3 126**	174
...	...	...	...	78.3**,y	78.9**,y	77.8**,y	0.99**,y	...	...	...	45**,y	22**,y	23**,y	175
66.7	71.0	62.3	0.88	78.8**	79.3**	78.2**	0.99**	63	27	35	44**	22**	23**	176
57.9**	59.8**	55.9**	0.93**	**59.0**	...	...	...	1 304**	626**	679**	**1 323**	...	...	177
45.3	53.6	36.7	0.69	65.5	72.6	58.1	0.80	681	293	388	455	183	272	178
...	...	...	...	...	...	...	...	...	...	...	...	...	...	179
65.8**	65.3**	66.3**	1.01**	66.5	66.4	66.5	1.00	2 077**	1 057**	1 020**	2 030	1 019	1 010	180
64.5	60.3	68.7	1.14	85.8	82.9	88.6	1.07	120	67	53	47	28	19	181
43.9	49.7	38.1	0.77	...	...	...	...	248	111	136	...	...	...	182
64.5	64.3	64.8	1.01	78.6	78.4	78.7	1.00	746	375	371	511	258	254	183
...	...	...	...	...	...	...	...	...	...	...	...	...	...	184
38.3**	44.5**	32.0**	0.72**	44.5	50.2	38.7	0.77	1 212**	553**	660**	1 231	559	671	185
93.2	93.1	93.2	1.00	96.6	95.6	97.6	1.02	8	4	4	4	3	2	186
47.3**	51.6**	43.0**	0.83**	55.3	57.7	52.7	0.91	1 277**	589**	687**	1 171	555	616	187
77.9	75.4	80.4	1.07	78.3	75.7	80.9	1.07	75	42	33	84	47	37	188
26.1	31.3	20.8	0.66	38.2	45.1	31.1	0.69	1 264	598	667	1 218	551	668	189
...	...	...	...	67.2**	73.9**	60.2**	0.82**	...	...	...	6 754**	2 731**	4 023**	190
...	...	...	...	86.7	85.1	88.3	1.04	...	...	...	178	99	79	191
85.5	86.5	84.4	0.98	97.1**,z	100.0**,z	94.2**,z	0.94**,z	3.2	1.5	1.2	0.7**,z	–**,z	0.7**,z	192
57.9	61.5**	54.1**	0.88**	68.5	71.2	65.8	0.92	635	293**	343**	507	234	273	193
99.1	100.0	98.3	0.98	99.6	100.0	99.1	0.99	0.1	–	0.1	0.04	–	0.04	194
...	...	...	...	...	...	...	...	...	...	...	...	...	...	195
...	...	...	...	...	...	...	...	...	...	...	...	...	...	196
91.3*	90.8*	91.8*	1.01*	89.0	88.7	89.3	1.01	608*	322*	286*	778	402	376	197
67.2	66.5	67.9	1.02	75.3	75.1	75.4	1.00	67	34	33	53	26	26	198
89.8	100.0	79.5	0.80	91.2	98.9	83.3	0.84	74	–	74	71	4	67	199
...	...	...	...	...	...	...	...	...	...	...	...	...	...	200
45.8	45.1	46.6	1.03	**77.4****	**78.3****	**76.4****	**0.98****	3 545	1 803	1 742	**1 635****	**786****	**849****	201
68.5	69.6	67.4	0.97	68.4	69.1	67.7	0.98	604	292	312	666	326	339	202
...	...	...	...	**79.2**	**78.5**	**79.8**	**1.02**	...	...	...	**530**	**274**	**256**	203

Weighted average								Sum						
83.6	86.5	80.6	0.93	84.6	86.5	82.6	0.96	106 724	45 316	61 408	99 876	45 030	54 846	I
85.4	85.9	84.9	0.99	89.1	89.3	88.9	1.00	2 304	1 135	1 170	1 468	736	732	II
96.6	96.6	96.6	1.00	95.6	95.4	95.9	1.01	2 367	1 210	1 157	2 949	1 593	1 356	III
82.0	85.2	78.6	0.92	83.2	85.3	80.9	0.95	102 052	42 971	59 081	95 459	42 701	52 758	IV
78.1	82.3	73.7	0.90	82.6	85.7	79.2	0.92	8 491	3 501	4 991	6 906	2 882	4 025	V
87.2	88.7	85.7	0.97	89.0	89.9	88.0	0.98	3 340	1 510	1 830	2 569	1 203	1 366	VI
88.9	89.4	88.3	0.99	89.9	90.8	89.0	0.98	775	375	400	635	294	341	VII
95.7	95.9	95.6	1.00	92.1	92.4	91.8	0.99	8 309	4 158	4 151	14 782	7 410	7 372	VIII
94.4	95.1	93.7	0.99	96.4	97.1	95.7	0.99	3 620	1 623	1 997	2 084	858	1 226	IX
96.3	96.3	96.3	1.00	95.3	95.0	95.6	1.01	1 885	967	918	2 421	1 320	1 101	X
78.6	85.5	71.3	0.83	82.5	85.7	79.1	0.92	35 722	12 534	23 189	30 109	12 698	17 411	XI
56.2	59.6	52.7	0.88	63.5	66.9	59.9	0.90	44 581	20 648	23 933	40 370	18 367	22 003	XII

4. Pending agreement on population data, the 2001 NER published herein in connection with China's primary education is for reference only.

5. Enrolment ratios were not calculated due to lack of United Nations population data by age.

6. Enrolment ratios were not calculated due to inconsistencies between enrolment and the United Nations population data.

(g) Projected at the national level (593 districts) on the basis of data by age collected for ISCED level 1 in a sample of 193 districts under the District Information System on Education.

Data in bold are for 2003/2004.

(z) Data are for 2001/2002.

(y) Data are for 2000/2001.

Table 6
Internal efficiency: repetition in primary education

	Country or territory	Duration[1] of primary education 2002/2003	REPETITION RATES BY GRADE IN PRIMARY EDUCATION (%), 2001/2002											
			Grade 1			Grade 2			Grade 3			Grade 4		
			Total	Male	Female	Total	Male	Female	Total	Male	Female	Total	Male	Female
	Arab States													
1	Algeria	6	10.9	12.3	9.3	9.8	11.6	7.7	9.5	11.9	6.7	10.9	13.6	7.9
2	Bahrain	6	0.4**	0.4**	0.4**	3.4**	3.2**	3.5**	3.1**	3.4**	2.8**	4.2**	4.7**	3.7**
3	Djibouti	6	**2.5****	**2.7****	**2.4****	**16.8****	**16.2****	**17.6****	...	...	...	...	...	...
4	Egypt	5	–	–	–	3.1**	3.8**	2.4**	3.7**	4.6**	2.7**	5.8**	7.2**	4.3**
5	Iraq	6	...	...	...	...	...	...	...	...	...	...	...	...
6	Jordan	6	0.3	0.3	0.3	0.1	0.1	0.2	0.1	0.1	0.1	0.5	0.4	0.5
7	Kuwait	4	3.7	3.8	3.5	1.9	1.9	1.9	3.1	3.6	2.6	1.6	1.9	1.3
8	Lebanon	6	4.7	5.5	3.8	6.3	7.6	4.9	6.7	8.2	5.1	18.8	21.7	15.6
9	Libyan Arab Jamahiriya	6	...	...	...	...	...	...	...	...	...	...	...	...
10	Mauritania	6	13.7	13.2	14.2	15.2	14.9	15.6	16.1	16.0	16.3	14.9	14.4	15.3
11	Morocco	6	17.2	18.2	16.1	14.9	16.6	12.9	15.4	17.7	12.8	12.4	14.8	9.4
12	Oman	6	0.2	0.2	0.1	0.1	0.2	0.1	0.1	0.1	0.1	1.2	1.5	0.9
13	Palestinian A. T.	4	0.8	0.6	1.0	1.2	1.3	1.2	0.4	0.4	0.4	2.4	2.6	2.3
14	Qatar	6	3.0**	3.4**	2.5**	...	...	...	...	...	...	...	...	...
15	Saudi Arabia	6	7.7	9.9	5.4	4.9	7.3	2.2	5.3	7.8	2.5	4.2	5.3	3.2
16	Sudan	6	5.3	4.6	6.2	4.7	3.9	5.6	4.8	4.6	5.0	5.7	5.4	6.0
17	Syrian Arab Republic	6	12.9	14.0	11.8	8.9	10.1	7.5	5.8	6.6	4.8	4.2	5.1	3.2
18	Tunisia	6	0.2	0.2	0.2	10.2	11.7	8.6	11.1	13.1	8.9	9.5	11.5	7.4
19	United Arab Emirates	5	2.8	2.9	2.7	2.4	2.6	2.2	2.1	2.3	1.9	3.1	4.3	1.8
20	Yemen	6	3.6	3.8	3.5	4.1	4.2	4.0	4.9	5.2	4.3	5.5	6.0	4.7
	Central and Eastern Europe													
21	Albania	4	5.2x	5.6x	4.7x	4.2x	5.0x	3.3x	3.0x	3.4x	2.7x	3.3x	3.8x	2.8x
22	Belarus	4	0.6	0.6	0.6	0.3	0.3	0.3	0.1	0.1	0.1	0.1	0.1	0.1
23	Bosnia and Herzegovina	4	...	...	...	...	...	...	...	...	...	...	...	...
24	Bulgaria	4	1.0	1.1	0.8	3.2	3.7	2.6	2.1	2.4	1.7	2.5	2.8	2.2
25	Croatia	4	0.9	1.0	0.8	0.3	0.3	0.2	0.2	0.2	0.1	0.1	0.1	0.1
26	Czech Republic	5	1.6	1.8	1.5	1.0	1.2	0.8	0.8	0.9	0.7	0.9	1.1	0.8
27	Estonia	6	1.4	1.6	1.2	0.9	1.3	0.6	1.7	2.3	1.0	2.0	2.7	1.1
28	Hungary	4	4.8	5.5	4.0	2.0	2.3	1.7	1.5	1.8	1.1	1.3	1.7	1.0
29	Latvia	4	3.7	4.9	2.5	1.4	1.8	0.9	1.1	1.4	0.7	1.0	1.4	0.7
30	Lithuania	4	1.3	1.6	1.0	0.3	0.4	0.3	0.3	0.4	0.2	0.4	0.6	0.2
31	Poland	6	0.7	...	...	0.3	...	...	0.4	...	...	0.7	...	...
32	Republic of Moldova	4	0.6	0.6	0.6	0.3	0.3	0.3	0.3	0.3	0.3	0.4	0.4	0.4
33	Romania	4	4.9	5.6	4.2	1.9	2.4	1.4	1.7	2.1	1.3	2.0	2.4	1.6
34	Russian Federation	3	0.9	...	...	0.7	...	...	0.6	...	...	.	.	.
35	Serbia and Montenegro	4	1.4**,x	1.4**,x	1.4**,x	1.3**,x	1.3**,x	1.3**,x	0.8**,x	0.8**,x	0.8**,x	0.7**,x	0.6**,x	0.7**,x
36	Slovakia	4	4.6	4.9	4.2	2.1	2.3	1.9	1.4	1.6	1.2	1.5	1.7	1.3
37	Slovenia	4	0.9	1.0	0.7	0.6	0.7	0.4	0.4	0.6	0.3	0.5	0.6	0.4
38	TFYR Macedonia	4	0.2	0.3	0.2	0.2	0.3	0.1	0.1	0.2	0.0	0.2	0.2	0.1
39	Turkey	6	...	...	...	...	...	...	...	...	...	...	...	...
40	Ukraine	4	0.3	0.3	0.2	0.1	0.1**	0.1**	0.1	0.1	0.1	...	...	...
	Central Asia													
41	Armenia	3	–	–	–	0.2	0.2	0.1	0.2	0.2	0.2	.	.	.
42	Azerbaijan	4	0.3	0.3	0.2	0.4	0.4	0.3	0.3	0.4	0.3	0.3	0.4	0.3
43	Georgia	4	0.2	0.3	0.2	0.1	0.2	0.1	0.1	0.2	0.1	0.2	0.3	0.1
44	Kazakhstan	4	0.1	0.1	0.0	0.2	0.3	0.1	0.1	0.2	0.1	0.1	0.2	0.1
45	Kyrgyzstan	4	0.1	0.2	0.1	0.2	0.2	0.1	0.2	0.2	0.1	0.1	0.2	0.1
46	Mongolia	4	1.3	1.4	1.2	0.7	0.7	0.6	0.4	0.4	0.3	0.3	0.3	0.3
47	Tajikistan	4	0.2	0.2	0.2	0.4	0.4**	0.4**	0.3	0.3**	0.3**	0.4	0.4**	0.4**
48	Turkmenistan	3	...	...	...	...	...	...	...	...	...	.	.	.
49	Uzbekistan	4	–	–	–	–	–	–	–	–	–	–	–	–
	East Asia and the Pacific													
50	Australia	7	...	...	...	...			...	...	...	...	...	...
51	Brunei Darussalam	6	.	.	.	.	.	.	.	.	.	.	.	.
52	Cambodia	6	17.9	18.5	17.1	11.0	11.9	9.9	8.0	9.0	6.8	5.5	6.2	4.6
53	China	5	1.4	1.6**	1.3**	0.2	0.2**	0.1**	0.1	0.2**	0.1**	0.1	0.1**	0.1**
54	Cook Islands	6	...	...	...	...	...	...	...	...	...	...	...	...
55	DPR Korea	4	...	...	...	...	...	...	...	...	...	...	...	...
56	Fiji	6	.	.	.	.	.	.	.	.	.	.	.	.

REPETITION RATES BY GRADE IN PRIMARY EDUCATION (%), 2001/2002									REPEATERS, ALL GRADES (%)						
Grade 5			Grade 6			Grade 7			1998/1999			2002/2003			
Total	Male	Female	Total	Male	Female	Total	Male	Female	Total	Male	Female	Total	Male	Female	
														Arab States	
11.2	14.0	8.0	15.9	19.0	12.4	.	.	.	11.9	14.6	8.7	11.6	14.1	8.8	1
3.9**	4.4**	3.4**	2.5**	3.4**	1.4**	.	.	.	3.8	4.6	3.1	2.9	3.2	2.5	2
…	…	…	…	…	…	.	.	.	16.6	16.7**	16.4**	**18.0**	**17.4**	**18.7**	3
9.6**	11.8**	7.2**	.	.	.	.	.	.	6.0**	7.1**	4.6**	4.5**	5.6**	3.3**	4
…	…	…	…	…	…	.	.	.	10.0	10.7	9.2	…	…	…	5
0.9	1.0	0.9	1.0	1.1	1.0	.	.	.	0.7	0.7	0.7	0.5	0.5	0.4	6
.	.	.	.	.	.	.	.	.	3.3	3.4	3.1	2.5	2.8	2.3	7
9.7	11.2	8.1	9.5	10.9	8.1	.	.	.	9.1	10.5	7.7	9.7	11.4	7.9	8
…	…	…	…	…	…	.	.	.	…	…	…	…	…	…	9
11.8	11.5	12.2	28.1	26.2	30.1	.	.	.	…	…	…	15.2	14.8	15.5	10
10.6	13.0	7.6	9.4	11.5	6.7	.	.	.	12.4	14.1	10.2	13.7	15.6	11.5	11
1.0	1.3	0.7	0.7	0.8	0.6	.	.	.	8.0	9.5	6.4	0.5	0.7	0.4	12
.	.	.	.	.	.	.	.	.	2.1	2.2	2.0	1.2	1.2	1.2	13
…	…	…	4.6**	7.0**	2.0**	.	.	.	2.7**	3.5**	1.9**	…	…	…	14
4.6	6.0	3.2	1.9	2.5	1.3	.	.	.	5.4	6.6	4.2	4.8	6.5	3.0	15
6.0	5.8	6.2	5.8	5.7	6.0	.	.	.	…	…	…	5.1	4.7	5.5	16
3.3	3.8	2.7	3.7	4.2	3.2	.	.	.	6.5	7.2	5.6	6.8	7.6	5.8	17
12.1	14.2	9.7	8.0	9.6	6.3	.	.	.	18.3	20.0	16.4	9.2	10.8	7.3	18
3.1	4.2	2.0	.	.	.	.	.	.	3.5	4.4	2.5	2.6	3.2	2.1	19
5.4	6.0	4.3	4.6	5.2	3.5	.	.	.	10.6	11.7*	8.7*	4.3	4.8	3.7	20
														Central and Eastern Europe	
.	.	.	.	.	.	.	.	.	3.9**	4.6**	3.3**	2.8	3.2	2.4	21
…	…	…	…	…	…	.	.	.	0.5	0.5	0.5	0.2	0.2	0.2	22
…	…	…	…	…	…	.	.	.	…	…	…	…	…	…	23
.	.	.	.	.	.	.	.	.	3.2	3.7	2.7	2.3	2.6	1.9	24
.	.	.	.	.	.	.	.	.	0.4	0.5	0.3	0.4	0.4	0.3	25
0.9	1.1	0.6	.	.	.	.	.	.	1.2	1.5	1.0	1.1	1.3	0.9	26
2.3	3.6	1.0	3.5	5.4	1.3	.	.	.	2.5	3.5	1.4	2.3	3.3	1.1	27
.	.	.	.	.	.	.	.	.	2.2	2.1	2.2	2.4	2.9	2.0	28
.	.	.	.	.	.	.	.	.	2.1	2.7**	1.3**	1.9	2.5	1.3	29
.	.	.	.	.	.	.	.	.	0.9	1.3	0.5	0.6	0.8	0.4	30
0.8	…	…	0.6	…	…	.	.	.	1.2	…	…	0.6	…	…	31
.	.	.	.	.	.	.	.	.	0.9	0.9**	0.9**	0.4	0.4	0.4	32
.	.	.	.	.	.	.	.	.	3.4	4.1	2.6	2.8	3.3	2.2	33
.	.	.	.	.	.	.	.	.	1.2	…	…	0.8	…	…	34
.	.	.	.	.	.	.	.	.	…	…	…	1.0y	1.0**,y	1.0**,y	35
.	.	.	.	.	.	.	.	.	2.3	2.6	2.0	2.5	2.7	2.2	36
.	.	.	.	.	.	.	.	.	1.0	1.3	0.7	0.6	0.7	0.4	37
.	.	.	.	.	.	.	.	.	0.0	0.1	0.0	0.2	0.2	0.1	38
…	…	…	…	…	…	.	.	.	…	…	…	…	…	…	39
.	.	.	.	.	.	.	.	.	0.8	…	…	0.1	0.2	0.1	40
														Central Asia	
.	.	.	.	.	.	.	.	.	…	…	…	0.1	0.1	0.1	41
.	.	.	.	.	.	.	.	.	0.4	0.4	0.4	0.3	0.4	0.3	42
.	.	.	.	.	.	.	.	.	0.3	0.5**	0.2**	0.2	0.2	0.1	43
.	.	.	.	.	.	.	.	.	0.3	…	…	0.1	0.2	0.1	44
.	.	.	.	.	.	.	.	.	0.3	0.4	0.2	0.1	0.2	0.1	45
.	.	.	.	.	.	.	.	.	0.9	1.0	0.8	0.6	0.7	0.6	46
.	.	.	.	.	.	.	.	.	0.5	0.5**	0.6**	0.3	0.3**	0.3**	47
.	.	.	.	.	.	.	.	.	…	…	…	…	…	…	48
.	.	.	.	.	.	.	.	.	–	–	–	–	–	–	49
														East Asia and the Pacific	
…	…	…	…	…	…	…	…	…	…	…	…	…	…	…	50
.	.	.	.	.	.	.	.	.	.	.	.	.	.	.	51
3.7	4.2	3.0	1.9	2.0	1.7	.	.	.	24.6**	25.5**	23.5**	10.1	10.8	9.3	52
0.1	0.1**	0.1**	.	.	.	.	.	.	…	…	…	0.3	0.4	0.3	53
…	…	…	…	…	…	.	.	.	0.6	0.9**	0.2**	…	…	…	54
.	.	.	.	.	.	.	.	.	…	…	…	…	…	…	55
.	.	.	.	.	.	.	.	.	.	.	.	.	.	.	56

Table 6 (continued)

	Country or territory	Duration[1] of primary education 2002/2003	REPETITION RATES BY GRADE IN PRIMARY EDUCATION (%), 2001/2002											
			Grade 1			Grade 2			Grade 3			Grade 4		
			Total	Male	Female	Total	Male	Female	Total	Male	Female	Total	Male	Female
57	Indonesia	6	7.5	7.4	7.7	4.6	4.6	4.7	3.9	3.9	3.9	3.0	3.0	3.0
58	Japan	6	...	...	...	...	...	...	...	...	...	...	...	...
59	Kiribati	6	...	...	...	...	...	...	...	...	...	...	...	...
60	Lao PDR	5	34.7	35.2	34.2	20.0	21.7	17.8	13.2	14.6	11.5	8.3	9.8	6.6
61	Macao, China	6	3.3	3.6	3.0	3.6	4.1	3.0	5.8	7.5	3.9	8.3	10.7	5.5
62	Malaysia	6	.	.	.	.	.	.	.	.	.	.	.	.
63	Marshall Islands	6	.	.	.	.	.	.	.	.	.	.	.	.
64	Micronesia (Federated States of)	6	...	...	...	...	...	...	...	...	...	...	...	...
65	Myanmar	5	1.2	1.2	1.2	0.7	0.7	0.7	0.6	0.6	0.6	0.5	0.5	0.5
66	Nauru	6	...	...	...	...	...	...	...	...	...	...	...	...
67	New Zealand	6	...	...	...	...	...	...	...	...	...	...	...	...
68	Niue	6	.	.	.	.	.	.	.	.	.	.	.	.
69	Palau	5	–[y]	–[y]	–[y]	–[y]	–[y]	–[y]	–[y]	–[y]	–[y]	–[y]	–[y]	–[y]
70	Papua New Guinea	6	–[y]	–[y]	–[y]	–[y]	–[y]	–[y]	–[y]	–[y]	–[y]	–[y]	–[y]	–[y]
71	Philippines	6	4.6	5.5	3.7	2.4	3.2	1.6	1.7	2.3	1.1	1.2	1.7	0.7
72	Republic of Korea	6	**0.4**	**0.4**	**0.4**	**0.2**	**0.2**	**0.2**	**0.2**	**0.2**	**0.2**	**0.2**	**0.2**	**0.2**
73	Samoa	6	2.6[y]	3.0[y]	2.2[y]	0.7[y]	1.1[y]	0.4[y]	0.4[y]	0.4[y]	0.5[y]	0.6[y]	0.9[y]	0.4[y]
74	Singapore	6	–	–	–	–	–	–	–	–	–	–	–	–
75	Solomon Islands	6	...	...	...	...	...	...	...	...	...	...	...	...
76	Thailand	6	...	...	...	...	...	...	...	...	...	...	...	...
77	Timor-Leste	6	...	...	...	...	...	...	...	...	...	...	...	...
78	Tokelau	6	...	...	...	...	...	...	...	...	...	...	...	...
79	Tonga	6	.	.	.	.	.	.	.	.	.	.	.	.
80	Tuvalu	6	...	...	...	...	...	...	...	...	...	...	...	...
81	Vanuatu	6	10.6[y]	11.8[y]	9.3[y]	...	...	...	...	...	...	...	...	...
82	Viet Nam	5	5.4**	6.2**	4.4**	2.6**	3.0**	2.1**	1.7**	2.0**	1.3**	1.6**	1.9**	1.2**
	Latin America and the Caribbean													
83	Anguilla	7	...	...	...	...	...	...	...	...	...	...	...	...
84	Antigua and Barbuda	7	...	...	...	–	...	...	–	...	...	...	...	...
85	Argentina	6	9.9	11.4	8.4	7.1	8.3	5.8	6.2	7.3	5.0	5.2	6.3	4.1
86	Aruba	6	14.7	18.1	10.9	11.7	12.3	11.1	9.0	10.9	6.9	7.9	8.8	7.0
87	Bahamas	6	.	.	.	.	.	.	.	.	.	.	.	.
88	Barbados	6	.	.	.	.	.	.	.	.	.	.	.	.
89	Belize	6	15.3**	...	...	...	...	...	...	...	...	...	...	...
90	Bermuda	6	–	–	–	.	.	.	.	.	.	.	.	.
91	Bolivia	6	2.0	2.0	1.9	1.8	1.9	1.7	1.9	2.1	1.8	1.9	2.0	1.7
92	Brazil	4	29.3	32.0**	26.2**	19.7	21.6**	17.6**	15.4	17.4**	13.4**	13.5	15.4**	11.5**
93	British Virgin Islands	7	7.2	...	...	...	...	...	...	...	...	...	...	...
94	Cayman Islands	6	0.4**,[y]	0.3**,[y]	0.4**,[y]	...	...	...	...	...	...	...	...	...
95	Chile	6	**0.9**	**1.0**	**0.8**	**3.0**	**3.5**	**2.5**	**0.6**	**0.7**	**0.5**	**2.2**	**2.7**	**1.7**
96	Colombia	5	11.8	12.8	10.8	6.3	6.9	5.7	5.2	5.7	4.7	4.1	4.7	3.6
97	Costa Rica	6	14.1	15.4	12.7	7.9	9.0	6.7	6.7	7.8	5.7	8.1	9.6	6.5
98	Cuba	6	–	–	–	1.9	2.5	1.3	–	–	–	1.5	2.1	0.9
99	Dominica	7	8.1	9.6	6.5	5.4	7.4	3.3	2.0	2.9	1.0	1.3	2.0	0.6
100	Dominican Republic	6	2.5**	2.9**	2.1**	2.8**	3.3**	2.4**	12.2**	...	...	7.3**	...	...
101	Ecuador	6	3.9	4.2	3.6	2.7	3.0	2.4	1.8	2.1	1.5	1.4	1.7	1.2
102	El Salvador	6	15.9	17.0	14.6	6.2	7.1	5.2	4.6	5.2	3.8	4.1	4.8	3.5
103	Grenada	7	4.2	5.6	2.7	2.0	2.1	1.9	2.2	3.1	1.4	1.9	2.6	1.2
104	Guatemala	6	27.6	28.7	26.5	14.8	15.6	14.0	11.4	12.1	10.7	8.1	8.7	7.3
105	Guyana	6	2.5[x]	2.7[x]	2.3[x]	1.6[x]	2.0[x]	1.3[x]	1.8[x]	2.1[x]	1.4[x]	1.3[x]	1.7[x]	0.8[x]
106	Haiti	6	...	...	...	...	...	...	...	...	...	...	...	...
107	Honduras	6	12.0**,[y]	12.0**,[y]	12.0**,[y]	...	...	...	...	...	...	...	...	...
108	Jamaica	6	3.7	4.1**	3.3**	1.1	1.2**	1.0**	0.9	...	...	4.0	3.4**	4.6**
109	Mexico	6	8.1	9.3	6.8	8.0	9.3	6.6	5.5	6.5	4.3	4.6	5.6	3.6
110	Montserrat	7	12.3**	8.3**	16.2**	...	...	...	...	...	...	...	...	...
111	Netherlands Antilles	6	18.9			...	...	...	...	...	...	...	...	...
112	Nicaragua	6	15.5	16.7	14.2	9.0	10.3	7.6	9.2	10.0	7.7	7.6	9.0	6.3
113	Panama	6	9.3	10.6	7.9	8.3	9.5	6.9	6.0	7.1	4.9	4.1	5.1	2.9
114	Paraguay	6	13.6	15.2	11.8	10.3**	11.9**	8.6**	7.5**	8.7**	6.2**	5.4**	6.3**	4.4**
115	Peru	6	5.2	5.4	5.0	16.6	17.0	16.2	13.5	13.8	13.2	9.6	9.8	9.4
116	Saint Kitts and Nevis	7		.	.	.	.	.	.	.	.	.	.	.
117	Saint Lucia	7	5.6	7.0	4.2	1.1	1.4	0.0		...	...	...	...	...

REPETITION RATES BY GRADE IN PRIMARY EDUCATION (%), 2001/2002									REPEATERS, ALL GRADES (%)						
Grade 5			Grade 6			Grade 7			1998/1999			2002/2003			
Total	Male	Female	Total	Male	Female	Total	Male	Female	Total	Male	Female	Total	Male	Female	
2.1	2.1	2.1	0.3	0.3	0.3	.	.	.	…	…	…	3.8	3.8	3.8	57
…	…	…	…	…	…	.	.	.	…	…	…	…	…	…	58
…	…	…	…	…	…	.	.	.	…	…	…	…	…	…	59
5.3	6.4	4.0	.	.	.	.	.	.	20.9	22.4	19.1	19.8	21.0	18.4	60
…	…	…	…	…	…	.	.	.	6.3	7.3	5.1	7.1	8.9	5.1	61
.	.	.	.	.	.	.	.	.	.	.	.	.	.	.	62
.	.	.	.	.	.	.	.	.	.	.	.	.	.	.	63
…	…	…	…	…	…	.	.	.	…	…	…	…	…	…	64
0.3	0.3	0.3	.	.	.	.	.	.	1.7	1.7**	1.7**	0.7	0.7	0.7	65
…	…	…	…	…	…	.	.	.	0.7**	0.9**	0.5**	…	…	…	66
…	…	…	…	…	…	.	.	.	…	…	…	…	…	…	67
.	.	.	.	.	.	.	.	.	.	.	.	.	.	.	68
–[y]	–[y]	–[y]	.	.	.	.	.	.	–	–	–	–	–	–	69
–[y]	–[y]	–[y]	–[y]	–[y]	–[y]	.	.	.	–	–	–	–	–	–	70
1.0	1.4	0.5	0.5	0.7	0.3	.	.	.	1.9	2.4	1.4	2.1	2.7	1.4	71
0.2	**0.2**	**0.2**	**0.2**	**0.2**	**0.2**	.	.	.	.	.	.	**0.2**	**0.2**	**0.2**	72
0.6[y]	…	…	0.3[y]	…	…	.	.	.	1.7	2.4**	0.9**	0.9[z]	1.1[z]	0.7[z]	73
–	–	–	–	–	–	.	.	.	–	–	–	–	–	–	74
…	…	…	…	…	…	.	.	.	…	…	…	…	…	…	75
…	…	…	…	…	…	.	.	.	3.5	3.4	3.5	…	…	…	76
…	…	…	…	…	…	.	.	.	…	…	…	…	…	…	77
…	…	…	…	…	…	.	.	.	…	…	…	.[y]	.[y]	.[y]	78
.	.	.	28.5**	31.0**	25.4**	.	.	.	7.4	7.9	6.9	6.2[z]	6.9[z]	5.4[z]	79
…	…	…	…	…	…	.	.	.	6.5**	7.4**	5.4**	…	…	…	80
…	…	…	…	…	…	.	.	.	10.9**	11.5**	10.2**	6.7[z]	7.5[z]	5.9[z]	81
0.2**	0.2**	0.2**	…	…	…	.	.	.	3.8	4.2	3.2	2.4**	2.8**	1.9**	82
Latin America and the Caribbean															
…	…	…	…	…	…	…	…	…	0.3	0.4	0.3	0.8**	1.0**	0.6**	83
…	…	…	…	…	…	…	…	…	…	…	…	…	…	…	84
4.3	5.2	3.3	3.6	4.5	2.7	.	.	.	5.3	6.2	4.3	5.9	7.0	4.8	85
7.7	8.8	6.6	3.5	3.9	3.2	.	.	.	7.7	9.5	5.9	9.0	10.3	7.5	86
.	.	.	.	.	.	.	.	.	.	.	.	.	.	.	87
.	.	.	.	.	.	.	.	.	.	.	.	.	.	.	88
…	…	…	8.8**	…	…	.	.	.	9.7	10.8	8.4	9.4**	11.0**	7.7**	89
.	.	.	.	.	.	.	.	.	…	…	…	.	.	.	90
1.9	2.0	1.7	3.8	4.4	3.2	.	.	.	6.5	6.9	6.2	2.1	2.3	1.9	91
.	.	.	.	.	.	.	.	.	…	…	…	20.6	23.0**	18.1**	92
…	…	…	…	…	…	…	…	…	4.3**	4.3**	4.2**	4.4	4.6	4.2	93
…	…	…	…	…	…	.	.	.	…	…	…	…	…	…	94
2.4	**3.1**	**1.6**	**2.2**	**2.9**	**1.5**	.	.	.	3.2	3.8	2.6	**2.0**	**2.4**	**1.5**	95
3.1	3.5	2.6	…	…	…	.	.	.	4.6	5.0	4.2	6.6	7.3	5.9	96
6.3	7.4	5.1	0.6	0.7	0.6	.	.	.	8.7**	9.6**	7.7**	7.5	8.5	6.3	97
0.8	1.1	0.5	0.3	0.4	0.2	.	.	.	1.9	2.6	1.1	0.8	1.1	0.5	98
0.9	1.1	0.6	1.1	1.7	0.3	6.9	8.9	4.7	3.6	3.8	3.5	3.8	5.0	2.5	99
5.5**	…	…	4.3**	…	…	.	.	.	4.1**	4.5**	3.7**	5.9**	7.1**	4.6**	100
0.9	1.1	0.8	0.5	0.6	0.4	.	.	.	2.7	3.0	2.4	2.0	2.3	1.8	101
3.3	4.0	2.6	3.0	3.7	2.4	.	.	.	7.5	8.3	6.7	7.0	7.8	6.1	102
1.4	…	…	2.1	…	…	4.0	…	…	…	…	…	2.7	3.3	2.1	103
5.1	5.6	4.4	1.8	2.1	1.5	.	.	.	14.9**	15.8**	13.8**	14.1	14.8	13.4	104
1.1[x]	1.4[x]	0.8[x]	1.3[x]	1.4[x]	1.1[x]	.	.	.	3.1	3.6	2.5	1.6[y]	1.9[y]	1.3[y]	105
…	…	…	…	…	…	.	.	.	…	…	…	…	…	…	106
…	…	…	…	…	…	.	.	.	…	…	…	…	…	…	107
1.0	…	…	6.2	…	…	.	.	.	…	…	…	2.8	…	…	108
3.1	3.9	2.3	0.5	0.6	0.4	.	.	.	6.6	7.6	5.5	5.1	6.1	4.1	109
…	…	…	…	…	…	…	…	…	0.9	…	–	17.0**	18.0**	15.7**	110
…	…	…	…	…	…	.	.	.	12.0**	14.5**	9.3**	12.6**	15.6**	9.6**	111
5.5	6.6	4.4	3.1	4.0	2.3	.	.	.	8.1	9.0	7.2	8.9	10.1	7.7	112
2.6	3.3	1.9	1.0	1.3	0.8	.	.	.	…	…	…	5.4	6.4	4.4	113
3.4**	4.1**	2.6**	1.7**	2.1**	1.2**	.	.	.	9.0**	10.4**	7.6**	7.6	8.8	6.3	114
8.1	8.4	7.8	3.9	4.1	3.8	.	.	.	9.8	10.0	9.5	9.9	10.2	9.7	115
.	.	.	.	.	.	.	.	.	.	.	.	.	.	.	116
…	…	…	…	…	…	…	…	…	2.4**	2.8**	2.0**	2.7	3.4	1.9	117

Table 6 (continued)

	Country or territory	Duration[1] of primary education 2002/2003	REPETITION RATES BY GRADE IN PRIMARY EDUCATION (%), 2001/2002											
			Grade 1			Grade 2			Grade 3			Grade 4		
			Total	Male	Female	Total	Male	Female	Total	Male	Female	Total	Male	Female
118	Saint Vincent/Grenad.	7	8.8 **	...	...	4.8 **	...	...	8.7	...	...	7.6	...	...
119	Suriname	6	...	...	...	...	...	...	...	...	...	...	...	...
120	Trinidad and Tobago	7	6.6 **,y	7.6 **,y	5.6 **,y	3.2 **,y	4.1 **,y	2.2 **,y	2.6 **,y	3.2 **,y	2.1 **,y	1.8 **,y	2.2 **,y	1.3 **,y
121	Turks and Caicos Islands	6	9.4	8.7	9.9	5.1	11.5	–	5.6	3.1	8.2	4.6	4.8	4.4
122	Uruguay	6	17.0	19.3	14.3	10.7	12.2	9.1	8.0	9.3	6.5	6.2	7.4	5.0
123	Venezuela	6	11.7	13.6	9.6	9.0	10.8	7.1	8.8	10.7	6.7	6.7	8.4	4.9
	North America and Western Europe													
124	Andorra	6	...	...	...	–	–	–	–	–	–	–	–	–
125	Austria	4	1.8 **,x	2.1 **,x	1.5 **,x	1.7 **,x	1.9 **,x	1.5 **,x	1.4 **,x	1.7 **,x	1.1 **,x	1.2 **,x	1.4 **,x	1.0 **,x
126	Belgium	6	...	...	...	...	...	...	...	...	...	...	...	...
127	Canada	6	...	...	...	...	...	...	...	...	...	...	...	...
128	Cyprus	6	1.3	1.6	1.0	0.1	0.2	0.0	0.1	0.1	0.0	0.0	0.1	–
129	Denmark	6	.	.	.	.	.	.	.	.	.	.	.	.
130	Finland	6	0.8	1.0	0.6	0.9	1.1	0.7	0.4	0.4	0.3	0.2	0.3	0.2
131	France	5	...	...	...	...	...	...	...	...	...	...	...	...
132	Germany	4	1.5	1.6	1.4	2.2	2.2	2.1	1.6	1.7	1.5	1.1	1.2	1.0
133	Greece	6	...	...	...	...	...	...	...	...	...	...	...	...
134	Iceland	7	–	–	–	–	–	–	–	–	–	–	–	–
135	Ireland	8	1.0	1.1	0.8	2.1	2.4	1.8	1.7	2.0	1.4	0.9	1.0	0.8
136	Israel	6	2.2 **	3.0 **	1.4 **	1.1 **	1.4 **	0.8 **	1.2 **	1.5 **	0.8 **	1.2 **	1.6 **	0.9 **
137	Italy	5	0.4 y	0.5 y	0.3 y	0.3 y	0.4 y	0.2 y	0.2 y	0.3 y	0.2 y	0.2 y	0.3 y	0.1 y
138	Luxembourg	6	6.7 **,y	7.4 **,y	5.8 **,y	5.1 **,y	6.1 **,y	4.1 **,y	6.6 **,y	8.1 **,y	5.1 **,y	4.0 **,y	4.8 **,y	3.2 **,y
139	Malta	6	0.8	0.8	0.8	0.7	0.9	0.5	0.7	0.6	0.7	0.8	0.9	0.6
140	Monaco	5	...	...	...	...	...	...	...	...	...	...	...	...
141	Netherlands	6	.	.	.	.	.	.	.	.	.	.	.	.
142	Norway	7	–	–	–	–	–	–	–	–	–	–	–	–
143	Portugal	6	...	...	...	...	...	...	...	...	...	...	...	...
144	San Marino	5	...	...	...	...	...	...	...	...	...	...	...	...
145	Spain	6	...	...	...	...	...	...	...	...	...	...	...	...
146	Sweden	6	...	...	...	...	...	...	...	...	...	...	...	...
147	Switzerland	6	...	...	...	...	...	...	...	...	...	...	...	...
148	United Kingdom	6	...	...	...	...	...	...	...	...	...	...	...	...
149	United States	6	...	...	...	...	...	...	...	...	...	...	...	...
	South and West Asia													
150	Afghanistan	6	...	...	...	...	...	...	...	...	...	...	...	...
151	Bangladesh	5	6.4	6.6	6.3	5.5	5.6	5.3	7.8	7.4	8.2	6.1	6.3	5.8
152	Bhutan	7	14.8 y	15.5 y	14.0 y	13.7 y	14.4 y	12.9 y	14.0 y	14.8 y	13.1 y	11.5 y	12.5 y	10.4 y
153	India	5	3.9	3.6	4.3	2.8	2.6	3.1	4.2	4.0	4.6	4.4	4.4	4.6
154	Iran, Islamic Republic of	5	5.5 **	6.5 **	4.4 **	3.4 **	...	...	2.3 **	...	...	2.3 **	...	...
155	Maldives	7	.	.	.	.	.	.	.	.	.	.	.	.
156	Nepal	5	36.8	36.9	36.6	17.2	16.4	18.3	13.7	13.6	13.9	14.0	13.6	14.6
157	Pakistan	5	...	...	...	...	...	...	...	...	...	...	...	...
158	Sri Lanka	5	**0.4** **	**0.5** **	**0.4** **	**0.7** **	**0.7** **	**0.6** **	**0.8** **	**0.9** **	**0.7** **	**0.9** **	**1.1** **	**0.8** **
	Sub-Saharan Africa													
159	Angola	4	...	...	...	...	...	...	...	...	...	...	...	...
160	Benin	6	16.8	17.0	16.6	16.8	16.4	17.4	18.5	17.8	19.3	23.5	22.5	25.0
161	Botswana	7	4.0 **	4.6 **	3.4 **	2.2 **	2.5 **	1.8 **	2.1 **	2.6 **	1.5 **	10.8 **	13.1 **	8.3 **
162	Burkina Faso	6	10.1 **	10.2 **	10.0 **	10.9 **	11.0 **	10.8 **	15.3 **	15.5 **	15.1 **	14.6 **	14.4 **	14.7 **
163	Burundi	6	27.1	26.4	28.0	26.6	26.4	26.8	24.8	24.2	25.6	24.3	23.5	25.2
164	Cameroon	6	31.5 **	31.9 **	31.1 **	21.9 **	22.7 **	21.0 **	30.6 **	30.9 **	30.2 **	21.6 **	22.1 **	20.9 **
165	Cape Verde	6	0.8	0.9	0.6	26.8	30.8	22.3	0.7	0.8	0.6	23.8	27.1	20.4
166	Central African Republic	6	...	...	...	...	...	...	...	...	...	...	...	...
167	Chad	6	29.4 **	29.3 **	29.5 **	26.3 **	26.0 **	26.8 **	26.1 **	25.9 **	26.5 **	24.2 **	23.4 **	25.5 **
168	Comoros	6	34.5 **,y	35.3 **,y	33.5 **,y	...			...	...	...	...	...	...
169	Congo	6	30.0	30.6	29.4	20.3	20.1	20.5	34.3	35.1	33.4	29.5	30.8	20.4
170	Côte d'Ivoire	6	13.3 **	14.0 **	12.5 **	...	...	...	...	...	...	...	...	...
171	Democratic Rep. of the Congo	6	...	...	...	...	...	...	...	...	...	...	...	...
172	Equatorial Guinea	5	48.1 **,y	44.6 **,y	51.7 **,y	40.2 **,y	38.1 **,y	42.2 **,y	33.6 **,y	32.8 **,y	34.4 **,y	32.5 **,y	33.0 **,y	32.0 **,y
173	Eritrea	5	29.8	29.4	30.3	19.6	19.2	20.1	19.0	18.2	20.0	22.5	21.5	23.7
174	Ethiopia	6	**20.3** **	**21.4** **	**18.9** **	**8.2** **	**7.3** **	**9.5** **	**6.9** **	**5.9** **	**8.4** **	**9.6** **	**8.1** **	**11.7** **

REPETITION RATES BY GRADE IN PRIMARY EDUCATION (%), 2001/2002									REPEATERS, ALL GRADES (%)						
Grade 5			Grade 6			Grade 7			1998/1999			2002/2003			
Total	Male	Female	Total	Male	Female	Total	Male	Female	Total	Male	Female	Total	Male	Female	
11.2	…	…	12.2	…	…	18.3	…	…	…	…	…	10.0	12.0	7.8	118
…	…	…	…	…	…	.	.	.	…	…	…	…	…	…	119
1.9**,y	2.1**,y	1.7**,y	3.7**,y	3.9**,y	3.5**,y	9.0**,y	8.2**,y	9.8**,y	4.7	4.9	4.4	5.0	5.9	4.0	120
4.3	5.4	3.2	18.0	20.0	15.7	.	.	.	…	…	…	9.7	10.9	8.5	121
5.0	6.1	3.8	2.2	2.6	1.8	.	.	.	8.4	9.9	6.9	8.4	9.7	6.9	122
4.6	5.7	3.4	1.8	2.3	1.2	.	.	.	6.7**	8.1**	5.2**	7.5	9.1	5.8	123
North America and Western Europe															
–	–	–	–	–	–	.	.	.	…	…	…	–	–	–	124
.	.	.	.	.	.	.	.	.	1.5	1.8	1.3	…	…	…	125
…	…	…	…	…	…	.	.	.	…	…	…	…	…	…	126
…	…	…	…	…	…	.	.	.	…	…	…	…	…	…	127
0.01	0.04	0.02	0.1	0.1	0.1	.	.	.	0.4	0.5	0.3	0.3	0.3	0.2	128
.	.	.	.	.	.	.	.	.	.	.	.	.	.	.	129
0.2	0.3	0.1	0.2	0.2	0.1	.	.	.	0.4	0.6	0.3	0.5	0.6	0.3	130
…	…	…	…	…	…	.	.	.	4.2	4.2**	4.2**				131
…	…	…	…	…	…	.	.	.	1.7	1.9	1.5	1.6	1.7	1.5	132
…	…	…	…	…	…	.	.	.	…	…	…	…	…	…	133
–	–	–	–	–	–	–	–	–	–	–	–	–	–	–	134
0.6	0.7	0.6	0.7	0.6	0.8	0.6	0.6	0.6	1.8	2.1	1.6	1.1	1.2	0.9	135
1.5**	1.8**	1.0**	1.0**	1.2**	0.8**	.	.	.	…	…	…	1.8	2.2	1.3	136
0.3y	0.4y	0.3y	…	…	…	.	.	.	0.4	0.5	0.3	0.3	0.3	0.2	137
4.1**,y	5.2**,y	2.9**,y	0.4**,y	0.5**,y	0.4**,y	.	.	.	…	…	…	4.5**,z	5.4**,z	3.6**,z	138
0.7	0.8	0.5	9.0	9.9	7.9	.	.	.	2.1	2.4	1.8	2.4	2.6	2.1	139
…	…	…	.	.	.	.	.	.	–	–	–	–	–	–	140
.	.	.	.	.	.	.	.	.	.	.	.	.	.	.	141
–	–	–	–	–	–	…	…	…	…	…	…	–	–	–	142
…	…	…	…	…	…	.	.	.	…	…	…	…	…	…	143
…	…	…	.	.	.	.	.	.	…	…	…	…	…	…	144
…	…	…	…	…	…	.	.	.	…	…	…	…	…	…	145
…	…	…	2.1x	2.1x	2.1x	.	.	.	.	.	.	…	…	…	146
…	…	…	…	…	…	.	.	.	1.8	1.9	1.6	1.6	1.8	1.5	147
…	…	…	…	…	…	.	.	.	…	…	…	…	…	…	148
…	…	…	…	…	…	.	.	.	…	…	…	…	…	…	149
South and West Asia															
…	…	…	…	…	…	.	.	.	…	…	…	…	…	…	150
5.0	6.1	4.0	.	.	.	.	.	.	6.7	6.9	6.5	6.2	6.5	6.0	151
15.0y	15.6y	14.4y	11.9y	11.6y	12.2y	11.8y	11.0y	12.8y	13.0	13.8	12.1	12.9**	13.5**	12.3**	152
4.6	4.5	4.7	…	…	…	.	.	.	4.0	4.0	4.1	3.6	3.6	3.6	153
1.1**	…	…	.	.	.	.	.	.	…	…	…	3.0**	3.6**	2.5**	154
.	.	.	.	.	.	.	.	.	…	…	…	.	.	.	155
11.0	10.9	11.1	…	…	…	.	.	.	24.5**	23.8**	25.5**	21.7	21.6	21.8	156
…	…	…	…	…	…	.	.	.	…	…	…	…	…	…	157
1.0**	**1.3****	**0.8****	.	.	.	.	.	.	5.1	6.0	4.2	**0.8****	**0.9****	**0.7****	158
Sub-Saharan Africa															
.	.	.	.	.	.	.	.	.	29.5**	29.3**	29.8**	…	…	…	159
28.9	27.6	31.0	34.6	34.5	34.7	.	.	.	…	…	…	19.9	19.9	20.0	160
1.4**	1.8**	1.1**	1.1**	1.4**	0.7**	0.1**	0.2**	0.1**	3.1	3.7	2.5	3.2**	4.0**	2.5**	161
16.7**	15.7**	18.2**	33.9**	33.1**	35.1**	.	.	.	17.7	17.5	18.0	15.1	15.0	15.2	162
34.9	34.0	36.1	45.3	44.5	46.4	.	.	.	20.3**	20.3**	20.4**	26.5	26.2	26.9	163
25.6**	26.2**	25.0**	22.8**	24.7**	20.6**	.	.	.	26.7**	26.8**	26.5**	25.8	26.4	25.1	164
0.8	1.0	0.6	15.3	17.2	13.4	.	.	.	11.6**	12.8**	10.3**	13.4	15.5	11.2	165
…	…	…	…	…	…	.	.	.	…	…	…	…	…	…	166
20.1**	19.3**	21.7**	23.3	23.8	22.0	.	.	.	25.9	25.7	26.3	25.3**	24.8**	25.9**	167
…	…	…	29.5**,y	32.4**,y	26.1**,y	.	.	.	26.0	26.4	25.5	28.0**	29.3**	26.3**	168
27.3	28.0	26.6	12.6	13.5	11.7	.	.	.	…	…	…	27.8	28.4	27.2	169
…	…	…	…	…	…	.	.	.	23.7	22.8**	24.9**	17.6*	17.5*	17.7*	170
…	…	…	…	…	…	.	.	.	…	…	…	…	…	…	171
33.5**,y	32.0**,y	35.0**,y	.	.	.	.	.	.	…	…	…	40.5z	38.1z	43.0z	172
16.1	15.1	17.3	.	.	.	.	.	.	19.4	18.2	20.8	20.7	20.1	21.5	173
9.3**	**7.3****	**12.5****	**5.6****	**4.5****	**7.6****	.	.	.	10.6	9.8	11.9	**10.6****	**10.1****	**11.2****	174

Table 6 (continued)

	Country or territory	Duration[1] of primary education 2002/2003	REPETITION RATES BY GRADE IN PRIMARY EDUCATION (%), 2001/2002 Grade 1 Total	Grade 1 Male	Grade 1 Female	Grade 2 Total	Grade 2 Male	Grade 2 Female	Grade 3 Total	Grade 3 Male	Grade 3 Female	Grade 4 Total	Grade 4 Male	Grade 4 Female
175	Gabon	6	48.1 **	49.1 **	47.0 **	33.2 **	33.7 **	32.6 **	37.0 **	38.3 **	35.6 **	24.8 **	25.1 **	24.5 **
176	Gambia	6	14.1 **	14.6 **	13.7 **	...	...	...	...	...	...	...	...	...
177	Ghana	6	**8.9** **	**9.1** **	**8.7** **	...	...	...	...	...	...	...	...	...
178	Guinea	6	22.5	22.3	22.8	17.9	16.9	19.3	19.9	18.8	21.4	20.3	18.7	22.7
179	Guinea-Bissau	6	...	...	...	...	...	...	...	...	...	...	...	...
180	Kenya	7	8.2 **	9.5 **	6.9 **	7.9 **	8.3 **	7.6 **	8.2 **	8.4 **	8.0 **	9.3 **	10.2 **	8.4 **
181	Lesotho	7	27.1	28.9	24.9	25.1	27.8	22.2	25.5	29.2	21.6	19.7	22.8	16.7
182	Liberia	6	...	...	...	...	...	...	...	...	...	...	...	...
183	Madagascar	5	41.2	42.4	39.9	31.3	33.0	29.3	33.1	34.4	31.8	26.6	27.1	26.1
184	Malawi	6	17.5	17.9	17.0	17.0	17.3	16.7	15.3	14.4	16.5	12.2	10.8	14.1
185	Mali	6	13.1	12.9	13.3	14.1	13.7	14.7	21.9	21.8	22.0	23.8	22.9	25.0
186	Mauritius	6	.	.	.	.	.	.	.	.	.	.	.	.
187	Mozambique	5	25.8	25.4	26.1	25.0	24.7	25.4	25.2	24.5	26.2	22.0	21.1	23.3
188	Namibia	7	15.2	15.9	14.5	11.9 **	14.1 **	9.6 **	11.4 **	13.7 **	9.1 **	13.0 **	...	...
189	Niger	6	0.9	0.9	0.8	5.5	5.3	5.7	7.2	7.0	7.7	8.4	8.1	9.0
190	Nigeria	6	...	...	...	...	...	...	...	...	...	...	...	...
191	Rwanda	6	19.3	19.6	19.0	14.8	15.2	14.5	15.3	15.4	15.2	17.9	17.6	18.2
192	Sao Tome and Principe	6	32.6 y	34.6 y	30.2 y	28.9 y	30.0 y	27.7 y	23.7 y	23.7 y	23.6 y	18.2 y	18.7 y	17.7 y
193	Senegal	6	10.7	10.7	10.6	12.4	12.4	12.4	12.1	12.1	12.2	14.3	14.1	14.5
194	Seychelles	6	.	.	.	.	.	.	.	.	.	.	.	.
195	Sierra Leone	6	...	...	...	...	...	...	...	...	...	...	...	...
196	Somalia	7	...	...	...	...	...	...	...	...	...	...	...	...
197	South Africa	7	9.2 **	9.5 **	9.0 **	...	...	...	...	...	...	...	...	...
198	Swaziland	7	18.6	21.1	15.9	15.3	18.4	11.8	17.7	20.9	14.2	15.6	18.0	13.0
199	Togo	6	28.9	29.2	28.6	23.1	22.8	23.4	25.0	24.4	25.8	20.4	19.5	21.4
200	Uganda	7	13.8	14.1	13.4	10.0	10.3	9.8	10.8	10.9	10.6	10.6	10.7	10.5
201	United Republic of Tanzania	7	**9.2** **	**9.2** **	**9.2** **	**7.0** **	**6.9** **	**7.0** **	**4.6** **	**4.4** **	**4.7** **	**12.1** **	**11.4** **	**12.8** **
202	Zambia	7	5.4 **	5.5 **	5.3 **	6.7 **	...	...	6.9 **	...	...	7.9 **	0.7	0.7
203	Zimbabwe	7	.	.	.	.	.	.	.	.	.	.	.	.
I	World[2]		4.0	4.6	3.4	2.6	2.7	2.6	2.1	2.5	1.6	2.7	3.0	2.5
II	Countries in transition		0.2	0.3	0.2	0.2	0.3	0.1	0.2	0.2	0.1	0.2	0.2	0.1
III	Developed countries		1.0	1.1	0.8	0.9	1.1	0.7	0.7	0.6	0.7	0.7	...	...
IV	Developing countries		7.6	8.7	6.5	5.4	7.4	3.3	5.4	6.0	4.8	5.4	6.3	4.5
V	Arab States		3.7	3.8	3.5	4.7	3.9	5.6	4.9	5.2	4.3	5.5	6.0	4.7
VI	Central and Eastern Europe		1.1	1.4	0.9	0.8	...	...	0.7	...	...	0.8	...	...
VII	Central Asia		0.1	0.2	0.1	0.2	0.2	0.1	0.2	0.2	0.1	0.2	0.3	0.1
VIII	East Asia and the Pacific		0.6	0.6	0.6	0.2	0.2	0.1	0.1	0.2	0.1	0.1	0.1	0.1
IX	Latin America and the Caribbean		8.1	9.3	6.8	5.0	...	...	5.2	5.7	4.7	4.1	4.7	3.5
X	North America and Western Europe		0.8	1.0	0.8	0.5	0.6	0.4	0.3	0.4	0.2	0.2	0.3	0.2
XI	South and West Asia		5.9	6.5	5.3	4.5	...	...	6.0	5.7	6.4	5.3	5.3	5.2
XII	Sub-Saharan Africa		16.8	17.0	15.9	15.3	18.4	11.8	15.3	14.4	16.5	17.9	17.6	18.2

1. Duration in this table is defined according to ISCED97 and may differ from that reported nationally.
2. All values shown are medians.
Data in bold are for 2002/2003 for repetition rates by grade, and 2003/2004 for percentage of repeaters (all grades).

(z) Data are for 2001/2002.
(y) Data are for 2000/2001.
(x) Data are for 1999/2000.

REPETITION RATES BY GRADE IN PRIMARY EDUCATION (%), 2001/2002									REPEATERS, ALL GRADES (%)						
Grade 5			Grade 6			Grade 7			1998/1999			2002/2003			
Total	Male	Female	Total	Male	Female	Total	Male	Female	Total	Male	Female	Total	Male	Female	
27.7**	27.4**	28.0**	19.3**	19.0**	19.6**	.	.	.	…	…	…	34.4**	35.1**	33.7**	175
…	…	…	…	…	…	.	.	.	10.6	10.7	10.5	…	…	…	176
…	…	…	…	…	…	.	.	.	4.2	4.3	4.1	5.9**	6.1**	5.7**	177
21.9	20.6	23.9	32.4	31.5	34.1	.	.	.	26.2	25.5	27.4	20.3	19.8	21.0	178
…	…	…	…	…	…	.	.	.	24.0**	23.6**	24.5**	…	…	…	179
9.6**	…	…	8.2**	…	…	11.1**	…	…	…	…	…	9.2**	9.7**	8.7**	180
14.7	17.1	12.6	12.6	13.9	11.6	11.9	11.4	12.2	20.3	23.3	17.4	21.2	23.8	18.6	181
…	…	…	…	…	…	.	.	.	…	…	…	…	…	…	182
31.1	31.1	31.1	.	.	.	.	.	.	28.3**	29.2**	27.4**	29.3	30.3	28.3	183
9.6	8.3	11.6	9.9	8.7	11.5	.	.	.	14.6	14.6	14.6	15.6	15.7	15.5	184
28.9	28.2	30.0	29.9	29.3	30.9	.	.	.	17.4	17.2	17.7	19.8	19.6	20.0	185
.	.	.	22.6	25.0	19.9	.	.	.	3.6	3.9	3.3	4.7	5.3	4.0	186
21.3	20.1	23.2	.	.	.	.	.	.	23.8**	23.3**	24.4**	23.2	22.9	23.6	187
18.7**	…	…	11.3**	…	…	10.2**	…	…	12.1	13.6	10.6	13.1**	14.6**	11.5**	188
12.5	11.9	13.4	27.9	27.3	28.7	.	.	.	12.2	12.4	11.8	7.3	7.2	7.5	189
…	…	…	…	…	…	.	.	.	…	…	…	2.6	2.5	2.6	190
19.8	19.2	20.4	20.8	20.4	21.1	.	.	.	29.1	29.2	29.0	16.5	16.7	16.4	191
18.5**,y	18.9**,y	18.2**,y	35.6**,y	37.1**,y	34.1**,y	.	.	.	30.7	32.6	28.7	25.8**,z	27.0**,z	24.5**,z	192
16.0	15.6	16.5	27.9	27.4	28.5	.	.	.	14.4	14.5**	14.2**	13.8	13.9	13.6	193
.	.	.	.	.	.	.	.	.	.	.	.	.	.	.	194
…	…	…	…	…	…	.	.	.	…	…	…	…	…	…	195
…	…	…	…	…	…	…	…	…	…	…	…	…	…	…	196
…	…	…	…	…	…	…	…	…	8.0*	9.0*	6.9*	7.4	8.5	6.3	197
14.0	15.3	12.7	13.3	14.2	12.5	8.5	9.0	8.0	15.3	17.7	12.8	15.5	17.5	13.2	198
21.5	20.6	22.7	19.0	17.6	21.0	.	.	.	31.2	30.9	31.6	23.7	23.2	24.3	199
10.5	10.4	10.7	11.0	10.8	11.1	8.9	9.7	7.8	…	…	…	10.5	10.8	10.3	200
0.4**	0.5**	0.3**	0.7**	0.7**	0.7**	0.01**	0.01**	0.01**	2.9	2.9	3.0	5.5**	5.4**	5.6**	201
7.9**	…	…	9.0**	…	…	…	…	…	5.8	6.1	5.6	7.6	8.0	7.1	202
.	.	.	.	.	.	.	.	.	.	.	.	.	.	.	203
1.4	…	…	1.1	1.4	0.7	.	.	.	3.6	3.8	3.5	3.0	3.4	2.5	I
.	.	.	.	.	.	.	.	.	0.5	0.5	0.5	0.2	0.2	0.1	II
.	.	.	–	–	–	.	.	.	1.2	1.5	1.0	0.8	0.9	0.7	III
4.1	4.2	4.1	3.5	3.9	3.2	.	.	.	6.5	7.1	5.8	6.2	6.5	6.0	IV
5.7	6.0	5.2	4.6	7.0	2.0	.	.	.	6.5	7.2	5.6	4.8	5.6	3.7	V
.	.	.	.	.	.	.	.	.	1.2	…	…	0.9	…	…	VI
.	.	.	.	.	.	.	.	.	0.3	0.5	0.2	0.2	0.2	0.1	VII
–	–	–	…	…	…	.	.	.	1.2	1.3	0.7	0.3	0.4	0.3	VIII
2.8	3.4	2.2	1.8	2.2	1.4	.	.	.	4.7	4.9	4.4	5.6	6.7	4.5	IX
…	…	…	…	…	…	.	.	.	0.4	0.5	0.3	0.3	0.3	0.2	X
4.8	5.3	4.4	…	…	…	.	.	.	6.7	6.9	6.5	4.9	5.0	4.8	XI
16.1	15.1	17.3	17.1	17.4	17.2	.	.	.	17.4	17.5	17.4	15.6	16.7	15.5	XII

Table 7. **Internal efficiency: survival in primary education and transition to secondary education**

Country or territory	Duration[1] of primary education 2002/2003	DROP-OUTS, ALL GRADES (%) 1998/1999 Total	Male	Female	2001/2002 Total	Male	Female	SURVIVAL RATE TO GRADE 5 (%) 1998/1999 Total	Male	Female	2001/2002 Total	Male	Female
Arab States													
Algeria	6	8.6	10.2	6.9	5.5	6.5	4.4	95.0	93.9	96.1	97.0	96.5	97.5
Bahrain	6	7.6**	8.7**	6.6**	1.3**	2.4**	–	97.4**	96.9**	97.9**	99.1**	98.2**	100.0**
Djibouti	6	...	...	...	...	...	...	76.7	71.2	84.9	80.2**	...	...
Egypt	5	...	...	...	2.0**	3.8**	–	...	...	...	98.0**	96.2**	100.0**
Iraq	6	50.6**	48.7**	52.8**	...	...	...	65.6**	67.4**	63.3**	...	...	...
Jordan	6	3.1	3.0	3.2	4.2	4.7	3.6	97.7	98.0	97.4	97.1	96.6	97.7
Kuwait	4	6.0	7.1	4.9	2.5	3.8	1.2	...	...	...	...	...	...
Lebanon	6	8.7	11.8	5.2	11.5	14.6	8.4	91.3	88.2	94.8	91.9	89.9	94.0
Libyan Arab Jamahiriya	6	...	...	...	...	...	...	...	...	...	...	...	...
Mauritania	6	42.9**	40.1**	45.8**	51.3	50.6	52.0	65.2**	67.9**	62.4**	60.6	60.8	60.3
Morocco	6	25.0	25.4	24.5	24.5	24.0	25.1	81.9	81.7	82.0	81.2	82.0	80.4
Oman	6	8.1	8.3	7.9	2.7	2.7	2.6	93.7	93.7	93.8	98.0	97.9	98.1
Palestinian A.T.	4	0.6	–	1.2	2.1	2.3	1.8	...	...	...	...	...	...
Qatar	6	...	...	...	...	...	...	...	...	...	...	...	...
Saudi Arabia	6	6.8	7.1	6.5	10.9	9.5	12.3	95.3	95.2	95.4	91.5	92.3	90.7
Sudan	6	22.9**	26.4**	18.5**	16.4	19.6	12.3	84.1**	80.7**	88.4**	84.3	81.0	88.4
Syrian Arab Republic	6	13.1	12.9	13.2	10.4	10.7	10.1	91.8	92.0	91.5	91.4	90.7	92.3
Tunisia	6	12.9	14.0	11.7	6.9	7.8	5.8	92.1	91.4	92.9	96.2	95.6	96.7
United Arab Emirates	5	10.3	9.9	10.7	7.5	7.4	7.5	92.4	92.8	91.9	92.5	92.6	92.5
Yemen	6	...	...	...	29.9	26.0	35.6	...			75.9	79.6	70.7
Central and Eastern Europe													
Albania	4	...	...	...	10.0x	13.5x	6.2x	...	...	...	...	...	...
Belarus	4	0.8	1.0	0.6	1.5	2.2	0.7	...	...	...	...	...	...
Bosnia and Herzegovina	4	...	...	...	...	...	...	...	...	...	...	...	...
Bulgaria	4	7.1	7.4	6.7	6.1	5.9	6.4	...	...	...	...	...	...
Croatia	4	0.3	0.6	–	0.4	0.9	–	...	...	...	...	...	...
Czech Republic	5	1.7	2.0	1.4	2.3	2.7	1.9	98.3	98.0	98.6	97.7	97.3	98.1
Estonia	6	1.5	2.2	0.7	2.3	2.9	1.6	99.1	98.6	99.5	98.4	97.6	99.2
Hungary	4	...	...	...	2.4	3.0	1.8	...	...	...	...	...	...
Latvia	4	3.0	3.4	2.6	2.2	1.9	2.5	...	...	...	...	...	...
Lithuania	4	0.7	1.3	–	2.1	1.9	2.4	...	...	...	...	...	...
Poland	6	1.7	...	...	0.8	...	...	98.6	...	...	99.3	...	...
Republic of Moldova	4	4.6	...	...	8.9	9.1	8.7	...	...	...	...	...	...
Romania	4	4.3	5.0	3.6	4.8	4.9	4.5	...	...	...	...	...	...
Russian Federation	3	...	...	...	0.8y	...	...	...	...	...	...	...	...
Serbia and Montenegro	4	...	...	...	4.4**,x	5.2**,x	3.5**,x	...	...	...	...	...	...
Slovakia	4	3.1	3.7	2.4	2.1	1.6	2.7	...	...	...	...	...	...
Slovenia	4	...	...	...	1.1	1.6	0.7	...	...	...	...	...	...
TFYR Macedonia	4	2.5	4.2	0.7	4.1	4.6	3.6	...	...	...	...	...	...
Turkey	6	...	...	...	...	...	...	...	...	...	...	...	...
Ukraine	4	4.0**	...	...	1.4y	1.1**,y	1.8**,y	...	...	...	...	...	...
Central Asia													
Armenia	3	...	...	...	3.7	3.8	3.6	...	...	...	...	...	...
Azerbaijan	4	1.6	2.5	0.6	3.4	2.1	4.7	...	...	...	...	...	...
Georgia	4	0.6	1.2	–	1.8	0.8	2.9	...	...	...	...	...	...
Kazakhstan	4	...	...	...	1.8	2.2	1.4	...	...	...	...	...	...
Kyrgyzstan	4	5.5*	4.9*	6.1*	6.5	7.9	5.1	...	...	...	...	...	...
Mongolia	4	12.8	15.3	10.3	8.0	8.2	7.7	...	...	...	...	...	...
Tajikistan	4	3.3	0.3**	6.4**	1.1	–	2.3**	...	...	...	...	...	...
Turkmenistan	3	...	...	...	...	...	...	...	...	...	...	...	...
Uzbekistan	4	...	...	...	3.9**	3.7**	4.2**	...	...	...	...	...	...
East Asia and the Pacific													
Australia	7	...	...			...	...	...			...		
Brunei Darussalam	6	...	...	...	...	...	...	...			[illegible]	[illegible]	93.7y
Cambodia	6	51.4**	48.1**	55.0**	45.0	45.8	44.1	56.3**	58.3**	54.0**	60.9	59.6	62.3
China	5	2.7	2.9	2.4	1.0	–	2.0**	97.3	97.1	97.6	99.0	100.0**	98.0**
Cook Islands	6	53.1	50.0	56.7	...	...	...	51.5	55.7	46.8	...	...	...
DPR Korea	4	...	...	...	...	...	...	...			...	...	...
Fiji	6	16.7**	18.3**	14.8**	15.2**,y	20.1**,y	9.6**,y	92.0**	90.5**	93.7**	88.5**,y	85.2**,y	92.1**,y

SURVIVAL RATE TO LAST GRADE (%)						TRANSITION TO SECONDARY EDUCATION (%)						
1998/1999			2001/2002			1998/1999			2001/2002			
Total	Male	Female	Total	Male	Female	Total	Male	Female	Total	Male	Female	Country or territory
												Arab States
91.4	89.8	93.1	94.5	93.5	95.6	71.9**	68.3**	76.1**	79.4	76.3	83.0	Algeria
92.4**	91.3**	93.4**	98.7**	97.6**	100.0**	98.5**	97.2**	100.0**	96.9**	95.3**	98.6**	Bahrain
...	...	...	...	...	...	42.3	42.6	41.9	58.0**	58.8**	57.0**	Djibouti
...	...	...	98.0**	96.2**	100.0**	...	...	...	84.3**	82.6**	86.3**	Egypt
49.4**	51.3**	47.2**	...	...	...	72.6**	78.9**	64.2**	...	...	...	Iraq
96.9	97.0	96.8	95.8	95.3	96.4	97.1	97.1	97.2	97.4	96.6	98.2	Jordan
94.0	92.9	95.1	97.5	96.2	98.8	96.7	97.4	96.1	98.9	97.8	100.0	Kuwait
91.3	88.2	94.8	88.5	85.4	91.6	85.4	83.7	87.1	86.1	83.5	88.9	Lebanon
...	...	...	...	...	...	...	...	...	...	...	...	Libyan Arab Jamahiriya
57.1**	59.9**	54.2**	48.7	49.4	48.0	40.6	42.5	38.5	47.3	50.5	44.0	Mauritania
75.0	74.6	75.5	75.5	76.0	74.9	80.7	79.3	82.8	79.2	78.2	80.5	Morocco
91.9	91.7	92.1	97.3	97.3	97.4	94.6	92.7	96.6	99.4	100.0	98.7	Oman
99.4	100.0	98.8	97.9	97.7	98.2	96.5	95.6	97.5	96.7	96.6	96.7	Palestinian A.T.
...	...	...	...	...	...	...	...	...	95.5**,x	91.4**,x	100.0**,x	Qatar
93.2	92.9	93.5	89.1	90.5	87.7	96.9	100.0	93.6	98.4	99.5	97.3	Saudi Arabia
77.1**	73.6**	81.5**	83.6	80.4	87.7	78.3**	...	...	90.4	90.5	90.2	Sudan
86.9	87.1	86.8	89.6	89.3	89.9	68.5	70.0	66.8	76.6	77.0	76.2	Syrian Arab Republic
87.1	86.0	88.3	93.1	92.2	94.2	68.0**	66.6**	69.6**	87.8	85.7	90.1	Tunisia
89.7	90.1	89.3	92.5	92.6	92.5	96.0	94.6	97.5	97.7	96.1	99.5	United Arab Emirates
...	...	...	70.1	74.0	64.4	...	...	...	...	...	...	Yemen
												Central and Eastern Europe
...	...	...	90.0x	86.5x	93.8x	93.0**	92.8**	93.3**	94.0x	93.2x	94.9x	Albania
99.2	99.0	99.4	98.5	97.8	99.3	99.9	99.7	100.0	99.9	100.0	99.8	Belarus
...	...	...	...	...	...	...	...	...	...	...	...	Bosnia and Herzegovina
92.9	92.6	93.3	93.9	94.1	93.6	...	...	...	95.8	96.2	95.3	Bulgaria
99.7	99.4	100.0	99.6	99.1	100.0	99.9	100.0	99.8	99.9	99.8	100.0	Croatia
98.3	98.0	98.6	97.7	97.3	98.1	...	...	...	99.1	99.0	99.1	Czech Republic
98.5	97.8	99.3	97.7	97.1	98.4	95.7	93.4	98.1	95.7	93.2	98.4	Estonia
...	...	...	97.6	97.0	98.2	99.3	99.9	98.6	98.8	98.6	99.0	Hungary
97.0	96.6	97.4	97.8	98.1	97.5	98.3	98.0	98.8	98.8	98.6	98.9	Latvia
99.3	98.7	100.0	97.9	98.1	97.6	100.0	99.9	100.0	98.9	99.1	98.7	Lithuania
98.3	...	...	99.2	...	...	100.0	...	...	98.3	...	...	Poland
95.4	...	...	91.1	90.9	91.3	99.0	99.0**	99.0**	98.0	97.4	98.6	Republic of Moldova
95.7	95.0	96.4	95.2	95.1	95.5	...	...	...	97.7	97.5	98.0	Romania
...	...	...	99.2y	...	...	...	...	...	90.0	...	...	Russian Federation
...	...	...	95.6**,x	94.8**,x	96.5**,x	...	...	...	...	...	...	Serbia and Montenegro
96.9	96.3	97.6	97.9	98.4	97.3	98.6**	98.5**	98.8**	98.2	98.1	98.3	Slovakia
...	...	...	98.9	98.4	99.3	...	...	...	99.3	99.2	99.5	Slovenia
97.5	95.8	99.3	95.9	95.4	96.4	99.0	99.8	98.1	97.7	98.0	97.3	TFYR Macedonia
...	...	...	...	...	...	...	...	...	...	...	...	Turkey
96.0**	...	...	98.6**,y	98.9**,y	98.2**,y	100.0**	...	...	99.4y	98.9**,y	100.0**,y	Ukraine
												Central Asia
...	...	...	96.3	96.2	96.4	...	...	...	97.9	98.6	97.1	Armenia
98.4	97.5	99.4	96.6	97.9	95.3	97.5	96.4	98.6	97.8	98.1	97.3	Azerbaijan
99.4	98.8	100.0	98.2	99.2	97.1	98.3	97.5	99.1	98.3	98.1	98.5	Georgia
...	...	...	98.2	97.8	98.6	...	...	...	99.4	99.5	99.4	Kazakhstan
94.5*	95.1*	93.9*	93.5	92.1	94.9	98.5*	97.1*	100.0*	98.4	96.8	100.0	Kyrgyzstan
87.2	84.7	89.7	92.0	91.8	92.3	94.4	92.5	96.4	99.0	98.3	99.6	Mongolia
96.7	99.7**	93.6**	98.9	100.0**	97.7**	97.1	97.2**	96.9**	98.2	99.7**	96.6**	Tajikistan
...	...	...	...	...	...	...	...	...	...	...	...	Turkmenistan
...	...	...	96.1**	96.3**	95.8**	...	...	...	99.6**	100.0**	99.2**	Uzbekistan
												East Asia and the Pacific
...	...	...	...	...	...	...	...	...	...	...	...	Australia
...	...	...	...	...	...	96.6	97.6	95.5	93.3	93.4	93.1	Brunei Darussalam
48.6**	51.9**	45.0**	55.0	54.2	55.9	77.4**	81.8**	71.4**	83.2	86.4	79.3	Cambodia
97.3	97.1	97.6	99.0	100.0**	98.0**	...	...	...	91.6	91.6**	91.6**	China
46.9	50.0	43.3	...	...	...	87.7	94.0	81.6	...	...	...	Cook Islands
...	...	...	...	...	...	...	...	...	...	...	...	DPR Korea
83.3**	81.7**	85.2**	84.8**,y	79.9**,y	90.4**,y	95.8**	97.8**	93.7**	98.4**,y	100.0**,y	96.6**,y	Fiji

Table 7 (continued)

Country or territory	Duration[1] of primary education	DROP-OUTS, ALL GRADES (%)						SURVIVAL RATE TO GRADE 5 (%)					
		1998/1999			2001/2002			1998/1999			2001/2002		
	2002/2003	Total	Male	Female	Total	Male	Female	Total	Male	Female	Total	Male	Female
Indonesia	6	…	…	…	13.6	14.3	12.9	…	…	…	89.1	88.3	89.9
Japan	6	…	…	…	…	…	…	…	…	…	…	…	…
Kiribati	6	…	…	…	…	…	…	…	…	…	…	…	…
Lao PDR	5	45.7	45.1	46.4	35.9	36.4	35.3	54.3	54.9	53.6	64.1	63.6	64.7
Macao, China	6	…	…	…	…	…	…	…	…	…	99.7	99.4	100.0
Malaysia	6	…	…	…	15.7	15.9	15.5	…	…	…	87.1	86.9	87.3
Marshall Islands	6	…	…	…	…	…	…	…	…	…	…	…	…
Micronesia (Federated States of)	6	…	…	…	…	…	…	…	…	…	…	…	…
Myanmar	5	…	…	…	35.4	36.3	34.4	…	…	…	64.6	63.7	65.6
Nauru	6	…	…	…	…	…	…	…	…	…	…	…	…
New Zealand	6	…	…	…	…	…	…	…	…	…	…	…	…
Niue	6	…	…	…	…	…	…	75.8	…	…	…	…	…
Palau	5	15.8	7.8	24.2	…	…	…	84.2	92.2	75.8	…	…	…
Papua New Guinea	6	38.6	38.5	38.8	56.2[y]	55.3[y]	57.3[y]	68.0	67.8	68.2	50.6[y]	51.5[y]	49.5[y]
Philippines	6	…	…	…	26.6	31.2	21.5	…	…	…	76.0	72.2	80.2
Republic of Korea	6	0.2	–	0.4	**0.1**	**0.2**	**–**	99.9	100.0	99.7	**99.9**	**99.8**	**100.0**
Samoa	6	19.8	…	…	…	…	…	82.6	…	…	93.8[y]	96.0[y]	91.5[y]
Singapore	6	…	…	…	…	…	…	…	…	…	…	…	…
Solomon Islands	6	…	…	…	…	…	…	…	…	…	…	…	…
Thailand	6	8.1**	10.3**	5.8**	…	…	…	94.1**	92.3**	96.0**	…	…	…
Timor-Leste	6	…	…	…	…	…	…	…	…	…	…	…	…
Tokelau	6	…	…	…	…	…	…	…	…	…	…	…	…
Tonga	6	…	…	…	…	…	…	…	…	…	…	…	…
Tuvalu	6	…	…	…	…	…	…	…	…	…	…	…	…
Vanuatu	6	9.9**	…	…	31.1[x]	33.0[x]	29.0[x]	95.3**	…	…	72.1[x]	72.4[x]	71.8[x]
Viet Nam	5	17.2	20.1	13.8	12.9**	12.6**	13.3**	82.8	79.9	86.2	87.1**	87.4**	86.7**
Latin America and the Caribbean													
Anguilla	7	…	…	…	…	…	…	…	…	…	…	…	…
Antigua and Barbuda	7	…	…	…	…	…	…	…	…	…	…	…	…
Argentina	6	7.7	9.5	5.8	10.1	11.7	8.4	94.7	93.3	96.1	92.2	91.1	93.4
Aruba	6	…	…	…	6.0	7.9	4.1	96.8	97.4	96.2	95.0	93.9	96.1
Bahamas	6	…	…	…	35.2**	…	…	…	…	…	75.2**	…	…
Barbados	6	…	…	…	3.2[y]	…	…	94.1	96.4	91.8	98.8	99.9	97.7
Belize	6	23.1	22.5	23.7	20.5[x]	21.4[x]	19.5[x]	77.8	76.2	79.5	81.5[x]	81.5[x]	81.5[x]
Bermuda	6	…	…	…	4.8[y]			…	…	…	96.3[y]	…	…
Bolivia	6	22.8	20.4	25.3	17.7	15.8	19.7	79.4	80.4	78.3	84.4	85.2	83.7
Brazil	4	…	…	…	20.1[y]	24.2**,[y]	15.5**,[y]	…	…	…	…	…	…
British Virgin Islands	7	…	…	…	…	…	…	…	…	…	…	…	…
Cayman Islands	6	…	…	…	…	…	…	…	…	…	…	…	…
Chile	6	0.5	1.0	–	**1.3**	**0.8**	**1.8**	99.8	99.6	100.0	**99.2**	**100.0**	**98.4**
Colombia	5	36.6	43.8	27.8	30.6	33.7	27.2	63.4	56.2	72.2	69.4	66.3	72.8
Costa Rica	6	…	…	…	11.6	13.0	10.1	…	…	…	91.6	90.2	93.1
Cuba	6	7.4	7.8	7.0	2.7	3.0	2.3	93.7	93.6	93.9	97.9	97.9	97.9
Dominica	7	…	…	…	21.3	25.1	17.2	…	…	…	83.7	80.3	87.2
Dominican Republic	6	29.4**	33.7**	24.8**	38.5**	…	…	75.1**	71.4**	79.1**	69.1**		
Ecuador	6	25.4	25.7	25.1	27.9	28.6	27.2	77.0	76.8	77.2	74.4	73.9	75.0
El Salvador	6	39.6**	39.8**	39.4**	34.7	36.7	32.6	61.3**	60.4**	62.3**	68.9	67.1	70.8
Grenada	7	…	…	…	…	…	…	…	…	…	79.0	73.0	85.4
Guatemala	6	45.2**	41.7**	49.0**	39.6	38.1	41.3	60.4**	64.1**	56.4**	65.2	66.6	63.6
Guyana	6	7.3	…	…	34.9[x]	38.5[x]	31.1[x]	97.4	…	…	77.2[x]	71.1[x]	84.0[x]
Haiti	6	…	…	…	…	…	…	…	…	…	…	…	…
Honduras	6	…	…	…	…	…	…	…	…	…	…	…	…
Jamaica	6	…	…	…	15.1	…	…	…	…	…	89.7	…	…
Mexico	6	12.8	14.0	11.5	8.7	9.6	7.7	89.0	88.0	90.0	93.0	92.3	93.7
Montserrat	7	…	…	…	…	…	…	…	…	…	…	…	…
Netherlands Antilles	0		…	…	16.9[y]	…	…	…	…	…	88.5[y]	…	…
Nicaragua	6	…	…	…	36.1	38.6	33.0			…	64.8	62.5	67.3
Panama	6	…	…	…	12.0	13.2	10.7	…	…	…	89.8	89.0	90.6
Paraguay	6	36.4**	37.7**	35.0**	36.4**	38.2**	34.6**	70.0**	68.9**	71.2**	69.7**	68.3**	71.2**
Peru	6	14.8	14.5	15.1	21.9	20.6	23.3	87.9	88.2	87.6	83.6	84.5	82.7
Saint Kitts and Nevis	7	…	…	…	27.5[y]	24.3[y]	29.8[y]	…	…	…	78.4[y]	74.5[y]	83.3[y]
Saint Lucia	7	…	…	…	…	…	…	90.1**	…	…	96.6[y]	…	…

SURVIVAL RATE TO LAST GRADE (%)						TRANSITION TO SECONDARY EDUCATION (%)						
1998/1999			2001/2002			1998/1999			2001/2002			
Total	Male	Female	Total	Male	Female	Total	Male	Female	Total	Male	Female	Country or territory
...	...	...	86.4	85.7	87.1	...	...	...	81.5	80.2	82.8	Indonesia
...	...	...	...	...	...	...	...	...	...	...	...	Japan
...	...	...	...	...	...	...	...	...	...	...	...	Kiribati
54.3	54.9	53.6	64.1	63.6	64.7	71.0	73.5	67.8	78.7	81.2	75.6	Lao PDR
...	...	...	...	...	...	84.2	83.3	85.2	89.8	87.2	92.5	Macao, China
...	...	...	84.3	84.1	84.5	...	...	...	99.7[y]	100.0[y]	99.5[y]	Malaysia
...	...	...	...	...	...	...	...	...	...	...	...	Marshall Islands
...	...	...	...	...	...	...	...	...	...	...	...	Micronesia (Federated States of)
...	...	...	64.6	63.7	65.6	68.2	65.9	70.6	69.9	73.9	65.8	Myanmar
...	...	...	...	...	...	...	...	...	...	...	...	Nauru
...	...	...	...	...	...	...	...	...	...	...	...	New Zealand
...	...	...	...	...	...	91.5	92.0	90.9	...	...	...	Niue
84.2	92.2	75.8	...	...	...	...	...	...	...	...	...	Palau
61.4	61.5	61.2	43.8[y]	44.7[y]	42.7[y]	70.3	70.9	69.4	74.4[**,y]	75.2[**,y]	73.5[**,y]	Papua New Guinea
...	...	...	73.4	68.8	78.5	...	...	...	97.5	98.2	96.8	Philippines
99.8	100.0	99.6	**99.9**	**99.8**	**100.0**	100.0	...	...	**99.1**	**99.0**	**99.2**	Republic of Korea
80.2	...	...	...	...	...	91.9	92.1	91.8	97.5[y]	95.7[y]	99.4[y]	Samoa
...	...	...	...	...	...	...	...	...	...	...	...	Singapore
...	...	...	...	...	...	...	...	...	...	...	...	Solomon Islands
91.9[**]	89.7[**]	94.2[**]	...	...	...	88.0[**]	86.8[**]	89.2[**]	91.7[**,y]	91.2[**,y]	92.2[**,y]	Thailand
...	...	...	...	...	...	...	...	...	82.1[**,y]	...	...	Timor-Leste
...	...	...	...	...	...	...	...	...	...	...	...	Tokelau
...	...	...	...	...	...	79.9	75.7	85.0	78.9[**,y]	80.1[**,y]	77.6[**,y]	Tonga
...	...	...	...	...	...	...	...	...	...	...	...	Tuvalu
90.1[**]	...	...	68.9[x]	67.0[x]	71.0[x]	...	...	...	42.7[y]	42.0[y]	43.4[y]	Vanuatu
82.8	79.9	86.2	87.1[**]	87.4[**]	86.7[**]	92.9	...	...	99.7[**]	99.4[**]	100.0[**]	Viet Nam
												Latin America and the Caribbean
...	...	...	...	...	...	...	...	...	...	...	...	Anguilla
...	...	...	...	...	...	...	...	...	...	...	...	Antigua and Barbuda
92.3	90.5	94.2	89.9	88.3	91.6	94.1[**]	92.7[**]	95.5[**]	93.9	92.7	95.0	Argentina
...	...	...	94.0	92.1	95.9	99.3	98.7	100.0	97.3	96.7	97.8	Aruba
...	...	...	64.8[**]	...	...	...	...	...	79.4[**]	81.0[**]	77.9[**]	Bahamas
...	...	...	96.8[y]	...	...	99.1	98.2	100.0	99.5	100.0	98.9	Barbados
76.9	77.5	76.3	79.5[x]	78.6[x]	80.5[x]	86.2	83.1	89.6	87.6[**]	87.2[**]	88.1[**]	Belize
...	...	...	95.2[y]	...	...	...	...	...	100.0[y]	...	...	Bermuda
77.2	79.6	74.7	82.3	84.2	80.3	89.6	88.8	90.5	89.8	88.8	90.8	Bolivia
...	...	...	79.9[y]	75.8[**,y]	84.5[**,y]	...	...	...	88.7[**]	...	...	Brazil
...	...	...	...	...	...	100.0	...	...	69.8[**,y]	62.6[**,y]	77.5[**,y]	British Virgin Islands
...	...	...	...	...	...	98.6[*]	100.0[*]	97.4[*]	90.8[y]	89.0[y]	92.9[y]	Cayman Islands
99.5	99.0	100.0	**98.7**	**99.2**	**98.2**	95.5[**]	94.2[**]	96.8[**]	**96.5**	**95.3**	**97.7**	Chile
63.4	56.2	72.2	69.4	66.3	72.8	94.2	94.3	94.1	92.3[**]	92.4[**]	92.2[**]	Colombia
...	...	...	88.4	87.0	89.9	79.5[**]	79.8[**]	79.2[**]	86.2	87.1	85.3	Costa Rica
92.6	92.2	93.0	97.3	97.0	97.7	94.3	92.4	96.2	97.9	97.5	98.3	Cuba
...	...	...	78.7	74.9	82.8	89.2	90.3	88.3	96.5	95.8	97.4	Dominica
70.6[**]	66.3[**]	75.2[**]	61.5[**]	...	...	87.8[**]	85.3[**]	90.2[**]	75.6[**]	72.4[**]	78.6[**]	Dominican Republic
74.6	74.3	74.9	72.1	71.4	72.8	68.3[*]	70.3[*]	66.3[*]	72.9	75.0	70.8	Ecuador
60.4[**]	60.2[**]	60.6[**]	65.3	63.3	67.4	...	...	...	92.9	93.4	92.5	El Salvador
...	...	...	...	...	...	...	...	...	...	...	...	Grenada
54.8[**]	58.3[**]	51.0[**]	60.4	61.9	58.7	84.0[**]	85.1[**]	82.6[**]	94.2	94.8	93.5	Guatemala
92.7	...	...	65.1[x]	61.5[x]	68.9[x]	67.6	64.7	70.7	...	...	...	Guyana
...	...	...	...	...	...	...	...	...	...	...	...	Haiti
...	...	...	...	...	...	...	...	...	...	...	...	Honduras
...	...	...	84.9	...	...	...	...	...	97.1	...	...	Jamaica
87.2	86.0	88.5	91.3	90.4	92.3	...	...	...	92.9	94.0	91.7	Mexico
...	...	...	...	...	...	...	...	...	...	...	...	Montserrat
...	...	...	83.1[y]	...	...	51.1	46.8	55.0	55.1[**]	52.6[**]	57.3[**]	Netherlands Antilles
...	...	...	63.9	61.4	66.5	...	...	...	...	...	...	Nicaragua
...	...	...	88.0	86.8	89.3	...	...	...	56.7[**]	55.5[**]	58.0[**]	Panama
63.6[**]	62.3[**]	65.0[**]	63.6[**]	61.8[**]	65.4[**]	87.1[**]	86.8[**]	87.4[**]	88.6[**]	89.0[**]	88.2[**]	Paraguay
85.2	85.5	84.9	78.1	79.4	76.7	92.5	93.6	91.3	94.0	95.7	92.2	Peru
...	...	...	72.5[y]	...	...	...	...	...	100.0[x]	...	...	Saint Kitts and Nevis
...	...	...	...	...	...	67.5[**]	57.4[**]	77.2[**]	65.7[**]	56.6[**]	74.6[**]	Saint Lucia

Table 7 (continued)

Country or territory	Duration[1] of primary education 2002/2003	DROP-OUTS, ALL GRADES (%) 1998/1999 Total	Male	Female	2001/2002 Total	Male	Female	SURVIVAL RATE TO GRADE 5 (%) 1998/1999 Total	Male	Female	2001/2002 Total	Male	Female
Saint Vincent/Grenad.	7	…	…	…	20.9	…	…	…	…	…	88.0	…	…
Suriname	6	…	…	…	…	…	…	…	…	…	…	…	…
Trinidad and Tobago	7	…	…	…	41.3**,y	44.7**,y	38.4**,y	100.0	…	…	71.2**,y	66.5**,y	76.2**,y
Turks and Caicos Islands	6	…	…	…	55.2	…	…	…	…	…	45.9	41.8	51.4
Uruguay	6	13.0	17.4	8.3	7.9	9.8	5.9	88.3	85.7	91.1	92.9	91.3	94.5
Venezuela	6	11.9	15.7	7.9	19.6	22.9	16.1	90.8	87.6	94.3	84.2	81.5	87.1
North America and Western Europe													
Andorra	6	…	…	…	…	…	…	…	…	…	…	…	…
Austria	4	…	…	…	6.1**,x	7.5**,x	4.7**,x	…	…	…	…	…	…
Belgium	6	…	…	…	…	…	…	…	…	…	…	…	…
Canada	6	…	…	…	…	…	…	…	…	…	…	…	…
Cyprus	6	4.0	5.3	2.6	…	…	…	96.1	94.8	97.4	99.3	98.6	100.0
Denmark	6	–	–	–	…	…	…	100.0	100.0	100.0	…	…	…
Finland	6	0.1	–	0.2	…	…	…	99.8	100.0	99.7	99.9	99.8	100.0
France	5	2.0	1.6**	2.5**	…	…	…	98.0	98.4**	97.5**	…	…	…
Germany	4	0.5	0.8	0.2	1.0	1.6	0.4	…	…	…	…	…	…
Greece	6	…	…	…	…	…	…	…	…	…	…	…	…
Iceland	7	…	…	…	0.4	…	…	99.8	100.0	99.7	99.7	100.0	99.4
Ireland	8	…	…	…	…	…	…	95.1	93.7	96.6	99.2	98.4	100.0
Israel	6	…	…	…	18.7**	18.3**	19.2**	…	…	…	85.2**	85.7**	84.7**
Italy	5	3.4	…	…	3.5y	4.0y	3.0y	96.6	…	…	96.5y	96.0y	97.0y
Luxembourg	6	…	…	…	12.4**,y	13.2**,y	11.7**,y	…	…	…	99.0**,y	99.2**,y	98.7**,y
Malta	6	–	…	…	1.0	1.4	0.5	99.4	100.0	98.8	99.3	98.8	99.9
Monaco	5	…	…	…	…	…	…	…			…		
Netherlands	6	0.2	–	0.5	…	…	…	99.9	99.8	100.0	99.8	99.7	100.0
Norway	7	…	…	…	0.6	–	1.3	…	…	…	99.5	100.0	99.1
Portugal	6	…	…	…	…	…	…	…	…	…	…	…	…
San Marino	5	…	…	…	…	…	…	…	…	…	…	…	…
Spain	6	…	…	…	…	…	…	…	…	…	…	…	…
Sweden	6	…	…	…	…	…	…	…	…	…	…	…	…
Switzerland	6	…	…	…	…	…	…	…	…	…	…	…	…
United Kingdom	6	…	…	…	…	…	…	…	…	…	…	…	…
United States	6	…	…	…	…	…	…	…	…	…	…	…	…
South and West Asia													
Afghanistan	6	…	…	…	…	…	…	…			…		
Bangladesh	5	45.3	49.9	40.0	46.1	50.7	41.0	54.7	50.1	60.0	53.9	49.3	59.0
Bhutan	7	23.6	25.6	21.1	18.7y	22.0y	14.9y	87.5	86.3	88.8	91.0y	89.2y	93.2y
India	5	38.0	36.7	39.6	38.6y	40.3y	36.5y	62.0	63.3	60.4	61.4y	59.7y	63.5y
Iran, Islamic Republic of	5	…	…	…	5.4**	…	…	…	…	…	94.6**	…	…
Maldives	7	…	…	…	…	…	…	…	…	…	…	…	…
Nepal	5	…	…	…	35.1	36.7	33.1	…	…	…	64.9	63.3	66.9
Pakistan	5	…	…	…	…	…	…	…	…	…	…		
Sri Lanka	5	…	…	…	**1.6****	**2.1****	**1.1****	…	…	…	**98.4****	**97.9****	**98.9****
Sub-Saharan Africa													
Angola	4	…	…	…	…	…	…	…	…	…	…		
Benin	6	…	…	…	41.4	38.5	45.7	…	…	…	68.3	70.3	65.6
Botswana	7	17.7	21.9	13.1	19.1**	23.1**	14.8**	87.6	84.2	91.1	87.6**	84.9**	90.5**
Burkina Faso	6	39.1	40.6	36.7	40.5**	42.5**	37.6**	68.3	66.9	70.4	66.2**	64.9**	68.2**
Burundi	6	…	…	…	37.6	38.9	35.9	…	…	…	67.5	65.8	69.7
Cameroon	6	22.3**	…	…	41.2**	40.4**	42.1**	80.7**	…	…	63.7**	63.9**	63.5**
Cape Verde	6	…	…	…	15.2	14.3	16.3	…	…	…	88.0	87.6	88.2
Central African Republic	6	…	…	…	…	…	…	…	…	…	…	…	…
Chad	6	53.2	49.8	59.1	67.3**	60.5**	76.7**	55.1	58.1	50.0	44.3**	50.8**	35.4**
Comoros	[illegible]		…	…	34.5**,x	…	…	…	…	…	71.7**,x	69.1**,x	74.8**,x
Congo	6	…	…	…	44.6	44.7	44.0		…	…	66.3	65.4	67.2
Côte d'Ivoire	6	38.1	33.3	44.4	14.4**,x	12.2**,x	17.8**,x	69.1	72.6	64.6	87.6**,x	88.3 [illegible]	[illegible]
Democratic Rep. of the Congo	6	…	…	…	…	…	…	…	…	…	…	…	…
Equatorial Guinea	5	…	…	…	70.5**,y	66.4**,y	75.0**,y	…	…	…	29.5**,y	33.6**,y	25.0**,y
Eritrea	5	4.7	2.5	7.2	13.7	10.5	17.9	95.3	97.5	92.8	86.3	89.5	82.1
Ethiopia	6	50.6	51.6	48.5	**46.7****	**45.6****	**47.9****	55.8	55.2	57.0	**61.5****	**63.0****	**59.7****

SURVIVAL RATE TO LAST GRADE (%)						TRANSITION TO SECONDARY EDUCATION (%)						
1998/1999			2001/2002			1998/1999			2001/2002			
Total	Male	Female	Total	Male	Female	Total	Male	Female	Total	Male	Female	Country or territory
...	...	...	79.1	...	...	...	...	...	51.1	44.2	57.8	Saint Vincent/Grenad.
...	...	...	...	...	...	...	...	...	12.5**	15.2**	10.0**	Suriname
...	...	...	58.7**,y	55.3**,y	61.6**,y	95.8	94.3	97.3	97.6**	...	...	Trinidad and Tobago
...	...	...	44.8	...	...	49.4	40.0	59.4	71.6	72.0	71.1	Turks and Caicos Islands
87.0	82.6	91.7	92.1	90.2	94.1	...	...	...	81.7	76.0	87.5	Uruguay
88.1	84.3	92.1	80.4	77.1	83.9	94.2	94.4	94.1	96.6	96.5	96.7	Venezuela
												North America and Western Europe
...	...	...	...	...	...	...	...	...	94.2	93.4	95.1	Andorra
...	...	...	93.9**,x	92.5**,x	95.3**,x	...	...	...	...	...	...	Austria
...	...	...	...	...	...	...	...	...	...	...	...	Belgium
...	...	...	...	...	...	...	...	...	...	...	...	Canada
96.0	94.7	97.4	...	...	...	99.8	99.7	100.0	99.4	99.8	98.9	Cyprus
...	...	...	...	...	...	99.9	99.9	100.0	99.6	100.0	99.1	Denmark
...	...	...	...	...	...	99.7	99.5	100.0	99.9	100.0	99.8	Finland
98.0	98.4**	97.5**	...	...	...	98.7**	99.1**	98.3**	98.9x	...	...	France
99.5	99.2	99.8	99.0	98.4	99.6	99.6	99.6	99.6	99.7y	100.0y	99.4y	Germany
...	...	...	...	...	...	...	...	...	...	...	...	Greece
...	...	...	99.6	...	...	99.8	100.0	99.5	99.6	99.2	100.0	Iceland
...	...	...	...	...	...	99.0	98.1	100.0	100.0	...	...	Ireland
...	...	...	81.3**	81.7**	80.8**	...	...	...	69.2**	69.1**	69.3**	Israel
96.6	...	...	96.5y	96.0y	97.0y	96.6	93.4	100.0	99.9	100.0	99.8	Italy
...	...	...	87.6**,y	86.8**,y	88.3**,y	...	...	...	...	...	...	Luxembourg
...	...	...	99.0	98.6	99.5	...	...	...	90.7	89.6	92.0	Malta
...	...	...	...	...	...	...	...	...	...	...	...	Monaco
99.8	...	...	...	...	...	...	...	...	98.9x	97.9x	100.0x	Netherlands
...	...	...	99.4	100.0	98.7	...	...	...	...	...	...	Norway
...	...	...	...	...	...	...	...	...	...	...	...	Portugal
...	...	...	...	...	...	...	...	...	...	...	...	San Marino
...	...	...	...	...	...	...	...	...	...	...	...	Spain
...	...	...	...	...	...	...	...	...	100.0y	100.0y	99.9y	Sweden
...	...	...	...	...	...	99.8	99.6	100.0	100.0	100.0	100.0	Switzerland
...	...	...	...	...	...	...	...	...	...	...	...	United Kingdom
...	...	...	...	...	...	...	...	...	...	...	...	United States
												South and West Asia
...	...	...	...	...	...	...	...	...	...	...	...	Afghanistan
54.7	50.1	60.0	53.9	49.3	59.0	75.5	69.9	81.7	89.3	83.0	95.7	Bangladesh
76.4	74.4	78.9	81.3y	78.0y	85.1y	87.6	87.8	87.4	82.5y	82.4y	82.6y	Bhutan
62.0	63.3	60.4	61.4y	59.7y	63.5y	88.8	90.7	86.1	86.7	84.9	89.0	India
...	...	...	94.6**	...	...	...	...	...	96.0	97.0	94.9	Iran, Islamic Republic of
...	...	...	...	...	...	...	...	...	...	...	...	Maldives
...	...	...	64.9	63.3	66.9	...	...	...	78.2	80.1	75.9	Nepal
...	...	...	...	...	...	...	...	...	...	...	...	Pakistan
...	...	...	98.4**	97.9**	98.9**	...	...	...	97.0**	96.4**	97.7**	Sri Lanka
												Sub-Saharan Africa
...	...	...	...	...	...	...	...	...	...	...	...	Angola
...	...	...	58.6	61.5	54.3	...	...	...	51.1	51.1	51.0	Benin
82.3	78.1	86.9	80.9**	76.9**	85.2**	95.8	95.2	96.4	93.9**	93.6**	94.3**	Botswana
60.9	59.4	63.3	59.5**	57.5**	62.4**	38.4	38.9	37.8	39.9**	40.7**	38.7**	Burkina Faso
...	...	...	62.4	61.1	64.1	...	...	...	32.3**,y	...	...	Burundi
77.7**	...	...	58.8**	59.6**	57.9**	...	...	...	26.7x	27.8x	25.4x	Cameroon
...	...	...	84.8	85.7	83.7	...	...	...	72.2	68.3	76.2	Cape Verde
...	...	...	...	...	...	...	...	...	...	...	...	Central African Republic
46.8	50.2	40.9	32.7**	39.5**	23.3**	47.2	48.4	43.8	43.8**,x	45.6**,x	39.0**,x	Chad
...	...	...	65.5**,x	...	...	...	...	...	58.2**	57.0**	59.6**	Comoros
...	...	...	55.4	55.3	55.4	...	...	...	60.0	73.6	46.0	Congo
61.9	66.7	55.6	85.6**,x	87.8**,x	82.2**,x	35.2	39.5	28.3	39.7y	41.9y	36.3y	Côte d'Ivoire
...	...	...	...	...	...	...	...	...	...	...	...	Democratic Rep. of the Congo
...	...	...	29.5**,y	33.6**,y	25.0**,y	...	...	...	...	...	...	Equatorial Guinea
95.3	97.5	92.8	86.3	89.5	82.1	84.5	86.9	81.5	82.8	86.7	77.6	Eritrea
49.4	48.4	51.5	53.3**	54.4**	52.1**	92.1	91.5	93.1	93.7**	95.0**	91.4**	Ethiopia

Table 7 (continued)

Country or territory	Duration[1] of primary education 2002/2003	DROP-OUTS, ALL GRADES (%) 1998/1999 Total	Male	Female	2001/2002 Total	Male	Female	SURVIVAL RATE TO GRADE 5 (%) 1998/1999 Total	Male	Female	2001/2002 Total	Male	Female
Gabon	6	…	…	…	44.5**	46.3**	42.6**	…	…	…	69.3**	67.9**	70.7**
Gambia	6	…	…	…	…	…	…	…	…	…	…	…	…
Ghana	6	…	…	…	40.0	44.7	34.7	…	…	…	63.3	61.8	64.7
Guinea	6	22.1	15.9	31.4	28.6	22.8	35.8	86.9	92.5	79.1	79.7	85.4	72.7
Guinea-Bissau	6	72.5**	69.5**	76.6**	…	…	…	38.1**	41.2**	33.8**	…	…	…
Kenya	7	…	…	…	43.8**	…	…	…			59.0**	60.9**	57.2**
Lesotho	7	46.1	53.9	38.3	41.3	50.1	32.2	68.9	61.7	76.1	73.0	65.8	80.5
Liberia	6	…	…	…	…	…	…	…	…	…	…	…	…
Madagascar	5	48.9	49.3	48.4	47.1	47.6	46.6	51.1	50.7	51.6	52.9	52.4	53.4
Malawi	6	62.4	59.9**	64.9**	78.2	83.4	69.1	44.1	49.5**	38.8**	32.8	29.2	38.1
Mali	6	34.4**	32.5**	37.2**	34.5	30.0	40.3	78.3**	79.2**	77.1**	74.6	77.9	70.5
Mauritius	6	0.7	1.4	–	2.4	3.8	0.9	99.4	98.9	100.0	98.9	98.2	99.5
Mozambique	5	58.2	54.8	62.5	50.8	47.3	55.1	41.8	45.2	37.5	49.2	52.7	44.9
Namibia	7	28.0	31.9	23.9	14.1**	…	…	83.4	79.8	87.1	94.7**	…	…
Niger	6	…	…	…	33.9	33.2	35.1	…	…	…	69.1	70.5	67.2
Nigeria	6	…	…	…	…	…	…	…	…	…	…	…	…
Rwanda	6	69.8	…	…	63.4	64.0	62.8	45.4	…	…	46.6	44.9	48.3
Sao Tome and Principe	6	…	…	…	42.3**,y	48.5**,y	35.8**,y	…	…	…	61.5**,y	58.3**,y	64.7**,y
Senegal	6	…	…	…	28.6	25.7	31.7	…	…	…	80.0	82.6	77.2
Seychelles	6	–	…	…	1.3	–	2.6	100.0	…	…	99.3	100.0	98.6
Sierra Leone	6	…	…	…	…	…	…	…	…	…	…	…	…
Somalia	7	…	…	…	…	…	…	…	…	…	…	…	…
South Africa	7	32.4*	34.1*	30.8*	42.6x	41.5x	43.7x	75.9*	75.1*	76.7*	64.8x	65.2x	64.2x
Swaziland	7	39.7	51.6	24.6	42.7	39.8	45.8	81.5	76.0	87.1	73.2	77.1	69.2
Togo	6	…	…	…	38.3	32.7	44.8	…	…	…	68.6	72.6	64.1
Uganda	7	…	…	…	59.3	58.6	60.1	…	…	…	63.6	62.9	64.4
United Republic of Tanzania	7	26.7	29.5	23.8	**26.1****	**26.0****	**26.1****	80.9	78.6	83.3	**82.0****	**81.6****	**82.5****
Zambia	7	36.4	28.7	43.9	12.5**	…	…	78.2	83.5	73.0	76.7**,y	78.7**,y	74.8**,y
Zimbabwe	7	…	…	…	**37.9****	**38.4****	**37.5****	…	…	…	**69.7****	**68.2****	**71.2****
World[2]	…	…	…	…	15.1	…	…	…	…	…	89.7	…	…
Countries in transition	…	3.3	0.3	6.4	1.8	0.8	2.9	…	…	…	…	…	…
Developed countries	…	…	…	…	2.3	2.8	1.7	…	…	…	…	…	…
Developing countries	…	…	…	…	25.5	27.6	23.3	…	…	…	81.2	82.0	80.4
Arab States	…	8.7	11.8	5.2	7.2	7.6	6.6	91.3	88.2	94.8	94.3	94.1	94.6
Central and Eastern Europe	…	2.5	4.2	0.7	2.2	2.4	2.0	…	…	…	…	…	…
Central Asia	…	3.3	0.3	6.4	3.5	3.0	4.1	…	…	…	…	…	…
East Asia and the Pacific	…	…	…	…	…	…	…	…	…	…	…	…	…
Latin America and the Caribbean	…	…	…	…	20.5	21.4	19.5	…	…	…	83.9	80.9	87.1
North America and Western Europe	…	…	…	…	…	…	…	…	…	…	…	…	…
South and West Asia	…	…	…	…	35.1	36.7	33.1	…	…	…	64.9	63.3	66.9
Sub-Saharan Africa	…	…	…	…	40.5	42.5	37.6	…	…	…	68.6	72.6	64.1

1. Duration in this table is defined according to ISCED97 and may differ from that reported nationally.
2. All values shown are medians.
Data in bold are for 2002/2003.

(y) Data are for 2000/2001.
(x) Data are for 1999/2000.

SURVIVAL RATE TO LAST GRADE (%)						TRANSITION TO SECONDARY EDUCATION (%)						
1998/1999			2001/2002			1998/1999			2001/2002			
Total	Male	Female	Total	Male	Female	Total	Male	Female	Total	Male	Female	**Country or territory**
...	...	...	55.5**	53.7**	57.4**	...	...	...	...	...	...	Gabon
...	...	...	...	...	...	83.5	84.2	82.7	78.5**,y	77.5**,y	79.8**,y	Gambia
...	...	...	60.0	55.3	65.3	92.6	92.1	93.3	**91.0****	**96.5****	**85.5****	Ghana
77.9	84.1	68.6	71.4	77.2	64.2	51.5	52.6	48.9	47.7	48.8	45.5	Guinea
27.5**	30.5**	23.4**	...	...	...	62.9**	65.5**	58.4**	...	...	...	Guinea-Bissau
...	...	...	56.2**	...	...	69.6	72.1	67.2	72.5**	74.6**	70.4**	Kenya
53.9	46.1	61.7	58.7	49.9	67.8	53.8	55.7	52.6	66.9	67.0	66.7	Lesotho
...	...	...	...	...	...	...	...	...	...	...	...	Liberia
51.1	50.7	51.6	52.9	52.4	53.4	47.5	48.8	46.2	44.6	45.6	43.7	Madagascar
37.6	40.1**	35.1**	21.8	16.6	30.9	80.3	82.6**	77.7**	...	...	...	Malawi
65.6**	67.5**	62.8**	65.5	70.0	59.7	52.7**	53.1**	52.1**	54.2	56.5	50.6	Mali
99.3	98.6	100.0	97.6	96.2	99.1	...	...	...	62.7	57.4	68.4	Mauritius
41.8	45.2	37.5	49.2	52.7	44.9	50.9	50.0	52.4	58.6	58.7	58.4	Mozambique
72.0	68.1	76.1	85.9**	...	...	82.1	80.9	83.3	83.3**	81.2**	85.2**	Namibia
...	...	...	66.1	66.8	64.9	29.6	30.0	28.9	42.1	43.1	40.6	Niger
...	...	...	...	...	...	...	...	...	...	...	...	Nigeria
30.2	...	...	36.6	36.0	37.2	...	...	...	...	...	...	Rwanda
...	...	...	57.7**,y	51.5**,y	64.2**,y	...	...	...	64.5**,y	66.4**,y	62.6**,y	Sao Tome and Principe
...	...	...	71.4	74.3	68.3	35.0	36.1**	33.5**	40.1	41.5	38.2	Senegal
100.0	...	...	98.7	100.0	97.4	98.6	100.0	97.2	99.0	98.9	99.1	Seychelles
...	...	...	...	...	...	...	...	...	...	...	...	Sierra Leone
...	...	...	...	...	...	...	...	...	...	...	...	Somalia
67.6*	65.9*	69.2*	57.4x	58.5x	56.3x	92.7**	...	...	91.9x	90.7x	93.0x	South Africa
60.3	48.4	75.4	57.3	60.2	54.2	81.3	80.2	82.4	78.1	76.6	79.6	Swaziland
...	...	...	61.7	67.3	55.2	...	...	...	62.5	65.7	57.8	Togo
...	...	...	40.7	41.4	39.9	23.8	22.9	25.2	42.2	40.7	44.1	Uganda
73.3	70.5	76.2	**73.9****	**74.0****	**73.9****	17.2**	17.9**	16.5**	**18.8****	**19.8****	**17.9****	United Republic of Tanzania
63.6	71.3	56.1	65.2**,y	68.7**,y	61.7**,y	31.2**	30.8**	31.7**	54.5**	53.5**	55.6**	Zambia
...	...	...	**62.1****	**61.6****	**62.5****	...	...	...	**69.7****	**69.3****	**70.2****	Zimbabwe
...	...	...	84.9	...	...	91.9	92.1	91.8	91.7	91.2	92.2	World[2]
96.7	99.7	93.6	98.2	99.2	97.1	98.5	97.1	100.0	98.3	98.1	98.5	Countries in transition
...	...	...	97.7	97.2	98.3	...	...	...	98.9	98.5	99.4	Developed countries
...	...	...	74.5	72.4	76.7	84.5	86.9	81.5	83.3	83.8	82.3	Developing countries
91.3	88.2	94.8	92.8	92.4	93.4	83.1	81.5	85.0	90.4	90.5	90.2	Arab States
97.5	95.8	99.3	97.8	97.6	98.0	99.1	99.9	98.4	98.3	...	...	Central and Eastern Europe
96.7	99.7	93.6	96.5	97.0	95.9	97.5	96.4	98.6	98.3	98.5	98.9	Central Asia
...	...	...	...	...	...	...	...	...	90.7	89.4	92.0	East Asia and the Pacific
...	...	...	79.5	78.6	80.5	89.6	88.8	90.5	90.8	89.0	92.9	Latin America and the Caribbean
...	...	...	...	...	...	...	...	...	99.6	99.6	99.6	North America and Western Europe
...	...	...	64.9	63.3	66.9	...	...	...	86.7	83.0	89.0	South and West Asia
...	...	...	59.5	57.5	62.4	53.8	55.7	52.6	60.0	73.6	46.0	Sub-Saharan Africa

Table 8
Participation in secondary[1] and post-secondary non-tertiary[2] education

	Country or territory	Age group	School-age population (000)	ENROLMENT IN SECONDARY EDUCATION						GROSS ENROLMENT RATIO (GER) IN SECONDARY EDUCATION (%)			
				Total enrolment				Enrolment in technical and vocational education					
				1998/1999		2002/2003		2002/2003		1998/1999			
		2002/2003	2002	Total (000)	% F	Total (000)	% F	Total (000)	% F	Total	Male	Female	GPI (F/M)
	Arab States												
1	Algeria	12-17	4 438	…	…	3 548	51	356	40	…	…	…	…
2	Bahrain	12-17	70	59	51	67	50	15	41	93.9	90.2	97.8	1.08
3	Djibouti	12-18	107	16	42	**27**	**40**	**2**	**49**	16.2	18.9	13.5	0.72
4	Egypt	11-16	9 828	7 671 **	47 **	8 384 **	47 **	2 514 **	45 **	80.8**	84.3**	77.2**	0.92 **
5	Iraq	12-17	3 460	1 105	38	1 478	40	63	19	35.7	43.6	27.5	0.63
6	Jordan	12-17	713	579	49	613	49	35	46	86.9	85.8	88.0	1.03
7	Kuwait	10-17	292	235 **	49 **	261	50	14	41	97.8**	96.8**	98.8	1.02 **
8	Lebanon	12-17	441	372	52	350	51	46	40	77.5	74.1	80.9	1.09
9	Libyan Arab Jamahiriya	12-17	762	…	…	798 **	50 **	178 **	53 **	…	…	…	…
10	Mauritania	12-17	373	63 **	42 **	84	44	3	35	18.7**	21.7**	15.8**	0.73 **
11	Morocco	12-17	3 904	1 470	43	1 758	45	106	42	37.7	42.0	33.3	0.79
12	Oman	12-17	347	229	49	279	48	.	.	71.7	71.9	71.5	0.99
13	Palestinian A.T.	10-17	663	444	50	583	50	4	29	78.8	77.5	80.3	1.04
14	Qatar	12-17	55	44	50	52	49	0.6	.	92.3	89.6	95.1	1.06
15	Saudi Arabia	12-17	2 981	1 774	46	1 995	46	68	10	67.9	72.7	62.9	0.87
16	Sudan	12-16	3 650	965 **	…	1 291	45	29	36	28.5**	…	…	…
17	Syrian Arab Republic	12-17	2 656	1 030	47	1 284	47	122	45	40.6	42.5	38.7	0.91
18	Tunisia	12-18	1 481	1 059	49	1 149	51	18	37	72.9	72.3	73.6	1.02
19	United Arab Emirates	11-17	348	202	50	273	49	2	.	82.1	79.0	85.5	1.08
20	Yemen	12-17	2 903	1 042	26	1 373	30	9	5	41.9	60.3	22.5	0.37
	Central and Eastern Europe												
21	Albania	10-17	489	363 **	49 **	396	48	20	49	75.8**	74.7**	77.1**	1.03 **
22	Belarus	10-16	1 098	1 143	49	998	50	5	34	97.2	97.4	97.0	1.00
23	Bosnia and Herzegovina	10-17	490	…	…					…	…	…	…
24	Bulgaria	11-17	719	700	48	707	48	199	39	89.4	90.3	88.5	0.98
25	Croatia	11-18	445	416	49	400	49	146	46	87.6	86.8	88.4	1.02
26	Czech Republic	11-18	1 032	928	50	1 000	49	391	47	82.5	80.9	84.3	1.04
27	Estonia	13-18	128	116	50	123	50	17	34	92.7	91.0	94.6	1.04
28	Hungary	11-18	973	1 007	49	1 030	49	67	39	95.3	94.5	96.0	1.02
29	Latvia	11-18	290	255	50	276	49	39	39	88.4	86.8	90.1	1.04
30	Lithuania	11-18	437	407	45	448	49	37	35	95.7	95.5	96.0	1.01
31	Poland	13-18	3 727	…	…	3 895	48	1 181	39	…	…	…	…
32	Republic of Moldova	11-17	560	415	50	411	50	23	37	72.2	71.8	72.6	1.01
33	Romania	11-18	2 620	2 218	49	2 218	49	650	44	78.9	78.3	79.4	1.01
34	Russian Federation	10-16	15 245	…	…	14 486 **	…	1 949 **	…	…	…	…	…
35	Serbia and Montenegro[3]	11-18	…	814	49	761 y	49 y	267 y	47 y	92.3	92.0	92.6	1.01
36	Slovakia	10-18	730	674	50	670	49	218	47	85.2	84.3	86.2	1.02
37	Slovenia	11-18	199	220	49	218	49	87	45	98.7	97.4	100.1	1.03
38	TFYR Macedonia	11-18	258	219	48	219	48	59	43	82.3	83.4	81.1	0.97
39	Turkey	12-16	7 263	…	…	5 742 **	42 **	1 261	36 **	…	…	…	…
40	Ukraine	10-16	4 980	…	…	4 824	49	326	33	…	…	…	…
	Central Asia												
41	Armenia	10-16	423	…	…	368	50	5	41	…	…	…	…
42	Azerbaijan	10-16	1 322	929	49	1 094	48	21	34	76.9	77.2	76.7	0.99
43	Georgia	10-16	562	440	49	450	49	9	27	72.8	73.1	72.3	0.99
44	Kazakhstan	11-17	2 252	1 966	49	2 067	49	91	36	87.4	87.8	87.1	0.99
45	Kyrgyzstan	11-17	805	633	50	739	50	26	36	85.4	84.3	86.4	1.02
46	Mongolia	12-17	374	205	55	313	53	17	50	58.3	51.4	65.2	1.27
47	Tajikistan	11-17	1 106	769	46	948	45	26	29	72.6	78.0	67.0	0.86
48	Turkmenistan	10-16	825	…	…	…	…		…	…	…	…	…
49	Uzbekistan	11-17	4 363	…	…	4 161	49	367	44	…	…	…	…
	East Asia and the Pacific												
50	Australia	12-17	1 635	2 433	50	2 514	48	1 102	46	154.8	151.7	158.0	1.04
51	Brunei Darussalam	12-18	43	33	51	39	49	2	36	81.6	77.7	85.6	1.10
52	Cambodia	12-17	2 222	318 **	34 **	560	38	15	34	16.0**	20.8**	11.0**	0.53 **

GROSS ENROLMENT RATIO (GER) IN SECONDARY EDUCATION (%)				NET ENROLMENT RATIO (NER) IN SECONDARY EDUCATION (%)								INTERNAL EFFICIENCY			POST-SECONDARY NON-TERTIARY EDUCATION		
												Repeaters in secondary general education (%)			Total enrolment		
2002/2003				1998/1999				2002/2003				2002/2003			2002/2003		
Total	Male	Female	GPI (F/M)	Total	Male	Female	GPI (F/M)	Total	Male	Female	GPI (F/M)	Total	Male	Female	Total (000)	% F	
Arab States																	
80.0	77.4	82.7	1.07	...	...	...	...	66.8**	65.1**	68.5**	1.05**	...	...	...	40	50	1
95.6	92.7	98.8	1.07	84.1	80.7	87.6	1.09	87.0	83.9	90.3	1.08	5.2	7.3	3.2	4	33	2
24.3	**28.9**	**19.8**	**0.68**	...	...	...	...	**21.2****	**25.0****	**17.3****	**0.69****	6.0**	6.1**	5.8**	**0.3**	**24**	3
85.3**	88.1**	82.4**	0.94**	...	...	...	...	80.8**,z	83.1**,z	78.5**,z	0.95**,z	7.4**	8.7**	6.1**	152	51	4
42.7	49.8	35.3	0.71	31.4	37.7	24.8	0.66	...				...	...	...	...	...	5
86.0	85.1	86.9	1.02	78.5**	76.0**	81.0**	1.07**	79.9	78.9	81.1	1.03	1.0	1.1	0.8	.	.	6
89.3	86.9	91.8	1.06	88.0**	87.3**	88.8**	1.02**	77.2**,z	75.2**,z	79.3**,z	1.05**,z	7.8	9.2	6.4	16	68	7
79.4	76.1	82.8	1.09	...	...	...	...	...	...	...	...	11.2	11.9	10.5	1**	41**	8
104.7**	101.5**	108.0**	1.06**	...	...	...	...	...	...	...	...	...	...	...	...	...	9
22.6	25.3	20.0	0.79	...	...	...	...	16.1**	18.2**	14.0**	0.77**	14.3	14.0	14.6	1	61	10
45.0	49.1	40.8	0.83	...	...	...	...	35.7**	38.5**	32.9**	0.86**	16.4	18.6	13.7	72	44	11
80.5	82.1	78.7	0.96	61.6	60.8	62.5	1.03	69.3	68.9	69.6	1.01	7.9	10.7	4.8	...	...	12
87.9	85.4	90.5	1.06	75.6	74.2	77.2	1.04	83.8	81.7	86.0	1.05	1.8	2.0	1.5	...	...	13
93.9	92.2	95.8	1.04	78.0	74.9	81.2	1.08	82.3**	79.8**	84.9**	1.06**	...	...	...	.	.	14
66.9	70.3	63.4	0.90	53.3**	58.1**	48.3**	0.83**	52.7**	53.9**	51.6**	0.96**	7.8	9.5	5.8	36z	41**,z	15
35.4	38.5	32.2	0.84	...	...	...	...	...				...	...	...	.	.	16
48.3	50.4	46.2	0.92	36.4	37.9	34.8	0.92	42.9	44.4	41.3	0.93	7.3	8.9	5.6	40	58	17
77.6	74.6	80.7	1.08	...	...	...	...	64.5	61.3	67.8	1.11	14.1	16.9	11.5	3	39	18
78.7	77.5	80.0	1.03	74.4	71.7	77.2	1.08	71.0	70.0	72.0	1.03	5.5	7.3	3.6	.	.	19
47.3	64.5	29.2	0.45	32.6*	45.8*	18.6*	0.41*	...				...	...	...	19y	16y	20
Central and Eastern Europe																	
81.1	80.9	81.3	1.00	71.5**	70.5**	72.7**	1.03**	77.0	76.4	77.7	1.02	4.2	4.5	3.8	.	.	21
90.9	89.6	92.3	1.03	...	...	...	...	84.8	83.3**	86.5**	1.04**	0.2	0.2	0.2	128	38	22
...	...	...	...	...	...	...	...	...				...	...	...			23
98.4	99.8	97.0	0.97	83.2	83.8	82.5	0.98	87.5	88.5	86.5	0.98	1.6	2.1	1.1	3	47	24
89.8	89.1	90.5	1.02	84.2	83.5	84.9	1.02	86.6	85.8	87.4	1.02	0.5	0.8	0.3	.	.	25
96.9	95.7	98.2	1.03	...	...	...	...	90.5	89.4	91.6	1.03	1.0	1.3	0.7	74	49	26
96.4	94.8	98.1	1.03	...	...	...	...	88.3	86.5	90.2	1.04	4.1	5.6	2.8	12	63	27
105.8	105.6	106.0	1.00	84.7**	84.2**	85.2**	1.01**	93.8	93.7	93.8	1.00	2.3	2.9	1.6	84	53	28
95.3	95.4	95.2	1.00	85.0**	83.8**	86.2**	1.03**	88.0	87.7	88.2	1.01	1.1	1.4	0.7	7	66	29
102.5	103.3	101.6	0.98	90.6**	90.2**	91.1**	1.01**	94.0	93.8	94.3	1.01	0.8	1.2	0.4	8	62	30
104.5	106.6	102.3	0.96	...	...	...	...	91.5	90.5	92.6	1.02	1.4	...	...	216	59	31
73.3	72.0	74.7	1.04	68.8**	...	...	...	69.0	67.6	70.5	1.04	0.4	0.4	0.4	.	.	32
84.7	84.1	85.3	1.01	74.4**	73.6**	75.3**	1.02**	80.5	79.5	81.6	1.03	2.0	2.8	1.2	62	62	33
95.0**	...	...	...	...	...	...	...	...	...	...	...	0.8**,y	...	...	234	59	34
88.7y	88.3y	89.2y	1.01y	...	...	...	...	87.6**,y	87.0**,y	88.1**,y	1.01**,y	2.1**,y	2.1**,y	2.1**,y	7y	5y	35
91.7	91.4	92.1	1.01	...	...	...	...	88.0	87.6	88.4	1.01	1.4	1.7	1.0	6	60	36
109.4	109.7	109.0	0.99	89.5	87.9	91.1	1.04	93.2	92.7	93.8	1.01	1.4	2.5	0.4	2	67	37
84.7	85.6	83.8	0.98	79.1**	80.1**	78.0**	0.97**	...	...	...	...	0.5	0.7	0.3	0.3	6	38
79.1**	90.3**	67.4**	0.75**	...	...	...	...	...	...	...	...	...	...	...	.	.	39
96.9	97.4	96.3	0.99	...	...	...	...	84.6	84.3**	84.8**	1.01**	0.1	0.1**	0.0**	176	53	40
Central Asia																	
86.9	85.9	88.0	1.02	...	...	...	...	83.3	82.1	84.6	1.03	0.2	0.3	0.1	29	68	41
82.8	84.3	81.2	0.96	73.8*	73.5*	74.2*	1.01*	75.9	76.7	74.9	0.98	0.6	0.8	0.5	51	69	42
80.2	79.9	80.4	1.01	71.1	71.2	71.1	1.00	77.6	77.3	78.0	1.01	0.3	0.4	0.1	28	61	43
91.8	91.7	91.9	1.00	...	...	...	...	86.8	86.7	86.9	1.00	0.2	0.3	0.1	211	56	44
91.9	91.5	92.3	1.01	...	...	...	...	...	...	...	...	0.1	0.2	0.1	26	65	45
83.7	77.6	89.9	1.16	55.4**	49.0**	62.0**	1.27**	77.4	71.6	83.3	1.16	0.1	0.1	0.1	3	46	46
85.8	93.7	77.8	0.83	68.0	72.1	63.8	0.89	83.3**	90.0**	76.4**	0.85**	0.5	0.5**	0.5**	25	51	47
...	...	...	...	...	...	...	...	...	...	...	...	...	...	...	...	...	48
95.4	96.7	94.0	0.97	...	...	...	...	...	...	...	...	–	–	–	...	...	49
East Asia and the Pacific																	
153.7	155.8	151.5	0.97	...	...	...	...	88.0**	87.0**	89.1**	1.02**	...	...	...	176	51	50
89.6	87.3	92.1	1.06	...	...	...	...	...	...	...	...	...	...	...	0.1	60	51
25.2	30.8	19.5	0.64	14.3**	18.6**	10.0**	0.54**	24.4**	29.7**	18.9**	0.64**	6.4	7.7	4.4	9	32	52

Table 8 (continued)

	Country or territory	Age group	School-age population (000)	ENROLMENT IN SECONDARY EDUCATION: Total enrolment 1998/1999		ENROLMENT IN SECONDARY EDUCATION: Total enrolment 2002/2003		Enrolment in technical and vocational education 2002/2003		GROSS ENROLMENT RATIO (GER) IN SECONDARY EDUCATION (%) 1998/1999			
		2002/2003	2002	Total (000)	% F	Total (000)	% F	Total (000)	% F	Total	Male	Female	GPI (F/M)
53	China	12-17	136 109	77 436	…	95 625	47	11 298	48	61.7	…	…	…
54	Cook Islands[4]	11-18	…	2	50	2 **,y	50 **,y	.	.	…	…	…	…
55	DPR Korea	10-15	2 364	…	…	…	…	…	…	…	…	…	…
56	Fiji	12-18	119	…	…	96 **,z	50 **,z	3 **,z	37**,z	…	…	…	…
57	Indonesia	13-18	26 141	…	…	15 873	49	2 100	43	…	…	…	…
58	Japan	12-17	7 971	8 959	49	8 131	49	1 048	44	101.8	101.1	102.4	1.01
59	Kiribati[3]	12-16	…	…	…	10	52	…	…	…	…	…	…
60	Lao PDR	11-16	809	240	40	353	42	5	40	33.4	39.4	27.3	0.69
61	Macao, China	12-17	49	32	51	44	50	3	48	75.5	71.8	79.4	1.10
62	Malaysia	12-18	3 273	2 154	51	2 300	51	141	42	69.4	65.9	73.1	1.11
63	Marshall Islands[3]	12-17	…	6	50	6 z	50 z	.	.	…	…	…	…
64	Micronesia (Fed. States of)	12-17	17	19	…	…	…	…	…	109.2	…	…	…
65	Myanmar	10-15	6 116	2 059	50	2 383	48	–	–	34.9	35.0	34.8	0.99
66	Nauru[3]	12-17	…	0.7**	51 **	…	…	…	…	53.9**	52.3**	55.6**	1.06 **
67	New Zealand	11-17	411	433	50	483	…	56	…	114.3	110.9	117.8	1.06
68	Niue[3]	11-16	…	0.3	47	0.2 z	50 z	.	.	101.4	111.9	91.7	0.82
69	Palau[3]	11-17	…	2	49	2 **,y	48 **,y	.	.	101.2	98.2	104.5	1.07
70	Papua New Guinea	13-18	723	133	40	185	41	17	27	20.4	23.2	17.3	0.75
71	Philippines	12-15	7 226	5 117	51	6 069	51	.	.	75.8	72.5	79.3	1.09
72	Republic of Korea	12-17	4 076	4 368	48	**3 646**	**47**	**546**	**48**	99.9	99.9	99.9	1.00
73	Samoa	11-17	30	22	50	23 **	50 **	.	.	74.9	71.2	78.9	1.11
74	Singapore	12-15	235	…	…	…	…	…	…	…	…	…	…
75	Solomon Islands	12-18	75	…	…	46	…	…	…	…	…	…	…
76	Thailand	12-17	6 596	…	…	**5 010**	**50**	**625**	**45**	…	…	…	…
77	Timor-Leste	12-17	138	…	…	47 z	…	– z	…	…	…	…	…
78	Tokelau	11-16	…	…	…	…	…	…	…	…	…	…	…
79	Tonga	11-16	14	14	51	15	50	…	…	93.3	87.8	99.3	1.13
80	Tuvalu[3]	12-17	…	0.8 **	45 **	0.9 z	46 z	…	…	78.3**	83.1**	73.1 **	0.88 **
81	Vanuatu	12-18	35	10 **	43 **	10	50	…	…	33.1**	36.1**	29.9**	0.83 **
82	Viet Nam	11-17	12 794	7 401	47	9 266	47	310	51	61.9	65.1	58.6	0.90
	Latin America and the Caribbean												
83	Anguilla[3]	12-16	…	1	53	1 **	51 **	0.1 **	58 **	…	…	…	…
84	Antigua and Barbuda	12-16	…	…	…	…	…	…	…	…	…	…	…
85	Argentina	12-17	3 986	3 556	51	3 976	51	1 271	52	89.0	85.7	92.5	1.08
86	Aruba[3]	12-16	…	6	51	7	52	1	38	100.6	98.6	102.7	1.04
87	Bahamas	11-16	35	…	…	32 **	50 **	.	.	…	…	…	…
88	Barbados	11-15	20	22 **	51 **	21	50	0.1	23	104.0**	101.3**	106.7**	1.05 **
89	Belize	11-16	36	22	51	28 **	51 **	1 **	59 **	64.8	62.3	67.4	1.08
90	Bermuda[3]	11-17	…	…	…	5 z	51 z	.	.	…	…	…	…
91	Bolivia	12-17	1 154	756	48	997 **	48 **	40 **	66 **	72.3	74.9	69.7	0.93
92	Brazil	11-17	24 345	…	…	26 789	52	484	70	…	…	…	…
93	British Virgin Islands[3]	12-16	…	2	47	2	54	0.3	53	98.8	103.3	94.1	0.91
94	Cayman Islands[4]	11-16	…	2	48	2 z	50 z	.	.	…	…	…	…
95	Chile	12-17	1 684	1 246	50	**1 557**	**49**	**387**	**46**	79.6	78.0	81.3	1.04
96	Colombia	11-16	5 261	3 549	52	3 723	52	286	55	70.6	66.9	74.5	1.11
97	Costa Rica	12-16	435	227	51	289	50	54	50	56.8	54.5	59.2	1.09
98	Cuba	12-17	1 013	740	50	938	48	272	39	79.4	77.1	81.8	1.06
99	Dominica[3]	12-16	…	7	53	8	52	0.4	61	85.5	78.5	92.8	1.18
100	Dominican Republic	12-17	1 122	610 **	55 **	658 **	54 **	30 **	55 **	56.1**	49.5**	63.0**	1.27 **
101	Ecuador	12-17	1 643	904	50	973	50	216	53	56.4	55.7	57.2	1.03
102	El Salvador	13-18	784	402	49	463	50	91 **	52 **	50.2	50.4	50.0	0.99
103	Grenada[3]	12-16	…	[illegible]	[illegible]	15	49	1	29	…	…	…	…
104	Guatemala	13-17	1 426	400 *	47 *	608	47	174	51	30.7	31.3	[illegible]	[illegible]
105	Guyana	12-16	73	66	50	69 **	50 **	…	…	81.1	80.5	81.8	1.02
106	Haiti	12-18	1 490	…	…	…	…	…	…	…	…	…	…
107	Honduras	13-18	940	…	…	…	…	…	…	…	…	…	…
108	Jamaica	12-16	273	231 **	50 **	230	50	0.4	42	84.1**	83.2**	85.1 **	1.02 **
109	Mexico	12-17	12 890	8 722	50	10 188	51	1 592	59	60.1	68.3	69.9	1.02

GROSS ENROLMENT RATIO (GER) IN SECONDARY EDUCATION (%)				NET ENROLMENT RATIO (NER) IN SECONDARY EDUCATION (%)								INTERNAL EFFICIENCY			POST-SECONDARY NON-TERTIARY EDUCATION		
												Repeaters in secondary general education (%)			Total enrolment		
2002/2003				1998/1999				2002/2003				2002/2003			2002/2003		
Total	Male	Female	GPI (F/M)	Total	Male	Female	GPI (F/M)	Total	Male	Female	GPI (F/M)	Total	Male	Female	Total (000)	% F	
70.3	71.2	69.2	0.97	…	…	…	…	…	…	…	…	0.3	0.3	0.2	612	38	53
…	…	…	…	…	…	…	…	…	…	…	…	4.3**,y	…	…	0.04**,y	69**,y	54
…	…	…	…	…	…	…	…	…	…	…	…	…	…	…	…	…	55
80.4**,z	77.6**,z	83.2**,z	1.07**,z	…	…	…	…	76.0**,z	73.4**,z	78.7**,z	1.07**,z	.	.	.	.	.	56
60.7	61.1	60.3	0.99	…	…	…	…	54.0	54.3	53.6	0.99	0.4	0.7	0.2	.	.	57
102.0	101.8	102.2	1.00	…	…	…	…	99.8**	…	…	…	…	…	…	14	63	58
104.4	98.0	111.1	1.13	…	…	…	…	…	…	…	…	…	…	…	…	…	59
43.7	50.0	37.2	0.74	26.7	29.9	23.5	0.79	35.1	38.3	31.8	0.83	2.0	2.8	1.0	20	42	60
90.9	88.0	94.0	1.07	61.9	58.4	65.6	1.12	74.3	70.7	78.0	1.10	11.2	13.3	9.1	.	.	61
70.3	66.7	74.1	1.11	68.9	65.4	72.6	1.11	70.0	66.4	73.8	1.11	…	…	…	173	46	62
75.7z	75.0z	76.4z	1.02z	…	…	…	…	64.9z	63.7z	66.2z	1.04z	3.1**,z	3.1**,z	3.2**,z	0.05z	27z	63
…	…	…	…	…	…	…	…	…	…	…	…	.z	.z	.z	…	…	64
39.0	40.1	37.8	0.94	31.2**	31.4**	31.0**	0.99**	35.1	36.2	33.9	0.94	2.2	2.2	2.3	.	.	65
…	…	…	…	…	…	…	…	…	…	…	…	…	…	…	…	…	66
117.5	…	…	…	92.1	91.5	92.6	1.01	92.7	91.3	94.1	1.03	…	…	…	45	53	67
93.8z	94.6z	93.0z	0.98z	…	…	…	…	93.8z	94.6z	93.0z	0.98z	.	.	.	.	.	68
88.8**,y	88.6**,y	88.9**,y	1.00**,y	…	…	…	…	…	…	…	…	…	…	…	…	…	69
25.5	28.4	22.3	0.79	20.4*	23.2*	17.3*	0.75*	23.7**,z	26.3**,z	20.7**,z	0.79**,z	–z	–z	–z	.	.	70
84.0	79.9	88.2	1.10	50.8	48.6	53.1	1.09	59.3	54.2	64.6	1.19	2.3	3.6	1.1	452	46	71
90.5	**90.3**	**90.7**	**1.00**	96.5	96.4	96.6	1.00	**87.9**	**87.8**	**88.0**	**1.00**	**0.3**	**0.3**	**0.2**	.	.	72
75.9**	72.5**	79.5**	1.10**	65.8	62.9	69.1	1.10	62.1**	59.1**	65.4**	1.11**	2.2z	2.4z	2.0z	0.2	60	73
…	…	…	…	…	…	…	…	…	…	…	…	–y	–y	–y	…	…	74
61.5	…	…	…	…	…	…	…	…	…	…	…	…	…	…	.	.	75
76.7	**76.6**	**76.7**	**1.00**	…	…	…	…	…	…	…	…	…	…	…	**17**	**72**	76
34.6z	…	…	…	…	…	…	…	20.3**,y	…	…	…	…	…	…	.	.	77
…	…	…	…	…	…	…	…	…	…	…	…	…	…	…	.	.	78
102.8	96.1	110.7	1.15	68.5	64.2	73.2	1.14	71.7**,z	67.5**,z	76.7**,z	1.14**,z	5.7z	5.8z	5.6z	1z	40z	79
84.4z	87.2z	81.3z	0.93z	…	…	…	…	…				6.3**,z	5.8**,z	6.8**,z	…	…	80
27.8	26.8	28.9	1.08	…	…	…	…	27.5z	…	…	…	.	.	.	2z	37z	81
72.4	75.2	69.6	0.93	55.2**	…	…	…	65.3**,z	…	…	…	1.3**	1.9**	0.7**	.	.	82
Latin America and the Caribbean																	
108.3**	108.4**	108.2**	1.00**	…	…	…	…	100.0**	…	…	…	–	–	–	0.1	73	83
…	…	…	…	…	…	…	…	…	…	…	…	–z	–z	–z	…	…	84
99.7	96.9	102.7	1.06	73.6**	71.0**	76.3**	1.07**	81.3	78.8	83.8	1.06	8.3	10.0	6.5	.	.	85
103.1	99.5	106.7	1.07	79.3	76.4	82.1	1.07	75.3	71.9	78.7	1.09z	14.7	15.5	14.0	.	.	86
91.3**	90.0**	92.6**	1.03**	…	…	…	…	75.8**	74.4**	77.3**	1.04**	.	.	.	…	…	87
105.8	105.0	106.6	1.02	88.2**	86.4**	90.0**	1.04**	89.8	89.9	89.7	1.00	–	–	–	4	50	88
77.8**	75.8**	79.8**	1.05**	56.4**	54.2**	58.7**	1.08**	69.0**	67.3**	70.7**	1.05**	7.0	7.7	6.3	2	59	89
86.1z	…	…	…	…	…	…	…	86.1z	…	…	…	.	.	.	.	.	90
86.4**	87.9**	84.8**	0.97**	…	…	…	…	71.2**	71.9**	70.5**	0.98**	3.5	4.1	2.8	…	…	91
110.0	104.9	115.3	1.10	…	…	…	…	74.9	71.9	77.9	1.08	17.4	…	…	.	.	92
94.7	87.8	101.5	1.16	79.8**	81.1**	78.4**	0.97**	77.6**	71.4**	83.7**	1.17**	9.5**	12.3**	7.1**	0.8**	69**	93
…	…	…	…	…	…	…	…	…	…	…	…	…	…	…	0.04*,z	54*,z	94
91.2	**90.6**	**91.8**	**1.01**	70.3	68.8	71.9	1.05	**80.8**	**80.2**	**81.4**	**1.01**	**2.2**	**2.7**	**1.7**	.	.	95
70.8	67.3	74.4	1.11	54.0**	…	…	…	55.3**	52.7**	57.9**	1.10**	4.5**	5.3**	3.7**	.	.	96
66.5	64.1	69.0	1.08	48.5**	46.5**	50.7**	1.09**	52.7	50.3	55.1	1.09	9.5	10.8	8.3	.	.	97
92.6	93.5	91.6	0.98	75.2	71.4	79.3	1.11	86.2	86.4	86.1	1.00	1.4	1.8	1.0	24	79	98
113.9	107.7	120.2	1.12	65.5	55.7	75.7	1.36	91.8**	86.0**	97.8**	1.14**	7.4	9.0	5.9	2	60	99
58.7**	52.6**	65.0**	1.23**	39.5**	34.6**	44.7**	1.29**	35.5**	30.5**	40.8**	1.34**	3.1**	4.0**	2.4**	.	.	100
59.2	58.7	59.7	1.02	46.1	45.4	46.8	1.03	50.4	49.6	51.2	1.03	3.9	4.7	3.1	.	.	101
59.0	58.8	59.2	1.01	39.6**	39.9**	39.4**	0.99**	48.6**	48.0**	49.2**	1.02**	2.4**,z	3.1**,z	1.7**,z	.	.	102
148.7	151.9	145.5	0.96	…	…	…	…	100.0**	…	…	…	8.5	10.7	6.3	1	66	103
42.7	44.3	41.0	0.93	21.3**	21.7**	20.8**	0.96**	29.7	30.4	28.9	0.95	3.1	3.5	2.5	.	.	104
94.7**	91.9**	97.7**	1.06**	74.2**	72.2**	76.3**	1.06**	76.4**,y	75.0**,y	77.9**,y	1.04**,y	7.2y	8.6y	5.8y	1**,z	73**,z	105
…	…	…	…	…	…	…	…	…	…	…	…	…	…	…	…	…	106
…	…	…	…	…	…	…	…	…	…	…	…	…	…	…	.	.	107
84.1	83.1	85.1	1.02	79.5**	78.8**	80.2**	1.02**	75.4**	73.9**	77.0**	1.04**	1.6	2.3**	0.8**	42z	59z	108
79.0	75.6	82.6	1.09	54.9**	55.1**	54.8**	1.00**	62.6	61.3	63.9	1.04	1.9	2.5	1.3	.	.	109

Table 8 (continued)

	Country or territory	Age group 2002/2003	School-age population (000) 2002	ENROLMENT IN SECONDARY EDUCATION: Total enrolment 1998/1999 Total (000)	1998/1999 % F	Total enrolment 2002/2003 Total (000)	2002/2003 % F	Enrolment in technical and vocational education 2002/2003 Total (000)	2002/2003 % F	GROSS ENROLMENT RATIO (GER) IN SECONDARY EDUCATION (%) 1998/1999 Total	Male	Female	GPI (F/M)
110	Montserrat[3]	12-16	...	0.3	47	0.3**	49**	.	.	...	...	...	...
111	Netherlands Antilles	12-17	21	15	54	15**	52**	6**	54**	74.9	69.0	80.9	1.17
112	Nicaragua	13-17	631	287**	54**	383	53	19	56	48.4**	44.3**	52.5**	1.18**
113	Panama	12-17	356	229**	51**	251	51	103	49	67.5**	65.0**	70.1**	1.08**
114	Paraguay	12-17	799	368	50	519	50**	45	48**	50.8	49.6	52.1	1.05
115	Peru	12-16	2 832	2 212	48	2 540	48	.	.	81.7	84.0	79.4	0.95
116	Saint Kitts and Nevis[3]	12-16	...	...	...	4	55	.	.	...	...	...	...
117	Saint Lucia	12-16	15	12	57	13	56	0.3	40	76.4	66.6	86.1	1.29
118	Saint Vincent/Grenad.	12-16	14	...	...	10	52	2	34	...	...	...	...
119	Suriname	12-17	56	...	...	41**	56**	18**	52**	...	...	...	...
120	Trinidad and Tobago	12-16	131	117**	52**	108**	51**	3**	53**	81.7**	78.5**	85.0**	1.08**
121	Turks and Caicos Islands[3]	12-16	...	1	51	1**	49**	0.1**	49**	...	...	...	...
122	Uruguay	12-17	314	...	...	332	52	28	45	...	...	...	...
123	Venezuela	12-16	2 670	1 439	54	1 866	53	57	51	56.9	51.2	62.8	1.23
	North America and Western Europe												
124	Andorra[4]	12-17	...	...	...	3	50	0.2	46	...	...	...	...
125	Austria	10-17	765	748	48	764	47	267	43	98.8	100.9	96.6	0.96
126	Belgium	12-17	735	1 033	51	1 181	51	693	51	142.4	137.3	147.7	1.08
127	Canada	12-17	2 514	2 565	49	2 622**,z	49**,z	102**,z	36**,z	105.3	105.6	105.0	0.99
128	Cyprus[3]	12-17	...	63	49	65	49	4	18	93.2	91.8	94.7	1.03
129	Denmark	13-18	346	422	50	447	50	118	46	125.6	122.1	129.2	1.06
130	Finland	13-18	388	480	51	497	51	178	50	120.9	115.8	126.2	1.09
131	France	11-17	5 379	5 955	49	5 859	49	1 457	45	109.6	109.5	109.6	1.00
132	Germany	10-18	8 447	8 185	48	8 447	48	1 730	43	98.2	99.0	97.3	0.98
133	Greece	12-17	732	771	49	714	49	134	41	93.9	93.3	94.5	1.01
134	Iceland	13-19	30	32	50	35	50	7	38	109.4	106.2	112.7	1.06
135	Ireland	12-16	300	346	50	321	51	.	.	105.4	102.2	108.7	1.06
136	Israel	12-17	647	569	49	603	48	125	42	90.8	91.0	90.6	1.00
137	Italy	11-18	4 561	4 450	49	4 528	48**	699	45	91.7	92.2	91.1	0.99
138	Luxembourg	12-18	36	...	...	35	50	12	48	...	...	...	...
139	Malta	11-17	40	...	...	38	48	2	24	...	...	...	...
140	Monaco[4]	11-17	...	3	51	3y	48y	0.5y	44y	...	...	...	...
141	Netherlands	12-17	1 161	1 365	48	1 415	49	489	47	124.4	127.1	121.6	0.96
142	Norway	13-18	336	378	49	385	49	124	45	120.3	118.9	121.7	1.02
143	Portugal	12-17	680	848	51	766	51	106	46	109.5	105.3	114.0	1.08
144	San Marino	11-18	...	...	...	...	...	...	...	...	...	...	...
145	Spain	12-17	2 599	3 299	50	3 053	50	410	48	108.9	105.4	112.6	1.07
146	Sweden	13-18	662	964	55	918	53	258	53	160.1	141.0	180.2	1.28
147	Switzerland	13-19	568	544	47	556	47	175	40	99.9	103.8	95.8	0.92
148	United Kingdom	11-17	5 437	8 053	52	9 706	54	5 302	58	156.9	148.3	165.7	1.12
149	United States	12-17	25 336	22 445	...	23 854	49	.	.	94.9	...	...	...
	South and West Asia												
150	Afghanistan	13-18	3 012	...	...	362z	–z	–z	–z	...	...	...	...
151	Bangladesh	11-17	23 212	9 134	47	11 024	51	126	26	42.4	43.3	41.5	0.96
152	Bhutan[5]	13-16	...	17	44	29**	45**	0.5**	39**	...	...	...	...
153	India	11-17	153 514	67 090	39	81 050	43	710	15	46.6	54.4	38.1	0.70
154	Iran, Islamic Republic of	11-17	12 869	9 727	47	10 024	47	819	38	77.4	80.2	74.4	0.93
155	Maldives	13-17	38	12	51	25	53	...	...	36.5	35.7	37.3	1.05
156	Nepal	10-16	4 047	1 265	40	1 822	42	16	22	35.5	41.2	29.3	0.71
157	Pakistan	10-16	25 462	...	...	5 734	40	83	18	...	...	...	...
158	Sri Lanka	10-17	2 721	...	...	2 320	[illegible]			...	...	...	...
	Sub-Saharan Africa												
159	Angola	10-16	2 241	292*	44*	414z	44z	77z	39z	14.7*	16.5*	13.0*	0.78*
160	Benin	12-18	1 131	213	31	312	32	29	25	21.1	29.1	13.2	0.45
161	Botswana	13-17	218	148	52	159**	51**	5**	30**	71.2	67.7	74.6	1.10
162	Burkina Faso	13-19	2 062	173	38	237	40	18	50	9.4	11.8	7.1	0.60

GROSS ENROLMENT RATIO (GER) IN SECONDARY EDUCATION (%)				NET ENROLMENT RATIO (NER) IN SECONDARY EDUCATION (%)								INTERNAL EFFICIENCY			POST-SECONDARY NON-TERTIARY EDUCATION		
												Repeaters in secondary general education (%)			Total enrolment		
2002/2003				1998/1999				2002/2003				2002/2003			2002/2003		
Total	Male	Female	GPI (F/M)	Total	Male	Female	GPI (F/M)	Total	Male	Female	GPI (F/M)	Total	Male	Female	Total (000)	% F	
103.4**	…	…	…	…	…	…	…	96.3z	…	…	…	0.3**	–	0.7**	0.02**	50**	110
71.0**	67.4**	74.8**	1.11**	70.8	65.2	76.3	1.17	63.1**	59.6**	66.7**	1.12**	–	–	–	0.4**	84**	111
60.7	55.9	65.5	1.17	…	…	…	…	39.0	35.8	42.2	1.18	6.4	7.8	5.2	.	.	112
70.6	68.3	72.9	1.07	60.1**	58.2**	62.2**	1.07**	63.0**	59.8**	66.3**	1.11**	5.1z	6.4z	3.8z	4	56	113
64.9	64.2**	65.7**	1.02**	42.1**	40.8**	43.5**	1.07**	51.1	49.7	52.6	1.06	1.1	1.4	0.7	1 *	…	114
89.7	92.8	86.5	0.93	62.2	62.9	61.6	0.98	69.2	70.2	68.1	0.97	5.6	6.4	4.6	264z	66z	115
105.9	92.4	120.7	1.31	…	…	…	…	94.7	…	…	…	2.5	2.3	2.6	1 **	48**	116
86.8	77.0	96.5	1.25	65.4	60.3	70.4	1.17	76.1**	67.6**	84.7**	1.25**	0.2**	0.2**	0.2**	2	62	117
69.2	65.8	72.7	1.11	…	…	…	…	58.4	55.9	60.8	1.09	16.2	19.7	13.5	1	69	118
73.8**	63.2**	84.8**	1.34**	…	…	…	…	63.7**	53.6**	74.1**	1.38**	–	–	–	.	.	119
82.4**	79.2**	85.6**	1.08**	72.5**	70.0**	74.9**	1.07**	72.0**	69.4**	74.7**	1.08**	0.9	0.9	1.0	8	63	120
94.0**	94.3**	93.7**	0.99**	…	…	…	…	79.1**	78.3**	79.9**	1.02**	1.9	2.2	1.6	0.6	67	121
105.6	99.4	112.1	1.13	…	…	…	…	73.2	69.8	76.8	1.10	12.4z	15.3z	9.9z	3	35	122
69.9	65.1	74.9	1.15	48.0	43.0	53.2	1.24	59.2	54.8	63.8	1.16	9.1	10.9	7.5	.	.	123
North America and Western Europe																	
…	…	…	…	…	…	…	…	…	…	…	…	–	–	–	.	.	124
100.0	102.3	97.5	0.95	…	…	…	…	88.9	89.3	88.5	0.99	…	…	…	55	61	125
160.8	153.1	168.9	1.10	…	…	…	…	97.2	96.7	97.8	1.01	…	…	…	54	49	126
105.3**,z	105.7**,z	104.9**,z	0.99**,z	94.0**	94.3**	93.7**	0.99**	97.6**,y	97.4**,y	97.9**,y	1.00**,y	…	…	…	298**,z	42**,z	127
98.4	97.6	99.3	1.02	87.8	86.2	89.6	1.04	92.8	91.4	94.3	1.03	1.7	2.6	0.9	.	.	128
129.1	125.9	132.4	1.05	89.0**	87.6**	90.4**	1.03**	95.9	94.3	97.6	1.04	.	.	.	1	25	129
128.2	121.7	134.9	1.11	94.9**	94.5**	95.2**	1.01**	94.6	94.2	95.0	1.01	0.3	0.4	0.3	11	46	130
108.9	108.4	109.5	1.01	93.3**	92.5**	94.3**	1.02**	94.4	93.5	95.3	1.02	8.7**,y	…	…	33	62	131
100.0	100.8	99.1	0.98	87.8**	87.6**	88.0**	1.0 **	88.0	87.8	88.2	1.00	3.1	3.5	2.6	463	49	132
97.5	97.6	97.3	1.00	84.9**	83.5**	86.4**	1.03**	86.1	85.2	87.1	1.02	…	…	…	33	55	133
114.4	110.4	118.6	1.07	84.7**	82.3**	87.2**	1.06**	86.0	84.0	88.1	1.05	–	–		1	40	134
106.8	102.2	111.6	1.09	82.1	80.1	84.1	1.05	83.4	80.4	86.6	1.08	2.4	2.1	2.6	51	55	135
93.2	94.2	92.3	0.98	86.8**	86.3**	87.3**	1.01**	89.0	89.1	88.9	1.00	1.9	3.0	0.9	14	51	136
99.3	100.0**	98.6**	0.99**	84.8**	84.4**	85.2**	1.01**	91.4	90.9	91.8	1.01	2.4	2.9**	1.8**	46	64	137
96.0	93.1	99.1	1.06	…	…	…	…	80.0	77.3	82.9	1.07	…	…	…	1	21	138
94.9	95.3	94.6	0.99	…	…	…	…	86.8	85.8	87.8	1.02	0.4	0.4	0.3	0.3	20	139
…	…	…	…	…	…	…	…	…	…	…	…	–	–	–	.	.	140
121.9	122.8	121.0	0.99	92.2**	91.8**	92.7**	1.01**	88.9	88.5	89.3	1.01	3.7	4.0	3.4	6	18	141
114.6	113.4	115.8	1.02	96.1**	95.7**	96.5**	1.01**	96.0	95.5	96.6	1.01	…	…	…	6	20	142
112.7	108.0	117.7	1.09	85.3**	81.8**	89.0**	1.09**	85.1	80.9	89.5	1.11	2.0**,y	2.0**,y	2.0**,y		.	143
…	…	…	…	…	…	…	…	…	…	…	…	–	–	–	…	…	144
117.5	114.4	120.7	1.06	…	…	…	…	95.6	93.7	97.6	1.04	…	…	…	.	.	145
138.7	127.3	150.6	1.18	97.8**	95.7**	100.0**	1.05**	99.5	99.2	99.8	1.01	…	…	…	11	50	146
97.9	100.9	94.7	0.94	88.2**	91.3**	85.0**	0.93**	87.0	89.3	84.5	0.95	2.2	2.4	2.1	29	69	147
178.5	159.0	199.1	1.25	94.8	94.7	94.9	1.00	95.2	93.8	96.6	1.03	…	…	…			148
94.2	94.2	94.1	1.00	88.3	…	…	…	88.4	87.7	89.0	1.01	…	…	…	423	66	149
South and West Asia																	
12.5z	24.0z	– z	– z	…	…	…	…	…	…	…	…	…	…	…	.	.	150
47.5	45.0	50.2	1.12	39.4	40.3	38.5	0.95	44.5	42.1	46.9	1.11	5.4	5.8	5.1	23	42	151
…	…	…	…	…	…	…	…	…	…	…	…	10.7z	9.2z	12.6z	4**	35**	152
52.8	58.5	46.7	0.80	…	…	…	…	…	…	…	…	4.8	5.2	4.3	522**	25	153
77.9	80.2	75.4	0.94	…	…	…	…	…	…	…	…	7.1y	9.8y	4.1y	881	16**	154
66.7	62.2	71.3	1.15	…	…	…	…	51.4**	47.9**	54.9**	1.15**	…	…	…	0.2z	…	155
45.0	50.4	39.2	0.78	…	…	…	…	…	…	…	…	11.7**	10.8**	12.9**	.	.	156
22.5	26.2	18.6	0.71	…	…	…	…	…	…	…	…	…	…	…	924*,y	45*,y	157
86.5**	**84.2****	**88.9****	**1.06****	…	…	…	…	…	…	…	…	…	…	…	.	.	158
Sub-Saharan Africa																	
19.1z	21.4z	16.8z	0.78z	…	…	…	…	…	…	…	…	…	…	…	.	.	159
27.6	37.9	17.4	0.46	15.7**	21.5**	9.9**	0.46**	20.1**,y	27.2**,y	12.9**,y	0.48**,y	23.1	22.8	23.8	…	…	160
72.7**	70.5**	74.9**	1.06**	52.7**	48.2**	57.4**	1.19**	53.6**	49.9**	57.4**	1.15**	0.5**	0.1**	0.9**	14z	49z	161
11.5	13.8	9.2	0.67	8.3	10.5	6.1	0.58	9.0	10.8	7.2	0.67	27.6	26.5	29.2	.	.	162

Table 8 (continued)

	Country or territory	Age group	School-age population (000)	ENROLMENT IN SECONDARY EDUCATION: Total enrolment 1998/1999		Total enrolment 2002/2003		Enrolment in technical and vocational education 2002/2003		GROSS ENROLMENT RATIO (GER) IN SECONDARY EDUCATION (%) 1998/1999			
		2002/2003	2002	Total (000)	% F	Total (000)	% F	Total (000)	% F	Total	Male	Female	GPI (F/M)
163	Burundi	13-19	1 183	...	...	131	42	12	31	...	...	...	...
164	Cameroon	12-18	2 627	626**	45**	820	45	151	40	26.5**	29.1**	24.0**	0.82**
165	Cape Verde	12-17	71	...	...	50	52	2	39	...	...	...	...
166	Central African Republic	12-18	617	...	...	...	...	...	...	...	...	...	...
167	Chad	12-18	1 316	123	21	191**	25**	4**	32**	10.7	17.1	4.4	0.26
168	Comoros	12-18	124	29	44	38	45	0.1	10	24.8	27.4	22.2	0.81
169	Congo	12-18	589	...	...	183**,z	42**,z	18**,z	52**,z	...	...	...	...
170	Côte d'Ivoire	12-18	2 891	592**	35**	737**,z	36**,z	...	...	22.5**	29.2**	15.7**	0.54**
171	D.R. Congo	12-17	7 322	1 235	34	...	...	...	...	18.4	24.2	12.7	0.52
172	Equatorial Guinea	12-18	74	20	38**	21**,z	36**,z	1z	20z	31.0	38.5**	23.5**	0.61**
173	Eritrea	12-17	575	115	41	161	39	2	23	23.3	27.6	19.1	0.69
174	Ethiopia	13-18	9 440	1 060	40	**2 141**	**36**	**87**	**47**	12.9	15.4	10.4	0.67
175	Gabon	12-18	212	87	46	105**,z	...	8z	...	45.7	49.2	42.3	0.86
176	Gambia	13-18	176	48	39	60**	41**	0.4**	67**	31.4	38.4	24.5	0.64
177	Ghana	12-17	2 979	1 024	44	**1 277**	**45**	**19**	**15**	36.7	41.2	32.2	0.78
178	Guinea	13-19	1 289	172**	26**	310**	31**	...	...	13.9**	20.2**	7.3**	0.36**
179	Guinea-Bissau	13-17	159	...	...	27**,y	35**,y	0.9**,y	27**,y	...	...	...	...
180	Kenya	13-17	4 222	1 156**	47**	1 390	48**	28	47	29.9**	31.5**	28.3**	0.90**
181	Lesotho	13-17	237	72	58	82	56	1	45	31.7	26.5	36.9	1.39
182	Liberia	12-17	463	114	39	...	...	...	...	30.5	37.0	23.9	0.65
183	Madagascar	11-17	2 721	347**	49**	...	...	...	...	14.3**	14.6**	14.0**	0.96**
184	Malawi	12-17	1 567	473	41**	518**	44**	.	.	32.9	38.8**	27.1**	0.70**
185	Mali	13-18	1 801	218	34	351	35	40	42	13.6	17.7	9.4	0.53
186	Mauritius	11-17	138	102**	49**	112	49	12	29	70.8**	70.7**	70.9**	1.00**
187	Mozambique	11-17	3 128	270**	40**	499	40	22	28	9.8**	11.7**	8.0**	0.68**
188	Namibia	13-17	221	110	53	138	53	.	.	57.3	53.2	61.4	1.15
189	Niger	13-19	1 783	105	38	125	39	0.9	24	6.7	8.1	5.2	0.63
190	Nigeria	12-17	17 328	...	...	6 313	44	–	–	...	...	...	...
191	Rwanda	13-18	1 174	91	50	189	47	...	...	9.6	10.2	9.0	0.88
192	Sao Tome and Principe	13-17	19	...	...	7**,z	45**,z	0.04z	25z	...	...	...	...
193	Senegal	13-19	1 601	239**	39**	310	41	4	45	16.7**	20.2**	13.0**	0.64**
194	Seychelles[3]	12-16	...	8	49	8	50	.	.	114.0	114.1	113.9	1.00
195	Sierra Leone	12-17	637	...	...	156y	42**,y	21y	44**,y	...	...	...	...
196	Somalia	...	...	...	...	...	...	...	...	...	...	...	...
197	South Africa	14-18	4 917	4 244*	53*	4 312**	52**	203**	42**	89.8*	84.5*	95.1*	1.13*
198	Swaziland	13-17	138	61	50	63	50	1.1	72	48.4	48.4	48.5	1.00
199	Togo	12-18	782	232	29	...	...	...	...	33.6	47.9	19.2	0.40
200	Uganda	13-18	3 487	304	39	688**	45**	32**	30**	9.8	12.0	7.7	0.64
201	United Republic of Tanzania	14-19	5 086	250**	45**	...	...	...	...	5.5**	6.1**	5.0**	0.82**
202	Zambia	14-18	1 261	226	43**	351	45	6	6	19.8	22.4**	17.1**	0.77**
203	Zimbabwe	13-18	2 057	...	...	**758**	**48**	.	.	...	...	...	...

			Sum	Sum	% F	Sum	% F	Sum	% F	Weighted average			
I	World	...	759 758	427 000	47	495 499	47	49 638	46	59.7	62.6	56.6	0.90
II	Countries in transition	...	33 537	31 127	50	31 112	49	2 862	35	88.9	88.3	89.5	1.01
III	Developed acountries	...	84 466	87 519	49	90 084	49	17 951	49	103.4	103.0	103.8	1.01
IV	Developing countries	...	641 754	308 354	46	374 303	47	28 825	46	51.8	55.4	47.9	0.86
V	Arab States	...	39 473	22 209	46	25 643	46	3 583	43	59.9	63.6	56.1	0.88
VI	Central and Eastern Europe	...	42 535	38 743	49	39 240	48	7 044	39	85.4	86.2	84.7	0.98
VII	Central Asia	...	12 028	9 688	49	10 707	48	576	41	85.7	87.0	84.5	0.97
VIII	East Asia and the Pacific	...	219 238	133 696	47	155 620	48	17 323	47	64.4	66.0	[illegible]	[illegible]
IX	Latin America and the Caribbean	...	66 486	41 894	51	58 662	51	5 355	55	71.7	68.6	74.9	1.09
X	North America and Western Europe	...	61 767	63 593	49	66 840	50	12 394	51	105.3	105.0	105.7	1.01
XI	South and West Asia	...	225 084	95 949	41	112 336	44	1 935	29	45.6	52.1	38.7	0.74
XII	Sub-Saharan Africa	...	93 147	21 228	46	26 452	44	1 427	37	24.5	27.2	21.8	0.80

1. Refers to lower and upper secondary education (ISCED levels 2 and 3).
2. Corresponds to ISCED level 4. Like secondary education, it includes general as well as technical and vocational programmes.
3. National population data were used to calculate enrolment ratios.
4. Enrolment ratios were not calculated due to lack of United Nations population data by age.

GROSS ENROLMENT RATIO (GER) IN SECONDARY EDUCATION (%)				NET ENROLMENT RATIO (NER) IN SECONDARY EDUCATION (%)								INTERNAL EFFICIENCY: Repeaters in secondary general education (%)			POST-SECONDARY NON-TERTIARY EDUCATION: Total enrolment		
2002/2003				1998/1999				2002/2003				2002/2003			2002/2003		
Total	Male	Female	GPI (F/M)	Total	Male	Female	GPI (F/M)	Total	Male	Female	GPI (F/M)	Total	Male	Female	Total (000)	% F	
11.1	12.8	9.4	0.73	...	...	...	...	8.6**	9.7**	7.6**	0.78**	36.6	31.7	43.0	.	.	163
31.2	33.9	28.5	0.84	...	...	...	...	...	...	...	...	17.5	17.2	17.8	...	...	164
69.7	66.8	72.7	1.09	...	...	...	...	58.0	55.0	61.1	1.11	20.4	21.9	19.1	0.8	66	165
...	...	...	...	...	...	...	...	...	...	...	...	...	...	...	...	...	166
14.5**	21.9**	7.2**	0.33**	7.5	11.6	3.4	0.29	10.4**	...	...	...	16.1**,y	16.1**,y	16.1**,y	.	.	167
31.0	33.8	28.1	0.83	...	...	...	...	...	...	...	...	18.5	18.3	18.7	0.7	46	168
32.0**,z	37.4**,z	26.6**,z	0.71**,z	...	...	...	...	...	...	...	...	30.2	30.3	30.0	...	...	169
25.9**,z	33.2**,z	18.5**,z	0.56**,z	18.2**	23.8**	12.6**	0.53**	20.8**,z	26.5**,z	15.1**,z	0.57**,z	15.8z	15.8z	15.8z	...	...	170
...	...	...	...	...	...	...	...	...	...	...	...	...	...	...	...	...	171
29.7**,z	37.8**,z	21.6**,z	0.57**,z	...	...	...	...	...	...	...	...	...	...	...	.	.	172
28.1	34.0	22.1	0.65	18.8**	20.8**	16.8**	0.80**	21.6	24.8	18.4	0.74	19.7	15.5	26.3	1	11	173
21.9	**27.8**	**15.9**	**0.57**	11.4	13.3	9.4	0.71	**18.4****	**23.4****	**13.4****	**0.57****	11.4	9.5	14.9	**29**	**39**	174
50.9**,z	...	...	...	...	...	...	...	...	...	...	...	21.7**,z	...	...	...	...	175
34.1**	40.5**	27.8**	0.69**	25.9	31.1	20.7	0.67	32.7**	38.8**	26.5**	0.68**	...	...	...	...	...	176
42.4	**46.8**	**38.0**	**0.81**	31.1**	34.1**	28.0**	0.82**	**36.2****	**39.1****	**33.3****	**0.85****	2.4**	2.4**	2.5**	19**	29**	177
24.1**	32.7**	15.2**	0.46**	12.0**	17.2**	6.5**	0.38**	20.8**	28.0**	13.4**	0.48**	24.8	26.1	21.8	...	...	178
17.8**,y	23.0**,y	12.5**,y	0.54**,y	...	...	...	...	...	...	...	...	...	...	...	.	.	179
32.9	34.2**	31.6**	0.92**	...	...	...	...	24.5**	24.7**	24.3**	0.98**	.	.	.	...	...	180
34.7	30.4	38.9	1.28	14.0**	9.7**	18.3**	1.89**	22.5**	17.8**	27.2**	1.53**	8.7	8.7	8.7	–	–	181
...	...	...	...	...	...	...	...	...	...	...	...	...	...	...	...	...	182
...	...	...	...	11.5**	11.3**	11.6**	1.03**	...	...	...	...	16.4	16.5	16.3	17**,z	34**,z	183
33.0**	37.5**	28.7**	0.76**	26.9**	30.3**	23.5**	0.78**	28.5**	31.5**	25.5**	0.81**	...	...	...	14y	35y	184
19.5	25.1	13.8	0.55	...	...	...	...	...	...	...	...	...	...	...	.	.	185
81.2	81.2	81.1	1.00	62.3**	62.1**	62.6**	1.01**	74.4**	74.3**	74.5**	1.00**	12.4	14.0	10.9	4**	23**	186
15.9	19.1	12.7	0.66	7.9**	9.3**	6.6**	0.72**	12.2	14.4	10.0	0.70	21.8	20.6	23.6	.	.	187
62.4	58.9	65.9	1.12	30.3	24.6	36.1	1.47	44.2	38.7	49.7	1.29	7.8**	6.9**	8.6**	2z	27z	188
7.0	8.4	5.5	0.66	5.8**	7.0**	4.6**	0.65**	6.1	7.3	4.9	0.67	21.0	18.9	24.4	3	36	109
36.4	40.3	32.5	0.81	...	...	...	...	29.1	32.2	25.9	0.80	3.6	3.7	3.5	...	...	190
16.1	17.9	14.5	0.81	...	...	...	...	...	...	...	...	13.2**,z	11.5**,z	15.0**,z	.	.	191
39.2**,z	42.4**,z	35.9**,z	0.84**,z	...	...	...	...	28.9**,z	31.6**,z	26.2**,z	0.83**,z	23.5**,z	20.7**,z	26.8**,z	...	...	192
19.4	22.8	15.8	0.69	...	...	...	...	...	...	...	...	11.4	11.3	11.5	...	...	193
110.9	110.8	111.0	1.00	99.4	98.8	100.0	1.01	99.9	100.0	99.7	1.00	.	.	.	2	56	194
26.4y	31.0**,y	21.8**,y	0.70**,y	...	...	...	...	...	...	...	...	7.8y	7.0y	8.9y	40y	57y	195
...	...	...	...	...	...	...	...	...	...	...	...	...	...	...	...	...	196
87.7**	84.5**	90.9**	1.08**	59.4*	55.4*	63.4*	1.15*	65.5**	62.7**	68.4**	1.09**	13.4	13.8	13.1	356	40	197
45.3	45.0	45.6	1.01	37.1	35.3	38.8	1.10	32.4**	29.3**	35.6**	1.21**	12.5z	12.6z	12.5z	0.4	28	198
...	...	...	...	23.1	32.1	14.1	0.44	...	...	...	...	24.2	24.2	24.0	...	...	199
19.7**	21.9**	17.6**	0.80**	...	...	...	...	16.5**	17.4**	15.6**	0.90**	2.0	1.9	2.0	.	.	200
...	...	...	...	...	...	...	...	...	...	...	...	**3.1****	**2.4****	**3.9****	–	–	201
27.9	30.5	25.3	0.83	15.9**	17.3**	14.6**	0.84**	22.8**	24.9**	20.6**	0.83**	12.3**,z	11.4**,z	13.4**,z	...	...	202
36.3	**38.1**	**34.6**	**0.91**	...	...	...	...	**33.8**	**35.1**	**32.6**	**0.93**	.	.	.	**0.9**	**11**	203
Weighted average				Weighted average								Median					
65.2	67.0	63.3	0.94	50.2	52.7	47.7	0.91	56.1**	57.8**	54.4**	0.94**	2.4	2.9	1.9	...	...	I
92.8	93.8	91.7	0.98	81.6	81.0	82.3	1.02	84.7	84.8	84.5	1.00	0.2	0.2	0.2	...	...	II
106.6	105.3	108.1	1.03	89.2	89.0	89.4	1.00	91.0	90.3	91.6	1.01	1.4	2.5	0.4	...	...	III
58.3	60.7	55.9	0.92	42.8	45.9	39.7	0.86	50.1	52.2	48.0	0.92	5.6	6.4	4.6	...	...	IV
65.0	68.1	61.7	0.91	51.2	53.9	48.5	0.90	56.1	58.1	54.0	0.93	7.6	9.0	5.8	...	...	V
92.3	94.6	89.8	0.95	78.2	78.6	77.8	0.99	83.4**	84.5**	82.2**	0.97**	1.2	1.6	0.9	...	...	VI
89.0	90.5	87.5	0.97	80.8	81.5	80.1	0.98	83.4	84.7	82.2	0.97	0.2	0.3	0.1	...	...	VII
71.0	71.7	70.2	0.98	53.4	54.9	51.7	0.94	64.3	64.8	63.8	0.98	1.3	1.9	0.7	...	...	VIII
88.2	85.1	91.5	1.08	52.8	50.7	55.0	1.09	65.7	63.7	67.7	1.06	3.1	3.8	2.5	...	...	IX
108.2	106.3	110.2	1.04	89.4	89.5	89.3	1.00	90.6	89.9	91.3	1.02	1.8	2.8	0.9	...	...	X
49.9	54.2	45.3	0.84	40.2	46.1	33.9	0.74	43.6	47.6	39.2	0.82	7.1	9.2	5.1	...	...	XI
28.4	31.9	24.9	0.78	17.9	19.6	16.2	0.83	22.1	24.5	19.7	0.80	13.4	13.8	13.1	...	...	XII

5. Enrolment ratios were not calculated due to inconsistencies between enrolment and the United Nations population data.

Data in bold are for 2003/2004.
(z) Data are for 2001/2002.
(y) Data are for 2000/2001.

Table 9A
Participation in tertiary education

	Country or territory	ENROLMENT IN TERTIARY EDUCATION									
		Total students enrolled (000)						Gross enrolment ratio (GER) (%)			
		1998/1999			2002/2003			1998/1999			
		Total	Male	Female	Total	Male	Female	Total	Male	Female	GPI (F/M)
	Arab States										
1	Algeria	456 **	...	...	683 **	...	...	15.1 **	...	...	...
2	Bahrain	11	4 **	7 **	19	7	12	20.7	15.0 **	27.8 **	1.86 **
3	Djibouti	0.2	...	...	**1.1**	**0.6**	**0.5**	0.3	...	...	...
4	Egypt	2 447 **	...	...	2 154	...	...	38.3 **	...	...	...
5	Iraq	272	179	93	318 **,z	210 **,z	108 **,z	12.9	16.7	9.1	0.54
6	Jordan	...	...	...	186	91	95	...	...	...	...
7	Kuwait	32 **	10 **	22 **	...	...	...	20.9 **	12.2 **	31.6 **	2.58 **
8	Lebanon	113	56	57	144	66	78	35.5	35.1	35.9	1.02
9	Libyan Arab Jamahiriya	308	158 **	150 **	375 **	182 **	193 **	56.1	56.8 **	55.4 **	0.98 **
10	Mauritania	13	...	...	9 **	7 **	2 **	5.5	...	...	...
11	Morocco	273	159	114	336	185	151	9.4	10.8	8.0	0.74
12	Oman	...	...	...	20 **,z	8 **,z	12 **,z	...	...	...	...
13	Palestinian Autonomous Territories	66	36	30	105	53	52	24.8	26.2	23.3	0.89
14	Qatar	9 **	3 **	6 **	8	2	6	25.2 **	11.7 **	45.7 **	3.89 **
15	Saudi Arabia	350	150	199	525	219	306	20.2	16.8	23.8	1.41
16	Sudan	201	106	95	...	...	...	6.8	7.1	6.5	0.92
17	Syrian Arab Republic	...	...	...	...	...	...	...	...	...	...
18	Tunisia	157 **	81 **	76 **	263	119	145	17.3 **	17.5 **	17.0 **	0.97 **
19	United Arab Emirates	40 **	13 **	27 **	68 **	23 **	45 **	19.7 **	10.6 **	34.0 **	3.22 **
20	Yemen	164	130	34	...	...	...	11.2	17.1	4.8	0.28
	Central and Eastern Europe										
21	Albania	...	...	...	44	16	27	...	...	...	...
22	Belarus	353	155	198	489	210	279	48.4	41.6	55.4	1.33
23	Bosnia and Herzegovina	...	...	...	...	...	...	...	...	...	...
24	Bulgaria	270	109	161	231	109	122	43.5	34.5	52.9	1.53
25	Croatia	96	45	51	122	57	65	31.9	29.6	34.2	1.16
26	Czech Republic	231	116	115	287	142	145	26.1	25.7	26.5	1.03
27	Estonia	49	21	28	64	24	39	51.0	42.3	60.0	1.42
28	Hungary	279	128	151	390	169	221	33.4	29.9	37.1	1.24
29	Latvia	82	32	51	119	46	73	50.5	38.5	62.6	1.63
30	Lithuania	107	43	64	168	67	101	45.5	36.1	55.0	1.52
31	Poland	1 399	601	798	1 983	837	1 147	45.7	38.5	53.1	1.38
32	Republic of Moldova	104	46	58	114	50	64	29.4	25.8	33.1	1.28
33	Romania	408	200	208	644	294	350	21.3	20.4	22.1	1.08
34	Russian Federation	...	...	...	8 151 **	3 572 **	4 579 **	...	...	...	...
35	Serbia and Montenegro[2]	197	92	106	209 y	97 y	112 y	34.0	31.1	37.0	1.19
36	Slovakia	123	59	64	158	74	84	26.5	25.2	27.9	1.11
37	Slovenia	79	35	44	101	44	57	52.8	45.3	60.7	1.34
38	The former Yugoslav Rep. of Macedonia	35	16	19	46	20	26	22.0	19.3	24.7	1.28
39	Turkey	...	...	...	1 918	1 108	811	...	...	...	...
40	Ukraine	1 737	821	916	2 296	1 061 *	1 235 *	47.3	44.1	50.5	1.15
	Central Asia										
41	Armenia	...	...	...	79	35	44	...	...	...	...
42	Azerbaijan	108	66	42	121	67	54	16.2	20.0	12.4	0.62
43	Georgia	130	63	68	155	80	76	32.2	30.4	34.1	1.12
44	Kazakhstan	324	151	173	603	261	342	23.7	22.0	25.5	1.16
45	Kyrgyzstan	131	65	67	201	92	109	30.4	29.8	30.9	1.04
46	Mongolia	65	23	42	98	37	61	26.1	18.1	34.1	1.88
47	Tajikistan	76	57	19	97	73	24	13.8	20.3	7.1	0.35
48	Turkmenistan			...	...	...	...	...	...	...	...
49	Uzbekistan	...	...	...	394	221	173	...	...	...	...
	East Asia and the Pacific										
50	Australia	869	399	470	1 012	466	547	63.9	57.4	70.7	1.23
51	Brunei Darussalam	3	1	2	4.4	1.6	2.8	9.4	6.5	12.4	1.90
52	Cambodia	...	...	...	43	31 **	12 **	...	...	...	...

ENROLMENT IN TERTIARY EDUCATION				DISTRIBUTION OF STUDENTS BY ISCED LEVEL						FOREIGN STUDENTS (000)						
Gross enrolment ratio (GER) (%)				Total students (%)			Percentage of female in each level									
2002/2003				2002/2003			2002/2003			1998/1999			2002/2003			
Total	Male	Female	GPI (F/M)	Level 5A	Level 5B	Level 6	Level 5A	Level 5B	Level 6	Total	Male	Female	Total	Male	Female	
															Arab States	
20.5**	...	...	...	...	...	...	...	...	...	...	...	...	...	...	...	1
33.2	23.5	44.4	1.89	82.1	17.9	0.02	63.6	54.0	50.0	...	...	...	1.3	0.9	0.4	2
1.8	**2.0**	**1.6**	**0.81**	**55.2**	**38.4**	**6.3**	**42.5**	**48.9**	**40.3**	–	–	–	–z	–z	–z	3
29.4	...	...	...	...	...	...	...	...	...	...	...	...	...	...	...	4
14.1**,z	18.2**,z	9.8**,z	0.54**,z	...	...	...	...	...	...	...	...	...	...	...	...	5
34.8	33.2	36.6	1.10	84.7	14.5	0.8	49.2	63.5	26.1	...	...	...	16	...	...	6
...	...	...	...	...	...	...	...	...	...	...	...	...	...	...	...	7
44.3	40.4	48.2	1.19	84.7	14.4	1.0	56.1	43.5	32.2	15.6	...	...	12.2	6.1	6.1	8
58.1**	55.5**	60.7**	1.09**	72.1**	25.7**	2.2**	52.4**	49.6**	38.0**	...	...	...	...	...	...	9
3.5**	5.5**	1.5**	0.27**	94.1**	4.9**	0.9**	21.8	18.5**	5.8	...	...	...	0.2	...	...	10
10.8	11.7	9.9	0.84	84.6	10.8	4.6	45.5	45.5	32.4	4.2	3.5	0.7	5.1	4.2	0.9	11
7.5**,z	5.7**,z	9.6**,z	1.67**,z	98.5**,z	.z	1.5**,z	58.5**,z	.z	22.2**,z	...	...	...	...	...	...	12
34.8	34.2	35.5	1.04	92.4	7.6	...	49.1	54.1	...	2.8	2.0	0.8	0.4y	0.2y	0.1y	13
22.0	11.9	32.3	2.71	98.5	1.3	0.2	72.7	81.9	23.1	...	...	...	1.6	0.7	1.0	14
25.4	20.7	30.4	1.47	84.8	13.1	2.1	65.4	15.6	34.0	6.1	4.5	1.5	11.0	7.9	3.1	15
...	...	...	...	...	...	...	...	...	...	...	...	...	...	...	...	16
...	...	...	...	...	...	...	...	...	...	...	...	...	...	...	...	17
26.7	23.5	30.0	1.28	73.3	19.3	7.4	...	...	...	2.7j	...	...	2.3	...	...	18
34.7**	20.7**	52.8**	2.55**	...	...	...	...	...	...	...	...	...	...	...	...	19
...	...	...	...	...	...	...	...	...	...	...	...	...	...	...	...	20
															Central and Eastern Europe	
16.2	11.7	20.9	1.78	98.7	1.3	./.[1]	62.1	81.4	./.[1]	...	...	...	0.5	0.4	0.1	21
61.6	51.7	72.1	1.39	65.8	32.9	1.3	57.5	56.6	49.3	2.7	...	...	1.0	...	...	22
...	...	...	...	...	...	...	...	...	...	...	...	...	...	...	...	23
39.0	35.9	42.2	1.18	91.7	6.4	1.9	52.5	56.9	50.9	8.4	4.9	3.5	8.0	4.7	3.3	24
39.4	36.1	42.8	1.18	65.5	34.3	0.2	55.2	49.5	36.5	0.5j	...	...	2.8	1.5	1.3	25
35.5	34.3	36.8	1.07	82.4	10.3	7.3	50.0	66.9	36.1	...	...	...	10.3	4.3	6.1	26
66.4	50.1	83.4	1.66	...	...	...	...	...	...	0.8	0.3	0.5	1.1	...	...	27
51.1	43.3	59.2	1.37	94.3	3.8	1.9	56.8	60.9	43.6	8.9j	4.1	4.8	12.2	6.6	5.7	28
72.5	54.7	90.9	1.66	80.1	18.8	1.1	63.4	54.9	58.3	1.8j	0.7**	1.1**	2.4	...	...	29
71.6	56.2	87.5	1.56	70.0	28.7	1.3	59.2	62.1	58.2	0.5	0.4	0.1	0.7	0.5	0.2	30
59.9	49.6	70.6	1.42	97.4	1.0	1.6	57.8	80.3	46.7	5.7j	3.0	2.7	7.6	3.5	4.1	31
29.8	25.7	34.0	1.32	84.9	13.4	1.7	56.1	57.5	59.3	1.7	...	...	2.4	1.6	0.8	32
34.9	31.3	38.7	1.24	87.8	7.9	4.2	54.0	60.2	49.9	13.3	8.0	5.3	9.7	5.4	4.3	33
69.4**	60.2**	78.8**	1.31**	72.9	25.1**	...	57.5	53.1**	...	41.2	...	...	71z	...	...	34
36.0y	32.8y	39.4y	1.20y	75.3y	24.4y	0.3y	55.4y	48.6y	35.7y	1.3	0.8	0.5	0.8y	0.5y	0.3y	35
33.7	31.0	36.4	1.17	89.7	3.9	6.4	52.6	80.8	42.8	...	...	...	1.7	1.0	0.6	36
68.4	58.4	79.0	1.35	49.8	50.2	–	59.6	52.9	–	0.7	0.4	0.3	1.0	0.5	0.5	37
27.5	23.6	31.6	1.34	93.6	6.4	–	56.8	46.8	–	0.3	0.2	0.1	0.1	0.0	0.1	38
28.0	31.9	24.1	0.76	68.8	30.0	1.2	42.1	42.8	37.4	18.3v	13.1	5.2	12.7	7.9	4.8	39
61.8	56.5*	67.2*	1.19*	73.5	25.4	1.2	54.1*	53.1*	49.7	18.3	...	...	18.2	...	...	40
															Central Asia	
27.3	24.2	30.5	1.26	98.3	.	1.7	55.8	.	35.4	...	...	...	3.0	...	...	41
16.5	18.6	14.4	0.78	99.1	.	0.9	44.8	.	29.4	1.7	1.1	0.6	1.9	1.4	0.5	42
37.9	38.3	37.5	0.98	98.9	.	1.1	48.6	.	61.1	0.3	...	...	0.9	...	...	43
44.7	38.7	50.7	1.31	99.1	.	0.9	56.6	.	61.1	7.5	...	...	6.5	...	...	44
42.2	38.5	45.9	1.19	99.0	.	1.0	54.0	.	61.9	1.1	0.5**	0.6**	13.4	7.2	6.3	45
37.0	27.6	46.5	1.69	94.2	4.1	1.6	62.2	69.1	59.4	0.3	0.1	0.1	0.2	0.1	0.1	46
16.4	24.4	8.3	0.34	99.1	.	0.9	24.9	.	36.6	5.0	3.7**	1.3**	2.2	1.8	0.4	47
...	...	...	...	...	...	...	...	...	...	...	...	...	...	...	...	48
15.7	17.5	13.9	0.80	59.0	40.2	0.8	38.9	51.4	38.9**	...	...	...	...	...	...	49
															East Asia and the Pacific	
74.3	66.8	82.2	1.23	77.9	18.8	3.3	55.1	50.3	48.5	...	...	...	179.6	94.6	85.0	50
13.0	9.5	16.7	1.76	64.5	35.3	0.2	63.2	63.5	28.6	0.1	0.05	0.05	0.04	0.02	0.02	51
3.4	4.9**	2.0**	0.40**	100.0	.	–	28.8**	.	–	0.02	0.02	0.01	0.04z	0.02z	0.02z	52

Table 9A (continued)

	Country or territory	ENROLMENT IN TERTIARY EDUCATION									
		Total students enrolled (000)						Gross enrolment ratio (GER) (%)			
		1998/1999			2002/2003			1998/1999			
		Total	Male	Female	Total	Male	Female	Total	Male	Female	GPI (F/M)
53	China	6 366	...	...	15 186	8 529	6 657	6.2	...	...	...
54	Cook Islands	.	.	.	.	.	.	.	.	.	.
55	Democratic People's Republic of Korea	...	...	...	...	...	...	...	...	...	...
56	Fiji	...	...	...	...	...	...	...	...	...	...
57	Indonesia	...	...	...	3 441	1 930	1 511	...	...	...	...
58	Japan	3 941	2 180	1 760	3 984	2 169	1 816	43.7	47.3	40.0	0.85
59	Kiribati	...	...	...	...	...	...	...	...	...	...
60	Lao People's Democratic Republic	12	8	4	28	18	10	2.6	3.4	1.7	0.49
61	Macao, China	7	4	3	26	17	10	27.6	31.4	24.1	0.77
62	Malaysia	443	216	226	632	284	348	22.9	22.0	23.8	1.08
63	Marshall Islands[2]	...	...	...	0.9 z	0.4 z	0.5 z	...	...	...	...
64	Micronesia (Federated States of)	2	...	...	...	...	...	15.3	...	...	...
65	Myanmar	...	...	...	555 **,z	...	...	...	...	...	...
66	Nauru	.	.	.	.	.	.	.	.	.	.
67	New Zealand	161	67	94	185	76	109	62.2	50.9	73.9	1.45
68	Niue	.	.	.	.	.	.	.	.	.	.
69	Palau[2]	...	...	...	0.5 **,z	0.2 **,z	0.3 **,z	...	...	...	...
70	Papua New Guinea	10	6	4	...	...	...	2.1	2.8	1.5	0.54
71	Philippines	2 209	995	1 213	2 427	1 086	1 341	29.4	26.0	32.8	1.26
72	Republic of Korea	2 636	1 713	923	**3 223**	**2 045**	**1 178**	64.7	81.8	46.7	0.57
73	Samoa	1.5	0.8	0.7	1.2 **,z	0.7 **,z	0.5 **,z	8.1	8.3	7.8	0.95
74	Singapore	...	...	...	...	...	...	...	...	...	...
75	Solomon Islands	.	.	.	.	.	.	.	.	.	.
76	Thailand	1 814	846	969	**2 251**	**1 043**	**1 208**	30.7	28.6	32.8	1.15
77	Timor-Leste	...	...	...	6 *,z	3 *,z	3 *,z	...	...	...	...
78	Tokelau	...	...	...	.	.	.	...	...	...	...
79	Tonga	...	...	...	0.4 **,z	0.2 **,z	0.2 **,z	...	...	...	...
80	Tuvalu	.	.	.	.	.	.	.	.	.	.
81	Vanuatu	...	...	...	0.7 z	...	...	...	...	...	...
82	Viet Nam	810	462	348	797 **	456 **	341 **	10.9	12.4	9.4	0.76
	Latin America and the Caribbean										
83	Anguilla	.	.	.	.	.	.	.	.	.	.
84	Antigua and Barbuda	.	.	.	.	.	.	.	.	.	.
85	Argentina	1 527	632 **	894 **	2 027	825	1 202	46.9	38.5 **	55.5 **	1.44 **
86	Aruba[2]	1.4	0.6	0.8	1.7	0.7	1.0	26.3	24.5	28.0	1.14
87	Bahamas	...	...	...	...	...	...	...	...	...	...
88	Barbados	7	2	5	8 y	2 y	6 y	32.0	19.6	44.6	2.28
89	Belize	...	...	...	0.5	0.2 *	0.3 *	...	...	...	...
90	Bermuda[2]	...	...	...	2.0 **,z	0.9 **,z	1.1 **,z	...	...	...	...
91	Bolivia	228	148 **	80 **	311	...	...	30.9	40.0 **	21.8 **	0.55 **
92	Brazil	2 204	992	1 211	3 579	1 558	2 021	13.6	12.3	15.0	1.22
93	British Virgin Islands	.	.	.	.	.	.	.	.	.	.
94	Cayman Islands[3]	0.4 **	0.1 **	0.3 **	0.4 y	0.1 y	0.3 y	...	...	...	...
95	Chile	407	219	187	**567**	**296**	**271**	33.8	36.0	31.5	0.88
96	Colombia	823 **	400 **	423 **	990	480	509	21.2 **	20.4 **	21.9 **	1.07 **
97	Costa Rica	58 **	27 **	30 **	77	37	40	16.8 **	15.5 **	18.2 **	1.18 **
98	Cuba	156 *	74 **	82 **	236	103	133	18.9 *	17.6 **	20.4 **	1.16 **
99	Dominica	.	.	.	.	.	.	.	.	.	.
100	Dominican Republic	...	...	...	287	111	176	...	...	...	...
101	Ecuador	...	...	...	...	...	...	...	...	...	...
102	El Salvador	118	53	65	113	52	62	18.3	16.4	20.2	1.23
103	Grenada	.	.	.	.	.	.	.	.	.	.
104	Guatemala	...	[illegible]		[illegible]	64	48	...	...	...	...
105	Guyana	...	...	...	5	2 **	3 **	...	[illegible]		
106	Haiti	...	...	...	...	...	...	...	...	...	...
107	Honduras	78	35 **	43 **	97 **,z	42 **,z	54 **,z	13.5	11.9 **	15.2 **	1.27 **
108	Jamaica	...	...	...	46 **	14 **	32 **	...	...	...	...
109	Mexico	[illegible]	[illegible]	888	2 237	1 126	1 110	18.3	19.2	17.4	0.91
110	Montserrat	.	.	.	.	.	.	.			.

ENROLMENT IN TERTIARY EDUCATION				DISTRIBUTION OF STUDENTS BY ISCED LEVEL						FOREIGN STUDENTS (000)						
Gross enrolment ratio (GER) (%)				Total students (%)			Percentage of female in each level									
2002/2003				2002/2003			2002/2003			1998/1999			2002/2003			
Total	Male	Female	GPI (F/M)	Level 5A	Level 5B	Level 6	Level 5A	Level 5B	Level 6	Total	Male	Female	Total	Male	Female	
15.8	17.1	14.4	0.84	50.8	48.5	0.7	44.0	44.0	28.1	...	...	...	...	...	...	53
.	.	.	.	.	.	.	.	.	.	.	.	.	.	.	.	54
...	...	...	...	...	...	...	...	...	...	...	...	...	...	...	...	55
...	...	...	...	...	...	...	...	...	...	...	...	...	...	...	...	56
16.4	18.2	14.5	0.80	72.4	25.9	1.7	42.4	48.8	34.7	0.3	...	...	0.4[z]	...	...	57
50.7	53.9	47.4	0.88	73.8	24.5	1.7	39.7	64.4	27.9	56.6	32.0	24.5	87	45	42	58
...	...	...	...	...	...	...	...	...	...	...	...	...	...	...	...	59
5.3	6.7	3.8	0.57	32.6	67.4	.	38.4	34.5	.	0.08	0.07	0.01	0.10	0.09	0.01	60
80.8	107.5	56.4	0.52	88.2	11.2	0.6	33.1	64.0	30.5	...	...	...	17.5	13.0	4.5	61
29.3	25.7	33.0	1.28	48.8	50.5	0.7	58.1	52.5	34.0	3.1[j]	...	...	28	...	...	62
18.1[z]	15.8[z]	20.4[z]	1.29[z]	13.6[z]	86.4[z]	.	56.9[z]	56.4[z]	.	...	...	...	...	...	...	63
...	...	...	...	...	...	...	...	...	...	...	...	...	...	...	...	64
11.5[**,z]	...	...	...	99.3[**,z]	0.5[**,z]	0.2[**,z]	...	...	...	...	...	...	...	...	...	65
.	.	.	.	.	.	.	.	.	.	.	.	.	.	.	.	66
73.9	58.8	90.1	1.53	72.5	25.5	2.0	58.7	59.8	48.7	...	...	...	17.7	8.8	8.9	67
.	.	.	.	.	.	.	.	.	.	.	.	.	.	.	.	68
39.3[**,z]	26.5[**,z]	54.4[**,z]	2.05[**,z]	100.0[**,z]	.	.	63.4[**,z]	.	.	...	...	...	0.01[y]	...	...	69
...	...	...	...	...	...	...	...	...	...	0.3	0.2	0.1	...	...	...	70
30.0	26.4	33.8	1.28	90.1	9.4	0.4	55.4	53.3	61.8	3.5	...	...	4.7	...	...	71
85.4	**105.1**	**64.5**	**0.61**	**58.8**	**40.0**	**1.1**	**36.9**	**36.2**	**29.5**	...	...	...	**8**	**4**	**4**	72
6.5[**,z]	6.8[**,z]	6.2[**,z]	0.90[**,z]	19.6[**,z]	80.4[**,z]	–[**,z]	39.8[**,z]	45.5[**,z]	–[**,z]	0.1	0.08	0.03	0.1[y]	...	...	73
...	...	...	...	...	...	...	...	...	...	...	...	...	...	...	...	74
.	.	.	.	.	.	.	.	.	.	.	.	.	.	.	.	75
38.8	**35.8**	**41.8**	**1.17**	**82.6**	**17.0**	**0.3**	**54.3**	**50.4**	**62.2**	1.9[j]	...	...	4.1[j,q,z]	...	...	76
12.0[*,z]	9.7[*,z]	15.3[*,z]	1.58[*,z]	...	...	...	...	...	...	...	...	...	...	...	...	77
.	.	.	.	.	.	.	.	.	.	.	.	.	.	.	.	78
3.6[**,z]	3.0[**,z]	4.2[**,z]	1.40[**,z]	...	...	...	...	...	...	...	...	...	...	...	...	79
.	.	.	.	...	...	...	...	...	...	.	.	.	.	.	.	80
4.0[z]	...	...	...	98.8[z]	.	1.2[z]	...	...	...	...	...	...	...	...	...	81
10.0[**]	11.4[**]	8.6[**]	0.76[**]	69.6[**]	27.7[**]	2.7[**]	51.7[**]	21.1[**]	36.7[**]	0.5	0.4	0.1	0.9[z]	0.7[z]	0.2[z]	82
Latin America and the Caribbean																
.	.	.	.	.	.	.	.	.	.	.	.	.	.	.	.	83
.	.	.	.	.	.	.	.	.	.	.	.	.	.	.	.	84
59.8	48.1	71.7	1.49	74.0	25.7	0.3	55.6	70.0	57.3	2.8[l]	...	...	3	...	...	85
30.3	25.0	35.4	1.42	22.8	77.2	.	79.0	53.5	.	...	...	...	0.09	0.08[**]	0.01[**]	86
...	...	...	...	...	...	...	...	...	...	...	...	...	...	...	...	87
38.1[y]	22.1[y]	54.6[y]	2.47[y]	49.4[y]	45.0[y]	5.6[**,y]	66.1[y]	77.3[y]	57.8[**,y]	...	...	...	0.6[y]	0.2[**,y]	0.4[**,y]	88
2.0	1.4[*]	2.6[*]	1.91[*]	100.0	.	.	64.9[*]	.	.	.	.	.	.	.	.	89
62.4[**,z]	...	...	...	.	100.0[**,z]	.	...	55.1[**,z]	...	...	...	...	...	...	...	90
39.4	...	...	...	...	...	...	...	...	...	1.1	...	...	...	...	...	91
20.6	17.8	23.4	1.32	...	...	2.8	...	...	55.4	...	...	...	...	...	...	92
.	.	.	.	.	.	.	.	.	.	.	.	.	.	.	.	93
...	...	...	...	79.5[y]	20.5[y]	.	71.6[y]	86.3[y]	.	...	...	...	0.1[y]	...	...	94
45.4	**46.7**	**44.1**	**0.94**	**83.0**	**16.7**	**0.3**	**48.2**	**46.2**	**39.9**	...	...	...	**5**	...	...	95
24.3	23.4	25.4	1.09	74.8[**]	19.2	6.0[**]	53.0[**]	46.1	49.2[**]	...	...	...	...	...	...	96
19.4	18.0	20.8	1.16	85.2	14.6	0.1	54.0	42.6	53.1	...	...	...	0.9	0.4[**]	0.5	97
33.7	28.9	38.7	1.34	98.9	.	1.1	56.4	.	36.6	3.7[hf]	...	...	17.2	...	...	98
.	.	.	.	.	.	.	.	.	.	.	.	.	.	.	.	99
34.5	26.0	43.4	1.67	91.0	8.4	0.6	64.8	25.1	39.5	...	...	...	...	...	...	100
...	...	...	...	...	...	...	...	...	...	...	...	...	...	...	...	101
17.4	15.8	19.1	1.21	...	...	...	...	...	...	0.6	...	...	0.5	0.2	0.3	102
.	.	.	.	.	.	.	.	.	.	.	.	.	.	.	.	103
9.3	10.5	8.2	0.78	95.4	4.6	.	41.9	66.1	.	...	...	...	...	...	...	104
6.1	4.7[**]	7.5[**]	1.58[**]	90.3	9.7	–	61.8[**]	53.0[**]	–	...	...	...	...	...	...	105
...	...	...	...	...	...	...	...	...	...	...	...	...	...	...	...	106
15.2[**,z]	13.2[**,z]	17.3[**,z]	1.31[**,z]	93.2[**,z]	5.1[**,z]	1.7[**,z]	56.2[**,z]	58.7[**,z]	41.0[**,z]	...	...	...	...	...	...	107
17.5[**]	10.4[**]	24.6[**]	2.36[**]	36.5[**]	56.2[**]	7.2[**]	72.7[**]	68.0[**]	71.1[**]	0.6	...	...	...	...	...	108
22.4	22.8	22.1	0.97	96.6	2.9	0.5	50.0	40.7	39.2	2.3	...	...	1.9[z]	...	...	109
.	.	.	.	.	.	.	.	.	.	.	.	.	.	.	.	110

Table 9A (continued)

	Country or territory	ENROLMENT IN TERTIARY EDUCATION									
		Total students enrolled (000)						Gross enrolment ratio (GER) (%)			
		1998/1999			2002/2003			1998/1999			
		Total	Male	Female	Total	Male	Female	Total	Male	Female	GPI (F/M)
111	Netherlands Antilles	2	1	1	2.3[z]	0.9[z]	1.4[z]	14.4	13.3	15.4	1.16
112	Nicaragua	...	...	...	100	48	52	...	...	...	...
113	Panama	...	...	...	118	45	73	...	...	...	...
114	Paraguay	...	...	...	147 **	62 **	85 **	...	...	...	...
115	Peru	...	...	...	831 **	407 **	425 **	...	...	...	...
116	Saint Kitts and Nevis	.	.	.	.	.	.	.	.	.	.
117	Saint Lucia	...	...	...	...	...	...	...	...	...	...
118	Saint Vincent and the Grenadines	.	.	.	...	...	...	.	.	.	.
119	Suriname	...	...	...	5[z]	2[z]	3[z]	...	...	...	...
120	Trinidad and Tobago	7.6	3.2	4.3	12	5	8	6.0	5.0	7.0	1.38
121	Turks and Caicos Islands[2]	0.03	–	0.03	0.01	0.01**	0.00**	...	...	...	...
122	Uruguay	94 **	34 **	60 **	99 **	34 **	64 **	34.8 **	24.6 **	45.3 **	1.84 **
123	Venezuela	...	...	...	983 **	482 **	502 **	...	...	...	...
	North America and Western Europe										
124	Andorra[3]	...	...	...	0.3	0.2	0.1	...	...	...	...
125	Austria	253	126	127	230	108	122	52.8	51.6	54.1	1.05
126	Belgium	352	168	183	375	175	200	55.9	52.6	59.2	1.13
127	Canada	1 193	529	664	1 193 **,[z]	525 **,[z]	668 **,[z]	58.9	51.0	67.1	1.31
128	Cyprus[2]	11	5	6	18	9	9	21.9	19.7	24.0	1.22
129	Denmark	190	83	107	202	85	117	54.6	46.8	62.7	1.34
130	Finland	263	121	142	292	136	156	83.3	75.1	91.9	1.22
131	France	2 012	917	1 095	2 119	953	1 166	51.4	46.1	57.0	1.24
132	Germany	2 185 **	1 163 **	1 022 **	2 335	1 191	1 144	48.4 **	50.4 **	46.3 **	0.92 **
133	Greece	388	193	195	561	275	286	49.0	47.5	50.6	1.07
134	Iceland	8	3	5	13	5	8	40.4	30.1	51.0	1.69
135	Ireland	151	70	81	182	80	101	44.5	40.5	48.7	1.20
136	Israel	247	105	142	301	134	168	49.1	40.5	58.2	1.44
137	Italy	1 797	806	991	1 913	837	1 076	45.3	39.9	50.9	1.28
138	Luxembourg	2.7	1.3	1.4	3	1	2	10.3	9.9	10.8	1.09
139	Malta	6	3	3	9	4	5	19.8	18.6	21.1	1.13
140	Monaco	.	.	.	.	.	.	.	.	.	.
141	Netherlands	470	238	232	527	258	269	48.9	48.6	49.1	1.01
142	Norway	187	80	108	212	86	127	64.8	54.2	75.8	1.40
143	Portugal	357	157	199	401	174	227	43.9	38.3	49.6	1.30
144	San Marino	...	...	...	...	...	...	...	...	...	...
145	Spain	1 787	839	948	1 841	863	978	52.9	48.6	57.5	1.18
146	Sweden	335	142	193	415	168	247	62.3	51.8	73.3	1.42
147	Switzerland	156	91	65	186	104	82	38.6	43.9	33.0	0.75
148	United Kingdom	2 081	974	1 107	2 288	1 009	1 279	59.2	55.2	63.2	1.15
149	United States	13 769	6 106 **	7 663 **	16 612	7 202	9 410	73.4	63.7 **	83.6 **	1.31 **
	South and West Asia										
150	Afghanistan	...	...	...	...	...	...	...	...	...	...
151	Bangladesh	709	480	229	877	596	281	5.6	7.3	3.7	0.51
152	Bhutan[4]	1.3**	0.9**	0.4**	1.9**,[z]	1.3**,[z]	0.6**,[z]	...	...	...	...
153	India	...	...	...	11 295	6 953	4 342	...	...	...	...
154	Iran, Islamic Republic of	1 308	740	568	1 714	844	870	20.2	22.4	17.9	0.80
155	Maldives	.	.	.	.	.	.	.	.	.	.
156	Nepal	...	...	...	125	95	30	...	...	...	...
157	Pakistan	...	...	...	401	228	173	...	...	...	...
158	Sri Lanka	...	...	...	...	...	...	...	...	...	...
	Sub-Saharan Africa										
159	Angola	8	5	3	13	8 *	5 *	0.8	0.9	0.6	0.69
160	Benin	16	13	3	...	...	...	3.3	5.3	1.4	0.26
161	Botswana	5.5	3.1	2.4	9 **	5 **	4 **	3.1	3.5	2.8	0.79
162	Burkina Faso	...	...	...	16 **	12 **	4 **	...	...	...	...
163	Burundi	5	4	1	12 **	8 **	4 **	1.0	1.5	0.6	0.40
164	Cameroon	67	...	...	81	50 **	32 **	5.1	...	...	...

ENROLMENT IN TERTIARY EDUCATION				DISTRIBUTION OF STUDENTS BY ISCED LEVEL						FOREIGN STUDENTS (000)						
Gross enrolment ratio (GER) (%)				Total students (%)			Percentage of female in each level									
2002/2003				2002/2003			2002/2003			1998/1999			2002/2003			
Total	Male	Female	GPI (F/M)	Level 5A	Level 5B	Level 6	Level 5A	Level 5B	Level 6	Total	Male	Female	Total	Male	Female	
14.0 z	11.3 z	16.7 z	1.48 z	15.1 z	64.2 z	20.7 z	44.2 z	59.1 z	72.9 z	…	…	…	…	…	…	111
18.3	17.5	19.2	1.10	95.5	4.5	.	51.8	59.3	.	…	…	…	…	…	…	112
43.2	32.2	54.6	1.69	86.2	13.8	0.0	64.2	49.1	63.0	…	…	…	…	…	…	113
27.0 **	22.6 **	31.5 **	1.39 **	79.1 **	20.6 **	…	54.7 **	68.6 **	…	…	…	…	…	…	…	114
31.9 **	30.8 **	33.0 **	1.07 **	54.1 **	45.8 **	–	47.0	55.9	–	…	…	…	…	…	…	115
.	.	.	.	.	.	.	.	.	.	.	.	.	.	.	.	116
…	…	…	…	…	…	…	…	…	…	…	…	…	…	…	…	117
…	…	…	…	…	…	…	…	…	…	.	.	.	.	.	.	118
12.2 z	9.2 z	15.4 z	1.69 z	62.7 **,z	37.3 **,z	.	49.1 **,z	83.6 **,z	.	…	…	…	…	…	…	119
8.9	6.9	10.9	1.59	54.5	27.9	17.6	60.0	66.1	56.5	1.0	0.5	0.5	1.2 z	0.4 *,z	0.8 *,z	120
0.7	1.0 **	0.4 **	0.44 **	.	100.0	.	.	33.3 **	.	.	.	.	.	.	.	121
37.4 **	25.5 **	49.7 **	1.95 **	76.3 **	23.6 **	…	59.9	82.9	…	…	…	…	2.1 y	…	…	122
40.2 **	38.8 **	41.8 **	1.08 **	61.6 **	34.3 **	4.1 **	47.3 **	57.6 **	…	…	…	…	0.1	…	…	123
North America and Western Europe																
…	…	…	…	28.1	71.9	.	64.0	42.7	.	…	…	…	0.03**	…	…	124
48.9	44.5	53.5	1.20	81.9	11.4	6.7	51.9	65.7	44.6	29.8	15.2	14.6	31	15	16	125
61.1	55.9	66.5	1.19	46.7	51.5	1.7	50.4	56.5	39.0	36.1	18.9	17.2	42	…	…	126
57.7 **,z	49.6 **,z	66.2 **,z	1.34 **,z	72.5 **,z	25.4 **,z	2.2 **,z	57.7 **,z	52.3 **,z	44.6 **,z	35.5 j	20.0	15.6	…	…	…	127
32.3	31.9	32.8	1.03	19.5	80.0	0.5	76.7	42.9	41.8	1.9	1.1	0.7	5	4	1	128
66.9	55.2	79.2	1.43	88.9	8.7	2.4	59.9	41.7	42.2	12.3	4.8	7.5	18	8	10	129
87.5	79.8	95.6	1.20	93.0	0.2	6.8	53.8	40.0	49.7	4.8	2.8	2.0	7	4	3	130
55.5	48.9	62.5	1.28	71.4	24.0	4.6	55.5	55.2	46.6	131.0 ±	…	…	222	114	108	131
51.0	51.1	51.0	1.00	81.5	14.6	…	47.3	61.5	…	178.2	96.2	82.0	241	122	119	132
74.2	70.8	77.7	1.10	64.0	32.5	3.4	52.5	48.7	42.8	…	…	…	12	…	…	133
62.7	44.8	81.2	1.81	94.1	5.6	0.3	64.5	50.9	53.3	0.2	0.1	0.1	0.6	0.2	0.4	134
51.6	44.6	59.0	1.32	62.2	35.7	2.1	57.1	53.8	46.9	7.2 eo	…	…	10	5	5	135
57.4	49.5	65.8	1.33	77.7	19.6	2.6	57.0	50.7	52.7	…	…	…	…	…	…	136
56.9	48.9	65.3	1.34	97.3	1.1	1.6	56.2	65.5	50.9	23.5	11.7	11.8	36	16	20	137
12.1	11.2	13.0	1.17	59.6	39.5	0.9	54.1	52.1	51.9	0.7 j	…	…	…	…	…	138
30.2	25.3	35.4	1.40	78.0	21.6	0.5	55.8	61.5	38.1	0.3 j	0.1	0.2	0.4	0.2	0.2	139
.	.	.	.	.	.	.	.	.	.	.	.	.	.	.	.	140
58.1	55.7	60.6	1.09	97.5	1.3	1.3	51.0	59.6	41.0	13.6	7.4	6.3	21	9	11	141
80.7	63.5	98.7	1.55	94.7	3.4	2.0	60.4	51.2	41.9	9.0	4.2	4.8	11	6	5	142
55.7	47.5	64.2	1.35	94.7	1.4	4.0	56.7	53.0	54.6	…	…	…	15	8	8	143
…	…	…	…	…	…	…	…	…	…	…	…	…	…	…	…	144
61.9	56.6	67.4	1.19	82.6	13.5	4.0	53.7	50.5	51.0	33.0	16.2	16.7	54	24	30	145
83.3	65.7	102.0	1.55	91.3	3.5	5.2	60.8	46.6	46.5	24.4	13.5	11.0	32	18	14	146
48.7	53.1	44.1	0.83	71.4	20.6	8.0	45.7	41.5	38.3	25.3	14.2	11.1	33	18	15	147
64.3	56.8	71.9	1.27	63.6	32.7	3.7	54.1	60.8	43.0	232.5	124.2	108.3	255	132	123	148
83.2	70.5	96.4	1.37	74.8	23.3	1.8	56.9	56.3	50.5	451.9	262.6	189.4	586	…	…	149
South and West Asia																
…	…	…	…	…	…	…	…	…	…	…	…	…	…	…	…	150
6.2	8.2	4.1	0.50	90.7	9.1	0.2	33.8	14.4	28.3	…	…	…	0.4	…	…	151
…	…	…	…	23.5 **,z	76.5 **,z	.	31.9 **,z	34.3 **,z	.	…	…	…	…	…	…	152
11.9	14.1	9.6	0.68	98.6	0.8	0.6	38.5	35.0	36.5	…	…	…	7.7	…	…	153
21.1	20.4	21.9	1.07	75.6	23.6	0.8	53.9	41.7	23.4	…	…	…	1.5	0.9	0.6	154
.	.	.	.	.	.	.	.	.	.	.	.	.	.	.	.	155
5.3	7.7	2.7	0.34	99.4	.	0.6	24.2	.	20.1	…	…	…	…	…	…	156
2.8	3.1	2.5	0.81	97.8	0.1	2.1	43.4	32.7	31.0	…	…	…	0.4	…	…	157
…	…	…	…	…	…	…	…	…	…	…	…	…	–	–	–	158
Sub-Saharan Africa																
1.0	1.2 *	0.8 *	0.65 *	100.0	.	.	39.9 *	.	.	0.05	0.02	0.03	…	…	…	159
…	…	…	…	…	…	…	…	…	…	…	…	…	…	…	…	160
4.7 **	5.4 **	4.0 **	0.75 **	88.5 **	11.4 **	0.1 **	44.6 **	28.5 **	60.0 **	…	…	…	…	…	…	161
1.4 **	2.1 **	0.7 **	0.34 **	…	…	…	…	…	…	…	…	…	…	…	…	162
2.0 **	2.8 **	1.3 **	0.45 **	…	…	…	…	…	…	0.1	…	…	0.5 z	…	…	163
5.5	6.7 **	4.2 **	0.63 **	…	…	…	…	…	…	…	…	…	…	…	…	164

Table 9A (continued)

		ENROLMENT IN TERTIARY EDUCATION									
		Total students enrolled (000)						Gross enrolment ratio (GER) (%)			
		1998/1999			2002/2003			1998/1999			
	Country or territory	Total	Male	Female	Total	Male	Female	Total	Male	Female	GPI (F/M)
165	Cape Verde	...	...	...	2.2	1.0	1.2	...	...	...	...
166	Central African Republic	6	5	1	...	...	...	1.9	3.3	0.6	0.18
167	Chad	...	...	...	...	...	...	...	...	...	...
168	Comoros	0.6	0.4	0.3	1.7	1.0	0.7	1.0	1.2	0.9	0.75
169	Congo	11 **	8 **	2 **	12 **	10 **	2 **	3.7 **	5.8 **	1.5 **	0.26 **
170	Côte d'Ivoire	97	71	25	...	...	...	7.1	10.4	3.7	0.36
171	Democratic Rep. of the Congo	60 **	...	...	...	...	...	1.4 **	...	...	...
172	Equatorial Guinea	...	...	...	...	...	...	...	...	...	...
173	Eritrea	4	3	1	6 **	5 **	1 **	1.2	2.2	0.3	0.16
174	Ethiopia	52	43	10	**172**	**129**	**43**	1.0	1.6	0.4	0.23
175	Gabon	7.5	4.8	2.7	...	...	...	6.8	8.9	4.8	0.54
176	Gambia	...	...	...	...	...	...	...	...	...	...
177	Ghana	...	...	...	**70**	**48**	**22**	...	...	...	...
178	Guinea	...	...	...	...	...	...	...	...	...	...
179	Guinea-Bissau	...	...	...	...	...	...	...	...	...	...
180	Kenya	...	...	...	99 **,z	64 **,z	34 **,z	...	...	...	...
181	Lesotho	4	1	3	6	2	4	2.2	1.7	2.7	1.61
182	Liberia	...	...	...	...	...	...	...	...	...	...
183	Madagascar	31	17	14	33	18	15	2.3	2.5	2.1	0.84
184	Malawi	3.2	2.3	0.9	4.5	3.2	1.3	0.3	0.5	0.2	0.37
185	Mali	19	...	...	28 **	...	...	1.8	...	...	...
186	Mauritius	7.6	4.1	3.5	17	7	10	7.1	7.6	6.6	0.87
187	Mozambique	...	...	...	...	...	...	...	...	...	...
188	Namibia	11	5	6	14 **	7 **	6 **	6.6	6.2	7.1	1.14
189	Niger	...	...	...	14 **,z	10 **,z	3 **,z	...	...	...	...
190	Nigeria	...	...	...	948	568 **	380 **	...	...	...	...
191	Rwanda	6	...	...	20	13	7	0.9	...	...	...
192	Sao Tome and Principe	.	.	.	0.2 **,z	0.1 **,z	0.1 **,z	.	.	.	.
193	Senegal	29	...	...	...	...	...	3.7	...	...	...
194	Seychelles	.	.	.	.	.	.	.	.	.	.
195	Sierra Leone	...	...	...	9 **,z	6 **,z	3 **,z	...	...	...	...
196	Somalia	...	...	...	...	...	...	...	...	...	...
197	South Africa	634	293	341	675	312	363	15.3	14.2	16.3	1.15
198	Swaziland	5	3	2	5 **	2 **	3 **	4.9	5.3	4.5	0.85
199	Togo	15	12	3	...	...	...	3.8	6.4	1.3	0.21
200	Uganda	41	27 **	14 **	74 **	49 **	26 **	2.0	2.7 **	1.4 **	0.52 **
201	United Republic of Tanzania	19	15	4	31	22	10	0.6	1.0	0.3	0.26
202	Zambia	23	16	7	25 **,y	17 **,y	8 **,y	2.3	3.2	1.5	0.46
203	Zimbabwe	...	...	...	**56 ****	**34 ****	**22 ****	...	...	...	...

		Sum						Median			
I	World	...	...	...	...	...	...	21.2	20.4	21.9	1.07
II	Countries in transition	...	...	...	...	...	...	29.9	27.8	32.0	1.15
III	Developed countries	...	...	...	...	...	...	48.4	43.9	52.9	1.21
IV	Developing countries	...	...	...	...	...	...	11.0	14.7	7.1	0.48
V	Arab States	...	...	...	...	...	...	19.7	10.6	34.0	3.22
VI	Central and Eastern Europe	...	...	...	...	...	...	38.7	32.8	43.8	1.34
VII	Central Asia	...	...	...	...	...	...	24.9	21.1	28.2	1.33
VIII	East Asia and the Pacific	...	...	...	...	...	...	...	...	...	...
IX	Latin America and the Caribbean	...	...	...	...	...	...	...	...	...	...
X	North America and Western Europe	...	...	...	...	...	...	49.1	40.5	58.2	1.44
XI	South and West Asia	...	...	...	...	...	...	...	...	...	...
XII	Sub-Saharan Africa	...	...	...	...	...	...	2.3	2.5	2.1	0.84

1. Data are included in ISCED level 5A.
2. National population data were used to calculate enrolment ratios.
3. Enrolment ratios were not calculated due to lack of United Nations population data by age.
4. Enrolment ratios were not calculated due to inconsistencies between enrolment and the United Nations population data.

(eo) Full-time only.
(hf) Data refer to ISCED level 5A only.
(j) Data refer to ISCED levels 5A and 6 only.

ENROLMENT IN TERTIARY EDUCATION				DISTRIBUTION OF STUDENTS BY ISCED LEVEL						FOREIGN STUDENTS (000)						
Gross enrolment ratio (GER) (%)				Total students (%)			Percentage of female in each level									
2002/2003				2002/2003			2002/2003			1998/1999			2002/2003			
Total	Male	Female	GPI (F/M)	Level 5A	Level 5B	Level 6	Level 5A	Level 5B	Level 6	Total	Male	Female	Total	Male	Female	
4.6	4.4	4.7	1.09	100.0	.	.	52.9	.	.	…	…	…	…	…	…	165
…	…	…	…	…	…	…	…	…	…	…	…	…	…	…	…	166
…	…	…	…	…	…	…	…	…	…	…	…	…	…	…	…	167
2.3	2.6	2.0	0.77	68.0	32.0	.	39.0	52.1	.	.	.	.	…	…	…	168
3.8**	6.5**	1.2**	0.19**	84.4**	15.0**	0.6**	16.3**	12.5**	31.2**	…	…	…	…	…	…	169
…	…	…	…	…	…	…	…	…	…	…	…	…	…	…	…	170
…	…	…	…	…	…	…	…	…	…	…	…	…	…	…	…	171
…	…	…	…	…	…	…	…	…	…	…	…	…	…	…	…	172
1.5**	2.6**	0.4**	0.15**	100.0**	.	.	13.3**	.	.	0.1	0.08	0.02	…	…	…	173
2.7	**4.1**	**1.4**	**0.33**	**100.0**	.	**0.0**	**25.2**	.	–	…	…	…	…	…	…	174
…	…	…	…	…	…	…	…	…	…	0.4	…	…	…	…	…	175
…	…	…	…	…	…	…	…	…	…	…	…	…	…	…	…	176
3.2	**4.3**	**2.0**	**0.46**	**86.7**	**13.0**	**0.3**	**32.5**	**25.6**	**17.0**	…	…	…	…	…	…	177
…	…	…	…	…	…	…	…	…	…	…	…	…	…	…	…	178
…	…	…	…	…	…	…	…	…	…	…	…	…	…	…	…	179
2.9**,z	3.8**,z	2.0**,z	0.53**,z	47.0**,z	49.6**,z	3.4**,z	39.2**,z	31.0**,z	25.4**,z	…	…	…	…	…	…	180
3.0	2.4	3.5	1.48	50.9	49.1	.	53.1	69.9	.	1.0	0.5	0.5	0.1	0.06	0.05	181
…	…	…	…	…	…	…	…	…	…	…	…	…	…	…	…	182
2.1	2.3	1.9	0.83	77.3	20.3	2.4	45.5	45.0	45.2	1.1	…	…	1.2z	0.9z	0.3z	183
0.4	0.6	0.2	0.41	100.0	.	.	…	29.2	…	…	…	…	…	…	…	184
2.5**	…	…	…	99.0**	.	1.0**	…	…	…	1.2	…	…	…	…	…	185
15.3	12.8	18.0	1.41	39.8	59.4	0.7	44.7	67.1	40.0	…	…	…	…	…	…	186
…	…	…	…	…	…	…	…	…	…	…	…	…	…	…	…	187
7.5**	7.9**	7.0	0.89**	55.3**	44.7**	0.0**	57.1**	35.0**	20.0	…	…	…	…	…	…	188
1.5**,z	2.2**,z	0.7**,z	0.34**,z	84.3**,z	14.9**,z	0.7**,z	23.9**,z	30.0**,z	25.2**,z	…	…	…	…	…	…	189
8.2	9.7**	6.7**	0.69**	61.0	37.7	1.3	37.1	44.8	44.8**	…	…	…	…	…	…	190
2.5	3.6	1.7	0.46	96.4	3.6	.	37.3	23.4	.	0.07	…	…	0.09y	0.06y	0.03y	191
1.0**,z	1.3**,z	0.7**,z	0.56**,z	100.0**,z	.	.	36.1**,z	.	.	.	.	.	.	.	.	192
…	…	…	…	…	…	…	…	…	…	1.3	…	…	…	…	…	193
.	.	.	.	…	…	…	…	…	…	.	.	.	.	.	.	194
2.2**,z	3.1**,z	1.2**,z	0.40**,z	43.9**,z	56.1**,z	.	16.0**,z	38.8**,z	.	…	…	…	…	…	…	195
…	…	…	…	…	…	…	…	…	…	…	…	…	…	…	…	196
15.0	14.0	16.1	1.15	86.6	12.2	1.1	52.3	65.7	38.7	15.5	8.4*	7.1*	…	…	…	197
4.7**	4.3**	5.0**	1.16**	…	…	…	…	…	…	0.1	…	…	0.1z	…	…	198
…	…	…	…	…	…	…	…	…	…	0.5	0.4	0.2	…	…	…	199
3.2**	4.3**	2.2**	0.52**	57.2**	42.7**	0.1**	37.5**	30.5**	–	…	…	…	…	…	…	200
0.9	1.3	0.6	0.44	70.6	25.4	4.0	32.0	25.4	40.7	…	…	…	0.4	0.3	0.1	201
2.4**,y	3.3**,y	1.5**,y	0.46**,y	58.4**,y	40.8**,y	0.8**,y	37.7**,y	23.3**,y	14.4**,y	…	…	…	…	…	…	202
3.9**	**4.7****	**3.0****	**0.63****	**37.5****	**59.2****	**3.3**	**32.1**	**43.7**	…	…	…	…	…	…	…	203

Median				Median						Sum						
26.7	23.5	30.0	1.28	82.1	17.9	0.02	53.7	45.2	50.4	…	…	…	…	…	…	I
37.9	38.3	37.5	0.98	98.3	.	1.7	54.1	.	49.5	…	…	…	…	…	…	II
57.7	49.6	66.2	1.34	79.0	20.2	0.8	55.5	55.0	44.6	…	…	…	…	…	…	III
13.0	9.5	16.7	1.76	82.3	17.5	0.1	49.1	54.1	…	…	…	…	…	…	…	IV
26.0	22.1	30.2	1.37	84.7	14.4	0.9	52.4	48.6	29.2	…	…	…	…	…	…	V
39.4	36.1	42.8	1.18	81.2	14.5	4.2	56.5	56.7	46.7	…	…	…	…	…	…	VI
32.2	26.0	34.0	1.31	98.9	.	1.1	51.3	.	49.1	…	…	…	…	…	…	VII
16.4	18.2	14.5	0.80	72.5	25.5	2.0	51.7	…	…	…	…	…	…	…	…	VIII
23.4	23.1	23.7	1.03	62.7	37.3	.	55.6	56.8	39.5	…	…	…	…	…	…	IX
57.7	49.6	66.2	1.34	77.8	20.6	1.6	63.5	52.2	44.6	…	…	…	…	…	…	X
6.2	8.2	4.1	0.50	94.3	4.6	1.1	36.1	33.5	25.9	…	…	…	…	…	…	XI
2.5	3.6	1.7	0.46	84.4	15.0	0.7	37.6	26.9	7.2	…	…	…	…	…	…	XII

(l) Data refer to ISCED level 5B only.
(v) Data do not include ISCED level 6.
(q) Data cover only 80% of students.

± Partial data.
Data in bold are for 2003/2004.

(z) Data are for 2001/2002.
(y) Data are for 2000/2001.

Table 9B. **Tertiary education: distribution of students by field of study and female share in each field, 2002/2003**

Country or territory	Total enrolment (000)	Total enrolment % F	PERCENTAGE DISTRIBUTION BY FIELD OF STUDY: Education	Humanities and arts	Social sciences, business and law	Science	Engineering, manufacturing and construction	Agriculture	Health and welfare	Services	Not known or unspecified
Arab States											
Algeria	683**	...	...	...	...	...	...	...	...	...	...
Bahrain	19	62	3	7	50	10	11	.	7	3	7
Djibouti	**1.1**	**45**	.	**21**	**51**	**20**	**2**	.	.	**6**	–
Egypt	2 154	...	...	...	...	...	...	...	...	...	100
Iraq	318**,z	34**,z	...	...	...	...	...	...	...	...	...
Jordan	186	51	15	15	26	18	12	1	10	1	2
Kuwait	...	...	...	...	...	...	...	...	...	...	...
Lebanon	144	54	3	19	39	16	12	0.4	8	3	0.5
Libyan Arab Jamahiriya	375**	51**	...	...	...	...	...	...	...	...	...
Mauritania	9**	21**	3**	24**	57**	10**	–	0.2**	1**	–	5**
Morocco	336	45	2	26	47	15	4	1	4	1	1
Oman	20**,z	58**,z	...	...	...	...	...	...	...	...	...
Palestinian A. T.	105	49	22	17	29	11	8	0.5	12	–	0.3
Qatar	8	73	17	15	41	12	4	.	3	.	8
Saudi Arabia	525	58	53	14	11	8	8	1	4	–	1
Sudan	...	...	...	...	...	...	...	...	...	...	...
Syrian Arab Republic	...	...	...	...	...	...	...	...	...	...	...
Tunisia	263	55	1	21	27	22	9	2	7	–	11
United Arab Emirates	68**	66**	...	...	...	...	...	...	...	...	...
Yemen	...	...	...	...	...	...	...	...	...	...	...
Central and Eastern Europe											
Albania	44	62	33	10	32	3	9	3	9	2	...
Belarus	489	57	...	...	...	...	...	...	...	...	...
Bosnia and Herzegovina	...	...	...	...	...	...	...	...	...	...	...
Bulgaria	231	53	9	9	41	5	22	2	6	6	0.1
Croatia	122	53	5	10	35	7	17	4	8	15	...
Czech Republic	287	51	12	9	27	10	20	4	13	4	0.4
Estonia	64	62	10	11	38	10	12	2	10	7	...
Hungary	390	57	13	7	40	7	14	3	7	7	...
Latvia	119	62	15	7	53	7	10	2	4	4	...
Lithuania	168	60	15	7	37	6	20	3	9	4	...
Poland	1 983	58	13	9	42	6	14	2	3	6	7
Republic of Moldova	114	56	...	...	...	...	...	...	...	...	...
Romania	644	54	3	11	43	5	22	3	6	3	3
Russian Federation	8 151**	56**	...	...	...	...	...	...	...	...	100z
Serbia and Montenegro	209y	54y	4y	10y	33y	5y	24y	5y	12y	7y	0.3y
Slovakia	158	53	16	6	28	9	18	4	12	7	...
Slovenia	101	56	10	7	44	5	17	3	7	7	...
TFYR Macedonia	46	56	13	11	28	8	20	5	10	6	...
Turkey	1 918	42	12	5	17	7	14	3	5	3	34
Ukraine	2 296	54*	8	5	42	4	22	5	6	5	2
Central Asia											
Armenia	79	55	17	4	35	0.3	6	2	8	2	26
Azerbaijan	121	45	...	...	...	...	...	...	...	...	...
Georgia	155	49	7	19	32	4	23	3	8	3	0.0
Kazakhstan	603	57	...	...	...	...	...	...	...	...	...
Kyrgyzstan	201	54	25	5	42	6	10	1	3	8	...
Mongolia	98	62	12	11	35	7	19	3	7	5	1
Tajikistan	97	25	14z	39z	20z	11z	8z	3z	4z	1z	...
Turkmenistan	...	...	...	...	...	...	...	...	...	...	...
Uzbekistan	[illegible]	[illegible]	...	...	...	...	...	...	...	...	...
East Asia and the Pacific											
Australia	1 012	54	8	11	36	13	11	2	13	4	2
Brunei Darussalam	4.4	63	55	11	13	4	3	.	12	.	3
Cambodia	43	29**	1z	11z	57z	14z	3z	3z	3z	5z	3z
China	15 186	44	...	...	...	...	...	...	...	...	...

PERCENTAGE OF FEMALES IN EACH FIELD									
Education	Humanities and arts	Social sciences, business and law	Science	Engineering, manufac-turing and construction	Agriculture	Health and welfare	Services	Not known or unspecified	**Country or territory**
									Arab States
...	...	...	...	...	...	...	...	...	Algeria
67	83	60	71	24	.	84	69	67	Bahrain
.	**52**	**52**	**18**	**25**	.	.	**52**	–	Djibouti
...	...	...	...	...	...	...	...	...	Egypt
...	...	...	...	...	...	...	...	...	Iraq
79	66	37	51	30	–	50	84	45	Jordan
...	...	...	...	...	...	...	...	...	Kuwait
94	72	56	42	21	49	64	31	78	Lebanon
...	...	...	...	...	...	...	...	...	Libyan Arab Jamahiriya
13	24	23	14	–	60	6	–	19**	Mauritania
55	51	45	34	22	25	64	46	32	Morocco
...	...	...	...	...	...	...	...	...	Oman
71	61	34	49	35	18	42	–	31	Palestinian Autonomous Territories
91	93	65	72	16	.	100	.	55	Qatar
86	31	30	41	1	32	40	–	8	Saudi Arabia
...	...	...	...	...	...	...	...	...	Sudan
...	...	...	...	...	...	...	...	...	Syrian Arab Republic
...	...	...	...	...	...	...	–	...	Tunisia
...	...	...	...	...	...	...	...	...	United Arab Emirates
...	...	...	...	...	...	...	...	...	Yemen
									Central and Eastern Europe
77	72	56	63	26	48	65	50	–	Albania
...	...	...	...	...	...	...	...	...	Belarus
...	...	...	...	...	...	...	...	...	Bosnia and Herzegovina
69	60	58	52	34	43	64	45	55	Bulgaria
92	71	65	46	25	43	72	29	–	Croatia
73	61	57	34	21	51	74	38	2	Czech Republic
88	75	63	39	28	50	87	49	–	Estonia
72	65	64	35	20	46	77	56	...	Hungary
84	80	64	33	22	44	86	49	–	Latvia
78	74	67	37	28	50	82	45	–	Lithuania
73	69	63	43	22	55	73	51	69	Poland
...	...	...	...	...	...	...	...	...	Republic of Moldova
75	66	62	59	29	38	66	52	40	Romania
...	...	...	...	...	...	...	...	57[z]	Russian Federation
85[y]	75[y]	60[y]	59[y]	29[y]	41[y]	73[y]	32[y]	36[y]	Serbia and Montenegro
75	54	59	34	29	36	77	36	.	Slovakia
79	73	63	30	23	54	78	45	.	Slovenia
77	68	61	58	29	34	73	43	.	The former Yugoslav Rep. of Macedonia
49	56	44	39	19	35	58	29	46	Turkey
...	...	...	...	...	...	...	...	...	Ukraine
									Central Asia
76	46	48	38	27	25	50	10	69	Armenia
...	...	...	...	...	...	...	...	...	Azerbaijan
64	77	39	70	31	25	72	11	73	Georgia
...	...	...	...	...	...	...	...	...	Kazakhstan
82	61	50	56	31	16	56	17	–	Kyrgyzstan
75	72	65	50	48	64	83	35	61	Mongolia
...	...	...	...	...	...	...	...	...	Tajikistan
...	...	...	...	...	...	...	...	...	Turkmenistan
...	...	...	...	...	...	...	...	...	Uzbekistan
									East Asia and the Pacific
74	65	56	35	20	46	76	52	52	Australia
67	51	60	48	40	.	75	.	56	Brunei Darussalam
31[z]	32[z]	32[z]	17[z]	4[z]	14[z]	30[z]	41[z]	22[z]	Cambodia
...	...	...	...	...	...	...	...	...	China

Table 9B (continued)

Country or territory	Total enrolment (000)	Total enrolment % F	Education	Humanities and arts	Social sciences, business and law	Science	Engineering, manufac-turing and construction	Agriculture	Health and welfare	Services	Not known or unspecified
			PERCENTAGE DISTRIBUTION BY FIELD OF STUDY								
Cook Islands	.	.	.	.	.	.	.	.	.	.	.
DPR Korea	...	...	...	...	...	...	...	...	...	...	...
Fiji	...	...	...	...	...	...	...	...	...	...	...
Indonesia	3 441	44	...	...	...	...	...	...	...	...	100
Japan	3 984	46	7	17	30	3	17	2	11	7	7
Kiribati	...	...	...	...	...	...	...	...	...	...	...
Lao PDR	28	36	29	.	20	1	7	9	2	4	28
Macao, China	26	36	4	4	82	3	2	–	4	1	...
Malaysia	632	55	7	13	27	16	24	2	4	0.2	7
Marshall Islands	0.9[z]	56[z]	...	...	...	...	...	...	...	...	...
Micronesia (Fed. States of)	...	...	...	...	...	...	...	...	...	...	...
Myanmar	555[**,z]	...	1[y]	32[y]	23[y]	37[y]	5[y]	1[y]	1[y]	0.0[y]	...
Nauru	.	.	...	...	...	...	...	...	...	...	...
New Zealand	185	59	10	19	30	13	6	1	11	4	5
Niue	.	.	...	...	...	...	...	...	...	...	...
Palau	0.5[**,z]	63[**,z]	...	...	...	...	...	...	...	...	...
Papua New Guinea	...	...	...	...	...	...	...	...	...	...	...
Philippines	2 427	55	17	3	31	12	12	3	9	4	7
Republic of Korea	**3 223**	**37**	**6**	**18**	**20**	**10**	**31**	**1**	**7**	**7**	**–**
Samoa	1.2[**,z]	44[**,z]	23[y]	8[y]	34[y]	9[y]	5[y]	11[y]	3[y]	3[y]	5[y]
Singapore	...	...	...	...	...	...	...	...	...	...	...
Solomon Islands	.	.	...	...	...	...	...	...	...	...	...
Thailand	**2 251**	**54**	...	...	...	...	...	...	...	...	100[z]
Timor-Leste	6[*,z]	53[*,z]	...	...	...	...	...	...	...	...	...
Tokelau	.	.	.	.	.	.	.	.	.	.	.
Tonga	0.4[**,z]	58[**,z]	...	...	...	...	...	...	...	...	...
Tuvalu	.	.	...	...	...	...	...	...	...	...	...
Vanuatu	0.7[z]	...	...	...	...	...	...	...	...	...	...
Viet Nam	797[**]	43[**]	23[z]	4[z]	39[z]	–[z]	20[z]	6[z]	4[z]	–[z]	5[z]
Latin America and the Caribbean											
Anguilla	.	.	.	.	.	.	.	.	.	.	.[z]
Antigua and Barbuda	.	.	.	.	.	.	.	.	.	.	.[z]
Argentina	2 027	59	3	7	35	7	7	3	10	1	26
Aruba	1.7	59	11	.	44	.	26	.	19	.	...
Bahamas	...	...	...	...	...	...	...	...	...	...	...
Barbados	8[y]	71[y]	...	...	...	...	...	...	...	...	...
Belize	0.5	65[*]	...	...	...	...	...	...	...	...	...
Bermuda	2.0[**,z]	55[**,z]	.[y]	12[y]	17[y]	8[y]	.[y]	.[y]	.[y]	.[y]	63[y]
Bolivia	311	...	...	...	...	...	...	...	...	...	...
Brazil	3 579	56	...	...	...	...	...	...	...	...	100
British Virgin Islands	.	.	...	...	...	...	...	...	...	...	...
Cayman Islands	0.4[y]	75[y]	...	...	...	...	...	...	...	...	...
Chile	**567**	**48**	**14**	**6**	**35**	**2**	**30**	**5**	**9**	**–**	**–**
Colombia	990	51	11[z]	3[z]	43[z]	3[z]	29[z]	2[z]	9[z]	...	...
Costa Rica	77	52	20	7	28	12	14	3	6	1	9
Cuba	236	56	...	...	...	...	...	...	...	...	...
Dominica	.	.	...	...	...	...	...	...	...	...	...
Dominican Republic	287	61	...	...	...	...	...	...	...	...	...
Ecuador	...	...	...	...	...	...	...	...	...	...	...
El Salvador	113	54	10	1	51	10	12	...	14	0.1	...
Grenada	.	.	...	...	...	...	...	...	...	...	...
Guatemala	112	43	13	1	44	2	17	2	6	.	16
Guyana	5	61[**]	...	...	...	...	...	...	...	...	...
Haiti	...	...		...	...	...	...	...	...	...	...
Honduras	97[**,z]	56[**,z]	...	...	...	...	...	...	...	...	...
Jamaica	46[**]	70[**]	...	...	...	...	...	...	...	...	100[z]
Mexico	2 237	50	11	4	42	13	19	2	8	2	0.3
Montserrat	.	.	...	...	...	...	...	...	...	...	...
Netherlands Antilles	2.3[z]	60[z]	5[y]	.[y]	41[y]	.[y]	32[y]	.[y]	22[y]	.[y]	...
Nicaragua	100	52	...	...	...	...	...	...	...	...	...

PERCENTAGE OF FEMALES IN EACH FIELD									
Education	Humanities and arts	Social sciences, business and law	Science	Engineering, manufac-turing and construction	Agriculture	Health and welfare	Services	Not known or unspecified	**Country or territory**
.	.	.	.	.	.	.	.	.	Cook Islands
...	...	...	...	...	...	...	...	...	Democratic People's Republic of Korea
...	...	...	...	...	...	...	...	...	Fiji
...	...	...	...	...	...	...	...	44	Indonesia
71	67	34	25	12	41	64	80	50	Japan
...	...	...	...	...	...	...	...	...	Kiribati
40	.	41	36	10	18	57	17	40	Lao People's Democratic Republic
...	...	...	...	...	...	...	...	...	Macao, China
65	61	68	50	31	66	70	64	67	Malaysia
...	...	...	...	...	...	...	...	...	Marshall Islands
...	...	...	...	...	...	...	...	...	Micronesia (Federated States of)
...	...	...	...	...	...	...	...	...	Myanmar
...	...	...	...	...	...	...	...	...	Nauru
82	65	57	40	32	47	80	51	45	New Zealand
...	...	...	...	...	...	...	...	...	Niue
...	...	...	...	...	...	...	...	...	Palau
...	...	...	...	...	...	...	...	...	Papua New Guinea
75	57	65	54	30	52	73	15	16	Philippines
70	**57**	**36**	**31**	**16**	**29**	**62**	**34**	–	Republic of Korea
67y	57y	37y	41y	4y	29y	81y	12y	44y	Samoa
...	...	...	...	...	...	...	...	...	Singapore
...	...	...	...	...	...	...	...	...	Solomon Islands
...	...	...	...	...	...	...	...	52z	Thailand
...	...	...	...	...	...	...	...	...	Timor-Leste
.	.	.	.	.	.	.	.	.	Tokelau
...	...	...	...	...	...	...	...	...	Tonga
...	...	...	...	...	...	...	...	...	Tuvalu
...	...	...	...	...	...	...	...	...	Vanuatu
56z	69z	49z	–z	14z	34z	40z	–z	43z	Viet Nam
									Latin America and the Caribbean
.	.	.	.	.	.	.	.	.	Anguilla
.	.	.	.	.	.	.	.	.	Antigua and Barbuda
78	63	58	45	30	43	67	47	69	Argentina
92	.	66	.	14	.	88	.	.	Aruba
...	...	...	...	...	...	...	...	...	Bahamas
...	...	...	...	...	...	...	...	...	Barbados
...	...	...	...	...	...	...	...	...	Belize
.y	67y	72y	4y	.y	.y	.y	.y	55y	Bermuda
...	...	...	...	...	...	...	...	...	Bolivia
...	...	...	...	...	...	...	...	56	Brazil
...	...	...	...	...	...	...	...	...	British Virgin Islands
...	...	...	...	...	...	...	...	...	Cayman Islands
73	**55**	**54**	**48**	**22**	**44**	**68**	–	–	Chile
64z	47z	58z	52z	33z	36z	71z	...	...	Colombia
74	57	54	35	25	35	65	47	63	Costa Rica
...	...	...	...	...	...	...	...	.	Cuba
...	...	...	...	...	...	...	...	...	Dominica
...	...	...	...	...	...	...	...	...	Dominican Republic
...	...	...	...	...	...	...	...	...	Ecuador
74	44	57	41	25	...	70	36	.	El Salvador
...	...	...	...	...	...	...	...	...	Grenada
61	53	45	72	19	24	55	.	44	Guatemala
...	...	...	...	...	...	...	...	...	Guyana
...	...	...	...	...	...	...	...	...	Haiti
...	...	...	...	...	...	...	...	...	Honduras
...	...	...	...	...	...	...	...	69z	Jamaica
68	55	57	41	24	30	62	55	45	Mexico
...	...	...	...	...	...	...	...	...	Montserrat
95y	.y	72y	.y	15y	.y	85y	.y	.y	Netherlands Antilles
...	...	...	...	...	...	...	...	...	Nicaragua

Table 9B (continued)

Country or territory	Total enrolment (000)	Total enrolment % F	Education	Humanities and arts	Social sciences, business and law	Science	Engineering, manufac-turing and construction	Agriculture	Health and welfare	Services	Not known or unspecified
			PERCENTAGE DISTRIBUTION BY FIELD OF STUDY								
Panama	118	62	16	7	42	4	18	1	7	3	2
Paraguay	147**	58**	...	...	...	...	...	...	...	...	100**
Peru	831**	51**	...	...	...	...	...	...	...	...	100**
Saint Kitts and Nevis	.	.	...	...	...	...	...	...	...	...	...
Saint Lucia	...	...	...	...	...	...	...	...	...	...	...
Saint Vincent/Grenad.	...	...	...	...	...	...	...	...	...	...	...
Suriname	5[z]	62[z]	38[z]	3[z]	35[z]	8[z]	10[z]	1[z]	.[z]	1[z]	3[z]
Trinidad and Tobago	12	61	11[z]	12[z]	25[z]	14[z]	21[z]	4[z]	11[z]	2[z]	0.0[z]
Turks and Caicos Islands	0.01	33**	...	...	...	...	...	...	...	...	...
Uruguay	99**	65**	...	...	...	...	...	...	...	...	...
Venezuela	983**	51**	...	...	...	...	...	...	...	...	...
North America and Western Europe											
Andorra	0.3	49	–	4	43	31	–	–	22	–	...
Austria	230	53	15	12	36	12	14	1	9	2	0.3
Belgium	375	53	13	10	30	8	11	2	17	1	8
Canada	1 193[**,z]	56[**,z]	...	...	...	...	...	...	...	...	...
Cyprus	18	49	12	10	44	13	3	0.1	4	14	...
Denmark	202	58	11	17	24	9	11	2	25	2	...
Finland	292	53	5	15	22	12	27	2	13	4	...
France	2 119	55	...	...	...	...	...	...	...	...	...
Germany	2 335	49	7	16	26	14	15	1	14	2	...
Greece	561	51	7[z]	14[z]	32[z]	16[z]	14[z]	6[z]	7[z]	5[z]	...
Iceland	13	64	20	14	35	11	7	1	12	2	...
Ireland	182	56	5	18	20	14	11	1	10	4	17
Israel	301	56	16	11	34	12	19	0.5	6	–	1
Italy	1 913	56	6	15	38	8	16	2	12	2	0.2
Luxembourg	3	53	22[z]	13[z]	41[z]	10[z]	8[z]	...	7[z]	...	...
Malta	9	57	20	11	37	5	8	0.3	18	1	...
Monaco	.	.	.	.	.	.	.	.	.	.	.
Netherlands	527	51	14	8	41	6	10	2	16	2	2
Norway	212	60	15	10	31	11	6	1	18	3	4
Portugal	401	57	12	9	32	8	21	2	11	5	...
San Marino	...	...	...	...	...	...	...	...	...	...	...
Spain	1 841	53	8	11	34	13	18	3	9	5	0.2
Sweden	415	60	15	13	26	10	17	1	16	2	0.2
Switzerland	186	44	10	13	38	12	14	1	9	3	0.4
United Kingdom	2 288	56	8	16	25	13	8	1	17	–	13
United States	16 612	57	...	...	...	...	...	...	...	...	100
South and West Asia											
Afghanistan	...	...	...	...	...	...	...	...	...	...	...
Bangladesh	877	32	3	41	38	11	2	1	2	0.1	2
Bhutan	1.9[**,z]	34[**,z]	...	...	...	...	...	...	...	...	...
India	11 295	38	1[z]	–[z]	52[z]	15[z]	5[z]	–[z]	1[z]	–[z]	25[z]
Iran, Islamic Republic of	1 714	51	...	...	...	...	...	...	...	...	...
Maldives	.	.	.	.	.	.	.	.	.	.	.
Nepal	125	24	...	...	...	...	...	...	...	...	...
Pakistan	401	43	...	...	...	...	...	...	...	...	...
Sri Lanka	...	...	...	...	...	...	...	...	...	...	...
Sub-Saharan Africa											
Angola	13	40*	35	.	37	10	9	.	7	.	3
Benin	...	...	...	...	...	...	...	...	...	...	...
Botswana	9**	43**	26[z]	22[z]	20[z]	11[z]	[illegible]	1[z]	[illegible]	0.4[z]	...
Burkina Faso	16**	25**	...	...	...	...	...	...	...	...	...
Burundi	12**	32**	25[z]	14[z]	28[z]	5[z]	5[z]	4[z]	6[z]	.[z]	13[z]
Cameroon	81	39**	...	...	...	...	...	...	...	...	...
Cape Verde	2.2	53	...	...	...	...	...	...	...	...	...
Central African Republic	...	...			...	...	...	...	...	...	...
Chad	...	...	...	...	...	...	...	...	...	...	...

PERCENTAGE OF FEMALES IN EACH FIELD									
Education	Humanities and arts	Social sciences, business and law	Science	Engineering, manufac-turing and construction	Agriculture	Health and welfare	Services	Not known or unspecified	Country or territory
79	65	67	53	29	33	78	67	79	Panama
...	...	...	...	...	...	...	.	58**	Paraguay
...	...	...	...	...	...	...	...	51	Peru
...	...	...	...	...	...	...	...	...	Saint Kitts and Nevis
...	...	...	...	...	...	...	...	...	Saint Lucia
...	...	...	...	...	...	...	...	...	Saint Vincent and the Grenadines
60[z]	81[z]	69[z]	67[z]	33[z]	67[z]	.[z]	79[z]	69[z]	Suriname
74[z]	78[z]	70[z]	57[z]	27[z]	58[z]	57[z]	72[z]	100[z]	Trinidad and Tobago
...	...	...	...	...	...	...	...	...	Turks and Caicos Islands
...	...	...	...	...	...	...	...	...	Uruguay
...	...	...	...	...	...	...	...	...	Venezuela
									North America and Western Europe
–	92	50	15	–	–	86	–	–	Andorra
75	65	55	35	20	60	67	52	58	Austria
71	59	53	30	20	50	73	47	45	Belgium
...	...	...	...	...	...	...	...	...	Canada
89	59	47	32	8	–	70	38	–	Cyprus
70	63	49	32	33	51	81	23	–	Denmark
81	71	63	42	19	49	84	67	...	Finland
...	...	...	...	...	...	...	...	...	France
69	65	47	33	19	46	73	54	...	Germany
68[z]	73[z]	54[z]	37[z]	27[z]	43[z]	72[z]	42[z]	.[z]	Greece
84	66	59	37	28	40	83	83	.	Iceland
81	66	60	43	18	41	79	53	56	Ireland
83	65	58	45	23	58	76	–	64	Israel
88	74	57	49	27	44	65	48	68	Italy
...	...	...	...	...	...	...	...	...	Luxembourg
74	58	53	33	28	30	65	33	.	Malta
.	.	.	.	.	.	.	.	.	Monaco
74	56	47	23	12	48	75	52	38	Netherlands
78	62	56	32	24	53	82	44	62	Norway
83	64	60	50	27	56	77	51	.	Portugal
...	...	...	...	...	...	...	...	...	San Marino
77	62	59	36	27	45	76	60	44	Spain
78	63	61	43	29	56	82	58	74	Sweden
70	59	44	26	14	43	66	54	43	Switzerland
72	62	56	36	19	58	78	–	55	United Kingdom
...	...	...	...	...	...	...	...	57	United States
									South and West Asia
...	...	...	...	...	...	...	...	...	Afghanistan
38	35	32	25	11	19	41	28	31	Bangladesh
...	...	...	...	...	...	...	...	...	Bhutan
43[z]	–[z]	42[z]	39[z]	25[z]	–[z]	41[z]	–[z]	35[z]	India
...	...	...	...	...	...	...	...	...	Iran, Islamic Republic of
.	.	.	.	.	.	.	.	.	Maldives
...	...	...	...	...	...	...	...	...	Nepal
...	...	...	...	...	...	...	...	...	Pakistan
...	...	...	...	...	...	...	...	...	Sri Lanka
									Sub-Saharan Africa
...	.	...	...	...	.	...	.	...	Angola
...	...	...	...	...	...	...	...	...	Benin
52[z]	56[z]	44[z]	24[z]	16[z]	14[z]	68[z]	34[z]	.[z]	Botswana
...	...	...	...	...	...	...	...	...	Burkina Faso
33[z]	19[z]	40[z]	18[z]	9[z]	15[z]	23[z]	.[z]	39[z]	Burundi
...	...	...	...	...	...	...	...	...	Cameroon
...	...	...	...	...	...	...	...	...	Cape Verde
...	...	...	...	...	...	...	...	...	Central African Republic
...	...	...	...	...	...	...	...	...	Chad

Table 9B (continued)

Country or territory	Total enrolment (000)	Total enrolment % F	Education	Humanities and arts	Social sciences, business and law	Science	Engineering, manufac-turing and construction	Agriculture	Health and welfare	Services	Not known or unspecified
			PERCENTAGE DISTRIBUTION BY FIELD OF STUDY								
Comoros	1.7	43	9	29	38	11	.	.	8	4	...
Congo	12[**]	16[**]	8[z]	27[z]	34[z]	10[z]	1[z]	3[z]	4[z]	0.2[z]	13[z]
Côte d'Ivoire	...	...	...	...	...	...	...	...	...	...	...
Democratic Rep. of the Congo	...	...	...	...	...	...	...	...	...	...	...
Equatorial Guinea	...	...	...	...	...	...	...	...	...	...	...
Eritrea	6[**]	13[**]	19[z]	1[z]	27[z]	17[z]	–[z]	6[z]	4[z]	–[z]	26[z]
Ethiopia	**172**	**25**	**24**	**3**	**42**	**9**	**10**	**6**	**5**	**0.3**	**1**
Gabon	...	...	...	...	...	...	...	...	...	...	...
Gambia	...	...	...	...	...	...	...	...	...	...	...
Ghana	**70**	**32**	**11**	**39**	**12**	**15**	**12**	**4**	**4**	**2**	**1**
Guinea	...	...	...	...	...	...	...	...	...	...	...
Guinea-Bissau	...	...	...	...	...	...	...	...	...	...	...
Kenya	99[**,z]	35[**,z]	23[y]	8[y]	21[y]	10[y]	19[y]	7[y]	9[y]	1[y]	1[y]
Lesotho	6	61	41	6	24	6	–	4	0.3	–	18
Liberia	...	...	...	...	...	...	...	...	...	...	...
Madagascar	33	45	3	10	54	13	7	2	9	0.1	1
Malawi	4.6	29	...	...	...	...	...	...	...	...	...
Mali	28[**]	...	...	...	...	...	...	...	...	...	...
Mauritius	17	58	37	15	20	12	13	1	0.4	1	0.3
Mozambique	...	...	...	...	...	...	...	...	...	...	...
Namibia	14[**]	47	32[z]	3[z]	40[z]	6[z]	4[z]	2[z]	5[z]	3[z]	3[z]
Niger	14[**,z]	25[**,z]	...	...	...	...	...	...	...	...	...
Nigeria	948	40[**]	...	...	...	...	...	...	...	...	...
Rwanda	20	37	...	...	...	...	...	...	...	...	...
Sao Tome and Principe	0.2[**,z]	36[**,z]	49[y]	21[y]	30[y]	.[y]	.[y]	.[y]	.[y]	.[y]	...
Senegal	...	...	...	...	...	...	...	...	...	...	...
Seychelles	.	.	.	.	.	.	.	.	.	.	.
Sierra Leone	9[**,z]	29[**,z]	43[y]	18[y]	11[y]	7[y]	1[y]	15[y]	4[y]	1[y]	...
Somalia	...	...	...	...	...	...	...	...	...	...	...
South Africa	675	54	21[y]	7[y]	47[y]	11[y]	7[y]	1[y]	5[y]	1[y]	...
Swaziland	5[**]	54[**]	14[**,y]	17[**,y]	32[**,y]	5[**,y]	6[**,y]	5[**,y]	4[**,y]	...	...
Togo	...	...	...	...	...	...	...	...	...	...	...
Uganda	74[**]	34[**]	44[y]	5[y]	33[y]	2[y]	5[y]	3[y]	3[y]	3[y]	2[y]
United Republic of Tanzania	31	31	...	...	...	...	...	...	...	...	...
Zambia	25[**,y]	32[**,y]	...	...	...	...	...	...	...	...	...
Zimbabwe	**56**[**]	**39**[**]	...	...	...	...	...	...	...	...	100

	Total enrolment (000)	Total enrolment % F	Education	Humanities and arts	Social sciences, business and law	Science	Engineering, manufac-turing and construction	Agriculture	Health and welfare	Services	Not known or unspecified
World[1]	...	...	...	...	...	...	...	...	...	...	...
Countries in transition	...	...	...	...	...	...	...	...	...	...	...
Developed countries	...	...	10	7	44	5	17	3	7	7	...
Developing countries	...	...	...	...	...	...	...	...	...	...	...
Arab States	...	...	3	13	44	13	11	0.2	8	3	4
Central and Eastern Europe	...	...	12	7	22	9	17	3	9	3	17
Central Asia	...	...	14	39	20	11	8	3	4	1	...
East Asia and the Pacific	...	...	...	...	...	...	...	...	...	...	...
Latin America and the Caribbean	...	...	...	...	...	...	...	...	...	...	...
North America and Western Europe	...	...	12	10	44	13	3	0.1	4	14	...
South and West Asia	...	...	...	...	...	...	...	...	...	...	...
Sub-Saharan Africa	...	...	...	...	...	...	...	...	...	...	...

1. All values shown are medians.
Data in bold are for 2003/2004.

(z) Data are for 2001/2002.
(y) Data are for 2000/2001.

PERCENTAGE OF FEMALES IN EACH FIELD									
Education	Humanities and arts	Social sciences, business and law	Science	Engineering, manufac-turing and construction	Agriculture	Health and welfare	Services	Not known or unspecified	**Country or territory**
53	36	47	27	.	.	55	57	.	Comoros
9[z]	13[z]	16[z]	16[z]	10[z]	31[z]	24[y]	44[z]	19[z]	Congo
...	...	...	...	...	...	...	...	...	Côte d'Ivoire
...	...	...	...	...	...	...	...	...	Democratic Rep. of the Congo
...	...	...	...	...	...	...	...	...	Equatorial Guinea
9[z]	32[z]	19[z]	7[z]	–[z]	10[z]	12[z]	–[z]	15[z]	Eritrea
19	**26**	**33**	**24**	**11**	**18**	**26**	**39**	**17**	Ethiopia
...	...	...	...	...	...	...	...	...	Gabon
...	...	...	...	...	...	...	...	...	Gambia
36	**37**	**42**	**27**	**8**	**20**	**37**	**22**	...	Ghana
...	...	...	...	...	...	...	...	...	Guinea
...	...	...	...	...	...	...	...	...	Guinea-Bissau
42[y]	33[y]	48[y]	28[y]	13[y]	27[y]	44[y]	35[y]	24[y]	Kenya
68	53	50	30	–	46	94	–	76	Lesotho
...	...	...	...	...	...	...	...	...	Liberia
45	59	49	31	20	37	52	51	40	Madagascar
...	...	...	...	...	...	...	...	...	Malawi
...	...	...	...	...	...	...	...	...	Mali
71	69	55	51	22	57	22	26	53	Mauritius
...	...	...	...	...	...	...	...	...	Mozambique
55[z]	60[z]	56[z]	40[z]	16[z]	35[z]	81[z]	62[z]	50[z]	Namibia
...	...	...	...	...	...	...	...	...	Niger
...	...	...	...	...	...	...	...	...	Nigeria
...	...	...	...	...	...	...	...	...	Rwanda
26[y]	61[y]	35[y]	.[y]	.[y]	.[y]	.[y]	.[y]	.[y]	Sao Tome and Principe
...	...	...	...	...	...	...	...	...	Senegal
.	.	.	.	.	.	.	.	.	Seychelles
33[y]	31[y]	21[y]	27[y]	25[y]	20[y]	29[y]	34[y]	.[y]	Sierra Leone
...	...	...	...	...	...	...	...	...	Somalia
71[y]	65[y]	53[y]	43[y]	17[y]	37[y]	72[y]	75[y]	...	South Africa
43[y]	62[y]	48[y]	41[y]	15[y]	33[y]	72[y]	...	...	Swaziland
...	...	...	...	...	...	...	...	...	Togo
33[y]	38[y]	38[y]	24[y]	18[y]	17[y]	42[y]	56[y]	48[y]	Uganda
...	...	...	...	...	...	...	...	...	United Republic of Tanzania
...	...	...	...	...	...	...	...	...	Zambia
...	...	...	...	...	...	...	...	41	Zimbabwe
...	...	...	...	...	...	...	...	...	World[1]
...	...	...	...	...	...	...	...	...	Countries in transition
75	65	59	47	25	49	66	52	49	Developed countries
...	...	...	...	...	...	...	...	...	Developing countries
...	...	...	...	...	...	...	...	...	Arab States
77	72	56	63	26	48	65	50	–	Central and Eastern Europe
...	...	...	...	...	...	...	...	...	Central Asia
...	...	...	...	...	...	...	...	...	East Asia and the Pacific
...	...	...	...	...	...	...	...	...	Latin America and the Caribbean
76	63	57	35	24	53	71	56	51	North America and Western Europe
...	...	...	...	...	...	...	...	...	South and West Asia
...	...	...	...	...	...	...	...	...	Sub-Saharan Africa

Table 10A
Teaching staff in pre-primary and primary education

Country or territory	PRE-PRIMARY EDUCATION											
	Total teachers				Trained teachers (%)						Pupil/teacher ratio	
	1998/1999		2002/2003		1998/1999			2002/2003			1998/1999	2002/2003
	Total (000)	% F	Total (000)	% F	Total	Male	Female	Total	Male	Female		
Arab States												
Algeria	1.3	93	1.8	83	...	...	...	...	...	...	28	28
Bahrain	0.7	100	0.8**	99**	18	–	18	...	...	...	21	21**
Djibouti	0.01	100	**0.04**	**77**	...	...	...	**87**	**67**	**93**	29	**21****
Egypt	13.7**	99**	18.9	99	...	...	...	86**,y	...	...	24**	24
Iraq	4.6	100	3.6	100**	...	...	...	...	...	...	15	15
Jordan	3.3	100	4.2	98	...	...	...	...	...	...	22	20
Kuwait	3.8	100	4.7	100	100	100	100	100	100	100	15	13
Lebanon	10.7	95	8.3	100	...	...	...	11	17	11	13	18
Libyan Arab Jamahiriya	1.2	100	1.8**	99**	...	...	...	...	...	...	8	10**
Mauritania	...	...	...	...	...	...	...	...	...	...	...	...
Morocco	40.1	40	41.1	52	...	...	...	...	...	...	20	17
Oman	0.4	100	0.4	100	93	.	93	92**,z	.**,z	92**,z	20	21
Palestinian A. T.	2.7	100	2.4	99	...	...	...	...	...	...	29	25
Qatar	0.4**	96**	0.7	95	...	...	...	...	...	...	21**	16
Saudi Arabia	8.7	100	9.2	100	...	...	...	72z	.z	72z	11	10
Sudan	12.3**	84**	14.2	83	...	...	...	46	...	...	30**	35
Syrian Arab Republic	4.6	96	6.4	94	87	84	87	...	...	...	24	22
Tunisia	3.9	95	5.7**	95**	...	...	...	100**,y	...	...	20	19**
United Arab Emirates	3.5	100	3.9	100	59	71	59	61z	80z	61z	19	19
Yemen	0.8	93	1.0	98	...	...	...	...	...	...	17	15
Central and Eastern Europe												
Albania	3.9**	100**	3.9	100	...	...	...	...	...	...	21**	21
Belarus	53.6	...	43.7	99	...	...	...	58	100	58	5	6
Bosnia and Herzegovina	...	...	...	...	...	...	...	...	...	...	...	...
Bulgaria	19.3	100**	17.1	100	...	...	...	...	...	...	11	12
Croatia	6.4	100	7.1	100	76	86	76	84	100	84	13	12
Czech Republic	17.0	100**	22.4	100	...	...	...	...	...	...	18	13
Estonia	6.9	100	6.9	100	...	...	...	...	...	...	8	8
Hungary	32.0	100	34.5	96	...	...	...	...	...	...	12	10
Latvia	1.3	100	1.2	98	...	...	...	...	...	...	46	51
Lithuania	12.7	99	11.1	100	...	...	...	...	...	...	7	8
Poland	77.1**	...	66.9**		...	...	...	...	...	...	12**	13**
Republic of Moldova	13.2	100	9.6	100	92**	–	92**	93	–	93	8	10
Romania	36.6	100**	34.3	100	...	...	...	...	...	...	17	18
Russian Federation	618.3	99**	490.1**	...	...	...	...	...	...	...	...	7
Serbia and Montenegro	11.8	100	11.9y	100y	96	–	96	95y	–y	95y	14	14y
Slovakia	16.3	100	15.5	100	...	...	...	...	...	...	10	10
Slovenia	3.2	99**	2.7	100	...	...	...	...	...	...	18	18
TFYR Macedonia	3.2	99	2.9	99	...	...	...	...	...	...	10	11
Turkey	17.1	99**	18.9	95	...	...	...	...	...	...	15	17
Ukraine	142.6	100	119.3	99	...	...	...	...	...	...	8	8
Central Asia												
Armenia	...	...	5.4	100	...	...	...	56	–	56	...	9
Azerbaijan	11.9	100	11.0	100	78	...	78	83	100	83	9	10
Georgia	5.8	100	7.2	100	...	...	...	98	–	98	13	10
Kazakhstan	18.5	...	23.1	99	...	...	...	...	...	...	9	12
Kyrgyzstan	2.6	100	2.3	100	32	–	32	36	33	36	18	21
Mongolia	3.0	100	3.3	99	99	75	99	98y	...	...	25	27
Tajikistan	5.2	100	4.4	100	...	...	...	85	–	85	11	13
Turkmenistan	...	...	...	...	...	...	...	...	...	...	...	...
Uzbekistan	...	...	65.8	95	...	...	...	100	100	100	...	10
East Asia and the Pacific												
Australia	...	...	...	...	...	...	...	...	...	...	...	...
Brunei Darussalam	0.5*	82*	0.6**	85**	...	...	...	...	...	...	21*	19**
Cambodia	2.2**	99**	3.5	99**	...	...	...	94z	...	...	27**	25
China	875.4	94	856.5y	94y	...	...	...	...	...	...	27	26y
Cook Islands	0.03	...	0.03**,y	100**,y	...	...	...	...	...	...	15	14**,y

PRIMARY EDUCATION

Total teachers				Trained teachers (%)						Pupil/teacher ratio		
1998/1999		2002/2003		1998/1999			2002/2003			1998/1999	2002/2003	
Total (000)	% F	Total (000)	% F	Total	Male	Female	Total	Male	Female			Country or territory
												Arab States
169.5	46	167.5	49	94	92	96	98	97	99	28	28	Algeria
...	...	5.0 **,z	76 **,z	...	...	...	...	...	...	...	16 **,z	Bahrain
1.0	28	1.3 **,z	30 **,z	...	...	...	...	...	...	40	34 **,z	Djibouti
346.0 **	52 **	354.9 **	54 **	...	...	...	100 **,y	...	...	23 **	22 **	Egypt
141.5	72	220.4	...	...	...	...	...	...	...	25	19	Iraq
...	...	39.4 **	64 **	...	...	...	...	...	...	...	20 **	Jordan
10.4	73	11.6	83	100	100	100	100	100	100	13	13	Kuwait
28.4	82	26.4	87	...	...	...	14	...	...	14	17	Lebanon
...	...	...	...	...	...	...	...	...	...	...	...	Libyan Arab Jamahiriya
7.4	26	9.6	25 **	...	...	...	...	...	...	47	41	Mauritania
123.0	39	145.6	44	...	...	...	...	...	...	28	28	Morocco
12.4	52	14.9 **	57 **	100	100	99	100 **,z	100 **,z	100 **,z	25	21 **	Oman
...	...	11.1	62	...	...	...	...	...	...	...	36	Palestinian A. T.
4.6	75	5.7	83	...	...	...	...	...	...	13	12	Qatar
184.8	54	198.2	51	...	...	...	93 y	100 y	87 y	12	12	Saudi Arabia
...	...	105.1 **	62 **	...	...	...	...	...	...	...	29 **	Sudan
110.5 **	68 **	120.9 **,z	68 **,z	...	...	...	88 y	87 y	89 y	25 **	24 **,z	Syrian Arab Republic
60.5	50	59.3	50	...	...	...	94 **,y	...	...	24	22	Tunisia
16.9	73	16.3	80	...	...	...	...	...	...	16	15	United Arab Emirates
77.2 **	21 **	...	...	...	...	...	...	...	...	30 **	...	Yemen
												Central and Eastern Europe
12.7 **	75 **	11.8	76	...	...	...	...	...	...	23 **	21	Albania
32.4	99	27.4	99	...	...	...	98	98	98	20	16	Belarus
...	...	...	...	...	...	...	...	...	...	...	...	Bosnia and Herzegovina
23.0	91 **	19.4	92	...	...	...	...	...	...	18	17	Bulgaria
10.6	89	10.8	90	100	100	100	100	100	100	19	18	Croatia
35.8	85 **	33.7	84	...	...	...	...	...	...	18	17	Czech Republic
8.1	...	7.7 **,z	...	...	...	...	...	...	...	16	14 **,z	Estonia
47.3	85	48.4	84	...	...	...	...	...	...	11	10	Hungary
9.2	97	7.5	97	...	...	...	...	...	...	15	14	Latvia
13.3	98	11.8	98	...	...	...	...	...	...	17	16	Lithuania
...	...	273.6 **		...	...	...	...	...	...	...	11 **	Poland
12.4	96	11.1	96	...	...	...	...	...	...	21	19	Republic of Moldova
68.6 **	85 **	56.6	87	...	...	...	...	...	...	19 **	17	Romania
349.0 **	98 **	321.1 **	97 **	...	...	...	...	...	...	18 **	17	Russian Federation
20.8 **	82 **	19.2 y	82 y	100 **	100 **	100 **	100 y	100 y	100 y	20 **	20 y	Serbia and Montenegro
16.9	93	14.7	92	...	...	...	...	...	...	19	18	Slovakia
6.5	96	6.9	96	...	...	...	...	...	...	14	13	Slovenia
5.9	66	5.8	69	...	...	...	...	...	...	22	20	TFYR Macedonia
...	...	...	...	...	...	...	...	...	...	...	...	Turkey
107.4	98	102.6	99	...	...	...	100	...	...	20	19	Ukraine
												Central Asia
...	...	7.6	99	...	...	...	...	...	...	...	18	Armenia
36.8	83	41.7	85	100	100	100	100	99	100	19	15	Azerbaijan
17.4	92	16.5	95	...	...	...	97	...	...	17	14	Georgia
...	...	60.5	98	...	...	...	...	...	...	...	19	Kazakhstan
19.2	95	18.4	97	48	49	48	52	52	52	24	24	Kyrgyzstan
7.8	93	7.8	93	...	...	...	93 y	93 y	93 y	32	31	Mongolia
31.4	56	31.1	62	...	...	...	82	...	...	22	22	Tajikistan
...	...	...	...	...	...	...	...	...	...	...	...	Turkmenistan
...	...	...	...	...	...	...	...	...	...	...	...	Uzbekistan
												East Asia and the Pacific
104.6	...	...	...	...	...	...	...	...	...	18	...	Australia
3.2 *	66 *	3.5 **	71 **	...	...	...	...	...	...	14 *	13 **	Brunei Darussalam
44.5 **	37 **	49.3	40	...	...	...	96 z	...	...	48 **	56	Cambodia
6 751.9	50 **	5 778.9	53	...	...	...	97 **,z	...	...	...	21	China
0.1	...	0.1 **,y	86 **,y	...	...	...	...	...	...	19	18 **,y	Cook Islands

Table 10A (continued)

Country or territory	PRE-PRIMARY EDUCATION													
	Total teachers				Trained teachers (%)						Pupil/teacher ratio	
	1998/1999		2002/2003		1998/1999			2002/2003			1998/1999	2002/2003
	Total (000)	% F	Total (000)	% F	Total	Male	Female	Total	Male	Female		
DPR Korea	...	...	...	...	...	...	...	...	...	...	...	...
Fiji	...	...	...	...	...	...	...	...	...	...	...	...
Indonesia	90.5**	98**	137.1	98	...	...	...	71**,y	...	...	17**	13
Japan	96.0	...	102.0	98**	...	...	...	...	...	...	31	30
Kiribati	...	...	...	...	...	...	...	...	...	...	...	...
Lao PDR	2.1	100	2.4	100	86	100	86	82	100	82	18	16
Macao, China	0.5	100	0.5	100	93	–	93	98	.	98	31	27
Malaysia	23.1	100	25.1	99	...	...	...	...	...	...	25	23
Marshall Islands	0.1	...	0.1z	60z	...	...	...	100z	100z	100z	11	12z
Micronesia (Federated States of)	...	...	...	...	...	...	...	...	...	...	...	...
Myanmar	1.9	...	...	...	...	...	...	...	...	...	22	...
Nauru	...	...	...	...	...	...	...	...	...	...	...	...
New Zealand	...	...	8.8	99	...	...	...	...	...	...	...	11
Niue	0.0	100	0.01z	100z	...	...	...	100z	.z	100z	14	6z
Palau	...	...	0.1**,y	98**,y	...	...	...	...	...	...	...	10**,y
Papua New Guinea	1.4	41	2.5z	42z	100	100	100	100z	100z	100z	34	30z
Philippines	18.0	...	23.7	96	100**	...	...	...	...	...	33	32
Republic of Korea	22.7	100	**26.1**	**99**	...	...	...	...	...	...	24	**21**
Samoa	...	...	0.1**	94**	...	...	...	...	...	...	...	41**
Singapore	...	...	...	...	...	...	...	...	...	...	...	...
Solomon Islands	...	...	...	...	...	...	...	...	...	...	...	...
Thailand	111.3	79	...	...	...	...	...	...	...	...	25	...
Timor-Leste	...	...	...	...	...	...	...	...	...	...	...	...
Tokelau	...	...	...	...	...	...	...	...	...	...	...	...
Tonga	0.1	100	0.1**,y	100**,y	50	–	50	...	...	...	10	18**,y
Tuvalu	...	...	0.04z	100z	...	...	...	33z	.z	33z	...	18z
Vanuatu	...	...	0.8z	99z	...	...	...	42z	–z	43z	...	10z
Viet Nam	94.0	100	103.2	100**	44	–	44	56y	.y	56y	23	21
Latin America and the Caribbean												
Anguilla	0.03	100	0.04	97	38	–	38	55	100	54	18	12
Antigua and Barbuda	...	...	...	...	...	...	...	...	...	...	...	...
Argentina	55.0	96	53.5	97	...	...	...	83**,y	...	...	21	24
Aruba	0.1	100	0.1	99	100	–	100	99	100	99	26	22
Bahamas	...	...	0.3**	100**	...	...	...	60z	.z	60z	...	11**
Barbados	0.3**	99**	0.4**	99**	84**	–	85**	84**	–**	85**	17**	16**
Belize	0.2	98	0.2	99	...	...	...	68**	50**	68**	19	18
Bermuda	...	...	0.1z	100z	...	...	...	100z	.z	100z	...	7z
Bolivia	4.8**	93**	5.1	95	...	...	...	84	66	85	42**	44
Brazil	265.7	98	297.5	96	...	...	...	87**,y	...	...	20	19
British Virgin Islands	0.1	98	0.1	100	...	...	...	20	.	20	7	13
Cayman Islands	0.1	96	0.1z	98z	...	...	...	97z	100z	97z	9	10z
Chile	...	...	**17.2**	**99**	...	...	...	91**,y	...	...	...	**23**
Colombia	58.3	94**	50.7	95	...	...	...	...	...	...	17	21
Costa Rica	3.3	97	5.6	96	...	...	...	79	...	...	20	18
Cuba	25.7	98	26.6	100	98	–	100	100	.	100	19	18
Dominica	0.1	100	0.1	100	75	–	75	75	.	75	18	12
Dominican Republic	8.2	95	7.1**	96**	...	...	...	75z	75**,z	75**,z	24	27**
Ecuador	10.2	90	12.3	88	...	...	...	71	60	72	18	17
El Salvador	...	...	...	...	...	...	...	...	...	...	...	...
Grenada	...	...	0.2	99	...	...	...	32	–	33	...	15
Guatemala	9.2*	...	17.0	...	...	...	...	100z	...	...	27*	23
Guyana	2.1	99	2.2**,z	99**,z	38	41	38	40y	10y	40y	18	16**,z
Haiti	...	...	...	...	...	...	...	...	...	...	...	...
Honduras		[illegible]	6.3**,z	...	...	...	...	...	...	...	...	19**,z
Jamaica	5.5	...	6.5	99	[illegible]			67**,y	...	...	25	21
Mexico	150.1	94	163.3	...	...	...	...	...	...	...	22	[illegible]
Montserrat	0.01	100	0.01**	100**	...	...	...	100z	.z	100z	12	11**
Netherlands Antilles	0.3	99	0.3**	100**	100	100	100	100z	100z	100z	21	19**
Nicaragua	4.7	97	7.2	97	35	24	36	30	15	30	31	25
Panama	2.1**	97**	3.9	[illegible]		...	...	54	...	...	22**	20

PRIMARY EDUCATION

Total teachers 1998/1999 Total (000)	Total teachers 1998/1999 % F	Total teachers 2002/2003 Total (000)	Total teachers 2002/2003 % F	Trained teachers (%) 1998/1999 Total	Trained teachers (%) 1998/1999 Male	Trained teachers (%) 1998/1999 Female	Trained teachers (%) 2002/2003 Total	Trained teachers (%) 2002/2003 Male	Trained teachers (%) 2002/2003 Female	Pupil/teacher ratio 1998/1999	Pupil/teacher ratio 2002/2003	Country or territory
...	...	...	...	...	...	...	...	...	...	...	...	DPR Korea
5.1**	57**	4.1**,z	57**,z	97**	97**	98**	97**,y	97**,y	98**,y	23**	28**,z	Fiji
...	...	1 431.5	54	...	...	...	94**,y	...	...	...	20	Indonesia
366.6	...	371.7	65**	...	...	...	...	...	...	21	20	Japan
0.7	64	0.7	71	...	...	...	...	...	...	24	22	Kiribati
27.1	43	28.6	44	76	69	85	78	71	86	31	31	Lao PDR
1.5	87	1.6	89	81	62	84	90	74	92	31	26	Macao, China
132.4	63	159.0	68	97**	...	...	...	...	...	22	19	Malaysia
0.6	...	0.5 z	34 z	...	...	...	...	...	...	15	17 z	Marshall Islands
...	...	...	...	...	...	...	...	...	...	...	...	Micronesia (Federated States of)
154.7	73	149.0	77	60	60	60	65	65	65	31	33	Myanmar
0.1**	82**	...	...	...	...	...	...	...	...	23**	...	Nauru
18.7	88	20.4	87**	...	...	...	...	...	...	19	18	New Zealand
0.01	100	0.02	...	...	...	...	100 z	.	100 z	24	15	Niue
0.1	82	...	...	...	...	...	...	...	...	15	...	Palau
16.1	38	17.7 z	39 z	100	100	100	100 z	100 z	100 z	36	35 z	Papua New Guinea
360.4	87	371.4	89	100**	...	...	...	...	...	35	35	Philippines
124.4	64	**139.1**	**73**	...	...	...	...	...	...	31	**30**	Republic of Korea
1.1**	73**	1.1**	54**	...	...	...	91 y	94 y	90 y	25**	27**	Samoa
...	...	...	...	...	...	...	...	...	...	...	...	Singapore
...	...	...	...	...	...	...	...	...	...	...	...	Solomon Islands
297.6	63	295.5**	58**	...	...	...	...	...	...	21	21**	Thailand
...	...	3.6 z	30 z	...	...	...	...	...	...	...	51 z	Timor-Leste
...	...	...	...	...	...	...	...	...	...	...	...	Tokelau
0.8	70	0.8	70	87	75	93	100 z	100 z	100 z	22	22	Tonga
...	...	0.1 z	84 z	...	...	...	...	...	...	...	25 z	Tuvalu
1.6**	44**	1.2 z	58 z	...	...	...	100 z	100 z	100 z	22**	29 z	Vanuatu
336.8	78	358.6	78	78	75	78	87 z	87 z	87 z	30	25	Viet Nam
												Latin America and the Caribbean
0.1	87	0.1	91	76	78	76	62	75	60	22	16	Anguilla
...	...	...	...	...	...	...	...	...	...	...	...	Antigua and Barbuda
234.1	89	283.4	86	...	...	...	67**,y	...	...	21	17	Argentina
0.5	78	0.5	92	100	100	100	100	100	100	19	18	Aruba
...	...	2.0**	93**	...	...	...	95 z	90 z	95 z	...	17**	Bahamas
1.4**	75**	1.4**	77**	84**	76**	87**	78**	88**	75**	20**	16**	Barbados
1.9**	64**	2.3	69	...	...	...	41**	37**	43**	24**	21	Belize
...	...	0.5 z	88 z	...	...	...	100 z	100**,z	100**,z	...	9 z	Bermuda
...	...	65.3**	62**	...	...	...	74**,y	70**,y	77**,y	...	24**	Bolivia
...	...	767.8**	90**	...	...	...	92**,y	...	...	...	25**	Brazil
0.2	86	0.2	89	72	55	75	79	78	79	18	14	British Virgin Islands
0.2	89	0.2 z	81 z	...	...	...	99 z	98 z	99 z	15	15 z	Cayman Islands
53.5	78	**50.3**	**77**	...	...	...	92**,y	...	...	33	**34**	Chile
220.5	77**	193.6	77	...	...	...	...	...	...	23	27	Colombia
19.2	81	24.1	80	...	...	...	88	...	...	28	23	Costa Rica
91.2	79	86.6	78	100	100	100	100	100	100	12	11	Cuba
0.6	77	0.6	84	64	49	68	60	45	63	20	19	Dominica
33.7**	75**	35.9**,z	82**,z	...	...	...	58**,z	58**,z	58**,z	39**	39**,z	Dominican Republic
70.6	68	83.7	69	...	...	...	70	70	70	27	24	Ecuador
...	...	...	...	...	...	...	...	...	...	...	...	El Salvador
...	...	0.9	78	...	...	...	68	66	68	...	19	Grenada
46.5*	...	68.9	...	...	...	...	100 z	...	...	36*	30	Guatemala
4.0	86	4.2**,z	85**,z	52	52	52	53 y	53 y	53 y	27	26**,z	Guyana
...	...	...	...	...	...	...	...	...	...	...	...	Haiti
...	...	32.8**,z	...	...	...	...	...	...	...	...	34**,z	Honduras
...	...	11.0	90	...	...	...	80**,y	...	...	...	30	Jamaica
539.9	66**	557.3	...	...	...	...	...	...	...	27	27	Mexico
0.02	84	0.03**	92**	...	...	...	91 z	100 z	91 z	21	19**	Montserrat
1.3	86	1.1**	86**	100	100	100	100 z	100 z	100 z	20	20**	Netherlands Antilles
21.1	83	26.2	82	74	62	76	74	53	79	37	35	Nicaragua
15.1**	75**	17.3	76	...	...	...	75	81	73	26**	24	Panama

Table 10A (continued)

Country or territory	PRE-PRIMARY EDUCATION											
	Total teachers				Trained teachers (%)						Pupil/teacher ratio	
	1998/1999		2002/2003		1998/1999			2002/2003			1998/1999	2002/2003
	Total (000)	% F	Total (000)	% F	Total	Male	Female	Total	Male	Female		
Paraguay	4.6**	92**	5.4	88	…	…	…	…	…	…	25**	26
Peru	35.2	96	39.8	98	…	…	…	…	…	…	29	27
Saint Kitts and Nevis	…	…	0.3	100	…	…	…	60**	.**	60**	…	9
Saint Lucia	0.5	100	0.3	100	…	…	…	58**	.**	58**	12	11
Saint Vincent/Grenad.	…	…	…	…	…	…	…	…	…	…	…	…
Suriname	…	…	0.7**	99**	…	…	…	100 z	100**,z	100**,z	…	24**
Trinidad and Tobago	1.7**	100**	1.8*	100*	20**	–	20**	20*	.*	20*	13**	13*
Turks and Caicos Islands	0.1**	97**	0.1	94	72**	50**	72**	77**	50**	79**	14**	12
Uruguay	3.1	98**	3.7	…	…	…	…	…	…	…	31	29
Venezuela	…	…	…	…	…	…	…	…	…	…	…	…
North America and Western Europe												
Andorra	…	…	0.2	93	…	…	…	…	…	…	…	15
Austria	14.1	99	14.5	99	…	…	…	…	…	…	16	15
Belgium	…	…	28.1	99	…	…	…	…	…	…	…	14
Canada	29.4	68**	27.9**,z	68**,z	…	…	…	…	…	…	18	18**,z
Cyprus	1.0	99	0.9	99	…	…	…	…	…	…	19	18
Denmark	45.2	92	45.4 y		…	…	…	…	…	…	6	6 y
Finland	10.4	96	11.3	97	…	…	…	…	…	…	12	12
France	128.4	78	137.2	81	…	…	…	…	…	…	19	18
Germany	…	…	…	…	…	…	…	…	…	…	…	…
Greece	9.0	…	10.7		…	…	…	…	…	…	16	13
Iceland	2.8	98	3.6	97	…	…	…	…	…	…	5	5
Ireland	0.2	92	…	…	…	…	…	…	…	…	18	…
Israel	…	…	…	…	…	…	…	…	…	…	…	…
Italy	119.2	99	134.2	99	…	…	…	…	…	…	13	12
Luxembourg	…	…	1.1	98	…	…	…	…	…	…	…	14
Malta	0.9	99	1.1 z	99 z	…	…	…	…	…	…	12	8 z
Monaco	0.1**	100**	0.1**,y	100**,y	…	…	…	…	…	…	18**	18 y
Netherlands	…	…	…	…	…	…	…	…	…	…	…	…
Norway	…	…	…	…	…	…	…	…	…	…	…	…
Portugal	…	…	14.4	92**	…	…	…	…	…	…	…	17
San Marino	…	…	…	…	…	…	…	…	…	…	…	…
Spain	67.5	93	89.6	88	…	…	…	…	…	…	17	14
Sweden	…	…	33.2		…	…	…	…	…	…	…	10
Switzerland	9.7	99	9.6**,z	99**,z	…	…	…	…	…	…	16	16**,z
United Kingdom	…	…	44.2	97	…	…	…	…	…	…	…	24
United States	326.6	95	387.6	91	…	…	…	…	…	…	22	19
South and West Asia												
Afghanistan	…	…	…	…	…	…	…	…	…	…	…	…
Bangladesh	64.7	32	61.6	34	…	…	…	…	…	…	38	38
Bhutan	0.02	81	0.04**	58**	88	…	…	72 z	73 z	71 z	22	16**
India	…	…	600.4	…	…	…	…	…	…	…	…	40
Iran, Islamic Republic of	9.5	98	15.6	90**	…	…	…	79**	…	…	23	26
Maldives	0.4	90	0.6	93	47	25	49	47	45	47	32	23
Nepal	9.9**	31**	12.2**	41**	–	–	–	–	–	–	24**	20**
Pakistan	…	…	…	…	…	…	…	…	…	…	…	…
Sri Lanka	…	…	…	…	…	…	…	…	…	…	…	…
Sub-Saharan Africa												
Angola	14.1**	24**	…	…	…	…	…	…	…	…	22**	…
Benin	0.6	61	0.6	65	100	100	100	100	100	100	28	34
Botswana	…	…	…	…	…	…	…	…	…	…	…	…
Burkina Faso			0.5**,z	66**,z	…	…	…	…	…	…	…	29**,z
Burundi	0.2**	99**	0.3*	90*	…	…				…	28**	30*
Cameroon	4.4	97	5.9	97	…	…	…	100	100	100	23	24
Cape Verde	…	…	0.8	100	…	…	…	8	.	8	…	26
Central African Republic	…	…	…	…	…	…	…	…	…	…	…	…
Chad	…	…	…	…	…	…	…	…	…	…	…	…
Comoros	0.1**	94**	0.1	95	…	…	…	…	…	…	26**	26

PRIMARY EDUCATION

Total teachers				Trained teachers (%)						Pupil/teacher ratio		
1998/1999		2002/2003		1998/1999			2002/2003			1998/1999	2002/2003	
Total (000)	% F	Total (000)	% F	Total	Male	Female	Total	Male	Female			**Country or territory**
48.9 **	76 **	35.7	72	...	...	...	...	...	...	19 **	27	Paraguay
170.2	60	170.7	67	...	...	...	78 **,y	...	...	25	25	Peru
...	...	0.4	85	...	...	...	56	55 **	56 **	...	17	Saint Kitts and Nevis
1.2	84 **	1.1	85	...	...	...	77	93	75	22	22	Saint Lucia
...	...	1.1 **	73 **	...	...	...	73 **	64 **	76 **	...	18 **	Saint Vincent and the Grenadines
...	...	3.3 **	85 **	...	...	...	100 z	100 z	100 z	...	19 **	Suriname
8.1	76	7.6	75	71	74	71	83	81	84	21	19	Trinidad and Tobago
0.1 **	93 **	0.1	87	61 **	67 **	60 **	80 **	...	...	20 **	15	Turks and Caicos Islands
17.7	92 **	17.2	...	...	...	...	...	...	...	21	21	Uruguay
...	...	...	...	...	...	...	...	...	...	...	...	Venezuela
												North America and Western Europe
...	...	0.3	78	...	...	...	...	...	...	...	12	Andorra
28.9	89	28.8	90	...	...	...	...	...	...	13	13	Austria
...	...	64.1	78	...	...	...	...	...	...	...	12	Belgium
156.9	67	142.5 **,z	68 **,z	...	...	...	...	...	...	15	17 **,z	Canada
3.5	67	3.3	83	...	...	...	...	...	...	18	19	Cyprus
37.1	63	39.9 y	64 y	...	...	...	...	...	...	10	10 y	Denmark
22.2	71	24.0	75	...	...	...	...	...	...	17	16	Finland
208.6	78	203.4	81	...	...	...	...	...	...	19	19	France
221.3	82	235.2	...	...	...	...	...	...	...	17	14	Germany
47.7	...	54.6	...	...	...	...	...	...	...	14	12	Greece
2.7 **	76 **	3.0 **	78 **	...	...	...	...	...	...	11 **	11 **	Iceland
21.1	85	24.0	...	...	...	...	...	...	...	22	19	Ireland
53.9	...	52.5	87	...	...	...	...	...	...	13	15	Israel
253.7	95	256.7	95	...	...	...	...	...	...	11	11	Italy
...	...	3.0	69	...	...	...	...	...	...	...	11	Luxembourg
1.8	87	1.7	85	...	...	...	...	...	...	20	18	Malta
0.1	87	0.1 y	87 y	...	...	...	...	...	...	16	16 y	Monaco
...	...	...	...	...	...	...	...	...	...	...	...	Netherlands
...	...	41.4	73 **	...	...	...	...	...	...	...	10	Norway
...	...	69.1	79 **	...	...	...	...	...	...	...	11	Portugal
...	...	...	...	...	...	...	...	...	...	...	...	San Marino
171.5	68	179.3	70	...	...	...	...	...	...	15	14	Spain
61.9	80	69.3	80	...	...	...	...	...	...	12	11	Sweden
39.5	72	39.4 **,z	73 **,z	...	...	...	...	...	...	13	14 **,z	Switzerland
244.5	76	262.4	81	...	...	...	...	...	...	19	17	United Kingdom
1 617.8	86	1 677.4	88	...	...	...	...	...	...	15	15	United States
												South and West Asia
32.6	–	53.4	24	...	...	...	...	...	...	32	61	Afghanistan
309.6	31	315.1	38	63	62	64	67	66	68	59	56	Bangladesh
2.1	41	2.4 **	36 **	100	100	100	92 z	92 z	91 z	38	38 **	Bhutan
3 135,3 *	33 *	3 038.2	44	...	...	...	...	...	...	...	41	India
327.0	53	297.7	54 **	...	...	...	100	100	100	27	24	Iran, Islamic Republic of
2.8	58	3.4	63	69	71	68	64	64	64	26	20	Maldives
82.0 **	22 **	110.2	29	52 **	55 **	41 **	16	17	13	41 **	36	Nepal
...	...	347.2	36	...	...	...	...	...	...	...	40	Pakistan
...	...	**72.7** **	**79** **	...	...	...	...	...	...	...	23 **	Sri Lanka
												Sub-Saharan Africa
32.1	24	...	...	...	...	...	...	...	...	42	...	Angola
16.3	23	19.8	19	58	52	77	62	60	72	53	62	Benin
11.7	82	12.4 **	80 **	92	87	93	89 **	84 **	91 **	28	27 **	Botswana
16.7	25	22.7	27	...	...	...	87	86	90	49	45	Burkina Faso
12.3 **	54 **	17.9	54	...	...	...	...	...	...	57 **	50	Burundi
41.1	36	49.0	33	...	...	...	68	67	71	52	57	Cameroon
3.2 **	62 **	3.1	65	...	...	...	69	61	74	29 **	28	Cape Verde
...	...	...	...	...	...	...	...	...	...	...	...	Central African Republic
12.4	9	16.5 **	11 **	...	...	...	...	...	...	68	68 **	Chad
2.4	26	2.9	...	...	...	...	...	...	...	35	37 **	Comoros

Table 10A (continued)

Country or territory	PRE-PRIMARY EDUCATION											
	Total teachers				Trained teachers (%)						Pupil/teacher ratio	
	1998/1999		2002/2003		1998/1999			2002/2003			1998/1999	2002/2003
	Total (000)	% F	Total (000)	% F	Total	Male	Female	Total	Male	Female		
Congo	0.6	100	1.0**	100**	...	...	...	34**	–**	34**	10	15**
Côte d'Ivoire	1.6	96	2.2*	80*	...	...	...	100*	100*	100*	23	22*
Democratic Rep. of the Congo	...	...	1.6**,z	88**,z	...	...	...	...	...	...	...	25**,z
Equatorial Guinea	0.4	36	0.6	80	...	...	...	36	46	33	43	39
Eritrea	0.3	97	0.4	95	65	22	66	66	58	66	36	36
Ethiopia	2.5	93	**4.3**	**91**	63	37	65	**74**	**60**	**75**	36	**32**
Gabon	...	...	0.5**,z	98**,z	...	...	...	...	...	...	...	30**,z
Gambia	...	...	0.8**	56**	...	...	...	...	...	...	...	38**
Ghana	24.2**	92**	**29.3**	**79**	27**	16**	28**	**12**	**10**	**12**	25**	**28**
Guinea	...	...	...	...	...	...	...	...	...	...	...	...
Guinea-Bissau	0.2**	73**	0.2**,y	73**,y	...	...	...	...	...	...	21**	21**,y
Kenya	37.8	99	54.5**	48**	...	...	...	44**	...	...	27	23**
Lesotho	2.0	100	2.0	99**	–	–	–	–	–	–	18	20
Liberia	...	...	...	...	...	...	...	...	...	...	...	...
Madagascar	...	...	3.4	91	...	...	...	...	...	...	...	48
Malawi	...	...	...	...	...	...	...	...	...	...	...	...
Mali	...	...	1.0**	73**	...	...	...	...	...	...	...	21**
Mauritius	2.6	100	2.4	100	100	–	100	91	.	91	17	15
Mozambique	...	...	...	...	...	...	...	...	...	...	...	...
Namibia	1.3**	88**	1.6**,z	89**,z	...	...	...	–	–	–	27**	27**,z
Niger	0.5	98	0.7	98	...	...	...	96	92	96	22	25
Nigeria	...	...	...	...	...	...	...	...	...	...	...	...
Rwanda	...	...	0.6**,z	86**,z	...	...	...	...	...	...	...	35**,z
Sao Tome and Principe	...	...	0.2**	94**	...	...	...	55z	75z	53z	...	25**
Senegal	1.3	78	1.4	82	...	...	...	100z	100z	100z	19	21
Seychelles	0.2	100	0.2	100	88	–	88	81**	.	81**	17	14
Sierra Leone	...	...	0.9y	83y	...	...	...	76y	95y	73y	...	19y
Somalia	...	...	...	...	...	...	...	...	...	...	...	...
South Africa	7.0**	79**	...	...	66**	68**	65**	...	...	...	36**	...
Swaziland	...	...	...	...	...	...	...	...	...	...	...	...
Togo	0.6	97	0.7	91	...	...	...	67	70	67	20	18
Uganda	2.6**	70**	3.2	84	...	...	...	77	56	81	25**	25
United Republic of Tanzania	...	...	**10.2** **	**59** **	...	...	...	...	...	...	...	**55** **
Zambia	0.7	57	...	...	100	100	100	...	...	...	43*	...
Zimbabwe	...	...	**19.6**	**100**	...	...	...	...	...	...	...	...
World[1]	...	99	...	98	...	...	...	...	...	...	19	18
Countries in transition	...	100	...	100	...	...	...	84	–	84	9	10
Developed countries	...	99	...	99	...	...	...	...	...	...	16	14
Developing countries	...	98	...	97	...	...	...	...	...	...	25	21
Arab States	...	100	...	99	...	...	...	...	...	...	20	19
Central and Eastern Europe	...	100	...	100	...	...	...	...	...	...	12	12
Central Asia	...	100	...	100	...	...	...	85	–	85	11	11
East Asia and the Pacific	...	...	...	99	...	...	...	...	...	...	23	19
Latin America and the Caribbean	...	98	...	99	...	...	...	76	63	77	20	18
North America and Western Europe	...	97	...	97	...	...	...	...	...	...	16	15
South and West Asia	...	81	...	58	...	...	...	...	...	...	24	24
Sub-Saharan Africa	...	94	...	89	...	...	...	...	...	...	25	25

1. All values shown are medians.
Data in bold are for 2003/2004.

(z) Data are for 2001/2002.
(y) Data are for 2000/2001.

PRIMARY EDUCATION

Total teachers				Trained teachers (%)						Pupil/teacher ratio		
1998/1999		2002/2003		1998/1999			2002/2003			1998/1999	2002/2003	
Total (000)	% F	Total (000)	% F	Total	Male	Female	Total	Male	Female			Country or territory
4.5	42	7.8	43	...	...	...	57	47	71	61	65	Congo
44.7	20	48.3 *	24 *	...	...	...	100 *	100 *	100 *	43	42 *	Côte d'Ivoire
154.6	21	...	...	...	...	...	...	...	...	26	...	Democratic Rep. of the Congo
...	...	1.8 **,y	24 **,y	...	...	...	...	...	...	...	43 **,y	Equatorial Guinea
5.6	35	7.7	36	73	75	69	81	88	68	47	47	Eritrea
112.4	28	**124.2** **	**34** **	...	...	...	**72** **	**65** **	**87** **	46	**67** **	Ethiopia
6.0	42	7.8	45	...	...	...	100	100	100	44	36	Gabon
4.6	29	4.7 **	29 **	72	72 **	72 **	73 y	69 y	83 y	33	38 **	Gambia
80.3	32	**82.8**	**39**	72	64	89	**68**	**58**	**84**	30	**32**	Ghana
15.5	25	23.9	24	...	...	...	...	...	...	47	45	Guinea
...	...	3.5 **,y	20 **,y	...	...	...	...	...	...	...	44 **,y	Guinea-Bissau
...	...	166.8 **	41 **	...	...	...	44 **	...	...	...	34 **	Kenya
8.3 **	80 **	8.9	80	77 **	74 **	77 **	73	59	76	44 **	47	Lesotho
10.0	19	...	...	...	...	...	...	...	...	39	...	Liberia
42.7	58	55.3	60	...	...	...	...	...	...	47	52	Madagascar
39.9 **	40 **	45.8	44	46 **	48 **	43 **	51 y	52 y	49 y	63 **	62	Malawi
15.4 *	23 *	22.6	24	...	...	...	...	...	...	62 *	57	Mali
5.1	53	5.3	57	100	100	100	100	100	100	26	25	Mauritius
31.5	24	40.2	28	33	33	33	60	57	66	...	67	Mozambique
12.0	67	14.3 **	61 **	29	29	29	50 **	50 **	49 **	32	28 **	Namibia
12.9	31	20.6	35	...	...	...	72	73	68	41	42	Niger
516.7 **	38 **	590.7	48	...	...	...	76	70	83	31 **	42	Nigeria
23.7	55	27.3	50	49	52	46	81 z	81 z	82 z	54	60	Rwanda
0.7	...	0.9 **,z	62 **,z	...	...	...	...	...	...	36	33 **,z	Sao Tome and Principe
21.3	23 **	26.3 **	23 **	...	...	...	91 z	96 z	72 z	49	49 **	Senegal
0.7	88	0.7	86	84	78	84	77 **	97 **	74 **	15	13	Seychelles
...	...	14.9 y	38 y	...	...	...	79 y	83 y	73 y	...	37 y	Sierra Leone
...	...	...	...	...	...	...	...	...	...	...	...	Somalia
216.0 **	78 **	211.0	80	63 **	66 **	62 **	81	91	79	37 **	35	South Africa
6.4	75	6.7	75	91	89	92	91	89	91	33	31	Swaziland
23.1	13	27.5	12	...	...	...	81 z	83 z	65 z	41	35	Togo
109.7	33	139.5	37	...	...	...	81	79	83	60	53	Uganda
106.3	44	**116.4** **	**46** **	...	...	...	100	100	100	38	**56** **	United Republic of Tanzania
34.8	47	40.5	49	89	86	92	100	100	100	45	43	Zambia
...	...	**61.3**	**51**	...	...	...	95 **,z	...	...	...	**39**	Zimbabwe
...	72	...	73	...	...	...	...	...	...	23	22	World[1]
...	95	...	97	...	...	...	98	...	...	20	18	Countries in transition
...	85	...	82				...	...	...	17	14	Developed countries
...	62	...	62	...	...	...	81	81	82	28	28	Developing countries
...	52	...	62	...	...	...	...	...	...	25	21	Arab States
...	92	...	92	...	...	...	...	...	...	19	17	Central and Eastern Europe
...	92	...	95	...	...	...	93	93	93	22	19	Central Asia
...	66	...	66	...	...	...	...	...	...	23	25	East Asia and the Pacific
...	78	...	82				78	...	...	22	21	Latin America and the Caribbean
...	78	...	79	...	...	...	...	...	...	15	14	North America and Western Europe
...	33	...	38	...	...	...	67	66	68	35	38	South and West Asia
...	35	...	41	...	...	...	79	83	73	43	43	Sub-Saharan Africa

Table 10B
Teaching staff in secondary and tertiary education

Country or territory	SECONDARY EDUCATION[1]						
	Total teachers				Trained teachers (%)		
	1998/1999		2002/2003		1998/1999		
	Total (000)	% F	Total (000)	% F	Total	Male	Female
Arab States							
Algeria	...	...	170.3**	48**	...	...	...
Bahrain	...	...	5.2**,z	54**,z	...	...	...
Djibouti	0.7	22	0.7**,z	23**,z	...	...	...
Egypt	454.0**	41**	485.2**	41**	...	...	...
Iraq	56.1**	69**	84.1	...	...	...	...
Jordan	...	...	...	...	...	...	...
Kuwait	22.3**	56**	23.7**,z	56**,z	100**	100**	100**
Lebanon	42.1**	51**	46.2	53	...	...	...
Libyan Arab Jamahiriya	...	...	...	...	...	...	...
Mauritania	2.4	10	3.2	12	...	...	...
Morocco	87.9**	33**	97.1**	33**	...	...	...
Oman	12.9	50	16.9**	50**	100	100	100
Palestinian Autonomous Territories	...	...	22.4	46	...	...	...
Qatar	4.4**	57**	5.1	56	...	...	...
Saudi Arabia	138.8	55	171.3	49	...	...	...
Sudan	...	...	50.6**	55**	...	...	...
Syrian Arab Republic	70.2**	47**	62.8**,y	51**,y	...	...	...
Tunisia	56.5**	40**	58.3**,z	46**,z	...	...	...
United Arab Emirates	16.3	55	20.1	54	52	46	56
Yemen	73.8**	19**	...	...	...	...	...
Central and Eastern Europe							
Albania	22.2**	54**	22.4	56	...	...	...
Belarus	106.9	77	105.9	79	...	...	...
Bosnia and Herzegovina	...	...	...	...	...	...	...
Bulgaria	56.0	73**	57.5	77	...	...	...
Croatia	33.4	64	36.8	67	100	100	100
Czech Republic	72.3	62**	93.1	67	...	...	...
Estonia	11.1	...	12.3**,z	...	...	...	...
Hungary	100.2	71	94.0	74	...	...	...
Latvia	24.8	80	24.8	82	...	...	...
Lithuania	36.3**	79**	41.2**	80**	...	...	...
Poland	...	...	315.2**	...	...	...	...
Republic of Moldova	33.0	72	31.0	75	...	...	...
Romania	177.3**	64**	164.6	66	...	...	...
Russian Federation	...	...	...	...	...	...	...
Serbia and Montenegro	58.8**	58**	55.9y	61y	100**	100**	100**
Slovakia	53.7**	72**	51.8	73	...	...	...
Slovenia	16.8	69	15.8	70	...	...	...
The former Yugoslav Rep. of Macedonia	13.4	49	14.0	52	...	...	...
Turkey	...	...	...	...	...	...	...
Ukraine	...	...	367.4	78	...	...	...
Central Asia							
Armenia	...	...	36.0	84	...	...	...
Azerbaijan	118.5	63	125.4	65	100	100	100
Georgia	57.8	77	49.0	82	...	...	...
Kazakhstan	...	...	176.1	84	...	...	...
Kyrgyzstan	48.1	68	52.7	71	...	...	...
Mongolia	11.0	69	14.5	70	...	...	...
Tajikistan	46.9	42	54.9	45	...	...	...
Turkmenistan	...	...	...	...	...	...	...
Uzbekistan	...	...	...	...	...	...	...
East Asia and the Pacific							
Australia	...	...	...	...	...	...	...
Brunei Darussalam	3.1*	47*	3.5	53	...	...	...
Cambodia	18.1**	27**	23.7	30	...	...	...
China	...	...	5 138.0	43	...	...	...
Cook Islands	...	...	...	...	...	...	...

SECONDARY EDUCATION[1]					TERTIARY EDUCATION				
Trained teachers (%)			Pupil/teacher ratio		Total teachers				
2002/2003			1998/1999	2002/2003	1998/1999		2002/2003		
Total	Male	Female			Total (000)	% F	Total (000)	% F	Country or territory
									Arab States
...	...	...	...	21 **	...	...	57.7 **	46 **	Algeria
...	...	...	...	12 **,z	...	...	0.9	36	Bahrain
...	...	...	23	28 **,z	0.02	30	**0.1**	**19**	Djibouti
83 **,y	...	...	17 **	17 **	...	...	72.6	...	Egypt
...	...	...	20 **	18	11.8	31	14.7 **,z	...	Iraq
...	...	...	...	...	...	...	6.9	20	Jordan
100 **,y	100 **,y	100 **,y	11 **	10 **,z	2.2 **	...	...	...	Kuwait
...	...	...	9 **	8	8.9	28	11.2	29	Lebanon
...	...	...	...	...	11.7	13 **	15.7 **	...	Libyan Arab Jamahiriya
...	...	...	26 **	26	...	...	0.4	4	Mauritania
...	...	...	17 **	18 **	16.2	23	18.0	23	Morocco
100 **,z	100 **,z	100 **,z	18	16 **	...	...	0.6 z	11 z	Oman
...	...	...	...	26	3.2	13	4.0	15 **	Palestinian Autonomous Territories
...	...	...	10 **	10	0.7 **	32 **	0.7	31	Qatar
...	...	...	13	12	19.7	36	23.4	34	Saudi Arabia
...	...	...	...	26 **	4.4	23	...	...	Sudan
...	...	...	15 **	18 **,y	...	...	...	...	Syrian Arab Republic
64 **,y	...	...	19 **	20 **,z	5.9	...	12.9	38	Tunisia
52 z	49 z	54 z	12	14	...	...	2.9 **,z	...	United Arab Emirates
...	...	...	14 **	...	4.9	1	...	...	Yemen
									Central and Eastern Europe
...	...	...	16 **	18	...	...	1.7	41	Albania
...	...	...	11	9	30.3	51	43.2	54	Belarus
...	...	...	...	...	...	...	...	...	Bosnia and Herzegovina
...	...	...	13	12	24.4	41 **	19.1	44	Bulgaria
100	100	100	12	11	6.7	35	8.1	37	Croatia
...	...	...	13	11	19.2	...	22.1	39	Czech Republic
...	...	...	10	10**,z	6.2	49	6.6	...	Estonia
...	...	...	10	11	21.3	...	23.8	39	Hungary
...	...	...	10	11	5.6	52	5.4	55	Latvia
...	...	...	...	11**	15.2	50	13.5	53	Lithuania
...	...	...	...	12**	...	...	86.5	...	Poland
...	...	...	13	13	7.1	50	7.2	54	Republic of Moldova
...	...	...	13 **	13	26.0	37	29.6	41	Romania
...	...	...	...	...	525.2 **	56 **	615.7 **	63 **	Russian Federation
100 y	100 y	100 y	14 **	14 y	12.8	36	11.6 y	38 y	Serbia and Montenegro
...	...	...	13 **	13	11.3 **	38 **	12.6	40	Slovakia
...	...	...	13	14	2.5	21	3.1	30	Slovenia
...	...	...	16	16	2.7	42	2.6	44	The former Yugoslav Rep. of Macedonia
...	...	...	...	...	60.1	...	76.1	37	Turkey
...	...	...	...	13	132.9	...	177.6	...	Ukraine
									Central Asia
...	...	...	...	10	...	...	12.1	46	Armenia
100	100	100	8	9	13.2	36	13.2	46	Azerbaijan
...	...	...	8	9	13.5	49 **	17.2	39	Georgia
...	...	...	...	12	27.1	58	37.6	59	Kazakhstan
72	71	72	13	14	7.7	32	13.2	48	Kyrgyzstan
...	...	...	19	22	5.7	47 **	5.4	53	Mongolia
94	...	...	16	17	5.9	29	6.5	30	Tajikistan
...	...	...	...	...	...	...	...	...	Turkmenistan
...	...	...	...	...	...	...	24.5	38	Uzbekistan
									East Asia and the Pacific
...	...	...	...	...	...	...	...	...	Australia
...	...	...	11 *	11	0.5	28	0.5	34	Brunei Darussalam
99 z	99 **,z	99 **,z	18 **	24	1.1	19	2.5	18 **	Cambodia
...	...	...	...	19	503.9	...	850.2 **	45 **	China
...	...	...	...	...	.	.	.	.	Cook Islands

Table 10B (continued)

Country or territory	SECONDARY EDUCATION[1]						
	Total teachers				Trained teachers (%)		
	1998/1999		2002/2003		1998/1999		
	Total (000)	% F	Total (000)	% F	Total	Male	Female
Democratic People's Republic of Korea	...	...	...	...	...	...	...
Fiji	...	...	5.8**,z	49**,z	...	...	...
Indonesia	...	...	1 115.1	41	...	...	...
Japan	629.8	...	615.2	31**	...	...	...
Kiribati	...	...	...	...	...	...	...
Lao People's Democratic Republic	11.8	40	13.8	42	98	97	98
Macao, China	1.4	56	1.8	57	59	50	66
Malaysia	111.2**	60**	129.8	63	...	...	...
Marshall Islands	0.3	...	0.4z	39z	...	...	...
Micronesia (Federated States of)	...	...	...	...	...	...	...
Myanmar	68.4	76	73.1	78	69**	73**	69**
Nauru	...	...	...	...	...	...	...
New Zealand	24.8	64	36.5z	59z	...	...	...
Niue	0.02	60	0.02**,z	50**,z	...	...	...
Palau	0.2	51	...	...	...	...	...
Papua New Guinea	6.0	35	7.6z	36z	100	100	100
Philippines	150.2	76	163.6	51	100**	...	...
Republic of Korea	192.5	40	**206.2**	**49**	...	...	...
Samoa	1.1**	56**	1.1**	59**	...	...	...
Singapore	...	...	...	...	...	...	...
Solomon Islands	...	...	...	...	...	...	...
Thailand	241.7	60	215.8**	54**	...	...	...
Timor-Leste	...	...	1.6z	...	...	...	...
Tokelau	...	...	...	...	...	...	...
Tonga	1.4	32	1.0**,y	50**,y	59	45	90
Tuvalu	...	...	0.04z	83z	...	...	...
Vanuatu	0.4**	47**	0.4y	49y	...	...	...
Viet Nam	258.3	65	362.1	65	...	...	...
Latin America and the Caribbean							
Anguilla	0.1**	65**	0.1**	63**	60**	65**	57**
Antigua and Barbuda	...	...	...	...	...	...	...
Argentina	257.8	69	229.2	66	...	...	...
Aruba	0.4**	49**	0.5	50	100**	100**	100**
Bahamas	...	...	2.1**	67**	...	...	...
Barbados	1.2**	58**	1.4**	59**	64**	63**	64**
Belize	0.9**	62**	1.2**	65**	...	...	...
Bermuda	...	...	0.7z	67z	...	...	...
Bolivia	...	...	41.0**	51**	...	...	...
Brazil	...	...	1 401.1	79	...	...	...
British Virgin Islands	0.1**	62**	0.2	65	...	...	...
Cayman Islands	0.2**	51**	0.2**,z	55**,z	...	...	...
Chile	...	...	**47.1****	**63****	...	...	...
Colombia	184.6**	50**	177.9	50	...	...	...
Costa Rica	12.0	53	15.4	54	...	...	...
Cuba	64.9	60	80.4	57	94	94	94
Dominica	0.3**	68**	0.5	61	30**	27**	31**
Dominican Republic	22.1**	58**	24.7**,z	72**,z	...	...	...
Ecuador	53.9**	50**	73.3*	49*	...	...	...
El Salvador	...	...	...	...	...	...	...
Grenada	...	...	0.7**	63**	...	...	...
Guatemala	27.2*	...	44.4	...	...	...	...
Guyana	3.6**	63**	3.4**	70**	58**	59**	58**
Haiti	...	...	...	...	...	...	...
Honduras	...	...	...	...	...	...	...
Jamaica	...	...	11.3	[illegible]	[illegible]	[illegible]	...
Mexico	...	...	594.4	...	...	...	...
Montserrat	0.03**	69**	0.03**	55**	...	...	...
Netherlands Antilles	1.0	53	1.2**	55**	100	100	100
Nicaragua	7.7*	58*	11.3*	56*	44*	36*	50*
Panama	14.3**	55**	15.6	57	...	...	...

SECONDARY EDUCATION[1]					TERTIARY EDUCATION				
Trained teachers (%)			Pupil/teacher ratio		Total teachers				
2002/2003			1998/1999	2002/2003	1998/1999		2002/2003		
Total	Male	Female			Total (000)	% F	Total (000)	% F	Country or territory
...	...	...	...	...	...	...	...	...	Democratic People's Republic of Korea
82**,y	80**,y	83**,y	...	17**,z	...	...	...	...	Fiji
53**,y	...	...	...	14	...	...	233.4	39	Indonesia
...	...	...	14	13	465.1	...	490.1	...	Japan
...	...	...	...	...	...	...	...	...	Kiribati
98	98	99	20	26	1.1	31	1.8	35	Lao People's Democratic Republic
63	50	73	23	25	0.7	...	1.2	33	Macao, China
53**,y	...	...	19**	18	...	...	35.0	44	Malaysia
...	...	...	22	17z	...	...	0.05z	52z	Marshall Islands
...	...	...	...	...	0.1	...	...	...	Micronesia (Federated States of)
68	69	67	30	33	...	...	10.5y	70**,y	Myanmar
...	...	...	...	...	.	.	.	.	Nauru
...	...	...	17	13z	10.5	42	13.4	45**	New Zealand
...	...	...	14	12**,z	.	.	.	.	Niue
...	...	...	13	...	...	...	0.05**,z	46**,z	Palau
100z	100z	100z	22	22z	1.1	20	...	...	Papua New Guinea
...	...	...	34	37	93.7	...	110.0	55	Philippines
...	...	...	23	**18**	126.6	25	**172.6**	**29**	Republic of Korea
84y	83y	84y	19**	21**	0.2	37	0.1**,z	43**,z	Samoa
...	...	...	...	...	...	...	...	...	Singapore
...	...	...	...	...	.	.	.	.	Solomon Islands
...	...	...	...	25**	50.2	53	65.5**	47**	Thailand
...	...	...	...	28z	...	...	0.1**,z	9**,z	Timor-Leste
...	...	...	...	...	...	...	.	.	Tokelau
...	...	...	10	15**,y	0.1**	21**	0.1**,y	22**,y	Tonga
...	...	...	...	25z	.	.	.	.	Tuvalu
85y	100y	70y	27**	27y	0.01	40	0.03z	...	Vanuatu
92**,z	91**,z	92**,z	29	26	28.0	37	38.6	40	Viet Nam
									Latin America and the Caribbean
66**	72**	63**	16**	14**	.	.	.	.	Anguilla
...	...	...	...	...	.	.	.	.	Antigua and Barbuda
65**,y	...	...	14	17	116.1	53	127.1	50	Argentina
96	95	97	16**	15	0.2	43	0.2	46	Aruba
100**,z	100**,z	100**,z	...	15**	...	...	...	...	Bahamas
78**	78**	77**	18**	15**	0.6**	41**	0.6**,y	51**,y	Barbados
41**	38**	43**	24**	23**	...	...	0.1	47**	Belize
100z	100z	100z	...	7z	...	...	0.1**,z	55**,z	Bermuda
77**,y	74**,y	80**,y	...	24**	11.5	...	16.3	...	Bolivia
79**,y	...	...	...	19	165.1	42	242.5	53	Brazil
72	63	77	10**	10	.	.	.	.	British Virgin Islands
100**,z	100**,z	100**,z	9**	10**,z	0.02	42	0.02y	32y	Cayman Islands
87**,y	...	...	...	33	...	...	...	...	Chile
...	...	...	19**	21	...	...	83.3	33	Colombia
84	...	...	19	19	...	...	3.9z	...	Costa Rica
85	85	84	11	12	23.5	47	44.7	37	Cuba
30	21	35	22**	17	.	.	...	...	Dominica
64**,z	67**,z	63**,z	28**	31**,z	...	...	11.1	41	Dominican Republic
70*	64*	76*	17**	13*	...	...	15.3y	...	Ecuador
...	...	...	...	...	7.2	32**	7.3	32	El Salvador
31**	34**	29**	...	20**	...	...	.	.	Grenada
100z	...	...	15*	14	...	...	4.0	...	Guatemala
60**,y	58**,y	61**,y	19**	20**	...	...	...	...	Guyana
...	...	...	...	...	...	...	...	...	Haiti
...	...	...	...	...	5.5	...	5.5**,z	36**,z	Honduras
...	...	...	...	20	1.5	...	2.0**	60**	Jamaica
...	...	...	...	17	192.4	...	231.6		Mexico
58**,z	33**,z	78**,z	10**	9**	.	.	.	.	Montserrat
100**,z	100**,z	100**,z	15	13**	0.2**	42**	0.3**,z	34**,z	Netherlands Antilles
65*	53*	75*	37**	34*	...	...	6.5	46	Nicaragua
81	76	85	16**	16	6.3	...	8.4	52	Panama

Table 10B (continued)

Country or territory	SECONDARY EDUCATION[1]						
	Total teachers				Trained teachers (%)		
	1998/1999		2002/2003		1998/1999		
	Total (000)	% F	Total (000)	% F	Total	Male	Female
Paraguay	…	…	43.8	61	…	…	…
Peru	128.4**	41**	134.3	44	…	…	…
Saint Kitts and Nevis	…	…	0.4**	67**	…	…	…
Saint Lucia	0.7**	64**	0.8**	63**	…	…	…
Saint Vincent and the Grenadines	…	…	0.4**	59**	…	…	…
Suriname	…	…	2.7**	61**	…	…	…
Trinidad and Tobago	5.4**	59**	5.7**	61**	56**	58**	54**
Turks and Caicos Islands	0.1**	61**	0.1**	64**	…	…	…
Uruguay	15.9	…	18.4**	…	…	…	…
Venezuela	…	…	…	…	…	…	…
North America and Western Europe							
Andorra	…	…	0.4	56	…	…	…
Austria	72.6	57	72.6	60	…	…	…
Belgium	…	…	117.7	57	…	…	…
Canada	136.7	…	148.0**,z	68**,z	…	…	…
Cyprus	4.9**	51**	5.3	60	…	…	…
Denmark	44.2	45	43.9y	48y	…	…	…
Finland	39.3	64	…	…	…	…	…
France	495.2	57	510.9	58	…	…	…
Germany	532.6	51	595.4	…	…	…	…
Greece	74.7	…	83.0	…	…	…	…
Iceland	2.5**	58**	2.8**	62**	…	…	…
Ireland	…	…	…	…	…	…	…
Israel	54.9	…	60.9	71	…	…	…
Italy	422.1	65	428.2	65	…	…	…
Luxembourg	…	…	3.3	43	…	…	…
Malta	3.6	48	3.8	53	…	…	…
Monaco	0.4	61	0.4y	61y	…	…	…
Netherlands	…	…	108.1	43	…	…	…
Norway	…	…	41.9	58**	…	…	…
Portugal	…	…	87.3	69**	…	…	…
San Marino	…	…	…	…	…	…	…
Spain	…	…	274.8	…	…	…	…
Sweden	63.1	…	72.1	56	…	…	…
Switzerland	50.3	39	48.0**,z	40**,z	…	…	…
United Kingdom	469.5	56	483.8	60	…	…	…
United States	1 503.9	56	1 599.3	61	…	…	…
South and West Asia							
Afghanistan	…	…	…	…	…	…	…
Bangladesh	251.5	13	320.8	14	28	26	43
Bhutan	0.5	33	0.9**	39**	100	100	100
India	…	…	2 490.6	35	…	…	…
Iran, Islamic Republic of	322.0	45	352.5	48**	…	…	…
Maldives	0.7	24	1.7	33	76	75	79
Nepal	39.9	9	52.5	14	…	…	…
Pakistan	…	…	…	…	…	…	…
Sri Lanka	…	…	**117.9****	**63****	…	…	…
Sub-Saharan Africa							
Angola	16.0*	33*	…	…	…	…	…
Benin	9.0**	12**	11.9**,y	11**,y	…	…	…
Botswana	8.5	46	…	…	80	83	78
Burkina Faso	6.2**	…	7.6	11	…	…	…
Burundi	…	…	6.9	21			…
Cameroon	26.4**	28**	38.8	…	…	…	…
Cape Verde	…	…	2.1	41	…	…	…
Central African Republic	…	…	…	…	…	…	…
Chad	3.6	5	4.4**,y	4**,y	…	…	…
Comoros	…	…	3.4	11	…	…	…

Trained teachers (%) Total 2002/2003	Trained teachers (%) Male 2002/2003	Trained teachers (%) Female 2002/2003	Pupil/teacher ratio 1998/1999	Pupil/teacher ratio 2002/2003	Total teachers 1998/1999 Total (000)	Total teachers 1998/1999 % F	Total teachers 2002/2003 Total (000)	Total teachers 2002/2003 % F	Country or territory
SECONDARY EDUCATION[1]					TERTIARY EDUCATION				
...	...	...	...	12	...	...	...	...	Paraguay
76 **,y	...	...	17 **	19	54.5	...	56.1	...	Peru
39 **	45 **	36 **	...	10 **	...	...	.	.	Saint Kitts and Nevis
61 **	63 **	59 **	18 **	16 **	...	...	...	...	Saint Lucia
...	...	...	...	22 **	.	.	...	...	Saint Vincent and the Grenadines
100 z	100 **,z	100 **,z	...	15 **	...	...	0.6 **	48 **	Suriname
58 **	61 **	56 **	21 **	19 **	0.5	31	1.0	33	Trinidad and Tobago
100 **	100 **	100 **	9 **	10 **	0.01	33	0.01 **	20 **	Turks and Caicos Islands
...	...	...	...	18 **	12.7	...	12.0	...	Uruguay
...	...	...	...	...	...	...	...	...	Venezuela
									North America and Western Europe
...	...	...	...	7	...	...	0.1	50	Andorra
...	...	...	10	11	25.7	...	28.7	29	Austria
...	...	...	...	10	...	...	25.4	39	Belgium
...	...	...	19 **	18 **,z	125.5	...	131.3 **,z	41 **,z	Canada
...	...	...	13 **	12	1.1	34	1.3	41	Cyprus
...	...	...	10	10 y	...	...	...	...	Denmark
...	...	...	12	...	17.5 **	46 **	18.0	45	Finland
...	...	...	12	11	102.3	...	134.1	34	France
...	...	...	15	14	271.7	...	284.1	33	Germany
...	...	...	10	9	17.2	...	23.8	...	Greece
...	...	...	13 **	12 **	1.4	43	2.0	48 **	Iceland
...	...	...	...	...	10.3	33	12.7	38	Ireland
...	...	...	10	10	...	...	...	...	Israel
...	...	...	11	11	73.0	...	87.2	33	Italy
...	...	...	...	11	...	...	...	...	Luxembourg
...	...	...	...	10	0.7	25	0.6	22	Malta
...	...	...	8	8 y	.	.	.	.	Monaco
...	...	...	...	13	...	...	44.1	34	Netherlands
...	...	...	...	9	14.1	...	15.2	...	Norway
...	...	...	...	9	...	...	36.2	41	Portugal
...	...	...	...	...	...	...	...	...	San Marino
...	...	...	...	11	107.7	...	136.4	38	Spain
...	...	...	15	13	28.9	...	36.4	...	Sweden
...	...	...	11	11 **,z	26.1	...	37.7	28	Switzerland
...	...	...	17	20	92.2	...	101.0	36	United Kingdom
...	...	...	...	15	991.8	41 **	1 167.3	42	United States
									South and West Asia
...	...	...	...	...	...	...	1.5 y	–	Afghanistan
29	27	42	36	34	44.9	14	61.3	15	Bangladesh
89 **,z	88 **,z	89 **,z	39	34 **	...	...	0.2 **,y	27 **,y	Bhutan
...	...	...	...	33	...	...	428.1	37	India
100	100 **	100 **	30	28	65.4	17	84.2	18	Iran, Islamic Republic of
81	79	86	17	15	.	.	.	.	Maldives
28 z	29 z	21 z	32	35	3.0 **	...	4.6 **,y	...	Nepal
...	...	...	...	...	...	...	...	...	Pakistan
...	...	...	...	20 **	...	...	...	...	Sri Lanka
									Sub-Saharan Africa
...	...	...	18 *	...	0.8	...	1.3 **	20 **	Angola
...	...	...	24 **	22 **,y	...	...	...	...	Benin
...	...	...	17	...	0.5 **	28 **	...	...	Botswana
...	...	...	28 **	31	...	...	...	...	Burkina Faso
37	39	28	...	19	0.4	...	0.8 **	...	Burundi
...	...	...	24 **	21	2.6	...	3.2 *	...	Cameroon
62	60	65	...	24	...	...	0.3	...	Cape Verde
...	...	...	...	...	0.3	5	...	...	Central African Republic
...	...	...	34	32 **,y	...	...	...	...	Chad
...	...	...	...	11	0.1	10	0.1	14	Comoros

Table 10B (continued)

Country or territory	SECONDARY EDUCATION[1] Total teachers 1998/1999 Total (000)	% F	2002/2003 Total (000)	% F	Trained teachers (%) 1998/1999 Total	Male	Female
Congo	...	...	7.7**,y	9**,y	...	...	...
Côte d'Ivoire	20.1**	...	...	...	...	...	...
Democratic Rep. of the Congo	89.5	10	...	...	...	...	...
Equatorial Guinea	0.9**	5**	...	...	...	...	...
Eritrea	2.3	12	3.0	11	56	55	66
Ethiopia	...	...	**45.1****	**9****	...	...	...
Gabon	3.1**	16**	...	...	...	...	...
Gambia	2.4**	15**	2.4**	17**	66**	65**	66**
Ghana	52.2	22	**67.9**	**24****	74	70	89
Guinea	5.8**	11**	...	...	...	...	...
Guinea-Bissau	...	...	...	...	...	...	...
Kenya	44.3**	35**	48.0**,y	35**,y	93**	91**	96**
Lesotho	3.1**	51**	3.5	54**	84**	85**	84**
Liberia	6.6	16	...	...	...	...	...
Madagascar	20.4**	44**	...	...	...	...	...
Malawi	7.5**	47**	11.4**	24**	...	...	...
Mali	7.7*	14*	...	...	...	...	...
Mauritius	5.1**	46**	5.9	50	...	...	...
Mozambique	...	...	14.8z	19z	...	...	...
Namibia	5.1**	47**	5.6**	58**	...	...	...
Niger	4.3	18	4.1	19	...	...	...
Nigeria	...	...	180.3	38	...	...	...
Rwanda	...	...	7.1	19	...	...	...
Sao Tome and Principe	...	...	...	...	...	...	...
Senegal	9.4**	14**	10.7**,z	14**,z	...	...	...
Seychelles	0.6	53	0.5	55	88	85	89
Sierra Leone	...	...	5.8y	27y	...	...	...
Somalia	...	...	...	...	...	...	...
South Africa	143.8**	50**	146.5**	51**	89**	86**	93**
Swaziland	3.4**	46**	3.9**	47**	99**	99**	99**
Togo	6.6	13	...	...	...	...	...
Uganda	...	...	31.0y	21**,y	...	...	...
United Republic of Tanzania	...	...	...	...	...	...	...
Zambia	10.0	26	9.9**	27**	...	...	...
Zimbabwe	...	...	**34.0**	**40**	...	...	...
World	...	51	...	55	...	...	...
Countries in transition	...	70	...	78	...	...	...
Developed countries	...	61	...	61	...	...	...
Developing countries	...	47	...	50	...	...	...
Arab States	...	48	...	50	...	...	...
Central and Eastern Europe	...	70	...	73	...	...	...
Central Asia	...	68	...	71	...	...	...
East Asia and the Pacific	...	56	...	50	...	...	...
Latin America and the Caribbean	...	58	...	61	...	...	...
North America and Western Europe	...	56	...	59	...	...	...
South and West Asia	...	24	...	35	...	...	...
Sub-Saharan Africa	...	22	...	22	...	...	...

1. Refers to lower and upper secondary education (ISCED levels 2 and 3).
2. All values shown are medians.

Data in bold are for 2003/2004.

(z) Data are for 2001/2002.
(y) Data are for 2000/2001.

SECONDARY EDUCATION[1]					TERTIARY EDUCATION				
Trained teachers (%)			Pupil/teacher ratio		Total teachers				
2002/2003			1998/1999	2002/2003	1998/1999		2002/2003		
Total	Male	Female			Total (000)	% F	Total (000)	% F	**Country or territory**
…	…	…	…	26**,y	0.4**	5**	0.9**	…	Congo
…	…	…	29**	…	…	…	…	…	Côte d'Ivoire
…	…	…	14	…	3.8	6	…	…	Democratic Rep. of the Congo
…	…	…	…	…	…	…	…	…	Equatorial Guinea
62y	61y	68y	51	54	0.2	13	0.2	13	Eritrea
…	…	…	…	**47****	2.2	6	**4.8**	**9**	Ethiopia
…	…	…	28**	…	0.6	17	…	…	Gabon
88**,y	87**,y	93**,y	20**	25**	0.1	13	…	…	Gambia
74y	70y	87y	20	**19**	2.3**	13**	**3.9**	**14**	Ghana
…	…	…	30**	…	…	…	…	…	Guinea
…	…	…	…	…	…	…	…	…	Guinea-Bissau
…	…	…	26**	26**,y	…	…	…	…	Kenya
–	–	–	23**	23	0.4	45**	0.5	50**	Lesotho
…	…	…	17	…	…	…	0.8**,y	16**,y	Liberia
…	…	…	17**	…	1.5	31	1.9	26	Madagascar
…	…	…	63**	46**	0.5	25	0.5	44**	Malawi
…	…	…	28*	…	1.0	…	…	…	Mali
…	…	…	20**	19	0.6**	26**	…	…	Mauritius
57z	55z	65z	…	27z	…	…	…	…	Mozambique
…	…	…	22**	24**	0.6	…	0.9	31	Namibia
67z	68z	63z	24	31	…	…	0.8y	15**,y	Niger
…	…	…	…	35	…	…	35.1	42**	Nigeria
…	…	…	…	27	0.4	10	1.3	13	Rwanda
…	…	…	…	…	.	.	0.03**,z	33**,z	Sao Tome and Principe
…	…	…	25**	27**,z	…	…	…	…	Senegal
84z	87z	82z	14	14	.	.	.	.	Seychelles
…	…	…	…	27y	…	…	1.2**,z	15**,z	Sierra Leone
…	…	…	…	…	…	…	…	…	Somalia
89**	88**	90**	30**	29**	…	…	40.8	49	South Africa
83**	73**	93**	18**	16**	0.2	32	0.3**	35**	Swaziland
…	…	…	35	…	0.4	10	…	…	Togo
…	…	…	…	…	2.2	17	5.1**	18**	Uganda
…	…	…	…	…	2.1	14	2.2	17	United Republic of Tanzania
…	…	…	23	36**	…	…	…	…	Zambia
79**,z	…	…	…	**22****	…	…	…	…	Zimbabwe
…	…	…	17	17	…	…	…	38	World[2]
…	…	…	12	12	…	50	…	47	Countries in transition
…	…	…	13	11	…	…	…	39	Developed countries
…	…	…	19	20	…	…	…	…	Developing countries
…	…	…	16	18	…	26	…	26	Arab States
…	…	…	13	12	…	42	…	41	Central and Eastern Europe
…	…	…	13	12	…	42	…	46	Central Asia
…	…	…	20	21	…	…	…	41	East Asia and the Pacific
77	…	…	17	17	…	…	…	46	Latin America and the Caribbean
…	…	…	12	11	…	…	…	38	North America and Western Europe
81	79	86	32	33	…	…	…	…	South and West Asia
…	…	…	24	26	…	…	…	18	Sub-Saharan Africa

Table 11
Private enrolment and education finance

	Country or territory	PRIVATE ENROLMENT AS % OF TOTAL ENROLMENT: Pre-primary education 1998/1999	Pre-primary education 2002/2003	Primary education 1998/1999	Primary education 2002/2003	Secondary education 1998/1999	Secondary education 2002/2003	EDUCATION FINANCE: Total public expenditure on education as % of GNP 1998	2002	Total public expenditure on education as % of total government expenditure 1998	2002	Public current expenditure on education as % of total public expenditure on education 1998	2002	Public current expenditure on primary education per pupil (unit cost) in constant 2002 US$ 1998	2002
	Arab States														
1	Algeria	.	.	.	.	.	.	...	...	...	...	...	...	...	...
2	Bahrain	100	99	19	22	13	15	...	...	...	...	...	...	...	1 731 **
3	Djibouti	100	**77**	9	**15**	14	**21**	3.4**	...	...	...	...	...	...	...
4	Egypt	54	48**,z	7**	8**,y	4**	...	...	...	...	...	...	...	...	...
5	Iraq	.	.	.	.	.	.	...	...	...	...	...	...	...	...
6	Jordan	100	97z	29	29	17	16	6.2**	...	...	...	...	...	216	239
7	Kuwait	24	32	32	31	27**	27	...	...	...	...	...	...	...	...
8	Lebanon	78	76	66	64	55	51	...	2.7	...	12.3	...	96.5	...	...
9	Libyan Arab Jamahiriya	.	15**	.	3**	.	3**	...	...	...	...	...	...	...	...
10	Mauritania	...	...	2	4	...	9	4.0**	...	16.6**	...	...	...	...	...
11	Morocco	100	100	4	5	5	5	6.1	6.6	26.1	26.4	90.8	92.3	210	217
12	Oman	100	100	5	4	0.9	1	4.3	4.8**	...	...	93.1	87.3**	800	880 **
13	Palestinian A. T.	100	100	9	8	5	4	...	...	...	...	...	...	...	...
14	Qatar	100	96	37	43	26	32	...	...	...	...	93.9*	...	...	...
15	Saudi Arabia	50	48	6	7	5	8	8.2	...	...	...	...	...	...	...
16	Sudan	90**	90	2**	4	9**	13**	...	...	...	...	...	...	...	...
17	Syrian Arab Republic	67	71	4	4	5	4	...	...	...	...	...	...	...	131
18	Tunisia	88	86z	0.7	0.9	8	4	7.9	6.7	...	18.2z	...	88.4	...	346 **
19	United Arab Emirates	68	70	44	54	31	38	...	...	...	22.5**	...	93.2**	...	1 532
20	Yemen	37	45	1	2	1	2	...	10.3**,z	...	32.8y	...	...	...	...
	Central and Eastern Europe														
21	Albania	.	2y	.	2	.	3	...	...	...	...	...	...	...	...
22	Belarus	.	.	0.1	0.1	0.04	0.1	6.0**	6.0**,y	...	...	...	...	...	...
23	Bosnia and Herzegovina	...	...	...	...	...	...	...	...	...	...	...	...	...	...
24	Bulgaria	0.1	0.3	0.3	0.4	0.6	0.8	3.3	3.6z	...	...	...	98.9**,z	223	305 **,z
25	Croatia	5	8	0.1	0.2	0.7	1	...	4.6	...	10.0	...	90.2	...	1 054 **
26	Czech Republic	2	2	0.8	1	6	7	4.0	4.6	...	9.6z	85.4	89.8	623	814
27	Estonia	0.7	1	1	2	1	2	6.4	6.0	...	...	...	86.1	605	935
28	Hungary	3	4	5	5	6	10	4.9	5.8	...	14.1y	91.3**	90.0	932 **	1 287
29	Latvia	1	3	1	0.9	0.8	1	6.3	5.8	...	...	...	94.2**,y	...	677 **,y
30	Lithuania	...	0.3	...	0.3	...	0.3	...	6.0	...	...	...	95.9	...	...
31	Poland	3	6	...	1	...	6	5.1	5.7	...	12.8	...	93.8	...	1 121
32	Republic of Moldova	...	0.8	...	1	...	1	...	4.5	...	21.4	...	92.7	...	65 **
33	Romania	...	1	...	0.1	...	0.6	3.6**	3.6	...	...	...	90.9	...	211 **
34	Russian Federation	...	2**	0.3	0.4	...	0.3**	3.8**	3.8	...	11.5z	...	...	...	...
35	Serbia and Montenegro	.	.	.	.	0.01	0.02y	...	3.3y	...	...	94.8	...	733	...
36	Slovakia	0.4	0.7	4	4	5	6	...	4.4	...	7.5z	...	94.4	...	520
37	Slovenia	1	1	0.1	0.1	0.8	2	...	...	...	...	...	...	...	...
38	TFYR Macedonia	.	.	.	.	...	0.5	...	3.5	...	...	...	...	...	...
39	Turkey	6	3.0	...	2**	...	2**	2.9	3.7z	...	...	...	94.4**,z	...	286 **,z
40	Ukraine	0.04	0.3	0.3	0.4	...	0.4	4.5	5.5	14.6	20.3	97.1	...	77 **	...
	Central Asia														
41	Armenia	...	2	...	0.9	...	0.7**	...	3.1**	...	...	...	98.6z	...	36 **,z
42	Azerbaijan	–	0.1	–	0.1	–	0.3	3.4	3.4	22.0	20.7	99.2**	98.0	...	54 **
43	Georgia	0.1	–	0.5	3	0.7	3	2.0	2.2	10.4	11.8	...	...	...	...
44	Kazakhstan	10	5	0.5	0.6	0.8	0.8	...	3.2	...	...	...	...	...	...
45	Kyrgyzstan	1	1	0.2	0.3	0.2	0.2	5.2	3.2**	...	18.6z	95.2	98.7**	...	...
46	Mongolia	1	2**,z	0.5	2	0.1	2	6.5	8.6	...	...	...	95.1	...	157
47	Tajikistan	.	.	.	.	.	.	2.6	2.9	...	17.0	[illegible]	[illegible]	[illegible]	[illegible]
48	Turkmenistan	...	...	...	...	...	...	...	...	...	...	...	...	...	...
49	Uzbekistan	.	.	.	.	.	.	...	...	...	...	...	...	...	...
	East Asia and the Pacific														
50	Australia	...	66	27	28	24	24z	4.9	5.0	...	...	95.9**	96.0	2 844 **	3 346
51	Brunei Darussalam	66	65	36	35	12	11	3.0	...	9.3**	9.1**,y	94.8	98.3y	...	...
52	Cambodia	22 **	24	2	0.9	0.6**	0.4z	1.3	1.9	10.2	15.3z	63.8	95.3z	7	18z

EDUCATION FINANCE

Public current expenditure on primary education per pupil (unit cost) at PPP in constant 2002 US$		Public current expenditure on primary education as % of GNP		Public current expenditure on primary education per pupil as % of GNP per capita		Public current expenditure on primary education as % of public current expenditure on education		Primary education textbooks and other teaching material as % of public current expenditure on primary education		Primary teachers' salaries as % of public current expenditure on primary education		Teachers' salaries as % of public current expenditure on education		Salaries of all personnel of primary education as % of public current expenditure on primary education		Salaries of all personnel in education as % of public current expenditure on education		
1998	2002	1998	2002	1998	2002	1998	2002	1998	2002	1998	2002	1998	2002	1998	2002	1998	2002	
																	Arab States	
…	…	…	…	…	…	…	…	…	…	…	…	…	…	…	92.8**	…	…	1
…	2 701**	…	2.1**	…	18.0**	…	…	4.2	4.0z	…	…	…	…	88.8	96.0z	…	…	2
…	…	…	…	…	…	…	…	…	…	…	…	…	…	…	…	…	…	3
…	…	…	…	…	…	…	…	…	…	…	…	…	…	…	…	…	…	4
…	…	…	…	…	…	…	…	…	…	…	…	…	…	…	…	…	…	5
477	561	1.9	2.0	13.0	13.5	…	…	…	…	…	89.3	…	…	…	95.6	…	…	6
…	…	…	…	…	…	…	…	…	…	…	…	…	…	…	…	…	…	7
…	…	…	…	…	…	…	…	…	…	…	…	…	…	…	…	…	98.3	8
…	…	…	…	…	…	…	…	…	…	…	…	…	…	…	…	…	…	9
…	…	…	…	…	…	…	…	…	…	…	…	…	…	…	…	…	…	10
561	679	2.3	2.5	18.6	18.4	41.0	41.1	…	…	…	…	…	…	95.2	95.8	89.6	91.9	11
1 572	1 466**	1.5	1.5**	12.0	12.8**	38.8	35.0**	…	1.4**	…	83.8**	…	…	…	98.6**	…	…	12
…	…	…	…	…	…	…	…	…	…	…	…	…	…	…	…	…	…	13
…	…	…	…	…	…	…	…	…	…	…	…	…	…	…	…	…	…	14
…	…	…	…	…	…	…	…	…	…	…	…	…	…	…	…	…	…	15
…	…	…	…	…	…	…	…	…	…	…	…	…	…	…	…	…	…	16
…	388	…	2.1	…	12.0	…	…	…	4.4	…	…	…	…	…	89.5	…	…	17
…	1 088**	…	2.2**	…	16.5**	…	36.7**	…	…	…	…	…	…	…	97.8y	…	90.4y	18
…	…	…	…	…	…	…	36.4**	…	1.0	…	82.7	…	…	…	85.7	…	…	19
…	…	…	…	…	…	…	…	…	…	…	…	…	…	…	…	…	…	20
																	Central and Eastern Europe	
…	…	…	…	…	…	…	…	…	…	…	…	…	…	…	…	…	…	21
…	…	…	…	…	…	…	…	…	…	…	…	…	…	…	…	…	…	22
…	…	…	…	…	…	…	…	…	…	…	…	…	…	…	…	…	…	23
796	1 213**,z	0.7	0.7**,z	14.6	17.1**,z	…	20.8**,z	…	…	…	53.3z	…	45.2z	…	76.2z	…	69.4z	24
…	2 148**	…	0.9**	…	21.1**	…	22.0**	…	…	…	…	…	…	…	68.4**	…	69.8	25
1 452	1 887	0.6	0.7	9.6	11.9	17.9	15.8	…	…	…	49.8	…	44.1	…	69.8	…	62.3	26
1 440	2 390	1.4	1.4	14.9	18.6	…	27.1	…	…	…	…	…	…	…	71.3	…	66.2	27
2 173**	2 660	0.9**	1.0	17.9**	20.8	20.1**	18.6	…	…	…	…	…	…	…	78.3	…	74.1	28
…	1 705**,y	…	1.1**,y	…	20.0**,y	…	20.8**,y	…	…	…	…	…	…	…	…	…	…	29
…	…	…	…	…	…	…	…	…	…	…	…	…	…	…	…	…	…	30
…	2 418	…	1.8	…	23.0	…	33.4	…	…	…	…	…	…	…	73.0	…	65.7	31
…	251**	…	0.8**	…	15.3**	…	18.6**	…	…	…	…	…	…	…	61.2**	…	48.3	32
…	673**	…	0.5**	…	10.4**	…	14.2**	…	…	…	…	…	…	…	83.4**	…	68.1	33
…	…	…	…	…	…	…	…	…	…	…	…	…	…	…		…		34
…	…	…	…	…	…	46.0	…	…	…	…	…	…	…	…	78.4y	…	71.8y	35
…	1 515	…	0.6	…	11.8	…	14.1	…	…	…	62.0	…	53.7	…	74.1	…	70.1	36
…	…	…	…	…	…	…	…	…	…	…	…	…	…	…	…	…	…	37
…		…	…	…	…	…	…	…	…	…	…	…	…	…	87.6**	…	88.9	38
…	800**,z	…	1.4**,z	…	11.8**,z	…	40.0**,z	…	…	…	…	…	69.3z	…	…	…	89.6z	39
337**	…	0.5**	…	11.3**	…	11.2**	…	…	…	…	…	…	23.9y	…	…	49.3	41.2y	40
																	Central Asia	
…	143**,z	…	0.2**,z	…	5.1**,z	…	7.9**,z	…	…	…	…	…	69.9	…	…	…	97.8	41
…	235**	…	0.6**	…	7.7**	…	18.0**	…	…	…	…	…	…	…	69.5**	…	63.9	42
…	…	…	…	…	…	…	…	…	…	…	…	…	…	…	…	…	…	43
…	…	…	…	…	…	…	…	…	…	…	…	…	…	…	…	…	63.7	44
…	…	0.9**	…	9.4**	…	18.8**	…	…	1.2**,z	…	55.7**,z	…	35.0z	…	71.5**,z	…	51.5z	45
…	586	…	3.2	…	34.0	…	39.0	0.2	0.1y	…	…	…	…	56.1	63.1y	39.8	43.8y	46
…	…	…	…	…	…	…	…	…	…	…	…	…	…	…	…	…	…	47
…	…	…	…	…	…	…	…	…	…	…	…	…	…	…	…	…	…	48
…	…	…	…	…	…	…	…	…	…	…	…	…	…	…	…	…	…	49
																	East Asia and the Pacific	
3 513**	4 542	1.5**	1.6	15.3**	16.1	32.1**	33.2	…	…	…	60.9	…	…	…	76.7	…	…	50
…	…	…	…	…	…	…	…	…	…	…	…	…	…	…	…	…	…	51
37	115z	0.5	1.3z	2.8	6.6z	56.7	73.1z	…	…	…	…	…	…	…	…	…	…	52

Table 11 (continued)

		PRIVATE ENROLMENT AS % OF TOTAL ENROLMENT						EDUCATION FINANCE							
		Pre-primary education		Primary education		Secondary education		Total public expenditure on education as % of GNP		Total public expenditure on education as % of total government expenditure		Public current expenditure on education as % of total public expenditure on education		Public current expenditure on primary education per pupil (unit cost) in constant 2002 US$	
	Country or territory	1998/1999	2002/2003	1998/1999	2002/2003	1998/1999	2002/2003	1998	2002	1998	2002	1998	2002	1998	2002
53	China	...	...	...	...	...	...	2.0	...	...	...	...	...	...	...
54	Cook Islands	26	...	15	...	11	...	0.4	...	13.1**	...	98.6	...	...	...
55	DPR Korea	...	...	...	...	...	...	...	...	...	...	...	...	...	...
56	Fiji	...	...	...	...	...	...	5.8**	5.9[**,z]	16.2**	19.4[**,z]	...	...	...	...
57	Indonesia	99**	99	...	16	...	43	...	1.3	...	9.0**	...	87.8	...	25
58	Japan	65	65	0.9	0.9	...	19	3.5	3.5[z]	9.3	10.5[y]	...	88.8[**,y]	...	5 962[**,y]
59	Kiribati	...	...	...	...	...	...	...	...	...	...	...	...	...	...
60	LPD Republic	18	19	2	2	0.7	0.8	2.5	2.8**	...	11.0**	...	40.3[z]	...	13[z]
61	Macao, China	94	92	95**	94	94	94	3.5	3.0[z]	10.8	16.1	...	91.0	...	...
62	Malaysia	53	41	0.9	0.9	...	3	5.1	8.7	14.0	20.3	73.9**	58.7	366**	479
63	Marshall Islands	...	18[z]	...	24[z]	...	34[z]	14.3	9.1**	...	...	...	97.2[z]	...	539[z]
64	Micronesia (Fed. States of)	...	...	...	...	...	...	5.1**	6.2[**,z]	...	...	...	...	...	...
65	Myanmar	90	...	.	–	.	–	0.6	1.3[y]	8.1	18.1[**,y]	63.8	66.5[y]	...	...
66	Nauru	...	...	...	...	...	...	...	...	7.0**	6.9[**,z]	...	95.3[**,y]	...	...
67	New Zealand	...	49	2	2	9	11[z]	7.3	7.1	...	15.1	95.1**	99.7	2 413**	2 779
68	Niue	.	.[z]	.	.[z]	.	.[z]	...	...	...	10.1[z]	99.7	97.3[z]	...	...
69	Palau	24	...	18	...	27	...	8.6**	10.7[**,z]	...	...	...	...	...	...
70	Papua New Guinea	...	1[z]	...	1[z]	...	2[z]	2.1**	2.4[**,y]	17.5**	17.5[**,y]	...	...	...	...
71	Philippines	47	46	8	7	26	20	4.0	2.9	...	17.8	90.4	96.9	121	105
72	Republic of Korea	75	**78**	2	**1**	41	**36**	3.8	4.2		15.5		80.0		1 523
73	Samoa	100	100[z]	15	17[z]	...	32[z]	4.5	4.8[**,z]	13.3	14.6[**,z]	98.9	100.0[y]	...	159[y]
74	Singapore	...	...	...	...	...	...	...	...	...	...	...	...	...	...
75	Solomon Islands	...	...	...	...	...	...	3.3	3.4[**,y]	15.4**	...	...	...	...	...
76	Thailand	19	22**	13	**15**	...	**9**	5.2	**4.7**	...	**27.5**	...	93.1[**,y]	...	312[**,y]
77	Timor-Leste	...	...	...	...	...	...	...	...	...	...	...	...	...	...
78	Tokelau	...	...	...	...	...	...	...	...	...	...	...	...	...	...
79	Tonga	...	...	...	9[z]	...	...	5.2**	5.0**	15.0**	13.2**	...	77.5[z]	...	171[z]
80	Tuvalu	...	...	...	...	...	...	...	...	...	...	...	...	...	...
81	Vanuatu	...	100[z]	...	4[z]	...	13[z]	8.9	11.2**	17.4	28.1**	...	59.3[z]	...	176[z]
82	Viet Nam	49	60	0.3	0.3	11	11**	...	...	...	...	...	...	...	...
	Latin America and the Caribbean														
83	Anguilla	100	100	5	10	.	.	...	...	14.4	10.4**	95.1	93.6	...	...
84	Antigua and Barbuda	...	...	...	...	...	...	...	4.0	...	...	...	96.2	...	...
85	Argentina	29	28	20	20	25	25	4.1	4.3	...	13.8	98.6	99.4**	364	290**
86	Aruba	83	79	83	80	91	92	...	...	17.5	15.6	73.9	87.6	...	2 467
87	Bahamas	...	79**	...	25**	...	28[z]	...	...	...	...	...	...	...	...
88	Barbados	18	20	9	11	8**	5	5.3	7.9	15.4	17.3	91.6	89.9	1 031**	1 955**
89	Belize	100	100	87**	87	54	74**	5.7**	5.7	17.1**	18.1	...	90.9	...	513
90	Bermuda	...	.	...	35[z]	...	41[z]	...	...	17.0	...	73.5	...	...	...
91	Bolivia	7	23	7	20	14**	28**	5.6	6.5	25.0	19.7	86.5	96.7	102**	138
92	Brazil	...	27	...	9	...	11[z]	5.3	4.4[z]	12.3	12.0[z]	94.1	92.7[z]	...	256[z]
93	British Virgin Islands	100	100	13	15	...	3	...	...	...	9.0[z]	...	79.8[z]	...	...
94	Cayman Islands	88	92[z]	36	38[z]	25	25[z]	...	...	...	...	...	...	...	...
95	Chile	45	**46**	44	47	46	50[y]	3.8	**4.3**	16.1	**19.1**	...	**90.3**	486	608
96	Colombia	45	38	20	17	33	24	4.0	5.4	18.1*	15.6	...	92.9	...	263**
97	Costa Rica	10**	15	7**	7	15**	12	...	5.2	...	22.4	...	80.2	...	656
98	Cuba	.	.	.	.	.	.	6.8	8.7[y]	12.2	18.7	...	83.5	...	...
99	Dominica	100	100	24	28	27	32	7.6	...	...	...	65.4*	...	633*	...
100	Dominican Republic	45	45	12**	15**	32**	24**	2.6**	2.4	15.7**	12.4	...	91.1	...	...
101	Ecuador	39	46	21	28	24	33	2.7	1.1[**,z]	14.2	8.0[**,z]	...	94.8[y]	...	...
102	El Salvador	22	10	11	10	25	20	2.4	2.9	16.4	20.0	96.8	95.3	182**	210**
103	Grenada	...	58	...	76	...	[illegible]		5.7	...	12.9	...	87.1**	...	393**
104	Guatemala	23**	19	15**	12	...	74	...	...	...	...			...	147[z]
105	Guyana	1	0.7[**,z]	1	0.9[**,z]	0.8	1[y]	9.5**	9.1	18.4**	18.4	...	84.4	...	194
106	Haiti	...	...	...	...	...	...	...	...	...	...	...	...	...	...
107	Honduras	...	...	...	...	...	...	4.2**	...	...	...	...	...	...	...
108	Jamaica	88	89	...	5		?	...	5.3	...	9.5	...	94.1	...	413
109	Mexico	9	10	7	8	15	16	4.3	5.4	...	21.3[z]	94.4**	97.3	554**	882

EDUCATION FINANCE

Public current expenditure on primary education per pupil (unit cost) at PPP in constant 2002 US$		Public current expenditure on primary education as % of GNP		Public current expenditure on primary education per pupil as % of GNP per capita		Public current expenditure on primary education as % of public current expenditure on education		Primary education textbooks and other teaching material as % of public current expenditure on primary education		Primary teachers' salaries as % of public current expenditure on primary education		Teachers' salaries as % of public current expenditure on education		Salaries of all personnel of primary education as % of public current expenditure on primary education		Salaries of all personnel in education as % of public current expenditure on education		
1998	2002	1998	2002	1998	2002	1998	2002	1998	2002	1998	2002	1998	2002	1998	2002	1998	2002	
…	…	…	…	…	…	…	…	…	…	…	…	…	…	…	…	…	…	53
…	…	0.2	…	…	…	53.0	…	…	…	…	…	…	…	…	…	…	…	54
…	…	…	…	…	…	…	…	…	…	…	…	…	…	…	…	…	…	55
…	…	…	…	…	…	…	…	…	…	…	…	…	…	…	…	…	…	56
…	98	…	0.4	…	3.2	…	38.7	…	…	…	78.3	…	80.7	…	80.8	…	89.6	57
…	4 124[**,y]	…	1.1[**,y]	…	18.9[**,y]	…	35.3[**,y]	…	…	…	…	…	…	…	88.1[z]	…	86.5[z]	58
…	…	…	…	…	…	…	…	…	…	…	…	…	…	…	…	…	…	59
…	68[z]	…	0.7[z]	…	4.5[z]	…	54.3[z]	…	…	…	…	…	…	…	…	…	…	60
…	…	…	…	…	…	…	…	…	…	…	…	…	…	…	88.9	…	…	61
858**	1 119	1.4**	1.6	10.7**	13.0	37.5**	31.8	…	…	…	71.2	…	55.6	…	83.8	…	67.3	62
…	…	…	4.0[z]	…	23.0[z]	…	45.0[z]	…	1.7[z]	…	68.6[z]	…	59.6[z]	…	78.9[z]	…	76.9[z]	63
…	…	…	…	…	…	…	…	…	…	…	…	…	…	…	…	…	…	64
…	…	…	…	…	…	…	…	…	…	…	…	…	…	…	…	…	…	65
…	…	…	…	…	…	…	45.6[**,y]	…	…	…	…	…	…	…	…	…	…	66
3 014**	4 062	1.8**	1.8	19.0**	19.2	26.7**	25.5	…	…	…	…	…	…	…	…	…	…	67
…	…	…	…	…	…	31.9	29.1[z]	…	…	…	…	…	…	…	…	…	…	68
…	…	…	…	…	…	…	…	…	…	…	…	…	…	…	…	…	…	69
…	…	…	…	…	…	…	…	…	…	…	…	…	…	…	…	…	…	70
496	449	2.2	1.6	12.6	9.9	59.8	57.6	…	…	…	87.5[y]	…	83.0[y]	…	92.0	…	89.6	71
2 580	…	1.2	…	13.2	…	34.2	…	…	…	63.8	…	56.1	…	73.2	…	68.0		72
…	596[y]	…	1.8[y]	…	11.2[y]	…	42.9[y]	…	…	…	…	…	…	…	…	…	…	73
…	…	…	…	…	…	…	…	…	…	…	…	…	…	…	…	…	…	74
…	…	…	…	…	…	…	…	…	…	…	…	…	…	…	…	…	…	75
…	985[**,y]	…	1.7[**,y]	…	16.4[**,y]	…	33.6[**,y]	…	…	…	…	…	…	…	…	…	…	76
…	…	…	…	…	…	…	…	…	…	…	…	…	…	…	…	…	…	77
…	…	…	…	…	…	…	…	…	…	…	…	…	…	…	…	…	…	78
…	807[z]	…	2.2[z]	…	13.2[z]	…	59.1[z]	…	…	…	…	…	…	…	…	…	…	79
…	…	…	…	…	…	…	…	…	…	…	…	…	…	…	…	…	…	80
…	472[z]	…	2.8[z]	…	15.4[z]	…	43.9[z]	…	1.2[z]	…	98.8[z]	…	94.5[z]	…	98.8[z]	…	97.9[z]	81
…	…	…	…	…	…	…	…	…	…	…	…	…	…	…	…	…	…	82
Latin America and the Caribbean																		
…	…	…	…	…	…	26.1	39.5	6.0	4.8	78.0	91.2	…	85.9	90.4	95.2	…	91.6	83
…	…	…	1.1	…	…	…	28.3	…	0.4	…	90.1	…	69.5	…	93.5	…	73.3	84
551	1 173**	1.4	1.5**	10.8	11.7**	35.2	35.4**	…	…	…	59.9	…	68.4	…	89.3	…	89.6	85
…	…	…	…	…	…	31.2	29.3	…	…	…	…	…	…	…	95.9	…	94.8	86
…	…	…	…	…	…	…	…	…	…	…	…	…	…	…	…	…	…	87
1 630**	3 173**	1.2**	1.8**	11.1**	21.6**	24.4**	25.9**	0.1	1.5**	…	…	…	…	93.9	75.0**	98.1	77.9	88
…	936	…	2.8	…	15.1	…	54.8	…	0.8[y]	…	…	…	…	…	97.5**	…	77.3**	89
…	…	…	…	…	…	43.0	…	…	…	…	…	…	…	…	…	…	…	90
224**	383	2.0**	2.8	11.3**	15.8	40.8**	44.9	…	…	…	…	…	…	…	…	…	…	91
…	663[z]	1.6	1.2[z]	…	10.6[z]	32.8	29.5[z]	…	…	…	…	…	…	…	78.7[z]	…	80.3[z]	92
…	…	…	…	…	…	…	29.5[z]	…	…	…	…	…	…	…	96.1[z]	…	…	93
…	…	…	…	…	…	…	…	…	…	…	…	…	…	…	…	…	…	94
864	1 452	1.5	**1.6**	12.5	**14.6**	…	**40.5**	…	…	…	…	…	…	…	**72.2**	…	**66.4**	95
…	906**	…	1.8**	…	14.8**	…	35.2**	…	…	…	…	…	91.0[z]	…	…	…	…	96
…	1 357	…	2.2	…	16.5	…	52.2	…	…	…	…	…	…	…	…	…	…	97
…	…	…	2.9[**,y]	…	32.0[**,y]	…	34.4	…	1.3	…	…	…	…	…	70.6	…	60.1	98
935*	…	3.0*	…	19.1*	…	61.0*	…	…	…	…	…	…	…	…	…	…	…	99
…	…	…	1.1[**,z]	…	6.4[**,z]	…	45.5[**,z]	…	1.7[z]	…	…	…	65.6	…	79.7[z]	…	82.2	100
…	…	…	…	…	…	…	…	…	…	…	…	…	…	…	…	…	82.4[y]	101
402**	462**	1.3**	1.5**	8.6**	9.7**	58.1**	53.4**	…	…	…	…	…	…	…	75.1**	…	73.5	102
…	705**	…	1.7**	…	10.6**	…	35.3**	…	–	…	93.5	…	79.6	…	96.1	…	90.8	103
…	330[z]	…	1.3[z]	…	7.7[z]	…	…	…	1.8[z]	…	…	…	…	…	89.1[z]	…	97.5[y]	104
…	884	…	3.2	…	22.2	…	42.4	…	…	…	63.5	…	61.5	…	63.5	…	64.2	105
…	…	…	…	…	…	…	…	…	…	…	…	…	…	…	…	…	…	106
…	…	…	…	…	…	…	…	…	…	…	…	…	…	…	…	…	…	107
…	547	…	1.7	…	13.8	…	34.5	…	…	…	77.4	…	63.1[z]	…	85.5	…	79.5[z]	108
1 011**	1 252	1.5**	2.1	9.5**	14.2	35.6**	39.3	…	…	…	85.7	…	77.6	…	95.9	…	90.9	109

Table 11 (continued)

		PRIVATE ENROLMENT AS % OF TOTAL ENROLMENT						EDUCATION FINANCE							
		Pre-primary education		Primary education		Secondary education		Total public expenditure on education as % of GNP		Total public expenditure on education as % of total government expenditure		Public current expenditure on education as % of total public expenditure on education		Public current expenditure on primary education per pupil (unit cost) in constant 2002 US$	
	Country or territory	1998/1999	2002/2003	1998/1999	2002/2003	1998/1999	2002/2003	1998	2002	1998	2002	1998	2002	1998	2002
111	Netherlands Antilles	75	75**	74	73**	79	81**	...	...	14.1**	12.8z	...	93.4z	...	...
112	Nicaragua	17 **	16	16 **	16	32 **	29	3.0	3.2	8.2	15.0	...	90.8	...	57
113	Panama	23 **	18	10 **	10	16 **	15	5.3**	4.6	...	7.7	96.1**	96.5z	535 **	425 z
114	Paraguay	32	28	15 **	16	29	26	4.5	4.4	...	11.4	...	95.7	...	112
115	Peru	...	16	...	14	...	17	3.3	3.1	...	17.1	86.2	93.8	136	134
116	Saint Kitts and Nevis	...	61	...	15	...	3	6.0	3.7	13.8	7.9**	...	99.7	...	603
117	Saint Lucia	100	100	2 **	3	...	5**	8.1	8.2**	20.7	...	81.4	...	...	...
118	Saint Vincent/Grenad.	...	...	...	5	...	33	4.9	10.5	6.5	20.3	...	93.0	...	604
119	Suriname	...	46**	...	48**	...	21**	...	...	...	...	...	...	...	...
120	Trinidad and Tobago	100 **	100*	5	28	8 **	28**	3.5	4.6**	13.1	13.4z	90.2	90.6z	581	994 **,z
121	Turks and Caicos Islands	47	64	18	24	9	12**	...	...	13.6	16.5	91.1	78.7	...	...
122	Uruguay	23	19	15	13	...	11	2.6	2.6	...	9.6	...	100.0**,z	...	441 **,z
123	Venezuela	20	17	15	14	30	25	...	...	...	...	...	...	...	...
	North America and Western Europe														
124	Andorra	...	2	...	1	...	4	...	...	...	...	...	...	...	...
125	Austria	25	26	4	4	8	9	6.4	5.8	...	11.1z	93.0**	96.2	5 481 **	5 683
126	Belgium	56	53	55	54	...	57	...	6.2	...	...	...	...	...	4 382 **,z
127	Canada	5	8**,z	5	6**,z	6	6**,z	6.0	5.4y	...	12.7y	98.4**	98.1**,y	...	...
128	Cyprus	54	42	4	5	10	12	...	6.4	...	...	...	88.4	...	2 757
129	Denmark	...	...	11	11z	12	11z	8.4	8.6	...	15.4z	95.2**	93.6	7 475 **	7 100
130	Finland	10	8	1	1	6	8	...	6.4	...	12.7z	...	92.4	...	3 977
131	France	13	13	15	15	25	25	5.8	5.6	...	11.4y	87.6	91.6	3 345	3 809
132	Germany	54	59	2	3	7	7	4.7	4.6z	...	9.5z	91.9**	92.7**,z	3 739 **	3 778 **,z
133	Greece	3	3	7	8	5	6	3.3	...	...	...	80.2**	...	1 253 **	...
134	Iceland	5	8	1	1	4	4	7.4	7.8**	...	...	87.5**	89.5**	...	6 429
135	Ireland	45	...	0.9	0.9	0.4	0.7	5.0	6.8	...	13.5y	93.3**	89.7	2 593 **	4 201
136	Israel	7	4	...	.	...	.	7.7	7.8	...	...	91.5**	94.2	3 076 **	3 426
137	Italy	30	31	7	7	6	5	4.8	4.8	...	10.3z	95.3**	93.4	4 325 **	4 775
138	Luxembourg	5	5	7	7	...	18	...	...	...	...	...	...	...	...
139	Malta	37	38	36	37	...	28	4.9	4.6	...	...	90.3	95.6	908	1 497
140	Monaco	26	25y	31	30y	23	25y	...	...	...	...	...	93.5y	...	...
141	Netherlands	69	69	68	69	85	83	4.9	5.2	...	10.7z	95.7**	94.6	3 545 **	4 183
142	Norway	40	40	1	2	7	6	7.6	7.6	...	16.2y	89.6	92.5	10 409 **	7 595 **
143	Portugal	52	49	9	11	12	15	...	...	...	12.7z	...	...	...	...
144	San Marino	...	.	...	.	...	.	...	...	...	...	...	...	...	...
145	Spain	32	35	33	33	28	29	4.6	4.5	...	11.3z	91.1**	91.4	2 500 **	2 809
146	Sweden	10	14	3	5	2	4z	7.8	7.7	...	12.8z	...	100.0**,z	...	6 013 **,z
147	Switzerland	6	7	3	4	8	7	5.0	5.5**	...	15.1y	90.2**	91.0**	7 769 **	8 069 **
148	United Kingdom	6	7	5	5	53	58	4.6	5.2z	11.4	11.5z	...	...	...	
149	United States	34	40	12	11	10	9	5.4	5.6z	...	17.1y	...	...	...	7 516 **,y
	South and West Asia														
150	Afghanistan	...	...	...	...	...	...	...	...	...	...	...	...	...	...
151	Bangladesh	...	...	36	39	95	96	2.3	2.3	15.7	15.5	63.7	84.5	13	24
152	Bhutan	100	100*,z	2	1z	–	0.3**,z	...	5.9y	...	12.9y	...	67.6y	...	...
153	India	...	4	...	17	...	42	3.2	4.1y	12.6	12.7y	...	99.5**,y	...	58 **,z
154	Iran, Islamic Republic of	...	8	...	4**	...	6**	4.6	4.9	18.7	17.7	90.9	89.9	...	179
155	Maldives	27	41	...	2	...	11	3.9**	...	11.2**	...	76.4**	...	...	...
156	Nepal	...	80	...	15	...	28	2.9**	3.4	12.5**	14.9	73.6**	76.8	16 **	18 **
157	Pakistan	...	25	...	29	...	25**	1.9**	1.8**,y	8.5**	7.8**,y	...	...	...	...
158	Sri Lanka	...	...		[illegible]	[illegible]	2**	3.1	...	...	...	82.7**	...	...	...
	Sub-Saharan Africa														
159	Angola	23	...	5	...	18 *	...	3.2	3.4**,z	...	...	88.7	93.7**,z	...	...
160	Benin	20	31**,z	7	6	18	19	2.5	3.3**	...	...	...	...	...	36 **
161	Botswana	...	...	4	5**	6	4**	...	2.3y	...	25.6y	...	...	...	147 y
162	Burkina Faso	34	...	11	13	33	34**,z	...	...	...	...	...	...	...	...
163	Burundi	49	60	0.8**	1**	...	...	4.0**	4.0	...	13.0	...	90.9	...	10

EDUCATION FINANCE

Public current expenditure on primary education per pupil (unit cost) at PPP in constant 2002 US$		Public current expenditure on primary education as % of GNP		Public current expenditure on primary education per pupil as % of GNP per capita		Public current expenditure on primary education as % of public current expenditure on education		Primary education textbooks and other teaching material as % of public current expenditure on primary education		Primary teachers' salaries as % of public current expenditure on primary education		Teachers' salaries as % of public current expenditure on education		Salaries of all personnel of primary education as % of public current expenditure on primary education		Salaries of all personnel in education as % of public current expenditure on education		
1998	2002	1998	2002	1998	2002	1998	2002	1998	2002	1998	2002	1998	2002	1998	2002	1998	2002	
...	...	...	...	...	...	...	...	...	...	...	...	...	...	...	...	...	...	111
...	187	...	1.3	...	7.8	...	46.4	...	10.2	...	...	...	...	...	85.0	...	88.2	112
784**	645[z]	1.9**	1.5[z]	14.1**	11.3[z]	38.3**	34.6[z]	...	...	...	...	...	...	...	90.6	...	86.0	113
...	518	...	2.0	...	11.7	...	46.6	...	...	...	74.3	...	74.8	...	85.2	...	88.1	114
275	318	1.1	1.0	6.7	6.5	40.4	36.1	...	...	...	89.1[z]	...	80.5[z]	...	93.7	...	82.8	115
...	966	...	1.3	...	7.9	...	33.7	0.7	0.6[**,z]	80.0	76.1[**,z]	78.9	73.3[**,z]	90.2	80.9[**,z]	88.6	85.4[z]	116
...	...	...	...	...	...	...	...	...	...	...	...	...	...	...	...	...	...	117
...	1 070	...	3.3	...	21.0	...	33.6	...	1.5	...	93.7	...	48.7	...	93.8	...	48.9	118
...	...	...	...	...	...	...	...	...	...	...	...	...	...	...	...	...	...	119
946	1 270[**,z]	1.3	1.7[z]	9.6	15.3[**,z]	41.3	41.9[z]	0.3	...	85.5	...	57.0	...	86.9	93.1[z]	85.9	87.3[z]	120
...	...	...	...	...	...	...	18.6**	...	1.7**	75.0**	67.9**	55.1	70.8	83.3**	83.3**	57.9	80.3	121
...	691[**,z]	...	1.2[**,z]	...	11.2[**,z]	...	37.2[**,z]	...	...	...	45.0	...	46.1	...	58.9	...	62.1	122
...	...	...	...	...	...	...	...	...	...	...	...	...	...	...	...	...	...	123
North America and Western Europe																		
...	...	...	...	...	...	...	...	...	1.2	...	92.6	...	79.2	...	98.8	...	98.8	124
5 243**	6 549	1.1**	1.1	23.8**	23.4	19.3**	19.7	...	...	...	67.1	...	59.8	...	74.0	...	73.9	125
...	5 399[**,z]	...	1.3[**,z]	...	17.9[**,z]	...	...	...	...	...	63.3	...	63.8	...	87.9	...	84.9	126
...	...	...	...	...	...	...	...	...	...	...	...	...	51.4[y]	...	...	...	73.7[y]	127
...		...	1.7	...	19.4	...	30.3	...	...	...	79.8	...	80.4	...	89.9	...	89.4	128
6 143**	6 827	1.8**	1.8	25.2**	22.4	22.2**	21.7	...	...	...	51.3	...	50.9	...	78.6	...	78.3	129
...	4 117	...	1.2	...	16.3	...	20.8	...	...	...	57.7	...	48.7	...	67.9	...	65.2	130
3 106	4 262	1.0	1.0	15.2	16.4	19.9	20.2	...	...	...	...	...	...	...	82.0	...	80.8	131
3 446**	4 511[**,z]	0.8**	0.6[**,z]	16.5**	15.5[**,z]	17.5**	14.9[**,z]	...	...	...	...	...	...	...	83.7[z]	...	82.4[z]	132
1 593**	...	0.7**	...	12.0**	...	26.9**	...	...	...	...	...	...	75.9[z]	...	...	...	...	133
...	6 429	...	2.4	...	22.3	...	35.1**	...	...	...	...	...	...	...	74.4	...	73.4[z]	134
2 613**	4 930	1.5**	2.0	12.4**	17.3	32.8**	32.5	...	...	...	79.8	...	68.2	...	89.9	...	80.0	135
3 291**	4 237	2.4**	2.6	19.2**	21.2	34.1**	35.4	...	...	...	...	...	...	...	72.5	...	72.6	136
4 797**	6 148	1.1**	1.2	22.8**	24.1	25.1**	26.1	...	...	...	71.8	...	60.6	...	82.1	...	77.3	137
...	...	...	...	...	...	...	...	...	...	...	75.5	...	70.0[z]	...	85.4	...	86.4[z]	138
1 560	2 709	1.0	1.1	10.5	13.4	21.7	24.7	...	...	...	60.5	...	59.9	...	93.4	...	85.8	139
...	...	...	...	...	...	...	16.2[y]	...	...	...	...	...	...	99.3	98.7[y]	98.7	97.6[y]	140
3 582**	4 703	1.2**	1.4	14.8**	17.0	25.2**	27.8	...	...	...	...	...	...	...	68.6	...	70.6	141
10 045**	6 622**	2.4**	1.7**	26.2**	18.0**	35.7**	24.5**	...	...	...	...	...	...	...	79.6**	...	76.0	142
...	...	...	...	...	...	...	...	...	...	...	...	...	...	...	...	...	...	143
...	...	...	...	...	...	...	...	...	...	...	...	...	...	...	...	...	...	144
3 061**	3 776	1.1**	1.1	17.9**	18.4	27.4**	27.1	...	...	...	78.0	...	72.5	...	86.7	...	83.9	145
...	6 177[**,z]	...	2.0[**,z]	...	22.7[**,z]	...	27.3[**,z]	...	...	...	52.6	...	...	...	70.9	...	63.9[z]	146
5 651**	6 600**	1.4**	1.5**	19.5**	20.5**	31.6**	30.5**	...	...	...	71.3	...	67.2	...	84.4	...	83.1	147
...	...	...	...	...	...	...	...	...	...	...	51.1[z]	...	54.3[z]	...	75.0[z]	...	75.7[z]	148
...	7 423[**,y]	...	1.8[**,y]	...	20.8[**,y]	...	...	...	...	...	55.5[z]	...	47.6[z]	...	81.1[z]	...	74.2[z]	149
South and West Asia																		
...	...	...	...	...	...	...	...	...	...	...	...	...	...	...	...	...	...	150
51	114	0.6	0.8	4.2	6.8	38.9	43.3	...	...	...	...	...	...	...	...	...	...	151
...	...	...	...	...	...	...	...	...	...	...	...	...	...	...	...	...	...	152
...	321[**,z]	...	1.4[**,z]	...	12.4[**,z]	...	37.6[**,y]	...	...	...	87.5[y]	...	...	...	92.6[y]	...	93.9[y]	153
...	727	...	1.1	...	10.7	...	25.0	...	...	...	...	...	...	...	...	...	...	154
...	...	...	...	...	...	...	...	...	...	...	...	...	...	...	...	...	...	155
88**	108**	1.1**	1.3**	7.5**	8.0**	52.7**	49.1**	...	...	...	...	...	...	...	...	...	...	156
...	...	...	...	...	...	...	...	...	...	...	...	...	...	...	...	...	...	157
...	...	...	...	...	...	...	...	...	...	...	...	...	...	...	...	...	...	158
Sub-Saharan Africa																		
...	...	...	...	...	...	...	...	...	...	...	...	...	...	...	...	...	...	159
...	94**	...	1.7**	...	8.9**	...	...	...	...	...	...	...	...	...	...	...	...	160
...	345[y]	...	1.1[y]	...	5.7[y]	...	...	...	...	...	...	...	...	...	...	...	...	161
...	...	...	...	...	...	...	...	...	...	...	...	...	...	...	...	...	...	162
...	64	...	1.5	...	11.0	...	40.5	...	...	...	...	...	...	...	99.6	...	80.4	163

Table 11 (continued)

	Country or territory	PRIVATE ENROLMENT AS % OF TOTAL ENROLMENT						EDUCATION FINANCE							
		Pre-primary education		Primary education		Secondary education		Total public expenditure on education as % of GNP		Total public expenditure on education as % of total government expenditure		Public current expenditure on education as % of total public expenditure on education		Public current expenditure on primary education per pupil (unit cost) in constant 2002 US$	
		1998/1999	2002/2003	1998/1999	2002/2003	1998/1999	2002/2003	1998	2002	1998	2002	1998	2002	1998	2002
164	Cameroon	57	62	28	23	32**	31	2.7**	4.1	10.9**	17.3	...	85.2	40	...
165	Cape Verde	–	–	–	–	–	–	4.4**	8.1	...	17.0	...	61.6	...	207
166	Central African Republic	...	...	...	...	...	...	1.9**	...	...	...	...	...	...	...
167	Chad	...	...	25	34**	14	17**	1.7**	...	...	...	...	...	...	...
168	Comoros	100	79	12	10**	46	42	3.8	3.9	23.5	24.1	...	100.0	...	40**
169	Congo	85	75**	10	24	...	13[**,z]	5.4	4.4**	21.2	12.6[z]	96.1	85.9**	...	66**
170	Côte d'Ivoire	46	46**	12	11**	...	...	4.0	4.8[**,z]	...	21.5[y]	88.3	94.0[y]	94	...
171	D.R. Congo	...	93[**,z]	...	...	...	...	...	...	...	...	...	...	...	...
172	Equatorial Guinea	37	37[**,z]	33	...	...	...	2.0	2.2[z]	...	1.6[z]	84.5	90.5	...	25[**,z]
173	Eritrea	97	86	11	8	7	6	3.9	3.3	...	...	69.5	48.2	40	...
174	Ethiopia	100	**100**	...	...	...	...	4.3**	4.6[**,z]	...	13.8[y]	...	63.9[**,z]	...	...
175	Gabon	...	73[**,z]	17	29	29	30[**,z]	3.8	4.6[**,y]	...	...	87.3	...	208	...
176	Gambia	...	100	...	3	...	21**	...	3.0	...	8.9	...	86.4	...	...
177	Ghana	26	**36**	13	**18**	7	**11**	...	...	...	...	...	...	...	...
178	Guinea	...	...	15	20	...	12**	1.8**	1.9[**,y]	25.8**	25.6[**,y]	...	...	...	...
179	Guinea-Bissau	62**	62[**,y]	...	19[**,y]	...	13[**,y]	...	...	...	...	...	...	...	...
180	Kenya	...	10	...	...	...	...	6.6	7.1	...	22.1	95.5	92.8	...	...
181	Lesotho	100	100	3	0.1	11	0.2	10.2	8.4[**,z]	25.5	18.4[y]	74.1	92.0[**,y]	74	80[**,z]
182	Liberia	39	...	38	...	37	...	...	...	...	...	...	...	...	...
183	Madagascar	93**	90	22	20	...	...	1.9	2.9[**,z]	10.2	...	79.6	71.7[**,z]	11	15[z]
184	Malawi	...	...	...	...	...	...	4.7	6.1	24.6	...	81.8	81.8	...	20
185	Mali	...	...	...	...	...	20	3.0	...	...	...	89.6	...	38	...
186	Mauritius	83	82	24	24	73**	73	4.2	4.7	17.7	13.3[y]	91.1	71.2	348	359
187	Mozambique	...	...	2**	2	10**	10	2.7	...	12.3	...	67.2	...	...	...
188	Namibia	100**	100	4	4	5	4	7.9	7.1	...	...	93.9	92.8[**,y]	305	302
189	Niger	33	29	4	4	16	15	...	2.4**	...	...	...	...	...	...
190	Nigeria	...	44	...	7	...	21	...	...	...	...	...	...	...	...
191	Rwanda	...	100[**,z]	...	0.8	49	44[**,z]	2.6**	2.8[**,y]	...	...	...	...	...	...
192	Sao Tome and Principe	–	–	–	–	–	–	...	...	...	...	...	...	...	...
193	Senegal	68	62	12	11	28**	25[**,z]	3.5*	3.7	...	3.5	...	91.8	...	47[**,z]
194	Seychelles	4	5	4	4	3	4	6.2	5.7	10.7	...	84.4	91.4	716	1 050**
195	Sierra Leone	...	59	...	...	...	2[y]	1.0	3.8[y]	...	...	98.5	...	...	...
196	Somalia	...	...	...	...	...	...	...	...	...	...	...	...	...	...
197	South Africa	17*	7	0.9*	2	1*	3**	6.2	5.4**	22.2	18.5[z]	98.1	98.1**	315*	317[**,z]
198	Swaziland	...	...	...	–	...	–	6.0	6.8	...	...	100.0	80.8	99	124
199	Togo	53	59	36	41	18	...	4.1	2.7	24.4	13.6	96.8	95.2	26	27[**,y]
200	Uganda	...	99	...	11	58**	...	...	...	...	...	...	...	...	...
201	United Republic of Tanzania	...	**1****	0.2	**0.5**	...	...	2.2**	...	...	...	...	...	...	...
202	Zambia	100*	...	2**	3	3**	3	2.5	2.1[**,z]	17.6	...	99.4	...	...	...
203	Zimbabwe	...	...	...	**87**	...	71	...	4.9[**,y]	...	...	...	...	...	112[**,z]
I	World[1]	38	40	7	7	11	11	4.3	4.6	...	14.1	...	92.7	...	...
II	Countries in transition	0.1	1	0.3	0.4	0.2	0.4	3.8	3.3	...	18.6	...	...	...	...
III	Developed countries	10	8	4	4	6	7	5.0	5.5	...	12.7	...	93.4	...	3 794
IV	Developing countries	52	59	11	11	16	15	4.0	4.5	...	15.5	...	91.8	...	...
V	Arab States	89	86	7	13	8	9	...	...	...	...	...	...	...	...
VI	Central and Eastern Europe	1	1	0.3	0.9	0.6	1	4.5	4.6	...	...	...	93.3	...	677
VII	Central Asia	1	1	0.5	0.8	0.2	0.8	3.4	3.2	...	...	...	98.0	...	...
VIII	East Asia and the Pacific	...	60	...	4	...	12	4.0	4.8	...	...	...	93.1	...	...
IX	Latin America and the Caribbean	42	41	13	16	25	25	4.4	4.6	14.9	14.4	...	93.0	...	413
X	North America and Western Europe	26	25	7	7	7	9	5.2	5.7	...	12.7	91.5	93.0	3 545	4 291
XI	South and West Asia	...	33	...	9	...	25	3.1	3.8	12.5	13.9	76.4	84.5	...	...
XII	Sub-Saharan Africa	51	62	10	8	16	13	3.8	4.0	...	...	...	...	...	...

1. All values shown are medians.
Data in bold are for 2003/2004.

(z) Data are for 2001/2002.
(y) Data are for 2000/2001.

EDUCATION FINANCE

Public current expenditure on primary education per pupil (unit cost) at PPP in constant 2002 US$		Public current expenditure on primary education as % of GNP		Public current expenditure on primary education per pupil as % of GNP per capita		Public current expenditure on primary education as % of public current expenditure on education		Primary education textbooks and other teaching material as % of public current expenditure on primary education		Primary teachers' salaries as % of public current expenditure on primary education		Teachers' salaries as % of public current expenditure on education		Salaries of all personnel of primary education as % of public current expenditure on primary education		Salaries of all personnel in education as % of public current expenditure on education		
1998	2002	1998	2002	1998	2002	1998	2002	1998	2002	1998	2002	1998	2002	1998	2002	1998	2002	
114	...	1.2	...	8.0	...	...	...	...	...	...	...	...	...	...	...	...	...	164
...	768	...	3.0	...	15.5	...	60.3	...	...	...	...	...	...	...	...	...	...	165
...	...	...	...	...	...	...	...	...	...	...	...	...	...	...	...	...	...	166
...	...	...	...	...	...	...	...	...	...	...	...	...	...	...	...	...	...	167
...	157**	...	1.7**	...	12.2**	...	45.2**	...	...	...	...	...	...	...	65.5	...	...	168
...	78**	...	1.5**	...	10.9**	...	40.2**	...	...	...	...	...	...	...	...	...	...	169
178	...	1.6	...	12.7	...	45.3	...	...	...	...	...	...	...	...	...	...	...	170
...	...	...	...	...	...	...	...	...	...	...	...	...	...	...	...	...	...	171
...	202**,z	...	0.4**,z	...	2.4**,z	...	27.1**,z	...	...	...	...	...	...	...	...	...	...	172
194	...	1.3	...	17.8	...	49.1	...	...	...	...	...	...	...	...	97.2	...	78.2	173
...	...	...	...	...	...	...	...	...	...	...	...	...	...	...	...	...	...	174
343	...	1.3	...	5.8	...	38.6	...	...	...	...	...	...	...	...	...	...	...	175
...	...	...	...	...	...	...	...	...	...	...	...	...	...	...	...	...	...	176
...	...	...	...	...	...	...	...	...	...	...	...	...	...	...	98.2z	...	96.8z	177
...	...	...	...	...	...	...	...	...	...	...	...	...	...	...	...	...	...	178
...	...	...	...	...	...	...	...	...	...	...	...	...	...	...	...	...	...	179
...	...	...	...	...	...	...	...	...	...	...	...	...	...	...	...	...	...	180
293	426**,z	3.2	3.9**,z	15.3	16.9**,z	42.8	46.7**,y	–	...	84.5	69.2y	57.3	56.3y	91.7	75.6y	63.7	62.6y	181
...	...	...	...	...	...	...	...	...	...	...	...	...	...	...	...	...	...	182
34	41z	0.5	0.7z	4.0	4.9z	34.7	34.7**,z	...	...	...	...	...	...	...	...	...	...	183
...	66	...	3.1	...	13.0	...	62.7	...	...	...	...	...	...	...	...	...	...	184
110	...	1.3	...	15.6	...	48.9	...	...	...	...	...	...	...	...	...	...	...	185
848	1 039	1.2	1.0	11.0	9.6	31.9	31.4	...	...	...	...	...	...	...	...	...	...	186
...	...	...	...	...	...	...	...	...	...	...	...	...	...	...	...	...	...	187
940	1 281	4.4	4.0	20.6	19.5	59.4	59.4**,y	...	...	...	...	...	...	...	...	...	...	188
...	...	...	...	...	...	...	...	...	...	...	...	...	...	...	...	...	...	189
...	...	...	...	...	...	...	...	...	...	...	...	...	...	...	...	...	...	190
...	...	...	...	...	...	...	...	...	...	...	...	...	...	...	...	...	...	191
...	...	...	...	...	...	...	...	...	...	...	...	...	...	...	...	...	...	192
...	155**,z	...	1.1**,z	...	9.2**,z	...	38.4**,z	...	...	...	...	...	...	...	...	...	...	193
...	...	1.1	1.5**	8.8	13.5**	20.8	29.4**	...	.	...	64.8	...	49.1	...	84.9	...	73.6	194
...	...	0.4	...	...	...	38.7	...	...	...	...	...	...	...	...	...	...	...	195
...	...	...	...	...	...	...	...	...	...	...	...	...	...	...	...	...	...	196
894*	1 227**,z	2.8	2.4**,z	14.8*	14.4**,z	45.2	43.9**,z	...	1.9y	...	90.2y	...	68.5y	...	95.9y	...	75.3y	197
316	515	2.0	2.1	9.4	10.7	33.2	38.2	...	...	...	...	...	...	...	...	...	...	198
115	145**,y	1.8	1.8**,y	7.9	8.7**,y	43.9	44.2**,y	...	2.3y	...	85.6y	...	74.1y	...	85.6y	...	79.9	199
...	...	...	...	...	...	...	...	...	...	...	...	...	...	...	...	...	...	200
...	...	...	...	...	...	...	...	...	...	...	...	...	...	...	...	...	...	201
...	...	...	...	...	...	...	...	...	...	...	...	...	...	...	95.3y	...	96.5y	202
...	376**,z	...	3.3**,z	...	16.7**,z	...	...	...	...	...	...	...	...	...	97.6z	...	96.9z	203
...	...	...	...	...	...	...	...	...	...	...	...	...	...	...	...	...	...	I
...	...	...	...	...	...	...	...	...	...	...	...	...	...	...	...	...	57.6	II
...	4 193	...	1.2	...	18.5	...	24.5	...	...	...	...	...	...	...	79.1		75.0	III
...	...	...	...	...	...	...	...	...	...	...	...	...	...	...	...	...	...	IV
...	...	...	...	...	...	...	...	...	...	...	...	...	...	...	...	...	...	V
...	1 705	...	0.9	...	17.1	...	20.8	...	...	...	...	...	...	...	74.1	...	69.4	VI
...	...	...	...	...	...	...	...	...	...	...	...	...	...	...	...	...	63.7	VII
...	...	...	...	...	...	...	...	...	...	...	...	...	...	...	...	...	...	VIII
...	794	...	1.7	...	12.8	...	35.4	...	...	...	...	...	...	...	89.1	...	82.2	IX
3 446	5 399	1.1	1.4	17.9	18.9	25.2	26.1	...	...	...	67.1	...	62.2	...	82.1	...	78.3	X
...	...	...	...	...	...	...	...	...	...	...	...	...	...	...	...	...	...	XI
...	...	...	...	...	...	...	...	...	...	...	...	...	...	...	...	...	...	XII

Table 12
Trends in basic or proxy indicators to measure EFA goals 1, 2 and 3

Country or territory	GOAL 1 Early childhood care and education GROSS ENROLMENT RATIO (GER) IN PRE-PRIMARY EDUCATION					
	1990/1991		1998/1999		2002/2003	
	Total (%)	GPI (F/M)	Total (%)	GPI (F/M)	Total (%)	GPI (F/M)
Arab States						
Algeria	…	…	2.5	1.01	3.8	0.99
Bahrain	27.1	1.02	32.9	0.95	36.7	0.94
Djibouti	0.7	1.46	0.4	1.50	**1.2**	**0.99**
Egypt	6.1	0.99	10.1	0.95	13.7	0.95
Iraq	7.8	0.95	5.2	0.98	3.8	0.98
Jordan	20.8	0.88	28.6	0.91	30.4	0.93
Kuwait	32.9	1.01	78.3	1.01	69.9	1.00
Lebanon	…	…	66.0	0.97	74.8	0.98
Libyan Arab Jamahiriya	…	…	5.0	0.98**	7.8 **	0.96**
Mauritania	…	…	…	…	1.9	…
Morocco	60.7	0.46	64.3	0.52	56.1	0.62
Oman	3.1	0.89	5.6	0.87	5.5	0.84
Palestinian Autonomous Territories	13.8	…	39.9	0.97	27.4	0.96
Qatar	28.3	0.93	25.6	0.98	33.9	0.92
Saudi Arabia	6.8	0.87	5.1	0.91	4.9	0.94**
Sudan[2]	19.7	0.57	21.3	…	26.6	0.86
Syrian Arab Republic	6.2	0.88	8.4	0.90	10.5	0.94
Tunisia	7.7	…	13.5	0.95	21.6 **	0.99**
United Arab Emirates	53.0	0.97	61.6	0.97	75.3	0.99
Yemen	0.7	0.94	0.7	0.87	0.7	0.93
Central and Eastern Europe						
Albania	58.6	…	41.7 **	1.09**	47.0	1.03
Belarus	84.1	…	81.2	0.92	101.9	0.98
Bosnia and Herzegovina	…	…	…	…	…	…
Bulgaria	91.6	1.01	64.3	0.99	75.5	0.98
Croatia	28.2	0.99	41.1	0.98	45.5	0.97
Czech Republic	95.0	0.97	90.5	1.06	102.0	1.00
Estonia	74.9	0.99	86.8	0.98	112.9	0.99
Hungary	113.4	0.97	79.4	0.98	80.5	0.97
Latvia	44.7	1.01	50.9	0.95	74.3	0.94
Lithuania	57.5	1.01	50.2	0.97	58.3	0.97
Poland	46.7	…	49.8	1.01	50.6	1.00
Republic of Moldova	72.7	0.95	40.3	0.96	46.9	0.97
Romania	76.0	1.04	61.8	1.02	76.4	1.03
Russian Federation[3]	74.0	…	…	…	93.9	0.94**
Serbia and Montenegro[4]	…	…	44.1	0.99	43.7 y	1.01 y
Slovakia	86.1	…	81.7	…	86.9	0.98
Slovenia	73.6	0.95	72.0	0.91	67.7	0.96
The former Yugoslav Rep. of Macedonia	…	…	27.3	1.01	28.5	1.01
Turkey	4.2	0.92	6.0	0.94	7.6	0.94
Ukraine	85.0	0.92	47.5	0.98	76.4	0.98
Central Asia						
Armenia	36.6	…	…	…	34.6	1.07
Azerbaijan	18.8	0.84	20.9	0.89	24.6	1.00
Georgia	58.9	…	35.4	0.99	42.7	1.06
Kazakhstan	72.4	…	13.9	0.95	29.4	0.98
Kyrgyzstan	33.5	1.02	10.5	0.78	11.3	0.95
Mongolia	39.1	1.24	24.7	1.21	33.8	1.14
Tajikistan	15.8	…	8.5	0.76	10.1	0.94
Turkmenistan	…	…	…	…	…	…
Uzbekistan	73.1	…	…	…	28.1	0.94
East Asia and the Pacific						
Australia	71.3	1.00	…	…	101.7	1.00
Brunei Darussalam	47.2	0.95	50.6	1.03	48.5	1.01
Cambodia	3.9	0.90	5.2 **	1.03**	7.0	1.05

GOAL 2						GOAL 3				
Universal primary education NET ENROLMENT RATIO (NER) IN PRIMARY EDUCATION						Learning needs of all youth and adults YOUTH LITERACY RATE (15-24)				
1990/1991		1998/1999		2002/2003		1990		2000-2004[1]		
Total (%)	GPI (F/M)	Total (%)	GPI (F/M)	Total (%)	GPI (F/M)	Total (%)	GPI (F/M)	Total (%)	GPI (F/M)	**Country or territory**
										Arab States
93.2	0.88	92.1	0.96	94.9	0.97	77.3	0.79	90.1*	0.92*	Algeria
99.0	1.00	93.9	1.02	89.9	1.02	95.6	0.99	99.3*	1.00*	Bahrain
31.3	0.71**	31.3	0.72	**35.6**	**0.80**	73.2	0.78	...	...	Djibouti
83.7**	0.84**	90.9**	0.93**	91.4**	0.96**	61.3	0.72	73.2*	0.85*	Egypt
94.2**	0.88**	91.2	0.85	90.5**,[y]	0.85**,[y]	41.0	0.44	...	...	Iraq
94.1	1.01	89.6	1.01	92.0	1.02	96.7	0.97	99.1*	1.00*	Jordan
49.0**	0.93**	88.2	1.00	83.4	1.02	87.5	0.99	93.1	1.02	Kuwait
77.8**	0.96**	87.5**	0.97**	90.6	0.99	92.1	0.93	...	...	Lebanon
96.1**	0.96**	...	...	...	...	91.0	0.84	97.0	0.94	Libyan Arab Jamahiriya
35.3**	0.74**	62.6**	0.94**	67.5	0.97	45.8	0.65	61.3*	0.82*	Mauritania
56.8	0.70	73.1	0.86	89.6	0.94	55.3	0.62	69.5	0.79	Morocco
69.3	0.95	75.9	1.00	71.9	1.01	85.6	0.79	98.5	0.98	Oman
...	...	96.9	1.01	90.9	1.00	...	...	98.7*	1.00*	Palestinian Autonomous Territories
89.4	0.98	97.1	1.01	94.5	1.00	90.3	1.05	98.6*	...	Qatar
58.7	0.81	56.8	0.93	54.4	0.99	85.4	0.86	95.9*	0.96*	Saudi Arabia
43.3**	0.75**	...	...	...	...	65.0	0.71	74.6*	0.85*	Sudan[2]
92.3	0.91	93.0**	0.93**	97.9	0.96	79.9	0.73	95.2*	0.96*	Syrian Arab Republic
93.9	0.92	94.0	0.98	97.3	1.00	84.1	0.81	94.3*	0.96*	Tunisia
99.1	0.98	78.2	0.98	83.1	0.98	84.7	1.08	91.4	1.08	United Arab Emirates
51.7**	0.38**	57.4	0.59	71.8	0.71	50.0	0.34	67.9	0.60	Yemen
										Central and Eastern Europe
95.1**	1.01**	99.1**	0.99**	94.9	0.98	94.8	0.94	99.4*	1.00*	Albania
86.2**	0.95**	...	...	94.3	0.99**	99.8	1.00	99.8*	1.00*	Belarus
...	...	...	...	...	...	...	...	99.6*	1.00*	Bosnia and Herzegovina
86.1	0.99	95.6	0.98	90.4	0.99	99.4	1.00	98.2*	1.00*	Bulgaria
74.2	1.00	88.4	0.98	89.3	0.99	99.6	1.00	99.6*	1.00*	Croatia
86.7**	1.00**	90.2	1.01	86.5	1.00	...	...	...	...	Czech Republic
99.5**	0.99**	97.0**	0.98**	94.9	0.99	99.8	1.00	99.8*	1.00*	Estonia
91.3	1.01	89.5	0.99	90.6	0.99	99.7	1.00	99.5*	1.00*	Hungary
92.1**	0.99**	91.0	0.99	85.6	0.99	...	...	99.7*	1.00*	Latvia
...	...	94.5	0.99	90.9	1.00	99.8	1.00	99.7*	1.00*	Lithuania
96.7	1.00	...	...	97.9	1.00	...	...	...	...	Poland
88.8**	0.99**	78.2**	...	79.0	0.99	99.8	1.00	98.7*	1.01*	Republic of Moldova
81.2**	1.00**	95.7	0.99	88.9	0.99	99.3	1.00	97.8*	1.00*	Romania
98.6**	1.00**	...	...	89.7**	1.02**	99.8	1.00	99.7*	1.00*	Russian Federation[3]
69.4	1.02	...	...	95.8[y]	1.00[y]	...	...	99.4*	1.00*	Serbia and Montenegro[4]
...	...	...	...	85.5	1.01	...	...	99.6*	1.00*	Slovakia
99.7**	1.01**	93.9	0.99	93.4	0.99	99.8	1.00	99.8	1.00	Slovenia
94.4	0.99	94.5	0.98	90.8	1.00	...	...	98.7*	0.99*	The former Yugoslav Rep. of Macedonia
89.5	0.92**	...	...	86.4	0.94	92.7	0.91	96.6*	0.96*	Turkey
80.2**	1.00**	...	...	84.3	1.00**	99.8	1.00	99.8*	1.00*	Ukraine
										Central Asia
...	...	...	...	94.4	0.98	99.5	1.00	99.8*	1.00*	Armenia
100.0**	1.00**	80.1**	1.00**	79.9	0.97	...	...	99.9*	1.00*	Azerbaijan
97.1**	1.00**	...	...	88.7	0.98	...	...	...	...	Georgia
87.6**	0.99**	...	...	91.5	0.99	99.8	1.00	99.8*	1.00*	Kazakhstan
92.3**	1.00**	91.0*	0.98*	89.3	0.96	...	...	99.7*	1.00*	Kyrgyzstan
90.1**	1.02**	89.4	1.04	79.0	1.03	...	...	97.7*	1.01*	Mongolia
76.7**	0.98**	94.3	0.94	...	...	99.8	1.00	99.8*	1.00*	Tajikistan
...	...	...	...	...	...	...	...	99.8*	1.00*	Turkmenistan
78.2**	0.99**	...	...	...	...	99.6	1.00	99.7	1.00	Uzbekistan
										East Asia and the Pacific
99.2	1.00	94.7	1.01	96.8	1.01	...	...	...	...	Australia
89.7**	0.95**	...	...	...	...	97.9	1.01	98.9*	1.00*	Brunei Darussalam
66.6**	0.83**	82.5**	0.91**	93.3	0.95	73.5	0.81	83.4*	0.90*	Cambodia

Table 12 (continued)

Country or territory	GOAL 1 — Early childhood care and education — GROSS ENROLMENT RATIO (GER) IN PRE-PRIMARY EDUCATION					
	1990/1991		1998/1999		2002/2003	
	Total (%)	GPI (F/M)	Total (%)	GPI (F/M)	Total (%)	GPI (F/M)
China[5,6]	22.7	0.99	37.9	0.97	36.4	0.92
Cook Islands[7]	...	...	...	...	...	...
Democratic People's Republic of Korea	...	...	...	...	...	...
Fiji	13.4	1.06	15.4 **	1.02**	...	...
Indonesia	18.1	...	17.5 **	1.01**	21.4	1.09
Japan	48.1	1.02	83.1	1.02**	84.9	1.03**
Kiribati	...	...	...	...	...	...
Lao People's Democratic Republic	7.3	0.87	7.9	1.11	8.0	1.05
Macao, China	88.8	0.98	86.9	0.95	85.3	0.95
Malaysia	35.0	1.02	109.5	0.99	98.8	1.08
Marshall Islands[4]	...	...	...	...	51.5 z	0.97z
Micronesia (Federated States of)	...	...	36.6	...	...	...
Myanmar	...	...	1.9	...	...	...
Nauru[4]	...	...	140.9 **	0.96**	...	...
New Zealand	74.5	1.00	84.5	1.00	88.4	1.01
Niue[4]	...	...	128.6	1.15	147.8 z	1.23z
Palau[4]	...	...	62.5	1.23	65.5 **,y	1.12**,y
Papua New Guinea	0.4	1.00	33.5	0.95	58.2	0.93
Philippines	11.7	...	30.7	1.05	38.5	1.04
Republic of Korea	55.4	0.98	79.8	1.00	**85.8**	**1.01**
Samoa	...	...	55.5	1.14	54.2 **	1.24**
Singapore	...	...	...	...	...	...
Solomon Islands	32.1	0.93	...	...	20.5	
Thailand	43.4	0.99	86.6	0.98	**88.2 ****	**0.99****
Timor-Leste	...	...	...	...	11.2 z	...
Tokelau	...	...	...	...	...	...
Tonga	...	...	21.7	1.15	29.4 **,y	1.21**,y
Tuvalu[4]	...	...	79.5 **	1.25**	82.4 z	1.16z
Vanuatu	...	...	73.2 **	1.11**	75.6 z	1.03z
Viet Nam	28.5	...	40.2	0.94	45.3	0.94
Latin America and the Caribbean						
Anguilla[4]	...	...	...	...	116.1 z	0.97z
Antigua and Barbuda	...	...	...	...	...	...
Argentina	...	...	57.0	1.02	60.5	1.01
Aruba[4]	...	...	96.9	1.00	100.2	0.99
Bahamas	...	...	...	...	30.4 **	0.99**
Barbados	...	...	82.2	0.98	88.5	1.00
Belize	23.2	1.13	27.8	1.03	28.8	1.07
Bermuda[4]	...	...	...	...	54.6 y	...
Bolivia	31.5	1.00	44.1	1.01	47.3	1.02
Brazil	46.5	...	53.5	1.01	57.2	1.00
British Virgin Islands[4]	...	...	61.6	1.16	86.4	0.95
Cayman Islands[7]	...	...	...	...	...	...
Chile	82.4	1.01	73.6	0.99	**45.8**	**0.99**
Colombia	13.0	...	34.8	1.02	37.1	1.01
Costa Rica	60.1	1.01	80.5	1.02	60.9	1.02
Cuba	101.0	0.82	102.0	1.04	114.6	0.99
Dominica[4]	...	...	76.1	1.11	51.0	0.88
Dominican Republic	...	...	35.2	1.01	34.3	1.01
Ecuador	41.9	...	63.6	1.04	74.4	1.03
El Salvador	...	...	40.2	1.05	48.6	1.06
Grenada[4]	...	...	...	...	85.8	0.99
Guatemala			37.3 *	0.99*	55.2 z	1.01z
Guyana	73.6	1.03	120.2	0.99	120.2	1.00
Haiti	34.2	0.95	...	...	...	...
Honduras	...	...	...	...	21.4 **,z	1.05**,z
Jamaica	78.1	1.03	83.6	1.08	85.7	1.05
Mexico	64.5	1.03	74.0	1.02	80.7	1.02
Montserrat[4]	...	...	...	...	82.9 z	...

GOAL 2						GOAL 3				
Universal primary education						Learning needs of all youth and adults				
NET ENROLMENT RATIO (NER) IN PRIMARY EDUCATION						**YOUTH LITERACY RATE (15-24)**				
1990/1991		1998/1999		2002/2003		1990		2000-2004[1]		
Total (%)	GPI (F/M)	Total (%)	GPI (F/M)	Total (%)	GPI (F/M)	Total (%)	GPI (F/M)	Total (%)	GPI (F/M)	**Country or territory**
97.4	0.96	…	…	94.6**,z	1.01**,z	95.3	0.95	98.9*	0.99*	China[5,6]
…	…	…	…	…	…	…	…	…	…	Cook Islands[7]
…	…	…	…	…	…	…	…	…	…	Democratic People's Republic of Korea
99.6**	1.01**	99.4**	1.00**	99.8**,z	1.00**,z	97.8	1.00	99.3*	1.00*	Fiji
96.7	0.96	…	…	92.4	0.98	95.0	0.97	98.0	0.99	Indonesia
99.7	1.00	100.0	1.00	99.9	1.00	…	…	…	…	Japan
…	…	…	…	…	…	…	…	…	…	Kiribati
62.6**	0.85**	80.2	0.92	85.0	0.93	70.1	0.76	78.5*	0.90*	Lao People's Democratic Republic
81.1**	0.98**	84.3	1.01	87.2	0.98	97.2	0.97	99.6*	1.00*	Macao, China
93.7**	1.00**	97.4	1.00	93.1	1.00	94.8	0.99	97.2*	1.00*	Malaysia
…	…	…	…	84.4z	0.99z	…	…	…	…	Marshall Islands[4]
…	…	…	…	…	…	…	…	…	…	Micronesia (Federated States of)
97.8**	0.96**	82.5**	0.99**	84.2	1.01	88.2	0.96	94.4*	0.98*	Myanmar
…	…	81.0**	1.04**	…	…	46.6	0.41	…	…	Nauru[4]
99.6	0.99	…	…	99.7**	0.99**	…	…	…	…	New Zealand
…	…	…	…	…	…	…	…	…	…	Niue[4]
…	…	96.8**	0.94**	96.1**,y	0.92**,y	…	…	…	…	Palau[4]
66.0**	0.86**	74.8*	0.93*	73.0**,z	0.90**,z	68.6	0.84	66.7*	0.93*	Papua New Guinea
96.5**	0.99**	…	…	93.7	1.02	97.3	1.00	95.1*	1.01*	Philippines
99.7	1.01	94.3	1.01	**99.8**	**1.00**	…	…	…	…	Republic of Korea
95.6**	1.09**	94.2	1.02	97.5**	0.98**	99.0	1.00	99.5	1.00	Samoa
96.4**	0.99**	…	…	…	…	99.0	1.00	99.5*	1.00*	Singapore
83.2**	0.86**	…	…	…	…	…	…	…	…	Solomon Islands
75.9**	0.97**	79.6**	0.95**	**85.4**	**0.97**	…	…	98.0*	1.00*	Thailand
…	…	…	…	…	…	…	…	…	…	Timor-Leste
…	…	…	…	…	…	…	…	…	…	Tokelau
91.8	0.96	91.7	1.00	99.9z	1.00z	…	…	99.3*	1.00*	Tonga
…	…	…	…	…	…	…	…	…	…	Tuvalu[4]
70.6**	1.01**	90.5**	1.00**	94.1**	1.02**	…	…	…	…	Vanuatu
90.5**	0.92**	96.1	…	94.0**,z	…	94.1	0.99	…	…	Viet Nam
										Latin America and the Caribbean
…	…	…	…	95.2	1.02	…	…	…	…	Anguilla[4]
…	…	…	…	…	…	…	…	…	…	Antigua and Barbuda
93.8**	1.00**	…	…	…	…	98.2	1.00	98.9*	1.00*	Argentina
…	…	97.8	1.01	99.0	0.99	…	…	…	…	Aruba[4]
89.6**	1.03**	…	…	86.4**	1.03**	96.5	1.02	…	…	Bahamas
80.1**	0.99**	99.7**	0.99**	100.0	1.00	99.8	1.00	99.8	1.00	Barbados
94.0**	0.99**	94.3**	1.00**	99.2	1.02	…	…	84.2*	1.01*	Belize
…	…	…	…	100.0**,z	…	…	…	…	…	Bermuda[4]
90.8	0.92	96.0	0.99	95.1	1.00	92.6	0.93	97.3*	0.98*	Bolivia
85.6	0.94**	…	…	97.3	…	91.8	1.03	96.6*	1.02*	Brazil
…	…	95.6**	1.02**	93.7	0.98	…	…	…	…	British Virgin Islands[4]
…	…	…	…	…	…	…	…	…	…	Cayman Islands[7]
87.7	0.98**	87.9	0.99	**84.8**	**0.99**	98.1	1.00	99.0*	1.00*	Chile
68.1**	1.15**	86.6	…	87.4	0.99**	94.9	1.01	97.6*	1.02*	Colombia
87.3	1.01	88.5**	1.02**	90.4	1.02	97.4	1.01	98.4	1.01	Costa Rica
91.7	1.00	98.9	0.98	93.5	0.99	99.3	1.00	100.0*	1.00*	Cuba
…	…	82.9**	0.93**	81.3	0.95	…	…	…	…	Dominica[4]
58.2**	2.20**	88.3**	1.02**	96.4	0.95**	87.5	1.02	94.0*	1.02*	Dominican Republic
97.8**	1.01**	97.0	1.01	99.5	1.01	95.5	0.99	96.4*	1.00*	Ecuador
72.8**	1.02**	81.0	1.17	90.4	1.00	83.8	0.97	88.9	0.98	El Salvador
…	…	…	…	84.2**,y	0.90**,y	…	…	…	…	Grenada[4]
64.0**	0.91**	76.5**	0.93**	87.3	0.97	73.4	0.82	82.2*	0.91*	Guatemala
88.9	1.00	95.7**	0.99**	99.2**	0.98**	99.8	1.00	…	…	Guyana
22.1	1.05	…	…	…	…	54.8	0.96	66.2	1.01	Haiti
89.9**	1.02**	…	…	87.4**,z	1.02**,z	79.7	1.03	88.9*	1.05*	Honduras
95.7	1.00	90.3**	1.00**	94.6	1.00	91.2	1.09	94.5	1.07	Jamaica
98.8	0.98**	99.5	1.01	99.4	1.01	95.2	0.98	97.6*	0.99*	Mexico
…	…	…	…	…	…	…	…	…	…	Montserrat[4]

Table 12 (continued)

Country or territory	GOAL 1 Early childhood care and education GROSS ENROLMENT RATIO (GER) IN PRE-PRIMARY EDUCATION					
	1990/1991		1998/1999		2002/2003	
	Total (%)	GPI (F/M)	Total (%)	GPI (F/M)	Total (%)	GPI (F/M)
Netherlands Antilles	...	...	100.3	1.03	86.2 **	0.99**
Nicaragua	12.1	1.09	24.7	1.02	27.7	1.03
Panama	53.4	1.00	37.7 **	0.96**	55.8	1.01
Paraguay	27.1	1.03	25.5	1.03	30.0	1.01
Peru	29.6	...	56.1	1.02	57.9	1.02
Saint Kitts and Nevis[4]	...	...	...	...	163.5	0.90
Saint Lucia	54.4	...	85.2	0.99	64.1	1.14
Saint Vincent and the Grenadines	44.6	1.11	...	...	...	...
Suriname	79.2	0.99	...	...	94.2 **	0.98**
Trinidad and Tobago	8.8	1.02	59.8 **	1.01**	66.4 *	1.03**
Turks and Caicos Islands[4]	...	...	...	...	125.0	1.00
Uruguay	42.6	1.03	56.0	1.01	63.4	1.02
Venezuela	40.8	1.02	44.2	1.03	52.7	1.01
North America and Western Europe						
Andorra[7]	...	...	...	...	...	...
Austria	68.9	0.99	81.5	0.99	86.4	1.00
Belgium	104.0	1.00	109.9	0.99	116.1	0.99
Canada	60.8	1.00	66.0	1.01	64.6 **,z	0.98**,z
Cyprus[4]	48.0	0.99	59.8	1.02	59.6	1.00
Denmark	99.0	1.00	91.0	1.00	91.6	1.00
Finland	33.6	...	48.3	0.99	56.0	0.99
France	83.3	1.00	110.6	1.00	112.7	1.00
Germany	...	...	93.6	0.98	99.6	0.95
Greece	56.7	1.00	68.4	1.02	67.7	1.04
Iceland	...	...	108.3	0.99	124.8	1.02
Ireland	101.2	0.98	...	...	...	...
Israel	85.4	...	106.0	0.98	112.2	1.00
Italy	93.9	1.01	95.4	0.98	101.4	0.98
Luxembourg	92.4	...	72.9	0.99	85.5	1.01
Malta	102.6	0.93	102.7	0.99	100.0	1.03
Monaco[7]	...	...	...	...	...	...
Netherlands	99.2	1.01	97.8	0.99	87.3	0.99
Norway	88.4	...	75.4	1.06	83.9	...
Portugal	52.7	0.99	66.3	1.00	72.9	1.02
San Marino	...	...	...	...	...	...
Spain	59.4	1.03	99.4	0.99	111.3	1.00
Sweden	64.7	...	76.1	1.01	81.1	1.00
Switzerland	59.7	1.00	93.9	0.99	99.7	1.00
United Kingdom	53.2	0.99	77.5	1.01	77.7	1.01
United States	62.7	0.97	57.4	0.97	58.2	...
South and West Asia						
Afghanistan	...	...	...	...	...	...
Bangladesh	...	...	22.3	1.08	20.6	1.07
Bhutan[8]	...	...	...	...	...	...
India[9]	3.4	0.89	19.5	0.99	34.0	1.01
Iran, Islamic Republic of	11.9	0.95	13.3	1.05	30.7	1.12
Maldives	...	...	45.9	1.00	46.6	1.02
Nepal	...	...	12.1 **	0.73**	17.6	0.86
Pakistan	...	...	...	...	47.3	0.88
Sri Lanka[2]	...	...	...	...	...	...
Sub-Saharan Africa						
Angola	54.4	0.51	25.5	[illegible]	[illegible]	[illegible]
Benin	2.6	0.83	4.6	0.94	5.2	0.95
Botswana	...	...	...	...	...	...
Burkina Faso	0.7	1.01	1.7	1.01	1.1 **,z	0.92**,z
Burundi	...	...	0.8	1.01	1.3	0.98
Cameroon	12.4	1.01	11.6	0.95	14.9	1.01

GOAL 2						GOAL 3				
Universal primary education NET ENROLMENT RATIO (NER) IN PRIMARY EDUCATION						Learning needs of all youth and adults YOUTH LITERACY RATE (15-24)				
1990/1991		1998/1999		2002/2003		1990		2000-2004[1]		
Total (%)	GPI (F/M)	Total (%)	GPI (F/M)	Total (%)	GPI (F/M)	Total (%)	GPI (F/M)	Total (%)	GPI (F/M)	**Country or territory**
...	...	96.1	1.01	88.4**	1.05**	97.5	1.00	98.3	1.00	Netherlands Antilles
72.2	1.04	77.9**	1.03**	85.5	1.00	68.2	1.01	86.2*	1.06*	Nicaragua
91.5	1.00	96.5**	0.99**	99.6	0.99	95.3	0.99	96.1*	0.99*	Panama
92.8	0.99	91.7	1.01	89.3	1.00	95.6	0.99	96.3*	1.00*	Paraguay
87.8**	0.99**	99.8	1.00	99.7	1.00	94.5	0.95	96.8*	0.98*	Peru
...	...	...	...	100.0	...	...	...	...	...	Saint Kitts and Nevis[4]
95.1**	0.97**	...	...	99.4	1.01	...	...	95.4*	1.01*	Saint Lucia
...	...	...	...	90.0	0.99	...	...	...	...	Saint Vincent and the Grenadines
78.4**	1.03**	...	...	97.0**	1.02**	...	...	93.5*	0.97*	Suriname
90.9	0.99	92.9	1.00	90.6	0.99	99.6	1.00	99.8	1.00	Trinidad and Tobago
...	...	...	...	73.5	0.98	...	...	...	...	Turks and Caicos Islands[4]
91.9**	1.01**	92.4	1.01	90.4	1.00	98.7	1.01	99.1	1.01	Uruguay
88.1	1.03	85.9	1.01	90.8	1.01	96.0	1.01	97.2*	1.02*	Venezuela
										North America and Western Europe
...	...	...	...	...	...	...	...	...	...	Andorra[7]
87.7**	1.02**	89.9	1.01	89.9	1.02	...	...	...	...	Austria
96.2	1.02	99.4	1.00	100.0	1.00	...	...	...	...	Belgium
97.7	1.00	96.9	1.00	99.6**,y	1.00**,y	...	...	...	...	Canada
86.9	1.00	95.5	1.00	96.1	1.00	99.7	1.00	99.8*	1.00*	Cyprus[4]
98.3	1.00	99.4	1.00	100.0	1.00	...	...	...	...	Denmark
98.3**	1.00**	98.7	1.00	100.0	1.00	...	...	...	...	Finland
100.0	1.00	100.0	1.00	99.3	1.00	...	...	...	...	France
...	...	...	...	...	...	...	...	...	...	Germany
94.6	0.99	93.4	1.00	98.5	1.00	99.5	1.00	99.5*	1.00*	Greece
99.6**	0.99**	98.3	0.98	99.6	0.99	...	...	...	...	Iceland
90.4	1.02	93.8	1.01	96.0	1.02	...	...	...	...	Ireland
91.9**	1.03**	99.9	1.00	99.3	1.00	98.7	0.99	99.6*	1.00*	Israel
99.8**	1.00**	99.7	0.99	99.5	0.99	...	...	...	...	Italy
81.4**	1.10**	96.0	1.02	90.3	1.01	...	...	...	...	Luxembourg
97.0	0.99	99.1	1.02	96.0	0.99	97.5	1.03	96.0*	1.04*	Malta
...	...	...	...	...	...	...	...	...	...	Monaco[7]
95.3	1.04	99.5	0.99	99.2	0.99	...	...	...	...	Netherlands
100.0	1.00	100.0	1.00	100.0	1.00	...	...	...	...	Norway
99.8	1.00	...	...	99.5	0.99	...	...	...	...	Portugal
...	...	...	...	...	...	...	...	...	...	San Marino
99.8	1.00	99.6	0.99	99.7	0.99	...	...	99.6*	1.00*	Spain
99.8	1.00	99.8	1.00	99.7	0.99	...	...	...	...	Sweden
83.7	1.02	97.9	0.99	98.9	0.99	...	...	...	...	Switzerland
98.3	0.97	99.6	1.01	100.0	1.00	...	...	...	...	United Kingdom
96.8	1.00	93.8	1.00	92.4	1.01	...	...	...	...	United States
										South and West Asia
26.5**	0.55**	...	...	...	...	...	...	...	...	Afghanistan
71.2	0.87	84.8**	0.98**	84.0	1.04	42.0	0.65	49.7	0.71	Bangladesh
...	...	...	...	...	...	...	...	...	...	Bhutan[8]
...	...	...	...	87.5(g)	0.94(g)	64.3	0.74	76.4*	0.80*	India[9]
92.3**	0.92**	81.4**	0.97**	86.3	0.97	86.3	0.88	...	...	Iran, Islamic Republic of
86.7**	1.00**	99.7**	1.01**	92.4	1.00	98.1	1.00	98.2*	1.00*	Maldives
...	...	68.5*	0.79*	70.5**,y	0.88**,y	46.6	0.41	70.1*	0.75*	Nepal
...	...	...	...	59.1**,y	0.74**,y	47.4	0.49	64.5*	0.72*	Pakistan
89.9**	0.96**	...	...	...	...	95.1	0.98	95.6*	1.01*	Sri Lanka[2]
										Sub-Saharan Africa
58.0**	0.95**	61.3**	0.86**	...	...	...	...	71.4*	0.76*	Angola
44.8**	0.52**	55.4*	0.66*	...	...	40.4	0.44	44.4*	0.56*	Benin
84.9	1.09	78.7	1.04	80.9**	1.04**	83.3	1.10	89.1	1.09	Botswana
26.2	0.63	33.5	0.68	36.2	0.73	...	...	19.4*	0.55*	Burkina Faso
53.2**	0.85**	...	...	57.4	0.84	51.6	0.77	72.3*	0.92*	Burundi
73.6**	0.87**	...	...	...	...	81.1	0.88	...	...	Cameroon

Table 12 (continued)

Country or territory	GOAL 1 — Early childhood care and education — GROSS ENROLMENT RATIO (GER) IN PRE-PRIMARY EDUCATION					
	1990/1991		1998/1999		2002/2003	
	Total (%)	GPI (F/M)	Total (%)	GPI (F/M)	Total (%)	GPI (F/M)
Cape Verde	...	...	...	...	59.2	1.02
Central African Republic	5.7	...	...	...	2.6	1.05
Chad	...	...	...	...	...	...
Comoros	...	...	2.2	1.07	2.4	0.91
Congo	2.3	1.00	1.8	1.59	4.1 **	1.06**
Côte d'Ivoire	0.9	0.94	2.6	0.97	3.5 *	0.97*
Democratic Rep. of the Congo	...	...	...	...	0.8 **,z	0.98**,z
Equatorial Guinea	...	...	30.9	1.04	...	...
Eritrea	...	...	5.3	0.89	5.9	1.00
Ethiopia	1.6	1.01	1.5	0.97	**2.1**	**0.95**
Gabon	...	...	...	...	13.9 **,z	...
Gambia	...	...	19.7	0.91	18.3	1.03
Ghana	...	...	37.0	0.99	**47.0**	**0.97**
Guinea	...	...	...	...	...	...
Guinea-Bissau	...	...	3.2 **	1.05**	3.2 **,y	1.05**,y
Kenya	32.9	1.13	38.3	1.07	48.2	0.99
Lesotho	...	...	24.9	1.13*	29.6	0.94
Liberia	...	...	43.3	0.74	...	...
Madagascar	...	...	3.4 **	1.02**	10.0	...
Malawi	...	...	...	...	...	...
Mali	...	...	1.9	1.08	1.6 **	1.00**
Mauritius	56.0	0.99	98.0	1.02	88.6	1.01
Mozambique	...	...	...	...	...	...
Namibia	14.2	1.13	20.1 **	1.11**	27.5	1.30
Niger	1.5	0.94	1.1	1.03	1.4	1.01
Nigeria	...	...	...	...	12.0	0.94
Rwanda	...	...	...	...	2.5 **,z	0.99**,z
Sao Tome and Principe	...	...	25.5 **	1.06**	25.8 **	1.11**
Senegal	2.4	1.04	2.9	1.00	3.4	1.10
Seychelles[4]	...	...	112.8	1.03	98.6	0.96
Sierra Leone	...	...	...	...	4.1 y	...
Somalia	...	...	...	...	...	...
South Africa	16.5	1.03	24.2 *	0.99*	31.6	1.02
Swaziland	14.0	1.83	...	...	...	...
Togo	3.2	0.98	2.7	1.00	2.8	0.99
Uganda	...	...	4.0	1.00	4.3	1.04
United Republic of Tanzania	...	...	...	...	**23.9 ****	**0.99****
Zambia	...	...	2.3 *	1.19*	...	...
Zimbabwe	...	...	...	...	**39.8**	...

	Median					
World	...	...	42.5	1.00	48.6	1.03
Countries in transition	72.4	...	28.1	0.95	34.6	1.07
Developed countries	72.5	0.98	76.1	1.01	81.1	1.00
Developing countries	...	...	32.9	0.95	34.3	1.01
Arab States	10.8	...	13.5	0.95	17.7	0.98
Central and Eastern Europe	74.0	...	50.5	0.96	74.3	0.94
Central Asia	37.9	...	17.4	0.91	28.8	0.96
East Asia and the Pacific	32.1	0.93	53.1	1.08	56.2	1.07
Latin America and the Caribbean	43.6	1.07	58.4	1.02	60.9	1.02
North America and Western Europe	68.9	0.99	81.5	0.99	86.8	0.99
South and West Asia	...		19.5	0.99	32.3	1.06
Sub-Saharan Africa	...	...	4.6	0.94	5.8	[illegible]

1. Data refer to the most recent year available during the period specified. See introduction to the Statistical annex for broader explanation of national literacy definitions, assessment methods, sources and years of data.
2. Literacy data for the most recent year do not include some geographic regions.
3. In countries where two or more education structures exist, indicators were calculated on the basis of the most common or widespread structure. In the Russian Federation this is three grades of primary education starting at age 7. However, a four-grade structure also exists, in which about one-third of primary pupils are enrolled.
4. National population data were used to calculate enrolment ratios.
5. Children enter primary school at age 6 or 7. Since 7 is the most common entrance age, enrolment ratios were calculated using the 7-11 age group for both enrolments and population.

GOAL 2						GOAL 3				
Universal primary education NET ENROLMENT RATIO (NER) IN PRIMARY EDUCATION						Learning needs of all youth and adults YOUTH LITERACY RATE (15-24)				
1990/1991		1998/1999		2002/2003		1990		2000-2004[1]		
Total (%)	GPI (F/M)	Total (%)	GPI (F/M)	Total (%)	GPI (F/M)	Total (%)	GPI (F/M)	Total (%)	GPI (F/M)	Country or territory
93.8**	0.95**	99.1**	0.98**	99.2	0.98	81.5	0.87	89.1	0.94	Cape Verde
53.5	0.66	...	...	...	...	52.1	0.60	58.5*	0.67*	Central African Republic
36.5**	0.45**	54.7	0.62	62.8**	0.68**	48.0	0.65	37.3*	0.42*	Chad
56.7**	0.73**	49.2	0.85	...	...	56.7	0.78	59.0	0.79	Comoros
79.3**	0.93**	...	...	54.0	0.96	92.5	0.95	97.8	0.99	Congo
45.6	0.71**	55.5	0.76	60.6*	0.81*	52.6	0.62	59.8*	0.74*	Côte d'Ivoire
54.5	0.78	...	...	...	...	68.9	0.72	68.7*	0.80*	Democratic Rep. of the Congo
90.5**	0.97**	88.0	0.83**	84.6z	0.85z	92.7	0.92	93.8*	1.00*	Equatorial Guinea
16.1**	0.99**	33.9	0.87	45.2	0.86	60.9	0.68	...	...	Eritrea
23.3**	0.75**	35.8	0.69	**51.1**	**0.85**	43.0	0.66	57.4	0.82	Ethiopia
86.0**	1.00**	...	...	78.3**,y	0.99**,y	...	...	...	...	Gabon
48.0**	0.71**	66.7	0.88	78.8**	0.99**	42.2	0.68	...	...	Gambia
52.4**	0.87**	57.9**	0.93**	**59.0**	...	81.8	0.86	...	...	Ghana
25.5**	0.51**	45.3	0.69	65.5	0.80	44.1	0.43	...	...	Guinea
38.0**	0.56**	...	...	...	...	...	...	...	...	Guinea-Bissau
74.3**	1.00**	65.8**	1.01**	66.5	1.00	89.8	0.93	80.3*	1.01*	Kenya
73.0	1.24	64.5	1.14	85.8	1.07	87.2	1.26	...	...	Lesotho
...	...	43.9	0.77	...	...	57.2	0.51	70.8	0.64	Liberia
64.8**	1.00**	64.5	1.01	78.6	1.00	72.2	0.86	70.1*	0.94*	Madagascar
49.8	0.92	...	...	...	...	63.2	0.68	76.3*	0.86*	Malawi
20.4	0.61	38.3**	0.72**	44.5	0.77	...	...	24.2*	0.52*	Mali
94.9	1.01	93.2	1.00	96.6	1.02	91.1	1.00	94.5*	1.02*	Mauritius
44.7	0.76**	47.3**	0.83**	55.3	0.91	48.8	0.48	62.8	0.64	Mozambique
83.2**	1.09**	77.9	1.07	78.3	1.07	87.4	1.04	92.3*	1.03*	Namibia
24.0	0.58	26.1	0.66	38.2	0.69	17.0	0.37	19.8*	0.54*	Niger
59.9**	0.78**	...	...	67.2**	0.82**	73.6	0.82	88.6	0.95	Nigeria
67.4	0.99	...	...	86.7	1.04	72.7	0.86	76.5*	0.98*	Rwanda
...	...	85.5	0.98	97.1**,z	0.94**,z	...	...	...	...	Sao Tome and Principe
47.1**	0.74**	57.9	0.88**	68.5	0.92	40.1	0.60	49.1*	0.70*	Senegal
...	...	99.1	0.98	99.6	0.99	...	...	99.1*	1.01*	Seychelles[4]
41.0**	0.73**	...	...	...	...	...	...	38.2*	0.64*	Sierra Leone
...	...	...	...	...	...	...	...	...	...	Somalia
87.9**	1.03**	91.3*	1.01*	89.0	1.01	88.5	1.00	93.9*	1.01*	South Africa
77.2	1.04	67.2	1.02	75.3	1.00	85.1	1.01	88.1*	1.03*	Swaziland
75.2	0.71	89.8	0.80	91.2	0.84	63.5	0.60	74.0*	0.76*	Togo
52.7**	0.82**	...	...	...	...	70.1	0.76	80.2	0.86	Uganda
49.6	1.02	45.8	1.03	**77.4****	**0.98****	83.1	0.87	78.4*	0.94*	United Republic of Tanzania
79.1**	0.96**	68.5	0.97	68.4	0.98	81.2	0.88	69.4*	0.91*	Zambia
85.7**	1.00**	...	...	**79.2**	**1.02**	93.9	0.95	97.6	0.97	Zimbabwe

Weighted average						Weighted average				
81.7	0.88	83.6	0.93	84.6	0.96	88.2	0.91	87.5	0.93	World
89.0	0.99	85.4	0.99	89.1	1.00	99.2	1.00	99.7	1.00	Countries in transition
96.2	1.00	96.6	1.00	95.6	1.01	99.7	1.00	99.7	1.00	Developed countries
79.5	0.86	82.0	0.92	83.2	0.95	85.8	0.88	85.0	0.91	Developing countries
74.8	0.81	78.1	0.90	82.6	0.92	77.3	0.71	78.3	0.85	Arab States
90.1	0.98	87.2	0.97	89.0	0.98	99.2	0.98	98.9	0.99	Central and Eastern Europe
84.8	0.99	88.9	0.99	89.9	0.98	97.8	1.00	99.7	1.00	Central Asia
95.9	0.96	95.7	1.00	92.1	0.99	97.2	0.96	97.9	0.99	East Asia and the Pacific
86.4	0.99	94.4	0.99	96.4	0.99	92.7	1.00	95.9	1.01	Latin America and the Caribbean
97.0	1.00	96.3	1.00	95.3	1.01	99.7	1.00	99.8	1.00	North America and Western Europe
72.7	0.67	78.6	0.83	82.5	0.92	71.1	0.72	73.1	0.80	South and West Asia
54.5	0.86	56.2	0.88	63.5	0.90	74.8	0.80	72.0	0.88	Sub-Saharan Africa

6. Pending agreement on population data, the 2001 NER published herein in connection with China's primary education is for reference only.

7. Enrolment ratios were not calculated due to lack of United Nations population data by age.

8. Enrolment ratios were not calculated due to inconsistencies between enrolment and the United Nations population data.

9. Literacy rates for the most recent year were derived from the absolute numbers of illiterates and literates provided to the UIS through its literacy questionnaire.

(g) Projected at the national level (593 districts) on the basis of data by age collected for ISCED level 1 in a sample of 193 districts under the District Information System on Education.

Data in bold are for 2003/2004.

(z) Data are for 2001/2002.

(y) Data are for 2000/2001.

Table 13
Trends in basic or proxy indicators to measure EFA goals 4 and 5

Country or territory	GOAL 4 Improving levels of adult literacy ADULT LITERACY RATE (15 and over)				GOAL 5 Gender parity in primary education GROSS ENROLMENT RATIO					
	1990		2000-2004[1]		1990/1991		1998/1999		2002/2003	
	Total (%)	GPI (F/M)	Total (%)	GPI (F/M)	Total (%)	GPI (F/M)	Total (%)	GPI (F/M)	Total (%)	GPI (F/M)
Arab States										
Algeria	52.9	0.64	69.8*	0.76*	100.5	0.85	106.8	0.92	108.7	0.93
Bahrain	82.1	0.86	87.7*	0.90*	110.0	1.00	100.7	1.01	97.1	1.00
Djibouti	53.0	0.59	...	...	37.7	0.71	38.1	0.71	**42.5**	**0.79**
Egypt	47.1	0.56	55.6*	0.65*	91.5	0.83	98.6**	0.92**	97.4**	0.95**
Iraq	35.7	0.38			115.6	0.84	99.5	0.82	110.1	0.83
Jordan	81.5	0.80	89.9*	0.89*	100.6	1.01	96.5	1.00	99.1	1.01
Kuwait	76.7	0.91	82.9	0.96	60.2	0.95	101.9	1.01	93.6	1.00
Lebanon	80.3	0.83	...	...	113.2**	0.96**	106.7	0.96	103.4	0.97
Libyan Arab Jamahiriya	68.1	0.62	81.7	0.77	104.7	0.94	115.7	0.98	114.1**	1.00**
Mauritania	34.8	0.52	51.2*	0.53*	50.3	0.73	86.5	0.94	88.1	0.97
Morocco	38.7	0.47	50.7	0.61	65.2	0.69	89.2	0.81	109.6	0.90
Oman	54.7	0.57	74.4	0.80	84.9	0.92	85.7	0.96	80.8	0.99
Palestinian Autonomous Territories	...	...	91.9*	0.91*	...	...	105.7	1.01	98.8	1.00
Qatar	77.0	0.98	89.2*	... *	100.5	0.93	108.0	0.97	105.7	0.97
Saudi Arabia	66.2	0.66	79.4*	0.80*	72.7	0.86	68.7	0.97	66.6	0.96
Sudan[2]	45.8	0.53	59.0*	0.72*	52.3	0.77	54.5**	0.85**	60.2	0.87
Syrian Arab Republic	64.8	0.58	82.9*	0.82*	102.2	0.90	103.6	0.92	114.9	0.95
Tunisia	59.1	0.65	74.3*	0.78*	113.7	0.89	114.9	0.95	110.7	0.96
United Arab Emirates	71.0	0.99	77.3	1.07	110.8	0.97	89.1	0.96	96.8	0.97
Yemen	32.7	0.23	49.0	0.41	65.4**	0.35**	73.3	0.56	83.5	0.69
Central and Eastern Europe										
Albania	77.0	0.77	98.7*	0.99*	100.2	1.00	108.2**	0.99**	103.5	0.98
Belarus	99.5	1.00	99.6*	1.00*	96.0	0.96**	108.9	0.98	101.9	0.99
Bosnia and Herzegovina	...	...	94.6*	0.93*	...	...	...	...	...	...
Bulgaria	97.2	0.98	98.2*	0.99*	97.6	0.97	103.4	0.97	100.3	0.98
Croatia	96.9	0.96	98.1*	0.98*	79.7	0.99	95.7	0.98	96.5	0.99
Czech Republic	...	...	...	...	96.4	1.00	104.0	0.99	102.0	0.98
Estonia	99.8	1.00	99.8*	1.00*	110.8	0.97	102.2	0.97	100.7	0.96
Hungary	99.1	1.00	99.3*	1.00*	94.5	1.00	103.5	0.98	100.3	0.99
Latvia	...	...	99.7*	1.00*	96.5	0.99	99.1	0.98	94.0	0.97
Lithuania	99.3	1.00	99.6*	1.00*	94.0	0.95	101.5	0.98	98.1	0.99
Poland	...	...	...	...	98.4	0.99	...	...	99.5	0.99
Republic of Moldova	97.5	0.97	96.2*	0.98*	93.1	1.00	84.3	1.00	86.0	0.99
Romania	97.1	0.97	97.3*	0.98*	91.3	1.00	104.3	0.98	99.0	0.98
Russian Federation[3]	99.2	0.99	99.4*	1.00*	109.2	1.00	100.5	0.99	118.2	1.00
Serbia and Montenegro[4]	...	...	96.4*	0.95*	72.0	1.02	103.9	0.99	98.3y	1.00y
Slovakia	...	...	99.6*	1.00*	...	...	102.5	0.99	100.7	0.99
Slovenia	99.6	1.00	99.7	1.00	108.3	...	97.7	0.99	107.8	0.99
The former Yugoslav Rep. of Macedonia	...	...	96.1*	0.96*	99.3	0.98	101.8	0.98	96.5	1.00
Turkey	77.9	0.74	88.3*	0.85*	99.1	0.92	...	...	91.4**	0.93**
Ukraine	99.4	0.99	99.4*	0.99*	88.8	1.00	105.7	0.99	92.7	1.00
Central Asia										
Armenia	97.5	0.97	99.4*	0.99*	...	...	...	...	98.5	0.98
Azerbaijan	...	...	98.8*	0.99*	110.6**	0.99**	90.9	1.00	92.3	0.97
Georgia	...	...	...	...	97.3	1.00	95.3	1.00	90.5	0.98
Kazakhstan	98.8	0.99	99.5*	1.00*	88.2	0.99**	93.0	1.00	101.5	0.99
Kyrgyzstan	...	...	98.7*	0.99*	92.8	1.00	101.1	0.98	100.9	0.97
Mongolia	...	...	97.8*	1.00*	97.2	1.02	98.2	1.04	100.8	1.02
Tajikistan	98.2	0.98	99.5*	1.00*	91.0	0.98	102.8	0.95	110.6	0.95
Turkmenistan	...	...	98.8*	0.99*	...	...	...	...	...	...
Uzbekistan	98.7	0.98	99.3	0.99	81.4	[illegible]			[illegible]	0.99
East Asia and the Pacific										
Australia	...	...	...	...	107.7	0.99	100.8	1.00	103.6	1.00
Brunei Darussalam	85.5	0.87	92.7*	0.95*	115.3	0.94	114.5	0.98	106.1	1.00
Cambodia	62.0	0.63	73.6	0.70*	[illegible]	[illegible]	96.5	0.86	123.8	0.90

GOAL 5						
Gender parity in secondary education GROSS ENROLMENT RATIO						
1990/1991		1998/1999		2002/2003		
Total (%)	GPI (F/M)	Total (%)	GPI (F/M)	Total (%)	GPI (F/M)	Country or territory
						Arab States
60.9	0.81	...	...	80.0	1.07	Algeria
99.7	1.03	93.9	1.08	95.6	1.07	Bahrain
11.6	0.66	16.2	0.72	**24.3**	**0.68**	Djibouti
70.8	0.79	80.8 **	0.92 **	85.3 **	0.94 **	Egypt
49.0	0.64	35.7	0.63	42.7	0.71	Iraq
63.3	1.04	86.9	1.03	86.0	1.02	Jordan
42.9	0.98	97.8 **	1.02 **	89.3	1.06	Kuwait
...	...	77.5	1.09	79.4	1.09	Lebanon
85.9	...	...	...	104.7 **	1.06 **	Libyan Arab Jamahiriya
13.4	0.46	18.7 **	0.73 **	22.6	0.79	Mauritania
35.5	0.73	37.7	0.79	45.0	0.83	Morocco
44.9	0.81	71.7	0.99	80.5	0.96	Oman
...	...	78.8	1.04	87.9	1.06	Palestinian Autonomous Territories
83.6	1.06	92.3	1.06	93.9	1.04	Qatar
43.7	0.79	67.9	0.87	66.9	0.90	Saudi Arabia
21.5	0.79	28.5 **	...	35.4	0.84	Sudan [2]
48.8	0.73	40.6	0.91	48.3	0.92	Syrian Arab Republic
44.4	0.79	72.9	1.02	77.6	1.08	Tunisia
65.4	1.21	82.1	1.08	78.7	1.03	United Arab Emirates
...	...	41.9	0.37	47.3	0.45	Yemen
						Central and Eastern Europe
78.3	0.86	75.8 **	1.03 **	81.1	1.00	Albania
95.3	...	97.2	1.00	90.9	1.03	Belarus
...	...	...	...	...	...	Bosnia and Herzegovina
75.2	1.04	89.4	0.98	98.4	0.97	Bulgaria
69.2	1.09	87.6	1.02	89.8	1.02	Croatia
91.2	0.97	82.5	1.04	96.9	1.03	Czech Republic
98.5	1.11	92.7	1.04	96.4	1.03	Estonia
78.6	1.01	95.3	1.02	105.8	1.00	Hungary
91.0	1.00	88.4	1.04	95.3	1.00	Latvia
91.7	...	95.7	1.01	102.5	0.98	Lithuania
81.5	1.05	...	...	104.5	0.96	Poland
80.0	1.09	72.2	1.01	73.3	1.04	Republic of Moldova
92.0	0.99	78.9	1.01	84.7	1.01	Romania
93.3	1.06	...	...	95.0 **	...	Russian Federation [3]
63.4	1.03	92.3	1.01	88.7 y	1.01 y	Serbia and Montenegro [4]
...	...	85.2	1.02	91.7	1.01	Slovakia
91.1	...	98.7	1.03	109.4	0.99	Slovenia
55.7	0.99	82.3	0.97	84.7	0.98	The former Yugoslav Rep. of Macedonia
48.2	0.63	...	...	79.1 **	0.75 **	Turkey
92.8	...	...	...	96.9	0.99	Ukraine
						Central Asia
...	...	...	...	86.9	1.02	Armenia
87.5	1.01	76.9	0.99	82.8	0.96	Azerbaijan
94.9	0.97	72.8	0.99	80.2	1.01	Georgia
97.5	1.04	87.4	0.99	91.8	1.00	Kazakhstan
100.1	1.02	85.4	1.02	91.9	1.01	Kyrgyzstan
82.4	1.14	58.3	1.27	83.7	1.16	Mongolia
102.1	...	72.6	0.86	85.8	0.83	Tajikistan
...	...	...	...	...	...	Turkmenistan
99.4	0.91	...	...	95.4	0.97	Uzbekistan
						East Asia and the Pacific
81.7	1.04	154.8	1.04	153.7	0.97	Australia
68.7	1.07	81.6	1.10	89.6	1.06	Brunei Darussalam
28.9	0.43	16.0 **	0.53 **	25.2	0.64	Cambodia

Table 13 (continued)

Country or territory	GOAL 4: Improving levels of adult literacy — ADULT LITERACY RATE (15 and over)				GOAL 5: Gender parity in primary education — GROSS ENROLMENT RATIO					
	1990		2000-2004[1]		1990/1991		1998/1999		2002/2003	
	Total (%)	GPI (F/M)	Total (%)	GPI (F/M)	Total (%)	GPI (F/M)	Total (%)	GPI (F/M)	Total (%)	GPI (F/M)
China[5]	78.3	0.79	90.9*	0.91*	125.2	0.93	…	…	115.2	1.00
Cook Islands[6]	…	…	…	…	…	…	…	…	…	…
Democratic People's Republic of Korea	…	…	…	…	…	…	…	…	…	…
Fiji	88.6	0.93	92.9*	0.97*	131.4	1.00**	110.5**	0.99**	108.8**,z	1.00**,z
Indonesia	79.5	0.84	87.9	0.90	114.3	0.98	…	…	111.7	0.98
Japan	…	…	…	…	99.7	1.00	101.4	1.00	100.4	1.00
Kiribati[4]	…	…	…	…	…	…	130.8	1.02	110.9	1.16
Lao People's Democratic Republic	56.5	0.61	68.7*	0.79*	103.4	0.79	116.7	0.85	116.4	0.87
Macao, China	90.5	0.92	91.3*	0.92*	98.6	0.96	99.1	0.95	104.0	0.93
Malaysia	80.7	0.86	88.7*	0.93*	93.7	1.00	97.4	1.00	93.1	1.00
Marshall Islands[4]	…	…	…	…	…	…	…	…	106.4z	0.93z
Micronesia (Federated States of)	…	…	…	…	…	…	…	…	…	…
Myanmar	80.7	0.85	89.7*	0.92*	108.6	0.95	90.1	0.98	91.9	1.01
Nauru[4]	30.4	0.30	…	…	…	…	81.0**	1.04**	…	…
New Zealand	…	…	…	…	105.6	0.98	102.6	1.00	101.7	0.99**
Niue[4]	…	…	…	…	…	…	102.9	0.87	117.6z	0.94z
Palau[4]	…	…	…	…	…	…	113.8	0.93	115.8**,y	0.93**,y
Papua New Guinea	56.6	0.75	57.3*	0.80*	66.2	0.86	74.8	0.93	73.4z	0.90z
Philippines	91.7	0.99	92.6*	1.00*	109.5	0.99	113.1	1.00	112.5	0.99
Republic of Korea	…	…	…	…	104.9	1.01	95.3	1.01	**105.5**	**0.99**
Samoa	98.0	0.99	98.7	0.99	121.7	1.09	99.4	1.01	105.4**	0.97**
Singapore	88.8	0.88	92.5*	0.92*	103.7	0.97	…	…	…	…
Solomon Islands	…	…	…	…	85.8	0.86	…	…	71.6	…
Thailand	…	…	92.6*	0.95*	98.1	0.96	94.1	0.95	**96.8**	**0.96**
Timor-Leste	…	…	…	…	…	…	…	…	143.3z	…
Tokelau	…	…	…	…	…	…	…	…	…	…
Tonga	…	…	98.9*	1.00*	105.8	0.96	110.4	0.97	112.3	0.97
Tuvalu[4]	…	…	…	…	…	…	103.6**	0.96**	102.2z	1.13z
Vanuatu	…	…	74.0*	…*	96.0	0.98	110.4	0.99	112.7	1.00
Viet Nam	…	…	90.3*	0.93*	106.9	0.93**	109.4	0.92	101.0	0.93
Latin America and the Caribbean										
Anguilla[4]	…	…	…	…	…	…	…	…	99.9	1.01
Antigua and Barbuda	…	…	…	…	…	…	…	…	…	…
Argentina	95.7	1.00	97.2*	1.00*	106.3	1.04**	119.7	1.00	119.4	1.00
Aruba[4]	…	…	…	…	…	…	112.2	0.98	115.1	0.94
Bahamas	94.4	1.02	…	…	95.6	1.03**	…	…	92.2**	1.01**
Barbados	99.4	1.00	99.7	1.00	93.0	1.00	104.3	0.99	108.7	0.99
Belize	…	…	76.9*	1.01*	111.5	0.98	118.1	0.97	122.0	0.98
Bermuda[4]	…	…	…	…	…	…	…	…	102.2z	…
Bolivia	78.1	0.80	86.5*	0.87*	94.8	0.91	112.5	0.98	115.3	0.99
Brazil	82.0	0.98	88.4*	1.00*	105.3	0.94**	…	…	147.0	0.95
British Virgin Islands[4]	…	…	…	…	…	…	111.6	0.97	106.6	0.94
Cayman Islands[6]	…	…	…	…	…	…	…	…	…	…
Chile	94.0	0.99	95.7*	1.00*	99.9	0.98	102.7	0.97	**98.0**	**0.97**
Colombia	88.4	0.99	94.2*	1.01*	102.2	1.15	113.7	0.97	110.3	0.99
Costa Rica	93.9	1.00	95.8	1.00	101.9	0.99	104.3	1.00	107.6	0.98
Cuba	95.1	1.00	99.8*	1.00*	97.7	0.97	105.3	0.96	97.8	0.96
Dominica[4]	…	…	…	…	…	…	98.8	0.95	88.2	0.93
Dominican Republic	79.4	0.99	87.7*	0.99*	94.8**	1.02**	116.7**	0.98**	124.3**	1.02**
Ecuador	87.6	0.94	91.0*	0.97*	116.5	0.99**	113.4	1.00	116.9	1.00
El Salvador	72.4	0.91	79.7	0.94	81.1	1.01	111.6	0.97	112.5	0.95
Grenada	…	…	…	…	…	…	…	…	119.6	0.98
Guatemala	61.0	[illegible]	69.1*	0.84*	77.6	0.88**	94.0*	0.89*	106.1	0.93
Guyana	97.2	0.98	…	…	93.6	0.98	116.9	0.98	124.8	0.98
Haiti	39.7	0.87	51.9	0.93	47.8	0.94	…	…	…	…
Honduras	68.1	0.98	80.0*	1.01*	109.0**	1.05**	…	…	105.8**,z	1.02**,z
Jamaica	82.2	1.10	87.6	1.09	101.3	0.99	95.4**	1.00**	99.8	0.99
Mexico	87.3	0.93	90.3*	0.96*	113.9	0.98	110.9	0.99	110.4	0.99
Montserrat[4]	…	…	…	…	…	…	…	…	118.3**	…

GOAL 5

Gender parity in secondary education

GROSS ENROLMENT RATIO

1990/1991 Total (%)	1990/1991 GPI (F/M)	1998/1999 Total (%)	1998/1999 GPI (F/M)	2002/2003 Total (%)	2002/2003 GPI (F/M)	Country or territory
48.7	0.75	61.7	...	70.3	0.97	China[5]
...	...	...	...	...	...	Cook Islands[6]
...	...	...	...	...	...	Democratic People's Republic of Korea
58.2 **	...	...	...	80.4 **,z	1.07 **,z	Fiji
45.5	0.83	...	...	60.7	0.99	Indonesia
97.1	1.02	101.8	1.01	102.0	1.00	Japan
...	...	...	...	104.4	1.13	Kiribati[4]
24.4 *	0.62 *	33.4	0.69	43.7	0.74	Lao People's Democratic Republic
65.1 *	1.11 *	75.5	1.10	90.9	1.07	Macao, China
56.3	1.07	69.4	1.11	70.3	1.11	Malaysia
...	...	...	...	75.7 z	1.02 z	Marshall Islands[4]
...	...	109.2	...	...	...	Micronesia (Federated States of)
22.4	0.98	34.9	0.99	39.0	0.94	Myanmar
...	...	53.9 **	1.06 **	...	...	Nauru[4]
89.1	1.02	114.3	1.06	117.5	...	New Zealand
...	...	101.4	0.82	93.8 z	0.98 z	Niue[4]
...	...	101.2	1.07	88.8 **,y	1.00 **,y	Palau[4]
11.5	0.59	20.4	0.75	25.5	0.79	Papua New Guinea
70.7	1.04	75.8	1.09	84.0	1.10	Philippines
89.8	0.97	99.9	1.00	**90.5**	**1.00**	Republic of Korea
36.1	1.22	74.9	1.11	75.9 **	1.10 **	Samoa
68.1	0.93	...	...	...	...	Singapore
14.0	0.63	...	...	61.5	...	Solomon Islands
30.8	0.94	...	...	**76.7**	**1.00**	Thailand
...	...	...	...	34.6 z	...	Timor-Leste
...	...	...	...	...	...	Tokelau
97.1	1.01	93.3	1.13	102.8	1.15	Tonga
...	...	78.3 **	0.88 **	84.4 z	0.93 z	Tuvalu[4]
16.7	0.79	33.1 **	0.83 **	27.8	1.08	Vanuatu
32.2	...	61.9	0.90	72.4	0.93	Viet Nam
						Latin America and the Caribbean
...	...	...	...	108.3 **	1.00 **	Anguilla[4]
...	...	...	...	...	...	Antigua and Barbuda
71.1	...	89.0	1.08	99.7	1.06	Argentina
...	...	100.6	1.04	103.1	1.07	Aruba[4]
...	...	...	...	91.3 **	1.03 **	Bahamas
...	...	104.0 **	1.05 **	105.8	1.02	Barbados
43.9	1.15	64.8	1.08	77.8 **	1.05 **	Belize
...	...	...	...	86.1 z	...	Bermuda[4]
36.7	0.85	72.3	0.93	86.4 **	0.97 **	Bolivia
38.4	...	...	...	110.0	1.10	Brazil
...	...	98.8	0.91	94.7	1.16	British Virgin Islands[4]
...	...	...	...	...	...	Cayman Islands[6]
73.5	1.08	79.6	1.04	**91.2**	**1.01**	Chile
49.8 *	1.13 *	70.6	1.11	70.8	1.11	Colombia
43.0	1.05	56.8	1.09	66.5	1.08	Costa Rica
88.9	1.14	79.4	1.06	92.6	0.98	Cuba
...	...	85.5	1.18	113.9	1.12	Dominica[4]
...	...	56.1 **	1.27 **	58.7 **	1.23 **	Dominican Republic
55.3 *	...	56.4	1.03	59.2	1.02	Ecuador
26.4 *	1.06 *	50.2	0.99	59.0	1.01	El Salvador
...	...	...	...	148.7	0.96	Grenada
...	...	30.7 *	0.92 *	42.7	0.93	Guatemala
78.7	1.06	81.1	1.02	94.7 **	1.06 **	Guyana
20.6 *	0.96 *	...	...	...	...	Haiti
...	...	...	...	...	...	Honduras
65.3	1.06	84.1 **	1.02 **	84.1	1.02	Jamaica
53.3	1.01	69.1	1.02	79.0	1.09	Mexico
...	...	...	...	103.4 **	...	Montserrat[4]

Table 13 (continued)

Country or territory	GOAL 4				GOAL 5					
	Improving levels of adult literacy				Gender parity in primary education					
	ADULT LITERACY RATE (15 and over)				GROSS ENROLMENT RATIO					
	1990		2000-2004[1]		1990/1991		1998/1999		2002/2003	
	Total (%)	GPI (F/M)	Total (%)	GPI (F/M)	Total (%)	GPI (F/M)	Total (%)	GPI (F/M)	Total (%)	GPI (F/M)
Netherlands Antilles	95.6	1.00	96.7	1.00	...	...	115.5	0.95	104.3**	1.00**
Nicaragua	62.7	1.00	76.7*	1.00*	93.5	1.06	99.9	1.03	108.5	0.99
Panama	89.0	0.98	91.9*	0.99*	106.4	0.96	108.1**	0.97**	112.0	0.97
Paraguay	90.3	0.96	91.6*	0.97*	105.4	0.97	109.6**	0.98**	110.1	0.96
Peru	...	...	87.7*	0.88*	118.9	0.97**	122.6	0.99	118.4	1.00
Saint Kitts and Nevis[4]	...	...	...	...	...	...	...	...	111.8	1.06
Saint Lucia	...	...	90.1*	1.01*	138.5	0.94	114.8	0.98	111.8	1.00
Saint Vincent and the Grenadines	...	...	...	...	111.6	0.99	...	...	107.3	0.97
Suriname	...	...	88.0*	0.91*	100.2	1.00	...	...	125.8**	0.98**
Trinidad and Tobago	96.8	0.98	98.5	0.99	96.7	0.99	101.7	0.99	100.1	0.97
Turks and Caicos Islands[4]	...	...	...	...	...	...	...	...	85.9	0.95
Uruguay	96.5	1.01	97.7	1.01	108.6	0.99	112.8	0.99	109.3	0.98
Venezuela	88.9	0.97	93.0*	0.99*	95.7	1.03	100.3	0.98	103.9	0.98
North America and Western Europe										
Andorra[6]	...	...	...	...	...	...	...	...	...	...
Austria	...	...	...	...	100.7	1.00	102.2	0.99	103.2	1.00
Belgium	...	...	...	...	99.9	1.01	103.8	0.99	105.3	0.99
Canada	...	...	...	...	103.8	0.98	97.7	1.00	101.3**,z	1.00**,z
Cyprus[4]	94.3	0.93	96.8*	0.96*	90.0	1.00	97.4	1.00	97.6	1.00
Denmark	...	...	...	...	98.3	1.00	101.9	1.00	103.9	1.00
Finland	...	...	...	...	98.8	0.99	99.2	1.00	102.0	0.99
France	...	...	...	...	108.4	0.99	105.6	0.99	104.3	0.99
Germany	...	...	...	...	101.0	1.01**	105.7	0.99	99.4	1.00
Greece	94.9	0.95	91.0*	0.94*	98.4	0.99	95.5	1.00	100.8	1.00
Iceland	...	...	...	...	101.3	0.99**	98.5	0.98	99.7	0.99
Ireland	...	...	...	...	102.5	1.00	104.1	1.00	105.6	1.00
Israel	91.4	0.93	96.9*	0.97*	97.9	1.03	112.9	0.99	112.2	1.00
Italy	...	...	...	...	103.7	1.00	102.5	0.99	101.1	0.99
Luxembourg	...	...	...	...	90.2	1.09	99.6	1.01	99.2	0.99
Malta	88.4	1.01	87.9*	1.03*	107.9	0.96	106.3	1.01	104.4	0.99
Monaco[6]	...	...	...	...	...	...	...	...	...	...
Netherlands	...	...	...	...	102.4	1.03	108.3	0.98	107.9	0.98
Norway	...	...	...	...	100.4	1.00	101.1	1.00	101.3	1.00
Portugal	...	...	...	...	123.0	0.95	123.1	0.96	115.3	0.95
San Marino	...	...	...	...	...	...	...	...	...	...
Spain	...	...	97.1*	0.98*	108.6	0.99	107.4	0.98	107.6	0.98
Sweden	...	...	...	...	99.8	1.00	109.7	1.03	110.5	1.03
Switzerland	...	...	...	...	90.3	1.01	106.3	0.99	107.7	0.99
United Kingdom	...	...	...	...	107.4	0.97	101.8	1.01	100.1	1.00
United States	...	...	...	...	103.1	0.98	100.6	1.03	98.1	1.00
South and West Asia										
Afghanistan	...	...	...	...	28.8	0.55	32.7	0.08**	92.3	0.52
Bangladesh	34.2	0.53	41.1	0.62	79.6	0.86	106.0	0.97	95.9	1.04
Bhutan[7]	...	...	...	...	...	...	...	...	...	...
India[8]	49.3	0.58	61.0*	0.65*	98.6	0.76	97.9	0.83	107.5	0.94
Iran, Islamic Republic of	63.2	0.75	77.0*	0.84*	109.3	0.90	95.6	0.95	91.9	0.97
Maldives	94.8	1.00	96.3*	1.00*	134.1**	0.97**	134.1	1.01	118.0	0.98
Nepal	30.4	0.30	48.6*	0.56*	113.8	0.61	112.3**	0.78**	119.3	0.89
Pakistan	35.4	0.41	48.7*	0.57*	...	...	...	...	68.5	0.71
Sri Lanka[2]	88.7	0.91	90.4*	0.96*	113.2	0.96	109.2	0.97	**110.5****	**0.99****
Sub-Saharan Africa										
Angola	...	...	66.8*	0.66*	92.0	0.92*	97.1	0.83	...	...
Benin	26.4	0.41	33.6*	0.49*	58.6	0.50	82.7	0.65	109.3	0.72
Botswana	68.1	1.07	78.9	1.07	103.0	1.08	102.8	1.00	103.3**	1.00**
Burkina Faso	...	...	12.8*	0.44*	32.5	0.63	41.8	0.68	46.2	0.74
Burundi	37.0	0.55	58.9*	0.78*	71.5	0.84	62.7**	0.80**	77.3	0.81
Cameroon	57.9	0.69	67.9*	0.78*	99.5	0.86	87.5	0.82	107.6	0.85

GOAL 5

Gender parity in secondary education

GROSS ENROLMENT RATIO

1990/1991 Total (%)	1990/1991 GPI (F/M)	1998/1999 Total (%)	1998/1999 GPI (F/M)	2002/2003 Total (%)	2002/2003 GPI (F/M)	Country or territory
92.9	1.19	74.9	1.17	71.0 **	1.11 **	Netherlands Antilles
40.4	1.37	48.4 **	1.18 **	60.7	1.17	Nicaragua
61.4	1.07	67.5 **	1.08 **	70.6	1.07	Panama
30.9	1.04	50.8	1.05	64.9	1.02 **	Paraguay
67.4	...	81.7	0.95	89.7	0.93	Peru
...	...	...	...	105.9	1.31	Saint Kitts and Nevis[4]
52.9	1.45	76.4	1.29	86.8	1.25	Saint Lucia
58.4	1.24	...	...	69.2	1.11	Saint Vincent and the Grenadines
52.1	1.15	...	...	73.8 **	1.34 **	Suriname
80.4	1.05	81.7 **	1.08 **	82.4 **	1.08 **	Trinidad and Tobago
...	...	...	...	94.0 **	0.99 **	Turks and Caicos Islands[4]
81.3	...	...	...	105.6	1.13	Uruguay
34.7	1.38	56.9	1.23	69.9	1.15	Venezuela
						North America and Western Europe
...	...	...	...	...	...	Andorra[6]
101.8	0.93	98.8	0.96	100.0	0.95	Austria
101.8	1.01	142.4	1.08	160.8	1.10	Belgium
100.8	1.00	105.3	0.99	105.3 **,z	0.99 **,z	Canada
72.1	1.02	93.2	1.03	98.4	1.02	Cyprus[4]
109.2	1.01	125.6	1.06	129.1	1.05	Denmark
116.4	1.19	120.9	1.09	128.2	1.11	Finland
98.5	1.05	109.6	1.00	108.9	1.01	France
98.2	0.97	98.2	0.98	100.0	0.98	Germany
93.8	0.98	93.9	1.01	97.5	1.00	Greece
99.6	0.96	109.4	1.06	114.4	1.07	Iceland
100.2	1.09	105.4	1.06	106.8	1.09	Ireland
88.1	1.08	90.8	1.00	93.2	0.98	Israel
83.2	1.00	91.7	0.99	99.3	0.99 **	Italy
76.5	...	...	...	96.0	1.06	Luxembourg
82.8	0.94	...	...	94.9	0.99	Malta
...	...	...	...	...	...	Monaco[6]
119.5	0.92	124.4	0.96	121.9	0.99	Netherlands
103.0	1.03	120.3	1.02	114.6	1.02	Norway
67.2	1.16	109.5	1.08	112.7	1.09	Portugal
...	...	...	...	...	...	San Marino
104.1	1.07	108.9	1.07	117.5	1.06	Spain
90.2	1.05	160.1	1.28	138.7	1.18	Sweden
99.1	0.95	99.9	0.92	97.9	0.94	Switzerland
88.0	1.00	156.9	1.12	178.5	1.25	United Kingdom
92.1	1.01	94.9	...	94.2	1.00	United States
						South and West Asia
10.2	...	...	...	12.5 z	– z	Afghanistan
20.2	0.52	42.4	0.96	47.5	1.12	Bangladesh
...	...	...	...	...	...	Bhutan[7]
44.5	0.60	46.6	0.70	52.8	0.80	India[8]
57.5	0.75	77.4	0.93	77.9	0.94	Iran, Islamic Republic of
...	...	36.5	1.05	66.7	1.15	Maldives
33.1	0.44	35.5	0.71	45.0	0.78	Nepal
25.1	0.48	...	...	22.5	0.71	Pakistan
76.8	1.09	...	...	**86.5** **	**1.06** **	Sri Lanka[2]
						Sub-Saharan Africa
12.1	...	14.7 *	0.78 *	19.1 z	0.78 z	Angola
11.7	0.41	21.1	0.45	27.6	0.46	Benin
37.6	1.12	71.2	1.10	72.7 **	1.06 **	Botswana
6.7	0.52	9.4	0.60	11.5	0.67	Burkina Faso
5.5	0.58	...	...	11.1	0.73	Burundi
27.5	0.71	26.5 **	0.82 **	31.2	0.84	Cameroon

Table 13 (continued)

Country or territory	GOAL 4: Improving levels of adult literacy — ADULT LITERACY RATE (15 and over)				GOAL 5: Gender parity in primary education — GROSS ENROLMENT RATIO					
	1990		2000-2004[1]		1990/1991		1998/1999		2002/2003	
	Total (%)	GPI (F/M)	Total (%)	GPI (F/M)	Total (%)	GPI (F/M)	Total (%)	GPI (F/M)	Total (%)	GPI (F/M)
Cape Verde	63.8	0.71	75.7	0.80	113.8	0.94**	125.6	0.96	120.6	0.95
Central African Republic	33.2	0.44	48.6*	0.52*	65.5	0.63	...	...	65.5	0.68
Chad	27.7	0.51	25.5*	0.31*	54.7	0.45	67.0	0.58	78.3**	0.64**
Comoros	53.8	0.76	56.2	0.77	75.0	0.73	75.2	0.85	89.6**	0.82**
Congo	67.1	0.75	82.8	0.87	116.8	0.90	49.6	0.95	80.4	0.93
Côte d'Ivoire	38.5	0.51	48.1*	0.64*	65.1	0.71	73.1	0.75	77.6*	0.80*
Democratic Rep. of the Congo	47.5	0.56	65.3*	0.65*	70.6	0.75	49.6	0.90	...	...
Equatorial Guinea	73.3	0.71	84.2*	0.83*	162.6**	0.95**	131.3	0.91**	126.2[z]	0.91[z]
Eritrea	46.4	0.59	...	...	21.3	0.94	53.2	0.83	63.4	0.81
Ethiopia	28.6	0.53	41.5	0.69	31.8	0.66	49.9	0.60	**70.0**	**0.77**
Gabon	...	...	...	...	141.8**	0.98**	134.1	1.00	132.2	0.99
Gambia	25.6	0.62	...	...	61.1	0.68	79.9	0.85	85.2	0.98**
Ghana	58.5	0.67	54.1*	0.73*	72.1	0.83	76.8	0.90	**83.0**	**0.91**
Guinea	27.2	0.30	...	...	34.0	0.47	58.4	0.63	81.5	0.77
Guinea-Bissau	...	...	...	...	49.9**	0.55**	...	...	69.7**[y]	0.67**[y]
Kenya	70.8	0.75	73.6*	0.90*	94.5	0.95	90.2	0.98	92.4	0.94
Lesotho	78.0	1.37	81.4*	1.23*	112.1	1.21	109.2	1.08	126.4	1.01
Liberia	39.2	0.41	55.9	0.54	...	...	89.6	0.74	...	...
Madagascar	58.0	0.75	70.6*	0.85*	93.6	0.98	95.6	0.97	119.6	0.96
Malawi	51.8	0.53	64.1*	0.72*	68.0	0.83	146.2	0.95**	140.1	0.96
Mali	...	...	19.0*	0.44*	25.3	0.60	48.8	0.71	58.4	0.76
Mauritius	79.8	0.88	84.3*	0.91*	109.2	1.00	107.6	1.00	103.8	1.01
Mozambique	33.5	0.37	46.5	0.50	63.9	0.76	81.2**	0.74**	103.4	0.81
Namibia	74.9	0.94	85.0*	0.96*	123.9	1.09	113.9	1.01	105.0	1.01
Niger	11.4	0.28	14.4*	0.48*	27.8	0.58	30.9	0.67	43.5	0.69
Nigeria	48.7	0.65	66.8	0.80	91.9	0.78	86.1**	0.76**	119.4	0.81
Rwanda	53.3	0.70	64.0*	0.84*	71.3	0.98	118.6	0.97	122.0	1.00
Sao Tome and Principe	...	...	...	...	...	...	107.1	0.96	126.4**[z]	0.94**[z]
Senegal	28.4	0.49	39.3*	0.57*	57.5	0.73	68.6	0.86**	79.9	0.92
Seychelles[4]	...	...	91.9*	1.01*	...	...	112.8	0.98	109.6	0.99
Sierra Leone	...	...	29.6*	0.52*	50.3	0.69	...	...	78.9[y]	0.70[y]
Somalia	...	...	...	...	...	...	...	...	...	...
South Africa	81.2	0.98	82.4*	0.96*	106.6	0.99	114.4*	0.97*	105.6	0.96
Swaziland	71.6	0.95	79.2*	0.97*	97.7	0.98	104.3	0.95	98.2	0.93
Togo	44.2	0.47	53.0*	0.56*	110.0	0.66	132.3	0.76	121.2	0.83
Uganda	56.1	0.63	68.9	0.75	68.7	0.80	143.3	0.90	140.7	0.98
United Republic of Tanzania	62.9	0.68	69.4*	0.80*	67.2	0.98	61.8	0.99	**90.8**	**0.96**
Zambia	68.2	0.75	67.9*	0.78*	93.7	0.91**	81.2	0.93	82.2	0.93
Zimbabwe	80.7	0.87	90.0	0.92	103.6	0.99	...	...	**92.9**	**0.98**

	Weighted average				Weighted average					
World	75.4	0.84	81.9	0.88	99.1	0.89	100.5	0.92	103.6	0.94
Countries in transition	99.2	0.99	99.4	0.99	97.0	0.99	100.5	0.99	105.6	0.99
Developed countries	98.0	0.99	98.7	0.99	101.9	0.99	102.1	1.00	100.6	1.00
Developing countries	67.0	0.76	76.4	0.83	98.8	0.87	100.3	0.91	103.9	0.93
Arab States	50.0	0.56	62.7	0.69	85.7	0.80	89.7	0.87	93.8	0.90
Central and Eastern Europe	96.2	0.97	97.4	0.97	98.0	0.98	97.3	0.96	99.5	0.97
Central Asia	98.7	0.99	99.2	0.99	89.4	0.99	98.9	0.99	101.6	0.98
East Asia and the Pacific	81.8	0.84	91.4	0.92	116.9	0.94	111.6	0.99	110.9	0.99
Latin America and the Caribbean	85.0	0.96	89.7	0.98	104.3	0.98	121.4	0.98	119.5	0.98
North America and Western Europe	97.9	0.99	[illegible]	[illegible]	104.0	0.99	102.5	1.01	100.8	1.00
South and West Asia	47.5	0.58	58.6	0.66	92.2	0.76	94.5	0.83	102.8	[illegible]
Sub-Saharan Africa	49.9	0.67	59.7	0.76	73.5	0.83	80.0	0.84	91.1	0.86

1. Data refer to the most recent year available during the period specified. See introduction to the Statistical annex for broader explanation of national literacy definitions, assessment methods, sources and years of data.

2. Literacy data for the most recent year do not include some geographic regions.

3. In countries where two or more education structures exist, indicators were calculated on the basis of the most common or widespread structure. In the Russian Federation this is three grades of primary education starting at age 7. However, a four-grade structure also exists, in which about one-third of primary pupils are enrolled. Gross enrolment ratios may be overestimated.

4. National population data were used to calculate enrolment ratios.

GOAL 5

Gender parity in secondary education

GROSS ENROLMENT RATIO

1990/1991 Total (%)	1990/1991 GPI (F/M)	1998/1999 Total (%)	1998/1999 GPI (F/M)	2002/2003 Total (%)	2002/2003 GPI (F/M)	Country or territory
20.9 *	…	…	…	69.7	1.09	Cape Verde
11.5	0.40	…	…	…	…	Central African Republic
7.0	0.20	10.7	0.26	14.5 **	0.33 **	Chad
17.6 *	0.65 *	24.8	0.81	31.0	0.83	Comoros
46.2	0.72	…	…	32.0 **,z	0.71 **,z	Congo
21.3	0.48	22.5 **	0.54 **	25.9 **,z	0.56 **,z	Côte d'Ivoire
…	…	18.4	0.52	…	…	Democratic Rep. of the Congo
…	…	31.0	0.61 **	29.7 **,z	0.57 **,z	Equatorial Guinea
…	…	23.3	0.69	28.1	0.65	Eritrea
13.5	0.75	12.9	0.67	**21.9**	**0.57**	Ethiopia
…	…	45.7	0.86	50.9 **,z	…	Gabon
18.4	0.49	31.4	0.64	34.1 **	0.69 **	Gambia
34.7	0.63	36.7	0.78	**42.4**	**0.81**	Ghana
9.5	0.33	13.9 **	0.36 **	24.1 **	0.46 **	Guinea
…	…	…	…	17.8 **,y	0.54 **,y	Guinea-Bissau
23.8	0.74	29.9 **	0.90 **	32.9	0.92 **	Kenya
25.4	1.47	31.7	1.39	34.7	1.28	Lesotho
…	…	30.5	0.65	…	…	Liberia
17.6	0.97	14.3 **	0.96 **	…	…	Madagascar
8.0	0.46	32.9	0.70 **	33.0 **	0.76 **	Malawi
6.6	0.51	13.6	0.53	19.5	0.55	Mali
52.9	1.01	70.8 **	1.00 **	81.2	1.00	Mauritius
6.9	0.57	9.8 **	0.68 **	15.9	0.66	Mozambique
38.9	1.26	57.3	1.15	62.4	1.12	Namibia
6.5	0.43	6.7	0.63	7.0	0.66	Niger
24.8	0.77	…	…	36.4	0.81	Nigeria
8.2	0.76	9.6	0.88	16.1	0.81	Rwanda
…	…	…	…	39.2 **,z	0.84 **,z	Sao Tome and Principe
16.3	0.53	16.7 **	0.64 **	19.4	0.69	Senegal
…	…	114.0	1.00	110.9	1.00	Seychelles[4]
16.6	0.57	…	…	26.4 y	0.70 **,y	Sierra Leone
…	…	…	…	…	…	Somalia
66.3	1.16	89.8 *	1.13 *	87.7 **	1.08 **	South Africa
41.3	0.93	48.4	1.00	45.3	1.01	Swaziland
22.7	0.34	33.6	0.40	…	…	Togo
12.5	0.56	9.8	0.64	19.7 **	0.80 **	Uganda
4.7	0.70	5.5 **	0.82 **	…	…	United Republic of Tanzania
19.6	…	19.8	0.77 **	27.9	0.83	Zambia
46.9	0.87	…	…	**36.3**	**0.91**	Zimbabwe

Median		Weighted average				
56.3	1.07	59.7	0.90	65.2	0.94	World
95.1	…	88.9	1.01	92.8	0.98	Countries in transition
91.7	…	103.4	1.01	106.6	1.03	Developed countries
39.7	…	51.8	0.86	58.3	0.92	Developing countries
48.8	0.73	59.9	0.88	65.0	0.91	Arab States
86.3	1.03	85.4	0.98	92.3	0.95	Central and Eastern Europe
97.5	1.04	85.7	0.97	89.0	0.97	Central Asia
52.5	0.91	64.4	0.93	71.0	0.98	East Asia and the Pacific
53.3	1.01	71.7	1.09	88.2	1.08	Latin America and the Caribbean
98.5	1.05	105.3	1.01	108.2	1.04	North America and Western Europe
33.1	0.44	45.6	0.74	49.9	0.84	South and West Asia
17.6	0.81	24.5	0.80	28.4	0.78	Sub-Saharan Africa

5. Children enter primary school at age 6 or 7. Since 7 is the most common entrance age, enrolment ratios were calculated using the 7-11 age group for both enrolments and population.
6. Enrolment ratios were not calculated due to lack of United Nations population data by age.
7. Enrolment ratios were not calculated due to inconsistencies between enrolment and the United Nations population data.
8. Literacy rates for the most recent year were derived from the absolute numbers of illiterates and literates provided to the UIS through its literacy questionnaire.

Data in bold are for 2003/2004.
(y) Data are for 2000/2001.
(z) Data are for 2001/2002.

Table 14
Trends in basic or proxy indicators to measure EFA goal 6

		GOAL 6. Educational quality in primary education														
		SCHOOL LIFE EXPECTANCY (expected number of years of formal schooling)									SURVIVAL RATE TO GRADE 5					
		1990/1991			1998/1999			2002/2003			1990/1991		1998/1999		2001/2002	
	Country or territory	Total	Male	Female	Total	Male	Female	Total	Male	Female	Total (%)	GPI (F/M)	Total (%)	GPI (F/M)	Total (%)	GPI (F/M)
	Arab States															
1	Algeria	10.3	...	...	...	...	...	12.4**	...	...	94.5	0.99	95.0	1.02	97.0	1.01
2	Bahrain	13.5	13.2	13.7	12.8**	12.3**	13.4**	13.5**	12.9**	14.2**	89.2	1.01	97.4**	1.01**	99.1**	1.02**
3	Djibouti	...	...	...	3.5**	...	...	**4.4****	**5.1****	**3.8****	87.3	...	76.7	1.19	80.2**	...
4	Egypt	9.7	10.8	8.5	12.4**	...	...	11.6**	...	...	...	...	...	...	98.0**	1.04**
5	Iraq	...	...	...	8.9**	10.1**	7.5**	...	...	...	...	...	65.6**	0.94**	...	...
6	Jordan	12.5	12.4	12.7	...	...	...	12.8**	12.7**	13.0**	99.1	1.02	97.7	0.99	97.1	1.01
7	Kuwait	...	...	...	13.5**	12.9**	14.3**	...	...	...	...	...	...	...	...	...
8	Lebanon	...	...	...	12.6**	12.4**	12.7**	13.2**	12.9**	13.5**	...	...	91.3	1.07	91.9	1.05
9	Libyan Arab Jamahiriya	13.0	...	...	...	...	...	16.4**	15.9**	17.0**	...	...	...	...	...	...
10	Mauritania	4.1	5.0	3.2	6.9**	...	...	7.1**	7.4**	6.7**	75.3	0.99	65.2**	0.92**	60.6	0.99
11	Morocco	6.6	7.8	5.4	8.2**	9.1**	7.3**	9.9**	10.5**	9.2**	75.1	1.02	81.9	1.00	81.2	0.98
12	Oman	8.2	8.8	7.7	...	...	...	10.4**,z	10.5**,z	10.4**,z	96.9	0.99	93.7	1.00	98.0	1.00
13	Palestinian A. T.	...	...	...	11.9	11.7	11.9	12.9	12.4	13.1	...	...	...	...	...	...
14	Qatar	12.3	11.8	13.2	13.3**	12.6**	14.3**	13.1**	12.6**	13.7**	64.1	1.02	...	...	...	...
15	Saudi Arabia	7.8	8.4	7.2	9.7**	9.8**	9.5**	9.6**	9.7**	9.5**	82.9	1.03	95.3	1.00	91.5	0.98
16	Sudan	4.4	5.0	3.9	5.1**	...	...	...	...	...	93.8	1.09	84.1**	1.10**	84.3	1.09
17	Syrian Arab Republic	10.0	10.9	8.9	...	...	...	...	...	...	96.0	0.98	91.8	0.99	91.4	1.02
18	Tunisia	10.4	11.3	9.5	12.7**	12.8**	12.5**	13.3**	13.0**	13.6**	86.6	0.83	92.1	1.02	96.2	1.01
19	United Arab Emirates	11.0	10.6	11.7	11.2**	10.7**	12.1**	12.1**	11.4**	13.1**	80.0	0.99	92.4	0.99	92.5	1.00
20	Yemen	...	...	...	7.8**	10.6**	4.9**	...	...	...	...	...	...		75.9	0.89
	Central and Eastern Europe															
21	Albania	11.5	11.7	11.3	...	...	...	11.4	11.2	11.6	...	...	...	...	...	...
22	Belarus	13.1	...	...	13.8**	13.6**	14.0**	14.2	13.7	14.6	...	...	...	...	...	...
23	Bosnia and Herzegovina	...	...	...	...	...	...	...	...	...	...	...	...	...	...	...
24	Bulgaria	12.3	12.3	12.3	12.7	12.2	13.1	12.8	12.7	12.8	90.6	0.99	...	...	...	...
25	Croatia	10.2	...	...	12.5	12.2	12.6	13.1	12.8	13.3	...	...	...	...	...	...
26	Czech Republic	11.9	12.1	11.7	...	...	...	14.9	14.6	15.1	...	...	98.3	1.01	97.7	1.01
27	Estonia	12.8	12.6	13.0	13.9	13.2	14.6	15.8	14.4	16.7	...	...	99.1	1.01	98.4	1.02
28	Hungary	11.4	11.4	11.4	14.0**	13.8**	14.3**	15.6	14.9	16.1	97.6	...	...	...	...	...
29	Latvia	12.4	12.2	12.5	13.7	12.8	14.4	15.2	13.8	16.1	...	...	...	...	...	...
30	Lithuania	...	...	...	...	...	...	15.8	14.9	16.5	...	...	...	...	...	...
31	Poland	12.2	12.0	12.4	...	...	...	15.6	14.9	16.1	97.8	...	98.6	...	99.3	...
32	Republic of Moldova	11.9	...	...	9.9**	9.7**	10.1**	10.1	9.8	10.4	...	...	...	...	...	...
33	Romania	11.5	11.5	11.4	11.8	11.6	12.0	12.7	12.3	13.0	...	...	...	...	...	...
34	Russian Federation	12.5	12.0	13.0	...	...	...	13.5**	...	...	...	...	...	...	...	...
35	Serbia and Montenegro	...	...	...	13.3	13.2	13.4	12.9**,y	12.7**,y	13.1**,y	...	...	...	...	...	...
36	Slovakia	...	...	...	13.1**	13.0**	13.3**	14.0	13.7	14.1	...	...	...	...	...	...
37	Slovenia	...	...	...	14.3**	13.6**	14.8**	16.3**	15.5**	16.8**	...	...	...	...	...	...
38	TFYR Macedonia	11.0	11.0	11.0	11.9	11.9	11.9	11.2**	11.0**	11.5**	...	...	...	...	...	...
39	Turkey	8.5	9.5	7.4	...	...	...	10.9**	11.8**	9.9**	97.6	0.99	...	...	...	...
40	Ukraine	12.3	...	...	...	...	...	13.4	13.0*	13.7*	97.7	...	...	...	...	...
	Central Asia															
41	Armenia	...	...	...	...	...	...	10.9	10.5	11.2	...	...	...	...	...	...
42	Azerbaijan	10.5	10.8	10.3	10.0	10.1	9.9	10.6	10.7	10.4	...	...	...	...	...	...
43	Georgia	12.4	12.3	12.4	10.8**	10.6**	10.9**	11.3**	11.2**	11.3**	...	...	...	...	...	...
44	Kazakhstan	12.4	...	...	11.5	11.3	11.7	13.5**	13.1**	13.9**	...	...	...	...	...	...
45	Kyrgyzstan	10.4	...	...	11.6	11.3	11.8	12.8	12.5	13.1	...	...	...	...	...	...
46	Mongolia	9.4	8.8	10.0	8.7**	7.8**	9.6**	11.0	10.0	11.9	...	...	...	...	...	...
47	Tajikistan	11.7	...	...	9.9	[illegible]	[illegible]	11.3	12.2	10.2	...	...	...	...	...	...
48	Turkmenistan	...	...	...	...	...	...	...	...	...	...				...	...
49	Uzbekistan	11.6	...	...	...	...	...	11.6**	11.8**	11.4**	...	...	...	...	...	...
	East Asia and the Pacific															
50	Australia	13.2	13.0	13.4	10.6**	19.0**	19.9**	20.6	19.4	20.8	...	...	...	...	...	...
51	Brunei Darussalam	...	...	...	13.1**	12.7**	13.4**	13.4**	13.1**	13.8**		...	...	...	93.0y	1.01y
52	Cambodia	7.0	...	...	...	...	...	9.1**	9.9**	8.3**	...	...	56.3**	0.93**	60.9	1.05

GOAL 6. Educational quality in primary education

PUPIL/TEACHER RATIO			% FEMALE TEACHERS			TRAINED TEACHERS as % of total		PUBLIC CURRENT EXPENDITURE ON PRIMARY EDUCATION AS % GNP			PUBLIC CURRENT EXPENDITURE ON PRIMARY EDUCATION PER PUPIL (unit cost) in constant 2002 US$			PUBLIC CURRENT EXPENDITURE ON PRIMARY EDUCATION PER PUPIL (unit cost) at PPP in constant 2002 US$			
1990/1991	1998/1999	2002/2003	1990/1991	1998/1999	2002/2003	1998/1999	2002/2003	1990	1998	2002	1990	1998	2002	1990	1998	2002	
																Arab States	
28	28	28	39	46	49	94	98	...	...	...	...	...	...	...	...	...	1
19	...	16**,z	54	...	76**,z	...	...	...	...	2.1**	...	...	1 731**	...	...	2 701**	2
43	40	34**,z	37	28	30**,z	...	...	2.0	...	...	411	...	...	...	...	...	3
24	23**	22**	52	52**	54**	...	100**,y	...	...	...	...	...	...	...	...	...	4
25	25	19	70	72	...	...	...	...	...	...	...	...	...	...	...	...	5
25	...	20**	62	...	64**	...	...	...	1.9	2.0	...	216	239	...	477	561	6
18	13	13	61	73	83	100	100	1.5	...	...	...	...	...	...	...	...	7
...	14	17	...	82	87	...	14	...	...	...	...	...	...	...	...	...	8
14	...	...	...	...	...	...	...	...	...	...	...	...	...	...	...	...	9
45	47	41	18	26	25**	...	...	1.3	...	...	50	...	...	111	...	...	10
27	28	28	37	39	44	...	...	...	2.3	2.5	...	210	217	...	561	679	11
28	25	21**	47	52	57**	100	100**,z	1.7	1.5	1.5**	677	800	880**	988	1 572	1 466**	12
...	...	36	...	...	62	...	...	...	...	...	...	...	...	...	...	...	13
11	13	12	72	75	83	...	...	...	...	...	...	...	...	...	...	...	14
16	12	12	48	54	51	...	93y	...	...	...	...	...	...	...	...	...	15
34	...	29**	51	...	62**	...	...	...	...	...	...	...	...	...	...	...	16
25	25**	24**,z	64	68**	68**,z	...	88y	...	...	2.1	...	...	131	...	...	388	17
28	24	22	45	50	50	...	94**,y	...	...	2.2**	...	...	346**	...	...	1 088**	18
18	16	15	64	73	80	...	...	...	...	...	...	...	1 532	...	...	...	19
...	30**	...	...	21**	...	...	...	...	...	...	...	...	...	...	...	...	20
																Central and Eastern Europe	
19	23**	21	55	75**	76	...	...	...	...	...	...	...	...	...	...	...	21
...	20	16	...	99	99	...	98	1.6	...	...	...	...	...	...	...	...	22
...	...	...	...	...	...	...	...	...	...	...	...	...	...	...	...	...	23
15	18	17	77	91**	92	...	...	2.6	0.7	0.7**,z	...	223	305**,z	...	796	1 213**,z	24
19	19	18	75	89	90	100	100	...	...	0.9**	...	...	1 054**	...	...	2 148**	25
23	18	17	...	85**	84	...	...	...	0.6	0.7	...	623	814	...	1 452	1 887	26
...	16	14**,z	...	...	...	...	...	...	1.4	1.4	...	605	935	...	1 440	2 390	27
13	11	10	84	85	84	...	...	2.3	0.9**	1.0	1 110	932**	1 287	3 146	2 173**	2 660	28
15	15	14	...	97	97	...	...	...	...	1.1**,y	...	...	677**,y	...	...	1 705**,y	29
18	17	16	94	98	98	...	...	...	...	...	...	...	...	...	...	...	30
16	...	11**	...	...	...	...	...	1.8	...	1.8	435	...	1 121	1 682	...	2 418	31
23	21	19	97	96	96	...	...	...	...	0.8**	...	...	65**	...	...	251**	32
22	19**	17	84	85**	87	...	...	1.2	...	0.5**	501	...	211**	1 616	...	673**	33
22	18**	17	99	98**	97**	...	...	...	...	...	...	...	...	...	...	...	34
...	20**	20y	...	82**	82y	100**	100y	...	...	...	...	733	...	...	...	...	35
...	19	18	...	93	92	...	...	...	...	0.6	...	...	520	...	...	1 515	36
...	14	13	...	96	96	...	...	...	...	...	...	...	...	...	...	...	37
21	22	20	...	66	69	...	...	...	...	...	...	...		...	...		38
30	...	...	43	...	...	...	...	1.1	...	1.4**,z	212	...	286**,z	336	...	800**,z	39
22	20	19	98	98	99	...	100	...	0.5**	...	...	77**	...	...	337**	...	40
																Central Asia	
...	...	18	...	...	99	...	...	...	...	0.2**,z	...	...	36**,z	...	...	143**,z	41
...	19	15	...	83	85	100	100	...	...	0.6**	...	...	54**	...	...	235**	42
17	17	14	92	92	95	...	97	...	...	...	...	...	...	...	...	...	43
21	...	19	96	...	98	...	...	...	...	...	...	...	...	...	...	...	44
...	24	24	81	95	97	48	52	...	0.9**	...	...	...	...	...	...	...	45
28	32	31	90	93	93	...	93y	...	...	3.2	...	...	157	...	...	586	46
21	22	22	49	56	62	...	82	...	...	...	...	...	...	...	...	...	47
...	...	...	...	...	...	...	...	...	...	...	...	...	...	...	...	...	48
24	...	...	79	...	...	...	...	...	...	...	...	...	...	...	...	...	49
																East Asia and the Pacific	
...	18	...	...	...	...	...	...	...	1.5**	1.6	...	2 844**	3 346	...	3 513**	4 542	50
...	14*	13**	...	66*	71**	...	...	0.5	...	...	...	...	...	...	...	...	51
33	48**	56	31	37**	40	...	96z	...	0.5	1.3z	...	7	18z	...	37	115z	52

Table 14 (continued)

GOAL 6. Educational quality in primary education

	Country or territory	SCHOOL LIFE EXPECTANCY (expected number of years of formal schooling)									SURVIVAL RATE TO GRADE 5					
		1990/1991			1998/1999			2002/2003			1990/1991		1998/1999		2001/2002	
		Total	Male	Female	Total	Male	Female	Total	Male	Female	Total (%)	GPI (F/M)	Total (%)	GPI (F/M)	Total (%)	GPI (F/M)
53	China	9.3	10.0	8.6	…	…	…	10.8**	10.9**	10.6**	86.0	…	97.3	1.00	99.0	0.98
54	Cook Islands	…	…	…	…	…	…	…	…	…	…	…	51.5	0.84	…	…
55	DPR Korea	…	…	…	…	…	…	…	…	…	…	…	…	…	…	…
56	Fiji	…	…	…	…	…	…	…	…	…	…	…	92.0**	1.04**	88.5**[y]	1.08**[y]
57	Indonesia	10.1	…	…	…	…	…	11.1	11.3	11.0	83.6	…	…	…	89.1	1.02
58	Japan	13.4	13.7	13.1	14.3**	14.5**	14.2**	14.7**	14.8**	14.5**	100.0	1.00	…	…	…	…
59	Kiribati	…	…	…	…	…	…	…	…	…	93.4	1.14	…	…	…	…
60	Lao PDR	…	…	…	8.4**	9.4	7.4**	9.1**	10.1**	8.1**	…	…	54.3	0.98	64.1	1.02
61	Macao, China	11.5	12.0	11.1	12.1**	12.3**	11.9**	15.1	13.9	14.0	…	…	…	…	99.7	1.01
62	Malaysia	9.9	9.8	10.0	12.0**	11.7**	12.2**	12.3	11.8	12.8	98.2	1.00	…	…	87.1	1.00
63	Marshall Islands	…	…	…	…	…	…	…	…	…	…	…	…	…	…	…
64	Micronesia (Fed. States of)	…	…	…	…	…	…	…	…	…	…	…	…	…	…	…
65	Myanmar	6.9	…	…	…	…	…	7.4**[z]	…	…	…	…	…	…	64.6	1.03
66	Nauru	…	…	…	8.1**	…	…	…	…	…	…	…	…	…	…	…
67	New Zealand	14.6	14.5	14.7	17.5**	17.0**	17.9**	18.9	…	…	92.2	1.02	…	…	…	…
68	Niue	…	…	…	12.3	…	…	12.8[z]	13.3[z]	12.4[z]	…	…	75.8	…	…	…
69	Palau	…	…	…	…	…	…	15.0**[y]	14.5**[y]	15.6**[y]	…	…	84.2	0.82	…	…
70	Papua New Guinea	…	…	…	5.7**	6.1**	5.3**	…	…	…	59.1	0.98	68.0	1.01	50.6[y]	0.96[y]
71	Philippines	10.8	10.6	11.1	11.7**	11.4**	11.9**	12.0**	11.7**	12.3**	…	…	…	…	76.0	1.11
72	Republic of Korea	13.7	14.4	12.9	14.9**	15.7**	14.0**	**16.9**	**17.5**	**15.9**	99.5	1.00	99.9	1.00	**99.9**	**1.00**
73	Samoa	…	…	…	11.7**	11.5**	12.0**	11.8**[z]	11.6**[z]	12.0**[z]	…	…	82.6	…	93.8[y]	0.95[y]
74	Singapore	11.9	12.3	11.5	…	…	…	…	…	…	…	…	…	…	…	…
75	Solomon Islands	…	…	…	…	…	…	8.7	…	…	84.9	…	…	…	…	…
76	Thailand	…	…	…	…	…	…	12.5**[y]	12.7**[y]	12.3**[y]	…	…	94.1**	1.04**	…	…
77	Timor-Leste	…	…	…	…	…	…	11.4**[z]	…	…	…	…	…	…	…	…
78	Tokelau	…	…	…	…	…	…	…	…	…	…	…	…	…	…	…
79	Tonga	…	…	…	…	…	…	13.5**[z]	13.3**[z]	13.7**[z]	89.6	0.89	…	…	…	…
80	Tuvalu	…	…	…	10.9**	…	…	10.8[z]	10.6[z]	11.1[z]	…	…	…	…	…	…
81	Vanuatu	…	…	…	…	…	…	9.4**[z]	…	…	…	…	95.3**	… **	72.1[x]	0.99[x]
82	Viet Nam	7.5	…	…	10.4**	10.9**	9.8**	10.6**	11.0**	10.1**	…	…	82.8	1.08	87.1**	0.99**
	Latin America and the Caribbean															
83	Anguilla	…	…	…	…	…	…	12.5[z]	…	…	…	…	…	…	…	…
84	Antigua and Barbuda	…	…	…	…	…	…	…	…	…	…	…	…	…	…	…
85	Argentina	…	…	…	14.9**	14.3**	15.6**	16.4	15.2	17.2	…	…	94.7	1.03	92.2	1.02
86	Aruba	…	…	…	13.3**	13.2**	13.4**	13.5[z]	13.2[z]	13.7[z]	…	…	96.8	0.99	95.0	1.02
87	Bahamas	…	…	…	…	…	…	…	…	…	…	…	…	…	75.2**	… **
88	Barbados	…	…	…	15.0**	14.4**	15.6**	14.3**[y]	13.6**[y]	15.1**[y]	…	…	94.1	0.95	98.8	0.98
89	Belize	…	…	…	…	…	…	12.5**	12.4**	12.7**	67.4	0.96	77.8	1.04	81.5[x]	1.00[x]
90	Bermuda	…	…	…	…	…	…	15.3**[z]	…	…	…	…	…	…	96.3[y]	…[y]
91	Bolivia	10.1	…	…	12.8**	13.5**	12.1**	14.2**	…	…	…	…	79.4	0.97	84.4	0.98
92	Brazil	10.3	…	…	…	…	…	14.7	14.1	15.0	…	…	…	…	…	…
93	British Virgin Islands	…	…	…	15.8**	…	…	14.7**	13.7**	15.8**	…	…	…	…	…	…
94	Cayman Islands	…	…	…	…	…	…	…	…	…	…	…	…	…	…	…
95	Chile	…	…	…	12.7**	12.8**	12.6**	**15.0****	**15.2****	**14.9****	…	…	99.8	1.00	**99.2**	**0.98**
96	Colombia	8.8	8.3	9.4	11.1**	10.9**	11.3**	11.0**	10.8**	11.3**	62.1	0.63	63.4	1.28	69.4	1.10
97	Costa Rica	9.7	…	…	10.1**	9.9**	10.3**	10.7**	10.6**	10.9**	82.4	1.04	…	…	91.6	1.03
98	Cuba	12.4	11.9	12.9	12.1**	…	…	13.3**	13.1**	13.4**	91.6	…	93.7	1.00	97.9	1.00
99	Dominica	…	…	…	11.8**	…	…	13.1**	12.6**	13.6**	…	…	…	…	83.7	1.09
100	Dominican Republic	…	…	…	…	…	…	12.7**	11.9**	13.6**	…	…	75.1**	1.11**	69.1**	**
101	Ecuador	11.4	…	…	…	…	…	…	…	…	…	…	77.0	1.01	74.4	1.02
102	El Salvador	[illegible]	[illegible]	8.9	10.7**	10.8**	10.6**	11.3**	11.4**	11.1**	…	…	61.3**	1.03**	68.9	1.06
103	Grenada	…	…	…	…	…	…	[illegible]			[illegible]	…	…	…	79.0	1.17
104	Guatemala	…	…	…	…	…	…	9.1**	9.5**	8.7**	…	…	60.4**	[illegible]	[illegible]	[illegible]
105	Guyana	…	…	…	…	…	…	…	…	…	93.1	0.99	97.4	…	77.2[x]	1.18[x]
106	Haiti	…	…	…	…	…	…	…	…	…	…	…	…	…	…	…
107	Honduras	…	…	…	…	…	…	…	…	…	…	…	…	…	…	…
108	Jamaica	11.0	11.0	11.1	…	…		11.8**	11.3**	12.3**	…	…	…	…	89.7	…
109	Mexico	10.8	11.0	10.6	11.8**	11.8**	11.7**	12.6	12.3	12.7	79.5	…	[illegible]	[illegible]	[illegible]	[illegible]
110	Montserrat	…	…	…	…	…	…	13.6[z]	…	…	…	…	…	…	…	…

GOAL 6. Educational quality in primary education

PUPIL/TEACHER RATIO			% FEMALE TEACHERS			TRAINED TEACHERS as % of total		PUBLIC CURRENT EXPENDITURE ON PRIMARY EDUCATION AS % GNP			PUBLIC CURRENT EXPENDITURE ON PRIMARY EDUCATION PER PUPIL (unit cost) in constant 2002 US$			PUBLIC CURRENT EXPENDITURE ON PRIMARY EDUCATION PER PUPIL (unit cost) at PPP in constant 2002 US$			
1990/ 1991	1998/ 1999	2002/ 2003	1990/ 1991	1998/ 1999	2002/ 2003	1998/ 1999	2002/ 2003	1990	1998	2002	1990	1998	2002	1990	1998	2002	
22	…	21	43	50 **	53	…	97 **,z	…	…	…	…	…	…	…	…	…	53
…	19	18 **,y	…	…	86 **,y	…	…	…	0.2	…	…	…	…	…	…	…	54
…	…	…	…	…	…	…	…	…	…	…	…	…	…	…	…	…	55
34	23 **	28 **,z	…	57 **	57 **,z	97 **	97 **,y	…	…	…	…	…	…	…	…	…	56
23	…	20	51	…	54	…	94 **,y	…	…	0.4	…	…	25	…	…	98	57
21	21	20	58	…	65 **	…	…	…	…	1.1 **,y	…	…	5 962 **,y	…	…	4 124 **,y	58
29	24	22	57	64	71	…	…	…	…	…	…	…	…	…	…	…	59
27	31	31	38	43	44	76	78	…	…	0.7 z	…	…	13 z	…	…	68 z	60
…	31	26	…	87	89	81	90	…	…	…	…	…	…	…	…	…	61
20	22	19	57	63	68	97 **	…	…	1.4 **	1.6	…	366 **	479	…	858 **	1 119	62
…	15	17 z	…	…	34 z	…	…	…	…	4.0 z	…	…	539 z	…	…	…	63
…	…	…	…	…	…	…	…	…	…	…	…	…	…	…	…	…	64
48	31	33	62	73	77	60	65	…	…	…	…	…	…	…	…	…	65
…	23 **	…	…	82 **	…	…	…	…	…	…	…	…	…	…	…	…	66
18	19	18	79	88	87 **	…	…	1.7	1.8 **	1.8	1 985	2 413 **	2 779	2 092	3 014 **	4 062	67
…	24	15	…	100	…	…	100 z	…	…	…	…	…	…	…	…	…	68
…	15	…	…	82	…	…	…	…	…	…	…	…	…	…	…	…	69
32	36	35 z	32	38	39 z	100	100 z	…	…	…	…	…	…	…	…	…	70
33	35	35	…	87	89	100 **	…	…	2.2	1.6	…	121	105	…	496	449	71
36	31	**30**	50	64	**73**	…	…	1.4	…	1.2	669		1 523	840		2 580	72
24	25 **	27 **	64	73 **	54 **	…	91 y	…	…	1.8 y	…	…	159 y	…	…	596 y	73
26	…	…	…	…	…	…	…	…	…	…	…	…	…	…	…	…	74
19	…	…	…	…	…	…	…	…	…	…	…	…	…	…	…	…	75
22	21	21 **	…	63	58 **	…	…	1.7	…	1.7 **,y	182	…	312 **,y	430	…	985 **,y	76
…	…	51 z	…	…	30 z	…	…	…	…	…	…	…	…	…	…	…	77
…	…	…	…	…	…	…	…	…	…	…	…	…	…	…	…	…	78
24	22	22	69	70	70	87	100 z	…	…	2.2 z	…	…	171 z	…	…	807 z	79
21	…	25 z	72	…	84 z	…	…	…	…	…	…	…	…	…	…	…	80
27	22 **	29 z	40	44 **	58 z	…	100 z	…	…	2.8 z	…	…	176 z	…	…	472 z	81
35	30	25	…	78	78	78	87 z	…	…	…	…	…	…	…	…	…	82
Latin America and the Caribbean																	
…	22	16	…	87	91	76	62	…	…	…	…	…	…	…	…	…	83
…	…	…	…	…	…	…	…	…	…	1.1	…	…	…	…	…	…	84
…	21	17	…	89	86	…	67 **,y	…	1.4	1.5 **	5	364	290 **	9	551	1 173 **	85
…	19	18	…	78	92	100	100	…	…	…	…	…	2 467	…	…	…	86
…	…	17 **	…	…	93 **	…	95 z	…	…	…	…	…	…	…	…	…	87
18	20 **	16 **	72	75 **	77 **	84 **	78 **	…	1.2 **	1.8 **	…	1 031 **	1 955 **	…	1 630 **	3 173 **	88
26	24 **	21	70	64 **	69	…	41 **	2.7	…	2.8	290	…	513	469	…	936	89
…	…	9 z	…	…	88 z	…	100 z	1.1	…	…	…	…	…	…	…	…	90
25	…	24 **	57	…	62 **	…	74 **,y	…	2.0 **	2.8	…	102 **	138	…	224 **	383	91
23	…	25 **	…	…	90 **	…	92 **,y	…	1.6	1.2 z	…	…	256 z	…	…	663 z	92
19	18	14	…	86	89	72	79	…	…	…	…	…	…	…	…	…	93
…	15	15 z	…	89	81 z	…	99 z	…	…	…	…	…	…	…	…	…	94
29	33	**34**	75	78	**77**	…	92 **,y	1.4	1.5	**1.6**	208	486	608	425	864	1 452	95
30	23	27	…	77 **	77	…	…	…	…	1.8 **	…	…	263 **	…	…	906 **	96
32	28	23	…	81	80	…	88	…	…	2.2	…	…	656	…	…	1 357	97
13	12	11	79	79	78	100	100	1.5	…	2.9 **,y	…	…	…	…	…	…	98
29	20	19	81	77	84	64	60	…	3.0 *	…	…	633 *	…	…	935 *	…	99
…	39 **	39 **,z	…	75 **	82 **,z	…	58 **,z	…	…	1.1 **,z	…	…	…	…	…	…	100
30	27	24	…	68	69	…	70	…	…	…	…	…	…	…	…	…	101
…	…	…	…	…	…	…	…	…	1.3 **	1.5 **	…	182 **	210 **	…	402 **	462 **	102
…	…	19	…	…	78	…	68	…	…	1.7 **	…	…	393 **	…	…	705 **	103
…	36 *	30	…	…	…	…	100 z	0.4	…	1.3 z	46	…	147 z	148	…	330 z	104
30	27	26 **,z	76	86	85 **,z	52	53 y	…	…	3.2	…	…	194	…	…	884	105
23	…	…	45	…	…	…	…	0.8	…	…	57	…	…	244	…	…	106
…	…	34 **,z	74	…	…	…	…	…	…	…	…	…	…	…	…	…	107
34	…	30	…	…	90	…	80 **,y	1.6	…	1.7	295	…	413	482	…	547	108
31	27	27	…	66 **	…	…	…	0.6	1.5 **	2.1	189	554 **	882	365	1 011 **	1 252	109
…	21	19 **	…	84	92 **	…	91 z	…	…	…	…	…	…	…	…	…	110

Table 14 (continued)

GOAL 6. Educational quality in primary education

	Country or territory	SCHOOL LIFE EXPECTANCY (expected number of years of formal schooling)									SURVIVAL RATE TO GRADE 5					
		1990/1991			1998/1999			2002/2003			1990/1991		1998/1999		2001/2002	
		Total	Male	Female	Total	Male	Female	Total	Male	Female	Total (%)	GPI (F/M)	Total (%)	GPI (F/M)	Total (%)	GPI (F/M)
111	Netherlands Antilles	…	…	…	12.3**	12.0**	12.6**	11.5z	11.0z	11.9z	…	…	…	…	88.5y	…
112	Nicaragua	8.3	7.7	8.8	…	…	…	10.5**	10.3**	10.8**	45.6	…	…	…	64.8	1.08
113	Panama	11.2	…	…	…	…	…	13.2**	12.6**	13.8**	…	…	…	…	89.8	1.02
114	Paraguay	8.6	8.7	8.5	…	…	…	12.1**	12.0**	12.3**	70.5	1.04	70.0**	1.03**	69.7**	1.04**
115	Peru	12.2	…	…	…	…	…	13.8**	13.8**	13.8**	…	…	87.9	0.99	83.6	0.98
116	Saint Kitts and Nevis	…	…	…	…	…	…	15.9**,y	…	…	…	…	…	…	78.4y	1.12y
117	Saint Lucia	12.9	12.6	13.1	…	…	…	…	…	…	…	…	90.1**	…**	96.6y	…
118	Saint Vincent/Grenad.	…	…	…	…	…	…	…	…	…	…	…	…	…	88.0	…
119	Suriname	…	…	…	…	…	…	12.5**,z	11.6**,z	13.4**,z	…	…	…	…	…	…
120	Trinidad and Tobago	11.1	11.1	11.2	11.8**	11.5**	12.0**	11.8**	11.6**	12.1**	97.9	1.04	100.0	…	71.2**,y	1.15**,y
121	Turks and Caicos Islands	…	…	…	…	…	…	12.8**,z	12.2**,z	13.3**,z	…	…	…	…	45.9	1.23
122	Uruguay	12.9	…	…	…	…	…	14.9**	14.0**	15.8**	94.5	1.03	88.3	1.06	92.9	1.04
123	Venezuela	10.8	…	…	…	…	…	11.8**	11.5**	12.0**	86.1	1.09	90.8	1.08	84.2	1.07
	North America and Western Europe															
124	Andorra	…	…	…	…	…	…	…	…	…	…	…	…	…	…	…
125	Austria	13.8	14.2	13.4	15.2**	15.2**	15.1**	14.9	14.5	15.1	…	…	…	…	…	…
126	Belgium	14.0	14.0	14.1	17.8**	17.4**	18.2**	19.2	18.3	19.9	…	…	…	…	…	…
127	Canada	16.9	16.4	17.3	16.0**	15.7**	16.3**	16.0**,z	15.7**,z	16.4**,z	…	…	…	…	…	…
128	Cyprus	10.3	10.3	10.4	12.5	12.3	12.7	13.4	13.3	13.5	99.9	…	96.1	1.03	99.3	1.01
129	Denmark	14.3	14.1	14.5	16.1**	15.6**	16.6**	16.9	15.8	17.6	94.2	1.00	100.0	1.00	…	…
130	Finland	15.2	14.5	16.0	17.5**	16.7**	18.2**	18.3	16.8	19.1	99.8	1.00	99.8	1.00	99.9	1.00
131	France	14.3	14.0	14.6	15.6**	15.3**	15.8**	15.6	15.1	15.9	96.4	…	98.0	0.99	…	…
132	Germany	14.5	…	…	16.0**	16.2**	15.8**	15.8	15.5	15.7	…	…	…	…	…	…
133	Greece	13.4	13.5	13.3	14.2**	14.0**	14.4**	15.8	15.5	16.0	99.7	1.00	…	…	…	…
134	Iceland	15.3	15.3	15.3	16.7**	16.0**	17.3**	18.3	16.6	19.4	…	…	99.8	1.00	99.7	0.99
135	Ireland	12.7	12.6	12.8	16.3**	15.6**	16.7**	17.0	16.1	17.7	99.5	1.01	95.1	1.03	99.2	1.02
136	Israel	13.2	12.9	13.4	14.8**	14.4**	15.2**	15.6	14.7	16.0	…	…	…	…	85.2**	0.99**
137	Italy	13.4	13.5	13.4	14.7**	14.5**	14.9**	15.6	15.1**	16.0**	99.6	1.01	96.6	…	96.5y	1.01y
138	Luxembourg	…	…	…	…	…	…	13.5**	13.3**	13.7**	…	…	…	…	99.0**,y	1.00**,y
139	Malta	12.9	13.2	12.5	…	…	…	14.5	14.1	14.6	99.3	1.01	99.4	0.99	99.3	1.01
140	Monaco	…	…	…	…	…	…	…	…	…	82.9	0.81	…	…	…	…
141	Netherlands	15.2	15.6	14.9	16.5**	16.7**	16.2**	16.6	16.4	16.6	…	…	99.9	1.00	99.8	1.00
142	Norway	14.4	14.1	14.7	17.5**	16.9**	18.0**	17.8	16.4	18.5	99.6	1.01	…	…	99.5	0.99
143	Portugal	12.5	12.2	12.7	15.8**	15.4**	16.1**	16.1	15.3	16.6	…	…	…	…	…	…
144	San Marino	…	…	…	…	…	…	…	…	…	88.1	1.27	…	…	…	…
145	Spain	14.6	14.3	14.8	15.7**	15.4**	16.0**	16.2	15.5	16.6	…	…	…	…	…	…
146	Sweden	13.1	12.8	13.4	19.0**	17.3**	20.8**	19.1	16.8	20.7	99.8	1.00	…	…	…	…
147	Switzerland	13.8	14.2	13.3	15.5**	16.0**	15.0**	15.9	15.8	15.6	79.7	0.98	…	…	…	…
148	United Kingdom	14.2	14.4	14.0	20.0**	19.3**	20.7**	22.0	19.8	23.5	…	…	…	…	…	…
149	United States	15.3	14.9	15.7	…	…	…	15.7**	14.4**	16.3**	…	…	…	…	…	…
	South and West Asia															
150	Afghanistan	2.5	…	…	…	…	…	…	…	…	…	…	…	…	…	…
151	Bangladesh	5.6	6.4	4.7	8.5**	8.7**	8.2**	8.4	8.2	8.5	…	…	54.7	1.20	53.9	1.20
152	Bhutan	…	…	…	…	…	…	…	…	…	…	…	87.5	1.03	91.0y	1.05y
153	India	8.1	9.6	6.6	…	…	…	9.7**	10.3**	8.9**	…	…	62.0	0.95	61.4y	…
154	Iran, Islamic Republic of	9.7	10.7	8.6	11.6**	12.2**	10.9**	11.6**	12.1**	11.1**	89.9	0.98	…	…	94.6**	…**
155	Maldives	…	…	…	11.6	…	…	11.9	11.8	12.1	…	…	…	…	…	…
156	Nepal	7.7	9.8	5.5	…	…	…	9.7**	10.6**	8.8**	…	…	…	…	64.9	1.06
157	Pakistan	4.7	6.1	3.2	…	…	…	5.4**	6.3**	4.5**	…	…	…	…	…	
158	Sri Lanka	12.0	11.9	12.1				…	…	…	94.4	1.01	…	…	**98.4****	**1.01****
	Sub-Saharan Africa															
159	Angola	4.8	…	…	5.2**	5.8**	4.6**	…	…	…	…	…	…	…	…	…
160	Benin	4.2	5.7	2.6	6.9**	8.7**	5.1**	…	…	…	55.1	1.02	…	…	68.3	0.93
161	Botswana	[illegible]	[illegible]	9.8	11.4**	11.3**	11.5**	11.3**	11.2**	11.3**	96.6	1.07	87.6	1.08	87.6**	1.07**
162	Burkina Faso	2.5	3.1	1.9	…	…	…	3.7**	4.3**	3.0**	[illegible]	[illegible]	[illegible]	1.05	66.2**	1.05**
163	Burundi	4.9	5.4	4.4	…	…	…	5.6**	6.3**	4.9**	61.8	0.89	…	…	67.5	1.06

GOAL 6. Educational quality in primary education

PUPIL/TEACHER RATIO			% FEMALE TEACHERS			TRAINED TEACHERS as % of total		PUBLIC CURRENT EXPENDITURE ON PRIMARY EDUCATION AS % GNP			PUBLIC CURRENT EXPENDITURE ON PRIMARY EDUCATION PER PUPIL (unit cost) in constant 2002 US$			PUBLIC CURRENT EXPENDITURE ON PRIMARY EDUCATION PER PUPIL (unit cost) at PPP in constant 2002 US$			
1990/ 1991	1998/ 1999	2002/ 2003	1990/ 1991	1998/ 1999	2002/ 2003	1998/ 1999	2002/ 2003	1990	1998	2002	1990	1998	2002	1990	1998	2002	
…	20	20**	…	86	86**	100	100z	…	…	…	…	…	…	…	…	…	111
33	37	35	87	83	82	74	74	…	…	1.3	…	…	57	…	…	187	112
23	26**	24	…	75**	76	…	75	1.8	1.9**	1.5z	354	535**	425z	586	784**	645z	113
25	19**	27	…	76**	72	…	…	0.5	…	2.0	33	…	112	100	…	518	114
29	25	25	…	60	67	…	78**,y	…	1.1	1.0	…	136	134	…	275	318	115
22	…	17	74	…	85	…	56	…	…	1.3	…	…	603	…	…	966	116
29	22	22	83	84**	85	…	77	2.6	…	…	396	…	…	551	…	…	117
20	…	18**	67	…	73**	…	73**	…	…	3.3	…	…	604	…	…	1 070	118
22	…	19**	84	…	85**	…	100z	5.0	…	…	534	…	…	…	…	…	119
26	21	19	70	76	75	71	83	1.6	1.3	1.7z	485	581	994**,z	657	946	1 270**,z	120
…	20**	15	…	93**	87	61**	80**	…	…	…	…	…	…	…	…	…	121
22	21	21	…	92**	…	…	…	1.1	…	1.2**,z	270	…	441**,z	526	…	691**,z	122
23	…	…	75	…	…	…	…	0.5	…	…	…	…	…	…	…	…	123
North America and Western Europe																	
…	…	12	…	…	78	…	…	…	…	…	…	…	…	…	…	…	124
11	13	13	82	89	90	…	…	0.9	1.1**	1.1	3 835	5 481**	5 683	3 355	5 243**	6 549	125
…	…	12	…	…	78	…	…	1.1	…	1.3**,z	3 220	…	4 382**,z	2 946	…	5 399**,z	126
15	15	17**,z	69	67	68**,z	…	…	…	…	…	…	…	…	…	…	…	127
21	18	19	60	67	83	…	…	1.1	…	1.7	1 039	…	2 757	1 273	…	…	128
…	10	10y	…	63	64y	…	…	…	1.8**	1.8	…	7 475**	7 100	…	6 143**	6 827	129
…	17	16	…	71	75	…	…	1.6	…	1.2	4 485	…	3 977	2 853	…	4 117	130
…	19	19	…	78	81	…	…	0.9	1.0	1.0	2 493	3 345	3 809	2 081	3 106	4 262	131
…	17	14	…	82	…	…	…	…	0.8**	0.6**,z	…	3 739**	3 778**,z	…	3 446**	4 511**,z	132
19	14	12	52	…	…	…	…	0.7	0.7**	…	715	1 253**	…	947	1 593**	…	133
…	11**	11**	…	76**	78**	…	…	2.5	…	2.4	5 106	…	6 429	4 151	…	6 429	134
27	22	19	77	85	…	…	…	1.5	1.5**	2.0	1 634	2 593**	4 201	1 500	2 613**	4 930	135
15	13	15	82	…	87	…	…	1.9	2.4**	2.6	1 567	3 076**	3 426	1 784	3 291**	4 237	136
12	11	11	91	95	95	…	…	0.8	1.1**	1.2	2 710	4 325**	4 775	2 457	4 797**	6 148	137
13	…	11	51	…	69	…	…	…	…	…	…	…	…	…	…	…	138
21	20	18	79	87	85	…	…	0.9	1.0	1.1	693	908	1 497	937	1 560	2 709	139
…	16	16y	…	87	87y	…	…	…	…	…	…	…	…	…	…	…	140
17	…	…	53	…	…	…	…	0.9	1.2**	1.4	2 602	3 545**	4 183	2 353	3 582**	4 703	141
…	…	10	…	…	73**	…	…	2.5	2.4**	1.7**	9 878	10 409**	7 595**	7 688	10 045**	6 622**	142
14	…	11	82	…	79**	…	…	1.6	…	…	1 414	…	…	2 109	…	…	143
6	…	…	89	…	…	…	…	…	…	…	…	…	…	…	…	…	144
22	15	14	73	68	70	…	…	0.9	1.1**	1.1	1 501	2 500**	2 809	1 473	3 061**	3 776	145
10	12	11	77	80	80	…	…	3.4	…	2.0**,z	10 157	…	6 013**,z	6 043	…	6 177**,z	146
…	13	14**,z	…	72	73**,z	…	…	2.0	1.4**	1.5**	12 542	7 769**	8 069**	8 676	5 651**	6 600**	147
20	19	17	78	76	81	…	…	1.2	…	…	2 938	…	…	2 833	…	…	148
…	15	15	…	86	88	…	…	…	…	1.8**,y	…	…	7 516**,y	…	…	7 423**,y	149
South and West Asia																	
41	32	61	59	–	24	…	…	…	…	…	…	…	…	…	…	…	150
63	59	56	19	31	38	63	67	…	0.6	0.8	…	13	24	…	51	114	151
…	38	38**	…	41	36**	100	92z	…	…	…	…	…	…	…	…	…	152
47	…	41	28	33*	44	…	…	…	…	1.4**,z	…	…	58**,z	…	…	321**,z	153
31	27	24	53	53	54**	…	100	…	…	1.1	…	…	179	…	…	727	154
…	26	20	…	58	63	69	64	…	…	…	…	…	…	…	…	…	155
39	41**	36	…	22**	29	52**	16	…	1.1**	1.3**	…	16**	18**	…	88**	108**	156
…	…	40	27	…	36	…	…	…	…	…	…	…	…	…	…	…	157
29	…	23**	…	…	79**	…	…	…	…	…	…	…	…	…	…	…	158
Sub-Saharan Africa																	
32	42	…	…	24	…	…	…	4.2	…	…	…	…	…	…	…	…	159
36	53	62	25	23	19	58	62	…	…	1.7**	…	…	36**	…	…	94**	160
32	28	27**	80	82	80**	92	89**	…	…	1.1y	…	…	147y	…	…	345y	161
57	49	45	27	25	27	…	87	…	…	…	…	…	…	…	…	…	162
67	57**	50	46	54**	54	…	…	1.6	…	1.5	19	…	10	67	…	64	163

Table 14 (continued)

GOAL 6. Educational quality in primary education

	Country or territory	SCHOOL LIFE EXPECTANCY (expected number of years of formal schooling) 1990/1991 Total	Male	Female	1998/1999 Total	Male	Female	2002/2003 Total	Male	Female	SURVIVAL RATE TO GRADE 5 1990/1991 Total (%)	GPI (F/M)	1998/1999 Total (%)	GPI (F/M)	2001/2002 Total (%)	GPI (F/M)
164	Cameroon	8.3	…	…	7.6**	…	…	9.2**	10.0**	8.4**	…	…	80.7**	…**	63.7**	0.99**
165	Cape Verde	…	…	…	…	…	…	11.8**	11.8**	11.8**	…	…	…	…	88.0	1.01
166	Central African Republic	4.9	6.2	3.6	…	…	…	…	…	…	24.0	0.90	…	…	…	…
167	Chad	…	…	…	…	…	…	…	…	…	53.1	0.75	55.1	0.86	44.3**	0.70**
168	Comoros	…	…	…	6.5**	7.0**	5.9**	7.9**	8.7**	7.2**	…	…	…	…	71.7**,x	1.08**,x
169	Congo	11.0	12.1	9.9	…	…	…	7.7**,z	8.4**,z	7.0**,z	62.7	1.15	…	…	66.3	1.03
170	Côte d'Ivoire	…	…	…	6.4**	7.7**	5.1**	…	…	…	73.0	0.94	69.1	0.89	87.6**,x	0.98**,x
171	D. R. Congo	…	…	…	4.4**	…	…	…	…	…	54.7	0.86	…	…	…	…
172	Equatorial Guinea	…	…	…	…	…	…	…	…	…	…	…	…	…	29.5**,y	0.74**,y
173	Eritrea	…	…	…	4.4**	5.0**	3.7**	5.1**	5.9**	4.3**	…	…	95.3	0.95	86.3	0.92
174	Ethiopia	2.8	3.4	2.3	4.0**	5.0**	3.0**	5.9**	6.9**	4.8**	…	…	55.8	1.03	61.5**	0.95**
175	Gabon	…	…	…	12.1**	12.5**	11.7**	…	…	…	…	…	…	…	69.3**	1.04**
176	Gambia	…	…	…	…	…	…	…	…	…	…	…	…	…	…	…
177	Ghana	6.5	7.5	5.6	…	…	…	7.3**	7.7**	6.9**	80.5	0.98	…	…	63.3	1.05
178	Guinea	2.8	4.0	1.7	…	…	…	…	…	…	58.8	0.76	86.9	0.86	79.7	0.85
179	Guinea-Bissau	…	…	…	…	…	…	…	…	…	…	…	38.1**	0.82**	…	…
180	Kenya	8.4	8.8	7.9	…	…	…	8.5**,z	8.7**,z	8.3**,z	…	…	…		59.0**	0.94**
181	Lesotho	9.8	8.8	10.8	9.7	9.2	10.3	10.8**	10.5	11.1**	70.7	1.42	68.9	1.23	73.0	1.22
182	Liberia	…	…	…	…	…	…	…	…	…	…	…	…	…	…	…
183	Madagascar	6.3	6.4	6.2	6.2**	6.3**	6.0**	…	…	…	21.7	0.95	51.1	1.02	52.9	1.02
184	Malawi	6.3	7.1	5.5	…	…	…	10.9**	11.4**	10.4**	64.5	0.80	44.1	0.78	32.8	1.30
185	Mali	2.0	2.5	1.4	3.9**	…	…	4.9**	…	…	72.5	0.95	78.3**	0.97**	74.6	0.90
186	Mauritius	10.3	10.4	10.3	11.9**	11.9**	11.8**	12.7**	12.5**	12.8**	98.4	1.00	99.4	1.01	98.9	1.01
187	Mozambique	…	…	…	…	…	…	…	…	…	32.9	0.76	41.8	0.83	49.2	0.85
188	Namibia	…	…	…	12.1**	12.0**	12.3**	11.5**	11.4**	11.6**	…	…	83.4	1.09	94.7**	…**
189	Niger	2.2	…	…	…	…	…	2.9**,z	3.5**,z	2.3**,z	62.4	1.06	…	…	69.1	0.95
190	Nigeria	…	…	…	…	…	…	10.2**	11.3**	9.0**	…	…	…	…	…	…
191	Rwanda	…	…	…	7.9**	…	…	8.6**	8.9**	8.4**	60.0	0.97	45.4	…	46.6	1.08
192	Sao Tome and Principe	…	…	…	…	…	…	9.6**,z	10.0**,z	9.2**,z	…	…	…	…	61.5**,y	1.11**,y
193	Senegal	4.8	…	…	5.6**	…	…	…	…	…	84.5	…	…	…	80.0	0.93
194	Seychelles	…	…	…	13.4	…	…	13.4**	13.3**	13.5**	…	…	100.0	…	99.3	0.99
195	Sierra Leone	4.8	…	…	…	…	…	6.8**,y	7.9**,y	5.7**,y	…	…	…	…	…	…
196	Somalia	…	…	…	…	…	…	…	…	…	…	…	…	…	…	…
197	South Africa	11.5	11.4	11.6	13.5**	13.3**	13.7**	13.1**	12.8**	13.1**	75.3	1.09	75.9*	1.02*	64.8x	0.99x
198	Swaziland	9.4	9.6	9.1	10.4**	10.8**	10.1**	9.6**	9.9**	9.3**	76.2	1.05	81.5	1.15	73.2	0.90
199	Togo	8.8	11.3	6.3	10.8**	13.1**	8.5**	…	…	…	50.7	0.81	…	…	68.6	0.88
200	Uganda	5.2	5.9	4.5	11.9**	12.7**	11.0**	12.0**	12.3**	11.7**	…	…	…	…	63.6	1.02
201	United Republic of Tanzania	5.3	…	…	5.0**	5.1**	4.9**	…	…	…	78.9	1.05	80.9	1.06	82.0**	1.01**
202	Zambia	7.8	…	…	6.9**	7.4**	6.5**	6.9**,y	7.3**,y	6.5**,y	…	…	78.2	0.87	98.5**	…**
203	Zimbabwe	9.8	…	…	…	…	…	10.1**	…	…	92.4	0.85	…	…	69.7**	1.04**

		Weighted average									Median					
I	World	9.3	9.9	8.4	9.8	10.3	9.4	10.5	10.8	10.2	…	…	…	…	89.7	…
II	Countries in transition	12.2	11.9	12.8	11.9	11.8	12.0	12.6	12.4	12.8	…	…	…	…	…	…
III	Developed countries	14.2	14.1	14.3	15.7	15.4	16.1	16.1	15.2	16.6	…	…	…	…	…	…
IV	Developing countries	8.4	9.2	7.4	9.1	9.7	8.5	9.9	10.3	9.4	…	…	…	…	81.2	0.98
V	Arab States	8.6	9.1	7.3	9.8	10.6	9.0	10.2	10.7	9.6	87.3	…	91.3	1.07	94.3	1.01
VI	Central and Eastern Europe	11.4	…	…	11.8	11.9	11.8	12.8	12.8	12.8	…	…	…	…	…	…
VII	Central Asia	11.6	…	…	10.9	11.0	10.0	11.5	11.6	11.4	…	…	…		…	…
VIII	East Asia and the Pacific	9.6	10.4	9.2	10.2	10.4	9.9	11.2	11.3	11.0	…	…	…	…		
IX	Latin America and the Caribbean	10.4	…	…	12.2	12.1	12.2	13.1	12.8	13.3	…	…	…	…	83.9	1.08
X	North America and Western Europe	14.7	14.6	15.0	16.2	15.8	16.6	16.4	15.3	17.0	99.5	1.01	…	…	…	…
XI	South and West Asia	7.6	9.0	6.2	8.4	9.4	7.4	9.1	9.7	8.4	…	…	…	…	64.9	1.06
XII	Sub-Saharan Africa	6.0	6.6	5.5	6.7	7.4	6.0	7.8	8.5	7.0	64.5	0.80	…	…	68.6	0.88

Data in bold are for 2003/2004. (z) Data are for 2001/2002. (y) Data are for 2000/2001. (x) Data are for 1999/2000.

GOAL 6. Educational quality in primary education

PUPIL/TEACHER RATIO			% FEMALE TEACHERS			TRAINED TEACHERS as % of total		PUBLIC CURRENT EXPENDITURE ON PRIMARY EDUCATION AS % GNP			PUBLIC CURRENT EXPENDITURE ON PRIMARY EDUCATION PER PUPIL (unit cost) in constant 2002 US$			PUBLIC CURRENT EXPENDITURE ON PRIMARY EDUCATION PER PUPIL (unit cost) at PPP in constant 2002 US$			
1990/1991	1998/1999	2002/2003	1990/1991	1998/1999	2002/2003	1998/1999	2002/2003	1990	1998	2002	1990	1998	2002	1990	1998	2002	
51	52	57	30	36	33	…	68	…	1.2	…	…	40	…	…	114	…	164
…	29**	28	…	62**	65	…	69	…	…	3.0	…	…	207	…	…	768	165
77	…	…	25	…	…	…	…	1.1	…	…	32	…	…	63	…	…	166
66	68	68**	6	9	11**	…	…	…	…	…	…	…	…	…	…	…	167
37	35	37**	…	26	…	…	…	…	…	1.7**	…	…	40**	…	…	157**	168
65	61	65	32	42	43	…	57	…	…	1.5**	…	…	66**	…	…	78**	169
37	43	42*	18	20	24*	…	100*	…	1.6	…	…	94	…	…	178	…	170
40	26	…	24	21	…	…	…	…	…	…	…	…	…	…	…	…	171
…	…	43^{**,y}	…	…	24^{**,y}	…	…	…	…	0.4^{**,z}	…	…	25^{**,z}	…	…	202^{**,z}	172
…	47	47	45	35	36	73	81	…	1.3	…	…	40	…	…	194	…	173
36	46	**67****	24	28	**34****	…	**72****	1.5	…	…	24	…	…	74	…	…	174
…	44	36	…	42	45	…	100	…	1.3	…	…	208	…	…	343	…	175
31	33	38**	31	29	29**	72	73^{y}	1.3	…	…	35	…	…	150	…	…	176
29	30	**32**	36	32	**39**	72	**68**	0.8	…	…	16	…	…	53	…	…	177
40	47	45	23	25	24	…	…	…	…	…	…	…	…	…	…	…	178
…	…	44^{**,y}	…	…	20^{**,y}	…	…	…	…	…	…	…	…	…	…	…	179
31	…	34**	38	…	41**	…	44**	3.2	…	…	57	…	…	143	…	…	180
55	44**	47	80	80**	80	77**	73	…	3.2	3.9^{**,z}	…	74	80^{**,z}	…	293	426^{**,z}	181
…	39	…	…	19	…	…	…	…	…	…	…	…	…	…	…	…	182
40	47	52	…	58	60	…	…	…	0.5	0.7^{z}	…	11	15^{z}	…	34	41^{z}	183
61	63**	62	31	40**	44	46**	51^{y}	1.1	…	3.1	11	…	20	20	…	66	184
47	62*	57	25	23*	24	…	…	…	1.3	…	…	38	…	…	110	…	185
21	26	25	44	53	57	100	100	1.2	1.2	1.0	235	348	359	550	848	1 039	186
55	…	67	23	24	28	33	60	1.0	…	…	13	…	…	40	…	…	187
…	32	28**	…	67	61**	29	50**	…	4.4	4.0	…	305	302	…	940	1 281	188
42	41	42	33	31	35	…	72	…	…	…	…	…	…	…	…	…	189
41	31**	42	43	38**	48	…	76	…	…	…	…	…	…	…	…	…	190
57	54	60	46	55	50	49	81^{z}	…	…	…	…	…	…	…	…	…	191
…	36	33^{**,z}	…	…	62^{**,z}	…	…	…	…	…	…	…	…	…	…	…	192
53	49	49**	27	23**	23**	…	91^{z}	1.7	…	1.1^{**,z}	80	…	47^{**,z}	117	…	155^{**,z}	193
…	15	13	…	88	86	84	77**	2.3	1.1	1.5**	701	716	1 050**	…	…	…	194
35	…	37^{y}	…	…	38^{y}	…	79^{y}	…	0.4	…	…	…	…	…	…	…	195
…	…	…	…	…	…	…	…	…	…	…	…	…	…	…	…	…	196
…	37**	35	…	78**	80	63**	81	4.1	2.8	2.4^{**,z}	472	315*	317^{**,z}	1 208	894*	1 227^{**,z}	197
33	33	31	79	75	75	91	91	1.4	2.0	2.1	72	99	124	217	316	515	198
58	41	35	19	13	12	…	81^{z}	1.6	1.8	1.8^{**,y}	29	26	27^{**,y}	82	115	145^{**,y}	199
29	60	53	30	33	37	…	81	…	…	…	…	…	…	…	…	…	200
35	38	**56**	41	44	**46****	…	100	…	…	…	…	…	…	…	…	…	201
44	45	43	…	47	49	89	100	…	…	…	…	…	…	…	…	…	202
36	…	**39**	39	…	**51**	…	95^{**,z}	4.3	…	3.3^{**,z}	164	…	112^{**,z}	423	…	376^{**,z}	203

Median			Median			Median		Median			Median			Median			
27	23	22	57	72	73	…	…	…	…	…	…	…	…	…	…	…	I
22	20	18	94	95	97	…	98	…	…	…	…	…	…	…	…	…	II
18	17	14	77	85	82		…	1.4	…	1.2	…	…	3794	…	…	4193	III
30	28	28	47	62	62	…	81	…	…	…	…	…	…	…	…	…	IV
25	25	21	51	52	62	…	…	…	…	…	…	…	…	…	…	…	V
20	19	17	84	92	92	…	…	…	…	0.9	…	…	677	…	…	1705	VI
21	22	19	85	92	95	…	93	…	…	…	…	…	…	…	…	…	VII
26	23	25	…	66	66	…	…	…	…	…	…	…	…	…	…	…	VIII
25	22	21	…	78	82		78	…	…	1.7	…	…	413	…	…	794	IX
15	15	14	77	78	79	…	…	1.2	1.1	1.4	2656	3545	4291	2405	3446	5399	X
40	35	38	28	33	38	…	67	…	…	…	…	…	…	…	…	…	XI
40	43	43	31	35	41	…	79	…	…	…	…	…	…	…	…	…	XII

Introduction to aid data annex tables

Most of the data on aid used in this Report are derived from the OECD's International Development Statistics (IDS) database, which records information provided annually by all member countries of the OECD Development Assistance Committee (DAC). IDS comprises the DAC database (aggregate data) and the Creditor Reporting System, which shows project and activity level data. IDS is available online at www.oecd.org/dac/stats/idsonline. It is updated frequently. The data presented in this Report were downloaded between January and June 2005.

Only public funding to developing countries is discussed here. Such funding is called Official Development Assistance. This and other terms used in describing aid data are explained below, to help in understanding the following annex tables and the data presented in Chapter 4.

Aid recipients and donors

Official Development Assistance (ODA) is public funding to developing countries to promote their economic and social development. It is concessional: that is, it takes the form either of a grant or of a loan carrying a lower interest rate and, usually, a longer repayment period than is available in the market. It may be provided directly by a government (**bilateral ODA**) or through an international agency (**multilateral ODA**). ODA includes **technical cooperation** (see below).

Developing countries are those in Part I of the DAC List of Aid Recipients, which essentially comprises all low and middle income countries and some central and eastern European countries in transition. Other countries in transition and several more advanced developing countries are in Part II of the list, and aid to them is referred to as Official Aid (OA). The data presented in this Report do not include OA unless indicated.

Bilateral donors are countries that provide development assistance directly to recipient countries. The majority (Australia, Austria, Belgium, Canada, Denmark, Finland, France, Germany, Greece, Ireland, Italy, Japan, Luxembourg, the Netherlands, New Zealand, Norway, Portugal, Spain, Sweden, Switzerland, the United Kingdom and the United States) are members of the DAC, a forum of major bilateral donors established to promote the volume and effectiveness of aid. Non DAC bilateral donors include the Republic of Korea and Arab countries. Bilateral donors also contribute to the work of multilateral donors through contributions recorded as multilateral ODA. The financial flows from multilateral donors to recipient countries are also recorded as ODA receipts.

Multilateral donors are international institutions with government membership that conduct all or a significant part of their activities in favour of developing countries. They include multilateral development banks (e.g. the World Bank and Inter-American Development Bank), United Nations agencies (e.g. UNDP and UNICEF) and regional groupings (e.g. the European Commission and Arab agencies).

Types of aid

Unallocated aid: some contributions are not susceptible to allocation by sector and are reported as **non sector allocable aid**. Examples are aid for general development purposes, balance-of-payments support, action relating to debt (including **debt relief**), and emergency assistance.

Basic education: the definition of basic education varies by agency. The DAC defines it as covering primary education, basic life skills for youth and adults, and early childhood education.

Education, level unspecified: the aid to education reported in the DAC database includes basic, secondary and post secondary education and a subcategory called 'education, level unspecified'. This subcategory covers aid related to education policy and research, as well as aid for buildings and teacher training where the level of education is unspecified. **Sector budget funding**, the contribution of funds directly to the budget of a ministry of education, is often reported by donors in this subcategory. Although this aid can in fact be used for specific levels of education, such information is not available in the DAC database. This lack has implications for accurately assessing the resources made available to a given level.

Technical cooperation (sometimes referred to as **technical assistance**): according to the DAC Directives, technical cooperation is the provision of know-how in the form of personnel, training, research and associated costs. It includes (a) grants to nationals of aid recipient countries receiving education or training at home or abroad; and (b) payments to consultants, advisers and similar personnel as well as teachers and administrators serving in recipient countries (including the cost of associated equipment). Where such assistance is related specifically to a capital project, it is included with project and programme expenditure and not separately reported as technical cooperation. The actual aid activities reported in this category vary by donor, as interpretations of the definition are broad.

Debt relief: this includes debt forgiveness, i.e. the extinction of a loan by agreement between the creditor (donor) and the debtor (aid recipient), and other action on debt, including debt swaps, buy-backs and refinancing. In the DAC database, debt forgiveness is reported as a grant. It raises gross ODA but not necessarily net ODA.

Aid data

Commitments and disbursements: a commitment is a firm obligation by a donor, expressed in writing and backed by the necessary funds, to provide specified assistance to a country or multilateral organization. The amount specified is recorded as a commitment. Disbursement is the release of funds to, or purchase of goods or services for, a recipient; in other words, the amount spent. Disbursements record the actual international transfer of financial resources or of goods or services valued by the donor. As the aid committed in a given year can be disbursed later, sometimes over several years, the annual aid figures based on commitments and disbursements differ.

Gross and net disbursements: gross disbursements are the total aid extended. Net disbursements are the total aid extended minus amounts of loan principal repaid by recipients or cancelled through debt forgiveness.

Current and constant prices: aid figures in the DAC database are expressed in US$. When other currencies are converted into dollars at the exchange rates prevailing at the time, the resulting amounts are at current prices and exchange rates. When comparing aid figures between different years, adjustment is required to compensate for inflation and changes in exchange rates. Such adjustments allow amounts to be expressed in constant dollars, i.e. in dollars fixed at the value they held in a given reference year, including their external value in terms of other currencies. Thus, 2002 constant dollars expresses amounts in terms of the purchasing power of dollars in 2002. In this Report, most data are presented in 2002 constant dollars. The indices used for adjusting currencies and years (called deflators) are derived from Table 36 of the statistical annex of the 2004 DAC annual report (OECD-DAC, 2005*b*). Figures in previous editions of the *EFA Global Monitoring Report* were based on the constant prices of different years (the 2005 Report was based on 2001 constant prices), so figures for a given country in a given year differ from those presented in this Report for the same year.

For more detailed and precise definitions of terms used in the DAC database, see the DAC Directives, available at www.oecd.org/dataoecd/36/32/31723929.htm#32,33

Source: OECD-DAC (2000, 2005*a*).

Table 1.1: Bilateral ODA from DAC countries: total ODA, aid to education, aid to basic education and education, level unspecified (commitments)

	Total ODA (constant 2002 US$ millions)						Per capita ODA (constant 2002 US$)	Total aid to education (constant 2002 US$ millions)					
Country	1999	2000	2001	2002	2003	Annual average 1999–2003	Annual average 1999–2003	1999	2000	2001	2002	2003	Annual average 1999–2003
Australia	678.9	753.1	713.7	773.7	793.8	742.6	38.2	131.7	135.0	82.5	63.5	61.4	94.8
Austria	591.7	399.3	439.7	458.5	226.8	423.2	57.9	117.2	59.2	61.8	68.9	62.0	73.8
Belgium	431.9	527.4	557.2	741.0	1 221.8	695.9	58.4	56.0	68.3	70.0	89.9	81.4	73.1
Canada	1 175.5	1 362.6	1 230.2	1 722.4	1 616.1	1 421.4	46.5	95.4	135.3	118.5	211.5	272.8	166.7
Denmark	729.7	992.4	982.9	844.3	693.1	848.5	164.7	9.0	79.4	20.7	75.7	30.2	43.0
Finland	249.8	212.5	299.2	311.6	322.9	279.2	53.4	18.4	19.3	26.1	33.6	34.3	26.3
France	4 622.8	3 615.8	3 463.5	4 743.0	5 920.3	4 473.1	71.2	1 381.5	800.9	832.4	925.8	1 042.7	996.6
Germany	4 004.3	3 123.2	3 734.2	4 596.7	4 665.4	4 024.8	48.7	670.7	582.1	613.4	692.3	811.5	674.0
Greece	74.3	107.6	90.3	107.0	183.9	112.6	8.9	4.7	6.2	8.9	8.4	64.8	18.6
Ireland	152.0	174.4	204.5	267.1	288.5	217.3	55.1	24.2	33.5	41.3	51.8	41.5	38.5
Italy	586.6	786.9	693.8	1 206.0	1 054.1	865.5	15.6	34.2	23.8	65.8	59.2	19.9	40.6
Japan	11 781.4	11 545.5	11 071.1	9 348.7	14 433.9	11 636.1	83.5	1 022.0	611.2	752.5	932.8	938.7	851.4
Luxembourg	83.6	97.8	...	...	...	...	...	15.7	23.0	...	...	...	...
Netherlands	1 837.6	3 157.4	2 601.5	4 456.4	2 599.0	2 930.4	206.5	152.1	183.6	228.1	315.3	183.9	212.6
New Zealand	95.1	90.8	93.5	91.7	101.7	94.6	24.3	33.4	29.1	31.1	26.3	24.2	28.8
Norway	1 315.3	881.0	1 205.4	1 101.8	1 276.6	1 156.0	249.8	136.2	54.0	84.7	124.9	115.6	103.1
Portugal	284.7	358.8	201.7	186.1	149.8	236.2	24.3	20.7	28.4	34.4	35.9	51.3	34.1
Spain	650.8	1 016.0	1 389.7	1 157.7	1 131.8	1 069.2	26.3	78.5	160.3	153.0	150.0	125.6	133.5
Sweden	1 020.0	1 065.2	1 150.9	1 264.6	1 449.1	1 190.0	130.1	59.5	44.0	43.3	78.3	68.3	58.7
Switzerland	714.5	694.8	708.4	768.6	821.9	741.6	101.9	25.9	31.3	29.5	34.2	34.1	31.0
United Kingdom	2 233.7	2 888.1	2 948.7	3 612.8	3 603.0	3 057.3	52.0	214.3	181.3	208.2	124.3	311.5	207.9
United States	10 717.9	10 383.7	9 708.8	12 125.6	20 604.2	12 708.0	38.3	347.8	264.0	322.9	283.1	273.2	298.2
All DAC countries	**44 032.1**	**44 234.3**	**43 489.0**	**49 885.3**	**63 157.6**	**48 923.4**	**53.9**	**4 649.0**	**3 553.4**	**3 829.2**	**4 385.5**	**4 649.0**	**4 205.5**

Sources: Total ODA, aid to education and aid to basic education: OECD-DAC database. Population data: United Nations Population Division statistics, 2002 revision, medium variant.

Table 1.2: Bilateral aid to education from DAC countries: commitments to education and basic education as percentage of gross national income

	ODA commitments to education as % of GNI						ODA commitments to basic education as % of GNI					
Country	1999	2000	2001	2002	2003	Annual average 1999–2003	1999	2000	2001	2002	2003	Annual average 1999–2003
Australia	0.037	0.037	0.022	0.016	0.015	0.025	0.006	0.009	0.009	0.007	0.007	0.007
Austria	0.061	0.030	0.031	0.034	0.030	0.037	0.002	0.001	0.000	0.001	0.001	0.001
Belgium	0.024	0.028	0.028	0.036	0.033	0.030	0.001	0.002	0.003	0.003	0.002	0.002
Canada	0.015	0.020	0.017	0.029	0.037	0.024	0.002	0.002	0.006	0.010	0.015	0.007
Denmark	0.006	0.048	0.012	0.044	0.018	0.026	0.000	0.029	0.004	0.013	0.006	0.010
Finland	0.015	0.015	0.020	0.026	0.026	0.021	0.000	0.000	0.004	0.005	0.002	0.003
France	0.104	0.059	0.059	0.064	0.072	0.071	0.001	0.009	0.011	0.011	0.012	0.009
Germany	0.035	0.030	0.031	0.035	0.041	0.034	0.004	0.003	0.002	0.004	0.004	0.003
Greece	0.004	0.005	0.007	0.006	0.047	0.015	...	0.000	...	...	0.019	...
Ireland	0.030	0.037	0.043	0.052	0.040	0.041	...	...	...	...	...	...
Italy	0.003	0.002	0.006	0.005	0.002	0.003	0.000	0.000	0.000	0.000	0.000	0.000
Japan	0.026	0.015	0.019	0.023	0.023	0.021	0.001	0.001	0.002	0.002	0.001	0.002
Luxembourg	0.092	0.127	...	...	...	...	0.016	0.044	...	...	...	...
Netherlands	0.038	0.044	0.054	0.077	0.045	0.052	0.018	0.026	0.043	0.052	0.031	0.034
New Zealand	0.071	0.060	0.064	0.048	0.042	0.056	0.004	0.003	0.005	0.005	0.005	0.004
Norway	0.077	0.029	0.045	0.065	0.060	0.055	0.048	0.009	0.009	0.032	0.032	0.026
Portugal	0.019	0.024	0.029	0.030	0.043	0.029	0.000	0.003	0.003	0.004	0.003	0.003
Spain	0.013	0.026	0.024	0.023	0.019	0.021	0.002	0.002	0.003	0.004	0.004	0.003
Sweden	0.029	0.020	0.019	0.033	0.028	0.026	0.014	0.012	0.003	0.007	0.009	0.009
Switzerland	0.009	0.011	0.010	0.012	0.012	0.011	0.003	0.003	0.003	0.004	0.004	0.003
United Kingdom	0.015	0.012	0.014	0.008	0.019	0.014	0.005	0.005	0.005	0.004	0.013	0.006
United States	0.001	0.002	0.003	0.003	0.003	0.003	0.001	0.002	0.002	0.002	0.002	0.002
All DAC countries	**0.020**	**0.015**	**0.016**	**0.018**	**0.018**	**0.017**	**0.002**	**0.003**	**[illegible]**	**0.004**	**0.005**	**0.004**

Notes:

- (···) indicate that data are not available.
- Aid to education and basic education as percentage of GNI *exclude* bilateral donors' contributions to multilateral agencies, but these are *included* in total ODA as percentage of GNI in Figure 4.16. The data thus are not comparable.
- Aid to basic education as % of GNI excludes the part of 'education, level unspecified' that is allocated to basic education.
- Totals do not include countries where data are not available.

Source: Derived from Table 4 of the statistical annex of OECD-DAC (2005).

Aid to basic education (constant 2002 US$ millions)						Education, level unspecified (constant 2002 US$ millions)						
1999	2000	2001	2002	2003	Annual average 1999–2003	1999	2000	2001	2002	2003	Annual average 1999–2003	
21.7	31.8	32.2	26.7	26.1	27.7	2.8	4.2	8.2	7.2	10.0	6.5	Australia
3.1	1.8	0.6	1.2	2.8	1.9	1.8	3.8	3.4	3.6	2.3	3.0	Austria
2.1	4.3	7.8	7.5	5.1	5.4	13.0	14.4	10.8	11.7	17.7	13.5	Belgium
9.9	15.5	43.8	68.8	112.2	50.0	25.9	40.8	16.2	53.9	89.6	45.3	Canada
0.7	47.3	6.6	22.6	9.5	17.3	3.2	11.6	2.7	51.1	16.4	17.0	Denmark
0.4	0.5	5.7	6.9	2.6	3.2	15.1	13.1	18.0	22.4	22.5	18.2	Finland
12.0	119.7	152.6	161.1	172.2	123.5	658.6	49.3	186.4	29.4	44.1	193.5	France
75.2	64.4	46.2	72.8	71.5	66.0	30.6	33.2	30.4	45.5	25.5	33.0	Germany
...	0.0	...	...	26.4	...	1.6	1.4	3.3	3.5	9.7	3.9	Greece
...	...	...	...	...	...	24.2	33.5	41.3	51.8	41.5	38.5	Ireland
0.3	0.3	0.1	0.3	0.1	0.2	24.4	8.6	40.7	48.6	7.2	25.9	Italy
45.3	37.3	76.7	101.3	54.9	63.1	764.7	540.8	162.3	107.2	198.6	354.7	Japan
2.7	7.9	...	...	...	...	7.4	8.6	...	...	...	...	Luxembourg
72.4	108.9	181.3	214.0	124.8	140.3	39.5	48.1	21.2	37.7	22.0	33.7	Netherlands
1.7	1.6	2.3	2.5	2.8	2.2	0.6	0.4	0.9	1.8	2.2	1.2	New Zealand
85.2	15.7	17.2	60.8	61.5	48.1	23.2	9.6	7.9	21.1	25.7	17.5	Norway
0.1	3.6	3.9	4.6	3.3	3.1	6.6	6.2	10.6	8.6	2.6	6.9	Portugal
14.5	11.9	17.3	25.4	23.7	18.5	18.3	98.7	68.1	36.3	19.0	48.1	Spain
29.9	25.8	5.9	17.8	21.9	20.3	13.8	15.3	19.8	40.0	34.5	24.7	Sweden
8.9	8.2	9.2	12.2	11.9	10.1	11.5	9.2	7.8	5.3	4.7	7.7	Switzerland
67.1	74.0	72.7	68.4	208.5	98.1	131.8	93.2	121.5	45.2	94.2	97.2	United Kingdom
126.8	196.1	207.5	218.2	221.2	194.0	29.1	...	3.4	13.3	6.1	...	United States
579.9	**776.7**	**889.5**	**1 093.0**	**1 163.0**	**893.0**	**1 847.7**	**1 043.8**	**784.9**	**645.0**	**696.0**	**1 002.9**	**All DAC countries**

Notes:

- Data for some donors for some years represent disbursements and others represent commitments.
- (...) indicate that data are not available.
- Totals do not include countries where data are not available.
- Aid to education does not count the part of general budget support that recipient countries may allocate to education.
- Aid to basic education does not count the part of education sector budget support (most of which is reported as 'level unspecified') that may benefit basic education.
- This table includes the data for Luxembourg, Ireland and Greece, which were not included in Table 4.2 of the main text because of limited data availability. Therefore, totals for DAC countries in this table are larger than those shown in Table 4.2.

Table 2: ODA from multilateral donors: total ODA, total aid to education and aid to basic education (commitments)

I. Annual averages for 1999–2003

Multilateral donors	Total ODA (constant 2002 US$ millions)	Total aid to education (constant 2002 US$ millions)	Education as % of total ODA	Aid to basic education (constant 2002 US$ millions)	Basic education as % of total aid to education
African Development Fund	968.5	90.7	10.4	39.4	73.5
Asian Development Fund	1 240.7	135.4	12.7	36.9	33.8
Caribbean Development Bank	47.9	5.3	19.2	1.0	25.0
European Commission	6 695.7	347.1	6.3	128.8	50.8
IDA	6 783.6	542.9	8.5	196.9	57.8
IDB Special Fund	391.1	21.0	6.3	6.0	74.6
Nordic Development Fund	64.6	2.5	4.1	0.0	0.0
UNDP	460.2	11.0	2.7	1.8	46.4
UNICEF	601.8	52.2	11.0	52.2	100.0
UNRWA	358.5	179.5	55.5	154.4	90.3
Total	**17 612.7**	**1 387.5**	**9.3**	**617.4**	**62.6**

Notes:

- The share of aid to education in total ODA is computed using total ODA minus multi-sector/cross-cutting and other general programme and commodity assistance.
- The shares of the various education levels in total aid to education are computed using total aid to education minus level unspecified.

Sources: Data for AfDF, AsDF, IDA, IDB Special Fund and UNDP are derived from CRS database, Table 2.
Data for Caribbean Development Bank, European Commission, UNICEF, UNRWA and Nordic Development Fund are from DAC database, Table 5.

Table 2 (continued)

II. Yearly data

Multilateral donors	Total ODA (constant 2002 US$ millions)					Total ODA to education (constant 2002 US$ millions)				
	1999	2000	2001	2002	2003	1999	2000	2001	2002	2003
African Development Fund	511.9	858.7	1 274.4	885.1	1 312.2	69.6	45.7	67.6	81.5	189.2
Asian Development Fund	1 120.0	1 006.7	1 401.3	1 039.6	1 635.8	131.8	80.7	35.2	238.8	190.3
Caribbean Development Bank	38.2	58.2	...	...	47.4	4.5	7.4	...	...	4.0
European Commission	...	7 748.4	6 067.2	5 938.6	7 028.6	...	420.1	235.4	253.9	478.8
IDA	5 426.4	5 927.0	7 194.7	8 108.4	7 261.7	641.0	398.4	545.1	605.5	524.6
IDB Special Fund	242.2	341.9	473.3	400.4	497.7	9.0	0.0	34.1	30.0	31.8
Nordic Development Fund	40.5	40.2	82.2	71.7	88.5	0.3	0.0	6.3	5.8	0.0
UNDP	460.2	...	...	...	...	11.0	...	...	...	...
UNICEF	601.3	600.4	612.2	571.4	623.9	45.5	53.4	57.2	47.8	57.0
UNRWA	302.3	311.4	363.5	392.2	423.2	172.3	177.0	176.3	183.1	188.8
Total	**8 743.1**	**16 893.0**	**17 468.6**	**17 407.4**	**18 919.0**	**1 085.0**	**1 182.9**	**1 157.2**	**1 446.4**	**1 664.6**

Multilateral donors	Total ODA to education (%)					Share of 'education, level unspecified' in aid to education				
	1999	2000	2001	2002	2003	1999	2000	2001	2002	2003
African Development Fund	18.0	5.5	6.2	10.4	14.8	78.5	64.3	78.2	19.0	17.6
Asian Development Fund	15.8	9.0	2.9	25.2	13.0	0.0	38.0	0.0	24.6	21.5
Caribbean Development Bank	18.9	27.7	...	...	12.5	0.0	0.0	...	...	87.8
European Commission	...	6.3	5.1	4.9	8.5	...	25.4	46.8	20.4	22.0
IDA	13.1	7.2	8.0	7.8	7.4	53.6	63.1	59.7	2.5	14.5
IDB Special Fund	4.5	0.0	9.1	8.4	7.3	100.0	...	70.0	0.0	100.0
Nordic Development Fund	0.8	0.0	7.7	9.0	0.0	100.0	...	0.0	100.0	...
UNDP	2.7	...	...	...	...	65.7	...	...	...	...
UNICEF	8.5	11.3	12.1	11.1	12.1	0.0	0.0	0.0	0.0	0.0
UNRWA	64.4	64.3	53.7	51.2	48.6	3.1	5.4	6.2	4.7	4.5
Total	**14.3**	**7.9**	**7.7**	**9.2**	**9.9**	**38.7**	**36.2**	**45.2**	**10.7**	**18.0**

Notes:

- (...) indicate that data are not available.
- The share of aid to education in total ODA is computed using total ODA minus multi-sector/cross-cutting and other general programme and commodity assistance.
- The shares of the various education levels in total aid to education are computed using total aid to education minus level unspecified.
- Totals do not include donors whose data are not available.

Sources: Data for AfDF, AsDF, IDA, IDB Special Fund and UNDP are derived from CRS database, Table 2.
Data for Caribbean Development Bank, European Commission, UNICEF, UNRWA and Nordic Development Fund are from DAC database, Table 5.

Basic education (constant 2002 US$ millions)					Secondary education (constant 2002 US$ millions)					Post-secondary education (constant 2002 US$ millions)				
1999	2000	2001	2002	2003	1999	2000	2001	2002	2003	1999	2000	2001	2002	2003
15.0	16.3	12.7	66.0	86.9	0.0	0.0	0.0	0.0	38.2	0.0	0.0	2.0	0.0	31.0
0.0	0.0	14.3	100.4	69.8	125.7	50.0	20.8	14.0	28.1	6.1	0.0	0.0	65.8	51.5
0.0	3.1	...	...	0.0	0.0	0.0	...	...	0.0	4.5	4.3	...	...	0.5
...	277.0	32.3	20.6	185.4	...	21.9	15.3	84.3	54.0	...	14.5	77.7	97.3	133.9
182.3	59.6	219.5	143.6	379.7	67.7	22.5	0.0	376.9	33.3	47.7	64.7	0.0	70.0	35.6
0.0	...	0.0	30.0	0.0	0.0	...	0.0	0.0	0.0	0.0	...	10.2	0.0	0.0
0.0	...	0.0	0.0	...	0.0	...	6.3	0.0	...	0.0	...	0.0	0.0	...
1.8	...	...	...	...	1.5	...	...	...	...	0.6	...	...	...	...
45.5	53.4	57.2	47.7	56.9	0.0	0.0	0.0	0.0	0.0	0.0		0.0	0.1	0.1
149.0	150.2	149.1	159.4	164.3	1.1	1.5	1.3	1.6	1.4	16.9	15.7	14.9	13.6	14.6
393.6	**559.7**	**485.0**	**567.6**	**943.0**	**195.9**	**96.0**	**43.8**	**476.7**	**155.1**	**75.7**	**99.2**	**104.8**	**246.7**	**267.2**

Basic education as % of total aid to education					Secondary education as % of total aid to education					Post-secondary education as % of total aid to education				
1999	2000	2001	2002	2003	1999	2000	2001	2002	2003	1999	2000	2001	2002	2003
100.0	100.0	86.5	100.0	55.7	0.0	0.0	0.0	0.0	24.5	0.0	0.0	13.5	0.0	19.8
0.0	0.0	40.7	55.7	46.7	95.4	100.0	59.3	7.8	18.8	4.6	0.0	0.0	36.5	34.5
0.0	41.8	...	...	0.0	0.0	0.0	...	...	0.0	100.0	58.2	...	...	100.0
...	88.4	25.8	10.2	49.7	...	7.0	12.2	41.7	14.5	...	4.6	62.0	48.1	35.9
61.2	40.6	100.0	24.3	84.6	22.7	15.3	0.0	63.8	7.4	16.0	44.1	0.0	11.9	7.9
0.0	...	0.0	100.0	0.0	0.0	...	0.0	0.0	0.0	0.0	...	100.0	0.0	0.0
0.0	...	0.0	0.0	...	0.0	...	100.0	0.0	...	0.0	...	0.0	0.0	...
46.4	...	...	...	...	39.0	...	...	...	...	14.6	...	...	...	...
100.0	100.0	100.0	99.9	99.9	0.0	0.0	0.0	0.0	0.0	0.0	0.0	0.0	0.1	0.1
89.2	89.7	90.2	91.3	91.1	0.6	0.9	0.8	0.9	0.8	10.1	9.4	9.0	7.8	8.1
59.2	**74.1**	**76.5**	**44.0**	**69.1**	**29.5**	**12.7**	**6.9**	**36.9**	**11.4**	**11.4**	**13.1**	**16.5**	**19.1**	**19.6**

Table 3: Aid to education and basic education by recipient country: total amounts and per capita/per primary-school-age child

Country	Aid to education (constant 2002 US$ millions)						Per capita aid to education (US$)	Aid to basic education (constant 2002 US$ millions)						Aid to basic education per primary-school-age child (US$)
	1999	2000	2001	2002	2003	Annual average 1999–2003	Annual average 1999–2003	1999	2000	2001	2002	2003	Annual average 1999–2003	Annual average 1999–2003
Arab States														
Algeria	67.0	64.7	66.5	72.0	96.1	73.3	2.4	0.0	0.0	0.2	0.0	0.3	0.1	0.0
Bahrain	0.1	0.1	0.1	0.2	0.3	0.2	0.2	...	...	...	...	...	...	...
Djibouti	18.6	12.7	12.9	14.9	19.7	15.8	23.3	4.9	0.0	0.0	2.5	6.8	2.9	17.5
Egypt	94.1	80.8	119.9	97.6	84.5	95.4	1.4	14.8	40.4	23.1	87.7	56.4	44.5	5.1
Iraq	3.5	4.7	4.9	1.9	7.5	4.5	0.2	0.0	0.0	0.0	0.0	0.6	0.1	0.0
Jordan	16.8	13.3	44.7	5.3	19.1	19.8	3.8	0.0	0.0	0.0	3.2	0.0	0.6	1.0
Lebanon	20.5	23.9	25.3	19.2	27.2	23.2	6.6	1.1	0.0	0.7	0.1	0.4	0.4	1.0
Libyan Arab Jamahiriya	2.2	0.0	0.0	0.0	0.0	0.4	0.1	...	...	...	...	...	...	...
Mauritania	10.8	10.5	10.7	9.4	11.1	10.5	3.8	0.1	1.8	0.2	1.8	0.4	0.8	2.2
Morocco	124.4	137.2	159.9	168.6	193.3	156.7	5.3	3.5	3.5	3.5	6.7	4.6	4.4	1.1
Oman	0.1	0.4	0.1	0.2	0.3	0.2	0.1	...	...	...	...	...	...	...
Palestinian A. T.	38.9	46.7	26.3	35.1	41.4	37.7	11.4	22.5	18.5	7.9	3.7	20.1	14.5	35.6
Saudi Arabia	1.0	0.9	1.0	0.7	2.9	1.3	0.1	...	...	...	...	...	...	...
Sudan	8.1	8.4	12.2	5.7	11.1	9.1	0.3	0.4	0.8	4.3	1.2	3.5	2.0	0.3
Syrian Arab Republic	16.5	17.3	18.6	12.9	25.4	18.1	1.1	0.0	0.2	0.0	0.0	0.8	0.2	0.0
Tunisia	40.4	67.0	48.1	44.2	85.9	57.1	5.9	0.0	0.2	0.2	1.7	0.2	0.5	0.5
Yemen	4.1	14.5	25.0	8.6	21.6	14.7	0.8	0.5	11.1	19.9	5.1	17.3	10.8	2.7
Central and Eastern Europe														
Albania	9.3	14.0	13.1	6.0	66.4	21.7	6.9	0.1	2.8	2.4	0.4	24.7	6.1	5.6
Bosnia/Herzegovina	15.3	14.3	27.0	16.9	19.0	18.5	4.6	1.0	2.1	2.2	11.3	0.2	3.4	21.8
Croatia	14.3	12.7	11.0	1.8	9.1	9.8	2.2	0.0	0.0	1.8	0.0	0.0	0.4	2.3
Republic of Moldova	1.7	2.0	2.5	2.4	4.4	2.6	0.6	0.0	0.0	0.0	0.0	0.2	0.1	...
Serbia and Montenegro	22.8	32.3	34.3	19.6	27.0	27.2	2.6	0.0	0.8	3.4	5.0	0.9	2.0	...
Slovenia	3.9	3.9	3.8	0.6	2.7	3.0	1.5	0.0	0.0	0.0	0.0	0.0	0.0	0.0
TFYR Macedonia	6.1	13.2	18.6	3.3	16.4	11.5	5.7	0.5	5.7	3.0	0.7	0.6	2.1	20.0
Turkey	68.6	55.3	56.5	22.1	71.7	54.8	0.8	0.4	2.2	1.6	1.3	1.3	1.3	0.2
Central Asia														
Armenia	6.1	6.0	5.8	1.5	6.1	5.1	1.6	0.0	0.1	0.0	0.0	1.4	0.3	0.1
Azerbaijan	1.2	2.2	1.7	1.1	3.4	1.9	0.2	0.0	0.0	0.0	0.0	0.1	0.0	0.0
Georgia	11.2	8.2	6.7	1.7	16.7	8.9	1.7	0.1	0.6	0.0	0.0	0.8	0.3	0.5
Kazakhstan	19.7	6.1	5.5	0.7	6.0	7.6	0.5	0.0	2.8	2.5	0.0	0.1	1.1	1.1
Kyrgyzstan	1.7	2.5	7.5	0.6	5.1	3.5	0.7	0.0	0.2	4.6	0.1	0.1	1.0	2.7
Mongolia	11.7	15.1	14.5	11.7	30.8	16.7	6.6	7.4	6.6	6.2	7.3	8.1	7.1	28.0
Tajikistan	5.0	2.4	2.6	1.2	3.0	2.8	0.5	0.0	2.1	2.1	0.2	0.2	0.9	1.7
Turkmenistan	4.9	0.6	1.1	0.2	0.5	1.5	0.3	0.0	0.4	0.8	0.0	0.0	0.2	0.8
Uzbekistan	14.1	5.5	59.3	5.1	17.0	20.2	0.8	0.0	1.2	2.1	0.0	0.1	0.7	0.3
East Asia and the Pacific														
Cambodia	17.3	12.1	15.0	29.9	18.0	18.5	1.4	8.5	1.8	0.5	4.6	2.4	3.6	1.7
China	83.2	84.0	136.0	319.9	741.9	273.0	0.2	20.0	1.1	0.4	2.8	86.1	22.1	0.1
Cook Islands	0.1	0.0	0.0	1.1	1.1	0.5	25.8	0.0	0.0	0.0	0.0	0.1	0.0	...
DPR Korea	0.8	0.9	0.7	0.8	1.3	0.9	0.0	0.0	0.0	0.0	0.0	0.0	0.0	0.0
Fiji	4.1	2.2	0.7	3.5	17.5	5.6	6.7	0.0	0.6	0.3	3.3	0.7	1.0	9.9
Indonesia	131.0	91.2	125.5	67.3	73.7	97.7	0.5	18.2	40.1	68.5	31.7	14.6	34.6	1.5
Kiribati	2.2	6.2	1.9	2.0	1.4	2.7	32.4	0.0	0.0	0.0	0.0	0.3	0.1	...
Lao PDR	9.1	23.9	12.1	22.4	13.8	16.2	3.0	0.6	0.8	0.6	14.2	4.0	4.0	5.4
Malaysia	289.8	5.3	3.0	11.0	21.2	66.1	2.9	0.0	0.0	0.0	0.0	0.1	0.0	0.0
Marshall Islands	0.5	0.0	0.0	0.2	1.0	0.3	6.5	0.0	0.0	0.0	0.0	0.2	0.0	...
Micronesia, F. S.	1.0	0.0	0.0	0.2	1.1	0.5	0.9	0.0	0.0	0.0	0.2	0.3	0.1	0.7
Myanmar	1.2	0.7	2.4	4.3	10.2	3.8	0.1	0.5	0.2	1.2	0.0	4.3	1.3	0.1
Nauru	0.1	0.0	0.0	0.0	0.0	0.0	2.0	...	...	...	...	...	...	...
Niue	0.4	0.0	0.0	0.5	0.4	0.3	128.0	0.0	0.0	0.0	0.0	0.0	0.0	...
Palau	0.4	0.0	0.2	0.2	1.0	0.4	17.5	0.0	0.0	0.0	0.0	0.5	0.1	...
Papua New Guinea	41.9	76.7	13.2	3.6	57.9	38.7	7.1	31.1	41.8	5.9	0.5	40.1	20.1	24.2
Philippines	94.9	15.2	13.5	31.0	28.9	36.7	0.5	11.7	0.2	3.2	1.0	9.1	5.0	0.4
Republic of Korea	35.2	0.0	0.0	0.0	0.0	7.0	0.2	...	...	...	...	...	...	...
Samoa	2.3	1.4	0.1	4.6	1.9	2.1	11.8	1.4	0.2	0.0	0.0	0.0	0.3	...
Solomon Islands	4.1	2.5	0.7	0.6	3.6	2.3	5.1	0.0	0.1	0.1	0.0	2.3	0.5	0.7
Thailand	17.7	9.8	12.4	4.7	36.1	16.2	0.3	0.0	0.0	0.0	0.0	0.1	0.0	0.0

Table 3 (continued)

Country	Aid to education (constant 2002 US$ millions)						Per capita aid to education (US$)	Aid to basic education (constant 2002 US$ millions)						Aid to basic education per primary-school-age child (US$)
	1999	2000	2001	2002	2003	Annual average 1999–2003	Annual average 1999–2003	1999	2000	2001	2002	2003	Annual average 1999–2003	Annual average 1999–2003
Timor-Leste	2.3	7.2	10.1	10.6	10.7	8.2	11.1	0.9	0.7	0.2	0.3	5.4	1.5	3.1
Tokelau	0.2	0.0	0.0	0.1	0.2	0.1	55.0	0.0	0.0	0.0	0.0	0.0	0.0	...
Tonga	1.7	0.9	0.2	1.5	2.6	1.4	13.3	0.0	0.4	0.0	0.0	0.4	0.1	...
Tuvalu	0.5	0.8	0.0	1.0	0.5	0.6	54.8	...	...	...	...	...	...	...
Vanuatu	5.6	4.0	1.6	3.3	7.6	4.4	21.8	0.0	0.0	0.2	0.0	0.5	0.1	1.5
Viet Nam	46.5	56.5	47.9	39.0	118.1	61.6	0.8	0.1	14.1	4.4	15.8	65.6	20.0	1.0
Latin America and the Caribbean														
Anguilla	4.3	0.3	0.0	0.6	0.1	1.0	92.8	0.0	0.2	0.0	0.0	0.0	0.0	...
Antigua and Barbuda	2.0	0.0	0.6	0.0	0.6	0.7	9.2	...	...	...	...	...	...	...
Argentina	10.0	9.3	9.9	11.7	13.6	10.9	0.3	0.3	0.1	0.1	0.5	0.3	0.3	0.1
Barbados	0.0	0.1	0.1	0.0	0.1	0.1	0.2	...	...	...	...	...	...	...
Belize	0.1	1.4	0.0	0.1	0.3	0.4	1.5	0.0	1.0	0.0	0.0	0.1	0.2	6.6
Bolivia	30.2	29.2	24.3	23.3	25.7	26.5	3.1	21.7	22.0	14.7	13.6	11.9	16.8	13.8
Brazil	24.0	27.8	29.3	22.8	38.2	28.4	0.2	3.7	2.9	1.5	1.0	1.9	2.2	0.2
Chile	11.7	9.5	7.0	5.7	10.1	8.8	0.6	0.4	0.4	0.2	0.1	0.0	0.2	0.1
Colombia	26.3	16.2	17.1	17.7	23.7	20.2	0.5	4.5	0.5	0.5	1.0	1.5	1.6	0.4
Costa Rica	2.7	2.2	13.2	1.8	3.0	4.6	1.1	0.3	0.0	0.1	0.4	0.0	0.2	0.4
Cuba	3.8	6.4	7.3	5.3	5.9	5.7	0.5	0.0	0.0	1.7	0.7	0.9	0.7	0.6
Dominica	0.3	0.2	0.3	0.2	0.3	0.2	3.0	...	...	...	...	...	...	...
Dominican Republic	4.2	6.6	12.2	9.9	5.5	7.7	0.9	1.7	0.2	8.9	6.5	1.4	3.7	3.9
Ecuador	7.2	5.8	9.7	22.3	13.6	11.7	0.9	0.9	0.2	1.9	1.3	1.8	1.2	0.6
El Salvador	14.6	8.5	12.8	13.5	7.8	11.5	1.8	6.1	4.2	8.7	9.8	4.3	6.6	8.4
Grenada	0.0	0.1	0.0	0.0	0.0	0.0	0.6	...	...	...	...	...	...	...
Guatemala	26.7	17.9	21.0	21.6	16.7	20.8	1.8	18.0	7.9	6.6	10.3	9.4	10.4	5.7
Guyana	5.9	0.6	0.5	0.7	25.2	6.6	8.6	0.0	0.0	0.0	0.0	23.5	4.7	0.0
Haiti	10.0	19.6	13.7	16.3	11.1	14.1	1.7	4.2	10.4	8.7	11.2	5.3	8.0	6.8
Honduras	26.9	8.2	12.2	26.7	26.1	20.0	3.0	3.2	4.7	4.9	11.4	8.2	6.5	5.7
Jamaica	9.4	13.8	3.1	3.8	5.3	7.1	2.7	8.4	13.3	2.8	3.6	4.6	6.6	21.3
Mexico	11.2	11.4	12.9	16.0	23.3	15.0	0.1	0.8	0.9	0.8	0.7	0.0	0.6	0.1
Montserrat	0.0	0.5	0.3	0.6	0.0	0.3	79.3	0.0	0.3	0.0	0.3	0.0	0.1	...
Nicaragua	23.5	33.2	16.4	12.6	15.4	20.2	3.9	10.2	25.1	4.6	2.2	5.9	9.6	13.0
Panama	14.7	3.3	1.5	2.9	6.5	5.8	1.9	0.2	1.0	0.1	0.2	0.0	0.3	1.1
Paraguay	2.7	2.9	2.8	2.6	6.5	3.5	0.6	0.9	1.1	0.7	1.0	1.8	1.1	1.1
Peru	18.9	18.7	18.8	15.5	29.0	20.2	0.8	6.3	2.2	3.9	4.9	7.8	5.0	1.2
Saint Kitts and Nevis	0.0	0.0	0.0	0.0	0.0	0.0	0.2	...	...	...	...	...	...	...
Saint Lucia	0.6	0.1	0.2	0.2	0.6	0.3	2.3	0.4	0.0	0.0	0.0	0.3	0.2	4.8
Saint Vincent/Grenadines	0.0	1.0	0.0	0.0	0.1	0.2	1.9	0.0	0.0	0.0	0.0	0.0	0.0	...
Suriname	0.7	0.8	0.7	2.6	1.3	1.2	2.8	0.0	0.0	0.0	1.9	0.0	0.4	9.5
Trinidad and Tobago	0.3	0.3	0.5	0.2	0.7	0.4	0.3	...	...	...	...	...	...	...
Turks and Caicos Islands	2.4	0.0	0.0	0.1	0.0	0.5	28.3	2.4	0.0	0.0	0.1	0.0	0.5	...
Uruguay	2.6	3.1	2.2	1.5	2.0	2.2	0.7	0.0	0.0	0.4	0.0	0.1	0.1	0.4
Venezuela	5.4	22.1	5.6	13.5	6.1	10.6	0.4	0.0	0.5	0.0	0.3	0.3	0.2	0.1
North America and Western Europe														
Malta	0.4	0.3	0.5	1.3	0.1	0.5	1.3	...	...	...	...	...	...	...
South and West Asia														
Afghanistan	5.1	3.9	4.7	23.8	25.3	12.5	0.5	0.4	0.3	0.2	4.6	16.4	4.4	0.4
Bangladesh	42.8	55.2	32.6	34.3	109.1	54.8	0.4	32.2	38.9	16.5	10.4	91.6	37.9	1.4
Bhutan	4.2	3.2	0.8	5.3	17.3	6.2	2.8	0.0	0.1	0.0	0.1	3.5	0.7	...
India	76.8	54.8	225.5	25.9	60.4	88.7	0.1	58.0	26.4	201.3	6.4	17.2	61.9	0.6
Iran, Islamic Republic of	62.7	45.1	40.4	7.5	42.6	39.7	0.6	0.0	0.0	0.0	0.0	0.0	0.0	0.0
Maldives	0.1	1.5	0.0	4.5	1.1	1.4	4.7	0.0	0.0	0.0	4.4	0.2	0.9	19.2
Nepal	41.6	14.7	11.0	5.8	20.2	18.7	0.8	34.9	7.7	7.0	0.6	8.3	11.7	4.0
Pakistan	6.6	14.5	10.6	38.7	49.1	23.9	0.2	0.6	2.5	2.3	29.2	36.5	14.2	0.4
Sri Lanka	18.0	3.1	6.8	7.2	14.3	9.9	0.5	10.6	0.2	1.8	1.1	0.5	2.9	2.1
Sub-Saharan Africa														
Angola	11.3	11.9	15.2	22.4	15.9	15.3	1.2	1.9	2.6	8.9	12.2	4.8	6.1	4.2
Benin	17.5	17.2	21.4	20.8	34.2	22.2	3.4	8.6	6.2	7.1	8.3	18.2	9.7	6.9
Botswana	2.5	1.0	0.6	0.6	1.1	1.2	0.7	0.2	0.0	0.0	0.0	0.2	0.1	0.2

Table 3 (continued)

Country	Aid to education (constant 2002 US$ millions)						Per capita aid to education (US$)	Aid to basic education (constant 2002 US$ millions)						Aid to basic education per primary-school-age child (US$)
	1999	2000	2001	2002	2003	Annual average 1999–2003	Annual average 1999–2003	1999	2000	2001	2002	2003	Annual average 1999–2003	Annual average 1999–2003
Burkina Faso	29.5	15.7	20.6	38.6	23.4	25.6	2.1	16.4	4.3	8.4	28.4	9.8	13.4	6.8
Burundi	2.1	1.2	1.5	2.5	2.7	2.0	0.3	0.0	0.1	0.0	1.0	0.3	0.3	0.2
Cameroon	51.9	50.4	63.5	34.4	78.4	55.7	3.6	8.2	0.7	8.5	8.6	12.1	7.6	2.5
Cape Verde	14.3	10.1	8.9	17.6	30.2	16.2	36.1	2.3	0.1	0.8	0.3	0.6	0.8	12.1
Central African Republic	4.9	5.9	5.3	11.5	5.7	6.7	1.8	0.1	0.5	0.0	5.7	0.1	1.2	2.5
Chad	6.0	6.1	4.6	7.5	5.2	5.9	0.7	1.9	2.1	0.8	3.2	0.7	1.7	1.5
Comoros	4.0	4.5	4.7	5.2	5.1	4.7	6.5	0.0	0.0	0.0	0.0	0.0	0.0	0.0
Congo	11.5	12.2	12.3	17.1	14.7	13.6	3.8	0.0	0.0	1.1	0.2	0.4	0.3	0.5
Cote d'Ivoire	34.8	31.6	22.2	28.1	25.2	28.4	1.8	11.9	3.6	2.4	2.0	1.3	4.2	1.9
Dem. Rep. of the Congo	7.6	9.2	9.6	17.3	17.8	12.3	0.2	0.6	0.6	0.3	1.1	2.4	1.0	0.1
Equatorial Guinea	5.7	6.8	5.1	5.0	5.8	5.7	12.1	1.9	1.7	0.6	2.3	0.6	1.4	26.6
Eritrea	6.0	41.5	4.4	3.7	11.0	13.3	3.5	0.3	34.9	0.7	0.0	0.2	7.2	17.1
Ethiopia	27.2	48.3	28.1	39.8	84.7	45.6	0.7	13.3	17.7	12.5	13.3	20.1	15.4	1.3
Gabon	16.4	17.4	16.7	16.4	17.2	16.8	13.1	3.3	1.7	1.6	1.4	1.4	1.9	9.6
Gambia	1.5	1.3	0.8	0.7	0.8	1.0	0.8	0.0	0.0	0.1	0.0	0.2	0.1	0.2
Ghana	90.4	15.7	13.7	11.1	81.3	42.4	2.1	73.9	7.7	7.6	7.3	56.0	30.5	7.7
Guinea	21.5	20.1	11.3	26.2	20.2	19.8	2.4	13.3	5.6	6.0	19.0	13.1	11.4	8.5
Guinea-Bissau	4.3	3.9	1.9	3.2	3.2	3.3	2.4	2.0	0.1	0.3	0.2	0.2	0.6	2.9
Kenya	13.7	35.0	19.7	9.1	37.7	23.0	0.7	7.1	26.3	0.3	4.4	22.9	12.2	1.6
Lesotho	0.6	4.6	6.9	2.1	3.5	3.5	2.0	0.2	1.6	0.7	1.1	1.9	1.1	2.7
Liberia	0.9	1.3	0.6	0.9	0.5	0.8	0.3	0.2	0.8	0.0	0.1	0.1	0.3	0.6
Madagascar	17.1	20.0	15.2	17.1	29.5	19.8	1.2	0.0	0.1	0.0	0.1	9.3	1.9	0.0
Malawi	12.8	142.0	15.8	36.3	26.1	46.6	4.0	0.4	102.1	11.7	33.5	8.0	31.1	19.3
Mali	24.9	24.6	36.7	83.5	43.7	42.7	3.4	14.6	10.6	29.0	47.1	10.9	22.4	11.7
Mauritius	7.9	9.4	9.1	9.7	10.5	9.3	7.8	0.0	0.0	0.0	0.1	0.0	0.0	0.1
Mozambique	30.1	59.5	48.2	88.9	64.0	58.1	3.2	11.5	32.5	24.6	26.0	23.6	23.6	9.2
Namibia	10.3	24.4	13.3	10.1	16.8	14.9	7.8	5.1	16.2	10.9	6.7	13.6	10.5	26.3
Niger	5.0	7.2	9.9	10.0	21.0	10.6	0.9	0.4	3.7	2.6	6.4	17.0	6.0	1.7
Nigeria	10.4	22.7	15.2	11.7	15.2	15.0	0.1	3.2	13.6	8.5	0.3	1.0	5.3	0.3
Rwanda	13.7	12.5	32.0	11.1	9.5	15.7	2.0	2.9	3.2	0.6	1.3	2.5	2.1	1.6
Sao Tome and Principe	1.9	3.2	2.6	3.4	3.7	2.9	19.2	0.3	0.3	0.3	0.4	0.4	0.3	...
Senegal	28.0	42.9	37.4	91.6	69.7	53.9	5.5	0.8	9.3	4.9	45.6	13.8	14.9	9.5
Seychelles	0.6	1.6	0.7	0.6	0.7	0.8	10.6	...	...	...	...	...	...	...
Sierra Leone	0.9	1.2	6.1	2.2	3.1	2.7	0.6	0.1	0.5	3.7	1.5	1.7	1.5	1.9
Somalia	5.7	0.7	14.0	2.9	2.4	5.1	0.6	0.1	0.0	0.1	2.4	0.7	0.7	...
South Africa	54.2	69.5	106.4	50.3	74.0	70.9	1.6	27.0	32.5	57.8	17.8	37.7	34.6	4.8
Swaziland	1.5	0.5	0.1	0.3	0.4	0.6	0.5	0.1	0.0	0.1	0.1	0.1	0.1	0.4
Togo	8.9	7.4	8.2	6.6	16.3	9.5	0.4	1.4	0.1	0.4	0.1	5.9	1.6	0.1
Uganda	33.1	55.3	61.8	40.4	45.3	47.2	1.3	28.4	11.3	45.4	23.6	29.7	27.7	3.9
U. R. Tanzania	17.7	19.8	46.0	154.5	78.2	63.2	13.3	10.2	4.0	27.8	130.2	12.4	36.9	54.0
Zambia	54.9	11.3	23.5	64.7	124.2	55.7	5.2	42.6	4.7	16.6	29.8	1.4	19.0	11.5
Zimbabwe	8.5	11.5	6.4	8.1	5.2	7.9	0.6	0.3	1.2	0.3	2.7	0.7	1.0	0.4
Other recipients[1]	2.5	0.2	1.9	0.3	7.5	2.5	3.6	0.0	0.0	1.5	0.0	0.0	0.3	...
Total	**2 776.1**	**2 498.0**	**2 643.3**	**2 628.2**	**3 979.7**	**2 907.5**	**0.6**	**698.5**	**746.2**	**793.9**	**849.9**	**1 016.7**	**821.0**	**1.4**
Total of 'country unspecified'[2]	**333.8**	**387.5**	**345.6**	**519.6**	**398.3**	...	...	**56.5**	**79.3**	**81.8**	**84.3**	**93.7**	...	...

Notes:

- (...) indicate that data are not available.
- Totals do not include countries where data are not available.

1. These are French Polynesia, Gibraltar, Mayotte, New Caledonia, Northern Marianas, Saint Helena, and Wallis and Futuna, which are included in the DAC database but do not figure in the table.
2. Country unspecified aid includes aid to least developed countries in general, to regions without specification of countries and to an area (e.g. West Indies, countries of former Yugoslavia).

Sources:

Aid commitments to basic education from all DAC countries: CRS, Table 2.
Population data: United Nations Population Division statistics, 2002 revision, medium variant.

Glossary

Achievement. Performance on standardized tests or examinations that measure knowledge or competence in a specific subject area. The term is sometimes used as an indication of education quality in an education system or when comparing a group of schools.

Adult education. Educational activities, offered through formal, non-formal or informal frameworks, targeted at adults and aimed at advancing, or substituting for, initial education and training. The purpose may be to (a) complete a given level of formal education or professional qualification; (b) acquire knowledge and skills in a new field (not necessarily for a qualification); and/or (c) refresh or update knowledge and skills. See also **Basic education** and **Continuing education**.

Adult literacy rate. Number of literate persons aged 15 and above, expressed as a percentage of the total population in that age group. Different ways of defining and assessing literacy yield different results regarding the number of persons designated as literate.

Aliterate. Young people or adults who have acquired the abilities to read, write and calculate, but who do not use these literacy skills.

Basic education. The whole range of educational activities, taking place in various settings (formal, non-formal and informal), that aim to meet **basic learning needs.** It has considerable overlap with the earlier concept 'fundamental education'. According to the **ISCED**, basic education comprises primary education (first stage of basic education) and lower secondary education (second stage).

Basic learning needs. Defined in the World Declaration on Education for All (Jomtien, Thailand, 1990) as essential tools for learning (e.g. literacy, oral expression, numeracy, problem-solving) as well as basic learning content (e.g. knowledge, skills, values, attitudes) that individuals should acquire in order to survive, develop personal capacities, live and work in dignity, participate in development, improve quality of life, make informed decisions and continue the learning process. The scope of basic learning needs, and how they should be met, varies by country and culture and changes over time.

Basic skills. Usually refers to some minimum competence in reading, writing and calculating (using numbers). The term is synonymous in many uses with **basic learning needs.**

Compulsory education. Educational programmes that children and young people are legally obliged to attend, usually defined in terms of a number of grades or an age range, or both.

Constant prices. A way of expressing values in real terms, enabling comparisons across a period of years. To measure changes in real national income or product, economists value total production in each year at constant prices using a set of prices that applied in a chosen base year.

Continuing (or **further**) **education.** A general term referring to a wide range of educational activities designed to meet the basic learning needs of adults. See also **Adult education** and **Lifelong learning**.

Curriculum. A course of study pursued in educational institutions. It consists of select bodies of knowledge, organized into a planned sequence, that are conveyed by educational institutions, primarily schools, to facilitate the interaction of educators and learners. When applied to adult, non-formal and literacy programmes, the term often implies a less formalized organization of learning materials and methods than in schools and tertiary institutions. Indeed, in programmes aimed at individual empowerment and social transformation, the curriculum may be developed as a dialogue with and between learners.

Drop-out rate by grade. Percentage of pupils or students who drop out from a given grade in a given school year. It is the difference between 100% and the sum of the promotion and repetition rates.

Early childhood care and education (ECCE). Programmes that, in addition to providing children with care, offer a structured and purposeful set of learning activities either in a formal institution (pre-primary or **ISCED** 0) or as part of a non-formal child development programme. ECCE programmes are normally designed for children from age 3 and include organized learning activities that constitute, on average, the equivalent of at least 2 hours per day and 100 days per year.

Education for All Development Index (EDI). Composite index aimed at measuring overall progress towards EFA. At present, the EDI incorporates four of the most easily quantifiable EFA goals – universal primary education as measured by the net enrolment ratio, adult literacy as measured by the adult literacy rate, gender as measured by the gender-specific EFA index, and quality of education as measured by the survival rate to Grade 5. Its value is the arithmetical mean of the observed values of these four indicators.

Elementary education. See **Primary education**.

Enrolment. Number of pupils or students enrolled at a given level of education, regardless of age. See also **gross enrolment ratio** and **net enrolment ratio**.

Entrance age (official). Age at which pupils or students would enter a given programme or level of education assuming they had started at the official entrance age for the lowest level, studied full-time throughout and progressed through the system without repeating or skipping a grade. The theoretical entrance age to a given programme or level may be very different from the actual or even the most common entrance age.

Family literacy (family literacy programmes). Organized educational programmes in various formats that combine learning by a mother (or parent) alongside that of her child. The term is often associated with, or used in place of, **intergenerational literacy programmes**.

Fields of study in tertiary or higher education.

Education: teacher training and education science.

Humanities and arts: humanities, religion and theology, fine and applied arts.

Social sciences, business and law: social and behavioural sciences, journalism and information, business and administration, law.

Science: life and physical sciences, mathematics, statistics and computer sciences.

Engineering, manufacturing and construction: engineering and engineering trades, manufacturing and processing, architecture and building.

Agriculture: agriculture, forestry and fishery, veterinary studies.

Health and welfare: medical sciences and health related sciences, social services.

Services: personal services, transport services, environmental protection, security services.

Foreign students. Students enrolled in an education programme in a country of which they are not permanent residents.

Functional literacy/illiteracy. A person is functionally literate/illiterate who can/cannot engage in all those activities in which literacy is required for effective functioning of his or her group and community and also for enabling him or her to continue to use reading, writing and calculation for his or her own and the community's development. (Definition originally approved in 1978 at UNESCO's General Conference, and still in use today.)

Gender parity index (GPI). Ratio of female to male values (or male to female, in certain cases) of a given indicator. A GPI of 1 indicates parity between sexes; a GPI above or below 1 indicates a disparity in favour of one sex over the other.

Gender-specific EFA index (GEI). Composite index measuring relative achievement in gender parity in total participation in primary and secondary education as well as gender parity in adult literacy. The GEI is calculated as an arithmetical mean of the gender parity indices of the primary and secondary gross enrolment ratios and of the adult literacy rate.

General education. Programmes designed mainly to lead students to a deeper understanding of a subject or group of subjects, especially, but not necessarily, with a view to preparing them for further education at the same or a higher level. These programmes are typically school-based and may or may not contain vocational elements. Their successful completion may or may not provide students with a labour-market-relevant qualification.

Gini coefficient. A commonly used measure of inequality. The coefficient varies between 0, which reflects complete equality, and 1, which indicates complete inequality (one person has all the income or consumption, all others have none).

Grade. Stage of instruction usually equivalent to one complete school year.

Graduate. A person who has successfully completed the final year of a level or sublevel of education. In some countries completion occurs as a result of passing an examination or a series of examinations. In other countries it occurs after a requisite number of course hours have been accumulated. Sometimes both types of completion occur within a country.

Gross enrolment ratio (GER). Total enrolment in a specific level of education, regardless of age, expressed as a percentage of the population in the official age group corresponding to this level of education. For the tertiary level, the population used is that of the five-year age group following on from the secondary school leaving age. The GER can exceed 100% due to early or late entry and/or grade repetition.

Gross intake rate (GIR). Total number of new entrants in the first grade of primary education, regardless of age, expressed as a percentage of the population at the official primary-school entrance age.

Gross domestic product (GDP). Sum of gross value added by all resident producers in the economy, including distributive trades and transport, plus any product taxes and minus any subsidies not included in the value of the products.

Gross national product (GNP). Gross domestic product plus net receipts of income from abroad. As these receipts may be positive or negative, GNP may be greater or smaller than GDP.

Gross national product per capita. GNP divided by the total population.

HIV prevalence rate in a given age group. Estimated number of people of a given age group living with HIV/AIDS at the end of a given year, expressed as a percentage of the total population of the corresponding age group.

Illiterate (see **Literate**)

Infant mortality rate. Number of deaths of children under age 1 per 1,000 live births in a given year.

Informal education. Learning that takes place in daily life without clearly stated objectives. The term refers to a lifelong process whereby every individual acquires attitudes, values, skills and knowledge from daily experiences and the educative influences and resources in his/her environment – e.g. family and neighbours, work and play, the marketplace, the library, the mass media.

Initial literacy (programme). A programme offering a first set of learning opportunities for youth or adults with no basic skills. It may be defined programmatically in terms of hours of teaching, learning content or a first set of skills considered critical to further literacy learning.

Intergenerational literacy (and **intergenerational literacy programmes**). Approaches to literacy programmes, similar to **family literacy**, where mothers are typically targeted for learning opportunities. Both family and intergenerational literacy approaches give stronger attention to action, in the home or in centres, to increase early childhood print-sensitivity and 'reading readiness'. It also emphasizes the importance of the home environment for children's future school success with reading and writing.

International Standard Classification of Education (ISCED). Classification system designed to serve as an instrument suitable for assembling, compiling and presenting comparable indicators and statistics of education both within countries and internationally. The system, introduced in 1976, was revised in 1997 (ISCED97).

Language (or **medium**) **of instruction.** Language(s) used to convey a specified curriculum in a formal or non-formal educational setting.

Language policy. Official government decisions regarding the use of language in the public domain, including courts, schools, government offices and health services.

Life expectancy at birth. Theoretical number of years a newborn infant would live if prevailing patterns of age-specific mortality rates in the year of birth were to stay the same throughout the child's life.

Lifelong learning. The concept of learning as a process that continues throughout life to address an individual's learning needs. The term is used widely in adult education to refer to learning processes in many forms and at many levels. See also **adult education** and **continuing education**.

Literacy. According to UNESCO's 1958 definition, it is the ability of an individual to read and write with understanding a simple short statement related to his/her everyday life. The concept of literacy has since evolved to embrace multiple skill domains, each conceived on a scale of different mastery levels and serving different purposes. See Chapter 6 for a detailed discussion.

Literacy campaign. Organized initiative, usually by a government, designed to promote the importance and acquisition of basic literacy skills. Such campaigns may offer literacy learning opportunities of short duration, either with volunteer or trained/regular tutors, and may be linked to further formal or non-formal educational opportunities to assure sustained learning.

Literacy educator. Instructor or facilitator in an adult literacy programme or campaign.

Literacy practices. The actual uses and applications of literacy skills in specific social settings (e.g. households, markets, workplaces, public offices, religious ceremonies, political movements).

Literacy projects/programmes. Limited-duration initiatives designed to impart initial or ongoing basic reading, writing and/or numeracy skills.

Literate/Illiterate. As used in the statistical annex, the term refers to a person who can/cannot read and write with understanding a simple statement related to her/his everyday life. (Based on UNESCO's 1958 definition.)

Literate environment. A rich literate environment is a public or private milieu with abundant written documents (e.g. books, magazines, newspapers), visual materials (e.g. signs, posters, handbills), or communication and electronic media (e.g. radios, televisions, computers, mobile phones). Whether in households, neighbourhoods, schools or workplaces, the quality of literate environments affects how literacy skills are acquired and practised.

Literate society. A society within which (a) the vast majority of the population acquires and uses basic literacy skills; (b) major social, political and economic institutions (e.g. offices, courts, libraries, banks) contain an abundance of printed matter, written records and visual materials, and emphasize the reading and writing of texts; and (c) the exchange of text-based information is facilitated and lifelong learning opportunities are provided.

Mother tongue. Main language spoken in the home environment and acquired as a first language. Sometimes called the home language.

Multiple literacies. The concept of a multiplicity of skills such as 'information literacy' 'visual literacy', 'media literacy' and 'scientific literacy'.

National language. Language spoken by a large part of the population of a country, which may or may not be designated an **official language** (i.e. a language designated by law to be employed in the public domain).

Neo-literate. An individual who has recently acquired a minimum level of literacy; also sometimes called a **newly literate** person. The term often refers to those who have recently completed a literacy training programme and have demonstrated the ability to continue to learn on their own, using the skills and knowledge they have obtained, without the direct guidance of a teacher.

Net attendance rate (NAR). Number of pupils in the official age group for a given level of education who attend school in that level, expressed as a percentage of the population in that age group.

Net enrolment ratio (NER). Enrolment of the official age group for a given level of education, expressed as a percentage of the population in that age group.

Net intake rate (NIR). **New entrants** to the first grade of primary education who are of the official primary-school entrance age, expressed as a percentage of the population of that age.

New entrants. Pupils entering a given level of education for the first time; the difference between enrolment and repeaters in the first grade of the level.

Non-formal education. Learning activities typically organized outside the formal education system. The term is generally contrasted with **formal** and **informal education**. In different contexts, non-formal education covers educational activities aimed at imparting adult literacy, basic education for out-of-school children and youth, life skills, work skills, and general culture. Such activities usually have clear learning objectives, but vary in duration, in conferring certification for acquired learning, and in organizational structure.

Number of children orphaned by HIV/AIDS. Estimated number of children up to age 17 who have lost one or both parents to AIDS.

Numeracy. Usually, the ability to add, subtract, multiply and divide. More broadly, it means the knowledge and skills required to effectively manage and respond to mathematical demands posed by diverse situations, involving objects, pictures, numbers, symbols, formulas, diagrams, maps, graphs, tables and text. Encompassing the ability to order and sort, count, estimate, compute, measure, and follow a model, it involves responding to information about mathematical ideas that may be represented in a range of ways.

Oral literacy. Transmission of knowledge by word of mouth from one generation to another. The term is derived from ethnography and anthropology.

Out-of-primary-school children. Children in the official primary school age range who are not enrolled in primary school.

Percentage of new entrants to the first grade of primary education with ECCE experience. Number of new entrants to the first grade of primary school who have attended the equivalent of at least 200 hours of organized ECCE programmes, expressed as a percentage of the total number of new entrants to the first grade.

Percentage of repeaters. Number of pupils enrolled in the same grade or level as the previous year, expressed as a percentage of the total enrolment in that grade or level.

Post-literacy programmes. Programmes designed to maintain and enhance basic reading, writing and numeracy skills. Like **initial literacy** programmes, they are usually of short duration (less than one year) and organized to develop specific skills for specific purposes. The 'post' is not intended to convey the idea that there is a 'pre' and 'post' state to literacy acquisition and skill development, but rather refers to the sequencing in programmatic terms for courses and programmes.

Post-secondary non-tertiary education (ISCED level 4). Programmes that lie between the upper secondary and tertiary levels from an international point of view, even though they might clearly be considered upper secondary or tertiary programmes in a national context. They are often not significantly more advanced than programmes at ISCED 3 (upper secondary) but they serve to broaden the knowledge of students who have completed a programme at that level. The students are usually older than those at ISCED level 3. ISCED 4 programmes typically last between six months and two years.

Pre-primary education (ISCED level 0). Programmes at the initial stage of organized instruction, primarily designed to introduce very young children, aged at least 3 years, to a school-type environment and provide a bridge between home and school. Variously referred to as infant education, nursery education, pre-school education, kindergarten or early childhood education, such programmes are the more formal component of ECCE. Upon completion of these programmes, children continue their education at ISCED 1 (primary education).

Primary education (ISCED level 1). Programmes normally designed on a unit or project basis to give pupils a sound basic education in reading, writing and mathematics and an elementary understanding of subjects such as history, geography, natural sciences, social sciences, art and music. Religious instruction may also be featured. These subjects serve to develop pupils' ability to obtain and use information they need about their home, community, country, etc. Also known as elementary education.

Private enrolment. Number of children enrolled in an institution that is not operated by a public authority but controlled and managed, whether for profit or not, by a private body such as a non-governmental organization, religious body, special interest group, foundation or business enterprise.

Public current expenditure on education as percentage of total public expenditure on education. Recurrent public expenditure on education expressed as a percentage of total public expenditure on education (current and capital). It covers public expenditure for both public and private institutions. Current expenditure includes expenditure for goods and services that are consumed within a given year and have to be renewed the following year, such as staff salaries and benefits; contracted or purchased services; other resources, including books and teaching materials; welfare services and items such as furniture and equipment, minor repairs, fuel, telecommunications, travel, insurance and rent. Capital expenditure includes expenditure for construction, renovation and major repairs of buildings and the purchase of heavy equipment or vehicles.

Public expenditure on education. Total public finance devoted to education by local, regional and national governments, including municipalities. Household contributions are excluded. Includes both current and capital expenditure.

Public expenditure on education as percentage of total government expenditure. Total current and capital expenditure on education at every level of administration, i.e. central, regional and local authorities, expressed as a percentage of total government expenditure (on health, education, social services, etc.).

Pupil. A child enrolled in pre-primary or primary education. Youth and adults enrolled at more advanced levels are often referred to as students.

Pupil/teacher ratio (PTR). Average number of pupils per teacher at a specific level of education, based on headcounts for both pupils and teachers.

Purchasing power parity (PPP). An exchange rate that accounts for price differences among countries, allowing international comparisons of real output and incomes.

Repetition rate by grade. Number of repeaters in a given grade in a given school year, expressed as a percentage of enrolment in that grade the previous school year.

School life expectancy (SLE). Number of years a child of school entrance age is expected to spend at school, including years spent on repetition. It is the sum of the age-specific enrolment ratios for primary, secondary, post-secondary non-tertiary and tertiary education.

School-age population. Population of the age group officially corresponding to a given level of education, whether enrolled in school or not.

Secondary education. Programmes at ISCED levels 2 and 3. Lower secondary education (ISCED 2) is generally designed to continue the basic programmes of the primary level but the teaching is typically more subject-focused, requiring more specialized teachers for each subject area. The end of this level often coincides with the end of compulsory education. In upper secondary education (ISCED 3), the final stage of secondary education in most countries, instruction is often organized even more along subject lines and teachers typically need a higher or more subject specific qualification than at ISCED level 2.

Survival rate by grade. Percentage of a cohort of pupils or students who are enrolled in the first grade of an education cycle in a given school year and are expected to reach a specified grade, regardless of repetition.

Teachers or teaching staff. Number of persons employed full time or part time in an official capacity to guide and direct the learning experience of pupils and students, irrespective of their qualifications or the delivery mechanism, i.e. face-to-face and/or at a distance. Excludes educational personnel who have no active teaching duties (e.g. headmasters, headmistresses or principals who do not teach) and persons who work occasionally or in a voluntary capacity.

Technical and vocational education. Programmes designed mainly to prepare students for direct entry into a particular occupation or trade (or class of occupations or trades). Successful completion of such programmes normally leads to a labour-market relevant vocational qualification recognized by the competent authorities (ministry of education, employers' associations, etc.) in the country in which it is obtained.

Tertiary or higher education. Programmes with an educational content more advanced than what is offered at ISCED levels 3 and 4. The first stage of tertiary education, ISCED level 5, includes level 5A, composed of largely theoretically based programmes intended to provide sufficient qualifications for gaining entry to advanced research programmes and professions with high skill requirements; and level 5B, where programmes are generally more practical, technical and/or occupationally specific. The second stage of tertiary education, ISCED level 6, comprises programmes devoted to advanced study and original research, and leading to the award of an advanced research qualification.

Total debt service. Sum of principal repayments and interest paid in foreign currency, goods or services on long-term debt, or interest paid on short-term debt, as well as repayments (repurchases and charges) to the International Monetary Fund.

Total fertility rate. Average number of children that would be born to a woman if she were to live to the end of her childbearing years (15 to 49) and bear children at each age in accordance with prevailing age-specific fertility rates.

Trained teacher. Teacher who has received the minimum organized teacher training (pre-service or in-service) normally required for teaching at the relevant level in a given country.

Trainer. In the context of adult education, someone who trains literacy educators, providing pre-service or in-service training in adult literacy teaching methods.

Transition rate to secondary education. New entrants to the first grade of secondary education in a given year, expressed as a percentage of the number of pupils enrolled in the final grade of primary education in the previous year.

Tutor. An individual teacher in a volunteer-delivered literacy programme or campaign, or a person who is paid to provide specialized instruction to a child outside school.

Youth literacy rate. Number of literate persons aged 15 to 24, expressed as a percentage of the total population in that age group.

References*

AAUW. 2001. *Hostile Hallways: Bullying, Teasing and Sexual Harassment in School*. Washington, DC, American Association of University Women.

Abadzi, H. 2003*a*. *Adult Literacy: A Review of Implementation Experience*. Operations Evaluation Department. Washington, DC, World Bank.

Abadzi, H. 2003*b*. *Improving Adult Literacy Outcomes: Lessons from Cognitive Research for Developing Countries*. Washington, DC, World Bank. (Directions in Development Series.)

Abadzi, H. 2004. Strategies and policies for literacy. Background paper for *EFA Global Monitoring Report 2006*.

Abdullaeva, M. 2005. Review of literacy in Central Asian countries. Background paper for *EFA Global Monitoring Report 2006*.

ActionAid. 2005. *Real Aid: An Agenda for Making Aid Work*. Johannesburg, ActionAid International.

ACCU. 1999. Cambodia national literacy survey. Tokyo, Asia/Pacific Cultural Centre for UNESCO. http://www.accu.or.jp/appreb/02/02-02/02-02country/02cam.html

Adams, M. 1993. Beginning to read: an overview. R. Beard (ed.), *Teaching Literacy Balancing Perspectives*. London, Hodder & Stoughton, pp. 204–15

Adams, S., Krolak, L., Kupidura, E. and Pahernik, Z. P. 2002. Libraries and resource centres: celebrating adult learners every week of the year. *Convergence*, Vol. 25 No. 2–3, pp. 27–39.

ADB. 2003. *Education: Our Framework Policies and Strategies*. Manila, Asian Development Bank. www.adb.org/Documents/Policies/Education/default.asp?p=educ

Aggio, C. 2005. Debt conversion for education: the case of Spain and Argentina. Background paper for *EFA Global Monitoring Report 2006*.

Aide et Action. 2005. Aide et Action's literacy approaches. Background paper for *EFA Global Monitoring Report 2006*.

Aid Harmonization and Alignment. 2003. Rome Declaration on Harmonization. http://www.aidharmonization.org/ah-wh/secondary-pages/why-RomeDeclaration

Altbach, P. G. 1992. *Publishing and development in the Third World*. London, Hans Zell Publishers.

Amadio, M., Frister J. and Sifuentes, D. 2005. Changing patterns in policies and strategies towards Education for All: an analysis of the National Reports presented at the 2001 and 2004 sessions of the International Conference on Education. Background paper for *EFA Global Monitoring Report 2006*.

Anderson, A. C. and Bowman, M. J. (eds). 1965. *Education and Economic Development*. Chicago, Ill., Aldine.

Anderson, A. C. and Bowman, M. J. 1976. Education and economic modernization in historical perspective. L. Stone (ed.), *Schooling and Society*. Baltimore, Md., Johns Hopkins University Press, pp 3–19.

Anderson-Levitt, K. M., Bloch, M. and Soumaré, A. M. 1998. Inside classrooms in Guinea: girls' experiences. K. M. Bloch, J. A. Beoku-Betts and B. R. Tabachnick (eds), *Women and Education in sub-Saharan Africa*. London, Lynne Rienner.

Anh, D. N. and Meyer, D. R. 1999. Impact of Human Capital on Joint-Venture Investment in Vietnam. *World Development*, Vol. 27, No. 8, pp. 1413–26.

Apple, M. 1996. *Cultural Politics and Education*. New York, Teachers' College Press.

Archer, D. and Cottingham, S. 1996*a*. *Action Research Report on REFLECT*. DFID Educational Paper No. 17. London, UK Department for International Development.

Archer, D. and Cottingham, S. 1996*b*. *The REFLECT Mother Manual: A New Approach to Adult Literacy*. London, ActionAid. http://217.206.205.24/resources/publications/mothermanual/background.htm

Arnove, R. 1987. The 1980 Nicaraguan literacy crusade. R. Arnove and H. Graff (eds). 1987. *National Literacy Campaigns: Historical and Comparative Perspectives*. New York, Plenum Press.

Arnove, R. and Graff, H. (eds). 1987. *National Literacy Campaigns: Historical and Comparative Perspectives*. New York, Plenum Press.

Arrien, J. B. 2005. La Alfabetización en Nicaragua [Literacy in Nicaragua]. Background paper for *EFA Global Monitoring Report 2006*.

Australian Bureau of Statistics. *Australian Indigenous Health Info Net 2003*. http://www.healthinfonet.ecu.edu.au/frames.htm

Azariadis, C. and Drazen, A. 1990. Threshold externalities in economic development. *Quarterly Journal of Economics*, Vol. 105, No. 2, pp 501–26.

Bagai, D. 2002. Education for All and Poverty Reduction Strategy Papers. Background paper for *EFA Global Monitoring Report 2002*.

Bailey, I. 2004. *Overview of the Adult Literacy System in Ireland and Current Issues in its Implementation*. Dublin, National Adult Literacy Agency.

Balescut, J. 2005. A historical perspective on disabilities: from Salamanca to the Convention on the Rights of Persons with Disabilities. Background paper for *EFA Global Monitoring Report 2006*.

* All background papers for *EFA Global Monitoring Report 2006* are available at www.efareport.unesco.org

Banerjee, A. and Kremer, M. 2002. Teacher-student ratios and school performance in Udaipur, India: a prospective evaluation. Cambridge, Mass., Harvard University. (Mimeograph)

Banister, J. 1987. *China's Changing Population*. Stanford, Calif., Stanford University Press.

Barrett, D. and Frank, D. J. 1999. Population control for national development: from world discourse to national policies. J. Boli and G. M. Thomas (eds), *Constructing World Culture: International Nongovernmental Organizations Since 1875*. Stanford, Calif., Stanford University Press.

Barro, R. 1991. Economic growth in a cross section of countries. *Quarterly Journal of Economics*, No. 106, pp. 407–43.

Barro, R. J. and Lee, J.-W. 1990. *International Data on Educational Attainment: Updates and Implications* (Center for International Development at Harvard University, Working Paper No. 42). www.cid.harvard.edu/ciddata/ciddata.html

Barton, D. 1994. *Literacy: An Introduction to the Ecology of Written Language*. Oxford, UK, Blackwell.

Barton, D. and Hamilton, M. 1998. *Local Literacies: Reading and Writing in One Community*. London, Routledge.

Barton, D. and Hamilton, M. 1999. Literacy practices. D. Barton, M. Hamilton. and R. Ivanic. (eds), *Situated Literacies: Reading and Writing in Context*. London, Routledge, pp. 7–15.

Barton, D., Hamilton, M. and Ivanic, R. (eds). 1999. *Situated Literacies: Reading and Writing in Context*. London, Routledge.

Baser, H. and Morgan, P. 2002. *Harmonising the Provision of Technical Assistance: Finding the Right Balance and Avoiding the New Religion* (ECDPM Discussion Paper 36). Maastricht, the Netherlands, European Centre for Development Policy Management.

Bashir, A.-H. M. and Darrat, A. F. 1994. Human capital, investment and growth: some results from an endogenous growth model. *Journal of Economics and Finance*, Vol. 18, No. 1, pp. 67–80.

Basu, K. and Foster, J. 1998. On measuring literacy. *Economic Journal*, Vol. 108, pp. 1733–49.

Bataille, L. (ed.). 1976. *A Turning Point for Literacy: Adult Education for Development. The Spirit and Declaration of Persepolis*. Oxford, UK, Pergamon.

Batchuluun Yembu and Khulan Munk-Erdene. 2005. Mongolia country study: policy options. Background Paper for *EFA Global Monitoring Report 2006*.

Baulch, B. 2004. *Aid Distribution and the MDGs*. CPRC Working Paper 48. Brighton, UK, Institute of Development Studies.

Bayou, J., Gouel, C. and Sauvageot, C. 2005. Projection of primary school children net enrolment ratios and of gender parity indices in primary and secondary education in 2015. Background paper for *EFA Global Monitoring Report 2006*.

Becker, W., Wesselius, F. and Fallon, R. 1976. *Adult Basic Education Follow-Up Study 1973–75*. Kenosa, Wis., Gateway Technical Institute.

Beder, H. 1999. *NCSALL Report No. 6. The Outcomes and Impacts of Adult Literacy in the United States*. Cambridge, Mass.: National Center for the Study of Adult Learning and Literacy, January 1999. htpp://gseweb.harvard.edu/~ncall/research/report6.pdf (Accessed 3 March 2005.)

Beder, H. 2003. *Quality Instruction in Adult Literacy Education: Summaries of Papers Presented at Twentieth Annual Rutgers Invitational Symposium on Education (RISE), National Center for the Study of Adult Learning and Literacy (NCSALL)*. Cambridge, Mass., Harvard Graduate School of Education.

Beisiegel, C. 1974. *Estado e educação popular: um estudo sobre a educação de adultos*. São Paulo, Pioneira.

Bekman, S. 1998. *Fair Chance: Evaluation Study of the Mother Child Education Program*. Istanbul, Mother Child Education Foundation. http://www.acev.org/english/about/partners.asp

Belenky, M. F., Clinchy, B. M., Goldberger, N. R. and Tarule, J. M. 1986. *Women's Ways of Knowing: The Development of Self, Voice, and Mind*. New York, Basic Books.

Benavot, A. 1996. Education and Political Democratization: Cross-National and Longitudinal Findings. *Comparative Education Review*, Vol. 40, No. 4, pp. 377–402.

Benavot, A. and Resnik, J. 2005. A Comparative Socio-Historical Analysis of Universal Basic and Secondary Education. A. Benavot, J. Resnik and J. Corrales (eds), *Global Educational Expansion: Historical Legacies, Political Obstacles*. Cambridge, Mass., American Academy of Arts and Sciences. (Occasional Paper)

Benavot, A. and Riddle, P. 1988. The expansion of primary education 1870–1940. *Sociology of Education,* Vol. 61, July, pp. 190–210.

Benin. 2001. Rapport national sur le développement de l'éducation préparé pour le BIE (UNESCO). Cotonou, Ministère de l'Education nationale et de la recherche scientifique du Bénin.

Bennell, P. 2005*a*. The impact of the AIDS epidemic on teachers in sub-Saharan Africa. *The Journal of Development Studies*, Vol. 41, No. 3, pp. 44066.

Bennell P. 2005*b*. The impact of the AIDS epidemic on the schooling of orphans and other directly affected children in sub-Saharan Africa. *The Journal of Development Studies*, Vol. 41, No. 3, pp. 467–88.

Benseman, J. and Tobias, R. 2003. *First Chance for a Real Education: An Impact Study of Adult Literacy. A Follow-Up study of Training Opportunities and Youth Training Adult Literacy Students in Christchurch, New Zealand*. Wellington, Tertiary Education Commission.

Benson, C. 2004. The importance of mother tongue-based schooling for educational quality. Background paper for *EFA Global Monitoring Report 2006*.

Bentaouet-Kattan, R. 2005. Primary school fees: an update. Background paper for *EFA Global Monitoring Report 2006*.

Bernard, A. 2005. Global Monitoring Report: East Asia Regional Analysis. Background paper for *EFA Global Monitoring Report 2006*.

Bernardo, A. B. I. 1998. *Literacy and the Mind: The Contexts and Cognitive Consequences of Literacy Practice*. Hamburg, Germany, Luzac Oriental.

Bett, J. 2003. Literacies and livelihood strategies: experience from Ulstan, El Salvador. *International Journal of Educational Development*, Vol. 23, No. 3, pp. 291–8.

Bhasin, K. 1984. The why and the how of literacy for women: some thoughts on the Indian context. *Convergence*, Vol. 17, No. 4, pp. 37-43.

Bhola, H. S. 1984. *Campaigns for Literacy: Eight national Experiences of the Twentieth Century, with a memorandum to decision-makers*. Paris, UNESCO.

Bhola, H. S. 1994. *A Sourcebook for Literacy Work: Perspective from the Grassroots*. Paris, UNESCO.

Bhola, H. S. 2005. Approaches to monitoring and evaluation in literacy programmes. Background paper for *EFA Global Monitoring Report 2006*.

Binder, M. 1999. Trends in schooling indicators during Mexico's 'Lost Decade'. *Economics of Education Review*, Vol. 18, pp. 183–99.

Bingman, M. 2000. *'I've Come a Long Way.' Learner-Identified Outcomes of Participation in Literacy Programs*. NCALL Report No. 13, February. Boston, Mass., National Center for the Study of Adult Learning and Literacy.

Biswal, K. and Govinda, R. 2005. Mapping literacy in India. Who are the illiterates and where do we find them? Background Paper for *EFA Global Monitoring Report 2006*.

Blum, A., Goldstein, H. and Guèrin-Pace, F. 2001. International Adult Literacy Survey (IALS): an analysis of international comparisons of adult literacy. *Assessment in Education*, Vol. 8, No. 2, pp. 225–46.

Blunch, N.-H. and Pörtner, C. C. 2004. Adult literacy programs in Ghana: an evaluation. Paper submitted at the conference Ghana's Economy at the Half Century. Institute of Statistical, Social and Economic Research (ISSER). http://www.isser.org/Adult%20Literacy.pdf

BMZ. 2004. *Position Paper: Basic Education for All as an International Development Goal – A Key Challenge for German Development Policy*. Bonn, Germany, Bundesministerium für wirtschaftliche Zusammenarbeit und Entwicklung [Federal Ministry for Economic Cooperation and Development].

Boggs, D., Buss, F. and Yarnell, S. 1979. Adult basic education in Ohio: program impact evaluation. *Adult Education*, Vol. 29, No. 2, pp. 123–40.

Boler, T. 2003. *Approaches to examining the impact of HIV/AIDS on teachers*. UK Working Group on Education and HIV/AIDS. London, Save the Children and ActionAid International, pp. 1–8. (Policy and Research: Series 1.)

Bondi, J. and Bondi, J. 1989. *Curriculum Development: A Guide to Practice*, 3rd edn. Columbus, Ohio, Merrill Publishing Company.

Bossuyt, J. 2001. *Mainstreaming Institutional Development: Why Is it Important and How Can it Be Done?* Maastricht, the Netherlands, European Centre for Development Policy Management.

Bougroum, M. 2005. Real options for policies and practices: Morocco. Background paper for *EFA Global Monitoring Report 2006*.

Bougroum, M., Oujour, H. and Kissami, M. A. 2005. Country study: Real options for policies and practices: Morocco. Background paper for *EFA Global Monitoring Report 2006*.

Bown, L. 1990. *Preparing the Future: Women, Literacy and Development*. ActionAid Development Report No. 4. London, ActionAid/ODA.

Boyle, S., Brock, A., Mace, J. and Sibbons M. 2002. *Reaching the Poor: The Costs of Sending Children to School*. London, UK Department for International Development.

Braithwaite, M., et. al. 2003. *Thematic Evaluation of the Integration of Gender in EC Development: Co-operation with Third Countries*. European Commission. (http://europa.eu.int/comm/europeaid/evaluation/reports/sector/951644_vol1.pdf) (http://europa.eu.int/comm/europeaid/evaluation/reports/sector/951644_vol2.pdf)

Brandt, D. and Clinton, K. 2002. Limits of the local: expanding perspectives on literacy as social practice. *Journal of Literacy Research*, Vol. 34, No. 3, pp. 337–56.

Bray, M. 2005. *Balancing the Books: Household Financing of Basic Education in Cambodia, Monograph No. 4*. Hong Kong, University of Hong Kong Comparative Education Research Centre.

Brock-Utne, B. 2000. *Whose Education For All?: The Recolonization of the African Mind*. New York, Falmer Press.

Brosh-Vaitz, S. 2005. On the state of literacy in Israel. Background paper for *EFA Global Monitoring Report 2006*.

Browne, S. 2002. *Developing Capacity through Technical Cooperation*. New York, Earthscan/UNDP.

Bruns, B., Mingat, A. and Rakotomalala, R. 2003. *A Chance for Every Child: Achieving Universal Primary Education by 2015*. Washington, DC, World Bank.

Buckland, P. 2005. *Reshaping the Future: Education and Postconflict Reconstruction*. Washington, DC, World Bank.

Bundy, D., Shaeffer, S., Jukes, M., Beegle, K., Gillespie, A., Drake, L., Lee, S., Hoffman, A-M., Jones, J., Mitchell, A., Barcelona, D., Camara, B., Golmar, C., Savioli, L., Takeuchi, T., Sembene, M. and Wright, C. 2006. School-based health and nutrition programs. D. Jamison, J. Breman, A. Measham, G. Alleyne, M. Claeson, D. Evans, P. Jha, A. Mills, P. Musgrove (eds), *Disease Control Priorities in Developing Countries*, 2nd edn. Oxford and New York, Oxford University Press for the World Bank.

Bunyi, G. W. 2005. Real options for literacy policy and practice in Kenya. Background paper for *EFA Global Monitoring Report 2006*.

Burakukaihou - Jinken kenkyuusho (Buraku Liberation and Human Rights Research Institute). 2005. *Data ni miru Burakusabestu* [Marginalization of Buraku as appears in data]. http://blhrri.org/nyumon/nyumon_jittai_seikatsu_1.htm (In Japanese.)

Burchfield, S. 1996. *An Evaluation of the Impact of Literacy on Women's Empowerment in Nepal*. Report for USAID ABEL project. Cambridge, Mass., Harvard Institute of International Development.

Burchfield, S. 1997. *An Analysis of the Impact of Literacy on Women's Empowerment in Nepal*. Cambridge, Mass., Harvard Institute for International Development.

Burchfield, S., Hua, H., Baral, D. and Rocha, V. 2002*a*. *A Longitudinal Study of the Effect of Integrated Literacy and Basic Education Programs on the Participation of Women in Social and Economic Development in Nepal*. Boston, Mass., World Education; Washington, DC, United States Agency for International Development Office of Women in Development.

Burchfield, S., Hua, H., Iturry, T. S. and Rocha, V. 2002*b*. *A Longitudinal Study of the Effect of Integrated Literacy and Basic Education Programs on the Participation of Women in Social and Economic Development in Bolivia*. Boston, Mass., World Education; Washington, DC, United States Agency for International Development Office of Women in Development.

Burgess, S. R. 1999. The development of phonological sensitivity. *Reading Research Quarterly*, Vol. 34, pp. 2-4.

Caillods, F. and Hallak, J. 2004. *Education and PRSPs: a Review of Experiences*. Paris, International Institute for Educational Planning.

Cambodia Ministry of Education, Youth and Sport (MoEYS). 2001. *Priority Action Program for Improving the Quality and Effectiveness of Basic education: Strategic Plan, Schedule of Activities and Budget Allocations*. Phnom Penh, MoEYS.

Cameron, J. and Cameron, S. 2005. Economic benefits of literacy. Background paper for *EFA Global Monitoring Report 2006*, through the University of East Anglia, Norwich.

Campaign for Popular Education. 1999. *Hope Not Complacency: State of Primary Education in Bangladesh*. 1999 Education Watch Report. Dhaka, University Press Ltd.

Campaign for Popular Education, 2001. *A Question of Quality: State of Primary Education in Bangladesh* (Vols 1, 2 and 3). 2000 Education Watch Report. Dhaka, University Press Ltd.

Campaign for Popular Education. 2002. *Renewed Hope: Daunting Challenges - State of Primary Education in Bangladesh*. 2001 Education Watch Report. Dhaka, University Press Ltd

Campaign for Popular Education. 2003. *Literacy in Bangladesh: Need for a New Vision - State of Primary Education in Bangladesh*. 2002 Education Watch Report. Dhaka, University Press Ltd.

Campaign for Popular Education. 2005. *Quality with Equity: The Primary Education Agenda*. 2003/4 Education Watch Report. Dhaka, University Press Ltd.

Canada, Government of. 2003. *The Kananaskis Summit Chair's Summary*. http://www.g8.gc.ca/2002Kananaskis/chairsummary-en.asp, last updated 14/07/2003

Canieso-Doronila, M. L. 1996. *Landscapes of Literacy: An Ethnographic Study of Functional Literacy in Marginal Philippine Communities*. Hamburg, Germany, UIE and Luzac Oriental.

Carey, S. (ed.). 2000. *Measuring Adult Literacy: The International Adult Literacy Survey in European Context*. London, Office for National Statistics.

Carnoy, M. and Marshall, J. 2005. Cuba's academic performance in comparative perspective. *Comparative Education Review*. Vol. 49, No. 2, pp. 230-61.

Carr-Hill, R. (ed.). 2001. *Adult Literacy Programs in Uganda: An Evaluation*. Washington, DC, World Bank.

Carr-Hill, R. 2005*a*. Assessment of international literacy and numeracy data (Phase II). Background paper for *EFA Global Monitoring Report 2006*.

Carr-Hill, R. 2005*b*. *Draft of Education for Nomads in Eastern Africa: Djibouti, Eritrea, Ethiopia, Kenya, Tanzania, Uganda*. Paris, UNESCO-IIEP, UNESCO-IICBA. New York, UNICEF.

Carr-Hill, R., Okech, A., Katahoire, A., Kakooza, T., Ndidde, A. and Oxenham, J. 2001. *Adult Literacy Programs in Uganda*. Washington, DC, Human Development, Africa Region, World Bank.

Carron, G., Wriria, K. and Righa, G. 1989. *The Functioning and Effects of the Kenya Literacy Programme*. IIEP Research Report No. 76. Paris, International Institute for Educational Planning.

Cawthera, A. 1997. *Let's Teach Ourselves: The Operation and Effectiveness of a People's Literacy Movement*. Manchester, UK, University of Manchester Centre for Adult and Higher Education.

Cawthera, A. 2003. *Nijera Shikhi and Adult Literacy: Impact on Learners after Five Years, Effectiveness When Operating as an NGO*. http://www.eldis.org/fulltext/nijerashikhi.pdf

Chabbott, C. 2003. *Constructing Education for Development: International Organizations and Education for All*. London, RoutledgeFarmer.

Chatry-Komarek, M. 2003. *Literacy at Stake: Teaching Reading and Writing in African Schools*. Windhoek, Namibia, Gamsberg Macmillan Publishers.

Chebanne, A., Nyati-Ramahobo, L. and Youngman, F. 2001. The development of minority language for adult literacy in Botswana: towards cultural diversity. Paper presented at the International Literacy Conference, Cape Town, 13-17 November.

Chhetri, N. and Baker, D. P. 2005. The environment for literacy among nations: concepts, past research, and preliminary analysis. Background paper for *EFA Global Monitoring Report 2006*.

Chile Ministry of Education and UNESCO-OREALC. 2002. *Educational Panorama of the Americas*. Santiago, Chile, Proyecto Regional de Indicadores Educativos [Regional Education Indicators Project]. http://www.prie.cl/ingles/seccion/documento/panorama1_5.pdf

Chilisa, B. M. 2003. Assessment of low levels of literacy in sub-Saharan Africa: conceptions and practices. Paper read at European Regional Meeting on Literacy, at Lyon, France, 2-5 April.

Choudhry, M. A. 2005. Country study: Pakistan – where and who are the world's illiterates? Background paper for *EFA Global Monitoring Report 2006*.

Chupil, T. 2003. *Creating Knowledge for Change: a Case Study of Sinui Pai Nanek Sengik's Educational Work with Orang Asli Communities in Malaysia*. Mumbai, India, Asian South Pacific Bureau of Adult Education. (ASPBAE indigenous adult education case study series.)

CIA. World Factbook. 2005. http://www.cia.gov/cia/publications/factbook/geos/af.html

CIDA. 2001. *Cida's Action Plan on Basic Education*. Gatineau, Qué., Canadian International Development Agency.

Cipolla, C. 1969. *Literacy and Development in the West*. Harmondsworth, Penguin Books.

Coalition to Stop the Use of Child Soldiers. 2001. *Global Report*. London, Coalition to Stop the Use of Child Soldiers.

Coben, D., with contributions by Colwell, D., Macrae, S., Boaler, J., Brown, M. and Rhodes, V. 2003. *Adult Numeracy: Review of Research and Related Literature*. London, National Research and Development Centre.

Cochrane, S. H. 1979. *Fertility and Education: What Do We Really Know?* Baltimore, Md., Johns Hopkins University Press.

Colclough, C., with Lewin, K. M. 1993. *Educating All the Children: Strategies for Primary Schooling in the South*. Oxford, UK, Clarendon Press.

Collins, J. 1995. Literacy and literacies. *Annual review of Anthropology*, Vol. 24, pp. 75–93.

Collins, J. and Blot, R. 2002. *Literacy and Literacies: Texts, Power and Identity*. New York, Cambridge University Press.

Collins, R. 2000. Comparative and historical patterns of education. M. T. Hallinan (ed.), *Handbook of the Sociology of Education*. New York, Kluwer.

Comings, J., Shrestha, C. K. and Smith, C. 1992. A secondary analysis of a Nepalese national literacy program. *Comparative Education Review*, Vol. 36, pp. 212–26.

Commeyras, M. and Chilisa, B. 2001. Assessing Botswana's first national survey on literacy with Wagner's proposed schema for surveying literacy in the 'Third World'. *International Journal of Educational Development*, Vol. 21, pp. 433–46.

Commission for Africa. 2005. *Our Common Interest: Report of the Commission for Africa*. London, Commission for Africa.

Cope, B. and Kalanztis, M. 2000. *Multiliteracies: Literacy Learning and the Design of Social Futures*. London, Routledge.

Corrêa, A. 1973. Mobral: Realizações e perspectivas. *Revista Educação*, Vol. 2, No. 7.

Coulmas, F. 1992. *Language and Economy*. Oxford, UK, Blackwell.

Coulmas, F. 2001. Literacy in Japan: Kanji, Kana, Romaji and Bits. D. R. Olson and N. Torrance (eds.), *The Making of Literate Societies*. Oxford, UK, Blackwell.

Coulombe, S., Tremblay, J. F. and Marchand, S. 2004. *Literacy Scores, Human Capital and Growth Across Fourteen OECD Countries*. (Catalogue No. 89-552, No. 11). Ottawa, Ont., Human Resources and Skills Development Canada, Statistics Canada.

Craig, J. 1981. The expansion of education. D. C. Berliner (ed.), *Review of Research in Education*. Washington, DC, American Educational Research Association.

Creed, C. and Perraton, H. 2001. *Distance Education in the E-9 Countries: The Development and Future of Distance Education Programmes in the Nine High-Population Countries*. Paris, UNESCO.

Cuban Libraries Solidarity Group. 2004. Cuba collaborates on literacy programs in New Zealand -20/11/2004. www.cubanlibrariessolidaritygroup.org.uk/articles.asp?ID=14

Curtin, P. D. 1990. *The Rise and Fall of the Plantation Complex: Essays in Atlantic History*. Cambridge, UK, Cambridge University Press.

Curtin, P. D. 2000. *The World and the West: The European Challenge and the Overseas Response in the Age of Empire*. Cambridge, UK, Cambridge University Press.

Damiba, A. 2005. Revue de plans d'action nationaux d'Education pour Tous: Pays francophones et lusophones d'Afrique et de la Guinée Equatorial. [Review of national Education for All action plans: French- and Portuguese-speaking countries of Africa and Equatorial Guinea.] Background paper for *EFA Global Monitoring Report 2006*.

De Ferranti, D., Perry, G. E., Gill, I. and Servén, L. 2000. *Securing our Future in a Global Economy*. Washington, DC, World Bank.

Dehn, J., Reinikka, R. and Svensson, J. 2003. Survey tools for assessing performance in service delivery. F. Bourguignon and L. Pereira da Silva (eds.), *The Impact of Economic Policies on Poverty and Income Distribution: Evaluation Techniques and Tools*. New York, Oxford University Press for the World Bank.

Deininger, K. 2003. Does cost of schooling affect enrolment by the poor? Universal primary education in Uganda. *Economics of Education Review*, Vol. 22, No. 3, pp. 291–305.

Delluc, A. 2005. Education and training policy for disadvantaged youth and adults in Senegal. Background paper for *EFA Global Monitoring Report 2006*.

Delors, J., Al Mufti, I., Amagi, I., Carneiro, R., Chung, F., Geremek, B., Gorham, W., Kornhauser, A., Manley, M., Padrón Quero, M., Savané, M.-A., Singh, K., Stavenhagen, R., Won Suhr, M. and Nanzhao, Z. 1996. *Learning: the Treasure Within – Report to UNESCO of the International Commission on Education for the Twenty-First Century*. Paris, UNESCO. http://www.unesco.org/delors

De Maeyer, M. 2005. Literacy for special target groups: prisoners. Background paper for *EFA Global Monitoring Report 2006*.

Department for Education and Skills (UK). 2001. *Skills for Life: The National Strategy for Improving Adult Literacy and Numeracy Skills*. London, UK Department for Education and Skills. http://publications.teachernet.gov.uk/eOrderingDownload/SFLLNES.pdf

Department of Adult Education and National Literacy Campaign Office (Ethiopia). 1989. *The Ethiopian National Literacy Campaign: Retrospect and Prospects (1979-1989)*. Addis Ababa, Ethiopia. Cited in: Shenkute, M. K. 2005. Literacy in Ethiopia. Background paper for *EFA Global Monitoring Report 2006*.

Desai, K. and Jukes, M. 2005. Education and HIV/AIDS. Background paper for *EFA Global Monitoring Report 2006*.

Desjardins, R. and Murray, R. S. 2004 (in press). Introduction to special issue on Literacy Proficiency: Investigations Using Direct Measures of Skills. *International Journal of Educational* Research, Vol. 39, No. 3, pp. 293-309.

DFID. 2000. *Literacy for Livelihoods*. Report on DFID Conference, Nepal. London, UK Department for International Development.

DFID. 2001. *Education for All: the challenge of Universal Primary Education.* Target Strategy Paper No. 6. London, UK Department for International Development.

Dickinson, D. K. and Tabors, P. O. 2001. *Beginning Literacy with Language: Young Children Learning at Home and School.* Baltimore, Md., Paul H. Brooks.

Dighe, A. 1995. *Women and Literacy in India: A Study in a Re-Settlement Colony in Delhi.* Reading, UK, Education for Development. (Education for Development Occasional Papers, Series 1, No. 2, August.)

Dighe, A. 2004. Pedagogical approaches to literacy acquisition and effective programme design. Background paper for *EFA Global Monitoring Report 2006*.

Direction de la Statistique (Morocco). 1991. *Enquête sur les niveaux de vie des ménages : 1990/1991*. Rabat, Direction de la Statistique.

Disability Awareness in Action. 1994. http://www.daa.org.uk/e_tribune/e_1994_02.htm.

Disability Awareness in Action. 1998. http://www.daa.org.uk/publications/Reskit6.htm.

Disability Awareness in Action. 2001. http://www.daa.org.uk/e_tribune/e_2001_09.htm#7.

Doronilla, M. L. 1996. *Landscapes of Literacy: An Ethnographic Study of Functional Literacy in Marginal Philippine Communities.* Hamburg, Germany, UNESCO Institute for Education.

Downing, J. 1987. Comparative Perspectives on World Literacy. D. Wagner (ed.), *The Future of Literacy in a Changing World, Volume I.* Oxford, UK, Pergamon Press.

Drèze, J. and Sen, A. 2002. *India: Development and Participation*. New Delhi, Oxford University Press.

D'Souza, N. 2003. *Empowerment and Action: Laya's Work in Tribal Education*. Mumbai, India, Asian South Pacific Bureau of Adult Education. (ASPBAE Case Study Series.)

Duke, C. and Hinzen, H. 2005. Basic and continuing adult education policies. Background paper for *EFA Global Monitoring Report 2006*.

Dumont, B. 1990. Post-literacy a Pre-requisite for Literacy. Geneva, UNESCO International Bureau of Education. (Literacy Lessons Series.)

Dunne, M., Leach, F., Chilisa, B., Maundeni, T., Tabulawa, R., Kutor, N., Dzama Forde, L. and Asamoah, A., 2005. *Gendered School Experiences: The Impact on Retention and Achievement in Botswana and Ghana*. Educational Papers. London, UK Department for International Development.

Duryea, S. and Arends-Kuenning, M. 2001. School attendance, child labor and local markets in urban Brazil. *World Development*, Vol. 31, No. 7, pp. 1165-78.

Dutcher, N. and Tucker, G. R.. 1997. *The Use of First and Second Languages in Education: A Review of International Experience.* Washington, DC, World Bank, East Asia and the Pacific Region, Country Department III.

Dyer, C. and Choksi, A. 2001. Literacy, schooling and development: Views of Rabari nomads, India. B. Street (ed.), *Literacy and Development: Ethnographic Perspectives*. London, Routledge.

Easton, P. B. 2005. Table in Limage, L. Literacy and empowerment: raising key issues. Paper presented at the Sixth Meeting of the Working Group on Education for All, UNESCO, 19-21 July 2005.

Egbo, B. 2000. *Gender, Literacy and Life Chances in Sub-Saharan Africa*. Cleveland/Buffalo/ Sydney, Multilingual Matters.

Elley, W. B. 1992. *How in the World Do Students Read?* The Hague, International Association for the Evaluation of Educational Achievement.

Elliot, J. L., Shin, H., Thurlow, M. L. and Ysseldyke, J. E. 1995. *A Perspective on Education and Assessment in Other Nations: Where are Students with Disabilities?* Minneapolis, Minn., National Center on Educational Outcomes. Cited in: Erickson, K. A. 2005. Literacy and persons with developmental disabilities: Why and how? Background paper for *EFA Global Monitoring Report 2006*

Eloundou-Enyegue, P., et al. 2000. *The Effects of High Fertility on Human Capital Formation under Structural Adjustment in Africa*. Paper prepared by the RAND Corporation under the POLICY Project. Santa Monica, Calif., RAND Corporation.

Erickson, K. A. 2005. Literacy and persons with developmental disabilities: why and how? Background paper for *EFA Global Monitoring Report 2006*.

European Association for International Education. 2003. *Mozambique Educational Structure*. Sixteenth Annual EAIE Conference, 15-18 September, Torino, Italy. http://www.eaie.nl/pdf/torino/905.pdf.

European Commission. 2002. *Communication from the Commission to the Council and the European Parliament on Education and Training in the Context of Poverty Reduction in Developing Countries.* Brussels, European Commission.

European Commission. 2003. *Tools for Monitoring Progress in the Education Sector*. Version 26.02.2003. http://europa.eu.int/comm/development/body/theme/human_social/docs/education/03-02_education_monitoring_tools_en.pdf

European Commission. 2005. *The European Commission Approves Proposals to Increase the Volume and Effectiveness of Development Aid.* Press Release IP/05/423. 12 April 2005. (http://europa.eu.int/rapid/pressReleasesAction.do?reference=IP/05/423&format=HTML&aged=0&language=EN&guiLanguage=en)

European Offenders Employment Forum. 2003. *What Works with Offenders? European Networking for the Identification of Successful Practices in Preparing Ex-Offenders for Employment Integration.* London, European Offenders Employment Forum. http://www.eoef.org/What%20Works%20with%20Offenders/EOEFreport03-English.pdf.

Evans, J. 2000. *Adults' Mathematical Thinking and Emotions: A Study of Numerate Practices.* London, Routledge/Falmer.

Ezeomah, C. (ed.). 1997. *The Education of Nomadic Populations in Africa*. Dakar, UNESCO Regional Office in Dakar.

Fagerberg-Diallo, S. 1999. Searching for signs of success: enlarging the concept of 'education' to include Senegalese languages. Dakar, Associates in Research & Education for Development, Inc. (Mimeograph)

Fairclough, N. 1991. Discourse and text: linguistics - an intertextual analysis within discourse analysis. Fairclough, N., *Critical Discourse Analysis: the Critical Study of Language*. London, Longman, pp. 187-213.

Farah, I. 2005. The cultural benefits of literacy. Background paper for *EFA Global Monitoring Report 2006*, through the University of East Anglia, Norwich.

Farrell, G. (ed.). 2004. *ICT and Literacy: Who Benefits? Experience from Zambia and India*. Final Report on the COL Literacy Project (COLLIT). Vancouver, BC, Commonwealth of Learning. http://www.col.org/Consultancies/04Literacy.htm. (Accessed 8 March 2005.)

Fast Track Initiative. 2004. EFA FTI Partnership Meeting Brasilia, 10-11 November, Minutes. http://www1.worldbank.org/education/efafti/documents/Brasilia/PartnershipMeetingBrasilia_Minutes.pdf

Fast Track Initiative. 2005*a*. *EFA FTI Report on the Catalytic Fund*. July 2005. Washington, DC, EFA FTI Secretariat.

Fast Track Initiative. 2005*b*. *Report from the EFA FTI Technical Meeting*. Croydon, UK, 17-19 March. http://www1.worldbank.org/education/efafti/documents/croydonreport.pdf

Fernandez, B. 2005. Literacy in francophone countries, situations and concepts. Background paper for *EFA Global Monitoring Report 2006*.

Ferraro, A. 2002. Alfabetismo e níveis de letramento no Brasil: o que dizem os Censos? *Educação e Sociedade*, Vol. 23, No. 81, pp. 21-47.

Fiedrich, M. and Jellema, A. 2003. *Literacy, Gender and Social Agency: Adventures in Empowerment*. DFID Research Report 53, September. London, UK Department for International Development.

Filmer, D. 1999. *The Structure of Social Disparities in Education: Gender and Wealth*. Policy research report on gender and development, Working Paper. No. 5. Washington, DC, World Bank.

Finnegan, R. 1988. *Literacy and Orality: Studies in the Technology of Communication*. New York, Basil Blackwell.

Fiszbein, A., Giovagnoli, P. and Adúriz, I. 2002. *Argentina's Crisis and its Impact on Household Welfare*. November, 2002. Washington, DC, World Bank.

FitzSimons, G. E. 2002. *What Counts as Mathematics? Technologies of power in adult and vocational education (Vol. 28)*. Dordrecht, the Netherlands: Kluwer Academic Publishers. Cited in: Coben, D. 2003. *Adult Numeracy: Review of research and related literature*. London, National Research and Development Centre.

Fonseca, Maria Conceição Ferreira. 2004. Letramento no Brasil: habilidades matemáticas. São Paulo, Global.

Fransman, J. 2005. Understanding literacy. Background paper for *EFA Global Monitoring Report 2006*.

Fredriksen, B. 2005*a*. External aid to 'hard core' EFA countries: the need to accompany financial aid with technical support. Background paper for *EFA Global Monitoring Report 2006*.

Fredriksen, B. 2005*b*. External aid to 'hard core' EFA countries: the need to redress the balance between technical and financial aid. Background paper for *EFA Global Monitoring Report 2006*.

Freire, P. 1985. *The Politics of Education: Culture, Power, and Liberation*. South Hadley, Mass., Bergin and Garvey.

Freire, P. 1993. Pedagogy of the City. Translated by D. Macedo. New York, Continuum.

Freire, P. 1995. *Pedagogy of Hope: Reliving Pedagogy of the Oppressed*. New York, Continuum.

Freire, P. and Macedo, D. 1987. *Literacy: Reading the Word and the World*. Westport, Conn., Begin and Garvey.

FTI Harmonization Working Group. 2004. *Harmonization in Education: Synthesis and Recommendations of the DIF Pilot*. FTI Harmonization Working Group. Paper for the FTI Partnership Meeting, Brasilia, 10-12 November . Washington, DC, Fast Track Initiative.

FTI Harmonization Working Group. 2005. Donors indicative framework, draft. http://www1.worldbank.org/education/efafti/documents/DIFjune04.xls

FTI Secretariat. 2004. *Education for All Fast Track Initiative, Status Report*. November 2004. http://www1.worldbank.org/education/efafti/documents/Brasilia/status_report_dec6.pdf

FTI Secretariat. 2005*a*. *Education Program Development Fund, Status Report*. March 2005. Prepared by the FTI Secretariat for the FTI Technical Meeting in 17-19 March 2003. http://www1.worldbank.org/education/efafti/documents/EPDFstatusreport_march05.pdf

FTI Secretariat. 2005*b*. *Guidelines for Appraisal of the Primary Education Component of an Education Sector Plan*. http://www1.worldbank.org/education/efafti/documents/assessmentguidelines.pdf (Accessed 17 July 2005)

Fuglesang, A. 1982. *About Understanding - Ideas and Observations on Cross-Cultural Communication*. Uppsala, Sweden, Dag Hammarskjold Foundation.

Fukuda-Parr, S., Lopes, C. and Malik, K. 2001. *Capacity for Development: New Solutions to Old Problems*. New York, Earthscan/UNDP.

Funkhouser, E. 1999. Cyclical economic conditions and school attendance in Costa Rica. *Economics of Education Review*, Vol. 18, No. 1, pp. 31-50.

Furet, F. and Ozouf, J. 1977. *Lire et écrire: L'alphabétisation des français de Calvin à Jules Ferry*. Vols. 1 and 2. Paris, Editions de Minuit.

G8 Gleneagles. 2005. The Gleneagles Communiqué. http://www.fco.gov.uk/Files/kfile/PostG8_Gleneagles_Communique.pdf

Gadotti, M. 1994. *Reading Paulo Freire: His Life and Work*. New York, SUNY Press.

Gal, I. 2000. The numeracy challenge. I. Gal (ed.), *Adult Numeracy Development: Theory, Research and Practice*. Cresskill, NJ, Hampton Press, pp. 9-31.

Garcia Garrido, J. L. 1986. *International Yearbook of Education XXXVIII: Primary Education on the Threshold of the Twenty-First Century.* Paris, UNESCO, International Bureau of Education.

Gautam, K. 1998. An Encounter with a 17th Century Manual. *PLA Notes*. Issue No. 32, pp. 40–42. London, International Institute for Environment and Development.

Gee, J. 1990. *Social Linguistics and Literacies: Ideology in Discourse.* London and Philadelphia, Falmer Press.

Gee, J. 1999. *An Introduction to Discourse Analysis: Theory and Method.* London, Routledge.

Gee, J., Hull, G. and Lankshear, C. 1996. *The New Work Order: Behind the Language of the New Capitalism*. London, Allen & Unwin.

Geva, E. and Ryan, E. B. 1993. Linguistic and academic correlates of academic skills in first and second languages. *Language Learning*, Vol. 43, pp. 5–42.

Ghebrezghi, D. 2003. The literacy programme, part and parcel of Eritrea's march towards Education for All. UNESCO (ed.), *Literacy as Freedom: a UNESCO Roundtable*. Paris, UNESCO.

Gibson, J. 1998. Literacy and intra-household externalities on measuring literacies. *Economic Journal*, Vol. 108 (November), pp. 1733–49.

Gibson, J. 2001. Literacy and intrahousehold externalities. *World Development*, Vol. 29, No. 1, pp. 155–66.

Giles, J., Hannum, E., Park, A. and Zhang, J. 2003. *Life Skills, Schooling, and the Labor Market in Urban China: New Insights from Adult Literacy Measurement*. Report to the International Centre for the Study of East Asian Development, Kitakyushu, Japan, ICSEAD. http://www.ssc.upenn.edu/china/lifeskills/documents/2003-21.pdf (Working Paper Series Vol. 2003-21.)

Global Campaign for Education. 2005. Deadly inertia? A cross-country study of educational responses to HIV/AIDS (working title). http://www.unesco.org/bpi/aids-iatt/deadly-inertia.pdf

Global Campaign for Education/ActionAid International. 2005. Global benchmarks for adult literacy. Background paper for *EFA Global Monitoring Report 2006*.

Goldstein, H. 2004. Education for All: the globalization of learning targets. *Comparative Education Review*, Vol. 40, N°. 1, pp. 7–14.

Goodman, K. 1996 *Ken Goodman on Reading.* Chapter 8: Learning and teaching reading and writing. Richmond Hill, Ont., Scholastic Canada Ltd., pp. 117–25

Goody, E. and Bennett, J. 2001. Literacy for Gonja and Birifor children in Northern Ghana. D. R. Olson and N. Torrance (eds), *The Making of Literate Societies*. Oxford, UK, Blackwell.

Goody, J. R. 1977. *The Domestication of the Savage Mind: Evolution and Communication*. Cambridge, UK, Cambridge University Press, pp. 10–18

Gordon, R. 1995. *Causes of Girls' Academic Underachievement: The Influence of Teachers' Attitudes and Expectations on the Academic Performance of Secondary School Girls*. Harare, Zimbabwe, HRCC, University of Zimbabwe.

Gordon, R. 2005. *Ethnologue: Languages of the World*. 15th edn SIL International. http://www.ethnologue.com/.

Govinda, R. and Biswal, K. 2005*a*. EFA in South and West Asia: an overview of progress since Dakar. Background paper for *EFA Global Monitoring Report 2006*.

Govinda, R. and Biswal, K. 2005*b*. Literacy: real options for policy and practice in India. Background paper for *EFA Global Monitoring Report 2006*.

Graff, H. 1987*a*. *The Labyrinths of Literacy*. New York, The Falmer Press.

Graff, H. 1987*b*. *The Legacies of Literacy: Continuities and Contradictions in Western Culture and Society*. Bloomington, Ind., Indiana University Press.

Graff, H. 1991. Literacy: Myths and lessons. L. Limage, L. Oppenheim and K. Pearl. (eds), *Adult Literacy in International Urban Perspective*. Proceedings of a conference co-organized by UNESCO, Literacy Assistance Center of New York, Mayor's Office of New York, and the City University of New York. New York, Bloomington, Ind., Indiana University Press.

Grant, K. B., Gorgens, M. and Kinghorn, A. 2004. *Mitigating the Impact of HIV on Service Providers: What Has Been Attempted, What is Working, What Has Not Worked, Where and Why?* Johannesburg, Health and Development Africa.

Grassly, N. C., Desai, K., Pegurri, E., Sikazwe, A., Malambo, I., Siamatowe, C. and Bundy, D. 2003. The economic impact of HIV/AIDS on the education sector in Zambia. *AIDS*, Vol. 17, pp. 1-6.

Gray, W. S. 1969. *The Teaching of Reading and Writing: an International Survey*. Glenview, Ill., UNESCO/Scott Foresman and Co.

Greaney, V., Khandker, S. R. and. Alam, M. 1998. *Bangladesh: Assessing Basic Learning Skills*. Washington, DC and Dhaka, World Bank.

Greenberg, D. 2002. *Women and Literacy Special Collections Project*. Funded by the National Institute for Literacy. http://www.litwomen.org?Research/Greenberg.html

Greenleigh Associates. 1968. *Participants in the Field Test of Four Adult Basic Education Systems: A Follow-Up Study*. New York, Greenleigh Associates.

Gregson, S., Waddell, H. and Chandiwana, S. 2001. School education and HIV control in sub-Saharan Africa: from discord to harmony. *Journal of Internationl Development*, Vol. 13, p. 467–85.

Grin, F. 2005. The economics of language policy implementation: Identifying and measuring costs. N. Alexander (ed.), *Mother Tongue-Based Bilingual Education in Southern Africa: the Dynamics of Implementation*. Proceedings of a symposium held at the University of Cape Town, 16–19 October. Cape Town,Volkswagen Foundation and PRAESA.

Groupe permanent de lutte contre l'illettrisme. 1998. Illettrisme: de l'enjeu social a l'enjeu citoyen. Collection 'en toutes lettres'. Paris, Ministère de l'emploi et de la solidarité, Groupe permanent de lutte contre l'illettrisme: La Documentation française.

Gunnarsson, C. 2001. *Capacity Building, Institutional Crisis and the Issue of Recurrent Costs.* Synthesis Report. Stockholm, Almkvist and Wiksell International.

Guy, T. 2005. Adult literacy in the United States: an overview of the federal system of adult education. Background paper for *EFA Global Monitoring Report 2006*.

Hagemann, E. 1988. *Statistik in China: ein Literaturbericht.* Berichte des Bundesinstituts für ostwissenshaftliche und internationale Studien, No. 5. Cologne.

Hamilton, M. and Barton, D. 2000. The international adult literacy survey: What does it really measure? *International Review of Education,* Vol. 46, No. 5, pp. 377-89.

Hammoud, H. R. 2005. Illiteracy in the Arab world. Background paper for *EFA Global Monitoring Report 2006*.

Hanemann, U. 2005*a*. Literacy in Botswana. Background paper for *EFA Global Monitoring Report 2006*, through UNESCO Institute for Education, Hamburg.

Hanemann, U. 2005*b*. Literacy in Conflict Situations. Background paper for *EFA Global Monitoring Report 2006*, through UNESCO Institute for Education, Hamburg.

Hanemann, U. and Mauch, W. 2005. Literacy for special target groups. Background paper for *EFA Global Monitoring Report 2006*.

Hannum, E. 2002. Ethnic differences in basic education in reform-era rural China. *Demography* Vol. 39, No. 1, pp. 95-117.

Hannum, E. and Buchman, C. 2003. *The Consequences of Global Educational Expansion.* Cambridge, Mass., American Academy of Arts and Sciences.

Hannum, E. and Xie, Y. 1998. Ethnic stratification in Northwest China: occupational differences between the Han Chinese and national minorities in Xinjiang, 1982–90. *Demography*, Vol. 35, No. 3, pp. 323–33.

Hanushek, E. A. and Kimko, D. D. 2000. Schooling, labor-force quality, and the growth of nations. *American Economic Review*, Vol. 90, No. 5, pp. 1184-1208.

Harmon, C., Oosterbeek, H. and Walker, I. 2003. The returns to education: microeconomics. *Journal of Economic Surveys*, Vol. 17, No. 2, pp. 115–56.

Hayes, E. 2003. Reconceptualizing adult basic education and the digital divide. A. Belzer and H. Beder (eds.), *Defining and Improving Quality in Adult Basic Education: Issues and Challenges.* Mahwah, NJ, Lawrence Erlbaum, pp. 27.

Hayford, C. W. 1987. Literacy movements in modern China. R. Arnove and H. Graff (eds). 1987. *National Literacy Campaigns: Historical and Comparative Perspectives*. New York, Plenum Press.

HEARD and MTT. 2005. Report on the Education Sector Global HIV/AIDS Readiness Survey 2004: A Review of the Comparative Readiness of the Education Sectors in 71 Countries to Respond to, Manage and Mitigate the Impact of HIV/AIDS. Survey by the Health Economics & HIV/AIDS Research Division of the University of KwaZulu Natal and the Mobile Task Team on the Impact of HIV/AIDS on Education, for the UNAIDS Inter-Agency Task Team on Education. Paris, International Institute for Educational Planning.

Heath, S. B. 1983. *Ways with Words: Language, Life and Work in Communities and Classrooms*. Cambridge, UK, Cambridge University Press.

Heath, S. B. 1993. The madness(es) of reading and writing ethnography. *Anthropology & Education Quarterly*, Vol. 24, No. 3, pp. 256–68.

Heltberg, R., Simler, K. and Tarp, F. 2001. *Public Spending and Poverty in Mozambique*. IFPRI Discussion Paper No. 167. Washington, DC, International Food Policy Research Institute.

Hendricks, P. A. 1996. *Developing Youth Curriculum Using the Targeting Life Skills Model: Incorporating Developmentally Appropriate Learning Opportunities to Assess Impact of Life Skill Development.* Ames, Iowa, Iowa State University Extension.

Henze, J. 1987. Statistical documentation in Chinese education: where reality ends and the myths begin. *Canadian and International Education*, Vol. 16, No. 1, pp. 198-210.

Herrera, L. 2004. Education, Islam and modernity: beyond westernization and centralization. *Comparative Education Review*, Vol. 48, No. 43, pp. 318–26.

Herrera, L. 2006. Higher education in the Arab world. J. Forest and P. Altbach (eds), *International Handbook of Higher Education*. Dordrecht, the Netherlands, Springer, pp. 409–21.

Herz, B. K. and Sperling, G. B. 2003. *What Works in Girls' Education, Evidence and Policies from the Developing World.* New York, Council on Foreign Relations.

Hough, K. 2003. *Language Policy and Democracy in South Africa: the Prospects of Equality within Rights-based Policy and Planning.* Stockholm, Stockholm University Centre for Research on Bilingualism.

Hinchliffe, K. 2004. *Notes on the Impact of the HIPC Initiative on Public Expenditures in Education and Health in African Countries.* Washington, DC, World Bank. (Africa Region Human Development Working Paper Series, No. 77.)

Homel, R. 1999. *Preventing Violence – A Review of the Literature on Violence and Violence Prevention.* New South Wales, Australia, Attorney General's Department. www.lawlink.nsw.gov.au/cpd.nsf/pages/violreport_index. (Accessed 27 May 2003.)

Horsman, J. 1990. *Something in My Mind Besides the Everyday: Women and Literacy*. Toronto, Ont., Women's Press.

Houston, R. 1985. *Scottish Literacy and Scottish Identity.* Cambridge, UK, Cambridge University Press.

Hull, G. 2003. Youth culture and digital media: new literacies for new times. *Research in the Teaching of English*, Vol. 38, No. 2, pp. 229-333.

Human Rights Watch. 1999. Kenya, Spare the Child: Corporal Punishment in Kenyan Schools. *Human Rights Watch Report*, Vol. 11, No. 6 (A).

Hunter, S. and Fall, D. 1998. *Orphans and HIV/AIDS in Zambia: An Assessment of Orphans in the Context of Children Affected by HIV/ AIDS*. Lusaka, UNICEF.

ILI/UNESCO. 1999. Assessing basic learning competencies in youth and adults in developing countries: analytic survey framework and implementation guidelines. *ILI/UNESCO Technical Report*. Philadelphia, Pa., International Literacy Institute.

ILI/UNESCO. 2001. *LAP First Experts' Meeting Report*. Philadelphia, Pa., International Literacy Institute.

ILI/UNESCO. 2002*a*. *Analytic Review of Four LAP Country Case Studies*. Philadelphia, Pa., International Literacy Institute.

ILI/UNESCO. 2002*b*. *LAP Second Experts' Meeting Report*. Philadelphia, Pa., International Literacy Institute.

ILO (World Commission on the Social Dimension of Globalization). 2004. *A Fair Globalization: Creating Opportunities for All*. http://www.ilo.org/public/english/fairglobalization/report/highlight.htm

IMF/IDA. 2003. *Heavily Indebted Poor Countries (HIPC) Initiative – Status of Implementation*. Washington, DC, International Monetary Fund and International Development Association.

IMF/IDA. 2004. *Heavily Indebted Poor Countries (HIPC) Initiative – Statistical Update*. Washington, DC, International Monetary Fund and International Development Association.

IMF/World Bank. 2005. *Development Committee Communiqué*. Joint Ministerial Committee of the Boards of Governors of the Bank and the Fund on the Transfer of Real Resources to Developing Countries, 17 April 2005. Washington, DC, IMF/World Bank.

INEE. 2004. *Minimum Standards for Education in Emergencies, Chronic Crises and Early Reconstruction: A Commitment to Access, Quality and Accountability*. Inter-Agency Network for Education in Emergencies. Paris, UNESCO.

International Association of Universities/UNESCO. 2005. *Country Reports: Mozambique*. IAU Online Databases. http://www.unesco.org/iau/onlinedatabases/

International Centre for Prison Studies. 2005. http://www.prisonstudies.org/ (Accessed 10 August 2005.)

International Organization for Migration. 2005. *World Migration 2005: Costs and Benefits of International Migration*. Geneva, IOM.

Ireland, T. D. 1994. Literacy skills as building bricks for trade union democracy: the experience of the construction workers trade union in Joao Pessoa, Brazil. *Adult Education and Development* Vol. 42, pp. 81-7.

Iskandar, L. 2005. Country study: Egypt: Where and who are the world's illiterates? Background paper for *EFA Global Monitoring Report 2006*.

Jalal, F. and Sardjunani, N. 2005. Increasing literacy for a better and more promising Indonesia. Background paper *for EFA Global Monitoring Report 2006*.

JBIC. 2002. *Medium-term Strategy for Overseas Economic Cooperation Operations*. Tokyo, Japan, Bank for International Cooperation.

Johansson, E. 1977. The History of Literacy in Sweden, in comparison with some other countries. *Educational Reports Umeå*, No. 12. Umeå, Sweden, Umeå School of Education, University of Umeå, pp. 151-60.

Johansson, E. 1981. The history of literacy in Sweden. H. Graff (ed.), *Literacy and Social Development in the West: A Reader*. Cambridge, UK, Cambridge University Press.

Johnston, B., FitzSimons, G., Maaβ, J., and Yasukawa, K. 2002. Editorial. *Literacy and Numeracy Studies*, Vol. 11, No. 2, pp. 1-7. Cited in: Coben, D. 2003. *Adult Numeracy: Review of Research and Related Literature*. London, National Research and Development Centre.

Joliffe, D. 2002. Whose education matters in the determination of household income? Evidence from a developing country. *Economic Development and Cultural Change*, Vol. 50, No. 2, pp. 287-312.

Jones, P. 1990*a*. *Literacy and Basic Education for Adults and Young people: Review of Experience*. Paris, UNESCO.

Jones, P. 1990*b*. UNESCO and the politics of global literacy. *Comparative Education Review*, Vol. 34, No. 1, pp. 41–60.

Jones, P. 1997. The World Bank and the literacy question: orthodoxy, heresy, and ideology. *International Review of Education*, Vol. 43, No. 4, pp. 367–75.

Jones, P., with Coleman, D. 2005. *The United Nations and Education: Multilateralism, Development and Globalization*. London and New York, Routledge/Falmer.

Jones, S., Riddell, R. and Katoglou, K. 2004. *Aid Allocation: Managing for Development Results and Difficult Partnerships*. Oxford, UK, Oxford Policy Management.

Jukes, M., Drake, L. and Bundy, D. Forthcoming. *Levelling the Playing Field: The Importance of School Health and Nutrition in Achieving Education for All*. Washington, DC, World Bank.

Juventud Rebelde. 2005. Libre de Analfabetismo Municipio de Ecuador con Programa Cubano. www.jrebelde.cubaweb.cu/2005/abril-junio/abril-25/libre.html

Kagitcibasi, C., Goksen, F. and Gulgoz, S. 2005. Functional adult literacy and empowerment of women: impact of a functional literacy program in Turkey. *Journal of Adolescent and Adult Literacy*, Vol. 48, No. 6, pp. 472-89.

Keeble, A. 2001. *In the Spirit of Wandering Teachers: Cuban Literacy Campaign, 1961*. Melbourne, Australia, Ocean Press.

Kell, C. 1995. Literacies of everyday life, development and schooling: a study of literacy practices in an informal settlement in South Africa. *Critical Forum*, Vol. 4, No. 1, pp. 2-42.

Kell, C. 1999. Teaching Letters: the recontextualisation of letter-writing practices in literacy classes for unschooled adults in South Africa. D. Barton and N. Hall (eds), *Letter Writing as a Social Practice*. Amsterdam and Philadelphia, John Benjamins.

Kenez, P. 1982. Liquidating illiteracy in revolutionary Russia. *Russian History*, Vol. 9, No. 2/3, p. 173.

Khandekar, S. 2004. 'Literacy brought us to the forefront': Literacy and empowering process of the Dalit community women in a Mumbai slum. A. Robinson-Pant (ed.), *Women, Literacy and Development: Alternative perspectives*. London, Routledge.

Kidd, R. and Khumar, K. 1981. Co-opting Freire. *Economic and Political Weekly*, Vol. 16, Nos. 1 and 2, pp. 27–40.

Killick, T. 2004. Politics, evidence and the new aid agenda. *Development Policy Review*, Vol. 22, No. 1, pp. 5–29.

King, E. M. and Alderman, H. 2001. *Empowering Women to Achieve Food Security*. (2020 Vision Focus, 6). Washington, DC, International Food Policy Research Institute.

Knight, J. and Sabot, R. 1990. *Education, Productivity, and Inequality: The East African Natural Experiment*. Oxford and New York, Oxford University Press for the World Bank.

Knowles, M. S. 1980. *The Modern Practice of Adult Education*. New York, Association Press.

Knowles, M. S. 1989. *The Making of an Adult Educator: An Autobiographical Journey*. San Francisco, Calif., Jossey-Bass.

Koirala, B. N. and Aryal, B. R. 2005. Options for policy and practice in Nepal. Background paper for *EFA Global Monitoring Report 2006*.

Koke, T. 2005. Baltic region: overview of progress towards EFA since Dakar. Background paper for *EFA Global Monitoring Report 2006*.

Kolb, D. 1984. *Experiential Learning: Experience as a Source of Learning and Development*. Englewood Cliffs, NJ, Prentice-Hall.

Koopman, H. 2005. Silent Partnership. Background paper for *EFA Global Monitoring Report 2006*.

Kosonen, K. 2004. Local languages in education in Southeast Asia: comparative analysis. Paper read at Comparative and International Education Society (CIES) annual conference, Salt Lake City, Utah, March 9–12.

Kratli, S. 2000. The bias behind nomadic education. *UNESCO Courier*, October, 2000.

Kress, G. and van Leeuwen, T. 2001. *Multimodal Discourse*. London, Arnold.

Krolak, L. 2005. The role of libraries for the creation of literate environments. Background paper for *EFA Global Monitoring Report 2006*.

Krueger, A. B. and Lindahl, M. 2000. *Education for Growth: Why and for Whom?* Working Paper No. 429. Princeton, NJ, Princeton University Industrial Relations Section.

Kutnick, P., Jules, V. and Layne, A. 1997. *Gender and School Achievement in the Caribbean*. Education Report No. 21. London, UK Department for International Development.

Lameta, E. 2005. Pacific region: overview of progress towards EFA since Dakar. Background paper for *EFA Global Monitoring Report 2006*.

Lankshear, C. and Knobel, M. 2003. New *Literacies: Changing Knowledge and Classroom Learning*. Buckingham, UK, Open University Press.

Lao People's Democratic Republic. Ministry of Education, Department of Non-formal Education. 2004. *Lao National Literacy Survey 2001. Final Report*. Bangkok, UNESCO Asia and Pacific Regional Bureau of Education.

Lauglo, J. 2001. *Engaging with Adults – The Case for Increased Support to Adult Basic Education in sub-Saharan Africa*. Washington, DC, World Bank. (Africa Region Human Development Working Paper Series.)

Lave, J. 1988. *Cognition in Practice*. Cambridge, UK, Cambridge University Press.

Lave, J. and Wenger, E. 1991. *Situated Learning: Legitimate Peripheral Participation*. Cambridge, UK, Cambridge University Press.

Lavy, V., Spratt, J. and Leboucher, N. 1995. *Changing Patterns of Illiteracy in Morocco: Assessment Methods Compared*. Washington, DC, World Bank. (Living Standards Measurement Study, Working Paper No. 115.)

Lawrence, J. 2004. *The Right to Education for Persons with Disabilities: Towards Inclusion*. Conceptual Paper, December. Paris, UNESCO.

Leach, F. 2003. Gender and violence in schools. Background paper for *EFA Global Monitoring Report 2003/4*.

Leach, F. and Machakanja. 2000. *Preliminary Investigation of the Abuse of Girls in Zimbabwean Junior Secondary Schools*. DFID Education Research Report No 39. London, UK Department for International Development.

Leach, F., Fiscian, V., Kadzamira, E., Lemani, E. and Nacgajabga, P. 2003. *An Investigative Study of the Abuse of Girls in African Schools*. DFID Educational Papers, No. 54. London, UK Department for International Development. http://www.id21.org/Education/e2fl1g2.html

Lehman, D. 2005. Shortening the distance to EFA in the African Sahel. World Bank Working Paper. (Mimeograph)

Leiner, M. 1987. The 1961 national literacy campaign. R. Arnove and H. Graff (eds). 1987. *National Literacy Campaigns: Historical and Comparative Perspectives*. New York, Plenum Press.

Lewin, K. M. and Caillods, F. 2001. *Financing Secondary Education in Developing Countries: Strategies for Sustainable Growth*. Paris, International Institute for Educational Planning.

Limage, L. 1986. Adult literacy policy in industrialized countries. *Comparative Education Review*, Vol. 30, No. 1, pp. 50–72 [Also in: R. Arnove and H. Graff (eds). 1987. *National Literacy Campaigns: Historical and Comparative Perspectives*. New York, Plenum Press, pp. 293–314.]

Limage, L. 2005*a*. Literacy Glossary for *EFA Global Monitoring Report 2006*.

Limage, L. 2005*b*. The growth of literacy in historic perspective: clarifying the role of formal schooling and adult learning opportunities. Background paper for *EFA Global Monitoring Report 2006*.

Limage, L. 2005*c*. The political economy and recent history of book publishing and print materials: considerations for literacy acquisition. Background paper for *EFA Global Monitoring Report 2006*.

Lind, A. 1988. *Adult Literacy Lessons and Promises: Mozambican literacy campaigns 1978-1982*. Studies in comparative and international education, Vol. 12. Stockholm, Institute of International Education, University of Stockholm.

Lind, A. 1996. *Free to Speak Up - Overall Evaluation of the National Literacy Programme in Namibia*. Edited by Directorate of Adult Basic Education, Ministry of Basic Education and Culture. Windhoek, Namibia, Gamsberg MacMillan.

Lind, A. and Johnston, A. 1990. *Adult Literacy in the Third World: A Review of Objectives and Strategies*. Stockholm, Swedish Agency for International Development Cooperation.

Lind, A. and Johnston, A. 1996. Adult literacy programs in developing nations. A. Tuijnman (ed.), *International Encyclopedia of Adult Education and Training*. Oxford, UK, Pergamon Press.

Lockridge, K. 1974. *Literacy in Colonial New England*. New York, Norton.

Loening, L. J. 2002. *The Impact of Education on Economic Growth in Guatemala*. Discussion Paper No. 87. Göttingen, Germany, Ibero-America Institute for Economic Research.

Lutz, W. and Goujon, A. 2005. Method of projecting literacy. Paris, UNESCO.

Maamouri, M. 1998. Language education and human development: Arabic diglossia and its impact on the quality of education in the Arab region. Paper read at World Bank Mediterranean Development Forum, Marrakech, Morocco, 3-6 September.

Maas, U. 2001. Literacy in Germany. D. Olson and N. Torrance (eds.), *The Making of Literate Societies*. Oxford, UK, Blackwell.

Maddox, B. 2001. Literacy and the market: the economic uses of literacy among the peasantry in north-west Bangladesh. B. Street (ed.), *Literacy and Development: Ethnographic Perspectives*. London, Routledge, pp. 137-51.

Maddox, B. 2005. Assessing the impact of women's literacies in Bangladesh: an ethnographic enquiry. *International Journal of Educational Development*, Vol. 25, No. 2, pp. 123-32.

Maimbolwa-Sinyangwe, I. M. and Chilangwa, B. Y. 1995. Learning from inside the classroom. Research Report for UNICEF and the Ministry of Education, Zambia.

Mammo, K. 2005. Where and who are the worlds illiterates: Ethiopia country study. Background paper for *EFA Global Monitoring Report 2006*.

Mancebo, M. E. 2005. Comparative study on national conceptions of literacy, numeracy and life skills. Background paper for *EFA Global Monitoring Report 2006*, through UNESCO International Bureau of Education, Geneva.

Mantes, J. C. 2005. Les nouvelles orientations de la coopération française dans le domaine de l'education [The New Focus of France's Aid Programme in the Area of Education]. Background paper for *EFA Global Monitoring Report 2006*.

Martin, M. O., Mullis, I. V. S., Gonzalez, E. J. and Chrostowski, S. J. 2004. *TIMSS 2003 International Mathematics Report: Findings from IEA's Trends in Mathematics and Science Study at the Fourth and Eighth Grades*. Chestnut Hill, Mass., Boston College.

Martinez Nateras, M. 2003. CONFINTEA thematic review: migrants. Paper read at CONFINTEA Mid-term Review, August.

Masagão Ribeiro, V. 2003. *Letramento no Brasil*. São Paulo, Global.

Masagão Ribeiro, V. and Gomes Batista, A. A. 2005. Commitments and challenges towards a literate Brazil. Background paper for *EFA Global Monitoring Report 2006*.

Maurer, M. 2005. An exploration study of conceptualisations of literacy, numeracy and life skills based on the 2004 series of National Reports. Background paper for *EFA Global Monitoring Report 2006*.

Mazrui, A. 1996. Language policy and the foundations of democracy: an African perspective. *International Journal of the Sociology of Language*, No. 118, pp. 107-24.

McClelland, D. 1961. *The Achieving Society*. Princeton, NJ, Van Nostrand.

McClelland, D. 1966. Does education accelerate economic growth? *Economic Development and Cultural Change*, Vol. 15, No. 3, pp. 257-78.

Mehrotra, S. 1998. Education for All: policy lessons from high-achieving countries. *International Review of Education*, Vol. 44, No. 5/6, pp. 1-24.

Meredith, K. and Steele, J. 2000. Education in transition: trends in Central and Eastern Europe. M. Kamill et al. (eds), *Handbook of Reading Research*, Mahwah, NJ, Lawrence Erlbaum.

Mezirow, J. 1996. Contemporary paradigms of learning. *Adult Education Quarterly*, Vol. 46, pp. 158-72.

Mifsud, C., Milton, J., Hutchinson, D., and Brooks, G. 2000*a*. *Prediction of Reading Attainment at Age Seven without a Baseline Pretest*. Msida, Malta, University of Malta Literacy Unit.

Mifsud, C., Milton, J., Hutchinson, D. and Brooks, G. 2000*b*. *Report on Using the Year 2 Reading Attainment Study as a Basis for a 'School Effectiveness' or 'Value Added' Study*. Msida, Malta, University of Malta Literacy Unit.

Miguel, E. and Kremer, M. 2004. Worms: identifying impacts on education and health in the presence of treatment externalities. *Econometrica*, Vol. 72, pp. 159-217.

Millennium Project. 2005*a*. *Investing in Development: A Practical Plan to Achieve the Millennium Development Goals*. New York, UNDP. http://www.unmilleniumproject.org/reports/fullreport.htm

Millennium Project. 2005*b*. Taking action: achieving gender equality and empowering women. Task Force on Education and Gender Equality. London, Earthscan. www.unmilleniumproject.org/reports/reports2.htm

Millennium Project. 2005*c*. Toward universal primary education: investments, incentives, and institutions. Task Force on Education and Gender Equality. London, Earthscan. www.unmillenniumproject.org/reports/reports2.htm

Miller, V. 1985. *Between Struggle and Hope: The Nicaraguan Literacy Crusade*. Boulder, Colo., Westview Press.

MINEDUC. 2003. *Education Sector Strategic Plan 2003-2008*. First draft, April. Kigali, Rwanda, Ministry of Education, Science, Technology and Scientific Research.

MINEDUC. 2005. *Functional Literacy for Youth and Adults in Rwanda: National Policy and Strategy*. Kigali, Rwanda, Ministry of Education, Science, Technology and Scientific Research, Non-formal Education Unit.

Ministère de la culture et de la communication. 2005. Communiqué: Publication du terme littérisme au Journal officiel du 30 août 2005. Paris, Délégation générale à la langue française et aux langues de France. www.culture.gouv.fr/culture/dglf/communique300805.htm

Mirsky, J. 2003. *Beyond Victims and Villains: Addressing Sexual Violence in the Education Sector.* London, Panos.

Miske, S. and Van Belle-Prouty, D. 1997. *Schools are for Girls Too: Creating an Environment of Validation*. Washington, DC, USAID, Bureau for Africa, Office of Sustainable Development.

Mitch, D. 1992. The rise of popular education in Europe. B. Fuller and R. Rubinson (eds), *The Political Construction of Education: The State, School Expansion, and Economic Change*. Westport, Conn., Greenwood.

Mohamed, O. 1975. *From Written Somali to a Rural Development Campaign*. Mogadishu, Somali Institute of Development Administration and Management.

Monga, N. 2000. Knowing her rights: case study from India. *Beyond Literacy: Case Studies from Asia and the South Pacific*. Mumbai, India, Asian South Pacific Bureau of Adult Education.

Monitoring Learning Achievement Project. 2002. Urban/rural disparities. Paris, UNESCO. (Mimeograph.)

Montagnes, I. 2000. *Textbooks & Learning Materials, 1990-1999: A Global Survey.* EFA 2000 Assessment. Thematic Studies for World Education Forum. Paris, UNESCO.

Mookherjee, D. 2001. Combating the crisis in government accountability: a review of recent international experience. R. C. Dutt Memorial Lectures. Calcutta, Center for Studies in Social Science.

Motivans, A. 2005. Countries with high pupil-teacher ratios: trends and projections. Background paper for *EFA Global Monitoring Report 2006*.

Moulton, J. 2001. Improving education in rural areas: guidance for rural development specialists. Draft paper. Washington, DC, World Bank.

Moye, M. 2001. *Overview of Debt Conversion*. London, Debt Relief International. Publication No. 4.

Mpopiya, P. and Prinsloo, M. 1996. Literacy, migrancy and disrupted domesticity: Khayelishan ways of knowing. M. Prinsloo and M. Breier (eds), *The Social Uses of Literacy*. Amsterdam, John Benjamins.

Mullis, I. V. S., Martin, M. O., Gonzalez, E. J. and Chrostowski, S. J. 2004. *TIMSS 2003 International Mathematics Report: Findings from IEA's Trends in Mathematics and Science Study at the Fourth and Eighth Grades*. Chestnut Hill, Mass., Boston College.

Mullis, I., Martin, M., Gonzalez, E. and Kennedy, A. 2003*a*. *PIRLS 2001 International Report: IEA's Study of Reading Literacy Achievement in Primary Schools in 35 Countries*. Chestnut Hill, Mass., Boston College.

Mullis, I., Martin, M., Gonzalez, E. and Kennedy, A. 2003*b*. *Trends in Children's Reading Literacy Achievement 1991-2001: IEA's Repeat in Nine Countries of the 1991 Reading Literacy Study*. Chestnut Hill, Mass, Boston College.

Murray, T. S. 1997. Proxy measurement of adult basic skills: lessons from Canada. A. Tuijnman, I. Kirsch and D. Wagner (eds), *Adult Basic Skills: Innovations in Measurement and Policy Analysis*. Cresskill, NJ, Hampton Press.

Murray Bradley, S. 1994. Visual literacy: an annotated bibliography. (Unpublished.)

Namibia Ministry of Education and Culture and University of Namibia. 1994. *Adult Literacy in Ondangwa and Windhoek: A Survey of Adult Learners' Literacy Skills and Education*. Windhoek, Ministry of Education and Culture, Directorate of Adult and Continuing Education, and University of Namibia, Social Sciences Division, Multi-Disciplinary Research Centre.

Napon, A. and Sanou/Zerbo, S. 2005. L'alphabétisation: les options réelles sur les politiques et les pratiques du Burkina [Literacy: real options for policy and practice in Burkina Faso]. Background paper for *EFA Global Monitoring Report 2006*.

National Literacy Campaign Coordinating Committee (Ethiopia). 1984. Every Ethiopian will be literate and will remain literate. Addis Ababa.

Naudé, W. A. 2004. The effects of policy, institutions and geography on economic growth in Africa: an econometric study based on cross-section and panel data. *Journal of International Development*, Vol. 16, pp. 821–49.

Netherlands Ministry of Foreign Affairs. 2002. Policy paper on silent partnership. Background paper for *EFA Global Monitoring Report 2006*.

Netherlands Ministry of Foreign Affairs. 2005. Dutch commitment to basic education: living up to promises. Background paper for *EFA Global Monitoring Report 2006*.

Neuman, S. and Celano, D. 2001. Access to print in low-income and middle-income communities: an ecological study of four neighbourhoods. *Reading Research Quarterly*, Vol. 36, No. 1, pp. 8-26.

Neuman, S. and Ruskos, K. 1997. Literacy knowledge in practice: contexts of participation for young writers and readers. *Reading Research Quarterly*, Vol. 32, No. 1, pp. 10–32.

Nicolai, S. and Triplehorn, C. 2003. *The Role of Education in Protecting Children in Conflict*. London, Overseas Development Institute. (Humanitarian Practice Network Paper No. 42.)

Nielsen, D.C. and Monson, D. L. 1996. Effects of Literacy Environment on Literacy Development of Kindergarten Children. *Journal of Educational Research,* Vol. 89, No. 5, pp. 259–71.

Ningwakwe / Rainbow Woman (Priscilla George). 2002. The Rainbow / Holistic Approach to Aboriginal Literacy. Paper read at Solidarity in Literacy Program, Literacy Week in Brazil, June 28, São Paulo.

Nirantar. 1997. Innovating for change: women's education for empowerment - an analysis of the Mahila Samakhya Program in Banda District (India). W. Mauch and U. Papen (eds), *Making a Difference: Innovations in Adult Education*. UNESCO Institute for Education, Hamburg; and German Foundation for International Development and Peter Lang, Frankfurt am Main, pp. 33-47

Norad. 2004. *From Earmarked Sector Support to General Budget Support: Development Partners' Experience*. Oslo, Direktoratet for utviklingssamarbeid [Norwegian Agency for Development Cooperation], Department for Governance and Macroeconomics, Public Finance Unit.

Nordtveit, B. H. 2004. *Managing Public-Private Partnerships: Lessons from Literacy Education in Senegal*. Washington, DC, World Bank.

Nordtveit, B. H. 2005*a*. Public-private partnerships and outsourcing. Background paper for *EFA Global Monitoring Report 2006*.

Nordtveit, B. H. 2005*b*. Senegal case study. Background paper for *EFA Global Monitoring Report 2006*.

Norwegian Ministry of Foreign Affairs. 2003. Education - Job No. 1: Norwegian Strategy for Delivering Education for All by 2015. Oslo, Utanriksdepartementet [Ministry of Foreign Affairs].

Norwood, G. 2003. Fighting oppression through literacy: a case study of the Karen's Women's Organisation. Mumbai, India, Asian South Pacific Bureau of Adult Education. ASPBAE Indigenous Adult Education Case Study Series.

Nyuumedia Jinken Kikou [Newmedia Human Rights Organization]. 2005. Burakusabetsutte nandesuka? [What is Burakusabetsu?]. http://www.jinken.ne.jp/buraku/kihon/index.html (In Japanese.)

NZAID. 2002. Policy statement: towards a safe and just world free of poverty. Wellington, New Zealand Agency for International Development.

Obura, A. 2003. *Never Again: Educational Reconstruction in Rwanda*. Paris, International Institute for Educational Planning.

OECD. 1999. *Trends in Income Distribution and Poverty in the OECD Area*. Paris, OECD.

OECD. 2000. *Literacy in the Information Age: Final Report of the International Adult Literacy Survey*. Paris, OECD.

OECD. 2001. *Knowledge and Skills for Life. First Results from PISA 2000*. Paris, OECD.

OECD. 2004. *Learning for Tomorrow's World: First Results from PISA 2003*. Paris, OECD.

OECD. 2005*a*. *Aid Activities in Support of Gender Equality 1999-2003*. Paris, OECD.

OECD. 2005*b*. *Promoting Adult Learning*. Paris, OECD. (Executive summary.).

OECD-DAC. 2000. DAC Statistical Reporting Directives. http://www.oecd.org/dataoecd/44/45/1894833.pdf

OECD-DAC. 2002. Reporting directives for the creditor system http://www1.oecd.org/scripts/cde/members/CRSAuthenticate.asp. OECD, Paris.

OECD-DAC. 2003. Report on harmonising donor practices for effective aid delivery. OECD, Paris.

OECD-DAC. 2005*a*. Comparison between commitments and disbursements. Personal communication, March 2005.

OECD-DAC. 2005*b*. 2004 development co-operation report, Vol. 6, No. 1. (*The DAC Journal* Development Co-operation Report 2004 (2005, Vol. 6, No. 1.). http://www.oecd.org/document/26/0,2340,en_2649_201185_34405978_1_1_1_1,00.html

OECD-DAC. 2005*c*. International development statistics. http://www.oecd.org/dataoecd/50/17/5037721.htm

OECD-DAC. 2005*d*. Official Development Assistance increases further - but 2006 targets still a challenge. Aid Statistics 11/04/2005. http://www.oecd.org/document/3/0,2340,en_2649_34447_34700611_1_1_1_1,00.html

OECD-DAC. 2005e. Paris Declaration on Aid Effectiveness: Harmonisation, Alignment, Results and Mutual Accountability. High Level Forum on Aid Effectiveness. Paris, 28 February to 2 March. http://www.oecd.org/dataoecd/11/41/34428351.pdf

OECD/HRDC/Statistics Canada. 1997. *Littératie et société du savoir [Literacy Skills for the Knowledge Society: Further Results from the International Adult Literacy Survey]*. Paris, OECD.

OECD/Statistics Canada. 1995. *Literacy, Economy and Society: Results of the First International Adult Literacy Survey*. Paris, OECD and Ottawa, Statistics Canada.

OECD/Statistics Canada. 2000. *Literacy in the Information Age: Final Report of the International Adult Literacy Survey*. Paris, OECD and Ottawa, Statistics Canada.

OECD/UNESCO Institute for Statistics. 2003. *Literacy Skills for the World of Tomorrow: Further Results from PISA 2000*. Montreal, UNESCO Institute for Statistics.

Ogawa, K. 2005. The EFA Fast Track Initiative: experience of Yemen. Background paper for *EFA Global Monitoring Report 2006*.

Okech, A. 2005. Uganda case study of literacy in Education for All 2005: a review of policies, strategies and practices. Background paper for *EFA Global Monitoring Report 2006*.

Okech, A., Carr-Hill, R., Katahoire, A. R., Kakooza, T., Ndidde, A. N. and Oxenham, J. 2001. Adult Literacy Programs in Uganda. Washington, DC, World Bank. Africa Region Human Development Series.

Olson, D. 1977. From utterance to text: the bias of language in speech and writing. *Harvard Educational Review*, Vol. 47, pp. 257-81.

Olson, D. 1994. *The World on Paper: The Conceptual and Cognitive Implications of Writing and Reading*. Cambridge, UK, Cambridge University Press.

Olson, D. and Torrance, N. (eds.) 2001. *The Making of Literate Societies*, Oxford, UK, Blackwell.

Ong, W. J. 1982. *Orality and Literacy: The Technologizing of the Word*. New York, Routledge.

Operations Evaluation Department. 2003. *Dept Relief for the Poorest: An OED Review of the HIPC Initiative*. Washington, DC, World Bank.

Operations Evaluation Department. 2004. *Books, Buildings, and Learning Outcomes: An Impact Evaluation of World Bank Support To Basic Education in Ghana*. Washington, DC, World Bank. (Report Number 28779.)

Organization of American States. 1948. Charter of the Organization of American States. http://www.oas.org/main/main.asp?sLang=E&sLink=http://www.oas.org/juridico/english/charter.html

Otto, A. 1997. Curriculum development for nonformal education. 4-H Center for Youth Development. (Monograph.) http://www.rrz.uni-hamburg.de/UNESCO-UIE/literacyexchange/course/bookshel.html

Ouane, A. 1989. *Handbook on Learning Strategies for Post-literacy and Continuing Education*. Hamburg, UNESCO Institute for Education.

Ouane, A. (ed.). 2003. *Towards a Multicultural Culture of Education*. Hamburg, UNESCO Institute for Education.

Ouane, A. and Glanz, C. 2005. why first literacy in mother tongue is advantageous in multilingual settings: findings from a stocktaking research on subSaharan Africa. Background paper for *EFA Global Monitoring Report 2006*.

Oxenham, J. 2003. *Review of World Bank Supported Projects in Adult Basic Education and Literacy, 1977-2002: Comparison of Costs*. Washington, DC, World Bank.

Oxenham, J. 2004*a*. ABET vs poverty: what have we learned? *Adult Education and Development*, No. 63, pp. 83-102.

Oxenham, J. 2004*b*. The quality of programmes and policies regarding literacy and skills development. Background paper for *EFA Global Monitoring Report 2005*.

Oxenham, J. and Aoki, A. 2002. Including the 900 million. Washington, DC, World Bank. (Draft.)

Oxenham, J., Diallo, A., Katahoire, A. R., Petkova-Mwangi, A. and Sall, O. 2002. *Skills and Literacy Training for Better Livelihoods: A Review of Approaches and Experiences*. Washington, DC, World Bank. Africa Region Human Development Series.

Papen, U. 2004. Reading the Bible and shopping on credit: literacy practices and literacy learning in a township in Windhoek, Namibia. A. Rogers (ed.), *Urban Literacy and Development*. Hamburg, UNESCO Institute for Education.

Papen, U. 2005. Literacy and development: what works for whom? or, how relevant is the social practices view of literacy for literacy education in developing countries? *International Journal of Educational Development*, Vol. 25, pp. 5-17.

Patel, I. 1987. Non-formal education for rural women in Gujarat: for development or domestication? (Mimeograph.)

Patel, I. 1991. *A Study of the Impact of New Communication Technologies on Literacy in India*. Singapore, Asian Mass Communication Research and Information Centre.

Patel, I. 2001. Literacy as freedom for women in India. UNESCO, *Literacy as Freedom: A UNESCO Roundtable*. Paris, UNESCO.

Patel, I. 2005. The human benefits of literacy. Background paper for *EFA Global Monitoring Report 2006*, through the University of East Anglia, Norwich.

Pavignani, E and Hauck, V. 2002. *Polling of Technical Assistance in Mozambique: Innovative Practices and Challenges*. Maastricht, the Netherlands, European Centre for Development Policy Management. (ECDPM Discussion Paper 39.)

Pennells, J. 2005. Literacy, distance learning and ICT. Background paper for *EFA Global Monitoring Report 2006*.

Petrakis, P. E. and Stamatakis, D. 2002. Growth and education levels: a comparative analysis. *Economics of Education Review*, Vol. 21, No. 5, pp. 513-21.

Poot, J. 2000. A synthesis of empirical research on the impact of government on long-run growth. *Growth and Change*, Vol. 31, No. 4, pp. 516-47.

Posner, G. J. and Rudnitsky, A. N. 1982. *Course Design: A Guide to Curriculum Development for Teachers*, 2nd edn. New York, Longman.

Pritchett, L. 2001. Where has all the education gone? *World Bank Economic Review*, Vol. 15, No. 3 (August), pp. 367-91.

Project Ploughshares. 2004. *Armed Conflicts Report 2004*. http://www.ploughshares.ca/libraries/ACRText/ACR-TitlePageRev.htm

ProLiteracy Worldwide. 2004. *Literacy in Action: Spreading the Light - International Programs Update 2004-05*. http://www.proliteracy.org/downloads/IP_04.pdf

Psacharopoulos, G. and Patrinos, H. 2002. Returns to investment in education: a further update. Washington, DC, World Bank. (Policy Research Working Paper 2881.)

Purcell-Gates, V. and Waterman, R. 2000. *Now We Read, We See, We Speak: Portrait of Literacy Development in an Adult Freirean-Based Class*. Mahwah, NJ, Lawrence Erlbaum.

Ramirez, F. and Boli, J. 1982. Global patterns of educational institutionalization. P. Altbach, R. Arnove and G. Kelly (eds), *Comparative Education Review*. New York, Macmillan.

Ramirez, F. and Boli, J. 1994. The political institutionalization of compulsory education: the rise of compulsory schooling in the western cultural context. J. A. Mangan (ed.), *A Significant Social Revolution: Cross-Cultural Aspects of the Evolution of Compulsory Education*. London, Woburn.

Ramirez, F. and Ventresca, M. 1992. Building the institution of mass schooling: isomorphism in the modern world. B. Fuller and R. Rubinson (eds), *The Political Construction of Education*. New York, Praeger.

Rampal, A., Ramanujan, R. and Saraswathi, L. S. 1997. *Numeracy Counts! A Handbook for Literacy Activists and Resource Persons*. Mussoorie, India, National Literacy Resource Centre.

Rao, N. and Robinson-Pant, A. 2003. CONFINTEA thematic review: adult learning and indigenous peoples. Paper read at CONFINTEA Mid-term Review, July.

Read, T. 1995. International Donor Agencies and Book Development. P. G. Altbach and E. S. Hoshino (eds), *International Book Publishing: An Encyclopedia*. London and Chicago, Fitzroy Dearborn Publishers.

Reh, M. (ed.). 1981. *Problems of Linguistic Communication in Africa*. Vol. 1, African linguistic bibliographies. Hamburg, Helmut Buske.

Richardson, J. G. 1980. Variation in date in enactment of compulsory school attendance laws: an empirical inquiry. *Sociology of Education*, Vol. LIII, pp. 153–63.

Riddell, A. 2001. Review of 13 evaluations of Reflect. London, ActionAid International, International Reflect Circle. http://www.reflect-action.org.

Ringold, D., Orenstein, M. A. and Wilkens, E. 2004. *Roma in an Expanding Europe: Breaking the Poverty Cycle*. Washington, DC, World Bank.

Robinson, C. 2003. The ongoing debate. UNESCO, *Literacy as Freedom: A UNESCO Roundtable*. Paris, UNESCO.

Robinson, C. 2005. Languages and literacies. Background paper for *EFA Global Monitoring Report 2006*.

Robinson-Pant, A. 2000. *Why Eat Green Cucumbers at the Time of Dying? Exploring the Link Between Women's Literacy and Development: A Nepal Perspective*. Hamburg, UNESCO Institute for Education.

Robinson-Pant, A. 2005. The social benefits of literacy. Background paper for *EFA Global Monitoring Report 2006*, through the University of East Anglia, Norwich.

Rockhill, K. 1987. Literacy as threat/desire: longing to be somebody. J. S. Gaskill and A. T. McLaren (eds), *Women in Education*. Calgary, Alta, Detselig.

Rogers, A. 2003. *What is the Difference? A New Critique of Adult Learning and Teaching*. Leicester, UK, National Institute of Adult Continuing Education.

Rogers, A. 2005. Training adult literacy educators in developing countries. Background paper for *EFA Global Monitoring Report 2006*.

Rogoff, B. 2003. *The Cultural Nature of Human Development*. New York, Oxford University Press.

Rogoff, B. and Lave, J. 1984. *Everyday Cognition: Its Development in Social Context*. Cambridge, Mass., Harvard University Press.

Rose, P. and Subrahmanian, R. 2005. *Evaluation of DFID Development Assistance: Gender Equity and Women's Empowerment - Phase II Thematic Evaluation: Education*. Glasgow, UK Department for International Development, Evaluation Department. (DFID Working Paper 11.) http://www.dfid.gov.uk/aboutdfid/performance/files/wp11.pdf

Rosenberg, D. (ed.). 2000. *Books for Schools: Improving Access to Supplementary Reading Materials in Africa*. Paris, Association for the Development of Education in Africa, ADEA Working Group on Books and Learning Materials. (Perspectives on African Book Development Series, No. 9.)

Ross, H., Lou, J., Lijing, Y., Rybakova, O. and Wakhunga, P. 2005. Where and who are the world's illiterates: China. Background paper for *EFA Global Monitoring Report 2006*.

Ross, K., Saito, M., Dolata, S., Ikeda, M. and Zuze, L. 2004. Data archive for the SACMEQ I and SACMEQ II Projects. Paris, International Institute for Educational Planning.

Rostow, W. W. 1960. *The Stages of Economic Growth: A Non-Communist Manifesto*. Cambridge, UK, Cambridge University Press.

Sachs, J. and Warner, A. 1997. Sources of slow growth in African economies. *Journal of African Economics*, Vol. 6, No. 3, pp. 335–76.

Sadembouo, E. and Watters, J. 1987. Proposition pour l'évaluation des niveaux de développement d'une langue écrite. *Journal of West African Languages*, Vol. 1, pp. 35–59.

Salzano, C. 2002. *Making Book Coordination Work!* Paris, UNESCO/DANIDA/ADEA Working Group on Books and Learning Materials. (Perspectives on African Book Development Series, No. 13.)

Sandiford, P. J., Cassel, M. and Sanchez, G. 1995 The impact of women's literacy on child health and its interaction with access to health services. *Population Studies*, Vol. 49, pp. 5–17.

Schaffner, J. 2005. Measuring literacy in developing country household surveys: issues and evidence. Background paper for *EFA Global Monitoring Report 2006*.

Schenker, I. 2005. HIV/AIDS literacy: an essential component in education. Background paper for *EFA Global Monitoring Report 2006*.

Schnuttgen, S. and Khan, M. 2004. Civil society engagement in EFA in the post-Dakar period: a self-reflective review. Working document for the fifth EFA Working Group Meeting, Paris, UNESCO, 20-21 July.

Schofield, R. S. 1968. The measurement of literacy in pre-industrial England. J. Goody (ed.), *Literacy in Traditional Societies*. Cambridge, UK, Cambridge University Press.

Schulz, T. P. 1993. Returns to women's education. E.M. King and M.A. Hill (eds), *Women's Education in Developing Countries*. Baltimore, Md., Johns Hopkins University Press.

Scribner, S. and Cole, M. 1978. Unpackaging literacy. *Social Science Information*, Vol. 17, No. 1, pp. 19–39.

Scribner, S. and Cole, M. 1981. *The Psychology of Literacy*. Cambridge, Mass., Harvard University Press.

Seeberg, V. 2000. *The Rhetoric and Reality of Mass Education in Mao's China*. Lewiston, NY, Edwin Mellen Press.

Sey, H. 1997. *Peeking Through the Windows: Classroom Observations and Participatory Learning for Action Activities*, Arlington, Va., Institute for International Research.

Shadrikov, V. and Pakhomov, N. 1990. From eradication of illiteracy to a new concept of literacy. Geneva, International Bureau of Education.

Sharma, J. and Srivastava, K. 1991. *Training Rural Women for Literacy*. Jaipur, India, Institute of Development Studies.

Sharma, R. K., Kumar, M. S. and Meher, S. 2002. Education, skills and the labour market in a globalised world: a case of India. *Indian Journal of Labour Economics*, Vol. 45, No. 4, pp. 1129–47.

Shavit, Y. and Kraus, V. 1990. Educational transition in Israel: a test of the industrialization and credentialism hypothesis. *Sociology of Education*, Vol. 63, No. 1, pp. 133–41.

Shenkut, M. K. 2005. Literacy in Ethiopia. Background paper for *EFA Global Monitoring Report 2006*.

Shikiji - Nihongo Sentaa (Centre for Adult Learning, Literacy and Japanese as a Second Language). 2005. Shikiji - Nihongo Sentaa donna tokoro? [Literacy and Japanese Centre: What is it?]. http://www.call-jsl.jp/annai/index.html (In Japanese.)

Shikshantar. 2003. The Dark Side of Literacy. R. M. Torres, D. C. Soni, L. Shlain, A. Meenakshi, P. Dey, G.Esteva, M. S. Prakash, M. Fasheh, J. Ellul, D. Stuchul, contributors. Udaipur, India, Shikshantar, The People's Institute for Rethinking Education and Development. http://www.swaraj.org/shikshantar/rethinking_literacy.htm

Sida. 2000. *Policy and Guidelines For Sector Programme Support*. Stockholm, Swedish International Development Cooperation Agency.

Sida. 2001*a*. *Education for All: A Human Right and Basic Need - Policy for Sida's Development Cooperation in the Education Sector*. Stockholm, Swedish International Development Cooperation Agency, Department for Democracy and Social Development, Education Division.

Sida. 2001*b*. *Education for All: A Way Out of Poverty*. Stockholm, Swedish International Development Cooperation Agency.

Sida. 2002. Principles and experiences of silent partnership: draft paper on activity levels in Sida's sector programmes. Stockholm, Swedish International Development Cooperation Agency.

Sida. 2003. *Adult Basic Learning and Education (ABLE): Sida's Cooperation in the Education Sector*. Stockholm, Swedish International Development Cooperation Agency.

SIL UK. 2004. Adult education and development in central and northern Ghana (CSCF 76): an evaluation: Unpublished. High Wycombe, UK, SIL UK.

Sinclair, M. 2003. Planning education in and after emergencies. Paris, International Institute for Educational Planning.

Siniscalco, M. 2005. Italy: some results from PISA 2003. Background paper for *EFA Global Monitoring Report 2006*.

Skutnabb-Kangas, T. 2000. *Linguistic Genocide in Education or Worldwide Diversity and Human Rights*. London, Lawrence Earlbaum Associates.

Skutnabb-Kangas, T. 2001. The globalisation of (educational) language rights. *International Review of Education*, Vol. 47, pp. 2001–219.

Smyth, J. A. 2005. UNESCO's international literacy statistics 1950-2000. Background paper for *EFA Global Monitoring Report 2006*.

Somers, M.-A. 2005. Disentangling schooling attainment from literacy skills and competencies. Background paper for *EFA Global Monitoring Report 2006*.

Sommers, M. 2002. *Children, Education and War: Reaching EFA Objectives in Countries Affected by Conflict*. Washington, DC, World Bank Social Development Department, Conflict Prevention and Reconstruction Unit. (CPR Working Paper 1.)

Sommers, M. and Buckland, P. 2004. *Parallel Worlds: Rebuilding the Education System in Kosovo*. Paris, International Institute for Educational Planning.

Sperling, G. and Balu, R. 2005. Designing a global compact on education. *Finance and Development*, Vol. 42, No. 2. http://www.imf.org/external/pubs/ft/fandd/2005/06/sperling.htm

Spolsky, B. 2004. *Language Policy*. Cambridge, UK, Cambridge University Press.

St Bernard, G. and Salim, C. 1995. *Adult Literacy in Trinidad and Tobago: A Study Based on the Findings of the National Literacy Survey 1995*. St. Augustine, Trinidad and Tobago, University of the West Indies, Institute of Social and Economic Research.

Stash, S. and Hannum, E. 2001. Who Goes to School? Educational Stratification by Gender, Caste and Ethnicity in Nepal. *Comparative Education Review*, Vol. 45, No. 3, pp. 354–78.

Statistical Institute of Jamaica. 1995. *National Literacy Survey 1994: Jamaica Final Report*. Kingston, Jamaica Movement for the Advancement of Literacy.

Statistics Canada/OECD. 2005. *Learning a Living: First Results of the Adult Literacy and Life Skills Survey*. Ottawa, Statistics Canada and Paris, OECD.

Stone, L. 1969. Literacy and education in England, 1640-1900. *Past and Present*, Vol. 42, pp. 69–139.

Strauss, J., Beegle, K., Sikoki, B., Dwiyanto, A., Herawati, Y. and Witoelar, F. 2004. The Third Wave of the Indonesia Family Life Survey (IFLS3): Overview and Field Report. Santa Monica, Calif., RAND Corporation. (WR-144/1-NIA/NICHD.)

Street, B. 1984. *Literacy in Theory and Practice*. Cambridge, UK, Cambridge University Press.

Street, B. (ed.). 1993. *Cross-cultural Approaches to Literacy*. Cambridge, UK, Cambridge University Press.

Street, B. 1996. Literacy, Economy, and Society. *Literacy Across the Curriculum* Vol. 12, pp. 8–15.

Street, B. 1998. New literacies in theory and practice: what are the implications for language in education? *Linguistics and Education*, Vol. 10, No. 1, pp. 1-21

Street, B. 2001*a*. Context for literacy work: the 'new orders' and the 'new literacy studies'. J. Crowther, M. Hamilton and L. Tett (eds), *Powerful Literacies*. Leister, UK, National Institute for Adult Continuing Education.

Street, B. (ed.). 2001*b*. *Literacy and Development: Ethnographic Perspectives*. London, Routledge.

Street, B. 2003. What's 'new' in New Literacy Studies? Critical approaches to literacy theory and practice. *Current Issues in Comparative Education*, Vol. 5, No. 2, 12 May. http://www.tc.columbia.edu/cice

Street, B. 2004. Understanding and defining literacy. Background paper for *EFA Global Monitoring Report 2006*.

Street, B. (ed.). 2005. *Literacy Across Educational Contexts: Mediating Learning and Teaching*. Philadelphia, Caslon.

Streumer, N. and Tuijnman, A. C. 1996. Curriculum in adult education. A. C. Tuijnman (ed.), *International Encyclopedia of Adult Education and Training*, 2nd edn. Oxford, Elsevier Science.

Stromquist, N. 1997. *Literacy for Citizenship: Gender and Grassroots Dynamics in Brazil*. Albany, NY, SUNY Press.

Stromquist, N. 2004. Women's rights to adult education as a means to citizenship. Paper for conference on Gender, Education and Development: Beyond Access, University of East Anglia, Norwich, June.

Stromquist, N. 2005. The political benefits of adult literacy. Background paper for *EFA Global Monitoring Report 2006*.

Subba, S. and Subba, D. 2003. *Learning in Our Own Language: Kirat Yakthung Chumlung Develop a Limbu Literacy Programme in Nepal*. Mumbai, India, Asian South Pacific Bureau of Adult Education. (ASPBAE Indigenous Adult Education Case Study Series.)

Sunanchai, S. 1988. Reading promotion in Thailand. *Adult Education and Development*, Vol. 31, September, pp. 63-9.

Sunanchai, S. 1989. Fifty years of adult education and non-formal education in Thailand. *Adult Education and Developmenti*, Vol. 33, September, pp. 7-26.

Swainson, N., Bendera, S., Gordon, R. and Kadzamira, E. 1998. Promoting Girls' Education in Africa: The Design and Implementation of Policy Interventions. London, UK Department for International Development.

Sylwester, K. 2000. Can educational expenditures reduce income inequality? *Economics of Education Review*, Vol. 21, No. 4, pp. 43-52.

Tarawa, N. 2003. *Reading our Land: a Case Study of Te Waka Pu Whenua, Maori Adult Education Center in New Zealand*. Mumbai, India, Asian South Pacific Bureau of Adult Education. (ASPBAE Indigenous Adult Education Case Study Series.)

Telles, E. 1994. Institutionalization and racial inequality in employment: the Brazilian example. American Sociological Review, Vol. 59, No. 1, pp. 46-63.

Terryn, B. 2003. The Literacy Assessment and Monitoring Programme (LAMP). Paper read at Association for Educational Assessment Conference, Lyon, France, 6 November.

Torres, R. M. 2004. *Lifelong Learning in the South: Critical Issues and Opportunities for Adult Education*. Stockholm, Swedish International Development Agency. (Sida Studies No. 11.)

Torres, R. M. 2005. Analfabetismo y alfabetización en el Ecuador: opciones para la política y la práctica [Illiteracy and literacy education in Ecuador: real options for policy and practice]. Background paper for *EFA Global Monitoring Report 2006*.

UIE. 1999. *Cultural Citizenship in the 21st Century: adult learning and indigenous people*. Hamburg, UNESCO Institute of Education.

UIE. 2004. *Sharpening the Focus, Evaluation of the Botswana National Literacy Programme*. Hamburg, UNESCO Institute of Education.

Umayahara, M. 2005. Regional overview of progress toward EFA since Dakar: Latin America. Background paper for *EFA Global Monitoring Report 2006*.

UNAIDS. 2005. *AIDS in Africa: Three Scenarios to 2025*. Geneva, UNAIDS.

UNAIDS/WHO. 2004. Global summary of the HIV and AIDS epidemic, December 2004. http://www.unaids.org/en/resources/epidemiology/epicore.asp

UNDP. 2004*a*. *Human Development Report 2004: Cultural Liberty in Today's World*. New York, UNDP.

UNDP. 2004*b*. Human Development Report. What is HD? HDR 2004. http://hdr.undp.org/hd/default.cfm

UNDP. 2004*c*. Iraq Living Conditions Survey: Volume I Tabulation Report. New York, UNDP.

UNDP. 2004*d*. Iraq Living Conditions Survey: Volume II Analytical Report. New York, UNDP.

UNDP. 2005. UNDP and Indigenous Peoples: A Practice Note on Engagement. http://www.undp.org/cso/policies/doc/IPPolicyEnglish

Undrakh, T. 2002. UNESCO project on non-formal education to meet basic learning needs of nomadic women in the Gobi Desert of Mongolia. http://www.literacyonline.org/products/ili/webdocs/undrakh.html

UNESCO. 1947. *Fundamental Education: Common Ground for All Peoples. Report of a Special Committee to the Preparatory Commission*. Paris, UNESCO.

UNESCO. 1953. *Progress of Literacy in Various Countries: A Preliminary Statistical Study of Available Census Data Since 1900*. Paris, UNESCO.

UNESCO. 1957. *World Illiteracy at Mid-Century: A Statistical Study*. Paris, UNESCO.

UNESCO. 1958. *Recommendations Concerning the International Standardization of Educational Statistics*. Paris, UNESCO.

UNESCO. 1960. Convention against Discrimination in Education. Paris, UNESCO.

UNESCO. 1970. *Literacy 1967-1969: Progress Achieved in Literacy throughout the World*. Paris, UNESCO.

UNESCO. 1975*a*. Declaration of Persepolis. International Symposium for Literacy, Persepolis, 3-8 September. www.unesco.org/education/pdf/PERSEP_E.PDF

UNESCO. 1975*b*. Literacy in the World since the 1965 Tehran Conference: Shortcomings, Achievements, Tendencies. L. Bataille (ed.), *A Turning Point for Literacy: Adult Education for Development. The Spirit and Declaration of Persepolis*. Oxford, UK, Pergamon.

UNESCO. 1978. *Literacy in Asia: A Continuing Challenge*. Report of the UNESCO Regional Experts Meeting on Literacy in Asia (Bangkok, 22-28 November 1977). Bangkok, UNESCO Regional Office for Education in Asia and Oceania.

UNESCO. 1980. *Literacy 1972-1976: Progress Achieved in Literacy throughout the World*. Paris, UNESCO.

UNESCO. 1988. *Compendium of Statistics on Illiteracy*. Paris, UNESCO.

UNESCO. 1990. World Declaration on Education for All.

UNESCO. 1995. *Compendium of Statistics on Illiteracy*. Paris, UNESCO.

UNESCO. 1997. The Hamburg Declaration on Adult Learning (CONFINTEA V).

UNESCO. 2000*a*. *A Synthesis Report of Education for All 2000: Assessment in the Trans-Caucasus and Central Asia Sub-Region*. Bangkok, UNESCO Regional office.

UNESCO. 2000*b*. *The Dakar Framework for Action: Education for All - Meeting our Collective Commitments*. World Education Forum, Dakar, Senegal, 26–28 April. Paris, UNESCO.

UNESCO. 2000*c*. *World Culture Report: Cultural Diversity, Conflict and Pluralism*. Paris, UNESCO.

UNESCO. 2001. *The Global Initiative towards Education for All: A Framework for Mutual Understanding*. Paris. UNESCO

UNESCO. 2002*a*. *Education for All: An International Strategy to Put the Dakar Framework for Action on Education for All into Operation*. Paris, UNESCO.

UNESCO, 2002*b*. *EFA Global Monitoring Report 2002: Education for All - Is the World on Track?* Paris, UNESCO.

UNESCO. 2003*a*. *Education in a Multilingual World*. UNESCO Education Position Paper. Paris, UNESCO.

UNESCO, 2003*b*. *EFA Global Monitoring Report 2003/4: Gender and Education for All - The Leap to Equality*. Paris, UNESCO.

UNESCO. 2003*c*. *Literacy as Freedom*. Paris, UNESCO. http://unesdoc.unesco.org/images/0013/001318/131823e.pdf

UNESCO. 2003*d*. *Literacy: a UNESCO Perspective*. Paris, UNESCO. http://unesdoc.unesco.org/images/0013/001318/131817eo.pdf

UNESCO. 2003e. The mother-tongue dilemma. *Education Today*, Vol. 6 (July-September).

UNESCO. 2003*f*. United Nations Literacy Decade 2003–2012. http://portal.unesco.org/education/en/ev.php-URL_ID=27158&URL_DO=DO_TOPIC&URL_SECTION=201.html

UNESCO. 2004*a*. *EFA Global Monitoring Report 2005, Education for All - The Quality Imperative*. Paris, UNESCO.

UNESCO. 2004*b*. *The Plurality of Literacy and Its Implication of Policies and Programmes*. UNESCO Education Sector Position Paper. Paris, UNESCO.

UNESCO. 2004*c*. Republic of Madagascar, Tanindrazana-Fahafahana-Fandrosoana. Programme overview, Joint Malagasy Government-United Nations System Programme for the Promotion of Basic Education for All Malagasy Children. Paris, UNESCO.

UNESCO. 2005*a*. B@bel Initiative. http://portal.unesco.org/education/en/ev.php-URL_ID=19749&URL_DO=DO_TOPIC&URL_SECTION=201.html.

UNESCO. 2005*b*. *Report by the Director-General on the Follow-Up to the EFA Strategic Review and UNESCO's Strategy for the 2005–2015 Period*. (Paper 171 EX/8 17 March 2005. 171st Session. UNESCO Executive Board). Paris, UNESCO. http://unesdoc.unesco.org/images/0013/001389/138915e.pdf

UNESCO. 2005*c*. United Nations Decade of Education for Sustainable Development, 2005–2014. (http://portal.unesco.org/education/en/ev.php-URL_ID=27234&URL_DO=DO_TOPIC&URL_SECTION=201.html)

UNESCO-BREDA. 1983. *Eradication of Illiteracy in Africa through the Combined Development of Primary and Adult Education*. Dakar, UNESCO Regional Office for Education in Africa.

UNESCO-IIEP. 2005*a*. An analysis of the place of literacy in poverty reduction papers. Background paper for *EFA Global Monitoring Report 2006*.

UNESCO-IIEP, 2005*b*. Country templates synthesis report. Background paper for *EFA Global Monitoring Report 2006*.

UNESCO-IIEP. 2005*c*. *Report on the Education Sector: Global HIV/AIDS readiness Survey 2004*. UNAIDS Inter Agency Task Team on Education. http://unesdoc.unesco.org/images/0013/001399/139972e.pdf

UNESCO-IIEP. 2005*d*. Scaling up training in educational planning and management for EFA. A note for the FTI Technical Meeting on 15 April. Paris, International Institute for Educational Planning.

UNESCO Institute for Statistics. 2004. *Global Education Digest 2004*. Montreal, PQ, UNESCO Institute for Statistics.

UNESCO Institute for Statistics. 2005. *Global Education Digest 2005*. Montreal, PQ, UNESCO Institute for Statistics.

UNESCO Institute for Statistics/OECD. 2005. *Education Trends in Perspective. World Education Indicators*. Montreal, PQ, UNESCO Institute for Statistics.

UNESCO-OREALC. 2001. *Overview of the 20 Years of the Major Project of Education in Latin America and the Caribbean*. Santiago, UNESCO/OREALC.

UNESCO-OREALC. 2004. *Education for All in Latin America: A Goal within Our Reach, Regional EFA Monitoring Report 2003*. Santiago, UNESCO/OREALC.

UNESCO-PROAP. 2001. *Final Report, Regional Workshop on Functional Literacy for Indigenous Peoples*. Kunming, Yunnan, People's Republic of China, October 2000. Bangkok, UNESCO Principal Regional Office for Asia and the Pacific.

UNESCO/UNDP. 1976. *The Experimental World Literacy Programme: A Critical Assessment*. Paris, UNESCO.

UNHCHR. 1951. Convention relating to the Status of Refugees. www.unhchr.ch/html/menu3/b/o_c_ref.htm

UNHCHR. 1969. Declaration on Social Progress and Development. http://www.unhchr.ch/html/menu3/b/m_progre.htm

UNHCHR. 1989. Convention on the Rights of the Child. http://www.unhchr.ch/html/menu2/6/crc/treaties/crc.htm

Education for All Global Monitoring Report 2006

UNHCHR. 1993. Vienna Declaration and Programme for Action. http://www.unhchr.ch/huridocda/huridoca.nsf/(Symbol)/A.CONF.157.23.En?OpenDocument

UNHCR. 2004. *Refugee Education Indicators 2003: Education Indicators and Gap Analysis covering 118 Refugee Camps in 23 Asylum Countries based on initial data from the camp indicator report*. Geneva, United Nations Office of the High Commissioner on Human Rights.

UNICEF. 2001. *Corporal Punishment in Schools in South Asia*. Kathmandu, UNICEF, Regional Office for South Asia.

UNICEF. 2002. Birth registration right from the start. *Innocenti Digest*, No. 9, March.

UNICEF. 2005*a*. *Girls' Education: Literacy*. http://www.unicef.org/girlseducation/index_focus_literacy.html. (Accessed 15 March 2005.)

UNICEF. 2005*b*. *Progress for Children: A Report Card on Gender Parity and Primary Education*. New York, UNICEF

UNICEF. 2005*c*. *The 'Rights' Start to Life: A Statistical Analysis of Birth Registration*. New York, UNICEF.

UNICEF. 2005*d*. Tsunami disaster-countries in crisis. http://www.unicef.org/emerg/disasterinasia/24615_newsline.html

United Nations. 1995. Beijing Declaration and Platform for Action. New York, United Nations Division for the Advancement of Women. http://www.un.org/womenwatch/daw/beijing/platform/

United Nations. 2002*a*. Final Outcomes of the International Conference on Financing for Development, The Monterrey Consensus. http://www.un.org/esa/ffd/0302finalMonterreyConsensus.pdf

United Nations. 2002*b*. Resolution 56/116 on United Nations Literacy Decade. http://portal.unesco.org/education/en/file_download.php/7a7d1ec1686411521f7840d7f41b2e9cResolution+English.pdf

United Nations. 2002*c*. United Nations Literacy Decade: Education for All; International Plan of Action; Implementation of General Assembly Resolution 56/116. Paris, UNESCO. http://portal.unesco.org/education/en/file_download.php/f0b0f2edfeb55b03ec965501810c9b6caction+plan+English.pdf

United Nations. 2005. *In Larger Freedom: Towards Development, Security and Human Rights for All. Report of the Secretary-General*. General Assembly A/59/2005. New York, United Nations.

United Nations Statistical Office. 1989. *Measuring Literacy through Household Surveys*. New York, United Nations Statistical Office. (Document No. DP/UN/INT-88-X01/10E.)

Unsicker, J. 1987. Tanzania's Literacy Campaign in Historical-Structural Perspectives. R. Arnove and H. Graff (eds), *National Literacy Campaigns: Historical and Comparative Perspectives*. New York, Plenum Press.

USAID. 1999. *Girls' Education: Good for Boys, Good for Development*. Gender Matters Information Bulletin, No. 5. Washington, DC, US Agency for International Development, Office of Women in Development.

USAID. 2005. *Education Strategy: Improving Lives through Learning*. Washington, DC, US Agency for International Development.

US Department of State. 2005. *Bush Malaria: Education Initiatives Support Africa's Future*. Briefing, 1 July. http://usinfo.state.gov/af/Archive/2005/Jul/01-739276.html

Vandermoortele, J. and Delamonica, E. 2000. The 'education vaccine' against HIV/AIDS. *Current Issues in Comparative Education*, Vol. 3, No. 1 (December).

Van Ravens, J. and Aggio, C. 2005. The costs of goal 4 and LIFE. Background paper for *EFA Global Monitoring Report 2006*.

Varavarn, K. 1989. Literacy campaigns and programmes in the context of literacy promotion: lessons learned from Thai experiences. *Adult Education and Development*, Vol. 33 (September), pp. 157–65.

Vélaz de Medrano, C. 2005. Literacy: real options for policy and practice in Spain. Background paper for *EFA Global Monitoring Report 2006*.

Verner, D. 2005. *What Factors Influence World Literacy? Is Africa Different?* World Bank Policy Research Working Paper 3496. Washington, DC, World Bank.

Verspoor, A. M. (ed.). Forthcoming. The Challenge of Learning: Improving the Quality of Basic Education in sub-Saharan Africa. Paris, Association for the Development of Education in Africa.

Vincent, D. 2000. *The Rise of Mass Literacy: Reading and Writing in Modern Europe*. Cambridge, Polity.

Wagner, D. A. 1993. *Literacy, Culture and Development: Becoming Literate in Morocco*. New York, Cambridge University Press.

Wagner, D. A. 2000. *EFA 2000: Thematic Study on Literacy and Adult Education*. Paris, UNESCO, International Literacy Institute.

Wagner, D. A. 2003. Smaller, quicker, cheaper: alternative strategies for literacy assessment in the UN Literacy Decade. *International Journal of Educational Research*, Vol. 39, pp. 293-309.

Wagner, D. A. 2004. Monitoring and measuring adult literacy: different models for different purposes. Background paper for *EFA Global Monitoring Report 2006*.

Wallet, P. 2005. Educational expansion and primary teacher training. Background paper for *EFA Global Monitoring Report 2006*.

Walter, S. L. 2004. Literacy, education, and language. Unpublished paper.

Waters, T. and Leblanc, K. 2005. Refugees and education: mass public schooling without a nation-state. *Comparative Education Review*, Vol. 49, No. 2, pp. 129–47.

Wheeler, D. 1980. *Human Resource Development and Economic Growth in Developing Countries: A Simultaneous Model*. Washington, DC, World Bank.

Whitehead, A. 2003. *Failing women, sustaining poverty: gender in poverty reduction strategy papers*. London, UK Gender and Development Network.

WHO. 2005. World Health Assembly Resolution WHA58.23 – Disability, including prevention, management and rehabilitation. http://www.who.int/ncd/disability/

Williams, E. and Cooke, J. 2002. Pathways and labyrinths: language and education in development. *TESOL Quarterly*, Vol. 36, No. 3, pp. 297–322.

Willms, J. D. and Somers, M-A. 2001. Family, classroom and school effects on children's educational outcomes in Latin America. *International Journal of School Effectiveness and Improvement*, Vol. 12, No. 4, pp. 409–45.

Willms, J. D. and Somers, M-A. 2005. Raising the learning bar in Latin America: measuring student outcomes. *Policy Brief,* March, pp. 1–4. Fredericton, NB, Canada, Canadian Research Institute for Social Policy.

Wils, A. 2002. On accelerating the global literacy transition. *Research and Assessment Systems for Sustainability Program* (Discussion Paper 2002-18). Cambridge, Mass., Belfer Center for Science and International Affairs, Kennedy School of Government, Harvard University.

Windows to the World. 1997. *Developing a Curriculum for Rural Women*. New Delhi, Niranter.

Women's Commission for Refugees and Children. 2004. *Global Survey on Education in Emergencies.* New York, Women's Commission for Refugees and Children. http://www.womenscommission.org/pdf/Ed_Emerg.pdf

World Bank. 1983. *China: Socialist Economic Development*. 3 vols. Washington, DC, World Bank.

World Bank. 1993. *Barriers and Solutions to Closing the Gender Gap.* Human Resources Development and Operations Policy, Note number 18, November 29. Washington, DC, World Bank. http://www.worldbank.org/html/extdr/hnp/hddflash/hcnote/hrn016.html

World Bank. 1999*a*. *Education Sector Strategy*. Washington, DC, World Bank. www1.worldbank.org/education/strategy.asp

World Bank. 1999*b*. *Ghana Living Standards Survey (GLSS) 1987–88 and 1988–89: Basic Information.* Washington, DC, Poverty and Human Resources Division, World Bank.

World Bank. 1999*c*. *New Approaches to Education: The Northern Areas Community Schools Program in Pakistan.* http://lnweb18.worldbank.org/sar/sa.nsf/0/908fc48b5cc644238525687b0061aa19?OpenDocument

World Bank. 2001. *Educational Attainment and Enrollment: Educational Attainment and Enrollment Profiles*. Washington, DC, World Bank. http://www.worldbank.org/research/projects/edattain/edattain.htm

World Bank. 2002*a*. User fees in primary education. Washington, DC, World Bank. (Mimeograph, review draft, February.)

World Bank. 2002*b*. *World Bank Support for Provision of Textbooks in sub-Saharan Africa*. Africa Region, Human Development Working Paper Series, No. 20. Washington, DC, World Bank.

World Bank. 2003*a*. *Lifelong Learning in the Global Knowledge Economy: Challenges for Developing Countries.* http://www1.worldbank.org/education/lifelong_learning/lifelong_learning_GKE.asp.

World Bank. 2003*b*. *Zambia Public Expenditure Management and Financial Accountability Review*. Poverty Reduction and Economic Management, Report No. 26162-ZA. Washington, DC, World Bank.

World Bank. 2004*a*. *Senegal: Public Expenditure Review*. Report No. 29357. Washington, DC, World Bank.

World Bank. 2004*b*. *The Norwegian Education Trust Fund: Annual Report 2004*. Washington, DC, The World Bank, Africa Region, Human Development Department. http://www.worldbank.org/afr/netf/pdf/netf_04_AR.pdf

World Bank. 2005*a*. *Edstats*. htpp://devdata.worldbank.org/edstats

World Bank. 2005*b*. *Global Monitoring Report: Millennium Development Goals, from Consensus to Momentum.* Washington, DC, World Bank.

World Bank. 2005*c*. Indonesia: preliminary damage and loss assessment, the December 26, 2004, natural disaster. http://siteresources.worldbank.org/INTINDONESIA/Resources/Publication/280016-1106130305439/damage_assessment.pdf

World Bank. 2005*d*. *Reshaping the Future: Education and Post-Conflict Reconstruction*. Washington, DC, World Bank.

World Bank. 2005*e*. *Secondary Education in the 21st Century: New Directions, Challenges and Priorities.* Washington, DC, World Bank.

World Economic Forum. 2005. *Global Governance Initiative: Annual Report 2005*. London and Washington, DC, World Economic Forum.

Wurm, S. A. 2001. *Atlas of the World's Languages in Danger of Disappearing*, 2nd edn. Paris, UNESCO.

Young, M. B., Fitzgerald, N. and Morgan, M. A. 1994. *National Evaluation of Adult Education Program's Fourth Interim Report: Learner Outcomes and Program Results.* Arlington, Va., Development Associates.

Young, M. B., Hipps, J., Hanberry, G., Hopstoch, P. and Golsmat, R. 1980. *An Assessment of the State-Administered Program of the Adult Education Act: Final Report.* Arlington, Va., Development Associates.

Yousif, A. A. 2003. Literacy: an overview of definitions and assessment. Paper presented to the Expert Meeting on Literacy Assessment, UNESCO, 10–12 June. Paris, UNESCO.

Zhang, T. and Wang, L. 2005. China country study: where and who? Background paper for *EFA Global Monitoring Report 2006*.

Zubair, S. 2001. Literacy, gender and power in rural Pakistan. B. Street (ed.), *Literacy and Development: Ethnographic Perspectives*. London, Routledge.

Zubair, S. 2004. Qualitative methods in researching women's literacy: a case study. A. Robinson-Pant (ed.), *Women, Literacy and Development: Alternative Perspectives*. London, Routledge.

Abbreviations

ACCU	Asia/Pacific Cultural Centre for UNESCO
ADEA	Association for the Development of Education in Africa
AfDF	African Development Fund
AIDS	Acquired immune deficiency syndrome
AKRSP	Aga Khan Rural Support Programme
ALL	Adult Literacy and Lifeskills Survey
APPEAL	Asia-Pacific Programme of Education for All
AsDF	Asian Development Fund
BCE	Before the Common Era
BEDP	Basic Education Development Project (Yemen)
BMZ	Bundesministerium für wirtschaftliche Zusammenarbeit und Entwicklung [Federal Ministry for Economic Cooperation and Development, Germany]
CAMPE	Campaign for Popular Education (Bangladesh)
CDE	Convention against Discrimination in Education
CEDAW	Convention on the Elimination of all Forms of Discrimination against Women
CIDA	Canadian International Development Agency
CLEBA	Centro Laubach de la Educación Popular Básica de Adultos [Laubach Centre of Popular Adult Basic Education] (Colombia)
CP	Cooperating partners
CRC	Convention on the Rights of the Child
CRS	Creditor Reporting System
CSO	Civil society organization
DAC	Development Assistance Committee (OECD)
Danida	Danish International Development Agency
DFID	Department for International Development (United Kingdom)
DIF	Donor indicative framework
EFA	Education for All
E-9	Nine high-population countries (Bangladesh, Brazil, China, Egypt, India, Indonesia, Mexico, Nigeria, Pakistan)
EC	European Commission
ECCE	Early childhood care and education
EDI	Education for All Development Index
EQJA	Éducation Qualifiante des Jeunes et des Adultes [Skill development for youth and adults] (Senegal)
ESD	Education for Sustainable Development
ESSP2	Education Sector Strategic Plan 2 (Mozambique)
EU	European Union
EWLP	Experimental World Literacy Programme
FAO	Food and Agriculture Organization of the United Nations

FRESH Focusing Resources on Effective School Health

FTI Fast Track Initiative

G8 Group of Eight (Canada, France, Germany, Italy, Japan, Russian Federation, United Kingdom and United States, plus EU representatives)

GCE Global Campaign for Education

GDP Gross domestic product

GEI Gender-specific EFA Index

GER Gross enrolment ratio

GIR Gross intake rate

GNI Gross national income

GNP Gross national product

GPI Gender parity index

HIPC Heavily indebted poor countries

HIV/AIDS Human immuno-deficiency virus/acquired immune deficiency syndrome

IALS International Adult Literacy Survey

IATT Inter-Agency Task Team on Education (UNAIDS)

IBE International Bureau of Education (UNESCO)

ICCPR International Covenant on Civil and Political Rights

ICT Information and communication technology

IDA International Development Association (World Bank)

IDB Inter-American Development Bank

IDS International Development Statistics (OECD-DAC)

IEA International Association for the Evaluation of Educational Achievement

IIEP International Institute for Educational Planning (UNESCO)

IIZ/DVV Institut für Internationale Zusammenarbeit des Deutschen Volkshochschul-Verbandes [Institute for International Cooperation of the German Adult Education Association]

ILI International Literacy Institute

ILO International Labour Office/Organization

IMF International Monetary Fund

INEE Inter-Agency Network for Education in Emergencies

I-PRSP Interim Poverty Reduction Strategy Paper

ISCED International Standard Classification of Education

LAC Latin America and the Caribbean

LAMP Literacy Assessment and Monitoring Programme

LDCs Least-developed countries

LIFE Literacy Initiative for Empowerment (UNESCO)

MDG Millennium Development Goal

MICS Multiple Indicator Cluster Surveys (UNICEF)

MINED Ministry of Education

NER Net enrolment ratio

NETF Norwegian Educational Trust Fund

NFLI National Functional Literacy Index (Brazil)

NGO Non-governmental organization

NIR	Net intake rate
NLS	New Literacy Studies
Norad	Norwegian Agency for Development Cooperation
NZAID	New Zealand Agency for International Development
OA	Official aid
ODA	Official Development Assistance
OECD	Organisation for Economic Co-operation and Development
PAP	Priority Action Program (Cambodia)
PC	Personal computer
PIRLS	Progress in Reading Literacy Study
PISA	Programme for International Student Assessment
PPP	Purchasing power parity
PROAP	Principal Regional Office for Asia and the Pacific (UNESCO)
PRODEC	Programme Décenal d'Éducation [10-Year Education Development Plan] (Mali)
PRSP	Poverty Reduction Strategy Paper
PTR	Pupil/teacher ratio
Reflect	Regenerated Freirean Literacy through Empowering Community Techniques
SACMEQ	Southern and Eastern Africa Consortium on Monitoring Educational Quality
Sida	Swedish International Development Cooperation Agency
SLE	School life expectancy
STD	Sexually transmitted disease
TIMSS	Trends in International Mathematics and Science Study
UIE	UNESCO Institute for Education
UIS	UNESCO Institute for Statistics
UNAIDS	Joint United Nations Programme on HIV/AIDS
UNDP	United Nations Development Programme
UNESCO	United Nations Educational, Scientific and Cultural Organization
UNFPA	United Nations Population Fund
UNGEI	United Nations Girls' Education Initiative
UNHCHR	United Nations High Commissioner for Human Rights
UNICEF	United Nations Children's Fund
UNLD	United Nations Literacy Decade
UOE	UNESCO/OECD/Eurostat
UPC	Universal primary completion
UPE	Universal primary education
USAID	United States Agency for International Development
USSR	Union of Soviet Socialist Republics
WEI	World Education Indicators project (UIS/OECD)
WHO	World Health Organization